National Lesbian and Gay Health Association
1734 14th St., NW
Washington, DC 20009
(202) 939-7880
An organization devoted to meeting the health needs of lesbians and gay men.

National Right to Life Committee, Inc.
512 Tenth St., NW
Washington, DC 20004
(202) 626-8800
www.nric.org
An organization based on the belief that human life begins at conception and that abortions should therefore be opposed.

National Women's Health Resource Center
2425 L Street NW, 3rd Floor
Washington, DC 20037
(202) 293-6045
A national clearinghouse on women's health information. Publishes a newsletter, *National Women's Health Report.*

Planned Parenthood Federation of America (PPFA)
434 West 33rd St.
New York, NY 10001
(212) 541-7800
www.plannedparenthood.org
PPFA is the nation's oldest and largest voluntary family planning agency. Through local clinics (call 1-800-230-PLAN for the clinic nearest you), it offers birth control information and services, pregnancy testing, voluntary sterilization, prenatal care, abortion, pelvic and breast exams, and other reproductive health services, including sexuality education.

Population Information Program
Johns Hopkins Center for Communication Programs
111 Market Place, Suite 310
Baltimore, MD 21202
Fax (410) 659-6266
Publishes *Population Reports,* frequent, up-to-date reports on contraception and family planning with emphasis on developing countries.

II. Sex Education, Sex Research, and Sex Therapy

The Alan Guttmacher Institute
120 Wall Street—21st Floor
New York, NY 10005
(212) 248-1111
email: info@guttmacher.org
www.agi-usa.org
A not-for-profit organization for reproductive health research, policy analysis, and public education. It produces many excellent, informative publications.

American Association of Sex Educators, Counselors, and Therapists (AASECT)
P.O. Box 5488
Richmond, VA 23220
email: aasect@aasect.org
www.aasect.org
This organization certifies sex educators, sex counselors, and sex therapists and provides other services associated with sexuality education and sex therapy.

Sexuality Information and Education Council of the United States (SIECUS)
130 West 42nd Street, Suite 350
New York, NY 10036
(212) 819-9770
email: siecus@siecus.org
www.siecus.org
Provides a library and information service on sexuality education, including curricula. Publishes bibliographies and maintains a database of titles of books and journals on human sexuality, currently consisting of over 8000 entries.

The Society for the Scientific Study of Sexuality
P.O. Box 416
Allentown, PA 18105-0416
(610) 530-2483
email: thesociety@inetmail.att.net
www.sexscience.org
An organization devoted to promoting quality sex research; publishes the *Journal of Sex Research.*

(continued on back inside cover)

Understanding
Human Sexuality

Understanding Human Sexuality

Tenth Edition

Janet Shibley Hyde
University of Wisconsin–Madison

John D. DeLamater
University of Wisconsin–Madison

McGraw-Hill
Higher Education

Boston   Burr Ridge, IL   Dubuque, IA   Madison, WI   New York   San Francisco   St. Louis
Bangkok   Bogotá   Caracas   Kuala Lumpur   Lisbon   London   Madrid   Mexico City
Milan   Montreal   New Delhi   Santiago   Seoul   Singapore   Sydney   Taipei   Toronto

McGraw-Hill
Higher Education

ISBN: 978-0-07-338262-3 (Student Edition)
MHID: 0-07-338262-0 (Student Edition)

ISBN: 978-0-07-335044-8 (Instructor's Edition)
MHID: 0-07-335044-3 (Instructor's Edition)

Editor in Chief: *Michael J. Ryan*
Publisher: *Beth Mejia*
Sponsoring Editor: *Suzanna Z. Ellison*
Marketing Manager: *James Headley*
Developmental Editor: *Judith Kromm*
Media Project Manager: *Ron Nelms, Jr.*
Production Editor: *Brett Coker*
Manuscript Editor: *Carole Crouse*
Art Director: *Jeanne M. Schreiber*
Interior Designers: *Jenny El-Shamy and Andrei Pasternak*
Cover Designer: *Lisa Buckley*
Art Editor: *Emma Ghiselli*
Illustrator: *Judith Waller*
Photo Research Coordinator: *Nora Agbayani*
Photo Research: *Editorial Image, LLC*
Production Supervisor: *Tandra Jorgensen*
Composition: *9.5 / 12 Utopia by Aptara*
Printing: *Tien Wah Press*

Cover image: *J. Pinderhughes*

Credits: The credits section for this book begins on page C-1 and is considered an extension of the copyright page.

Library of Congress Cataloging-in-Publication Data

Hyde, Janet Shibley.
    Understanding human sexuality / Janet Shibley Hyde, John D. DeLamater. – 10th ed.
        p. cm.
    Includes bibliographical references and index.
    ISBN-13: 978-0-07-338262-3
    ISBN-10: 0-07-338262-0
    1. Sex. 2. Sex customs. 3. Hygiene, Sexual. 4. Sex (Psychology) I. DeLamater, John D.
    II. Title.
        HQ12. H82 2008
        306.7—dc22

                                                            2007028059

www.mhhe.com

Author Biographies

Janet Shibley Hyde, the Helen Thompson Woolley Professor of Psychology and Women's Studies at the University of Wisconsin–Madison, received her education at Oberlin College and the University of California, Berkeley. She has taught a course in human sexuality since 1974, first at Bowling Green State University, then at Denison University, and now at the University of Wisconsin. Her research interests are in gender differences and gender development in childhood and adolescence. Author of the textbook *Half the Human Experience: The Psychology of Women,* she is a past president of the Society for the Scientific Study of Sexuality and is a Fellow of the American Psychological Association and the American Association for the Advancement of Science. She has received many other honors, including an award for excellence in teaching at Bowling Green State University, the Chancellor's Award for teaching at the University of Wisconsin, and the Kinsey Award from the Society for the Scientific Study of Sexuality for her contributions to sex research. In 2000–01 she served as one of the three scientific editors for U.S. Surgeon General David Satcher's report *Promoting Sexual Health and Responsible Sexual Behavior.* She is married to John DeLamater.

John D. DeLamater, Professor of Sociology at the University of Wisconsin–Madison, received his education at the University of California, Santa Barbara, and the University of Michigan. He created the human sexuality course at the University of Wisconsin in 1975 and has since taught it regularly. His current research and writing are focused on the effects of life-course transitions on sexuality. He has published papers on the effects of having a child, of dual-career couples, and of divorce, and is studying the effects of menopause and later-life transitions on sexual attitudes and behavior. He is the co-author of the textbook *Social Psychology.* He is a Fellow of the Society for the Scientific Study of Sexuality and the 2002 recipient of the Kinsey Award from the Society for Career Contributions to Sex Research. He has received awards for excellence in teaching from the Department of Sociology and Interfraternity Council–Panhellenic Association and is a Fellow and past Chair of the Teaching Academy at the University of Wisconsin. He regularly teaches a seminar for graduate students on teaching undergraduate courses. He is married to Janet Hyde.

Contents in Brief

Contents

Preface

In our not entirely objective opinion, there is no more exciting course to teach or to take than human sexuality. One of the things that makes it so exciting is the fantastic pace of change we see nearly every day in scientific knowledge, social attitudes, laws, current events, and countless other facets of our lives involving sex. Today we have "friends with benefits" and same-sex marriage. Every year, advances are made in the prevention and treatment of AIDS. New methods of contraception are developed and made available. Viagra bursts on the scene, transforming the sexual experience for thousands of men and their partners, and we wonder what can be done to help women with sexual disorders. Much has changed in the new edition of this textbook as well. At the same time, we have retained the features that instructors and students have praised since the book was first published.

Objectives of the Book and the Course

First and foremost, we try to keep in mind at all times that students *want* to learn about sexuality and that our job as writers is to help them learn. This book uses presentational strategies that we have honed in our extensive experience teaching this course over many years. We use language and illustrations that enlighten rather than intimidate, and we convey as much information as possible, simply and clearly. We present the best, most current, and most authoritative scholarhip about sexuality in a format that empowers students to make more informed personal choices and to take an educated view of their own and others' sexuality and the role of sexuality in our society.

The book does not assume that students have taken prior college courses in biology, psychology, or sociology. It is designed as an introduction and adheres to the four major objectives that guide our own courses in human sexuality:

1. To provide practical information needed for everyday living (information about sexual anatomy, contraception, and sexually transmitted infections, for example) and to deal with problems in sexual functioning (such as early ejaculation or inability to have an orgasm).
2. To help students appreciate the fabulous diversity of human sexuality along many dimensions, including age, sexual orientation and identity, ethnicity within the United States (a multiethnic perspective), and culture around the world (a multicultural perspective).
3. To help students feel more at ease with thinking and talking about sex, both to minimize their own personal discomfort with a tension-causing topic and to help them become responsible decision makers in an important aspect of their personal lives and in their roles as citizens and voters.
4. To familiarize students with methods used in research on sexuality, and particularly with problems inherent in some of these methods, so that they can read research reports critically and intelligently.

Our own courses are surveys, designed to provide students with a broad range of information about sexuality. Reflecting that approach, we wrote this book to be both comprehensive and balanced in its coverage, so that students will want to save it for use as a reference in future years. For instructors who lack the time or resources to cover the entire book or who prefer to rearrange the order of topics, we have written all of the chapters to be fairly independent of one another.

Certainly some aspects of sexuality today are very serious. Nonetheless, we believe that, in modern American culture, we are in danger of taking some aspects of sexuality far too seriously. We may not be serious about it in the same way as were our Victorian ancestors, but we are serious nonetheless—serious about whether we are using the best and most up-to-date sexual techniques, serious about whether our partners are having as many orgasms as possible, and so on. To counteract this tendency, we have tried to incorporate a light touch, with occasional humor. We hope that this approach will help us all keep things in perspective.

One thing we are serious about is the quality of research. The quality of sex research is highly variable, to put it mildly. Some journalists think they are sex researchers if they have interviewed 10 people and written a book about it! We see other sexuality textbooks that give equal weight to an article from the local newspaper and a refereed journal article from the *New England Journal of Medicine* or the *Journal of Sex Research*—and readers have to do a lot of detective work to find out what the real source is for a statement. We believe that it is our responsibility as textbook authors to sift through available studies and present only those that are of the best quality and the greatest relevance to this course. We are thrilled to observe that the quality of sex research improves every decade. In this edition we were able to prune away many older studies of lesser quality and rely much more on recent studies that are of excellent quality in terms of sampling, research design, and measurements.

What's New in the 10th Edition

A major change in this new edition is that, at the request of many instructors, we have reduced the number of chapters and significantly streamlined the size of the book without sacrificing important content. Previously we had 23 chapters and now we have 20. We removed the chapter on menstruation and menopause; the material on menstruation is now in Chapter 5, Sex Hormones, Sexual Differentiation, Puberty, and the Menstrual Cycle and the material on menopause is now in Chapter 10, Sexuality and the Life Cycle: Adulthood. We eliminated the chapter on techniques of arousal and communication; the material on techniques of arousal now appears in Chapter 8, Sexual Arousal, which also contains all the material (updated) from the old chapter on the physiology of sexual response. The material on communication is covered in Chapter 11, Attraction, Love, and Communication.

In keeping with our focus on top-quality research coverage, we have highlighted some of the most important new research trends. First and foremost, we discuss cutting-edge research on the biology of sexuality, written so that the average undergraduate can understand it. This coverage includes fMRI studies of brain activity, neuroscience research, and the latest findings in endocrinology. For an example, see the new Focus box, Endocrine Disrupters, in Chapter 5, Sex Hormones, Sexual Differentiation, Puberty, and the Menstrual Cycle. We believe that we can justifiably say that this edition has the best coverage of biology of any text in the field.

The emerging concept of sexual health, as defined by the World Health Organization, is now introduced in Chapter 1. This content can then be used in considering other issues later in the course.

Focus boxes have been reorganized into three themes: Milestones in Sex Research, which features important classic and new studies; First Person, which describes case histories, biographies of individuals who were important in the history of sex research, and personal growth exercises for the student; and A Sexually Diverse World, which covers multicultural studies and studies of sexual minorities.

Important, too, is our extensive updating and integration of Internet issues and Web-based research. See especially the discussion of two-person cybersex in Chapter 8, Sexual Arousal, and on the application of scientific theories by Internet matching services in Chapter 11, Attraction, Love, and Communication.

Following is a brief tour of the highlights of new material in each chapter of *Understanding Human Sexuality*, 10th Edition.

Chapter 1. Sexuality in Perspective
- New section on sexual health and sexual rights.
- Data on mass media thoroughly updated.

Chapter 2. Theoretical Perspectives on Sexuality
- Entire chapter streamlined to be more accessible to students.

Chapter 3. Sex Research
- Streamlined with removal of older material, such as the Bell, Weinberg, and Hammersmith study of homosexuals and heterosexuals.

Chapter 4. Sexual Anatomy
- Data from the latest international Demographic and Health Surveys on female genital cutting (FGC) added to the Focus box on FGC.

- The latest on circumcision and HIV infection is presented, including halted clinical trials in Kenya and Uganda.
- Information added on the new vaccine against human papillomavirus (HPV) infection and cervical cancer.
- Statistics on cancer and information on treatment have been updated.

Chapter 5. Sex Hormones, Sexual Differentiation, Puberty, and the Menstrual Cycle

- A new Focus box, Endocrine Disrupters, added with the latest research on environmental pollutants that affect the endocrine system and the behavior of humans and other species.
- Figure 5.5, on the functions of genes linked to sexual differentiation in mammals, updated and expanded. For those teaching a biology-oriented course, or for biologically sophisticated students, the genes are explained and citations to current research on them is provided so that students can pursue this work in more detail. The material is set off in a figure caption so that it can be omitted in courses that do not have a biology focus.
- New terminology for intersex—disorders of sex development—included.
- Material on menstruation streamlined and placed at the end of this chapter.
- Updated Table 5.2 on ages of menarche and other aspects of pubertal development.

Chapter 6. Conception, Pregnancy, and Childbirth

- Introduces the "pregnancy as silent struggle" perspective, which argues that mother and fetus are in continuing struggle for adequate nourishment and nutrients.
- Updated statistics and discussion of cesarean section deliveries and vaginal birth after cesarean (VBAC).
- Updated coverage of postpartum depression.
- The latest coverage of infertility and new reproductive technologies.

Chapter 7. Contraception and Abortion

- New data on the economics of contraception added to the introduction.
- Updates from the World Health Organization on contraceptive use—for example, what to do when a pill is missed.
- The latest in developments on male contraception.

Chapter 8. Sexual Arousal

- Includes material previously covered in chapter on physiology of sexual response, as well as material on techniques of arousal, previously in chapter on arousal and communication.
- In keeping with contemporary trends to modify Masters and Johnson's model, dropped the distinction between the excitement phase and the plateau phase.
- The latest research on the brain, spinal cord, and sex, including MRI studies.
- Substantially updated discussion of pheromones with new research on humans and other primates.
- New discussion of two-person cybersex.

Chapter 9. Sexuality and the Life Cycle: Childhood and Adolescence

- Added data from 2002 National Survey of Family Growth (NSFG) and 2005 Youth Risk Behavior Survey (CDC) throughout chapter.
- Added detailed coverage of APA Task Force Report on the Sexualization of Girls.
- Updated statistics on childhood and adolescent sexual experience throughout.
- Updated Focus box on mass media; added new content analyses on sex in the media.

Chapter 10. Sexuality and the Life Cycle: Adulthood

- Expanded discussion of research on effects of cohabitation on stability of subsequent marriage.
- New research on patterns in couples' level of sexual desire/lust.
- New research on polyamory.
- New research on sexuality in later life.

Chapter 11. Attraction, Love, and Communication

- New discussion of the use of scientific theories by Internet matching services.
- Expanded discussion of the theory of evolutionary roots of attraction and mating processes.
- The material on communication, previously in chapter on techniques of arousal and communication, moved to the end of this chapter.

Chapter 12. Gender and Sexuality

- Research on the media and gender socialization thoroughly updated.

- New research on MRI scans of brains before and during the gender reassignment process.
- New genetic study of transsexuals added.
- The latest on controversies about the treatment of gender identity disorder discussed.

Chapter 13. Sexual Orientation: Gay, Straight, or Bi?

- New data on gay men and lesbians in civil unions.
- All statistics on attitudes and behaviors thoroughly updated.
- New research on the genetics of sexual orientation.
- Section on psychoanalytic theory deleted in response to instructors' recommendations.
- New research on differences between gay men and lesbians.

Chapter 14. Variations in Sexual Behavior

- Added discussion of Bancroft and colleagues' high-arousal, low-inhibition perspective on variations.
- New section on asexuality.

Chapter 15. Sexual Coercion

- Updated statistics on rape, marital rape, and sexual harassment.

Chapter 16. Sex for Sale

- Added coverage of live sex shows.
- Added discussion of sex industry efforts to upgrade its legitimacy by forming Chamber of Commerce.
- New data from Kinsey Institute survey of users of pornography added (Table 16.2).

Chapter 17. Sexual Disorders and Sex Therapy

- The New View of Women's Sexual Problems (Tiefer, Basson) explained and integrated throughout (e.g., the concept of "responsive desire" added in the section on desire disorders).
- New Focus: First Person, on a case of low sexual desire, which illustrates an application of the New View.
- The concept of sexual health, introduced in Chapter 1, is revisited in the section on practical advice for preventing sexual disorders and in a Question for Thought, Discussion, and Debate.

Chapter 18. Sexually Transmitted Infections

- Statistics updated throughout.
- The latest research on HPV, including high-risk and low-risk types, as well as the HPV vaccine.

- New data on the prevalence of HSV-2 and HSV-1 infection in the United States.
- Scientific advances regarding genes that confer resistance to HIV infection.
- The latest developments in microbicides.

Chapter 19. Ethics, Religion, and Sexuality

- Discussion of Buddhism expanded to include a new discussion of Tantric Buddhism.
- Focus: Dissent over Sexual Ethics in the Roman Catholic Church has been updated.
- Data on attitudes about abortion updated.
- Section on religious positions on homosexuality updated and reorganized into rejectionist, love-the-sinner-but-hate-the-sin, and full acceptance.
- Statements by religions updated and Web sites provided when available.

Chapter 20. Sex and the Law

- Updated Table 20.2, Americans' Attitudes toward Gay Rights.
- Updated coverage of gays in the armed forces.
- Discussion of activities by owners of adult-oriented businesses to counter attempts to enforce sex laws.
- Added coverage of effects of parental consent requirements on teen abortion rates.

Epilogue. Looking to the Future: Sexuality Education

- Enhanced coverage of Canadian research on sexuality education.
- Revised discussion of guidelines of the Sexuality Information and Education Council of the United States (SIECUS) to reflect changes made by SIECUS.
- Completely rewritten discussion of sex education curricula and research on effectiveness.
- Material streamlined considerably.

Resources for Instructors and Students

A number of supplementary materials are available for learning and extending the concepts of the book. Please contact your local McGraw-Hill representative for details concerning policies, prices, and availability as some restrictions may apply.

SexSource Online, a resource for instructors and students using McGraw-Hill human sexuality textbooks, provides more than 60 high-quality educational video clips carefully chosen by instructors and researchers to illustrate core concepts in human sexuality. Each clip is accompanied by postviewing questions that can be used to generate in-class discussion or completed independently by students. For courses taught wholly online or those supported by course Web sites, the content is fully integrated within course management cartridges, complete with suggested assessment items for instructional use.

Supplements for the Instructor

The supplements listed here accompany *Understanding Human Sexuality,* 10th Edition. Please contact your McGraw-Hill representative for more information.

Instructor's Edition

The Instructor's Edition was prepared by Janet Hyde and John DeLamater. It is based on their experience conducting workshops on the teaching of human sexuality at the conference of the Society for the Scientific Study of Sexuality over the past 12 years, and teaching classes of all sizes at the University of Wisconsin–Madison. It contains tips and techniques for leading discussions, introducing difficult topics, and encouraging group work, along with many other useful strategies for new or experienced instructors. The authors welcome feedback on this new instructional resource. Please send comments to Janet Hyde (jshyde@wisc.edu).

Online Learning Center for Instructors

This extensive Web site, designed specifically to accompany *Understanding Human Sexuality,* 10th Edition, offers an array of resources for both instructor and student. Among the features included on the instructor's side of the Web site, which is password protected, are downloadable versions of the Instructor's Manual, PowerPoint slides, CPS Questions, and Test Bank files. These resources and more can be found by logging on to the text site at www.mhhe.hyde10. Contact your McGraw-Hill representative for your instructor password.

Instructor's Manual

Written by Sylvester Allred, Northern Arizona University, the Instructor's Manual includes chapter outlines, lecture topics and suggestions, ideas for classroom activities and demonstrations, ques-

tions for use in classroom discussions, ideas for student research papers, and lists of current research articles. New to this edition are suggested discussion topics and activities to help instructors incorporate the material on SexSource into classroom instruction. The manual is organized by chapter and has been designed to assist instructors new to the teaching of human sexuality as well as more experienced professors.

Test Bank and Dual Platform Computerized Test Bank

Written by Lisa Wade, Occidental College, this comprehensive Test Bank includes more than 1,700 multiple-choice questions, as well as more than 100 essay questions. The test questions are organized by chapter and are designed to test factual, applied, and conceptual understanding. Questions on SexSource video clips are also included.

All questions in the Test Bank are compatible with EZ Test, McGraw-Hill's flexible and easy-to-use electronic testing program. The program allows instructors to create tests from book-specific items and accommodates a wide range of question types; instructors may also add their own questions. Multiple versions of the test can be created, and any test can be exported for use with course management systems such as WebCT or BlackBoard. The program is available for Windows and Macintosh environments. **EZ Test Online** is a new service that gives you a way to easily administer your EZ Test–created exams and quizzes online.

PowerPoint Presentations

Developed by Valerie Smith, Coast Community College District, Central Park Campus, these presentations cover the key points of the chapter and include charts and graphs from the text where relevant. They can be used as is or modified to meet your specific needs.

Classroom Performance System (CPS) by eInstruction

This revolutionary system brings ultimate interactivity to the lecture hall or classroom. It is a wireless electronic response system that gives the instructor and students immediate feedback from the entire class. Questions specific to this text, written by Lance Jones at Bowling Green State University, include class-tested polling questions, designed to prompt self-reflection and class discussion. CPS is also a superb way to give interactive quizzes, test understanding, and take attendance.

Annual Editions: Human Sexuality

This McGraw-Hill publication offers articles on topics related to the latest research and thinking in human sexuality from more than 300 public press sources. These editions are updated annually and contain helpful features such as a topic guide, an annotated table of contents, unit overviews, and a topical index. An Instructor's Guide containing assessment materials is also available.

Sources: Notable Selections in Human Sexuality

This is a collection of articles, book excerpts, and research studies that have shaped the study of human sexuality and our contemporary understanding of it. The selections are organized topically around major areas of study within human sexuality. Each selection is preceded by a headnote that establishes the relevance of the article or study and provides biographical information on the author.

Taking Sides: Clashing Views on Controversial Issues in Human Sexuality

This debate-style reader introduces students to controversial viewpoints on the field's most crucial issues. Each topic is carefully framed for the students, and the pro and con essays represent the arguments of leading scholars and commentators in their fields. An Instructor's Guide containing testing materials is also available.

Supplements for the Student

Online Learning Center

This extensive Web site, created by Kim Foreman and designed specifically to accompany *Understanding Human Sexuality*, 10th Edition, offers an array of learning tools to support student comprehension and reflection. Included on the student side of the Online Learning Center are chapter outlines, learning objectives, matching exercises for key terms, quiz questions, and Web links for each chapter. These resources and more can be found by logging on to the text site at www.mhhe.com/hyde10.

Acknowledgments

We are delighted to take this opportunity to thank the many friends and colleagues who have helped us in so many ways as we've worked on this revision. We are particularly indebted to the students in our classes, who keep us up to date on what college students are thinking and wondering about sexuality. We would also like to thank all the members of our team at McGraw-Hill, especially executive editor Suzanna Ellison, lead project manager Brett Coker, and senior developmental editor Judith Kromm, for their efforts in bringing the tenth edition to fruition.

Over the course of the first nine editions, numerous reviewers contributed to the development of *Understanding Human Sexuality*. Space limitations prevent us from listing them all, but their contributions endure, as does our gratitude to them. In addition, we are enormously grateful to the following reviewers who helped shape this edition:

Sylvester Allred, *Northern Arizona University*

Linde Althaus, *University of Minnesota*

Andrew E. Behrendt, *Drexel University and Chestnut Hill College*

Wendy C. Chambers, *University of Georgia*

Herbert L. Coleman, *Austin Community College*

David L. Delmonico, *Duquesne University*

Joseph P. Fanelli, *Syracuse University*

Nicole Hillier, *University of Illinois at Urbana–Champaign*

Karen L. Horner, *Catawba College*

Kim Hyatt, *Weber State University*

Kris Koehne, *University of Tennessee*

Shirley Ogletree, *Texas State University–San Marcos*

Amy Sweetman, *Los Angeles City College*

Virginia Wray Totaro, *Virginia Commonwealth University*

Soni Verma, *Sierra College*

Lester W. Wright, Jr., *Western Michigan University*

We love teaching our human sexuality courses, and we've loved writing this text. We hope you will enjoy reading it, learning from it, and teaching with it.

Janet Shibley Hyde

John D. DeLamater

Student's Guide to *Understanding Human Sexuality*

This trusted text examines the biological, psychological, and social science of human sexuality and provides practical information you can apply in your everyday life. Janet Hyde, a psychologist, and John DeLamater, a sociologist, take an interdisciplinary approach to the topic, which ensures full exposure to key aspects of this intriguing field of study.

Comprehensive and scientific, the text covers a broad range of information about sexuality. Providing thorough coverage of biological foundations, sexual behavior, and sexual problems, the authors strike a balance between a rigorous scientific presentation and a sensitive approach designed to make you more comfortable with issues relevant to your own sexuality.

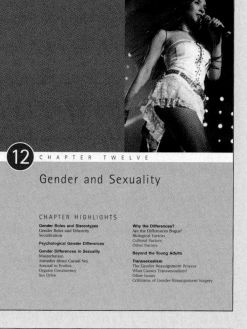

Designed for Easy Reading and Review

Each chapter opens with a chapter outline identifying key topics, and ends with a brief summary and questions for review. Key terms are defined in the margins.

Focus: Milestones in Sex Research
Alfred C. Kinsey

Alfred C. Kinsey was born in 1894 in New Jersey. In high school he did not date, and a classmate recalled that he was "the shyest guy around girls you could think of."

His father was determined that Kinsey become a mechanical engineer. From 1912 to 1914 he tried studying mechanical engineering at Stevens Institute, but he showed little talent for it. At one point he was close to failing physics, but a compromise was reached with the professor, who agreed to pass him if he would not attempt any advanced work in the field. In 1914 Kinsey made his break and enrolled at Bowdoin College in Maine to pursue his real love: biology. Because this went against his father's wishes, Kinsey was put on his own financially.

In 1916 he began graduate work at Harvard. There he developed an interest in insects, specializing in gall wasps. While still a graduate student he wrote a definitive book on the edible plants of eastern North America.

In 1920 he went to Bloomington, Indiana, to take a job as assistant professor of zoology at Indiana University. That fall he met Clara McMillen, whom he married six months later. They soon had four children.

With his intense curiosity and driving ambition, Kinsey quickly gained academic success. He published a high school biology text in 1926, which received enthusiastic reviews. By 1936 he had published two major books on gall wasps; they established his reputation as a leading authority in the field and contributed not only to the knowledge of gall wasps but also to genetic theory.

Kinsey came to the study of human sexual behavior as a biologist. His shift to the study of sex

began in 1938, when Indiana University began a "marriage" course; Kinsey chaired the faculty committee teaching it. When confronted with teaching the course, he became aware of the appalling lack of information on human sexual behavior. Thus, his research resulted in part from his realization of the need of people, especially young people, for sex information. In 1939 he made his first field trip to collect sex histories in Chicago. His lifetime goal was to collect 100,000 sex histories.

His work culminated with the publication of the Kinsey reports in 1948 (*Sexual Behavior in the Human Male*) and 1953 (*Sexual Behavior in the Human Female*). While the scientific community generally received them as a landmark contribution, they also provoked hate mail.

In 1947 Kinsey founded the Institute for Sex Research (known popularly as the Kinsey Institute) at Indiana University. It was financed by a grant from the Rockefeller Foundation and, later, by book royalties. But in the 1950s Senator Joseph McCarthy, the communist baiter, was in power. He made a particularly vicious attack on the Institute and its research, claiming that its effect was to weaken American morality and thus make the nation more susceptible to a communist takeover. Under his pressure, the Rockefeller Foundation terminated its support.

Kinsey's health began to fail, partly as a result of the heavy workload he set for himself, and partly because he saw the financial support for the research collapsing. He died in 1956 at the age of 62 of heart failure while honoring a lecture engagement when his doctor had ordered him to convalesce.

By 1957 McCarthy had been discredited and the grant funds returned. The Institute was then

contributed to *Sexual Behavior in the Human Female* (1953). Though some Blacks were interviewed, only interviews with whites were included in the publications. The interviews were conducted between 1938 and 1949.

Initially, Kinsey was not much concerned with sampling issues. His goal was simply to collect sex histories from as wide a variety of people as possible. He began conducting interviews on the Indiana University campus and then moved on to large cities such as Chicago.

Kinsey later became more concerned with sampling issues and developed a technique called *100*

percent sampling. In this method he contacted a group, obtained its cooperation, and then got every one of its members to give a history. Once the cooperation of a group had been secured, peer pressure ensured that all members would participate. Unfortunately, although he was successful in getting a complete sample from such groups, the groups themselves were by no means chosen randomly. Thus, among the groups from which 100 percent samples were obtained were 2 sororities, 9 fraternities, and 13 professional groups.

In the 1953 volume on females, Kinsey said that he and his colleagues had deliberately chosen not

52

Fascinating Focus Boxes Highlight Noteworthy Topics Related to Chapter Content

"Focus: Milestones in Sex Research" looks at important scientists and research studies; "Focus: A Sexually Diverse World" highlights the variety of sexual experiences and outlooks worldwide; and "Focus: First Person" looks at sexuality on a personal level.

Focus: A Sexually Diverse World
The Debate over the Treatment of Intersex Individuals

When Chris was born, her clitoris was 1.7 cm long. That's about halfway between the length of the average newborn clitoris and the average newborn penis. She had a scrotum but no testes in it, and the physician was unsure whether she was a girl or a boy. A blood test revealed that her sex chromosomes were XY. After 24 hours of consultations, during which her parents were in agony, the physician decided that Chris should be a girl because it would be impossible for her to function as a boy with such strange genitals. While a baby, she had several surgeries, one to remove her testes, which were still in her abdomen. Her clitoris was surgically reduced in size when she was age 5, old enough to remember it. Today she is 27 and angry about what she considers the mutilations of her body. She now knows that she has androgen-insensitivity syndrome. So much of her clitoris was removed that she is not able to orgasm.

Chris (a composite of several case histories in the scientific literature) is an intersex individual; that is, her genitals have combined male, female, or ambiguous elements. She was treated according to a protocol that became standard beginning in the 1960s and persists today. This protocol was based on the pioneering research of Dr. John Money and others. According to him, individuals such as Chris, whom he called "pseudohermaphrodites," could successfully be assigned to either gender, provided that it was done before 18 months of age and that the necessary surgeries and follow-up medical treatments (such as hormone treatment) occurred. Money's research indicated that individuals treated with the standard protocol grew up to be healthy and well adjusted.

In the last decade, however, intersex individuals have come out of the closet and formed an activist

organization, the Intersex Society of North America (ISNA).* Intersex activists argue that they have cases of genital variability, not genital abnormality. The medical standard is that an infant's organ that is 0.9 cm or less is a clitoris and 2.5 cm or more is a penis. Activists argue that these cutoffs are arbitrary. What is wrong with a clitoris that is 1.7 cm long? Perhaps the only thing wrong with it is that it makes doctors, and perhaps parents, embarrassed. Issues of medical ethics are raised: Should essentially cosmetic surgery be performed on a baby who cannot give informed consent? Should parents be encouraged to lie to their child?

Sex researcher Milton Diamond conducted long-term follow-ups on several individuals treated using Money's standard protocol. He found that, contrary to the glowing picture of perfect adjustment painted by Money and others, these intersex individuals had serious adjustment problems that they traced directly to the medical "management" of their condition. Diamond's research has sparked a debate over the proper treatment of intersex individuals. Diamond has proposed a protocol in which he urges physicians, in cases of intersex infants, (1) to make their most informed judgment about the child's eventual gender identity (CAH girls, for example, almost invariably have a female identity) and counsel the parents to rear the child in that gender; (2) not to perform surgeries that might later need to be reversed; and (3) to provide honest counseling and education to the parents and child as he or she grows up so that the child

*For information about the ISNA and other sexuality organizations, including the ISNA Web site, see the Directory of Resources at the end of this book.

girls exist. A girl may be stuck with a date who barely reaches her armpits, while a boy may have to cope with someone who is better qualified to be on his basketball team than he is.

Second, there are large individual differences (differences from one person to the next) in the age at which the processes of puberty take place. For this reason there is no one "normal" time to begin menstruating or growing a beard. Instead, we give age ranges in describing the timing of this process.

Changes in Girls

A summary of the physical changes of puberty in males and females is provided in Table 5.2 on page 104. The first sign of puberty in the female is the beginning of breast development, on average around 9 to 10 years of age (Sun et al., 2002). The ducts in the nipple area swell, and there is growth of fatty and connective tissue, causing the small, conical buds to increase in size. These changes are produced by increases in the levels of the sex hormones by a process that is described in the following pages.

102

Focus: First Person
A Gay Couple: Lee and Bob

Lee and Bob have been living together as a couple for 10 years. Lee is 30 and Bob is 53; they live in a small town in northern Wisconsin.

Lee feels that he never had a real home while growing up. His father worked in construction, and they moved frequently, living in motel rooms. His mother remarried soon, but the man turned out to be a wife batterer, so they divorced when Lee was in the fifth grade. His mother, now single, turned to drugs and partying. Home life had no structure and was chaotic, although Lee feels that she loved him. Then his mom was "saved" and joined a repressive, fundamentalist church. She married again, to someone with like beliefs, and is still married to that man.

Lee knew that he liked boys more than girls by the first grade, but he also knew that he shouldn't talk about it. He didn't completely self-label as gay until his first semester in college. At that time he had his first affair, with his boss at Burger King. The affair was tempestuous, and he was heartbroken when it ended badly. His mother sensed that something was up. When he told her that he was gay, she insisted that he go to a psychiatrist to be cured. He agreed to try not to be gay and did try, but of course it didn't work. He and his mother had one more fight about it, and she kicked him out of the house. After two years they reconciled somewhat but not completely, and his stepfather is still rejecting.

Bob, in contrast, had an unremarkable childhood. His parents are still married after 54 years, and he speaks to them every day, although he has

never told them that he is gay and they have never asked. Raised as a Catholic in northern Wisconsin, he is nonpracticing today.

Bob began to find boys to be more attractive than girls in high school, but in the 1950s and 1960s no label of "gay" was available. He first acted on his impulses in college and had dated five or six people before meeting Lee.

They met, improbably, in northern Wisconsin when the first gay bar opened in one small town. They dated briefly and quickly settled down as a couple. They have an agreement to be monogamous, which Bob has never breached and Lee has breached only once.

When asked what they liked best about their relationship, Bob said it was the stability of knowing that there's someone to share life with. The relationship seems to him like an investment built up over time. Lee likes being in a relationship because he loves Bob and knows Bob loves him in return. He also appreciates the depth of the relationship, which seems to him to be a major accomplishment. They worry a bit about their age gap. Bob is beginning to think about retirement, whereas Lee is getting ready to launch his career and anticipates a major move in the next few years. They also regret their emotional distance from their families.

Today Lee is working on his Ph.D. in clinical psychology, hoping to become a therapist. Bob is a commercial pilot for a major airline.

Source: Based on an interview conducted by Janet Hyde.

flooded with same-gender couples seeking marriage licenses (Belluck, 2004).

Beginning in 2000, gay men and lesbians were able to form legal civil unions in Vermont, and we now have an initial round of research on couples entering these unions (Solomon et al., 2004). In the first year of the policy in Vermont, 2,475 civil union certificates were issued. Among those couples, only 21 percent were actually from Vermont; two-thirds of the couples were female. Those seeking civil unions were on average 43-44 years old; lesbians on average had been living together for 9 years, and gay men had been living together for 12 years. Among the lesbian couples, 34 percent had children, 15 percent from the current relationship and 19 percent from a prior relationship. For male couples, 18 percent had

children, 8 percent from the current relationship and 11 percent from a prior relationship.

Gay and lesbian couples—like heterosexual couples—must struggle to find a balance that suits both persons. Three aspects of the relationship typically have to be negotiated and can be sources of conflict: money, housework, and sex (Solomon et al., 2005).

In one study, gay couples, lesbian couples, and heterosexual couples were brought to the laboratory and told to discuss a problem (Julien et al., 2003). Each couple's interactions were videotaped and later coded for both positive and negative behaviors by each partner. The results showed no differences between lesbian, gay, and heterosexual couples on any of the interaction measures.

345

Current, High-Quality Research

In keeping with the high standards of research introduced in Chapter 2, the authors base this book on both classical and contemporary studies that are of excellent quality in terms of sampling, research design, and measurements. The new edition includes updated research and new studies published since the ninth edition was prepared.

Research using the longitudinal Add Health survey measured the effects of parent–adolescent relationships on likelihood of first intercourse (Ream & Savin-Williams, 2005). Decreases in feelings of closeness to parents and in shared activities with them were associated with initiation of sexual intercourse, and followed first intercourse as well (parents may or may not have been aware that the youth had intercourse). Research with a sample of Asian American adolescents found that high levels of parental attachment were associated with reduced odds of first intercourse for women but not men (Hahm et al., 2006). Other research using Add Health data considered the influence of friends (Sieving et al., 2006) on whether virgins at Time 1 (1994–1995) engaged in intercourse for the first time between Times 1 and 2 (1996). The higher the proportion of a youth's friends who were sexually experienced at Time 1, the more likely the person was to engage in intercourse for the first time by Time 2.

to lose it with a lover or soul mate; those who viewed it as a stigma often lost it with a stranger or nonlover.

Premarital Sex with a Prostitute

In the 1940s and 1950s, premarital sex with a prostitute was fairly common among males, and many young men received their sexual initiation in this manner. Among the college-educated men under age 35 in one study (Hunt, 1974), 19 percent said they had had their first intercourse with a prostitute. Today, however, having premarital sex with a commercial sex worker is much less common. In the NHSLS survey of 3,432 adults, 3 percent of the men and $\frac{1}{10}$ of 1 percent of the women reported that their first intercourse had involved a paid partner (Laumann et al., 1994).

Techniques in Premarital Sex

Paralleling the increase in the incidence of premarital intercourse is an increase in the variety of tech-

Online Learning Center and SexSource Online

Visit www.mhhe.com/hyde10 for practice tests on core content in each chapter of the book that will help you prepare for exams. In addition, *SexSource Online,* available from within the OLC, contains over 60 high-quality educational video clips carefully chosen to illustrate core concepts in human sexuality. Each clip is accompanied by postviewing questions to draw out key points from viewing.

SexSource Online
www.mhhe.com/hyde10

CHAPTER ONE

Sexuality in Perspective

CHAPTER HIGHLIGHTS

Y ou're so beautiful," he whispered. "I want a picture of you like this with your face flushed and your lips wet and shiny." . . . He tore open a foil packet he'd retrieved from his pocket. Mesmerized, she watched him sheath himself, amazed at how hard he was. She reached out to touch him, but he moved back, made sure she was ready, and then slid neatly inside her, so deeply she gasped. She contracted her muscles around him, and he closed his eyes and groaned, the sound so primal, it made her skin tingle.*

Human sexual behavior is a diverse phenomenon. It occurs in different physical locations and social contexts, consists of a wide range of specific activities, and is perceived differently by different people. An individual engages in sexual activity on the basis of a complex set of motivations and organizes that activity on the basis of numerous external factors and influences. Thus, it is unlikely that the tools and concepts from any single scientific discipline will suffice to answer all or even most of the questions one might ask about sexual behavior.†

*Debbi Rawlins. (2003). *Anything goes.* NY: Harlequin Blaze.
†Laumann et al. (1994).

Strikingly different though they may seem, both of the above quotations are talking about the same thing—sex. The first quotation is from a romance novel. It is intended to stimulate the reader's fantasies and arousal. The second is from a scholarly book about sex. It aims to stimulate the brain but not the genitals. From reading these two brief excerpts we can quickly see that the topic of sexuality is diverse, complex, and fascinating.

Why study sex? Most people are curious about sex, particularly because exchanging sexual information is somewhat taboo in our culture, so curiosity motivates us to study sex. Sex is an important force in many people's lives, so there are practical reasons for wanting to learn about it. Finally, most of us at various times experience problems with our sexual functioning or wish that we could function better, and we hope that learning more about sex will help us. This book is designed to address all of these needs. So let's consider various perspectives on sexuality—the effects of religion, science, and culture on our understanding of sexuality, as well as the sexual health perspective. These perspectives will give you a glimpse of the forest before you study the trees: sexual anatomy and physiology (the "plumbing" part), and sexual behavior (the "people" part), which are discussed in later chapters. But first we must draw an important distinction, between sex and gender.

Sex and Gender

Sometimes the word *sex* is used ambiguously. In some cases it refers to being male or female, and sometimes it refers to sexual behavior or reproduction. In

Gender: The state of being male or female.

most cases, of course, the meaning is clear from the context. If you are filling out a job application form and one item says, "Sex:," you don't write, "I like it" or "As often as possible." It is clear that your prospective employer wants to know whether you are a male or a female. In other cases, though, the meaning may be ambiguous. For example, when a book has the title *Sex and Temperament in Three Primitive Societies,* what is it about? Is it about the sexual practices of primitive people and whether having sex frequently gives them pleasant temperaments? Or is it about the kinds of personalities that males and females are expected to have in those societies? Not only does this use of *sex* create ambiguities, but it also clouds our thinking about some important issues.

To remove—or at least reduce—this ambiguity, the term *sex* will be used in this book in contexts referring to sexual anatomy and sexual behavior, and the term **gender** will be used to refer to the state of being male or female.

This is a book about sex, not gender; it is about sexual behavior and the biological, psychological, and social forces that influence it. Of course, although we are arguing that sex and gender are conceptually different, we would not try to argue that they are totally independent of each other. Certainly gender roles—the ways in which males and females are expected to behave—exert a powerful influence on the way people behave sexually, and so one chapter will be devoted to gender roles and their effects on sexuality.

How should we define *sex,* aside from saying that it is different from *gender*? A biologist might define sexual behavior as "any behavior that increases the likelihood of gametic union [union of sperm and egg]" (Bermant & Davidson, 1974).

This definition emphasizes the reproductive function of sex. However, particularly in the last few decades, medical advances such as the birth control pill have been developed that allow us to separate reproduction from sex. Most Americans now use sex not only for procreation but also for recreation.[1]

The noted sex researcher Alfred Kinsey defined *sex* as behavior that leads to orgasm. Although this definition has some merits (it does not imply that sex must be associated with reproduction), it also presents some problems. If a wife has intercourse with her husband but does not have an orgasm, was that not sexual behavior for her?

To try to avoid some of these problems, **sexual behavior** will be defined in this book as *behavior that produces arousal and increases the chance of orgasm*.[2]

The History of Understanding Sexuality: Religion and Science

Religion

Throughout most of recorded history, at least until about 100 years ago, religion (and rumor) provided most of the information that people had about sexuality. Thus, the ancient Greeks openly acknowledged both heterosexuality and homosexuality in their society and explained the existence of the two in a myth in which the original humans were double creatures with twice the normal number of limbs and organs; some were double males, some were double females, and some were half male and half female (LeVay, 1996). The gods, fearing the power of these creatures, split them in half, and forever after each one continued to search for its missing half. Heterosexuals

were thought to have resulted from the splitting of the half male, half female; male homosexuals, from the splitting of the double male; and female homosexuals, from the splitting of the double female. It was through this mythology that the ancient Greeks understood sexual orientation and sexual desire.

Fifteenth-century Christians believed that "wet dreams" (nocturnal emissions) resulted from intercourse with tiny spiritual creatures called *incubi* and *succubi,* a notion put forth in a papal bull of 1484 and a companion book, the *Malleus Maleficarum* ("witch's hammer"); the person who had wet dreams was considered guilty of sodomy (see Chapter 19) as well as witchcraft.

Over the centuries, Muslims have believed that sexual intercourse is one of the finest pleasures of life, reflecting the teachings of the great prophet Muhammad.

People of different religions hold different understandings of human sexuality, and these religious views often have a profound impact. A detailed discussion of religion and sexuality is provided in Chapter 19.

Science

It was against this background of religious understandings of sexuality that the scientific study of sex began in the nineteenth century, although, of course, religious notions continue to influence our ideas about sexuality. In addition, the groundwork for an understanding of the biological aspects of sexuality had already been laid by the research of physicians and biologists. The Dutch microscopist Anton van Leeuwenhoek (1632–1723) had discovered sperm swimming in human semen. In 1875 Oskar Hertwig (1849–1922) first observed the actual fertilization of the egg by the sperm in sea urchins, although the ovum in humans was not directly observed until the twentieth century.

A major advance in the scientific understanding of the psychological aspects of human sexuality came with the work of the Viennese physician Sigmund Freud (1856–1939), founder of psychiatry and psychoanalysis. His ideas are discussed in detail in Chapter 2.

It is important to recognize the cultural context in which Freud and the other early sex researchers crafted their research and writing. They began their work in the Victorian era, the late 1800s, both in the United States and in Europe. Norms about sexuality were extraordinarily rigid and oppressive. Historian Peter Gay

[1]Actually, even in former times sex was not always associated with reproduction. For example, a man in 1850 might have fathered 10 children; using a very conservative estimate that he engaged in sexual intercourse 1,500 times during his adult life (once a week for the 30 years from age 20 to age 50), one concludes that only 10 in 1,500 of those acts, or less than 1 percent, resulted in reproduction.

[2]This definition, though an improvement over some, still has its problems. For example, consider a woman who feels no arousal at all during intercourse. According to the definition, intercourse would not be sexual behavior for her. However, intercourse would generally be something we would want to classify as sexual behavior. It should be clear that defining *sexual behavior* is difficult.

Sexual behavior: Behavior that produces arousal and increases the chance of orgasm.

(a)

(b)

Figure 1.1   Two important early sex researchers. (*a*) Sigmund Freud. (*b*) Henry Havelock Ellis.

characterized this repressive aspect of Victorian cultural norms as

> a devious and insincere world in which middle-class husbands slaked their lust by keeping mistresses, frequenting prostitutes, or molesting children, while their wives, timid, dutiful, obedient, were sexually anesthetic and poured all their capacity for love into their housekeeping and their child-rearing. (Gay, 1984, p. 6)

Certainly traces of these Victorian attitudes remain with us today. Yet at the same time the actual sexual behavior of Victorians was sometimes in violation of societal norms (see Focus: Milestones in Sex Research, p. 6). In his history of sexuality in the Victorian era, Gay documented the story of Mabel Loomis Todd, who, though married, carried on a lengthy affair with Austin Dickinson, a community leader in Amherst, Massachusetts. Many people actually knew about the "secret" affair, yet Mrs. Loomis did not become an outcast (Gay, 1984). Doubtless, this wide discrepancy between Victorian sexual norms and actual behavior created a great deal of personal tension. That tension probably propelled a good many people into Dr. Freud's office, providing data for his theory, which emphasizes sexual tensions and conflict.

An equally great—though not so well known—early contributor to the scientific study of sex was Henry Havelock Ellis (1859–1939). A physician in Victorian England, he compiled a vast collection of information on sexuality—including medical and anthropological findings, as well as case histories—which was published in a series of volumes entitled *Studies in the Psychology of Sex* beginning in 1896. Havelock Ellis was a remarkably objective and tolerant scholar, particularly for his era. He believed that women, like men, are sexual creatures. A sexual reformer, he believed that sexual deviations from the norm are often harmless, and he urged society to accept them. In his desire to collect information about human sexuality rather than to make judgments about it, he can be considered the forerunner of modern sex research (for his autobiography, see Ellis, 1939; numerous biographies exist).

Another important figure in nineteenth-century sex research was the psychiatrist Richard von Krafft-Ebing (1840–1902). His special interest was "pathological" sexuality. He managed to collect more than 200 case histories of pathological individuals, which appeared in his book entitled *Psychopathia Sexualis*. His work tended to be neither objective nor tolerant. Nonetheless, it has had a

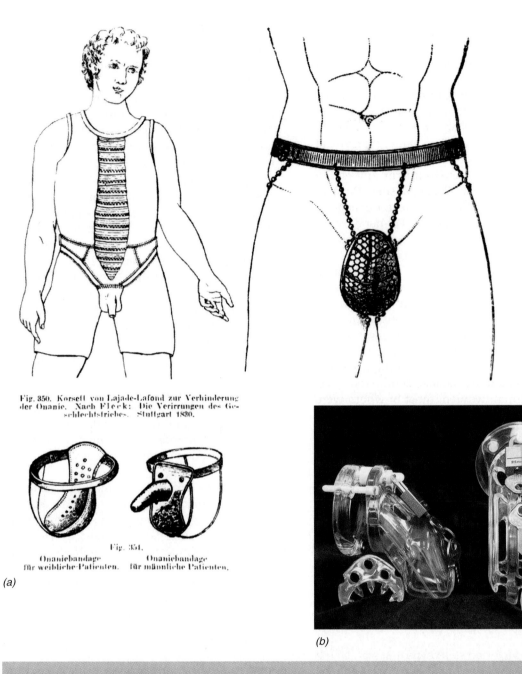

Fig. 350. Korsett von Lajade-Lafond zur Verhinderung der Onanie. Nach Fleck: Die Verirrungen des Geschlechtstriebes. Stuttgart 1830.

Fig. 351.

Onaniebandage für weibliche Patienten.   Onaniebandage für männliche Patienten.

(a)

(b)

Figure 1.2 Devices designed to prevent masturbation. (*a*) The Victorian era, from which Freud and Ellis emerged, was characterized by extreme sexual repression. Here are some apparatuses that were sold to prevent onanism (masturbation). (*b*) Are things so different today? Here are current devices for sale on the Web, for the same purpose.

lasting impact. He coined the concepts of sadism, masochism, and pedophilia, and the terms *heterosexuality* and *homosexuality* entered the English language in the 1892 translation of his book (Oosterhuis, 2000). One of his case histories is presented in Chapter 14.

One other early contributor to the scientific understanding of sexuality deserves mention, the German Magnus Hirschfeld (1868–1935). He founded the first sex research institute and administered the first large-scale sex survey, obtaining data from 10,000 people on a 130-item questionnaire. (Unfortunately, most of the information he amassed was destroyed by the Nazis.) Hirschfeld also established the first journal devoted to the study of sex, established a marriage counseling

Focus: Milestones in Sex Research
A Victorian Sex Survey

In the late 1800s Queen Victoria reigned in England, and both there and in the United States the ideal was to repress sexuality as much as possible. Women, particularly, were to have no sexual desires. Standards of modesty were so great that pianos had "limbs" rather than vulgar "legs."

Out of the Victorian environment emerged a remarkable woman, Dr. Clelia Mosher. Born in Albany, New York, in 1863, she began college at Wellesley and finished at Stanford. For her master's degree from Stanford, she collected data to debunk a popular myth of the time: that women could breathe only high in the chest, whereas men breathed deeply. Mosher concluded, quite reasonably, that any differences resulted purely from women being laced into tight-fitting corsets. Mosher began medical school at Johns Hopkins when she was 32 and earned her M.D. degree four years later.

Over a period of 30 years, beginning when she was an undergraduate, Mosher conducted a sex survey of Victorian women, most of whom were born around the time of the Civil War. In all, she administered her nine-page questionnaire to 47 women. (This sample was, admittedly, small and nonrandom; the criteria for valid survey research are discussed in Chapter 3.) Many of the women were faculty wives at universities, or women from Mosher's medical practice, and surely they were a select sample to agree to answer the questions; 81 percent had attended college, a high level of education for women in those days. Nonetheless, the survey is remarkable because—despite the accepted ideas about Victorian women—this is the only actual survey of them known to exist. Here are some interesting findings from the study:

- Despite the Victorian stereotype that women felt no sexual desire, 80 percent of the women who answered the question said that they felt a desire for sexual intercourse.

- Thirty-four of the women (72 percent) indicated that they experienced orgasm. Interestingly, Mosher worded the question "Do you always have a venereal orgasm?" thus assuming that orgasm was to be expected.

- Mosher suspected that women's relative slowness at reaching orgasm might be a cause of marital conflicts. Many of her respondents supported this idea. One said that sex had been unpleasant to her for years because of her "slow reaction," but "orgasm [occurs] if time is taken." Another complained that "men have not been properly trained." And for some, not reaching orgasm was psychologically devastating (one can't help thinking that things haven't changed so much from the 1890s to the present).

- At least 30 of the women (64 percent) used some form of birth control. Douching was the most popular method, followed by withdrawal and "timing." Several women's husbands used a "male sheath," and two women used a "rubber cap over the uterus." One woman used cocoa butter. She did not explain how or why.

Clelia Mosher's survey is fascinating because it demonstrates that despite the Victorian era's repressive teachings, some women still managed to enjoy sex. True, some were affected by Victorian mores; three of the women said their ideal would be to abstain from intercourse entirely. But the majority of the respondents still expressed sexual desires, experienced orgasms, and seemed to enjoy sex with their husbands.

Source: Jacob (1981).

---

service, worked for legal reforms, and gave advice on contraception and sex problems. His special interest, however, was homosexuality. Doubtless some of his avant-garde approaches resulted from the fact that he was himself both homosexual and a transvestite. His contributions as a pioneer sex researcher cannot be denied (Bullough, 1994).

In the twentieth century, major breakthroughs in the scientific understanding of sex came with the massive surveys of human sexual behavior in the United States conducted by Alfred Kinsey and his colleagues in the 1940s and with Masters and Johnson's investigations of sexual disorders and the physiology of sexual response. At about the same time that the Kinsey research was being conducted, some anthropologists—most notably Margaret Mead and Bronislaw Malinowski—were beginning to collect data on sexual behavior in other cultures.

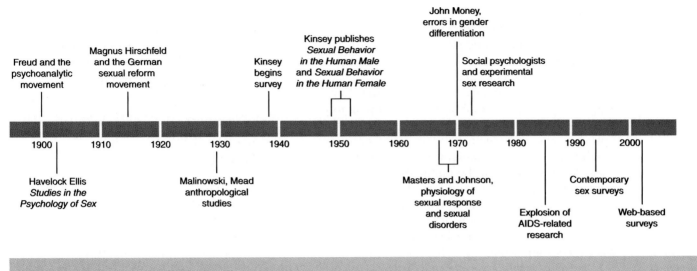

Figure 1.3   Milestones in the history of scientific research on sex.

Other, smaller investigations also provided important information. By the 1990s we had a rich array of sex research, including major national surveys (e.g., Laumann et al., 1994), detailed investigations of sexual disorders and sexual orientation, and studies of the biological processes underlying sexual response.

The scientific study of sex has not emerged as a separate, unified academic discipline like biology or psychology or sociology. Rather, it tends to be interdisciplinary—a joint effort by biologists, psychologists, sociologists, anthropologists, and physicians (see Figure 1.3). This approach to understanding sexuality gives us a better view of humans in all their sexual complexity.

STD (sexually transmitted disease) prevention and pregnancy prevention—are rare. Only 2 percent of sexual scenes portray any sexual precautions (Kunkel et al., 2005).

In short, the average American's views about sexuality are likely to be much more influenced by the mass media than by scientific findings. Communications theorists believe that the media can have three types of influence (Brown, 2002). The first, called **cultivation,** refers to the notion that people begin to think that what they see on television and in

> **Cultivation:** In communications theory, the view that exposure to the mass media makes people think that what they see there represents the mainstream of what really occurs.

The Media

In terms of potency of influence, the mass media in America today may play the same role that religion did in previous centuries. American children spend 6 to 7 hours per day with some form of mass media (Rideout, 2005). Across a typical week in 2005, 35 percent of television programs showed some sexual behavior—ranging from kissing to intercourse—up from 23 percent in 1998 (Kunkel et al., 2005). In a study of sex on the soaps, the most frequent sexual activity was heterosexual intercourse between unmarried persons (Greenberg & Busselle, 1996)—although this pattern is far from what occurs in the real world, where marital sex is most frequent. References to safer sex—both for

Figure 1.4   Sexual portrayals in the media have become much more explicit, as in this scene from *General Hospital.*

other media really represents the mainstream of what happens in our culture (Gerbner et al., 2002). For example, college students who watch the soaps are more likely than nonviewing students to overestimate the incidence of divorce.

The second influence is **agenda setting.** News reporters select what to report and what to ignore and, within the stories they report, what to emphasize. For example, in 1998 the media chose to highlight the sexual dalliances of President Bill Clinton, suggesting to the public that these matters were important. In contrast, the illicit sexual activities of President John F. Kennedy were not revealed during his presidency. The media in many ways tell us what the agenda is to which we should pay attention.

The third influence is **social learning,** a theory we will take up in detail in Chapter 2. The contention here is that characters on television, in the movies, or in romance novels may serve as models whom we imitate, perhaps without even realizing it. Research has found, for example, that teens who watch more sexy television engage in first intercourse earlier than do other teens (Brown, 2002).

The *Internet* is the newest, and perhaps most powerful, mass media influence. Computer and Internet use is spreading more rapidly than any previous technology, and it is estimated that by 2010 most U.S. homes with children will have Internet access (Brown, 2002). In 2004, 69 percent of adults were online (Taylor, 2004). The most frequent search term on AOL for 2006 was Paris Hilton (AOL Search, 2006). As we discuss in later chapters, the Internet has the potential for both positive and negative effects on sexual health. A number of sites, such as that for the American Social Health Association, www.iwannaknow.org, provide excellent information about sexuality and promote sexual health. At the same time, a well-sampled study of youth between the ages of 10 and 17 who use the Internet regularly indicated that approximately 20 percent had received at least one sexual solicitation or approach over the Internet in the last year, and 3 percent had received an aggressive sexual solicitation, in which the initiator asked to meet the recipient somewhere or sent them money or gifts (Finkelhor et al., 2000).

In the chapters that follow, we examine the content of the media on numerous sexual issues and we

Agenda setting: In communications theory, the idea that the media define what is important and what is not by which stories they cover.
Social learning: In communications theory, the idea that the media provide role models whom we imitate.
Culture: Traditional ideas and values passed down from generation to generation within a group and transmitted to members of the group by symbols (such as language).
Ethnocentrism: The tendency to regard one's own ethnic group and culture as superior to others and to believe that its customs and way of life are the standards by which other cultures should be judged.
Incest taboo: A regulation prohibiting sexual interaction between blood relatives, such as brother and sister or father and daughter.

consider what the effects of exposure to this media content might have on viewers.

Let us now consider the perspectives on sexuality that are provided by scientific observations of humans in a wide variety of societies.

Cross-Cultural Perspectives on Sexuality

Humans are a cultural species (Heine & Norenzayan, 2006). Although some other species are capable of learning from others, humans are unique in the way that cultural learning accumulates over time. What do anthropologists mean by the term *culture*? Generally, **culture** refers to traditional (that is, passed down from generation to generation) ideas and values transmitted to members of the group by symbols (such as language). These ideas and values then serve as the basis for patterns of behavior observed in the group (Frayser, 2004; Kroeber & Kluckhohn, 1963).

Ethnocentrism tends to influence our understanding of human sexual behavior. Most of us have had experience with sexuality in only one culture—the United States, for example—and we tend to view our sexual behavior as the only pattern in existence, and certainly as the only "natural" pattern. But anthropologists have discovered that there are wide variations in sexual behavior and attitudes from one culture to the next. Considering these variations should help us to put our own sexual behavior in perspective.

The major generalization that emerges from cross-cultural studies is that all societies regulate sexual behavior in some way, though the exact regulations vary greatly from one culture to the next (DeLamater, 1987). Apparently no society has seen fit to leave sexuality totally unregulated, perhaps fearful that social disruption would result. As an example, **incest taboos** are nearly universal: Sex is regulated in that intercourse between blood relatives is prohibited (Gregersen, 1996). Most societies also condemn forced sexual relations such as rape.

Beyond this generalization, though, regulations vary greatly from one society to the next, and sexual behavior and attitudes vary correspondingly (see Focus: A Sexually Diverse World, p. 10). Let's look at the ways in which various societies treat some key areas of human sexual behavior.

Variations in Sexual Techniques
Kissing is one of the most common sexual techniques in our culture. It is also very common in

Figure 1.5 Margaret Mead, an anthropologist who contributed much to the early cross-cultural study of sexuality.

most other societies (Gregersen, 1996). There are a few societies, though, in which kissing is unknown. For example, when the Thonga of Africa first saw Europeans kissing, they laughed and said, "Look at them; they eat each other's saliva and dirt." There is also some variation in techniques of kissing. For example, among the Kwakiutl of Canada and the Trobriand Islanders, kissing consists of sucking the lips and tongue of the partner, permitting saliva to flow from one mouth to the other. Many Americans might find such a practice somewhat repulsive, but other peoples find it sexually arousing.

Cunnilingus (mouth stimulation of the female genitals) is fairly common in our society, and it occurs in a few other societies as well, especially in the South Pacific. A particularly interesting variation is reported on the island of Ponape; the man places a fish in the woman's vulva and then gradually licks it out prior to coitus.

Inflicting pain on the partner is also a part of the sexual technique in some societies. The Apinaye woman of the Brazilian highlands may bite off bits of her partner's eyebrows, noisily spitting them aside. Ponapean men usually tug at the woman's eyebrows, occasionally yanking out tufts of hair. People of various societies bite their partners to the point of drawing blood and leaving scars; most commonly, men and women mutually inflict pain on each other (Frayser, 1985).

The frequency of intercourse for married couples varies considerably from one culture to the next. The lowest frequency seems to be among the Irish natives of Inis Beag, discussed in Focus: A Sexually Diverse World on page 10, who engage in intercourse perhaps only once or twice a month; however, the anthropologists who studied them were unable to determine exactly how often couples did have sex because so much secrecy surrounds the act. At the opposite extreme, the Mangaians (described in Focus: A Sexually Diverse World on p. 10) have intercourse several times a night, at least among the young. The Santals of southern Asia copulate as often as five times per day every day early in marriage (Gregersen, 1996). Surveys of U.S. sexuality in the 1990s indicated that our frequency of intercourse was then about in the middle compared with other societies (e.g., Laumann et al., 1994).

Very few societies encourage people to engage in sexual intercourse at particular times (Frayser, 1985). Instead, most groups have restrictions that forbid intercourse at certain times or in certain situations. For example, almost every society has a postpartum sex taboo, that is, a prohibition on sexual intercourse for a period of time after a woman has given birth, with the taboo lasting from a few days to more than a year (Gregersen, 1996).

Masturbation

Attitudes toward **masturbation,** or sexual self-stimulation of the genitals, vary widely across cultures. Some societies tolerate or even encourage masturbation during childhood and adolescence, whereas others condemn the practice at any age. Almost all human societies express some disapproval of adult masturbation, ranging from mild ridicule to severe punishment (Gregersen, 1996). However, at least some adults in all societies appear to practice it.

Female masturbation certainly occurs in other societies. The African Azande woman uses a phallus made of a wooden root; however, if her husband catches her masturbating, he may beat her severely. The following is a description of the Lesu of the South Pacific, one of the few societies that express no disapproval of adult female masturbation:

A woman will masturbate if she is sexually excited and there is no man to satisfy her. A couple may

Masturbation: Self-stimulation of the genitals to produce sexual arousal.

Focus: A Sexually Diverse World
Sexuality in Three Societies

Inis Beag

Inis Beag is a small island off the coast of Ireland. It is probably one of the most naive and sexually repressive societies in the world.

The people of Inis Beag seem to have no knowledge of a number of sexual activities such as French kissing, mouth stimulation of the breast, or hand stimulation of the partner's penis, much less oral sex or homosexuality. Sex education is virtually nonexistent; parents do not seem to be able to bring themselves to discuss such embarrassing matters with their children, and they simply trust that, after marriage, nature will take its course.

Menstruation and menopause are sources of fear for the island women because they have no idea of their physiological significance. It is commonly believed that menopause can produce insanity; in order to ward off this condition, some women have retired from life in their mid-forties, and a few have confined themselves to bed until death years later.

The men believe that intercourse is hard on one's health. They will desist from sex the night before they are to do a job that takes great energy. They do not approach women sexually during menstruation or for months after childbirth; a woman is considered dangerous to the man at these times.

The islanders abhor nudity. Only babies are allowed to bathe while nude. Adults wash only the parts of their bodies that extend beyond their clothing—face, neck, lower arms, hands, lower legs, and feet. The fear of nudity has even cost lives. Sailors who never learned to swim because it involved wearing scanty clothing drowned when their ships sank.

Premarital sex is essentially unknown. In marital sex, foreplay is generally limited to kissing and rough fondling of the buttocks. The husband invariably initiates the activity. The male-on-top is the only position used, and both partners keep their underwear on during the activity. The man has an orgasm quickly and falls asleep immediately. Female orgasm either is believed not to exist or is considered deviant.

Mangaia

In distinct contrast to Inis Beag is Mangaia, an island in the South Pacific. For the Mangaians, sex—for pleasure and for procreation—is a principal interest.

The Mangaian boy first hears of masturbation when he is about 7, and he may begin to masturbate at age 8 or 9. At around age 13 he undergoes the superincision ritual (in which a slit is made on the top of the penis, along its entire length). This ritual initiates him into manhood; more important,

be having intercourse in the same house, or near enough for her to see them, and she may thus become aroused. She then sits down and bends her right leg so that her heel presses against her genitalia. Even young girls of about six years may do this quite casually as they sit on the ground. The women and men talk about it freely, and there is no shame attached to it. It is a customary position for women to take, and they learn it in childhood. They never use their hands for manipulation. (Powdermaker, 1933, pp. 276–277)

Premarital and Extramarital Sex

Societies differ considerably in their rules regarding premarital sex (Frayser, 1985). At one extreme are the Marquesans of eastern Polynesia. Both boys and girls in that culture have participated in a wide range of sexual experiences before puberty. Their first experience with intercourse occurs with a heterosexual partner who is 30 to 40

years old. Mothers are proud if their daughters have many lovers. Only later does marriage occur. In contrast are the Egyptians of Siwa. In this culture a girl's clitoris is removed at age 7 or 8 in order to decrease her potential for sexual excitement and intercourse. Premarital intercourse is believed to bring shame on the family. Marriage usually occurs around the age of 12 or 13, shortening the premarital period and any temptations it might contain.

These two cultures are fairly typical of their regions. According to one study, 90 percent of Pacific Island societies permit premarital sex, as do 88 percent of African and 82 percent of Eurasian societies; however, 73 percent of Mediterranean societies prohibit premarital sex (Frayser, 1985).

Extramarital sex is complex and conflicted for most cultures. Extramarital sex ranks second only to incest as the most strictly prohibited type of sexual contact. One study found that it was forbidden for

however, the expert who performs the superincision gives him sexual instruction. He shows the boy how to perform oral sex, how to kiss and suck breasts, and how to bring his partner to orgasm several times before he has his own. About two weeks after the operation, the boy has intercourse with an experienced woman, which removes the superincision's scab. She provides him with practice in various acts and positions and trains him to hold back until he can have simultaneous orgasms with his partner.

After this, the Mangaian boy actively seeks out girls, or they seek him out; soon he has coitus every night. The girl, who has received sexual instruction from an older woman, expects demonstration of the boy's virility as proof of his desire for her. What is valued is the ability of the male to continue vigorously the in-and-out action of coitus over long periods of time while the female moves her hips "like a washing machine." Nothing is despised more than a "dead" partner who does not move. A good man is expected to continue his actions for 15 to 30 minutes or more.

The average "nice" girl will have three or four successive boyfriends between the ages of 13 and 20; the average boy may have 10 or more girlfriends. Mangaian parents encourage their daughters to have sexual experiences with several men. They want them to find marriage partners who are congenial.

At around age 18, the Mangaians typically have sex most nights of the week, with about three orgasms per night. By about age 48, they have sex two or three times per week, with one orgasm each time.

All women in Mangaia apparently learn to have orgasms. Bringing his partner to orgasm is one of the man's chief sources of sexual pleasure.

Mehinaku

Between Inis Beag, where there is little sex and plenty of anxiety, and Mangaia, where there is plenty of sex and little anxiety, is Mehinaku, where there is plenty of sex and plenty of anxiety.

In the central Brazilian village of Mehinaku, sex is believed to be very fascinating and the culture is highly eroticized. There is an openness with children about sex, and children can easily list the names of their parents' extramarital lovers, who are typically many. The men have a very high libido, leading them to compete with each other for women's sexual favors by bringing small gifts such as fish.

On the other hand, the culture is very gender-segregated. There is a men's house, and if a woman enters it and sees what she is forbidden to see, she is taken to the woods and gang raped, in a culture that is otherwise very nonviolent. Mehinaku women are believed to have a much weaker sex drive than men, and there seems to be no recognition of female orgasm. Women's menstruation is believed to be dangerous.

The dreams and mythic stories told by the people testify to their sexual anxieties—for example, those in myths who engage in extramarital sex typically die in fantastic ways. In reality, the people continue with a great deal of sexual activity while feeling intense ambivalence and anxiety about it.

Sources: Gregor (1985); Marshall (1971); Messenger (1993).

---

one or both partners in 74 percent of the cultures surveyed (Frayser, 1985). Even when extramarital sex is permitted, it is subjected to regulations; the most common pattern of restriction is to allow extramarital sex for husbands but not wives.

Sex with Same-Gender Partners

A wide range of attitudes toward same-gender sexual expression—what we in the United States call *homosexuality*—exists in various cultures (Murray, 2000). At one extreme are societies that strongly disapprove of same-gender sexual behavior for people of any age. In contrast, some societies tolerate the behavior for children but disapprove of it in adults. Still other societies actively encourage all their male members to engage in some same-gender sexual behavior, usually in conjunction with puberty rites (Herdt, 1984). A few societies have a formalized role for the adult gay man that gives him status and dignity.

While there is wide variation in attitudes toward homosexuality and in same-gender sexual behavior, three general rules do seem to emerge (Ford & Beach, 1951; Murray, 2000; Whitam, 1983): (1) No matter how a particular society treats homosexuality, the behavior always occurs in at least some individuals—that is, same-gender sexuality is found universally in all societies; (2) males are more likely to engage in same-gender sexual behavior than females; and (3) same-gender sexual behavior is never the predominant form of sexual behavior for adults in any of the societies studied.

In the United States and other Western nations, we hold an unquestioned assumption that people have a sexual identity, whether gay, lesbian, bisexual, or heterosexual. Yet sexual identity as an unvarying, lifelong characteristic of the self is unknown or rare in some cultures, such as Indonesia (Stevenson, 1995). In those cultures the self and individualism, so prominent in American culture,

(a)   (b)

Figure 1.6 Cross-cultural differences, cross-cultural similarities. *(a)* Woman of West Africa. *(b)* North American beauty queen. The custom of female adornment is found in most cultures, although the exact definition of beauty varies from culture to culture.

SexSource Online
www.mhhe.com/hyde10

"BEAUTIFUL" IN
PERSPECTIVES ON
SEXUALITY

are downplayed. Instead, a person is defined in relation to others and behavior is seen as much more the product of the situation than of lifelong personality traits. In such a culture, having a "gay identity" just doesn't compute.

Sex with same-gender partners is discussed in detail in Chapter 13.

Standards of Attractiveness

In all human societies physical characteristics are important in determining whom one chooses as a sex partner. What is considered attractive varies considerably, though. For example, the region of the body that is judged for attractiveness varies from one culture to the next. For some peoples, the shape and color of the eyes are especially significant. For others, the shape of the ears is most important. Some societies go directly to the heart of the matter and judge attractiveness by the appearance of the external genitals. In a few societies, elongated labia majora (the

pads of fat on either side of the vaginal opening in women) are considered sexually attractive, and it is common practice for a woman to pull on hers in order to make them longer. Among the Nawa women of Africa, elongated labia majora are considered a mark of beauty and are quite prominent.

Our society's standards are in the minority in one way: In most cultures, a plump woman is considered more attractive than a thin one.

One standard does seem to be a general rule: A poor complexion is considered unattractive in the majority of human societies.

Research on sexual attraction is discussed in detail in Chapter 11.

Social-Class and Ethnic-Group Variations in the United States

The discussion so far may have seemed to imply that there is one uniform standard of sexual behavior in the United States and that all Americans

Table 1.1 Social-Class Variations in Sexual Behavior in the United States (education is used as an indicator of social class)

	Less than High School	High School Graduates	Some College	College Graduates	Graduate Degree
Percent who masturbated in last year					
Men	45%	55%	67%	76%	81%
Women	25	32	49	52	59
Percent who have performed oral sex					
Men	59	75	80	84	81
Women	41	60	78	79	79
Percent of conceptions terminated					
by abortion	5	10	11	11	14
Percent who have had two or more sexual					
partners in the last 12 months	17	15	18	19	13

Source: Laumann et al. (1994), Table 3.1 (p. 82), Table 3.6 (p. 98), Table 12.6A (p. 458), Table 5.1A (p. 177).

behave alike sexually. In fact, though, there are large variations in sexual behavior within our culture. Some of these subcultural variations can be classified as social-class differences and some as ethnic differences.

Social Class and Sex

Table 1.1 shows data on some social-class variations in sexuality. Education is used as an indicator of social class. The more educated the respondents, the more likely they are to have masturbated within the last year. This trend is true for both men and women, and the differences are large. Those who have advanced degrees are approximately twice as likely to have masturbated as those who did not finish high school.

The pattern for oral sex is different. Among men there are no important social-class variations, except that those who did not graduate from high school are less likely to have performed oral sex. Oral sex has become a standard sexual technique in the United States, and about three-quarters of all people engage in it. Most of those who don't are in the lowest educational groups.

Among women, the percentage of conceptions that are terminated by abortion rises steadily from 5 percent for those who did not complete high school to 14 percent for those who hold advanced degrees. These findings raise the possibility that, especially for women, social class and sexuality exert a mutual influence on each other. That is, thus far we have assumed that one's social class affects one's sexual behavior. But it may also be true that one's sexuality influences one's social class. In this case, choosing to have an abortion may allow women to continue their education.

Finally, there are some social-class similarities. The percentage of people who have had two or more sex partners in the past 12 months (which puts them in a high-risk category for acquiring a sexually transmitted disease) is about the same at all educational levels (Table 1.1).

In summary, some social-class variations in sexuality have been found. For example, the percentage of people who masturbate rises steadily with the level of education. At the same time, there are some social-class similarities.

Ethnicity and Sexuality in the United States

The U.S. population is composed of many ethnic groups, and there are some variations among these groups in sexual behavior. These variations are a result of having different cultural heritages, as well as of current economic and social conditions. Here we discuss the cultural heritages and their influence on sexuality of five groups: African Americans, Latinos, Asian Americans, American Indians, and whites. A summary of some ethnic-group variations in sexuality is shown in Table 1.2.

In examining these data on ethnic-group variations in sexuality, it is important to keep in mind two points: (1) There are ethnic-group variations, but there are also ethnic-group similarities. The sexuality of these groups is not totally different. (2) Cultural context is the key. The sexuality of any particular group can be understood only by understanding the cultural heritage of that group as well as its current social and economic conditions. The sexuality of white Euro-Americans, for example, is influenced by the heritage of European cultures, such as the Victorian era in England. In the following sections, we briefly discuss the cultural contexts

Table 1.2 Comparison of the Sexuality of Whites, African Americans, Latinos, and Asian Americans

	Whites	African Americans	Latinos/ Latinas	Asian Americans
Sex ratio (number of males per 100 females), 30- to 34-year-olds*	100	84	104	101
Percent who masturbated in the last year				
Men	67%	40%	67%	61%
Women	44	32	35	NA†
Percent who have performed oral sex				
Men	81	51	71	64
Women	75	34	60	NA†
Percent of 30- to 34-year-olds who have never been married*				
Men	28	46	29	30
Women	18	44	18	23
Percent of conceptions terminated by abortion	10	9	11	21
Had sex with a same-gender partner				
Men	10	8	8	3
Women	5	3	4	0
Percent who have had two or more sexual partners in the last 12 months	15	27	20	8

*Source: U.S. Bureau of the Census (2000 a, b).

†Not available, because the number of respondents in this category was too small for statistics to be computed.

Source: Laumann et al. (1994), Table 3.6 (p. 98), Table 12.6A (p. 458), Table 8.2 (p. 305), Table 5.1A (p. 177).

for African Americans, Latinos, Asian Americans, and American Indians and examine how these cultural contexts are reflected in their sexuality.

African Americans. The sexuality of African Americans is influenced by many of the same factors influencing the sexuality of Euro-Americans, such as the legacies of the Victorian era and the influence of the Judeo-Christian tradition. In addition, at least three other factors act to make the sexuality of Blacks somewhat different from that of whites: (1) the African heritage (Savage & Tchombe, 1994), (2) the forces that acted upon Blacks during slavery, and (3) current economic and social conditions (Sudarkasa, 1997).

Like other U.S. ethnic groups, Black Americans are not homogeneous. They vary in whether they are of Caribbean origin (Afro-Caribbeans) or are descendants of persons brought to the United States as slaves (African Americans); in whether they are rural and southern or urban; and in social class. These variations are reflected in sexual attitudes. Afro-Caribbeans emphasize sexual propriety and teach girls to be modest; this group tends to view African Americans as morally suspect and sexually undisciplined (Lewis & Kertzner, 2003; Reid & Bing, 2000).

Table 1.2 shows some data comparing the sexuality of African Americans with whites, Latinos, and Asian Americans. In some cases, differences between Blacks and whites are striking. For example, Black men are considerably less likely than white men to have masturbated in the last year, and both Black men and Black women are less likely than whites to have performed oral sex. These differences, though, must be balanced against the similarities. For example, African American women and white women are about equally likely to terminate a conception with an abortion.

Notice that the marriage rate is lower for African Americans than for other groups. This is due to a number of factors. First, there is not an equal gender ratio among Blacks. As shown in Table 1.2, the gender ratio is nearly equal among whites, Asian Americans, and Latinos; that is, there are about 100 men for every 100 women. Among African Americans, however, there are only about 84 men for every 100 women. This creates lower marriage rates among African American women because there are simply not enough Black men to go around [among both Blacks and whites, 98 percent of marriages are between two people of the same race (Thornton & Wason, 1995)]. Second, lower marriage rates among African American men are also due to the obstacles that they have encountered in seeking and maintaining the jobs necessary to support a family. Since World War II, the number of manufacturing jobs, which once were a major source of employment for working-class Black men, has declined dramatically. The result has been a decline in the Black working class and an expansion of the Black underclass.

In later chapters, we discuss other issues having to do with race/ethnicity and sexuality, always bearing in mind the cultural context that shapes and gives meaning to different sexual patterns.

Latinos.   **Latinos** are people of Latin American heritage; therefore, the category includes many different cultural groups, such as Mexican Americans, Puerto Ricans, and Cuban Americans. *Latinos* can refer to the entire group or specifically to men; the term *Latinas* refers exclusively to women of Latin American origin.

Latinos have a cultural heritage distinct from that of both African Americans and Anglos, although forces such as the Judeo-Christian religious tradition affect all three groups. In traditional Latin American cultures, gender roles are sharply defined (Rafaelli & Ontai, 2004). Such roles are emphasized early in the socialization process for children. Boys are given greater freedom and are encouraged in sexual exploits. Girls are expected to be passive, obedient, and weak. Latinos in the United States today have a cultural heritage that blends these traditional cultural values with the contemporary values of the dominant Anglo culture.

The gender roles of traditional Latino culture are epitomized in the concepts of *machismo* and *marianismo* (Comas-Diaz, 1987). The term *machismo,* or *macho,* has come to be used loosely in American culture today. Literally, *machismo* means "maleness" or "virility." More generally, it refers to the "mystique of manliness" (Ruth, 1990). The cultural code of *machismo* among Latin Americans mandates that the man must be responsible for the well-being and honor of his family, but in extreme forms it also means tolerating men's sexual infidelities. *Marianismo,* the female counterpart of *machismo,* derives from Roman Catholic worship of Mary, the virgin mother of Jesus. Thus, motherhood is highly valued while virginity until marriage is closely guarded. In Mexico, for example, 62 percent of males report having had premarital intercourse by age 19, compared with only 14 percent of females (Liskin, 1985).

The data in Table 1.2 reveal a striking similarity in the data for Latinos and whites. The incidence of masturbation is approximately the same for both groups, although Latinas have a slightly lower incidence than white women. Marriage rates and abortion rates are also approximately equal between the two groups.

(a)

(b)

Figure 1.7   The sexuality of members of different ethnic groups is profoundly shaped by their cultures. *(a)* Roman Catholicism has a powerful impact on Latinos. *(b)* There is strong emphasis on the family among American Indians.

Latinos: People of Latin American heritage.

Focus: A Sexually Diverse World
Sex in China

The first 4,000 years of recorded Chinese history were characterized by open, positive attitudes about human sexuality, including a rich erotic literature. Indeed, the oldest sex manuals in the world come from China, dating from approximately 200 B.C.E. The most recent 1,000 years, however, have been just the opposite, characterized by repression of sexuality and censorship.

A major philosophical concept in Chinese culture, yin and yang, originated around 300 B.C.E. and is found in important writings on Confucianism and Taoism. According to the yin-yang philosophy, all objects and events are the products of two elements: yin, which is negative, passive, weak, and destructive; and yang, which is positive, active, strong, and constructive. Yin is associated with the female, yang with the male. For several thousand years, the Chinese have used yin and yang in words dealing with sexuality. For example, *yin fu* (the door of yin) means "vulva," and *yang ju* (the organ of yang) means "penis." *Huo yin yang* (the union of yin and yang) is the term used for sexual intercourse. This philosophy holds that the harmonious interaction between the male and female principles is vital, creating positive cultural attitudes toward sexuality.

Of the three major religions of China—Confucianism, Taoism, and Buddhism—Taoism is the only truly indigenous one, dating from the writings of Chang Ling around A.D. 143. Taoism is one of the few religions to advocate the cultivation of sexual techniques for the benefit of the individual. To quote from a classic Taoist work, *The Canon of the Immaculate Girl*,

> Said P'eng, "One achieves longevity by loving the essence, cultivating the spiritual, and partaking of many kinds of medicines. If you don't know the ways of intercourse, taking herbs is of no benefit. The producing of man and woman is like the begetting of Heaven and Earth. Heaven and Earth have attained the method of intercourse and, therefore, they lack the limitation of finality. Man loses the method of intercourse and therefore suffers the mortification of early death. If you can avoid mortification and injury and attain the arts of sex, you will have found the way of nondeath." (Ruan, 1991, p. 56)

The tradition of erotic literature and openness about sexuality began to change about 1,000 years ago, led by several famous neo-Confucianists, so that negative and repressive attitudes became dominant. In 1422 there was a ban on erotic literature, and a second major ban occurred in 1664. A commoner involved in printing a banned book could be beaten and exiled.

When the communist government founded the People's Republic of China in 1949, it imposed a strict ban on all sexually explicit materials. The policy was quite effective in the 1950s and 1960s. By the late 1960s, however, erotica was being produced much more in Western nations and in China there was increased openness to the West. By the late 1970s, X-rated videotapes were being smuggled

---

Asian Americans. The broad category of Asian Americans includes many different cultural groups, such as Japanese Americans, Chinese Americans, and Indian Americans, as well as the relative newcomer groups such as Vietnamese Americans and the Hmong. As discussed in Focus: A Sexually Diverse World, above, traditional Asian cultures, such as the Chinese, have been repressive about sexuality. Traditional Cambodian society, for instance, believed that a lack of information about sexuality would prevent the premarital sex that would tarnish a family's honor (Okazaki, 2002).

Several core Asian values persist in the United States and doubtless affect sexual expression. Among the core values that are relevant to sexuality are the following (Kim et al., 2005):

1. *Collectivism.* Others' needs, especially those of the family, should be considered before one's own. Open expression of some forms of sexuality would represent a threat to the highly interdependent social structure as well as to the family (Okazaki, 2002).

2. *Conformity to norms.* The individual should conform to the expectations of the family and society. Shame and the threat of loss of face, which can apply both to the individual and to his or her family, are powerful forces shaping good behavior.

3. *Emotional control.* Emotions should not be openly expressed. Emotions such as love or passion should be muted and controlled.

Given all these forces, it is not surprising that Asian Americans today tend to be the sexual conservatives of the various ethnic groups. For example, they have the lowest incidence of multiple sexual partners

into China from Hong Kong and other countries, and they quickly became a fad. Small parties were organized around the viewing of these tapes. The government reacted harshly, promulgating a new antipornography law in 1985. According to the law, "Pornography is very harmful, poisoning people's minds, inducing crimes . . . and must be banned." (Ruan, 1991, p. 100). Publishing houses that issued pornography were given stiff fines, and by 1986, 217 illegal publishers had been arrested and 42 forced to close. In one incident, a Shanghai railway station employee was sentenced to death for having organized sex parties on nine different occasions, during which pornographic videotapes were viewed and he engaged in sexual activity with women.

Male homosexuality is recognized in historical writings in China as early as 2,000 years ago. Homosexuality was then so widespread among the upper classes that the period is known as the Golden Age of Homosexuality in China. One historical book on the Han dynasty contained a special section describing the emperors' male sexual partners. There were also tolerant attitudes toward lesbianism. But with the founding of the People's Republic in 1949, homosexuality, like all other sexuality, was severely repressed. Most Chinese in the 1980s claimed that they had never known a homosexual and argued that there must be very few in Chinese society.

In the early 1980s, China was characterized by a puritanism that probably far exceeded that observed by the original Puritans. It was considered scandalous for a married couple to hold hands in public. Prostitution, premarital sex, homosexuality, and variant sexual behaviors were all illegal, and the laws were enforced. Even sexuality in marriage was given little encouragement.

A moderate sexual liberation began in the 1980s. Open displays of affection, such as holding hands in public, are now no longer treated as signs of promiscuity. High schools now include sex education in the curriculum. The rationale is that a scientific understanding of sexual development is essential to the healthy development of young people and to the maintenance of high moral standards and well-controlled social order. Sexual images are found today much more often in the media, although censors continue to monitor the content. There is open discussion of the importance of women's sexual pleasure.

Noted American sex researcher Edward Laumann (see Chapter 3) has extended his surveys to China, conducting a well-sampled study in 1999–2000 (Laumann & Parish, 2004). The results indicate that the liberalizing trends are occurring mainly in the larger cities, whereas the majority of Chinese live in more rural areas that are still extremely conservative. In regard to premarital sex, 72 percent of the men and 85 percent of the women in the sample said they were virgins when they first married, and strong disapproval of premarital sex continues. However, among the younger generation, rates of premarital sex are up: Some 41 percent of men and 21 percent of women in the youngest cohort reported engaging in premarital sex. These rates are still low compared with Western nations such as the United States. It will be interesting to see whether liberalization continues or an eventual swing back to repression occurs.

Sources: Evans (1995); Ruan (1991); Ruan & Lau (1998).

(see Table 1.2). A similar pattern has been documented for Asians in Canada (Meston et al., 1996).

Table 1.2 shows that Asian Americans have the lowest incidence of same-gender sexual experience. This is consistent with the widespread denial by the Chinese that homosexuality even exists in China. Moreover, it is consistent with the Asian emphasis on family, defined as a mother, father, and children. Gays and lesbians, then, are seen as violating not only a sexual norm but also the paramount cultural norm of the family.

Among the ethnic groups shown in Table 1.2, Asian Americans have the highest rate of terminating conceptions by abortion. Again, this is consistent with cultural heritage. In China, for example, abortion is considered a reasonable backup method of birth control, the intrauterine device (IUD) being the primary method (Ruan & Lau, 1998). China's severe overpopulation problem has led to a policy of per-

mitting only one child per family, and the survival of all Chinese is thought to rest on everyone's complying with this policy. Under these circumstances, abortion is considered ethical and, in fact, desirable in order to avoid mass starvation. In addition, most Asians are not Christian and therefore are not part of that religious tradition, which in some quarters questions the morality of abortion. In this context it is not surprising that Asian Americans, the largest subgroup of whom are Chinese Americans, are more accepting of abortion than are other ethnic groups.

American Indians. American Indians, like other U.S. ethnic groups, are diverse among themselves, as a result of the different heritages of more than 500 tribes, such as the Navajo, Hurons, Mohicans, and Cheyenne. In addition, there are distinctions between those who are city dwellers and those who live on reservations (Tafoya, 1989; Weaver, 1999).

The popular media over the last century have portrayed American Indian men as noble savages who are both exotic and erotic (Bird, 1999). They have been shown nearly naked, emphasizing well-developed masculine bodies. In romance novels of the 1990s, American Indian males became cultural icons for vanishing standards of masculinity. They are handsome and virile, yet tender and vulnerable, and magnificent lovers for white women (Van Lent, 1996).

American Indian women have been less visible in the popular media. When present, they are stereotyped as princesses or squaws (Bird, 1999). The princess is noble, beautiful, and erotic. The Disney animated film *Pocahontas* features such a voluptuous princess. The stereotypical squaw, in contrast, is unattractive, uninteresting, and ignored.

Unfortunately, the major national sex surveys such as that from which Table 1.2 was drawn have had such small samples of American Indians that they have not been able to report reliable statistics for this group.

The Significance of Cross-Cultural Studies

What relevance do cross-cultural data have to an understanding of human sexuality? They are important for two basic reasons. First, they give us a notion of the enormous variation that exists in human sexual behavior, and they help us put our own standards and behavior in perspective. Second, these studies provide impressive evidence concerning the importance of culture and learning in the shaping of our sexual behavior; they show us that human sexual behavior is not completely determined by biology or drives or instincts. For example, a woman of Inis Beag and a woman of Mangaia presumably have vaginas that are similarly constructed and clitorises that are approximately the same size and have the same nerve supply. But the woman of Inis Beag never has an orgasm, and all Mangaian women orgasm.[3] Why? Their cultures are different, and they and their partners learned different things about sex as they were growing up. Culture is a major determinant of human sexual behavior.

The point of studying sexuality in different cultures is *not* to teach that there are a lot of exotic people out there doing exotic things. Rather, the point is to remind ourselves that each group has its own culture, and this culture has a profound influence on the sexual expression of the women and men who grow up in it. We offer more examples in many of the chapters that follow.

Cross-Species Perspectives on Sexuality

Humans are just one of many animal species, and all of them display sexual behavior. To put our own sexual behavior in evolutionary perspective, it is helpful to explore the similarities and differences between our own sexuality and that of other species.

There is one other reason for this particular discussion. Some people classify sexual behaviors as "natural" or "unnatural," depending on whether other species do or do not exhibit those behaviors. Sometimes, though, the data are twisted to suit the purposes of the person making the argument, and so there is a need for a less biased view. Let's see exactly what some other species do.

Masturbation

Humans are definitely not the only species that masturbates. Masturbation is found among many species of mammals, particularly among the primates (monkeys and apes). Male monkeys and apes in zoos can be observed masturbating, often to the horror of the proper folk who have come to see them. At one time it was thought that this behavior might be the result of the unnatural living conditions of zoos. However, observations of free-living primates indicate that they, too, masturbate. Techniques include hand stimulation of the genitals or rubbing the genitals against an object. In terms of technique, monkeys and nonhuman apes have one advantage over humans: Their bodies are so flexible that they can perform mouth-genital sex on themselves. A unique form of male masturbation is found among red deer; during the rutting season they move the tips of their antlers through low-growing vegetation, producing erection and ejaculation (Beach, 1976).

Female masturbation is also found among many species besides our own. The prize for the most inventive technique probably should go to the female porcupine. She holds one end of a stick in her paws and walks around while straddling the stick; as the stick bumps against the ground, it vibrates against her genitals (Ford & Beach, 1951). Human females are apparently not the only ones to enjoy vibrators.

---

[3]We like to use the word *orgasm* not only as a noun but also as a verb. The reason is that alternative expressions, such as "to *achieve* orgasm" and "to *reach* orgasm," reflect the tendency of Americans to make sex an achievement situation (an idea to be discussed further in Chapter 8). To avoid this, we use "to have an orgasm" or "to orgasm."

Same-Gender Sexual Behavior

Same-gender behavior is found in many species besides our own (Bagemihl, 1999; Vasey, 2002a; Wallen & Parsons, 1997). Indeed, observations of other species indicate that our basic mammalian heritage is bisexual, composed of both heterosexual and homosexual elements (Bagemihl, 1999).

Males of many species will mount other males, and anal intercourse has been observed in some male primates (Wallen & Parsons, 1997). Among domestic sheep, 9 percent of adult males strongly prefer other males as sex partners (Ellis, 1996; Roselli et al., 2002). In a number of primate species, including bonobos and Japanese macaques, females mount other females (Vasey et al., 2006).

Sexual Signaling

Female primates engage in sexual signaling to males, in effect, flirting (Dixson, 1990). For example, females in one species of macaque engage in parading in front of males to signal their interest. Among baboons, spider monkeys, and orangutans, the female makes eye contact with the male. The female patas monkey puffs out her cheeks and drools. The parading and eye contact sound very familiar—they could easily be observed among women at a singles bar. The puffing and drooling probably wouldn't play as well, though.

Human Uniqueness

Are humans in any ways unique in their sexual behavior? The general trend, as we move from lower species such as fish or rodents to higher ones like primates, is for sexual behavior to be more hormonally (instinctively) controlled among the lower species and to be controlled more by the brain (and therefore by learning and social context) in the higher species (Beach, 1947; Wallen, 2001). Thus, environmental influences are much more important in shaping primate—especially human—sexual behavior than they are in shaping the sexual behavior of other species.

An illustration of this fact is provided by studies of the adult sexual behavior of animals raised in deprived environments. If mice are reared in isolation, their adult sexual behavior will nonetheless be normal (Scott, 1964). But if rhesus monkeys are reared in isolation, their adult sexual behavior is severely disturbed, to the point where they may be incapable of reproducing (Harlow et al., 1963). Thus, environmental experiences are crucial in shaping the sexual behavior of higher species, particularly humans; for us, sexual behavior is a lot more than just "doin' what comes naturally."

Female sexuality provides a particularly good illustration of the shift in hormonal control from lower to higher species. Throughout most of the

(a)

(b)

Figure 1.8 (*a*) The sexual behavior of primates: Females have various ways of expressing choice. Here a female Barbary macaque presents her sexual swelling to a male. He seems to be interested. (Photograph by Frans de Waal.) (*b*) Same-gender sexuality in animals: Two male giraffes "necking." They rub necks and become aroused. (Photograph by Stephen G. Maka.)

animal kingdom, female sexual behavior is strongly controlled by hormones. In virtually all mammals, females do not engage in sexual behavior at all except when they are in "heat" (estrus), which is a particular hormonal state. In contrast, human females are capable of engaging in sexual behavior—and actually do engage in it—during any phase of their hormonal (menstrual) cycle. Thus, the sexual behavior of the human female is not nearly as much under hormonal control as that of females of other species.

Traditionally it was thought that female orgasm is unique to humans and does not exist in other species. Then some studies found evidence of orgasm in rhesus macaques (monkeys), as indicated by the same physiological responses indicative of orgasm in human females—specifically, increased heart rate and uterine contractions (Burton, 1970; Goldfoot et al., 1980; Zumpe & Michael, 1968). Thus, humans can no longer claim to have a corner on the female orgasm market. This fact has interesting implications for understanding the evolution of sexuality. Perhaps the higher species, in which the females are not driven to sexual activity by their hormones, have the pleasure of orgasm as an incentive.

In summary, then, there is little in human sexuality that is completely unique to humans, except for elaborate, complex cultural influences. In other respects, we are on a continuum with other species.

The Nonsexual Uses of Sexual Behavior

Two male baboons are locked in combat. One begins to emerge as the victor. The other "presents" (the "female" sexual posture, in which the rump is directed toward the other and is elevated somewhat).

Two male monkeys are members of the same troop. Long ago they established which one is dominant and which subordinate. The dominant one mounts (the "male" sexual behavior) the subordinate one.

These are examples of animals sometimes using sexual behavior for nonsexual purposes (Small, 1993; Wallen & Zehr, 2004). Commonly such behavior signals the end of a fight, as in the first example. The loser indicates his surrender by presenting, and the winner signals victory by mounting. Sexual behaviors can also symbolize an animal's rank in a dominance hierarchy. Dominant animals mount subordinate ones. As another example, male squirrel monkeys sometimes use an exhibitionist display of their erect penis as part of an aggressive display

Sexual health: A state of physical, emotional, mental, and social well-being in relation to sexuality.

against another male in a phenomenon called *phallic aggression* (Wickler, 1973).

All this is perfectly obvious when we observe it in monkeys. But do humans ever use sexual behavior for nonsexual purposes? Consider the rapist, who uses sex as an expression of aggression against and power over a woman (Holmstrom & Burgess, 1980), or over another man in the case of homosexual rape. Another example is the exhibitionist, who uses the display of his erect penis to shock and frighten women, much as the male squirrel monkey uses such a display to shock and frighten his opponent. Humans also use sex for economic purposes; the best examples are male and female prostitutes.

There are also less extreme examples. Consider the couple who have a fight and then make love to signal an end to the hostilities.[4] Or consider the woman who goes to bed with an influential—though unattractive—politician because this gives her a vicarious sense of power.

You can probably think of other examples of the nonsexual use of sexual behavior. Humans, just like members of other species, can use sex for a variety of nonsexual purposes.

The Sexual Health Perspective

The important new concepts of sexual health and sexual rights provide yet another broad and thought-provoking perspective on sexuality. **Sexual health** is a social and political movement that is gaining momentum worldwide. Although many discussions of sexual health are actually about sexual disease, such as HIV infection, sexual health is a much broader concept that involves a vision of positive sexual health (Edwards & Coleman, 2004; Parker et al., 2004). The World Health Organization (WHO) definition, adopted in 2002, is as follows:

> Sexual health is a state of physical, emotional, mental and social well-being in relation to sexuality; it is not merely the absence of disease, dysfunction or infirmity. Sexual health requires a positive and respectful approach to sexuality and sexual relationships, as well as the possibility of having pleasurable and safe sexual experiences, free of coercion,

---

[4]It has been our observation that this practice may not always mean the same thing to the man and the woman. To the man it can mean that everything is fine again, but the woman can be left feeling dissatisfied and not at all convinced that the issues are resolved. Thus, this situation can be a source of miscommunication between the two.

discrimination and violence. For sexual health to be attained and maintained, the sexual rights of all persons must be respected, protected and fulfilled. (World Health Organization, 2002)

Notice that this definition includes not only sexual physical health but also sexual mental health and positive sexual relationships. Therefore, public health efforts to prevent HIV or chlamydia infection, programs to enhance romantic relationships, and activism to end discrimination and violence against gays and lesbians all fall under the umbrella of sexual health. Notice also that the definition includes both negative and positive rights. Negative rights are freedoms *from*—for example, freedom from sexual violence. Positive rights are freedoms *to*—for example, freedom to experience sexual pleasure or to express one's sexuality with same-gender partners.

With the growth of the sexual health movement, the concept of **sexual rights** has also come to center stage; in fact, the term is used in the WHO definition. The idea here is that all human beings have certain basic, inalienable rights regarding sexuality, just as in America's Declaration of Independence the writers asserted that all people have the right to life, liberty, and the pursuit of happiness (that last one is interesting in the context of sexuality, wouldn't you say?). The question then is, What are humans' basic sexual rights? The principles are new and evolving, but they generally include elements such as a right to reproductive self-determination and freedom from sexual abuse and sexual violence, as well as the right to sexual self-expression (provided, of course, that it doesn't interfere with someone else's sexual rights) (Sandfort & Ehrhardt, 2004). Some would argue that same-sex marriage, in this context, is a basic sexual right, and these arguments are gaining momentum worldwide. Argentina, Australia, Belgium, Canada, France, the Netherlands, Spain, and Switzerland are among the nations now offering a legally recognized relationship for both heterosexual and same-gender couples. And South Africa's constitution of 1996 bars discrimination on the basis of sexual orientation (Parker et al., 2004).

> **Sexual rights:** Basic, inalienable rights regarding sexuality, both positive and negative, such as rights to reproductive self-determination and sexual self-expression and freedom from sexual abuse and violence.

SUMMARY

Sexual behavior is activity that produces arousal and increases the chance of orgasm. *Sex* (sexual behavior and anatomy) is distinct from *gender* (being male or female).

Throughout most of human history, religion was the main source of information concerning sexuality. In the late 1800s and early 1900s, important contributions to the scientific understanding of sex were made by Sigmund Freud, Havelock Ellis, Richard von Krafft-Ebing, and Magnus Hirschfeld. These early researchers emerged from the Victorian era, in which sexual norms were highly rigid—although many people's actual behavior violated these norms. By the 1990s, major, well-conducted sex surveys were available. Today, the mass media are a powerful influence on most people's understanding of sexuality.

Studies of various human cultures around the world provide evidence of the enormous variations in human sexual behavior. For example, the frequency of intercourse may vary from once a week in some cultures to three or four times a night in others. All societies regulate sexual behavior in some way. Attitudes regarding premarital and extramarital sex, masturbation, same-gender sexual behavior, and gender roles vary considerably from one culture to the next. The great variations provide evidence of the importance of learning in shaping sexual behavior.

Within the United States, sexual behavior varies with one's social class and ethnic group. For example, African Americans are less likely to perform oral sex than whites are. In other areas, though, Blacks and whites are quite similar. Traditional Latino cultures are characterized by sharply defined gender roles and restrictions on female—but not male—sexuality. Asian cultures tend to be conservative about sexuality for both males and females.

Studies of sexual behavior in various animal species show that masturbation, mouth-genital stimulation, and same-gender sexual behavior are by no means limited to humans. They also illustrate how sexual behavior may be used for a variety of nonsexual purposes, such as expressing dominance.

A new international movement is focusing on sexual health and the principles of sexual rights.

QUESTIONS FOR THOUGHT, DISCUSSION, AND DEBATE

1. In the wide spectrum of sexual practices in different cultures, from the conservatism of Inis Beag to the permissiveness of Mangaia, where would you place the United States today? Are we permissive, restrictive, or somewhere in between? Why?

2. Research indicates that masturbation, mouth-genital stimulation, and same-gender sexual behaviors are present in other species besides humans. What is the significance of this finding?

3. Sally is a newspaper reporter in the state capital. She learns, through a trusted friend, that the highly popular governor, George Smith, has been having a long-term affair with a local woman attorney, despite the fact that each of them is apparently happily married. Should Sally break the news in an article? In terms of communications theories, what effects might she expect her article to have on the public's attitudes about sexuality?

4. How does premarital sexual behavior in the United States compare with premarital sex in Mangaia and Inis Beag (see Focus: A Sexually Diverse World, p. 10)? Which of these three cultures do you think it is best for adolescents to grow up in? Why? In which of those three cultures do you think adults are likely to have the most positive feelings about their sexuality? Why?

SUGGESTIONS FOR FURTHER READING

Bagemihl, Bruce. (1999). *Biological exuberance: Animal homosexuality and natural diversity.* New York: St. Martin's. The author documents the blindness of scientists to the homosexual behavior they observed and at the same time catalogs the extensiveness of homosexual behaviors in hundreds of species.

Gregersen, Edgar. (1996). *The world of human sexuality.* New York: Irvington. Gregersen, an anthropologist, has compiled a vast amount of information about sexuality in cultures around the world. The book also includes a treasure trove of fascinating illustrations.

Peiss, Kathy (Ed.). (2002). *Major problems in the history of American Sexuality.* Boston: Houghton Mifflin. This book contains a fascinating collection of documents and essays, ranging from Virginia's regulations on sex among servants, slaves, and masters, 1642–1769, to Black entertainer Mabel Hampton recalling lesbian life in the 1920s and 1930s.

Zuk, Marlene. (2002). *Sexual selections: What we can and can't learn about sex from animals.* Berkeley: University of California Press. Zuk, a biologist, carefully analyzes what can be inferred from studies of the sexual behavior of animals.

CHAPTER TWO

Theoretical Perspectives on Sexuality

CHAPTER HIGHLIGHTS

O ne of the discoveries of psychoanalysis consists in the assertion that impulses, which can only be described as sexual in both the narrower and the wider sense, play a peculiarly large part, never before sufficiently appreciated, in the causation of nervous and mental disorders. Nay, more, that these sexual impulses have contributed invaluably to the highest cultural, artistic, and social achievements of the human mind.*

From an evolutionary perspective, no single decision is more important than the choice of a mate. That single fork in the road determines one's ultimate reproductive fate.[†]

*Freud (1924), pp. 26–27.
[†]Buss (2000), p. 10.

Imagine, for a moment, that you are sitting in a bedroom, watching two people making love. Imagine, too, that sitting with you in the room, thinking your same thoughts, are Sigmund Freud (creator of psychoanalytic theory), E. O. Wilson (a leading sociobiologist), Albert Bandura (a prominent social learning theorist), and John Gagnon (a proponent of script theory). The scene you are imagining may evoke arousal and nothing more in you, but your imaginary companions would have a rich set of additional thoughts as they viewed the scene through the specially colored lenses of their own theoretical perspectives. Freud might be marveling at how the biological sex drive, the *libido,* expresses itself so strongly and directly in this couple. Wilson, the sociobiologist, would be thinking how mating behavior in humans is similar to such behavior in other species of animals and how it is clearly the product of evolutionary selection for behaviors that lead to successful reproduction. Bandura might be thinking how sexual arousal and orgasm act as powerful positive reinforcers that will lead the couple to repeat the act frequently and how they are imitating a technique of neck nibbling that they saw in an X-rated film last week. Finally, Gagnon's thoughts might be about the social scripting of sexuality; this couple begins with kissing, moves on to petting, and finishes up with intercourse, following a script written by society.

Some of the major theories in the social sciences have had many—and different—things to say about sexuality, and it is these theories that we consider in this chapter. Theories provide us with answers to the question "why?" We often wonder why others do or do not engage in particular sexual behaviors and relationships. We sometimes ask the "why" question about our own sexuality. Creative minds have developed theories to answer such questions. Given the diversity in human sexuality, we need a range of theories to understand it.

Evolutionary Perspectives

Sociobiology

Sociobiology is a controversial theory. **Sociobiology** is defined as the application of evolutionary biology to understanding the social behavior of animals, including humans (Barash, 1982). Sexual behavior is, of course, a form of social behavior, and so the sociobiologists try, often through observations of other species, to understand why certain patterns of sexual behavior have evolved in humans.

Before we proceed, we should note that in terms of **evolution,** what counts is producing lots of healthy, viable offspring who will carry on one's genes. Evolution occurs via **natural selection,** the process by which the animals that are best adapted to their environment are more likely to survive, reproduce, and pass on their genes to the next generation.

How do humans choose mates? One major criterion is the physical attractiveness of the person (see Chapter 11). The sociobiologist argues that many of the characteristics we evaluate in judging attractiveness—for example, physique and complexion—are indicative of the health and vigor of the individual. These in turn are probably related to the person's reproductive potential; the unhealthy are less likely to produce many vigorous offspring. Natural selection would favor individuals preferring mates who would have maximum reproductive success. Thus, perhaps our concern with physical attractiveness is a product of evolution and natural

Sociobiology: The application of evolutionary biology to understanding the social behavior of animals, including humans.
Evolution: A theory that all living things have acquired their present forms through gradual changes in their genetic endowment over successive generations.
Natural selection: A process in nature resulting in greater rates of survival of those plants and animals that are adapted to their environment.

selection. (See Barash, 1982, for an extended discussion of this point and the ones that follow.) We choose an attractive, healthy mate who will help us produce many offspring. Can you guess why it is that the sociobiologist thinks most men are attracted to women with large breasts?

From this viewpoint, dating, going steady, getting engaged, and similar customs are much like the courtship rituals of other species (see Figure 2.1). For example, many falcons and eagles have a flying courtship in which objects are exchanged between the pair in midair. The sociobiologist views this courtship as an opportunity for each member of the prospective couple to assess the other's fitness. For example, any lack of speed or coordination would be apparent during the airborne acrobatics. Evolution would favor courtship patterns that permitted individuals to choose mates who would increase their reproductive suc-

cess. Perhaps that is exactly what we are doing in our human courtship rituals. The expenditure of money by men on dates indicates their ability to support a family. Dancing permits the assessment of physical prowess, and so on.

Sociobiologists can also explain why the nuclear family structure of a man, a woman, and their offspring is found in every society. Once a man and a woman mate, there are several obstacles to reproductive success, two being infant vulnerability and maternal death. Infant vulnerability is greatly reduced if the mother provides continuing physical care, including breast feeding. It is further reduced if the father provides resources and security from attack for mother and infant. Two mechanisms that facilitate these conditions are a *pair-bond* between mother and father, and *attachment* between infant and parent (Miller & Fishkin, 1997). Thus, an offspring's chances of survival are greatly

(a)

(b)

Figure 2.1 (*a*) The courtship rituals of great egrets. (*b*) Dancing is a human dating custom. According to sociobiologists, human customs of dating and becoming engaged are biologically produced and serve the same functions as courtship rituals in other species: They allow potential mates to assess each other's fitness.

increased if the parents bond emotionally, that is, love each other, and if the parents have a propensity for attachment. Further, an emotional bond might lead to more frequent sexual interaction; the pleasurable consequences of sex in turn will strengthen the bond. Research with small mammals, including mice and moles, demonstrates the advantages of biparental care of offspring and the critical role of bonding (Morell, 1998).

According to this theory, parents are most interested in the survival and reproductive success of their genetic offspring. *Parental investment* refers to the behavior and resources invested in offspring to achieve this end. Because of the high rates of divorce and remarriage in the United States, many men have both biological children and stepchildren. This situation leads to the prediction that men will tend to invest more in their genetic children than in their stepchildren. Research indicates that fathers invest the most money on the genetic children of their current union and the least money on stepchildren from a past relationship. However, they spend an equal amount on their genetic children and the stepchildren of their current relationship, perhaps to cement the pair-bond with their current partner (Anderson et al., 2001).

In addition to natural selection, Darwin also proposed a mechanism that is not as much a household word, **sexual selection** (Gangestad & Thornhill, 1997). Sexual selection is selection that results from differences in traits affecting access to mates. It consists of two processes: (1) competition among members of one gender (usually males) for mating access to members of the other gender, and (2) preferential choice by members of one gender (usually females) for certain members of the other gender. In other words, in many—though not all—species, males compete among themselves for the right to mate with females; and females, for their part, prefer certain males and mate with them while refusing to mate with other males.[1] Researchers are currently testing with humans some of the predictions that come from the theory of sexual selection. For example, the theory predicts that men should compete with each other in ways that involve displaying material resources that should be attractive to women, and men should engage in these displays more than women do (Buss, 1988). Examples might be giving impressive gifts to potential mates, flashy showing of possessions (e.g., cars, stereos), or displaying personality

characteristics that are likely to lead to the acquisition of resources (e.g., ambition). Research shows that men engage in these behaviors significantly more than women do, and that both men and women believe these tactics are effective (Buss, 1988).

Many criticisms of sociobiology have been made. Some critics object to the biological determinism that it implies. Also, sociobiology has been criticized for resting on an outmoded version of evolutionary theory that modern biologists consider naive (Gould, 1987). For example, sociobiology has focused mainly on the individual's struggle for survival and efforts to reproduce; modern biologists focus on more complex issues such as the survival of the group and the species. Further, sociobiologists assume that the central function of sex is reproduction; this may have been true historically but is probably not true today. Given the emphasis in the theory on reproduction, proponents of the theory have a difficult time explaining homosexuality. Finally, recent research does not support some of the evidence that is widely cited in support of the theory. One sociobiologist reported that the winners of the Miss America contest and *Playboy*'s centerfold models have consistently had a waist-to-hip ratio of .7, arguing that this reflects a universal standard related to reproductive fitness (Singh, 1993). A closer look at the data shows that the average for Miss America winners has steadily declined since 1921, from .78 to .64 in 1986, contradicting the claim that a preference for .70 was hardwired by evolution thousands of years ago (Freese & Meland, 2002).

Evolutionary Psychology

A somewhat different approach is taken by **evolutionary psychology,** which focuses on psychological mechanisms that have been shaped by natural selection (Buss, 1991). If behaviors evolved in response to selection pressures, it is plausible to argue that cognitive or emotional structures evolved in the same way. Thus, a man who accurately judged whether a woman was healthy and fertile would be more successful in reproducing. If his offspring exhibited the same ability to judge accurately, they in turn would have a competitive advantage.

One line of research has concentrated on *sexual strategies* (Buss & Schmitt, 1993). According to this theory, females and males face different adaptive problems in short-term, or casual, mating and in long-term mating and reproduction. These differences lead to different strategies, or behaviors designed to solve these problems. In short-term mating, a female may choose a partner who offers

SexSource Online
www.mhhe.com/hyde10

"EVOLUTIONARY PSYCHOLOGY" IN SEXUALITY OVER THE LIFE-SPAN

Sexual selection: Selection that results from differences in traits affecting access to mates.
Evolutionary psychology: The study of psychological mechanisms that have been shaped by natural selection.

[1]Sociobiologists use this mechanism to explain gender differences.

her immediate resources, such as food or money. In long-term mating, a female may choose a partner who appears able and willing to provide resources for the indefinite future. A male may choose a sexually available female for a short-term liaison but avoid such females when looking for a long-term mate.

Based on research with college students, Buss (1994) argues that men generally relax their standards when seeking a short-term partner, requiring of them less education, honesty, and emotional stability, for example; relaxing one's standards is assumed to make it more likely one will find a mate. Women's preferences change less than men's when looking for a short-term mate, but they are more likely to seek someone who has resources and is generous with them.

Buss (1994) and others have reported research data that support a number of specific predictions based on this theory. However, research using the same measures with both men and women, and controlling for confounding effects, finds that men and women are very similar in their mating preferences. Both prefer long-term strategies and few or no short-term partners (Pedersen et al., 2002). Another criticism of evolutionary psychology is that it assumes that every characteristic that we observe must have some adaptive significance, but in fact some human traits may be simply "design flaws" (de Waal, 2002).

Psychological Theories

Four of the major theories in psychology are relevant to sexuality: psychoanalytic theory, learning theory, social exchange theory, and cognitive theory.

Psychoanalytic Theory

Sigmund Freud's **psychoanalytic theory** has been one of the most influential of all psychological theories. Because Freud saw sex as one of the key forces in human life, his theory gives full treatment to human sexuality.

Freud termed the sex drive or sex energy **libido,** which he saw as one of the two major forces motivating human behavior (the other being *thanatos,* or the death instinct).

Id, Ego, and Superego

Freud described the human personality as being divided into three major parts: the id, the ego, and the superego. The **id** is the basic part of personality and is present at birth. It is the reservoir of psychic energy (including libido). Basically it operates on the *pleasure principle.*

While the id operates only on the pleasure principle and can thus be pretty irrational, the **ego** operates on the *reality principle* and tries to keep the id in line. The ego functions to make the person have realistic, rational interactions with others.

Finally, the **superego** is the conscience. It contains the values and ideals of society that we learn, and it operates on *idealism.* Thus its aim is to inhibit the impulses of the id and to persuade the ego to strive for moral goals rather than realistic ones.

To illustrate the operation of these three components of the personality in a sexual situation, consider the case of the CEO of a corporation who is at a meeting of the board of directors; the meeting is also attended by her gorgeous, muscular colleague, Mr. Hunk. She looks at Mr. Hunk, and her id says, "I want to throw him on the table and make love to him immediately. Let's do it!" The ego intervenes and says, "We can't do it now because the other members of the board are also here. Let's wait until 5 P.M., when they're all gone, and then do it." The superego says, "I shouldn't make love to Mr. Hunk at all because I'm a married woman." What actually happens? It depends on the relative strengths of this woman's id, ego, and superego.

The id, ego, and superego develop sequentially. The id contains the set of instincts present at birth. The ego develops later, as the child learns how to interact realistically with his or her environment and the people in it. The superego develops last, as the child learns moral values.

Erogenous Zones

Freud saw the libido as being focused in various regions of the body known as **erogenous zones.** An erogenous zone is a part of the skin or mucous membrane that is extremely sensitive to stimulation; touching it in certain ways produces feelings of pleasure. The lips and mouth are one such erogenous zone, the genitals a second, and the rectum and anus a third.

Stages of Psychosexual Development

Freud believed that the child passes through a series of stages of development. In each of these stages a different erogenous zone is the focus.

The first stage, lasting from birth to about 1 year of age, is the *oral*

Psychoanalytic theory: A psychological theory originated by Sigmund Freud; it contains a basic assumption that part of human personality is unconscious.
Libido (lih-BEE-doh): In psychoanalytic theory, the term for the sex energy or sex drive.
Id: According to Freud, the part of the personality containing the libido.
Ego: According to Freud, the part of the personality that helps the person have realistic, rational interactions.
Superego: According to Freud, the part of the personality containing the conscience.
Erogenous (eh-RAH-jen-us) zones: Areas of the body that are particularly sensitive to sexual stimulation.

stage. The child's chief pleasure is derived from sucking and otherwise stimulating the lips and mouth. Anyone who has observed children of this age knows how they delight in putting anything they can into their mouths. The second stage, which occurs during approximately the second year of life, is the *anal stage.* During this stage, the child's interest is focused on elimination.

The third stage of development, lasting from age 3 to perhaps age 5 or 6, is the *phallic stage.* The boy's interest is focused on his phallus (penis), and he derives great pleasure from masturbating.[2] Perhaps the most important occurrence in this stage is the development of the **Oedipus complex,** which derives its name from the Greek story of Oedipus, who killed his father and married his mother. In the Oedipus complex, the boy loves his mother and desires her sexually. He hates his father, whom he sees as a rival for the mother's affection. The boy's hostility toward his father grows, but eventually he comes to fear that his father will retaliate by castrating him—cutting off his prized penis. Thus, the boy feels *castration anxiety.* Eventually the castration anxiety becomes so great that he stops desiring his mother and shifts to identifying with his father, taking on the father's gender role and acquiring the characteristics expected of males by society. Freud considered the Oedipus complex and its resolution to be one of the key factors in human personality development.

As might be expected from the name of this stage, the girl will have a considerably different, and much more difficult, time passing through it, since she has none of what the stage is all about. For a girl, the phallic stage begins with her traumatic realization that she has no penis, perhaps after observing that of her father or a brother. She feels envious and cheated, and she suffers from *penis envy,* wishing that she too had a wonderful wand. (Presumably she thinks her own clitoris is totally inadequate, or she is not even aware that she has it.) She begins to desire her father, forming her version of the Oedipus complex, sometimes called the **Electra complex.** In part, her incestuous desires for her father result from a desire to be impregnated by him, to substitute for the unobtainable penis. Unlike the boy, the girl does not have a strong motive of castration anxiety for resolving the Oedipus complex; she has already lost her penis. Thus, the girl's resolution of the Electra complex is

Oedipus (EH-di-pus) complex: According to Freud, the sexual attraction of a little boy for his mother.
Electra (eh-LEK-tra) complex: According to Freud, the sexual attraction of a little girl for her father.

[2]Masturbation to orgasm is physiologically possible at this age, although males are not capable of ejaculation until they reach puberty (see Chapter 5).

not so complete as the boy's resolution of the Oedipus complex, and for the rest of her life she remains somewhat immature compared with men.

Freud said that following the resolution of the Oedipus or Electra complex, children pass into a prolonged stage known as *latency,* which lasts until adolescence. During this stage, the sexual impulses are repressed or are in a quiescent state, and so nothing much happens sexually. The postulation of this stage is one of the weaker parts of Freudian theory, because it is clear from the data of modern sex researchers that children do continue to engage in behavior with sexual components during this period (see Chapter 9).

With puberty, sexual urges reawaken, and the child moves into the *genital stage.* During this stage, sexual urges become more specifically genital, and the oral, anal, and genital urges all fuse together to promote the biological function of reproduction.

According to Freud, people do not always mature from one stage to the next as they should. A person might remain permanently fixated, for example, at the oral stage; symptoms of such a situation would include incessant cigarette smoking and fingernail biting, which gratify oral urges. Most adults have at least traces of earlier stages remaining in their personalities.

Freud on Women

Feminists have been critical of Freudian theory. Let us first review what Freud had to say about women and then discuss what feminists object to in his theory (Callan, 2001; Lerman, 1986).

Essentially, Freud assumed that the female is biologically inferior to the male because she lacks a penis. He saw this absence as a key factor in her personality development. As Freud said, "Anatomy is destiny."

Freud also originated the distinction between *vaginal orgasm* and *clitoral orgasm* in women. During childhood little girls rub their clitorises to produce orgasm (clitoral orgasm). Freud believed, though, that as they grow to adulthood women need to shift their focus to having orgasm during heterosexual intercourse, with the penis stimulating the vagina (vaginal orgasm). Thus, not only did he postulate two kinds of orgasm for women, but he also maintained that one kind was better (more mature) than the other. The evidence that Masters and Johnson have collected on this issue is reviewed in Chapter 8; suffice it to say for now that there seems to be little or no physiological difference between the two kinds of orgasm. The assertion that the vaginal orgasm is more mature is not supported by Masters and Johnson's and others' findings that most adult women orgasm as a result of clitoral stimulation.

Feminists understandably object to several aspects of Freud's theory. A chief objection is to the whole notion that women are anatomically inferior to men because they lack a penis. What is so intrinsically valuable about a penis that makes it better than a clitoris, a vagina, or a pair of ovaries? In a creative approach, psychoanalyst Karen Horney (1926/1973) coined the concept of "womb envy," arguing that males have a powerful envy of females' reproductive capacity, more than females envy the penis. Feminists argue that psychoanalytic theory is essentially a male-centered theory that may cause harm to women, particularly those who seek psychotherapy from therapists who use a traditional psychoanalytic approach.

Evaluation of Psychoanalytic Theory

From a scientific point of view, one of the major problems with psychoanalytic theory is that most of its concepts cannot be evaluated scientifically to see whether they are accurate. Freud postulated that many of the most important forces in personality are unconscious, and thus they could not be studied using the scientific techniques common to the twentieth century. Recent advances in our ability to image brain activity, for example, with high-powered magnetic resonance imaging, have opened the possibility of testing some of Freud's ideas (Figure 2.2). He believed that dreams provide a window into the person's id, that during sleep the activity of the ego and superego is reduced. Research in the developing area of *neuropsychoanalysis* suggests that it is activity in the prefrontal area of the brain that constrains the sometimes bizarre imagery that is generated by the limbic and postcortical regions. During rapid eye movement, or REM, sleep, there is a reduction of activity in the former (the ego?) and vivid and bizarre dreams are at times associated with activity in the latter (the id?) (Solms, 1997).

Another criticism is that Freud derived his data almost exclusively from his work with patients who sought therapy from him. Thus, his theory may provide a view not so much of the human personality as of *disturbances* in the human personality.

Finally, many modern psychologists feel that Freud overemphasized the biological determinants of behavior and instincts and that he gave insufficient recognition to the importance of the environment and learning.

Nonetheless, Freud did make some important contributions to our understanding of human

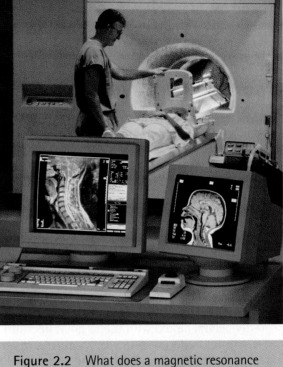

Figure 2.2 What does a magnetic resonance imaging machine have to do with psychoanalytic theory? The answer is that by studying patterns in brain waves, we can test some of Freud's ideas about the relationship between the id and the ego.

behavior. He managed to rise above the sexually repressive Victorian era of which he was a member and teach that the libido is an important part of personality (although he may have overestimated its importance). His recognition that humans pass through stages in their psychological development was a great contribution. Perhaps most important from the perspective of this text, Freud took sex out of the closet, brought it to the attention of the general public, and suggested that we could talk about it and that it was an appropriate topic for scientific research.

Learning Theory

While psychoanalytic and sociobiological theories are based on the notion that much of human sexual behavior is biologically controlled, it is also quite apparent that much of it is learned. Some of the best evidence for this point comes from studies of sexual behavior across different human societies, which were considered in Chapter 1. Here the various principles of modern learning theory will be reviewed, because they can help us understand our own sexuality (for a more detailed discussion, see Hogben & Byrne, 1998).

Classical Conditioning

Classical conditioning is a concept usually associated with the work of the Russian scientist Ivan Pavlov (1849–1936). Think of the following situations: You salivate in response to the sight or smell of food, you blink in response to someone poking a finger in your eye, or you experience sexual arousal in response to stroking the inner part of your thigh. In all these cases, an unconditioned stimulus (US; for example, appealing food) automatically, reflexively elicits an unconditioned response (UR; for example, salivation). The process of learning that occurs in classical conditioning takes place when a new stimulus, the conditioned stimulus (CS; for example, the sound of a bell) repeatedly occurs paired with the original unconditioned stimulus (food). After this happens many times, the conditioned stimulus (the ringing bell) can eventually be presented without the unconditioned stimulus (food) and will evoke the original response, now called the conditioned response (CR, salivation).

As an example, suppose that Nadia's first serious boyfriend in high school always wears Erotik cologne when they go out. As they advance in their sexual intimacy, they have many pleasant times, where he strokes her thighs and other sexually responsive parts of her body and she feels highly aroused, always with the aroma of Erotik in her nostrils. One day she enters an elevator full of strangers in a department store and someone is wearing Erotik. Nadia instantly feels sexually aroused, although she is not engaged in any sexual activity. From the point of view of classical conditioning, this makes perfect sense, although Nadia may wonder why she is feeling so aroused in the elevator. The thigh-stroking and sexy touching were the US. Her arousal was the UR. The aroma of the cologne, the CS, was repeatedly paired with the US. Eventually, the aroma occurred by itself, evoking arousal, the CR.

Classical conditioning of sexual arousal has been demonstrated in an experiment using male students as participants (Lalumiere & Quinsey, 1998). All of the participants were first shown 20 slides of partially clothed women; a slide rated as 5 on a scale of sexual attractiveness ranging from 1 to 10 was selected as the target slide. Ten participants were shown the target slide, followed by a 40-second segment of a sexually explicit videotape, for 11 trials; men in the control group saw only the target slide for 11 trials. Arousal was measured by a penile strain gauge, which measures the extent of engorgement or erection of the penis (see Chapter 12). Each man then rated the 20 original slides again. In the experimental group, the target slide was associated with an increase in arousal as measured by the strain gauge; in the control group, men were less aroused by the target slide following the repeated exposure. Subsequent research demonstrated classical conditioning of sexual arousal in women (Hoffmann et al., 2004).

Classical conditioning is useful in explaining a number of phenomena in sexuality. One example is fetishes, explained in Chapter 14.

Operant Conditioning

Operant conditioning, a concept that is often associated with the psychologist B. F. Skinner, refers to the following process. A person performs a particular behavior (the operant). That behavior may be followed by either a reward (positive reinforcement) or a punishment. If a reward follows, the person will be likely to repeat the behavior again in the future; if a punishment follows, the person will be less likely to repeat the behavior. Thus, if a behavior is repeatedly rewarded, it may become very frequent, and if it is repeatedly punished, it may become very infrequent or even be eliminated.

Some rewards are considered to be primary reinforcers; that is, there is something intrinsically rewarding about them. Food is one such primary reinforcer; sex another. Rats, for example, can be trained to learn a maze if they find a willing sex partner at the end of it. Thus, sexual behavior plays dual roles in learning theory: It can itself be a positive reinforcer, but it can also be the behavior that is rewarded or punished.

Simple principles of operant conditioning can help explain some aspects of sex (McGuire et al., 1965). For example, if a woman repeatedly experiences pain when she has intercourse (perhaps because she has a vaginal infection), she will probably want to have sex infrequently or not at all. In operant conditioning terms, sexual intercourse has repeatedly been associated with a punishment (pain), and so the behavior becomes less frequent.

Another principle of operant conditioning that is useful in understanding sexual behavior holds that consequences, whether reinforcement or punishment, are most effective in shaping behavior when

Classical conditioning: The learning process in which a previously neutral stimulus (conditioned stimulus) is repeatedly paired with an unconditioned stimulus that reflexively elicits an unconditioned response. Eventually the conditioned stimulus itself will evoke the response.

Operant (OP-ur-unt) conditioning: The process of changing the frequency of a behavior (the operant) by following it with positive reinforcement (which will make the behavior more frequent in the future) or punishment (which should make the behavior less frequent in the future).

they occur immediately after the behavior. The longer they are delayed after the behavior has occurred, the less effective they become. As an example, consider a young man who has had gonorrhea three times yet continues to have unprotected sexual intercourse. The pain associated with gonorrhea is certainly punishing, so why does he persist in having sex without a condom? The delay principle suggests the following explanation. Each time he engages in intercourse, he finds it highly rewarding; this immediate reward maintains the behavior; the punishment, gonorrhea, does not occur until several days later and so is not effective in eliminating that behavior.

A third principle that has emerged in operant conditioning studies is that, compared with rewards, punishments are not very effective in shaping behavior. Often, as in the case of the child who is punished for taking an illicit cookie, punishments do not eliminate a behavior but rather teach the person to be sneaky and engage in it without being caught. As an example, some parents, as many commonly did in earlier times in our culture, punish children for masturbating; yet most of those children continue to masturbate, perhaps learning instead to do it under circumstances (such as in a bathroom with the door locked) in which they are not likely to be caught.

One important difference between psychoanalytic theory and learning theory should be noticed. Psychoanalytic theorists believe that the determinants of human sexual behavior occur in early childhood, particularly during the Oedipal complex period. Learning theorists, in contrast, believe that sexual behavior can be learned and changed at any time in one's life span—in childhood, in adolescence, in young adulthood, or later. When we try to understand what causes certain sexual behaviors and how to treat people with sex problems, this distinction between the theories will have important implications.

Behavior Modification

Behavior modification involves a set of techniques, based on principles of classical or operant conditioning, that are used to change (or modify) human behavior. These techniques have been used to modify everything from problem behaviors of children in the classroom to the behavior of schizophrenics. In particular, these methods can be used to modify problematic sexual behaviors—that is, sexual disorders such as orgasm problems (see Chapter 17) or deviant sexual behavior such as child molesting. Behavior modification methods differ from more traditional methods of psychotherapy

such as psychoanalysis in that the behavioral therapist considers only the problem behavior and how to modify it using learning-theory principles; the therapist does not worry about a depth analysis of the person's personality to see, for example, what unconscious forces might be motivating the behavior.

One example of a technique used in modifying sexual behavior is *olfactory aversion therapy* (Abel et al., 1992). In aversion therapy, the problematic behavior is punished using an aversive stimulus. Repeated pairing of the behavior and the aversive stimulus should produce a decline in the frequency of the behavior, or its **extinction.** In olfactory aversion therapy, the problematic sexual behavior is punished using an unpleasant odor, such as the odor of spirits of ammonia, as the aversive stimulus. With the help of a therapist, the patient first identifies the behavior chain or sequence that leads up to the problem behavior. Then the patient imagines one event in the chain and is simultaneously exposed to the odor. The odor can be administered by the patient, using a breakable inhaler. This form of therapy not only punishes the behavior but also creates the perception in the patient that the behavior is under his or her control.

Social Learning

Social learning theory (Bandura, 1977; Bandura & Walters, 1963) is a somewhat more complex form of learning theory. It is based on principles of operant conditioning, but it also recognizes two other processes at work: *imitation* and *identification.* These two processes are useful in explaining the development of gender identity, or one's sense of maleness or femaleness (see Figure 2.3). For example, it seems that a little girl acquires many characteristics of the female role by identifying with her mother and imitating her, as when she plays at dressing up after observing her mother getting ready to go to a party. Also, various forms of sexuality may be learned through imitation. In high school, for example, the sexiest girl in the senior class may find that other girls are imitating her behaviors and the way she dresses. Or a boy might see a movie in which the hero's technique seems to "turn women on"; then he tries to use this technique with his own dates. The latter example points to the importance of mass media as a source of images of sexuality that young people imitate and personalities that they identify with (see Chapter 9, Focus: Milestones in Sex Research).

> **Behavior modification:** A set of operant conditioning techniques used to modify human behavior.
> **Extinction:** The process of repeatedly pairing a behavior with an aversive stimulus, leading to a decline in the frequency of the behavior.

| Figure 2.3 | According to social learning theory, children learn about sex and gender in part by imitation. These children may be imitating their parents or a scene they have watched on TV. |

Once a behavior is learned, the likelihood of its being performed depends on its consequences. The young man who imitates actor Brad Pitt's romantic technique may not succeed in arousing his companion. If the behavior is not reinforced, he will stop performing it. If it is reinforced, he will repeat it. Successful experiences with an activity over time create a sense of competence, or **self-efficacy** (Bandura, 1982), at performing the activity. If a woman feels efficacious at using the female condom, she will expend more effort (going to the drugstore to buy one) and will show greater persistence in the face of difficulty (continuing to adjust it until it fits properly) than she did before. The concept of self-efficacy has been widely used in designing health intervention programs such as those that encourage individuals to use condoms to prevent transmission of sexually transmitted diseases and HIV infection (e.g., DeLamater et al., 2000). These programs provide opportunities for participants to practice the behaviors that are being promoted and be successful.

Social Exchange Theory

An important process based on the principle of reinforcement is social exchange. **Social exchange theory** (Cook, 2004) uses the concept of reinforcement to explain stability and change in relationships between people. The theory assumes that we have freedom of choice and often face choices among alternative actions. Every action provides some rewards and entails certain costs. There are many kinds of rewards—money, goods, services, sexual gratification, approval by others—and costs—time, effort, money, embarrassment. The theory states that we are *hedonistic,* that we try to maximize rewards and minimize costs when we act. Thus, we choose actions that produce profits (profits equaling rewards less costs) and avoid actions that produce losses.

As its name indicates, social exchange theory views social relationships primarily as exchanges of goods and services among persons. People participate in relationships only if they find that the relationships provide profitable outcomes. An individual judges the attractiveness of a relationship by comparing the profits it provides against the profits available in alternative relationships. The level of outcomes in the best alternative relationship is called the *comparison level for alternatives* (Thibaut & Kelley, 1959). These ideas have been applied to personal relationships. Studies of heterosexual couples in long-term dating relationships have found that the concepts of rewards and costs can explain whether persons stay in or exit from such relationships (Rusbult, 1983; Rusbult et al., 1986). Individuals are more likely to stay in when the partner is physically and personally attractive, when the relationship does not entail undue costs (such as high monetary commitments, broken promises, or arguments), and when romantic relationships with others are not available. In other words, they are more likely to stay in a relationship when its rewards are high, its costs are low, and the comparison level for alternatives is low.

Social exchange theory also predicts the conditions under which people try to change their relationships. A central concept is *equity* (Walster [Hatfield] et al., 1978). A state of equity exists when participants in a relationship believe that the rewards they receive from it are proportional to the costs they bear. If a participant feels that the allocation of rewards and costs is inequitable, then the relationship is unstable. People find inequity unpleasant and may feel cheated or angry. As we will see in Chapter 10, a married person experiencing inequity may cheat on the spouse as a result.

This perspective leads to the *matching hypothesis* (see Chapter 11), which predicts that men and women will choose as mates people who match them on physical and social characteristics. People who match will provide each other with similar rewards on dimensions such as attractiveness, social status, and wealth. We noted earlier that sociobiologists predict that we will choose attractive mates—if

Self-efficacy: A sense of competence at performing an activity.
Social exchange theory: A theory, based on the principle of reinforcement, that assumes that people will choose actions that maximize rewards and minimize costs.

Focus: A Sexually Diverse World
Learning Theory and Sexual Orientation in a Non-Western Society

The Sambia are a tribe living in Papua New Guinea in the South Pacific, which has been extensively studied by anthropologists (see Focus: A Sexually Diverse World in Chapter 13, p. 357). The Sambia are interesting for a number of reasons, the chief one being that young males are expected to spend 10 or more years of their lives in exclusively homosexual relations. During this time they are taught to fear women and believe that women have polluting effects on them. After that stage of their lives, they are expected to marry women. They do, and their sexual behavior becomes exclusively heterosexual. These observations defy our Western notions that one's sexual orientation is a permanent characteristic throughout life. Indeed, the very concepts of having a "heterosexual identity" or "homosexual identity" are not present in Sambia culture.

Can social learning theory explain these patterns of sexual behavior? It can, according to the analysis of John and Janice Baldwin. The thing that is puzzling is how the Sambia male, who has had years of erotic conditioning to homosexual behavior just at puberty when he is most easily aroused and sensitive to conditioning, would then switch to heterosexual behavior and do so happily.

According to the Baldwins' analysis, several factors in social learning theory explain this switch. First, positive conditioning in the direction of heterosexuality occurs early in life. The boy spends the first 7 to 10 years of his life with his family. He has a close, warm relationship with his mother. In essence, he has been conditioned to positive feelings about women.

Second, observational learning occurs. In those same first 7 to 10 years, the boy observes closely the heterosexual relationship between two adults, his mother and father. This observational learning can be used a decade later when it is time for him to marry and form a heterosexual relationship.

Third, the boy is provided with much cognitive structuring, a notion present in social learning theory as well as cognitive psychology. He is instructed that a boy must pass through a series of stages to become a strong, masculine man. This includes first becoming the receptive partner to fellatio, then being the inserting partner to fellatio, marrying, defending himself from his wife's first menstruation (girls are usually married before puberty and undergo no homosexual stage of development), and then fathering a child by her. Essentially he is given all the cognitive structures necessary to convince him that it is perfectly natural, indeed desirable, to engage in sex with men for 10 years and then switch to women. Finally, there is some aversive conditioning to the homosexual behavior that leads it to be not particularly erotic. The boy performs fellatio for the first time after several days of initiation, when he is exhausted. The activities are staged so that the boy feels fearful about it. He must do it in darkness with an older boy who may be an enemy, and he is required to do it with many males in succession. In essence, unpleasantness or punishment is associated with homosexual behavior.

In summary, then, social learning theory provides a sensible explanation of the seemingly puzzling shift that Sambia males make from exclusively homosexual expression to exclusively heterosexual expression.

Sources: Baldwin & Baldwin (1989); Herdt (1984).

---

true, men would fight for the most attractive woman in the area and unattractive women would not have partners. In fact, people at all levels of attractiveness find partners, reflecting the operation of matching.

Social exchange theories have been criticized for applying ideas of rewards and costs to romantic relationships. Some people believe that love is not and should not be about what one can get out of a relationship (i.e., its rewards). A related criticism is that social exchange theories downplay other motivations. Because of the emphasis on rewards and costs, such theories cannot explain, for example, selfless behaviors such as altruism and martyrdom.

Cognitive Theory

In the 1980s and 1990s, a "cognitive revolution" swept through psychology. In contrast to the older behaviorist tradition (which insisted that psychologists should study only behaviors that could be directly observed), cognitive psychologists believe that it is very important to study people's thoughts—that is, the way people perceive and think.

Cognition and Sexuality

Cognitive psychology can readily explain some aspects of human sexuality (Walen & Roth, 1987). A basic assumption is that what we think influences what we feel. If we think happy, positive thoughts, we will tend to feel better than if we think negative ones. Therapists using a cognitive approach believe that psychological distress is often a result of unpleasant thoughts that are usually not tuned to reality and include misconceptions, distortions, exaggerations of problems, and unreasonably negative evaluations of events.

To the cognitive psychologist, how we perceive and evaluate a sexual event makes all the difference in the world (Walen & Roth, 1987). For example, suppose that a man engaged in sexual activity does not get an erection. Starting from that basic event, his thoughts might take one of two directions. In the first, he thinks that it is quite common for men in his age group (fifties) not to get an erection every time they have sex; this has happened to him a few times before, once every two or three months, and it's nothing to worry about. At any rate, the oral sex was fun, and his partner had an orgasm from that, so all in all it was a nice enough encounter. In the second possibility, he began the activity thinking that he had to have an erection, had to have intercourse, and had to have an orgasm. When he didn't get an erection, he mentally labeled it *impotence* and imagined that he would never again have an erection. He thought of the whole episode as a frustrating disaster because he never had an orgasm.

As cognitive psychologists point out, our perception, labeling, and evaluating of events are crucial. In one case, the man perceived a slight problem, labeled it a temporary erection problem, and evaluated his sexual experience as pretty good. In the other case, the man perceived a serious problem, labeled it impotence, and evaluated the experience as horrible.

We shall see cognitive psychology several times again in this book, as theorists use it to understand the cycle of sexual arousal (see Chapter 8), the causes of some sexual variations such as fetishes (see Chapter 14), and the causes and treatment of sexual disorders (see Chapter 17). Before we leave cognitive psychology, however, we will look at one cognitive theory, schema theory, that has been used especially to understand issues of sex and gender.

Schema (SKEE-muh): A general knowledge framework that a person has about a particular topic.

Gender Schema Theory

Psychologist Sandra Bem (1981) has proposed a schema theory to explain gender-role development and the impact of gender on people's daily lives and thinking. *Schema* is a term taken from cognitive psychology. A **schema** is a general knowledge framework that a person has about a particular topic. A schema organizes and guides perception; it helps us remember, but it sometimes also distorts our memory, especially if the information is inconsistent with our schema. Thus, for example, you might have a "football game schema," the set of ideas you have about what elements should be present at the game (two teams, spectators, bleachers, and so on) and what kinds of activities should occur (opening kickoff, occasional touchdown, band playing at half-time, and so on).

It is Bem's contention that all of us possess a *gender schema*—a cognitive structure comprised of the set of attributes (behaviors, personality, appearance) that we associate with males and females. Our gender schema, according to Bem, predisposes us to process information on the basis of gender. That is, we tend to think of things as gender-related and to dichotomize them on the basis of gender. A good example is the case of the infant whose gender isn't clear when we meet him or her. We eagerly seek out the information or feel awkward if we don't, because we seem to need to know the baby's gender in order to continue to process information about it.

Bem (1981) has done a number of experiments that provide evidence for her theory, and there are confirming experiments by other researchers as well, although the evidence is not always completely consistent (Ruble & Stangor, 1986). In one of the most interesting of these experiments, 5- and 6-year-old children were shown pictures like those in Figure 2.4, showing males or females performing either stereotype-consistent activities (such as a girl baking cookies) or stereotype-inconsistent activities (such as girls boxing) (Martin & Halverson, 1983). One week later the children were tested for their recall of the pictures. The results indicated that the children distorted information by changing the gender of people in the stereotype-inconsistent pictures, while not making such changes for the stereotype-consistent pictures. That is, children tended to remember a picture of girls boxing as having been a picture of boys boxing. These results are just what would be predicted by gender schema theory. The schema helps us remember schema-consistent (stereotype consistent) information well, but it distorts our memory of information that is inconsistent with the schema (stereotype inconsistent).

(a)   (b)

Figure 2.4 Pictures like these were used in the Martin and Halverson research on gender schemas and children's memory. (*a*) A girl engaged in a stereotype-consistent activity. (*b*) Girls engaged in a stereotype-inconsistent activity. In a test of recall a week later, children tended to distort the stereotype-inconsistent pictures to make them stereotype consistent; for example, they remembered that they had seen boys boxing.

One of the interesting implications of gender schema theory is that stereotypes—whether they are about males and females, or heterosexuals and homosexuals, or other groups—may be very slow to change. The reason is that our schemas tend to filter out stereotype-inconsistent (that is, schema inconsistent) information so that we don't even remember it.

Sociological Perspectives

Sociologists are most interested in the ways in which society or culture shapes human sexuality. (For a detailed articulation of the sociological perspective, see DeLamater, 1987; the arguments that follow are taken from that source.)

Sociologists approach the study of sexuality with three basic assumptions: (1) Every society regulates the sexuality of its members. (For a discussion of the reasons why, see Horrocks, 1997.) (2) Basic institutions of society (such as religion and the family) affect the rules governing sexuality in that society. (3) The appropriateness or inappropriateness of a particular sexual behavior depends on the culture in which it occurs.

The Influence of Society

Sociologists view societal influences on human sexuality as occurring on several levels, including the macro level, or society as a whole, and the subcultural level, at which one's social class or ethnic group may have an impact on one's sexuality. Our discussion in this section emphasizes the macro level of influence.

Social Institutions

According to the sociological perspective, at the macro level our sexuality is influenced by powerful social institutions, including religion, the economy, the family, medicine, and the law. Each major institution supports a sexual ideology, or discourse, about sexual activity. This ideology influences the beliefs and behaviors of those affiliated with the institution.

Religion

In our culture, the Judeo-Christian religious tradition has been a powerful shaper of sexual norms. A detailed discussion of that religious tradition and its teachings on sexuality is provided in Chapter 19. Suffice it to say here that the Christian religion has contained within it a tradition of asceticism, in which abstinence from sexual pleasures—especially by certain persons such as monks and priests—is seen as virtuous. The tradition, at least until recently, has also been oriented toward procreation—that is, a belief that sexuality is legitimate only within traditional heterosexual marriage and only with the goal of having children, a *procreational ideology.* This view has created within our culture a set of norms, or standards for behavior, that say, for example, that premarital sex, extramarital sex, and homosexual sex are wrong. The procreational ideology is our basis for asserting that marriage is exclusively for a man and a woman, since only a heterosexual couple can procreate.

The Economy

The nature and structure of the economy is another macro-level influence on sexuality. Before the Industrial Revolution, most work was done in the family unit in the home or farm. This kind of togetherness permitted rather strict surveillance of family members' sexuality and thus strict norms could be enforced. However, with the Industrial Revolution, people—most frequently men—spent many hours per day at work away from the home. Thus, they were under less surveillance, and scripts such as extramarital affairs and same-gender sex could be acted out more often.

Today we see much evidence of the extent to which economic conditions, and especially the unemployment rate, can affect the structure of the family and thus sexuality (see Figure 2.5). For example, when a group of men—such as lower-class Black men—have less access to jobs and thus have a high unemployment rate, they are reluctant to marry because they cannot support a family. The result is many female-headed households, with sexuality occurring outside marriage and children born without a legal father, although the father may be present in the household, providing care for the children. The point is that a culture's economy may have a profound effect on patterns of sexuality, marriage, and childbearing (Teachman et al., 2000).

In a capitalist economy such as the United States, goods and services become commodities that can be sold for a price (an exchange). Not surprisingly, this includes sexual images and sexual gratification, giving rise to the sale of sexually explicit materials, in stores and on the Internet, and commercial sex work. The increasing globalization

Figure 2.5   According to sociologists, a culture's economy may have a profound effect on patterns of sexuality, marriage, and childbearing. High rates of male unemployment may lead to an increase in the number of female-headed households.

of the economy has led to the development of sex tourism, in which well-to-do men and women travel to other cultures, such as Thailand, to purchase sexual gratification from "exotic" (e.g., Asian) sex workers (see Chapter 16).

The Family

The family is a third institution influencing sexuality. As we noted earlier, before the Industrial Revolution the family was an important economic unit, producing the goods necessary for survival. As that function waned after the Industrial Revolution, there was increased emphasis on the quality of interpersonal relationships in the family. At the same time, love was increasingly seen as an important reason for marriage. By 1850, popular American magazines sang the praises of marriage based on romantic love (Lantz et al., 1975). Thus, a triple linkage between love, marriage, and sex was formed. Ironically, the linkage eventually became a direct one between love and sex (removing marriage as the middleman) so that, by the 1970s, some people were arguing that sex outside of marriage, if in the context of a loving relationship, was permissible, as was same-gender sex, again if the relationship was a loving one. This is the *relational ideology.*

The family exerts a particularly important force on sexuality through its *socialization* of children. That is, parents socialize their children—teach them appropriate norms for behavior—in many areas, including sexuality. Others, of course, such as the peer group, also have important socializing influences.

Medicine

The institution of medicine has become a major influence on our sexuality over the last 100 years. Physicians tell us what is healthy and what is unhealthy. In the late 1800s, physicians warned that masturbation could cause various pathologies. Today sex therapists tell us that sexual expression is natural and healthy and sometimes even "prescribe" masturbation as a treatment.

Another example is provided by childbirth; until after the Civil War, most babies were born at home, with an experienced woman (a midwife) providing assistance to the laboring woman and her partner. Today the vast majority of births occur in hospitals or birthing facilities, with medical personnel in charge. We tend to have great confidence in medical advice, so the pronouncements of the medical establishment, based on a *therapeutic ideology,* have an enormous impact on sexuality.

The increasing influence of medicine on sexuality has not been taken lying down. The domination of contemporary theory and research by the biomedical model is referred to as the **medicalization of sexuality** (Tiefer, 2004). Medicalization has two components: Certain behaviors or conditions are defined in terms of health and illness, and problematic experiences or practices are given medical treatment. The medicalization of male sexuality is being hastened by the development of drugs to treat erectile dysfunction, and many physicians and pharmaceutical companies are seeking to medicalize female orgasmic dysfunction by finding a pill that will "cure" it.

The Law

The legal system is another institution influencing sexuality at the macro level. A detailed discussion of laws relating to sexuality is provided in Chapter 20. The point to be made here is that from a sociological perspective, the law influences people's sexual behaviors in a number of ways. First, laws determine norms. Generally we think that what is legal is right and what is illegal is wrong. Thus, a society in which prostitution is illegal will have much different views of it than a society in which it is legal.

Second, laws are the basis for the mechanisms of social control. They may specify punishments for certain acts and thus discourage people from engaging in them. An example is public sexual acts such as exhibitionism or nudity on beaches. One wonders how many people would prefer to be nude at the beach if they did not fear arrest because the behavior is generally illegal and if they did not fear possible embarrassing publicity such as having their names in the paper as the result of an arrest.

Third, the law reflects the interests of the powerful, dominant groups within a society. In part, the law functions to confirm the superiority of the ideologies of these dominant groups. Consider the Mormons in the United States. In the past, their religion approved of polygyny (a man having several wives). Mormons did not become the dominant group in American society—although they might have, with the kind of reproduction one could achieve with polygyny. Rather, the Judeo-Christian tradition was the ideology of the dominant group, and that tradition takes a very dim view of polygyny. Accordingly, polygyny is illegal in the United States, and Mormons have been arrested for their practice. Also, one wonders what kinds of laws we would have on prostitution or sexual harassment if the compositions of the state legislatures were 90 percent women rather than 90 percent men. Would

Medicalization of sexuality: The process by which certain sexual behaviors or conditions are defined in terms of health and illness, and problematic experiences or practices are given medical treatment.

prostitution, for example, be legal? Or would it still be illegal, but would the male customer be held as guilty as or guiltier than the female prostitute?

In summary, then, the sociological perspective focuses on how society or culture shapes and controls our sexual expression, at levels from institutions such as religion and the law to the interpersonal level of socialization by family and peers.

Symbolic Interaction Theory

An important sociological theory is **symbolic interaction theory** (Charon, 1995; Stryker, 1987). Its basic premise is that human nature and the social order are products of symbolic communication among people. A person's behavior is constructed through his or her interaction with others. People can communicate successfully with one another only to the extent that they ascribe similar meanings to objects and people. An object's meaning for a person depends not on the properties of the object but on what a person might do with it; an object takes on meaning only in relation to a person's plans. Thus, the theory views people as proactive and goal seeking. Achieving most goals requires the cooperation of others.

This is especially true of many forms of sexual expression. For example, suppose a woman invites a person she is dating to her apartment; what meaning does this invitation have? Does she want to prolong the conversation, or engage in intimate sexual activity? The two people will have to achieve an agreement about the purpose of the visit before joint activity is possible. In terms of the theory, they have to develop a *definition of the situation.* Thus, to fit their actions together and achieve agreement, people interacting with each other must continually reaffirm old meanings or negotiate new ones.

Central to social interaction is the process of *role taking,* in which an individual imagines how he or she looks from the other person's viewpoint. By viewing the self and potential actions from the perspective of the other person, we are often able to anticipate what behavior will enable us to achieve our goal. One consequence of role taking is self-control; we see ourselves from the viewpoint of others and so strive to meet their standards, in the process exercising control over our behavior. This perspective emphasizes the importance of symbolic communication (see Chapter 11). It also alerts us to the mutual effort required to arrive at a definition of the situation. Criticisms of this theory include the

fact that it emphasizes rational, conscious thought, whereas in the realm of sexuality emotions may be very important in many interactions. Also, this perspective portrays humans as *other-directed individuals,* concerned primarily with meeting others' standards. A third criticism is that we don't always consciously role take and communicate in an effort to achieve agreement. Sometimes we rely on past experience and habit. Situations such as these are the province of script theory.

Sexual Scripts

The outcome of these social influences is that each of us learns a set of *sexual scripts* (Gagnon, 1977, 1990; Gagnon & Simon, 1973). The idea is that sexual behavior (and virtually all human behavior, for that matter) is scripted much as a play in a theater is. That is, sexual behavior is a result of elaborate prior learning that teaches us an etiquette of sexual behavior (see Figure 2.6). According to this concept, little in human sexual behavior is spontaneous. Instead, we have learned an elaborate script that tells us who, what, when, where, and why we do what we do sexually. For example, the "who" part of the script tells us that sex should occur with someone of the other gender, of approximately our own age, of our own race, and so on. Even the sequence of sexual activity is scripted. *Scripts,* then, are plans that people carry around in their heads for what they are doing and what they are going to do; they are also devices for helping people remember what they have done in the past (Gagnon, 1977, p. 6).

How could we study these scripts? How could we find out if there are widely shared beliefs about how one should behave in a specific situation? One way is to ask people to describe what one should do in such a situation. Researchers asked male and female college students to make a list of the things that a man or woman would typically do on a first date (Rose & Frieze, 1993). The hypothetical script written by many of the participants included a core sequence of acts: dress, pick up, get to know, evaluate, eat, make out, and go home. This is the first-date script. This script is also influenced by contemporary views of gender roles. Males were portrayed as proactive, taking the initiative: pick up the female, pay for the date, attempt to make out, and ask for another date. Females were portrayed as reactive: be picked up, be treated, accept or reject the male's attempt to make out, and accept or reject an invitation to another date. The widely shared nature of this script enables relative strangers to interact smoothly on their first date.

Symbolic interaction theory: A theory based on the premise that human nature and the social order are products of communication among people.

Figure 2.6   According to some people's sexual scripts, a man taking a woman to dinner is one scene of the first act in a sexual script that features intercourse as Act V.

One study attempted to identify the sequence of sexual behaviors that is scripted for males and females in a heterosexual relationship in our culture (Jemail & Geer, 1977). People were given 25 sentences, each describing an event in a heterosexual interaction. They were asked to rearrange the sentences in a sequence that was "most sexually arousing" and then to do it again to indicate what was "the most likely to occur." There was a high degree of agreement among the participants about what the sequence should be. There was also high agreement between males and females. The standard sequence was kissing, hand stimulation of the breasts, hand stimulation of the genitals, mouth-genital stimulation, intercourse, and orgasm. Does this sound familiar? Interestingly, not only is this the sequence in a sexual encounter, it is also the sequence that occurs as a couple progresses in a relationship. These results suggest that there are culturally defined sequences of behaviors that we all have learned, much as the notion of a "script" suggests.

Can you imagine a young man, on the first date, attempting oral stimulation of the young woman's genitals before he has kissed her? The idea seems amazing, and perhaps humorous or shocking. Why? Because the young man has performed Act IV before Act I.

While the first-date script provides guidelines, each couple will enact that script in a unique way. Where they go, what they talk about, what they eat or drink will reflect the desires and expectations of each, and the course of their interaction. Each couple creates their own first date, which may be memorable and become a story they tell their grandchildren, or a disaster that becomes their only date.

Scripts also tell us the meaning we should attach to a particular sexual event (Gagnon, 1990). Television programs and films frequently suggest but do not show sexual activity between people. How do we make sense out of these implicit portrayals? A study of how women interpret such scenes in films found that they utilize scripts. If the film showed a couple engaging in two actions that are part of the accepted script for sexual intercourse (e.g., kissing and undressing each other) and then faded out, viewers inferred that intercourse had occurred (Meischke, 1995).

The Social Importance of Sexuality

Ira Reiss (1986) has proposed a sociological theory of human sexuality. Borrowing from script theory, he defines sexuality as "erotic and genital responses produced by the cultural scripts of a society" (p. 37). As he points out, a sociological theory, because it focuses on societal influences on sexuality, must be able to account for both cross-cultural variations in sexuality and cross-cultural universals in sexuality.

One cross-cultural universal is that all societies believe that sexuality is important. Even in cultures that are sexually repressive, sexuality is still accorded great importance as something that is dangerous and must be controlled. Why is sexuality considered so important? Many theorists have claimed that it is the link of sexuality to making babies, which is undeniably important for any society. Reiss argues against this notion, however, citing instances of societies that do not understand the link between sex and reproduction yet still find sex important. Indeed, in North America today effective methods of contraception have allowed us to separate much of sexuality from reproduction, but we still think sex—even nonreproductive sex—is important.

Reiss's explanation for the universal importance of sexuality points to two components: (1) sexuality is associated with great physical pleasure, and (2) sexual interactions are associated with great personal self-disclosure, involving not only disclosure of one's body but, in an intimate interaction, of one's thoughts and feelings as well (see Figure 2.7). Humans seem to find intrinsic value in the physical pleasures of sex and in the psychic satisfaction of the self-disclosures associated with sex. Societies consider them important because they are key elements of social bonding. Recall our discussion of the importance of the pair bond to the welfare of children. Socially, the pair bond is the foundation of social structure.

According to Reiss, sexuality is linked to the structures of any society in three areas: the kinship system, the power structure, and the ideology of the society.

First, because sexuality is the source of reproduction, it is always linked to *kinship,* and all societies seek to maintain social order through stable kinship systems. This linkage is the explanation for sexual jealousy, which is universal cross-culturally although it exists in varied forms. Jealousy is a way of setting boundaries on a relationship that is considered very important, essential enough so that it should not be breached. Marriage is typically such a relationship, and jealousy in marriage about extramarital affairs

Figure 2.7 According to Reiss's sociological theory, sex is important to us because it is associated with great physical pleasure and self-disclosure.

exists in all human societies. Kin define what relationships are and are not acceptable and enforce the resulting rules. Furthermore, all societies have structured ways of dealing with such jealousy. Even in societies that practice polygyny, rituals develop to minimize jealousy among the wives—for example, the husband must sleep one night with one wife, the next with another, and so on, and has violated norms if he spends two nights with the same wife. Reiss argues, therefore, that no society will be able to eliminate sexual jealousy, because jealousy is a statement of the value or importance that kinship groups and individuals attach to a particular relationship such as marriage.

Second, sexuality is always linked to the *power structure* of a society. Reiss defines power as the ability to influence others and achieve one's objectives even if there is opposition from the other person.

Powerful groups in any society generally seek to control the sexuality of the less powerful. Males are more powerful than females in most societies, so sexuality becomes linked to gender roles and males exercise control over female sexuality. Cross-cultural research shows, interestingly, that the closer females are in power to males in a society, the more sexual freedom women have; in societies in which women have little power, their sexuality is greatly restricted.

Third, sexuality is closely linked to the *ideologies* of a culture. Reiss defines *ideology* as fundamental assumptions about human nature. Societies define carefully what sexual practices are normal and abnormal, and which are right and wrong. Some cultures define homosexuality as abnormal, whereas others define it as normal—but the point is that all cultures define it one way or the other. Similarly, some cultures take a permissive attitude toward premarital sex for both males and females, some are permissive for males but not for females, and some are permissive for neither. A culture's ideologies define what is right and wrong sexually.

In summary, Reiss's sociological theory of sexuality argues that societies regard sexuality as important because it is associated with physical pleasure and with self-disclosure. Sexuality is tightly woven into the fabric of any society because of its links to the kinship system, to power structures, and to the ideologies of the society.

SUMMARY

Theories provide explanations for sexual phenomena. Sociobiologists view human sexual behaviors as the product of natural selection in evolution and thus view these behavioral patterns as being genetically controlled. Contemporary evolutionary theorists view behavior as the result of an interaction between evolved mechanisms and environmental influence.

Among the psychological theories, Freud's psychoanalytic theory views the sex energy, or libido, as a major influence on personality and behavior. Freud introduced the concepts of erogenous zones and psychosexual stages of development. Learning theory emphasizes how sexual behavior is learned and modified through reinforcements and punishments according to principles of operant conditioning. Behavior modification techniques—therapies based on learning theory—are used in treating sexual variations and sexual disorders. Social learning theory adds the concepts of imitation, identification, and self-efficacy to learning theory. Exchange theory highlights the role of rewards and costs in relationships. Cognitive psychologists focus on people's thoughts and perceptions—whether positive or negative—and how these influence sexuality.

Sociologists study the ways in which society influences our sexual expression. At the macro level of analysis, sociologists investigate the ways in which institutions such as religion, the economy, the family, medicine, and the law influence sexuality. Symbolic interaction theory calls attention to processes of communication and interaction. Sexual scripts provide us with guidelines for behavior in many situations. Reiss argues that all societies regard sexuality as important because it is associated with great physical pleasure and self-disclosure.

QUESTIONS FOR THOUGHT, DISCUSSION, AND DEBATE

1. Compare and contrast how a sociobiologist, a psychoanalyst, and a sociologist would explain why people engage in premarital intercourse.

2. Of the theories described in this chapter, which do you think provides the most insight into human sexuality? Why?

3. You are visiting your married sister and her family for the holidays. Her 6-year-old asks you a question: "Why do mommies stay home with kids?" Drawing on the knowledge you gained from Chapter 2, how would you answer this question? Which ideas about parental investment, social learning, or social norms and scripts would you use to explain why, in most cultures, women perform the childrearing activities?

4. From a sociologist's point of view, how have social institutions controlled female sexuality?

5. Could script theory explain the pattern of homosexual and heterosexual behavior of

Sambia males described in Focus: A Sexually Diverse World, page 33? Explain your answer.

6. In Chapter 1, we identified a number of differences in the sexual behavior of whites, African Americans, Latinos, and Asian Americans (see Table 1.2, p. 14). Which of the theories discussed in Chapter 2 can most easily explain these differences? Pick one specific difference and construct an explanation for it using that theory. How well does the theory help you to understand cultural differences in sexuality?

SUGGESTIONS FOR FURTHER READING

Baker, Robin (1996). *Sperm wars: The evolutionary logic of love and lust.* New York: Basic Books. Baker uses a series of vignettes describing sexual interactions to illustrate the many ways evolutionary mechanisms may influence our selection of mates, frequency of intercourse, success and failure to conceive, and infidelity.

Buss, David M. (1994). *The evolution of desire.* New York: Basic Books. A detailed presentation of sexual strategy theory and data that are consistent with the theory.

Freud, Sigmund. (1943). *A general introduction to psychoanalysis.* Garden City, NY: Garden City Publishing. (Original in German, 1917.) Good for the reader who wants a basic introduction to Freud. For a good one-chapter summary, see Hall, C. S., and Lindzey, G. (1970). *Theories of personality* (2nd ed.). New York: Wiley.

Gagnon, John H., & Simon, William. (1987). The sexual scripting of oral-genital contacts. *Archives of Sexual Behavior, 16,* 1–26. An interesting discussion and application of script theory.

CHAPTER THREE

Sex Research

CHAPTER HIGHLIGHTS

W hat is research, but a blind date with knowledge.

—William Henry

In the last several decades, sex research has made increasing advances, and the names of Kinsey and Masters and Johnson have become household words. How do sex researchers do it? How valid are their conclusions?

There are many different types of sex research, but basically the techniques vary in terms of the following: (1) whether they rely on people's self-reports of their sexual behavior or whether the scientist observes the sexual behavior directly; (2) whether large numbers of people are studied (surveys) or whether a small number or just a single individual is studied (in laboratory studies or case studies); (3) whether the studies are conducted in the laboratory or in the field; and (4) whether sexual behavior is studied as it occurs naturally or whether some attempt is made to manipulate it experimentally.

Examples of studies using all these techniques will be considered and evaluated later in this chapter. First some issues in sex research will be discussed.

It is important to understand the techniques of sex research and their strengths as well as their limitations. This knowledge will help you evaluate the studies that are cited as evidence for various conclusions in later chapters and will also help you decide how willing you are to accept these conclusions. Perhaps more important, this knowledge will help you evaluate future sex research. Much sex research has been conducted already, but much more will be done in the future. The information in this chapter should help you understand and evaluate sex research that appears 10 or 20 years from now. Moreover, the mass media often report poor-quality research as enthusiastically as high-quality research. You should be equipped to tell the difference.

Issues in Sex Research

Sampling

One of the first steps in conducting sex research is to identify the appropriate **population** of people to be studied. Does the population in question consist of all adult human beings, all adolescents in the United States, all people guilty of sex crimes, or all married couples who engage in swinging? Generally, of course, the scientist is unable to get data for all the people in the population, and so a **sample** is taken.

At this point, things begin to get sticky. If the sample is a **random sample** or representative sample of the population in question and if it is a reasonably large sample, then results obtained from it can safely be generalized to the population that was originally identified. That is, if a researcher has really randomly selected 1 out of every 50 adolescents in the United States, then the results obtained from that sample are probably true of all adolescents in the United States. One technique that is sometimes used to get such a sample is **probability sampling.**[1] But if the sample consists only of adolescents with certain characteristics—for example, only those whose parents agree to let them participate in sex research—then the results obtained from that sample may not be true of all adolescents. Sampling has been a serious problem in sex research.

Typically, sampling proceeds in three phases: the population is identified, a method for obtaining a sample is adopted, and the people in the sample are contacted and asked to participate. What is perhaps the thorniest problem occurs in

---

[1] A detailed discussion of probability sampling is beyond the scope of this book. For a good description of this method as applied to sex research, see Cochran et al. (1953). In brief, with a random sample, each individual in the population has an equal probability of being chosen. With a probability sample, the researchers can set a higher probability of inclusion for certain groups, a technique called *oversampling*. For example, if we had funds to interview 1,000 people in the United States, a random sample would yield only about 120 Blacks and 130 Latinos because these groups constitute about 12 percent and 13 percent of the population, respectively. We might not feel confident reaching conclusions about Blacks or Latinos based on only 120 or 130 people, so we could decide to use probability sampling and give Blacks and Latinos a double probability of inclusion compared with whites. The resulting sample of 1,000 would include 240 Blacks, 260 Latinos, and 500 Euro-Americans, and we would feel more confident about making conclusions about each group. We could do even more oversampling of Asian Americans and American Indians, who constitute even smaller percentages of the U.S. population.

Population: A group of people a researcher wants to study and make inferences about.
Sample: A part of a population.
Random sample: An excellent method of sampling in research, in which each member of the population has an equal chance of being included in the sample.
Probability sampling: An excellent method of sampling in research, in which each member of the population has a known probability of being included in the sample.

the last phase: getting the people identified for the sample to participate. If any of the people refuse to participate, then the great probability sample is ruined. This is called the **problem of refusal or nonresponse.** As a result, the researcher is essentially studying volunteers, that is, people who agree to be in the research. The outcomes of the research may therefore contain **volunteer bias.** In casually conducted research such as the Hite report (Hite, 1976, 1981), the response rate was only 3 percent, making it impossible to reach any conclusions about the population based on the sample. The problem of refusal in sex research is difficult, since there is no ethical way of forcing people to participate when they do not want to.

The problem of volunteer bias would not be so great if those who refused to participate were identical in their sexual behavior to those who participated. But it seems likely that those who refuse to participate differ in some ways from those who agree to, and that means the sample is biased. Evidence suggests that volunteers who participate in sex research hold more permissive attitudes about sexuality and are more sexually experienced than those who don't; for example, they masturbate more frequently and have had more sexual partners (Morokoff, 1986; Strassberg & Lowe, 1995; Wiederman, 1993; Wiederman et al., 1994). In addition, women are less likely to volunteer for sex research than men are (Wiederman et al., 1994), so that female samples are even more highly selected than male samples. In sum, volunteer bias is potentially a serious problem when we try to reach conclusions based on sex research.

Table 3.1 shows how different the results of sex surveys can be, depending on how carefully the sampling is done (Greeley, 1994). The table shows results from the Janus report (Janus & Janus, 1993), which used sampling methods so haphazard that the researchers ended up with what some call a "convenience sample." It included volunteers who came to sex therapists' offices and friends recruited by the original volunteers. This report contrasts with the probability sample obtained in the General Social Survey conducted in 1993 by the University of Chicago. Notice that a considerably higher level of sexual activity is reported by the convenience sample in the Janus report, compared with the probability sample. This difference is especially pronounced among the elderly. Convenience samples simply do not give us a very good picture of what is going on in the general population.

Reliability of Self-Reports of Sexual Behavior

Most sex researchers have not directly observed the sexual behavior of their research participants. Instead, most have relied on respondents' self-reports of their sexual practices. The question is, How accurately do people report their own sexual behavior? Inaccuracies may occur in several ways.

Purposeful Distortion

If you were an interviewer in a sex research project and a 90-year-old man said that he and his wife made love twice a day, would you believe him, or would you suspect that he might be exaggerating slightly? If a

> **Problem of refusal or nonresponse:** The problem that some people will refuse to participate in a sex survey, thus making it difficult to study a random sample.
> **Volunteer bias:** A bias in the results of sex surveys that arises when some people refuse to participate, so that those who are in the sample are volunteers who may in some ways differ from those who refuse to participate.

Table 3.1 The Percentage of People Reporting Having Sex at Least Once a Week: Comparing a Convenience Sample with a Probability Sample

Age	Men		Women	
	Convenience Sample (Janus Report)	Probability Sample (General Social Survey)	Convenience Sample (Janus Report)	Probability Sample (General Social Survey)
18–26	72%	57%	68%	58%
27–38	83	69	78	61
39–50	83	56	68	49
51–64	81	43	65	25
Over 65	69	17	74	6

Source: Greeley (1994).

Figure 3.1   The reliability of self-reports of sexual behavior. If you were interviewing this man in a sex survey and he said that he had never masturbated, would you believe him, or would you think that he was concealing a taboo behavior?

35-year-old woman told you that she had never masturbated, would you believe her, or would you suspect that she had masturbated but was unwilling to admit it?

Respondents in sex research may, for one reason or another, engage in **purposeful distortion,** intentionally giving self-reports that are distortions of reality. These distortions may be in either of two directions. People may exaggerate their sexual activity (a tendency toward *enlargement*), or they may minimize their sexual activity or hide the fact that they have done certain things (*concealment*).

Distortion is a basic problem when using self-reports. To minimize distortion, participants must be impressed with the fact that because the study will be used for scientific purposes, their reports must be as accurate as possible. They must also be assured that their responses will be completely anonymous; this is necessary, for example, so that a politician would not be tempted to

Purposeful distortion: Purposely giving false information in a survey.

hide an extramarital affair or a history of sex with animals for fear that the information could be used to defeat him in the next election.

But even if all respondents were very truthful and tried to give information as accurate as possible, two factors might still cause their self-reports to be inaccurate: memory and difficulties with estimates.

Memory

Some of the questions asked in sex surveys require respondents to recall what their sexual behavior was like many years before. For example, some of the data we have on sexual behavior in childhood come from the Kinsey study, in which adults were asked about their childhood sex behavior. This might involve asking a 50-year-old man to remember at what age he began masturbating and how frequently he masturbated when he was 16 years old. It might be difficult to remember such facts accurately. The alternative is to ask people about their current sexual behavior, although getting data like this from children raises serious ethical and practical problems.

Difficulties with Estimates

One of the questions sex researchers have asked is, How long, on the average, do you spend in precoital foreplay? If you were asked this question, how accurate a response do you think you could give? It is rather difficult to estimate time to begin with, and it is even more difficult to do so when engaged in an absorbing activity. The point is that in some sex surveys people are asked to give estimates of things that they probably cannot estimate very accurately. This may be another source of inaccuracy in self-report data.

Evidence on the Reliability of Self-Reports

Scientists have developed several methods for assessing how reliable or accurate people's reports are (Catania et al., 1995). One is the method of **test-retest reliability,** in which the respondent is asked a series of questions and then is asked the same set of questions after a period of time has passed, for example, a week or a month. The correlation[2] between answers at the two times (test and retest) measures the reliability of responses. If people answer identically both times, the correlation would be 1.0, meaning perfect reliability. If there were absolutely no relationship between what they said the first time and what they said the second time, the correlation would be 0, meaning that the responses are not at all reliable.

In one study, urban African American and Latina girls between the ages of 12 and 14 were interviewed about their sexual experiences and then were reinterviewed three weeks later (Hearn et al., 2003). The test-retest reliability was .84 for their age when they had their first crush and .95 for the age at which they first touched a penis, which indicates excellent reliability. Other research generally indicates that respondents give their best estimates about short, recent time intervals (Catania et al., 1990).

Another method for assessing reliability involves obtaining independent reports from two different people who share sexual activity, such as husbands and wives. We used this method of checking for agreement between spouses (Hyde et al., 1996). On a simple item such as whether they had engaged in intercourse in the last month, there was 93 percent agreement. When reporting on

something that requires somewhat more difficult estimation, the number of times they had intercourse in the past month, the correlation was .80, which still indicates good reliability.

Interviews versus Questionnaires

In the large-scale sex surveys, three methods of collecting data have been used: the face-to-face interview, the phone interview, and the written questionnaire. Each of these methods has some advantages when compared with the others (Catania et al., 1995).

The advantage of the interview method, particularly the face-to-face interview, is that the interviewer can establish rapport with the respondent and try to convince that person of the research's worth and of the necessity for being honest. An interviewer can also vary the sequence of questions, depending on the person's response. For example, if a person mentioned having had a homosexual experience, this response would be followed by a series of questions about the experience; those questions would be omitted if the person reported having had no homosexual experiences. It is hard to get this kind of flexibility in a printed questionnaire. Finally, interviews can be administered to persons who cannot read or write. However, it is possible that respondents would be more honest in answering a questionnaire because they are more anonymous.

What do the data say about which method works best for sex research? Several researchers have compared the results obtained through use of two different methods. For example, in one study, the rate of reporting rape was nearly double (11 percent) in a face-to-face interview compared with a telephone interview (6 percent) (Koss et al., 1994, p. 174). This finding seems to indicate that interviewers can establish rapport and trust better in person than over the telephone. In a study assessing risky sexual behavior among gay men, both face-to-face interviews and written questionnaires were administered to all respondents (Siegel et al., 1994). Riskier behaviors were more likely to be reported on the questionnaire than in the interview. People evidently feel a bit freer to report particularly sensitive information on the more private written questionnaire than to an interviewer. Many experts in sex research recommend that a face-to-face interview to build rapport be combined with a written

> **Test-retest reliability:** A method for testing whether self-reports are reliable or accurate; participants are interviewed (or given a questionnaire) and then interviewed a second time sometime later to determine whether their answers are the same both times.

[2]The statistical concept of correlation is discussed in the last section of this chapter.

questionnaire administered during the interview to tap particularly sensitive information (Laumann et al., 1994; Siegel et al., 1994).

A recent innovation is the **computer-assisted self-interview method (CASI),** which can be combined with an audio component so that the respondent not only reads but hears the questions. This method offers the privacy of the written questionnaire while accommodating poor readers. The computer can be programmed to follow varying sequences of questions depending on respondents' answers, just as a human interviewer does. In one survey, among 15-year-old boys, 16 percent reported in a personal interview that they had engaged in vaginal intercourse, but 25 percent said they had when CASI was used (Mosher et al., 2005). These findings indicate that CASI gives much more honest responses.

Web-Based Surveys

The possibility of having surveys administered on Web sites has opened a whole new era in sex research. Compared with other methods for administering surveys, Web-based surveys have many advantages but also some disadvantages (Bowen, 2005; Gosling et al., 2004; Kraut et al., 2004; Mustanski, 2001; Ochs et al., 2002).

Web-based sex surveys can recruit much larger samples than can traditional interview or questionnaire studies. For example, one Web survey of gays, lesbians, and bisexuals yielded 2,800 completed surveys in just two months (Mustanski, 2001). And Web surveys can potentially produce broader samples than traditional survey methods can. For example, if you were conducting a survey on college students' sexuality using traditional methods, you would probably sample students at your own college or university. If, instead, you administered the questionnaire on the Web, you could sample students from colleges and universities across the nation and, indeed, around the world. In what is perhaps the most spectacular example to date, the *BBC Internet Study* obtained data from 255,000 persons on questions about gender and sexuality (Reimers, 2007). The researchers are only in the early stages of data analysis, but we will report some of their findings in later chapters. These new methods open up exciting possibilities for cross-cultural research.

Web-based surveys have particular advantages for studying special populations defined by their sexual behavior, particularly if the behavior is taboo. For example,

Computer-assisted self-interview (CASI): A method of data collection in which the respondent fills out questionnaires on a computer. Headphones and a soundtrack reading the questions can be added for young children or poor readers.

traditional studies of gays and lesbians have used methods such as recruiting the sample through gay activist organizations and gay bars. These methods have been criticized because they omit from the sample closeted gays and those who do not actively participate in organizations or go to bars. Closeted gays have equal access to Web-based surveys and can answer them in a highly anonymous way, respecting their own decisions to remain closeted. Therefore, Web methods can access this population that had previously been studied very little and can yield a much wider sample of gays and lesbians. Web methods can also locate stigmatized sexual minorities, such as those involved in sadomasochism, bondage, and discipline, by recruiting participants through virtual communities and Web sites designed for that particular sexual group.

Web-based surveys, then, have substantial strengths on the issue of sampling. Nonetheless, they still rely on self-reports, which, as we saw earlier, can be inaccurate to some degree.

Web-based surveys have the ability to eliminate extraneous influences on responding (discussed in the next section). For example, the gender or ethnicity of the interviewer may influence an individual's responses, but these factors are eliminated in a Web-administered questionnaire.

Do all these substantial advantages come with any disadvantages? Some bias is introduced because not everyone has Internet access. Access grows every day, but Internet users still, on average, have incomes above the national average. Internet samples are nonetheless considerably more diverse than the college-student samples used in much research. The researcher lacks control of the environment in which the respondent completes the survey—something that can be controlled in personal interviews but cannot in mailed-out questionnaires. One can imagine, for example, a group of fraternity brothers filling out a Web sex survey together and having fun faking the answers. Individuals might respond multiple times or might try to sabotage or skew the results to show a particular outcome. Internal checks can be built into the sequence of questions that can detect faked patterns of answers, and methods have been devised to detect repeat responders. Nonetheless, these issues continue to be a concern.

On balance, then, Web-based surveys offer substantial advantages over traditional survey methods. Researchers will have to continue to monitor and control potential problems such as repeat responders.

Self-Reports versus Direct Observations

As we noted earlier, one of the major ways of classifying techniques of sex research is by whether the scientist relied on people's self-reports of their behavior or observed the sexual behavior directly.

The problems of self-reports have just been discussed. In a word, self-reports may be inaccurate. Direct observations—such as those done by Masters and Johnson in their work on the physiology of sexual response—have a major advantage over self-reports in that they are accurate. No purposeful distortion or inaccurate memory can intervene. On the other hand, direct observations have their own set of problems. They are expensive and time consuming, with the result that generally only a rather small sample is studied. Furthermore, obtaining a random or probability sample of the population is even more difficult than in survey research. While some people are reticent about completing a questionnaire concerning their sexual behavior, even more would be unwilling to come to a laboratory where their sexual behavior would be observed by a scientist or where they would be hooked up to recording instruments while they engaged in sex. Thus, results

obtained from the unusual group of volunteers who would be willing to do this might not be generalizable to the rest of the population. One study showed that volunteers for a laboratory study of male sexual arousal felt less guilty and were less sexually fearful and more sexually experienced than nonvolunteers (Farkas et al., 1978; for similar results with females, see Wolchik et al., 1983).

Direct observations of sexual behavior in the laboratory, such as those made by Masters and Johnson, involve one other problem: Is sexual behavior in the laboratory the same as sexual behavior in the privacy of one's own bedroom? For example, might sexual response in the laboratory be somewhat inhibited?

Extraneous Factors

Various extraneous factors may also influence the outcomes of sex research. Extraneous factors such as the gender, race, or age of the interviewer may influence respondents' answers. Questionnaires do not get around these problems, since such simple factors as the wording of a question may influence the results. In one study, respondents were given either standard or supportive wording of some items (Catania et al., 1995). For

"Another one of those damned sex surveys, I suppose."

Figure 3.2 Sex researchers have tried to devise some ingenious methods for overcoming the problems of self-reports.

Source: © Punch/Rothco.

the question about extramarital sex, the standard wording was as follows:

> At any time while you were married during the past 10 years, did you have sex with someone other than your (husband/wife)?

The supportive wording was as follows:

> Many people feel that being sexually faithful to a spouse is important, and some do not. However, even those who think being faithful is important have found themselves in situations where they ended up having sex with someone other than their (husband/wife). At any time while you were married during the past 10 years, did you have sex with someone other than your (husband/wife)?

The supportive wording significantly increased reports of extramarital sex from 12 percent with the standard wording to 16 percent with the supportive wording, if the interviewer was of the same gender as the respondent; the wording made no difference when the interviewer and respondent were of different genders. Sex researchers must be careful to control these extraneous factors so that they influence the results as little as possible.

Ethical Issues

There is always a possibility of ethical problems involved in doing research. Ethical problems are particularly difficult in sex research, because people are more likely to feel that their privacy has been invaded when you ask them about sex than when you ask them to name their favorite presidential candidate or memorize a list of words. The ethical standards specified by the U.S. government and university regulations involve three basic principles: informed consent, protection from harm, and justice (see, for example, U.S. National Commission, 1978).

Informed Consent

According to the principle of **informed consent,** participants have a right to be told, before they participate, what the purpose of the research is and what they will be asked to do. They may not be forced to participate or be forced to continue. An investigator may not coerce people to be in a study, and it is the scientist's responsibility to see to it that all participants understand exactly what they are agreeing to do. In the case of children who may be too young to give truly informed consent, it is usually given by the parents.

> **Informed consent:** An ethical principle in research, in which people have a right to be informed, before participating, of what they will be asked to do in the research.
>
> **Cost-benefit approach:** An approach to analyzing the ethics of a research study, based on weighing the costs of the research (the participants' time, stress to participants, and so on) against the benefits of the research (gaining knowledge about human sexuality).

The principle of informed consent was adopted by scientific organizations in the 1970s. It was violated in some of the older sex studies, as discussed later in this chapter.

Protection from Harm

Investigators should minimize the amount of physical and psychological stress to people in their research. Thus, for example, if an investigator must shock participants during a study, there should be a good reason for doing this. Questioning people about their sexual behavior may be psychologically stressful to them and might conceivably harm them in some way, so sex researchers must be careful to minimize the stress involved in their procedure. The principle of *anonymity* of response is important to ensure that participants will not suffer afterward for their participation in research.

Justice

The principle of justice in research ethics holds that the risks of participating in research and the benefits of the results of the research should be distributed fairly across groups in society. For example, early testing of the birth control pill was done on poor women in Puerto Rico, not on wealthy women in Manhattan. The risks were not distributed fairly, and a particular group bore a disproportionate burden. As a second example, research on the potential benefits of taking aspirin for preventing heart attacks was conducted with an all-male sample. Whether this effect worked for women as well remained unknown. Thus, the benefits of the research did not extend fairly to everyone. Researchers have an obligation to make sure that they conduct their work in a way that benefits as wide a range of persons as possible.

A Cost–Benefit Approach

Considering the possible dangers involved in sex research, is it ethical to do such research? Officials in universities and government agencies sponsoring sex research must answer this question for every proposed sex research study. Typically they use a **cost-benefit approach.** That is, the stress to the research participants should be minimized as much as possible, but some stresses will remain; they are the cost. The question then becomes, Will the benefits that result from the research be greater than the cost? That is, will the participants benefit in some way from being in the study, and will science and society in general benefit from the knowledge resulting from the study?

Do these benefits outweigh the costs? If they do, the research is justifiable; otherwise, it is not.

As an example, Masters and Johnson considered these issues carefully and concluded that their research participants benefited from being in their research; they collected data from former participants that confirmed this belief. Thus, a cost-benefit analysis would suggest that their research was ethical, even though their participants might have been temporarily stressed by it. Even in a study as ethically questionable as Laud Humphreys's study of the tearoom trade (discussed later in this chapter), the potential cost to the participants should be weighed against the benefits that accrue to society from being informed about this aspect of sexual behavior.

Political Issues

In October 2003, during a major committee meeting, a member of the U.S. House of Representatives, Rep. Mike Ferguson (R–NJ), waved a list of research projects funded by the National Institutes of Health (NIH) that he claimed were ridiculous and a terrible use of taxpayers' money. As it turned out, the hit list had been compiled by the Traditional Values Coalition, a right-wing religious group, which asserted that U.S. taxpayers would deplore these "smarmy" projects. Earlier in July, Rep. Patrick Toomey (R–PA) had introduced a measure dubbed the Toomey amendment to halt the funding of five specific grants, effectively trying to stop the research. The amendment was defeated by a narrow margin of two votes.

One of the projects on the list was a study conducted at the Kinsey Institute at Indiana University, in which physiological responses of sexually aroused adults were studied in the laboratory. The methods are similar to those used by Masters and Johnson (discussed in Chapter 8) and Heiman (see Chapter 12). The rationale for the Kinsey Institute study involved the fact that some serious problems in society today, such as pedophilia, adult sexual attraction to children, involve people being aroused by inappropriate stimuli. If we are to do something about this social evil, we must understand the basic processes of sexual arousal and identify the stimuli that elicit arousal, which were exactly the issues this research worked on. The Traditional Values Coalition, however, could not understand the merits of the research.

A second study involved research on Asian American female sex workers in San Francisco. The project investigated these women's HIV risk behaviors and their drug use and evaluated an intervention designed to reduce the chance of HIV transmission.

The Traditional Values Coalition thought that taxpayer money shouldn't fund research such as this on Asian American sex workers. Scientists believe, however, that we must halt the AIDS epidemic and that these sex workers represent one vector of transmission that has not been studied and deserved intervention efforts.

Some members of Congress stood up to their colleagues, especially Rep. Henry Waxman (D–CA), accusing the Traditional Values Coalition of scientific McCarthyism. And scientific organizations such as the American Association for the Advancement of Science (AAAS) and the American Psychological Association (APA) were also quick to line up in support of the research and in opposition to the political interference.

Also in the fall of 2003, the Special Investigations Division of the U.S. House of Representatives' Committee on Government Reform issued a report entitled *Politics and Science in the Bush Administration*. This report detailed the misuse of scientific findings to suit the political goals of the Bush administration, not only in areas such as HIV/AIDS and condoms, but also on topics such as environmental health, global warming, and lead poisoning.

These incidents raise a number of serious questions. How can we fight such problems as the AIDS epidemic or pedophilia when we lack accurate knowledge of the factors that contribute to them? Should politicians be permitted to interfere with the integrity of the scientific peer review process? Are elected officials qualified to judge the difference between high-quality and low-quality research?

The Major Sex Surveys

In the major sex surveys, the data were collected from a large sample of people by means of questionnaires or interviews. The best known of these studies is the one done by Alfred C. Kinsey, so we will consider it first. His data were collected in the late 1930s and 1940s, and thus the results are now largely of historical interest. However, Kinsey documented his methods with extraordinary care, so his research is a good example to study for both the good and the bad points of surveys.

The Kinsey Report
The Sample
Kinsey (see Focus: Milestones in Sex Research, p. 54) and his colleagues interviewed a total of 5,300 males, and their responses were reported in *Sexual Behavior in the Human Male* (1948); 5,940 females

Focus: Milestones in Sex Research
Alfred C. Kinsey

Alfred C. Kinsey was born in 1894 in New Jersey. In high school he did not date, and a classmate recalled that he was "the shyest guy around girls you could think of."

His father was determined that Kinsey become a mechanical engineer. From 1912 to 1914 he tried studying mechanical engineering at Stevens Institute, but he showed little talent for it. At one point he was close to failing physics, but a compromise was reached with the professor, who agreed to pass him if he would not attempt any advanced work in the field! In 1914 Kinsey made his break and enrolled at Bowdoin College in Maine to pursue his real love: biology. Because this went against his father's wishes, Kinsey was put on his own financially.

In 1916 he began graduate work at Harvard. There he developed an interest in insects, specializing in gall wasps. While still a graduate student he wrote a definitive book on the edible plants of eastern North America.

In 1920 he went to Bloomington, Indiana, to take a job as assistant professor of zoology at Indiana University. That fall he met Clara McMillen, whom he married six months later. They soon had four children.

With his intense curiosity and driving ambition, Kinsey quickly gained academic success. He published a high school biology text in 1926, which received enthusiastic reviews. By 1936 he had published two major books on gall wasps; they established his reputation as a leading authority in the field and contributed not only to the knowledge of gall wasps but also to genetic theory.

Kinsey came to the study of human sexual behavior as a biologist. His shift to the study of sex began in 1938, when Indiana University began a "marriage" course; Kinsey chaired the faculty committee teaching it. When confronted with teaching the course, he became aware of the appalling lack of information on human sexual behavior. Thus, his research resulted in part from his realization of the need of people, especially young people, for sex information. In 1939 he made his first field trip to collect sex histories in Chicago. His lifetime goal was to collect 100,000 sex histories.

His work culminated with the publication of the Kinsey reports in 1948 (*Sexual Behavior in the Human Male*) and 1953 (*Sexual Behavior in the Human Female*). While the scientific community generally received them as a landmark contribution, they also provoked hate mail.

In 1947 Kinsey founded the Institute for Sex Research (known popularly as the Kinsey Institute) at Indiana University. It was financed by a grant from the Rockefeller Foundation and, later, by book royalties. But in the 1950s Senator Joseph McCarthy, the communist baiter, was in power. He made a particularly vicious attack on the Institute and its research, claiming that its effect was to weaken American morality and thus make the nation more susceptible to a communist takeover. Under his pressure, the Rockefeller Foundation terminated its support.

Kinsey's health began to fail, partly as a result of the heavy workload he set for himself, and partly because he saw the financial support for the research collapsing. He died in 1956 at the age of 62 of heart failure while honoring a lecture engagement when his doctor had ordered him to convalesce.

By 1957 McCarthy had been discredited and the grant funds returned. The Institute was then

SexSource Online
www.mhhe.com/hyde10

"THE ALFRED KINSEY RESEARCH" IN PERSPECTIVES ON SEXUALITY

contributed to *Sexual Behavior in the Human Female* (1953). Though some Blacks were interviewed, only interviews with whites were included in the publications. The interviews were conducted between 1938 and 1949.

Initially, Kinsey was not much concerned with sampling issues. His goal was simply to collect sex histories from as wide a variety of people as possible. He began conducting interviews on the Indiana University campus and then moved on to large cities such as Chicago.

Kinsey later became more concerned with sampling issues and developed a technique called *100 percent sampling*. In this method he contacted a group, obtained its cooperation, and then got every one of its members to give a history. Once the cooperation of a group had been secured, peer pressure ensured that all members would participate. Unfortunately, although he was successful in getting a complete sample from such groups, the groups themselves were by no means chosen randomly. Thus, among the groups from which 100 percent samples were obtained were 2 sororities, 9 fraternities, and 13 professional groups.

In the 1953 volume on females, Kinsey said that he and his colleagues had deliberately chosen not

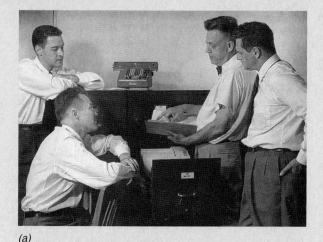

(a)

(b)

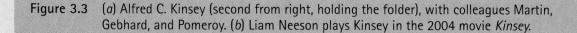

Figure 3.3 (*a*) Alfred C. Kinsey (second from right, holding the folder), with colleagues Martin, Gebhard, and Pomeroy. (*b*) Liam Neeson plays Kinsey in the 2004 movie *Kinsey.*

headed by Paul Gebhard, an anthropologist who had been a member of the staff for many years. The Institute continues to do research today; it also houses a large library on sex and an archival collection including countless works of sexual art.

In a highly publicized, tell-all biography of Kinsey, James Jones (1997) argued that, although Kinsey's public self was a stable, married man, he was in fact homosexual (more accurately, bisexual) and practiced masochism. According to Jones, this discredits Kinsey's research. Jones's logic is poor, though, because one can evaluate the quality of the research methods independently of Kinsey's personal sex life. Moreover, Kinsey's sexual experimenting may have contributed importantly to the innovativeness of his research.

Sources: Bancroft (2004); Christensen (1971); Gathorne-Hardy (2000); Gebhard (1976); Jones (1997).

to use probability sampling methods because of the problems of nonresponse. This is a legitimate point. But as a result, we have almost no information on how adequate the sample was. One might say that the sampling was haphazard but not random. For example, there were more respondents from Indiana than from any other state. Generally, the following kinds of people were overrepresented in the sample: college students, young people, well-educated people, Protestants, people living in cities, and people living in Indiana and the Northeast. Underrepresented groups included manual laborers, less well-educated people, older people, Roman Catholics, Jews, members of racial minorities, and people living in rural areas.

The Interviews
Although scientists generally regard Kinsey's sampling methods with some dismay, his face-to-face interviewing techniques are highly regarded. More than 50 percent of the interviews were done by Kinsey himself and the rest by his associates, whom he trained carefully. The interviewers made every attempt to establish rapport with the people they spoke to, and they treated all reports matter-of-factly. They were also skillful at phrasing

questions in language that was easily understood. Questions were worded so as to encourage people to report anything they had done. For example, rather than asking, "Have you ever masturbated?" the interviewers asked, "At what age did you begin masturbating?" They also developed a number of methods for cross-checking a person's report so that false information would be detected. Wardell Pomeroy recounted an example:

> Kinsey illustrated this point with the case of an older Negro male who at first was wary and evasive in his answers. From the fact that he listed a number of minor jobs when asked about his occupation and seemed reluctant to go into any of them [Kinsey] deduced that he might have been active in the underworld, so he began to follow up by asking the man whether he had ever been married. He denied it, at which Kinsey resorted to the vernacular and inquired if he had ever "lived common law." The man admitted he had, and that it had first happened when he was 14.
>
> "How old was the woman?" [Kinsey] asked.
>
> "Thirty-five," he admitted, smiling.
>
> Kinsey showed no surprise. "She was a hustler, wasn't she?" he said flatly.
>
> At this the subject's eyes opened wide. Then he smiled in a friendly way for the first time, and said, "Well, sir, since you appear to know something about these things, I'll tell you straight."
>
> After that, [Kinsey] got an extraordinary record of this man's history as a pimp. (Pomeroy, 1972, pp. 115–116)

Kinsey took strict precautions to ensure that responses were anonymous and remained anonymous. The data were stored on IBM cards, but using a code that was never written down and had been memorized by only a few people directly involved in the project. The research team had even made contingency plans for destroying the data in the event that the police tried to demand access to the records for prosecuting people.

Put simply, the interviewing techniques were probably very successful in minimizing purposeful distortion. However, other problems of self-report remained: the problems of memory and of an inability to estimate some of the numbers requested.

How Accurate Were the Kinsey Statistics?

When all is said and done, how accurate were the statistics presented by Kinsey? The American Statistical Association appointed a blue-ribbon panel to evaluate the Kinsey reports (Cochran et al., 1953; for other evaluations see Terman, 1948; Wallin, 1949). While the panel members generally felt that the interview techniques had been

excellent, they were dismayed by Kinsey's failure to use probability sampling and concluded, somewhat pessimistically,

> In the absence of a probability-sample benchmark, the present results must be regarded as subject to systematic errors of unknown magnitude due to selective sampling (via volunteering and the like). (Cochran et al., 1953, p. 711)

However, they also felt that this was a nearly insoluble problem for sex research in that even if a probability sample were used, refusals would still create serious problems.

The statisticians who evaluated Kinsey's methods felt that one aspect of his findings might have been particularly subject to error: the generally high levels of sexual activity, and particularly the high incidence of homosexual behavior. These conclusions might, they felt, have been seriously influenced by sampling problems, particularly Kinsey's tendency to seek out persons with unusual sexual practices.

Kinsey's associates felt that the most questionable statistic was the incidence of male homosexuality. Wardell Pomeroy commented, "The magic 37 percent of males who had one or more homosexual experiences was, no doubt, overestimated" (1972, p. 466).

In sum, it is impossible to say how accurate the Kinsey statistics are; some may be very accurate and some may contain serious errors. Probably the single most doubtful figure is the high incidence of homosexuality. Also, at this point the Kinsey survey is more than 50 years old; for accurate information about sexuality today, we need to look to more recent research.

The NHSLS

Since the time of the Kinsey report, many sex surveys have been conducted, most using slipshod sampling methods. What was needed was a large-scale, national survey of sexuality using probability sampling methods to tell us what Americans' patterns of sexual behavior are today. Such a study appeared in 1994. The research team was headed by Edward Laumann, a distinguished sociologist at the University of Chicago, and was conducted by the National Opinion Research Center (NORC), one of the best-respected survey organizations in the country. The survey was called the National Health and Social Life Survey; to keep things simple, we will call this study the NHSLS (Laumann et al., 1994; Michael et al., 1994).

The research method involved a probability sampling of households in the United States. This excluded less than 3 percent of Americans but did exclude people living in institutions (e.g., prisons, college dormitories) and the homeless. People were eligible if they were adults between the ages of 18 and 59.

The researchers obtained an impressive 79 percent cooperation rate. Apparently, the great majority of people are willing to respond to a carefully conducted sex survey. The response rate is particularly impressive in view of the fact that today, even surveys of more neutral topics such as political opinions generally have a response rate of only about 75 percent.

The researchers had originally planned to poll a sample of 20,000 people. However, federal funding for the project was blocked by the same political processes described earlier in the chapter. They were able to obtain funding from private foundations, but only enough to interview a sample of 3,432 people.

The data were obtained in face-to-face interviews supplemented by brief written questionnaires, which were handed to the respondents for particularly sensitive topics (such as masturbation) and sealed in a "privacy envelope" when they had been completed. The researchers chose the face-to-face interview because they felt that it would yield a higher response rate than a written questionnaire alone, and it allowed the researchers to ask more complex, detailed sequences of questions than would have been possible with just a written questionnaire or a phone interview.

Laumann's team was careful to obtain the respondents' informed consent. About a week before an interviewer went to a household, a letter was sent explaining that the purpose of the survey was to help "doctors, teachers, and counselors better understand and prevent the spread of diseases like AIDS and better understand the nature and extent of harmful and of healthy sexual behavior in our country" (Laumann et al., 1994, p. 55). The purpose was therefore clearly and honestly described to participants before their consent was requested. In order to protect confidentiality, all identifying information about the respondent was destroyed after the interview. Each respondent was paid $35 for the interview, which lasted, on average, 90 minutes.

The NHSLS is the best sex survey of the general population of the United States that we have today, and its findings are referred to in many chapters in this book. The researchers made outstanding efforts to use the best sampling methods and interview techniques.

Nonetheless, the study has some limitations. It sampled only people between ages 18 and 59, giving us no information about the sexuality of older adults. The sample did not include enough people from some statistically small minority groups—in particular, American Indians—to compute reliable statistics for them, so their data were omitted from most tables of the results. This problem would probably not have occurred if there had been funding for the full sample of 20,000. On the other hand, for other ethnic minority groups—African Americans, Latinos, and Asian Americans—there are lots of interesting findings. No doubt some respondents engaged in concealment and perhaps also in enlargement, because self-reports were used. The skill of the interviewers and their ability to build rapport is crucial in overcoming such problems. The researchers reported training the interviewers extensively, but nonetheless the extent of concealment, or underreporting, remains unknown.

Ironically, the most controversial statistic in the study was the same as in Kinsey's research—the incidence of homosexuality. In Kinsey's case, people thought the numbers were too high. In the case of the NHSLS, some people thought they were too low. We will return to this issue in Chapter 13.

Sexual Behavior in France and Britain

Again stimulated by a need for far better information about sexual behavior in order to deal with the AIDS crisis, a team of French researchers, called the ACSF Investigators, conducted a major French sex survey (ACSF Investigators, 1992). The data were collected in 1991 and 1992. These researchers chose the method of telephone interviews, preceded by a letter notifying potential respondents that they had been identified for the representative sample. The response rate was 76.5 percent. The result was a sample of 20,055 adults ranging in age from 18 to 69.

The findings indicate, for example, that 13 percent of French men, compared with 6 percent of French women, had two or more sex partners in the past 12 months and therefore were at higher risk of HIV infection.

A similar British survey was conducted by Anne Johnson and her colleagues (1992, 2001), yielding data for 18,876 men and women aged 16 to 59, living in England, Wales, and Scotland. The data indicated that, for the entire sample, 14 percent of the men

Figure 3.4 Sociologist Edward Laumann, head of the research team that conducted the NHSLS study.

Figure 3.5 Research conducted among racial and ethnic minority groups in the United States must be culturally sensitive. Ideally, for example, interviewers should be of the same cultural background as research participants.

and 7 percent of the women had had multiple sex partners in the past 12 months, figures quite similar to those of the French survey. However, when one looks just at 16- to 24-year-olds, 27 percent of the men and 16 percent of the women had had two or more partners in the past 12 months—a considerably greater proportion.

Many of the statistics in the French and British surveys match quite closely those from the U.S. NHSLS study.

A Sex Survey of African American and Hispanic Youth

Kathleen Ford and Anne Norris (1997) conducted a major sex survey of African American and Latino youth between the ages of 15 and 24 years, residing in low-income areas of Detroit. They used excellent sampling methods, contacting a probability sample

of households in low-income neighborhoods. More than 95 percent of the 60 interviewers were themselves ethnic minority residents of Detroit. The interviewers were given extensive training in skills for interviewing people about sensitive topics such as sexuality.

The study focused on the respondents' networks of sexual relationships. Although both Latinos and African Americans were found to form sexual partnerships with another member of their ethnic group the majority of the time, Latinos were far more likely than African Americans to have a partner outside their ethnic group. Among both African Americans and Latinos, women were likely to have partners older than themselves. We see in these results a pattern of both ethnic-group differences and ethnic-group similarities.

In other writings, Ford and Norris (1991) have provided extensive discussions of methodological points that must be kept in mind as researchers move beyond studying all or mostly white samples and focus increasingly on ethnic minorities in the United States (see also Matsumoto, 1994). Here are some of the issues they raise.

Respondents should be interviewed by an interviewer of the same gender and ethnic background as themselves. This practice is important for building rapport and establishing trust during the interview, both of which are critical in obtaining honest answers.

Language is another important issue in constructing interviews. Many people, Anglos included, do not know the scientific terms for sexual concepts. Interviewers therefore have to be ready with a supply of slang terms so that they can switch to these if a respondent does not understand a question. The problem becomes more complex when interviewing people whose first language is not English. Ford and Norris had the interview questions translated into Spanish by experts. They were then checked by both Mexican and Puerto Rican persons.

Cultural differences may mean that people from different ethnic groups attach different meanings to sexual concepts. An example is the apparently simple question, "Would you classify yourself as homosexual, heterosexual, or bisexual?" In Latino cultures, men who engage in anal intercourse with other men are typically not categorized as homosexual as long as they are the inserting partner (the receiving partner is definitely categorized as homosexual) (see Chapter 13). Therefore, a Latino male who frequently has sex with other men but is always the inserter might quite truthfully answer that he does not classify himself as homosexual.

The Hispanic women presented some special challenges for these researchers. Hispanic culture is characterized by sharply defined gender roles, a high valuation on virginity in unmarried women, and protection of women from sexual discussions and sexual knowledge. In keeping with these cultural traditions, the Latinas in this sample seemed to have the least sexual knowledge of all the groups and were especially sensitive about sexual topics, making it difficult to interview them.

In conclusion, doing sex research with ethnic minorities in the United States requires more than just administering the same old surveys to samples of minorities. It also dictates revisions to methodology that are culturally sensitive on issues such as the ethnicity of the interviewer, the language used in the interview, and the special sensitivity of some groups regarding certain topics.

Magazine Surveys

Many large-scale sex surveys have been conducted through magazines. Often the survey is printed in one issue of the magazine and readers are asked to respond. The result can be a huge sample—perhaps 20,000 people—which sounds impressive. But are these magazine surveys really all they claim to be?

Sampling is just plain out of control with magazine surveys. The survey is distributed just to readers of the magazine, and different magazines have different clienteles. No one magazine reaches a random sample of Americans. If the survey appeared in *Redbook,* it would go to certain kinds of women; if it were in *Ladies' Home Journal,* it would go to others. It would be risky to assume that women who read *Redbook* have the same sexual patterns as those who read *Ladies' Home Journal.* To make matters worse, the response rate is unknown. We can't know how many people saw the survey and did not fill it out, compared with the number who did. The response rate could be something like 3 percent. One does not, therefore, even have a random sample of readers of that magazine.

As an example, let's consider a survey that was reported in the August 2000 issue of *Cosmopolitan* (Gilbert, 2000). The headline on the cover announces "Our Biggest Sex Survey Ever. Thousands of Guys Reveal What Sends Them over the Edge (Their Answers Will Shock You)". The description of the methods in the article says that *Cosmo* polled 60,000 "loose-lipped men and women." That's a much larger sample than the NHSLS, but in sex surveys as in some other aspects of sexuality, bigger is not always better. How did *Cosmo* distribute the surveys? If they were printed in a previous issue, which seems like a good guess, how can we know the response rate? And how did so many men receive the survey, given that *Cosmo* is a magazine carefully aimed at a female audience? Among the respondents, how many were married? Single? What about their ethnic backgrounds? How old were they? Of course these details are not the sort of thing that *Cosmo* probably thinks will entertain its readers. Nonetheless, they could have printed the information in a small box at the end of the article. More important, these details are crucial in evaluating whether one can take their claims seriously.

For example, one question asked what a guy thinks of a girl who has sex on a first date. Of the men who were polled, 44 percent said they were happy when a woman went with her desires and wouldn't think negatively about her, as long as she was comfortable with her decision. From this, can we conclude that 44 percent of U.S. men don't think ill of a woman who goes to bed with them on a first date? This conclusion would require a leap of logic that is too big for safety. *Cosmo* wasn't even close to having a random sample in this survey.

For all these reasons, it would not be legitimate to infer that these statistics characterize U.S. men in general. We could continue with more examples of magazine surveys, but the general conclusion should be clear by now. Although they may appear impressive because of their large number of respondents, magazine sex surveys are poor in quality because the sample is generally seriously biased.

Studies of Special Populations

In addition to the large-scale studies of the U.S. population discussed earlier, many studies of special populations have been done. One example is the Coxon study of gay men in the AIDS era.

British sociologist Tony Coxon (1996) conducted a study, called Project SIGMA, to understand gay men's sexual behavior in the AIDS era. He took on two exceptionally difficult issues: sampling and the accuracy of self-reports.

In regard to sampling, he first defined the population not as gay men (that is, men who think of themselves as gay, are "out," and so on) but rather as men who have sex with men (MSM) in England and Wales. How does a researcher obtain a random sample of such a population, when no one has a convenient list of all the members of the population? To overcome this difficulty, Coxon divided the population conceptually into two subgroups: those who were relatively more "out" and active and could be contacted through gay bars, gay activist organizations, and so on; and those who were hidden, perhaps heterosexually married, and not easily accessible. He recruited respondents from the first group, which he referred to as easily accessible, through gay pubs and clubs. He then used these respondents to nominate persons in the second, hard-to-reach category. Once he had a few persons in the second category, he asked them to nominate others in their category, a technique known as *snowballing*. A total of 385 men were recruited using these methods.

In order to overcome some of the difficulties with self-reports, discussed earlier in this chapter,

and to maximize accuracy, Coxon used the *daily diary* method. Each participant was provided with a multiple-page diary, with one page for each week and horizontal boxes to record the events for each day. The instructions at the top of the page reminded the respondent to record, for each sexual session, the time, the place, and the partner (from a list of partners kept by the respondent but referred to only as P1, P2, and so on, in the diary to preserve anonymity), a description of the session in his own words, whether he had an orgasm, whether condoms were used, and whether any "accompaniments" were used, such as drugs or sex toys.

The diary method overcomes problems with relying on memory in self-reports (McAuliffe et al., 2007). It also allows a much richer, contextualized description of people's sexual experiences. In this case, the resulting book gives a fascinating account of gay men's sex lives. We will discuss it in more detail in Chapter 13.

When doing research with sexual minorities, it is important to show the same kind of cultural sensitivity as in research with ethnic minorities (Bauer & Wayne, 2005). For example, interviewers should themselves be sexual minorities.

Media Content Analysis

To this point we have focused on methods used to analyze people's responses. Yet we have also recognized the profound impact of the mass media on Americans' sexuality. To be able to understand this impact, we need to be able to analyze the media; the standard technique for this is called **content analysis** (Reinharz, 1992; Weber, 1990).

Content analysis refers to a set of procedures used to make valid inferences about text. The "text" might be romance novels, advice columns in *Cosmopolitan* magazine, lyrics from rap music, or prime-time television programs. As it turns out, many of the same methodological issues discussed earlier also come into play with content analysis.

Sampling is one such issue. Suppose that you want to do a content analysis of advice columns in *Playboy* magazine. First, you need to define the population. Do you want to sample only from *Playboy,* or do you want to sample from all sex-oriented magazines? If you want to focus only on *Playboy,* then you will surely want to collect your sample of columns from more than one issue. You will have to define the span of years of magazine issues in order to define the population. Finally, you will have to decide whether you will analyze all advice columns

Content analysis: A set of procedures used to make valid inferences about text.

Figure 3.6   Precise methods have been developed for analyzing the content of the media.

from those years, sample from only certain years, or sample some columns in some issues.

The next step is to create a coding scheme. First, you must define the recording unit—is it the word, the sentence, the entire text, or perhaps themes that run across several sentences? Then, perhaps most important, you need to define the coding categories. Creating the coding scheme involves defining the basic content categories, the presence or absence of which will be recorded, for example, in the advice columns. These coding categories will depend on the question you want to ask. For example, suppose your question about prime-time television shows is, What is the frequency on these shows of nonmarital compared with marital sex? In creating a coding scheme, you would have to define carefully what observable behaviors on television count as "sex." Suppose you include kissing, fondling of the breasts or genitals, sexual intercourse actually shown, and implied sexual intercourse. You could then code each of these behaviors as they occurred on a sample of prime-time shows and indicate, for each act, whether it was between married or unmarried persons.

The reliability of the data must be demonstrated in content analysis just as it must in research with human participants. Without a demonstration of reliability, a critic might accuse you of bias, for example, seeing far more acts of sex on the programs than actually occurred. Usually a measure called **intercoder reliability** is used. The researcher trains another person in the exact use of the coding scheme. Then the researcher and the trained coder each independently code a sample of the texts in the study—for example, 20 of the advice columns or 20 of the prime-time shows. The researcher then computes a correlation or percent of agreement between the two coders' results, which gives the measure of intercoder reliability. If the two coders agree exactly, the correlation will be 1.0.

Content analysis is a powerful scientific technique that allows us to know how the media portray sexuality. As an example, let's suppose that your friend Rachel says that it is deeply disturbing that women are shown in nothing but traditional roles on prime-time TV, and this situation hasn't improved a bit over the years. Your other friend Tanisha disagrees, saying that there may still be some traditional images of women, but there are many examples of women in nontraditional roles such as doctors, and that the media's portrayals of women have changed a lot over the years. How can you decide who is

Intercoder reliability: In content analysis, the correlation or percent of agreement between two coders independently rating the same texts.

right? Arguing won't settle the debate. What is needed is a content analysis of current prime-time shows, counting instances of women in traditional and nontraditional roles, together with an analysis of archived prime-time shows from 10 and 20 years ago. We will see examples of content analyses such as these in Chapter 12.

Laboratory Studies Using Direct Observations of Sexual Behavior

The numerous problems associated with using self-reports of sexual behavior in scientific research have been discussed. The main alternative to using self-reports is to make direct observations of sexual behavior in the laboratory. These direct observations overcome the major problems of self-reports: purposeful distortion, inaccurate memory, and inability of people to estimate correctly or describe certain aspects of their behavior. The pioneering example of this approach is Masters and Johnson's work on the physiology of sexual response.

Masters and Johnson: The Physiology of Sexual Response

William Masters began his research on the physiology of sexual response in 1954. No one had ever studied human sexual behavior in the laboratory before, so he had to develop all the necessary research techniques from scratch. He began by interviewing 188 female prostitutes, as well as 27 male prostitutes working for a homosexual clientele. They gave him important preliminary data in which they "described many methods for elevating and controlling sexual tensions and demonstrated innumerable variations in stimulative techniques," some of which were useful in the later program of therapy for sexual disorders.

Meanwhile, Masters began setting up his laboratory and equipping it with the necessary instruments: an electrocardiograph to measure changes in heart rate over the sexual cycle, an electromyograph to measure muscular contractions in the body during sexual response, and a pH meter to measure the acidity of the vagina during the various stages of sexual response.

SexSource Online
www.mhhe.com/hyde10

"MASTERS AND JOHNSON'S RESEARCH" IN SEXUAL RESPONSE

Sampling

Masters made a major breakthrough when he decided that it should be possible to recruit normal participants from the general population and have them engage in sexual behavior in the laboratory, where their behavior and physiological responses could be carefully observed and measured. This approach had never been used before, as even the daring Kinsey had settled for people's verbal reports of their behavior.

Masters let it be known in the medical school and university community that he needed volunteers for laboratory studies of human sexual response. Some people volunteered because of their belief in the importance of the research. Some, of course, came out of curiosity or because they were exhibitionists; they were weeded out in the initial interviews. Participants were paid for their hours in the laboratory, as is typical in medical research, so many medical students and graduate students participated because it was a way to earn money.

Initially, all prospective participants were given detailed interviews by Masters and his colleague Virginia Johnson. People who had histories of emotional problems or who seemed uncomfortable with the topic of sex either failed to come back after this interview or were eliminated even if they were willing to proceed. Participants were also assured that the anonymity and confidentiality of their participation would be protected carefully. In all, 694 people participated in the laboratory studies reported in *Human Sexual Response*. The men ranged in age from 21 to 89, while the women ranged from 18 to 78. A total of 276 married couples participated, as well as 106 women and 36 men who were unmarried. The unmarried persons were helpful mainly in the studies that did not require sexual intercourse—for example, studies of the ejaculatory mechanism in males and of the effects of sexual arousal on the positioning of the diaphragm in the vagina.

Certainly the group of people Masters and Johnson studied were not a random sample of the population of the United States. In fact, one might imagine that people who would agree to participate in such research would be rather unusual. The data indicate that they were more educated than the general population and the sample was mostly white, with only a few ethnic minority persons participating. Paying the participants probably helped broaden the sample, since it attracted some people who simply needed the money. The sample omitted two notable types of people: those who were not sexually experienced or did not respond to sexual stimulation and those who were unwilling to have their sexual behavior studied in the laboratory. Therefore, the results Masters and Johnson obtained might not generalize to such people.

Just exactly how critical is this sampling problem to the validity of the research? Masters and Johnson were not particularly concerned about it, because they assumed that the processes they were studying are normative; that is, they work in essentially the same way in all people. This assumption is commonly made in medical research. For example, a researcher who is studying the digestive process does not worry that the sample is composed of all medical students, since the assumption is that digestion works the same way in all human beings. If this assumption is also true for the physiology of sexual response, then all people respond similarly, and it does not matter that the sample is not random. Whether this assumption is correct remains to be seen (see Chapter 8 for further critiques). The sampling problem, however, does mean that Masters and Johnson could not make statistical conclusions on the basis of their research; for example, they could not say that X percent of all women have multiple orgasms. Any percentages would be specific to their sample and could not be generalized to the rest of the population.

In defense of their sampling techniques, even if they had identified an initial probability sample, they would still almost surely have had a very high refusal rate, probably higher than in survey research, and the probability sample would have been ruined. At present, this seems to be an unsolvable problem in this type of research.

Data Collection Techniques

After they were accepted for the project, participants then proceeded to the laboratory phase of the study. First, they had a "practice session," in which they engaged in sexual activity in the laboratory in complete privacy, with no data being recorded and no researchers present. The purpose of this was to allow the participants to become comfortable with engaging in sexual behavior in a laboratory setting.

The physical responses of the participants were then recorded during sexual intercourse, masturbation, and "artificial coition." Masters and Johnson made an important technical advance with the development of the artificial coition technique. In it, a female participant stimulates herself with an artificial penis constructed of clear plastic; it is powered by an electric motor, and the woman can adjust the depth and frequency of the thrust. There is a light and a recording apparatus inside the artificial penis, so the changes occurring inside the vagina can be photographed.

Measures such as these avoid the problems of distortion that are possible with self-reports. They also answer much different questions. That is, it would be impossible from such measures to tell whether the person had had any homosexual experiences or how frequently he or she masturbated. Instead, they ascertain how the body responds to sexual stimulation, with a kind of accuracy and detail that would be impossible to obtain through self-reports.

One final potential problem also deserves mention. It has to do with the problems of laboratory studies: Do people respond the same sexually in the laboratory as they do in the privacy of their own homes?

Ethical Considerations

Masters and Johnson were attentive to ethical principles. They were careful to use informed consent. Potential participants were given detailed explanations of the kinds of things they would be required to do in the research and were given ample opportunity at all stages to withdraw from the research if they so desired. Furthermore, Masters and Johnson eliminated people who appeared too anxious or distressed during the preliminary interviews.

It is also possible that participating in the research itself might have been harmful in some way to some people. Masters and Johnson were particularly concerned with the long-term effects of participating in the research. Accordingly, they made follow-up contacts with the participants at five-year intervals. In no case did a participant report developing a sexual disorder. In fact, many of the couples reported specific ways in which participating in the research enriched their marriages. Thus, the available data seem to indicate that such research does not harm the participants and may in some ways benefit them, not to mention the benefit to society that results from gaining information in such an important area.

In sum, direct observations of sexual behavior of the type done by Masters and Johnson have some distinct advantages but also some disadvantages, compared with survey-type research. Their research avoids the problems of self-reports and is capable of answering much more detailed physiological questions than self-reports could. But the research is costly and time consuming, making large samples impractical; furthermore, a high refusal rate is probably inevitable, so probability samples are impossible to obtain.

Participant-Observer Studies

A research method used by anthropologists and sociologists is the **participant-observer technique.** In this type of research, the scientist actually becomes a part of the

Participant-observer technique: A research method in which the scientist becomes part of the community to be studied and makes observations from inside the community.

community to be studied, and she or he makes observations from inside the community. In the study of sexual behavior, the researcher may thus be able to get direct observations of sexual behavior combined with interview data.

Examples of this type of research are studies of sexual behavior in other cultures, such as those done in Mangaia, Mehinaku, and Inis Beag, which were discussed in Chapter 1. Two other examples are Laud Humphreys's study of the tearoom trade and Charles Moser's study of S/M (sadomasochistic) parties.

Humphreys: The Tearoom Trade

Sociologist Laud Humphreys (1970) conducted a participant-observer study of impersonal sex between men in public places. The study is discussed in detail in Focus: Milestones in Sex Research, page 343 in Chapter 13. Briefly, Humphreys acted as a lookout while men engaged in sex acts in public rest rooms ("tearooms"); his job was to sound a warning if police or other intruders approached. This permitted Humphreys to make direct observations of the sexual behavior. He also got the license-plate numbers of the men involved, traced them, and later interviewed them in their homes under the pretext of conducting a routine survey.

Humphreys obtained a wealth of information from the study, but in doing so he violated several ethical principles of behavioral research. He had no informed consent from his subjects; they were never even aware of the fact that they were participants in research, much less of the nature of the research. Thus, this study was quite controversial.

S/M Parties

Sex researcher Charles Moser observed S/M interactions in semipublic settings, attending more than 200 S/M parties (Moser, 1998). Such parties are typically highly scripted. The person who gives the party may advertise it widely (e.g., on the Internet) or may issue personal invitations to only a very select list. The parties may have a particular theme, such as female dominant/male submissive only or women only. The party might be held at a person's home or in a rented space; some cities have spaces dedicated for S/M party rental.

Each party has a particular set of rules—which vary from one party to another—and guests may be required to sign a written agreement to them. Issues covered

in these rules include who may talk to whom (can a submissive be spoken to?), who may play with whom, who may have sex with whom, prohibited S/M or sexual behaviors, what constitutes safer sex, not blocking equipment by sitting on it, and so on. Drunkenness is never acceptable; some parties allow wine or beer, but others ban all alcohol.

Some individuals plan to have a first "date" at a party. Parties clearly have the function of ensuring safety for participants, since others are always present if an interaction goes too far. Potential partners negotiate what kind of interaction they desire—for example, pain versus humiliation.

Perhaps most interesting is the fact that coitus or genitally focused activity designed to produce orgasm is very rare at these parties. The participants describe the S/M experiences as highly sexual, but orgasm typically is not the goal.

Moser did not report that he obtained informed consent from the people he observed. However, their behavior was public, leading to a relaxation of human subjects regulations. In his report he was careful not to divulge any identifying information about individuals.

Experimental Sex Research

All the studies discussed so far have had one thing in common: They were all studies of people's sexual behavior as it occurs naturally, conducted by means of either self-reports or direct observations. Such research is **correlational;** that is, the data obtained can tell us that certain factors are related. They cannot, however, tell us what *causes* various aspects of sexual behavior.

For instance, suppose we conduct a survey and find that women who masturbated to orgasm before marriage are more likely to have a high consistency of orgasm in marriage than women who did not. From this it would be tempting to conclude that practice in masturbating causes women to have more orgasms in heterosexual sex. Unfortunately, this is not a legitimate conclusion to draw from the data, since many other factors might also explain the results. For example, it could be that some women have a higher sex drive than others, which causes them to masturbate and also have orgasms in heterosexual sex. Therefore, the most we can conclude is that masturbation experience is related to (or correlated with) orgasm consistency in marital sex.

Correlational study: A study in which the researcher does not manipulate variables but rather studies naturally occurring relationships (correlations) among variables.

Figure 3.7 An innovation in surveys of children is the use of "talking computers" to ask questions, with the child entering her answers using the mouse or the keyboard.

An alternative method that does allow researchers to determine the causes of various aspects of behavior is the **experiment.** According to its technical definition, in an experiment one factor must be manipulated while all other factors are held constant. Thus, any differences among the groups of people who received different treatments on that one factor can be said to be caused by that factor. For obvious reasons, most experimental research is conducted in the laboratory.

As an example of an experiment, let us consider a study that investigated whether being interviewed face to face causes children to underreport their sexual experiences (Romer et al., 1997). The participants were approximately 400 low-income children between the ages of 9 and 15. Some were assigned to a face-to-face interview with an experienced adult interviewer of their own gender. Others were assigned to be interviewed by a "talking computer," which had the same questions programmed into it. The questions appeared on the screen and, simultaneously, came through headphones, for those who were not good readers. Presumably in the talking computer condition, the child feels more of a sense of privacy and anonymity and therefore responds more truthfully.

Among 13-year-old boys interviewed by the talking computer, 76 percent said they had "had sex," compared with only 50 percent of the boys in the face-to-face interview. Forty-eight percent of 13-year-old girls interviewed by computer said they had had sex, compared with 25 percent of those interviewed by a human. The children clearly reported more sexual activity to the computer than to a human interviewer.

In the language of experimental design, the *independent variable* (manipulated variable) was the type of interview (computer or human interviewer). The *dependent variable* (the measured variable) was whether they had had sex (there were a number of other dependent variables as well, but a discussion of them would take us too far afield).

The results indicated that those interviewed by humans reported significantly less sexual activity than those interviewed by computer. Because the research design was experimental, we can make causal inferences. We can say confidently that the type of interview had an effect on children's answers. We might also say that a face-to-face interview causes children to underreport their activity. That statement is a bit shakier than the previous one, because it assumes that the answers given to the talking computer were "true." It is possible that children overreported or exaggerated in responding to the computer and that their answers to the human interviewer were accurate, although this interpretation seems rather far-fetched.

Experimental sex research permits us to make much more powerful statements about the causes of various kinds of sexual phenomena. As for disadvantages, much of the experimental sex research, including the study described here, still relies on self-reports. Experimental sex research is time consuming and costly, and it can generally be done only on small samples of participants. Sometimes in their efforts to control all variables except the independent variable, researchers control too much. Finally, experiments cannot address some of the most interesting—but most complex—questions in the field of sexual behavior, such as what factors cause people to develop heterosexual or homosexual orientations.

Experiment: A type of research study in which one variable (the independent variable) is manipulated by the experimenter while all other factors are held constant; the research can then study the effects of the independent variable on some measured variable (the dependent variable); the researcher is permitted to make causal inferences about the effects of the independent variable on the dependent variable.

Some Statistical Concepts

Before you can understand reports of sex research, you must understand some basic statistical concepts.

Average

Suppose we get data from a sample of married couples on how many times per week they have sexual intercourse. How can we summarize the data? One way to do this is to compute some average value; this will tell us how often, on the average, these people have intercourse. In sex research, the number that is usually calculated is either the mean or the median; both of these give us an indication of approximately where the average value for that group of people is. The **mean** is simply the average of the scores of all the people. The **median** is the score that splits the sample in half, with half the respondents scoring below that number and half scoring above it.

Variability

In addition to having an indication of the average for the sample of respondents, it is also interesting to know how much variability there is from one respondent to the next in the numbers reported. That is, it is one thing to say that the average married couple in a sample had intercourse three times per week, with a range in the sample from two to four times per week, and it is quite another thing to say that the average was three times per week, with a range from zero to fifteen times per week. In both cases the mean is the same, but in the first there is little variability, and in the second there is a great deal of variability. These two alternatives are shown graphically in Figure 3.8. There is great variability in virtually all sexual behavior.

Average versus Normal

It is interesting and informative to report the average frequency of a particular sexual behavior, but this also introduces the danger that people will confuse "average" with "normal." That is, there is a tendency, when reading a statistic like "the average person has intercourse twice per week," to think of one's own sexual behavior, compare it with that average, and then conclude that one is abnormal if one differs much from the average. If you read that statistic and your frequency of intercourse is only once a week, you may begin to worry that you are undersexed or that you are not getting as much as you should. If you are having intercourse seven times per week, you might begin worrying that you are oversexed. Such conclusions are a mistake, first because they can make you miserable and second because there is so much variability in sexual behavior that any behavior (or frequency or length of time) within a wide range is perfectly normal. Don't confuse average with normal.

Mean: The average of respondents' scores.
Median: The middle score.

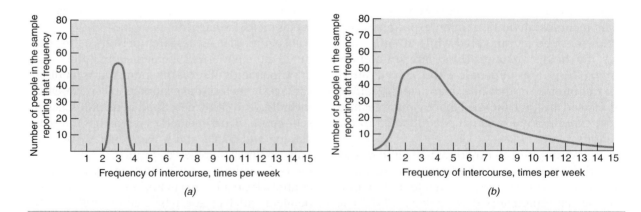

Figure 3.8 Two hypothetical graphs of the frequency of intercourse for married couples in a sample. In both the average frequency is about three times per week, but in (*a*) there is little variability (almost everyone has a frequency between two and four times per week), whereas in (*b*) there is great variability (the frequency ranges from zero to fifteen or more times per week). The graph for most sexual behavior looks like (*b*), with great variability.

Incidence versus Frequency

In sex statistics, the terms *incidence* and *frequency* are often used. **Incidence** refers to the percentage of people who have engaged in a certain behavior. **Frequency** refers to how often people do something. Thus we might say that the incidence of masturbation among males is 92 percent (meaning that 92 percent of all males masturbate at least once in their lives), whereas the average frequency of masturbation among males between the ages of 16 and 20 is about once per week.

A closely related concept is that of cumulative incidence. If we consider a sexual behavior according to the age at which each person in the sample first engaged in it, the *cumulative incidence* refers to the percentage of people who have engaged in that behavior before a certain age. Thus, the cumulative incidence of masturbation in males might be 10 percent by age 11, 25 percent by age 12, 82 percent by age 15, and 95 percent by age 20. Graphs of cumulative incidence always begin in the lower left-hand corner and move toward the upper right-hand corner. An example of a cumulative-incidence curve is shown in Figure 3.9.

Correlation

In this chapter the concept of correlation has already been mentioned several times—for example, test-retest reliability is measured by the correlation between people's answer to a question with their answer to the same question a week or two later—and the concept of correlation will reappear in later chapters.

The term *correlation* is used by laypeople in contexts such as the following: "There seems to be a correlation here between how warm the days are and how fast the corn is growing." But what do statisticians mean by the term *correlation*? A **correlation** is a number that measures the relationship between two variables. A correlation can be positive or negative. A positive correlation occurs when there is a positive relationship between the two variables; that is, people who have high scores on one variable tend to have high scores on the other variable; low scores go with low scores. A negative correlation occurs when there is an opposite relationship between the two variables; that is, people with high scores on one variable tend to have low scores on the other variable. We might want to know, for example, whether there is a correlation between the number of years a couple has been married and the frequency with which they have sexual intercourse. In this case we might expect that there would be a negative correlation, and that is just what researchers have found. That is, the *greater* the number of years

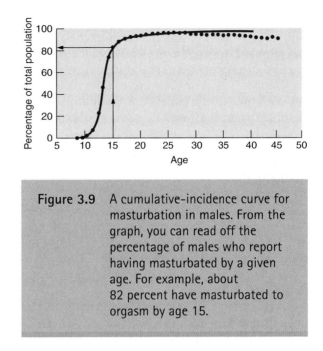

Figure 3.9 A cumulative-incidence curve for masturbation in males. From the graph, you can read off the percentage of males who report having masturbated by a given age. For example, about 82 percent have masturbated to orgasm by age 15.

of marriage, the *lower* the frequency of intercourse. As another example, we might want to know whether there is a correlation between people's sexual attitudes and their sexual behavior, specifically whether people who hold more permissive attitudes about premarital sex have more premarital partners. In this case we expect a positive correlation in the sense that the people who score high on the measure of permissive attitudes are expected to have more partners and that people who score low on the measure of permissiveness are expected to have fewer partners.

Correlations range between +1.0 and −1.0. A correlation of +1.0 indicates a perfect positive relationship between two variables, meaning that the person in the sample who scores highest on one variable also has the highest score on the other variable, the person with the second highest score on the first variable also has the second highest score on the other variable, and so on. A correlation of 0 indicates no relationship between the two variables. Knowing a person's score on one variable tells us nothing about whether the person will have a high or a low score on the other variable. Positive correlations between 0 and +1.0, for example, +.62, say that the relationship is positive but not a perfect relationship.

Returning to the example of test-retest reliability discussed earlier in this chapter, suppose we administer a questionnaire to a sample of adults. One of the questions asks, "How many times did

Incidence: The percentage of people giving a particular response.
Frequency: How often a person does something.
Correlation: A number that measures the relationship between two variables.

you masturbate to orgasm during the month of September?" We ask this question of the sample on October 1 and again on October 8. If each person in the sample gives us exactly the same answer on October 1 and on October 8, the correlation between the two variables (the number given on October 1 and the number given on October 8) would be $+1.0$ and the test-retest reliability would be a perfect $+1.0$. In fact, test-retest reliabilities for questions about sex typically range between $+.60$ and $+.90$, indicating that people's answers on the two occasions are not identical but are very similar.

SUMMARY

Knowledge of the major methods that have been used in sex research and of the problems and merits associated with each is necessary for understanding and evaluating sex research.

Ideally, sex research should employ probability sampling techniques.

Large-scale surveys of sexual behavior generally rely on people's self-reports, which may be inaccurate because of purposeful distortion, problems of memory, or an inability to estimate some of the information requested. Direct observations of sexual behavior avoid these problems, but they lead to an even more restricted sample. They also answer questions that are somewhat different from those answered by surveys. Web-based surveys offer new opportunities for sex research.

In all behavioral research, the ethical principles of informed consent, protection from harm, and justice must be observed, although historically some sex researchers did not do this.

One major sex survey was Kinsey's large-scale interview study of the sexual behavior of Americans, done during the 1940s. The 1994 NHSLS is a large-scale survey of the sexual behavior of Americans; it was based on probability sampling. Other large surveys have been done, including some through magazines; the samples in magazine surveys, however, are so restricted that we cannot draw general conclusions from them.

Studies of special populations include Coxon's daily diary study of the sexual behavior of gay men.

In media content analysis, researchers use systematic coding categories to analyze what is represented in the media, such as on television, in romance novels, or in magazine ads.

In participant-observer studies, the scientist becomes a part of the community to be studied and uses a combination of direct observations and interviewing. Examples are studies of sexual behavior in other cultures and Humphreys's study of the tearoom trade.

In experimental sex research, the goal is to discover what factors cause or influence various aspects of sexual behavior. The researcher manipulates an independent variable and measures a dependent variable.

The following statistical terms were introduced: *mean*, *median*, *variability*, *incidence*, *frequency*, and *correlation*.

QUESTIONS FOR THOUGHT, DISCUSSION, AND DEBATE

1. Find a recent sex survey in a magazine. Evaluate the quality of the study, using concepts you have learned in this chapter.
2. Of the research techniques in this chapter—surveys, laboratory studies using direct observations, media content analysis, participant-observer studies, experiments—which do you think is best for learning about human sexuality? Why?
3. You want to conduct a survey, using face-to-face interviews, to determine whether there are differences between Asian American and white American teenagers ages 15 to 19 in their sexual behavior and attitudes. In what ways would you tailor the research methods to make them culturally sensitive?
4. Imagine that you have been hired by your college or university to produce a report on the patterns of sexual behavior of the students there, with the goal of helping the administration plan better in areas such as health services and counseling. You are given a generous budget for data collection. How would you go about collecting the data you would need to produce a truly excellent report?

SUGGESTIONS FOR FURTHER READING

Matsumoto, David. (1994). *Cultural influences on research methods and statistics.* Pacific Grove, CA: Brooks/Cole. This concise book, written for undergraduates, explains principles of cross-cultural research and how one should modify research methods depending on the culture being studied.

Michael, Robert T., Gagnon, John H., Laumann, Edward O., & Kolata, Gina. (1994). *Sex in America: A definitive survey.* Boston: Little, Brown. This book reports the results of the NHSLS and is written for the general public.

Wiederman, Michael W. (2001). *Understanding sexuality research.* Belmont, CA: Wadsworth. This slim volume, written for undergraduates, takes up where the present chapter leaves off and offers an excellent analysis of methodological issues in sex research, with interesting examples.

CHAPTER FOUR

Sexual Anatomy

CHAPTER HIGHLIGHTS

Men and women, all in all, behave just like our basic sexual elements. If you watch single men on a weekend night they really act very much like sperm—all disorganized, bumping into their friends, swimming in the wrong direction.

"I was first."

"Let me through."

"You're on my tail."

"That's my spot."

We're like the Three Billion Stooges.

But the egg is very cool: "Well, who's it going to be? I can divide. I can wait a month. I'm not swimming anywhere."*

*Jerry Seinfeld. (1993). *SeinLanguage.* New York: Bantam Books, p. 17.

The women's health movement has emphasized that women need to know more about their bodies. Actually, that is a good principle for everyone to follow. The current trend is away from the elitist view that only a select group of people—physicians—should understand the functioning of the body and toward the view that everyone needs more information about his or her own body. The purpose of this chapter is to provide basic information about the structure and functions of the parts of the body that are involved in sexuality and reproduction. Some readers may anticipate that this will be a boring exercise. Everyone, after all, knows what a penis is and what a vagina is. But even today, we find some bright college students who think a woman's urine passes out through her vagina. And how many know what the epididymis and the seminiferous tubules are? If you don't know, keep reading. You may even find out a few interesting things about the penis and the vagina that you were not aware of.

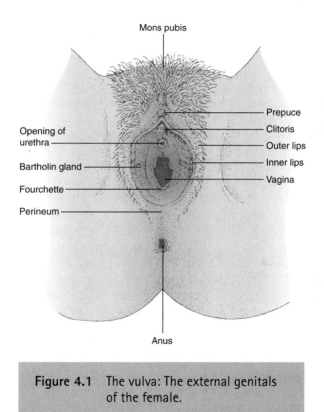

Figure 4.1   The vulva: The external genitals of the female.

Female Sexual Organs

The female sexual organs can be classified into two categories: the *external organs* and the *internal organs.*

External Organs

The external genitals of the female consist of the clitoris, the mons pubis, the inner lips, the outer lips, and the vaginal opening (see Figure 4.1). Collectively, they are known as the **vulva** ("crotch"; other terms such as "cunt" and "pussy" may refer either to the vulva or to the vagina, and some ethnic groups use "cock" for the vulva—slang, alas, is

not so precise as scientific language).[1] *Vulva* is a wonderful term but, unfortunately, it tends to be underused—the term, that is. The appearance of the vulva varies greatly from one woman to another (see Figure 4.2).

[1]For a discussion of slang terms for female and male genitals, see Braun and Kitzinger (2001).

SexSource Online
www.mhhe.com/hyde10

"SELF-AWARENESS" IN SEXUAL ANATOMY AND PHYSIOLOGY

Vulva (VULL-vuh): The collective term for the external genitals of the female.

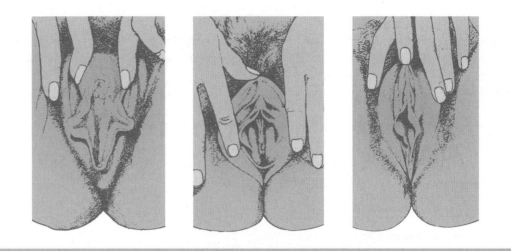

Figure 4.2   The shape of the vulva varies widely from one woman to the next.

The Clitoris

The **clitoris** is a sensitive organ that is exceptionally important in female sexual response (Figure 4.3). It consists of the tip (glans), a knob of tissue situated externally in front of the vaginal opening and the urethral opening; a shaft consisting of two corpora cavernosa (spongy bodies similar to those in the male's penis) that extends perhaps an inch into the body; and two crura (singular "crus"), longer spongy bodies that lie deep in the body and run from the tip of the clitoris to either side of the vagina, under the major lips (Clemente, 1987). Some refer to the entire structure as having a "wishbone" shape. Close to the crura are the vestibular bulbs, which will be discussed in the section on internal organs.

As we will see in Chapter 5, female sexual organs and male sexual organs develop from similar tissue before birth; thus we can speak of the organs of one gender as being *homologous* (in the sense of developing from the same source) to the organs of the other gender. The female's clitoris is homologous to the male's penis; that is, both develop from the same embryonic tissue. The clitoris has a structure similar to that of the penis in that both have corpora cavernosa. The clitoris varies in size from one woman to the next, much as the penis varies in size from man to man. Also, the clitoris, like the penis, is erectile. Its erection is possible because its internal structure contains corpora cavernosa that fill with blood, as the similar structures in the penis do. The corpora cavernosa and the

mechanism of erection will be considered in more detail in the discussion of the male sexual organs. Like the penis, the clitoris has a rich supply of nerve endings, making it very sensitive to stroking. Most women find it to be more sensitive to erotic stimulation than any other part of the body.

The clitoris is unique in that it is the only part of the sexual anatomy with no known reproductive function. All the other sexual organs serve sexual and reproductive functions. For example, not only is the vagina used for sexual intercourse, but it also receives the sperm and serves as the passageway through which the baby travels during childbirth. The penis not only produces sexual arousal and pleasure but also is responsible for ejaculation and impregnation. The clitoris clearly has an important function in producing sexual arousal. Unlike the other sexual organs, however, it appears to have no direct function in reproduction.

The Mons

Other parts of the vulva are the mons pubis, the inner lips, and the outer lips. The **mons pubis** (also called the *mons* or the *mons veneris,* for "mountain of Venus") is the rounded, fatty pad of tissue, covered with pubic hair, at the front of the body. It lies on top of the pubic bones.

The Labia

The **outer lips** (or *labia majora,* for "major lips") are rounded pads of fatty tissue lying along both sides of the vaginal opening; they are covered with pubic hair. The **inner lips** (or *labia minora,* for "minor lips") are two hairless folds of skin lying between the outer lips and running right along the edge of

Clitoris (KLIT-or-is): A small, highly sensitive sexual organ in the female, found in front of the vaginal entrance.
Mons pubis (PYOO-bis): The fatty pad of tissue under the pubic hair.
Outer lips: Rounded pads of fatty tissue lying on either side of the vaginal entrance.
Inner lips: Thin folds of skin lying on either side of the vaginal entrance.

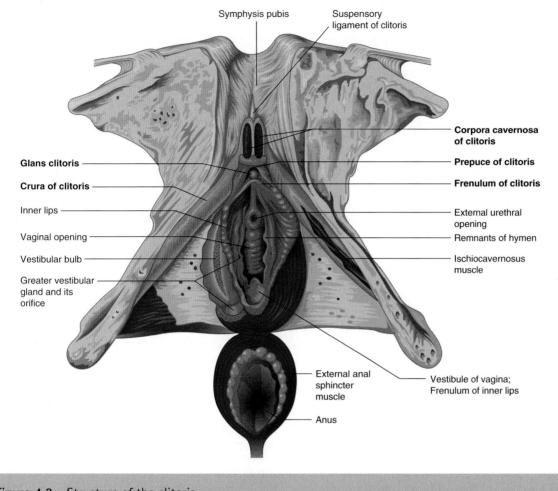

Symphysis pubis

Suspensory ligament of clitoris

Corpora cavernosa of clitoris

Glans clitoris

Prepuce of clitoris

Crura of clitoris

Frenulum of clitoris

Inner lips

External urethral opening

Vaginal opening

Remnants of hymen

Vestibular bulb

Ischiocavernosus muscle

Greater vestibular gland and its orifice

External anal sphincter muscle

Vestibule of vagina; Frenulum of inner lips

Anus

Figure 4.3   Structure of the clitoris.

the vaginal opening. Sometimes they are folded over, concealing the vaginal opening until they are spread apart. The inner lips extend forward and come together in front, forming the clitoral hood. The inner and outer lips are well supplied with nerve endings and thus are also important in sexual stimulation and arousal.

A pair of small glands, the **Bartholin glands,** lie just inside the inner lips (Figure 4.1). Their function is unknown, and they are of interest only because they sometimes become infected.[2]

[2]And there is a limerick about them:

There was a young man from Calcutta
Who was heard in his beard to mutter,
"If her Bartholin glands
Don't respond to my hands,
I'm afraid I shall have to use butter."

Actually, there is a biological fallacy in the limerick. Can you spot it? If not, see Chapter 8.

A few more landmarks should be noted (Figure 4.1). The place where the inner lips come together behind the vaginal opening is called the *fourchette.* The area of skin between the vaginal opening and the anus is called the **perineum** (Latin for "around the anus"). The vaginal opening itself is sometimes called the **introitus.** Notice also that the urinary opening lies about midway between the clitoris and the vaginal opening. Thus urine does not pass out through the clitoris (as might be expected from analogy with the male) or through the vagina, but instead through a separate pathway, the **urethra,** with a separate opening.

Self-Knowledge

One important difference between the male sex organs and the female sex organs—and a difference that has some important psychological

Bartholin glands: Two tiny glands located on either side of the vaginal entrance.
Perineum (pair-ih-NEE-um): The skin between the vaginal entrance and the anus.
Introitus: Another word for the vaginal entrance.
Urethra: The tube through which urine passes from the bladder out of the body.

Focus: A Sexually Diverse World
Female Genital Cutting

Today a worldwide sexual health controversy rages over female genital cutting (FGC, also known as female genital mutilation, or FGM). FGC is practiced in 25 African nations as well as in several countries in the Middle East and among Muslim populations in Indonesia and Malaysia. It is estimated to affect between 80 million and 110 million women worldwide. Typically, girls are subjected to the procedure between the ages of 4 and 10, although sometimes it is done during infancy. Often the procedure is performed by a native woman, with no anesthetic and under unsanitary conditions. If these practices seem remote to many North Americans, it is important to recognize that immigrant women from these countries now reside in North America. Moreover, some of these practices were performed in Britain and North America in the 1800s, during the Victorian era, to cure various "female weaknesses" such as masturbation. And currently there is a cult in the United States that practices genital surgeries such as removal of the outer lips, because they believe that the vulva is more beautiful and erotic that way.

FGC is practiced in several forms, depending on the customs of the particular culture. The mildest form, called *sunna,* refers to the removal of just the clitoral hood (prepuce), not the clitoris; it is the only procedure that could legitimately be called "female circumcision," analogous to male circumcision. In its mildest form, it may involve only making a slit in the prepuce, not removing it. A second form of FGC is *excision* (sometimes known as *clitoridectomy*), which refers to complete removal of the clitoris and perhaps some of the inner lips. The most extreme form is *infibulation* or pharaonic circumcision (named for the pharaohs of Egypt, under whose reign the practice is said to have originated thousands of years ago). It involves the removal of the clitoris, all of the inner lips, and part of the outer lips; the raw edges of the outer lips are then stitched together to cover the urethral opening and the vaginal entrance, with only a small opening left for the passage of urine and menstrual fluid.

Infibulation poses severe health problems for women. Hemorrhaging may occur, leading to shock and even to bleeding to death. Because of the unsanitary conditions present during the procedure, tetanus and other infections are risks. Because the same instrument may be used on multiple girls, HIV and hepatitis B can be transmitted.

A common problem is that the pain of the wound is so severe and the stitching so tight that the girl avoids urinating or cannot urinate properly, leading to urinary infections and other complications. A tightly infibulated woman can only urinate drop by drop, and her menstrual period may take 10 days and be extremely painful. Women who have undergone FGC are at higher risk of infections such as herpes and bacterial vaginosis.

The sexual and reproductive health consequences are no less severe. Infibulation is an effective method for ensuring virginity until marriage, but on the wedding night the man must force an opening through stitching and scar tissue. This is painful and may take days; a midwife may be called to cut open the tissue. Some men report wounds to the penis as a result of attempts at intercourse with wives who had had FGC. Orgasm would be only a remote possibility for a woman whose clitoris has been removed. Infibulated women have a substantial risk of complications during childbirth. The scar must always be cut open to permit delivery and, if done too late, the baby may die.

In Egypt, 77 percent of women support the continuation of FGC (Yoder et al., 2004). If these procedures are so harmful, why do they persist? Why do girls submit to them, and even ask for them, and why do their parents permit or even encourage it? The answer lies in the complex and powerful interplay of culture and gender. Being infibulated indicates not only virginity but also a woman's loyalty to and identification with her culture and its traditions, a particularly sensitive issue for people long dominated by European colonizers. A woman who is not infibulated is not marriageable in these cultures, in which marriage is the only acceptable way of life for an adult woman. When those are the rules of the game, it is less surprising that girls submit or even want to be circumcised and that their parents require them to do it. Particular communities may also hold certain beliefs that make these procedures seem necessary. For example, in some areas there is a belief that the clitoris contains poison and can harm men during sexual intercourse and kill children during birth. Some Muslims mistakenly believe that it is required by their faith, although it is not mentioned in the Koran. In practice, FGC is only loosely associated with Islam. In Mali, for example, 92 percent of Muslim women had FGC, but so did 76 percent of Christian women (Yoder et al., 2004).

Figure 4.4 Twenty-five African nations practice some form of ritualized genital cutting of young girls as an initiation into womanhood. Clitoridectomy is also practiced in Muslim countries outside Africa, and was practiced in the United States during the Victorian era.

Infibulation raises a number of dilemmas for North Americans. In universities, we generally encourage the approach of *cultural relativism,* an openness to and appreciation of the customs of other cultures. FGC is definitely a custom of other cultures. If we apply standards of cultural relativism, we should say, "Great, if that's what those people want." But should there be limits to cultural relativism? Can one oppose certain practices that pose well-documented, serious health risks? Medical personnel in North America face difficult dilemmas. A physician may cut open an infibulated woman to permit childbirth. But what if the woman then requests that she be restitched? Should the physician comply, knowing the risks? Immigrant women whose daughters are born in North America may request that a physician perform an excision or infibulation, knowing that the procedure will be far safer if done by a physician in a hospital. Should the physician comply, knowing that the realistic alternative is that the procedure will be performed by someone, possibly untrained and inexperienced, from that culture under unsanitary conditions?

On a more hopeful note, a grassroots movement of women that is dedicated to eliminating these practices has sprung up in a number of African nations, including Kenya, Gambia, Sudan, Somalia, and Nigeria. Furthermore, to put matters into perspective, only about 15 percent of cultures that practice FGC do the severe form, infibulation. The remaining cultures practice the milder forms ranging from a slit in the prepuce to clitoridectomy. To add additional perspective, far more cultures practice male genital modifications than female genital modifications. An example is the United States, where male circumcision is widespread but FGC is extremely rare and occurs almost exclusively among a subgroup of immigrants, who come from Islamic cultures.

Sources: Almroth et al. (2001); Council on Scientific Affairs (1995); Gregersen (1996); Gruenbaum (2000); Horowitz & Jackson (1997); Kiragu (1995); Leonard (2000); Lightfoot-Klein (1989); Morison (2001); Schroeder (1994); Toubia (1994, 1995); Williams & Sobieszczyk (1997); Yoder et al. (2004).

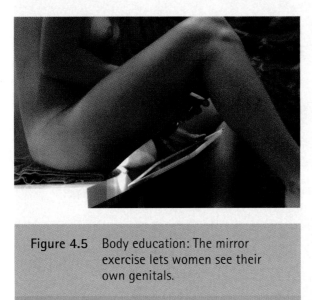

Figure 4.5   Body education: The mirror exercise lets women see their own genitals.

consequences—is that the female's external genitals are much less visible than the male's. A male can view his external genitals directly either by looking down at them or by looking into a mirror while naked. Either of these two strategies for the female, however, will result at best in a view of the mons. The clitoris, the inner and outer lips, and the vaginal opening remain hidden. Indeed, many adult women have never taken a direct look at their own vulva. This obstacle can be overcome by simply using a mirror. The genitals can be viewed either by putting a mirror on the floor and sitting in front of it or by standing up and putting one foot

Hymen (HYE-men): A thin membrane that may partially cover the vaginal entrance.

on the edge of a chair, bed, or something similar and holding the mirror up near the genitals (see Figure 4.5). We recommend that all women use a mirror to identify on their own bodies all the parts shown in Figure 4.1.

The Hymen

The **hymen** ("cherry," "maidenhead") is a thin membrane which, if present, partially covers the vaginal opening. The hymen may be one of a number of different types (see Figure 4.6), although it generally has some openings in it; otherwise, the menstrual flow would not be able to pass out.[3] At the time of first intercourse, the hymen may be broken or stretched as the penis moves into the vagina. This may cause bleeding and possibly some pain. Typically, though, it is an untraumatic occurrence and goes unnoticed in the excitement of the moment. For a woman who is very concerned about her hymen and what will happen to it at first coitus, there are two possible approaches. A physician can cut the hymen neatly so that it will not tear at the time of first intercourse, or the woman herself can stretch it by repeatedly inserting a finger into the vagina and pressing on it.

The hymen, and its destruction at first intercourse, has captured the interest of people in many cultures. In Europe during the Middle Ages, the lord might claim the right to deflower a peasant bride on her wedding night before passing her on

---

[3]The rare condition in which the hymen is a tough tissue with no opening is called *imperforate hymen* and can be corrected with fairly simple surgery.

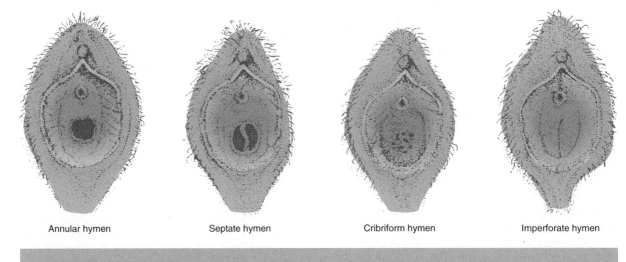

Annular hymen   Septate hymen   Cribriform hymen   Imperforate hymen

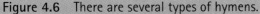

Figure 4.6   There are several types of hymens.

to her husband (the practice is called *droit du seigneur* for "right of the lord" in French and *jus primae noctis* for "law of the first night" in Latin). The hymen has been taken as evidence of virginity. Thus, bleeding on the wedding night was proof that the bride had been delivered intact to the groom; the parading of the bloody bedsheets on the wedding night, a custom of the Kurds of the Middle East, is one ritual based on this belief.

Such practices rest on the assumption that a woman without a hymen is not a virgin. However, we now know that this is not true. Some girls are simply born without a hymen, and others may tear it in active sports such as horseback riding. Unfortunately, this means that some women have been humiliated unjustly for their lack of a hymen.

Internal Organs

The internal sex organs of the female consist of the vagina, the vestibular bulbs, the Skene's glands, the uterus, a pair of ovaries, and a pair of fallopian tubes (see Figure 4.7).

The Vagina

The **vagina** is the tube-shaped organ into which the penis is inserted during coitus; it also receives the ejaculate. Because it is the passageway through which a baby travels during birth, it is sometimes also called the *birth canal.* In the resting or unaroused state, the vagina is about 8 to 10 centimeters (3 to 4 inches) long and tilts slightly backward from the bottom to the top. At the bottom it ends in the vaginal opening, or *introitus.* At the top it connects with the cervix (the lower part of the uterus). It is a very flexible organ that works somewhat like a balloon. In the resting state its walls lie against each other like the sides of an uninflated balloon; during arousal it expands like an inflated balloon, allowing space to accommodate the penis.

The walls of the vagina have three layers. The inner layer, the *vaginal mucosa,* is a mucous membrane similar to the inner lining of the mouth. The middle layer is muscular, and the outer layer forms a covering. The walls of the vagina are extremely elastic and are capable of expanding to the extent necessary during intercourse and childbirth, although with age they become thinner and less flexible.

The nerve supply of the vagina is mostly to the lower one-third, near the introitus. That part is sensitive to erotic stimulation. The inner two-thirds of the vagina contains almost no nerve endings and is therefore relatively insensitive except to feelings of deep pressure. Some women have a spot on the front wall of the vagina that is more sensitive than the rest of the vagina, but even it is not nearly so sensitive as the inner lips, outer lips, or clitoris (Schultz et al., 1989). This spot is referred to by some as the G spot (see Chapter 8).

The number of slang terms for the vagina (for example, "beaver," "cunt") and the frequency of their usage testify to its power of fascination across the ages. One concern has been with size: whether some vaginas are too small or too large. As noted earlier, though, the vagina is highly elastic and expandable. Thus, at least in principle, any penis can fit into any vagina. The penis is, after all, not nearly so large as a baby's head, which manages to fit through the vagina. The part of the vagina that is most responsible for a man's sensation that it is "tight," "too tight," or "too loose" is the introitus. One of the things that can stretch the introitus is childbirth; indeed, there is a considerable difference in the appearance of the vulva of a woman who has never had a baby *(nulliparous)* and the vulva of a woman who has *(parous)* (see Figure 4.8).

Surrounding the vagina, the urethra, and the anus is a set of muscles called the *pelvic floor muscles.* One of these muscles, the **pubococcygeus muscle,** is particularly important. It may be stretched during childbirth, or it may simply be weak. However, it can be strengthened through exercise, which is recommended by sex therapists (see Chapter 17) as well as by many popular sex manuals and magazines.

The Vestibular Bulbs

The **vestibular bulbs** (or bulbs of the clitoris) are two organs about the size and shape of a pea pod (Figure 4.3). They lie on either side of the vaginal wall, near the entrance, under the inner lips (O'Connell & DeLancey, 2005). They are erectile tissue and lie close to the crura of the clitoris.

The Skene's Gland or Female Prostate

The **Skene's gland,** or female prostate (also called the *paraurethral gland),* lies between the wall of the urethra and the wall of the vagina (Zaviačič et al., 2000b). Its ducts empty into the urethra, but it can be felt on the front wall of the vagina. The evidence indicates that it secretes fluid that is biochemically similar to male prostate fluid. Many women find it to be a region of special erotic sensitivity on the wall of the vagina. The size of the female prostate varies considerably from one woman to the next, as does the amount of its

Vagina (vuh-JINE-uh): The tube-shaped organ in the female into which the penis is inserted during coitus and through which a baby passes during birth.
Pubococcygeus muscle (pyoo-bo-cox-ih-GEE-us): A muscle around the vaginal entrance.
Vestibular bulbs: Erectile tissue running under the inner lips.
Skene's gland: Female prostate.

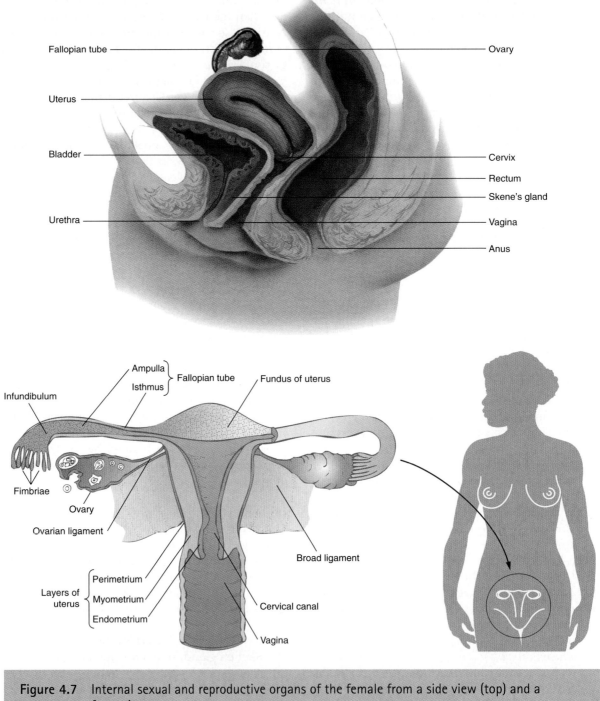

Figure 4.7 Internal sexual and reproductive organs of the female from a side view (top) and a front view.

secretions. Some women experience no secretion, whereas others have an actual ejaculation when they orgasm. This is the organ, dubbed the G spot, that is responsible for female ejaculation, discussed in Chapter 8.

Uterus (YOO-tur-us): The organ in the female in which the fetus develops.

The Uterus

The **uterus** (womb) is about the size and shape of an upside-down pear. It is usually tilted forward and is held in place by ligaments. The narrow lower third, called the *cervix*, opens into the vagina. The top is the *fundus*, the main part the

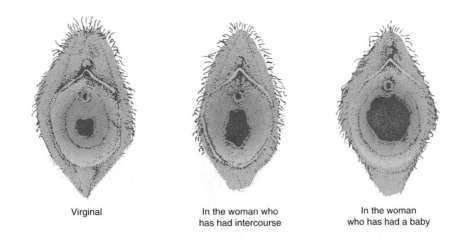

Virginal

In the woman who
has had intercourse

In the woman
who has had a baby

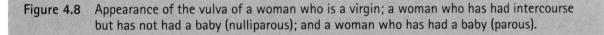

Figure 4.8   Appearance of the vulva of a woman who is a virgin; a woman who has had intercourse but has not had a baby (nulliparous); and a woman who has had a baby (parous).

body. The entrance to the uterus through the cervix is very narrow, about the diameter of a drinking straw, and is called the *os* (or *cervical canal*). The major function of the uterus is to hold and nourish a developing fetus.

The uterus, like the vagina, consists of three layers. The inner layer, or *endometrium,* is richly supplied with glands and blood vessels. Its state varies according to the age of the woman and the phase of the menstrual cycle. It is the endometrium that is sloughed off at menstruation and creates the menstrual discharge. The middle layer, the *myometrium,* is muscular. The muscles are very strong, creating the powerful contractions of labor and orgasm, and also highly elastic, capable of stretching to accommodate a nine-month-old fetus. The outer layer—the *perimetrium*—forms the external cover of the uterus.

The Fallopian Tubes

Extending out from the sides of the upper end of the uterus are the **fallopian tubes,** also called the *oviducts* ("egg ducts") or *uterine tubes* (see Figure 4.7). The fallopian tubes are extremely narrow and are lined with hairlike projections called *cilia.* The fallopian tubes are the pathway by which the egg travels toward the uterus and the sperm reach the egg. Fertilization of the egg typically occurs in the infundibulum, the section of the tube closest to the ovary; the fertilized egg then travels the rest of the way through the tube to the uterus. The infundibulum curves around toward the ovary; at its end are numerous fingerlike projections called *fimbriae* that extend toward the ovary.

The Ovaries

The **ovaries** are two organs about the size and shape of unshelled almonds; they lie on either side of the uterus. The ovaries have two important functions: they produce eggs (ova), and they manufacture the sex hormones *estrogen* and *progesterone.*

Each ovary contains numerous follicles. A *follicle* is a capsule that surrounds an egg (not to be confused with hair follicles, which are quite different). A female is born with an estimated 1 million immature eggs (Federman, 2006). Beginning at puberty, one or several of the follicles mature during each menstrual cycle. When the egg has matured, the follicle bursts open and releases the egg. The ovaries do not actually connect directly to the fallopian tubes. Rather, the egg is released into the body cavity and reaches the tube by moving toward the fimbriae. If the egg does not reach the tube, it may be fertilized outside the tube, resulting in an abdominal pregnancy (see the section on ectopic pregnancy in Chapter 6). There have also been cases recorded of women who, although they were missing one ovary and the opposite fallopian tube, nonetheless became pregnant. Apparently, in such cases the egg migrates to the tube on the opposite side.

The Breasts

Although they are not actually sex organs, the *breasts* deserve discussion here because of their erotic and reproductive significance. The breast consists of about 15 or 20 clusters of *mammary glands,* each with a separate opening to the nipple, and of fatty

Fallopian tubes (fuh-LOW-pee-un): The tubes extending from the uterus to the ovary; also called the oviducts.
Ovaries: Two organs in the female that produce eggs and sex hormones.

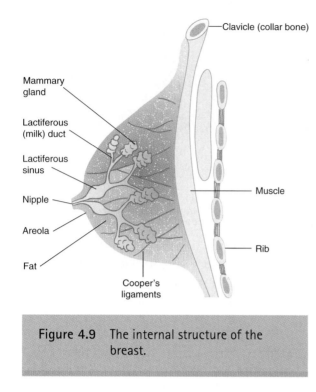

- Clavicle (collar bone)
- Mammary gland
- Lactiferous (milk) duct
- Lactiferous sinus
- Nipple
- Areola
- Fat
- Muscle
- Rib
- Cooper's ligaments

Figure 4.9 The internal structure of the breast.

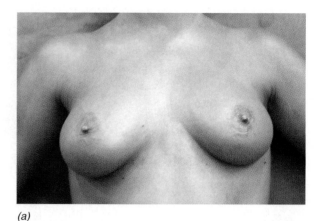

(a)

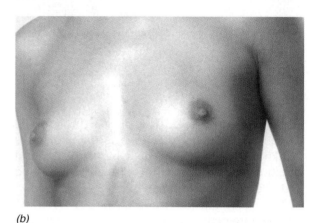

(b)

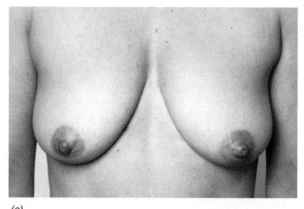

(c)

Figure 4.10 Breasts come in many sizes and shapes.

and fibrous tissues that surround the clusters of glands (see Figure 4.9). The nipple, into which the milk ducts open, is at the tip of the breast. It is richly supplied with nerve endings and therefore very important in erotic stimulation for many women. The nipple consists of smooth muscle fibers; when they contract, the nipple becomes erect. The darker area surrounding the nipple is called the *areola.*

There is wide variation among women in the size and shape of breasts (Figure 4.10). One thing is fairly consistent, though: Few women are satisfied with the size of their breasts. Most women think they are either too small or too large; almost no woman thinks hers are just right. It is well to remember that there are the same number of nerve endings in small breasts as in large breasts. It follows that small breasts are actually more erotically sensitive per square inch than are large ones.

Breasts may take on enormous psychological meaning; they can be a symbol of femininity or a means of attracting men. Ours is a very breast-oriented culture. Many American men develop a powerful interest in, and attraction to, women's breasts. The social definition of beauty is a compelling force; many women strive to meet the ideal and a few overadapt, going too far in their striving (Mazur, 1986). Breast augmentation surgery has increased steadily, while other women have been

SexSource Online
www.mhhe.com/hyde10

"BREASTS" IN SEXUAL ANATOMY AND PHYSIOLOGY

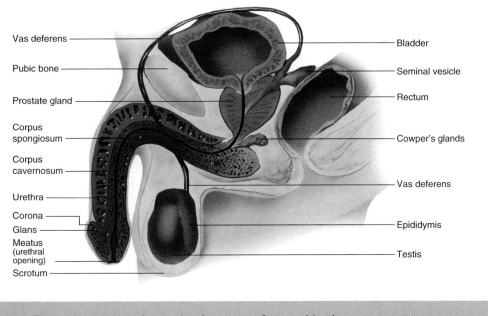

Vas deferens

Pubic bone

Prostate gland

Corpus spongiosum

Corpus cavernosum

Urethra

Corona

Glans

Meatus (urethral opening)

Scrotum

Bladder

Seminal vesicle

Rectum

Cowper's glands

Vas deferens

Epididymis

Testis

Figure 4.11   The male sexual and reproductive organs from a side view.

undergoing breast reduction surgery, in both cases to meet a socially defined standard of beauty.

Male Sexual Organs

Externally, the most noticeable parts of the male sexual anatomy are the penis and the scrotum, or scrotal sac, which contains the testes (see Figure 4.11).

External Organs

The Penis

The **penis** (phallus, "prick," "cock," "johnson," and many other slang terms too numerous to list) serves important functions in sexual pleasure, reproduction, and elimination of body wastes by urination. It is a tubular organ with an end or tip called the *glans*. The opening at the end of the glans is the *meatus*, or *urethral opening*, through which urine and semen pass. The main part of the penis is called the *shaft*. The raised ridge at the edge of the glans is called the *corona* ("crown"). While the entire penis is sensitive to sexual stimulation, the corona and the rest of the glans are the most sexually excitable region of the male anatomy.

Internally, the penis contains three long cylinders of spongy tissue running parallel to the *urethra,* which is the pathway through which semen and urine pass (see Figure 4.12). The two spongy bodies lying on top are called the **corpora cavernosa,** and

the single one lying on the bottom of the penis is called the **corpus spongiosum** (the urethra runs through the middle of it). During erection, the corpus spongiosum can be seen as a raised column on the lower side of the penis. As the names suggest, these bodies are tissues filled with many spaces and cavities, much like a sponge. They are richly supplied with blood vessels and nerves. In the flaccid (unaroused, not erect) state, they contain little blood. *Erection,* or *tumescence,* occurs when they become filled with blood (engorged) and expand, making the penis stiff.

Contrary to popular belief, the penis does not contain a muscle, and no muscle is involved in erection. Erection is purely a vascular phenomenon; that is, it results entirely from blood flow. It is also commonly believed that the penis of the human male contains a bone. This is not true either, although in some other species—for example, dogs—the penis does contain a bone, which aids in intromission (insertion of the penis into the vagina). In human males, however, there is none.

The skin of the penis usually is hairless and is arranged in loose folds, permitting expansion during erection. The **foreskin,** or *prepuce,* is an additional layer of skin that forms a sheathlike covering over the glans; it may be present or absent in the adult male, depending

Penis: The male external sexual organ, which functions both in sexual activity and in urination.

Corpora cavernosa: Spongy bodies running the length of the top of the penis.

Corpus spongiosum: A spongy body running the length of the underside of the penis.

Foreskin: A layer of skin covering the glans or tip of the penis in an uncircumcised male; also called the prepuce.

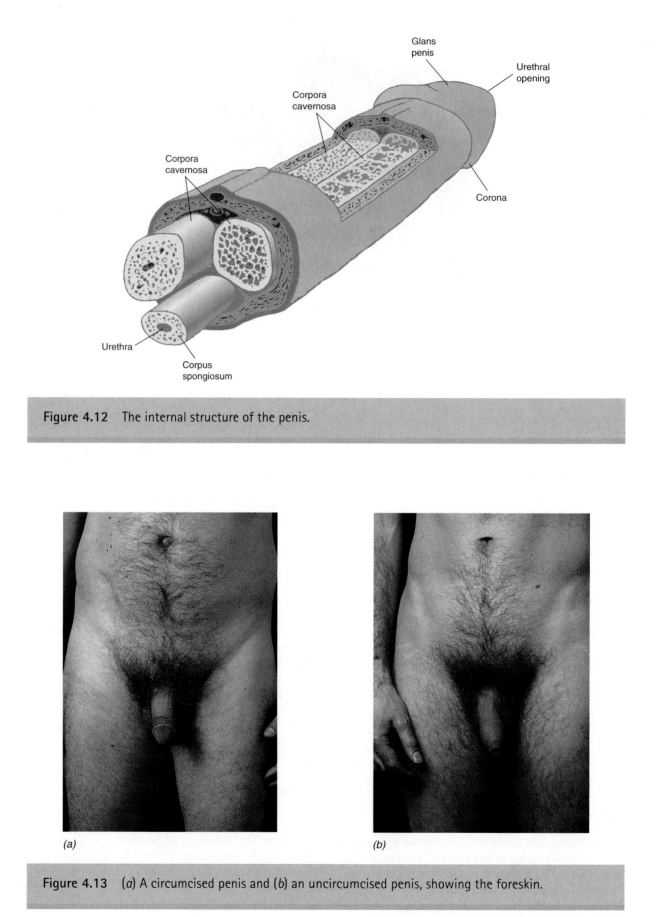

Figure 4.12   The internal structure of the penis.

(a)   *(b)*

Figure 4.13   (*a*) A circumcised penis and (*b*) an uncircumcised penis, showing the foreskin.

on whether he has been circumcised (see Figure 4.13). Under the foreskin are small glands (Tyson's glands) that produce a substance called *smegma,* which is cheesy in texture. The foreskin is easily retractable,[4] this being extremely important for proper hygiene. If the foreskin is not pulled back and the glans washed thoroughly, the smegma may accumulate, producing a very unpleasant smell.

Circumcision refers to the surgical cutting away or removal of the foreskin. Circumcision is practiced in many parts of the world and, when parents so choose, is done to boys in the United States within a few days after birth.

Circumcision may be done for cultural and religious reasons. Circumcision has been a part of Jewish religious practice for thousands of years. It symbolizes the covenant between God and the Jewish people and is done on the eighth day after birth, according to scriptural teaching (Genesis 17: 9–27). Circumcision is also common in Muslim cultures. In some cultures circumcision is done at puberty as an initiation ritual, or *rite de passage.* The ability of the young boy to stand the pain may be seen as a proof of manhood.

In the 1980s, an anticircumcision movement began gaining momentum in the United States. Its proponents argue that circumcision does not have any health benefits and does entail some health risk as well as psychological trauma. According to this view, circumcision is nothing more than cruel mutilation. (For a statement of this anticircumcision position, see Wallerstein, 1980.) In fact, as early as 1971 the American Academy of Pediatrics had gone on record saying that there is no medical need for routine circumcision of newborn boys. Reflecting this advice and the growth of controversy about circumcision, only 59 percent of infant boys were circumcised in the United States in 1986, compared with 90 percent in 1970 (Lindsey, 1988).

New evidence accumulated, though, and in 1999 the American Academy of Pediatrics, changing its 1971 statement, declared that there are potential medical benefits and advantages to circumcision as well as some potential risks. The new evidence indicates, for example, that uncircumcised male babies are 11 times more likely to get urinary tract infections than are circumcised babies (Wiswell et al., 1987). There is also evidence that uncircumcised men have a higher risk of infection with HIV, the AIDS virus. It is thought that the foreskin can harbor HIV and other viruses. In a study of different geographic and ethnic groups in Africa, some of which practice circumcision and some of which do not, it was found that HIV infection rates were very low among groups that practice circumcision and high among those that do not (Moses et al., 1990). In a five-nation study, including Spain, Colombia, Brazil, Thailand, and the Philippines, circumcised men showed lower rates of HPV infection (Castellsagué et al., 2002). HPV is the virus that causes genital warts and predisposes women to cervical cancer (see Chapter 18). In this same study, the monogamous women partners of the circumcised men had lower rates of cervical cancer. In a randomized controlled trial in Kenya and Uganda, adult men who wanted to be circumcised were circumcised (or not in the control group) (Roehr, 2007). Over the next two years, the circumcised men had half the rate of infection of the uncircumcised men. The trial was actually halted over ethical concerns about withholding circumcision from those who wanted it.

Other arguments have focused on whether the circumcised or the uncircumcised man receives more pleasure from sexual intercourse. In fact, Masters and Johnson (1966) found that there is no difference in excitability between the circumcised and the uncircumcised penis.

Other forms of male genital cutting are done throughout the world. In fact, male genital cutting is done in more cultures than is female genital cutting (Gregersen, 1996). A common form, across most of Polynesia, is **supercision** (also known as *superincision*), which involves making a slit the length of the foreskin on the top, with the foreskin otherwise remaining intact (Gregersen, 1996). With **subincision,** which is common in some tribes in central Australia, a slit is made on the lower side of the penis along its entire length and to the depth of the urethra. Urine is then excreted at the base rather than at the tip of the penis.

To say the least, the penis has been the focus of quite a lot of attention throughout history. In some cultures, the attention has become so pronounced that the male genitals have become the object of religious worship (phallic worship). Not surprisingly, the male genitals were often seen as symbols of fertility and thus were worshipped for their powers of procreativity. In ancient Greece, phallic worship centered on Priapus, the son of Aphrodite (the goddess of love) and Dionysus (the god of fertility and wine). Priapus is usually represented as a grinning man with a huge penis.

---

[4]In a rare condition, the foreskin is so tight that it cannot be pulled back; this condition, called *phimosis,* requires correction by circumcision.

Circumcision: Surgical removal of the foreskin of the penis.
Supercision (superincision): A form of male genital cutting in which a slit is made the length of the foreskin on top.
Subincision: A form of male genital cutting in which a slit is made on the lower side of the penis along its entire length.

In contemporary American society, phallic concern often focuses on the size of the penis. E-mail spam leers at us with various products that ostensibly increase penis size. It is commonly believed that a man with a large penis is a better lover and can satisfy a woman more than can the man with a small penis. Masters and Johnson (1966), however, found that this is not true. While there is considerable variation in the length of the penis from one man to the next—the average penis is generally somewhere between 6.4 centimeters (2.5 inches) and 10 centimeters (4 inches) in length when flaccid (not erect)—there is a tendency for the small penis to grow more in erection than one that starts out large. As a result, there is little correlation between the length of the penis when flaccid and its length when erect. As the saying has it, "Erection is the great equalizer." The average erect penis is about 15 centimeters (6 inches) long, although erect penises longer than 33 centimeters (13 inches) have been measured (Dickinson, 1949). Furthermore, as noted earlier, the vagina has relatively few nerve endings and is relatively insensitive. Hence penetration to the far reaches of the vagina by a very long penis is not essential and may not even be noticeable. Many other factors are more important than penis size in giving a woman pleasure (see Chapters 8 and 17).

Phallic concern has also included an interest in the variations in the shape of the penis when flaccid and when erect, as reflected in this limerick:

> There was a young man of Kent
> Whose kirp in the middle was bent.
> To save himself trouble
> He put it in double,
> And instead of coming, he went.

The Scrotum

The other major external genital structure in the male is the **scrotum;** this is a loose pouch of skin, lightly covered with hair, that contains the testes ("balls" or "nuts" in slang).[5] The testes themselves are considered part of the internal genitals.

Internal Organs

Scrotum (SKROH-tum): The pouch of skin that contains the testes in the male.
Testes: The pair of glands in the scrotum that manufacture sperm and sex hormones.
Seminiferous tubules (sem-ih-NIFF-ur-us): Tubes in the testes that manufacture sperm.
Interstitial cells (int-er-STIH-shul): Cells in the testes that manufacture testosterone.

The **testes** are the *gonads*, or reproductive glands, of the male, which are analogous to the female's

[5]This brings to mind another limerick:

There once was a pirate named Gates
Who thought he could rhumba on skates.
He slipped on his cutlass
And now he is nutless
And practically useless on dates.

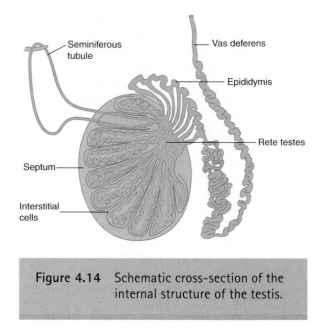

Figure 4.14   Schematic cross-section of the internal structure of the testis.

ovaries. Like the ovaries, they serve two major functions: to manufacture germ cells (sperm) and sex hormones, in particular *testosterone*. Both testes are about the same size, although the left one usually hangs lower than the right one.

In the internal structure of the testes, two parts are important: the seminiferous tubules and the interstitial cells (see Figure 4.14). The **seminiferous tubules** carry out the important function of manufacturing and storing sperm, a process called *spermatogenesis*. They are a long series of threadlike tubes curled and packed densely into the testes. There are about 1,000 of these tubules, which if they were stretched out end to end would be several hundred feet in length.

The **interstitial cells** (or *Leydig's cells*) carry out the second important function of the testes, the production of testosterone. These cells are found in the connective tissue lying between the seminiferous tubules. The cells lie close to the blood vessels in the testes and pour the hormones they manufacture directly into the blood vessels. Thus, the testes are endocrine (hormone secreting) glands.

One of the clever tricks that the scrotum and testes can perform, as any male will testify, is to move up close to the body or down away from it. These changes are brought about mainly by changes in temperature (although emotional factors may also produce them). If a man plunges into a cold lake, the scrotum will shrivel and move close to the body. If the man is working in an extremely hot place, the scrotum will hang down and away from the body. This mechanism is important because the testes should remain at a fairly constant temperature, slightly lower than normal body temperature. This constancy of temperature is necessary to protect the sperm, which may be injured by extremes of temperature. Thus if the air is cold, the testes move closer to the body to maintain warmth, but if the air is too hot, they move away from it to keep cool. The mechanics of this movement are made possible by the *cremasteric reflex,* named for the cremaster muscle connecting the scrotum to the body wall. Reflex contraction of this muscle pulls the testes up.

Many people believe that taking hot baths, wearing tight athletic supporters, or having a high fever can cause infertility. Indeed, in some countries the men take long, hot baths as a method of contraception. Such a practice has some basis in biological fact, because sperm can be destroyed by heat. However, as a method of contraception this practice has not been particularly effective. In one study, it was found that the use of a special jockstrap raised the temperature of the scrotum by nearly 1°C (1.7°F) and that wearing the device daily for seven weeks caused about a 25 percent reduction in the number of sperm produced (Robinson & Rock, 1967). Thus such practices might decrease a man's fertility somewhat, but they are far from 100 percent effective as contraceptives. On the other hand, men with problems of infertility can sometimes cure them by getting out of their tight jockstraps and jockey shorts.

Following initial cell division in the seminiferous tubules, the male germ cells go through several stages of maturation. At the earliest stage, the cell is called a *spermatogonium.* Then it becomes a *spermatocyte* (first primary and then secondary) and then a *spermatid.* Finally, when fully mature it is a *spermatozoan,* or **sperm.** *Spermatogenesis,* the manufacture of sperm, occurs continuously in adult men. An average ejaculate contains about 200 million sperm (Bang et al., 2005).

A mature sperm is very tiny—about 60 micrometers, or 60/10,000 millimeter (0.0024 inch), long—and consists of a head, a neck, a midpiece, and a tail. A normal human sperm carries 23 chromosomes in the head. These 23 are half the normal number in the other cells of the human body. When the sperm unites with the egg, which also carries 23 chromosomes, the full complement of 46 for the offspring is produced. (See Chapter 6 for a discussion of the sperm's role in conception.)

After the sperm are manufactured in the seminiferous tubules, they proceed into the *rete testes,* a converging network of tubes on the surface of the testis toward the top. The sperm then pass out of the testis and into a single tube, the epididymis.

The **epididymis** is a long tube (about 6 meters, or 20 feet, in length) coiled into a small crescent-shaped region on the top and side of the testis. The sperm are stored in the epididymis, in which they ripen and mature, possibly for as long as six weeks.

Upon ejaculation, the sperm pass from the epididymis into the **vas deferens** (it is the vas that is cut in a vasectomy—see Chapter 7). The vas passes up and out of the scrotum and then follows a peculiar circular path as it loops over the pubic bone, crosses beside the urinary bladder, and then turns downward toward the prostate. As the tube passes through the prostate it narrows and at this point is called the *ejaculatory duct.* The ejaculatory duct opens into the *urethra,* which has the dual function of conveying sperm and transporting urine; sperm are ejaculated out through the penis via the urethra.

Sperm have little motility (capability of movement) of their own while in the epididymis and vas. Not until they mix with the secretions of the prostate are they capable of movement on their own (Breton et al., 1996). Up to this point, they are conveyed by the cilia and by contractions of the epididymis and vas.

The **seminal vesicles** are two saclike structures that lie above the prostate, behind the bladder, and in front of the rectum. They produce about 70 percent of the seminal fluid, or ejaculate. The remaining 30 percent is produced by the prostate. They empty their fluid into the ejaculatory duct to combine with the sperm.

The **prostate** lies below the bladder and is about the size and shape of a chestnut. It is composed of both muscle and glandular tissue. The prostate secretes a milky alkaline fluid that is part of the ejaculate. It is thought that the alkalinity of the secretion provides a favorable environment for the sperm and helps prevent their destruction by the acidity of the vagina. The prostate is fairly small at birth, enlarges at puberty, and typically shrinks in old age. It may become enlarged enough so that it interferes with urination, in which case surgery or drug therapy is required. Its size can be determined by rectal examination.

Cowper's glands, or the *bulbourethral glands,* are located just below the prostate and empty into the urethra. During sexual arousal these glands secrete a small amount of a clear alkaline fluid, which appears as droplets at the tip of the penis before ejaculation occurs. It is thought that the

Sperm: The mature male reproductive cell, capable of fertilizing an egg.
Epididymis (ep-ih-DIH-dih-mus): A highly coiled tube located on the edge of the testis, where sperm mature.
Vas deferens: The tube through which sperm pass on their way from the testes and epididymis, out of the scrotum, and to the urethra.
Seminal vesicles: Saclike structures that lie above the prostate and produce about 70 percent of the seminal fluid.
Prostate: The gland in the male, located below the bladder, that secretes some of the fluid in semen.
Cowper's glands: Glands that secrete a clear alkaline fluid into the male's urethra.

function of this secretion is to neutralize the acidic urethra, allowing safe passage of the sperm. Generally it is not produced in sufficient quantity to serve as a lubricant in intercourse. The fluid often contains some stray sperm. Thus it is possible (though not likely) for a woman to become pregnant from the sperm in this fluid even though the man has not ejaculated.

Cancer of the Sex Organs

Breast Cancer

Cancer of the breast is the second most common form of cancer in women, exceeded only by skin cancer. About one out of every nine American women has breast cancer at some time in her life. Every year, 40,000 women in this country die of breast cancer (American Cancer Society, 2007). The risk is higher for the woman whose mother, sister, or grandmother has had breast cancer.

Causes

Approximately 5 to 10 percent of the cases of breast cancer in women are due to genetic factors (American Cancer Society, 2007). The remaining cases may be related to a particular virus or to diet. In countries such as Japan and Romania where the diet is low in fat, breast cancer rates are less than half that of the United States, where the diet is high in fat.

There have been great breakthroughs in research into the genetics of breast cancer. Scientists have identified two breast cancer genes: BRCA1 (for BReast CAncer 1) on chromosome 17 and BRCA2 on chromosome 13 (Ezzell, 1994; Miki et al., 1994; Shattuck-Eidens et al., 1995). Mutations of these genes create a high risk of breast cancer. BRCA1 and BRCA2 mutations also increase susceptibility to ovarian cancer (Miki et al., 1994). In one study, of women having a mutation in BRCA1 or BRCA2, 82 percent eventually developed breast cancer and 54 percent developed ovarian cancer (King et al., 2003). In fact, among men carrying mutations of these genes, 16 percent develop prostate cancer. Genetic screening tests are available that detect BRCA mutations in women who have a family history of breast cancer. If a BRCA mutation is found, the woman can be monitored closely, and if it is not found, she can feel relieved! Researchers are currently exploring gene therapy (Marot et al., 2006). In such studies genetically engineered cells containing normal BRCA1 genes are injected into the woman.

Radical mastectomy (mast-ECT-uh-mee): A surgical treatment for breast cancer in which the entire breast, as well as underlying muscles and lymph nodes, is removed.

Diagnosis

Women can do breast self-exams, and it is good for all women to know how their breasts feel normally so that they can detect any changes. However, exams by clinicians and mammograms are more accurate than self-exams.

There are three kinds of breast lumps: *cysts* (fluid-filled sacs, also called *fibrocystic* or *cystic mastitis*), *fibroadenomas,* and *malignant tumors.* The important thing to realize is that 80 percent of breast lumps are cysts or fibroadenomas and are benign—that is, not dangerous. Therefore, if a lump is found in your breast, the chances are fairly good that it is not malignant; of course, you cannot be sure of this until a doctor has performed a biopsy.

The main technique available for early detection of breast cancer is mammography. Basically, *mammography* involves taking an X ray of the breast. This technique is highly accurate, although some errors are still made. The major advantage, though, is that it is capable of detecting tumors that are so small that they cannot yet be felt; thus it can detect cancer in very early stages, making recovery more likely. Nonetheless, mammography involves some exposure to radiation, which itself may increase the risk of cancer. The question is, Which is more dangerous—having mammography or not detecting breast cancer until a later stage? Experts have concluded that the benefits outweigh the risks. The American Cancer Society now says that a woman should have her first baseline mammogram at around age 35 and then should have one done regularly at one-year intervals from age 40 on. Women in their 20s should also learn how their breasts normally feel and should report any changes to their doctor.

Once a lump is discovered, one of several diagnostic procedures may be carried out. One is *needle aspiration,* in which a fine needle is inserted into the breast; if the lump is a cyst, the fluid in the cyst will be drained out. If the lump disappears after this procedure, then it was a cyst; the cyst is gone, and there is no need for further concern. If the lump remains, it must be either a fibroadenoma or a malignant tumor.

Most physicians feel that the only definitive way to differentiate between a fibroadenoma and a malignant tumor is to do a *biopsy.* A small slit is made in the breast and the lump is removed. A pathologist then examines it to determine whether it is cancerous. If it is simply a fibroadenoma, it has been removed and there is no further need for concern.

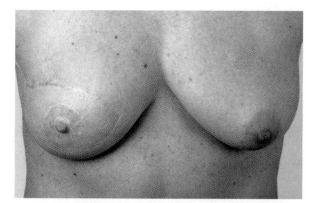

Figure 4.15   Appearance of a breast reconstructed after a mastectomy.

Mastectomy

Several forms of surgery may be performed when a breast lump is found to be malignant. Radiation therapy, chemotherapy, and hormone therapy may also be used. The most serious surgery is **radical mastectomy,** in which the entire breast and the underlying pectoral muscle and the lymph nodes are removed. Advocates of this procedure argue that if the cancer has spread to the adjoining lymph nodes, the procedure ensures that all the affected tissue is removed. The disadvantages of the procedure are that it is disfiguring and there may be difficulty in arm movement following removal of the pectoral muscles. In *modified radical mastectomy* the breast and lymph nodes, but not the muscles, are removed. In *simple mastectomy* only the breast (and possibly a few lymph nodes) is removed. In **lumpectomy,** only the lump itself and a small bit of surrounding tissues are removed. The breast is thus preserved. Research indicates that in cases of early breast cancer when the cancer has not spread beyond the breast (e.g., to the lymph nodes), lumpectomy followed by radiation therapy is as effective as radical mastectomy (American Cancer Society, 2007) and is obviously much preferable. Drug therapy (e.g., tamoxifen) may also be used.

Treatments generally are highly effective. If the cancer is localized, the survival rate is more than 98 percent five years after treatment (American Cancer Society, 2007).

Psychological Aspects

A lot more is at stake with breast cancer and mastectomy than technical details about diagnosis and surgery. The psychological impact of breast cancer and mastectomy can be enormous (for an excellent review see Meyerowitz, 1980). There seem to be two sources of the trauma: Finding out that one has cancer of any kind is traumatic, and the surgery and possibly amputation of the breast is additionally stressful.

The typical emotional response of the mastectomy patient is depression, often associated with anxiety (Compas & Luecken, 2002). These responses are so common that they can be considered normal. The woman must make a number of physical and psychological adaptations, including different positions for sleeping and lovemaking and, for many women, a change to less revealing clothing. It is common for women to have difficulty showing their incisions to their sexual partners. Marital tensions and sexual problems may increase. Many women experience a fear of recurring cancer and its treatment and of death, as well as concerns about mutilation from mastectomy and a possible loss of femininity. Our culture is very breast oriented, and a woman who has defined her identity in terms of her beauty and voluptuous figure may have a more difficult time adjusting.

Long-term studies, however, indicate that most women gradually adapt to the stresses they have experienced. One study found that breast cancer survivors did not differ from controls on measures of depression (Cordova et al., 2001). Many women manage to find meaning in the cancer experience and some show *posttraumatic growth,* such as finding new meaning in relationships and appreciating life more.

Educational classes providing relevant information can be very helpful. However, peer support groups, though popular, have not fared well in tests of their effectiveness in improving mental health (Helgeson et al., 2001). For women who are more severely distressed, cognitive behavioral therapy with a trained therapist can be very effective (Antoni et al., 2001).

Cancer of the Cervix, Endometrium, and Ovaries

Cancers of the cervix, endometrium, and ovaries are the most common cancers in women after breast cancer, accounting for about 11 percent of all new cancers in women. Each year about 27,000 U.S. women die of these cancers (American Cancer Society, 2007). Other cancers of the female sexual-reproductive organs include cancer of the vulva, vagina, and fallopian tubes; these are all relatively rare.

Lumpectomy: A surgical treatment for breast cancer in which only the lump and a small bit of surrounding tissue are removed.

Focus: First Person
The Pelvic Exam

All adult women should have a checkup every year that includes a thorough pelvic exam. Among other things, such an exam is extremely important in the detection of cervical cancer, and early detection is the key to cure. Some women neglect to have the exam because they feel anxious or embarrassed about it or because they think they are too young or too old; however, having regular pelvic exams can be a matter of life and death. Actually, the exam is quite simple and need not cause any discomfort. The following is a description of the procedures in a pelvic exam (Boston Women's Health Book Collective, 2005).

First, the health care provider inspects the vulva, checking for irritations, discolorations, bumps, lice, skin lesions, and unusual vaginal discharge. Then there is an internal check for *cystoceles* (bulges of the bladder into the vagina) and *rectoceles* (bulges of the rectum into the vagina), for pus in the Skene glands, for cysts in the Bartholin glands, and for the strength of the pelvic floor muscles and abdominal muscles. There is also a test for stress incontinence; the physician asks the patient to cough and checks to see whether urine flows involuntarily.

Next comes the speculum exam. The *speculum* is a plastic or metal instrument that is inserted into the vagina to hold the vaginal walls apart to permit examination. Once the speculum is in place (it should be prewarmed to body temperature if it is metal), the health care provider looks for any unusual signs, such as lesions, inflammation, or unusual discharge from the vaginal walls, and for any signs of infection or damage to the cervix. The health care provider then uses a small metal spatula to scrape a tiny bit of tissue from the cervix for the Pap test for cervical cancer. If this is done properly, it should be painless. A battery of tests for sexually transmitted diseases can also be run.

If the woman is interested in seeing her own cervix, she can ask the doctor to hold up a mirror so that she can view it through the speculum. Indeed, some women's groups advocate that women learn to use a speculum and give themselves regular exams with it; early detection of diseases would thus be much more likely. (For a more detailed description, see the Boston Women's Health Book Collective, 2005.)

Next, the health care provider does a bimanual vaginal exam. She or he slides the index and middle fingers of one hand into the vagina and then, with the other hand, presses down from the outside on the abdominal wall. The health care provider then feels for the position of the uterus, tubes, and ovaries and for any signs of growths, pain, or inflammation.

Approximately 95 percent of cases of cervical cancer are caused by the human papillomavirus, HPV (see Chapter 18) (Janicek & Averette, 2001). Early initiation of heterosexual intercourse during the teenage years is a known risk factor for cervical cancer, as is intercourse with multiple partners. Both early intercourse *and* multiple partners, of course, increase the risk of HPV infection. Research shows that tumor suppressor genes are active in normal cells, preventing them from becoming cancerous. HPV interferes with the activity of those tumor suppressor genes (Janicek & Averette, 2001).

It is encouraging to note that the death rate from cervical cancer has decreased sharply since the mid-1960s, mainly as a result of the *Pap test* (invented by G. N. Papanicolaou) and more regular checkups (American Cancer Society, 2004). The Pap test is performed during a pelvic examination (described in Focus: First Person, above). Because this highly accurate test can detect cancer long before the person has any symptoms, all women over age 18 should have one annually, and they should begin even earlier if they are sexually active.

The most exciting news is that a vaccine is now available that prevents the most common HPV infections that cause cervical cancer. It is approved for use in females between the ages of 9 and 26, and all girls and women in this group should receive the vaccine.

Endometrial and ovarian cancers have multiple symptoms, making diagnosis difficult. Endometrial cancer may be suspected when a woman has vaginal bleeding during times in the menstrual cycle other than her period, or after menopause. Ovarian cancer symptoms—abdominal bloating and cramping, vomiting and diarrhea—can be, and usually are, indicative of much less serious conditions like a stomach virus or irritable bowel syndrome. Imaging techniques such as pelvic sonogram and MRI, and minimally invasive surgical

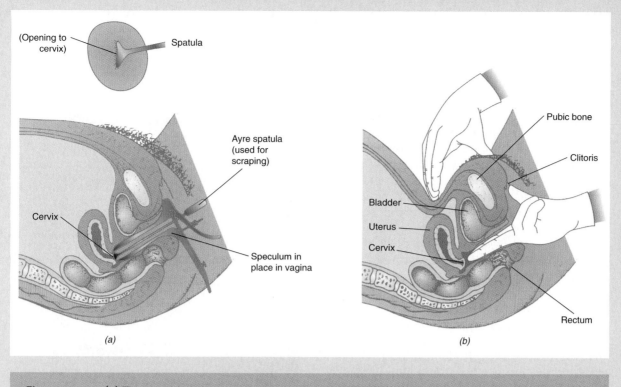

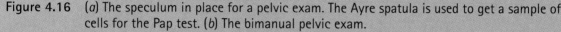

Figure 4.16 (*a*) The speculum in place for a pelvic exam. The Ayre spatula is used to get a sample of cells for the Pap test. (*b*) The bimanual pelvic exam.

Finally, the health care provider may do a recto-vaginal exam by inserting one finger into the vagina and one into the rectum; this provides further information on the positioning of the pelvic organs and can include a test for colon cancer.

Once again, it is important to emphasize that these are not painful procedures and that having them performed regularly is extremely important to a woman's health.

techniques such as hysteroscopy, can help diagnose these cancers.

Treatment for cervical cancer varies according to how advanced it is when diagnosed. If it is detected very early, it is quite curable with methods such as cryotherapy, a nonsurgical technique that uses extreme cold to destroy just the abnormal cells. Another common treatment is cone biopsy, in which a segment of the cervix is surgically removed, leaving the cervix largely intact. For women with advanced cervical cancer that has spread beyond a small, localized spot, **hysterectomy** (surgical removal of the uterus) is the usual treatment, although radiation therapy may be an alternative.

For women with endometrial cancer, hysterectomy is the standard treatment. Ovarian cancer is treated by *oophorectomy* (surgical removal of the ovaries), often accompanied by hysterectomy. These surgeries are typically followed by radiation treatments or chemotherapy.

It is important to note some facts about hysterectomy. Although it carries risks similar to those of any major surgery, hysterectomy does not leave a woman "masculinized," with a beard and deep voice. Beard growth is influenced by testosterone, not estrogen or progesterone. And it is the ovaries that manufacture estrogen and progesterone. They are not removed in a hysterectomy except in rare cases when the cancer has spread to them. Women who have their ovaries removed before age 50 usually take hormone replacement therapy (HRT) to avoid the effects of premature menopause. Another fallacy about hysterectomy is that it prevents a woman from enjoying, or even having, sex. In fact, though, the vagina is left intact, so intercourse is quite possible (for more detail, see Chapter 10).

Cancer of the Prostate

Cancer of the prostate is the second leading cause of cancer death

Hysterectomy (his-tuh-REK-tuh-mee): Surgical removal of the uterus.

Focus: First Person
Testicular Examination

D octors agree that examination of a man's testicles is an important part of a general physical examination. The American Cancer Society includes the examination in its recommendations for routine cancer-related checkups. The issue of regular testicular self-examination is more controversial. The ACS does not feel that there is any medical evidence to suggest that, for men with average testicular cancer risk, monthly examination is any more effective than simple awareness and prompt medical evaluation. However, the choice of whether or not to perform this examination should be made by each man, so instructions for testicular examination are included in this section.

If you plan to perform the self-exam, the best time to do so is during or after a bath or shower, when the skin of the scrotum is relaxed. Stand in front of a mirror and hold the penis out of the way. Examine each testicle separately. Hold the testicle between the thumbs and fingers with both hands and roll it gently between the fingers. Look and feel for any hard lumps or *nodules* (smooth rounded masses) or any change in the size, shape, or consistency of the testes. Contact your doctor if you detect any troublesome signs. Be aware that the testicles contain blood vessels, supporting tissues, and tubes that conduct sperm and that some men may confuse these with a cancer. If you have any doubts, ask your doctor.

These are warning signs of testicular cancer:

1. A painless or an uncomfortable lump on a testicle
2. A testicular enlargement or swelling
3. A sensation of heaviness or aching in the lower abdomen or scrotum
4. In rare cases, men with germ cell cancer notice breast tenderness or breast growth

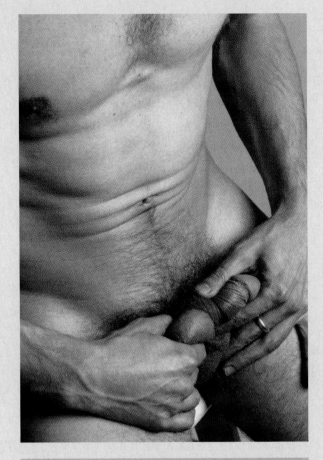

Figure 4.17 The technique used in the testicular self-exam.

See a physician promptly if you have any of these symptoms.

---

in men, the most common being lung cancer. Most cases are not lethal, however, and survival rates are high, because most of the tumors are small and spread (metastasize) only very slowly. On the other hand, a certain percentage of prostate tumors do spread and are lethal. Prostate cancer causes 27,000 deaths a year (American Cancer Society, 2007). A prostate cancer gene (HPC1, for Hereditary Prostate Cancer) has been

discovered, but it accounts for only about 3 percent of all cases (Pennisi, 1996; Smith et al., 1996).

Early symptoms of prostate cancer are frequent urination (especially at night), difficulty in urination, and difficulty emptying the bladder. These are also symptoms of benign prostate enlargement, which itself may require treatment by surgery or drugs (Oesterling, 1995). These symptoms result from the pressure of the prostate tumor on the urethra. In the early stages there may be frequent erections and an increase in sex drive; however, as the disease progresses, there are often problems with sexual functioning.

Preliminary diagnosis of prostate cancer is by a rectal examination, which is simple and causes no more than minimal discomfort. The physician (wearing a lubricated glove) inserts one finger into the rectum and palpates (feels) the prostate. All men over 50 should have a rectal exam at least once a year. If the rectal exam provides evidence of a tumor, further laboratory tests can be conducted as confirmation. The rectal exam has its disadvantages, though. Some men dislike the discomfort it causes, and it is not 100 percent accurate. A blood test for PSA (prostate-specific antigen) is also available and should be done as well.

Treatment often involves surgical removal of some or all of the prostate, plus some type of hormone therapy, radiation therapy, or anticancer drugs. Because prostate cancer is often a slow-growing cancer, it may be left untreated, particularly if the man is elderly. Surgery may result in erection problems (Perez et al., 2002). Just as research has found that a greater number of sexual partners increases women's risk of cervical cancer, new research indicates that men with a greater number of female sex partners have an increased risk of prostate cancer (Rosenblatt et al., 2001).

Cancer of the penis is another cancer of the male sexual-reproductive system, but it is rare compared with prostate cancer. It seems to be much more common among uncircumcised men than among circumcised men, suggesting that the accumulation of smegma under the foreskin may be related to its cause. Treatment may consist of surgery or radiation therapy.

Cancer of the Testes

Cancer of the testes is not a particularly common form of cancer. About 8,000 new cases are diagnosed each year (American Cancer Society, 2007). However, it tends to be a disease of young men, and it is the most common form of cancer in men between the ages of 29 and 35.

The first sign is usually a painless lump in the testes, or a slight enlargement or change in consistency of the testes. There may be pain in the lower abdomen or groin. Unfortunately, many men do not discover the tumor, or if they do they do not see a physician soon, so that in most cases the cancer has spread to other organs by the time a physician is consulted. When a lump is reported to a physician early, the five-year survival rate is 96 percent. Lance Armstrong, the great cyclist, was treated for testicular cancer and went on to win the Tour de France multiple times. However, if the lump is not discovered or the man waits to see a physician and the cancer has progressed to Stage III, the survival rate is 70 percent (American Cancer Society, 2007).

It is also true that not every lump in the testes is cancerous. Some lumps are varicoceles, that is, varicose veins.

Diagnosis is made by a physician's examination of the testes (see Focus: First Person, p. 88) and by ultrasound. Final diagnosis involves surgical removal of the entire testis. This is also the first step in treatment. Fortunately, the other testicle remains, so that hormone production and sexual functioning can continue unimpaired. An artificial, gel-filled testicle can be implanted to restore a normal appearance.

The cause of testicular cancer is not known for certain. An undescended testis has a much greater risk of developing cancer.

SUMMARY

The external sexual organs of the female are the clitoris, the mons, the inner lips, the outer lips, and the vaginal opening. Collectively these are referred to as the vulva. The clitoris is an extremely sensitive organ and is very important in female sexual response. Clitoridectomy and infibulation are rituals that involve cutting of the clitoris and other parts of the vulva and are practiced widely in some African nations and elsewhere. Another external structure is the hymen, which has taken on great symbolic significance as a sign of virginity, although its absence is not a reliable indicator that a woman is not a virgin. The important internal structures are the vagina, which receives the penis during coitus; the uterus, which houses the developing fetus; the ovaries, which produce eggs and manufacture sex hormones; and the fallopian tubes, which convey the egg to the uterus. The breasts of the female also function in sexual arousal and may have great symbolic significance.

The external sexual organs of the male are the penis and the scrotum. The penis contains three spongy bodies that, when filled with blood, produce an erection. Circumcision, or surgical removal of the foreskin of the penis, is a practice debated in the United States but may have some health advantages. The scrotum contains the testes, which are responsible for the manufacture of sperm (in the seminiferous tubules) and sex hormones (in the interstitial cells). Sperm pass out of the testes during ejaculation via the vas deferens, the ejaculatory duct, and the urethra. The seminal vesicles manufacture most of the fluid that mixes with the sperm to form semen. The prostate also contributes secretions.

Breast cancer is the second most common form of cancer in women. All woman should do a monthly self-exam, because the earlier a lump is detected, the greater the chances of complete recovery. The Pap test is used to detect cervical cancer. Prostate cancer is the second most common form of cancer in men, but it generally affects older men. Cancer of the testes, although rare, is the most common cancer in men between the ages of 29 and 35. Men should do a monthly testicular self-exam.

QUESTIONS FOR THOUGHT, DISCUSSION, AND DEBATE

1. Form two groups of students to debate the following: Resolved: Circumcision should not be performed routinely. You can draw on many resources to provide evidence for your debate, including interviews with doctors and nurses, library materials (books and journal articles on the effects of circumcision), and interviews with parents of infants.

2. You are a gynecologist practicing in New York. An immigrant woman from Somalia makes an appointment with you. She wants you to perform infibulation on her 8-year-old daughter. She pleads with you, saying that she wants the girl to have the procedure performed under safe, sanitary conditions in a hospital. She firmly believes that she would betray her culture, to which they will return in two years, if she does not carry out this ancient custom with her daughter. What should you do?

3. Clitoridectomy and infibulation are practiced widely today, particularly in East Africa. Scientific evidence indicates that these practices can cause serious negative health consequences for women and girls. Some argue that people throughout the world should work to eradicate this practice, perhaps with the help of an institution such as the World Health Organization. Others argue that this practice is deeply rooted in the cultures of these countries, and that outsiders have no right to judge it, much less try to stop it. What do you think? Why?

SUGGESTIONS FOR FURTHER READING

Boston Women's Health Book Collective. (2005). *Our bodies, ourselves.* New York: Simon & Schuster. A good, easy-to-read source on female biology and sexuality.

Gruenbaum, Ellen. (2000). *The female circumcision controversy: An anthropological perspective.* Philadelphia: University of Pennsylvania Press.

Gruenbaum tells of her fieldwork in Sudan, where the most severe forms of FGC are practiced.

Morgentaler, Abraham. (1993). *The male body: A physician's guide to what every man should know about his sexual health.* New York: Simon & Schuster. An authoritative book on men's health.

CHAPTER FIVE

Sex Hormones, Sexual Differentiation, Puberty, and the Menstrual Cycle

CHAPTER HIGHLIGHTS

This Way

I have AIS, I guess,
because there is a god,
and he or she or both,
peered deep into my heart
to see
that all that I can be
is best expressed
in female form.

The alternative for me
would be XY, and I
would be virilized;
so all that's soft and tender
would instead surrender
to a strand of DNA.
In the lie of X and Y
I came to challenge the
immutability
of "he" and the certainty
of "she." Blended and infused,
a ruse of gender
that upends
a different fate.

Non-functioning receptors
have rescued me
Not a failed mess
But a smashing success of nature!*

*Sherri Groveman, an intersex individual with androgen insensitivity syndrome (AIS). In *Hermaphrodites with Attitude*, 1995, p. 2 (contact Info@isna.org).

Prenatal period (pree-NAY-tul): The time from conception to birth.
Hormones: Chemical substances secreted by the endocrine glands into the bloodstream.
Testosterone: A hormone secreted by the testes in the male (and also present at lower levels in the female).
Androgens: The group of male sex hormones, one of which is testosterone.
Estrogens (ESS-troh-jens): The group of female sex hormones.
Progesterone (pro-JES-tur-ohn): A female sex hormone secreted by the ovaries.
Pituitary gland (pih-TOO-ih-tair-ee): A small endocrine gland located on the lower side of the brain below the hypothalamus; the pituitary is important in regulating levels of sex hormones.
Hypothalamus (hy-poh-THAL-ah-mus): A small region of the brain that is important in regulating many body functions, including the functioning of the sex hormones.

One of the marvels of human biology is that the complex and different male and female anatomies—males with a penis and scrotum, and females with a vagina, uterus, and breasts—arise from a single cell, the fertilized egg, which varies only in whether it carries two X chromosomes (XX) or one X and one Y (XY). Many of the structural differences between males and females arise before birth, during the **prenatal period,** in a complex and delicate process called *prenatal sexual differentiation.* Further differences develop during puberty.

Yet as the chapter opening poem suggests, gender is not always a simple matter. Sex and gender and their development are complex and vulnerable to disturbances. Further variety in the human condition results.

In this chapter, we examine the process of sexual differentiation—both prenatally and during puberty. We also consider the biological and psychological aspects of the menstrual cycle. Let's start, however, with another biological system, the endocrine or hormonal system, paying particular attention to the sex hormones. They play a major role in the differentiation process.

Sex Hormones

Hormones are powerful chemical substances manufactured by the *endocrine glands* and secreted directly into the bloodstream. Because they go into the blood, their effects are felt fairly rapidly and at places in the body quite distant from where they were manufactured. The most important sex hormones are **testosterone** (one of a group of hormones called **androgens**) and **estrogens** and **progesterone.** The thyroid, the adrenals, and the pituitary are examples of endocrine glands. We are interested here in the gonads, or sex glands: the testes in the male and the ovaries in the female.

The **pituitary gland** and a closely related region of the brain, the **hypothalamus,** are also important to our discussion, because the hypothalamus regulates the pituitary, which regulates the other glands, in particular the testes and ovaries. Because of its role, the pituitary has been called the *master gland* of the endocrine system. The pituitary is a small gland, about the size of a pea, which projects down from the lower side of the brain. It is divided into two lobes: the anterior and the posterior. The anterior lobe interacts with the gonads. The hypothalamus is a region at the base of the brain just above the pituitary (see Figure 5.1). It plays a part in regulating many vital behaviors, such as eating, drinking, and sexual behavior.[1] It is important in regulating the pituitary.

These three structures—the hypothalamus, the pituitary, and gonads (testes or ovaries)—function together. They influence such important sexual functions as the menstrual cycle, pregnancy, the changes of puberty, and sexual behavior.

---

[1]One psychologist summarized the functions of the hypothalamus as being the four F's: fighting, feeding, fleeing, and, ahem, sexual behavior.

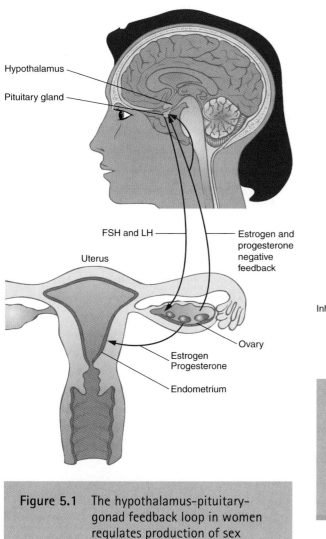

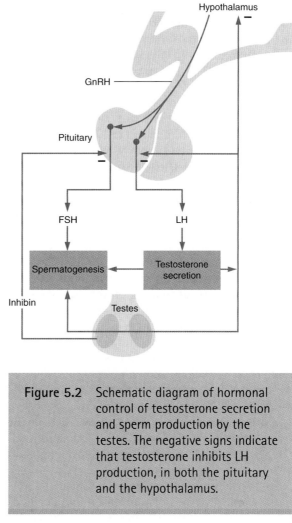

Figure 5.2 Schematic diagram of hormonal control of testosterone secretion and sperm production by the testes. The negative signs indicate that testosterone inhibits LH production, in both the pituitary and the hypothalamus.

Figure 5.1 The hypothalamus-pituitary-gonad feedback loop in women regulates production of sex hormones.

Sex Hormone Systems in the Male

The pituitary and the testes both produce hormones. The important hormone produced by testes is *testosterone*. A "male" or masculinizing sex hormone, testosterone has important functions in stimulating and maintaining the secondary sex characteristics (such as beard growth), maintaining the genitals and their sperm-producing capability, and stimulating the growth of bone and muscle.

The pituitary produces several hormones, two of which are important in this discussion: **follicle-stimulating hormone (FSH)** and **luteinizing hormone (LH).** These hormones affect the functioning of the testes. FSH controls sperm production, and LH controls testosterone production.

Testosterone levels in males are relatively constant. The hypothalamus, pituitary, and testes

operate in a negative feedback loop that maintains these constant levels (Figure 5.2). The levels of LH are regulated by a substance called **GnRH (gonadotropin-releasing hormone),** which is secreted by the hypothalamus. (FSH levels are similarly regulated by GnRH.) The system comes full circle because the hypothalamus monitors the levels of testosterone present, and in this way testosterone influences the output of GnRH. This feedback loop is sometimes called the **HPG axis,** for *h*ypothalamus-*p*ituitary-*g*onad axis.

This negative feedback loop operates much like a thermostat-controlled heating system. When a room cools down, certain changes occur in the thermostat, which then signals the furnace to turn on. The action of the furnace warms the air in the room. Eventually the

Follicle-stimulating hormone (FSH): A hormone secreted by the pituitary; it stimulates follicle development in females and sperm production in males.
Luteinizing hormone (LH): A hormone secreted by the pituitary; it regulates estrogen secretion and ovum development in the female and testosterone production in the male.
GnRH (gonadotropin-releasing hormone): A hormone secreted by the hypothalamus that regulates the pituitary's secretion of gonad-stimulating hormones.
HPG axis: Hypothalamus-pituitary-gonad axis, the negative feedback loop that regulates sex-hormone production.

air becomes so warm that another change is produced in the thermostat, which sends a signal to the furnace to turn off. The temperature in the room then gradually falls until it triggers another change in the thermostat, which turns on the furnace, and the cycle is repeated. This cycle is a *negative* feedback loop because *increases* in temperature turn *off* the furnace, and *decreases* in temperature turn *on* the furnace.

The hypothalamus, pituitary, and testes work together in a similar negative feedback loop, ensuring that testosterone is maintained at a fairly constant level, just as a thermostat can keep room temperature fairly constant. The pituitary's production of LH stimulates the testes to produce testosterone. But when testosterone levels get high, the hypothalamus reduces its production of GnRH, in turn causing the pituitary to reduce production of LH, and consequently decreasing production of testosterone by the testes. When testosterone levels fall, the hypothalamus again increases the production of GnRH, and the process starts again. Although the level of testosterone in men is fairly constant, there is some cycling, with variations according to the time of day, and possibly to the time of month, as we discuss later in this chapter.

Inhibin is another hormone produced in the testes (by cells called Sertoli cells). It acts to regulate FSH levels in a negative feedback loop, just as testosterone does with LH (Plant et al., 1993). Interest in inhibin has been intense because the hormone shows great promise, at least theoretically, as a male contraceptive. In other words, because inhibin suppresses FSH production, sperm production in turn is inhibited. Future developments in this field should be interesting.

Sex Hormone Systems in the Female

The ovaries produce two important hormones, *estrogen*[2] and *progesterone*. Estrogen brings about many of the changes of puberty (stimulating the growth of the uterus and vagina, enlarging the pelvis, and stimulating breast growth). Estrogen is also responsible for maintaining the mucous membranes of the vagina and stopping the growth of bone and muscle, which accounts for females being generally smaller than males.

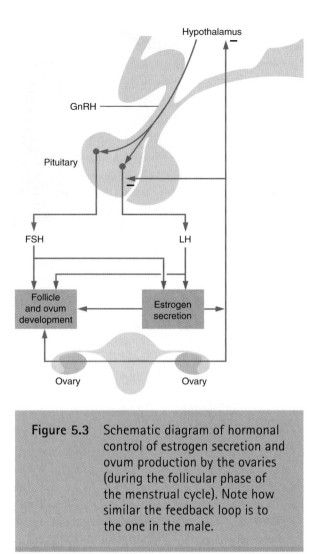

Figure 5.3 Schematic diagram of hormonal control of estrogen secretion and ovum production by the ovaries (during the follicular phase of the menstrual cycle). Note how similar the feedback loop is to the one in the male.

In adult women the levels of estrogen and progesterone fluctuate according to the phases of the menstrual cycle and during various other stages such as pregnancy and menopause. The two pituitary hormones, FSH and LH, regulate the levels of estrogen and progesterone. In this way the levels of estrogen and progesterone are controlled by a negative feedback loop of the hypothalamus, pituitary, and ovaries that is similar to the negative feedback loop in the male (see Figures 5.1, 5.3). For example, as shown on the right side of Figure 5.3, increases in the level of GnRH increase the level of LH, and the increases in LH eventually produce increases in the output of estrogen. Finally, the increases in the level of estrogen inhibit (decrease) the production of GnRH and LH.

The pituitary produces two other hormones, *prolactin* and *oxytocin*. Prolactin stimulates production of milk by the mammary glands after a

[2]We really should say *estrogens* because they are a group of hormones like the androgens. Estradiol is one of the estrogens. To keep things simple, we will just use the term *estrogen*.

Inhibin: A substance secreted by the testes and ovaries that regulates FSH levels.

woman has given birth to a child. Oxytocin stimulates ejection of that milk from the nipples. Oxytocin also stimulates contractions of the uterus during childbirth.

The female sex hormone system functions much like the male sex hormone system. The ovaries and testes produce many of the same hormones, but in different amounts. The ovaries, like the testes, produce inhibin, which in turn forms a negative feedback loop with FSH production (Burger, 1993). We consider the functioning of the female sex hormone system and the menstrual cycle in more detail later in this chapter.

Prenatal Sexual Differentiation

Sex Chromosomes

At the time of conception the future human being consists of only a single cell, the fertilized egg. The specific sex chromosomes carried in that fertilized egg are the deciding factor in whether it will become a male or a female. If there are two X chromosomes, the result will typically be a female, but if there are one X and one Y, the result will typically be a male. Although incredibly tiny, the sex chromosomes carry a wealth of information that they transmit to various organs throughout the body, giving instructions on how to differentiate in the course of development. Because the Y chromosome is smaller, it has fewer genes and carries less information than the X. The Y chromosome has about 80 genes, compared with 1,090 on the X (Federman, 2006).

Occasionally, individuals receive at conception a sex chromosome combination other than XX or XY. Such abnormal sex chromosome complements may lead to a variety of clinical syndromes, such as *Klinefelter's syndrome.* In this syndrome, a genetic male has an extra X chromosome (XXY). As a result, the testes are abnormal, no sperm are produced, and testosterone levels are low (Winter & Couch, 1995).

During development, the single cell divides repeatedly, becoming a two-celled organism, then a four-celled organism, then an eight-celled organism, and so on. By 28 days after conception, the embryo is about 1 centimeter (less than a half inch) long, but male and female embryos are still identical, except for the sex chromosomes. In other words, the embryo is still in the undifferentiated state. However, by the 7th week after conception, some basic structures have been formed that will eventually become either a male or a female reproductive system. At this point, the embryo has a pair of gonads (and each gonad has two parts—an outer cortex and an inner medulla), two sets of ducts (the *Müllerian ducts* and the *Wolffian ducts*), and rudimentary external genitals (the *genital tubercle,* the *urethral folds,* and the *genital swelling*) (see Figure 5.4, top).

Gonads

In the 7th week after conception, the sex chromosomes direct the gonads to begin differentiation. In the male, the undifferentiated gonad develops into a testis at about 7 weeks. In the female, the process occurs somewhat later, with the ovaries developing at around 13 or 14 weeks.

An important gene that directs the differentiation of the gonads, located on the Y chromosome, is called **SRY**, for *sex-determining region, Y chromosome* (Page et al., 1987; Skaletsky et al., 2003). If SRY is present, it causes the manufacture of a substance called *testis-determining factor* (TDF), which makes the gonads differentiate into testes, and male development occurs. (See Figure 5.5 on p. 98 for a summary of all the genes that regulate sexual differentiation.) The X chromosome carries genes that control normal functioning of the ovaries (Winter & Couch, 1995). Surprisingly, a number of genes on the X chromosome also affect cells in the testes that manufacture sperm (Wang et al., 2001).

Prenatal Hormones and the Genitals

Once the ovaries and testes have differentiated, they begin to produce different sex hormones, which then direct the differentiation of the rest of the internal and external genital system (see Figure 5.4, middle).

In the female the Wolffian ducts degenerate, and the **Müllerian ducts** turn into the fallopian tubes, the uterus, and the upper part of the vagina. The tubercle becomes the clitoris, the folds become the inner lips, and the swelling develops into the outer lips.

The testes secrete Müllerian inhibiting substance (MIS) (Vilain, 2000). MIS causes the Müllerian ducts to degenerate, while the **Wolffian ducts,** supported by testosterone, turn into the epididymis, the vas deferens, and the ejaculatory duct. The tubercle becomes the glans penis, the folds form the shaft of the penis, and the swelling develops into the scrotum.

SRY: Stands for sex-determining region, Y chromosome.
Müllerian ducts: Ducts found in both male and female fetuses; in males they degenerate and in females they develop into the fallopian tubes, the uterus, and the upper part of the vagina.
Wolffian ducts: Ducts found in both male and female fetuses; in females they degenerate and in males they develop into the epididymis, the vas deferens, and the ejaculatory duct.

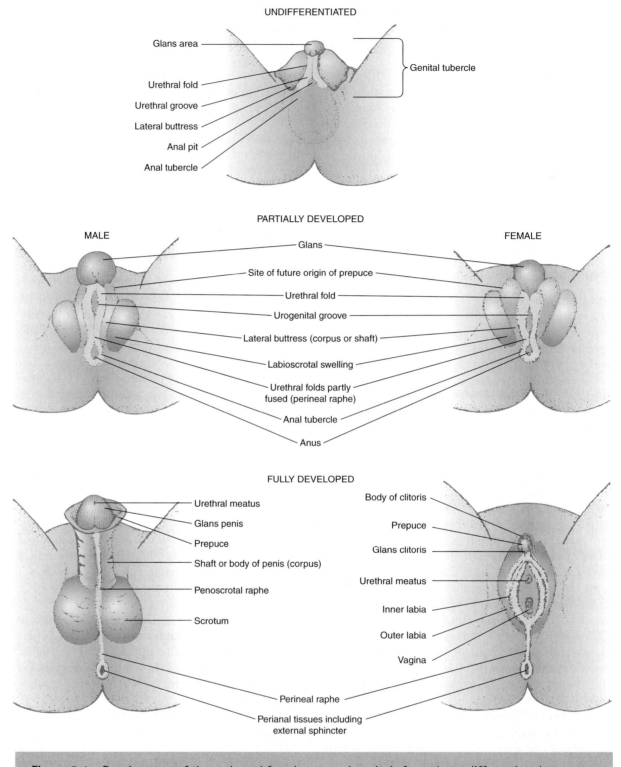

Figure 5.4   Development of the male and female external genitals from the undifferentiated stage during prenatal development. Note homologous organs in the female and male.

Focus: Milestones in Sex Research
Endocrine Disrupters

Florida panthers have low sperm counts and the same levels of estradiol as females. Frogs are born hermaphroditic, with mixed male and female organs. Male turtledoves display reduced courtship and nesting behaviors. A preschool girl begins growing pubic hair. These cases and dozens of others have appeared in the news in the last decade. Are they unrelated bizarre occurrences, or is there a common link?

Scientists believe that underlying all these troubling cases is the phenomenon of **endocrine disrupters,** which are chemicals found in the environment that affect the endocrine system as well as biological functioning and behavior of animals, including humans. Evidence of the effects of endocrine disrupters (also called endocrine disrupting chemicals, or EDCs) comes both from studies of animals in the wild and from carefully controlled laboratory experiments.

What chemicals are the culprits? Some are pesticides such as atrazine and DDT, used by farmers and others to kill unwanted insects and weeds. Bisphenol A is used in making plastics such as baby bottles. PCBs, which were banned from production in the United States in 1976, were used in making products such as paints, plastics, and printing ink. Some have a half-life of over 1,000 years and thus are still abundant in the environment despite being banned.

How do these chemicals exert their effects on sexual biology and behavior? All of them affect the endocrine system and, specifically, the sex hormone system. Many have multiple effects. Atrazine, for example, affects both estrogen and testosterone and inhibits their binding to estrogen receptors and androgen receptors. It also depresses the LH surge that causes ovulation, described later in this chapter in the discussion of the menstrual cycle. The insecticide DDT affects estrogen, progesterone, and testosterone by mimicking estrogen and binding to estrogen receptors, as well as by altering the metabolism of both progesterone and testosterone. PCBs are both anti-estrogens and anti-androgens. These chemicals are in the food we eat and the water and milk that we drink.

Why should we care about a few hermaphroditic frogs or preschoolers with pubic hair? Scientists see these cases as examples of the proverbial canary in the mine shaft—that is, they are small signs that something terribly dangerous is happening. The European Union is beginning to take steps to regulate these chemicals, but we have seen little action on the issue in the United States. In 1996, Congress directed the Environmental Protection Agency to develop a program to detect endocrine disrupters, but nothing happened, perhaps because representatives of the chemical industry are members of the relevant advisory board.

Meanwhile, on a Chippewa Indian reservation in a part of Ontario that is heavily populated with chemical manufacturing plants, only 35 percent of the babies born today are boys.

Sources: Hayes et al. (2002); Iwaniuk et al. (2006); Propper (2005); Sanghavi (2006); Zala & Penn (2004).

The process by which the internal and external genitals differentiate is the subject of much exciting new research. At least six different genes are involved in prenatal sexual differentiation (Figure 5.5), and a mutation in any one of them can cause an error in development (Vilain, 2000).

By 4 months after conception, the gender of the fetus is clear from the appearance of the external genitals (Figure 5.4, bottom).

Descent of the Testes and Ovaries

As these developmental changes are taking place, the ovaries and testes are changing in shape and position. At first, the ovaries and testes lie near the top of the abdominal cavity. By the 10th week they have grown and have moved down to the level of the upper edge of the pelvis. The ovaries remain there until after birth, and later they shift to their adult position in the pelvis.

The male testes must make a much longer journey, down into the scrotum via a passageway called the *inguinal canal.* Normally this movement occurs around the 7th month after conception. The inguinal canal closes off after the testes descend.

Two problems may occur in this process. First, one or both testes may fail to descend into the scrotum by the time of birth, a condition known as *undescended testes,* or **cryptorchidism** (Santen, 1995). This condition occurs in about 2 percent of all males. Most frequently, only

Endocrine disrupters: Chemicals found in the environment that affect the endocrine system as well as the biological functioning and behavior of animals, including humans. **Cryptorchidism:** Undescended testes; the condition in which the testes do not descend to the scrotum as they should during prenatal development.

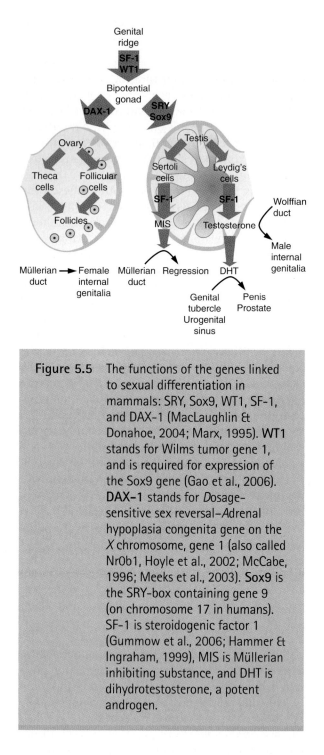

Figure 5.5 The functions of the genes linked to sexual differentiation in mammals: SRY, Sox9, WT1, SF-1, and DAX-1 (MacLaughlin & Donahoe, 2004; Marx, 1995). **WT1** stands for Wilms tumor gene 1, and is required for expression of the Sox9 gene (Gao et al., 2006). **DAX-1** stands for *Dosage-sensitive sex reversal–Adrenal hypoplasia congenita gene on the X chromosome, gene 1* (also called NrOb1, Hoyle et al., 2002; McCabe, 1996; Meeks et al., 2003). **Sox9** is the SRY-box containing gene 9 (on chromosome 17 in humans). SF-1 is steroidogenic factor 1 (Gummow et al., 2006; Hammer & Ingraham, 1999), MIS is Müllerian inhibiting substance, and DHT is dihydrotestosterone, a potent androgen.

one testis is undescended, and the other is in the normal position. In most of these cases, the testes do descend by puberty, and so only about 1 in 500 adult men has undescended testes. If the testes do not descend spontaneously, however, the condition must be corrected by surgery or hormonal therapy. The optimum time for doing this is before age 5. Otherwise, if both testes fail to descend, the man will be sterile, because, as we discussed in Chapter 4, the

high temperature of the testes inside the body inhibits the production of sperm. Undescended testes are also more likely to develop cancer.

The second possible problem occurs when the inguinal canal does not close off completely. It may then reopen later in life, creating a passageway through which loops of the intestine can enter the scrotum. This condition, called *inguinal hernia,* can be remedied by simple surgery.

Brain Differentiation

During the prenatal period, when sex hormones are having a big impact on genital anatomy, they are also acting on the brain (Arnold, 2003). The results of many experiments with animals indicate that in certain regions there are differences between male and female brains. The primary sex-differentiated structure is the hypothalamus, in particular a region of it called the *preoptic area* (Fitch & Bimonte, 2002). The hypothalamus is gender-differentiated in humans as well (Cahill, 2005; Swaab et al., 2001).

One of the most important effects of this early sexual differentiation is the determination of the estrogen sensitivity of certain cells in the hypothalamus, cells that have *estrogen receptors* (Choi et al., 2001; McEwen, 2001). If testosterone is present during fetal development, these specialized cells in the hypothalamus become insensitive to estrogen. If estrogen is present, these cells become highly sensitive to levels of estrogen in the bloodstream. This sensitivity is crucial to the hypothalamic-pituitary-gonad feedback loop discussed earlier. Male hypothalamic cells are relatively insensitive to estrogen levels, but female hypothalamic cells are highly sensitive to them. Male hypothalamic cells have more androgen receptors (Donahue et al., 2000).

New magnetic resonance imaging (MRI) studies are giving us a view into the brain of alive, awake humans, in contrast to earlier techniques that dissected the brains of, well, dead people and animals. The trade-off, at least for now, is that the MRI measures are relatively crude, simple assessments of the volume or size of certain regions. One of these studies found a larger volume of the hypothalamus and amygdala—both brain regions with high densities of estrogen and androgen receptors—in men than in women (Goldstein et al., 2001). Regions of the brain that have few estrogen and androgen receptors did not show these gender differences in size. Interestingly, a different MRI technique—the functional MRI, or fMRI—has detected increased activation in one region of the

Table 5.1 Homologous and Analogous Organs of the Male and Female Reproductive Systems

Embryonic Source	Homologous Organs		Analogous Organs	
	In the Adult Male	In the Adult Female	In the Adult Male	In the Adult Female
Gonad (medulla plus cortex)	Testes (from medulla)	Ovaries (from cortex)	Testes (from medulla)	Ovaries (from cortex)
Genital tubercle	Glans penis	Clitoris	Glans penis	Clitoris
Genital swelling	Scrotum	Outer lips		
Müllerian duct	Degenerates, leaving only remnants	Fallopian tubes, uterus, part of vagina		
Wolffian duct	Epididymis, vas deferens, seminal vesicles	Degenerates, leaving only remnants		
Urethral primordia	Prostate, Cowper's glands	Skene's glands, Bartholin glands	Prostate, Cowper's glands	Skene's glands, Bartholin glands

hypothalamus in men who were sexually aroused (Arnow et al., 2002).

The brains of men and women are quite similar in many regions, but a few brain structures show some gender differentiation. These structures include the hippocampus, which is important for memory and spatial navigation, and the amygdala, important in emotion (Cahill, 2005).

Homologous Organs

Our discussion of sexual differentiation highlights the fact that the reproductive organs of men and women have similar origins, even though adult men and women appear to have very different reproductive anatomies. When an organ in the male and an organ in the female both develop from the same embryonic tissue, the organs are said to be **homologous.** When the two organs have similar functions, they are said to be **analogous.** Table 5.1 summarizes the major homologies (similar origins) and analogies (similar functions) of the male and female reproductive systems. For example, ovaries and testes are homologous (because they develop from an undifferentiated gonad) and analogous (because they produce gametes and sex hormones).

Atypical Prenatal Gender Differentiation

Gender is not a simple matter, as you may have noticed from the preceding discussion. Most people, however, assume that it is. In other words, people typically assume that if a person is female, she will be feminine; will think of herself as a woman; will be sexually attracted to men; will have a clitoris, vagina, uterus, and ovaries; and will have sex chro-

mosomes XX. They also assume that all males are masculine; think of themselves as male; are sexually attracted to women; have a penis, testes, and scrotum; and have sex chromosomes XY.

A great deal of research over the last several decades challenges these assumptions and provides much information about sexuality and gender and their development. Before we consider the results of this research, however, some background information is helpful.

We can distinguish among the following eight variables of gender (adapted from Money, 1987)[3]:

1. *Chromosomal gender.* XX in the female; XY in the male.
2. *Gonadal gender.* Ovaries in the female; testes in the male.
3a. *Prenatal hormonal gender.* Testosterone and MIS in the male but not the female before birth.
3b. *Prenatal and neonatal brain differentiation.* Testosterone present for masculinization, absent for feminization.
4. *Internal organs.* Fallopian tubes, uterus, and upper vagina in the female; prostate and seminal vesicles in the male.
5. *External genital appearance.* Clitoris, inner and outer lips, and vaginal opening in the female; penis and scrotum in the male.

[3]The distinction between the terms *gender* and *sex,* discussed in Chapter 1, is being maintained here.

Homologous organs (huh–MOLL–uh–gus): Organs in the male and female that develop from the same embryonic tissue.
Analogous organs (an–AL–uh–gus): Organs in the male and female that have similar functions.

6. *Pubertal hormonal gender.* At puberty, estrogen and progesterone in the female; testosterone in the male.

7. *Assigned gender.* The announcement at birth, "It's a girl" or "It's a boy," based on the appearance of the external genitals; the gender the parents and the rest of society believe the child to be; the gender in which the child is reared.

8. *Gender identity.* The person's private, internal sense of maleness or femaleness.

These variables might be subdivided into biological variables (the first six) and psychological variables (the last two).

In most cases, of course, all the variables are in agreement in an individual. In other words, the person is a "consistent" female or male. If the person is a female, she has XX chromosomes, ovaries, a uterus and vagina, and a clitoris; she is reared as a female; and she thinks of herself as a female. If the person is a male, he has the parallel set of appropriate characteristics.

However, as a result of any one of a number of factors during the course of prenatal sexual development, the gender indicated by one or more of these variables may disagree with the gender indicated by others. When the contradictions occur among several of the biological variables (1 through 6), the person is said to have an **intersex** condition or **disorder of sex development (DSD)** (Berenbaum, 2006; Hughes et al., 2006). Biologically, the gender of such a person is ambiguous. The reproductive structures may be partly male and partly female, or they may be incompletely male or female. Approximately 2 percent of births have an intersex condition (Blackless et al., 2000).

A number of syndromes can cause an intersex condition. Some of the most common are congenital adrenal hyperplasia, progestin-induced pseudohermaphroditism, and the androgen-insensitivity syndrome. In **congenital adrenal hyperplasia (CAH)** (also called *adrenogenital syndrome*), a genetic female develops ovaries normally as a fetus, but later in the course of prenatal development, the adrenal gland begins to function abnormally (as a result of a recessive genetic condition unconnected with the sex chromosomes) and produces an excess amount of androgens. Prenatal sexual differentiation

Figure 5.6   Dr. John Money, a controversial pioneer in research on and treatment of intersex individuals.

then does not follow the normal female course. As a result, the external genitals are partly or completely male in appearance. The labia are partly or totally fused (so there is no vaginal opening), and the clitoris is enlarged to the size of a small penis or even a full-sized one. For this reason, at birth these genetic females are sometimes identified as males. Long-term follow-ups indicate that CAH girls have a female gender identity, tend toward male-stereotyped toy and game preferences, and generally function well as girls and women (Meyer-Bahlburg et al., 2004, 2006).

Progestin-induced pseudohermaphroditism is a similar syndrome that resulted from a drug, progestin, that was at one time given to pregnant women to help them maintain the pregnancy if they were prone to miscarriage. (The drug is no longer prescribed because of the following effects.) As the drug circulated in the mother's bloodstream, the developing fetus was essentially exposed to a high dose of androgens. (Progestin and androgens are quite similar biochemicals, and in the body the progestin acted like androgen.) In genetic females this produced an abnormal, masculinized genital development similar to that found in CAH.

The reverse case occurs in **androgen-insensitivity syndrome (AIS)** (Wisniewski et al., 2000). In this syndrome a genetic male produces normal levels of testosterone, but as a result of a genetic condition, the body tissues are insensitive to the testosterone, and prenatal development is feminized.

Intersex: A condition in which the individual has a mixture of male and female reproductive structures, so that it is not clear at birth whether the individual is a male or a female. Formerly called a *pseudohermaphrodite.*

Disorders of sex development (DSD): A newer term for intersex conditions.

Congenital adrenal hyperplasia (CAH): A condition in which a genetic female produces abnormal levels of androgens prenatally and therefore has male-appearing genitals at birth.

Androgen-insensitivity syndrome (AIS): A genetic condition in which the body is unresponsive to androgens so that a genetic male may be born with a female-appearing body.

For this reason, the individual is born with the external appearance of a female: a small vagina (but no uterus) and undescended testes. The individual whose poem appeared at the beginning of this chapter has AIS.

Intersex persons provide good evidence of the great complexity of sex and gender and their development. Many variables are involved in gender and sex, and there are many steps in gender differentiation, even before birth. Because the process is complex, it is vulnerable to disturbances, creating conditions such as intersex.

Indeed, the research serves to question our basic notions of what it means to be male or female. In CAH, is the genetic female who is born with male external genitals a male or a female? What makes a person male or female—chromosomal gender? External genital appearance? Gender identity?

A related phenomenon was first studied in a small community in the Dominican Republic (Imperato-McGinley et al., 1974). Due to a genetic-endocrine problem, a large number of genetic males there appeared to be females at birth. The syndrome is called *5-Alpha Reductase Syndrome*. These infants had a vaginal pouch instead of a scrotum and a clitoris-sized penis. The uneducated parents, according to the researchers, were unaware that there were any problems, and these genetic males were treated as typical females. At puberty, a spontaneous biological change caused a penis to develop. Significantly, the psychological identity of these individuals also changed. Despite their rearing as females, their gender identity switched to male, and they developed heterosexual interests. In their culture, these people are called Guevodoces ("penis at 12").

Anthropologist Gilbert Herdt (1990) is critical of the research and interpretations about the Guevodoces. The major criticism is that the Western researchers assumed that this culture is a two-gender society, like the United States, and that people have to fall into one of only two categories, either male or female. Anthropologists, however, have documented the existence of three-gender societies—that is, societies in which there are three, not two, gender categories—and the society in which the Guevodoces grow up is a three-gender society. The third gender is the Guevodoces. Their gender identity is not male or female but Guevodoce. The 5-Alpha Reductase Syndrome has also been found among the Sambia of New Guinea, who also have a three-gender culture. Again we see the profound effect of culture on our most basic ideas about sex and gender.

Sexual Differentiation during Puberty

What is puberty? Puberty is not a point in time but rather a process during which there is further sexual differentiation. It is the stage in life during which the body changes from that of a child into that of an adult, with secondary sexual characteristics (such as breasts or a beard) and the ability to reproduce sexually.

Puberty can be scientifically defined as the time during which there is sudden enlargement and maturation of the gonads, other genitalia, and secondary sex characteristics, leading to reproductive capacity (Tanner, 1967). It is the second important period—the first being the prenatal period—during which sexual differentiation takes place. Perhaps the most important single event in the process is the first ejaculation for the male and the first menstruation for the female. Note that first menstruation is not necessarily a sign of reproductive capability, since girls typically do not produce mature eggs until a year or two after the first menstruation.

The physiological process that underlies puberty in both genders is a marked increase in levels of sex hormones. For this reason, the hypothalamus, pituitary, and gonads control the changes.

Adolescence is a socially defined period of development that bears some relationship to puberty. Adolescence represents a psychological transition from the behavior and attitudes of a child to the behavior, attitudes, and responsibilities of an adult. In the United States it corresponds roughly to the years from age 10 to age 20. Modern American culture has an unusually long period of adolescence (Steinberg, 2005). A century ago, adolescence was much shorter. The lengthening of the educational process has served to prolong adolescence. In some cultures, in fact, adolescence does not exist. Instead, the child shifts to being an adult directly, with only a *rite of passage* in between.

Before describing the changes that take place during puberty, we should note two points. First, the timing of the pubertal process differs considerably for males and females. Girls begin the change around 8 to 12 years of age, while boys do so about 2 years later. Girls reach their full height by about age 16, while boys continue growing until about age 18 or later. The phenomenon of males and females being out of step with each other at this stage creates no small number of crises for the adolescent. Girls are interested in boys long before boys are aware that

Puberty: The time during which there is sudden enlargement and maturation of the gonads, other genitalia, and secondary sex characteristics, so that the individual becomes capable of reproduction.

Focus: A Sexually Diverse World
The Debate over the Treatment of Intersex Individuals

W hen Chris was born, her clitoris was 1.7 cm long. That's about halfway between the length of the average newborn clitoris and the average newborn penis. She had a scrotum but no testes in it, and the physician was unsure whether she was a girl or a boy. A blood test revealed that her sex chromosomes were XY. After 24 hours of consultations, during which her parents were in agony, the physician decided that Chris should be a girl because it would be impossible for her to function as a boy with such strange genitals. While a baby, she had several surgeries, one to remove her testes, which were still in her abdomen. Her clitoris was surgically reduced in size when she was age 5, old enough to remember it. Today she is 27 and angry about what she considers the mutilations of her body. She now knows that she has androgen-insensitivity syndrome. So much of her clitoris was removed that she is not able to orgasm.

Chris (a composite of several case histories in the scientific literature) is an intersex individual; that is, her genitals have combined male, female, or ambiguous elements. She was treated according to a protocol that became standard beginning in the 1960s and persists today. This protocol was based on the pioneering research of Dr. John Money and others. According to him, individuals such as Chris, whom he called "pseudohermaphrodites," could successfully be assigned to either gender, provided that it was done before 18 months of age and that the necessary surgeries and follow-up medical treatments (such as hormone treatment) occurred. Money's research indicated that individuals treated with the standard protocol grew up to be healthy and well adjusted.

In the last decade, however, intersex individuals have come out of the closet and formed an activist organization, the Intersex Society of North America (ISNA).* Intersex activists argue that they have cases of genital *variability,* not genital abnormality. The medical standard is that an infant's organ that is 0.9 cm or less is a clitoris and 2.5 cm or more is a penis. Activists argue that these cutoffs are arbitrary. What is wrong with a clitoris that is 1.7 cm long? Perhaps the only thing wrong with it is that it makes doctors, and perhaps parents, embarrassed. Issues of medical ethics are raised: Should essentially cosmetic surgery be performed on a baby who cannot give informed consent? Should parents be encouraged to lie to their child?

Sex researcher Milton Diamond conducted long-term follow-ups on several individuals treated using Money's standard protocol. He found that, contrary to the glowing picture of perfect adjustment painted by Money and others, these intersex individuals had serious adjustment problems that they traced directly to the medical "management" of their condition. Diamond's research has sparked a debate over the proper treatment of intersex individuals. Diamond has proposed a protocol in which he urges physicians, in cases of intersex infants, (1) to make their most informed judgment about the child's eventual gender identity (CAH girls, for example, almost invariably have a female identity) and counsel the parents to rear the child in that gender; (2) not to perform surgeries that might later need to be reversed; and (3) to provide honest counseling and education to the parents and child as he or she grows up so that the child

*For information about the ISNA and other sexuality organizations, including the ISNA Web site, see the Directory of Resources at the end of this book.

girls exist. A girl may be stuck with a date who barely reaches her armpits, while a boy may have to cope with someone who is better qualified to be on his basketball team than he is.

Second, there are large individual differences (differences from one person to the next) in the age at which the processes of puberty take place. For this reason there is no one "normal" time to begin menstruating or growing a beard. Instead, we give age ranges in describing the timing of the process.

Changes in Girls

A summary of the physical changes of puberty in males and females is provided in Table 5.2 on page 104. The first sign of puberty in the female is the beginning of breast development, on average around 9 to 10 years of age (Sun et al., 2002). The ducts in the nipple area swell, and there is growth of fatty and connective tissue, causing the small, conical buds to increase in size. These changes are produced by increases in the levels of the sex hormones by a process that is described in the following pages.

percent of the individuals raised as women were dissatisfied with their genitals, and 40 percent had no sexual interest or experience. Whether reared male or female, all were satisfied with their gender. In this case, it seems that rearing as a male worked better.

Another study examined the success of "feminizing" genital surgery—that is, performing surgery to reduce the size of an overlarge clitoris or to create or enlarge a vagina, as might happen with CAH girls (Creighton et al., 2001). Of the surgeries done in childhood, 41 percent were judged as having a poor outcome, supporting Diamond's recommendations against these early surgeries. Another study of intersex women—many of them with CAH—who had had clitoral surgery in childhood indicated approximately twice as many of them (39 percent) being unable to orgasm, compared with a control group (20 percent) of intersex women who had not had clitoral surgery (Minto et al., 2003).

Recognizing these new developments, the American Academy of Pediatrics (2000) issued guidelines for primary care pediatricians on how to care for newborns with ambiguous genitals. They include what tests to run to determine the cause of the ambiguous genitals, when the baby should be referred to a center specializing in intersexuality, and what factors should be used to decide the sex of rearing. These factors include fertility potential (for example, a CAH girl is potentially fertile and should be raised as a girl) and capacity for normal sexual functioning. Only with long-term studies will we learn whether these new treatments will yield better results for intersex individuals.

Sources: American Academy of Pediatrics (2000); Creighton et al. (2001); Creighton & Minto (2001); Diamond (1996, 1999); Diamond & Sigmundson (1997); Kessler (1998); Meyer-Bahlburg et al. (2004); Money & Ehrhardt (1972); Wisniewski et al. (2000, 2001).

Figure 5.7 Cheryl Chase, an intersex activist.

can eventually make an informed decision regarding treatment.

Diamond's research on intersex individuals was quickly followed by more systematic studies. Micropenis is a condition in which a genetic XY male is born with a very small penis. One study followed up 18 of these individuals in adulthood; 13 had been reared as boys and 5 as girls (Wisniewski et al., 2001). All of the individuals raised as men reported good or fair erections, but 50 percent were dissatisfied with their genitals. In contrast, 80

As the growth of fatty and supporting tissue increases in the breasts, a similar increase takes place at the hips and buttocks, leading to the rounded contours that distinguish adult female bodies from adult male bodies. Individual females have unique patterns of fat deposits, so there are also considerable individual differences in the resulting female shapes.

Another visible sign of puberty is the growth of pubic hair, which occurs shortly after breast development begins. About two years later, axillary (underarm) hair appears.

Body growth increases sharply during puberty, during the approximate age range of 9.5 to 14.5 years. The growth spurt for girls occurs about two years before the growth spurt for boys (Figure 5.8). This timing is consistent with girls' general pattern of maturing earlier than boys. Even prenatally, girls show an earlier hardening of the structures that become bones.

Estrogen eventually stops the growth spurt in girls. The presence of estrogen also causes the growth period to end sooner in girls than in boys, in this way accounting for the lesser average

Table 5.2   Summary of the Changes of Puberty and Their Sequence

Girls			Boys		
Characteristic	Average Age of First Appearance (Years)	Major Hormonal Influence	Characteristic	Average Age of First Appearance (Years)	Major Hormonal Influence
1. Growth of breasts	9–10	Pituitary growth hormone, estrogens, progesterone, thyroxine	1. Growth of testes, scrotal sac	9–10	Pituitary growth hormone, testosterone
2. Growth of pubic hair	9–10	Adrenal androgens	2. Growth of pubic hair	11–12	Testosterone
3. Body growth	9.5–14.5	Pituitary growth hormone, adrenal androgens, estrogens	3. Body growth	10.5–16	Pituitary growth hormone, testosterone
4. Menarche	12–12.5	GnRH, FSH, LH, estrogens, progesterone	4. Growth of penis	11–14.5	Testosterone
5. Underarm hair	About 2 years after pubic hair	Adrenal androgens	5. Change in voice (growth of larynx)	About the same time as penis growth	Testosterone
6. Oil- and sweat-producing glands (acne occurs when glands are clogged)	About the same time as underarm hair	Adrenal androgens	6. Facial and underarm hair	About 2 years after pubic hair	Testosterone
			7. Oil- and sweat-producing glands, acne	About the same time as underarm hair	Testosterone

height of adult women as compared with adult men.

At about 12 years of age, the **menarche** (first menstruation) occurs. The girl, however, is not capable of becoming pregnant until ovulation begins, typically about two years after the menarche. The first menstruation is not only an important biological event but also a significant psychological one. Various cultures have ceremonies recognizing its importance. In some families, it is a piece of news that spreads quickly to the relatives. Girls themselves display a wide range of reactions to the event, ranging from negative ones, such as fear, shame, or disgust, to positive ones, such as pride and a sense of maturity and womanliness.

Some of the most negative reactions occur when the girl has not been prepared for the menarche, which is still the case surprisingly often. Parents who are concerned about preparing their daughters for the first menstruation should remember that there is a wide range in the age at which it occurs.

It is not unusual for a girl to start menstruating in the fifth grade, and instances of the menarche during the fourth grade, while rare, do occur.

What determines the age at which a girl first menstruates? One explanation is the *percent body fat hypothesis* (Frisch & McArthur, 1974; Hopwood et al., 1990). During puberty, deposits of body fat increase in females. According to the percent body fat hypothesis, the percentage of body weight that is fat must rise to a certain level for menstruation to occur for the first time and for it to be maintained. For this reason, very skinny adolescent girls would tend to be late in the timing of first menstruation. **Leptin,** a hormone manufactured in the body, seems to be related to the onset of puberty in both girls and boys, although scientists have not yet sorted out the details (Apter, 2003; Phillip & Lazar, 2003; Wilson et al., 2003). In prepubertal girls and boys, leptin levels rise as body fat increases. Leptin stimulates the growth of skeletal bone and the release of LH.

The percent body fat hypothesis also helps to make sense of two related phenomena: the cessation

Menarche (MEN–ar–key): First menstruation.
Leptin: A hormone produced in the body that is related to the onset of puberty.

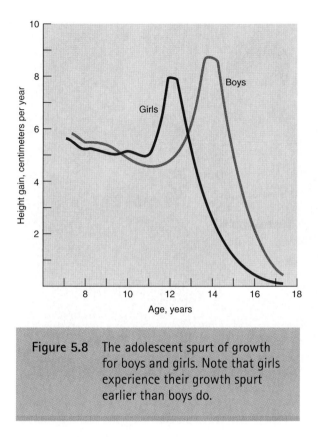

Figure 5.8 The adolescent spurt of growth for boys and girls. Note that girls experience their growth spurt earlier than boys do.

of menstruation in anorexics and the cessation of menstruation in women distance runners. *Anorexia nervosa* is a condition in which the person—most commonly an adolescent girl—engages in compulsive, extreme dieting, perhaps to the point of starving herself to death. As anorexia progresses, the percentage of body fat declines and menstruation ceases. It is also fairly common for women who are runners, and all women who exercise seriously to the point where their body fat is substantially reduced, to cease menstruating. For both anorexics and female runners, it seems that when the percentage of body fat falls below a critical value, the biological processes that control the menstrual cycle shut down menstruation.[4]

Before leaving the topic of running, we should note that there is some evidence that serious exercise also affects the male reproductive system. One study of male distance runners found that their testosterone levels were only about 68 percent as high, on the average, as a control group's testosterone levels (Wheeler et al., 1984). There are some reports of male long-distance runners complaining of a loss of sex drive, but it is unclear

[4]On the other hand, programs of moderate, regular aerobic exercise have been shown to reduce menstrual problems such as cramps (Golub, 1992).

whether this results from reduced testosterone levels or from the perpetual feelings of fatigue that such runners have from their intensive training (Wheeler et al., 1984).

Other body changes in girls during puberty include a development of the blood supply to the clitoris, a thickening of the walls of the vagina, and a rapid growth of the uterus, which doubles in size between ages 10 and 18. The pelvic bone structure grows and widens, contributing to the rounded shape of the female and creating a passageway large enough for an infant to move through during birth.

The dramatic changes that occur during puberty are produced, basically, by the endocrine system and its upsurge in sex hormone production during puberty. The process begins with an increase in secretion of FSH by the pituitary gland. FSH in turn stimulates the ovaries to produce estrogen. Estrogen is responsible for many of the changes that occur. It stimulates breast growth and the growth of the uterus and vagina.

Also involved in puberty are the paired **adrenal glands,** which are located just above the kidneys. In the female, the adrenal glands are the major producer of androgens, which exist at low levels in females. Adrenal androgens stimulate the growth of pubic and axillary hair and are related to the female sex drive. **Adrenarche**—the time of increasing secretion of adrenal androgens—generally begins slightly before age 8 (Grumbach & Styne, 1998).

Changes in Boys

As noted earlier, puberty begins at about 10 or 11 years of age in boys, a year or two later than it does in girls. The physical causes of puberty in boys parallel those in girls. They are initiated by increased production of FSH and LH by the pituitary. At the beginning of puberty, the increase in LH stimulates the testes to produce testosterone, which is responsible for most of the changes of puberty in the male.

The first noticeable pubertal change in males is the growth of the testes and scrotal sac, which begins on average at around 9 to 10 years of age as a result of testosterone stimulation. The growth of pubic hair begins at about the same time. About a year later the penis begins to enlarge, first thickening and then lengthening. This change also results from testosterone stimulation. As the testes enlarge, their production of testosterone increases even more,

Adrenal glands (uh-DREE-nul): Endocrine glands located just above the kidneys; in the female they are the major producers of androgens.

Adrenarche (AD-ren-ar-key): A time of increased secretion of adrenal androgens, usually just before age 8.

(a)   *(b)*

Figure 5.9   There is great variability in the onset of puberty and its growth spurt. Both girls are the same age. All boys are the same age.

leading to rapid growth of the penis, testes, and pubic hair at ages 13 and 14.

The growth of facial and axillary hair begins about two years after the beginning of pubic hair growth. The growth of facial hair begins with the appearance of fuzz on the upper lip, but adult beards do not appear until two or three years later. Indeed, by age 17, 50 percent of American males have not yet shaved. These changes also result from testosterone stimulation, which continues to produce growth of facial and chest hair beyond 20 years of age.

Erections increase in frequency. The organs that produce the fluid of semen, particularly the prostate, enlarge considerably at about the same time the other organs are growing. By age 13 or 14, the boy is capable of ejaculation.[5] By about age 15, the ejaculate contains mature sperm and the male is now fertile. The pituitary hormone FSH is responsible for initiating and maintaining the production of mature sperm.

[5]Note that orgasm and ejaculation are two separate processes, even though they generally occur together, at least in males after puberty. But orgasm may occur without ejaculation, and ejaculation may occur without orgasm.

Beginning about a year after the first ejaculation, many boys begin having nocturnal emissions, or "wet dreams." For the boy who has never masturbated, a wet dream may be his first ejaculation.

At about the same time penis growth occurs, the larynx ("voice box") also begins to grow in response to testosterone. As the larynx enlarges, the boy's voice drops, or "changes." Typically the transition occurs at around age 13 or 14. Because testosterone is necessary to produce the change in voice, castration before puberty results in a male with a permanently high voice. This principle was used to produce the *castrati*, who sang in the great choirs of Europe during the eighteenth century. They began as lovely boy sopranos, and their parents or the choirmaster, hating to see their beautiful voices destroyed at puberty, had them castrated so that they remained permanent sopranos. Contrary to popular belief, castration in adulthood will not produce a high voice, because the larynx has already grown.

A great spurt of body growth begins in males at around 11 to 16 years of age (Figure 5.8). Height increases rapidly. Body contours also change. While the changes in girls involve mainly the increase in fatty tissue in the breasts and hips, the changes in

(a)   *(b)*

Figure 5.10   Most cultures celebrate puberty, but cultures vary widely in the nature of the celebration. (*a*) American Jewish youth celebrate a bar mitzvah (for boys) or bat mitzvah (for girls). (*b*) The Samburu youth of Kenya celebrate a male circumcision ritual.

boys involve mainly an increase in muscle mass. Eventually testosterone brings the growth process to an end, although it permits the growth period in boys to continue longer than it does in girls.

Puberty brings both changes and problems. One problem is *acne,* a distressing skin condition that is stimulated by androgens and affects boys more frequently than girls. It is caused by a clogging of the sebaceous (oil-producing) glands, resulting in pustules, blackheads, and redness on the face and possibly the chest and back. Generally, acne is not severe enough to be a medical problem, although its psychological impact may be great. In order to avoid scarring, severe cases should be treated by a physician. The treatment is typically ultraviolet light, the drug Retin-A, and/or antibiotics. The drug Accutane is highly effective for severe cases. However, it must be used cautiously because it may have serious side effects, including birth defects if taken by a pregnant woman.

Gynecomastia (breast enlargement) may occur temporarily in boys, creating considerable embar-

rassment. About 80 percent of boys in puberty experience this growth, which is probably caused by small amounts of female sex hormones being produced by the testes. Obesity may also be a temporary problem, although it is more frequent in girls than boys.

In various cultures around the world, puberty rites are performed to signify the adolescent's passage to adulthood (Figure 5.10). In the United States the only remaining vestiges of such ceremonies are the Jewish bar mitzvah for boys and bat mitzvah for girls and, in Christian churches, confirmation. In a sense, it is unfortunate that we do not give more formal recognition to puberty. Puberty rites probably serve an important psychological function in that they are a formal, public announcement of the fact that the boy or girl is passing through an important and difficult period of change. In the absence of such rituals, the young person may think that his or her body is doing strange things and may feel very much alone. The lack of recognition may be particularly problematic for boys, who lack an obvious sign of puberty like the first menstruation (the first ejaculation is probably the closest analogy) to help them identify the stage they are in.

The Menstrual Cycle

Women's sexual and reproductive lives have a rhythm of changes. One notable sign that marks the changes is menstruation. The events surrounding it are not only biological but psychological as well.

Biology of the Menstrual Cycle

The menstrual cycle is regulated by fluctuating levels of sex hormones, which produce certain changes in the ovaries and uterus (Buffet et al., 1998). The hormone cycles are regulated by the HPG axis and by means of the negative feedback loops discussed earlier in this chapter.

Humans are nearly unique among species in having a menstrual cycle. Only a few other species of apes and monkeys also have menstrual cycles. All other species of mammals (for example, horses and dogs) have *estrous* cycles. There are several differences between estrous cycles and menstrual cycles, and it is important to note them because some people mistakenly believe that women's cycles are like those of a dog or a cat, when in fact the cycles are quite different.

First, in animals that have estrous cycles there is no menstruation. There is either no bleeding or only a slight spotting of blood, which is not a real menstruation. Second, the timing of ovulation in relation to bleeding (if there is any) is different in the two cycles. For estrous animals, ovulation occurs while the animal is in "heat," or estrus, which is also the time of slight spotting. In the menstrual cycle, however, ovulation occurs about midway between the periods of menstruation. A third difference is that female animals with estrous cycles engage in sexual behavior only when they are in heat, that is, during the estrus phase of the cycle. In contrast, females with menstrual cycles are capable of engaging in sexual behavior throughout the cycle.

The Phases of the Menstrual Cycle

The menstrual cycle has four phases, each characterized by a set of hormonal, ovarian, and uterine changes (see Figure 5.11). Because menstruation is the easiest phase to identify, it is tempting to call it the first phase, but biologically, it is actually the last phase. (Note, however, that in numbering the days of the menstrual cycle, the first day of menstruation is counted as day 1 because it is the most identifiable day of the cycle.)

The first phase of the menstrual cycle is called the **follicular phase** (or sometimes the *proliferative phase*). At the beginning of this phase, the pituitary secretes relatively high levels of FSH (follicle-stimulating hormone). As the name of this hormone implies, its function is to stimulate follicles in the ovaries. At the beginning of the follicular phase, it signals one follicle (occasionally more than one) in the ovaries to begin to bring an egg to the final stage of maturity. At the same time, the follicle secretes estrogen.

The second phase of the cycle is **ovulation,** which is the phase during which the follicle ruptures open, releasing the mature egg (see Figure 5.12, p. 110). By this time, estrogen has risen to a high level, which inhibits FSH production, and so FSH has fallen back to a low level. The high levels of estrogen also stimulate the hypothalamus to produce GnRH, which causes the pituitary to begin production of LH (luteinizing hormone).[6] A surge of LH triggers ovulation.

The third phase of the cycle is called the **luteal phase** (sometimes also the *secretory phase*). After releasing an egg, the follicle, under stimulation of LH, turns into a glandular mass of cells called the **corpus luteum**[7] (hence the names *luteal phase* and *luteinizing hormone*). The corpus luteum manufactures progesterone, so progesterone levels rise during the luteal phase. But high levels of progesterone also inhibit the pituitary's secretion of LH, and as LH levels decline, the corpus luteum degenerates. With this degeneration comes a sharp decline in estrogen and progesterone levels at the end of the luteal phase. The falling levels of estrogen stimulate the pituitary to begin production of FSH, and the whole cycle begins again.

The fourth and final phase of the cycle is **menstruation.** Physiologically, menstruation is a shedding of the inner lining of the uterus (the

---

Follicular phase (fuh-LIK-you-lur): The first phase of the menstrual cycle, beginning just after menstruation, during which an egg matures in preparation for ovulation.

Ovulation: Release of an egg from the ovaries; the second phase of the menstrual cycle.

Luteal phase (LOO-tee-uhl): The third phase of the menstrual cycle, following ovulation.

Corpus luteum: The mass of cells of the follicle remaining after ovulation; it secretes progesterone.

Menstruation: The fourth phase of the menstrual cycle, during which the endometrium of the uterus is sloughed off in the menstrual discharge.

---

[6]This statement may seem to contradict the earlier statement that high estrogen levels cause a decline in LH. Both of these effects occur, but at different times in the menstrual cycle (Molitch, 1995). There are two centers in the hypothalamus: one produces a negative feedback loop between estrogen and LH; the other produces a positive feedback loop between the two.

[7]*Corpus luteum* is Latin for "yellow body." The corpus luteum is so named because the mass of cells is yellowish in appearance.

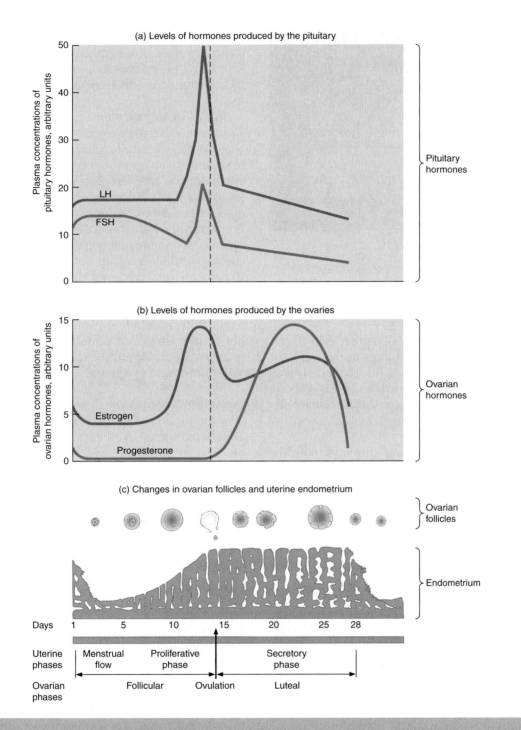

Figure 5.11 The biological events of the menstrual cycle. Changes in the levels of hormones produced by the pituitary (*a*) and the ovaries (*b*) bring about changes (*c*) in the ovarian follicles and the endometrium of the uterus.

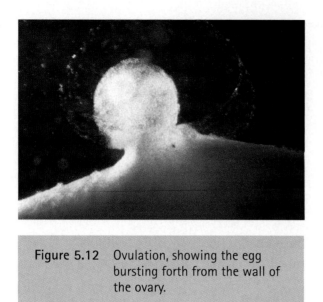

Figure 5.12 Ovulation, showing the egg bursting forth from the wall of the ovary.

endometrium), which then passes out through the cervix and the vagina. During this phase, estrogen and progesterone levels are low and FSH levels are rising. Menstruation is triggered by the sharp decline in estrogen and progesterone levels at the end of the luteal phase.

What has been happening in the uterus while the ovaries and endocrine system were going through the four phases that we just described? During the first, or follicular, phase, the high levels of estrogen stimulate the endometrium (the inner layer) of the uterus to grow, thicken, and form glands that will eventually secrete substances to nourish the embryo. In other words, the endometrium proliferates (giving us the alternative name for this first phase, the *proliferative phase*). Then, during the luteal phase, the progesterone secreted by the corpus luteum stimulates the glands of the endometrium to start secreting the nourishing substances (giving us the name *secretory phase*). If the egg is fertilized and the timing goes properly, about 6 days after ovulation the fertilized egg arrives in a uterus that is well prepared to cradle and nourish it.

The corpus luteum continues to produce estrogen and progesterone for about 10 to 12 days. If pregnancy has not occurred, its hormone output declines sharply at the end of this period. The uterine lining cannot be maintained and is shed, resulting in menstruation. Immediately afterward, a new lining starts forming in the next proliferative phase.

The menstrual fluid itself is a combination of blood (from the endometrium), degenerated cells, and mucus from the cervix and vagina.

Normally the discharge for an entire period is only about 2 ounces (4 tablespoons). Common practice is to use sanitary napkins, which are worn externally, or tampons, which are worn inside the vagina, to absorb the fluid.

Toxic shock syndrome, sometimes abbreviated TSS, is caused by the bacterium *Staphylococcus aureus*. It is associated with tampon use, which seems to encourage an abnormal growth of the bacteria. Symptoms of toxic shock syndrome include high fever (102°F or greater) accompanied by vomiting or diarrhea. Any woman who experiences these symptoms during her period should discontinue tampon use immediately and see a doctor. Toxic shock syndrome leads to death in approximately 10 percent of cases. It is recommended that women change tampons frequently, at least every 6 to 8 hours during their periods (although the effectiveness of this is debated). Women are also advised not to use tampons continuously throughout a menstrual period, and to minimize their use of super-absorbent tampons.

Length and Timing of the Cycle

How long is a normal menstrual cycle? Generally, anywhere from 20 to 36 days is considered within the normal range. The average is about 28 days, but somehow this number has taken on more significance than it deserves. There is enormous variation from one woman to the next in the average length of the cycle, and for a given woman there can be considerable variation in length from one cycle to the next.

What is the timing of the four phases of the cycle? In a perfectly regular 28-day cycle, menstruation begins on day 1 and continues until about day 4 or 5. The follicular phase extends from about day 5 to about day 13. Ovulation occurs on day 14, and the luteal phase extends from day 15 to the end of the cycle, day 28 (see Figure 5.11c).

But what if the cycle is not a perfect 28-day one? In cycles that are shorter or longer than 28 days, the principle is that the length of the *luteal* phase is relatively constant. In other words, the time from ovulation to menstruation is always 14 days, give or take only a day or two. It is the follicular phase that is of variable length. For this reason, if a woman has a 44-day cycle, for example, she ovulates on about day 30. If she has a 22-day cycle, she ovulates on about day 8.

Some women report that they can actually feel themselves ovulate, a phenomenon called *Mittelschmerz* ("middle pain"). The sensation described is a cramping on one or both sides of the lower abdomen, lasting for about a day, which is sometimes confused with appendicitis.

Toxic shock syndrome (TSS): A sometimes fatal bacterial infection associated with tampon use during menstruation.

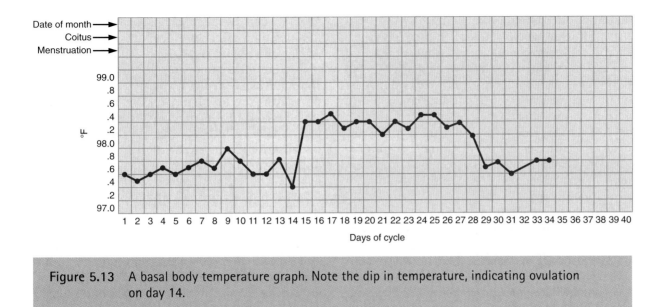

Figure 5.13 A basal body temperature graph. Note the dip in temperature, indicating ovulation on day 14.

It is also true that ovulation does not occur in every menstrual cycle. In other words, menstruation may take place without ovulation. When this happens, the woman is said to have an *anovulatory cycle.* Such cycles occur once or twice a year in women in their twenties and thirties and are fairly common among girls during puberty and among women in their forties.

Other Cyclic Changes

Two other biological processes fluctuate with the menstrual cycle: the cervical mucus cycle and the basal body temperature cycle.

The cervical mucus cycle involves glands in the cervix that secrete mucus throughout the menstrual cycle. One function of the mucus is to protect the entrance to the cervix, helping to keep bacteria out. These glands respond to the changing levels of estrogen during the cycle. As estrogen increases at the start of a new cycle, the mucus is alkaline, thick, and viscous. When LH production begins, just before ovulation, the cervical mucus changes markedly. It becomes even more alkaline, thin, and watery. These changes make the environment for sperm passage most hospitable just at ovulation. After ovulation, the mucus returns to its former viscous, less alkaline state.

If a sample of mucus is taken just before ovulation and allowed to dry, the dried mucus takes on a fern-shaped pattern. After ovulation, during the luteal phase, the fernlike patterning will not occur. For this reason, the "fern test" is one method for detecting ovulation.

A woman's *basal body temperature,* taken with a thermometer, also fluctuates with the phases of the menstrual cycle. The temperature is low during the follicular phase and takes a dip on the day of ovulation. Then, on the day after ovulation, it rises noticeably, generally by 0.4°F or more, and then continues at the higher level for the rest of the cycle (Figure 5.13). Progesterone raises body temperature, so the higher temperature during the luteal phase is due to the increased production of progesterone during that time (Baker et al., 2002). This change in basal body temperature is important when a couple are using the rhythm method of birth control (Chapter 7) and when a woman is trying to determine the time of ovulation so that she may become pregnant (Chapter 6).

Menstrual Problems

The most common menstrual problem is painful menstruation, called **dysmenorrhea.** Almost every woman experiences at least some menstrual discomfort at various times in her life, but the frequency and severity of the discomfort vary considerably from one woman to the next. Cramping pains in the pelvic region are the most common discomfort. Other symptoms may include headaches, backaches, nausea, and a feeling of pressure and bloating in the pelvis.

Dysmenorrhea is caused by **prostaglandins,** hormonelike substances produced by many tissues

Dysmenorrhea (dis-men-oh-REE-uh): Painful menstruation.
Prostaglandins: Chemicals secreted by the uterus that cause the uterine muscles to contract; they are a likely cause of painful menstruation.

of the body, including the lining of the uterus (Deligeoroglou, 2000). Prostaglandins can cause smooth muscle to contract and can affect the size of blood vessels. Women with severe menstrual pain have unusually high levels of prostaglandins. The high levels cause intense uterine contractions, which in turn choke off some of the supply of oxygen-carrying blood to the uterus. Prostaglandins may also cause greater sensitivity in nerve endings. The combination of the uterine contractions, lack of oxygen, and heightened nerve sensitivity produces menstrual cramps.

Household remedies for painful menstruation are available and may be helpful to some women. Aspirin appears to be the best, and cheapest, painkiller available, and it can help to relieve menstrual pain.

A somewhat more provocative remedy suggested by, among others, Masters and Johnson is masturbation. This makes good physiological sense because part of the discomfort of menstruation— the pressure and bloating—results from pelvic edema. During sexual arousal and orgasm, pelvic edema increases, but after orgasm, the edema dissipates (see Chapter 8). For this reason, orgasm, whether produced by masturbation or some other means, should help to relieve the pelvic edema causing menstrual discomfort. And it's a lot more fun than taking medicine!

Mefenamic acid, an antiprostaglandin drug, is powerful and effective in the treatment of menstrual pain. The drug is sold with brand names such as Naprosyn and Anaprox. About 80 to 85 percent of women who take this drug report significant relief from menstrual pain and symptoms such as nausea, vomiting, dizziness, and weakness (Golub, 1992). Interestingly, aspirin is also an antiprostaglandin.

Dietary changes and aerobic exercise may also be helpful (Golub, 1992; Hatcher et al., 1998). Caffeine should be avoided. A diet high in carbohydrates and low in protein, during the luteal phase, is helpful for some.

A menstrual problem that may be mistaken for dysmenorrhea is **endometriosis.** The endometrium, or the lining of the uterus, grows during each menstrual cycle and is sloughed off in menstruation. Endometriosis occurs when the endometrium grows in a place other than the uterus—for example, the ovaries, fallopian tubes, rectum, bladder, vagina, vulva, cervix, or lymph glands. The symptoms vary, depending on the location of the

growth, but very painful periods that last an unusually long time are the most common symptom. Endometriosis is fairly serious and should be treated by a physician. If left untreated, it can lead to sterility. Hormones are generally used in treatment, but if the problem is severe, surgery may be required. Laser surgery is one treatment option.

Another menstrual problem is **amenorrhea,** or the absence of menstruation. It is called *primary amenorrhea* in girls who have not yet menstruated by about age 18. It is called *secondary amenorrhea* in girls who have had at least one period. Some of the causes of amenorrhea include pregnancy, congenital defects of the reproductive system, hormonal imbalance, cysts or tumors, disease, stress, and emotional factors related to puberty. As we discussed earlier in the chapter, amenorrhea can also result from programs of strenuous exercise and from anorexia.

Psychological Aspects of the Menstrual Cycle

"Why do I get so emotional?" screams the ad for Midol PMS in *Teen* magazine. It is part of the folk wisdom of our culture that women experience fluctuations in mood over the phases of the menstrual cycle. In particular, women are supposed to be especially cranky and depressed just before and during their periods. In France, if a woman commits a crime during her premenstrual phase, she may use the fact in her defense, claiming "temporary impairment of sanity."

What is the scientific evidence concerning the occurrence of such fluctuations in mood, and, if they do occur, what causes them?

Fluctuations in Mood: Do Women Become Extra Emotional?

The term **premenstrual syndrome (PMS)** refers to cases in which the woman has a particularly severe combination of physical and psychological symptoms that occur premenstrually. These symptoms may include depression, irritability, breast pain, and water retention (Stanton et al., 2002). In the last several decades much research has been done on moods during the premenstrual period and on whether moods fluctuate during the cycle (Taylor, 2006).

Research based on women's daily self-reports throughout the cycle generally finds positive moods around the time of ovulation (that is, midcycle), and various symptoms, such as anxiety, irritability, depression, fatigue, and headaches, premenstrually (Golub, 1992). However, the fluctuations are not large on average. In one study, the average depression score of women was 6.84 around ovulation and

Endometriosis: A condition in which the endometrium grows abnormally outside the uterus; the symptom is unusually painful periods with excessive bleeding.
Amenorrhea: The absence of menstruation.
Premenstrual syndrome (PMS): A combination of severe physical and psychological symptoms, such as depression and irritability, occurring just before menstruation.

9.30 premenstrually, compared with a mean of 16.03 for depressed psychiatric patients (Golub, 1992). Premenstrual women are not ready for the psychiatric ward!

The evidence supporting mood fluctuation and PMS has been challenged, though. Of the numerous criticisms that have been made (Chrisler et al., 2006; Stanton et al., 2002), three deserve special mention here. First, much of the evidence depends on subjective, retrospective reports of mood and symptoms, which are probably not very reliable.

Second, the interpretation of the direction of the differences might be questioned. The typical interpretation is that women show a psychological "deficit" premenstrually, as compared with the "normal" state at ovulation and during the rest of the cycle. However, the opposite interpretation might also be made: that women are "normal" premenstrually and experience unusual well-being psychologically at midcycle. What, then, defines the "normal" or "average" mood? Men's moods? Support for a reinterpretation might come from the statistics on violent crimes committed by women. While it may be true that women are somewhat more likely to commit crimes during the eight premenstrual and menstrual days, even during this period they are far less likely to commit crimes than men are.

Third, PMS is a stereotype in our culture. The stereotype includes beliefs that premenstrual women have sharp mood swings and crying spells and are bloated from water retention. Women in fact report far fewer symptoms for themselves than they think the average woman experiences (Chrisler et al., 2006). PMS may therefore be largely a stereotype that does not match most women's actual experience.

Taking into account the criticisms and available evidence, it seems reasonable to conclude the following:

1. Women do, on average, experience some fluctuations in mood over the phases of the menstrual cycle.

2. Present evidence does not clearly indicate how the direction of the shifts should be interpreted—whether women are unusually "low" premenstrually or unusually "high" around the time of ovulation.

3. There is a great deal of variation from one woman to the next in the size of these shifts and the way they are expressed. Some women experience no shifts or shifts so slight that they are not noticeable. Others may

experience large shifts. It would be interesting to know how many do show mood fluctuations and how many do not. Unfortunately, the various studies that have tried to provide this information show substantial variation, with the percentage of women reporting symptoms ranging between 25 percent and 80 percent (Stanton et al., 2002). It is important to make a distinction between women who have full-blown PMS and women who experience no fluctuation or only moderate fluctuations in mood over the cycle.

The American Psychiatric Association has formalized PMS with the diagnosis **premenstrual dysphoric disorder (PMDD)** in the DSM-IV (American Psychiatric Association, 2000a). It isn't in the main DSM, but rather, it's in an appendix, meaning that it isn't officially "in" yet. Symptoms must occur during the last week of the luteal phase and include feeling sad or hopeless, tense or anxious, tearfulness, irritability, difficulty concentrating, and changes in appetite. The symptoms have to have occurred most months for the past year. This new diagnostic category is very controversial, however (Caplan, 1995). Some argue that it represents nothing but a medicalizing of women's experience. Others point out that the scientific basis for PMDD is nonexistent and that some studies fail to confirm it (Gallant et al., 1992).

Fluctuations in Performance: Can a Woman Be President?

So far our discussion has concentrated on fluctuations in psychological characteristics such as depression, anxiety, and irritability. However, in some situations performance is of more practical importance than mood. For example, is a woman secretary's clerical work less accurate premenstrually and menstrually? Is a female athlete's coordination or speed impaired during the premenstrual–menstrual period?

Research on performance—such as intellectual or athletic performance—generally shows no fluctuations over the cycle. Research has found no fluctuations in academic performance, problem solving, memory, or creative thinking (Epting & Overman, 1998; Golub, 1992; Stanton et al., 2002).

In one study, 31 percent of female athletes said they believed that they experienced a decline in performance during the premenstrual or menstrual phase. Yet when their actual performance was measured, they showed no deficits in strength (weight lifters)

Premenstrual dysphoric disorder (PMDD): A tentative diagnostic category in the DSM, characterized by symptoms such as sadness, anxiety, and irritability in the week before menstruation.

or swimming speed (swimming team members) (Quadagno et al., 1991). There is no reliable evidence indicating that the kinds of performance required in a work situation or an athletic competition fluctuate over the menstrual cycle.

Fluctuations in Sex Drive

Another psychological characteristic that has been investigated for fluctuations over the cycle is women's sex drive or arousability. Observations of female animals that have estrous cycles indicate that sexual behavior depends a great deal on cycle phase and the corresponding hormonal state. Females of these species engage in sexual behavior enthusiastically when they are in the estrus, or "heat," phase of the cycle and do not engage in sexual behavior at all during any other phase. This pattern makes good biological sense, since the females engage in sex precisely when they are fertile.

Human females, of course, engage in sexual behavior throughout the menstrual cycle. But might some subtle cycling in drive remain, expressed, perhaps, in fluctuations in frequency of intercourse? Studies have yielded contradictory results. Some have found a peak frequency of intercourse around ovulation, which would be biologically functional. But others have found peaks just before and just after menstruation (reviewed by Zillmann et al., 1994).

Moreover, we should be cautious about using frequency of intercourse as a measure of a woman's sex drive. Intercourse requires some agreement between partners, and for this reason reflects not only a woman's desires but her partner's as well. One study assessed both sexual activity with a partner and self-rated sexual desire (Bullivant et al., 2004). The results indicated that sexual activity initiated by the woman—but not by the man—peaked during the three days before and three days after ovulation. Sexual desire showed the same pattern.

In a sophisticated study, women kept daily diaries of their moods and sexual interest and provided blood samples for hormone assays (Van Goozen et al., 1997). In addition to levels of estrogen and progesterone, this study assessed testosterone levels—an important addition because the evidence is strongest for an association between testosterone and sex drive in women. The results indicated that testosterone levels peaked at ovulation. The women seemed to fall into two subgroups, with different patterns of sexual interest. About half the women reported that they suffered from premenstrual symptoms, and their sexual interest peaked at ovulation, exactly when testosterone levels are high. The other half of the women said they did not suffer from premenstrual symptoms and their peak in sexual interest occurred premenstrually, perhaps in anticipation of a deprivation during menstruation.

If there is a link between phase of the menstrual cycle and sexual interest, it most likely reflects an association between testosterone levels and sexuality with a peak in sexual interest around the time of ovulation. But with humans, psychological and social factors—such as some couples' dislike of intercourse when the woman is menstruating—play a strong role as well.

What Causes the Fluctuations in Mood: Why Do Some Women Get Emotional?

The answer to the question of what causes mood fluctuations during the menstrual cycle touches off a nature–nurture, or biology–environment, controversy. In other words, some researchers argue that the mood fluctuations are caused primarily by biological factors—in particular, fluctuations in levels of hormones. Others argue that environmental factors such as menstrual taboos and cultural expectations are the primary cause.

On the biology side, changes in mood appear to be related to changes in hormone levels during the cycle. The fact that depression is more frequent in women premenstrually and postpartum (after having a baby) suggests that there is at least some relationship between sex hormones and depression. The exact hormone–mood relationship is not known, but low or declining levels of estrogen and/or progesterone are the likeliest culprits. Neither is it known exactly what the process is by which hormones influence mood. Research does indicate that the estrogen–progesterone system interacts with the production of the neurotransmitters norepinephrine, serotonin, and dopamine, and neurotransmitter levels are linked to mood disorders such as depression (Halbreich, 1996; Mortola, 1998).

Critics of the hormone point of view note that causality is being inferred from correlational data. In other words, the data show a correlation between cycle phase (hormone levels) and mood, but it is unwarranted to infer that the hormone levels cause the mood shifts.

Those arguing the other side—that the fluctuations are due to cultural forces—note the widespread cultural expectations and taboos surrounding menstruation (for reviews, see Golub, 1992; Stanton et al., 2002). In some nonindustrialized cultures, women who are menstruating are isolated from the community and may have to stay in a menstrual hut at the edge of town during their period. Often the menstrual blood itself is thought to have supernatural, dangerous powers, and the woman's isolation is considered necessary for the safety of the community. Among the Lele of the Congo, for example,

> A menstruating woman was a danger to the whole community if she entered the forest. Not only was her menstruation certain to wreck any enterprise in the forest that she might undertake, but it was thought to produce unfavorable conditions for men. Hunting would be difficult for a long time after, and rituals based on forest plants would have no efficacy. Women found these rules extremely irksome, especially as they were regularly short-handed and late in their planting, weeding, harvesting, and fishing. (Douglas, 1970, p. 179)

Such practices do not occur only among non-Western people. Note that there is a history of similar practices in our own culture as well. For example, the following passage is from the book of Leviticus in the Bible:

> When a woman has a discharge of blood which is her regular discharge from her body, she shall be in her impurity for seven days, and whoever touches her shall be unclean until the evening. . . . And whoever touches her bed shall wash his clothes, and bathe himself in water, and be unclean until the evening; whether it is the bed or anything upon which she sits, when he touches it he shall be unclean until the evening. (Leviticus 15:19–23)

Among the most common menstrual taboos are those prohibiting sexual intercourse with a menstruating woman. For example, the passage from Leviticus quoted above continues,

> And if any man lies with her, and her impurity is on him, he shall be unclean seven days; and every bed on which he lies shall be unclean. (Leviticus 15:24)

Couples who violated the taboo could be stoned. To this day, Orthodox Jews abstain from sex during the woman's period and for seven days afterward. At the end of this time the woman goes to the *mikvah* (ritual bath) to be cleansed, and only after this cleansing may she resume sexual relations.

Advocates of the cultural explanation argue, then, that women become anxious and depressed around the time of menstruation because of the many cultural forces, such as menstrual taboos, that create negative attitudes toward menstruation. In addition, women's expectations may play a role (Stanton et al., 2002). Our culture is filled with teachings that women are supposed to behave strangely just before and during their periods. Recall, for example, the drug company ads that ask

"Why am I so emotional?" According to this line of reasoning, women are taught that they should be depressed around the time of menstruation, and because they expect to become depressed, they do become depressed. In addition, women who experience painful cramps may well spend the several days before they know their period is due anticipating the pain, which makes them feel anxious and depressed.

Surely such forces do exist in our culture. But is there any evidence that they really have an effect on women's moods and behavior? Psychologist Diane Ruble did a clever experiment to determine whether women's culturally induced expectations influence their reporting of premenstrual symptoms (1977; see also Klebanov & Jemmott, 1992). College students were tested on the sixth or seventh day before the onset of their next menstrual period. They were told that they would participate in a study on a new technique for predicting the expected date of menstruation using an electroencephalogram (EEG), a method that had already been successfully tested with older women. After the EEG had been run (it actually wasn't), each woman was informed of when her next period was to occur, depending on which of three experimental groups she had randomly been assigned to: (1) the woman was told she was "premenstrual" and her period was due in 1 or 2 days; (2) the woman was told she was "intermenstrual" or "midcycle" and her period was not expected for at least a week to 10 days; or (3) she was given no information at all about the predicted date of menstruation (control group). The women then completed a self-report menstrual distress questionnaire.

The results indicated that women who had been led to believe they were in the premenstrual phase reported significantly more water retention, pain, and changes in eating habits than did women who had been led to believe they were around midcycle. (In fact, women in these groups did not differ significantly in when their periods actually arrived.) There were no significant differences between the groups in ratings of negative moods, however. This study indicates that, probably because of learned beliefs, women overstate the changes in body states that occur over the menstrual cycle. When they think they are in the premenstrual phase, they report more problems than when they think they are at midcycle.

This nature–nurture argument will not be easily resolved, particularly because there is evidence for both points of view. Perhaps the best solution is to say that both biology and culture contribute to women's mood fluctuations during the menstrual cycle. In other words, some women probably do

Figure 5.14 Does advertising for menstrual drugs contribute to negative stereotypes about women and PMS?

experience mood shifts caused by hormonal and possibly other physical factors, and for many others, slight biological influences are magnified by psychological and cultural influences. A woman's premenstrual hormonal state may act as a sort of trigger. It may, for example, provide a state conducive to depression, and if the environment then provides further stimuli to depression, the woman becomes depressed.

Cycles in Men

The traditional assumption, of both laypeople and scientists, has been that monthly biological and psychological cycles are for women only and that men experience no monthly cycles. These assumptions are made, at least in part, because men have no obvious signs like menstruation to call attention to the fact that some kind of periodic change is occurring. Yet their hormone levels do fluctuate—over the day, possibly the month, and over the year. One study, in fact, found no differences between men and women in day-to-day mood changes. Men were neither more nor less changeable than women (McFarlane et al., 1988; see also McFarlane & Williams, 1994).

SUMMARY

The major sex hormones are testosterone, which is produced in the male by the testes, and estrogen and progesterone, which are produced in the female by the ovaries. Levels of the sex hormones are regulated by two hormones secreted by the pituitary: FSH (follicle-stimulating hormone) and LH (luteinizing hormone). The gonads, pituitary, and hypothalamus regulate one another's output through a negative feedback loop. Inhibin regulates FSH levels.

At conception males and females differ only in the sex chromosomes (XX in females and XY in males). As the male fetus grows, the SRY gene on the Y chromosome directs the gonads to differentiate into the testes. In the absence of the SRY gene, ovaries develop. Different hormones are then produced by the gonads, and these stimulate further differentiation of the internal and external reproductive structures of males and females. A male organ and a female organ that derive from the same embryonic tissue are said to be homologous to each other.

Intersex conditions are generally the result of various syndromes (such as CAH) and accidents that occur during the course of prenatal sexual differentiation. Currently there is a debate over the best medical treatment of these individuals. The Guevodoces provide an interesting case of gender change at puberty.

Puberty is initiated and characterized by a great increase in the production of sex hormones. Pubertal changes in both males and females include body growth, the development of pubic and axillary hair, and increased output from the oil-producing glands. Changes in the female include breast development and the beginning of menstruation. Changes in the male include growth of the penis and testes, the beginning of ejaculation, and a deepening of the voice.

Biologically, the menstrual cycle is divided into four phases: the follicular phase, ovulation, the luteal phase, and menstruation. Corresponding to these phases, there are changes in the levels of pituitary hormones (FSH and LH) and in the levels of ovarian hormones (estrogen and progesterone), as well as changes in the ovaries and the uterus. A fairly common menstrual problem is dysmenorrhea, or painful menstruation.

Research indicates that some, though not all, women experience changes in mood over the phases of the menstrual cycle. For those who experience such changes, their mood is generally positive around the middle of the cycle (around ovulation), and negative moods characterized by depression and irritability are more likely just before and during menstruation. These negative moods and physical discomforts are termed the premenstrual syndrome (PMS). However, research indicates that there are no fluctuations in performance over the cycle. Some evidence suggests that fluctuations in mood are related to changes in hormone levels, but data also suggest that mood fluctuations are related to cultural factors. Research attempting to document whether men experience monthly biological and/or psychological cycles is now in progress.

QUESTIONS FOR THOUGHT, DISCUSSION, AND DEBATE

1. Of the physical changes of puberty, which are the most difficult to cope with?

2. The society in the Dominican Republic into which the Guevodoces are born (see p. 101) is a three-gender society, unlike the two-gender society of the dominant U.S. culture. What would the United States be like if it was a three-gender society? Who would be classified in the third gender? Would their lives be better or worse as a result? Could we have a four-gender society? Who would be classified in the fourth gender? (For further information, see Herdt, 1990.)

3. Teresa has just given birth to her first baby. The doctor approaches her with a worried expression and says that her baby's genitals are unusual and some decisions will have to be made. The phallus is too big for a clitoris, but too small for a penis. What should Teresa do? What other information should she obtain from the doctor before making a decision?

4. Are women's fluctuations in mood over the menstrual cycle caused by biological factors or by environmental/cultural factors?

5. Your 10-year-old daughter tells you that she has heard about PMS and wonders whether she will get it when she begins her periods. What would you tell her?

SUGGESTIONS FOR FURTHER READING

Fausto-Sterling, Anne. (2000). *Sexing the body.* New York: Basic Books. The author, a developmental geneticist, has written a provocative book that calls into question our most basic understandings of differentiation of the sexes, both physical and psychological.

Kessler, Suzanne J. (1998). *Lessons from the intersexed.* New Brunswick, NJ: Rutgers University Press. Kessler, a psychologist, reports on her years of research with intersex individuals and the medical and psychological professionals who treat them, and proposes new approaches in dealing with the condition.

Larsen, P. Reed, et al. (2003). *Williams textbook of endocrinology.* 10th ed. Philadelphia: Saunders. An outstanding endocrinology text, with a particularly good chapter on sexual differentiation.

Steinberg, Laurence. (2005). *Adolescence.* 7th ed. New York: McGraw-Hill. This is the definitive textbook on adolescence, written by a leading researcher.

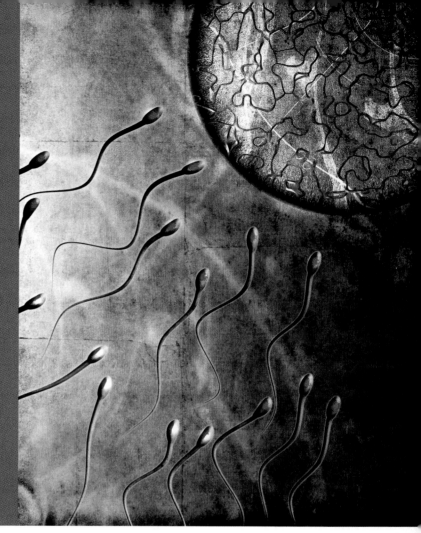

6 CHAPTER SIX

Conception, Pregnancy, and Childbirth

CHAPTER HIGHLIGHTS

I remember feeling very sexy. We were trying all these different positions. Now that we were having a baby, I felt a lot looser. I used to feel uptight about sex for its own sake, but when I was pregnant I felt a lot freer.

I thought it would never end. I was enormous. I couldn't bend over and wash my feet. And it was incredibly hot.*

*Boston Women's Health Book Collective (2005), pp. 434, 443.

Chapter 5 described the remarkable biological process by which a single fertilized egg develops into a male or a female human being. This chapter is about some equally remarkable processes involved in creating human beings: conception, pregnancy, and childbirth.

Conception

Sperm Meets Egg: The Incredible Journey

On about day 14 of an average menstrual cycle the woman ovulates. The egg is released from the ovary into the body cavity. Typically it is then picked up by the fimbriae (long, fingerlike structures at the end of the fallopian tube—see Figure 6.1) and enters the fallopian tube. It then begins a leisurely trip down the tube toward the uterus, reaching it in about five days, if it has been fertilized. Otherwise, it disintegrates in about 48 hours. The egg, unlike the sperm, has no means of moving itself and is propelled by the cilia (hairlike structures) lining the fallopian tube. The egg has begun its part of the journey toward conception.

Meanwhile, the couple have been having intercourse. The woman's cervix secretes mucus that flushes the passageways to prepare for the arrival of the sperm. The man has an orgasm and ejaculates inside the woman's vagina. The sperm are deposited in the vagina, there to begin their journey toward the egg. Actually, they have made an incredible trip even before reaching the vagina. Initially they were manufactured in the seminiferous tubules of the testes (see Chapter 4). They then collected and were stored in the epididymis. During ejaculation they moved up and over the top of the bladder in the vas deferens; then they traveled down through the ejaculatory duct, mixed with seminal fluid, and went out through the urethra.

The sperm is one of the tiniest cells in the human body. It is composed of a *head*, a *midpiece*, and a *tail* (see Figure 6.2, p. 122). The head is about

5 micrometers long, and the total length, from the tip of the head to the tip of the tail, is about 60 micrometers (about 2/1,000 inch, or 0.06 millimeter). The DNA, which is the sperm's most important contribution when it unites with the egg, is contained in the nucleus, which is in the head of the sperm. Sperm also contain RNA, carrying the instructions for early embryonic development, and a large number of proteins (Ainsworth, 2005). The *acrosome*, a chemical reservoir, is also in the head of the sperm. The midpiece contains mitochondria, tiny structures in which chemical reactions occur that provide energy. This energy is used when the sperm lashes its tail back and forth. The lashing action (called *flagellation*) propels the sperm forward.

A typical ejaculate has a volume of about 3 milliliters, or about a teaspoonful, and contains about 200 million sperm. Although this might seem to be a wasteful amount of sperm if only one is needed for fertilization, the great majority of the sperm never even get close to the egg. Some of the ejaculate, including one-half of the sperm, will flow out of the vagina as a result of gravity. Other sperm may be killed by the acidity of the vagina, to which they are very sensitive. Of those that make it safely into the uterus, half swim up the wrong fallopian tube (the one containing no egg).

But here we are, several hours later, with a hearty band of sperm swimming up the fallopian tube toward the egg, against the currents that are bringing the egg down. Sperm are capable of swimming 1 to 3 centimeters (about 1 inch) per hour, although it has been documented that sperm may arrive at the egg within $1\frac{1}{2}$ hours after ejaculation, which is much sooner than would be expected, given their swimming rate. It is thought that muscular contractions in the uterus may help speed them along. By the time a sperm reaches the egg, it has swum approximately 3,000 times its own length. This would be comparable to a swim of more than 3 miles for a human being.

Contrary to the popular belief that conception occurs in the uterus, typically it occurs in the outer

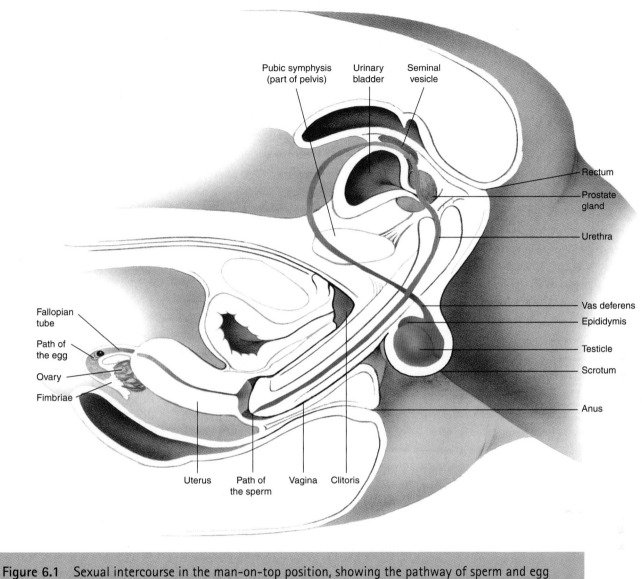

Figure 6.1 Sexual intercourse in the man-on-top position, showing the pathway of sperm and egg from manufacture in the testes and ovary to conception, which typically occurs in the fallopian tube.

third (the part near the ovary) of the fallopian tube. Of the original 200 million sperm, only about 2,000 reach the tube containing the egg. As they approach, a chemical secreted by the egg attracts the sperm to the egg. Chemical receptors on the surface of the sperm respond to the attractant, and the sperm swims toward the egg (Spehr et al., 2003). The egg is surrounded by a thin, gelatinous layer called the *zona pellucida*. Sperm swarm around the egg and secrete an enzyme called **hyaluronidase** (produced by the acrosome located in the head of the sperm—see Figure 6.2); this enzyme dissolves the zona pellucida, permitting one

sperm to penetrate the egg.[1] Conception has occurred (see Figure 6.3).

The fertilized egg, called the **zygote,** continues to travel down the fallopian tube. About 36 hours after conception, it begins the process of cell division, by which the original one cell becomes a mass

[1]Thus, while only one sperm is necessary to accomplish fertilization, it appears important for it to have a lot of buddies along to help it get into the egg. Therefore, maintaining a high sperm count seems to be important for conception.

Hyaluronidase: An enzyme secreted by the sperm that allows one sperm to penetrate the egg.
Zygote: A fertilized egg.

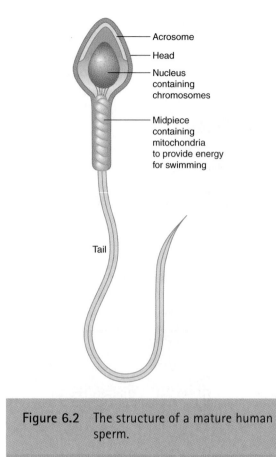

Figure 6.2 The structure of a mature human sperm.

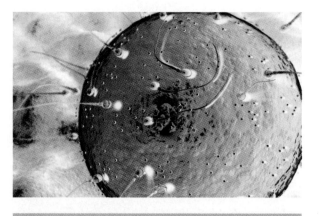

Figure 6.3 The egg is fertilized by one sperm as many sperm cluster about.

of two cells, then four cells, then eight cells, and so on. About five to seven days after conception, the mass of cells implants itself in the lining of the uterus, there to be nourished and grow. For the first eight weeks of gestation the *conceptus* (product of conception) is called an *embryo;* from then until birth it is called a *fetus.*

Improving the Chances of Conception: Making a Baby

While this topic may seem rather remote to a 20-year-old college student, whose principal concern is probably *avoiding* conception, some couples do want to have a baby. The following are points for them to keep in mind.

The whole trick, of course, is to time intercourse so that it occurs around the time of ovulation. To do this, it is necessary to determine when the woman ovulates. If she is that idealized woman with the perfectly regular 28-day cycle, then she ovulates on day 14. But for the vast majority of women, the time of ovulation can best be determined by keeping a *basal body temperature chart.* To do this, the woman takes her tempera-

ture every morning immediately upon waking (that means before getting up and moving around or drinking a cup of coffee). She then keeps a graph of her temperature (like the one shown in Figure 5.13 on page 111). During the preovulatory phase, the temperature will be relatively constant (the temperature is below 98.6°F because temperature is low in the early morning). On the day of ovulation the temperature drops, and on the day following ovulation it rises sharply, by 0.4° to 1.0°F above the preovulatory level. The temperature should then stay at that high level until just before menstruation. The most reliable indicator of ovulation is the rise in temperature the day after it occurs. From this, the woman can determine the day of ovulation, and that determination should be consistent with menstruation occurring about 14 days later. After doing this for a couple of cycles, the woman should have a fairly good idea of the day in her cycle on which she ovulates. Two other methods for determining when a woman is ovulating are the cervical mucus and sympto-thermal methods, described in Chapter 7.

Sperm live inside the woman's body for up to five days (Wilcox et al., 1995). The egg is capable of being fertilized for about the first 12 to 24 hours after ovulation. Allowing the sperm some swimming time, this means that intercourse should be timed right at ovulation or one or two days before.

Assuming you have some idea of the time of ovulation, how frequent should intercourse be? While more may be merrier, more is not necessarily more effective. The reason for this is that it is important for the man's sperm count to be maintained. It takes a while to manufacture

200 million sperm—at least 24 hours. And, as discussed earlier, maintaining a high sperm count appears to be important in accomplishing the task of fertilizing the egg. For purposes of conceiving, then, it is probably best to have intercourse about every 24 to 48 hours, or about four times during the week in which the woman is to ovulate. Abstaining for more than 48 hours may lead to a low sperm count.

It is also important to take some steps to ensure that, once deposited in the vagina, the sperm get a decent chance to survive and to find their way into the fallopian tubes. Position during and after intercourse is important. For purposes of conceiving, the best position for intercourse is with the woman on her back (man-on-top, or "missionary," position—see Chapter 8). If the woman is on top, much of the ejaculate may run out of the vagina because of the pull of gravity. After intercourse, she should remain on her back, possibly with her legs pulled up and a pillow under her hips, preferably for about a half hour to an hour. This allows the semen to remain in a pool in the vagina, which gives the sperm a good chance to swim up into the uterus. Because sperm are very sensitive to the pH (acidity-alkalinity) of the vagina, this factor also requires some consideration. Acidity kills sperm. Douching with commercial preparations or with acidic solutions (such as vinegar) should be avoided. If anything, the woman may want to douche before intercourse with a slightly basic solution made by adding two or three tablespoons of baking soda to a quart of water. Finally, lubricants and/or suppositories should not be used; they may kill sperm or block their entrance into the uterus.

Development of the Conceptus

For the nine months of pregnancy, two organisms—the conceptus and the pregnant woman—coexist. In the past, the relationship between the two was viewed as harmonious. In recent years, a new perspective has been gaining support, pregnancy as a "silent struggle" (Haig, 1996). Both fetus and mother need a variety of nutrients, such as calcium, and may be competing for them. Nature should favor the development of characteristics of each that would give it the edge in such competitions, enabling it to win, for example, struggles over calcium. Such a struggle can explain aspects of pregnancy that are inconsistent with the view of harmonious coexistence, such as gestational diabetes and preeclampsia.

For nine months, the two organisms undergo parallel, dramatic changes. The changes that occur in the developing conceptus are discussed in this section; a later section discusses the changes that take place in the pregnant woman.

Typically the nine months of pregnancy are divided into three equal periods of three months, called *trimesters*. Thus the first trimester is months 1 to 3, the second trimester is months 4 to 6, and the third (or last) trimester is months 7 to 9.

The Embryo and Its Support Systems

We left the conceptus, which began as a single fertilized egg cell, dividing into many cells as it passed down the fallopian tube, finally arriving in the uterus and implanting itself in the uterine wall.

During the embryonic period of development (the first eight weeks), most of the fetus's major organ systems are formed in processes that occur with amazing speed (see Figure 6.4a and b). The inner part of the ball of cells implanted in the uterus now differentiates into two layers, the endoderm and the ectoderm. Later a third layer, the mesoderm, forms between them. The various organs of the body differentiate themselves out of these layers. The *ectoderm* will form the entire nervous system and the skin. The *endoderm* differentiates into the digestive system—from the pharynx to the stomach and intestines to the rectum—and the respiratory system. The muscles, skeleton, connective tissues, and reproductive and circulatory systems derive from the *mesoderm*. Fetal development generally proceeds in a cephalocaudal order—that is, the head develops first, the lower body last. For this reason the head of a fetus is enormous compared with the rest of the body.

Meanwhile, another group of cells has differentiated into the *trophoblast*, which has important functions in maintaining the embryo and which will eventually become the placenta. The **placenta** is the mass of tissues that surrounds the conceptus early in development and nurtures its growth. Later it moves to the side of the fetus. The placenta has a number of important functions, perhaps the most important being that it serves as a site for the exchange of substances between the woman's blood and the fetus's blood. It is important to note that the woman's circulatory system and the fetus's circulatory system are completely separate. That is, with only rare exceptions, the woman's blood never circulates

> **Placenta (plah-SEN-tuh):** An organ formed on the wall of the uterus through which the fetus receives oxygen and nutrients and gets rid of waste products.

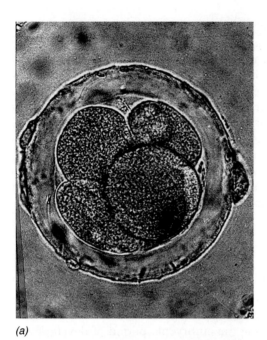

(a)

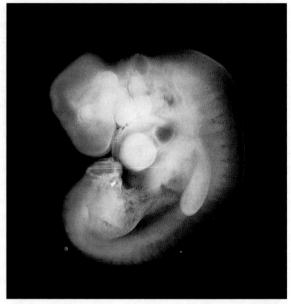

(b)

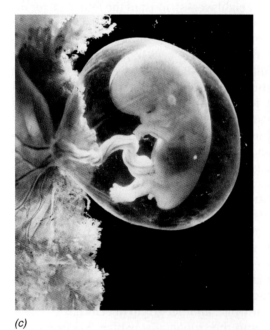

(c)

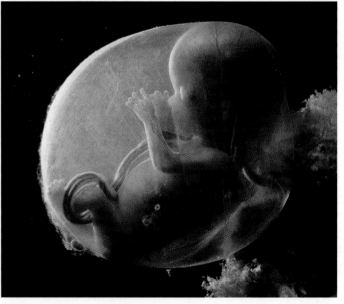

(d)

Figure 6.4 *(a)* This embryo has divided into four cells and would still be traveling down the fallopian tube. *(b)* The embryo after 4 weeks of development. The major organs are forming; the bright red, blood-filled heart is just below the lower jaw. *(c)* At 9 weeks the human fetus is recognizable as a primate. Limbs have formed and ears are clearly visible. *(d)* By about 3 months the fetus is approximately 8 centimeters long and weighs about 28 grams. Muscles have formed, which move the limbs and body.

inside the fetus, nor does the fetus's blood circulate in the woman's blood vessels. Instead, the fetus's blood passes out of its body through the umbilical cord to the placenta. There it circulates in the numerous *villi* (tiny fingerlike projections in the placenta). The woman's blood circulates around the outside of these villi. Thus there is a membrane barrier between the two blood systems. Some substances are capable of passing through this barrier, whereas others are not. Oxygen and nutrients can pass through the barrier, and thus the woman's blood supplies oxygen and nutrients to the fetus, providing substitutes for breathing and eating. Carbon dioxide and waste products similarly pass back from the fetal blood to the woman's blood. Some viruses and other disease-causing organisms can pass through the barrier, including those for German measles (rubella) and syphilis. But some other organisms cannot pass through the barrier; for instance, the woman may have a terrible cold, but the fetus will remain completely healthy. Various drugs can also cross the placental barrier, and the woman should therefore be careful about drugs taken during pregnancy (see Effects of Substances Taken during Pregnancy, later in this chapter).

Another major function of the placenta is that it secretes hormones. The placenta produces large quantities of estrogen and progesterone. Many of the physical symptoms of pregnancy may be caused by these elevated levels of hormones. Another hormone manufactured by the placenta is **human chorionic gonadotropin (hCG),** the hormone that is detected in pregnancy tests.

The **umbilical cord** is formed during week 5 of embryonic development. The fully developed cord is about 55 centimeters (20 inches) long. Normally, it contains three blood vessels: two arteries and one vein. Some people believe that the fetus's umbilical cord attaches to the woman's navel; actually, the umbilical cord attaches to the placenta, thereby providing for the interchanges of substances described earlier.

Two membranes surround the fetus, the *chorion* and the *amnion,* the amnion being the innermost. The amnion is filled with a watery liquid called **amniotic fluid,** in which the fetus floats and can readily move. It is the amniotic fluid that is sampled when an amniocentesis is performed. The amniotic fluid maintains the fetus at a constant temperature and, most important, cushions the fetus against possible injury. Thus, even if the woman falls down a flight of stairs, the fetus will remain undisturbed. Indeed, the amniotic fluid might be considered the original waterbed.

Fetal Development

Fetal Development during the First Trimester

In a sense, the development of the fetus during the first trimester is more remarkable than its development during the second and third trimesters. That's because during the first trimester the small mass of cells implanted in the uterus develops into a fetus with most of the major organ systems present and with recognizable human features.

By the third week of gestation, the embryo appears as a small bit of flesh and is about 0.2 centimeter ($\frac{1}{12}$ inch) long. During weeks 3 and 4, the head undergoes great development. The central nervous system begins to form, and the beginnings of eyes and ears are visible. The backbone is constructed by the end of week 4. A "tail" is noticeable early in embryonic development but has disappeared by week 8.

From weeks 4 to 8, the external body parts—eyes, ears, arms, hands, fingers, legs, feet, and toes—develop. By the end of week 10 they are completely formed. Indeed, by week 10 the embryo has not only a complete set of fingers but also fingernails.

By the end of week 7, the liver, lungs, pancreas, kidneys, and intestines have formed and have begun limited functioning. The gonads have also formed, but the gender of the fetus is not clearly distinguishable until week 12.

At the end of week 12 (end of the first trimester), the fetus is unmistakably human and looks like a small infant (see Figure 6.4d). It is about 10 centimeters (4 inches) long and weighs about 19 grams ($\frac{2}{3}$ ounce). From this point on, development consists mainly of the enlargement and differentiation of structures that are already present.

Fetal Development during the Second Trimester

Around the end of week 14, the movements of the fetus can be detected (*quickening*). By week 18, the woman has been able to feel movement for two to four weeks, and the physician can detect the fetal heartbeat. The latter is an important point, because it helps the physician determine the length of gestation. The baby should be born about 20 weeks later.

The fetus first opens its eyes around week 20. By about week 24, it is sensitive to light and can hear sounds *in utero.* Arm and leg movements are vigorous at this time, and the fetus alternates between periods of wakefulness and sleep.

Fetal Development during the Third Trimester

At the end of the second trimester the fetus's skin is wrinkled and

Human chorionic gonadotropin (hCG): A hormone secreted by the placenta; it is the hormone detected in pregnancy tests.

Umbilical cord: The tube that connects the fetus to the placenta.

Amniotic fluid: The watery fluid surrounding a developing fetus in the uterus.

covered with downlike hair. At the beginning of the third trimester, fat deposits form under the skin; these will give the infant the characteristic chubby appearance of babyhood. The downlike hair is lost.

During month 7 the fetus turns in the uterus to assume a head-down position. If this turning does not occur by the time of delivery, there will be a *breech presentation*. Women can try assuming various positions to aid the turning (Boston Women's Health Book Collective, 2005). Physicians and midwives can also perform certain procedures to turn the fetus.

The fetus's growth during the last two months is rapid. At the end of month 8 it weighs an average of 2,500 grams (5 pounds 4 ounces). The average full-term baby weighs 3,300 grams (7.5 pounds) and is 50 centimeters (20 inches) long.

The Stages of Pregnancy

The Trimesters

The First Trimester (The First 12 Weeks)

Symptoms of Pregnancy.   For most women, the first symptom of pregnancy is a missed menstrual period. Of course, there may be a wide variety of reactions to this event. For the teenager who is not married or for the married woman who feels that she already has enough children, the reaction may be negative—depression, anger, and fear. For the woman who has been trying to conceive for several months, the reaction may be joy and eager anticipation.

In fact, there are many other reasons besides pregnancy for a woman to have a late period or miss a period. Illness or emotional stress may delay a period, and women occasionally skip a period for no apparent reason.

It is also true that a woman may continue to experience some cyclic bleeding or spotting during pregnancy. This is not particularly a danger sign, except that in a few cases it is a symptom of a miscarriage.

If the woman has been keeping a basal body temperature chart, it can provide a very early sign that she is pregnant. If her temperature rises abruptly at about the time ovulation would normally occur and then stays up for more than two weeks—say, about three weeks—the chances are fairly good that she is pregnant. The increased temperature results from the high level of progesterone manufactured by the corpus luteum and, later, the placenta.

Other early symptoms of pregnancy are tenderness of the breasts—a tingling sensation and special sensitivity of the nipples—and nausea and vomiting (called *morning sickness,* although these symptoms may happen anytime during the day). More frequent urination, feelings of fatigue, and a need for more sleep are other early signs of pregnancy.

Pregnancy Tests.   It is important that early, accurate pregnancy tests be available and that women make use of them. This is true for several reasons. A woman needs to know that she is pregnant as early as possible so that she can see a physician or midwife and begin getting good prenatal care. She also needs to know so that she can get the nutrition she requires during pregnancy (see p. 131). And if she does not want to carry the baby to term, she needs to know as soon as possible, because abortions are much safer and simpler when performed in the first trimester than in the second.

A pregnancy test may be done by a physician, at a Planned Parenthood or family planning clinic, or at a medical laboratory. The most common pregnancy test is an immunologic test based on detecting the presence of hCG (human chorionic gonadotropin, secreted by the placenta) in the woman's urine. It can be done in a matter of minutes and is very accurate. It involves mixing a drop of urine with certain chemicals, either on a slide or in a tube.

The laboratory tests for pregnancy are 98 to 99 percent accurate. A laboratory test may produce a false negative (tell the woman she is not pregnant when she really is) if it is done too early or if errors are made in processing. Also, some women simply do not show positive signs in the tests or do not do so until the second or third test. The modern urine tests are 98 percent accurate seven days after implantation (just when a period is missed).

A different type of test, called the *beta-hCG radioimmunoassay,* assesses the presence of beta-hCG in a blood sample. It can detect hCG at very low levels, so it can reliably detect pregnancy seven days after fertilization. It is much more expensive than the urine tests and is available only in laboratories associated with hospitals or large clinics.

Home pregnancy tests are also available, sold under such brand names as First Response, Answer, and ClearBlue. These are all urine tests designed to measure the presence of hCG; they cost $10 to $15. Their charm lies in their convenience and the privacy of getting the results. Manufacturers claim the test will accurately detect a pregnancy on the first day of the missed period. Laboratory tests of 18 brands found that only 1 of the 18 detected low levels of hCG, and only 8 detected high levels of hCG (Cole et al., 2004). Thus 10 of 18 would produce a false negative result. This compares with an error rate of 1 to 2 percent for laboratory tests. The home pregnancy tests also have a 16 percent rate of false positives (Hatcher et al., 2004). To guard against false negatives, the manufacturers recommend repeating the test one week later if the results are negative the first time, although this increases the cost by $3 to $4. A high rate of false negatives is very serious because it leads a pregnant woman to think she is not pregnant, and thus she might take substances that would harm the fetus, and she will not begin getting prenatal care; such dangerous conditions as ectopic pregnancy might therefore go undetected. Performing the tests also requires a certain amount of coordination and care. All in all, they are probably not as good an idea as they seem, although they may be improved in the future.

The signs of pregnancy may be classified as *presumptive signs, probable signs,* and *positive signs.* Amenorrhea, breast tenderness, nausea, and so on, are presumptive signs. The pregnancy tests discussed previously all provide probable signs. Three signs are interpreted as positive signs, that is, as definite indications of pregnancy: (1) beating of the fetal heart, (2) active fetal movement, and (3) detection of a fetal skeleton by ultrasound. These signs cannot be detected until month 4, with the exception of ultrasound, which can be used in the first trimester.

Once the pregnancy has been confirmed, the woman generally is very interested in determining her expected delivery date (called EDC for a rather antiquated expression, "expected date of confinement"). The EDC is calculated using *Nägele's rule.* The rule says to take the date of the first day of the last menstrual period, subtract three months, add seven days, and than add one year. Thus, if the first day of the last menstrual period was September 10, 2008, the expected delivery date would be June 17, 2009: subtracting three months from September 10 gives June 10, adding seven days yields June 17, and adding one year gives June 17, 2009. In cases where the date the last menstrual period began is not known, an ultrasound procedure may be used to determine gestational age (Afriat, 1995).

Physical Changes. The basic physical change that takes place in the woman's body during the first trimester is a large increase in the levels of hormones, especially estrogen and progesterone, that are produced by the placenta. Many of the other physical symptoms of the first trimester arise from these endocrine changes.

The breasts swell and tingle. This results from the development of the mammary glands, which is stimulated by hormones. The nipples and the area around them (areola) may darken and broaden.

There is often a need to urinate more frequently. This is related to changes in the pituitary hormones that affect the adrenals, which in turn change the water balance in the body so that more water is retained. The growing uterus also contributes by pressing against the bladder.

Some women experience morning sickness—feelings of nausea, perhaps to the point of vomiting, and of revulsion toward food or its odor. The nausea and vomiting may occur on waking or at other times during the day. Their exact cause is not known. One theory is that nausea and vomiting cause pregnant women to expel and subsequently avoid foods containing toxic chemicals (Flaxman & Sherman, 2000). Supporting evidence includes a lower rate of miscarriage among women who experience morning sickness. While these symptoms are quite common, about 33 percent of pregnant women experience no vomiting at all.

Vaginal discharges may also increase at this time, partly because the increased hormone levels change the pH of the vagina and partly because the vaginal secretions are changing in their chemical composition and quantity.

The feelings of fatigue and sleepiness are probably related to the high levels of progesterone, which is known to have a sedative effect.

Psychological Changes. Our culture is full of stereotypes about the psychological characteristics of pregnant women. According to one view, pregnancy is supposed to be a time of happiness and calm. Radiant contentment, the "pregnant glow," is said to emanate from the woman's face, making this a good time for her to be photographed. According to another view, pregnancy is a time of emotional ups and downs. The pregnant woman swings from very happy to depressed and crying, and back again. She is irrational, sending her partner out in a blizzard for kosher dill spears. One study compared 70 pregnant women (planned pregnancies) with 92 nonpregnant women. The researchers assessed both the women's physical and psychological states at three points during the pregnancy (or nine months for the nonpregnant women). On the whole, they found that pregnancy is a time of neither heightened well-being nor heightened emotional turmoil (Striegel-Moore et al., 1996).

Research indicates that the situation is more complex than these stereotypes suggest. A woman's emotional state during pregnancy, often assessed with measures of depression, varies according to several factors. First, her attitude toward the pregnancy makes a difference; women who desire the pregnancy are less anxious than women who do not (Kalil et al., 1993). A second factor is social class. Several studies have found that low income is associated with depression during pregnancy. For example, a study involving interviews with 192 poor, inner-city pregnant women found that they were twice as likely as their middle-income counterparts to be depressed (Hobfoll et al., 1995). This may be due to the economic situation these women face; also, there may be more unwanted pregnancies among low-income women. A third influence is the availability of social support. Women with a supportive partner are less likely to be depressed, perhaps because the partner serves as a buffer against stressful events (Chapman et al., 1997).

Research also shows that a woman's emotional state during pregnancy may have an effect on the developing fetus. In one study, women who experienced multiple stressful events during pregnancy had babies who showed small cognitive deficits at 18 months (Bergman et al., 2007). This may occur because the stress hormone cortisol crosses the placenta (Talge et al., 2007).

During the first trimester, the variables that distinguish pregnant from nonpregnant women are nausea, associated with morning sickness, and fatigue (Streigel-Moore et al., 1996). Depression is not uncommon during this time. Women who led very active lives prior to becoming pregnant may find fatigue and lack of energy especially distressing. Depression during the first trimester is more likely among women experiencing other stressful life events, such as moving, changes in their jobs, changes in relationships, or illnesses (Kalil et al., 1993). In this trimester, women's anxieties often center on concerns about miscarriage.

The Second Trimester (Weeks 13 to 26)

Physical Changes. During month 4, the woman becomes aware of the fetus's movements (quickening). Many women find this to be a very exciting experience.

The woman is made even more aware of the pregnancy by her rapidly expanding belly. There are a variety of reactions to this. Some women feel that it is a magnificent symbol of womanhood, and they rush out to buy maternity clothes and wear them before they are even necessary. Other women

feel awkward and resentful of their bulky shape and may begin to wonder whether they can fit through doorways and turnstiles.

Most of the physical symptoms of the first trimester, such as morning sickness, disappear, and discomforts are at a minimum. Physical problems at this time include constipation and nosebleeds (caused by increased blood volume). **Edema**—water retention and swelling—may be a problem in the face, hands, wrists, ankles, and feet; it results from increased water retention throughout the body.

By about midpregnancy, the breasts, under hormonal stimulation, have essentially completed their development in preparation for nursing. Beginning about week 19, a thin amber or yellow fluid called **colostrum** may come out of the nipple, although there is no milk yet.

Psychological Changes. While the first trimester can be relatively tempestuous, particularly with morning sickness, the second is usually a period of relative calm and well-being. The discomforts of the first trimester are past; the tensions associated with labor and delivery are not yet present. Fear of miscarriage diminishes as the woman feels fetal movement (Leifer, 1980).

Depression is less likely during the second trimester if the pregnant woman has a cohabiting partner or spouse (Hobfoll et al., 1995). Furthermore, women who report more effective partner support report less anxiety in the second trimester (Rini et al., 2006). Interestingly, women who have had a previous pregnancy are more distressed during this time than women who have not (Wilkinson, 1995). This may reflect the impact of the demands associated with the care of other children when one is pregnant. Research also indicates that feelings of nurturance, or maternal responsiveness to the infant, increase steadily from the prepregnant to the postpartum period (Fleming et al., 1997). This increase does not appear to be related to changes in hormone levels during pregnancy.

The Third Trimester (Weeks 27 to 38)

Physical Changes. The uterus is very large and hard by the third trimester. The woman is increasingly aware of her size and of the fetus, which is becoming more and more active. In fact, some women are kept awake at night by its somersaults and hiccups.

The extreme size of the uterus puts pressure on a number of other organs, causing some discomfort. There is pressure on the lungs, which may cause shortness of breath. The stomach is also being squeezed, and indigestion is common. The

Edema (eh-DEE-muh): Excessive fluid retention and swelling.
Colostrum: A watery substance that is secreted from the breasts at the end of pregnancy and during the first few days after delivery.

navel is pushed out. The heart is being strained because of the large increase in blood volume. At this stage most women feel low in energy (Leifer, 1980).

The weight gain of the second trimester continues. The Mayo Clinic (2007) recommends that the amount of weight gained should range from 15 to 40 pounds, depending on the woman's weight prior to pregnancy. Women who are slim should gain relatively more, 28 to 40 pounds, whereas women who are heavy should gain less, 15 to 25 pounds. The average infant at birth weighs 7.5 pounds; the rest of the weight gain is accounted for by the placenta (1–2 pounds), the amniotic fluid (about 2 pounds), enlargement of the uterus (about 2 pounds), enlargement of the breasts (1–3 pounds), and the additional fat and water retained by the woman (8 or more pounds). Physicians restrict the amount of weight gain because the incidence of complications such as high blood pressure and strain on the heart is much higher in women who gain an excessive amount of weight. Also, excessive weight gained during pregnancy can be very hard to lose afterward.

The woman's balance is somewhat disturbed because of the large amount of weight that has been added to the front part of her body. She may compensate for this by adopting the characteristic "waddling" walk of the pregnant woman, which can result in back pains.

The uterus tightens occasionally in painless contractions called **Braxton-Hicks contractions.** These are not part of labor. It is thought that they help to strengthen the uterine muscles, preparing them for labor.

In a first pregnancy, around two to four weeks before delivery the baby turns and the head drops into the pelvis. This is called *lightening, dropping,* or *engagement.* Engagement usually occurs during labor in women who have had babies before.

Some women are concerned about the appropriate amount of activity during pregnancy—whether some things constitute "overdoing it." Traditionally, physicians and textbooks warned of the dangers of physical activities and tried to discourage them. It appears now, however, that such restrictions were based more on superstition than on scientific fact. Current thinking holds that for a healthy pregnant woman, moderate activity is not dangerous and is actually psychologically and physically beneficial. Modern methods of childbirth encourage sensible exercise for the pregnant woman so that she will be in shape for labor (see Childbirth Options later in this chapter). The matter, of course, is highly individual.

Psychological Changes. The patterns noted earlier continue into the third trimester. Psychological well-being is greater among women who have social support (often in the form of a cohabiting partner or husband), have higher incomes, are middle class, and experience fewer concurrent stressful life events. One study assessed the relationship between social support and birth outcomes. Women who reported less support during pregnancy were more likely to have low-birth-weight babies (McWilliams, 1994).

What happens to the relationship of the pregnant woman with her husband? A comparison of women pregnant for the first time with women who had experienced previous pregnancies found that first-time mothers reported a significant increase in dissatisfaction with their husbands from the second to the third trimester (Wilkinson, 1995). Another study included 54 women who were pregnant for the first time and their husbands (Zimmerman-Tansella et al., 1994). Wives who reported that higher levels of affection were exchanged between husband and wife reported lower levels of anxiety and of insomnia in the third trimester.

The Father's Experience in Pregnancy

Physical Changes. Some men experience pregnancy symptoms, including indigestion, gastritis, nausea, change in appetite, and headaches (Kiselica & Scheckel, 1995), referred to as *couvade syndrome.* These may be caused by hormonal changes in the male. A longitudinal study of 34 couples collected blood samples from both before and after the birth of the infant (Storey et al., 2000). Men and women displayed stage-specific hormone differences, including high levels of prolactin prenatally and low levels of testosterone postnatally. Men with more pregnancy symptoms had higher levels of prolactin prenatally.

In some cultures this phenomenon takes a more dramatic form, known as *couvade ritual.* In this ritual, the husband retires to bed while his wife is in labor. He suffers all the pains of delivery, moaning and groaning as she does. Couvade is still practiced in parts of Asia, South America, and Oceania (Gregersen, 1996).

Psychological Changes. In twenty-first-century American culture, many men expect to be actively involved in fathering. In fact, it has even been claimed that there is a "father instinct" (Biller & Meredith, 1975). Recall the discussion in Chapter 2 of the reproductive advantages of

> **Braxton-Hicks contractions:** Contractions of the uterus during pregnancy that are not part of actual labor.

a father–infant bond. The likelihood of such a bond depends partly on the father's responsiveness to the infant. The study of hormonal changes during pregnancy presented videotapes with auditory and visual cues from newborns after the blood sample was drawn. Men who showed higher levels of responsiveness had higher levels of prolactin prenatally and lower levels of testosterone postnatally (Storey et al., 2000). Lower levels of testosterone may facilitate paternal behavior.

One study of emotional changes found that 70 percent of expectant fathers were initially ambivalent about fathering but gradually became more positive, in anticipation of the satisfactions to be derived from being a father (Obzrut, 1976). The men reported engaging in many activities in preparation for becoming fathers, including attending parenting classes, planning father–child activities, observing and talking to other fathers, and daydreaming about the baby (see Figure 6.5). Most of these activities, of course, parallel those done by expectant mothers. It has been theorized that men who display this active involvement will do best in the father role after the baby is born (Antle, 1978).

Preparing for the Baby.   Fathers or other partners play an important role in preparing for a baby. The birth or arrival of a first child may require finding a larger home or making physical changes to the present one. There will be visits to medical personnel, tests to be taken, and arrangements to be made. Fathers or partners who participate in these activities provide support to their partner and become more involved themselves. Many couples take some form of classes in preparation for childbirth. The classes often specifically address the partner's role in late pregnancy and during labor and delivery. These joint activities contribute to the bond between the partners, which in turn provides a better foundation for the arrival of the new member of the family.

Figure 6.5   Dad changes his daughter's diaper at a "Bootee Camp" in Irvine, California, which helps new or prospective fathers adjust to their new role.

Table 6.1 Percentage of Women Having Various Frequencies of Coitus at Different Stages of Pregnancy

Number of Acts of Coitus per Week	Baseline Prepregnancy %	12 Weeks Pregnant, %	24 Weeks Pregnant, %	36 Weeks Pregnant, %
None	0	11	8	36
<1	7	24	25	26
1–3	54	52	55	33
4 or more	40	14	13	5

Source: Kumar et al. (1981).

Diversity in the Contexts of Pregnancy

There are lots of family contexts in which women have babies these days besides the traditional one of being married to the baby's father. These include living in a stable relationship with the baby's father but not being married; not being married to or living with the baby's father but seeing him regularly; being a single mother-to-be who has no contact with the baby's father; being a single mother-to-be who is pregnant as a result of artificial insemination or other reproductive technologies; and being a woman in a stable relationship with another woman, who is pregnant as a result of artificial insemination or other technologies. Because it is too complicated to mention these alternatives constantly, in the sections that follow our language is based on a situation in which the woman is married to the baby's father, which is still statistically the most common context in which babies are born in the United States. Readers should, however, keep in mind all these other possible family scenarios.

Sex during Pregnancy

Many women and men are concerned about whether it is safe or advisable for a pregnant woman to have sexual intercourse, particularly during the latter stages of pregnancy. Traditionally, physicians believed that intercourse might (1) cause an infection or (2) precipitate labor prematurely or cause a miscarriage. Current medical opinion, however, is that—given a normal, healthy pregnancy—intercourse can continue safely until four weeks before the baby is due (Cunningham et al., 1993). There is no evidence that intercourse or orgasm is associated with preterm labor (Sayle et al., 2001; Schaffir, 2006). In fact, a study involving interviews with pregnant women at 28 weeks gestation and again following delivery, found that recent intercourse and orgasm was associated with reduced risk of preterm birth (Sayle et al., 2001). The only exception is a case where a miscarriage or preterm labor is threatened. Whether and how frequently to have intercourse is a matter for a couple to decide, perhaps in consultation with a physician or midwife.

Most pregnant women continue to have intercourse throughout the pregnancy (Reamy & White, 1987). The most common pattern is a decline in the frequency of intercourse during the first trimester, variation in the second trimester, and an even greater decline in the third trimester (see Table 6.1). One study included male partners of pregnant women; the men reported the same pattern (Bogren, 1991).

During the latter stages of pregnancy, the woman's shape makes intercourse increasingly awkward. The man-on-top position is probably best abandoned at this time. The side-to-side position (see Chapter 8) is probably the most suitable one for intercourse during the late stages of pregnancy. Couples should also remember that there are many ways of experiencing sexual pleasure and orgasm besides having intercourse; hand–genital stimulation or oral–genital sex may be good alternatives.[2] The best guide in this matter is the woman's feelings. If intercourse becomes uncomfortable for her, alternatives should be explored.

Nutrition during Pregnancy

During pregnancy, another living being is growing inside the woman, and she needs lots of energy, protein, vitamins, and minerals at this time. Therefore, diet during pregnancy is extremely important.

---

[2]There is, however, some risk associated with cunnilingus for the pregnant woman, as discussed in Chapter 8.

If the woman's diet is good, she has a much better chance of remaining healthy during pregnancy and of bearing a healthy baby; if her diet is inadequate, she stands more of a chance of developing one of a number of diseases during pregnancy herself and of bearing a child whose weight is low at birth. This is a result of the silent struggle between mother and fetus for nutrition, discussed earlier. Babies with low birth weights do not have as good a chance of survival as ones with normal birth weights. According to a study done in Toronto, mothers in a poor-diet group had four times as many serious health problems during pregnancy as a group of mothers whose diets were supplemented with highly nutritious foods. Those with the poor diets had seven times as many threatened miscarriages and three times as many stillbirths; their labor lasted five hours longer on average (Newton, 1972).

It is particularly important that a pregnant woman get enough protein, folic acid, calcium, magnesium, and vitamin A (Luke, 1994). Protein is important for building new tissues. Folic acid is also important for growth; symptoms of folic acid deficiency are anemia and fatigue. A pregnant woman needs much more iron than usual, because the fetus draws off iron for itself from the blood that circulates to the placenta. Muscle cramps, nerve pains, uterine ligament pains, sleeplessness, and irritability may all be symptoms of a calcium deficiency. Severe calcium deficiency during pregnancy is associated with increased blood pressure, which may lead to a serious condition called eclampsia, discussed later in this chapter (Repke, 1994). Deficiencies of calcium and magnesium are associated with premature birth. Sometimes even an excellent diet does not provide enough iron, calcium, or folic acid, in which case the pregnant woman should take supplements. Surveillance data collected in 19 states indicate that women with less than 12 years of education and Black and Hispanic women were less likely to report multivitamin use during pregnancy (Williams et al., 2003).

Effects of Substances Taken during Pregnancy

We are such a pill-popping culture that we seldom stop to think about whether we should take a certain drug. The pregnant woman, however, needs to know that when she takes a drug, not only does it circulate through her body, but it may also circulate

Teratogen: A substance that produces defects in a fetus.

through the fetus. Because the fetus develops so rapidly during pregnancy, drugs may produce severe consequences, including serious malformations. Drugs that produce such defects are called **teratogens.**[3] Of course, not all drugs can cross the placental barrier, but many can. The drugs that pregnant women should be cautious in using are discussed below.

Antibiotics

Long-term use of antibiotics by the woman may cause damage to the fetus. Tetracycline may cause stained teeth and bone deformities. Gentamycin, kanamycin, neomycin, streptomycin, and vancomycin may cause deafness. Nitrofurantoin may cause jaundice. Accutane (isotretinoin), used to treat acne, can cause severe birth defects if taken by a pregnant woman. Some drugs taken by diabetics may cause various fetal anomalies.

Alcohol

WARNING: ACCORDING TO THE SURGEON GENERAL, WOMEN SHOULD NOT DRINK ALCOHOLIC BEVERAGES DURING PREGNANCY BECAUSE OF THE RISK OF BIRTH DEFECTS.

A substantial amount of research has documented the risks to a child of maternal drinking during pregnancy. Alcohol consumed by the woman circulates through the fetus, so it can have pervasive effects on fetal growth and development (Jones, 2006).

The effects of prenatal alcohol consumption are dose dependent; that is, the more alcohol the mother drinks, the larger the number and severity of effects on the child. Male infants whose mothers had five or more drinks per week were more likely to be born with cryptorchidism, or undescended testes (Damgaard et al., 2006). Consuming the equivalent of one drink or two glasses of wine per day was associated with slower information-processing times in a study of 6-month-old infants (Jacobson et al., 1993). A study of 403 Black children at 1 year found that slower reaction times, increased visual fixation, and reduced complexity of play were associated with maternal alcohol consumption during the second and third trimesters of pregnancy (Jacobson et al., 1994). The children of mothers who had taken at least one drink per day in midpregnancy had poorer gross and fine motor skills (e.g., catching and throwing a ball) at age 4 (Barr et al., 1990). Deficits of 10 points or

[3]Teratogen is from the Greek words *teras*, meaning "monster," and *gen*, meaning "cause."

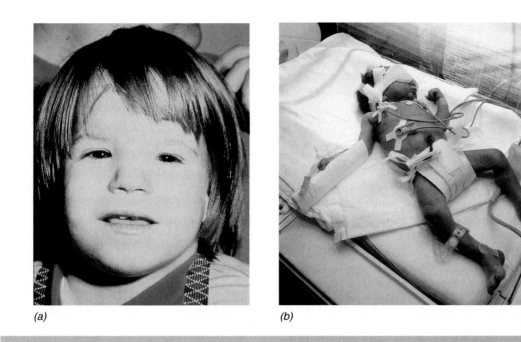

(a)   (b)

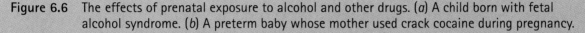

Figure 6.6   The effects of prenatal exposure to alcohol and other drugs. (*a*) A child born with fetal alcohol syndrome. (*b*) A preterm baby whose mother used crack cocaine during pregnancy.

more in intelligence test scores at 1 year and lower scores at 4 years of age are associated with prenatal drinking (O'Connor et al., 1993; Barr et al., 1990). Data from the Seattle longitudinal study indicate that maternal drinking (an average of 3.6 drinks per occasion, eight occasions per month) is associated with numerous academic and behavioral problems among children at age 14 (Streissguth et al., 1999).

The abuse of alcohol during pregnancy may result in offspring who display a pattern of malformations termed the **fetal alcohol syndrome (FAS)** (for reviews, see Mattson & Riley, 1998; see Figure 6.6a). Among the characteristics of the syndrome are both prenatal and postnatal growth deficiencies, a small brain, small eye openings, and joint, limb, and heart malformations. Perhaps the most serious effect is mental retardation. About 85 percent of children with FAS score 2 or more standard deviations below the mean on intelligence tests—that would be an IQ of about 70 or below. Indeed, FAS is the leading preventable cause of mental retardation (Braun, 1996).

Research indicates that "risk drinking" (seven or more drinks per week, or five or more drinks on one occasion) poses a serious health threat to the fetus (Centers for Disease Control, 2002). It is clear that women who drink moderately may have children who are affected to some degree (Abel, 1980).

The effects have been documented in the children even when they reach adulthood (Streissguth et al., 1999). "Safe" limits for alcohol consumption during pregnancy have not been established, so the best advice about drinking for women who are, or may be or want to be, pregnant is Don't. Perhaps understandably, there are many reports of well-intentioned bartenders, wait staff, and patrons approaching pregnant women consuming alcohol and asking them not to drink.

Cocaine

Cocaine use during pregnancy is associated with an increased risk of premature birth (Handler et al., 1991) and low birth weight (Phibbs et al., 1991) (see Figure 6.6b). The only regularly noted physical abnormality is smaller head circumference (Cherukuri et al., 1988); cocaine-exposed children are more likely to be microcephalic, which is in turn associated with poorer growth and lower intelligence-test scores in school-age children. Infants exposed to cocaine in utero display neurological deficits and central nervous system anomalies (O'Shea, 1995). A carefully done longitudinal study measuring infant development at 6, 12, and 24 months compared 218 cocaine-exposed and 197 unexposed infants on cognitive outcomes (Singer

Fetal alcohol syndrome (FAS): Serious growth deficiency and malformations in the child of a mother who abuses alcohol during pregnancy.

et al., 2002). Cocaine exposure was associated with a 6-point deficit in scores on a cognitive measure at 2 years of age. While the effects of exposure are serious, careful assessments suggest that relatively few infants are exposed to cocaine in utero (Bauer et al., 2002).

Steroids

Synthetic hormones such as progestin can cause masculinization of a female fetus, as discussed in Chapter 5. Corticosteroids are linked with low birth weight, cleft palate, and stillbirth in some studies but not in others (Ostensten, 1994). Excessive amounts of vitamin A are associated with cleft palate. Excesses of vitamins D, B_6, and K have also been associated with fetal defects. A potent estrogen, diethylstilbestrol (DES), has been shown to cause cancer of the vagina in girls whose mothers took the drug while pregnant (Herbst, 1972). Long-term exposure to DES is associated with an increased risk of low birth weight (Zhang & Bracken, 1995). At one time, DES was used as a "morning after" treatment, following unprotected intercourse, but such use is no longer approved (Hatcher et al., 1994).

Other Substances

According to the U.S. Public Health Service, maternal smoking during pregnancy exerts a retarding influence on fetal growth, indicated by decreased infant birth weight and increased incidence of prematurity. A study of 18,000 live births assessed infants for evidence of 22 types of congenital defects; infants whose mothers smoked were more likely to be born with cardiovascular anomalies, conditions involving arteries, veins, or the heart (Woods & Raju, 2001). A study involving 58,800 births in Finland replicated the finding that infants of smokers were more likely to be preterm and low birth weight. A seven-year follow-up found that these children were more likely to have developed asthma; the risk was greater for children whose mothers smoked from 1 to 10 cigarettes per day, and greater still for those whose mothers smoked more than 10 per day during pregnancy (Jaakkola & Gissler, 2004). A study comparing the risk due to smoking, drinking, and limited prenatal care found that the largest and most consistent effect on children of white women was associated with smoking (Li & Poirier, 2001).

Some antihistamines may produce malformations. Even plain aspirin may cause blood problems (Cunningham et al., 1989).

The psychoactive chemical in marijuana crosses the placental barrier (Harbison & Mantilla-Plata, 1972; Idänpään-Heikkilä et al., 1969). There is some evidence that marijuana inhibits ovulation (Abel, 1984); thus its use might make it more difficult to become pregnant. In one Canadian study, women who used marijuana during pregnancy were compared with a control group of nonusers. There were no differences between the two groups in rate of miscarriage, complications during birth, or incidence of birth defects. However, the newborns of the marijuana users had more tremors and had a higher rate of visual problems in the preschool years (Fried, 1986). A longitudinal study of 668 children found that children of users attained lower scores on the Stanford-Binet Intelligence Scale at ages 3 and 6. Six-year-olds who had been exposed to marijuana in utero performed poorly on tasks requiring attention (Day & Richardson, 1994).

Tricyclic antidepressant medications such as amitriptyline and imipramine have been associated with birth defects in some studies but not others. One study of children whose mothers took tricyclics during pregnancy found no significant differences in language development, measured intelligence, mood, or temperament at 16 to 86 months of age (Nulman et al., 1997). Use during pregnancy of certain antimanic drugs, including lithium, valproic acid, and carbamazepine, should be avoided; they are risk factors for teratogenesis in humans. Use is especially risky from day 18 to day 55 following conception. On the other hand, chlorpromazine, halperidol, fluphenazine, and clozapine can be used safely during pregnancy (Iqbal et al., 2001).

Selective serotonin reuptake inhibitors such as fluoxetine (Prozac) are frequently used to treat depression. A meta-analysis of prospective cohort studies found that newborns exposed to SSRIs are more likely to be low birth weight, and to be admitted to special or intensive care nurseries at birth (Lattimore et al., 2005). They were also more likely to show signs of poor neonatal adaptation, including respiratory distress and jaundice.

As with alcohol, the best rule for the pregnant woman considering using a drug is, When in doubt, don't.

Although not classified as a drug, X rays deserve mention here because they can damage the fetus, particularly during the first 42 days after conception.

Dads and Drugs

Most research has focused on the effects of drugs taken by the pregnant woman. However, new theorizing suggests that drugs taken by men before a conception may also cause birth defects, probably because the drugs damage the sperm and their genetic contents (Narod et al., 1988). In addition, one study found evidence that a mother's smoking during the first trimester of pregnancy increased her offspring's risk of cancer in childhood; but a father's smoking during the pregnancy in the absence of the mother's smoking also increased the risk of childhood cancer (John et al., 1991).

Birth

The Beginning of Labor

The signs that labor is about to begin vary from one woman to the next. There may be a discharge of a small amount of bloody mucus (the "bloody show"). This is the mucus plug that was in the cervical opening during pregnancy, its purpose being to prevent germs from passing from the vagina up into the uterus. In about 10 percent of all women the membranes containing the amniotic fluid rupture (the bag of waters bursts), and there is a gush of warm fluid down the woman's legs. Labor usually begins within 24 hours after this occurs. More commonly, the amniotic sac does not rupture until the end of the first stage of labor. The Braxton-Hicks contractions may increase before labor and may be mistaken for labor. Typically, they are distinct from the contractions of labor in that they are very irregular.

The biological mechanism that initiates and maintains labor is not completely understood. The progesterone-withdrawal theory is the leading hypothesis (Schwartz, 1997). Progesterone is known to inhibit uterine contractions. It has been proposed that some mechanism such as increased production of antiprogesterone reduces the inhibiting effect of progesterone and labor begins.

The Stages of Labor

Labor is typically divided into three stages, although the length of the stages may vary considerably from one woman to the next. The whole process of childbirth is sometimes referred to as *parturition.*

First-Stage Labor

First-stage labor begins with the regular contractions of the muscles of the uterus. These contractions are responsible for producing two changes in the cervix, both of which must occur before the baby can be delivered. These changes are called **effacement** (thinning out) and **dilation** (opening up). The cervix must dilate until it has an opening 10 centimeters (4 inches) in diameter before the baby can be born.

First-stage labor itself is divided into three stages: early, late, and transition. In *early first-stage labor,* contractions are spaced far apart, with perhaps 15 to 20 minutes between them. A contraction typically lasts 45 seconds to a minute. This stage of labor is fairly easy, and the woman is quite comfortable between contractions. Meanwhile, the cervix is effacing and dilating.

Late first-stage labor is marked by the dilation of the cervix from 5 to 8 centimeters (2 to 3 inches). It is generally shorter than the early stage, and the contractions are more frequent and more intense.

The final dilation of the cervix from 8 to 10 centimeters (3 to 4 inches) occurs during the **transition** phase, which is both short and difficult. The contractions are very strong, and it is during this stage that women report pain and exhaustion.

The first stage of labor can last anywhere from 2 to 24 hours. It averages about 12 to 15 hours for a first pregnancy and about 8 hours for later pregnancies. (In most respects, first labors are the hardest, later ones easier.) The woman is usually told to go to the hospital when the contractions are 4 to 5 minutes apart. Once there, she is put in the labor room or birthing room for the rest of first-stage labor.

Second-Stage Labor: Delivery

Second-stage labor (Figure 6.7) begins when the cervix is fully dilated and the baby's head (or whichever part comes first, depending on the baby's position; see Figure 6.8) begins to move into the vagina, or birth canal. It lasts from a few minutes to a few hours and is generally much shorter than the first stage.

During this stage, many women feel an urge to push or bear down, and if done properly, this may be of great assistance in pushing the baby out. With each contraction the baby is pushed farther along.

When the baby's head has traversed the entire length of the vagina, the top of it becomes visible at the vaginal entrance; this is called *crowning.* It is at this point that many physicians perform an

Effacement: A thinning out of the cervix during labor.
Dilation: An opening up of the cervix during labor; also called *dilatation.*
First-stage labor: The beginning of labor, during which there are regular contractions of the uterus; the stage lasts until the cervix is dilated 8 centimeters (3 inches).
Transition: The difficult part of labor at the end of the first stage, during which the cervix dilates from 8 to 10 centimeters (3 to 4 inches).
Second-stage labor: The stage during which the baby moves out through the vagina and is delivered.

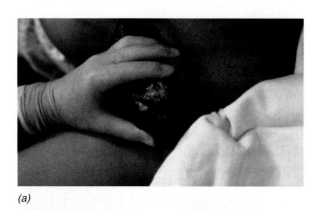

(a)

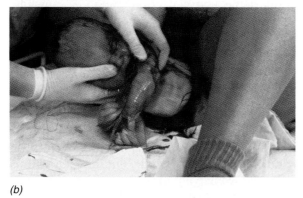

(b)

Figure 6.7 Second-stage labor. (*a*) Baby's head crowning and then (*b*) moving out.

Episiotomy (ih-pee-see-AH-tuh-mee): An incision made in the skin just behind the vagina, allowing the baby to be delivered more easily.

episiotomy (see Figure 6.9), in which an incision or slit is made in the perineum, the skin just behind the vagina. Most women do not feel the episiotomy being per-

formed because the pressure of the baby against the pelvic floor provides a natural anesthetic. The incision is stitched closed after the baby is born. The reasons physicians give for performing an episiotomy are that it will prevent impaired sexual functioning in later life, reduce the severity of perineal lacerations, and reduce postdelivery pain and medication use. However, a review of relevant research conducted between 1950 and 2004 found no evidence that any of these benefits result from episiotomies (Hartmann et al., 2005). Critics claim that it is unnecessary and is done merely for the doctor's convenience, while causing the woman discomfort later as it is healing. They note that episiotomies are usually not performed in western European countries, where delivery still takes place quite nicely.

The baby is finally eased completely out of the mother's body. At this point, the baby is still connected to the mother by the umbilical cord, which runs from the baby's navel to the placenta, and the placenta is still inside the mother's uterus. As the baby takes its first breath of air, the functioning of its body changes dramatically. Blood begins to flow to the lungs, there to take on oxygen, and a flap closes between the two atria (chambers) in the heart. This process generally takes a few minutes, during which time the baby changes from a somewhat bluish color to a healthy, pink hue. At this point, the baby no longer needs the umbilical cord, which is clamped and cut off about 7 centimeters (3 inches) from the body. The stub gradually dries up and falls off.

To avoid the possibility of transmitting gonorrhea or other eye infections from the mother to the baby, drops of silver nitrate or a similar drug are placed in the baby's eyes (see Chapter 18).

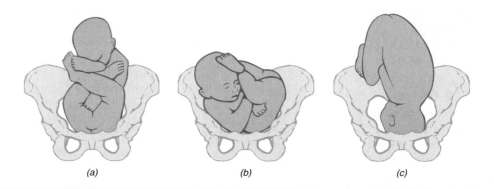

(a)   (b)   (c)

Figure 6.8 Possible positions of the fetus during birth. (*a*) A breech presentation (4 percent of births). (*b*) A transverse presentation (less than 1 percent). (*c*) A normal, headfirst or cephalic presentation (96 percent of births).

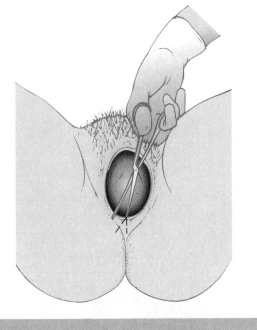

Figure 6.9   Episiotomy. A mediolateral or median cut may be performed.

Third-Stage Labor

During **third-stage labor,** the placenta detaches from the walls of the uterus, and the afterbirth (placenta and fetal membranes) is expelled. This stage may take from a few minutes to an hour. Several contractions may accompany the expulsion of the placenta. The episiotomy and/or any tears are sewn up.

Cesarean Section (C-Section)

Cesarean section is a surgical procedure for delivery; it is used when normal vaginal birth is impossible or undesirable. Cesarean section may be required for a number of different reasons: if the baby is too large or if the mother's pelvis is too small to allow the baby to move into the vagina; if the labor has been very long and hard and the cervix is not dilating or if the mother is nearing the point of total exhaustion; if the umbilical cord *prolapses* (moves into a position such that it is coming out through the cervix ahead of the baby); if there is an Rh incompatibility; or if there is excessive bleeding or the mother's or the infant's condition takes a sudden turn for the worse. Another condition requiring a C-section is *placenta previa,* in which the placenta is attached to the wall of the uterus over or close to the cervix.

In the cesarean section, an incision is made first through the abdomen and then through the wall of the uterus. The physician lifts out the baby and then sews up the uterine wall and the abdominal wall.

Cesarean delivery rates in the United States stood at 24 percent in 1989 (Taffel et al., 1991), which is a rate considerably higher than in most western European countries. For example, the cesarean rate was 10 percent of deliveries in the Netherlands, 12 percent of deliveries in Norway, and 10 percent of deliveries in England and Wales (Notzon, 1990). Rates among an American Indian population in New Mexico are one-third of the overall rate in the United States (Leeman & Leeman, 2003). Overall rates of cesarean birth in the United States declined from 22.6 percent in 1991 to 20.7 in 1996, but then rose steadily to 27.6 in 2005 (Menacker, 2005). Much of the variability during these years was due to fluctuations in the number of repeat cesareans, from 80 percent in 1991 to 71.7 in 1996, to 89.4 in 2003. These fluctuations reflect changes in medical practice (Declercq et al., 2006).

Contrary to popular opinion, it is not true that once a woman has had one delivery by cesarean, she must have all subsequent deliveries by the same method. Vaginal births after cesareans (VBAC) are possible (Taffel et al., 1991). And up to 60 percent of women with a prior cesarean delivery attempt a subsequent vaginal birth. There is a risk of uterine rupture during the attempt, particularly when labor is induced using drugs (Lydon-Rochelle et al., 2001).

There is concern about the high U.S. cesarean rates. A study of VBAC in California noted no change in neonatal or maternal mortality despite the increase in rates of repeat cesareans, that is, increasing the rate of C-sections did not lower mortality (Zweifler et al., 2006). An analysis of 540,174 primary C-sections and 371,863 repeat cesarean births in 2001 classified 11 percent of the former and 55 percent of the latter as potentially unnecessary (Kabir et al., 2005).

Programs in two hospitals indicate that cesarean rates can be decreased dramatically. In one hospital, prenatal education was expanded, guidelines for cesareans were tightened, women were encouraged to remain active during labor (for example, to walk at regular intervals), and physicians were given statistics each month about their own deliveries. In May 1988, when the study began, the rate of cesarean births was 31 percent. For the period January to June 1994, it was 15 percent (Hollander, 1996).

Third-stage labor: The stage during which the afterbirth is expelled.
Cesarean section (C-section): A method of delivering a baby surgically, by an incision in the abdomen.

Childbirth Options

Pregnant women and their partners can choose from a variety of childbirth options. Foremost among these is taking childbirth classes to prepare mentally and physically for labor and delivery. In addition, there are several options regarding the use of anesthesia during childbirth. Third, women can often choose to give birth at home, in a birthing or maternity center, or in a hospital delivery suite.

The Lamaze Method

English obstetrician Grantly Dick-Read coined the term *natural childbirth* in 1932. He postulated that fear causes tension and tension causes pain. Thus, to attempt to eliminate the pain of childbirth, he recommended a program consisting of education (to eliminate the woman's fears of the unknown) and the learning of relaxation techniques (to eliminate tension).

One of the most widely used methods of *prepared childbirth* was developed by French obstetrician Fernand Lamaze. Classes teaching the Lamaze method or variations of it are now offered in most areas of the country. The **Lamaze method** involves two basic techniques, *relaxation* and *controlled breathing* (Figure 6.10). The woman learns to relax all the muscles in her body. Knowing how to do this has a number of advantages, including conservation of energy during an event that requires considerable endurance and, more important, avoidance of the tension that increases the perception of pain. The woman also learns a series of controlled breathing exercises, which she will use to help her during each contraction.

Some other techniques are taught as well. One, called *effleurage,* consists of a light, circular stroking of the abdomen with the fingertips. There are also exercises to strengthen specific muscles, such as the leg muscles, which undergo considerable strain during labor and delivery. Finally, because the Lamaze method is based on the idea that fear and the pain it causes are best eliminated through education, the Lamaze student learns a great deal about the processes involved in pregnancy and childbirth.

One other important component of the Lamaze method is the requirement that the woman be accompanied during the classes and during childbirth itself by her partner or some other person, who serves as coach. The coach plays an integral role in the woman's learning of the

Lamaze method: A method of "prepared" childbirth involving relaxation and controlled breathing.

Figure 6.10 Practice in relaxation and breathing techniques is essential in preparing for a Lamaze childbirth.

techniques and her use of them during labor. He (we shall assume that it is the baby's father) is present during labor and delivery. He times contractions, checks on the woman's state of relaxation and gives her feedback if she is not relaxed, suggests breathing patterns, helps elevate her back as she pushes the baby out, and generally provides encouragement and moral support. Aside from the obvious benefits to the woman, this principle of the Lamaze method represents real progress in that it allows the partner to play an active role in the birth of the child and to experience more fully one of the most basic and moving of all human experiences.

One common misunderstanding about the Lamaze method is that the use of anesthetics is prohibited. In fact, the Lamaze method is more flexible than that. Its goal is to teach each woman the techniques she needs to control her reactions to labor so that she will not need an anesthetic;

however, her right to have an anesthetic if she wants one is affirmed. The topic of anesthetics in childbirth, which has become quite controversial in recent years, is discussed next.

A number of studies indicate that childbirth training, such as the Lamaze method, has several desirable results. These include reduction in the length of labor, decreased incidence of birth complications, a decrease in the use of anesthetics, a more positive attitude after birth, increased self-esteem, and a heightened sense of being in control (e.g., Felton & Segelman, 1978; Zax et al., 1975). Lamaze training is associated with increased tolerance for pain and reduced anxiety both before birth and for four weeks after birth (Markman & Kadushin, 1986; McClure & Brewer, 1980; Worthington et al., 1983).

There is no doubt that the Lamaze method has improved the childbirth experiences of thousands of women and men. On the other hand, some Lamaze advocates are so idealistic that they may create unrealistic expectations about delivery, especially for women having their first baby (**primiparas**). The use of the Lamaze method reduces pain in childbirth but does not eliminate it completely. For primiparas there is often a discrepancy between their positive expectations for delivery and the actual outcomes (Booth & Meltzoff, 1984). Thus, while the Lamaze method produces excellent outcomes and helps women control pain, childbirth still involves some pain, as well as unexpected complications in some cases.

The Use of Anesthetics in Childbirth

Throughout most of human history, childbirth has been "natural"; that is, it has taken place without anesthetics and in the woman's home or other familiar surroundings. The pattern in the United States began to change about 225 years ago, at the time of the Revolutionary War, when male physicians rather than midwives started to assist during birth (Wertz & Wertz, 1977). The next major change came around the middle of the nineteenth century, with the development of anesthetics for use in surgery. When their use in childbirth was suggested, there was some opposition from physicians, who felt they interfered with natural processes, and some opposition from the clergy, who argued that women's pain in childbirth was prescribed in the Bible, quoting Genesis 3:16: "In sorrow thou shalt bring forth children." Opposition to the use of anesthetics virtually ceased, however, when Queen Victoria gave birth under chloroform anesthesia in 1853. Since then, the use

of anesthetics has become routine (too routine, according to some) and effective. Before discussing the arguments for and against the use of anesthetics, let us briefly review some of the common techniques of anesthesia used in childbirth.

Tranquilizers (such as Valium) or narcotics may be administered when labor becomes fairly intense. They relax the woman and take the edge off the pain. Barbiturates (Nembutal or Seconal) are administered to put the woman to sleep. Scopolamine may sometimes be used for its amnesic effects; it makes the woman forget what has happened, and thus she has no memory afterward of any pain during childbirth. Regional and local anesthetics, which numb only the specific region of the body that is painful, are used most commonly. An example is the pudendal block (named for the pudendum, or vulva), in which an injection numbs only the external genitals. Other examples are spinal anesthesia (a *spinal*), in which an injection near the spinal cord numbs the entire birth area, from the waist down, and the caudal block and epidural anesthesia, which are both administered by injections in the back and produce regional numbing from the belly to the thighs (for more information, see Coustan, 1995).

The routine use of anesthetics has been questioned by some. Proponents of the use of anesthetics argue that, with modern technology, women no longer need to experience pain during childbirth and that it is therefore silly for them to suffer unnecessarily. Opponents argue that anesthetics have a number of well-documented dangerous effects on both mother and infant. Anesthetics in the mother's bloodstream pass through the placenta to the infant. Thus, while they have the desired effect of depressing the mother's central nervous system, they also depress the infant's nervous system. Anesthetics prevent the mother from using her body as effectively as she might to help push the baby out. If administered early in labor, anesthetics may inhibit uterine contractions, slow cervical dilation, and prolong labor. They also numb a woman to one of the most fundamental experiences of her life.

Research shows that the negative effects of epidural anesthesia, such as the increased likelihood of the use of instruments during delivery, and longer second stage of labor, can be reduced by using low dosages and techniques that allow the woman to move around (COMET, 2001).

Perhaps the best resolution of this controversy is to say that a pregnant woman should participate in prepared childbirth classes and should use

Primipara: A woman having her first baby.

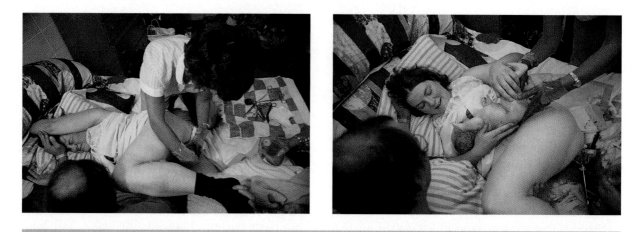

Figure 6.11   A home birth.

those techniques during labor. If, when she is in labor, she discovers that she cannot control the pain and wants an anesthetic, she should feel free to request it and to do so without guilt; the anesthetic should then be administered with great caution.

Home Birth versus Hospital Birth

Home birth has become increasingly popular. Either a physician or a nurse midwife may assist in a home birth. Advocates of home birth argue that the atmosphere in a hospital—with its forbidding machines, rules and regulations, and general lack of comfort and "homeyness"—is stressful to the woman and detracts from what should be a joyous, natural human experience (see Figure 6.11). Furthermore, hospitals are meant to deal with illness, and the delivery of a baby should not be viewed as an illness; hospital births encourage the use of procedures such as forceps deliveries and episiotomies that are themselves dangerous. Birth at home is likely to be more relaxed and less stressful; friends and other children are allowed to be present. Some studies indicate that, for uncomplicated pregnancies, home delivery is as safe as hospital delivery (Hahn & Paige, 1980; for a detailed discussion, see Hoff & Schneiderman, 1985).

On the other side of the argument, if unforeseen emergency medical procedures are necessary, home birth may be downright dangerous for the mother, the baby, or both. Furthermore, hospital practices in labor and delivery have changed radically, particularly with the increased popularity of the Lamaze method; thus hospitals are not the forbidding, alien environments they once were. Most hospitals, for example, allow fathers to be present

for the entire labor and delivery, and many allow the father to be present in the operating room during cesarean deliveries. Many hospitals have created birthing centers that contain a set of homelike rooms, with comfortable beds and armchairs, that permit labor and delivery to occur in a relaxed atmosphere, while being only a minute away from emergency equipment if it is required.

For any home birth, careful medical screening is essential. Only women with normal pregnancies and anticipated normal deliveries should attempt a home birth. A qualified physician or nurse midwife must be part of the planning. Finally, there must be access to a hospital in case an emergency arises.

After the Baby Is Born: The Postpartum Period

Physical Changes

With the birth of the baby, the woman's body undergoes a drastic physiological change. During pregnancy the placenta produces high levels of both estrogen and progesterone. When the placenta is expelled, the levels of these hormones drop sharply, and thus the postpartum period is characterized by low levels of both estrogen and progesterone. The levels of these hormones gradually return to normal over a period of a few weeks to a few months. Other endocrine changes include an increase in hormones associated with breast-feeding.

In addition, the body undergoes considerable stress during labor and delivery, and the woman may feel exhausted. Discomfort from an episiotomy is common in the first postpartum weeks.

Psychological Changes

For a day or two after parturition, the woman typically remains in the hospital, although many women leave the hospital less than 24 hours after delivery. For the first two days, women often feel elated; the long pregnancy is over, they have been successful competitors in a demanding athletic event and are pleased with their efforts, and the baby is finally there, to be cuddled and loved.

Following childbirth, many women experience some degree of depression. The depressed mood and other experiences range from mild to severe; the medical literature identifies three types. In the mildest, *postpartum blues,* or "baby blues," women experience mood swings, with periods of feeling depressed, being irritable, and crying alternating with positive moods. The symptoms usually begin a few days after delivery, are most intense at one-week postpartum, and lessen or disappear by two weeks postpartum. Between 50 and 80 percent of women experience these mild baby blues (Kennedy & Suttenfield, 2001). **Postpartum depression** is more severe, characterized by depressed mood, insomnia, tearfulness, feelings of inadequacy, and fatigue. It usually begins two to three weeks postpartum but may occur any time after delivery. Between 8 and 15 percent of women will experience it, with symptoms lasting six to eight weeks (Morris-Rush & Bernstein, 2002; O'Hara & Swain, 1996). The most severe disturbance is *postpartum psychosis,* for which early symptoms include restlessness, irritability, and sleep disturbance; later ones include disorganized behavior, mood swings, delusions, and hallucinations. Its onset can be dramatic, within 72 hours of delivery, or four to six weeks postpartum. It is very rare, affecting only 1 or 2 women out of 1,000 (Kennedy & Suttenfield, 2001).

It appears that many factors contribute to this depression. Being in a hospital in and of itself is stressful, as noted earlier. Once the woman returns home, another set of stresses faces her. She has probably not yet returned to her normal level of energy, yet she must perform the exhausting task of caring for a newborn infant. For the first several weeks or months she may not get enough sleep, rising several times during the night to tend to a baby that is crying because it is hungry or sick, and she may become exhausted. Clearly she needs help and support from her partner and friends at this time. Some stresses vary depending on whether this is a first child or a later one. The first child is stressful because of the woman's inexperience; while she is in the hospital, she may become anxious, wondering whether she will be capable of caring for the infant when she returns home. In the case of later-born children, and some firstborns, the mother may become depressed because she did not really want the baby.

Physical stresses are also present during the postpartum period; hormone levels have declined sharply, and the body has been under stress. Thus it appears that postpartum depression is caused by a combination of physical and social factors.

Risk factors for more severe depression include personal or family history of psychiatric disorder, unwanted pregnancy, serious complications following birth, and lack of social support (Morris-Rush & Bernstein, 2002).

Postpartum depression and psychosis should be treated; depression improves in response to antidepressant drugs, individual psychotherapy, partner and peer support, and nurse home visits (Gjerdingen, 2003; Mehta & Sheth, 2006). A review of the research using randomized controlled trials to assess psychological interventions reported that the most promising is intensive professional postpartum support (Dennis, 2005).

Fathers, too, sometimes experience depression after the birth of a baby. In one study, 89 percent of the mothers and 62 percent of the fathers had experienced the blues during the 3 months after the birth (Zaslow et al., 1985). A study in Great Britain assessed depression in both mothers and fathers 8 weeks after delivery. Ten percent of the mothers and 4 percent of the fathers attained high scores. Paternal depression at 8 weeks was related to adverse emotional and behavioral outcomes for children at 3.5 years of age, controlling for mother's depression score (Ramchandani et al., 2005).

Attachment to the Baby

While much of the traditional psychological research has focused on the baby's developing attachment to the mother, more recent interest has been about the development of the mother's attachment (bond) to the infant. Research clearly shows that this process begins even before the baby is born. Two studies of women expecting their first child found that feelings of nurturance grew during pregnancy and increased further at birth (Fleming et al., 1997). In this sense,

Postpartum depression: Mild to moderate depression in women following the birth of a baby.

Table 6.2   Sexual Behaviors within the Previous Month, Reported by Mothers during Pregnancy and the Year Postpartum

Behavior	Pregnancy 2nd Trimester	Postpartum 1 month	Postpartum 4 months	Postpartum 12 months
Intercourse	89%	17%	89%	92%
Mean frequency of intercourse/month	4.97	0.42	5.27	5.1
Fellatio	43%	34%	48%	47%
Cunnilingus	30%	8%	44%	49%
Satisfaction with sexual relationship*	3.76	3.31	3.36	3.53

*Satisfaction with the relationship was rated on a scale from 1 (very dissatisfied) to 5 (very satisfied).

Source: Hyde et al., 1996, pp. 143–151.

pregnancy is, in part, a psychological preparation for motherhood.

In the 1970s, pediatricians Marshall Klaus and John Kennell popularized the idea that there is a kind of "critical period" or "sensitive period" in the minutes and hours immediately after birth, during which the mother and infant should bond to each other (Klaus & Kennell, 1976). Scientists later concluded that there is little or no evidence for the sensitive-period-for-bonding hypothesis (e.g., Goldberg, 1983; Lamb, 1982; Lamb & Hwang, 1982; Myers, 1984). That outcome is fortunate. Otherwise, mothers who give birth by cesarean section (and may therefore be asleep under a general anesthetic for an hour or more after the birth) and adoptive parents would have to be presumed to have inadequate bonds with their children. We know that, in both cases, strong bonds of love form between parents and children despite the lack of immediate contact following birth.

Sex during Postpartum

The birth of a child has a substantial effect on a couple's sexual relationship. Following the birth, the mother is at some risk of infection or hemorrhage (Cunningham et al., 1993), so the couple should wait at least two weeks before resuming intercourse. When coitus is resumed, it may be uncomfortable or even painful for the woman. If she had an episiotomy, she may experience vaginal discomfort; if she had a cesarean birth, she may experience abdominal discomfort. Fatigue of both the woman and her partner also may influence when they resume sexual activity.

A longitudinal study of the adjustment of couples to the birth of a child collected data from 570 women (and 550 partners) four times: during the second trimester of pregnancy, and at one, four, and twelve months postpartum (Hyde et al., 1996). Data on the sexual relationship are displayed in Table 6.2. In the month following birth, only 17 percent resumed intercourse; by the fourth month, nine out of ten couples had, the same percentage as reported intercourse during the second trimester. Reports of cunnilingus showed a similar pattern, while reports of fellatio did not indicate a marked decline. Note that although sexual behavior was much less frequent in the month following birth, satisfaction with the sexual relationship remained high. A major influence on when the couple resumed intercourse was whether the mother was breast-feeding. At both one month and four months after birth, breast-feeding women reported significantly less sexual activity and lower sexual satisfaction. One reason is that lactation suppresses estrogen production, which in turn results in decreased vaginal lubrication; this makes intercourse uncomfortable. This problem can be resolved by the use of vaginal lubricants.

Breast-Feeding

Biological Mechanisms

Two hormones, both secreted by the pituitary, are involved in lactation (milk production). One, *prolactin*, stimulates the breasts to produce milk. Prolactin is produced fairly constantly for whatever length of time the woman breast-feeds. The other hormone, *oxytocin*, stimulates the breasts to eject milk. Oxytocin is produced reflexively by the pituitary in response to the infant's sucking of the breast. Thus sucking stimulates nerve cells in the nipple; this nerve signal is transmitted to the brain, which then relays the message to the pituitary, which sends out the messenger oxytocin, which stimulates the breasts to eject milk. Interestingly, research with animals indicates that oxytocin stimulates maternal behavior (Jenkins & Nussey, 1991).

Actual milk is not produced for several days after delivery. For the first few days, the breast secretes colostrum, discussed earlier, which is high in protein and gives the baby a temporary immunity to infectious diseases. Two or three days after delivery, true lactation begins; this may be accompanied by discomfort for a day or so because the breasts are swollen and congested.

It is also important to note that, much as in pregnancy, substances ingested by the mother may be transmitted through the milk to the infant. The nursing mother thus needs to be cautious about using alcohol and other substances.

Physical and Mental Health

The National Institutes of Health strongly encourages mothers to breast-feed, because breast milk is the ideal food for a baby and has even been termed the "ultimate health food." It provides the baby with the right mixture of nutrients, it contains antibodies that protect the infant from some diseases, it is free from bacteria, and it is always the right temperature. Breast-feeding is associated with a reduced risk of obesity at ages 5 and 6 (von Kries et al., 1999). Thus there is little question that it is superior to cow's milk and commercial formulas. The American Academy of Pediatrics (1997) agrees. The Academy's Policy Statement on breast-feeding concludes that "breast-feeding ensures the best possible health as well as the best developmental and psychosocial outcomes for the infant" (see Figure 6.12).

The percentage of infants who were breast-fed has been rising since the late 1980s. In 2004, 71 percent of white babies and 50 percent of Black babies were breast-fed initially. Among those, 54 percent of white mothers and 43 percent of Black mothers continued breast-feeding until at least six months. Within each race, the percent of infants breast-fed was 23 to 26 percent higher in

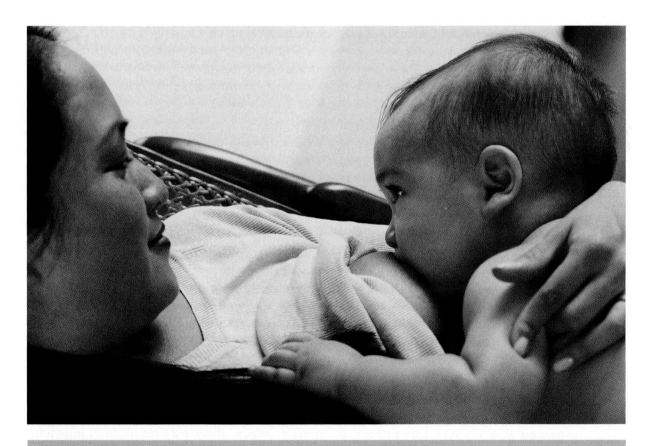

Figure 6.12   Breast-feeding.

the highest income group (*Morbidity and Mortality Weekly Report*, 2006). A systematic review of programs designed to promote breast-feeding concludes that educational sessions that review benefits, lactation, common problems and solutions, and provide skills training as well as in-person or telephone support programs improve rates of the initiation and maintenance of breast-feeding at six months (Guise et al., 2003). Programs that involve only giving out materials at the time the new mother leaves the hospital may actually reduce the likelihood that she will breast-feed. Direct encouragement by a physician or nurse is associated with a much greater likelihood of breast-feeding; provider encouragement was especially significant for young African American single mothers (Lu et al., 2001).

From the mother's point of view, breast-feeding has several advantages. These include a quicker shrinking of the uterus to its normal size and a faster loss of the weight gained during pregnancy. Breast-feeding reduces the likelihood of pregnancy by inhibiting ovulation. Full breast-feeding, short intervals between feedings, night feeds, and the absence of supplemental feeding are all associated with greater delay in ovulation (Hatcher et al., 2004). However, it is important to note that a woman can become pregnant again before she has a period; recall from Chapter 5 that ovulation precedes menstruation. Research indicates that breast-feeding reduces negative moods, and breast-feeding mothers report having less perceived stress (Mezzacappa & Katkin, 2002). Breast-feeding is also associated with reduced risk of breast cancer; the relative risk decreases by 4.3 percent for every 12 months of breast-feeding (Collaborative Group, 2002).

Some women report sexual arousal during breast-feeding, and a few even report having orgasms. Unfortunately, this sometimes produces anxiety in the mother, leading her to discontinue breast-feeding. However, there is nothing "wrong" with this arousal, which appears to stem from activation of hormonal mechanisms. Clearly, from an adaptive point of view, if breast-feeding is important to the infant's survival, it would be wise for nature to design the process so that it is rewarding to the mother.

The La Leche League is devoted to encouraging women to breast-feed their babies and has helped spread information on breast-feeding. The organization tends to be a bit militant in its advocacy of breast-feeding, however. A few women are physically unable to breast-feed, while some others feel psychologically uncomfortable with the idea. And breast-feeding can be very inconvenient for the woman who works outside the home.

Problem Pregnancies

Ectopic Pregnancy

An **ectopic pregnancy** (misplaced pregnancy) occurs when the fertilized egg implants somewhere other than the uterus. Most commonly, ectopic pregnancies occur when the egg implants in the fallopian tube (tubal pregnancy; Schenker & Evron, 1983). In rare cases, implantation may also occur in the abdominal cavity, the ovary, or the cervix.

A tubal pregnancy may occur if, for one reason or another, the egg is prevented from moving down the tube to the uterus, as when the tubes are obstructed as a result of a sexually transmitted infection. Early in a tubal pregnancy, the fertilized egg implants in the tube and begins development, forming a placenta and producing the normal hormones of pregnancy. The woman may experience the early symptoms of pregnancy, such as nausea and amenorrhea, and think she is pregnant; or she may experience some bleeding, which she mistakes for a period, and think that she is not pregnant. It is therefore quite difficult to diagnose a tubal pregnancy early.

A tubal pregnancy may end in one of two ways. The embryo may spontaneously abort and be released into the abdominal cavity, or the embryo and placenta may continue to expand, stretching the tube until it ruptures. Symptoms of a rupture include sharp abdominal pain or cramping, dull abdominal pain and possibly pain in the shoulder, and vaginal bleeding. Meanwhile, hemorrhaging is occurring, and the woman may go into shock and, possibly, die. It is extremely important for a woman displaying these symptoms to see a doctor quickly.

The rate of ectopic pregnancy increased 600 percent in the United States from 1980 to 2004, to a rate of approximately 2 percent of all pregnancies (Dialani & Levine, 2004). Part of the increase is due to improved diagnostic techniques, but most of the increase is real. Similar increases have been observed in a number of western European nations. It is thought that these changes are due to (1) increased rates of sexually transmitted infections (STIs), some of which lead to blocking of the fallopian tubes; and (2) increased use of contraceptives such as the IUD and progestin-only methods

Ectopic pregnancy: A pregnancy in which the fertilized egg implants somewhere other than the uterus.

that prevent implantation in the uterus but do not necessarily prevent conception. A study of pregnant women in France found that a history of STIs and heavy smoking (more than 20 cigarettes per day) was associated with ectopic pregnancy (Bouyer et al., 2003).

Pseudocyesis (False Pregnancy)

In **pseudocyesis,** or *false pregnancy*, the woman believes that she is pregnant and shows the signs and symptoms of pregnancy without really being pregnant. She may stop menstruating and may have morning sickness. She may begin gaining weight, and her abdomen may bulge. The condition may persist for several months before it goes away, either spontaneously or as a result of psychotherapy. In rare cases it persists until the woman goes into labor and delivers nothing but air and fluid.

Pregnancy-Induced Hypertension

Pregnancy may cause a woman's blood pressure to rise to an abnormal level. *Pregnancy-induced hypertension* includes three increasingly serious conditions: (1) hypertension, (2) preeclampsia, and (3) eclampsia. Hypertension refers to elevated blood pressure alone. **Preeclampsia** refers to elevated blood pressure accompanied by generalized edema (fluid retention and swelling) and proteinuria (protein in the urine). The combination of hypertension and proteinuria is associated with an increased risk of fetal death. In severe preeclampsia the earlier symptoms persist and the woman may also experience vision problems, abdominal pain, and severe headaches. In *eclampsia*, the woman has convulsions, may go into a coma, and may die (Cunningham et al., 1993).

Preeclampsia may reflect the "silent struggle" between mother and fetus for resources. It is hypothesized that the fetus, perhaps due to insufficient nutrition, releases a protein that increases the mother's blood pressure and, therefore, the flow of nutrients to the placenta. Indeed, research finds elevated levels of the protein sFlt1 associated with preeclampsia (Widmer et al., 2007).

Preeclampsia usually does not appear until after week 20 of pregnancy. It is more likely to occur in women who have not completed a pregnancy before. It is especially common among teenagers. Latina and Black women are much more likely than non-Hispanic white women to experience preeclampsia. The risk of preeclampsia rises steadily as prepregnancy *body mass index* increases. For overweight women, a reduction in prepregnancy weight may reduce their risk

(Bodnar et al., 2004). The possibility of preeclampsia emphasizes the need for proper medical care before and during pregnancy, especially for teenage and minority women. Hypertension and preeclampsia can be managed well during their early stages. Most maternal deaths occur among women who do not receive prenatal medical care.

Viral Illness during Pregnancy

Certain viruses may cross the placental barrier from the woman to the fetus and cause considerable harm, particularly if the illness occurs during the first trimester of pregnancy. The best-known example is rubella, or German measles. If a woman gets German measles during the first month of pregnancy, there is a 50 percent chance that the infant will be born deaf or mentally deficient or with cataracts or congenital heart defects. The risk declines after the first month, so that by the third month of pregnancy the chance of abnormalities is only about 10 percent. While most women have an immunity to rubella because they had it when they were children, a woman who suspects that she is not immune can receive a vaccination that will give her immunity; she should do this well before she becomes pregnant.

Herpes simplex is also *teratogenic*, that is, capable of producing defects in the fetus. Symptoms of herpes simplex are usually mild: cold sores or fever blisters. Genital herpes (see Chapter 18) is a form of herpes simplex in which sores may appear in the genital region. Usually the infant contracts the disease by direct contact with the sore; delivery by cesarean section can prevent this. Women with herpes genitalis also have a high risk of aborting spontaneously.

Birth Defects

As has been noted, a number of factors, such as substances taken during pregnancy and illness during pregnancy, may cause defects in the fetus. Other causes include genetic defects (e.g., phenylketonuria, PKU, which causes retardation) and chromosomal defects (e.g., Down syndrome, which causes retardation).

Of all babies born in the United States, 2 to 3 percent have a significant birth defect. About one-fourth of miscarried fetuses are malformed. The cause of more than half of these defects is unknown (O'Shea, 1995).

In most cases, families have simply had to learn, as best they could, to live with a child who had a birth defect. Now, however, amniocentesis, chorionic villus sampling

> **Pseudocyesis:** False pregnancy, in which the woman displays the signs of pregnancy but is not actually pregnant.
> **Preeclampsia:** A serious disease of pregnancy, marked by high blood pressure, severe edema, and proteinuria.

(explained below), and genetic counseling are available to help prevent some of the sorrow, provided that abortion is ethically acceptable to the parents.

Amniocentesis involves inserting a fine tube through the pregnant woman's abdomen and removing some amniotic fluid, including cells sloughed off by the fetus, for analysis. The technique is capable of providing an early diagnosis of most chromosomal abnormalities, some genetically produced biochemical disorders, and sex-linked diseases carried by females but affecting males (hemophilia and muscular dystrophy), although it cannot detect all defects. If a defect is discovered, the woman may then decide to terminate the pregnancy with an abortion.

Amniocentesis should be performed between weeks 13 and 16 of pregnancy. This timing is important for two reasons. First, if a defect is discovered and an abortion is to be performed, it should be done as early as possible (see Chapter 7). Second, there is a 1 percent chance that the amniocentesis itself will cause the woman to lose her baby, and the risk becomes greater as the pregnancy progresses.

Because amniocentesis itself involves some risk, it is generally thought (although the matter is controversial) that it should be performed only on women who have a high risk of bearing a child with a birth defect. A woman is in this category if (1) she has already had one child with a genetic defect; (2) she believes that she is a carrier of a genetic defect, which can usually be established through genetic counseling; and (3) she is over 35, in which case she has a greatly increased chance of bearing a child with a chromosomal abnormality.

Chorionic villus sampling (CVS) may eventually replace amniocentesis for prenatal diagnosis of genetic defects (Doran, 1990; Kolker, 1989). A major problem with amniocentesis is that it cannot be done until the second trimester of pregnancy; if genetic defects are discovered, there may have to be a late abortion. Chorionic villus sampling, in contrast, can be done in the first trimester of pregnancy, usually around 9 to 11 weeks postconception. Chorionic villus sampling can be performed in one of two ways: transcervically, in which a catheter is inserted into the uterus through the cervix as shown in Figure 6.13, and transabdominally, in which a needle (guided by ultrasound) is inserted through the abdomen. In either case a sample of cells is

Amniocentesis (am-nee-oh-sen-TEE-sus): A test done to determine whether a fetus has birth defects; done by inserting a fine tube into the woman's abdomen in order to obtain a sample of amniotic fluid.
Chorionic villus sampling (CVS): A technique for prenatal diagnosis of birth defects, involving taking a sample of cells from the chorionic villus and analyzing them.

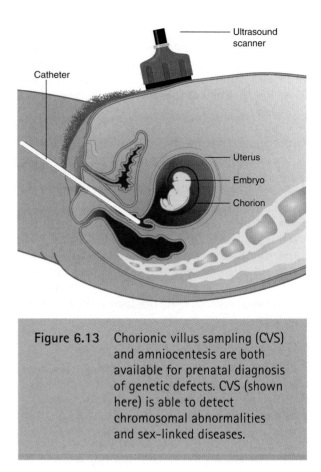

Figure 6.13 Chorionic villus sampling (CVS) and amniocentesis are both available for prenatal diagnosis of genetic defects. CVS (shown here) is able to detect chromosomal abnormalities and sex-linked diseases.

taken from the chorionic villi (the chorion is the outermost membrane surrounding the fetus, the amnion, and the amniotic fluid), and these cells are analyzed for evidence of genetic defects. Studies indicate that CVS is as accurate as amniocentesis. Like amniocentesis, it carries with it a slight risk of fetal loss (due, for example, to miscarriage). For amniocentesis, the fetal loss rate is around 1 percent; for CVS, it is about 2 percent (Wass et al., 1991).

Amniocentesis and CVS (when followed by abortion) raise a number of serious ethical questions, some of which are discussed in later chapters. However, it is important to note here the extreme psychological stress to which families of children with birth defects are often subjected.

Rh Incompatibility

The Rh factor is a substance in the blood; if it is present, the person is said to be Rh positive (Rh+); if it is absent, the person is said to be Rh negative (Rh−). The Rh factor is genetically transmitted, with Rh+ being dominant over Rh−.

The presence or absence of the Rh factor does not constitute a health problem except when an Rh− person receives a blood transfusion or when an Rh− woman is pregnant with an Rh+ fetus (which can happen only if the father is Rh+). A blood test is done routinely early in pregnancy to determine whether a woman is Rh−. Fortunately, about 85 percent of whites and 93 percent of Blacks are Rh+; thus the problems associated with being Rh− are not very common.

If some Rh+ blood gets into Rh− blood, the Rh− blood forms antibodies as a reaction against the Rh factor in the invading blood. Typically, as has been noted, there is little interchange between the woman's blood and the fetus's blood; the placenta keeps them separate. However, during parturition there can be considerable mixing of the two. Thus during birth, the blood of an Rh+ baby causes the formation of antibodies in an Rh− woman's blood. During the next pregnancy, some of the woman's blood enters the fetus and the antibodies attack the fetus's red cells. The baby may be stillborn, severely anemic, or retarded. Thus there is little risk for an Rh− woman with the first pregnancy because antibodies have not yet formed; however, later pregnancies can be extremely dangerous.

Fortunately, techniques for dealing with this situation have been developed. An injection of a substance called *Rhogam* prevents the woman's blood from producing antibodies. If necessary the fetus or newborn infant may get a transfusion.

Miscarriage (Spontaneous Abortion)

Miscarriage, or *spontaneous abortion,* occurs when a pregnancy terminates through natural causes, before the conceptus is viable (capable of surviving on its own). It is not to be confused with *induced abortion,* in which a pregnancy is terminated by mechanical or medicinal means (what is commonly called *abortion*—see Chapter 7), or with *prematurity,* in which the pregnancy terminates early, but after the infant is viable.

It is estimated that 20 percent of all pregnancies end in spontaneous abortion (Frishman, 1995). This is probably an underestimate, since very early spontaneous abortions may not be detected. The woman may not know that she is pregnant and may mistake the products of the miscarriage for a menstrual period. Thus the true incidence may be closer to 40 percent (Cunningham et al., 1993). Most spontaneous abortions—80 percent—occur during the first trimester of pregnancy.

Most spontaneous abortions occur because the conceptus is defective. Studies of spontaneously aborted fetuses indicate that 61 percent showed abnormalities that were incompatible with life; for example, many had gross chromosomal abnormalities (Ljunger et al., 2005). Thus, contrary to popular belief, psychological and physical traumas are not common causes of miscarriage. In fact, spontaneous abortions seem to be functional in that they naturally eliminate many defective fetuses.

Preterm Birth

A major complication during the third trimester of pregnancy is premature labor and delivery of the fetus. When delivery occurs prior to 37 weeks gestation, it is considered *preterm.* Because the date of conception cannot always be accurately determined, preterm birth (prematurity) may be defined in terms of the birth weight of the infant; an infant weighing less than 2,500 grams ($5\frac{1}{2}$ pounds) is considered to be in the low-birth-weight category. However, this is inappropriate. The principal concern should be the functional development of the infant rather than his or her weight. The National Center for Health Statistics (Martin et al., 2006) reports that 12.5 percent of all births in the United States in 2004 were preterm. The rate was 11.5 for white infants, 11.0 for Hispanic infants, and 17.9 for Black infants. The overall rate has increased 18 percent since 1990.

Preterm birth is a cause for concern because the premature infant is much less likely to survive than the full-term infant. It is estimated that more than half of the deaths of newborn babies in the United States are due to preterm birth. Preterm infants are particularly susceptible to respiratory infections and must receive expert care. Advances in medical techniques have considerably improved survival rates for preterm infants. Currently, 99 percent of infants weighing 2,500 grams at birth survive, as do 64 percent of those weighing 1,000 grams (Cunningham et al., 1993). However, prematurity may cause damage to an infant who survives. A longitudinal study found that low-birth-weight infants scored significantly lower on math and reading tests at age 6 to 14 (Boardman et al., nd).

Maternal factors such as poor health, poor nutrition, heavy smoking, cocaine use, and genital or systemic infections are associated with prematurity.[4] Pregnancy-induced hypertension can also lead to preterm birth. Young teenage mothers, whose bodies are not yet ready to bear children, are also very susceptible to premature labor and delivery. The more risks a pregnant woman is exposed to, the greater the risk of prematurity (Dew et al., 2007).

---

[4]An analysis of 3,130 births found that extreme prematurity, birth at less than 32 weeks gestation, was associated with alcohol use (proportion of drinking days per week) and cocaine use (Solcol et al., 2007).

Miscarriage: The termination of a pregnancy before the fetus is viable, as a result of natural causes (not medical intervention).

Infertility

Infertility refers to a woman's inability to conceive and give birth to a living child, or a man's inability to impregnate a woman. It is estimated that 14 percent of all couples in the United States have an infertility problem at some time (Sciarra, 1991). When fertile couples are purposely attempting to conceive a child, about 20 percent succeed within the first menstrual cycle, and about 70 percent succeed within the first six cycles (Hatcher et al., 2004). A couple is considered infertile if they have not conceived after one year of frequent, unprotected intercourse, or after six months if the woman is over 35. The term *sterile* refers to an individual who has an absolute factor preventing conception.

Causes of Infertility

Among couples with an identifiable cause, in about 40 percent, male factors are responsible; female factors are responsible in an additional 40 percent. In the remaining 20 percent, both have problems (see Hatcher et al., 2004).

Causes in the Female. The most common cause of infertility in women is pelvic inflammatory disease (PID) caused by a sexually transmitted infection, especially gonorrhea or chlamydia. Other causes include failure to ovulate, blockage of the fallopian tubes, and "hostile mucus," meaning cervical mucus that blocks the passage of sperm. Less common causes include poor nutrition, eating disorders, exposure to toxic chemicals such as lead or pesticides, smoking, and use of alcohol, narcotics, or barbiturates. Age may also be a factor; fertility declines in women after 35 years of age, the decline being especially sharp after age 40.

Causes in the Male. The most common cause of infertility in men is infections in the reproductive system caused by sexually transmitted diseases. Another cause is low sperm count (often due to varicoceles—varicose veins in the testes). Couples concerned about low sperm count may decide to abstain from vaginal intercourse in the hope of increasing the count, but research indicates this does not work. In men with low sperm counts, the sperm become less mobile and begin to show signs of becoming stale after only 24 hours of abstinence (Levitas, 2003). Another cause is low motility of the sperm, which means the sperm are not good swimmers. Less common causes include exposure to toxic agents such as lead, smoking, alcohol and marijuana use, and use of some prescription drugs (Hatcher et al., 1994). Recent research has shown that exposure to environmental estrogens causes sperm to mature too fast, reducing their fertilizing capacity (Adeoya-Osiguwa et al., 2003). Exposure to environmental estrogens comes through contact with substances such as beer and pesticides.

Research also reports that the quality of male semen declines with age. As men age, the volume of the semen and the number and motility of the sperm decline (Eskenazi et al., 2003). Also, the rate of sperm with various genomic abnormalities increases with age (Wyrobek et al., 2006). Finally, women whose partners are over 40 are more likely to experience a spontaneous abortion (Kleinhaus et al., 2006).

Combined Factors. In some situations a combination of factors in both the man and the woman causes the infertility. One such factor is an immunologic response. The woman may have an allergic reaction to the man's sperm, causing her to produce antibodies that destroy or damage the sperm. Or her immune system may react to the fetus or placenta. According to one controversial theory, an immune reaction may create the high blood pressure that is associated with preeclampsia (Fox, 2002). Immune reactions occur in response to novel cells entering the body; if the body has been exposed to the cells frequently in the past, the reaction is less likely. Frequent prior exposure of a woman to a specific man's semen would reduce the likelihood of rejecting his sperm. So frequent vaginal intercourse (Robertson & Sharkey, 2001) or oral sex in which the woman swallows the ejaculate (Koelman et al., 2000) prior to the attempt to get pregnant may increase the chances of a successful pregnancy.

Sperm have a chemical sensor that causes them to swim toward the egg, attracted by a chemical on the surface of the egg (Spehr et al., 2003). Researchers have already identified one chemical that disrupts this process by shutting down the receptor. This chemical, or chemicals, that influence the surface of the egg can cause infertility. Finally, a couple may also simply lack knowledge; for instance, they may not know how to time intercourse correctly so that conception may take place.

Psychological Aspects of Infertility

It is important to recognize the psychological stress to which an infertile couple may be subjected (Liebmann-Smith, 1987). Because the male role is defined partly in our society by the ability to father children, the man may feel that his masculinity or

Infertility: A woman's inability to conceive and give birth to a living child, or a man's inability to impregnate a woman.

virility is in question. Similarly, the female role is defined largely by the ability to bear children and be a mother, so the woman may feel inadequate.[5] Historically, in most cultures fertility has been encouraged and, indeed, demanded; hence, pressures on infertile couples may be high, leading to more psychological stress. As emphasis on population control increases in our society, and as childlessness[6] becomes an acceptable and more recognized option, the stress on infertile couples may lessen.

Research indicates that among couples entering infertility treatment programs, the women perceive themselves as experiencing greater emotional and social stress than do the men (unless the man is diagnosed as responsible for the infertility) (Leiblum, 1993). At the same time, women expect to receive more social support in coping with these stresses. Infertility does not significantly reduce marital satisfaction, but it does cause conflict (Abbey et al., 1992). It does affect the couple's sexual relationship; it reduces spontaneity (especially for couples in treatment programs that include scheduled intercourse) and is associated with lower sexual satisfaction (Zoldbrod, 1993). Couples whose first attempt at treatment is unsuccessful show elevated levels of anxiety and depression (Schmidt, 2006).

Treatment of Infertility

There are physicians and clinics that specialize in the evaluation and treatment of infertility. An infertility evaluation should include an assessment of the couple's knowledge of sexual behavior and conception, and lifestyle factors such as regular drug use. Infertility caused by such factors can be easily treated.

If the infertility problem stems from the woman's failure to ovulate, the treatment may involve the so-called fertility drugs. The drug of first choice is clomiphene (Clomid). It stimulates the pituitary to produce LH and FSH, thus inducing ovulation. The treatment produces a pregnancy in about half the women who are given it. Multiple births occur about 8 percent of the time with Clomid, compared with 1.2 percent with natural pregnancies. If treatment with Clomid is not successful,

a second possibility is injections with HMG (human menopausal gonadotropin).

If the infertility is caused by blocked fallopian tubes, delicate microsurgery can sometimes be effective in removing the blockage.

If the infertility is caused by varicoceles in the testes, the condition can usually be treated successfully by a surgical procedure known as varicocelectomy.

Finally, a number of new reproductive technologies, such as in vitro fertilization, are now available for those with fertility problems, as discussed in the next section.

A Canadian study is helpful in putting issues of the treatment of infertility into perspective. Among infertile couples seeking treatment, 65 percent subsequently achieved a pregnancy with *no treatment* (Rousseau et al., 1983). For some couples, conception just takes a bit longer. Thus the risks associated with treatments need to be weighed against the possibility that a pregnancy can be achieved without treatment.

New Reproductive Technologies

Reproductive technologies developed in the last three decades offer many ways to conceive and birth babies besides sexual intercourse and pregnancy.

Artificial Insemination

Artificial insemination involves artificially placing semen in the vagina to produce a pregnancy; thus it is a means of accomplishing reproduction without having sexual intercourse. Artificial insemination in animals was first done in 1776. In 1949, when British scientists successfully froze sperm without any apparent damage to them, a new era of reproductive technology for animals began. Today cattle are routinely bred by artificial insemination.

In humans there are two kinds of artificial insemination: artificial insemination by the husband (AIH) and artificial insemination by a donor (AID, not to be confused with the disease AIDS). AIH can be used when the husband has a low sperm count. Several samples of his semen are collected and pooled to make one sample with a higher count. This sample is then placed in the woman's vagina at the time of ovulation. AID is used when the husband is sterile. A donor provides

> **Artificial insemination:** Procedure in which sperm are placed into the vagina by means other than sexual intercourse.

---

[5]A survey of infertile couples found that the stress of infertility was associated with reduced self-esteem in both husband and wife (Abbey et al., 1992).

[6]Semantics can make a big difference here. Many couples who choose not to have children prefer to call themselves *child-free* rather than *childless*.

Figure 6.14 "I already know about the birds and the bees, Mom; I want to know about artificial insemination, invitro fertilization and surrogate mothering!"

Source: Renault/*Sacramento Bee*, CA/Rothco.

semen to impregnate the wife. Estimates are that between 10,000 and 20,000 babies are born every year in the United States as a result of AID.

Sperm Banks

Because it is now possible to freeze sperm, it is possible to store it, which is just what some people are doing: using frozen human *sperm banks*. The sperm banks open up many new possibilities for various life choices. For example, suppose that a couple decide, after having had two children, that they want a permanent method of contraception. The husband then has a vasectomy. Two years after he has the vasectomy, however, one of their children dies, and they very much want to have another baby. If the man has stored semen in a sperm bank, they can.

Young men can use sperm banks to store sperm before they undergo radiation therapy for cancer. They can later father children without fearing that they will transmit damaged chromosomes (as a result of the radiation) to their offspring.

Embryo transfer: A procedure in which an embryo is transferred from the uterus of one woman into the uterus of another.

In vitro fertilization (IVF): A procedure in which an egg is fertilized by sperm in a laboratory dish.

Since the mid-1990s, sperm banks have gone online, making their services available to millions of people around the world (Springen & Noonan, 2002). There are an estimated 110 sperm banks in the United States, and the larger ones have developed websites. These sites allow prospective parents to browse through a good deal of information about each potential donor, enabling them to select not only on the basis of height, weight, and eye and hair color but also education and family medical history. As recipients demand more information about prospective donors, it becomes harder to maintain the donor's anonymity. Some donors of eggs or sperm advertise directly on the Internet; while the cost may be lower than the costs associated with clinic services, as is often true on the Internet, there is no guarantee that the donor has given accurate information. It is estimated that some 70 percent of the money spent on sperm-bank services in 2002 ($65 million) was for purchases via the Internet.

Embryo Transfer

With **embryo transfer,** a fertilized, developing egg (embryo) is transferred from the uterus of one woman to the uterus of another woman. Dr. John Buster of UCLA perfected the technique for use with humans, and the first two births resulting from the procedure were announced in 1984 (Brotman, 1984; Associated Press, 1984).

This technique may enable a woman who can conceive but who always miscarries early in the pregnancy to transfer her embryo to another woman who serves as the *surrogate mother*—that is, the person who provides the uterus in which the fetus grows (and whom the media, somewhat callously, have called a "rent-a-womb"). The embryo transfer procedure also essentially can serve as the opposite of artificial insemination. That is, if a woman produces no viable eggs, her husband's sperm can be used to artificially inseminate another woman (who donates her egg), and the fertilized egg is then transferred from the donor to the mother.

Test-Tube Babies

It is possible for scientists to make sperm and egg unite outside the human body (in a "test tube"). The scientific term for this procedure is **in vitro fertilization,** or **IVF** (*in vitro* is Latin for "in glass"). The fertilized egg or embryo can then be implanted in the uterus of a woman and carried to term (see Figure 6.15). This technique can be of great benefit to couples who are infertile because the woman's fallopian tubes are blocked.

A milestone was reached with the birth of Louise Brown, the first test-tube baby, in England

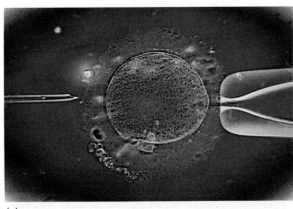

(a)

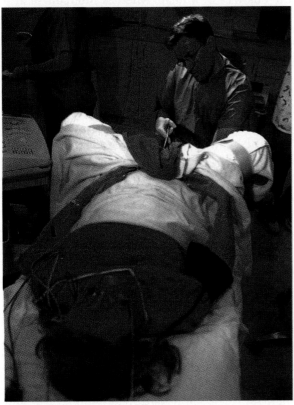

(b)

Figure 6.15   New reproductive technologies.
(*a*) With in vitro fertilization,
conception is more likely if the
egg is scratched, allowing the
sperm to enter more easily.
(*b*) Vicken Sahakian, MD, medical
director of a fertility center,
collects eggs from Deborah, 38.
She and her husband, Eric,
came in for in vitro fertilization.
Out of 13 eggs produced by her,
5 became fertilized and were
reintroduced into Deborah.

on July 25, 1978. Obstetrician Patrick Steptoe and physiologist Robert Edwards had fertilized the mother's egg with her husband's sperm in a laboratory dish and implanted the embryo in the mother's uterus. The pregnancy went smoothly, and Louise was born healthy and normal. The procedure is now performed in a number of countries, with 70 clinics in the United States alone.

According to data collected by the Centers for Disease Control and Prevention, 74 percent of the procedures performed in the United States in 2004 were IVF using freshly fertilized embryos from the patients' eggs (Wright et al., 2007). A survey of 411 infertility clinics in 2004 indicated that about 42 percent of all procedures were successful; that is, they resulted in a live birth. The procedure is expensive, around $12,400 per attempt, not counting preliminary procedures. It is estimated that the average IVF baby costs between $10,000 and $18,000 to produce.

There is evidence that babies born as a result of IVF are more likely to be low in birth weight and have congenital abnormalities. A study in Finland found a 30 percent greater risk of abnormalities in IVF babies (Klemetti et al., 2005). It is not clear whether the increased risk is due to the procedure, or to related factors—for example, mothers are typically older (Kovacs, 2002a). These adverse outcomes are more common in babies born after procedures using donor eggs (Wright et al., 2007).

It is also possible to freeze eggs that have been fertilized in vitro, resulting in frozen embryos. This procedure creates the possibility of donated embryos; the birth of a baby resulting from this procedure was first announced in 1984 in Australia. Research finds that babies born after procedures using thawed embryos were less likely to be low birth weight but more likely to be preterm (Wright et al., 2007). The legal and moral status of the frozen embryo is a difficult question, and some worry about *embryo wastage.*

GIFT

GIFT (for gamete intrafallopian transfer) is an improvement, in some cases, over IVF. Sperm and eggs (gametes) are collected and then inserted together into the fallopian tube, where natural fertilization can take place, followed by natural implantation. Less than 1 percent of the procedures performed in 2004 were of this type (Wright et al., 2007). Because the number is so small, success rates are not reported.

Yet another improvement is ZIFT (zygote intrafallopian transfer), which involves fertilizing the egg

GIFT: Gamete intrafallopian transfer, a procedure in which sperm and eggs are collected and then inserted together into the fallopian tube.

with sperm in a laboratory dish and then placing the developing fertilized egg (zygote) into the fallopian tube, again allowing natural implantation. Less than 1 percent of the procedures performed in 2004 involved this technique (Wright et al., 2007).

Assisted reproduction is more likely to be successful if the woman is younger (under 34) and if fresh embryos rather than frozen ones are used. Success rates do not vary by cause of the infertility.

Assisted reproduction is likely to result in multiple births. Of about 50,000 infants born through ART (assisted reproductive technology) in 2004, 50 percent were born in multiple-birth deliveries (Wright et al., 2007). These deliveries are associated with greater health risks for mother and infants. The multiple births result from the common practice of transferring several embryos at one time. Medical and public health authorities are increasingly concerned about the problem. One university-based infertility clinic has instituted a mandatory single-embryo transfer policy with no decline in pregnancy rates (Ryan et al., 2007).

Cloning

Cloning is the reproduction of an individual from a single cell taken from a "donor" or "parent." The technique involves replacing the nucleus of an ovum with the nucleus from a donor, thus producing an embryo that is genetically identical to the donor. Normally, of course, a child has only half its genes in common with the mother; the other half come from the father. Therefore, children are never genetically identical to either parent. But in cloning, no sperm is necessary and the result is an individual who is genetically identical to the donor.

The first successful cloning was of a mouse, in 1981. In 1997, researchers announced the birth of Dolly, a sheep cloned from a single cell of an adult ewe. In 2000, six cloned piglets were born, significant because pigs are physiologically close to humans (Prather, 2000). Cloning has great potential as a source of organs that could be transplanted to replace failing ones, or as an alternative in cases of infertility. But it has great risks as well; fewer than 3 percent of cloning efforts succeed, and those that do sometimes suffer from grave, unpredictable genetic defects (Kolata, 2001).

Gender Selection

There is much interest in techniques that will allow couples to choose whether to have a boy or a girl. Such a technology would be useful to parents who have six girls and really want a boy, or for people who would like to have two children, one of each gender. Problems might arise, though. Some scientists fear that the result of being able to choose gender would be a great imbalance in our population, with many more males than females, because many couples prefer their first child to be a boy.

There is a good deal of "conventional wisdom" about various home methods of increasing the likelihood that a fetus will be male or female. One technique is timing intercourse in relation to ovulation, based on the belief that sperm carrying a Y chromosome swim faster; thus intercourse at the time of ovulation should increase the chances of a male, whereas intercourse at a time before and remote from ovulation should favor the slow but hardy sperm carrying X chromosomes, resulting in a female. Several studies have tried to test these ideas, relying on indirect measures of time of ovulation (cervical mucus changes, BBT); they suggest that a female is more likely when intercourse coincides with ovulation. Thus conventional wisdom is wrong. Studies have also investigated the effect of douching; conventional wisdom has it that douching with vinegar will change the vaginal pH, increasing the chances of a boy. Neither of these, or other, "natural" methods will reliably affect the offspring's gender (Kovacs, 2002b).

As usual, entrepreneurs are taking advantage of people's desire to pick the baby's sex and selling kits that promise results. Some of the kits capitalize on the natural methods, providing the purchaser with thermometers, douching solutions, and other paraphernalia. At least one company is selling kits via the Internet. Again, there is no evidence that these kits will produce the expected result. *Caveat emptor* (buyer beware)!

Several scientific laboratory procedures can be used to separate sperm containing male and female chromosomes. Older techniques involved separation based on swimming speed or immunologic characteristics; these work with 70 to 80 percent accuracy. The latest sorting technique, the Micro-Sort method, uses the fluorescence-activated sorter, which can select sperm with an X chromosome with 90 percent accuracy; this technique greatly reduces sperm count and requires ART. There is little data on the long-term outcomes of using this procedure (Kovacs, 2002b).

The most reliable method of gender selection is preimplantation genetic diagnosis (PGD). This technique involves the removal of eggs from the woman and fertilizing them via IVF. After three days, a cell is taken from each embryo, and its chromosomal makeup is determined. An embryo of the preferred type would then be implanted via ART. This method is very invasive of the woman's body and very expensive. The likelihood that the implanted egg would result in the live birth of a healthy infant is the same as for other ART pregnancies. PGD is banned in Britain and Canada, and is controversial in the United States (Check, 2005).

The technologies discussed here, especially GIFT and ZIFT, require expert practitioners and appropriate facilities. Consequently, they are very expensive (Hatcher et al., 2004). As noted, their success rates are low. For these and other reasons, these procedures raise complex legal questions (discussed in Chapter 20) and ethical concerns (discussed in Chapter 19).

SUMMARY

Sperm are manufactured in the testes and ejaculated out through the vas deferens and urethra into the vagina. Then they begin their swim through the cervix and uterus and up a fallopian tube to meet the egg, which has already been released from the ovary. When the sperm and egg unite in the fallopian tube, conception occurs. The single fertilized egg cell then begins dividing as it travels down the tube, and finally it implants in the uterus. Various techniques for improving the chances of conception are available.

The placenta, which is important in transmitting substances between the woman and the fetus, develops early in pregnancy. The most remarkable development of the fetus occurs during the first trimester (first three months), when most of the major organ systems are formed and human features develop.

For the woman, early signs of pregnancy include amenorrhea, tenderness of the breasts, and nausea. The most common pregnancy tests are designed to detect hCG in the urine or blood. Physical changes during the first trimester are mainly the result of the increasing levels of estrogen and progesterone produced by the placenta. Despite cultural myths about the radiant contentment of the pregnant woman, some women do have negative feelings during the first trimester. During the second trimester the woman generally feels better, both physically and psychologically.

Despite people's concerns, sexual intercourse is generally quite safe during pregnancy. Nutrition is exceptionally important during pregnancy because the woman's body has to supply the materials to create another human being. Pregnant women must also be very careful about ingesting drugs because some can penetrate the placental barrier and enter the fetus, possibly causing damage.

Labor is typically divided into three stages. During the first stage, the cervix undergoes effacement (thinning) and dilation. During the second stage, the baby moves out through the vagina. The placenta is delivered during the third stage. Cesarean section is a surgical method of delivering a baby.

The Lamaze method of "prepared" childbirth has become very popular; it emphasizes the use of relaxation and controlled breathing to control contractions and minimize the woman's discomfort. Anesthetics may not be necessary, which seems desirable, since they are potentially dangerous.

During the postpartum period, hormone levels are very low. Postpartum depression may arise from a combination of this hormonal state and the many environmental stresses on the woman at this time.

Two hormones are involved in lactation: prolactin and oxytocin. Breast-feeding has a number of psychological as well as health advantages.

Problems of pregnancy include ectopic (misplaced) pregnancy, pseudocyesis (false pregnancy), preeclampsia and eclampsia, illness (such as German measles), a defective conceptus, Rh incompatibility, spontaneous abortion, and preterm birth.

The most common cause of infertility in men and women is sexually transmitted infections.

Assisted reproductive technologies include artificial insemination, frozen sperm banks, embryo transplants, in vitro fertilization (test-tube babies), and GIFT (gamete intrafallopian transfer), all of which are now a reality. These procedures are expensive and have low success rates. In addition, the practice of transferring multiple embryos often results in multiple births, which are riskier for both mother and infants.

QUESTIONS FOR THOUGHT, DISCUSSION, AND DEBATE

1. Taking the point of view of a pregnant woman, which would you prefer to have, a home birth or a hospital birth? Why?

2. For readers who are men, what role would you envision for yourself in parenting if you had a child? Do you feel that you are adequately prepared for that role? For readers who are women, what role would you ideally like an imaginary partner to take in the parenting of your imaginary children?

3. A close friend confides in you that she is afraid of pregnancy. She has heard that pregnant women experience unpleasant physical (aches and pains, fatigue, illness) and psychological (crying spells, depression) symptoms. She is especially concerned that pregnancy might have a bad effect on her relationship with her partner. What information would you give her about these fears?

SUGGESTIONS FOR FURTHER READING

Dorris, Michael. (1989). *The broken cord.* New York: Harper & Row. The true story of a man and the child he adopted, who turned out to have fetal alcohol syndrome and all the behavior disturbances that go with it.

Kane, Elizabeth. (1988). *Birth mother: The story of America's first legal surrogate mother.* San Diego: Harcourt Brace Jovanovich. An insightful, first-person account by the woman who was the first to have a contract to bear a child for another couple but later developed serious misgivings.

Nilsson, A. L., et al. (1986). *A child is born.* New York: Dell. Contains exceptional photographs of prenatal development.

Zoldbrod, Aline P. (1993). *Men, women and infertility: Intervention and treatment strategies.* New York: Lexington. Explores the impact of infertility on personality, the couple's relationship, and sexuality.

CHAPTER SEVEN

Contraception and Abortion

CHAPTER HIGHLIGHTS

For a short time I worked in an abortion clinic. One day I was counseling a woman who had come in for an abortion. I began to discuss the possible methods of contraception she could use in the future (she had been using rhythm), and I asked her what method she planned to use after the abortion. "Rhythm," she answered. "I used it for 11 months and it worked!"*

*Weideger (1976), p. 42.

The average student of today grew up in the pill era and takes for granted that highly effective methods of contraception are available. We tend to forget that contraception was once a hit-or-miss affair at best. Contraception is less controversial than it once was, and yet the use of contraceptives was illegal in Connecticut until 1965 (the Supreme Court decision in the case of *Griswold v. Connecticut*, 1965, is discussed in Chapter 20).

Today, individuals use contraceptives for a variety of reasons. Both babies and mothers are healthier if pregnancies are spaced three to five years apart (Setty-Venugopal & Upadhyay, 2002). Most couples want to limit the size of their family—usually to one or two children. Unmarried persons typically wish to avoid pregnancy. In some cases a couple know, through genetic counseling, that they have a high risk of bearing a child with a birth defect, and they therefore wish to prevent pregnancy. And in this era of successful career women, many women feel that it is essential to be able to control when and whether they have children.

At the level of society as a whole, there are also important reasons for encouraging the use of contraceptives. There are approximately 750,000 adolescent pregnancies annually in the United States (Guttmacher Institute, 2006), which constitute a major social problem. On the global level, overpopulation is a serious problem. In 1900 the world population was 1.6 billion—and it had taken millions of years to reach that level (Townsend, 2003). By 1950 it had increased to 2.5 billion. In 1999 world population hit 6 billion, an alarming increase, and experts estimate that it will reach 8.9 billion by 2050. With the resulting destruction of the environment and increased consumption of natural resources, grave concerns arise about the ability of the planet to sustain such a large population, even in the near future. Most experts believe that we must limit the size of the U.S. population as well as assist other countries in limiting theirs (Upadhyay & Robey, 1999). For a summary of contraceptive practices around the world, see Table 7.1.

Contraception is also economical! California instituted a program to provide contraceptives and related medical services at no cost to low-income women. An analysis of the data indicated that, in one year, 205,000 unwanted pregnancies were averted (Foster et al., 2006). The researchers estimated that those 205,000 pregnancies would have resulted in 79,000 abortions and 94,000 births (as well as many miscarriages), and 21,400 of those births would have been to adolescent mothers. The births would have cost government agencies an estimated $1.1 billion over two years, in health care, social services, and education. According to the researchers' calculations, for every $1 California spent on these contraceptive services, it saved $2.76—a great investment.

In this chapter we discuss various methods of birth control, how each works, how effective each is, what side effects it has, and its relative advantages and disadvantages. We also discuss abortion and advances in contraceptive technology.

The Pill, the Patch, and the Ring

The Combination Pill

With **combination birth control pills** (sometimes called *oral contraceptives*) such as Loestrin and Ovcon, the woman takes a pill that contains estrogen and progestin (a synthetic progesterone), both at doses higher than natural levels, for 21 days. Then she takes no pill or a placebo for 7 days, after which she repeats the cycle.

The traditional 21-on, 7-off pattern is still very common, but variations have been introduced. One is Seasonale, which provides 84 days of combined hormones and 7 days of placebo. This pattern means that the woman has a period only once in three months.

How It Works

The pill works mainly by preventing ovulation. Recall from Chapter 5 that in a natural menstrual cycle the low levels of estrogen during and just after

Combination birth control pills: Birth control pills that contain a combination of estrogen and progestin (progesterone).

Table 7.1 Contraception around the World, Reported by Currently Married Women (the great variations reflect differences among cultures in such factors as availability of medical services, people's education about contraception, and gender roles)

| Region, Country | Voluntary Sterilization | | Percentage Using Contraceptive Method | | | | | |
	Men	Women	Pill	IUD	Male Condom	Injectables*	Vaginal Methods[†] & Rhythm	All Methods
North America								
United States	11	28	27	1	20	4	4	—
Europe								
France	NA	NA	38	21	5	NA	NA	80
Netherlands	9	4	47	3	8	NA	NA	74
Africa (Sub-Saharan)								
Kenya	0	6	9	3	1	12	6	39
Asia								
Bangladesh	1	7	23	1	4	7	5	54
India	2	34	2	2	3	0	3	48
Latin America								
Colombia	1	27	12	12	6	4	7	77
Middle East and North Africa								
Egypt	0	1	10	36	1	6	1	56
Morocco	0	3	38	5	1	<1	3	58

NA: Statistics not available.

*Includes injections such as Depo-Provera.

[†]Includes diaphragm, cervical cap, and spermicides.

Sources: Piccinino & Mosher (1998); U.S. Bureau of the Census, International Data Base (2004), www.census.gov/ipd/www/idbprint.html; Zlidar et al. (2003).

the menstrual period trigger the pituitary to produce FSH, which stimulates the process of ovulation. When a woman starts taking the birth control pills, estrogen levels are high. This high level of estrogen inhibits FSH production, and the message to ovulate is never sent out. The high level of progesterone inhibits LH production, further preventing ovulation.

The progestin provides additional backup effects. It keeps the cervical mucus very thick, making it difficult for sperm to get through, and it changes the lining of the uterus in such a way that even if a fertilized egg were to arrive, implantation would be unlikely.

When the estrogen and progestin are withdrawn (after day 21 in the traditional pill), the lining of the uterus disintegrates, and withdrawal bleeding or menstruation occurs. The flow is typically reduced because the progestin has inhibited development of the endometrium.

Effectiveness

Before we discuss the effectiveness of the pill, let's define several technical terms that are used in communicating data on the effectiveness of contraceptives in general. If 100 women use a contraceptive method for one year, the number of them who become pregnant during that first year of use is called the **failure rate** or *pregnancy rate*. In other words, if 5 women out of 100 become pregnant during a year of using contraceptive A, then A's failure rate is 5 percent. *Effectiveness* is 100 minus the failure rate; thus contraceptive A would be said to be 95 percent effective.

There are two kinds of failure rate: the *failure rate for perfect users* and the *failure rate for typical users.* The perfect-user failure rate refers to studies of the best possible use of the method—for example, when the user has been well taught about the method, uses it with perfect consistency, and so on. The failure rate for typical users is just that—the failure rate when people actually use the method, perhaps imperfectly when they forget to take a pill or do not use a condom every time. The good news is that if you are very responsible about contraception, you can anticipate close to the perfect-user failure rate for yourself.

Failure rate: The pregnancy rate occurring using a particular contraceptive method; the percentage of women who will be pregnant after a year of use of the method.

Focus: First Person
Margaret Sanger—Birth Control Pioneer

Margaret Higgins Sanger (1879–1966) was a crusader for birth control in the United States; to reach her goals, she had to take on a variety of opponents, including the U.S. government, and she served one jail term.

Sanger was born in Corning, New York, the daughter of a tubercular mother who died young after bearing 11 children. Her father was a free spirit who fought for women's suffrage. After caring for her dying mother, Sanger embarked on a career in nursing. She married William Sanger in 1902.

She became interested in women's health and began writing articles on the subject. Later these were published as books entitled *What Every Girl Should Know* (1916) and *What Every Mother Should Know* (1917).

Perhaps Sanger's strongest motivation came from her work as a nurse. Her patients were poor maternity cases on New York's Lower East Side. Among these women, pregnancy was a "chronic condition." Margaret Sanger saw them, weary and old at 35, resorting to self-induced abortions, which killed many of them. Frustrated at her inability to help them, she renounced nursing:

> I came to a sudden realization that my work as a nurse and my activities in social service were entirely palliative and consequently futile and useless to relieve the misery I saw all about me.

She determined, instead, to "seek out the root of the evil." Though she was often accused of wanting to lower the birthrate, she instead envisioned families, rich and poor alike, in which children were wanted and given every advantage.

Impeding her work was the Comstock Act of 1873 (see Chapter 20), which classified contraceptive information as obscene and made it illegal to send it through the mail. In 1914 she founded the National Birth Control League, launching the birth control movement in the United States. Though her magazine, *Woman Rebel*, obeyed the letter of the law and did not give contraceptive information, she was nonetheless indicted on nine counts and made liable to a prison term of 45 years.

Margaret Sanger left the United States on the eve of the trial. Touring Europe, in Holland she visited the first birth control clinics to be established anywhere. There she got the idea of opening such clinics in the United States. Meanwhile, the charges against her had been dropped.

She returned to the United States and, in 1916, opened the first U.S. birth control clinic, in Brooklyn. The office was closed by the police after 9 days of operation, and Margaret Sanger was put in jail for 30 days. On appeal, however, her side was upheld by the courts, and in 1918 a decision was handed

Combination pills are one of the most effective methods of birth control. The perfect-user failure rate is 0.3 percent (that is, the method is essentially 100 percent effective), and the typical-user failure rate is 8 percent (Hatcher et al., 2004). Failures occur primarily as a result of forgetting to take a pill for 2 or more days. If a woman forgets to take a pill, she should take it as soon as she remembers and take the next one at the regular time. This does not appear to increase the pregnancy risk appreciably. If she forgets for 2 days, she should do the same thing—take one as soon as possible and then continue taking one a day. If she forgets for 3 or more days, she should follow the same instructions, taking one pill as soon as possible and then one pill a day, but in addition she should use condoms or abstain from sex until she has taken hormonal pills for 7 days in a row, at which point she will again be well protected (Salem, 2005).

Side Effects

You may have seen reports in the media on the dangerous side effects of birth control pills. Some of these reports are no more than scare stories with little or no evidence behind them. However, some well-documented risks are associated with the use of the pill, and women who are using it or who are contemplating using it should be aware of them.

Among the serious side effects associated with use of the pill are slight but significant increases in certain diseases of the circulatory system. One of these is problems of blood clotting (thromboembolic disorders). Women who use the pill have a higher chance than nonusers of developing blood clots (thrombi). Often these form in the legs, and they may then move to the lungs. A stroke may occur if the clot goes to the brain. The clots may lead to pain, hospitalization, and (in rare cases) death.

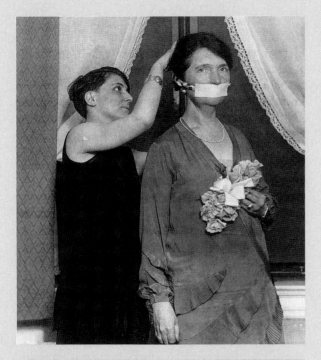

Figure 7.1 Margaret Sanger, a pioneer of the birth control movement, shown here in 1929. She was forbidden by Boston authorities to speak on birth control, so she taped her mouth in protest and wrote on a chalkboard.

down allowing doctors to give contraceptive information to women for the "cure and prevention of disease."

The birth control movement was gaining followers, and the first National Birth Control Conference was held in 1921 in New York, attended by doctors, scientists, and lay supporters. In 1931 the Pope approved the rhythm method for use by Roman Catholics.

Women were also at the forefront of the birth control movement in Canada. In Hamilton, Ontario, Mary Elizabeth Hawkins organized the Hamilton Birth Control Society in 1932. Dr. Elizabeth Bagshaw, one of Hamilton's few female physicians at the time, served the clinic for the next 30-odd years. Providing information about birth control was technically illegal in Canada too at the time, unless it served "the public good," and an Ottawa social worker was actually charged (but acquitted in 1937) for her family-planning activity.

Margaret Sanger's role in getting birth control information to American women and in making it legal for them to use the information is unquestioned. When Heywood Broun once remarked that Margaret Sanger had no sense of humor, she replied, "I am the protagonist of women who have nothing to laugh at."

Sources: Chesler (1992); *Current Biography* (1944); Van Preagh (1982).

Symptoms of blood clots are severe headaches, severe leg or chest pains, and shortness of breath. Most cases of clots occur in women over 35 who smoke. For some women, the pill can cause high blood pressure. For this reason it is important to have regular checkups so that this side effect can be detected if it occurs.

There have been many reports in the media of the pill causing cancer. However, the scientific data do not provide evidence that the pill causes cancer of the cervix, uterus, or breast. The good news is that the pill actually protects women from endometrial cancer and ovarian cancer (Hatcher et al., 2004). However, the pill may aggravate already existing cancer such as breast cancer.

For women who have taken the pill for more than five years, the risk of benign liver tumors increases (Hatcher et al., 2004). Although these problems are relatively rare, they underline the importance of the doctor's giving a thorough examination before

prescribing birth control pills and of the woman's having regular checkups while using them.

The pill increases the amount of vaginal discharge and the susceptibility to vaginitis (vaginal inflammations such as monilia—see Chapter 18) because it alters the chemical balance of the lining of the vagina. Women on the pill have an increased susceptibility to chlamydia. In one study women using the pill had a 73 percent higher rate of acquiring chlamydia and a 70 percent higher rate of acquiring gonorrhea than did comparison groups of women using sterilization or an IUD (Louv et al., 1989).

The pill may cause some nausea, although this almost always goes away after the first month or two of use. Some brands of pills can also cause weight gain, by increasing appetite or water retention, but this side effect can often be reversed by switching to another brand.

Finally, there may be some psychological effects. About 20 percent of women on the pill report increased irritability and depression, which become worse with the length of time they use the pill. These side effects are probably related to the progesterone in the pill; switching to a different brand may be helpful. There may also be changes in sexual desire. Some women report an increase in sexual interest (McCoy & Matyas, 1996), but others report a decrease in sexual desire as well as a decrease in vaginal lubrication (Graham et al., 1995). Once again, switching brands may be helpful.

Because of the side effects discussed previously, women in the following groups should *not* use the pill (Hatcher et al., 2004): those with poor blood circulation or blood-clotting problems; those who have had a heart attack or who have coronary artery disease; those with liver tumors; those with cancer of the breast; nursing mothers (the pill tends to dry up the milk supply, and the hormones may be transmitted through the milk to the baby); and pregnant women. Women over 35 who are cigarette smokers should use the pill only with caution, because the risk of heart attack is considerably higher in this group.

After all this discussion, just how dangerous is the pill? The answer to this question depends on who you are and how you look at it. If you have blood-clotting problems, the pill is dangerous to you; if you have none of the contraindications listed above, it is very safe (Hatcher et al., 2004). One's point of view and standard of comparison also matter. While a death rate of 1.6 per 100,000 sounds high, it is important to consider that one alternative to the pill is intercourse with no contraceptive, which can mean pregnancy, with its own set of side effects and a death rate all its own. For example, the death rate for the pill is 1.6 per 100,000, but the death rate for pregnancy and delivery is 12 per 100,000 (Cheng et al., 2003). From this perspective, in many ways the pill is no more dangerous than the alternative, pregnancy, and actually may be safer. Another possible standard of comparison is drugs that are commonly taken for less serious reasons. Aspirin, for example, is routinely used for headaches. Recent reports indicate that aspirin has side effects, and the birth control pill may be no more dangerous than drugs we take without worrying much.

In short, the pill does have some serious potential side effects, particularly for high-risk individuals, but for many others it is an extremely effective means of contraception that poses little or no danger.

Advantages and Disadvantages

The pill has a number of advantages. It is close to 100 percent effective if used properly. It does not interfere with intercourse, as do some other methods—the diaphragm, the condom, and foam. It is not messy. Some of its side effects are also advantages. For example, it reduces the amount of menstrual flow and thus reduces cramps. Indeed, it is sometimes prescribed for the noncontraceptive purpose of regulating menstruation and eliminating cramps. Iron-deficiency anemia is less likely to occur among pill users. The pill can clear up acne, and it has a protective effect against some rather serious things, including pelvic inflammatory disease (PID) and ovarian and endometrial cancer (Hatcher et al., 2004).

The side effects of birth control pills, discussed earlier, are of course major disadvantages. Another disadvantage is the cost, which is about $35 a month (or as little as $2 to $4 per month through a Planned Parenthood clinic) for as long as they are used. They also place the entire burden of contraception on the woman. In addition, taking them correctly is a little complicated; the woman must understand when they are to be taken, and she must remember when to take them and when not to take them. This effort would not be too taxing for today's college student, but for an illiterate peasant woman in a developing nation who thinks the pills are to be worn like an amulet on a chain around the neck, or for individuals with mental retardation (who need contraceptives, too), currently available birth control pills may be too complicated.

One other criticism of the pill is that for a woman who has intercourse only infrequently (say, once or twice a month or less), it represents contraceptive overkill. In other words, the pill makes her infertile every day of the month (with the side effects of taking it every day), and yet she needs it only a few days each month. Women in this situation might consider a method, such as the diaphragm, that is used only when needed.

Finally, it is important to recognize that, although it is an excellent contraceptive, the pill provides absolutely no protection against sexually transmitted infections.

Reversibility

When a woman wants to become pregnant, she simply stops taking pills after the end of one cycle. Some women experience a brief delay (two or three months) in becoming pregnant, but pregnancy rates are about the same as for women who never took the pill.

Drug Interactions

If you are taking birth control pills, you are taking a prescription drug that may interact with other prescription drugs you take (Hatcher et al., 2004). Some antituberculosis drugs, for example, decrease the effectiveness of the pill.

The pill may also increase the metabolism of some drugs, making them more potent (Hatcher et al., 2004). Examples include some antianxiety drugs, corticosteroids used for inflammations, and theophylline (a drug used for asthma and an ingredient in, for example, Primatene). For this reason, women using the pill may require lower doses of these drugs.

Some over-the-counter drugs may also interact with the pill. St. John's wort, for instance, can substantially decrease the effectiveness of the pill.

Other Kinds of Pills

To this point, our discussion has centered chiefly on the *combination pill,* so named because it contains both estrogen and progestin. This variety of pill is the most widely used, but there are many kinds of combination pills and several kinds of pills other than combination ones (Figure 7.2).

Combination pills vary from one brand to the next in the dosages of estrogen and progestin. The dose of estrogen is important because higher doses are more likely to induce blood-clotting problems. Most women do well on pills containing no more than 20 to 35 micrograms of estrogen, such as Alesse, Mircette, and Desogen. Because of concerns about side effects due to the estrogen in the pill, current pills have considerably lower levels of

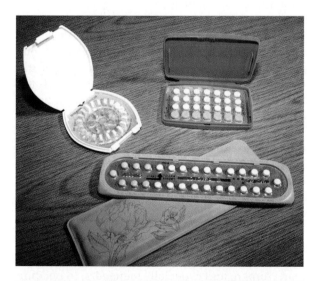

Figure 7.2 Different types of birth control pills.

estrogen than early pills; for example, Ortho-Novum 1/35 has one-third the amount of estrogen of the early pill Enovid 10. High-progestin brands are related to symptoms such as vaginitis and depression. Depending on what side effects the woman wants to avoid, she can choose a brand for its high or low estrogen or progestin level. (See Hatcher et al., 2004, page 428, for a list of symptoms related to dosages of estrogen and progestin.)

Triphasic pills (e.g., Ortho Tri-Cyclen) contain a steady level of estrogen like the combination pill does, but there are three phases in the levels of progesterone. The idea is to reduce total hormone exposure, although it may be about marketing more than anything else.

Progestin-only pills (such as Micronor, Nor-Q D, and Ovrette) have also been developed. They are sometimes called *minipills.* The pills contain only a low dose of progestin and no estrogen, and were designed to avoid the estrogen-related side effects of the standard pills. The woman takes one beginning on the first day of her period and one every day thereafter, at the same time each day. Progestin-only pills work by changing the cervical mucus such that sperm cannot get through, inhibiting implantation, and inhibiting ovulation (although while taking minipills, about 40 percent of women ovulate consistently).

Progestin-only pills have a typical-user failure rate that is higher than that of combination pills. Their major side effect seems to be that they produce very irregular menstrual cycles. The minipill is probably most useful for women who cannot take combination pills—for example, women over 35 who smoke, or women with a history of high blood pressure or blood-clotting problems.

Progestin-only pills are also useful for women who are breast-feeding and cannot use combination pills because they reduce milk production. Neither kind of pill should be used in the first six weeks after birth when breast-feeding, because trace amounts of the hormones can reach the infant through the breast milk. After that time, though, progestin-only pills are a good choice.

The Patch

The patch (Ortho Evra) contains the same hormones as combination birth control pills but is administered transdermally—that is, through the skin. The patch itself, which has been shown in many TV commercials, is thin, beige, and about the size of a double Band-Aid. It consists of an outer, protective layer of polyester, an adhesive layer that

Triphasic pill: A birth control pill containing a steady level of estrogen and three phases of progesterone, intended to mimic more closely women's natural hormonal cycles.

contains the hormones, and a polyester liner that is removed before applying.

The patch lasts for seven days, so the woman places a new one on once a week for three weeks and then has a patch-free week. The first time it is used it takes a couple of days for the hormones to reach effective levels in the bloodstream, so a backup method such as a condom should be used for a while. One advantage is that women using it do not have to remember to take a pill every day, only to replace the patch every week. In addition, with the patch, the hormones enter the body through the skin rather than going to the stomach and needing to be digested.

The patch is new, so we do not have extensive data on it at this point. Because the hormones are the same as in the pill, the expectation is that the benefits and side effects will be quite similar to those of the pill (Hatcher et al., 2004). A trial over 13 months with real users indicated an actual-user failure rate of less than 1 percent, making it extremely effective, somewhat more so than the pill (Audet et al., 2001; Smallwood et al., 2001).

The Vaginal Ring

It's not the latest in body piercing. Rather, the vaginal ring (NuvaRing) is a flexible, transparent ring made of plastic and filled with the same hormones as those in the combination pill, at slightly lower doses (Figure 7.3). The ring is placed high up in the vagina and remains in place for 21 days. It is removed and the

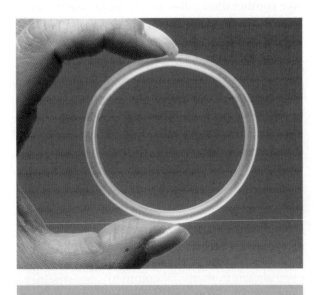

Figure 7.3 NuvaRing, the vaginal contraceptive ring.

woman goes ring-free for—you guessed it—7 days. She then inserts a new ring. This method requires even less remembering than the patch does.

The ring, too, was only recently introduced, so the scientific data on it are limited. Because the hormones in it are the same as those in the combination pill, the side effects should be the same. Research shows that it is extremely effective at stopping ovulation (Mulders & Dieben, 2001). It is expected to be even more effective than the pill because it removes the problem of missed pills. One study of 2,300 women using it over a year found an actual-user pregnancy rate of less than 1 percent (21 pregnancies), with half the pregnancies resulting from major failures to use the method correctly (Dieben et al., 2002).

Emergency Contraception

Emergency contraception is available in pill form for situations such as rape or a condom breaking (Hatcher et al., 2004; Trussell et al., 2000; von Hertzen & Van Look, 1996). The treatment is most effective if begun within 12 to 24 hours and cannot be delayed longer than 120 hours (5 days). Regular birth control pills containing levonorgestrel (a progestin) are taken at higher doses. Plan B, a product produced specifically for emergency contraception, contains the same important hormone. Nausea is a common side effect, but a drug can be taken to prevent it. In 2006 the FDA approved Plan B for sale in the United States over the counter, without prescription. Women can keep a supply on hand for . . . emergencies.

Emergency contraception may work in any of several ways, depending on when in the cycle it is taken. It may stop ovulation, inhibit the functioning of sperm, prevent fertilization, or inhibit the development of a nourishing endometrium. Its action is almost always to prevent pregnancy, not to cause abortion.

Emergency contraception is between 75 and 89 percent effective (Hatcher et al., 2004). These statistics underestimate its actual effectiveness, though, because they refer to the effectiveness during the most fertile part of the cycle. Actual pregnancy rates are between 0.5 and 2.0 percent (von Hertzen et al., 2002). Emergency contraception, then, is highly effective.

Opponents of Plan B had argued that it would lead women, and especially teenagers, to become irresponsible about contraception and their sexual behavior if emergency contraception were widely available. Research, however, indicates that making Plan B available to teenagers has no effect on whether they had unprotected intercourse or on their number of sexual partners (Harper et al., 2005).

Depo-Provera Injections

Depo-Provera (DMPA) is a progestin administered by injection. The injections must be repeated every three months for maximum effectiveness. Depo-Provera became available in the United States in 1992.

How It Works

Depo-Provera works like the other progestin-only methods, by inhibiting ovulation, thickening the cervical mucus, and inhibiting the growth of the endometrium.

Effectiveness

Depo-Provera is highly effective, with a typical-user failure rate of 3 percent, making it more effective than the pill.

Side Effects

No lethal side effects of Depo-Provera have been found, although long-term studies have not yet been done.

Advantages and Disadvantages

Depo-Provera has many advantages. It does not interfere with lovemaking. It requires far less reliance on memory than birth control pills do, although the woman must remember to have a new injection every three months. It is available for women who cannot use the combination pill, such as those over 35 who smoke and those with blood pressure problems.

A disadvantage of Depo-Provera is that most users experience amenorrhea (no menstrual periods). Sometimes there is just some spotting. However, this may be an advantage. It can relieve anemia due to heavy menstrual periods, and Depo-Provera can be used in the treatment of endometriosis.

Reversibility

The method is reversible simply by not getting another injection. Many women are infertile for 6 to 12 months after stopping its use, but then are able to become pregnant at normal rates (Lande, 1995).

The IUD

The **intrauterine device (IUD)** is a small piece of plastic and comes in various shapes (Figure 7.4). Metal or a hormone may also be part of the device. An IUD is inserted into the uterus by a doctor or nurse practitioner and then remains in place until the woman wants to have it removed. One or two plastic strings hang down from the IUD through the cervix, enabling the woman to check to see whether it is in place.

The basic idea for the IUD has been around for some time. In 1909 Burton Richter reported on the use of an IUD made of silkworm gut. In the 1920s the German physician Ernst Gräfenberg reported data on 2,000 insertions of silk or silver wire rings. In spite of the high effectiveness of these devices (98.4 percent), his work was poorly received. Not until the 1950s, with the development of plastic and stainless-steel devices, did the method gain much popularity. In the 1980s the use of the IUD in the United States was sharply reduced by numerous lawsuits against manufacturers by persons claiming to have been damaged by the device, specifically by the IUD

> **Intrauterine device (IUD):** A plastic device sometimes containing metal or a hormone that is inserted into the uterus for contraceptive purposes.

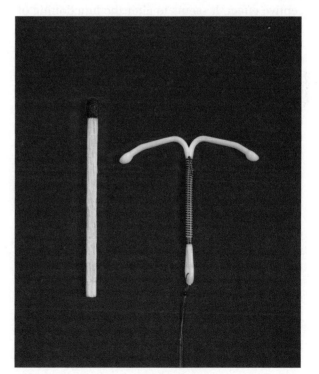

Figure 7.4   Copper T IUD (shown enlarged).

known as the Dalkon Shield, which was taken off the market (Hubacher, 2002). Some companies stopped producing IUDs, and others declared bankruptcy.

As a result, only two IUDs are available in the United States today. Both are T-shaped; one contains copper (the copper T, or Paragard), the other progesterone (Mirena LNG-IUS). Currently 106 million women worldwide are using IUDs, 40 million of them in the People's Republic of China, and experts predict a resurgence of enthusiasm for them in the United States (Hubacher, 2002).

How It Works

The IUD works by preventing fertilization. It produces changes in the uterus and fallopian tubes, and in this environment, sperm that reach the uterus are immobilized and cannot move into the fallopian tube (Treiman et al., 1995). The egg may also move more swiftly through the fallopian tube, reducing the chances of fertilization.

The Mirena releases progesterone directly into the uterus. One effect is to reduce the endometrium. This results in reduced menstrual flow and reduced risk of anemia, overcoming two undesirable side effects of other IUDs.

The small amount of copper that is added to the copper T is thought to have an additional contraceptive effect. It seems to alter the functioning of the enzymes involved in implantation. The progestin thickens cervical mucus, disrupts ovulation, and changes the endometrium.

Effectiveness

The IUD is extremely effective. It is in the same category as Depo-Provera and the pill (and sterilization) in effectiveness. The pregnancy rate for the copper T is 0.7 percent for the first year of use, and after that, the failure rate is even lower (Hatcher et al., 2004). The copper T is effective for 10 years, and Mirena is effective for 5 years.

Most failures occur during the first 3 months of use, either because the IUD is expelled or for other, unknown reasons. Expulsion is most likely in women who have never been pregnant, in younger women, and in women during menstruation. The expulsion rate is about 1 to 7 percent in the first year (Treiman et al., 1995).

Side Effects

The most common side effects of the copper T are increased menstrual cramps, irregular bleeding, and increased menstrual flow. These symptoms occur in 10 to 20 percent of women using

Diaphragm: A cap-shaped rubber contraceptive device that fits inside a woman's vagina over the cervix.

it and are most likely immediately after insertion. Mirena, in contrast, reduces menstrual flow and about 20 percent of users stop bleeding altogether.

There is no evidence that the IUD causes cancer.

Advantages and Disadvantages

One disadvantage of the IUD is its initial cost, which is about $300 for a full-paying client at Planned Parenthood, for the IUD plus insertion. Even at that rate, though, the IUD is a cheap means of contraception over a long period of use. The cost is incurred only once and the copper T, for example, lasts 10 years.

The effectiveness of the copper-T IUD is a major advantage. The typical-user failure rate is only 0.7 percent, making it more effective than combination birth control pills and Depo-Provera.

Once inserted, the IUD is perfectly simple to use. The woman has only to check periodically to see that the strings are in place. It has an advantage over methods like the diaphragm or condom in that it does not interrupt intercourse in any way. It has an advantage over the pill in that the woman does not have to remember to use it. The IUD can be used safely by women after having a baby and while breast-feeding.

Contrary to what some people think, the IUD does not interfere with the use of a tampon during menstruation, nor does it have any effect on intercourse.

Reversibility

When a woman who is using an IUD wants to become pregnant, she simply has a physician remove the device. She can become pregnant immediately.

Diaphragms and Caps

The Diaphragm

The **diaphragm** is a circular, dome-shaped piece of thin rubber with a rubber-covered rim of flexible metal (Figure 7.5). It is inserted into the vagina and, when properly in place, fits snugly over the cervix. In order for it to be used effectively, a contraceptive cream or jelly (such as Delfen) must be applied to the diaphragm. The cream is spread on the rim and the inside surface (the surface that fits against the cervix). The diaphragm may be inserted up to 6 hours before intercourse, and it must be left in place for at least 6 hours afterward and may be left in for as long as 24 hours. Wearing it longer than that is thought to increase the risk of toxic shock syndrome.

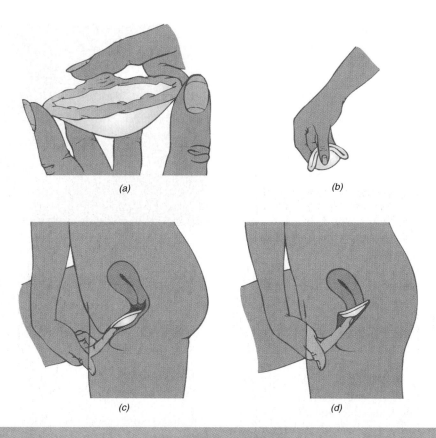

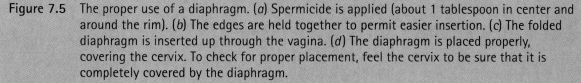

Figure 7.5 The proper use of a diaphragm. (*a*) Spermicide is applied (about 1 tablespoon in center and around the rim). (*b*) The edges are held together to permit easier insertion. (*c*) The folded diaphragm is inserted up through the vagina. (*d*) The diaphragm is placed properly, covering the cervix. To check for proper placement, feel the cervix to be sure that it is completely covered by the diaphragm.

The diaphragm was the earliest of the highly effective methods of contraception for women. It was popularized in a paper in 1882 by the German researcher Mensinga. In 1925 Margaret Sanger's husband funded the first U.S. company to manufacture diaphragms, and they were the mainstay of contraception until about 1960.

How It Works
The primary action of the diaphragm itself is mechanical. It blocks the entrance to the uterus so that sperm cannot swim up into it. The contraceptive cream kills any sperm that manage to get past the barrier. Any sperm remaining in the vagina die after about 6 hours (this is why the diaphragm should not be removed until at least 6 hours after intercourse).

Effectiveness
The typical-user failure rate of the diaphragm has been estimated to be about 16 percent. Most failures are due to improper use—for example, it is not used every time, it is not left in long enough, or contraceptive cream is not used. Even with perfect use, there is still a failure rate. For example, Masters and Johnson found that expansion of the vagina during sexual arousal (see Chapter 8) may cause the diaphragm to slip. To get closer to 100 percent effectiveness, the diaphragm can be combined with a condom around the time of ovulation or throughout the cycle.

Failure rates for the diaphragm and cervical cap (which we discuss later) are often stated as ranges, for example, 17 to 25 percent, because failure rates for these methods depend so much on the fertility characteristics of the user. For example, a woman under 30 who has intercourse four or more times weekly has twice the average failure rate of a woman over 30 who has intercourse less than four times a week.

Because proper fit of the diaphragm is essential to its effectiveness, it is important for the woman to be individually fitted for one by her physician.

She must be refitted after the birth of a child, an abortion, extreme weight gain or loss, or any similar occurrence that would alter the shape and size of the vagina.

Side Effects

The diaphragm has few side effects. One is the possible irritation of the vagina or the penis. This irritation is caused by the cream or jelly and can be relieved by switching to another brand. Another side effect is the rare occurrence of toxic shock syndrome that has been reported in women who left the diaphragm in place for more than 24 hours. For the reason, users should be careful not to leave the diaphragm in place for much more than the necessary 6 to 8 hours, especially during menstruation.

Advantages and Disadvantages

Some people think that the diaphragm is undesirable because it must be inserted before intercourse and therefore ruins the spontaneity of sex. People with this attitude, of course, should not use the diaphragm as a means of birth control, since they probably will not use it all the time, in which case it will not work. However, a student told us that she and her partner made the preparation and insertion of the diaphragm a ritual part of their foreplay; he inserts it, and they both have a good time! Couples who maintain this kind of attitude are much more likely to use the diaphragm effectively. In addition, the diaphragm can be inserted an hour or more before sex.

Some women dislike touching their genitals and sticking their fingers into their vagina. Use of the diaphragm is not a good method for them.

The diaphragm requires some thought on the woman's part. She must remember to have it with her when she needs it and to have a supply of cream or jelly. She also needs to avoid becoming so carried away with passion that she forgets about it or decides not to use it.

A disadvantage is that the cream or jelly may leak out after intercourse.

The cost of a diaphragm is about $35 plus the cost of the office visit and the cost of the contraceptive cream. With proper care, a diaphragm should last about two years, so it is not expensive.

The major advantages of the diaphragm are that it has few side effects and, when used properly, is very effective. For this reason, women who are worried about the side effects of the pill should seriously consider the diaphragm as an alternative. There is also evidence of a reduction in the rate of cervical cancer among longtime

Male condom: A contraceptive sheath that is placed over the penis.

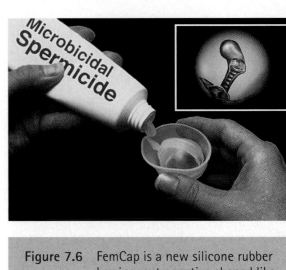

Figure 7.6 FemCap is a new silicone rubber barrier contraceptive shaped like a sailor's hat, with a dome that covers the cervix and a brim that conforms to the vaginal walls.

users of the diaphragm. And the diaphragm provides some protection against sexually transmitted infections such as chlamydia, because it covers and protects the cervix.

Reversibility

If a woman wishes to become pregnant, she simply stops using the diaphragm. Its use has no effect on her later chances of conceiving.

FemCap and Lea's Shield

FemCap and Lea's Shield are both vaginal barrier devices similar to the diaphragm. Lea's Shield is a one-size, cup-shaped silicone device that has a small one-way valve to allow air to escape as it is being inserted, and to help provide suction to keep it properly in place over the cervix. FemCap is shaped like a sailor's cap (see Figure 7.6), is also made of silicone, and comes in three sizes. Both should be used with a spermicide or one of the new microbicides. Each was recently approved by the FDA, and both are now available (Hatcher et al., 2004). They must be obtained through a health care provider.

The Male Condom

The **male condom** ("rubber," "prophylactic," "safe") is a thin sheath that fits over the penis (Figure 7.7). It comes rolled up in a little packet and must be unrolled onto the penis before use. It may be made

Figure 7.7 A variety of male condoms.

of latex ("rubber"), polyurethane, or the intestinal tissue of lambs ("skin"). The polyurethane condom (Avanti, Trojan Supra) is a recent innovation that is helpful to people who are allergic to latex (Walsh et al., 2003).

The widespread use of the modern condom, both for contraception and for protection against diseases, dates from about 1843, when vulcanized rubber was developed, but the use of a sheath to cover the penis has been known throughout most of recorded history.[1] The legendary Italian adventure and lover Casanova (1725–1798) was one of the first to popularize it for its contraceptive ability as well as its protective value. Condoms have become increasingly popular because they help protect against sexually transmitted infections (STIs). Approximately 440 million are sold each year in the United States (Hatcher et al., 2004).

To be effective, the condom must be used properly (Figure 7.8). It must be unrolled onto the erect penis before the penis ever enters the vagina—*not* just before ejaculation, because long before then some drops containing a few thousand sperm may have been produced. To be effective in preventing STIs, too, it must be put on before the penis enters the vagina.

Condoms come in two shapes: those with plain ends and those with a protruding tip that catches the semen. If a plain-ended one is used, about $\frac{1}{2}$ inch of air-free space should be left at the tip to catch the ejaculate. Care should be taken that the condom does not slip during intercourse. After the man has ejaculated, he must hold the rim of the condom against the base of the penis as he withdraws. It is best to withdraw soon after ejaculation, while the man still has an erection, in order to minimize the chances of leakage. A new condom must be used with each act of intercourse.

[1]Condoms have also been the stimulus for humor throughout history, an example being this limerick:

There was a young man of Cape Horn
Who wished he had never been born
   And he wouldn't have been
   If his father had seen
That the end of the rubber was torn.

(a)   (b)

Figure 7.8   Putting on a condom correctly. (*a*) The tip is pinched to keep air out. (*b*) The condom is then rolled down over the erect penis.

Condoms may be either lubricated or unlubricated. Some further lubrication for intercourse may be necessary. A contraceptive foam or jelly works well and provides additional protection. A sterile lubricant such as K-Y Jelly may also be used.

How It Works
The condom catches the semen, preventing it from entering the vagina. For condoms coated with a spermicide, the spermicide kills sperm and in theory provides extra protection. Spermicide-coated condoms are not necessarily to be preferred, though. They may create allergies to the spermicide for the man or his partner, and the amount of spermicide is probably not sufficient to be very effective. For couples who want to improve on the effectiveness of the condom, it is probably wiser for the woman to use a contraceptive foam or, better yet, a diaphragm.

Effectiveness
Condoms are much more effective as a contraceptive than most people think. The perfect-user

failure rate is about 2 percent. The typical-user failure rate is about 15 percent, but many failures result from improper or inconsistent use. The FDA controls the quality of condoms carefully, so the chances of a failure due to a defect in the condom itself are small. Combined with a contraceptive foam or cream or a diaphragm, the condom is close to 100 percent effective.

Side Effects
The condom has no side effects, except that some users are allergic to latex. For them, nonlatex condoms made of polyurethane or other plastics are available.

Advantages and Disadvantages
One disadvantage of the condom is that it must be put on just before intercourse, raising the spontaneity problem again. If the couple can make an enjoyable, erotic ritual of putting it on together, they can minimize this problem.

Some men complain that the condom reduces their sensation, lessening their pleasure in intercourse ("It's like taking a shower with a raincoat on"). The reduction in sensation, however, may be an advantage for some. For example, it may help men who tend to ejaculate prematurely. Polyurethane condoms are thinner and should provide more sensation.

There are several advantages to condoms. They are the only contraceptive currently available for men except sterilization. They are cheap (around $1.00 to $1.50 for three), readily available without prescription at any drugstore and some convenience stores, and fairly easy to use. The man (or woman) must plan ahead, however, so they will have one available when it is needed.

Finally, a major advantage of condoms is that they provide protection against many sexually transmitted infections (Cates, 2001). Over the past several years, far-right political groups have mounted a campaign to convince the public that condoms are completely ineffective at STI prevention. However, the scientific data say otherwise. Condoms are highly effective protection against STIs that are transmitted mainly through genital secretions (semen, cervical and vaginal secretions) because they keep the secretions away from the other person. STIs in this category include chlamydia, gonorrhea, trichomoniasis, hepatitis B, and HIV (Hatcher et al., 2004).

Condoms also provide some, although not perfect, protection against STIs that are transmitted mainly by skin-to-skin contact, such as herpes, syphilis, and human papillomavirus. They won't protect against these diseases, of course, if the area producing the microbe is not covered by the condom—for example, if herpes blisters are on the scrotum. Latex and polyurethane condoms are the effective ones. Animal-skin condoms are much less effective because they have larger pores that allow some viruses, such as HIV, to pass through them. For a more complete discussion, see Chapter 18.

Reversibility
The method is easily and completely reversible. The man simply stops using condoms if conception is desired.

The Female Condom

The female condom, originally called Reality and now called FC, became available in 1994. It is made of polyurethane and resembles a clear balloon (Figure 7.9). There are two rings in it, one at either end. One ring is inserted into the vagina much like

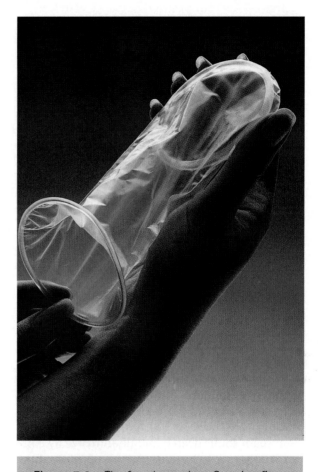

Figure 7.9 The female condom. One ring fits over the cervix, and the other goes outside the body, over the vulva, so that the condom lines the vagina and partly covers the vulva.

a diaphragm, while the other is spread over the vaginal entrance. The inside is prelubricated, and additional lubrication may be applied if desired. The penis must be guided into the female condom so that the penis does not slip in between the condom and the vaginal wall. The condom is removed immediately after intercourse, before the woman stands up. The outer ring is squeezed together and twisted to keep the semen inside. A new female condom must be used with each act of intercourse.

How It Works
The female condom works by preventing sperm from entering the vagina and by blocking the entrance to the uterus.

Effectiveness
The female condom is new, so we have less data on its effectiveness compared with other methods.

The data we have do not look impressive. The typical-user failure rate is 21 percent (Hatcher et al., 2004), which is unacceptably high for many women. The perfect-user failure rate is 5 percent.

Side Effects

There are few if any side effects with the female condom. A few women experience vaginal irritation and a few men experience irritation of the penis as a result of using it.

Advantages and Disadvantages

The female condom is made of polyurethane, not the latex used in most male condoms. Polyurethane is less susceptible to tearing and does not deteriorate with exposure to oil-based substances in the way that latex does. It does not create the allergic reactions that some people have to latex.

One major advantage is that the female condom is a method that a woman can use herself to reduce her risk of contracting an STI. The polyurethane is impermeable to the HIV virus and to the viruses and bacteria that cause other STIs.

In regard to disadvantages, the spontaneity problem presents itself again. The female condom, at least in its present form, is awkward and makes rustling noises while in use. It makes the male condom seem sophisticated and unobtrusive by comparison. Also, it is the least effective of the methods discussed so far in this chapter. Another disadvantage is the cost, about $5 per condom, which is considerably higher than the cost for male condoms.

Newer female condoms are under development, including FC2, which is made of synthetic latex rather than polyurethane, and is expected to be cheaper (Upadhyay et al., 2005). Another is the VA feminine condom (also called Reddy and V-Amour), which contains a sponge to hold it in place in the vagina rather than the internal ring of FC. Yet another is PATH, which has urethane foam on the condom pouch so that the condom clings lightly to the vaginal wall.

Reversibility

The method is easily and completely reversible. The woman simply stops using the condom.

Spermicides

Contraceptive foams (Delfen, Emko), creams, and jellies are all classified as **spermicides,** that is, sperm killers (Figure 7.10). They come in a tube or a can, along with a plastic applicator. The applicator is filled and inserted into the

Spermicide (SPERM-ih-side): A substance that kills sperm.

vagina. The applicator's plunger is then used to push the spermicide out into the vagina near the cervix, so the spermicide is inserted much as a tampon is. It must be left in for 6 to 8 hours after intercourse. One application provides protection for only one act of intercourse.

Spermicides are not to be confused with the various feminine hygiene products (vaginal deodorants) on the market. Hygiene products are not effective as contraceptives.

How They Work

Spermicides consist of a spermicidal chemical in an inert base. They work in two ways: chemical and mechanical. The chemicals in them kill sperm, while the inert base itself mechanically blocks the entrance to the cervix so that sperm cannot swim into it.

Effectiveness

Failure rates for spermicides can be as high as 25 percent (Raymond et al., 2004). Put simply, they are not very effective. Foams tend to be more effective, creams and jellies less so. Spermicidal tablets and suppositories are also available, but they are the least effective. Spermicides are highly effective only when used with a diaphragm or a condom.

Side Effects

Some people experience an allergic reaction—irritation of the vagina or penis—to spermicides. Because we couldn't find any scientific studies on the incidence of these allergies, we surveyed our sexuality classes. We found that, of the students who had used spermicides, about 2 percent of the men and 26 percent of the women reported an allergic reaction.

Advantages and Disadvantages

The major advantage of spermicides is that they are readily available, without a prescription, in any drugstore. For this reason, they can be used as a stopgap method until the woman can see a physician and get a more effective contraceptive. Their failure rate is so high, though, that we cannot recommend using them by themselves. Always combine them with a second method such as a condom.

Spermicides provide no protection against bacterial STIs such as chlamydia and gonorrhea. Neither do they protect against HIV, and there is some evidence that their frequent use increases susceptibility to HIV (Hatcher et al., 2004).

Their major disadvantage is that by themselves they are not very effective. They also interrupt the spontaneity of sex, although only briefly. Some

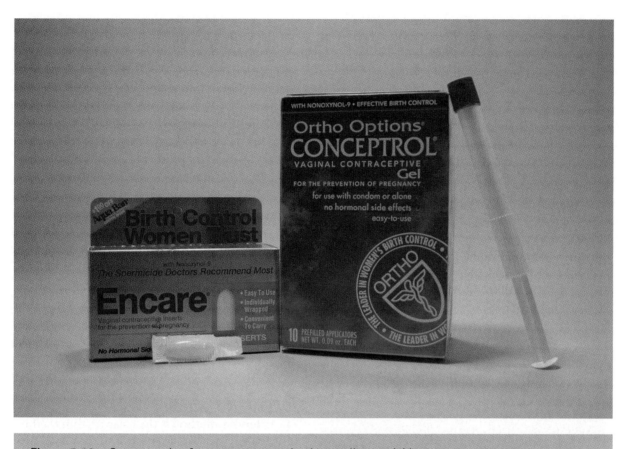

Figure 7.10 Contraceptive foams, creams, and gels are all spermicides.

women dislike the sensation of the spermicide leaking out after intercourse, and some are irritated by the chemicals. Finally, some people find that they taste terrible, and so their use interferes with oral sex.

Douching

Some people mistakenly believe that **douching** (flushing the vagina with a liquid) with any one of a variety of solutions is an effective contraceptive technique. A popular rumor among teenagers is that douching with Coca-Cola after intercourse will prevent pregnancy. Unfortunately, while it is true that acidic solutions will kill sperm, it takes only seconds for some of the sperm to reach the cervical mucus, and once there, they are free to continue moving up into the uterus, and no douching solution will reach them. The woman would have to be a championship sprinter to get herself up and douched soon enough. And the douche itself may even push some sperm up into the uterus. Douching, for these reasons, is just not effective as a contraceptive method.

Withdrawal

Withdrawal (*coitus interruptus,* "pulling out") is probably the most ancient form of birth control. (A reference to it is even found in Genesis 38:8–9, in the story of Onan. For this reason it is sometimes called *onanism,* although this term is also used for masturbation.) Withdrawal is still widely used throughout the world. The man withdraws his penis from his partner's vagina before he has an orgasm and ejaculates outside the vagina. For this method to be effective as contraception, the ejaculation must occur completely away from the woman's vulva. Reliance on withdrawal highlights the key issue of male responsibility in birth control (Figure 7.11).

Effectiveness

Withdrawal is not very effective as a method of birth control. The failure rate is around 27 percent. Failures occur for several reasons: The few drops of fluid that come out of

Douching (DOOSH-ing): Flushing out the inside of the vagina with a liquid.
Withdrawal: A method of birth control in which the man withdraws his penis from his partner's vagina before he ejaculates.

My scholarship is

Now I need a job to support my baby.

USELESS

sex has consequences | www.teenpregnancy.org

Figure 7.11 Male responsibility is a key issue in birth control.

the penis during arousal may carry enough sperm for conception to occur. If ejaculation occurs outside the vagina but near or on the vulva, sperm may still get into the vagina and continue up into the uterus. And sometimes the man simply does not withdraw in time.

Side Effects
Withdrawal produces no direct physical side effects. However, over long periods of time it may contribute to sexual dysfunctions in the man, such as premature ejaculation, and also sexual dysfunctions in the woman.

Advantages and Disadvantages
The major advantage of withdrawal is that it is the only last-minute method. It can be used when nothing else is available, although if the situation is that desperate, the couple might consider abstinence or some other form of sexual expression, such as mouth–genital sex, as alternatives. Obviously, withdrawal requires no prescription and is free.

Rhythm (fertility awareness) method: A method of birth control that involves abstaining from intercourse around the time the woman ovulates.
Calendar method: A type of rhythm method of birth control in which the woman determines when she ovulates by keeping a calendar record of the length of her menstrual cycles.

One major disadvantage is that withdrawal is not very effective. In addition, it requires exceptional motivation on the part of the man, and it may be psychologically stressful to him. He must constantly maintain a kind of self-conscious control. The woman may worry about whether he really will withdraw in time, and the situation is certainly less than ideal for her to orgasm.

Fertility Awareness (Rhythm) Methods

Rhythm (fertility awareness) methods are the only form of "natural" birth control and are the only methods officially approved by the Roman Catholic Church. They require abstaining from intercourse during the woman's fertile period (around ovulation). There are several rhythm methods, in each of which the woman's fertile period is determined in a different way (Kambic, 1999).

The Calendar Method
The **calendar method** is the basic rhythm method. It is based on the assumption that ovulation occurs about 14 days before the onset of menstruation. It works best for the woman with the perfectly regular 28-day cycle. She should ovulate on day 14, and almost surely on one of days 13 to 15. Three days are added in front of that period (because previously deposited sperm may result in conception), and 2 days are added after it (to allow for long-lasting eggs), so the couple must abstain from sexual intercourse from day 10 to day 17. For these reasons, even for the woman with perfectly regular cycles, 8 days of abstinence are required in the middle of each cycle. Research shows that sperm can live up to 5 days inside the female reproductive tract, and eggs live less than a day (Wilcox et al., 1995).

The woman who is not perfectly regular must keep a record of her cycles for at least 6 months, and preferably for a year. From this she determines the length of her shortest cycle and the length of her longest cycle. The preovulatory safe period is then calculated by subtracting 18 from the number of days in the shortest cycle, and the postovulatory safe period is calculated by subtracting 11 from the number of days in the longest cycle (see Table 7.2). For a woman who is somewhat irregular—say, with cycles varying from 26 to 33 days in length—a period of abstinence from day 8 to day 22 (a total of 15 days) would be required.

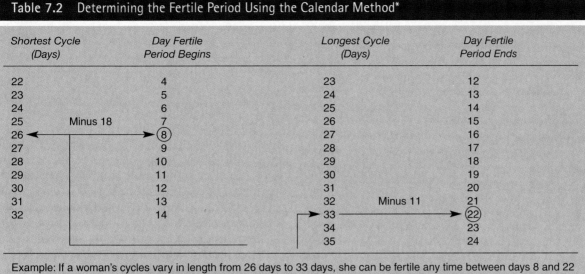

Table 7.2   Determining the Fertile Period Using the Calendar Method*

Shortest Cycle (Days)	Day Fertile Period Begins	Longest Cycle (Days)	Day Fertile Period Ends
22	4	23	12
23	5	24	13
24	6	25	14
25	Minus 18 7	26	15
26 ←	→ ⑧	27	16
27	9	28	17
28	10	29	18
29	11	30	19
30	12	31	20
31	13	32 Minus 11	21
32	14	→ 33	→ ㉒
		34	23
		35	24

Example: If a woman's cycles vary in length from 26 days to 33 days, she can be fertile any time between days 8 and 22 of the cycle. To avoid getting pregnant, she must abstain from sexual intercourse from day 8 to day 22.

*See text, "The Calendar Method," for further explanation.

The Standard Days Method

The standard days method (SDM) is a variation on the calendar method, designed to make it simpler (Hatcher et al., 2004). Proponents of this method say that 80 percent of women have cycle lengths between 26 and 32 days. For those women the fertile period is very likely to fall between days 8 and 19. For this reason, if a woman knows that she is regular and that her cycle length is between 26 and 32 days, all she needs to do is keep track of the day of the cycle and abstain from days 8 to 19. Of course, abstaining for 12 days each month would not be an enticing prospect for many women or their partners. In trials, the perfect-user failure rate was 5 percent and the typical-user failure rate was 12 percent (Arévalo et al., 2002).

The Basal Body Temperature Method

A somewhat more accurate method for determining ovulation is the **basal body temperature (BBT) method.** We discussed the principle behind this method in Chapter 5. The woman takes her temperature every day immediately upon waking. During the preovulatory phase her temperature will be at a fairly constant low level. On the day of ovulation it drops (although this does not always occur), and on the day after ovulation it rises sharply and then stays at that high level for the rest of the cycle. Intercourse would be safe beginning about three days after ovulation.

We have noted some of the psychological stresses involved in using this method. As a form of contraception, the BBT method has a major disadvantage in that it determines safe days only *after* ovulation, and theoretically, according to the method, there are no safe days before ovulation. For this reason the BBT method is best used in combination with the calendar method or the cervical mucus method, which determine the preovulatory safe period, while the BBT method determines the postovulatory safe period.

The Cervical Mucus (Ovulation) Method

Another rhythm method is based on variations over the cycle in the mucus produced by the cervix. The **cervical mucus method** works in the following way.

There are generally a few days just after menstruation during which no mucus is produced and there is a general sensation of vaginal dryness. This period is relatively safe. Then there are a number of days of mucus discharge around the middle of the cycle. On the first days, the mucus is white or cloudy and tacky. The amount increases, and the mucus becomes clearer, until there are one or two *peak days,* when the mucus is like raw egg white—clear, slippery, and stringy. There is also a sensation of vaginal lubrication. Ovulation occurs within 24 hours after the last peak day. Abstinence is required from the first day of mucus discharge until 4 days after the peak days. After that, the mucus, if present, is cloudy or white, and intercourse is safe.

Basal body temperature (BBT) method: A type of rhythm method of birth control in which the woman determines when she ovulates by keeping track of her temperature.

Cervical mucus method: A type of rhythm method of birth control in which the woman determines when she ovulates by checking her cervical mucus.

The Sympto-Thermal Method

The **sympto-thermal method** combines two rhythm methods to produce better effectiveness. The woman records changes in her cervical mucus (symptoms) as well as her basal body temperature (thermal). The combination of the two should give a more accurate determination for the time of ovulation.

Home Ovulation Tests

Recently, home tests for the detection of ovulation have been developed. Most such tests have been designed for use by couples wanting to conceive, but a few are now available for contraception (Hatcher et al., 2004). One kind (PG53, PC 2000, and Maybe Baby) involves minimicroscopes to examine saliva or cervical mucus. Others involve temperature computers that work on the BBT method. Hormone computers (for example, Persona) assess hormone levels in urine. Costs range between $50 and $500. The effectiveness of these tests is not yet well enough researched for them to be recommended as reliable.

Effectiveness

The effectiveness of the rhythm method varies considerably, depending on a number of factors, but basically it is not very effective with typical users (giving rise to its nickname, "Vatican roulette," and a number of old jokes like, "What do they call people who use the rhythm method?" Answer: "Parents"). Although the typical-user failure rate is around 25 percent for all methods, ideal-user failure rates vary considerably. They are 5 percent for the calendar method, 2 percent for BBT, 2 percent for the sympto-thermal method, and 3 percent for the cervical mucus method (Hatcher et al., 2004).

Failure rates are lower when the woman's cycle is very regular and when the couple are highly motivated and have been well instructed in the methods. The effectiveness of the rhythm method also depends partly on one's purpose in using it: whether for preventing pregnancy absolutely or for spacing pregnancies. If absolute pregnancy prevention is the goal (as it probably would be, for example, for an unmarried teenager), the method is just not effective enough. But if the couple simply wish to space pregnancies further apart than would occur naturally, the method will probably accomplish this. Knowing when the woman's fertile times occur can also improve the effectiveness of other methods of contraception. Combining the sympto-thermal method with use of a condom or diaphragm during fertile days can lead to better effectiveness with no need for abstinence.

Advantages and Disadvantages

For many users of the rhythm method, its main advantage is that the Roman Catholic Church considers it an acceptable method of birth control.

The method has no side effects except possible psychological stress, and it is cheap. It is easily reversible. It also helps the woman become more aware of her body's functioning. The method requires cooperation from both partners, which may be considered either an advantage or a disadvantage.

Its main disadvantages are its high failure rate and the psychological stress it may cause. Periods of abstinence of at least 8 days, and possibly as long as 2 or 3 weeks, are necessary, which is an unacceptable requirement for many couples. Actually, the rhythm method would seem best suited to people who do not like sex very much.

A certain amount of time, usually several months, is required to collect the data needed to make the method work. Thus one cannot simply begin using it on the spur of the moment.

Sterilization

Sterilization, or voluntary surgical contraception (VSC), is a surgical procedure whereby an individual is made permanently sterile, that is, unable to reproduce. Sterilization is a rather emotion-laden topic, for a number of reasons. Some people confuse sterilization with castration, though the two are quite different. This is also an emotional topic because sterilization means the end of one's capacity to reproduce. The ability to impregnate and the ability to bear a child are very important in cultural definitions of manhood and womanhood. We hope that as gender roles become more flexible in our society and as concern about reproduction is replaced by a concern for limiting population size, the word *sterilization* will no longer carry such emotional overtones.

Most physicians are conservative about performing sterilizations; they want to make sure that the patient has made a firm decision on his or her own and will not be back a few months later wanting to have the procedure reversed. The physician has an obligation to follow the principle of informed consent. This means explaining the procedures involved, telling the patient about

Sympto-thermal method: A type of rhythm method of birth control combining the basal body temperature method and the cervical mucus method.
Sterilization: A surgical procedure by which an individual is made sterile, that is, incapable of reproducing.

the possible risks and advantages, discussing alternative methods, and answering any questions the patient has.

Despite this conservatism, both male sterilization and female sterilization have become increasingly popular as methods of birth control. Sterilization is the most common method of birth control in the United States today, used by 39 percent of contracepting fertile-aged couples (Hatcher et al., 2004).

Male Sterilization

The male sterilization operation is called a **vasectomy,** so named for the vas deferens, which is tied or cut. It can be done in a physician's office under local anesthesia and requires only about 20 minutes to perform. In the traditional procedure, the physician makes a small incision on one side of the upper part of the scrotum. The vas is then separated from the surrounding tissues, tied off, and cut. The procedure is then repeated on the other side, and the incisions are sewn up. For a day or two the man may have to refrain from strenuous activity and be careful not to pull the incision apart.

Now a *no-scalpel vasectomy* procedure has been developed (Hatcher et al., 2004). It involves making just a tiny pierce in the scrotum (Figure 7.12). This procedure has an even lower rate of complications than a standard vasectomy.

Typically, the man can return to having intercourse within a few days. It should not be assumed that he is sterile yet, however. Some stray sperm may still be lurking in his ducts beyond the point of the incision. Men should not rely completely on the vasectomy until 3 months after it was performed (Salem, 2005). Until then, an additional method of birth control should be used.

Misunderstandings about the vasectomy abound. In fact, a vasectomy creates no physical changes that interfere with erection. Neither does it interfere in any way with sex hormone production; the testes continue to manufacture testosterone and secrete it into the bloodstream. Nor does a vasectomy interfere with the process or sensation of ejaculation. As we noted earlier, virtually all the fluid of the ejaculate is produced by the seminal vesicles and prostate, and the incision is made long before that point in the duct system. Thus the ejaculate is completely normal, except that it does not contain any sperm.

How It Works

The vasectomy makes it impossible for sperm to move beyond the cut in the vas. Thus the vasectomy prevents sperm from being in the ejaculate.

Effectiveness

The vasectomy is essentially 100 percent effective; it has a failure rate of 0.1 percent. Failures occur because stray sperm are still present during the first few months after surgery, because the physician did not completely sever the vas, or because the ends of the vas have grown back together.

Side Effects

The physical side effects of the vasectomy are minimal. In about 5 percent of cases there is a minor

> **Vasectomy (va-SEK-tuh-mee):** A surgical procedure for male sterilization involving severing of the vas deferens.

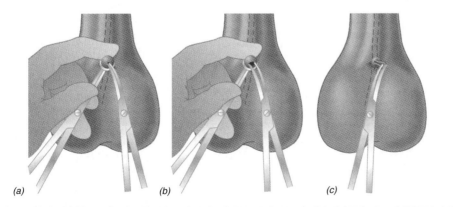

(a)   (b)   (c)

Figure 7.12   The no-scalpel vasectomy. (*a*) The vas (dotted line) is grasped by special ring forceps and the scrotum is pierced by sharp-tipped forceps. (*b*) The forceps stretch the opening slightly, and (*c*) the vas is lifted out and then tied off. The other vas is then lifted out through the same small hole and the procedure is repeated.

complication from the surgery, such as infection of the vas (Hatcher et al., 2004).

Some psychologically based problems may arise. Thus the man's attitude toward having a vasectomy is extremely important. Only about 5 percent regret having had a vasectomy (Hatcher et al., 2004).

Reversibility

Quite a bit of effort has been devoted to developing techniques for reversing vasectomies (the surgical procedure for reversal is termed *vasovasostomy*) and to developing vasectomy techniques that are more reversible. At present, with sophisticated microsurgery techniques, pregnancy rates following reversal are around 50 percent (Hatcher et al., 2004). In making a decision about whether to have a vasectomy, though, a man should assume that it is irreversible.

After a vasectomy some men begin forming antibodies to their own sperm. Because these antibodies destroy sperm, they might contribute further to the irreversibility of the vasectomy.

Advantages and Disadvantages

The major advantages of the vasectomy are its effectiveness and its minimal health risks. Once performed, it requires no further thought or planning on the man's part. As a permanent, long-term method of contraception, it is very cheap. The operation itself is simple—simpler than the female sterilization procedures—and requires no hospitalization or absence from work. Finally, it is one of the few methods that allow the man to assume contraceptive responsibility.

The permanency of the vasectomy may be either an advantage or a disadvantage. If permanent contraception is desired, the method is certainly much better than something like birth control pills, which must be used repeatedly. But if the couple change their minds and decide that they want to have a child, the permanence is a distinct disadvantage. Some men put several samples of their sperm into a frozen sperm bank so that artificial insemination can be performed if they do decide to have a child after a vasectomy.

Another disadvantage of the vasectomy is the various psychological problems that might result if the man sees sterilization as a threat to his masculinity or virility. However, long-term studies of vasectomized men provide no evidence of such psychological problems (Population Information Program, 1983). In studies done around the world, the majority of vasectomized men say that they have no regrets about having had the sterilization performed, that they would recommend it to others, and that there has been no change or else an improvement in their happiness and sexual satisfaction in marriage. Fewer than 5 percent of vasectomized men report psychological problems such as decreased libido or depression. This rate is no higher than in control samples of unvasectomized men.

Finally, if a married couple use the vasectomy as a permanent method of birth control, the woman is not protected if she has intercourse with someone other than her husband.

Female Sterilization

Several surgical techniques are used to sterilize a woman, including minilaparotomy, laparoscopy, and the transcervical approach (sometimes called tubal ligation or "having the tubes tied"). These techniques differ in terms of the type of procedure used (Figure 7.13). They are performed under local or general anesthesia, and involve blocking the

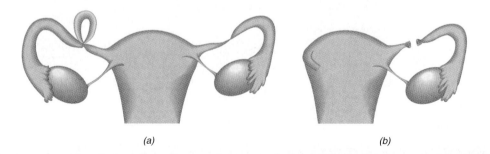

(a)   (b)

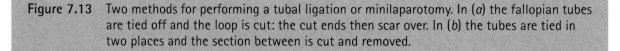

Figure 7.13   Two methods for performing a tubal ligation or minilaparotomy. In (a) the fallopian tubes are tied off and the loop is cut: the cut ends then scar over. In (b) the tubes are tied in two places and the section between is cut and removed.

fallopian tubes in some way so that sperm and egg cannot meet.

In a **minilaparotomy** ("minilap"), a small incision (less than 3 centimeters, or about 1 inch long) is made in the abdomen. Each fallopian tube is in turn gently pulled to the opening. Each tube is blocked, either by cutting and tying off the ends or by applying a small clip, and the tubes are then allowed to slip back into place. With the *laparoscopy,* a magnifying instrument is inserted into the abdomen. The doctor uses it to identify the fallopian tubes and then blocks them by electrocoagulation or by clips. Either procedure takes only about 10 to 20 minutes and does not require that the woman spend the night in the hospital.

The newest procedure is the *transcervical approach,* which does not require an incision. Instead, the instruments enter through the cervix and uterus, and a blockage device is placed in the fallopian tubes. Several transcervical methods are under development (Upadhyay et al., 2005). One involves inserting a tiny microcoil called Essure into each fallopian tube. Scar tissue forms around it, blocking the fallopian tube.

The female sterilization procedures do not interfere with the ovaries. For this reason, the production of sex hormones continues normally so female sterilization does not bring on premature menopause. Some misunderstandings arise from confusing female sterilization procedures with hysterectomy (surgical removal of the uterus) or oophorectomy (surgical removal of the ovaries, which does impair hormonal functioning). These two operations do produce sterility, but they are generally performed for purposes other than sterilization, such as treatment of cancer.

How It Works

Female sterilization procedures make it impossible for the egg to move down the fallopian tube toward the uterus. They also prevent sperm from reaching the egg.

Effectiveness

These procedures are essentially 100 percent effective. The failure rate of 0.5 percent is due to an occasional rejoining of the ends of the fallopian tubes, and rare cases in which the woman was pregnant before the sterilization procedure was performed.

Side Effects

Occasionally there are side effects arising from the surgery, such as infections, hemorrhaging, and problems related to the anesthetic. Generally, only 1 percent of women undergoing the surgery experience complications.

Reversibility

Highly refined microsurgery techniques make it possible to reverse female sterilization in some cases. The success rate varies considerably, depending on the method that was used to perform the sterilization. Pregnancy rates range between 38 percent and 82 percent (Hatcher et al., 2004). However, in deciding whether to have sterilization surgery, a woman should assume that it is irreversible. Five years after sterilization, only 7 percent of women regret having had the procedure (Jamieson et al., 2002).

Advantages and Disadvantages

Female sterilization has some of the same advantages as male sterilization in terms of effectiveness, permanence, and cheapness when used for long-term contraception. One disadvantage is that it offers no protection from sexually transmitted infections.

Psychological Aspects: Attitudes toward Contraception

It is a favorite old saying among Planned Parenthood workers that contraceptives are only as effective as the people who use them. In other words, no contraceptive method is effective if it is not used or if it is used improperly. For this reason the user is at least as important as all the technology of contraception.

Each year in the United States, 750,000 teenagers become pregnant (Guttmacher Institute, 2006). It is not an overstatement to say that teenage pregnancy is at epidemic proportions. Approximately 29 percent of these unwanted pregnancies are terminated by abortion, 57 percent result in live births (to single teenagers or to couples joined in "shotgun" matrimony), and the rest end in miscarriage (Guttmacher Institute, 2006).

The great majority of these unwanted pregnancies occur because sexually active persons fail to use contraceptives responsibly. Among sexually active teenage girls, 17 percent used no method of contraception the last time they had sex (Guttmacher Institute, 2006). In a study of U.S. women having abortions, 46 percent had used no method of contraception in the month when the conception occurred, and many of the rest had been inconsistent (Jones et al., 2002).

Minilaparotomy: A method of female sterilization.

If we are to understand this problem and take effective steps to solve it, we must understand the psychology of contraceptive use and nonuse. Many researchers have been investigating this issue.

When adolescents are asked why they do not use contraceptives, the reasons they give tend to fall into the following categories (Morrison, 1985):

1. Beliefs about their own fertility. "I thought I (or my partner) couldn't get pregnant."
2. Wanting to become pregnant, or at least not minding if they did become pregnant.
3. Problems in obtaining contraception. Many factors may be involved, such as not knowing where to get contraceptives, feeling that it is a hassle to get contraceptives, or expecting that they would be too expensive to buy.
4. Intercourse is unplanned and therefore contraception is not planned.
5. Negative attitudes and feelings about contraception. For example, some feel that contraceptives are messy or embarrassing; others have religious objections; and some believe that contraceptives are dangerous.

Social scientists have developed several theories to explain teenagers' use and nonuse of contraceptives. These theories tend to fall into three categories: (1) theories that view contraceptive behavior as a result of a decision-making process; (2) theories that see contraceptive behavior as the outcome of psychological development; and (3) theories that focus on personality and emotions, such as Donn Byrne's work on erotophobia. Let us look at each of these three categories.

An example of a decision-making theory was formulated by Kristin Luker (1975). She argues that teenage girls essentially engage in a cost-benefit analysis—perhaps not a very deliberate one—in which they weigh (1) the costs of contraception (for example, it may be difficult to obtain, partner may not like the idea); (2) the benefits of contraception (not getting pregnant); (3) the costs of pregnancy, which may not seem large for a young woman with few bright hopes for the future; and (4) the benefits of pregnancy (feeling like a woman, having a baby who loves you). The woman also makes some estimate of the probability of getting pregnant, and she generally underestimates it. As a result, she engages in contraceptive risk-taking—much like deciding not to fasten one's seatbelt in a car—because the costs of contraception seem to outweigh the benefits, or perhaps because there seem to be benefits to pregnancy.

Developmental models look at the process of psychological development during adolescence (e.g., Jorgensen, 1980; Morrison, 1985). Teenagers may find their values to be firmly in line with their parents' values, but their behavior increasingly conforms to the norms of their peer group. A conflict between values and behavior results (Zabin et al., 1984). More specifically, teenagers may hold their parents' conservative values about premarital sex, which prize abstinence and therefore the nonuse of contraceptives. Meanwhile, their actual behavior conforms to that of their peer group, and they engage in premarital intercourse. The hope is that as adolescents mature, their behavior and values will become more consistent with each other.

Social psychologist Donn Byrne (1983; Fisher et al., 1988) focuses on a dimension of personality that he calls *erotophobia–erotophilia*. According to his analysis, there are five steps in effective contraception:

1. The person must acquire and remember accurate information about contraception.
2. The person must acknowledge that there is a likelihood of engaging in sexual intercourse. Contraceptive preparation, of course, makes sense only if one has some expectations of having intercourse. Gender-role socialization has made it particularly difficult for women to acknowledge such expectations.
3. The person must obtain the contraceptive. This may involve a visit to a doctor or to a drugstore or Planned Parenthood clinic.
4. The person must communicate with his or her partner about contraception. Otherwise, each may assume that the other will take care of it.
5. The person must actually use the method of contraception.

According to Byrne's analysis, a number of psychological factors can intervene in any of these five steps, making the person either more likely or less likely to use contraceptives effectively. These factors include attitudes and emotions, information, expectations, and fantasies.

Attitudes and emotions play an important role. One particular dimension is erotophilia–erotophobia (Byrne, 1983; Fisher et al., 1983). **Erotophobes** don't discuss sex, have sex lives that are influenced by guilt and fear of social disapproval, have intercourse infrequently with few partners, and are shocked by sexually explicit films. **Erotophiles** are just the opposite—they discuss sex, they are relatively uninfluenced by sex guilt, they have

Erotophobes: People who feel guilty and fearful about sex.
Erotophiles: People who feel comfortable with sex, lacking in feelings of guilt and fear about sex.

intercourse more frequently with more partners, and they find sexually explicit films to be arousing.

Research shows that erotophiles are more likely to be consistent, reliable contraceptive users. At every one of the five steps of contraceptive use, the erotophobes are more likely to fail. Research shows that they have less sex information than erotophiles do and that, when they are exposed to the same sex information, erotophobes learn less than erotophiles do (Fisher et al., 1983). Because of their fearfulness, erotophobes are less likely to acknowledge that intercourse may occur, which makes contraceptive planning difficult (although extreme erotophobes are likely to abstain from sex completely, which definitely reduces the risk of unwanted pregnancy). Erotophobes also have more difficulty going to a doctor or a drugstore to obtain contraceptives. Erotophobes don't discuss sex or contraception very much, and therefore effective communication with their partner is unlikely to occur. Finally, erotophobes have trouble with actually using the contraceptive. An erotophobic male isn't going to be thrilled about pulling out a condom. An erotophobic female won't be thrilled with inserting a diaphragm or thinking about sex every day as she takes her pill.

Information is also an important factor in contraceptive use and nonuse. People who lack information about contraceptives and their correct use can scarcely use them effectively.

Expectations play an important role. When thinking about sex and contraception, people have some expectations about how likely it is that intercourse will result in pregnancy. Research shows that many people think that the chance is zero or close to it, expressing the expectation that "it can't happen to me." People with this expectation are unlikely to use contraceptives.

Although it is generally recognized that *fantasy* is an important part of sexual expression, fantasy may also play an important role in contraceptive behavior (Byrne, 1983). Most of us have fantasies about sexual encounters, and we often try to make our real-life sexual encounters turn out like the scripts of our fantasies. An important shaper of our fantasies is the mass media. Through movies, television, and romance novels we learn idealized techniques for kissing, holding, lovemaking. But the media's idealized versions of sex almost never include a portrayal of the use of contraceptives. In the popular series *Grey's Anatomy*, intern Cristina has sex with resident Burke with no contraception in sight—and they're doctors!

Positive examples come from the series *Sex and the City*. In one sequence, Miranda had "mercy sex"

with her ex-boyfriend Steve, who had just undergone treatment for testicular cancer. They didn't use a condom, and Miranda got pregnant. After that, she frequently reminded her friends to use a condom, using herself as an example of the consequences if one didn't. These episodes were excellent in showing that negative consequences do occur when contraception is not used, and they provide examples of honest discussions of contraception. Nonetheless, this show was on HBO, and it remains to be seen whether the major networks would air such open and truthful approaches. If teenagers saw lots of instances of their heroes and heroines behaving responsibly about contraception, it would probably influence their behavior. But right now that is not what the media gives them.

What are the solutions? Can this research and theorizing on the social psychology of contraceptive use be applied to reducing the teenage pregnancy problem? The most direct solution would be to have better programs of sex education in the schools. Many districts have no sex education programs, and those that do often skip the important issue of contraception, fearing that it is too controversial. Sex education programs would need to include a number of components that are typically missing. These include legitimizing presex communication about sex and contraception; legitimizing the purchase and carrying of contraceptives; discussing how one weighs the costs and benefits of pregnancy, contraception, and abortion; legitimizing noncoital kinds of sexual pleasure, such as masturbation and oral–genital sex; and encouraging males to accept equal responsibility for contraception. For further information on sexuality education, see Looking to the Future: Sexuality Education, at the end of this book.

Abortion

In the past several decades, **abortion** (the termination of a pregnancy) has been a topic of considerable controversy in North America. Pro-choice groups talk of the woman's right to control her own body, whereas members of right-to-life groups speak of the fetus's rights. In 1973 the U.S. Supreme Court made two landmark decisions (*Roe v. Wade* and *Doe v. Bolton*) that essentially decriminalized abortion by denying the states the right to regulate early abortions. The conservative Supreme Court of the 1990s made some rulings that partly reversed

Abortion: The termination of pregnancy.

Table 7.3   Abortion Rates around the World

Country	Number of Abortions per Year	Abortion Rate*	Abortion Ratio*
Australia	63,200	16.6	20.4
Bulgaria	119,900	64.7	50.7
Canada	63,600	10.2	14.7
China	10,394,500	38.8	31.4
India[†]	588,400	3.0	2.2
Israel[†]	15,500	16.2	13.5
Italy[†]	191,500	15.3	25.7
Japan[†]	497,800	18.6	27.0
South Korea	528,000	53	43
Sweden	34,700	19.8	24.9
U.S.S.R.[†]	6,818,000	111.9	54.9
U.S.	1,588,600	28.0	29.7
Vietnam[†]	170,600	14.6	8.2

*"Abortion rate" is the number of abortions per 1,000 women aged 15 to 44. "Abortion ratio" is the number of abortions per 100 known pregnancies.

[†]Data are from 1989 and are of unknown accuracy.

Source: Henshaw (1990).

these decisions (see Chapter 20). Nevertheless, 1.3 million legal abortions are performed each year in the United States (Guttmacher Institute, 2007).

In other countries, policies on abortion vary widely. It is legal and widely practiced in Russia and Japan, parts of eastern and central Europe, and South America. The use of abortion in the developing nations of Africa and Asia is limited because of the scarcity of medical facilities. Table 7.3 gives rates of abortion in various countries.

In this section we discuss methods of abortion and the psychological aspects of abortion. We explore the ethical and legal aspects in Chapters 19 and 20.

Abortion Procedures

Several methods of abortion are available. Which one is used depends on how far the pregnancy has progressed.

Vacuum Aspiration

The **vacuum aspiration method** (also called *suction curettage*) can be performed during the first trimester of pregnancy and up to 14 weeks' gestation. It is done on an outpatient basis with a local anesthetic. The procedure itself takes only about 10 minutes, and the woman stays in the doctor's office, clinic, or hospital for a few hours. It is the most widely used abortion procedure in the United States today.

Vacuum aspiration: A method of abortion that is performed during the first trimester and involves suctioning out the contents of the uterus. Also called *suction curettage*.

The woman is prepared as she would be for a pelvic exam, and an instrument is inserted into the vagina; the instrument dilates (stretches open) the opening of the cervix. A tube is then inserted into this opening until one end is in the uterus (see Figure 7.14). The other end is attached to a suction-producing apparatus and the contents of the uterus, including the fetal tissue, are sucked out.

Vacuum aspiration has become the most common method of early (first trimester) abortion because it is simple and entails little risk. There are rare risks of uterine perforation, infection, hemorrhaging, and failure to remove all the fetal material. In the U.S. today, 88 percent of abortions are performed by suction curettage, and 88 percent of abortions are performed in the first 12 weeks of gestation (CDC, 2006a).

Dilation and Evacuation

Dilation and evacuation (D and E) is similar to vacuum aspiration, but it must be done in a hospital under a general anesthetic. It is used especially for later abortions, from 14 to 24 weeks' gestation (Autry et al., 2002). It is somewhat similar to vacuum aspiration, but it is more complicated because the fetus is relatively large by the second trimester.

Induced Labor

During the late part of the second trimester, abortion is usually performed by inducing labor and a miscarriage. The most commonly used version of

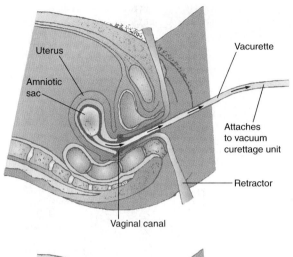

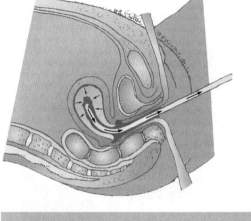

Figure 7.14   A vacuum aspiration abortion.

Table 7.4	Summary of Death Rates Associated with Legal Abortion and with Normal Childbirth
Deaths per 100,000 legal abortions*	
Curettage	0.1
Induced labor	7.0
Hysterotomy	51.6
Deaths per 100,000 normal childbirths	13
Blacks	30.0
Whites	8.1
Other	9.8

*Centers for Disease Control (2006a).
Sources: Cheng et al. (2003); Hatcher et al. (2004).

this method is the *saline-induced abortion*. A fine tube is inserted through the abdomen into the amniotic sac and saline solution is injected. Within several hours, the solution causes labor to begin. A variation on this technique is the *prostaglandin abortion*. Prostaglandins (hormonelike substances that cause contractions) are injected and cause labor. The prostaglandin misoprostol can also be used to induce labor for second-trimester abortions (Autry et al., 2002).

Induced labor, which is used for abortion only if pregnancy has progressed late into the second trimester, accounts for only 1 percent of abortions in the United States (Koonin et al., 1991). This method is both more hazardous and more costly than the other methods.

Hysterotomy

Hysterotomy is a surgical method of abortion that can be done 16 to 24 weeks after the woman's last menstrual period. Essentially, a cesarean section is performed and the fetus is removed. Hysterotomy is more serious and more expensive (more than $1,000) than the other methods, and there is greater risk of complications. It is done only rarely, but it may be used if the pregnancy has progressed to the late second trimester and the woman's health is such that the induction methods should not be used.

A summary of statistics on death rates associated with the various methods of abortion is shown in Table 7.4.

Mifepristone

In 1986 French researchers announced the development of a new drug called **RU-486, or mifepristone** (Couzinet et al., 1986; Ulmann et al., 1990). It can induce a very early abortion. It has a powerful antiprogesterone effect, causing the endometrium of the uterus to be sloughed off and thus bringing about an abortion. It is administered as a tablet followed 2 days later by a small dose of prostaglandin (misoprostol), which increases contractions of the uterus, helping to expel the embryo (Figure 7.15). It is used within 10 days of an expected but missed menstrual period. Research shows that it is effective in 92 to 96 percent of cases when combined with prostaglandin (Silvestre et al., 1990; Spitz et al., 1998; Ulmann et al., 1990). It is most effective when the woman has been pregnant less than 49 days. Early research has found little evidence of side effects, although the woman experiences some cramping as the uterine contents are expelled.

In France today, more than half of women who decide to terminate an early pregnancy choose RU-486 rather than conventional abortion methods (Jones & Henshaw, 2002). However, until 1994 the drug was

Hysterotomy: A surgical method of abortion done in the late second trimester.
Mifepristone (RU-486): The "abortion pill."

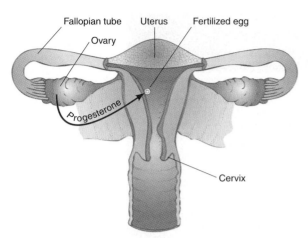

Progesterone, a hormone produced by the ovaries, is necessary for the implantation and development of a fertilized egg.

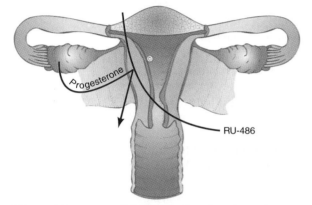

Taken early in pregnancy, RU-486 blocks the action of progesterone and makes the body react as if it isn't pregnant.

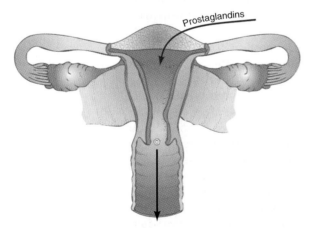

Prostaglandins, taken two days later, cause the uterus to contract and the cervix to soften and dilate. As a result, the embryo is expelled in 97% of the cases.

(a)

(b)

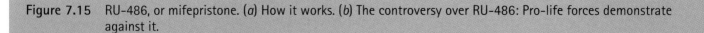

Figure 7.15   RU–486, or mifepristone. (*a*) How it works. (*b*) The controversy over RU–486: Pro-life forces demonstrate against it.

blocked from use in the United States by pressure from antiabortion groups. Because the drug can be easily administered in any doctor's office and reduces the use of abortion clinics, these groups fear that it will become more difficult to protest abortions. The drug was finally approved in 2000 and is now widely available.

Scientists who developed mifepristone, as well as pro-choice groups, prefer not to call it an abortion method, but rather a method for the induction of menstruation or a contragestational drug. It cannot properly be called a contraceptive because it prevents gestation, not conception. Mifepristone and the drug discussed below, methotrexate, are referred to as medical methods of abortion, compared with the more traditional surgical methods.

Methotrexate

Another alternative in drug-induced early abortion involves the use of a combination of the drug methotrexate, which is toxic to the embryo, with misoprostol, which causes uterine contractions that expel the embryo (Hatcher et al., 2004). Both of these drugs are already widely used for other purposes, methotrexate for the treatment of cancer and misoprostol for ulcers. Like mifepristone, they permit the early induction of abortion in a physician's office rather than an abortion clinic, allowing women to avoid sidewalk picketers and potential violence by protestors at abortion clinics. Methotrexate is also used to treat ectopic pregnancy, which is a life-threatening condition.

Psychological Aspects

The discovery of an unwanted pregnancy triggers a complicated set of emotions, as well as a complex decision-making process. Initially women tend to feel anger and some anxiety. They then embark on the decision-making process studied by psychologist Carol Gilligan (1982). In this process women essentially weigh the need to think of themselves and protect their own welfare against the need to think of the welfare of the fetus. Even focusing only on the welfare of the fetus can lead to conflicting conclusions: Should I complete the pregnancy, because the fetus has a right to life; or should I have an abortion, because the fetus has a right to be born into a stable family with married parents who have completed their education and can provide good financial support? Many women in Gilligan's study showed considerable psychological growth over the period in which they wrestled with these issues and made their decision.

Is there a "postabortion syndrome"? Antiabortion activists claim that women are psychologically

traumatized by having an abortion (Bazelon, 2007). What do the scientific data say? The best scientific evidence indicates that most women do not experience severe negative psychological responses to abortion (Major et al., 2000; Schmiege & Russo, 2005). When women are interviewed a year or so after their abortion, most show good adjustment. Typically they do not feel guilt or sorrow over the decision. Instead, they report feeling relieved, satisfied, and relatively happy, and say that if they had the decision to make over again they would do the same thing. Nonetheless, some women benefit from talking about their experience, and it is important that postabortion support groups be available.

Research in this area raises many interesting questions. Women generally show good adjustment after having an abortion, but good adjustment compared with what? That is, what is the appropriate control or comparison group? One comparison group that could be studied is women who requested an abortion but were denied it. It would be important to know the consequences for their adjustment.

One group that has been studied is children who were born because an abortion request was denied. It is impossible to do this research in the United States now because abortion has been legal since 1973. However, in some other countries access to abortion depends on obtaining official approval. One such country was the former Czechoslovakia. Researchers followed up 220 children born to women denied abortion (the study group) and 220 children born to women who had not requested abortion; the children were studied when they were 9 years old and again when they were 14 to 16 years old, 21–23, 30, and 35 (David et al., 2003). By age 14, 43 children from the study group, but only 30 of the controls, had been referred for counseling. Although there were no differences between the groups in tested intelligence, children in the study group did less well in school and were more likely to drop out. Teachers described them as less sociable and more hyperactive compared with the control group. At age 16, the boys (but not the girls) in the study group more frequently rated themselves as feeling neglected or rejected by their mothers, and felt that their mothers were less satisfied with them. By their early twenties, the study group reported less job satisfaction, more conflicts with coworkers and supervisors, and fewer and less satisfying friendships. Several other studies have found results similar to the Czech one (David et al., 2003). These results point to the serious long-term consequences for

Focus: A Sexually Diverse World
Abortion in Cross-Cultural Perspective

Beliefs about abortion show dramatic variations in different cultures around the world. The following is a sampling from two very different cultures.

Ekiti Yoruba

The Ekiti Yoruba, many of whom have a high school or college education, live in southwest Nigeria. For them, abortion is not a distinct category from contraception but rather is on a continuum with it (Renne, 1996).

Traditionally in the Ekiti Yoruba culture the ideal was for a woman to have as many children as possible, spaced at two- to three-year intervals. The spacing of children is made possible by a period of sexual abstinence for two years postpartum. The Ekiti Yoruba believe that sexual intercourse while a woman is still breast-feeding a baby causes illness or death to the child; men whose children have died in infancy have been blamed for breaking the postpartum sex taboo and causing the death. Because of the high value placed on fertility, use of contraceptives and abortion must be kept secret. Even though condoms, foam, and birth control pills are available at a local clinic, few people take advantage of the service because they would not want others to know that they engaged in such practices. Abortion then becomes the chief method of birth control. Estimates are that between 200,000 and 500,000 pregnancies are aborted each year in Nigeria and that about 10,000 women die each year from botched abortions.

If a woman has an unwanted pregnancy, she generally will consult a local divine healer or herbalist first, in order to "keep the pregnancy from staying." They generally provide pills or substances to insert in the vagina. If the treatment does not work, the woman then goes to a clinic and has a dilation and curettage (D&C; a procedure similar to D&E).

Women who abort generally fall into two categories: unmarried high school or college students who want to finish their education, and married women who are pregnant because of an affair. Here is one woman's story:

> In 1991, when awaiting entrance into university, I became pregnant by one boyfriend whom I later decided not to marry in favor of another. Since I did not want my chosen fiancé to know of the pregnancy, I decided to abort it. I first used 3 Beecodeine tablets, Andrew's Liver Salt, and Sprite, mixing them together and then drinking them. When this did not work, I went to a clinic in a neighboring town for D&C. The abortion cost N80 and was paid for by my boyfriend. There were no aftereffects. (Renne, 1996, p. 487)

The ease with which Ekiti Yoruba people rely on abortion is related in part to their understanding of prenatal development. Many believe that the "real child" is not formed until after the fourth month of pregnancy, and before that the being is lizardlike.

Greece

Birth control for women was legalized in Greece only in 1980, and abortion was not legalized until 1986. Yet Greece has had a sharply declining birthrate since World War II, accounted for, in large part, by abortion (Georges, 1996). Among European nations, Greece is unique in its combination of very little use of medical contraception, a low fertility rate, and the highest abortion rate in Europe.

Three powerful institutions—the government, the Greek Orthodox Church, and the medical profession—have exerted a strong pronatalist (in favor of having babies) influence. The Greek Orthodox Church equates abortion with murder and prohibits all methods of birth control except rhythm and abstinence. The government, for its part,

children whose mothers would have preferred to have an abortion.

Men and Abortion

Only women become pregnant, and only women have abortions, but where do men enter the picture? Do they have a right to contribute to the decision to have an abortion? What are their feelings about abortion?

Sociologist Arthur Shostak (1984) surveyed 1,000 male "abortion veterans." The most common reaction from the men was a sense of helplessness. Although most men are used to being in control, but in this situation they are not, and the feeling of powerlessness is difficult for them. Most of the men also felt isolated, angry at themselves and their partners, and fearful of emotional and physical damage to the woman. Most

encourages large families by a variety of measures, including paying a monthly subsidy to families with more than three children, making day care centers widely available, and keeping female methods of contraception illegal (until 1980). Despite all this, Greek women achieved a low fertility rate, which is regarded by the government as a threat to the Greek "race," Greek Orthodoxy, and the military strength of Greece in relation to hostile neighbors such as the extremely fertile Turks.

Despite the illegality of abortion in Greece until 1986, abortion was widespread and a very open secret. Abortions were not back-alley affairs but rather were performed by gynecologists in private offices. Physicians, as members of a powerful and prestigious profession, were successful at legal evasion. As a result, Greek women did not have to face the life-threatening risks that occur with illegal abortion in other countries. They had access to safe, illegal abortion.

Why is there so much reliance on abortion and so little access to contraception in this modern European nation? As noted earlier, the Greek Orthodox Church opposes all medical contraception and the Greek government kept contraception illegal until 1980. But even then, contraception did not become widespread. In 1990 only 2 percent of women of reproductive age were using the pill. Some blame this on the medical profession, which is thought to block access to contraception in order to continue a thriving abortion practice that is more lucrative. Greek women, too, resist contraception. They distinguish between "contraception" (such as birth control pills) and "being careful" (withdrawal and condoms). They reject contraception, but being careful—especially the use of withdrawal—is widespread. Rhythm is not widely used and would not be very successful if it were, since Greek women commonly believe that they are most fertile for the four to seven days just before and after the menstrual period. The mass media have spread scare messages about the pill, and many women believe that it causes cancer.

How do Greek women, the great majority of whom are Orthodox, deal with the contradiction between their church's teaching—that abortion is murder and that a woman who has had an abortion may not receive communion—and their actual practice of having abortions? First, the Greek Orthodox Church is not as absolutist in its application of doctrines regarding abortion as the Roman Catholic Church is. Some attribute this to the fact that Orthodox priests can be married and are therefore more in touch with the realities of life. In some cases, women do abstain from receiving communion following an abortion but then later make a confession to the priest. Priests typically are forgiving.

In Greece, motherhood is highly esteemed and idealized, yet abortion is not considered contradictory to the high value placed on motherhood. Good motherhood today is thought to require an intense investment of time and energy in one's children; by definition, then, the good mother limits family size, and abortion is a means to achieve that goal.

Cross-Cultural Patterns

Several patterns emerge from the study of abortion in these quite distinct cultures and other cultures (e.g., Gursoy, 1996; Johnson et al., 1996; Rigdon, 1996; Rylko-Bauer, 1996). First, no matter how strict the prohibitions against abortion, some women in all cultures choose and manage to obtain abortion. Second, the meaning of abortion is constructed in any particular culture based on factors such as beliefs about prenatal development, when life starts, and how much large families are valued. Third, the legality and morality of abortion in any culture is determined in part by political forces, such as the Greek government's desire to expand the size of the Greek population.

Sources: Georges (1996); Gursoy (1996); Johnson et al. (1996); Renne (1996); Rigdon (1996); Rylko-Bauer (1996).

---

of them tried to hide their stress and remain unemotional. Nonetheless, 26 percent thought of abortion as murder, and 81 percent said they thought about the child who might have been born. However, few men wanted to be able to overrule the woman's decision; they only wanted to share in it.

Although counseling for women undergoing abortion is a standard procedure, counseling is rarely available for the men who are involved. Given Shostak's findings, it is clear that such counseling is badly needed (see Coyle & Enright, 1997, for an example). On a political level, some men's activists argue that, just as women should not be forced to carry a pregnancy to term, so men should not be subjected to forced fatherhood and an 18-year financial commitment (Marsiglio & Diekow, 1998).

New Advances in Contraception

According to some, a really good method of contraception is not yet available. The highly effective methods either are permanent (sterilization) or have associated health risks (the pill). Other, safer methods (such as the condom and the diaphragm) have failure rates that cannot be ignored. Most of the methods are for women, not men. Because of the limitations of the currently available methods, contraception research continues. Unfortunately, its pace has been slow in the last few years because pharmaceutical companies are weary of lawsuits. There is little incentive for conducting highly innovative research and much incentive for companies to be cautious. Nonetheless, research and innovation continue, even if at a slow pace. Below we discuss some of the more promising possibilities for the future.

Male Methods

Several possibilities for new or improved male contraception are being explored (Hatcher et al., 2004; Institute of Medicine, 2004; Wenk & Nieschlag, 2006).

New Condoms

Several new models of condoms are being tested. To deal with the problem of allergies to latex, polyurethane condoms have been developed, as noted earlier. They are thinner than latex, so they should provide more sensation. Another model is one that could be put on before erection.

Male Hormonal Methods

The basic idea underlying the development of male hormonal methods is to suppress the production of LH and FSH by the pituitary, so that sperm would not be produced or would not develop properly (Wenk & Nieschlag, 2006). Unfortunately, many of the hormone preparations that have been tried shut down sperm production but also shut down the user's sex drive, making them unacceptable to most men. Current drugs being tested involve a combination of testosterone and a progestin (such as DMPA, used in the Depo-Provera shot for women); the latter would suppress FSH and LH production leading to the suppression of spermatogenesis (Page et al., 2006). Another group of drugs are GnRH antagonists. By reducing GnRH activity, they would reduce the production of FSH and LH, which would stop spermatogenesis.

Immunocontraceptives

Scientists have been working on a contraceptive vaccine that would induce the individual's immune system to react in a way that would interrupt one of the steps in the fertility system—for example, one of the stages in the production or maturation of sperm. One option is a vaccine targeting sperm antigens. Another is a vaccine for men that would target pituitary FSH, which would block sperm production without stopping the manufacture of testosterone. None of these are in trials yet.

Female Methods

Microbicides

Microbicides are substances that kill microbes (bacteria and viruses) and, preferably, sperm. Experts had hoped that current contraceptive foams and gels, which contain nonoxynol-9 (N-9), would be effective microbicides, but it turns out that N-9 is ineffective and may actually make women more vulnerable to infection. What we need is a microbicide that is highly effective at killing the viruses and bacteria that cause STIs *and* is also effective at killing sperm. Several promising microbicides are in clinical trials now (Hatcher et al., 2004). They include BufferGel, Invisible Condom, Savvy, and PRO 2000. These microbicides could be used by themselves or with a diaphragm or condom.

Vaginal Rings

The NuvaRing, discussed earlier, is already available and contains a combination of estrogen and progestin. Two new progestin-only vaginal rings are under development (Upadhyay et al., 2005). They are somewhat less effective than the combination hormone ring, but they could be used by breast-feeding women.

Spray-On Contraception

Nestorone, a progestin, is now under development in spray form, the Nestorone Metered Dose Transdermal System (Upadhyay et al., 2005). It is sprayed on the skin (transdermally) once a day, is quickly absorbed through the skin, and then slowly diffuses into the bloodstream.

Implants and Injectables

Norplant, a progestin-only method, was approved by the FDA in 1990 and involves implanting six small rods under the skin in the upper arm. Although it was highly effective, users expressed much dissatisfaction, and it proved difficult to remove the rods when the woman wanted to become pregnant. Newer, improved implants are being developed, including Jadelle and Implanon (Upadhyay et al., 2005). They have only one or two rods or capsules implanted in the upper arm. Their initial cost, unfortunately, is high.

The contraceptive injection used in the United States today is Depo-Provera, which contains

Focus: Milestones in Sex Research
History of the Development of Sophisticated Methods of Contraception

Late 1700s	Casanova (1725–1798) popularizes and publicizes use of the sheath, or "English riding coat."
1798	Malthus urges "moral restraint" or abstinence.
1840s	Goodyear vulcanizes rubber. Production of rubber condoms soon follows.
1883	Mensinga invents the diaphragm.
1893	Harrison performs the first vasectomy.
1909	Richter uses the intrauterine silkworm gut.
1910–1920	Sanger pioneers in New York City; the term *birth control* is coined.
1930	Gräfenberg publishes information documenting his 21 years of experience with the ring (silver and copper) and catgut as IUDs.
1930–1931	Knaus and Ogino elucidate "safe and unsafe" periods of the woman's menstrual cycle: the rhythm method.
1934	Corner and Beard isolate progesterone.
1937	Makepeace demonstrates that progesterone inhibits ovulation.
1950s	Abortions are utilized extensively in Japan.
1950–1960	Hormonal contraceptive research results in FDA approval of the use of the pill as a contraceptive in 1960.
1960s	Many Western nations liberalize abortion laws. Modern IUDs become available. Contraceptive sterilization becomes more acceptable. The laparoscopic tubal ligation technique is developed.
1973	The United States Supreme Court rules on abortion.
1970s	Depo-Provera contraceptive injections become available in more than 50 nations (though not in United States until 1992).
1990	Norplant becomes available.
1994	Female condom becomes available over the counter.
2001	NuvaRing and Ortho Evra patch approved by FDA.
2003	Seasonale approved by FDA.
2006	Plan B emergency contraception approved by FDA for sale over the counter.

Sources: Hatcher et al. (1976); Institute of Medicine (2004).

---

progestin only. Newer injections, such as Cyclofem, Lunelle, and Mesigyna, are being developed that contain a combination of estrogen and progestin much like the combination pill (Upadhyay et al., 2005).

New IUDs
Several new IUDs are under development. One, GyneFix, is similar to the copper T, but without the T—that is, it is frameless. It simply carries copper tubes on a string and would last for at least five years, but the top of it must be anchored into the fundus of the uterus. It has been approved in Europe and is available in China.

Reversible, Nonsurgical Sterilization
This method involves injecting liquid silicone into the fallopian tubes. The silicone hardens and forms a plug. The plugs could later be removed if the woman wished to become pregnant. This method has not yet been approved by the FDA but is being studied in the Netherlands. It might also be used to plug the vas in men.

SUMMARY

Table 7.5 provides a comparative summary of the various methods of birth control discussed in this chapter.

Table 7.5 Summary of Information on Methods of Contraception and Abortion

Method	Effectiveness Rating	Failure Rate, Perfect Use, %	Failure Rate, Typical Use, %	Death Rate (per 100,000 Women)	Yearly Costs, $*	Advantages	Disadvantages
Depo-Provera	Excellent	0.3	3		300	Requires less memory	
Combination birth control pills	Excellent	0.3	8	1.6	455	Highly effective; not used at time of coitus; improved menstrual cycles	Cost; possible side effects; must take daily
Patch	Excellent	0.3	1.3		455	Requires less memory than pill	
Vaginal Ring	Excellent	0.5	5	—	455		
IUD, Copper T	Excellent	0.6	0.8	1.0	250[†]	Requires no memory or motivation	May be expelled
Progesterone T	Excellent	0.1	0.1		250		
Condom, male	Very good	2	15	1.7	75	Easy to use; protection from STIs	Used at time of coitus; continual expense
Condom, female	Good	5	21	2.0	375	Protection from STIs	Awkward
Diaphram with spermicide	Good	6	16	2.0[‡]	100	No side effects, inexpensive	Aesthetic objections
Femcap with spermicide					100	No side effects, inexpensive	—
Parous women	Fair	26	32	2.0[‡]			
Nulliparous women	Good	9	16	2.0[‡]			
Vaginal foam, cream	Fair	18	29	2.0[‡]	50	Easy to use; availability	Messy, continual expense
Withdrawal	Good	4	27	2.0	None	No cost	Requires high motivation
Rhythm	Poor to fair	2–9	25	2.0	None	No cost, accepted by Roman Catholic Church	Requires high motivation, prolonged abstinence; not all women can use
Unprotected intercourse	Poor	85	85	9[‡]	None[§]		
Legal abortion, first trimester	Excellent	0	0	0.5	350–700	Available when other methods fail	Expensive; moral or psychological unacceptability
Sterilization, male	Excellent	0.10	0.15	0.3	1,500**	Permanent; highly effective	Permanence; expense
Sterilization, female	Excellent	0.5	.5	1.5	1,500–6,000**	Permanent; highly effective	Permanence; expense

*Based on 150 acts of intercourse. Prices are provided by Planned Parenthood, 2007, for full-paying clients (http://www.plannedparenthood.org/birth-control-pregnancy). Prices are reduced for those with low incomes. Prices are higher for private physicians.

[†]Based on a cost of $500 for the IUD including insertion by a physician, and the assumption that the IUD will be used for two years. The cost per year is much less if the IUD is used for more than two years.

[‡]Based on the death rate for pregnancies resulting from the method. Of every 100,000 live births in the United States, 12 women die (Cheng et al., 2003).

[§]But having a baby is expensive.

**These are one-time-only costs.

Source: Hatcher et al. (2004).

QUESTIONS FOR THOUGHT, DISCUSSION, AND DEBATE

1. Do you think you are an erotophobe or an erotophile? In what ways do you think your erotophobia or erotophilia has affected or will affect your use of birth control?

2. Debate the following topic. Resolved: The birth control pill is a safe and effective method of birth control for most women.

3. In the United States, few IUDs are available because of lawsuits against companies that make them and concern over possible health risks. In contrast, in the People's Republic of China they are the mainstay of contraception, with 40 million in use. Which country has the better policy?

4. On your campus, as on all campuses, students are probably inconsistent in their use of birth control or use nothing even though they are sexually active. Design a program to improve birth control practices on your campus.

5. Knowing that you are taking a human sexuality course and have gained a lot of expertise, Latoya, your best friend, comes to you in a state of crisis. She and her boyfriend had unprotected intercourse last night, and she is terrified that she is pregnant. What options would you explain to her, and which one would you recommend?

SUGGESTIONS FOR FURTHER READING

Hatcher, Robert A., et al. (2004). *Contraceptive technology.* 18th ed. New York: Ardent Media. This authoritative book is updated frequently and provides the most recent information on all methods of contraception.

Tone, Andrea. (2001). *Devices and desires: A history of contraceptives in America.* New York: Hill & Wang. This book provides a fascinating and enlightening social history of the development of birth control in America, from the widespread manufacture of rubber condoms in the mid-1800s, through Comstock's attempts to outlaw contraceptives, Margaret Sanger's efforts to make birth control widely accessible, and the introduction of the pill.

Ulmann, André, Teutsch, Georges, and Philibert, Daniel. (June 1990). RU-486. *Scientific American, 262,* 42–48. An interesting, behind-the-scenes article by three of the French scientists involved in the development of RU-486 (mifepristone).

CHAPTER EIGHT

Sexual Arousal

CHAPTER HIGHLIGHTS

H ere are some colors of different people's orgasms: champagne, all colors and white and gray afterward, red and blue, green, beige and blue, red, blue and gold. Some people never make it because they are trying for plaid.*

*Berne (1970), p. 238.

In this chapter we focus on the way the body responds during sexual arousal and orgasm and the processes behind these responses. This information is very important in developing good techniques of lovemaking, which we discuss later in this chapter, and in analyzing and treating sexual disorders such as premature ejaculation (see Chapter 17).

First we examine how the body responds physiologically during orgasm. Much of what we know about these processes is based on the classic research of Masters and Johnson. Their research has been criticized, though, so in the next section we present some alternative models. Next we focus on how hormones, the brain, and the spinal cord contribute to sexual behavior and response. We consider research on pheromones and their influence on sexual behavior in animals and humans. Finally, we discuss sexual techniques.

The Sexual Response Cycle

Sex researchers William H. Masters and Virginia E. Johnson provided one of the first models of the physiology of human sexual response. Their research culminated in 1966 with the publication of *Human Sexual Response,* which reported data on 382 women and 312 men observed in more than 10,000 sexual cycles of arousal and orgasm. Recent biological research has confirmed many of their findings, while questioning a few and augmenting many. All of this research is the basis for the sections that follow.

Sexual response typically progresses in three stages: *excitement, orgasm,* and *resolution.* The two basic physiological processes that occur during these stages are vasocongestion and myotonia. **Vasocongestion** occurs when a great deal of blood flows into the blood vessels in a region, in this case the genitals, as a result of dilation of the blood vessels in the region. **Myotonia** occurs when muscles contract, not only in the genitals but also throughout the body. Let us now consider in detail what occurs in each of the stages.

Excitement

The **excitement** phase is the beginning of erotic arousal. The basic physiological process that occurs during excitement is vasocongestion. This produces the obvious arousal response in the male—erection. Erection results when the corpora cavernosa and the corpus spongiosum fill (becoming engorged) with blood (see Figure 8.1). Erection may be produced by direct physical stimulation of the genitals, by stimulation of other parts of the body, or by erotic thoughts. It occurs very rapidly, within a few seconds of the stimulation, although it may take place more slowly as a result of a number of factors including age, intake of alcohol, and fatigue. As the man gets closer to orgasm, a few drops of fluid (for some men, quite a few), secreted by the Cowper's gland, appear at the tip of the penis. Although they are not the ejaculate, they may contain active sperm.

Research in the last decade—stimulated, in part, by the search for drugs to treat erectile disorder—has given us much more detailed information about the physiological processes involved in erection (Adams et al., 1997; Heaton, 2000). Several arteries supply the corpora cavernosa and spongiosum. For an erection to occur, these arteries must dilate (vasodilation), allowing a strong flow of blood into the corpora. At the same time, the veins carrying blood away from the penis are compressed, restricting outgoing blood flow. The arteries dilate because the smooth muscle surrounding the arteries relaxes. Multiple neurotransmitters are involved in this process, including, especially, nitric oxide (NO). Dopamine is involved as well. The drug Viagra acts on the NO system.

Nice as they are, erections would become a pain if they lasted forever, so there is a reverse process, vasoconstriction, that makes an erection go away, for example, following orgasm. The neurotransmitters epinephrine and norepinephrine are involved. These processes occur in the resolution phase, which we discuss below.

An important response of females in the excitement phase is

Vasocongestion (vay-so-con-JES-tyun): An accumulation of blood in the blood vessels of a region of the body, especially the genitals; a swelling or erection results.
Myotonia (my-oh-TONE-ee-ah): Muscle contraction.
Excitement: The first stage of sexual response, during which erection in the male and vaginal lubrication in the female occur.

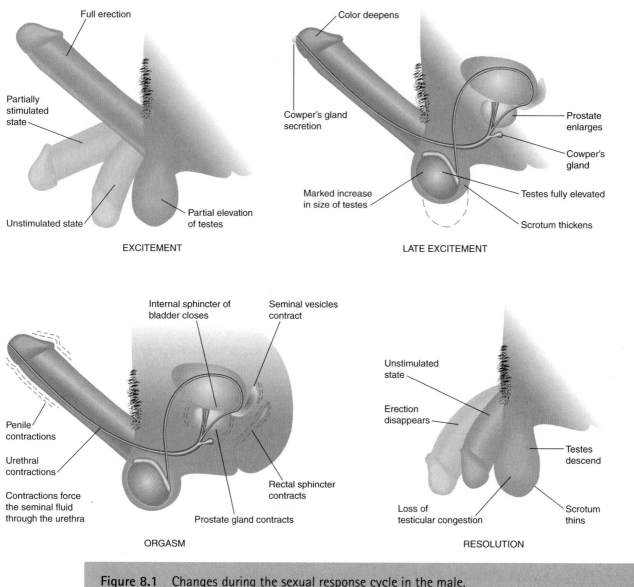

Full erection

Partially stimulated state

Unstimulated state

Partial elevation of testes

EXCITEMENT

Color deepens

Cowper's gland secretion

Marked increase in size of testes

Prostate enlarges

Cowper's gland

Testes fully elevated

Scrotum thickens

LATE EXCITEMENT

Internal sphincter of bladder closes

Seminal vesicles contract

Penile contractions

Urethral contractions

Contractions force the seminal fluid through the urethra

Prostate gland contracts

Rectal sphincter contracts

ORGASM

Unstimulated state

Erection disappears

Loss of testicular congestion

Testes descend

Scrotum thins

RESOLUTION

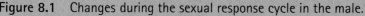

Figure 8.1   Changes during the sexual response cycle in the male.

lubrication of the vagina. Although this response might seem much different from the male's, actually they both result from the same physiological process: vasocongestion. During excitement, the capillaries in the walls of the vagina dilate and blood flow through them increases (Levin, 2005). Vaginal lubrication results when fluids seep through the semipermeable membranes of the vaginal walls, producing lubrication as a result of vasocongestion in the tissues surrounding the vagina. This response to arousal is also rapid, though not quite so fast as the male's; lubrication begins 10 to 30 seconds after the onset of arousing stimuli.[1] Like the male sexual response, female responding can be affected by factors such as age, intake of alcohol, and fatigue.

As the woman becomes more aroused and gets closer to orgasm, the **orgasmic platform** forms. This response is a tightening and thickening of the wall of the outer third of the vagina (Figure 8.2). As a

Orgasmic platform: A tightening of the entrance to the vagina caused by contractions of the bulbospongiosus muscle (which covers the vestibular bulbs) that occur during the excitement stage of sexual response.

[1]Before the Masters and Johnson research, it was thought that the lubrication was due to secretions of the Bartholin glands, but it is now known that these glands contribute little if anything. At this point, you might want to go back to the limerick about the Bartholin glands in Chapter 4 and see whether you can spot the error in it.

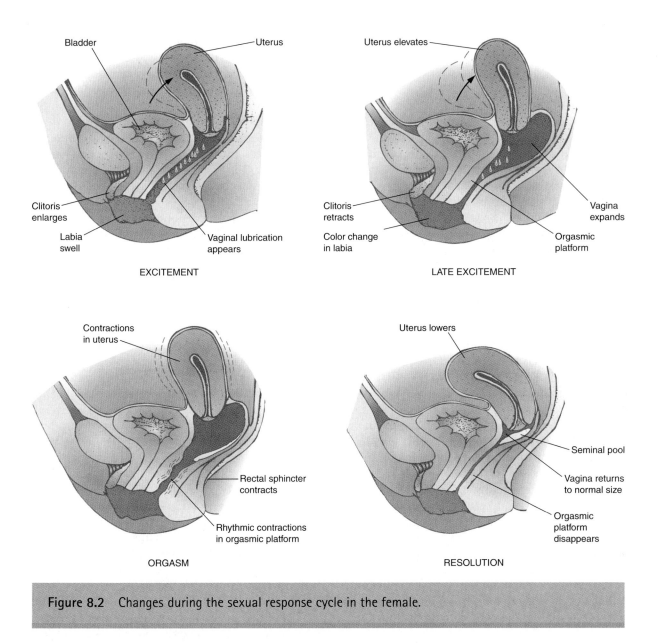

Bladder — Uterus

Clitoris enlarges

Labia swell

Vaginal lubrication appears

EXCITEMENT

Uterus elevates

Clitoris retracts

Color change in labia

Vagina expands

Orgasmic platform

LATE EXCITEMENT

Contractions in uterus

Rectal sphincter contracts

Rhythmic contractions in orgasmic platform

ORGASM

Uterus lowers

Seminal pool

Vagina returns to normal size

Orgasmic platform disappears

RESOLUTION

Figure 8.2   Changes during the sexual response cycle in the female.

result, the size of the vaginal entrance actually becomes smaller, and there may be a noticeable increase in gripping of the penis.

During the excitement phase, the glans of the clitoris (the tip) swells. This swelling results from engorgement of its corpora cavernosa and is similar to erection in the male. The clitoris can be felt as larger and harder than usual. The crura of the clitoris, lying deeper in the body (see Figure 4.3), also swell as a result of vasocongestion. The vestibular bulbs, which lie along the wall of the vagina, are also erectile and swell during the excitement phase. Late in the excitement phase, elevation of the clitoris may occur. The clitoris essentially retracts or draws up into the body.

Vasocongestion in females results from the same underlying physiological processes as those in males. That is, relaxation of the smooth muscle surrounding the arteries supplying the glans and crura of the clitoris and the vestibular bulbs occurs, allowing a great deal of blood flow to the region (Berman et al., 2000). As in the male, nitric oxide is a key neurotransmitter involved in the process (Traish et al., 2002). Estrogen helps the vasodilation.

During excitement the nipples become erect. This response results from contractions of the muscle fibers (myotonia) surrounding the nipple. The breasts themselves swell and enlarge somewhat in the late part of the excitement phase (a vasocongestion response). The nipples may not actually look erect but may appear somewhat flatter against the breast because the breast has swollen. Many males also have nipple erection during the excitement phase.

In the unaroused state the inner lips are generally folded over, covering the entrance to the vagina, and the outer lips lie close to each other. During excitement the inner lips swell and open up (a vasocongestion response).

The vagina shows an important change during excitement. Think of the vagina as being divided into two parts, an upper (or inner) two-thirds and a lower (or outer) one-third. In the unaroused state the walls of the vagina lie against each other, much like the sides of an uninflated balloon. During the excitement phase, the upper two-thirds of the vagina expands dramatically in what is often called a "ballooning" response. In other words, it becomes more like an inflated balloon (Figure 8.2). This ballooning helps accommodate the entrance of the penis. As part of the ballooning, the cervix and uterus also pull up.

During excitement a "sex flush" may appear on the skin of both men and women, though more commonly of women. The sex flush resembles a measles rash; it often begins on the upper abdomen and spreads over the chest. It may also appear later in the sexual response cycle.

Pulse rate, breathing rate, and blood pressure also increase in both men and women.

In men, the skin of the scrotum thickens. The scrotal sac tenses, and the scrotum is pulled up and closer to the body (see Figure 8.1). The spermatic cords shorten, pulling the testes closer to the body.

Late in the excitement phase, the processes of vasocongestion and myotonia continue to build until there is sufficient tension for orgasm.

Orgasm

In the male, **orgasm** consists of a series of rhythmic contractions of the pelvic organs at 0.8-second intervals. Male orgasm occurs in two stages. In the preliminary stage, the vas, seminal vesicles, and prostate contract, forcing the ejaculate into a bulb at the base of the urethra (see Figure 8.1). Masters and Johnson call the sensation in this stage one of *ejaculatory inevitability* ("coming"). In other words, there is a sensation that ejaculation is just about to happen and cannot be stopped. And, indeed, it cannot be, once the man has reached this point. In the second stage, the urethral bulb and the penis itself contract rhythmically,

> **Orgasm:** The second stage of sexual response; an intense sensation that occurs at the peak of sexual arousal and is followed by release of sexual tensions.

forcing the semen through the urethra and out the opening at the tip of the penis.

In both males and females, pulse rate, blood pressure, and breathing rate increase sharply during orgasm.[2] Muscles contract throughout the body. The face may be contorted in a grimace; the muscles of the arms, legs, thighs, back, and buttocks may contract; and the muscles of the feet and hands may contract in *carpopedal spasms.* Generally, in the passion of the moment, a person is not really aware of these occurrences, but an aching back or buttocks may serve as a reminder the next day.

The process of orgasm in females is basically similar to that in males. It is a series of rhythmic muscular contractions of the orgasmic platform. The contractions generally occur at about 0.8-second intervals; there may be three or four in a mild orgasm or as many as a dozen in a very intense, prolonged orgasm. The uterus also contracts rhythmically. Other muscles, such as those around the anus, may also contract.

Female orgasm is a funny thing. As with love, you can almost never get anyone to give you a solid definition of what it is. Instead, people usually fall back on, "You'll know what it is when you have one." This evasiveness is probably related to several factors, most notably that female orgasm leaves no tangible evidence of its occurrence like ejaculation—except for those women who do ejaculate. Also, women often do not reach orgasm as quickly as men do, a point to be discussed in more detail in Chapter 12. In fact, some women, particularly young women, may think they are having an orgasm when they are not. If they have never had an orgasm, they mistake intense arousal for orgasm.

Just what does orgasm in the female feel like? The main feeling is a spreading sensation that begins around the clitoris and then spreads outward through the whole pelvis. There may also be sensations of falling or opening up. The woman may be able to feel the contraction of the muscles around the vaginal entrance. The sensation is more intense than just a warm glow or a pleasant tingling. In one study, college men and women gave written descriptions of what an orgasm felt like to them (Vance & Wagner, 1976). Interestingly, a panel of experts (medical students, obstetrician–gynecologists, and clinical psychologists) could not reliably figure out which of the descriptions were written by women

---

[2]With all the current attention to aerobics and exercising the heart, we have yet to hear anyone suggest orgasm aerobics. It seems to us that it should work. Kickboxing, watch out. Here comes sexercise!

"Did you come?"

Figure 8.3

Source: Tom Chency/*Penthouse Magazine.* © 1996 by Tom Chency. Reprinted by permission.

and which by men. This result suggests that the sensations are quite similar for males and females.

Some of the men in our classes have asked how they can tell whether a woman has really had an orgasm. Their question in itself is interesting. In part it reflects a cultural skepticism about female orgasm. There is usually obvious proof of male orgasm: ejaculation. But there is no consistent proof of female orgasm—except that some women do ejaculate.

The question also reflects the fact that men know that women sometimes fake orgasm. Faking orgasm is a complex issue. Basically, it is probably not a very good idea, because it is dishonest. It also leads the woman's partner to think that his or her technique of stimulation is more effective than it is. On the other hand, one needs to be sympathetic to the variety of reasons women do it. It is often difficult for women to reach orgasm, and our culture currently places a lot of emphasis on everyone's having orgasms. The woman may feel that she is expected to have an orgasm, and realizing that it is unlikely to happen this time, she fakes it in order to meet expectations. She may also do it to please her partner.[3]

But back to the question: How can a woman's partner tell? There really is not any very good way.

[3]Indeed, many of the old sex manuals, as well as physicians' textbooks, counseled women to fake orgasm. For example: "It is good advice to recommend to the women the advantage of innocent simulation of sex responsiveness, and as a matter of fact many women in their desire to please their husbands learned the advantage of such innocent deception" (Novak & Novak, 1952, p. 572).

From a scientific point of view, a good method would be to have the woman hooked up to an instrument that registers pulse rate. There is a sudden sharp increase in the pulse rate at orgasm, and that would be a good indicator. We doubt, though, that most men have such equipment available, and we are even more doubtful about whether most women would agree to be so wired up. Probably rather than trying to check up on each other, it would be better for partners to establish good, honest communication and avoid setting performance goals in sex, points that we will discuss further in later chapters.

Resolution

Following orgasm is the **resolution** phase, during which the body returns physiologically to the unaroused state. Orgasm triggers a massive release of muscular tension and of blood from the engorged blood vessels. Resolution represents a reversal of the processes that build up during the excitement stage.

The first change in women is a reduction in the swelling of the breasts. In the 5 to 10 seconds after the end of the orgasm, the clitoris returns to its normal position, although it takes longer for it to shrink to its normal size. The orgasmic platform relaxes and begins to shrink. The ballooning of the vagina diminishes, and the uterus shrinks. The resolution phase generally takes 15 to 30 minutes, but it may take much longer—as much as an hour—in women who have not had an orgasm.

In both males and females, resolution brings a gradual return of pulse rate, blood pressure, and breathing rate to the unaroused levels.

In men, the most obvious occurrence in the resolution phase is detumescence, the loss of erection in the penis. Detumescence happens in two stages. The first occurs rapidly but leaves the penis still enlarged. This first loss of erection results from an emptying of the corpora cavernosa. The second stage occurs more slowly, as a result of the slower emptying of the corpus spongiosum and the glans.

During the resolution phase, men enter a **refractory period,** during which they are refractory to further arousal. In other words, they are incapable of being aroused again, having an erection, or having an orgasm. The length of this refractory period varies considerably from one man to the next. In some it may last only a few minutes, and in others it may go on for 24 hours. The refractory period tends to become longer as men grow older.

Resolution: The third stage of sexual response, in which the body returns to the unaroused state.
Refractory period (ree-FRAK-toh-ree): The period following orgasm during which the male cannot be sexually aroused.

Women do not have a refractory period, making possible the phenomenon of multiple orgasm in women, which we discuss in the next section.

What about the role of hormones? Oxytocin is secreted during sexual arousal, and a surge of prolactin occurs at orgasm in both women and men (Exton et al., 1999; Levin, 2003; Krüger et al., 2002). Some think that prolactin is the offswitch to sexual arousal and that it creates the refractory period in males, although that does not explain why females do not have a refractory period. Interestingly, in both women and men, much more prolactin is secreted following orgasm from intercourse than orgasm from masturbation (Kruger, 2006). Does that make orgasms from intercourse more satiating or satisfying?

More on Women's Orgasms

Some people believe that women can have two kinds of orgasm: **clitoral orgasm** and **vaginal orgasm.** The words *clitoral* and *vaginal* refer to the region of stimulation: an orgasm resulting from clitoral stimulation versus an orgasm resulting from vaginal stimulation. The distinction originated with Sigmund Freud. Freud believed that in childhood little girls masturbate and for this reason have orgasms by means of clitoral stimulation, or clitoral orgasms. He thought that as women grow older and mature, they ought to shift from having orgasms as a result of masturbation to having them as a result of heterosexual intercourse, in other words, by means of vaginal stimulation. For this reason the vaginal orgasm was considered "mature" and the clitoral orgasm "immature" or "infantile." Not only did there come to be two kinds of orgasm, but one was regarded as "better" (that is, more mature) than the other.

Freud's formulation is of more than theoretical interest, since it has had an impact on the lives of many women. Over several decades many women undertook psychoanalysis and spent countless hours agonizing over why they were not able to achieve the elusive vaginal orgasm and why they enjoyed the "immature" clitoral one so much. Women who could have orgasms only through clitoral stimulation were called "vaginally frigid" or "fixated" at an infantile stage.

According to the results of Masters and Johnson's research, though, there is no difference between clitoral and vaginal orgasms. This conclusion is based on two findings. First, their results indicate that all female orgasms are physiologically the same, regardless of the site of stimulation. An orgasm always consists of contractions of the orgasmic platform, whether the stimulation is clitoral or vaginal. Indeed, they found a few women who could orgasm purely through breast stimulation, and that orgasm was the same as the other two, consisting of contractions of the orgasmic platform and the muscles around the vagina. Physiologically there is only one kind of orgasm. (Of course, this does not mean that psychologically there are not different kinds. The experience of orgasm during intercourse may be quite different from the experience of orgasm during masturbation.)

Second, clitoral stimulation is almost always involved in producing orgasm, even during vaginal intercourse. The deep structure of the clitoris (see Figure 4.3) ensures that the crura of the clitoris are stimulated as the penis moves through the vaginal entrance. For this reason even the purely vaginal orgasm results from quite a bit of clitoral stimulation. Clitoral stimulation is usually the trigger to orgasm, and the orgasm itself occurs in the vagina and surrounding tissues.

Traditionally it was believed that orgasmically women behaved like men in that they could have one orgasm and then would have a refractory period before they could have another. Masters and Johnson, however, discovered that women do not enter a refractory period, and they can have **multiple orgasms** within a short period of time. Actually, women's capacity for multiple orgasms was originally discovered by Kinsey in his interviews with women (Kinsey et al., 1953; see also Terman et al., 1938). The scientific establishment, however, dismissed these reports as another instance of Kinsey's supposed unreliability.

The term *multiple orgasm,* then, refers to a series of orgasms occurring within a short period of time. Multiple orgasms do not differ physiologically from single orgasms. Each is a "real" orgasm, and they are not minor experiences. One nice thing, though, is that the later ones generally require less effort than the first one.

How does multiple orgasm work physiologically? Immediately following an orgasm, both males and females move into the resolution phase. In this phase, males typically enter into a refractory period, during which they cannot be aroused again. But the female does not enter into a refractory period. That is, if she is stimulated again, she can immediately be aroused and move back into the excitement phase and have another orgasm.

Clitoral orgasm: Freud's term for orgasm in the female resulting from stimulation of the clitoris.
Vaginal orgasm: Freud's term for orgasm in the female resulting from stimulation of the vagina in heterosexual intercourse; Freud considered vaginal orgasm to be more mature than clitoral orgasm.
Multiple orgasm: A series of orgasms occurring within a short period of time.

Multiple orgasm is more likely to result from hand–genital or mouth–genital stimulation than from intercourse, since most men do not have the endurance to continue thrusting for such long periods of time. Regarding capacity, Masters and Johnson found that women in masturbation might have 5 to 20 orgasms. In some cases, they quit only when physically exhausted. When a vibrator is used, less effort is required, and some women were capable of having 50 orgasms in a row.

We should note that some women who are capable of multiple orgasms are completely satisfied with one, particularly in intercourse, and do not wish to continue. We should be careful not to set multiple orgasm as another of the many goals in sexual performance.

Some men are capable of having multiple orgasms (e.g., Hartman & Fithian, 1984; Zilbergeld, 1992). In one study, 21 men were interviewed, all of whom had volunteered for research on multiply orgasmic men (Dunn & Trost, 1989). Some of the men reported having been multiply orgasmic since their sexual debut, whereas others had developed the pattern later in life, and still others had worked actively to develop the capacity after reading about the possibility. The respondents reported that multiple orgasm did not occur every time they engaged in sexual activity. For these men, detumescence did not always follow an orgasm, allowing for continued stimulation and an additional orgasm. Some men reported that some of the orgasms included ejaculation and others in the sequence did not. This study cannot tell us the incidence of multiply orgasmic men in the general population, but it does provide evidence that multiply orgasmic men exist.

Cognitive–Physiological Models

Some experts on human sexuality are critical of Masters and Johnson's model. One important criticism is that the Masters and Johnson model ignores the cognitive and subjective aspects of sexual response (Zilbergeld & Ellison, 1980). Masters and Johnson focused almost entirely on the physiological aspects of sexual response, ignoring what the person is thinking and feeling emotionally. Desire and passion are not part of the model.

A second important criticism concerns how research participants were selected and how this process may have created a self-fulfilling prophecy for the outcome (Tiefer, 1991). To participate in the research, participants were required to have a history of orgasm both through masturbation and through coitus. Essentially, anyone whose pattern of sexual response did not include orgasm—and therefore did not fit Masters and Johnson's model—was excluded from the research. For this reason, the model cannot be generalized to the entire population. Masters and Johnson themselves commented that every one of their participants was characterized by high and consistent levels of sexual desire. Yet sexual desire is certainly missing among some members of the general population, or it is present sometimes and absent at others. The research, in short, claims to be objective and universal when it is neither (Tiefer, 1991).

Once these difficulties with the Masters and Johnson research and model of sexual response were recognized, several alternative models were proposed. We will examine two of them in the following sections. Both of them add a cognitive component to Masters and Johnson's physiological model.

Kaplan's Triphasic Model

On the basis of her work on sex therapy (discussed in Chapter 17), Helen Singer Kaplan (1974, 1979) proposed a **triphasic model** of sexual response. Rather than thinking of the sexual response as having successive stages, she conceptualized it as having three relatively independent phases, or components: *sexual desire, vasocongestion* of the genitals, and the reflex *muscular contractions* of the orgasm phase. Notice that two of the components (vasocongestion and muscular contractions) are physiological, whereas the other (sexual desire) is psychological. Kaplan's model adds the desire component that was missing in Masters and Johnson's model. Desire can occur either spontaneously, motivating the person toward sexual activity and excitement, or excitement can come first, activating desire (Levin, 2005).

There are a number of justifications for Kaplan's approach. First, the two physiological components are controlled by different parts of the nervous system. Vasocongestion—producing erection in the male and lubrication in the female—is controlled by the parasympathetic division of the autonomic nervous system. In contrast, ejaculation and orgasm are controlled by the sympathetic division.

Second, the two components involve different anatomical structures—blood vessels for vasocongestion and muscles for the contractions of orgasm.

Third, vasocongestion and orgasm differ in their susceptibility to

Triphasic model: Kaplan's model of sexual response in which there are three phases: vasocongestion, muscular contractions, and sexual desire.

Focus: First Person
William Masters and Virginia Johnson

William Howell Masters was born in 1915. He attended Hamilton College in Clinton, New York, graduating in 1938 with a B.S. degree. At Hamilton he specialized in science courses and yet managed to play on the varsity football, baseball, basketball, and track teams and participate in the Debate Club. The college yearbook called him "a strange, dark man with a future. . . . Has an easy time carrying three lab courses but a hard time catching up on lost sleep. . . . Bill is a boy with purpose and is bound to get what he is working for." His devotion to athletics persisted, and in 1966 a science writer described him as "a dapper, athletically trim gynecologist who starts his day at 5:30 with a two-mile jog."

He entered the University of Rochester School of Medicine in 1939, planning to train himself to be a researcher rather than a practicing physician. In his first year there he worked in the laboratory of the famous anatomist Dr. George Washington Corner. Corner was engaged in research on the reproductive system in animals and humans, which eventually led to important discoveries about hormones and the reproductive cycle. He had also published *Attaining Manhood: A Doctor Talks to Boys About Sex* and the companion volume, *Attaining Womanhood.*

The first-year research project that Corner assigned to Masters was a study of the changes in the lining of the uterus of the rabbit during the reproductive cycle. In this way his interest was focused early on the reproductive system.

Masters was married in 1942 and received his M.D. in 1943. He and his wife had two children.

After Masters received his degree, he had to make an important decision: To what research area should he devote his life? Apparently his decision to investigate the physiology of sex was based on his shrewd observation that almost no prior research had been done in the area and that he thus would have a good opportunity to make some important scientific discoveries. In arriving at this decision he consulted with Dr. Corner, who was aware of Kinsey's progress and also of the persecution he had suffered (see Chapter 3). For this reason Corner advised Masters not to begin the study of sex until he had established himself as a respected researcher in some other area, was somewhat older, and could conduct the research at a major university or medical school.

Masters followed the advice. He completed his internship and residency and then established himself on the faculty of the Washington University

Figure 8.4 Virginia Johnson and William H. Masters.

School of Medicine in St. Louis. From 1948 to 1954 he published 25 papers on various medical topics, especially on hormone-replacement therapy for postmenopausal women.

In 1954 he began his research on sexual response at Washington University, supported by grants from the U.S. Public Health Service. The first paper based on that research was published in 1959, but the research received little attention until the publication, in 1966, of *Human Sexual Response* and, in 1970, of *Human Sexual Inadequacy* (a topic discussed in Chapter 17), both of which received international acclaim.

Virginia Johnson was born Virginia Eshelman in 1925 in the Missouri Ozarks. She was raised with the realistic attitude toward sex that rural children often have, as well as many of the superstitions found in that area. She began studying music at Drury College but transferred to Missouri University, where she studied psychology and sociology. She was married in 1950 and had two children, one in 1952 and the other in 1955. Shortly after that, she and her husband separated, and she went to the Washington University placement office to find a job. Just at that time, Masters had put in a request for a woman to assist him in research interviewing, preferably a married woman with children who was interested in people. Johnson was referred to him and became a member of the research and therapy team in 1957.

In 1971, following the divorce of Masters and his first wife, he and Virginia Johnson were married. They divorced in 1993. In 1994, at the age of 79, Masters retired and closed his research institute. He died in 2001.

Source: Brecher & Brecher (1966).

being disturbed by injury, drugs, or age. For example, the refractory period following orgasm in the male lengthens with age. Accordingly, orgasm decreases in frequency with age. In contrast, for many men the capacity for erection is relatively unimpaired with age, although the erection may be slower to make its appearance. An elderly man may have nonorgasmic sex several times a week, with a firm erection, although he may have an orgasm only once a week.

Fourth, the reflex of ejaculation in the male can be brought under voluntary control by most men, but the erection reflex generally cannot.

Finally, impairment of the vasocongestion response or the orgasm response produces different disturbances (sexual disorders). Erection problems in men are caused by an impairment of the vasocongestion response, whereas premature ejaculation and retarded ejaculation are disturbances of the orgasm response. Similarly, many women show a strong arousal and vasocongestion response, yet have trouble with orgasm.

Kaplan's triphasic model is useful both for understanding the nature of sexual response and for understanding and treating disturbances in it. Her writing on the desire phase is particularly useful in understanding disorders of sexual desire, which we discuss in Chapter 17.

Walen and Roth: A Cognitive Model

As noted earlier, an important criticism of the Masters and Johnson model is that it ignores the cognitive and subjective aspects of sexual response. In Chapter 2 we discussed the importance of cognitive approaches in understanding the psychology of human sexuality. Susan R. Walen and David Roth (1987) applied such an approach to understanding the sexual response. Their model is shown in Figure 8.5.

Recall from Chapter 2 that according to the cognitive approach, how we feel depends tremendously on what we are thinking: how we perceive what is occurring and how we evaluate it. For this reason, the first step in the cognitive model is *perception:* the perception of a stimulus as sexual. What we perceive to be sexy stimuli—whether they are visual stimuli, touch stimuli, or odors—depends greatly on the culture in which we've grown up and on our prior learning. If you've just begun a sexual relationship with someone, the very sight of that person may make you feel turned on. At the same time, looking at 10 other people in the same room produces no turn-on. To a person with a fetish, the sight of black, leather, high-heeled women's boots may produce instant arousal. According to the model, perception is the first step.

The second step in the cognitive model is *evaluation.* If we feel positive about the sexual stimulus, that will lead to the next step, arousal, but if our evaluation of the stimulus is negative, the arousal cycle stops. For example, if you are a married woman and your husband, with whom you normally have a great sex life, begins to kiss you when his breath smells of a cigarette he has just smoked, your evaluation of the sexual stimulus is likely to be negative and you will not feel aroused.

Let's suppose, though, that the evaluation of the sexual stimulus is positive. Physiological *arousal—* as described in the Masters and Johnson model discussed earlier in this chapter—is the third step. But again, the cognitive approach says that it is not so much what happens physically, but how we perceive it, that counts. So the *perception of arousal,* step 4, is critical. For example, some research shows that women are sometimes not aware of their own physical arousal probably because vaginal lubrication can be a rather subtle response (Heiman, 1975, discussed in Chapter 12). Or a man might pay so much attention to whether his technique is pleasing his partner that he fails to perceive his own arousal and thus does not experience as much sexual pleasure as he might. People can

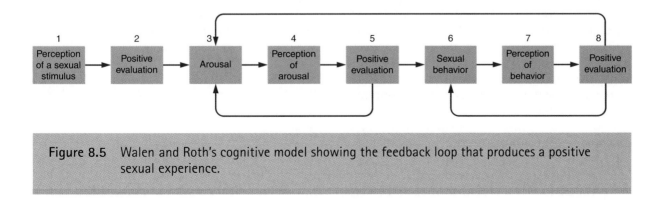

Figure 8.5   Walen and Roth's cognitive model showing the feedback loop that produces a positive sexual experience.

Figure 8.6   Can the cognitive model of sexual arousal explain our response to this? Here a man touches a woman's breast, but it is not sexual. Why not? The context, a medical office, leads us not to perceive the woman's breast as a sexual stimulus, nor the man's touch as sexual.

create sexual problems for themselves if they set too high criteria for deciding that they are aroused. How much lubrication, or how firm an erection, is enough? You can augment your sexual response by perceiving even a little bit of lubrication, or the first stirrings of an erection, or some other sign (such as increased heart rate) as an indication of arousal.

Again, the cognitive approach argues that it is not only the perception of arousal but also a positive evaluation of the arousal that is important if the sexual response cycle is to continue. Accordingly, *evaluation* of the arousal is step 5. As before, if the evaluation is negative, the response cycle stops. An example would be an adult who feels himself becoming aroused when looking at a child. He realizes that this response is totally inappropriate, evaluates the arousal negatively, and feels anxiety rather than arousal. On the other hand, if the evaluation of the arousal is positive—you like the feeling of being turned on in this particular situation that you are in—there is feedback to step 3, so that physical arousal increases further. Essentially,

feeling good about being turned on makes you feel even more turned on.

All this propels you to step 6, *sexual behavior.* Again, cognitive psychologists believe that two further steps—*perception of the behavior* and a *positive evaluation* of it, steps 7 and 8—are critical for the arousal cycle to continue. If the evaluation is positive, two kinds of feedback occur: The sexual behavior is likely to continue, and arousal increases.

In sum, the cognitive model of the sexual response cycle stresses the importance of our perception and evaluation of sexual events. In many ways, the greatest erogenous zone is the brain.

Neural and Hormonal Bases of Arousal

Up to this point we have focused on the genital and cognitive responses that occur during sexual activity. But what about the underlying neural and hormonal processes that make the sexual response cycle possible?

The Brain, the Spinal Cord, and Sex

The brain and the spinal cord both have important interacting functions in sexual response. First, we discuss the relatively simple reflexes involved in sexual response, and then we consider the more complex brain processes.

Spinal Reflexes

Several important components of sexual behavior, including erection and ejaculation, are controlled by fairly simple spinal cord reflexes (see the lower part of Figure 8.7). A reflex has three basic components. The *receptors* are sensory neurons that detect stimuli and transmit the message to the spinal cord (or brain). The *transmitters* are centers in the spinal cord (or brain) that receive the message, interpret it, and send out a message to produce the appropriate response. The *effectors* are neurons or muscles that respond to the stimulation. The jerking away of the hand when it touches a hot object is a good example of a spinal reflex.

Erection

Erection is produced by a spinal reflex that works in a similar way (McKenna, 2000). The penis has lots of receptor neurons, and tactile stimulation (stroking or rubbing) of the penis or nearby regions such as the scrotum or thighs produces a neural signal that is transmitted to an *erection center* in the sacral, or lowest, part of the spinal cord. (There may also be another erection center higher in the cord.) This center then sends out a message via the parasympathetic division of the autonomic nervous system to the muscles (the effectors) around the walls of the arteries in the penis. In response to the message, the muscles relax, and the arteries then expand, permitting a large volume of blood to flow into them. Erection results. In addition, the valves in the veins and the compression of the veins caused by the swelling in the tissue around them reduce the blood flow out of the penis (Adams et al., 1997).

How do we know this reflex exists? Its existence is confirmed by the responses of men who have had their spinal cords completely severed, as a result of accidents, at a level above that of the reflex center (see Focus: A Sexually Diverse World, p. 202). They are capable of having erections and ejaculations produced by rubbing their genitals, although it is clear that no brain effects can be operating, since signals from the brain cannot move past the

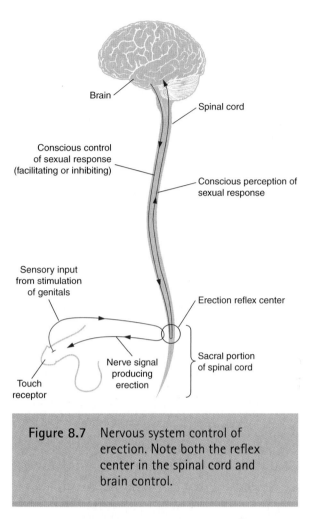

Brain

Spinal cord

Conscious control of sexual response (facilitating or inhibiting)

Conscious perception of sexual response

Sensory input from stimulation of genitals

Erection reflex center

Touch receptor

Nerve signal producing erection

Sacral portion of spinal cord

Figure 8.7 Nervous system control of erection. Note both the reflex center in the spinal cord and brain control.

point at which the spinal cord was severed. (In fact, these men cannot "feel" anything because neural signals cannot be transmitted up the spinal cord either.) Erection can be produced simply by tactile stimulation of the genitals, which triggers the spinal reflex.

Besides tactile stimulation of the genitals, other conditions may also produce erection. For example, fantasy or other purely psychological factors may produce erection. We explore the importance of the brain in producing erection in a later section.

Ejaculation

The ejaculation reflex is much like the erection reflex—except that there are two ejaculation centers and they are located higher in the spinal cord, both the sympathetic and parasympathetic divisions of the nervous system are involved, and the response is muscular, not vasocongestion (Giuliano & Clement, 2005; Rowland & Slob, 1997).

Focus: A Sexually Diverse World
Sexuality and Disability

I t is commonly believed that a person in a wheelchair is sexless. People with physical disabilities are thought not to be interested in sex, much less to be capable of engaging in sexual activity. Contrast those stereotypes with the following ideas:

> A stiff penis does not make a solid relationship, nor does a wet vagina. . . .
> Absence of sensation does not mean absence of feelings. . . .
> Inability to move does not mean inability to please. (Cole & Cole, 1978, p. 118)

About 10 percent of adults in the United States have a physical disability that imposes a substantial limitation on their activities. Given a chance to express themselves, these people emphasize the importance of their sexuality and sex drive, which are not necessarily altered by their disability.

Space does not permit a complete discussion of all types of disabilities and their consequences for sexuality. Instead, we will concentrate on two illustrative examples: spinal-cord injury and mental retardation.

Spinal-Cord Injury

Paraplegia (paralysis of the lower half of the body on both sides) and quadriplegia (paralysis of the body

from the neck down) are both caused by injuries to the spinal cord. Many able-bodied people find it difficult to understand what it feels like to be paralyzed. Imagine that your genitals and the region around them have lost all sensation. You would not know they were being touched unless you saw it happen. Furthermore, there is loss of bladder and bowel control, which may produce embarrassing problems if sexual activity is attempted.

The capacity of a man with a spinal-cord injury to have erections depends on the level of the spinal cord at which the injury (lesion) occurred and whether the spinal cord was completely or only partially severed. According to most studies, a majority of men with a spinal-cord injury are able to have erections. In some cases only reflex erections are possible. In other words, erections are produced

(a)

(b)

Figure 8.8 In the last 20 years we have become aware of the capacity of people with disabilities for sexual expression. (*a*) There is a need for sex education for children with disabilities. (*b*) Ellen Stohl, the first woman with disabilities to appear in *Playboy* (July, 1987). She has quadriplegia, having suffered several broken bones in her neck in an automobile accident. She was completely paralyzed initially, but her injury was incomplete. She gradually recovered use of her arms and hands. Although she has no movement below the waist, she has some sensitivity in her legs and is hypersensitive in the genitals. She enjoys sex very much and is orgasmic.

by direct stimulation of the genitals, even though the man may not be able to feel the sensation. In a few cases, particularly if the injury was not severe, the man is able to produce an erection by erotic thoughts, but this capacity is typically lost with spinal-cord injury. When the injury is severe, the man is not able to ejaculate, although ejaculation may be possible if the cord was only partially severed. Generally men's fertility is impaired by spinal-cord injury. In sum, many men with a spinal-cord injury experience the same sexual responses as other men—including erection, elevation of the testes, and increases in heart rate—except that they generally cannot ejaculate, nor can they feel the physical stimulation.

Women with a spinal-cord injury experience many of the same sexual responses as other women, including engorgement of the clitoris and labia, erection of the nipples, and increases in heart rate. Approximately 50 percent of women with spinal-cord injuries are able to have orgasms from stimulation of the genitals. Some women with a spinal-cord injury develop a capacity for orgasm from stimulation of the breasts or lips.

Because sexuality in our culture is so orgasm-oriented, orgasm problems among people with spinal-cord injury may appear to be devastating. But many of them report that they have been able to cultivate a kind of "psychological orgasm" that is as satisfying as the physical one. Fantasy is a perfectly legitimate form of sexual expression that their injury does not rule out.

For women with spinal-cord injuries whose menstrual cycling returns, their ability to conceive a baby is normal. Most pregnancies proceed normally, although there is a higher risk of some complications. Vaginal deliveries are usually possible and can be done without anesthetic.

Mental Retardation

Persons with IQs below 70 are generally classified as having mental retardation. There is a great range in the capacities of individuals with mental retardation, from some who require institutionalization and constant care to others who function quite normally in the community, who can read and write and hold simple jobs. It is important to recognize that the great majority of persons with mental retardation have only moderate retardation (IQs between 50 and 70) and function nearly normally.

Four issues are especially important when considering the sexuality of persons with mental retardation: their opportunity for sexual expression, the need for sexuality education, the importance of contraception, and the possibility of sexual abuse.

Individuals with mental retardation have normal sexual desires and seek to express them. Unfortunately, because children with mental retardation are often slower to learn the norms of society, they may express themselves sexually in ways that may shock others, such as masturbating in public. For this reason and others, careful sexuality education for persons with mental retardation is essential. They must be taught about the norms of privacy for sexuality. At the same time, they must be allowed their privacy, a right that institutions often fail to recognize.

It is important that individuals with mental retardation be educated about contraception and that contraceptives be made available to them. Because they have normal sexual desires, they may engage in sexual intercourse. In one study, 24 percent of boys with mental retardation and 8 percent of girls with mental retardation had engaged in intercourse by age 16 (Cheng & Udry, 2003). If these youth lack sexuality education, they may not realize that pregnancy can result. An unwanted pregnancy for a woman or couple with mental retardation may be a difficult situation. They may be able to function well when taking care of themselves, but not with the added burden of a baby. On the other hand, some persons with mental retardation do function sufficiently well to care for a child. The important thing is that they make as educated a decision as possible. Many experts recommend the IUD for women with mental retardation because it does not require memory and forethought for effective use.

The topic of contraception and individuals with mental retardation raises the ugly issue of involuntary sterilization. Until the mid-1950s, persons with mental retardation in institutions were routinely sterilized, although certainly not with their informed consent. We now view this as a violation of the rights of these persons especially if they have only mild mental retardation. It is now very difficult to gain legal permission to sterilize a person with mental retardation.

A final concern is that persons with mental retardation may be particularly vulnerable to sexual abuse.

In summary, there are three general points to be made about sexuality and persons with disabilities: (1) They generally do have sexual needs and desires; (2) they are often capable of a sexual response quite similar to that of able-bodied people of average intelligence; and (3) there is a real need for more information, and communication, about what people with various disabilities can and cannot do sexually.

Sources: Ames (1991); Baladerian (1991); Bérard (1989); Beretta et al. (1989); Cheng & Udry (2003); Kempton & Kahn (1991); Komisaruk et al. (1997); McCabe (2002); McCabe & Taleporos (2003); Phelps et al. (2001); Rawicki & Hill (1991); Siosteen et al. (1990); Sipski & Alexander (1997); Sipski et al. (2001); Sipski et al. (2004).

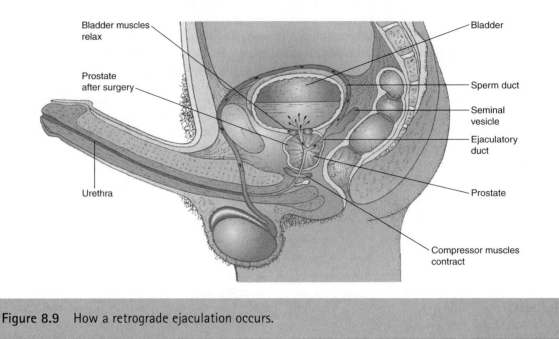

Bladder muscles relax

Prostate after surgery

Urethra

Bladder

Sperm duct

Seminal vesicle

Ejaculatory duct

Prostate

Compressor muscles contract

Figure 8.9 How a retrograde ejaculation occurs.

In the ejaculation reflex, the penis responds to stimulation by sending a message to the *ejaculation center*, which is located in the lumbar portion of the spinal cord. This center then sends out a message via the nerves in the sympathetic nervous system, and this message triggers muscle contractions in the internal organs that are involved in ejaculation.

Ejaculation can often be controlled voluntarily. This fact highlights the importance of brain influences on the ejaculation reflex (Truitt & Coolen, 2002).

The three main problems of ejaculation are premature ejaculation, male orgasmic disorder (retarded ejaculation), and retrograde ejaculation. We discuss premature ejaculation, which is by far the most common problem, and male orgasmic disorder in Chapter 17. **Retrograde ejaculation** occurs when the ejaculate empties into the bladder, rather than going out through the tip of the penis (Kothari, 1984). A *dry orgasm* results, since no ejaculate is emitted. This problem can be caused by some illnesses, by tranquilizers and drugs used in the treatment of psychoses, and by prostate surgery. The way it happens is fairly simple (Figure 8.9). Two sphincters are involved in ejaculation: an internal one, which closes off the entrance to the bladder during a normal ejaculation, and an external one, which opens during a normal ejac-

Retrograde ejaculation: A condition in which orgasm in the male is not accompanied by an external ejaculation; instead, the ejaculate goes into the urinary bladder.

Gräfenberg spot (GRAY-fen-berg) or **G-spot:** A small region on the front wall of the vagina, emptying into the urethra, and responsible for female ejaculation.

ulation, allowing the semen to flow out through the penis. In retrograde ejaculation, the action of these two sphincters is reversed. The external one closes, and thus the ejaculate cannot flow out through the penis, and the internal one opens, permitting the ejaculate to go into the bladder. The condition itself is quite harmless, although some men are disturbed by the lack of sensation of emitting semen.

Reflexes in Women

Unfortunately, there is far less research on similar reflexes in women. We know that sensory input—such as touch—to the clitoris travels along the dorsal nerve of the clitoris and continues within the pudendal nerve to a reflex center in the sacral portion of the spinal cord (Berman et al., 2000). Research with nonhumans—mainly male and female rats—has investigated the urethrogenital reflex, which results in muscle contractions similar to orgasm in humans (Meston et al., 2004). This research suggests that the neural circuits for orgasm in women are very similar to those for orgasm and ejaculation in men. The clitoris receives both sympathetic and parasympathetic nerve fibers. The vagina, too, is supplied by both sympathetic and parasympathetic nerves. The limbic system of the brain, which we discuss shortly, is crucial to female sexual arousal just as it is to male sexual arousal.

Research indicates that *female ejaculation* occurs in some women (Addiego et al., 1981; Belzer, 1981; Perry & Whipple, 1981). The region responsible is the **Gräfenberg spot** (or **G-spot**), also called

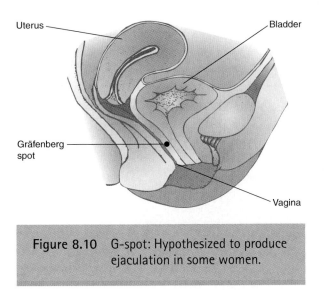

Uterus — Bladder

Gräfenberg spot

Vagina

Figure 8.10 G-spot: Hypothesized to produce ejaculation in some women.

the *female prostate* or the *Skene's glands* (Schubach, 2002). It is located on the top side of the vagina (with the woman lying on her back, which is the best position for finding it), about halfway between the pubic bone and the cervix (see Figure 8.10). Its ducts open into the urethra. Stroking it produces an urge to urinate, but if the stroking continues for a few seconds more, it begins to produce sexual pleasure. The original researchers, Perry and Whipple, argued that continued stimulation of it produces a *uterine orgasm,* characterized by deeper sensations of uterine contractions than the clitorally induced vulvar orgasm investigated in the Masters and Johnson research.

In one survey of 1,289 adult women, 40 percent reported having experienced ejaculation at the time of orgasm at least once, and 66 percent reported having an especially sensitive area on the front wall of the vagina (Darling et al., 1990). The most recent biochemical analyses indicate that the female prostate produces prostate-specific antigen (PSA) just as the male prostate does (Zaviačič et al., 2000).

Brain Control of Sexual Response
Sexual responses are controlled by more than simple spinal reflexes. Sexual responses may be brought under voluntary control and may be initiated by purely psychological forces, such as fantasy. Environmental factors, such as having been taught as a child that sex is dirty and sinful, may also affect a person's sexual response. All these phenomena point to the critical influence of the brain and its interaction with the spinal reflexes in producing sexual response (see Figure 8.7).

Brain control of sexual response is complex and only partly understood at the present time. It appears that the most important influences come from a set of structures called the **limbic system** (see Figure 8.11). The limbic system forms a border between the central part of the brain and the outer part (the cerebral cortex), and it includes the amygdala, the hippocampus, the cingulate gyrus, the hypothalamus, and the septum. Other structures—the thalamus, the pituitary, and the reticular formation—are not properly part of the limbic system, but they are closely connected to it.

Several lines of evidence point to the importance of the limbic system in sexual behavior. A particular region of the anterior portion of the hypothalamus (the medial preoptic area, or MPOA) has been implicated in male sexual behavior (McKenna, 2005). If this area of the hypothalamus is given electrical stimulation, male rats increase their sexual behavior, and if this region is destroyed, they no longer engage in copulation with females. The paraventricular nucleus (PVN) of the hypothalamus is another sexual hotspot. If the genitals are stroked, cells in the PVN fire, and neurons from the PVN project down the spinal cord to sexual reflex sites (McKenna, 2005).

Exciting new research using the brain-scanning technique called functional MRI (fMRI) confirms the importance of the limbic system in sexual responding. Healthy men were shown erotic or nonerotic films while in the MRI chamber (Park et al., 2001). Several structures in the limbic system—including the cingulate gyrus and thalamus—were activated by the erotic films (see Focus: Milestones in Sex Research, p. 207). In another fMRI study, the amygdala responded when men were shown sexually arousing photographs (Hamann et al., 2004).

Many of the brain centers for sex are also close to the olfactory centers. This brings up the topic of pheromones and their role in sexual behavior, which we discuss later in the chapter.

Hormones and Sex
The sex hormones are another important physiological force that interacts with the nervous system to influence sexual response.

Organizing versus Activating Effects
Endocrinologists generally make a distinction between the organizing effects of hormones and the activating effects of hormones. As we discussed in Chapter 5, hormones present during prenatal development have important influences on genital anatomy, creating male or female genitals. Hormone

Limbic system: A set of structures in the interior of the brain, including the amygdala, hippocampus, and fornix; believed to be important for sexual behavior in both animals and humans.

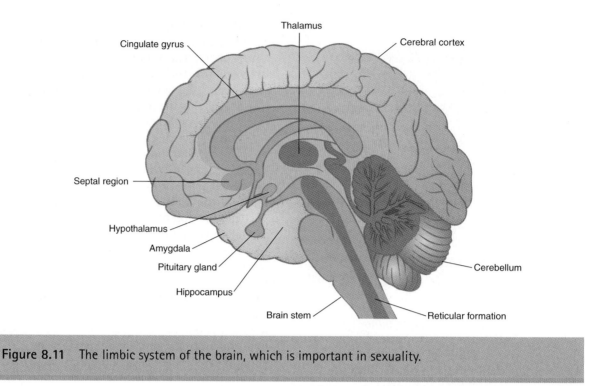

Figure 8.11   The limbic system of the brain, which is important in sexuality.

effects such as these are called **organizing effects,** because they cause a relatively permanent change in the organization of some structures, whether in the nervous system or in the reproductive system. Typically there are critical periods during which these hormone effects may occur.

It has also been known for some time that if an adult male mouse or rat is castrated (has the testes removed, which removes the source of testosterone), it will cease engaging in sexual behavior (and will be less aggressive). If that animal is then given injections of testosterone, it will start engaging in sex again. Hormone effects such as these are called **activating effects** because they activate (or deactivate) certain behaviors.

The organizing effects of sex hormones on sexual behavior have been well documented (Keefe, 2002). In a classic experiment, testosterone was administered to pregnant female guinea pigs. The female offspring that had been exposed to testosterone prenatally[4] were, in adulthood, incapable of displaying female sexual behavior (in particular, lordosis, which is a sexual posturing involving arching of the back and raising of the hindquarters so that intromission

of the male's penis is possible) (Phoenix et al., 1959). It is thought that this result occurred because the testosterone "organized" the brain tissue (particularly the hypothalamus) in a male fashion. These female offspring were also born with masculinized genitals—evidence that their reproductive systems had also been organized in the male direction. But the important point here is that the prenatal doses of testosterone had masculinized their sexual behavior. Experiments with many other species have obtained similar results.

These hormonally masculinized females in adulthood displayed mounting behavior, a male[5] sexual behavior. When they were given testosterone in adulthood, they showed about as much mounting behavior as males did. In this way, the testosterone administered in adulthood *activated* male patterns of sexual behavior.

The analogous experiment on males would be castration at birth, followed by administration of ovarian hormones in adulthood. When this experiment was done with rats, female sexual behavior resulted. These males responded to mating

Organizing effects of hormones: Effects of sex hormones early in development, resulting in a permanent change in the brain or reproductive system.
Activating effects of hormones: Effects of sex hormones in adulthood, resulting in the activation of behaviors, especially sexual behaviors and aggressive behaviors.

[4]Note the similarity of these experiments to John Money's observations of human intersex individuals (Chapter 5).

[5]The term *male sexual behavior* is being used here to refer to a sexual behavior that is displayed by normal males of the species and either is absent in females of that species or is present at a much lower frequency. Normal females do mount, but they do so less frequently than males do. *Female sexual behavior* is defined similarly.

Focus: Milestones in Sex Research
Mapping the Sexual Brain

Exciting advances in the technology of neuroimaging are giving us inside views of the human brain during various activities. Methods such as PET (positron emission tomography) and fMRI (functional magnetic resonance imaging) show which regions of the brain "light up" (have neurons most actively firing) while the individual is solving a math problem or thinking about something sad (Figure 8.12).

Sex researchers have quickly adopted these techniques with the goal of learning which regions of the brain are most involved in various aspects of sexuality. One of the challenges they have faced is that the subject cannot move while in an MRI scanner, making it difficult to achieve sexual arousal using most of the normal methods. Researchers have solved the problem by showing erotic videos to the person inside the scanner.

In one experiment, heterosexual men viewed erotic video clips, relaxing clips, and sports clips, in random order (Arnow et al., 2002). Meanwhile, their brains were being scanned in an MRI machine and the erection of the penis was measured. One has to admire these men for being able to become aroused while in an MRI scanner! When the men were exposed to erotic clips and were sexually aroused, as indicated by erection, intense brain activity was found in the right insula and claustrum, striatum (left caudate nucleus and putamen), cingulate gyrus, and—you guessed it—the hypothalamus! The insula is known to be involved in sensory processing, particularly of touch sensations. The cingulate cortex has been demonstrated in other studies to be involved in attentional processes and in guiding responsiveness to new environmental stimuli. Doubtless it was activated because of the men's attention to the erotic film.

Another study used fMRI to assess brain activation in both men and women while viewing erotic video segments (Karama et al., 2002). This study found brain activation in roughly the same regions as the study discussed previously. Almost all regions responded similarly in women and men. This study also found evidence of activation of the amygdala during sexual arousal. The amygdala is part of the limbic system, and, as noted earlier in this chapter, plays a role in sexual responding. The amygdala is known to be involved in emotion, and its activation speaks to the strong emotions—sometimes positive, sometimes negative—that are evoked by sexual stimuli.

Research with women with spinal-cord injury (see Focus: A Sexually Diverse World, p. 202) indicates that they experience sexual arousal and orgasm as a result of genital stimulation (Komisaruk & Whipple, 2005). The neural signals do not travel up the spinal cord, which has been damaged, but rather pass up to the brain through the vagus nerves. fMRI scans indicate that the brain regions activated during arousal include the hypothalamus, amygdala, hippocampus, and the rest of the list of structures identified in fMRI research on people who are able-bodied.

These studies are fascinating in themselves, as they allow us to view the workings of the brain during sexual responding. As research advances, future studies will help us understand the brain regions and associated neurotransmitters involved in sexual dysfunction, which will lead to more effective treatments for these problems. They will also allow us to better understand and treat arousal problems such as those suffered by individuals with pedophilia, who are aroused by completely inappropriate stimuli—children.

Sources: Arnow et al. (2002); Holstege et al. (2003); Karama et al. (2002); Komisaruk & Whipple (2005); Schultz et al. (1999).

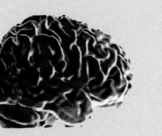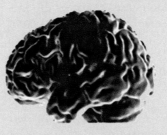

Figure 8.12 fMRI scans of the brain are opening up exciting opportunities to learn how the brain is involved in sexual response.

attempts by other males essentially in the same way females do (Harris & Levine, 1965). Their brain tissue had been organized in a female direction during an early, critical period when testosterone was absent, and the female behavior patterns were activated in adulthood by administration of ovarian hormones.

It seems, then, that males and females initially have capacities for both male and female sexual behaviors. If testosterone is present early in development, the capacity for exhibiting female behaviors is suppressed. Sex hormones in adulthood then activate the behavior patterns that were differentiated early in development.

How relevant is this research to humans? Generally the trend is for the behavior of lower species to be more under hormonal control and for the behavior of higher species to be more under brain (neural) control. Accordingly, human sexual behavior is less under hormonal control than is rat sexual behavior, and human sexual behavior is controlled more by the brain. For these reasons, learning from past experiences and cultural conventions, which are stored in the brain, is more likely to have a profound effect (Wallen, 2001).

Let us now consider in more detail the known activating effects of sex hormones on the sexual behavior of adult humans.

Testosterone and Sexual Desire

Testosterone has well-documented effects on libido, or sexual desire, in humans (Carani et al., 1990; Carter, 1992; Everitt & Bancroft, 1991). In men deprived of their main source of testosterone by castration or by illness, there is a dramatic decrease in sexual behavior in some, but not all, cases (Feder, 1984). Sexual desire is rapidly lost if a man is given an antiandrogen drug. Thus testosterone seems to have an activating effect in maintaining sexual desire in men. However, in cases of castration, sexual behavior may decline very slowly and may be present for several years after the source of testosterone is gone. Such cases point to the importance of experience and brain control of sexual behavior in humans.

Research has also demonstrated that levels of testosterone are correlated with sexual behavior in boys around the time of puberty (Udry et al., 1985). Boys in the eighth, ninth, and tenth grades filled out a questionnaire about their sexual behavior and gave blood samples from which their level of testosterone could be measured. Among the boys whose testosterone level was in the highest quartile (25 percent of the sample), 69 percent had engaged in sexual intercourse, whereas only

16 percent of the boys whose testosterone level was in the lowest quartile had done so. Similarly, of the boys with testosterone levels in the highest quartile, 62 percent had masturbated, compared with 12 percent for the boys in the lowest quartile. These effects were uncorrelated with age, so it wasn't simply a matter of the older boys having more testosterone and more sexual experience. The authors concluded that at puberty, testosterone affects sexual motivation directly.

Research indicates that androgens are related to sexual desire in women also (Hutchinson, 1995; Sherwin, 1991). If all sources of androgens (the adrenals and the ovaries) are removed, women lose sexual desire. Women who have undergone oophorectomy (surgical removal of the ovaries, typically because of cancer) report marked decreases in sexual desire. If they are treated with testosterone, their sexual desire increases (Shifren et al., 1998, 2000). Moreover, androgens are used successfully in the treatment of women who have low sexual desire (Kaplan & Owett, 1993). Androgen levels decline with age in women, and research shows that administration of DHEA (a pretestosterone hormone) to women over 60 results in their having increased sexual desire (Baulieu et al., 2000; Spark, 2002).

Sex Offenders—Castration or Incarceration?

In 2004, James Jenkins, imprisoned for sexually molesting three young girls, asked a guard for a razor, saying that he wanted to be clean-shaven for a court appearance the next day. He then got the blade out of the holder, castrated himself, and flushed his testes down the toilet. Today he is happy with the outcome, saying that he is now free of sexual urges and deviant sexual fantasies (Rondeaux, 2006). In a 2001 case, a Florida judge ordered a convicted first-time rapist to complete a 20-year prison sentence and then undergo chemical castration.

Physical castration refers to surgical removal of the testes, technically known as *bilateral orchiectomy. Chemical castration* refers to injections of a drug such as Depo-Provera, an antiandrogen drug that sharply reduces the levels of testosterone in the body.

Cases such as these raise a host of questions, some of them legal, others within the province of the sciences (Scott & Holmberg, 2003; Weinberger et al., 2005). Legally, a castration sentence could be challenged on the grounds that it is cruel and unusual punishment. And what is the goal of such a punishment? Was the judge in the second case

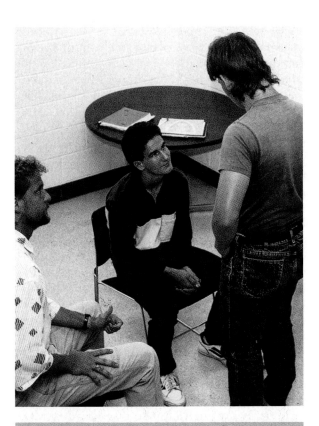

Figure 8.13   Sex offenders in a therapy group. Research shows that treatment of sex offenders, whether with the drug Depo-Provera or not, should always include psychotherapy.

simply being punitive and letting the punishment fit the crime? Or is castration intended to ensure that the man would never commit the crime again? The scientific data become pertinent in addressing this last point.

With either physical castration or chemical castration, the man is left with little natural testosterone in his body. Numerous experiments with other species have demonstrated that the effect of this low level of testosterone is a sharply reduced sex drive and the virtual elimination of sexual behavior. However, the effects in humans are not so clear, because we are not as hormone dependent as other species. There are documented cases of castrated men continuing to engage in sexual intercourse for years after the castration. Castration may reduce sexual behavior in humans, but its effects are not completely predictable. Furthermore, testosterone is available artificially, either by pill or by injection, so a physically castrated criminal might secretly obtain replacement testosterone.

In cases of rape, more than sexual behavior is involved. Many experts believe that rape is better conceptualized as an aggressive or violent crime that happens to be expressed sexually than seen as a sex crime per se. For this reason, the scientific question may be restated from "Does castration eliminate sexual behavior?" to "Does castration eliminate aggressive behavior?" Here, too, there are numerous experiments documenting—in other species—that castration greatly reduces aggressive behavior by lowering testosterone levels. But once again, the hormone effects are not as clear or consistent in humans. So castration might be effective in reducing sexual or aggressive behaviors and for this reason might reduce the chances of the man committing rape again, but such effects cannot be guaranteed.

It seems clear that physical or chemical castration should be only part of the treatment, which should also include intensive psychotherapy (Gijs & Gooren, 1996).

Pheromones

Scientists and laypeople alike are intrigued by the role that pheromones play in sexual behavior (Cutler, 1999; McClintock, 2000). Pheromones are somewhat like hormones. Recall that hormones are biochemicals that are manufactured in the body and secreted into the bloodstream to be carried to the organs they affect. **Pheromones,** in contrast, are biochemicals that are secreted outside the body. Through the sense of smell, they are an important means of communication between animals. An animal's urine often contains pheromones. The dog that does scent marking by urinating on a tree is actually depositing pheromones. Some pheromones appear to be important in sexual communication, and some have even been called *sex attractants* (Figure 8.14).

Much of the research on pheromones has been done with animals and demonstrates the importance of pheromones in sexual and reproductive functioning. For example, pheromones present in female urine influence male sexual behavior. If urine from an ovulating monkey is in the cage of a pregnant (and thus not ovulating) female and her mate, the male shows more frequent erections and more mounting (Snowdon et al., 2006). Males also show an increase in testosterone levels following exposure to the urine of the ovulating female.

Pheromones (FARE-oh-mones): Biochemicals secreted outside the body that are important in communication between animals and that may serve as sex attractants.

(a)

(b)

Figure 8.14 Pheromones. (a) Pheromones are a major means of communication between animals. (b) Are there human pheromones that are sex attractants?

The sense of smell, olfaction, is essential for pheromone effects to occur. Removal of the olfactory bulbs, and specifically a region called the *vomeronasal organ* (VNO), dramatically reduces the sexual behavior of males from species such as mice and guinea pigs (Thorne & Amrein, 2003). The VNO, located inside the nose, is a chemoreceptor— that is, it is activated by chemicals such as pheromones. Neuroscientists have even recorded the activity of single neurons in the VNO of male mice and found that certain neurons fire when the animal comes into contact with another male, but different neurons fire when he comes into contact with a female (Luo et al., 2003). Activation of the VNO then activates cells in the hypothalamus (Keverne, 1999), and as discussed earlier, the hypothalamus is crucial to sexuality. The VNO is a kind of second olfactory pathway. Sometimes called the *accessory olfactory bulb*, the VNO functions in addition to the main sense of smell.

What relevance does all this have for humans? Humans are not, by and large, "smell animals." Olfaction is much less important for us than for most other species. We tend to rely mostly on vision and, secondarily, hearing. Compare this with a dog's ability to gain a wealth of information about who and what has been in a park simply by sniffing around for a few minutes. Does this mean that pheromones have no influence on our sexual behavior?

It is now clear that human pheromones exist and may play an important role in sexuality (Wyatt, 2003). Indeed, pheromones may be exactly the "body chemistry" that attracts people to each other. Perfumes with musky scents have become popular and presumably increase sexual attractiveness, perhaps because they smell like pheromones. The perfume industry has eagerly tried to capitalize on pheromone research (Berliner et al., 1991). In fact, a perfume called Pheromone was introduced to the market.

What scientific evidence is there regarding the existence and effects of pheromones in humans? First, the vomeronasal organ—which, as noted earlier, is related to olfaction and sexual behavior in other species and essentially seems to function as a pheromone sensor—is present in most humans (Garcia-Velasco & Mondragon, 1991). (It might make sense to wonder whether plastic surgery to create a pretty nose could inadvertently harm the person's sex life.)

It is clear that humans do secrete pheromones. Androstenol, an odorous steroid that is well documented as a pheromone in pigs, has been isolated in the underarm sweat of humans (Gower & Ruparelia, 1993). Short-chain fatty acids known to be sex-attractant pheromones to male rhesus monkeys have been isolated in human vaginal secretions (Cowley & Brooksbank, 1991).

Research provides important indications that pheromones may play a role in human sexuality. In one experiment, for example, a synthesized female pheromone was added to women's perfume, and a placebo was added to perfume for women in the control group (McCoy & Pitino, 2002; Rako & Friebely, 2004). The women recorded their sexual behaviors over the next three months. Compared with the control group, pheromone-treated women showed a significantly greater frequency of intercourse, dates, and petting and kissing. They did not differ in frequency of masturbation. The researchers concluded that the pheromone had increased the women's attractiveness to men.

The classic research of Martha McClintock (1971) documented the existence of a phenomenon known as **menstrual synchrony:** the convergence, over several months, of the dates of onset of menstrual periods among women who are in close contact with each other (McClintock, 1998; Weller et al., 1995). This phenomenon is now thought to be due to pheromones produced by the women.

In perhaps the most dramatic experiment to date in humans, the results indicated that the timing of ovulation could be experimentally manipulated with human pheromones (Stern & McClintock, 1998). Odorless secretions from women's armpits were collected in the late follicular phase, just before ovulation. Other women exposed to these secretions showed an accelerated appearance of the LH surge that triggers ovulation. Underarm secretions from the same donors collected later in the menstrual cycle had the opposite effect: they delayed the LH surge in other women and lengthened the time to menstruation.

Other pheromone research has found that people's preference for human body odors and their brain responses to pheromones differ according to sexual orientation (Berglund et al., 2006; Martins et al., 2005). In one study, armpit secretions were collected from heterosexual men, heterosexual women, gay men, and lesbians (Martins et al., 2005). Odor evaluators then rated the pleasantness of these odors without knowing the source of them. Heterosexual men gave the lowest pleasantness ratings to the pheromones from gay men. In contrast, gay men gave low ratings to the pheromones of heterosexual men. The researchers concluded that human "odor prints" may help us identify groups of people who are potential sex partners.

The smell of pheromones does not necessarily have to be consciously perceived in order to have an effect (McClintock, 2000). The olfactory system can respond to odors even when they are not con-sciously perceived. For this reason, pheromones that we are not even aware of may have important influences.

If these indications about the effects of pheromones on human sexual behavior are correct, our hyperclean society may be destroying the scents that attract people to each other. The normal genital secretions (assuming reasonable cleanliness to eliminate bacteria) may contain sex attractants. Ironically, "feminine hygiene" deodorants may destroy precisely the odors that turn men on.

Future research on human pheromones should indeed be interesting.

Sexual Techniques

Earlier in this chapter, we discussed some of the wonderful things that happen to the body during sexual arousal and orgasm. How do we get to these marvelous states, for both ourselves and our partners?

We live in the era of sex manuals. Books like *Electrify Your Sex Life* and *The Illustrated Guide to Extended Massive Orgasm,* as well as feature articles and advice columns in many magazines, give us information on how to produce bigger and longer orgasms in ourselves and our partners. The "read all about it" boom has produced not only benefits but also problems. It may turn our attention so much to mechanical techniques that we forget about love and the emotional side of sexual expression. The sex manuals may also set up impossible standards of sexual performance that none of us can meet.

On the other hand, we live in a society that has a history of leaving the learning of sexual techniques to nature or to chance, in contrast to some other societies in which adolescents are given explicit instruction in methods for producing sexual pleasure. For humans, sexual behavior is a lot more than "doin' what comes naturally." We all need some means for learning about sexual techniques, and the sex manuals may help to fill that need. In the sections that follow, we consider sexual techniques.

Erogenous Zones

Although the notion of **erogenous zones** originated in Freud's work, the term is now part of our general vocabulary. It refers to parts of the body that are sexually sensitive. Stroking them or otherwise

Menstrual synchrony: The convergence, over several months, of the dates of onset of menstrual periods among women who are in close contact with each other.
Erogenous zones (eh-RAH-jen-us): Areas of the body that are particularly sensitive to sexual stimulation.

stimulating them produces sexual arousal. The genitals and the breasts are good examples. The lips, neck, and thighs are generally also erogenous zones. But even some rather unlikely regions—such as the back, the ears, the stomach, and the feet—can also be quite erogenous. One person's erogenous zones can be quite different from another's. For this reason it is impossible to give a list of sure "turn-ons." The best way to find out is to communicate with your partner, verbally or nonverbally.

One-Person Sex

It does not necessarily take two to have sex. Individuals can produce their own sexual stimulation. Sexual self-stimulation is called **autoeroticism.**[6] The best examples are masturbation and fantasy.

Masturbation

Here we reserve the term *hand–genital stimulation* for stimulation of another's genitals and the term **masturbation** for self-stimulation, either with the hand or with some object, such as a pillow or a vibrator. Masturbation is a very common sexual behavior. Almost all men and the majority of women in the United States masturbate to orgasm at least a few times during their lives. In the NHSLS survey, 62 percent of the men and 42 percent of the women reported that they had masturbated in the preceding year (Laumann et al., 1994, Table 3.1). Twenty-seven percent of the men and 8 percent of the women said that they masturbated at least once a week. The techniques used by males and females in masturbation are interesting in part because they provide information to their partners concerning the best techniques to use in lovemaking (Figure 8.15).

Most commonly, women masturbate by manipulating the clitoris and the inner lips. They may rub up and down or in a circular motion, sometimes lightly and sometimes applying more pressure to the clitoris. Some prefer to rub at the side of the clitoris, while a few stimulate the glans of the clitoris directly. The inner lips may also be stroked or tugged. One woman described her technique as follows:

> I use the tips of my fingers for actual stimulation, but it's better to start with patting motions or light rubbing motions over the general area. As excitement increases I begin stroking above the clitoris and finally reach a climax with a rapid, jerky circu-

(a)

(b)

Figure 8.15   (a) Male masturbation using hand stimulation of the penis. (b) Female masturbation using clitoral stimulation.

lar motion over the clitoral hood. Usually my legs are apart, and occasionally I also stimulate my nipples with the other hand. (Hite, 1976, p. 20)

Of the women in Kinsey's sample who masturbated, 84 percent used clitoral and labial manipulation. Inserting fingers or objects into the vagina was the second most commonly used technique, but it was practiced by only 20 percent of the women. Other techniques used by women in masturbation include breast stimulation, thigh pressure exerted by crossing the legs and pressing them together rhythmically to stimulate the clitoris, and pressing the genitals against some object, such as a pillow, or massaging them with a stream of water while in the shower. A few women are capable of using fantasy alone to produce orgasm; fantasy-induced orgasms are accompanied by the same

---

Autoeroticism: Sexual self-stimulation; for example, masturbation.
Masturbation: Stimulation of one's own genitals with the hand or with some object, such as a pillow or vibrator.

[6]For those of you who are interested in the roots of words, *autoeroticism* does not refer to sex in the backseat of a car. The prefix *auto* means "self" (as in *autobiography*); hence self-stimulation is autoeroticism.

physiological changes as orgasms produced by masturbation (Whipple et al., 1992).

Almost all males report masturbating by hand stimulation of the penis. Those interested in speed can reach an orgasm in only a minute or two. Most men use the technique of circling the hand around the shaft of the penis and using an up-and-down movement to stimulate the shaft and glans. Because the penis produces no natural lubrication of its own, some men like to use lubrication, such as soapsuds while showering. The tightness of the grip, the speed of movement, and the amount of glans stimulation vary from one man to the next. Most increase the speed of stimulation as they approach orgasm, slowing or stopping the stimulation at orgasm because further stimulation would be uncomfortable (Masters & Johnson, 1966). At the time of ejaculation, they often grip the shaft of the penis tightly. Immediately after orgasm, the glans and corona are hypersensitive, and the man generally avoids further stimulation of the penis at that time.

Media and Masturbation

Some men and women incorporate use of mass media into their autoerotic activity. Some people masturbate as they view erotic images in magazines, on DVD, or on the Internet. In one survey, half of the men and one-third of the women reported viewing pornographic videos and erotic magazines, and 32 percent of the men and 15 percent of the women reported viewing pornography on Web sites (Adam & Eve, 2004). Some of these viewers used these materials as aids to sexual arousal and masturbation. Up to 10 percent of the male students in our human sexuality classes report that their most recent sexual activity was masturbation while viewing erotic materials.

The Internet plays an important role in another form of autoerotic expression. Some people have sexual desires or needs that they are afraid to express in their relationships. They may fear embarrassment and rejection, or risks to their physical or emotional health if they act on these needs and desires. Because of its anonymity, the Internet provides a relatively safe context for exploring these needs and desires (Ross, 2005). A study of men and women recruited in chat rooms found that persons who reported lacking real relationships and expressed fear of disclosing aspects of their sexuality were more likely to use the Internet as an important form of sexual self-expression (McKenna et al., 2001).

Fantasy

Sexual fantasy refers to sexual thoughts or images that alter the person's emotions or physiological state (Maltz & Boss, 1997). Almost all men and women report that they have experienced sexual fantasies (Leitenberg & Henning, 1995).

The themes of sexual fantasies reported by men and women are similar. The most common are touching and kissing sensuously, watching a partner undress, giving or receiving oral sex, and seducing someone or being seduced (Hsu et al., 1994). Other common themes are having sex in an unusual location, having sex in an unusual position, and having sex that lasts for hours.

There are some gender differences in the content of fantasies. Men's fantasies focus on sexual activity. They may fantasize having oral sex with a virgin, an experienced older woman, or with two partners at the same time. Women are more likely to focus on playing a role during sexual activity, such as the shy maiden, the victim, the dominatrix, or the voyeur (Maltz & Boss, 1997). For many women, the relationship with the partner is the key, not the activity.

In a survey of a national sample of British adults, men were more likely to report fantasies of sex with multiple and anonymous partners, whereas women reported fantasies involving a same-gender or famous male partner (Wilson, 1997). These differences are consistent with predictions based on evolutionary theory.

One study comparing the fantasies of gays and lesbians with those of heterosexual men and women found that the reported contents were very similar, except that the partner was someone of the same gender (Price et al., 1985). However, heterosexuals may fantasize sexual activity with someone of the same gender, and gay and lesbian fantasies may include persons of the other gender.

Where do sexual fantasies come from? The images may come from past experience, dreams, media portrayals you have read or viewed, or stories someone told you. The activity may be dreamlike and sensuous, or explicit and vigorous. Like all fantasy, sexual fantasies represent a fusion of mind, body, and emotion. Sexual fantasies may represent earlier or childhood experiences, pleasant or abusive (Maltz & Boss, 1997).

Sexual fantasy can have a variety of functions for the person doing the fantasizing (Maltz & Boss, 1997). These include enhancing self-esteem and attractiveness, increasing the person's own sexual arousal (e.g., during masturbation or partnered sex), and facilitating orgasm. A very important role is enabling the person to mentally rehearse future possibilities. Such a rehearsal may enable the person to change behavior, initiate communication with a partner, or change partners.

Sexual fantasy: Sexual thoughts or images that alter the person's emotions or physiological state.

More men than women report having had sexual fantasies during masturbation. The results of 13 studies indicate that about 87 percent of men and 69 percent of women fantasized during masturbation (Leitenberg & Henning, 1995). Here is an adolescent male's description of one of his favorite fantasies during masturbation:

> We would be riding in the back seat of the car and I would reach over and fondle her breasts. She would reach into my pants and begin to caress my penis and finally suck me off. (Jensen, 1976, p. 144)

This is the fantasy of one college woman as she imagines seducing her French teacher:

> At exactly 8:00 I knocked on the door. When this guy saw what I was wearing I thought his eyes were going to pop out. Calmly he asked me to come in and sit down. . . .
> "Please call me Jim." Now I was getting somewhere. . . . I slipped out of my shoes and loosened my dress. When Jim returned I was ready and waiting. . . . Well the man finally got the hint; he reached around and unzipped my dress. While I was slowly undoing his zipper, he buried his head between my breasts. As his mouth slowly descended down my body I could feel the heat rising from between my legs. . . . To add to my desire he started speaking French to me. You didn't have to be fluent to understand this. As his mouth continued to nibble away, his tongue zeroed in on my clit and sent me to a mind-boggling orgasm. As my pleasure subsided I began to return the favor. . . . Although I had enjoyed several orgasms by now the night was far from over. Jim then got on top of me and made love to me for what seemed like an eternity. (Moffatt, 1989, pp. 190–191)

The content of male and female sexual fantasies seems to be influenced by cultural stereotypes of male and female sexuality.

Vibrators, Dildos, and Such

Various sexual devices, such as vibrators and dildos, are used by some people in masturbation or by couples as they have sex together (Figure 8.16).

Both male and female artificial genitals can be purchased. A **dildo** is a rubber or plastic cylinder, often shaped like a penis. It can be inserted into the vagina or the anus. Dildos are used by some women in masturbation, by men, by lesbians, by gays, and by heterosexual couples. Artificial vaginas, and even inflatable replicas of the entire body, male or female, can also be purchased.

Some *vibrators* are shaped like a penis, but others are not. Some models have a cord that plugs into an electric outlet; others are cordless and use bat-

Dildo: A rubber or plastic cylinder, often shaped like a penis.

Figure 8.16 Vibrators and dildos, used for sexual stimulation.

teries. Women may use vibrators to masturbate, stimulating the clitoral and mons area or inserting them into the vagina. Men may use them to stimulate the genitals or the anus. They can be purchased in "respectable" stores (where they are sometimes euphemistically called "face massagers"), in sex stores, and by mail.

Vibrators designed for women are not recent. They were invented in the 1880s and sold as a medical device (Maines, 1999). Physicians prescribed their use for the treatment of various female "maladies," especially hysteria. Vibrators disappeared from medical use after they were used in pornographic films in the 1920s. Today they are back in full force, with women throwing Passion Parties or Slumber Parties, which are Tupperware-style home parties where you and your friends can buy sex toys from the local salesperson (Jefferson, 2005).

Body oils are also popular for sexual use. In fact, their use has been encouraged by experts in the field. For example, sex therapists recommend them for the touching or sensate focus exercises that they prescribe for their patients in sex therapy (see Chapter 17). Oils have a sensuous quality that heightens erotic feelings. Furthermore, if you are being stroked or massaged for any extended period of time, the oil helps ensure that the part of your body that is being stimulated will not end up feeling like it has been sandpapered. The sex stores sell oils in a variety of exotic scents, but plain baby oil will also do nicely. Be aware that Vaseline and some other lubricants cause condoms to break.

Two-Person Sex

When many of us think of techniques of two-person sex, the image that flashes across our mind generally reflects several assumptions. One assumption is that one of the people is a male and the other a female—that is, that the sex is heterosexual. This image reflects a belief that heterosexual sex is normative. We also tend to assume that the man is supposed to do certain things during the act and the woman is to do certain other things, reflecting the sexual scripts of our culture. He, for example, is supposed to take the initiative in deciding what techniques are to be used, while she is to follow his lead. Although there is nothing particularly evil in these assumptions, they do tend to impose limitations on our own sexual expression and to make some think that their own sexual behavior is "not quite right." For these reasons we will make an attempt to avoid these assumptions in the sections that follow.

Kissing

Kissing (or what we might call, technically, "mouth-to-mouth stimulation") is an activity that virtually everyone in our culture has engaged in. In simple kissing, the partners keep their mouths closed and touch each other's lips. In deep kissing ("French kissing"), both people part their lips slightly and insert their tongues into each other's mouths (somehow these clinical descriptions do not make it sound like as much fun as it is). There are endless variations on these two basic approaches, such as nibbling at the partner's lips or tongue or sucking at the lips; they depend only on your imagination and personal preference. There are also plenty of other regions of the body to kiss: the nose, the forehead, the eyelids, the earlobes, the neck, the breasts, the genitals, and even the feet, to give a few examples.

Touching

Enjoying touching and being touched is essential to sexual pleasure. Caresses or massages, applied to virtually any area of the body, can be exciting. The regions that are exciting vary a great deal from one person to the next and depend on how the person is feeling at the moment. For this reason it is important to communicate what sort of touching is most pleasurable to you. (For specific exercises on touching and being touched, see Chapter 17.)

As we noted earlier, one of the best ways to find out how to use your hands in stimulating the genitals of another person is to find out how that person masturbates.

As a technique of lovemaking, hand stimulation of the male genitals can be used as a pleasurable

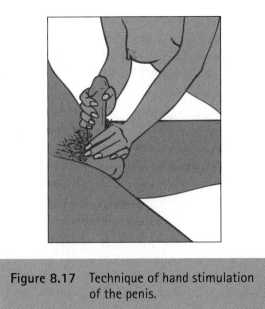

Figure 8.17 Technique of hand stimulation of the penis.

preliminary to intercourse, as a means of inducing orgasm itself, or as a means of producing an erection after the man has had one orgasm and wants to continue for another round of lovemaking ("rousing the dead").

Alex Comfort, in *The New Joy of Sex*, recommends the following techniques (see Figure 8.17):

> If he isn't circumcised, she will probably need to avoid rubbing the glans itself, except in pursuit of very special effects. Her best grip is just below the groove, with the skin back as far as it will go, and using two hands—one pressing hard near the root, holding the penis steady, or fondling the scrotum, the other making a thumb-and-first-finger ring, or a whole hand grip. She should vary this, and, in prolonged masturbation, change hands often. (1991, p. 85)

One of the things that make hand stimulation most effective is for the man's partner to have a playful delight in, and appreciation of, the man's penis. Most men think their penis is pretty important. If the partner cannot honestly appreciate it and enjoy massaging it, hand stimulation might as well not be done.

The hands can be used to stimulate the woman's genitals to produce orgasm, as a preliminary method of arousing the woman before intercourse, or simply because it is pleasurable.

Generally it is best, particularly if the woman is not already aroused, to begin with gentle, light stroking of the inside of the thighs and the inner and outer lips, moving to light stroking of the clitoris. As she becomes more aroused, the stimulation of the clitoris can become firmer. The clitoris

is very sensitive and this sensitivity can be either exquisite or painful. Some care has to be used in stimulating it; it cannot be manipulated like a piece of Silly Putty. Generally, the clitoris should not—except, perhaps, for some light stroking—be rubbed while it is dry, for the effect can be abrasive. If the woman is already somewhat aroused, lubrication can be provided by touching the fingers to the vaginal entrance and then spreading the lubrication on the clitoris. If she is not aroused or does not produce much vaginal lubrication, saliva works well, too. Moisture makes the stimulation not only more comfortable but also more sensuous. Some women find direct stimulation of the clitoral glans to be painful in some states of arousal. These women generally prefer stimulation on either side of the clitoris instead.

With these caveats in mind, the clitoris can be stimulated with circular or back-and-forth movements of the finger. The inner and outer lips can also be stroked or rubbed. These techniques, if done with skill and patience, can bring the woman to orgasm. Another technique that can be helpful in producing orgasm is for the partner to place the heel of the hand on the mons, exerting pressure on it while moving the middle finger in and out of the vaginal entrance. If it isn't clear by now, the partner needs to have close-trimmed nails without jagged edges. This is sensitive tissue we are dealing with.

The Other Senses

So far in this chapter, we have been focused on tactile (touch) sensations in sexual arousal. However, the other senses—vision, smell, and hearing—can also make contributions.

What you see can contribute to your arousal. Men seem, in general, to be turned on by a variety of visual stimuli, such as an attractive person or partially dressed or nude bodies. Both men and women respond with physiological arousal to portrayals of partnered sexual activity (Laan & Everaerd, 1995). Just as erotica may be used during autoerotic activity, viewing sexual activity on a video or on the Internet may contribute to partnered sexual activities. Some men, and a few women, have mild fetishes (see Chapter 14 for more detail) and like to see their partner wearing certain types of clothing, such as leather or rubber clothing or schoolgirl dresses. A good rule here, as elsewhere, is to communicate with your partner to find out what he or she would find arousing.

The decor of the room can also contribute to visual stimulation. Large mirrors, hung either

behind the bed or on the ceiling above it, can be a visual turn-on, since they allow you to watch yourself make love. Candlelight is soft and contributes more to an erotic atmosphere than an electric light, which is harsh, or complete darkness, which offers no visual stimulation at all.

Perhaps the biggest visual turn-on comes simply from looking at your own body and your partner's. According to the NHSLS, watching a partner undress is one of the most appealing sexual activities (Michael et al., 1994, Table 12).

Odors can be turn-ons or turn-offs. The scent of a body that is clean, having been washed with soap and water, is a natural turn-on. It does not need to be covered up with an "intimate deodorant."[7] In a sense, the scent of your skin, armpits, or genitals is your "aroma signature" and can be quite arousing.

A body that has not been washed or a mouth that has not been cleaned or has recently been used for smoking cigarettes can be a real turn-off. Breath that reeks of garlic may turn a desire for closeness into a desire for distance. Ideally, the communication between partners is honest and trusting enough so that if one offends, the other can request that the appropriate cleanup be done.

Music—whether your preference is for rock or classical music—can contribute to an erotic atmosphere. Another advantage of playing music is that it helps muffle the sounds of sex, which can be important if you live in an apartment with thin walls or are worried about your children hearing you.

Fantasy during Two-Person Sex

Fantasies can be done solo or can heighten the experience of sex with another person. Particularly in a long-term, monogamous relationship, sexual monotony can become a problem. Fantasies are one way to introduce some variety and excitement without violating an agreement to be faithful to the other person. It is important to view such fantasies in this way, rather than as a sign of disloyalty to, or dissatisfaction with, one's sexual partner.

Fantasies during two-person sex are generally quite similar to the ones people have while masturbating. In one study, 84 percent of males and 82 percent of females reported that they fantasized at least some of the time during intercourse (Cado & Leitenberg, 1990). This kind of fantasizing

[7]With the popularity of mouth–genital sex, some women worry that the scent of their genitals might be offensive. The advertisements for feminine hygiene deodorant sprays prey upon these fears. These sprays should not be used, because they may irritate the vagina. Besides, there is nothing offensive about the scent of a vulva that has been washed; some people, in fact, find it arousing.

is quite common. Some sexual partners enjoy sharing their fantasies with each other. Describing a sexual fantasy to your partner can be a turn-on for both of you. Some couples act out all or part of a fantasy and find it very gratifying. One man said,

> I fantasized about being a fourteen-year-old girl. This is a long-lived fantasy of mine. The girl is pretty, with a petite body, probably five-one, five-two, cute ass, maybe light blond or dark brown pussy hair. Small to medium size breasts. Kind of sweet-looking, virginal. . . . Anyway, Sue got into it, like we were two girlfriends sleeping over and she was a couple years older and she was going to show me some things. I happen to be very sensitive around my nipples, so she'd say, "Oh, you have nice little nipples, you're going to have very pretty breasts." Then she'd massage my crotch like she was massaging a vagina: "Do you like it when I pet you down there?" And she'd show me what to do to pleasure her, how to masturbate her and go down on her. We played around with that for a few months. (Maurer, 1994, p. 231)

Genital–Genital Stimulation: Positions of Intercourse

One of the most common heterosexual techniques involves the insertion of the penis into the vagina. This technique is called **coitus**[8] or *sexual intercourse*. Ancient love manuals and other sources illustrate many positions of intercourse (Figure 8.18).

Some authorities state that there are only four positions of intercourse. Personally, we prefer to believe that there are an infinite number. Consider how many different angles your arms, legs, and torso may be in, in relation to those of your partner, and all the various ways in which you can intertwine your limbs—that's a lot of positions. We trust that given sufficient creativity and time, you can discover them all for yourself.

We would agree, though, that there are a few basic positions. One basic variation depends on whether the couple face each other (face-to-face position) or whether one partner faces the other's back (rear-entry position). If you try the other obvious variation, a back-to-back position, you will quickly find that you cannot accomplish much that way. The other basic variation depends on whether one partner is on top of the other or whether the couple are side by side. Let us consider four basic positions that illustrate these variations. As cookbooks often do, we'll give you the basic recipes and let you decide on the embellishments.

The face-to-face, *man-on-top position* ("missionary" position—see Figure 8.19) is probably the one

[8]From the Latin word *coire*, meaning "to go together."

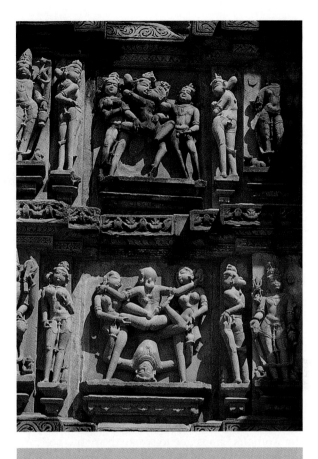

Figure 8.18 Erotic sculptures at the Temple of Kandariya Mahadevo, India, built in A.D. 1000.

used most frequently by couples in the United States. In this position the man and woman stimulate each other until they are aroused, he has an erection, and she is producing vaginal lubrication. Then he moves on top of her as she spreads her legs apart, either he or she spreads the vaginal lips apart, and he inserts his penis into her vagina. He supports himself on his knees and hands or elbows and moves his penis in and out of the vagina in what is sometimes called pelvic thrusting. Some men worry that their heavy weight will crush the woman under them, but because the weight is spread out over so great an area, most women do not find this to be a problem at all, and most find the sensation of contact to be pleasurable.

The woman can have her legs in a number of positions that create variations. She may have them straight out horizontally, a position that produces a tight rub on the penis but does not permit it to go deeply into the vagina. She may bend her legs and elevate them to varying degrees, or she

Coitus: Sexual intercourse; insertion of the penis into the vagina.

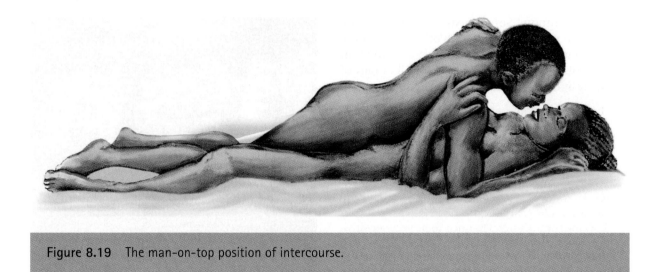

Figure 8.19   The man-on-top position of intercourse.

may hook them over the man's back or over his shoulders. The last approach permits the penis to move deeply into the vagina. The woman can also move her pelvis, either up and down or side to side, to produce further stimulation.

The man-on-top position has some advantages and some disadvantages. It is the best position for ensuring conception, if that is what you want. It leaves the woman's hands free to stroke the man's body (or her own, for that matter). The couple may feel better able to express their love or to communicate other feelings, since they are facing each other. This position, however, does not work well if the woman is in the advanced stages of pregnancy or if either she or the man is extremely obese. Sex therapists have also found that it is not a very good position if the man wants to control his ejaculation; the woman-on-top position is better for this purpose (see Chapter 17).

For the *woman-on-top position* (Figure 8.20), the woman kneels over the man, with one knee on either side of his hips. Then his hand or hers guides the erect penis into the vagina as she lowers herself onto it. She then moves her hips to produce the stimulation. Beyond that, there are numerous variations, depending on where she puts her legs. She can remain on her knees, or she can straighten out her legs behind her, putting them outside his legs or between them. Or she can turn around and face toward his feet.

This position has a number of advantages. It provides a lot of clitoral stimulation, and the woman can control the kind of stimulation she gets. For this reason, many women find it the best position for having an orgasm. It is also a good position for the man who wants to delay his ejaculation, and for this reason it is used in sex therapy. This position is also a good one if the man is tired and the woman is going to supply most of the

movement. Furthermore, the couple face each other, facilitating better communication, and each has the hands free to stroke the other.

In the *rear-entry position*, the man faces the woman's back. One way to do this is for the woman to kneel with her head down. The man kneels behind her and inserts his penis into her vagina (Figure 8.21, p. 220). (This is sometimes called the "doggie position," because it is the way in which dogs and most other animals copulate.) Rear entry can also be accomplished when the couple are in the side-to-side position.

In this position the man's hands are free to stimulate the woman's clitoris or any other part of her body. The couple do not face each other, however, and some couples dislike this aspect of the position. A small amount of air may enter the vagina when this position is used, producing interesting noises when it comes out.

In the *side-to-side position*, the man and woman lie beside each other, either face to face or in a rear-entry position (Figure 8.22). There are many variations beyond this, depending on where the arms and legs go—so many, in fact, that we won't even attempt to list them.

The side-to-side position is good for leisurely or prolonged intercourse or if one or both of the partners are tired. It is also good for the pregnant and the obese. At least some hands are free to stimulate the clitoris, or whatever.

Other Variations

Aside from the variations in these basic positions that can be produced by switching the position of the legs, there are many other possibilities. For example, the man-on-top position can be varied by having the woman lie on the edge of a bed with her

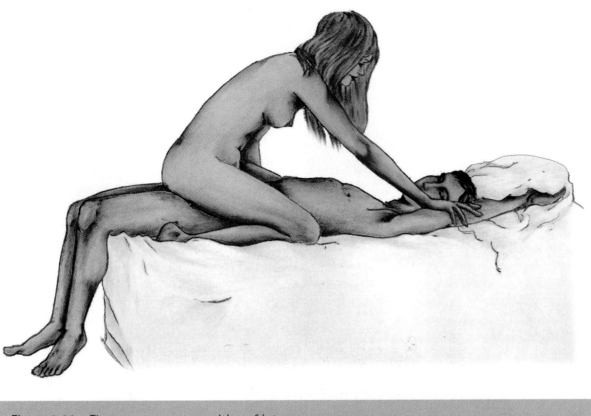

Figure 8.20   The woman-on-top position of intercourse.

feet on the floor while the man kneels on the floor. Or the woman can lie on the edge of a table while the man stands (don't forget to close the curtains first). Both these positions produce a somewhat tighter vagina and therefore more stimulation for the penis. Or the man can sit on a chair and insert the penis as the woman sits on his lap, using either a face-to-face or a rear-entry approach. Or, with both partners standing, the man can lift the woman onto his erect penis as she wraps her legs around his back, or she can put one leg over his shoulder (you have to be pretty athletic to manage this one, however).

Mouth–Genital Stimulation

One of the most striking features of the sexual revolution of the last few decades is the increased popularity of mouth–genital, or oral–genital, techniques. There are two kinds of mouth–genital stimulation ("going down on" one's partner): cunnilingus and fellatio.

In **cunnilingus,** or "eating" (from the Latin words *cunnus,* meaning "vulva," and *lingere,* meaning "to lick"), the woman's genitals are stimulated by her partner's mouth. Cunnilingus can be performed by either heterosexuals or lesbian couples. Generally the focus of stimulation is the cli-

toris. The tongue stimulates it and the surrounding area with quick darting or thrusting movements, or the mouth can suck at the clitoris. A good prelude to cunnilingus can be kissing of the inner thighs or the belly, gradually moving to the clitoris. The mouth can also suck at the inner lips, or the tongue can stimulate the vaginal entrance or be inserted into the vagina. During cunnilingus, some women also enjoy having a finger inserted into the vagina or the anus for added stimulation. The best way to know what she wants is through communication between partners, either verbal or nonverbal.

Many women are enthusiastic about cunnilingus and say that it is the best way—perhaps the only way—for them to orgasm. Such responses are well within the normal range of female sexuality. As one woman put it,

> A tongue offers gentleness and precision and wetness and is the perfect organ for contact. And, besides, it produces sensational orgasms. (Hite, 1976, p. 234)

In one large, well-sampled study of Australians, respondents reported the specific sexual practices that were used in their most recent heterosexual

Cunnilingus (cun-ih-LING-us): Mouth stimulation of the female genitals.

Figure 8.21   The rear-entry position of intercourse.

encounter (Richters et al., 2006). If women had intercourse only, 50 percent had an orgasm, but when they had cunnilingus plus intercourse, 73 percent had an orgasm. In contrast, among men who engaged only in intercourse, 95 percent had an orgasm. It just isn't fair.

Cunnilingus, like fellatio, discussed next, can transmit some sexually transmitted infections such as gonorrhea. Oral sex can also result in transmission of HPV (human papillomavirus, which causes genital warts) from the genitals of an infected person to the mouth of the partner. Some cases of oral cancers involve the HPV16 strain, which may have been transmitted by oral sex (Herrero et al., 2003). For these reasons, you need to be as careful about whom you engage in mouth–genital sex with as about whom you would engage in intercourse with. A small

sheet of plastic, called a *dental dam,* can be placed over the vulva for those wanting to practice safer sex.

One other possible problem should be noted, as well. Some women enjoy having their partner blow air forcefully into the vagina. While this technique is not dangerous under normal circumstances, when used on a pregnant woman it has been known to cause death (apparently as the result of air getting into the uterine veins), damage to the placenta, and embolism (Sadock & Sadock, 1976). For these reasons, it should not be used on a pregnant woman.

In **fellatio**[9] ("sucking," "a blow job") the man's penis is stimulated by his partner's mouth. Fellatio

---

Fellatio (feh–LAY-shoh): Mouth stimulation of the male genitals.

[9]Fellatio is from the Latin word *fellare,* meaning "to suck." Partners should not take the "sucking" part too literally. The penis, particularly at the tip, is a delicate organ and should not be treated like a straw in an extra-thick milkshake.

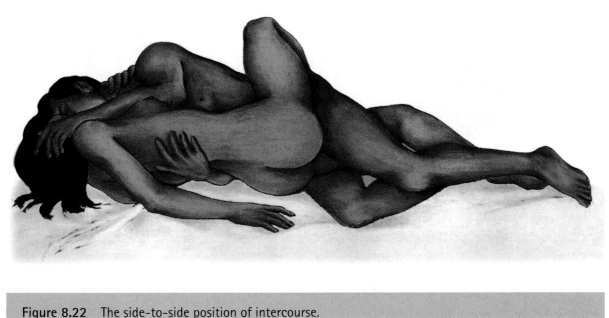

Figure 8.22   The side-to-side position of intercourse.

can be performed by either heterosexuals or gay male couples. The partner licks the glans of the penis, its shaft, and perhaps the testes. The penis is gently taken into the mouth. If it is not fully erect, an erection can generally be produced by stronger sucking combined with hand stimulation along the penis. After that, the partner can produce an in-and-out motion by moving the lips down toward the base of the penis and then back up, always being careful not to scrape the penis with the teeth. Or the tongue can be flicked back and forth around the tip of the penis or along the corona.

To bring the man to orgasm, the in-and-out motion is continued, moving the penis deeper and deeper into the mouth and perhaps also using the fingers to encircle the base of the penis and give further stimulation. Sometimes when the penis moves deeply toward the throat, it stimulates a gag reflex, which occurs any time something comes into contact with that part of the throat. To avoid this, the partner should relax the throat muscles while firming the lips to provide more stimulation to the penis.

When a couple are engaged in fellatio, the big question in their minds may concern ejaculation. The man may, of course, simply withdraw his penis from his partner's mouth and ejaculate outside it. Or he may ejaculate into it, and his partner may even enjoy swallowing the ejaculate. The ejaculate resembles partially cooked egg white in texture. It does not have a very distinctive flavor but often leaves a salty aftertaste. Because some people have

mixed feelings about having the semen in their mouths, it is probably a good idea for the couple to discuss ahead of time (or during the activity) what they plan to do, particularly because ejaculation into the mouth is an unsafe practice in the AIDS era (see Chapter 18).

Most men find fellatio to be a highly stimulating experience, which no doubt accounts for the high frequency with which prostitutes are asked to do it. Enjoyment of fellatio is certainly within the normal range of male sexuality.

Fellatio and cunnilingus can be performed simultaneously by both partners. This is often called **sixty-nining**[10] because the numerals "69" suggest the position of the two bodies during simultaneous mouth–genital sex. Sixty-nining may be done either side to side or with one person on top of the other, each with the mouth on the other's genitals (Figure 8.23).

Simultaneous mouth–genital sex allows both people to enjoy the pleasure of that stimulation at the same time. It can give a feeling of total body involvement and total involvement between partners. Some couples, however, feel that this technique requires doing too many things at once and is more complicated than enjoyable. For example, the woman may be distracted from enjoying the marvelous clitoral stimulation she is receiving because

---

[10]If you want to be elegant and impress your friends, you can call it *soixante-neuf,* which is just "sixty-nine" in French.

Sixty-nining: Simultaneous mouth–genital stimulation; also called *soixante-neuf.*

Figure 8.23   Simultaneous mouth–genital stimulation in the sixty-nine position.

she has to concentrate at the same time on using her mouth to give good stimulation to the penis. If sixty-nine is done in the man-on-top position, some women also feel that they have no control over the movement and that they may be choked.

Anal Intercourse

In **anal intercourse** the man inserts his penis into his partner's rectum (Morin, 1981). In legal terminology it is sometimes called *sodomy* (although this term may also refer to other sexual practices such as intercourse with animals), and it is sometimes referred to as having sex "Greek style." It may be done by either heterosexual couples or gay male couples.

Anal intercourse is somewhat more difficult than penis-in-vagina intercourse because the rectum has no natural lubrication and because it is surrounded by fairly tight muscles. The man should therefore begin by moistening the partner's anus, either with saliva or with a sterile surgical lubricant such as K-Y Jelly (*not* Vaseline). He should also lubricate his penis. He then inserts it gently into the rectum and begins controlled pelvic thrusting. It is typically done in the rear-entry position or in the man-on-top position. The more the partner can relax, the less uncomfortable it is. Discomfort can also be reduced by allowing the receiving partner to be in control. If it is done properly, it need involve no pain. While some heterosexual couples find the idea repulsive, others delight in it. Some women report orgasm during anal intercourse, particularly

when it is accompanied by hand stimulation of the clitoris. Men also report orgasms from anal intercourse, primarily due to stimulation of the prostate.

Some health risks are associated with anal intercourse. It can cause damage or injury to the tissue of the rectal lining and anal sphincter. It can lead to infections with various organisms. Of greatest concern, HIV can be transmitted through anal intercourse. For these reasons, safer sex consists of either refraining from engaging in anal intercourse or using a condom (or doing it only in a monogamous relationship with an uninfected partner). Furthermore, for heterosexuals the penis should never be inserted into the vagina after anal intercourse unless it has been washed thoroughly. The reason for this is that the rectum contains bacteria that do not belong in the vagina and that can cause a dandy case of vaginitis if they happen to get there. Also, sex toys or other objects inserted in the anus should be thoroughly washed following removal from the anus.

Another variation is **anilingus** (*feuille de rose* in French, "rimming" in slang), in which the tongue and mouth stimulate the anus. The anus may also be stimulated by the hand, and some people report that having a finger inserted into the rectum near the time of orgasm provides a heightened sexual sensation. Anilingus carries with it some risk of AIDS, hepatitis, or *E. coli* infections.

Techniques of Lesbians and Gays

Some people have difficulty imagining exactly what gays and lesbians do in bed—after all, the

Anal intercourse: Insertion of the penis into the partner's rectum.
Anilingus (ay-nih-LING-us): Mouth stimulation of the partner's anus.

Figure 8.24   Female–female sexual expression.

important ingredients for sex are one penis and one vagina, aren't they?

The preliminaries consist, as they do for heterosexuals, of kissing, hugging, and petting. Gay men engage in mutual masturbation, oral–genital sex (fellatio), and, less frequently, anal intercourse. Gay men sometimes also engage in **interfemoral intercourse,** in which a man's penis moves between the thighs of the partner. Lesbians engage in mutual masturbation, oral–genital sex (cunnilingus), and a practice called **tribadism** ("dry hump"), which is similar to heterosexual intercourse, with one partner lying on top of the other and making thrusting movements so that both receive genital stimulation. Another practice is the use of a dildo by one person to stimulate the other.

An important point to note about these practices is that they are all behaviors in which heterosexuals also engage. In other words, homosexuals do the same things sexually that heterosexuals do. The only thing that is distinctive about homosexual lovemaking is that the partners are of the same gender.

Masters and Johnson (1979), in their laboratory studies, made direct observations of the lovemaking techniques of gays and lesbians and compared them with those of straights. They found that, in masturbation techniques, there were no differences.

However, in couple interactions there were some substantial differences. The major one was that homosexuals "took their time"—in other words, they seemed to have less of a goal orientation. Heterosexual couples, on the other hand, seemed to be performance oriented—they seemed to strive toward a goal of orgasm for each partner. In the initial approach to stimulating the female, heterosexuals and lesbians began with holding and kissing, but this lasted only about 30 seconds for the heterosexuals, who quickly moved on to genital stimulation. Lesbians, on the other hand, spent more time in holding and kissing and then went on to a long period of breast stimulation, which sometimes resulted in orgasm in the absence of genital stimulation. Lesbians also appeared to communicate more with each other. In the initial approach to stimulating the male, gays did extensive stimulation of the nipples, generally producing erection, but such a technique was rare among heterosexuals (done by only 3 of 100 couples). Gay men were also much more likely to stimulate the frenulum (the area of the penis on the lower side, just below the corona). They also used a "teasing technique" in which the man brings his partner near orgasm,

Interfemoral intercourse: A sexual technique used by gay men in which one man moves his penis between the thighs of the other.
Tribadism (TRY-bad-izm): A sexual technique used by lesbians in which one woman lies on top of another and moves rhythmically in order to produce sexual pleasure, particularly clitoral stimulation.

Figure 8.25   Male–male sexual expression.

then relaxes the stimulation, then increases the stimulation again, and so on, essentially prolonging the pleasure. Among heterosexuals, the man's most frequent complaint was that the woman did not grasp the shaft of the penis tightly enough. Masters and Johnson argued that heterosexuals can learn from gays and lesbians; the technique of gays and lesbians benefits from stimulating another body like their own.

Two-Person Cybersex

The Internet provides not only visual sexual images for people wanting to masturbate, it also creates the opportunity for two-person cybersex. People report forming relationships on the Internet that they consider to be sexually intimate, even though they have never actually met the person face-to-face (Ross, 2005). It has also created a new sexual space that is somewhere between fantasy and action. Essentially, a person can type sexual acts without actually doing them (Ross, 2005).

These Internet activities challenge us to think more clearly about our definitions of sexual activity. For example, a wife accuses her husband of having a cybersex affair with another woman and he replies that he was only typing. Who is right?

Aphrodisiacs

Is There a Good Aphrodisiac?

An **aphrodisiac** is a substance—such as a food, a drug, or a perfume—that excites sexual desire. Throughout history people have searched for the surefire aphrodisiac. Before arousing your hopes, we should say that the search has been unsuccessful. There is no known substance that works well as an aphrodisiac.

One popular idea is that oysters are an aphrodisiac. This notion appears to reflect the myth that foods that resemble sexual organs have

> **Aphrodisiac** (ah–froh–**DIZ**–ih–ak): A substance that increases sexual desire.

sexual powers. For example, bananas and asparagus resemble the penis and have been thought to be aphrodisiacs. Another example is the Asian belief that powdered rhinoceros horn is an aphrodisiac (perhaps this is also the origin of the term *horny*) (Taberner, 1985). Perhaps oysters are thought to have such powers because of their resemblance to the testes (MacDougald, 1961). Oysters, however, contain no substances that can in any way influence sexual functioning (Neiger, 1968). Other foods thought to be aphrodisiacs include caviar, truffles, and skink (a kind of lizard).

Doubtless some substances gain a continued reputation as aphrodisiacs because simply believing that something will be arousing can itself be arousing. For example, the belief that a bull's testicles ("prairie oysters") or peanuts or clams have special powers may produce a temporary improvement of sexual functioning, not because of the chemicals contained in them but because of a belief in them.

Alcohol also has a reputation as an aphrodisiac. Briefly, drinking small quantities of alcohol may, for some people, decrease psychological inhibitions and for this reason increase sexual desire. Moderate to large quantities, however, rapidly lead to an inability to function sexually. We will discuss the effects of alcohol on sexual functioning in more detail in Chapter 17.

Users of marijuana report that it acts as a sexual stimulant. Probably this effect is due, in part, to the fact that marijuana produces the sensation that time is being stretched out, thus prolonging and intensifying sensations, including sexual sensations. There is no scientific documentation of the aphrodisiac effects of marijuana except for the reports of users. We consider possible negative effects of marijuana on sexual functioning in Chapter 17.

The current interest in nutrition, and in natural and organic foods and supplements, has created a market for "natural" aphrodisiacs. According to one industry source, the popular herbs purchased for this purpose include yohimbe, cayenne, arginine, aventa sativa, and damiana. Some companies sell herbal combinations and edible syrups and "brews" that are claimed to increase sexual desire, sexual performance, sexual stamina, or all three. Again, there is no evidence that any of these affect sexual desire, though the belief that they do may enhance sexual functioning.

Unfortunately, some of the substances that are thought to enhance sexual functioning are quite dangerous. For example, cantharides (Spanish fly) has a reputation as an aphrodisiac, but it is poisonous (Kaplan, 1974; Leavitt, 1974; Taberner, 1985).

Amyl nitrite ("poppers") is popular among some people. Because it relaxes the sphincter muscle of the anus, it is used by those engaging in anal intercourse (Taberner, 1985). Users report that it produces heightened sensations during orgasms (Everett, 1975). Probably it acts by dilating the blood vessels in the genitals. It may, however, have side effects, including dizziness, headaches, fainting, and, in rare cases, death, so it can be dangerous (Taberner, 1985).

Butyl nitrite—sold under such trade names as Rush, Locker Room, and Climax—is a chemical relative of amyl nitrite. It is used to heighten sexual pleasure. Although no deaths have been reported from inhaling it, there are reported deaths from swallowing it (UPI, 1981).

In contrast to these street drugs, several prescription drugs have been approved by the Food and Drug Administration for use in treating male sexual dysfunction. *Viagra* is designed to increase the flow of blood to the penis and maintain the resulting erection. *Cialis* is intended to create the ability to have an erection up to 36 hours after taking it. Note that neither drug increases desire. (For more information, see Chapter 17.) There is no evidence that these drugs increase sexual desire or performance in women.

Anaphrodisiacs

Just as people have searched for aphrodisiacs, so they have sought **anaphrodisiacs,** substances or practices that would diminish sexual desire. Cold showers are reputed to have such effects, as is potassium nitrate (saltpeter). This substance contains nothing that decreases sexual drive, but it does act as a diuretic. In other words, it makes the person want to urinate frequently, which may be distracting enough so that he or she is not much interested in sex.

There has been some medical interest in finding drugs that would decrease sex drive for use in treating aggressive sexual offenders. One such drug is cyproterone acetate, which is an antiandrogen. (For more information, see Chapter 14.)

We discus other drugs that may lead to a loss of sexual functioning in Chapter 17.

Should Intercourse and Orgasm Be the Goal?

Our culture has traditionally held the belief that a sexual encounter should "climax" with intercourse and orgasm, at least orgasm for the man. In our

> **Anaphrodisiac (an-ah-froh-DIZ-ih-ak):** A substance that decreases sexual desire.

modern era of multiple orgasms for women and general sexual liberation, the view that intercourse is the important part of sex and that orgasm is the goal toward which both partners must strive is pervasive. This belief system is reflected in the term *foreplay*, which implies that activities like hand stimulation of the genitals, kissing, and mouth–genital sex are only preliminaries that take place before intercourse, which is viewed as the "real sex." Similar beliefs are reflected in a commonly used phrase, *achieving orgasm*, as if orgasm were something to be achieved like a promotion on the job.[11]

Psychologist Rollo May felt that men particularly, by concentrating on "achieving" orgasm and *satisfying* their desire, miss out on the more important part of the sexual experience: prolonging the feeling of desire and pleasure, building it higher and higher. As he put it,

> The pleasure in sex is described by Freud and others as the reduction of tension [orgasm]; in eros, on the contrary, we wish not to be released from the excitement but rather to hang on to it, to bask in it, and even to increase it. (1974, pp. 71–72)

Another one of the goals of sex that has emerged is the simultaneous orgasm. Some people consider this an event to be worked for rather than a pleasant thing that sometimes happens.

The legacy of the Protestant ethic in our culture is that our achievement drives now seem to be channeled into our sexual behaviors. There is nothing intrinsically wrong with expressing achievement drives in sex, except that any time there is an achievement situation, there is also the potential for a failure. If she does not have an orgasm or if he cannot get an erection, the couple feel as if the whole experience was a disaster. The problem with setting up sexual goals, then, is that the possibility of sexual failures or sexual disorders is also being set up.

Men are stereotyped as preferring quick "foreplay" leading to intercourse, whereas women are stereotyped as preferring much more extended foreplay. Contrary to these stereotypes, a study of heterosexual couples indicated that there were no differences between women and men in their ideal duration of foreplay (Miller & Byers, 2004). Men's ideal duration of intercourse itself was considerably longer (18 minutes, on average) than their estimates of their actual duration of intercourse (8 minutes, on average). The men essentially wanted to "perform" longer than they actually did.

The best approach is to enjoy all the various aspects of lovemaking for themselves, rather than as techniques for achieving something, and to concentrate on sex as a feast of the senses, rather than as an achievement competition. We need to broaden our view of sexual expression to recognize that a broad continuum of activities may provide sexual pleasure—a dream, a thought, a conversation, cuddling, kissing, sensual massage, dancing, oral–genital stimulation and intercourse (Chalker, 1995). In short, we need to view the entire body as erogenous and focus on *outercourse* as much as intercourse.

From Inexperience to Boredom

After an initial lack of experience with sex, some people shift rather quickly to becoming bored with it, with perhaps only a brief span of self-confident, pleasurable sexuality in between. Most of us, of course, are sexually inexperienced early in our lives, and most of us feel bored with the way we are having sex at times. How can we deal with these problems?

Sexual Inexperience

In our culture we expect men to be "worldly" about sex—to have had experience with it and to be skillful in the use of sexual techniques. A man or a boy who is sexually inexperienced (perhaps even a virgin) or who has had only a few sexual experiences, with little opportunity to practice, may have a real fear about whether he will be able to "perform" (the achievement ethic again) in a sexual encounter. With the sexual revolution has come an increasing expectation that women should also have a bag of sexual tricks ready to use, and so they, too, are increasingly expected to be experienced.

How can one deal with this problem of inexperience? First, it is important to question society's assumption that one should be experienced. Everyone has to begin sometime, and there is absolutely nothing wrong with inexperience.

Second, there are many good books and articles on sexual techniques that are definitely worth reading, although it is important to be selective, since a few of these may be more harmful than helpful. This chapter should be a good introduction. You also might want to consult *The New Joy of Sex* or any of the self-help manuals listed at the end of Chapter 17. Do not become slavishly attached to the techniques you read about in books, though. They should serve basically as a stimulus to your

---

[11]To avoid this whole notion, we never use the phrase *to achieve orgasm* in this book. Instead, we prefer *to have an orgasm* or simply *to orgasm*. Why not turn it into a verb so that we will not feel we have to work at achieving it?

Focus: First Person
A Personal Growth Exercise—Getting to Know Your Own Body

Most experts on sexual communication agree that before you can begin to communicate your sexual needs to your partner, you must get to know your own body and its sexual responsiveness. This exercise is designed to help you do that. Set aside some time for yourself, preferably 30 minutes or more. You'll need privacy and a mirror, preferably a full-length one.

1. Undress and stand in front of the mirror. Relax your body completely.

2. Take a good look at your body, top to bottom. Look at the colors, the curves, the textures. Take your time doing this. Try to discover things you haven't noticed before. What pleases you about your body? What don't you like about your body? Can you say these things aloud?

3. Look at your body. What parts of it influence how you feel about yourself sexually?

4. Run your fingers slowly over your body, from head to toe. How does it feel to you? Are some parts soft? Are some sensitive? Are you hurrying over some places? Why? How do you feel about doing this?

5. Explore your genitals. *If you're a man,* look at them. Do you like the way they look? Now explore your genitals with your fingers. Gently stroke your penis, scrotum, and the area behind the scrotum. Pay close attention to the various sensations you're producing. Which areas feel particularly good when they're stroked? Try different kinds of touching—light, hard, fast, slow. Which kind feels best? If you get an erection, that's okay. Just take your time and learn as much as you can. Are there differences in sensitivities between the aroused state and the unaroused state? *If you're a woman,* take a hand mirror and look at your genitals. Do you like the way they look? Now explore your genitals with your fingers. Touch your outer lips, inner lips, clitoris, vaginal entrance. Which areas feel particularly good? Try different kinds of touching—light, hard, fast, slow. Which kind feels best? If you get aroused, that's okay. Are there differences in sensitivities between the aroused state and the unaroused state? Just take your time and learn as much as you can.

6. Now you're ready to communicate some new information to your partner!

For more exercises like this, see Zilbergeld's *The New Male Sexuality* (1992) and Heiman, LoPiccolo, and LoPiccolo's *Becoming Orgasmic: A Sexual Growth Program for Women* (1976).

Sources: Brenton (1972); Heiman et al. (1976); Zilbergeld (1992).

---

imagination, not as a series of steps that must be followed.

Third, communicate with your partner. Because individual preferences vary so much, no one, no matter how experienced, is ever a sexual expert with a new partner. The best way to please a partner is to find out what that person likes, and communication accomplishes this better than prior experience. Chapter 11 gives some specific tips on communication. Interestingly, one study found that the best sexual predictor of relationship satisfaction was not frequency of sex or techniques but mutual agreement on sexual issues (Markman, personal communication).

Boredom

The opposite problem to inexperience is the feeling of boredom in a long-term sexual relationship.

Boredom, of course, is not always a necessary consequence of having sex with the same person over a long period of time. Certainly there are couples who have been married for 40 or 50 years and who continue to find sexual expression exciting. Unfortunately, the major sex surveys have not inquired about the phenomenon of boredom, so it is not possible to estimate the percentage of people who eventually become bored or who experience occasional spells of boredom. However, such experiences are surely common. As someone once said, a rut is no place to be making love. How can we deal with the problem of boredom?

Communication can help in this situation, as it can in others. Couples sometimes evolve a routine sexual sequence that leads to boredom, and sometimes that sequence is not really what either person wants. By communicating to each other what they really would like to do and then doing it, two people can introduce some variety into their relationship. The various love manuals can also give ideas on new techniques. Finally, a couple's sexual relationship often mirrors the other aspects of their relationship, and sexual boredom may sometimes mean that they are generally bored with each other. Rejuvenating the rest of the relationship—perhaps taking up a hobby or a sport together or going on a good vacation, during which they really try to build their relationship in general—may do wonders for their sexual relationship.

One might also question the meaning of *boredom*. Perhaps our expectations for sexual experience are too high. Encouraged by the media, we tend to believe that every time we have intercourse the earth should move. We do not expect that every meal we eat will be fantastic or that we will always have a huge appetite and enjoy every bite. Yet we do tend to have such expectations with regard to sexuality. Perhaps when boredom seems to be a problem it is not the real issue. Rather, the problem may be unrealistically high expectations.

SUMMARY

William Masters and Virginia Johnson conducted an important program of research on the physiology of human sexual response. They found that two basic physiological processes occur during arousal and orgasm: vasocongestion and myotonia. The sexual response cycle occurs in three stages: excitement, orgasm, and resolution.

Their research indicates that there is no physiological distinction between clitoral and vaginal orgasms in women, which refutes an early idea of Freud's. They also provided convincing evidence of the existence of multiple orgasm in women.

Criticisms of Masters and Johnson's model are that (1) they ignored cognitive factors and (2) their selection of research participants may have led to a self-fulfilling prophecy in their results.

Two cognitive physiological models are Kaplan's three-component model, focusing on desire, vasocongestion, and muscular contraction, and Walen and Roth's model, which emphasizes cognitive aspects of sexual response, namely perception and evaluation.

The nervous system and sex hormones are important in sexual response. The nervous system functions in sexual response by a combination, of spinal reflexes (best documented for erection and ejaculation) and brain influences (particularly of the limbic system). There is evidence that some women ejaculate. Hormones are important to sexual behavior, both in their influences on prenatal development (organizing effects) and in their stimulating influence on adult sexual behavior (activating effects). Testosterone seems to be crucial for maintaining sexual desire in both men and women.

Pheromones are biochemicals secreted outside the body that play an important role in sexual communication and attraction. Much of the evidence is based on research with animals, but evidence in humans is accumulating rapidly.

Sexual pleasure is produced by stimulation of various areas of the body called erogenous zones.

Sexual self-stimulation, or autoeroticism, includes masturbation and sexual fantasies. Many people have sexual fantasies while masturbating. Common themes of these fantasies are kissing and touching sensuously, oral sex, and seduction. Similar sexual fantasies are also common during intercourse.

An important technique in two-person sex is hand stimulation of the partner's genitals. A good guide to technique is to find out how the partner masturbates. Touching other areas of the body and kissing are also important. The other senses—sight, smell, and hearing—can also be used in creating sexual arousal.

While there are infinite varieties in the positions for intercourse, there are four basic positions: man on top (the missionary position), woman on top, rear entry, and side to side.

The two kinds of mouth–genital stimulation are cunnilingus (mouth stimulation of the female genitals) and fellatio (mouth stimulation of the male genitals). Both are engaged in frequently and are considered pleasurable by many people. Lesbians and gays use techniques similar to those of straights (e.g., hand–genital stimulation and oral–genital sex). Gays and lesbians, though, seem less goal oriented, take more time, and communicate more than heterosexuals do.

Anal intercourse involves inserting the penis into the rectum. This activity and the insertion of other objects in the anus must be done carefully to avoid injury or transmission of STIs.

An aphrodisiac is a substance that arouses sexual desire. There is no known reliable aphrodisiac, and some of the substances that are popularly thought to act as aphrodisiacs can be dangerous to a person's health.

We have a tendency in our culture, perhaps a legacy of the Protestant ethic, to view sex as work and to turn sex into an achievement situation, as witnessed by expressions such as "achieving orgasm." Such attitudes make sex less pleasurable and may set the stage for sexual failures or sexual disorders.

QUESTIONS FOR THOUGHT, DISCUSSION, AND DEBATE

1. Debate the following topic. Resolved: Castration is an appropriate and effective treatment for convicted rapists.

2. Do you think that pheromones might play more of a role in human sexual behavior in cultures that do not stress personal hyper-cleanliness as much as we do in the United States? If so, what do you think the effects of pheromones would be in those other cultures?

3. Your little sister is a sophomore in college and is in the fourth month of what looks like will be a wonderful long-term relationship. Katie and her boyfriend now seem to have a full sexual relationship. As a benevolent older brother/ sister, you want her to enjoy much sexual pleasure in this relationship. What information from this chapter would you tell your sister about, if you hoped to ensure her sexual satisfaction and sexual pleasure?

4. What do you think about sexual fantasizing? Is it harmful, or is it a good way to enrich someone's sexual expression? Are your ideas consistent with the results of the research discussed in this chapter?

5. You have been in an intimate relationship for two years. You find you are getting bored with your sexual activity. List three things that could make your sexual relationship more satisfying. How would you communicate your desire to do each of these to your partner?

SUGGESTIONS FOR FURTHER READING

Comfort, Alex. (1991). *The new joy of sex: A gourmet guide to lovemaking for the nineties.* New York: Crown. Alex Comfort rewrote his bestseller to maintain the joy of sex while recognizing the risk of AIDS.

Dodson, Betty. (1987). *Sex for one: The joy of self-loving.* New York: Harmony Books (Crown Publishers). An inspiring ode to masturbation.

Kroll, Ken, et al. (1995). *Enabling romance: A guide to love, sex, and relationships for the disabled (and the people who care for them).* Bethesda, MD: Woodbine House. With the recognition of disabled persons' sexuality comes a need for self-help books, and this one is designed for that purpose.

Laqueur, Thomas W. (2003). *Solitary sex: A cultural history of masturbation.* New York: Zone Books.

Maines, Rachel P. (1999). *The technology of orgasm: "Hysteria," the vibrator, and women's sexual satisfaction.* Baltimore: Johns Hopkins University Press. A delicious history of the vibrator, originally developed for physicians in the Victorian era to use in curing women of a mental disorder termed "hysteria."

Tiefer, Leonore. (2004). *Sex is not a natural act and other essays.* 2nd ed. Boulder, CO: Westview. Tiefer is both knowledgeable and a witty writer. This book contains some of her insightful criticisms of the Masters and Johnson model of sexual response.

Wyatt, Tristram. (2003). *Pheromones and animal behavior.* New York: Cambridge University Press. The definitive book on pheromones.

CHAPTER NINE

Sexuality and the Life Cycle: Childhood and Adolescence

CHAPTER HIGHLIGHTS

My son Jeremy . . . naively decided to wear barrettes to nursery school. Several times that day, another little boy insisted that Jeremy must be a girl because "only girls wear barrettes." After repeatedly asserting that "wearing barrettes doesn't matter; being a boy means having a penis and testicles," Jeremy finally pulled down his pants as a way of making his point more convincingly. The boy was not impressed. He simply said, "Everybody has a penis; only girls wear barrettes."*

*Berm (1989).

Stop for a moment and think of the first sexual experience you ever had. Some of you will think of the first time you had sexual intercourse, while others will remember much earlier episodes, like "playing doctor" with the other kids in the neighborhood. Now think of the kind of sex life you had, or expect to have, in your early twenties. Finally, imagine yourself at 65 and imagine the kinds of sexual behavior you will be engaging in then.

In recent years, scientists have begun thinking of human sexual development as a process that occurs throughout the life span. This process is influenced by biological, psychological, social, and cultural factors. This represents a departure from the Freudian heritage, in which the crucial aspects of development were all thought to occur in childhood. This chapter and Chapter 10 are based on the newer **life-span,** or life-cycle, approach to understanding the **development** of our sexual behavior throughout the course of our lives. The things you were asked to remember and imagine about your own sexual functioning in the preceding paragraph will give you an idea of the sweep of this approach to development.

Data Sources

What kinds of scientific data are available on the sexual behavior of people at various times in their lives? One source we have is the Kinsey report (Kinsey et al., 1948, 1953). The scientific techniques used by Kinsey were discussed and evaluated in Chapter 3. A number of more recent surveys of adults also provide relevant data.

In these surveys, adults are questioned about their childhood sexual behavior, and their responses form some of the data to be discussed in this chapter. These responses may be even more problematic than some of the other kinds of data from those studies, though. For example, a 50- or 60-year-old man is asked to report on his sexual behavior at age 10. How accurately will he remember things that happened 40 or 50 years ago? Surely there will be some forgetting. Thus the data on childhood sexual behavior may be subject to errors that result from adults being asked to recall things that happened a very long time ago.

An alternative would be to interview children about their sexual behavior or perhaps even to observe their sexual behavior. Few researchers have done either, for obvious reasons. Such a study would arouse tremendous opposition from parents, religious leaders, and politicians, who might argue that it is unnecessary, or that it would harm the children who were studied. These reactions reflect in part the widespread beliefs that children are not yet sexual beings and should not be exposed to questions about sex. Such research also raises ethical issues: at what age can a child give truly informed consent to be in such a study?

In a few studies children have been questioned directly about their sexual behavior. Kinsey interviewed 432 children, aged 4 to 14, and the results of the study were published after his death (Elias & Gebhard, 1969). A recent innovation is the use of a "talking" computer to interview children (Romer et al., 1997). The computer is programmed to present the questions through headphones, and the child enters his or her answers using the keyboard. This process preserves confidentiality even when others are present, because only the child knows the question. This procedure was used to gather data from samples of high-risk youth ages 9 to 15. More children reported sexual experience to the computer than did children in face-to-face interviews.

Many studies of adolescent sexual behavior have also been done. Particularly notable are several surveys using nationally representative samples, including the National Longitudinal Study of Youth (NLSY), the National Survey of Family Growth 2002 (NSFG), and the National Longitudinal Study of Adolescent Health (Add Health). Sociological studies of premarital sexual behavior have been done by Reiss (1967), DeLamater and MacCorquodale (1979), and Bancroft, Herbenick,

Life-span development: Development from birth through old age.

and Reynolds (2003). These are well-sampled studies of adolescent sexuality, and we can have confidence in their results.

The studies of child and adolescent sexual behavior have all been surveys, which have used either questionnaires or interviews. No one has made systematic, direct observations of children's sexual behavior.

Infancy (0 to 2 Years)

Before 1890, it was thought that sexuality was something that magically appeared at puberty. Sigmund Freud first expressed the notion that children—in fact, infants—have sexual urges and engage in sexual behavior.

The capacity of the human body to show a sexual response is present from birth. Male infants, for example, get erections. Indeed, boy babies are sometimes born with erections. Ultrasound studies indicate that reflex erections occur in the male fetus for several months before birth (Masters et al., 1982). And vaginal lubrication has been found in baby girls in the 24 hours after birth (Masters et al., 1982).

The first intimate relationship most children experience is with their mothers (Figure 9.1). The

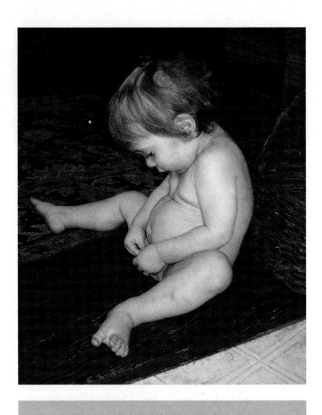

Figure 9.2   Infant self-stimulation.

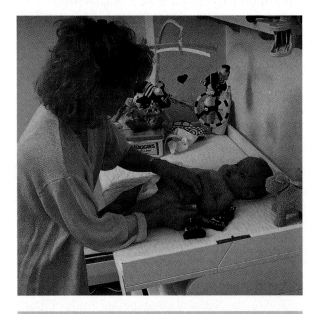

Figure 9.1   Some activities associated with nurturing an infant are potentially sensuous, because they involve pleasant physical contact.

mother–infant relationship involves a good deal of physical contact and typically engages the infant's tactile, olfactory, visual, and auditory senses (Frayser, 1994).

> Most activities associated with nurturing and hygienic care of babies are intimate and sensuous since they involve contact with sensitive organs—lips, mouth, anus, and genitals—that can produce in the infant a physiological response of a sensuous and sexual nature. These activities include (in addition to breast feeding) toilet training, bathing, cleaning, and diapering. The highly physiological and emotionally charged first encounters of mother and infant play an indispensable part in the development process. (Martinson, 1994, p. 11)

Self-Stimulation

Infants have been observed fondling their own genitals (Figure 9.2). There is some question as to how conscious they are of what they are doing, but at the least they seem to be engaging in some pleasurable, sexual self-stimulation. The rhythmic manipulation of the genitals associated with adult masturbation does not occur until age $2\frac{1}{2}$ to 3 years (Martinson, 1994). A survey of sexual behavior in other cultures suggested that, if permitted, most boys and girls will progress from absent-minded fingering of their genitals to systematic masturbation by ages 6 to 8 (Ford & Beach, 1951). In fact, in some cultures adults fondle infants' genitals to keep them quiet, a remarkably effective pacifier.

Orgasms from self-stimulation are possible even at this early age, although before puberty boys are not capable of ejaculation. Masturbation is a normal, natural form of sexual expression in infancy. It is definitely not a sign of pathology, as some previous generations believed. Indeed, in one study comparing infants who had optimal relationships with their mothers and infants who had problematic relationships with their mothers, it was the infants with the optimal maternal relationships who were more likely to masturbate (Spitz, 1949).

Infant–Infant Sexual Encounters

Infants and young children are very self-centered (what the psychologist Jean Piaget called *egocentric*). Even when they seem to be playing with another child, they may simply be playing alongside the other child, actually in a world all their own. Their sexual development parallels the development of their other behaviors. Thus their earliest sex is typically one-person sex—self-stimulation. Not until later do they develop social, two-person sex, either heterosexual or homosexual.

Nonetheless, particularly in later infancy there may be some infant–infant encounters, either affectionate or sexual. In these encounters, children may kiss, hug, pat, stroke, and gaze at each other, behaviors that are part of erotic intimacy later in life.

Nongenital Sensual Experiences

Many of the sensual experiences that infants and young children have are diffuse and not easily classified as some type of sexual activity. For example, as Freud noted, infants delight in putting things in their mouths. Thus sucking at the mother's breast, or sucking on his or her own fingers, may be a sensuous experience for the infant.

Being cuddled or rocked can also be a warm, sensuous experience. Indeed, the infant's experiences in such early intimate encounters might influence her or his reactions to intimacy and cuddling in adulthood. It seems that some infants are cuddlers, some noncuddlers (Schaffer & Emerson, 1964). Cuddlers enjoy physical contact, while noncuddlers show displeasure and restlessness when they are handled or held. As soon as they are old enough to do so, they show resistance to such situations or crawl or walk away from them. Cuddling and non-cuddling seem to be basically different personality patterns. It would be interesting to know whether these patterns remain consistent into adulthood.

Attachment

The quality of the relationship with the parents at this age can be very important to the child's capacity for later sexual and emotional relationships. In psychological terms, an **attachment** (or bond) forms between the infant and the mother, the father, or other caregiver. The bond begins in the hours immediately following birth and continues throughout the period of infancy (Coustan & Angelini, 1995). It is facilitated by cuddling and other forms of physical contact. Later, attachments form to other familiar people. These are the individual's earliest experiences with love and emotional attachment. The quality of these attachments—whether they are stable, secure, and satisfying or unstable, insecure, and frustrating—affects the person's capacity for emotional attachments in adulthood. Recent research with humans (discussed in Chapter 11) indicates that adults' styles of romantic attachment are similar to the kinds of attachment they remember having with their parents in childhood.

Knowing about Boy–Girl Differences

By age 2½ or 3, children know what gender they are (see Chapter 12); this is the first step in developing a gender identity. Awareness of being male or female motivates them to be like other members of that group (Martin & Ruble, 2004). They know that they are like the parent of the same gender and different from the parent of the opposite gender and from other children of the opposite gender. At first, infants think that the difference between girls and boys is a matter of clothes or haircuts. But by age 3 there may be some awareness of differences in the genital region and increasing interest in the genitals of other children (Martinson, 1994). At ages 4 to 6 ideas about gender are very rigid, as reflected in the opening vignette. As the child gains experience, these gender beliefs become more flexible (Martin & Ruble, 2004).

Early Childhood (3 to 7 Years)

Between the ages of 3 and 7, there is a marked increase in sexual interest and activity, just as there is in activity and interest in general (Figure 9.3).

Attachment: A psychological bond that forms between an infant and the mother, the father, or other caregiver.

Figure 9.3 Between the ages of 3 and 7 there is a marked increase in sexual interest.

Masturbation

Children increasingly gain experience with masturbation during childhood. In a study of 1,114 children, the mothers of 60 percent of the boys ages 2 to 5 and of 44 percent of the girls reported that the child touched his or her genitals (Friedrich et al., 1998). In a study of college students, 15 percent of the males and 20 percent of the females recalled that their first masturbation experience occurred between ages 5 and 8 (Arafat & Cotton, 1974).

Children also learn during this period that masturbation is something that one does in private.

Heterosexual Behavior

By the age of 4 or 5, children's sexuality has become more social. There is some heterosexual play. Boys and girls may hug each other or hold hands in imitation of adults. "Playing doctor" can be a popular game at this age (Gundersen et al., 1981). It generally involves no more than exhibiting one's own genitals, looking at those of others, and perhaps engaging in a little fondling or touching. One woman recalled,

> It was at the age of 5 that I, along with my three friends who were sisters and lived next door, first viewed the genitals of a boy. They had a male cousin who came to visit and we all ended up behind the furnace playing doctor. No matter what he would say his symptoms were, we were so fascinated with his penis that it was always the center of our examinations. I remember giggling as I punched it and dunked it in some red food-colored water that we were using for medicine. This seemed to give him great enjoyment. One girl put hand lotion and a bandage on his penis and in the process he had an erection. We asked him to do it again, but their [sic] was no such luck. (Martinson, 1994, p. 37)

By about the age of 5, children have formed a concept of marriage—or at least of its nongenital aspects. They know that a member of the other gender is the appropriate marriage partner, and they are committed to marrying when they get older (Broderick, 1966a, b). They practice marriage roles as they "play house."

Some children first learn about heterosexual behavior by seeing or hearing their parents engaging in sexual intercourse, or the *primal scene experience*. Freud believed that this experience could inhibit the child's subsequent psychosexual development; some contemporary writers share this belief. Limited empirical data suggest that the experience is not damaging. In surveys, about 20 percent of middle-class parents report that their child observed them when the child was 4 to 6 years of age. Parents report such reactions as curiosity ("Why are you bobbing up and down?"), amusement and giggling, or embarrassment and closing the door (Okami, 1995).

Same-Gender Sexual Behavior

During late childhood and preadolescence, sexual play with members of one's own gender may be more common than sexual play with members of the other gender (Martinson, 1994). Generally the activity involves no more than touching the other's genitals (Broderick, 1966a). One girl recalled,

> I encountered a sexual experience that was confusing at kindergarten age. . . . Some afternoons we would meet and lock ourselves in a bedroom and take our pants off. We took turns lying on the bed and put pennies, marbles, etc. between our labia. . . . As the ritual became old hat, it passed out of existence. (Martinson, 1994, p. 62)

Sex Knowledge and Interests

At age 3 or 4, children begin to have some notion that there are genital differences between males and females, but their ideas are very vague. By age 7, 30 percent of U.S. children understand what the differences are (Goldman & Goldman, 1982). Children generally react to their discovery of genital differences calmly, though of course there are exceptions.

At age 3, children are very interested in different postures for urinating. Girls attempt to urinate while standing. Children are also very affectionate at this age. They enjoy hugging and kissing their parents and may even propose marriage to the parent of the other gender.

At age 4, children are particularly interested in bathrooms and elimination. Games of "show" are also common at this age. They become less common at age 5 as children become more modest. The development of modesty reflects the child's learning of the restrictions that American society places on sexual expression. Often as early as age 3 the child is taught by his or her parents not to display or touch certain parts of his or her body, at least in public. Children are often taught not to touch the bodies of others. Many parents also restrict conversation about sex. These restrictions come at precisely the time the child is becoming more aware of and curious about sexuality. One young man recalled,

> One of my favorite pastimes was playing doctor with my little sister. During this doctor game we would both be nude and I would sit on her as if we were having intercourse. On one occasion, I was touching my sister's genital area and mother discovered us. We were sternly switched and told it was dirty and to never get caught again or we would be whipped twice as bad. So, we made sure we were never caught again. (Starks & Morrison, 1996)

As a result, children turn to sex play and their peers for information about sex (Martinson, 1994). Cross-cultural data suggest that in less restrictive societies children continue to show overt interest in sexual activities through childhood and preadolescence (Frayser, 1994). In the rare society that puts no restrictions on childhood sex play, intercourse may occur as young as age 6 or 7. In the United States, the first attempts at intercourse may occur three to four years later.

It is important to remember that children's sex play at this age is motivated largely by curiosity and is part of the general learning experiences of childhood. One man illustrated this well as he recalled,

> At the age of six or seven my friend (a boy) and I had a great curiosity for exploring the anus. It almost seemed *more like scientific research.* (Martinson, 1994, p. 59, italics added)

A longitudinal study of the impact of childhood sex play obtained reports from mothers when the child was 6 and assessed the sexual adjustment of the person at age 17 or 18 (Okami et al., 1997). Forty-seven percent of the mothers reported that their child had engaged in interactive sex play. Looking at a range of outcomes, including social relationships and sexual behavior and "problems," there were no significant differences between males and females whose mothers reported such play, and males and females whose mothers did not report such activity.

Preadolescence (8 to 12 Years)

Preadolescence is a period of transition between the years of childhood and the years of puberty and adolescence. Freud used the term *latency* to refer to the preadolescent period following the resolution of the Oedipus complex. He believed that the sexual urges go "underground" during latency and are not expressed. The evidence indicates, however, that Freud was wrong and that children's interest in and expression of sexuality remain lively throughout this period, perhaps more so than their parents are willing to believe. For many, "sexual awakening" does not occur until the teens, but for others it is a very real and poignant part of preadolescence (Martinson, 1994).

At around age 9 or 10, the first bodily changes of puberty begin: the formation of breast buds in girls and the growth of pubic hair. The growth of pubic hair occurs in response to *adrenarche,* the maturation of the adrenal glands, leading to increased levels of androgens. In three recent studies, one of adolescents and two of adults, the average age at which participants reported first experiencing sexual attraction to another person was at age 10 (McClintock & Herdt, 1996). The samples included gays, lesbians, and heterosexual men and women. This experience may reflect the maturation of the adrenal gland and the increase in testosterone and estradiol (a steroid responsible for the development of female reproductive organs) that results. This research suggests that "adult" sexual development starts as early as age 9 or 10, not at puberty as previously thought.

The first experience of sexual attraction may lead children to consider their sexual orientation.

Boys and girls attracted to someone of the opposite gender probably conclude they are heterosexual, that is, typical. Boys and girls attracted to someone of the same gender may experience a period of *sexual questioning*—a time of assessment and interpretation of features of their experience that violates sexual norms (Savin-Williams & Diamond, 1999). A study of fourth through eighth graders asked each child how likely it was that he or she would fall in love with a woman/man, marry, be a wife/husband, be a mother/father, and have a family someday. These items were used to create a scale; a low score (uncertainty that these events would occur) is interpreted as indicating that the child was questioning his/her orientation. Compared to children who were confident that these events would occur, questioning children attained lower scores on global self-worth and perceived themselves as less socially competent than their peers. They were also less attracted to same-sex activities, and rated themselves as more gender atypical (Carver et al., 2004).

Masturbation

During preadolescence, more and more children gain experience with masturbation. In a sample of college women, 40 percent recalled masturbating before puberty.[1] The comparable figure for men is 38 percent (Bancroft et al., 2003). Other data, as well as those on adolescents, indicate that boys generally start masturbating earlier than girls do. A study of 269 high school seniors in Sweden inquired about solitary sexual activities in childhood. Forty-two percent of the boys and 20 percent of the girls reported masturbating to orgasm by age 12; an additional 27 percent of the boys and 18 percent of the girls reported masturbating without orgasm (Larrson & Svedin, 2002).

Interestingly, boys and girls learn about masturbation in different ways. Typically boys are told about it by their male peers, they see their peers doing it, or they read about it; girls most frequently learn about masturbation through accidental self-discovery (Langfeldt, 1981). One man recalled,

> An older cousin of mine took two of us out to the garage and did it in front of us. I remember thinking that it seemed a very strange thing to do, and that people who were upright wouldn't do it, but it left a powerful impression on me. A couple of years later, when I began to get erections, I wanted to do it, and felt I shouldn't, but I remembered how he

[1]These are cumulative-incidence figures, to use the terminology introduced at the end of Chapter 3.

> had looked when he was doing it, and the memory tempted me strongly. I worried, and held back, and fought it, but finally I gave in. The worry didn't stop me, and doing it didn't stop my worrying. (Hunt, 1974, p. 79)

Heterosexual Behavior

There is generally little heterosexual behavior during the preadolescent period, mainly because of the social division of males and females into separate groups. However, children commonly hear about sexual intercourse for the first time during this period. For example, in a sample of adult women, 61 percent recalled having learned about intercourse by age 12 (Wyatt et al., 1988). Children's reactions to this new information are an amusing combination of shock and disbelief—particularly disbelief that their parents would do such a thing. A college woman recalled,

> One of my girlfriends told me about sexual intercourse. It was one of the biggest shocks of my life. She took me aside one day, and I could tell she was in great distress. I thought she was going to tell me about menstruation, so I said that I already knew, and she said, "No, this is *worse!*" Her description went like this: "A guy puts his thing up a girl's hole, and she has a baby." The hole was, to us, the anus, because we did not even know about the vagina and we knew that the urethra was too small. I pictured the act as a single, violent and painful stabbing at the anus by the penis. Somehow, the idea of a baby was forgotten by me. I was horrified and repulsed, and I thought of that awful penis I had seen years ago. At first I insisted that it wasn't true, and my friend said she didn't know for sure, but that's what her cousin told her. But we looked at each other, and we knew it was true. We held each other and cried. We insisted that "my parents would never do that," and "I"ll never let anyone do it to me." We were frightened, sickened, and threatened by the idea of some lusty male jabbing at us with his horrid penis. (From a student essay)

In the study of Swedish high school seniors, more than 80 percent reported having consensual sexual experiences with another child when they were 6 to 12 years of age (Larsson & Svedlin, 2002). The most common activities were talking about sex, kissing and hugging, looking at pornographic videos, and teasing other children sexually. With the exception of kissing and hugging, these activities were more often reported when they were ages 11 and 12 than when they were 6 to 10. Turning to the gender of the partner, 57 percent of the boys reported such experiences with girls, 11 percent with another boy, and 33 percent with both boys and girls. For girls, the percentages were 31 with a boy,

29 with a girl, and 40 with both. Thus sexual experiences are very common, especially at ages 11 and 12, and involve consensual experiences with both boys and girls.

The age at which youth have their first sexual experience has been declining (see Figure 9.7). Some boys and girls have their first experience during the preadolescent period. The research that used the talking computer studied children ages 9 to 15 who lived in public housing projects. The results indicate that 63 percent of the boys and 14 percent of the girls had "had sex with someone" by age 12 (Romer et al., 1997). A study of college students using computer-assisted self-interviewing found that 9 percent of the women and 16 percent of the men reported oral–genital contact, 3 percent of both reported inserting objects in the anus, 18 percent of women and 22 percent of men reported inserting objects in the vagina, and 2 percent of the women and 5 percent of the men reported having vaginal intercourse prior to entering high school (Reynolds et al., 2003).

For some preadolescents, heterosexual activity occurs in an incestuous relationship, whether brother–sister or parent–child. This topic is discussed in detail in Chapter 15.

Same-Gender Sexual Behavior

It is important to understand same-gender sexual activity as a normal part of the sexual development of children. In preadolescence, children have a social organization that is **gender segregated.** That is, boys play separately from girls, and thus children socialize mainly with members of their own gender. This separation begins at around age 8. According to one study of children's friendship patterns, the segregation reaches a peak at around 10 to 12 years of age. At ages 12 to 13 children are simultaneously the most segregated by gender and the most interested in members of the opposite gender (Broderick, 1966b).

Observational research suggests that there is greater segregation at school than in neighborhood play groups (Thorne, 1993). Some of the social separation of the genders during preadolescence is actually comical; boys, for example, may have been convinced that girls have "cooties" and that they must be very careful to stay away from them.

Given that children are socializing with other members of their own gender, sexual exploring at this age is likely to be with partners of the same gender. These activities generally involve masturbation, exhibitionism, and the fondling of others' genitals. Boys, for example, may engage in a "circle jerk," in which they masturbate in a group.

Girls do not seem so likely to engage in such group activities, perhaps because the spectacle of them masturbating is not quite so impressive or perhaps because they already sense the greater cultural restrictions on their sexuality and are hesitant to discuss sexual matters with other girls.

A study of psychosexual development among lesbian, gay, and bisexual youth ages 14 to 21 found that the participants reported their first experience of sexual attraction at age 10 or 11 (Rosario et al., 1996). Their first experience of sexual fantasies occurred several months to one year later. The first sexual activity with another person occurred on average at age 12 or 13. All of the young men and women reported experiencing sexual attraction to and fantasies about a person of the same gender, and one-half also reported them about a person of the other gender.

Dating and Romantic Relationships

Pre- and early adolescence is a period of transition in the nature of social relationships. We noted above that preadolescent activities are often homosocial. Around age 10 or 11, children begin to spend time in mixed-gender or heterosocial groups. These groups engage in a variety of activities, including "hanging out" in parks or at malls, going to clubs, sporting events, or movies, and later going to parties or dances. A study of fifth through eighth graders found that the frequency of these mixed-gender activities increased steadily over the four grades (Connolly et al., 2004). It is in these mixed-group settings that youth first experience dyadic pairings, and the first romantic or sexual behaviors often occur in this context (Figure 9.4).

According to the study, *dating*, defined as spending time or going out with a boy or girl whom the youth liked, loved, or had a crush on, emerged in seventh grade. Some adolescents begin to go out at night with boys and girls, to double-date, or to go on dates. However, the mixed-gender activities remain very common through eighth grade. Another survey of 12- and 13-year-olds reports that light sexual activity, that is, holding hands, hugging and kissing, was reported by about one-half of the 13-year-olds (Williams et al., 2004). Heavy sexual activity, petting below the waist and intercourse, was reported by less than 10 percent of the 13-year-olds; those who reported heavy activity also reported going out on dates alone (without friends). Results from three surveys of nationally representative samples indicate that by age 14, about 20 percent of boys and girls have

Gender-segregated social organization: A general form of social grouping in which males play and associate with other males, and females play and associate with other females; that is, the genders are separate from each other.

Figure 9.4 Group dating, heterosexual parties, and hanging out emerge during preadolescence and may include making out.

engaged in heterosexual intercourse. Many are in a dating or "romantic" relationship with a partner. Almost half of the sexually active youth had sex two times or less in the prior 12 months (Albert et al., 2003). Thus the progression from mixed-gender activities to dyadic dating is paralleled by a progression in the development of physical intimacy.

Note that romantic dyadic relationships involved a small percentage of youth. There is obviously great variability in the timing of these developments, and probably variation by culture, ethnicity, and perhaps religious affiliation. In some cultures, boys and girls are married at age 13.

Sexualization of Girls

A major concern of some parents, educators, and researchers is the sexualization of girls in U.S. society. **Sexualization** occurs when

- a person's value comes only from his or her sexual appeal or behavior.
- a person is held to a standard that equates physical attractiveness with being sexy.
- a person is sexually objectified.

Sexualization occurs when a person is valued only for sex appeal or behavior; is held to a standard that equates physical attractiveness with being sexy; is sexually objectified; or sexuality is inappropriately imposed upon a person.

- sexuality is inappropriately imposed upon a person. (American Psychological Association, 2007)

When children or preadolescents are sexualized, it is imposed upon them at a time when it may have wide-ranging effects.

An American Psychological Association Task Force report stated that sexualization of girls involves cultural contributions, including sexualized representations of girls and women on television and the Internet, and in movies, MTV, cartoons, magazines, and sports media. The cultural contribution also involves sexualized products—dolls (Barbie, Bratz), toys, books, and clothing.

It also involves an interpersonal contribution, when girls are treated like sexual objects by family, friends, teachers, and other adults. "Fat talk" and expressions of concern about her weight and appearance can create a self-consciousness that can be debilitating. As a result of learning to view themselves as sexual objects, many girls and women engage in self-sexualization, including purchasing clothing because it is sexy, and undergoing cosmetic surgery before they are physically mature. Research documents each of these contributions, especially in white U.S. culture.

People are concerned because sexualization may lead to reduced self-esteem (because one does not meet the standard), impaired cognitive functioning (e.g., at math) and physical performance (e.g., at athletics), anxiety about appearance in interaction with others, body-image dissatisfaction, and reduced educational and occupational aspirations. Viewing oneself as a sexual object may lead girls and young women to initiate sexual intimacy (see Focus: Milestones in Sex Research, p. 240), to engage in unwanted sexual activity and relationships, and to engage in risky sexual behavior (e.g., unprotected vaginal intercourse).

The report suggests many ways to counteract sexualization. Within the schools, we can provide media literacy training programs, a broader range of athletic opportunities, and comprehensive sexuality education (see Appendix). Within the family, we can encourage parents to watch TV and movies and to navigate the Internet with children, commenting on appropriate and inappropriate content. Creating alternative media including "zines," blogs, and alternative magazines and books may help. Creation of girl empowerment groups to support girls in a variety of ways can be very effective. Finally, parents, educators, and boys and girls can engage in activism and resistance, such as campaigning against companies that use sexualized images to sell products.

Adolescence (13 to 19 Years)

A surge of sexual interest occurs around puberty and continues through adolescence (which is equated here roughly with the teenage years, ages 13 to 19). This heightened sexuality may be caused by a number of factors, including bodily changes and an awareness of them, rises in levels of sex hormones, and increased cultural emphasis on sex and rehearsal for adult gender roles. We can see evidence of this heightened sexuality particularly in the data on masturbation. But before examining those data, let's consider some theoretical ideas about how hormones and social forces might interact as influences on adolescent sexuality.

Udry (1988) has proposed a theoretical model that recognizes that both sociological factors and biological factors are potent in adolescent sexuality. He studied eighth-, ninth-, and tenth-graders (13 to 16 years old), measuring their hormone levels (testosterone, estrogen, and progesterone) and a number of sociological factors (for example, whether they were in an intact family, their parents' educational level, the teenager's response to a scale measuring sexually permissive attitudes, and the teenager's attachment to conventional institutions such as involvement in school sports and church attendance). Thirty-five percent of the males had engaged in sexual intercourse, as had 14 percent of the females.

For boys, testosterone levels had a very strong relationship to sexual activity (including coitus, masturbation, and the extent of feeling sexually "turned on"). Sexually permissive attitudes, a social variable, were related to sexuality among boys, although they had a much smaller effect than testosterone did. For girls, the relationship between testosterone level and sexual activity was not as strong as it was for boys, but it was a significant relationship, and it was testosterone—not estrogen or progesterone—that was related to sexuality. Pubertal development (developing a "curvy" figure) had an effect, probably by increasing the girl's attractiveness. And the effects of testosterone were accentuated among girls in father-absent families. When girls were asked to rate their plans about sexuality, testosterone level was an important predictor of their ratings, as were the social variables of permissive attitudes and church attendance.

The bottom line in this study is that it shows testosterone level to have a substantial impact on the sexuality of adolescent boys and girls. Social variables (such as permissive attitudes, father absence for girls, and church attendance) then interact with the biological effects, in some cases magnifying them (father absence for girls) and in some cases suppressing them (church attendance).

Two longitudinal studies, of 12- to 15-year-old girls (O'Sullivan & Brooks-Gunn, 2005) and seventh- and eighth-grade girls and boys (L'Engle et al., 2006) report evidence that cognitive changes mediate the effects of these biological and social changes on sexual behavior. Girls who initiated sexual intimacy—breast fondling, genital contact—had weaker abstinence values, and lower arousability and sexual self-esteem scores. Youth who reported that they were likely to engage in sexual intimacy within the next year were more likely to initiate sexual intercourse. These measures of cognitive readiness were in turn related to reports of greater sexual feelings and competency than age-mates who were not ready.

Masturbation

According to the Kinsey data, there is a sharp increase in the incidence of masturbation for boys between the ages of 13 and 15. This is illustrated in Figure 9.5. Note that the curve is steepest between the ages of 13 and 15, indicating that most boys begin masturbating to orgasm during that period. By age 15, 82 percent of the boys in Kinsey's study had masturbated. Many girls also begin masturbating in adolescence, but note that the curve on the graph is flatter for them, indicating that many other girls do not begin masturbating until later.

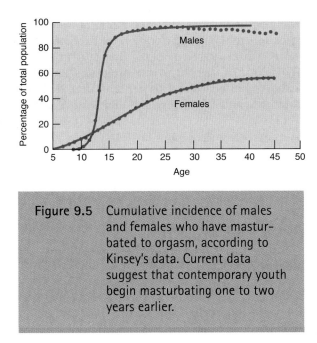

Figure 9.5   Cumulative incidence of males and females who have masturbated to orgasm, according to Kinsey's data. Current data suggest that contemporary youth begin masturbating one to two years earlier.

Focus: Milestones in Sex Research
The Impact of the Mass Media on Adolescent Sexuality

A major developmental task of adolescence is learning how to manage physical and emotional intimacy in relationships with others. It is not surprising, therefore, that young people are curious about sex and about sexual intimacy. An increasingly important source of information is the mass media. In a survey of youth ages 10 to 15, the most frequently named source of information about sexuality and relationships was the mass media, including TV, movies, magazines, and music (Kaiser Family Foundation, 1997). Youth who watch talk shows learn about impotence and ways to deal with it. *CSI* provides information about prostitution and prostitutes, and young women who appear in porn videos. Soap operas deal, sometimes explicitly, with sexual themes like frigidity, menopause, abortion, and infidelity. How much sexual content is there in the mass media? To what extent are children and adolescents exposed to it? And what is the impact of this exposure?

Research, much of it done since 1990, has been devoted to the question of how much sexual content there is in the mass media in the United States. *Sexual material* is defined as verbal references to sexual activity, sexually suggestive behavior, and explicit portrayals of sex. A major project analyzed sexual material on television in 2004–2005. The sample included 1,154 programs on the four commercial networks, public television, four cable networks (including HBO), and one independent broadcaster. The sample included all types of programs broadcast between 6:00 A.M. and 10:00 P.M. Concrete definitions of sexual material were used by coders to analyze the content of each program (Kunkel et al., 2005). Looking first at prime-time television, 70 percent of the programs included sexual material; 4.6 scenes per hour included talk about sex, and 2.0 scenes per hour included sexual

behavior. These represent substantial increases since 1998, when a similar project was carried out. Only 4 percent of the scenes containing sexual content depicted risks or responsibilities of sex. Interestingly, the characters portrayed as having intercourse in 2005 were older than in earlier years.

Adolescents see feature films in theatres, on pay TV, or on video or DVD. Many of these films are rated R and contain more frequent—and more explicit—depictions of sexual behavior, an average of 17.5 per hour, than depictions of sexual behavior on prime-time television (Greenberg & Busselle, 1996). Cable movie networks have the largest proportion of programs with sexual content (Fisher et al., 2004). The most frequent portrayals are of unmarried heterosexual intercourse, often in a context of alcohol and drug use; there are no safer sex messages here!

We have already mentioned the variety of sexual situations, most of them problematic, that are included in soap operas. In 2004–2005 each hour of a soap opera contained 4.9 scenes with sexual content, with 3.1 scenes including sexual behavior; only 13 percent of the programs analyzed included discussion of risks and responsibilities (Kunkel et al., 2005). Finally, there are music videos. The visual elements in many MTV videos are implicitly or explicitly sexual (Browne & Steele, 1996) and frequently combine sexuality with implicit aggression (Sommers-Flanagan et al., 1993). MTV videos also objectify women, presenting them in revealing clothing and portraying them as receptive to sexual advances. A study of Black high school students found that those who watched music videos more often expressed stereotypic views of gender than those who did not watch them. In a related experiment, youth exposed to four music videos with stereotypic male and female characters expressed

Thus the increase in their masturbation behavior is much more gradual than for boys and continues past adolescence.

More recent data indicate that children and adolescents begin to masturbate earlier today, and thus the Kinsey data need to be pushed back about one or two years. However, the general shape of the curves still holds (Bancroft et al., 2003).

One man recalled his adolescent experiences with masturbation and the intense feelings involved as follows:

When I was fourteen I was like Portnoy—always rushing off to the bathroom when the urge came over me. I did it so much that my dick would get swollen and sore, and even that didn't stop me. By the time I was nineteen I was screwing, but there'd be times when I wouldn't be able to get

more traditional views of gender and sexual relationships (Ward et al., 2005).

Clearly, the mass media are providing a great deal of sexual content. But is anybody watching? Children ages 9 to 13 are heavy TV viewers (Comstock, 1991). During middle and late adolescence, TV viewing declines, and time spent listening to music, reading magazines, and surfing the Internet increases (for a discussion of the sexual material available on the Internet, see Chapter 16). There are gender differences in exposure to mass media: teenage girls spend more time reading magazines and watching soap operas, while their male counterparts spend more time surfing the Internet. Media use also varies by social class and ethnicity; children and adolescents from less affluent families watch more television, and African American youth watch more TV than do their European American peers.

What effect do these portrayals have? There has been less research on this issue, partly because it is difficult to isolate the effects of media exposure from other influences on adolescents' sexual attitudes and behavior. Media images can have an immediate effect on the user's emotional state: Portrayals may induce arousal, which can influence behavior or activate thoughts or associations (see the discussion of sexual fantasy in Chapter 8). Media portrayals may have long-term effects in that children may learn schemas and scripts that influence their later sexual decision making and behavior (Kaiser Family Foundation, 1998). A longitudinal study surveyed a national sample of 12- to 17 year-olds. In baseline and 1-year-follow-up interviews, 1,792 youth reported their TV viewing behavior and their social behavior. The interview also assessed other variables known to influence adolescent sexual activity. Youth who reported viewing more sexual content at baseline were more likely to progress to more advanced activities and to initiate intercourse in the following year (Collins et al., 2004).

There is also evidence from experiments about the impact of mass media. One experimental study indicated that teenagers exposed to 15 hours of portrayals of nonmarital sexual relationships had more permissive attitudes toward nonmarital sex than did teens exposed to portrayals of nonsexual relationships (Bryant & Rockwell, 1994). Another experiment assessed the frequency and involvement of college students' TV viewing, and randomly assigned them to watch clips from TV portraying sexual stereotypes (e.g., women as sex objects) or nonsexual content. Those who reported greater frequency and involvement of viewing, and who viewed a stereotypic clip, were more likely to endorse the stereotype (Ward, 2002). Men and women who more frequently watch reality dating programs report more adversarial gender attitudes, endorse beliefs that men are sex-driven, and endorse a sexual double standard (Zurbriggen & Morgan, 2006). Thus media portrayals reinforce stereotyped views of sexual behavior and sexual relationships (Brown, 2002). The media may also influence standards of physical attractiveness and contribute to the dissatisfaction that many, especially women, feel about their bodies.

The evidence that mass media portrayals have an important impact on adolescent sexual knowledge, attitudes, and behavior is not conclusive. On the other hand, we noted at the outset that both children and adolescents believe that mass media are the most important source of their knowledge. The problem lies in the fact that these portrayals are unrealistic. In sharp contrast to the high rates of nonmarital sex portrayed in the media, most sexual activity involves persons who are married (see Chapter 10). Many couples in real life, whether married or not, are responsible users of birth control. Many youth and adults use various forms of prophylaxis to prevent STIs. It is unfortunate that these realities are missing from mass media portrayals of sexual behavior. It is also unfortunate that the media have generally not taken advantage of their opportunity to provide positive sexuality education.

anything, and I'd go back to jacking off—and then I felt really guilty and ashamed of myself, like I was a failure, like I had a secret weakness. (Hunt, 1974, p. 95)

Boys typically masturbate two or three times per week, whereas girls do so about once per month (Hass, 1979). Interestingly, the frequency of masturbation among boys decreases during periods when they are having sexual intercourse; among girls, however, this situation is accompanied by an increased frequency of masturbation (Sorensen, 1973).

Attitudes toward Masturbation

Attitudes toward masturbation underwent a dramatic change in the twentieth century. As a result, adolescents today are given much different information about masturbation than were earlier adolescents, which may affect both their behavior and their feelings about masturbation. For example, a popular handbook *What a Boy Should Know,* written in 1913 by two doctors, advised its readers,

> Whenever unnatural emissions are produced . . . the body becomes "slack." A boy will not feel so vigorous and springy; he will be more easily tired. . . . He will probably look pale and pasty, and he is lucky if he escapes indigestion and getting his bowels confined, both of which will probably give him spots and pimples on his face. . . .

> The results on the mind are the more severe and more easily recognized. . . . A boy who practices this habit can never be the best that Nature intended him to be. His wits are not so sharp. His memory is not so good. His power of fixing his attention on whatever he is doing is lessened. . . . A boy like this is a poor thing to look at. . . .

> The effect of self-abuse on a boy's character always tends to weaken it, and in fact, to make him untrustworthy, unreliable, untruthful, and probably even dishonest. (Schofield and Vaughan-Jackson, 1913, pp. 30–42)

Masturbation, in short, was once believed to cause everything from warts to insanity.[2]

Attitudes toward masturbation are now considerably more positive, and today few people would subscribe to notions like those expressed earlier. By

[2]In case you're wondering why boys' advice books were saying such awful things, there is a rather interesting history that produced those pronouncements (Money, 1987). Swiss physician Simon André Tissot (1728–1797) wrote an influential book, *Treatise on the Diseases Produced by Onanism,* taking the term from the biblical story of Onan (Genesis 38:9). In this work he articulated a degeneracy theory, in which loss of semen was believed to weaken a man's body; Tissot had some very inventive physiological explanations for his idea. Benjamin Rush, a famous U.S. physician of the 1800s, was influenced by Tissot and spread degeneracy theory in the United States. The theory became popularized by Sylvester Graham (1794–1851), a religious zealot and health reformer, who was a vegetarian and whose passion for health foods gave us the names for Graham flour and Graham crackers. To be healthy, according to Graham, one needed to follow the Graham diet and practice sexual abstinence. Then John Harvey Kellogg (1852–1943) of—you guessed it—cornflakes fame entered the story. He was an ardent follower of Graham and his doctrines of health food and sexual abstinence. While experimenting with healthful foods, he invented cornflakes. His younger brother, Will Keith Kellogg, thought to add sugar and made a fortune. John Harvey Kellogg contributed further to public fears about masturbation by writing (during his honeymoon, no less) *Plain Facts for Old and Young: Embracing the Natural History and Hygiene of Organic Life,* which provided detailed descriptions of the horrible diseases supposedly caused by masturbation. These ideas then found their way into the advice books for boys of the early 1900s.

the 1970s only about 15 percent of young people believed that masturbation was wrong (Hunt, 1974, p. 74). Indeed, masturbation is now recommended as a remedy in sex therapy. As psychiatrist Thomas Szasz said, the shift in attitudes toward masturbation has been so great that in a generation it has changed from a disease to a form of therapy.

While approval of masturbation is now explicit, people can still have mixed feelings about it. An example of a lingering negative attitude is that of the man quoted earlier who likened his adolescent masturbation to Portnoy's,[3] accompanied as it was by feelings of guilt and shame. Another example is the firing of Surgeon General Joycelyn Elders in 1994, by President Clinton, for speaking publicly about masturbation.

Same-Gender Sexual Behavior

According to the NSFG, small percentages of teens ages 15 to 19 report sexual contact with a partner of the same gender. The percentage varies by gender and race. Among males, 5.4 percent of Hispanics, 4.6 percent of whites, and 5.7 percent of Blacks report "any oral or anal sex" with a male. Among females, 9.1 percent of Hispanics, 14.2 percent of whites, and 10.2 percent of Blacks report "any sexual experience" with a female. So, while the percentages are at least twice as large for women, they were asked a much broader question (Mosher et al., 2005).

In college, about 10 percent of men and 6 percent of women report having had one same-gender partner in high school (Bancroft et al., 2003). Of those who have had homosexual experiences, 24 percent had their first experience with a younger person, 39 percent with someone of their own age, 29 percent with an older teenager, and 8 percent with an adult (Sorensen, 1973). Thus there is no evidence that adolescent homosexual experiences result from being seduced by adults; most such encounters take place between peers. In many cases the person has only one or a few homosexual experiences, partly out of curiosity, and the behavior is discontinued. Such adolescent homosexual behavior does not seem to be predictive of adult homosexual orientation.

Comparing the results reported by Bancroft and colleagues (2003) with those reported by DeLamater and MacCorquodale (1979), there was no increase in the incidence of adolescent homosexual behavior

[3]Of Philip Roth's novel *Portnoy's Complaint* (1968), which poignantly and humorously describes an adolescent boy's obsessive masturbation.

from 1973 to 1999. It seems safe to conclude from various studies, taken together, that about 10 percent of adolescents have same-gender sexual experiences.

Teenagers can be quite naive about homosexual behavior and societal attitudes toward it. In some cases they have been taught that heterosexual sex is "bad"; having been told nothing about homosexual sex, they infer that it is permissible. In some cases, homosexual relationships naively develop from a same-gender friendship of late childhood and adolescence. One woman recalled,

> I did not even know what homosexuality was. I had never heard the term, although I had read extensively. One day at a friend's house, we were listening to music in her bedroom, she came on to me in a very surprising way. We were good friends and spent much time together, but this particular night was different. Her eyes had a new sparkle, she got very close to me, her touch lingered; she was different than she ever had been before. I was 16 and she was 15. I did not understand, but I knew that I was aroused. We were good church-going kids who had never heard anything about this. (Starks & Morrison, 1996, p. 97)

Heterosexual Behavior

Toward the middle and end of the adolescent years, more and more young people engage in heterosexual sex, with more and more frequency. Thus heterosexual behavior gains prominence and becomes the major sexual outlet.

In terms of the individual's development, the data indicate that there is a very regular progression

Figure 9.6 Sexuality in early adolescence is often playful and unsophisticated.

from kissing, through French kissing and breast and genital fondling, to intercourse and oral–genital contact; this generally occurs over a period of four or more years (DeLamater & MacCorquodale, 1979; DeLamater, 2003). To use terminology introduced in Chapter 2, these behaviors tend to follow a sexual script. The sexual scripts of many youth specify a heterosexual couple with some emotional or psychological commitment as appropriate for sexual intimacy. A large longitudinal study followed boys and girls from sixth grade to ninth grade. Boys and girls who reported a same-age girlfriend/boyfriend were more likely to report sexual intercourse in the ninth grade. The association was mediated by participation in situations that could lead to sex, such as being alone with the partner and attending unsupervised parties (Martin et al., 2006).

Premarital Sex[4]

One of the most dramatic changes to occur in sexual behavior and attitudes in recent decades is in the area of premarital sexual behavior.

How Many People Have Premarital Intercourse?

On the basis of the data he collected in the 1940s, Kinsey concluded that about 33 percent of all females and 71 percent of all males have had premarital intercourse by the age of 25. According to the NHSLS (Laumann et al., 1994), 70 percent of women and 78 percent of men interviewed reported engaging in vaginal intercourse before marriage. Thus in the 50 years between these two large-scale surveys, the incidence of premarital intercourse doubled among women, while increasing only slightly among men. Today, about three-fourths of Americans engage in premarital sex.

As premarital intercourse has become common, attention has shifted to "teen sex," the incidence of sexual intercourse among teenagers. The National Survey of Family Growth periodically interviews a national sample of women of childbearing age. The Centers for Disease Control and Prevention conducts a Youth Risk Behavior Survey of high school

[4]Note that the very term *premarital sex* contains some hidden assumptions, most notably that marriage is normative and that proper sex occurs in marriage. Thus sex among never-married (young) persons is considered *pre*marital—something done before marrying. A more neutral term would be *nonmarital sex*, although this fails to distinguish between premarital sex, extramarital sex, and postmarital sex.

Table 9.1   Percentage of High School Students Who Have Engaged in Intercourse

	NSFG	CDC	
Year of Study	Females, 15 to 19	Females, 9th–12th grade	Males, 9th–12th grade
1975	36%	—	—
1982	47	—	—
1990	55	—	—
1991	—	51%	57%
1995	50	52	54
1999	54	48	52
2001	—	43	48
2002	53	—	—
2005	—	46	48

students every few years. Data from these surveys are shown in Table 9.1. These data indicate that rates of adolescent intercourse reached a peak about 1990 and have been declining since then (Smith, 2003).

Not only are more young women having sex than in the 1940s, but young men and women today are engaging in intercourse for the first time at younger ages, compared to persons born 40 years earlier. Figure 9.7 provides data from a cross-temporal

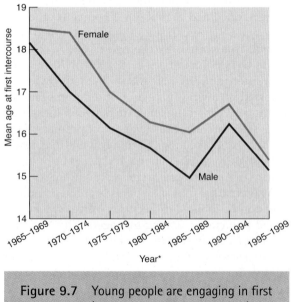

Figure 9.7   Young people are engaging in first intercourse at younger ages than men and women 50 years ago.

*Year refers to year data collected. The age of participants in all studies included in the analysis was 12 to 27, mean = 17.

Source: Wells, B., & Twenge, J. (2005). Changes in young people's sexual behavior and attitudes, 1943–1999: A cross-temporal meta-analysis. *Review of General Psychology, 9,* 249–261 (Figure 2).

meta-analysis (Wells & Twenge, 2005), including 530 samples of young people ages 12 to 27 (mean = 17). Looking at the mean age of first intercourse, among men it declined from 18 in data collected in the 1960s to 15 in data collected in 2000. Among women, it declined from 18.5 to 15.5 in the same period. Similar declines are reported by a large-scale survey of persons 16 to 59 in Australia (Smith et al., 2003). These trends reflect, in part, the impact of the "sexual revolution" of the 1960s and 1970s, which encouraged greater openness about sexuality and acceptance of premarital and other forms of sexual expression. As we saw earlier, the incidence of premarital intercourse among men has been high since Kinsey collected his data. The impact of the social changes in the 1960s and 1970s was greater on women.

In the United States, patterns of premarital intercourse vary substantially by ethnic group. Table 9.2 shows data on this point from a population sample of youth who were interviewed in 1992–1995 (Upchurch et al., 1998). The sample was drawn from Los Angeles County, so the social context is similar for the youth. Look first at the differences between men and women of the same race or ethnicity in median age of first intercourse. In two groups, men begin having sex at younger ages than women; among Blacks, the average age for males is about 15 months younger than that for females, whereas among Hispanics (primarily Mexican American), the difference is about 9 months. Among whites, the median age is

Table 9.2   Ethnicity and Age of First Intercourse in a Sample of 12- to 17-Year-Old Youth

	Subgroup	Median Age of First Intercourse (Years)
Asian American	Male	18.1
	Female	*
Black	Male	15.0
	Female	61.3
Hispanic	Male	16.5
	Female	17.3
White	Male	16.6
	Female	16.6
Other	Male	16.8
	Female	*

*Number of females too small to compute reliable median.

Source: Upchurch et al. (1998).

the same for men and women. There are also differences by race or ethnicity. African Americans have sex for the first time at about 15.7 years of age, whites at 16.6, Hispanics at 17, and Asian American men at 18.1. Similar results are reported by the NSFG in 2002 (Mosher et al., 2005). Among 15- to 19-year-old men, 45 percent of whites, 56 percent of Hispanics, and 66 percent of Blacks have had original intercourse. Among woman 15 to 19, the incidence is 52 percent, 49 percent, and 62 percent, respectively.

The differences by race or ethnicity reflect in part differences between these groups in family structure and socioeconomic opportunities. Living in an intact family, having a highly educated mother, and attending church regularly are all associated with later age of first intercourse (Day, 1992). Living in a neighborhood where average incomes are high and the female unemployment rate is low—that is, where there are good economic opportunities—is also associated with later age of first intercourse (Brewster, 1994). In Chapter 1 we discussed variations in the incidence of masturbation and oral sex by ethnicity.

What accounts for these variations among European Americans, Black Americans, and Hispanics? Are there ethnic differences in the factors associated with being sexually active as a teenager? A questionnaire study of 15,000 youth ages 12 to 17 in Michigan assessed a variety of these factors (Perkins et al., 1998). In all three ethnic groups, age, alcohol use, lower grade point average, and greater time spent at home unsupervised by an adult were associated with having had sexual intercourse. Religiosity was the only factor whose relationship to sexual activity varied by ethnicity; it was associated with sexual activity among European Americans and Latinos but not among African Americans. This research suggests that differences in cultural norms regarding sexual activity account for the variations noted by ethnicity.

There are substantial variations in patterns of premarital intercourse in different cultures around the world, as the data in Table 9.3 indicate. Most of the data were collected by the Demographic and Health Surveys Program, which interviews women in developing countries. Several interesting points emerge from the data. First, the percentage of young women who report recent intercourse is smaller in Latin and South American countries than in African nations, due partly to the greater influence of the Catholic Church in the former (Figure 9.8). Second, the United States has the highest percentage of respondents having had premarital intercourse in the preceding four weeks. Third, there is less variation

Table 9.3 A Global Perspective on Female Premarital Intercourse

Country and Year	Age of Respondents (Years)	Percentage Having Had Intercourse (Last Four Weeks)*	Median Age of First Coitus (Years)
Africa			
Cameroon, 1998	15–19	33.7	16.3
Kenya, 1998	15–19	19.4	17.3
Nigeria, 1999	15–19	24.6	18.1
Tanzania, 1996	15–19	28.2	17.4
Zambia, 1996	15–19	26.9	16.6
Mexico & Central America			
Mexico, 1985	15–19	13.0	17.0
Nicaragua, 1998	15–19	21.7	18.1
South America			
Bolivia, 1998	15–19	8.6	19.6
Brazil, 1996	15–19	21.5	18.7
United States, 1999	15–18	36.3[†]	17.4[‡]
2005	15–18	34.6	17.4

*These percentages are of all women, so some of these women are married.

[†]Had intercourse in the last three months.

[‡]Mean age of first intercourse.

Source: Data for the United States are from the 1999 and 2005 Youth Risk Behavior Surveys conducted by the Centers for Disease Control and Prevention. The data for other countries are from the Demographic and Health Surveys Program, which collects comparable data from many countries around the world. The results are published in individual volumes for each country by Macro International, Inc., Calverton, MD. The typical reference is Kenya: Demographic and Health Survey, 1998. Calverton, MD: Macro International, 1999.

in the average age of first intercourse; it is 16, 17, or 18 in all but one of the countries.

In many countries around the world, the incidence of premarital intercourse has risen in the last few decades. Around the globe, especially where modernization has been rapid, adolescents are less and less under the influence of family, community, and religion and more and more responsive to peers and the mass media (Liskin, 1985). On a trip to Ukraine in 1995, we were struck by the prominence of U.S. programs and films on local television.

To summarize, the trends in premarital intercourse in the last four decades are (1) both in the United States and in most other countries, more adolescents engaging in premarital intercourse; (2) in the United States, a greater increase in incidence for females, thereby narrowing the gap between males and females; (3) first intercourse occurring at somewhat younger ages; (4) moderate ethnic-group variations in the United States; and (5) substantial variations from one country to another (Day, 1992; Liskin, 1985).

Figure 9.8   In South America, the percentage of unmarried young women who engage in premarital intercourse is lower than in the United States owing to the strong influence of the Catholic Church.

The increase in premarital sexual intercourse reflects two long-term trends. First, the age of menarche has been falling steadily since the beginning of the twentieth century. The average age has now reached about 12.5 years for whites and 12.0 for Blacks (Chumlea et al., 2003). Second, the age of first marriage has been rising. In 1960, first marriages occurred at age 20.8 for women and 23.2 for men. In 2003, it was 25.3 for women and 27.1 for men (U.S. Bureau of the Census, 2006). The effect is a substantial lengthening of the time between biological readiness and marriage; the gap is typically 12 to 14 years today. Recall that Udry found that hormone levels are a major influence on the initiation of sexual intercourse. Not surprisingly, many more young people are having sex before they get married now than in 1960. Since many of these young people do not consistently use birth control, there has been a corresponding rise in the rate of premarital pregnancy (see Focus: Milestones in Sex Research, p. 248).

First Intercourse

First sexual intercourse is a major transition, with both psychological and social significance. If it follows puberty, first intercourse marks the passage from child to adult in the reproductive realm. If others in the community are aware that puberty has occurred, they may perceive the person as sexually available and behave appropriately, which the person may or may not welcome. From a health perspective, the person is at risk for pregnancy and STIs, as well as various emotional and mental health sequelae such as joy, excitement, and anticipation of the future, or regret and depression.

Because of the significance of first intercourse, much research has been done in an effort to identify the influences on whether one engages in intercourse for the first time. The research by Udry (1988), discussed earlier, identifies biological influences—that is, testosterone levels—and social ones, such as permissive attitudes among boys and girls, and church attendance among girls, as influential.

Research using the longitudinal Add Health survey measured the effects of parent–adolescent relationships on likelihood of first intercourse (Ream & Savin-Williams, 2005). Decreases in feelings of closeness to parents and in shared activities with them were associated with initiation of sexual intercourse, and followed first intercourse as well (parents may or may not have been aware that the youth had intercourse). Research with a sample of Asian American adolescents found that high levels of parental attachment were associated with reduced odds of first intercourse for women but not men (Hahm et al., 2006). Other research using Add Health data considered the influence of friends (Sieving et al., 2006) on whether virgins at Time 1 (1994–1995) engaged in intercourse for the first time between Times 1 and 2 (1996). The higher the proportion of a youth's friends who were sexually experienced at Time 1, the more likely the person was to engage in intercourse for the first time by Time 2.

Researchers have also analyzed the emotional reactions to first coitus of college students (Sprecher et al., 1995). Men reported significantly greater pleasure and significantly less guilt than did women. Both men and women who experienced an orgasm rated the experience as more pleasurable than men and women who did not. Men and women who reported a close relationship with the partner reported stronger emotional reactions than those in casual relationships.

The typical female reaction to first intercourse has been described as the **Peggy Lee syndrome** (named for her song "Is That All There Is?"). Despite our culture's romanticized high expectations that the first intercourse experience will be like firecrackers popping on the Fourth of July, it turns out to be much less thrilling than that for most females. For example, the women studied by Sprecher and her colleagues gave the experience on the average only a 2.95 on a pleasure scale that ranged from 1 for "not at all" to 7 for "a great deal."

Many people assume that having penile–vaginal intercourse for the first time equals losing one's virginity. However, a qualitative study involving in-depth interviews with 61 men and women found that virginity loss is socially constructed (Carpenter, 2001). Many believed that virginity could not be lost by rape and, conversely, that behaviors other than vaginal intercourse could constitute loss of virginity. Carpenter identified three distinct interpretations of virginity: as a gift, a stigma, or a process. Each was associated with distinctive individual choices about the transition to nonvirginity. Men and women who viewed it as a gift were likely to lose it with a lover or soul mate; those who viewed it as a stigma often lost it with a stranger or nonlover.

Premarital Sex with a Prostitute

In the 1940s and 1950s, premarital sex with a prostitute was fairly common among males, and many young men received their sexual initiation in this manner. Among the college-educated men under age 35 in one study (Hunt, 1974), 19 percent said they had had their first intercourse with a prostitute. Today, however, having premarital sex with a commercial sex worker is much less common. In the NHSLS survey of 3,432 adults, 3 percent of the men and $\frac{1}{10}$ of 1 percent of the women reported that their first intercourse had involved a paid partner (Laumann et al., 1994).

Techniques in Premarital Sex

Paralleling the increase in the incidence of premarital intercourse is an increase in the variety of techniques that are used in premarital sex. One of the most dramatic changes has been the increased use of oral–genital techniques. In the Kinsey sample, 33 percent of the males had experienced fellatio premaritally and 14 percent had engaged in cunnilingus. According to data from the NSFG, in 2002, among persons ages 18 and 19, 52 percent of men have given oral sex while 66 percent have received it. Among women, the percentages are 63 and 67, respectively. In our classes we generally find that about 5 percent of the women students have engaged in fellatio and/or cunnilingus but not in intercourse—perhaps because they know that mouth–genital sex cannot cause pregnancy. A survey of ethnically diverse ninth graders found that they perceived oral sex as less risky than vaginal sex in both health and emotional consequences (Halpern-Felsher et al., 2005). Young people today also use a greater variety of positions, not just the traditional man-on-top.

Doubtless some of this increased variety in techniques is a result of today's "performance ethic" in sexual relations, which is discussed in Chapter 8. Adolescents and young adults may feel pressured to be gold medalists in the sexual Olympics. One man said,

> Sometimes I'm really good; I can make a girl have orgasms until she's about half dead. But if I don't like the girl, or if I'm not feeling confident, it can be hard work— and sometimes I can't even cut the mustard, and that bothers me a lot when that happens. (Hunt, 1974, p. 163)

Peggy Lee syndrome: The feelings of disappointment experienced by teenage girls at first intercourse when it is not as thrilling as they expected.

Focus: Milestones in Sex Research
Teen Pregnancy and Parenthood

In the United States in 2002, some 746,000 young women under 20 years of age, or about 9 percent of all teenage girls, became pregnant (Alan Guttmacher Institute, 2006). The rate of teenage pregnancy in the United States is the highest of any Western nation; teenagers in this country are twice as likely to become pregnant as are Canadian teens, four times as likely as French teen women, and almost six times as likely as teens in Sweden (Darroch et al., 2001). About 57 percent of these U.S. women gave birth to a child, and the vast majority chose to keep the baby. U.S. teenage birth rates vary by ethnicity. The rate for whites (27 per 1,000 for 15- to 19-year-olds in 2002) is much lower than the rate for Blacks (63) or Hispanics (83).

It is important to note that the teen pregnancy rate has declined 28 percent since it peaked in 1990. More effective contraceptive use is responsible for an estimated 75 percent of the decline, and a reduction in the number of adolescents having intercourse is responsible for the remaining 25 percent (Darroch et al., 2001). This underlines the importance of having comprehensive sexuality education in the schools, covering both abstinence and the use of contraception by those who choose to be sexually active.

Why is teenage pregnancy considered a major social problem? Because most of these births are *nonmarital;* most of these babies will be raised for at least a few years by single mothers. Nonmarital births have increased dramatically, from 15 percent in 1960 to 80 percent of all teenage births in 1998 (USDHHS, 1999). Several factors have contributed to the incidence of nonmarital pregnancy and childbearing. First, the age at which puberty occurs has declined dramatically in the past century, from about 17 to about 12 years of age. On the other hand, the average age of marriage has increased from 22 to 26 years of age in the past 40 years. Thus young men and women are at risk for nonmarital pregnancy for up to 14 years. Second, teen childbearing is associated with economic conditions; teenage women who give birth are much more likely to live in a low-income family (National Campaign to Prevent Teen Pregnancy, 2007). Poverty and high rates of unemployment in poor neighborhoods lower young people's educational and occupational aspirations (Coley & Chase-Lansdale, 1998). Girls growing up in these circumstances perceive a greater likelihood that they will have a nonmarital birth (East, 1998). In fact, it has been suggested that for African American adolescent girls with poor employment prospects, motherhood is a career choice (Merrick, 1995).

Sociologist Frank Furstenberg and his colleagues (1987) did an important study of teenage pregnancy that gave essential information on its effects on the mother and her child. The study is particularly impressive because it followed up the women and their children in 1984, 17 years after the women were initially interviewed while pregnant in 1966–1967. There were approximately 400 respondents, most of them black, all of them initially residing in Baltimore.

Furstenberg and his colleagues concluded that although there are many negative consequences to teenage childbearing, they have been exaggerated and there has not been enough attention paid to the women who, despite the odds against them, manage to cope with adversity and succeed.

Let's focus first on the findings for the mothers. When they were first followed up, 5 years after the pregnancy, they looked very disadvantaged. For example, 49 percent had not graduated from high school. Approximately one-third of them were on welfare at some point during the 17 years of the study. However, by the time of the 1984 follow-up, an impressive proportion of women had staged a substantial recovery. At that point, an additional 38 percent had graduated from high school, a further 25 percent had obtained some education beyond high school, and 5 percent had graduated from college. Of those who had been on welfare at some time during the study, two-thirds had managed to get off it by 1984; 67 percent were employed, and fully a quarter had incomes in excess of $25,000 per year.

The study shows clearly that there is great diversity in the outcomes for adolescent mothers. Some remain locked in poverty for the rest of their lives, whereas others manage to succeed despite their circumstances. The most important factor is differential resources. Women with better-educated parents who have more income tend to do better because they have more resources on which to draw. The second most important factor is competence and motivation. The women who were doing well in school at the time of their pregnancy and had high educational aspirations were more likely to do well following the birth. A third factor is intervention programs such as special schools for pregnant teenagers and hospital intervention programs. When these programs are successful, they help the women complete high school and postpone other births, two factors that are crucial to recovering from the adverse circumstances of a teenage pregnancy. If there are additional births soon after the first, the woman essentially becomes locked out of the job market.

Turning now to the children, the results indicate that they are at risk in many ways. At birth, 11 percent were at low birth weight (2,500 grams or less), which puts them at risk for a variety of other problems (see Chapter 6). However, it seems that the excess of low-birth-weight babies is more a function of the adequacy or inadequacy of medical care during pregnancy than it is a function of the mother's being a teenager. By 1984 the school record showed evidence of academic failure and behavior problems. Half of the children had had to repeat at least one grade. Thirty-five percent had had to bring their parents to school in the last year because of a behavioral problem, and 44 percent had been suspended or expelled in the past five years. The study sample was also more sexually active than randomly chosen national samples. By age 16, 78 percent (84 percent of the boys, 60 percent of the girls) had engaged in sexual intercourse. By age 17, 26 percent of the girls reported having been pregnant. Thus, the cycle of teen pregnancy tends to repeat itself.

Many teen mothers are from disadvantaged socioeconomic backgrounds. This raises the question of the relative contribution of teenage parenting and poverty to the outcomes that Furstenberg observed. One attempt to control for the effects of context compared teens who became pregnant but miscarried with teens who gave birth and kept the child (Hotz et al., 1999). Their results parallel those reported by Furstenberg; there were serious short-term consequences for the teen mothers, but by the time they were in their late twenties they had only slightly more children, were slightly more likely to be a single mother, and did not differ in their level of educational attainment. Moreover, the teen mothers were less likely to be living in poverty and receiving welfare. The results led the authors to conclude that "*the cost of teenage childbearing to U.S. taxpayers is negligible*" (emphasis added).

Thus programs to reduce teen pregnancy will improve the lives of young people but will not have a substantial effect on the costs of welfare programs. What can be done?

Furstenberg's results enable us to identify factors crucial to successful outcomes and to design

Figure 9.9   An important factor in life success for a pregnant teenager is the existence of special programs that allow her to complete high school.

social programs to provide these resources to other teen mothers. Two factors critical to success, for example, are finishing high school (and preferably going for even more education) and postponing other births. Social programs need to be set up to assist adolescent mothers in finishing high school (including special schools for pregnant teenagers, and child care for mothers while attending school) (Figure 9.9). Information on and access to contraception is essential. Programs such as Head Start that help prepare the children of teen mothers for school are critical, because they are at high risk for academic failure. Marriage to a man with some financial resources was also a route to success for some women in this study. However, the high rate of unemployment among young, Black, urban men makes such marriages less likely. This points out the importance of social programs aimed at males as well as females.

In summary, teenage pregnancy is a serious problem, but not an unsolvable one. By studying women who stage a recovery from the experience, we can gain important insights into how we can break the cycle of poverty and teen pregnancy.

Attitudes toward Premarital Intercourse

Attitudes toward premarital intercourse have also undergone marked changes, particularly among young people. Sociologist Ira Reiss (1960) distinguished among four kinds of standards for premarital coitus:

1. **Abstinence** Premarital intercourse is considered wrong for both males and females, regardless of the circumstances.
2. **Permissiveness with affection** Premarital intercourse is permissible for both males and females if it occurs in the context of a stable relationship that involves love, commitment, or being engaged.
3. **Permissiveness without affection** Premarital intercourse is permissible for both males and females, regardless of emotional commitment, simply on the basis of physical attraction.
4. **Double standard** Premarital intercourse is acceptable for males but is not acceptable for females. The double standard may be either *orthodox* or *transitional*. In the orthodox case, the double standard holds regardless of the couple's relationship; in the transitional case, sex is con-

sidered acceptable for the woman if she is in love or engaged.

Historically in the United States, the prevailing standard has been either abstinence or the double standard. However, today, particularly among young people, the standard is one of permissiveness with affection.

We can see evidence of this new standard, and of the shift it represents from previous generations, by comparing the data on current attitudes toward premarital intercourse with those from previous decades, as shown in Table 9.4. Note that in surveys conducted in 1937 and 1959, few people approved of premarital intercourse. By 1982 more people approved than disapproved, representing a real shift in norms. Note that adult attitudes have essentially remained the same from 1982 to 2004.

Abstinence

The data presented in Table 9.1 indicate that less than one-half of U.S. high school students have had intercourse. Among those who have not, some will by the time they graduate, but others will remain abstinent. According to a recent survey among teens 15 to 17 who had not had intercourse, 74 percent said they had "made a conscious decision to wait" (Kaiser Family Foundation, 2000b). A study of two samples of adolescents, one a national sample of 12,000 seventh to twelfth graders and the other a sample of 300 seventh and eighth graders

Abstinence: A standard in which premarital intercourse is considered wrong, regardless of the circumstances.
Permissiveness with affection: A standard in which premarital intercourse is considered acceptable if it occurs in the context of a loving, committed relationship.
Permissiveness without affection: A standard in which premarital intercourse is acceptable without emotional commitment.
Double standard: A standard in which premarital intercourse is considered acceptable for males but not for females.

Table 9.4 Percentages of People Agreeing That Premarital Intercourse Is Acceptable in 1937, 1959, 1972, 1982, 1990, 1998, 2004

Do you think it is all right for either or both parties to a marriage to have had previous sexual intercourse?

	1937	1959
All right for both	22%	22%
All right for men only	8	8
All right for neither	56	54
Don't know or refused to answer	14	16

If a man and a woman have sex relations before marriage, do you think it is . . .

	1972	1982	1990	1998	2004
Always wrong	35%	28%	25%	25%	26%
Almost always wrong	11	9	9	9	9
Wrong only sometimes	23	21	22	20	17
Not wrong at all	26	40	39	42	45
Don't know	4	3	4	3	2

Source: Hunt (1974), pp. 115–116; National Opinion Research Center, *General Social Survey, 1972, 1982, 1990, 1998, 2004.*

in North Carolina, reported that those most likely to abstain had the highest intelligence test scores (Halpern et al., 2000). High intelligence was associated not only with postponing intercourse but also with delaying other partnered sexual activities as well. One explanation is that smart teens are more committed to long-term educational and career goals and are aware that being involved in a pregnancy or contracting an STI could interfere with or render impossible the achievement of their goals.

Some school- and community-based sex-education programs have launched campaigns to persuade teens to declare publicly their intent to abstain by signing virginity pledges. In theory, a public commitment will reduce the likelihood that the young person will yield to the desire to have sex or to peer pressure to do so. In addition, signing the pledge provides one with a social identity and the social support of others who have signed. One longitudinal study of a large sample of youth found that signers of a pledge were 34 percent less likely to have intercourse than nonsigners; the pledge was most effective among youth ages 16 and 17, and in situations where about 30 percent of the teens in the school or community signed the pledge (Bearman & Bruckner, 2001). If more than 30 percent signed the pledge, the youth were less likely to delay having intercourse, perhaps because they didn't feel special or unique.

Motives for Having Premarital Intercourse

Young people mention a variety of reasons for engaging in physical intimacy (Sprecher & McKinney, 1993). A survey of ninth graders (mean age 14.1) in two California schools measured the importance of three relationship goals—intimacy, sexual pleasure, and social status—and the extent to which the adolescent believed vaginal intercourse would achieve each goal (Ott et al., 2006). Many adolescents believed that vaginal sex would achieve all three goals. Girls considered intimacy significantly more important as a goal, and pleasure significantly less important. Sexually experienced girls valued social status significantly less than inexperienced girls; there were no differences by experience among boys. Impett and colleagues (2005) identify five approach motives and four avoidance motives that might influence one's decision to engage in sexual activity. The approach motives are promoting intimacy, own pleasure, expressing love, pleasing partner, and feeling good about the self; avoidance motives are avoiding conflict, and preventing partner from becoming upset, getting angry, or losing interest. Using daily diaries completed by college students in relationships, they found that having sex for approach motives was positively associated with well-being. Having sex for avoidance reasons was negatively associated with well-being, and with greater likelihood of breaking up in the following month. Respondents to the NHSLS gave two additional reasons for having intercourse the first time: it was their wedding night (7 percent of the men, 21 percent of the women), and the person wanted to get pregnant (less than 1 percent of the respondents) (Laumann et al., 1994).

Dating and Going Steady, or Friends with Benefits

The social forces that have produced changes in premarital sexual behavior and standards are complex. But among them seems to be a change in courtship stages—in the process of dating, leading to going steady, and establishing a special romantic relationship with another partner. Dating and going steady occur at much younger ages now than in previous generations. Dating earlier and going steady earlier create both more of a demand for premarital sex and more of a legitimacy for it. For many, sexual intimacy is made respectable by going steady.

Sorensen (1973) found the most common premarital sexual pattern to be **serial monogamy** without marriage. In such a relationship there is an intention of being faithful to the partner, but the relationship is of uncertain duration. Of those in the sample who had premarital intercourse, 40 percent were serial monogamists. Though they averaged about four partners, nearly half of them had had only one partner, and about half of them had been involved in their current relationship for a year or more. In 2002, the NSFG interviewed 12,571 men and women ages 15 to 44. Of the single never-married men, 31 percent reported having more than one partner in the preceding year; by race the percentages were 22 percent of Hispanics, 16 percent of whites, and 33 percent of Blacks. Among single never-married women, the percentages were 13, 13, and 22, respectively (Mosher et al., 2005).

A qualitative study of Puerto Rican youth living in New York City explored the concept of serial monogamy among these youth (Ascensio, 2002). Most of the young people endorsed monogamy and viewed infidelity as wrong. But many also believed that one was required to be faithful only in a

Serial monogamy: A premarital sexual pattern in which there is an intention of being faithful to the partner, but the relationship may end and the person will then move on to another partner.

serious relationship, with seriousness not being related to the length of the relationship or to whether the couple had engaged in vaginal intercourse. Men were more likely to differentiate between a relationship and a "serious" relationship, whereas many women defined their relationships as "serious." As a result, men's and women's expectations of fidelity did not always coincide. And both men and women expressed greater tolerance for male infidelity. Thus the attitudes of these young people are complex, reflecting their particular construction of monogamy, fidelity, and the double standard.

The preceding paragraphs describe one trajectory for romantic and sexual relationships in adolescence in the contemporary United States, starting with mixed-gender activities that progress to dyadic dating, and then to going steady, probably involving a series of special relationships with the pattern continuing into adulthood. An alternative pattern is evident in some youth subcultures. Here, many adolescents remain actively involved in mixed-gender social groupings and do not make a transition to primarily dyadic dating relationships. Instead, romantic and sexual activities occur within the context of the group, often during parties. When sexual intimacy occurs, it may involve another member of the group, another friend, or someone met on the Net. Such relationships are often referred to as *friends with benefits* (Denizet-Lewis, 2004).

Friends with benefits are an alternative to going steady, being in a relationship.

> "Being in a real relationship just complicates everything," says Brian, a 16-year-old from New England. "When you're friends with **benefits,** you go over, hook up, then play video games or something. It rocks." (Denizet-Lewis, 2004, p. 33—emphasis in original)

Brian is really describing casual sex, and that is what some adolescents and young adults say they want. Men and women with solid education and career plans want to focus on achieving their goals and not get sidetracked by a relationship, an unintended pregnancy, or a life-threatening STI. Others, however, are secretly looking for a more committed, longer-term relationship, and some admit that they are hurt by the failure of the partner to call them the next day or the next week.

On college campuses across the United States, these casual encounters are referred to as **hooking up,** a sexual encounter that usually occurs on one occasion involving

Hooking up: A sexual encounter that usually occurs on one occasion involving people who are strangers or acquaintances.

people who are strangers or acquaintances (Paul et al., 2000). The encounter may or may not involve sexual intercourse; oral sex may occur as one alternative. A study of 555 undergraduates classified each into one of three groups: no hookup experience, hookup experience without intercourse (HU), and hookup experience including intercourse (HU-Sex). Of interest is the fact that those without hookup experience were much more likely to be in long-term romantic relationships. No hookup persons attained significantly higher scores on a measure of self-esteem. Those who had hookup experience reported an average of 10.8 experiences in their lives. Males were significantly more likely to report hookups involving intercourse. Twenty-eight percent of the HU and 49 percent of the HU-Sex participants reported that they never saw the partner again. The major difference between those in the HU group and those in the HU-Sex group was that the latter experience significantly more symptoms of alcohol intoxication when they drink.

Conflicts

We are currently in an era in which there are tensions between a restrictive sexual ethic and a permissive one. In such circumstances, conflicts are bound to arise. One is between parents and children as parents hold fast to conservative standards while their children adopt permissive ones.

These conflicts within our society are mirrored in the messages of the mass media.

> We are a nation that is deeply ambivalent about sex. On the one hand, sex is so much a part of the landscape that we almost take it for granted, and the message we get is that everybody else seems to be doing it and we are missing the party if we don't get moving. We should liberate our sexual natures, polish up the hot buttons, follow our hormones, and seek fulfillment somewhere across a crowded room. Sex is the ultimate expression of the American dream of freedom, liberation, and mobility. On the other hand, we hear just how frightening sex can be. Some of that comes from the powerful hold of our puritan heritage, but with a uniquely modern twist. AIDS, urban anonymity, sexual abuse and assault, all make sex a dangerous pastime. And this dovetails nicely with the old morality that co-exists with our alleged libertine behavior. (Michael et al., 1994, p. 8)

With such conflicting messages so prevalent, it is no wonder that many young people feel conflicts about premarital sex.

Young people may also experience conflicts between their own behaviors and their attitudes or standards. Behaviors generally change faster than attitudes do. As a result, people may engage in premarital sex while still disapproving of it. For example, in one study of inner-city junior high and senior high school students, of those who were sexually active 83 percent gave an ideal age for first intercourse that was older than when they themselves had first had intercourse (Zabin et al., 1984). And among those who had engaged in premarital intercourse, 25 percent believed that premarital sex is wrong. These inconsistencies between behavior and attitudes can create feelings of conflict.

How Sexuality Aids in Development

Erik Erikson has postulated a model of psychosocial development according to which we experience crises at each of eight stages of our lives (1950, 1968). Each one of these crises may be resolved in one of two directions. Erikson notes that social influences are particularly important in determining the outcomes of these crises.

The stages postulated by Erikson are listed in Table 9.5. Note that the outcomes of several of them may be closely linked to sexuality. For example, in early childhood there is a crisis between autonomy and shame, and later between initiative and guilt. The child who masturbates at age 5 is showing autonomy and initiative. But if the parents react to this activity by severely punishing the child, their actions may produce shame and guilt. Thus they may be encouraging the child to feel ashamed and consequently to suffer a loss of self-esteem.

In adolescence, the crisis is between identity and role confusion. Gender roles are among the most important; in later adolescence, the person may emerge with a stable, self-confident sense of manhood or womanhood or, alternatively, may feel in conflict about gender roles. A choice of career is extremely important in this developing sense of identity, and gender roles influence career choice. A sexual identity also emerges—one's status as, for example, heterosexual or homosexual, popular or unpopular.

In young adulthood, the crisis is between intimacy and isolation. Sexuality, of course, can function in an important way as people develop their capacity for intimacy.

Adolescent relationships provide the context in which the individual develops the skills and learns the scripts needed to sustain long-term intimate relationships (O'Sullivan & Meyer-Bahlburg, 2003). Research indicates that the process begins, at ages 9 to 12, with a first boyfriend or girlfriend; often there is little direct interaction between the two, but the relationship does provide an opportunity to assume an "adult" role. Later comes group dating and perhaps mixed-sex social events at schools. These situations provide an opportunity for conversation and for peers to observe and instruct the person in sexual scripts. In mid- to late adolescence, youth begin to spend time in mixed-sex, unsupervised interaction, which provides an opportunity for physical intimacy, leading often to sexual intercourse. Qualitative research finds that this process generally occurs at younger ages for African Americans compared to Latinas, because the latter are generally under closer monitoring by parents (O'Sullivan & Meyer-Bahlburg, 2003).

Research using longitudinal data from Add Health focused on Asian American youth and found variations in rate of first intercourse by ethnicity. Percent of youth initiating intercourse between ages 16 and 17 (the average age of the sample at two waves) varied from 11 percent of Vietnamese and Indian women, 27 percent of Korean, to 40 percent of Chinese and Filipino women. Those women who reported close attachment to parents at wave 1 were less likely to initiate intercourse by wave 2 (Hahm et al., 2006).

Furman (2002) proposes that this behavioral sequence parallels a developmental one. Early relationships reflect simple interest. Subsequent ones fulfill primarily affiliative and sexual reproductive needs as young people explore their sexual feelings. As the person moves into late adolescence and early adulthood, longer-term relationships become the site of the fulfillment of needs for attachment and mutual care taking. One important consequence of this process is the development of

SexSource Online
www.mhhe.com/hyde10

"LEARNING TO BE STRAIGHT" IN SEXUALITY OVER THE LIFE-SPAN

Table 9.5	Erikson's Stages of Psychosocial Development
Approximate Stage in the Life Cycle	*Crisis*
Infancy	Basic trust vs. mistrust
Ages 1½ to 3 years	Autonomy vs. shame and doubt
Ages 3 to 5½ years	Initiative vs. guilt
Ages 5½ to 12 years	Industry vs. inferiority
Adolescence	Identity vs. role confusion
Young adulthood	Intimacy vs. isolation
Adulthood	Generativity vs. stagnation
Maturity	Ego integrity vs. despair

a sexual identity, with regard to orientation and sexual attractiveness. Obviously, the timing of this process varies from one person to another, one influence being culture and its associated variation in the degree of parental control over adolescents. Furman points out that many social and cultural arrangements facilitate the emergence of heterosexual relationships and at the same time deter gay and lesbian relationships. Mixed-sex gatherings in adolescence are usually heterosexual, and monitoring by peers would likely result in harassment of same-gender romantic activity. Diamond's (2003) research indicates the relative fluidity of the sexual self-identities of some young women from adolescence to their midtwenties.

Thus we can see that sexuality is an integral part of our psychological development.

SUMMARY

A capacity for sexual response is present from infancy. According to contemporary data, about 40 percent of U.S. children have masturbated by the time they reach puberty. Recent studies indicate that children begin masturbating at somewhat earlier ages now than a generation or so ago. Children also engage in some heterosexual play, as well as some same-gender activity.

During adolescence there is an increase in sexual activity. According to one theory, this activity is influenced by the interaction of biological factors (increasing testosterone level) and social and psychological factors (for example, sexually permissive attitudes). By age 15, nearly all boys have masturbated. Girls tend to begin masturbating somewhat later than boys, and fewer of them do masturbate. Attitudes toward masturbation are considerably more permissive now than they were a century ago. About 10 percent of adolescents have same-gender experiences to orgasm.

Today the majority of males and of females alike have premarital sex. This is a considerable increase over the incidence reported in the Kinsey studies, done 60 years ago. Adolescents today are considerably more likely to use a variety of sexual techniques, including mouth–genital sex. There is variation in the incidence of premarital intercourse among various racial and ethnic groups in the United States, and even greater variability from one country to another.

The predominant sexual standard today is one of "permissiveness with affection"; that is, sex is seen as acceptable outside marriage, provided there is an emotional commitment between the partners.

Following Erik Erikson's theory, experiences with sexuality can serve important functions in a person's psychological development. They may be important, for example, in the process of becoming independent of parents and in establishing a viable moral system.

QUESTIONS FOR THOUGHT, DISCUSSION, AND DEBATE

1. Do you see evidence of conservative trends in sexual attitudes and behaviors, reversing the trends from 1940 to 1990?

2. Does "permissiveness with affection" characterize the standard for premarital intercourse among the 18- to 22-year-olds you know?

3. The mother of a 5-year-old child tells you that her son has been masturbating while he watches TV in the family room. She asks you what she should do about his behavior. What would you tell her?

4. In this chapter, we presented data on ethnic differences in adolescent sexual experiences and in teenage pregnancy and parenting (Focus: Milestones in Sex Research, p. 248). In Chapter 1, we presented data on ethnic differences in masturbation and oral sex (Table 1.2). Using these data, create a brief description of adolescent sexuality among both Black and white youth in the United States. In what ways are they similar? In what ways are they different?

SUGGESTIONS FOR FURTHER READING

Eder, Donna, with Catherine Evans & Stephen Parker. (1995). *School talk: Gender and adolescent culture.* New Brunswick, NJ: Rutgers University Press. A study of adolescent peer groups and relationships in one middle school.

McCormick, Naomi B. (1979). Come-ons and put-offs: Unmarried students' strategies for having and avoiding intercourse. *Psychology of Women Quarterly, 4,* 194–211. An interesting discussion of college students' reported techniques for inviting or avoiding intercourse, and how these techniques relate to gender-role stereotypes.

Starks, Kay, & Morrison, Eleanor. (1996). *Growing up sexual* (2nd ed.). New York: HarperCollins. A fascinating view of sexual development with many first-person quotes, based on student autobiographies for a human sexuality course.

CHAPTER TEN

Sexuality and the Life Cycle: Adulthood

CHAPTER HIGHLIGHTS

G row old along with me!
The best is yet to be.*

*Robert Browning. (1864). *Rabbi Ben Ezra.*

This chapter continues to trace the development of sexuality across the life span. We look at various aspects of sexuality in adulthood: sex and the single person, cohabitation, marital sexuality, extramarital sexuality, postmarital sexuality, and sex among the elderly. We consider lifestyles involving same-gender partners in Chapter 13. Each of these lifestyles is an option, reflecting the diversity of choices available in the contemporary United States.

Sex and the Single Person

Sexual Unfolding

Late adolescence and early adulthood are times of sexual unfolding as the individual moves toward mature, adult sexuality. First, there is a need to deal with issues of sexual orientation and define one's sexual identity. Heterosexuality is the norm in our society, and some people slip into it easily without much thought. Others sense that their orientation is gay or lesbian and must struggle with society's negative messages about these groups. Others sense that they are attracted to both males and females. Still others feel that their orientation is heterosexual but wonder why they experience homosexual fantasies, thinking that a person's sexual orientation must be perfectly consistent in all areas (research shows that heterosexuals sometimes have homosexual fantasies, and vice versa). These struggles over sexual orientation seem to be more difficult for males than for females because heterosexuality is such an important cornerstone of the male role in many societies, including ours (see Chapter 12).

Another step toward maturity is identifying our sexual likes and dislikes and learning to communicate them to a partner. Learning what one likes and dislikes may occur naturally as the individual experiences various behaviors over time. Alternatively, some people intentionally seek opportunities to engage in novel behaviors or in sexual intimacy with novel partners. Learning to communicate with sexual partners is difficult for many persons, perhaps because there are few role models in our society showing us how to engage in direct, honest communication with them.

Two more issues are important in achieving sexual maturity: becoming responsible about sex, and developing a capacity for intimacy. Taking responsibility includes being careful about contraception and sexually transmitted infections, being responsible for yourself and for your partner. Intimacy (see Chapter 11) involves a deep emotional sharing between two people that goes beyond casual sex or manipulative sex.

The Never Married

The term *never married* refers to adults who have never been married. This group includes those who intend to marry someday and those who have decided to remain single. The National Survey of Family Growth interviewed more than 12,000 men and women ages 15–44 in 2002–2003. At age 30, 27 percent of the women and 39 percent of the men were never married. By age 40, the percentages were 18 and 25, respectively (Martinez et al., 2006).

Most adults in our society do marry. The median age of first marriage in 2003 was 25.3 years for women and 27.1 years for men (U.S. Bureau of the Census, 2004), so the typical person who marries spends several adult years in the never-married category. Some of these men and women spend this entire time in one relationship that eventually leads to marriage. According to the NHSLS, among married persons 20 to 29 years old, 46 percent of the men and 65 percent of the women are in this category (Laumann et al., 1994). Other young adults continue the pattern of *serial monogamy,* which (as we saw in Chapter 9) is common in adolescence; they are involved in two or more sexually intimate relationships prior to marriage. According to the NHSLS, among married persons 20 to 29, 40 percent of the men and 28 percent of the women had two or more sexual partners before they married.

The person who passes age 30 without getting married gradually enters a new world. The social structures that supported dating—such as college—are gone, and more people of the same age are married. Dating and sex are no longer geared to mate selection, and it no longer seems reasonable to call her or his sexual activity *premarital sex.*

The attitudes of singles about their status vary widely. Some young men and women decide to live both celibate (unmarried) and chaste (abstaining from sexual intercourse). Little research has been done on celibacy, and published studies often do not distinguish voluntary from involuntary celibates. One study found that such persons were introverted and ambitious and that celibate women had high educational and occupational status (Kiernan, 1988). Research using a questionnaire posted on the Internet identified three types of involuntary celibates (Donnelly et al., 2001). *Virgins* had never had intercourse, had rarely ever dated, and often had not engaged in any partnered sexual intimacy; the data suggest that they failed to make the developmental transitions discussed at the end of Chapter 9. *Singles* had had sexual experience but often reported that it was not satisfying; they were unable to find and maintain relationships. Both their residential and work arrangements made it difficult for persons in either group to meet potential partners. Other research suggests that one's competence in romantic relationships in adulthood—being close to and getting along with a partner—is predicted by one's competence in the social and academic domains in late adolescence (Roisman et al., 2004). The third type are *partnered,* persons in sexless relationships. Typically, the relationship had included sex in the past, but the frequency gradually declined over time.

Some young people plan to be celibate but not chaste. They find the single lifestyle exciting and enjoy their freedom. Census data suggest that about 9 percent of the population will never marry; this, of course, includes involuntary celibates and persons who are not heterosexual. Other men and women are searching for a spouse, with increasing desperation as the years go by. According to one researcher, their desperation is fueled by **singleism,** the stigmatizing and stereotyping of people who are not in a socially recognized couple relationship (De Paulo, 2006). She argues that singles can and do live "happily ever after."

Being Single

At one extreme, there is the *singles scene*. It is institutionalized in such forms as singles apartment complexes and singles bars. Fitness centers, church groups, school, and parties also provide opportunities for meeting others (Figure 10.1). A survey of a cross-section of Cook County, Illinois, residents found that 24 percent of men and 20 percent of women met their most recent sex partner at school, 19 percent of men and 23 percent of women met him/her at work, and 13 percent of men and 18 percent of women met her/him at bars or clubs (Laumann et al., 2004). The singles group, of course, is composed of the divorced and the widowed as well as the never married.

Singleism: The stigmatizing and stereotyping of people who are not in a socially recognized couple relationship.

Figure 10.1   School is one place where people look for Mr. or Ms. Right.

The singles bar is a visible symbol of the singles scene. Everyone is there for a similar purpose: to meet Mr. or Ms. Right. However, most will settle for a date, and it is fairly well understood that coitus will be a part of the date. The singles bar is somewhat like a meat market; the people there try to display themselves to their best advantage and are judged and chosen on the basis of their physical appearance—and perhaps rejected for too high a percentage of fat.

Many singles, however, do not go to singles bars. Some are turned off by the idea; some feel that they cannot compete, that they are too old, or that they are not attractive enough; and some live in rural areas where they have no access to such places. An alternative way of meeting people is through singles ads, found in most daily newspapers. One woman said,

> Most of the men I've dated I've met . . . through personals ads. The reason I prefer guys I meet through ads is because I get to know them before meeting them. I get the chance to really get to know them before I actually see them. (Louis, 1997, p. 10)

Singles ads can also be found on the Internet. There are hundreds of sites, for example, American

Singles and Match.com, where one can post ads or create a personal Web page. Persons wishing to place ads are encouraged to indicate the type of partner they are searching for, as well as their age, ethnicity, height, and area of residence. Those seeking partners can search the ads and home pages on these characteristics. Contacts made online can lead to an offline relationship or to a continuing online one. The relationship may evolve to include *cybersex,* where participants engage in sexual talk online for the purposes of sexual pleasure (Daneback et al., 2004). It may or may not involve masturbation.

The visibility of singles ads, singles bars, cruises, and other activities geared toward single adults suggests a fun-loving lifestyle with frequent sexual activity. Undoubtedly some single persons live such a life. As Figure 10.2 indicates, 26 percent of the single men and 22 percent of the single women interviewed for the NHSLS reported having sexual intercourse two or more times per week. But the reality is different for other singles; 22 percent of the single men and 30 percent of the single women

interviewed did not have sex in the year prior to the interview. The National Survey of Family Growth (NSFG) (Mosher et al., 2005) reports that 24 percent of the never-married men and women in the United States had no sexual contact in the preceding year.

As we noted in Chapter 1, Black men and women are more likely to remain single than are their white counterparts (Kreider, 2006). In 2005, 52 percent of Black family households were headed by a single woman, compared with 18 percent of white, 25 percent of Hispanic, and 13 percent of Asian households. In part, these family arrangements reflect choice. And, they reflect the fact that there are more adult Black women than men (Kiecolt et al., 1995). But they also reflect the structural circumstances of Blacks in U.S. society. It is difficult for many Black men to find a job that provides the wages and benefits needed to support a family (Anderson, 1989). As a consequence, some Black women are unable to find a suitable Black man (Chapman, 1997). When they do, they are more likely than white or Hispanic women to report that

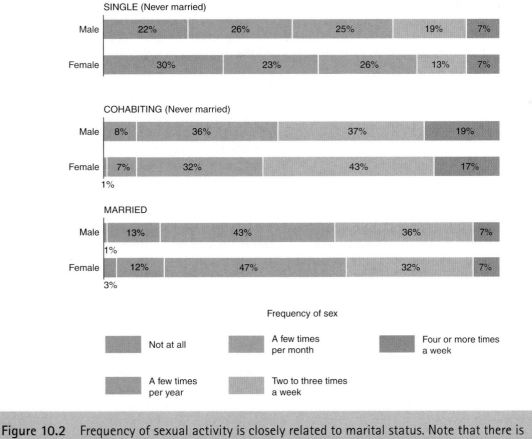

Figure 10.2 Frequency of sexual activity is closely related to marital status. Note that there is substantial variability in frequency within each status as well (Laumann et al., 1994).

they are the ones who decide whether sex will occur and that they control what behaviors the couple engages in (Quadagno et al., 1998).

A qualitative study of heterosexually active men provides insight into their motives and the importance of scripts in their interactions with women (Seal & Ehrhardt, 2003). The men were ethnically diverse and were recruited from inner-city neighborhoods in New York City. Desire for sexual intimacy was a major motivation for their involvement in courtship rituals. Desire for sex was associated with playing the courtship game via the traditional script of male initiates and female controls. If romance—for example, professions of love—was involved, the goal was sexual intimacy. On other occasions, men were motivated by a desire for intimate relationships; in these interactions, men moved from superficial to in-depth mutual disclosure. These interactions were governed by a script characterized by mutual initiation and control; sexual intimacy was a secondary goal. A third motive was a desire for sexual passion, for immersion in the partner and the experience of high levels of arousal and lust. These interactions were usually spontaneous, and could not be planned. The narratives of courtship told by the men suggested that their selection and pursuit of partners varied according to their motive. A man motivated by a desire for sex sought a physically attractive, sexually available woman; a man motivated by a desire for intimacy sought Ms. Right, a woman who was not sexually available.

Cohabitation

In early adulthood, it is common for couples to experiment with various levels of commitment, such as an exclusive dating relationship or living together. Even when living together, there are different levels of commitment, from "living together apart" to "some days and nights" to "all the time." Living together is an important turning point not only because it represents commitment but also because it is a public declaration of a sexual relationship. It is rare for a man and woman to live together just because it will save on rent. Cohabiting is an opportunity to try out marriage, at least to some extent.

Among heterosexuals, cohabitation has become an increasingly common alternative to marriage. In 2005, 9 percent of all men and women

ages 15 to 44 were cohabiting (Martinez et al., 2006). Twenty-five percent of people aged 19 to 24 and 42 percent of people aged 25 to 29 have cohabited at least once. These arrangements tend to be short lived; one-third last less than 1 year, and only one out of ten lasts 5 years (Bumpass et al., 1991). Almost three-fourths of the men and women who are cohabiting have plans to marry or think they will marry their partner. In fact, 60 percent of these couples do marry. Contrary to what many people think, these marriages are more likely to end in divorce than are marriages not preceded by cohabitation (Smith, 2003). A longitudinal study compared couples who cohabited before they got engaged, couples who cohabited after engagement/before marriage, and couples who did not live together until after marriage (Kline et al., 2004). Couples were assessed twice, following engagement and after 10 months of marriage. At both times, couples who lived together before engagement had more negative interactions (e.g., criticizing a partner), lower commitment, and lower relationship quality. Thus, the seeds of divorce are sown in the pre-engagement relationship. A related study found that men in pre-engagement cohabiting relationships were less committed to the partner (Rhoades et al., 2006).

The popular image of cohabitation is that it involves young, never-married couples without children. About one-third of cohabiting couples fit this image, but 40 percent have children. In one-third of these families, the two adults are the biological parents of the children. In the other two-thirds, the children were born into a previous union of one of the adults (Bumpass et al., 1991). Some formerly married people choose to live with someone instead of remarrying.

With regard to sexual behavior, an analysis of data from a large, representative sample of adults found that married persons reported having intercourse 8 to 11 times per month, whereas cohabiting persons reported a frequency of 11 to 13 times per month (Call et al., 1995). The NHSLS found that cohabiting men and women reported more frequent sex than did married men and women (see Figure 10.2). However, notice the wide variation; some cohabitors report having sexual intercourse only a few times per year. It is interesting that on average cohabiting couples have sex more often than married couples. Cohabitors are concerned about the stability of the relationship (Bumpass et al., 1991); they may have sex more frequently in the hope that it will strengthen the relationship (Blumstein & Schwartz, 1983).

Marital Relationships

Marriage is a sexual turning point (Sarrel & Sarrel, 1984) for a number of reasons (Figure 10.3). The decision to get married is a real decision these days, in contrast to earlier decades when everyone assumed that they would marry and the only question was to whom. Today, many couples have had a full sexual relationship, sometimes for years, before they marry. Some psychological pressures seem to intensify with marriage, and these pressures may result in problems where there were none previously. Marriage is a tangible statement that one has left the family of origin (the family in which you grew up) and shifted to the family of procreation (in which you become the parents rearing children); for some, this separation from parents is difficult. The pressure for sexual performance may become more intense once married; when just living together, a couple can always say to themselves that if things don't work out in bed, they can simply switch to another partner. And finally, marriage still carries with it an assumption of fidelity or faithfulness, a promise that is hard for some to keep.

In marriage, there is a need to work out issues of gender roles. Who does what? Some of the decisions are as tame as who cooks supper. But who initiates sex is a far more sensitive issue, and who has the right to say no to sex is even more so.

This is the era of two-career couples, or at least dual-earner couples. There are issues here of finding time for sex and for just being with each other.

As a marriage progresses, it can't stay forever as blushingly beautiful as it seemed on the day of the wedding. The nature of love changes (see Chapter 11), and for some couples there is a gradual disenchantment with sex. Couples need to take steps to avoid boredom in the bedroom. Sexual disorders (see Chapter 17) occur in many marriages, and couples need to find ways to resolve them.

(a)

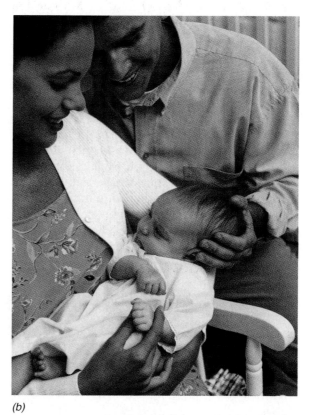

(b)

Figure 10.3   Sexual turning points. (*a*) Marriage and the commitment it represents is a major turning point. (*b*) The birth of a baby is a turning point that can have a negative impact on sexual aspects of the relationship, but couples who are aware of this possibility can work to overcome these problems and keep the romance going.

Frequency of Marital Intercourse

About 92 percent of all people aged 54 or younger are or have been married (U.S. Bureau of the Census, 2000b). Of those who divorce, 80 percent remarry (Norton, 1987). In our society, marriage is also the context in which sexual expression has the most legitimacy. Therefore, sex in marriage is one of the commonest forms of sexual expression for adults.

The average American married couple have coitus two to three times per week when they are in their twenties, with the frequency gradually declining as they get older. The data on this point from three studies are shown in Table 10.1. Several things can be noted from the table. Specifically, the frequency of marital sex remained about the same from the 1940s to the 2000s. In each survey, people in their twenties reported having intercourse about every three days. Also, the frequency of intercourse declines with age; however, in 2003, among couples in their fifties, the frequency was still once per week. Social characteristics such as race, social status, and religion are generally not related to marital sexual frequency (Christopher & Sprecher, 2000).

Two general explanations have been suggested for the age-related decline in frequency: biological aging, and habituation to sex with the partner (Call et al., 1995). With regard to aging, there may be physical factors associated with age that affect sexual frequency, such as a decrease in vaginal lubrication in females, or increased likelihood of poor health. The habituation explanation states that we lose interest in sex as the partner becomes more and more familiar. Recent data indicate a sharp decline in frequency after the first year and a slow, steady decline thereafter. The decline after the first year may reflect habituation (Call et al.,

1995). It is often assumed that this decline in frequency reflects a loss of interest in sex, meaning a decline in quality. However, there is an alternative possibility: that learning about your partner's sexual desires, preferences, and habits results in increased marital sexual quality, if not frequency (Liu, 2003). But analysis of the data on satisfaction with the marital sexual relationship from the NHSLS found a significant decline with length of marriage, controlling for age, consistent with the habituation hypothesis. A third factor is the arrival of children, discussed later.

It is important to note that there is wide variability in these frequencies. For example, 2 percent of couples in their twenties report not engaging in intercourse at all; 6 percent of all married couples had not had sex in the 12 months prior to the interview (Smith, 2003). Research on a sample of 6,029 married couples found that sexual inactivity was associated with unhappiness with the marriage, lack of shared activity, the presence of children, increased age, and poor health (Donnelly, 1993). In contrast, a married couple in Seattle have claimed the world record, having had intercourse more than 900 times in 700 days! Data from the NHSLS also confirm this wide variability, as shown in Figure 10.2.

Techniques in Marital Sex

The NHSLS (Laumann et al., 1994) included a number of questions about specific aspects of sexual interactions. For example, it asked respondents to estimate the duration of their last sexual interaction. Sixteen percent of the married people reported that it lasted 15 minutes or less; about 9 percent reported that it lasted 1 hour or more. Incidentally, one-third of the never-married respondents said it lasted 1 hour or more.

Table 10.1 Marital Coitus: Frequency per Week (male and female estimates combined), 1938–1949, 1970, and 2003

1938–1949 (Kinsey)		1970 (Westoff)		2003 (Smith)	
Age	Mean Frequency per Week	Age	Mean Frequency per Week	Age	Mean Frequency per Week
16–25	2.45	20–24	2.5	18–29	2.1
26–35	1.95	25–34	2.1	30–39	1.7
36–45	1.40	35–44	1.6	40–49	1.4
46–55	0.85			50–59	1.0
56–60	0.55			60–69	0.6
				70+	0.3

The increased popularity of mouth–genital techniques is one of the most dramatic changes in marital sex to have occurred in the past 50 years. According to Kinsey's data, 54 percent of the married women reported that they had received cunnilingus, and 49 percent reported that they had engaged in fellatio (Kinsey et al., 1948). In the NHSLS data, 74 percent reported that their partners had stimulated their genitals orally, and 70 percent of them had stimulated their partners orally. Women who have attended college are twice as likely to report both techniques as women who did not complete high school.

Much larger percentages of women under age 50 as compared to those over 50 have given or received oral sex in their lifetime. And those in the oldest age group were less than half as likely to have had or received oral sex the last time they had sex. This is suggestive evidence that oral sex came into vogue in the 1960s (Michael et al., 1994).

Kinsey did not report data on anal intercourse. According to the NHSLS data, 27 percent of the married men and 21 percent of the married women reported having engaged in this activity (Laumann et al., 1994).

Negotiating Sex

Before any of these techniques are executed, there is typically a "mating dance" between the partners. Sexual scripts are played out in marriages as in other aspects of sex (Gagnon, 1977, pp. 208–209). Some scripts involve direct verbal statements. One person may say, "I'd love to go to bed with you right now." The partner might reply, "What are we waiting for?" or "Not now. Dinner is almost ready." Some scripts are behavioral. One woman said, "We'd get into bed, and he'd roll over to me and kind of bing me in the back end with his penis, so I'd know, Okay, tonight's the night" (Maurer, 1994, p. 180). For other couples, deciding to have intercourse involves preliminary negotiations, which are phrased in indirect or euphemistic language, in part so that the person's feelings can be salvaged if her or his partner is not interested. For example, the husband may say, "I think I'll go take a shower" or "I think I'll go take a nap" (that means "I want to, do you?"). The wife might respond with, "I think I'll take one too" (that means yes) or "The kids will be home any moment" or "I have a headache" (that means no). Or conversely, she may put on a lot of his favorite perfume and parade around in front of him (that is *her* offer). He may respond with, "I

had an exhausting day at work" (his no) or "I'll meet you upstairs" (his yes). To avoid some of the risk of rejection inherent in such negotiations, some couples ritualize sex so they both understand when it will and when it will not occur—Thursday night may be their time, or perhaps Sunday afternoon.

A survey of married couples found that for 33 percent of them the husband and wife are about equally likely to initiate sex; for 51 percent the husband is more likely to be the initiator, and in only 16 percent of the couples is the wife usually the initiator (Blumstein & Schwartz, 1983). Thus there is some evidence of liberation (the couples where both are initiators), but traditional roles persist, with the majority of couples having the male in the initiating role. Women seem to be particularly careful not to initiate sex when they believe their spouse is feeling psychologically vulnerable. The traditional gender-typing of initiation patterns may also be related to how people deal with a refusal. If the man initiates and the woman refuses, he can simply attribute it to her lesser sexual appetite, according to traditional stereotypes. If the woman initiates and the man refuses, she has no stereotype to rescue her, and she is likely to conclude that he is not interested in *her* (Blumstein & Schwartz, 1983). The recent emphasis on a woman's right to sexual fulfillment has lessened this difference and made refusal by the woman threatening to the man's self-esteem (Duncombe & Marsden, 1994). Both men and women in equalitarian relationships may have to work at sustaining (the appearance of) a sexually fulfilling relationship.

Masturbation in Marriage

Many people masturbate; the NHSLS found that 63 percent of the men and 42 percent of the women reported masturbating in the past year. Seventeen percent of the married men and 5 percent of the married women masturbate at least once a week (Laumann et al., 1994).

Many adults continue to masturbate even though they are married and have ready access to heterosexual sex. This behavior is perfectly normal, although it often evokes feelings of guilt and may be done secretly. According to the NHSLS, married people were more likely to report that they masturbated than were single people (Michael et al., 1994). Masturbation can serve very legitimate sexual needs in marriage. It can provide sexual gratification while allowing the partner to remain faithful to a spouse when husband and wife are separated or cannot have sex for some reason such as illness.[1]

Masturbation can also be a pleasant adjunct to marital sex. According to a 49-year-old man,

> One of the other things we do a lot is masturbation. We have it developed to a fine art. We rent a porno movie, take a bath, rub each other down with baby oil. My wife and I not only masturbate each other at the same time, but we get pleasure watching each other masturbate individually as well. It's a terrifically exciting thing. (Janus & Janus, 1993, p. 383)

Satisfaction with Marital Sex

Satisfaction with sex has two components: satisfaction with the sexual activity, and emotional satisfaction. In the NHSLS, 51 percent of the married men and 40 percent of the married women said they were "extremely" or "very" physically satisfied by their sexual relationship. Similarly, 48 percent of the husbands and 42 percent of the wives said they were "extremely satisfied" emotionally (Laumann et al., 1994). Analyses of the data indicate that married men and women are significantly more satisfied than are cohabiting or single men and women in a continuing relationship (Waite & Joyner, 2000). The results indicate that this greater satisfaction reflects the stronger emotional commitment and sexual exclusivity associated with marriage.

Sexual satisfaction is an important contributor to marital quality. Longitudinal data from 283 married couples found that sexual satisfaction predicted marital quality for both men and women (Yeh et al., 2006). Sexual satisfaction and marital quality both predicted marital stability. Thus, sexuality and relational education programs that increase sexual satisfaction have the potential to lower the divorce rate.

In-depth interviews with 52 people, ages 12 to 69, straight, gay, lesbian, and bisexual, provide a different but related picture (Maurer, 1994). Reflecting on what differentiated those who were happy with their sex lives, the researcher identified four factors. First, there is a sense of calm about, an acceptance of their sexuality. Second, happy people are generous; they delight in giving their partners sexual pleasure. Third, these people *listen* to their partners and are aware of the partner's quirks, moods, likes and dislikes. Fourth, they *talk*, both in and out of bed, even though it is often difficult.

These interviews remind us that good communication is essential to a satisfying relationship (see Chapter 11).

Sexual Patterns in Marriage

Sexual patterns in marriage are influenced by the level of sexual desire experienced by each person. A study of 24 couples obtained daily ratings of relationship affect (positive or negative), relationship status (closeness, equality of power), and lust from each partner (Ridley et al., 2006). Researchers identified four patterns in ratings of desire: stable and low; slight fluctuations (1 point on a 1 to 5 scale) and low; moderate fluctuations and average; and highly fluctuating and average. On days when positive affect toward the spouse was high, lust was high; when negative affect was high, lust was low. Interestingly, on days when people reported high closeness to spouse, the link between positive (negative) affect and lust was stronger. Finally, there was a significant positive association between own lust and partner's lust each day.

Sexual patterns can change during the course of a marriage. After 10 years of marriage they may be quite different from what they were during the first year. One stereotype is that sex becomes duller as marriage wears on, and certainly there are some marriages in which that happens. In a survey of a national sample of adults, 23 percent of the sexually active men and women reported that their sexual relationship was often or always "routine." Thirty-eight percent said it was never or hardly ever routine (Kaiser Family Foundation, 1998) (Table 10.2). As we noted in Chapter 8, a boring sexual relationship can be spiced up by telling each other what you really want to do and then doing it, or by consulting a how-to manual such as *The New Joy of Sex*. One such book changed one 23-year-old married woman's sexual relationship:

> To say that our sex life had been going through the doldrums would be putting it mildly. Sometimes a whole month would go past and I would have another period and realize that during that whole month we hadn't made love once, not even *once*, whereas when we first dated we used to make love six or seven times a week. [I read] *Sex Secrets of the Other Woman*, how "the other woman" takes the trouble to have her hair done well and to look extra good. I went downtown and had my hair highlighted and cut. I bought some really sexy lingerie. When David came home from work that evening, I had a martini ready for him, like I always do. But I wasn't dressed in my usual jeans and sweater. I was wearing my new negligee, and when he sat down I opened it up for him and did a twirl.

---

[1]An old navy saying has it, "If your wife can't be at your right hand, let your right hand be your wife."

I was frightened. But he smiled and shook his head and said "Heyyy, that's pretty!" (Masterton, 1993, pp. 86–88)

There are also relationships in which the sex remains very exciting. A 36-year-old engineer said,

[Though my wife's career] is tremendously important to her, she manages to look attractive, and to dress chicly, and though she is not what many would call a beautiful woman, she is, to me, a handsome woman. In bed, she is the hottest, most exciting woman I have ever known. We have been married seven years. . . . When we get to bed, and she lets herself go, we get wild together. (Janus & Janus, 1993, p. 191)

Having a baby—what researchers call the transition to parenthood—has an impact on a marriage and on the sexual relationship of the couple. According to one 44-year-old mother of three children, "There's the passionate period when you can't get enough of each other, and after a few years it wanes, and after kids it really wanes" (Maurer, 1994, p. 403). Trying to get pregnant and the threat of infertility, which are so much publicized, can be potent forces on one's identity as a sexual being. Pregnancy itself can influence a couple's sexual interactions, particularly in the last few months (see Chapter 6).

For the first few weeks after the baby is born, intercourse is typically uncomfortable for the woman. While estrogen levels are low—which lasts longer when breast-feeding—the vagina does not lubricate well. Then, too, the mother and sometimes the father feel exhausted with 2:00 A.M. feedings. The first few months after a baby is born are usually not the peak times in a sexual relationship, so that, too, must be negotiated between partners.

Not all couples have children. Based on data collected in June 2002, the Census Bureau reports that a record number of women ages 15 to 44 are childless (Downs, 2003). There were 26.7 million childless women in 2002, compared to 24.3 million in 1990. Some of these women are delaying childbearing while they complete their education and establish their careers. There is some risk in this strategy; fertility declines with age, so some of these women may be unable to have a child when they want to. Other women in this group have made a decision to remain childfree. A third group of women are those who chose to adopt; adopting an infant probably has effects on one's relationships and sexual activities similar to those of having a baby. Childlessness varies by race; among women 15 to 44, 51 percent of Asian American, 46 percent of white, 39 percent of Black, and 36 percent of Hispanic women do not have children.

Some people will experience fundamental changes in their sexual experience at least once over the course of the marriage. The change may result from developing a capacity to give as well as receive sexual pleasure. A man may outgrow performance anxiety and enlarge his focus to include his partner. A woman may learn that she can take care of her own sexual needs as well as her partner's. Aging may produce change in sexual experience, a topic we consider later in this chapter. There are changes due to illness, such as breast cancer or testicular cancer, which can lead to disaster or triumph depending on how the couple copes with it.

Sex and the Two-Career Family

In our busy, achievement-oriented society, it is possible that work commitments—particularly with the increased incidence of wives holding jobs—may interfere with a couple's sex life. One couple, both of whom are professionals, commented to us

Table 10.2 Frequency of Activities to Enhance Sexual Interactions Reported by Adults*

	Very Often	Often	Sometimes	Hardly Ever	Never	DK
Do romantic things like eat by candlelight	8	18	35	30	6	3
Act out your fantasies together	4	10	28	39	12	7
Wear sexy lingerie (women†)	9	10	28	35	12	6
Try different sexual positions	11	19	35	23	4	8
Read books or watch videos about improving your sex life	2	3	14	52	26	3
Go out on special evenings or dates or go away on weekends alone	11	22	37	22	5	3

*Number of respondents = 1,109.

†Number of female respondents = 564.

Source: Kaiser Family Foundation (1998).

that they actually have to make an appointment with each other to make love.

Research shows that there is little cause for concern. A longitudinal study followed 570 women and 550 of their husbands for one year following the birth of a baby (Hyde et al., 1998). The women were categorized according to the number of hours worked per week: homemakers, employed part-time (6 to 31 hours/week), full-time (32 to 44 hours), and high full-time (45 or more hours). There were no significant differences among the four groups in frequency of sexual intercourse, sexual satisfaction, or sexual desire. It was not the number of hours of work, but rather the quality of work that was associated with sexual outcomes. Women and men who had satisfying jobs reported that sex was better, compared with people who expressed dissatisfaction with their jobs. For women, fatigue was associated with decreased sexual satisfaction, but that was true for both homemakers and employed women; and homemakers reported the same level of fatigue as employed women.

Problems may occur at the extremes, though. Two-profession couples, when both partners are committed to working 60 to 80 hours per week, don't have much time for sex. The issue with such couples is not so much having a career as being workaholics (Sarrel & Sarrel, 1984). An addiction to one's work can spell the death of sex just as readily as addiction to a drug can (Figure 10.4).

Keeping Your Mate

Most couples who establish a long-term relationship intend to stay together. However, we all know that not all couples succeed. What makes men and women susceptible to infidelity? A study of 107 couples married less than one year asked each partner how likely he or she was to be unfaithful in the next year (Buss & Shackelford, 1997b). Each was asked the likelihood that she or he would flirt, kiss passionately, and have a romantic date, a one-night stand, a brief affair, or a serious affair with someone of the opposite sex. Thirty-seven percent of the men and 38 percent of the women predicted they would flirt, while 5 percent of the men and 7 percent of the women said they would kiss. Two percent (of men and of women) predicted a one-night stand, and less than 1 percent (of men and women) thought they would have a serious

(a)

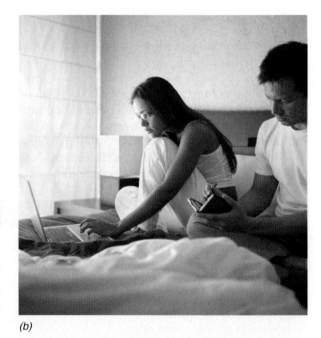

(b)

Figure 10.4   Sex and the two-career family. (a) Research indicates that marital/sexual relationships do not suffer if the woman works outside the home. (b) However, for those working 60 or more hours per week, some experts are concerned because these workaholics literally take their work to bed with them.

affair. In addition, researchers measured a variety of personality, mate value, and relationship characteristics. Among the personality variables, high scorers on narcissism and impulsiveness gave a higher probability of infidelity. Characteristics of the relationship associated with greater likelihood of infidelity included reports of conflict, especially that the partner sexualized others, engaged in sexual withholding, and abused alcohol. Finally, among both men and women, dissatisfaction with the marriage and with marital sex was associated with susceptibility to infidelity.

The role of dissatisfaction with the relationship is obvious in this explanation for a serious affair. "I'm definitely not looking for more sex. The affair I'm having is for emotional reasons. Freddie [her husband] is very self-centered. He's not an emotional support. He's distant, and we have nothing in common" (Maurer, 1994, p. 391).

How would you know if your partner was being emotionally or sexually unfaithful? Researchers asked those two questions of undergraduates (Shackelford & Buss, 1997). The participants identified 170 behaviors they thought would be cues of infidelity. In a subsequent study, one-half of a similar sample was asked how likely it is that, if the behavior occurred, the partner was being emotionally/sexually unfaithful. The other half was asked how likely it was that, if the partner was being unfaithful, the behavior would occur. Cues thought to be associated with sexual infidelity included physical signs (partner contracts STI), changes in "normal" sexual behavior with partner, increased or decreased sexual interest, and partner discloses the infidelity. Emotional infidelity was evidenced by expressions of relationship dissatisfaction, emotional disengagement from one's partner, inconsiderateness, being angry and critical toward one's partner, and acting guilty.

Our awareness of the possibility of infidelity sometimes leads us to engage in behaviors designed to preserve the relationship, or *mate retention tactics* (Buss & Shackelford, 1997a). Such tactics may be elicited by our own fear that the partner is losing interest or is dissatisfied, or because we observe some cues to infidelity. Members of the sample of 107 married couples described earlier were given a list of 104 mate-retention behaviors and asked how often they had performed each in the past year. There were marked gender differences in the reported actions. Men reported greater use of resources display (giving her money) and more frequent submission to the partner. Women reported more frequent use of enhancing their appearance or attractiveness and use of

possessive verbal statements. Evolutionary theory predicts that we make greater effort to retain mates who have greater reproductive value. Indeed, men married to young and physically attractive women reported greater use of these tactics, whereas women married to men who had higher incomes and engaged in resource display and social networking reported greater use of the tactics.

Extramarital Sex

Extramarital sex, or adultery, refers to sexual activity between a married person and someone other than that person's spouse. Extramarital sex can occur under several different circumstances (Pittman, 1993). Sometimes it is *accidental,* unintended and not characteristic of the person; it "just happens." One or both persons may be drunk, or having a bad day, or lonely. More serious is *romantic infidelity,* when the two people fall in love and consider or establish a long-term relationship; this situation can be very destructive to spouses, children, and careers. We noted earlier in this chapter that dissatisfaction with the relationship is especially likely to lead to romantic infidelity. A third type is the *open marriage,* in which the partners agree in advance that each may have sex with other persons. (In contrast, accidental and romantic infidelities begin without the spouse's knowledge, and may remain secret.) Finally, there are *philanderers—*gay, lesbian, or straight—who repeatedly engage in sexual liaisons outside their committed relationship. These men and women are not motivated by the desire for sexual gratification; they are searching for self-affirmation (Pittman, 1993).

How Many People Engage in Extramarital Sex?

Extramarital sexual activity is not as common as many people believe. According to the NHSLS, about 25 percent of the married men and 15 percent of the married women surveyed reported having engaged in extramarital sex at least once (Laumann et al., 1994). According to the NSFG, 7.6 percent of married men and 5.8 percent of married women ages 15–44 report more than one sexual partner in the preceding 12 months (Mosher et al., 2005).

According to the General Social Survey data, it varies by ethnicity: 23 percent of Blacks report extramarital sexual activity, compared to 16 percent of whites (Smith, 2003). Data from the

Extramarital sex: Sexual activity between a married person and someone other than that person's spouse; adultery.

NHSLS suggest that Hispanics have the same rate of extramarital sex as whites (Laumann et al., 1994). Extramarital sex is more common among persons with low incomes, and those who rarely or never attend religious services (Smith, 2003).

All these percentages are of persons who had sex with someone other than their spouse while married. At the time of the survey, some of these people were divorced. Others were remarried, perhaps for the second or third time. Thus we can ask a more specific question: How many people engage in extramarital sex during their first marriage? Data from the NHSLS (1994) indicate that from 10 to 23 percent of the men were unfaithful, compared to 6 to 12 percent of the women, depending on the person's age.

For women, at least, there is no indication that extramarital sex is casual or promiscuous. In one survey, of married women who had had extramarital sex, 43 percent had done so with only one partner (Blumstein & Schwartz, 1983).

Attitudes toward Extramarital Sex

While, as we have seen, attitudes toward premarital sex have changed substantially during the last several decades, attitudes toward extramarital sex have remained relatively unchanged; most people in the United States disapprove of extramarital sex. In 1998, according to the General Social Survey, 78 percent of adult Americans believed it is always wrong for a married person to have sexual relations with someone other than the marriage partner (National Opinion Research Center, 2004a). This statistic has increased somewhat since 1973, when it was 69 percent (Davis & Smith, 1991). Some people view unfaithfulness to a partner in any type of committed relationship as the equivalent of adultery. And some don't limit the term to cases of sexual intimacy. "Adultery is absolutely anything," said one young woman.

A study of couples seeking therapy compared couples in which one member admitted being unfaithful with couples who did not report infidelity (Atkins et al., 2005). Couples in which one (or both) admitted infidelity reported higher levels of dishonesty, more arguments about trust, and more time spent apart. Men who reported participation in affairs were older and more sexually dissatisfied.

Attitudes toward extramarital sex are not very good predictors of extramarital sexual behavior (Thompson, 1983). That is, the person who approves of extramarital sex is not more likely to actually engage in extramarital sex than the

Swinging: A form of extramarital sex in which married couples exchange partners with each other.

person who disapproves of it. Several other factors are related to attitudes toward sex outside one's primary relationship, including gender (men are more tolerant of it), education (those with more education are more accepting of it), and social class (upper-middle-class persons are more tolerant about it) (Willetts et al., 2004).

Because our society condemns extramarital sex, the individual who engages in it typically has confused, ambivalent feelings. A young married woman described her feelings:

> I don't like the illicit part of the affair. Mostly, it's a nuisance, because it's very difficult to find time, and I don't like lying to Freddie and sneaking around. If he wouldn't mind, I'd tell him. I don't think he would go for that. He'd show up with a gun. (Maurer, 1994, p. 393)

Swinging

One form of extramarital sex is **swinging,** in which married couples exchange partners with other couples, or engage in sexual activity with a third person, with the knowledge and consent of all involved.[2]

Swingers may find their partners in several ways. Often they advertise, in tabloid newspapers, in swingers' magazines such as the *Swing Times,* or on specialized bulletin boards and Web sites on the Internet. The following is an example:

> We are engaged bicouple lookin to meet bim, bif and bicouples for friendship and fun . . . we are into nudism, motorcycling, fishin, volleyball, pool and campin . . . she is 22 5'5 180# 38-d blond blue . . . he is 24 5'10 145# blond green 7″ and very thick. email: (www. . . /~gnkfoxx/nefriend.htm)

Swingers may also meet potential partners at swingers' clubs, parties, or resorts. Many of these places advertise in swingers' magazines and newsletters and are listed on specialized Web sites.

Several organizations and many local groups or couples sponsor parties. The date and general location of the party is publicized in magazines and on the Internet. Interested persons call or e-mail a contact person who screens them. If they pass, they are told the exact location of the party, often a private home or a hotel. A fee of $50 or more per couple may be charged for membership or entry to the party. The Lifestyle Organization in Southern

---

[2]Swinging was originally called *wife swapping.* However, because of the sexist connotations of that term and the fact that women were often as eager to swap husbands as men were to swap wives, the more equitable *mate swapping* or *swinging* was substituted.

California sponsors parties and dances at hotels and motels, and it publicizes the exact location in advance. It merely hosts the gathering. Couples who want to swing must connect with others on their own. They are free to rent a room in the hotel or motel or travel to some other location to engage in sexual activity.

A man who frequently hosts parties described what happens:

A lot of people have the idea that swinger parties are big orgies, where everybody jumps on everybody else. It isn't that way. People are selective, like they are anyplace else. [It starts with the eyes.] So if the interest continues from eye contact to talking, and to desire, there's touching. You just go with it. So you go from talking to touching, and at a swinging party you can go from touching to bed. (Maurer, 1994, p. 120)

Swinging may be closed or open. In *closed swinging,* the couples meet and exchange partners, and each pair goes off separately to a private place to have intercourse, returning to the meeting place at an agreed-upon time. In *open swinging,* the pairs get back together for sex in the same room for at least part of the time. In 75 percent of the cases, this includes the women having sex with each other, although male homosexual sex almost never occurs (Bartell, 1970; Gilmartin, 1975).

What kind of people are swingers? A review of 15 published studies, most of them involving small, convenience samples, concludes that the majority are upper or middle class, above average in education and income, and employed in the professions and in management (Jenks, 1998). Although one might expect them to be politically liberal, in one study 50 percent voted Republican and only 27 percent described themselves as politically liberal—the rest were moderate or conservative (Jenks, 1985). In this same sample, 93 percent were white; African Americans and other minorities are rare among swingers. The evidence indicates that at least two-thirds were raised in a religious home, but as adults they did not attend services and were not affiliated with a denomination.

Why do people become swingers? One of the main reasons is the desire for variety in sexual partners and experiences. Another reason given is pleasure or excitement, in part because exchanging partners is culturally forbidden. A third reason is to meet new people, which led one researcher to conclude that swingers must lead boring lives (Bartell, 1970). Researchers have noted that a major aspect of open swinging is the opportunity to

be a voyeur, to watch other people engage in sexual activity, which turns on some people (Jenks, 1998).

Swinging appears to involve a small minority of people. Published estimates range from less than 1 to 2 percent, although none of these are current.

Internet Infidelity

The proliferation of Web sites designed to connect people looking for romantic or sexual partners and chat rooms and other forms of digital communication has created new opportunities for people in committed relationships to be unfaithful. A **cyberaffair** is a romantic or sexual relationship initiated by online contact and maintained primarily via online communication (Young et al., 2000). Once a relationship is established, the online contacts can turn into mutual erotic dialogue, which may be accompanied by masturbation. In some cases, the participants arrange to meet face-to-face and may then engage in sexual intimacy.

There has been little empirical study of cyberaffairs. Professionals engaged in relationship and sexual counseling report working with couples whose problems include loss of trust by one person over another's online relationships. Some partners define such a relationship as infidelity even if it did not involve sexual conversation or activity. Note that these can be heterosexual or same-sex couples, who are married, cohabiting, or "committed" to each other. An online survey of Internet users, recruited by a banner that appeared on a major Web portal, included questions about *cybersex,* the practice of engaging in sexual talk online. One-third of 1,828 participants reported engaging in this activity; 46 percent of those reporting the activity—both men and women—said they were also in a committed relationship. Interestingly, those who reported engaging in cybersex reported more offline sexual activity as well (Daneback et al., 2004).

Equity and Extramarital Sex

Equity theory is a social–psychological theory designed to predict and explain many kinds of human relations (Hatfield et al., 1978). In particular, it has been applied to predicting patterns of extramarital sex (Hatfield, 1978).

The basic idea in equity theory is that in a relationship, people mentally tabulate their inputs to it and what they get out of it (benefits

Cyberaffair: A romantic or sexual relationship initiated by online contact and maintained primarily via online communication.
Equity theory: A theory that states that people mentally calculate the benefits and costs for them in a relationship; their behavior is then affected by whether they feel there is equity or inequity, and they will act to restore equity if there is inequity.

Focus: Milestones in Sex Research
Have Adults Changed Their Sexual Behavior in the AIDS Era?

I n June 2006 we acknowledged the twenty-fifth anniversary of the AIDS epidemic; in 1981 the first case of the illness was diagnosed. Beginning in 1985, the mass media published and broadcast a steady stream of features about AIDS, including its risks and recommendations for safer sex practices. Public health and community-based groups engaged in large-scale outreach efforts to educate gay men. Has all this publicity and activity had any impact on people's sexual behavior? (See Chapter 18 for a discussion of safer sex practices.)

In order to assess whether behavior has actually changed, we need longitudinal research, where the same people are surveyed or the same questions are asked of comparable samples over time. Unfortunately, there are few such studies; most of the data are from cross-sectional surveys.

If you ask adults whether they have changed their behavior because of AIDS, some say they have. Moreover, the percent saying yes has increased over time. In several surveys conducted between 1986 and 1988, 7 to 13 percent reported changing their behavior; in surveys conducted between 1989 and 1991, 14 to 23 percent said yes (Smith, 2003). In the representative sample interviewed by the NHSLS in 1992, 35 percent of the men and 25 percent of the women reported that they had changed their behavior (Feinleib & Michael, 2001). Men reported reducing their number of sexual partners (14 percent), increasing condom use (12 percent), and selecting partners more carefully (10 percent). Smaller percentages of women reported these same changes.

A review of three comparable surveys conducted in 1990, 1992, and 1996, with representative samples of heterosexual men and women ages 18 to 49, found a significant increase in condom use by at-risk persons (Catania et al., 2001). The largest increases were among African Americans and Hispanics.

Research shows that in the decade from 1985 to 1995 gay men showed substantial behavior change (Ehrhardt et al., 1991). Many gay men reduced the number of their sex partners, had fewer anonymous sexual encounters, and engaged less in anal intercourse or used condoms consistently. These changes, undertaken by both straights and gays, contributed to a decline in the number of new cases of AIDS each year from 150,000 in the mid-1980s to about 43,000 in 2002 (CDC, 2000b, 2003b). Furthermore, several studies suggest that some men and

or rewards); then they calculate whether these are equitable or not. In an equitable relationship between person A and person B, it would be true that

$$\text{Rewards}_A - \text{Inputs}_A = \text{Rewards}_B - \text{Inputs}_B$$

In a traditional marriage, the wife's inputs might include her beauty, keeping a charming house, cooking good meals, and so on. The husband's inputs might include his income and his pleasant temperament. His rewards from the relationship might include feeling proud when he is accompanied by his beautiful wife, enjoying her cooking, and so on. Notice that this is not an egalitarian relationship in the modern sense; however, it is an equitable relationship (as defined by equity theory) because both partners derive equal benefits from it.

According to equity theory, if individuals perceive a relationship as inequitable (if they feel they are not getting what they deserve), they become distressed. The more inequitable the relationship, the more distressed they feel. In order to relieve the distress, they make attempts to restore equity in the relationship. For example, people who feel they are putting too much into a relationship and not getting enough out of it might let their appearance go, or not work as hard to earn money, or refuse sexual access, or refuse to contribute to conversations. The idea is that such actions will restore equity.

If these equity processes do occur, they might help to explain patterns of extramarital sex. That is, engaging in extramarital sex would be a way of restoring equity in an inequitable relationship (Figure 10.5, p. 272). Social psychologist Elaine Hatfield (1978) tested this notion. Her prediction was that people who felt underbenefited in their marriages (that is, they felt that there was an inequity and that they were not getting as much as they deserved) would be the ones to engage in extramarital sex. Confirming this notion, people who felt they were underbenefited began engaging in extramarital sex earlier in their marriages and had more extramarital partners than did people who felt equitably treated or overbenefited. Apparently, feeling that one is not getting all one deserves in a

women who are diagnosed with HIV/AIDS become celibate—that is, live without a romantic or intimate relationship (Siegel & Scrimshaw, 2003). This reduces the likelihood of transmission to uninfected persons.

Perhaps because of the decline, and because of the effectiveness of the antiretroviral therapies in reducing the impact of the illness, there has been less media attention to HIV and AIDS in recent years, and perhaps less effort by public health and medical personnel. There are signs that this recent complacency has led to a slowing of the earlier gains.

Substantial numbers of heterosexuals are not practicing safe sex. As part of its continuing surveillance of HIV infection/AIDS, the Centers for Disease Control conducts a telephone survey of civilian, noninstitutionalized adults. In 1997, the survey included questions on risky behavior in 23 states. The median prevalence of having multiple sex partners in the preceding year was 11 percent (range: 5 percent to 18 percent); the median prevalence of condom use at last sex was 65 percent (range: 53 percent to 79 percent) (CDC, 2001).

As the number of new AIDS cases has declined, an increasing percentage of the new cases are among minority persons. In 2005 there were 40,608 new cases in the United States, 73 percent involving men. Of these, 34 percent were white, 44 percent Black, and 20 percent Hispanic or Latino. New cases among women were even more disproportionately among Blacks (66 percent) compared with whites (16 percent) and Hispanic/Latina (16 percent)

(CDC, 2007). Rates of several sexually transmitted infections (STIs) declined in Canada through 1997 but then increased (Patrick et al., 2000). The increase parallels a decline in safe-sex campaigns and sex education programs, suggesting that continuing efforts to increase awareness of the risk of HIV/AIDS and other STIs and the importance of safer-sex practices are very important to efforts to control these illnesses. In the United States, these efforts must target minority youth.

Research evaluating various intervention programs provides a solid base for designing and implementing such programs. Community-based programs targeting specific groups have demonstrated significant effects on condom use and safer sex (Ross & Williams, 2002). The use of opinion leaders and role models and the delivery of the intervention by peer educators are associated with the success of such programs. Also important to success is the establishment of ties to the target community and a "buy-in" by the community. Clinic-based programs can also be successful in increasing consistent condom use (Fortenberry, 2002). Extensive, personal counseling can lead to some reduction in the rates of new STIs. Thus we can further reduce the incidence of HIV/AIDS, but it requires continuing media attention and redoubled efforts by public health and medical personnel, with the active participation of the community.

marriage is related to engaging in extramarital sex. (As an aside, equitable marriages were rated as happier than inequitable ones.)

Equity theory includes rewards and costs of all kinds, as indicated by our examples. The *interpersonal exchange model* focuses on the rewards and costs associated with the sexual relationship (Lawrence & Byers, 1995). Research based on this model assesses the perceived rewards and costs, the perceived rewards and costs relative to what one expects, and the perceived rewards and costs relative to one's partner. In a longitudinal study of 244 adults in heterosexual relationships, all six of these measures were related to the participants' reported sexual satisfaction with their relationships three months later. The results also indicated that relationship satisfaction was associated with sexual satisfaction. A study of 193 married Chinese men and 231 women living in Beijing and Shanghai yielded similar results (Renaud & Byers, 1997). In addition to the association of rewards and costs with sexual satisfaction, greater sexual satisfaction was related to higher frequencies of affectionate

and sexual behavior, and fewer sexual concerns and problems.

Clearly, our assessments of the rewards and costs in our intimate relationships are associated with both our satisfaction with those relationships and the likelihood that we will become involved in extramarital (or extrarelationship) sexuality.

Evolution and Extramarital Sex

Extramarital sex is not unique to the United States. In fact, it occurs in virtually every society. When sociobiologists observe a behavior that occurs in all societies, they are inclined to explain that behavior in terms of evolutionary processes.

From an evolutionary perspective, the genes that enable their bearers to produce larger numbers of offspring are more likely to survive from one generation to the next than genes that don't. A man who mates with one woman for life could produce a maximum of 6 to 12 offspring, depending on the length of time infants are breast-fed, postpartum sex taboos, and so on. If that same man

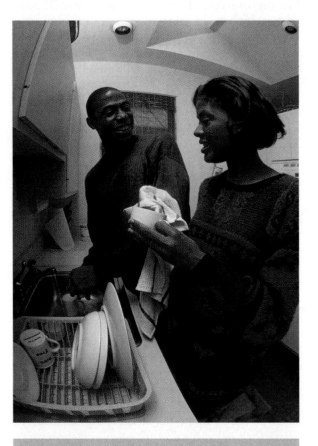

Figure 10.5   Equitable sharing of household tasks in a marriage. According to equity theory, if a person perceives that the marital relationship is inequitable and feels underbenefited, he or she is more likely to engage in extramarital sex.

that enhanced her offspring's chances for survival. Second, adultery could serve as "insurance"; if her husband died, she would have another man to turn to for food, shelter, and protection. Third, a woman married to a timid, unproductive hunter could "upgrade her genetic line" by mating with another man. Finally, having children with multiple partners increases the genetic diversity of one's offspring, increasing the chances that some of them will survive. A study of 48 couples found that as the number of similar genes at the MHC complex increased, the number of extra-pair sexual partners they reported increased (Garver-Apgar et al., 2006). Given the lower status of women in most societies, a married woman who had extramarital liaisons would have had to be careful; if caught she risked death.

Genetic research on species that appear to be monogamous reveals that some of the offspring being raised by a male–female pair were fathered by another male. These tests also reveal that females paired with lesser-quality males engage in extrapair mating, whereas females paired with high-quality males do not (Morell, 1998). These results provide solid support for the sociobiological hypothesis about the adaptive value of female infidelity.

According to this sociobiological perspective, then, extramarital sex occurs because some men and women carry in their genetic makeup something that motivates them to be unfaithful. If there are environments in which adultery is adaptive in contemporary society, people with those genes will have a selective advantage.

Polyamory

Polyamory is "the nonpossessive, honest, responsible, and ethical philosophy and practice of loving multiple people simultaneously" (Ve Ard & Veaux, 2003). There are several forms of such relationships, including the *intentional family*, involving three or more persons; the *group relationship*, with committed, loving relationships involving three or more partners; and *group marriage*, involving three or more persons. One specific type of group relationship is a triad involving a married couple and an additional man or woman who share sexual intimacy; the third person and one or both members of the couple may be bisexual. Other arrangements involve two or more men and two or more women. Unlike the extramarital affair, there is (ideally) full disclosure of the network of relationships to all participants. Unlike swinging, the emphasis is on long-term intimate relationships.

occasionally has sex with a second woman (or a series of other women), he could produce 12 to 24 offspring. We think you get the picture. Men who seek out the "other woman" will produce more offspring, who in turn will produce more offspring carrying the genetic makeup that leads to extrarelationship liaisons (Fisher, 1992).

What about women? They cannot increase the number of their offspring by increasing the number of their sexual partners. However, there are ways in which adultery might have been biologically adaptive for women in the past (Greiling & Buss, 2000). First, sexual liaisons with other men might have enabled a woman to acquire extra goods and services

Polyamory: The nonpossessive, honest, responsible, and ethical philosophy and practice of loving multiple people simultaneously.

Research involving in-depth interviews with 20 men and 20 women provided information about participants in one geographic area (Sheff, 2005). Those interviewed were in their mid thirties to late fifties, usually college educated, and employed in professional occupations; they were overwhelmingly white. Their high social status and access to resources may be a prerequisite for participating in the polyamory lifestyle. The interviewees noted that persons outside the polyamorous community, including members of their family of origin (parents, siblings), often react negatively and with hostility toward community members. Their status insulates them against some potential sanctions.

Women involved in polyamory report expanding their familial, gender, and sexual roles. For example, some of these women rejected monogamy in favor of a network of intimate partner relationships. With respect to gender, the women adopted a much more assertive style in their relationships with men. In the realm of sexuality, the women often recognized their high sex drive, the emotional and sexual value of intimacy with other women, and their bisexual interests or identities. Moving away from traditional roles was reported to be both liberating and frightening; creating new roles was often difficult.

In multiethnic settings such as Hong Kong, polyamorous relationships may cross ethnic, racial, and social class boundaries (Sik Ying Ho, 2006). For example, a 37-year-old woman described concurrent sexual relationships with both men and women of different races and social classes. Such relationships provide novel experiences that may both be anxiety provoking and expand one's understanding of sexual diversity.

Postmarital Sex

From the point of view of developmental psychologists, the sexual relationship in a second union, perhaps following a divorce or the death of one's partner, is especially interesting. In what ways is it the same, and how does it differ from the sexual relationship in the first marriage? It represents the blending of things that are unique and consistent about the person with things that are unique to the new situation and new partner. As we develop sexually throughout the life span, these two strands continue to be intertwined—the developmental continuities (the things that are us and always will be) and the developmental changes (things that differ at various times in our lives, either because we are older or have experienced more, or because our partner or the situation is different).

The Divorced and the Widowed

Divorced and widowed people are in a somewhat unusual situation in that they are used to regular sexual expression and suddenly find themselves in a situation in which the socially acceptable outlet for that expression—marital sex—is no longer available. Partly recognizing this dilemma, our society places few restrictions on postmarital sexual activity, although it is not as approved as marital sex.

Most divorced women, but fewer widowed women, return to having an active sex life. The NHSLS found that 46 percent of divorced and widowed men and 58 percent of divorced and widowed women had sex a few times per year or not at all (Laumann et al., 1994). In another study, 77 percent of the widowed had been sexually abstinent in the last year, compared with 29 percent of the divorced (Smith, 2003).

The lower incidence of postmarital sex among widows, compared with divorced women, is due in part to the fact that widows are, on the average, older than divorced women; but even when matched for age, widows are still less likely than divorcees to engage in postmarital sex. There are probably several reasons for this (Gebhard, 1968). Widows are more likely to be financially secure than divorced women and therefore have less motivation for engaging in sex as a prelude to remarriage. They have the continuing social support system of in-laws and friends, and so they are less motivated to seek new friendships. There is also a belief that a widow should be loyal to her dead husband, and having a sexual relationship with another man is viewed as disloyalty. Many widows believe this or tell themselves that they will "never find another one like him."

Divorced women face complex problems of adjustment (Song, 1991). These problems may include reduced income, a lower perceived standard of living, and reduced availability of social support. Some divorced men face similar problems. These problems may increase the motivation to establish a new long-term relationship.

Widowed and divorced women who have postmarital sex often begin a relationship within one year of the end of the marriage. The evidence suggests that these are long-term relationships. According to a study of a national sample of adults, 74 percent of the divorced men and women reported either zero or one sexual partner in the year prior to the survey (Stack & Gundlach, 1992).

Divorced men were more sexually active than were divorced women. The average frequency of intercourse reported was twice a month. A survey of professional women who held teaching and administrative posts in academic institutions found that divorced women had a larger number of sexual partners and more frequent activity than their never-married counterparts (Davidson & Darling, 1988).

Earlier in this chapter we noted that substantial numbers of men and women cohabit. Like marriages, these relationships break up. What are the similarities and differences between formerly married and formerly cohabiting men and women? To answer this question, researchers used the NHSLS data to analyze the rate of acquisition of new partners following the dissolution of a relationship (Wade & DeLamater, 2002). The results indicate that these newly single men and women do not acquire new sexual partners at a high rate, and there were no significant differences between formerly married and formerly cohabiting men and women. Newly single persons acquire new partners at a significantly higher rate than single, never-married persons in the year following a breakup. Men with custody of children and men and women with low incomes have higher rates of new partner acquisition, perhaps reflecting the impact of instability associated with the dissolution. The results suggest that the postdissolution experience is similar across various demographic groups; given the high rates of breaking up in U.S. society, dissolution may be considered a significant life stage with its own specific characteristics.

Sex and Seniors

When Freud suggested that young children, even infants, have sexual thoughts and feelings, his ideas met with considerable resistance. When, 50 years later, researchers began to suggest that elderly men and women also have sexual thoughts and feelings, there was similar resistance (Pfeiffer et al., 1968). This section deals with the sexual behavior of older men and women, the physical changes they undergo, and the attitudes that influence them.

Physical Changes in Women
Biological Changes

The *climacteric* is a period lasting about 15 or 20 years (from about ages 45 to 60) during which a

> **Menopause:** The cessation of menstruation.

woman's body makes the transition from being able to reproduce to not being able to reproduce; the climacteric is marked particularly by a decline in the functioning of the ovaries. But climacteric changes occur in many other body tissues and systems as well. **Menopause** (the "change of life," the "change") refers to one specific event in this process, the cessation of menstruation; this occurs, on average, over a 2-year period beginning at around age 50 (with a normal menopause occurring anywhere between the ages of 40 and 60).

Biologically, as a woman grows older, the pituitary continues a normal output of FSH and LH; however, as the ovaries age, they become less able to respond to the pituitary hormones. In addition, the brain—including the hypothalamus–pituitary unit—ages (Lamberts et al., 1997). With the aging of the ovaries, there is an accompanying decline in the output of their two major products: eggs and the sex hormones estrogen and progesterone (Figure 10.6).

Physical symptoms of menopause may include "hot flashes" or "hot flushes," headaches, and dizziness. For some women, a long-range effect of the decline in estrogen levels is *osteoporosis* (porous and brittle bones). The hot flash is probably the best known of the symptoms. Typically it is described as a sudden wave of heat from the waist up. The woman may get red and perspire a lot; when the flush goes away, she may feel chilled and sometimes shiver. The flashes may last from a few seconds to half an hour and occur several or many times a day. They may also occur at night, causing insomnia; the resulting perspiration can actually soak the sheets.

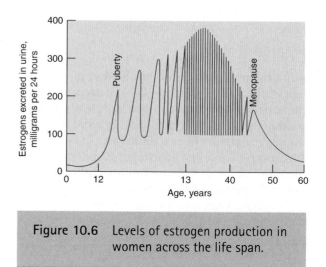

Figure 10.6   Levels of estrogen production in women across the life span.

Do all women experience these menopausal symptoms? The Massachusetts Women's Health Study (Avis & McKinlay, 1995; McKinlay et al., 1992) followed a large sample of middle-aged women for several years, beginning when they were pre-menopausal and continuing through menopause to the postmenopausal period. The peak in report-ing of hot flashes and night sweats occurred just be-fore the onset of menopause, with 50 percent of women reporting them. About one-quarter of the sample (23 percent) did not report a hot flash at any of the interview times. Furthermore, 69 percent of the women reported not being bothered by the hot flashes and night sweats. So about one-quarter of women do not experience hot flashes and 50 to 75 percent of women do, but the majority report that they are not bothered by them.

Hormone-replacement therapy (HRT) may be helpful to many menopausal women, particularly for relief of physical discomfort such as hot flashes and some sexual problems such as lack of vaginal lubrication. The treatment today often includes both estrogen and progesterone, and testosterone may be added as well. The therapy is somewhat controversial, and its benefits need to be weighed against its potential risks. HRT conveys some benefits. It protects women from osteoporosis (which may cause a broken hip leading to death in an elderly woman) (Kamel et al., 2001). However, HRT increases the risk of breast cancer and en-dometrial cancer (Chen et al., 2002; Rosenberg, 1993; Steinberg et al., 1991).

In a startling move in 2002, the National Insti-tutes of Health (NIH) stopped a large, national clinical trial of Prempro with menopausal women (Enserink, 2002). Prempro contains a combination of estrogen and progesterone. The NIH did not stop the other treatment group in the study, who were taking estrogen only. The reason for the dra-matic action was that women in the Prempro group were having a higher incidence of heart at-tack, stroke, breast cancer, and blood clots, com-pared with the placebo control group. That is, Prempro was increasing rather than decreasing the rates of heart attack and stroke. Does this mean that all women should stop HRT? Not necessarily. The trial was of a particular drug, Prempro. Some other formulation of estrogen and progesterone might be fine. The estrogen-only group was doing well, so no concerns were raised about estrogen (ERT). The study, which was investigating the long-term use of HRT, stopped the Prempro group at five years. The short-term use of HRT for one or two years is probably safe for most women. Moreover, the increase in risk from Prempro might seem

small to women who are having serious difficulty with menopausal symptoms. The study found that, per 10,000 women on Prempro, the increased risk was 7 more women with heart disease compared with the control group.

The picture on ERT and HRT is complex and speaks to the importance of individualized evalua-tion and treatment for each woman, taking into ac-count her particular pattern of symptoms and how distressed she is by them.

Sexuality and Menopause

During the climacteric, physical changes occur in the vagina. The lack of estrogen causes the vagina to become less acidic, which leaves it more vulnerable to infections. Estrogen is also responsi-ble for maintaining the mucous membranes of the vaginal walls. With a decline in estrogen, there is a decline in vaginal lubrication during arousal, and the vaginal walls become less elastic. Either or both of these may make intercourse painful for the woman. Several remedies are available, including hormone-replacement therapy, the use of arti-ficial lubricants, and estrogen creams for the vagina by prescription. On the other hand, some women report that intercourse is even better after menopause, when the fear of pregnancy no longer inhibits them.

Experts reviewing the research on women's sex-uality during and after menopause have reached the following conclusions (Dennerstein et al., 2003; McCoy, 1996, 1997): (1) The majority of women continue to engage in sexual activity and enjoy it both during and after menopause. (2) There is some decline in sexual functioning, on average, during menopause and particularly after the last period. (3) Estrogen is related to the decline in sex-ual functioning, in part because low estrogen levels cause vaginal dryness. There is some evidence that higher estrogen levels are associated with better sexual functioning. (4) Testosterone is also impor-tant; a woman's sexual desire may decline as her levels of ovarian testosterone decline. Testosterone replacement therapy may be helpful in such cases (Warnock et al., 1997).

One study analyzed the data from an AARP sur-vey of 1,384 persons age 45 and older (DeLamater & Moorman, 2007). The AARP survey, discussed in more detail later in the chapter, included questions about various factors that might affect the fre-quency of sexual behavior, including diagnosed physical and emotional illnesses, use of medica-tions, attitudes toward sexuality, and the presence of a sexual partner. Physical limitations such as prior stroke and arthritis, emotional problems

Figure 10.7   Affection, romance, and sex are not just for the young.

such as depression, and use of various medications can interfere with sexual activity. While both men and women reported these conditions, they were relatively uncommon and were not significantly related to the frequency of oral sexual activity or vaginal intercourse (Figure 10.7). The factors that were significantly related were high scores on an index of sexual desire (frequent sexual thoughts, desire), positive attitudes toward sex for oneself, and the presence of a partner with no limitations related to sexuality. Men and women who reported that their partner had limitations that interfered with sexual expression were significantly more likely to report masturbating.

Some people believe that having a **hysterectomy** means the end of a woman's sex life. In fact, sex hormone production is not affected as long as the ovaries are not removed (surgical removal of the ovaries is called **oophorectomy** or ovariectomy). The majority of women report that a hysterectomy had no effect on their sex lives. However, approximately one-third of women who have had hysterectomies report

Hysterectomy (hiss–tur–EK–tuh–mee): Surgical removal of the uterus.
Oophorectomy (OH–uh–fuh–REK–tuh–mee): Surgical removal of the ovaries.

problems with sexual response (Zussman et al., 1981). There are two possible physiological causes for these problems. If the ovaries have been removed, hormonal changes may be responsible; specifically, the ovaries produce androgens, and they may play a role in sexual response. The other possibility is that the removal of the cervix, and possibly the rest of the uterus, is an anatomical problem if the cervix serves as a trigger for orgasm.

Changes in Men

Testosterone production declines gradually over the years (Schiavi, 1990) (see Figure 10.8). Vascular diseases such as hardening of the arteries are increasingly common with age in men, but good circulation is essential to erection (Riportella-Muller, 1989). A major change is that erections occur more slowly. It is important for men to know that this is a perfectly natural slowdown so that they will not jump to the conclusion that they are developing an erection problem. It is also important for partners to know about this so that they will use effective techniques of stimulating the man and not mistake slowness for lack of interest.

The refractory period lengthens with age; thus for an elderly man there may be a period of 24 hours after an orgasm during which he cannot get an erection. (Note that women do not undergo a similar change; most women do not enter into a refractory period and are still capable of multiple

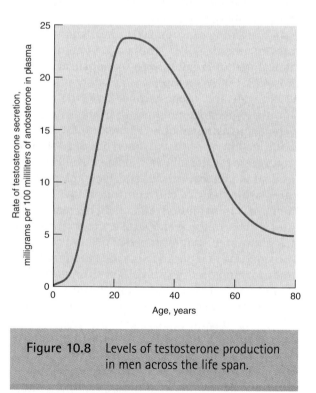

Figure 10.8   Levels of testosterone production in men across the life span.

orgasm at age 80.) Other signs of sexual excitement—the sex flush and muscle tension—diminish with age.

The volume of the ejaculate gradually decreases, and the force of ejaculation lessens. The testes become somewhat smaller, but viable sperm are produced by even very old men. Ninety-year-old men have been known to father children.

One advantage is that middle-aged and elderly men may have better control over orgasm than young men; thus they can prolong coitus and may be better sexual partners.

A study of healthy men ages 45 to 74, all married, assessed their biological, psychological, and behavioral functioning (Schiavi et al., 1994). Satisfaction with sexual functioning was significantly related to whether the man had erectile difficulties. Men who reported erectile difficulties were less satisfied with their sexual functioning. General satisfaction was related negatively to erectile problems, and positively to sexual information and marital adjustment. Accurate information is important, because it may result in more realistic expectations for sexual performance.

Some people believe that prostate surgery or removal of the prostate, **prostatectomy,** means the end of a man's sex life. It is true that the volume of the ejaculate will decrease. Prostatectomy can cause damage to the nerves supplying the penis, creating erectile problems. In other cases, retrograde ejaculation may result. Whether there are such problems depends on which of several available methods of surgery is used.

In sum, the evidence suggests that there need be no time limit on sexual expression for either men or women.

A 73-year-old man reported,

> I can't begin to tell you how happy I am. I am married to a wonderful woman who loves me as much as I love her. My children gave me a hard time of it at first, especially because she is a bit younger than me. [My son] was telling me that marrying again and *trying* to have a lot of sex—imagine that, saying to me *trying* to have sex—could be dangerous to the marriage. So, I said to him with a straight face, "Do you think she'll survive it?" He was so shocked, he laughed. (Janus & Janus, 1993, p. 8)

Attitudes about Sex and the Elderly

Our society has a negative attitude toward sexual expression among the elderly.[3] Somehow it seems indecent for two 70-year-old people to have sex with each other, and even more indecent for a 70-year-old to masturbate. These negative attitudes become particularly obvious in nursing homes, where staff members may frown on sexual activity among the residents. Somehow what is "virility" at 25 becomes "lechery" at 75.

Cross-cultural research indicates that the sexual behavior of the elderly is related to these cultural expectations (Winn & Newton, 1982). The elderly continue to be sexually active in 70 percent of societies and in precisely those societies where they are expected to be sexually active. Indeed, in 22 percent of societies, women are expected to become more uninhibited about sexuality when they become old.

Why does our society have such negative attitudes toward sex among the elderly? In part, these attitudes are due to the fact that ours is a youth-oriented culture. We value youth, and the physical characteristics that are considered "sexy" are youthful ones, such as a trim, firm body and smooth skin. It is therefore hard to believe that someone with old, wrinkled skin could be sexually active. According to one youthful-looking 59-year-old woman,

> No one looks at me today with any kind of sexual interest. I mean, I don't even get the time of day from any man. I'm an older woman. I want men to be aggressive now. I'm not going to approach a man, because I'm afraid to be rejected. So I've just given up. (Maurer, 1994, p. 475)

A study of heterosexual, midlife women assessed menopause status, self-rated attractiveness, sexual desire, and frequency of sexual intercourse (Koch et al., 2005). Regardless of menopause status, women who perceived themselves as less attractive than 10 years earlier reported a decline in both sexual desire and sexual behavior. Women who perceived themselves as more attractive reported an increase in sexual desire, frequency of sex, and frequency of orgasm.

Our negative attitudes may be a holdover from the belief that sex was for reproductive purposes only—and those past the age of reproduction should therefore not engage in it (Pfeiffer, 1975). The incest taboo may also be involved in our negative attitudes. We tend to identify old people with our parents or grandparents and find it hard to think of them as sexual beings. This attitude is encouraged by the fact that many parents take great pains to hide their sexual activity from their children.

These attitudes affect the way elderly people are treated, and the

Prostatectomy (pros-tuh-TEK-tuh-mee): Surgical removal of the prostate.

[3]These attitudes are reflected in jokes such as "Once you're 80, your sex life is less like the Fourth of July and more like Thanksgiving."

elderly may even hold such attitudes themselves. One remedy that has been proposed for these negative attitudes is a "coming out of the closet." As one 67-year-old commented,

> The common view that the aging and aged are nonsexual, I believe, can only be corrected by a dramatic and courageous process—the *coming-out-of-the-closet* of sexually active older women and men, so that people can see for themselves what the later years are really like. (Brecher, 1984, p. 21)

Various specific misunderstandings may influence sexuality. For example, a man might believe that sex will precipitate a heart attack or, if he has already had a heart attack, that it will bring on another one. Although Masters and Johnson found that the heart rate accelerated during sexual intercourse, another study showed that the mean heart rate during orgasm was only 117 beats per minute, which is about that attained during many common forms of daily exercise (Hellerstein & Friedman, 1969). This rate is about the equivalent of climbing two flights of stairs at a moderate pace. Thus the demands of sex on the heart are not unreasonable. A study of patients who had had a heart attack questioned them about their activities immediately prior to the attack and in the year prior to the attack (Muller et al., 1996). The results indicate that the increase in risk caused by sexual activity is one chance in one million for a healthy individual. Furthermore, the relative risk is no greater in patients with a history of cardiac disease.

Some men also mistakenly believe that sexual activity saps their "vital strength." In some cases men may believe that they can have only a fixed number of orgasms during their lifetimes (as a woman is born with a fixed number of ova) and therefore adopt a strategy of saving them now so that they will have some left later on. One woman wrote,

> My husband has reached the age of sixty-five. He has decided that, in order to ensure a longer life and health, he will no longer engage in sex activity. He is convinced that intercourse and the emission of semen are quite debilitating, particularly in his years. (I. Rubin, 1966, p. 258)

Ideas such as this, as well as factors such as illness or hospitalization, may lead to a period of sexual inactivity. But being sexually inactive is one of the most effective ways of diminishing sexuality. Masters and Johnson emphasized that two factors are critical in maintaining sexual capacity in old age:

1. *Good physical and mental health.* An excellent study confirms this notion (Persson, 1980). A representative sample of 70-year-olds in one town in Sweden were selected, and 85 percent agreed to participate in the detailed interviews. In the entire sample, 46 percent of the men and 16 percent of the women still had sexual intercourse; when only those who were currently married were considered, the figures rose to 52 percent for men and 36 percent for women. For both men and women, those who continued to have sexual intercourse had better mental health as rated by a psychiatrist and more positive attitudes toward sexual activity among the aged.

2. *Regularity of sexual expression.* As noted earlier, evidence exists that some physical changes of the sex organs in old age are related to sexual inactivity. As the saying goes, "If you don't use it, you lose it." In fact, a longitudinal study suggests that, for men, frequency of orgasm is positively associated with longevity. The study involved men aged 45 to 59. At the beginning of the study, the men completed a standard medical history and a questionnaire that assessed sexual behavior. Ten years later, the researchers found out who had died, and compared their questionnaire answers with those of the survivors. Men who reported less than one orgasm per month at the beginning of the study were more than twice as likely to die as the men who reported two orgasms per month (Smith et al., 1997).

Apparently some elderly people have caught on to this fact. As one 80-year-old husband said of his relationship with his 75-year-old wife,

> My wife and I both believe that keeping active sexually delays the aging process . . . if we are troubled with an erection or lubrication, we turn to oral methods or masturbation of each other. We keep our interest alive by a great deal of caressing and fondling of each other's genitals. We feel it is much better to wear out than to rust out. (Brecher, 1984, p. 33)

Reformers urge us to change our attitudes about sex and the senior citizen. Nursing homes particularly need to revise their practices (Figure 10.9); even such simple changes as knocking before entering a resident's room would help (people masturbate, you know). Other reforms would include making provisions for spouses to stay

Figure 10.9 Romance is important even for nursing-home residents.

overnight and allowing couples—married or unmarried—to share a bedroom. Indeed, some experts even advocate sex as a form of therapy for persons in nursing homes (Rice, 1974):

> Sex relations can provide a much needed and highly effective resource in the later years of life, when so often men face the loss of their customary prestige and self-confidence and begin to feel old, sometimes long before they have begun to age significantly. The premature cessation of sexual functioning may accelerate physiological and psychological aging since disuse of any function usually leads to concomitant changes in other capacities. After menopause, women may find that continuation of sexual relations provides a much needed psychological reinforcement, a feeling of being needed and of being capable of receiving love and affection and renewing the intimacy they earlier found desirable and reassuring. (Frank, 1961, pp. 177–178)

Sexual Behavior of the Elderly

While sexual behavior and sexual interest do decline somewhat with age, there are still substantial numbers of elderly men and women who have active sex lives, even in their eighties. In a sample of healthy 80- to 102-year-olds, 62 percent of the men and 30 percent of the women reported that they still engaged in sexual intercourse (Bretschneider & McCoy, 1988). There does not seem to be any age beyond which all people are sexually inactive.

Some older people do, for various reasons, stop having intercourse after a certain age. For women, this occurs most often in the late fifties and early sixties, while it occurs somewhat later for men

(Pfeiffer et al., 1968). Contrary to what one might expect, though, when a couple stop having intercourse, the husband is most frequently the cause; both wives and husbands agree that this is true. In some cases, the husband has died (and we can hardly blame him for that), but even excluding those cases, the husband is still most frequently the cause. Thus the decline in female sexual expression with age may be directly related to the male's decline. Death of the spouse is more likely to put an end to intercourse for women than it is for men, in part because women are less likely to remarry (Riportella-Muller, 1989).

One of the most important influences on sexuality in the elderly, then, is that there are far more elderly women than elderly men. Because of both men's earlier mortality and their preference for younger women, elderly women are more likely to be living alone and to have less access to sexual partners. For example, in 1999, among those 75 and over, 71 percent of the men were married and likely living with their spouse, compared with only 31 percent of the women (U.S. Bureau of the Census, 2000b). Some innovative solutions have been proposed, such as elderly women forming lesbian relationships.

The best survey to date on the sexuality of people over 50 was conducted by a research firm for the American Association of Retired Persons (1999). The AARP staff designed a questionnaire focused on the role of sexuality in the lives of older adults. A research firm that maintains a large panel of households selected 3,450 panel members age 45 and older, telephoned them, and invited them to participate in the study. A questionnaire was mailed to the 1,709 persons who agreed to participate; 1,384 persons returned completed questionnaires. The result is a volunteer sample, with certain likely biases. Specifically, elderly people who are sick or in care facilities, or whose sight has failed, are highly unlikely to have completed the survey. Thus, we must regard this as a survey of elderly people who are above average in health, activity, and intelligence, and who are doubtless more sexually active than some other elderly persons. Nonetheless, it is a very important source of information about sex and the elderly, a topic about which there is a shortage of knowledge.

Some statistics from the survey are included in Table 10.3. They are presented by age group; as we would expect, the numbers of participants decline as age advances. Note that women over 60 are much less likely to have a sexual partner available, so they report much lower frequencies of partnered activities. About 24 percent of the women

Table 10.3   Sexual Activity in a Sample of Persons Age 45 and Over

	45 to 59	60 to 74	75 and over
Women	**368**	**253**	**119**
Have a sexual partner	77.8%	52.6%	21.4%
Feel sexual desire daily	8.4	1.6	0.6
Have sexual intercourse at least once a week*	49.6	24.2	6.6
Have oral sex at least weekly*	19.5	2.2	0.8
Masturbate once a week or more often*	4.5	2.0	0.6
Always experience an orgasm from sexual activity	31.6	26.0	25.0
Men	**341**	**205**	**90**
Have a sexual partner	84.2%	79.2%	57.9%
Feel sexual desire daily	39.7	13.9	3.4
Have sexual intercourse at least once a week*	54.8	30.9	19.1
Have oral sex at least weekly*	20.1	6.5	8.8
Masturbate once a week or more often*	33.5	14.2	5.2
Always experience an orgasm from sexual activity	76.6	57.0	48.1

*Within the preceding six months.
Source: AARP (1999).

and 31 percent of the men ages 60 to 74 have intercourse at least weekly. More than 25 percent of the women and half the men at all ages report that they always have an orgasm from sexual activity.

In spite of the differences in frequency of activity, men and women were equally likely to report that they were satisfied with their sexual lives. Among 45- to 59-year-olds, 63 and 61 percent reported satisfaction, while among 60- to 74-year-olds, 50 percent said they were satisfied. About 36 percent of men and women 75 or older were satisfied. Asked what changes in their lives would increase their satisfaction, men and women

45 to 59 were most likely to say less stress and more free time, while older men said better health for themselves and their partners. Women 60 years of age or older said better health for their partners and finding a partner. Thus, these results illustrate the fact that among many older couples it is the health of the male that determines sexual activity, and that for many older women the problem is absence of a partner.

We see, then, that among older people who are healthy and have regular opportunities for sexual expression, sexual activity continues well past 70 years of age.

SUMMARY

Sexuality continues to develop throughout the life span. It may be expressed in singlehood, cohabitation, marriage, extramarital relationships, relationships following divorce, or in a variety of contexts as the individual ages.

Young adults grow toward sexual maturity. Many do so in the context of a single relationship that results in marriage. Others are involved in two or more relationships before they begin to live with or marry someone. Never-married people over 25 may find themselves part of the "singles scene." Blacks are more likely to remain single than whites.

Cohabitation is a stage that up to 40 percent of people experience. The time couples spend living together varies from a few months to several years.

Sixty percent of cohabiting couples marry. Some cohabiting couples have children, either together or with previous partners. Men and women who are living together engage in sexual activity more often, on average, than those who are married or dating.

Marriage represents a major turning point as couples face new responsibilities and problems, and try to find time for each other. Married couples in their twenties engage in sexual intercourse two or three times per week on average, with the frequency declining to two or three times per month among couples over 60. Perhaps the most dramatic change in marital sex practices in recent decades is the increased popularity of oral–genital sex. Many people continue to masturbate even though they are married. Most people today—both women and men—express general satisfaction with their marital sex life. Sexual patterns in marriage, however, show great variability.

About 25 percent of all married men and 15 percent of all married women engage in extramarital sex at some time. Extramarital sex is disapproved of in our society and is generally carried on in secrecy. In a few cases, it is agreed that both husband and wife can have extramarital sex, as in open marriage, swinging, and polyamory. Equity theory and the sociobiological perspective may be helpful in understanding patterns of extramarital sex.

Virtually all widowed and divorced men return to an active sex life, as do most divorced women and about half of widowed women.

Research indicates that gay men have modified their sexual practices somewhat in the AIDS era. They have reduced their number of partners and have shifted away from risky sex practices. Among heterosexuals there is some evidence of a reduction in the number of partners, and slight improve-

ments in condom use. Blacks and single persons are more likely to have changed in this regard. Most heterosexuals do not consider themselves at risk for HIV infection, however, so they are less concerned with safer sex practices.

While sexual activity declines somewhat with age, it is perfectly possible to remain sexually active into one's eighties or nineties. Problems with sex or the cessation of intercourse may be related to physical factors. In women, declining estrogen levels result in a thinner, less elastic vagina and less lubrication; in men, there is lowered testosterone production and increased vascular disease, combined with slower erections and longer refractory periods. Psychological factors can also be involved, such as the belief that the elderly cannot or should not have sex. Masters and Johnson emphasized that two factors are critical to maintaining sexual capacity in old age: good physical and mental health, and regularity of sexual expression. The AARP survey indicates that all sexual behaviors—including heterosexual intercourse and masturbation—may continue past age 70.

QUESTIONS FOR THOUGHT, DISCUSSION, AND DEBATE

1. What is your response when you see an elderly couple expressing affection physically with each other, perhaps kissing or holding hands? Why do you think you respond that way?

2. What is your opinion about extramarital sex? Is it ethical or moral? What are its effects on a marriage—does it destroy marriage or improve it, or perhaps have no effect?

3. If you are currently in a relationship, apply equity theory to your relationship. Do you feel

that it is equitable or inequitable? If you view it as inequitable, what effects does that have on your behavior?

4. You and your partner are talking about establishing a long-term relationship. Your partner says that his main concern is that living together will lead to a decline in how often you have sex. Is that a realistic concern? If so, what could the two of you do to prevent that from occurring?

SUGGESTIONS FOR FURTHER READING

Brecher, Edward M. (1984). *Love, sex, and aging.* Mount Vernon, NY: Consumers Union. This large-scale survey offers a liberated view of sexuality in the elderly.

Fisher, Helen. (1992). *Anatomy of love: The mysteries of mating, marriage, and why we stray.* New York: Fawcett Columbine. This book presents a provocative, sociobiological account of human sexual behavior, including extramarital sex.

Maurer, Harry. (1994). *Sex: Real people talk about what they really do.* New York: Penguin Books.

Maurer interviewed 52 people of diverse ages, preferences, and orientations about their sexual experiences. He presents lengthy excerpts organized around themes, such as Awakenings, Wild Oats, and the Long Haul.

Sarrel, Lorna, & Sarrel, Philip. (1984). *Sexual turning points: The seven stages of adult sexuality.* New York: Macmillan. This book, written for a general audience, provides an interesting theory of adult sexual development.

CHAPTER ELEVEN

Attraction, Love, and Communication

CHAPTER HIGHLIGHTS

Attraction
The Girl Next Door
Birds of a Feather
Physical Attractiveness
The Interpersonal Marketplace
From the Laboratory to Real Life
Attraction Online
Explaining Our Preferences

Intimacy

Love
Triangular Theory of Love
Attachment Theory of Love

Love as a Story
The Biology of Love

Research on Love
Measuring Love
Gender Differences
Love and Adrenaline
Cross-Cultural Research

Communication
Communication and Relationships
Being an Effective Communicator
Fighting Fair
Checking Out Sexy Signals

The intimacy in sex is never only physical. In a sexual relationship we may discover who we are in ways otherwise unavailable to us, and at the same time we allow our partner to see and know that individual. As we unveil our bodies, we also disclose our persons.*

*Dr. Thomas Moore, "Soul Mates," *Psychology Today*, March–April 1994, downloaded from http://faculty.uccb.ns.ca/pmacintyre/psych365/quotes.htm.

Many people believe that there is, or should be, a close connection between love and sex. The sexual standard for many is that sex is appropriate if one loves the other person (see Chapter 9), and sex seems to be the logical outcome of a loving relationship. For this reason, it is important in a text on sexuality to spend some time considering the emotion we link so closely to sex: love.

This chapter is organized in terms of the way relationships usually progress—if they progress. We begin by talking about attraction, what brings people together in the first place. Then we consider intimacy, which develops as relationships develop. Next, we look at four different views of what love is. We discuss some of the research on love, including cross-cultural research. Finally, we conclude with one of the requirements for fulfilling, long-term relationships: communication.

Attraction

What causes you to be attracted to another person? Social psychologists have done extensive research on interpersonal attraction. We consider the major results of this research in this section.

The Girl Next Door

Our opportunities to meet people are limited by geography and time. You may meet that attractive person sitting two rows in front of you in "human sex," as the course is referred to at the University of Wisconsin, but you will never meet the wealthy, brilliant engineering student who sits in your seat two classes later. You are much more likely to meet and be attracted to the boy or girl next door than the one who lives across town. The NHSLS (introduced in Chapter 3) asked participants where they met their current dating partner, cohabitant, or spouse. More than half met at school, work, church, or a party (Michael et al., 1994, Fig. 2).

Among those who work in the same place or take the same class, we tend to be more attracted

to people with whom we have had contact several times than we are to people with whom we have had little contact (Harrison, 1977). This tendency has been demonstrated in laboratory studies in which the amount of contact between participants was systematically varied. At the end of the session, people gave higher "liking" ratings to those with whom they had had much contact and lower ratings to those with whom they had had little contact (Saegert et al., 1973). This is the **mere-exposure effect:** Repeated exposure to any stimulus, including a person, leads to greater liking for that stimulus (Bornstein, 1989). For this reason, the chance of a man falling in love with the "girl next door" is greater than the chance of falling in love with someone he seldom meets.

Birds of a Feather

We tend to like people who are similar to us. We are attracted to people who are approximately the same as we are in age, race or ethnicity, and economic and social status. Similarity on these *social* characteristics is referred to as **homophily,** the tendency to have contact with people equal in social status. Data on homophily from the NHSLS are displayed in Table 11.1. Note that the greatest homophily is by race, followed by education and age. Couples are least likely to share the same religion. It is interesting that short-term partnerships are as homophilous as marriages.

A social psychologist has done numerous experiments demonstrating that we are attracted to people whose attitudes and opinions are similar to ours (Byrne, 1971). In these experiments, the researcher typically has people fill out an opinion questionnaire. They are then shown a questionnaire that was supposedly filled out by another person and are asked to rate how much they think they would like that person. In fact, the questionnaire was filled out to show either high or low agreement with the participant's responses. Participants report more liking for a person whose responses are similar to

Mere–exposure effect: The tendency to like a person more if we have been exposed to him or her repeatedly.
Homophily: The tendency to have contact with people who are equal in social status.

Table 11.1   Percentage of Relationships That Are Homophilous, by Type of Relationship

Type of Homophily	Type of Relationship			
	Marriages*	Cohabitations*	Long-Term Partnerships	Short-Term Partnerships
Racial/ethnic	93%	88%	89%	91%
Age[†]	78	75	76	83
Educational[‡]	82	87	83	87
Religious[§]	72	53	56	60

*Percentages of marriages and cohabitational relationships that began in the ten years prior to the survey.

[†]Age homophily is defined as a difference of no more than five years in partners' ages.

[‡]Educational homophily is defined as a difference of no more than one educational category. The educational categories used were less than high school, high school graduate, vocational training, four-year college, and graduate degree.

[§]Cases in which either partner was reported as "other" or had missing data are omitted.

Source: Laumann et al. (1994), Table 6.4.

theirs than for one whose responses are quite different.

Why are we attracted to a person who is similar to us in, say, attitude? There are a number of reasons (Huston & Levinger, 1978). We get positive reinforcement from that person agreeing with us. The other person's agreement bolsters our sense of rightness. And we anticipate positive interactions with that person.

Folk sayings are sometimes wise and sometimes foolish. The interpersonal-attraction research indicates that the saying "Birds of a feather flock together" contains some truth. This tendency for men and women to choose as partners people who match them on social and personal characteristics is called the **matching phenomenon** (Feingold, 1988).

At the same time, "opposites attract" may be more accurate with regard to interpersonal style. In one study, dominant people paired with submissive people reported greater satisfaction with their relationship than dominant or submissive people paired with a similar partner (Dryer & Horowitz, 1997).

People vary on a large number of characteristics. Perhaps similarity on some is important to attraction and relationship success, while similarity on others is not. Attitudes are one set of characteristics, personality traits (e.g., the Big Five—Neuroticism, Openness, etc.) are another, and attachment style (secure, anxious, etc.) is another. The research discussed so far argues that similarity in attitudes is important, but similarity in personality is not.

These predications were tested in research involving newly married couples (Luo & Klohnen, 2005). The average participant was 28 years old, white, fairly well educated, and Christian. The researchers calculated couple similarity scores on numerous measures in the three domains. They compared these real-couple scores with the mean scores of randomly paired couples. As predicted, real couples were significantly more similar on values, religiosity, and political attitudes, but no more similar than random couples on personality. The NHSLS found that couples are similar in age, race, and education. Could this homophily account for similarity in attitudes? Researchers tried to predict similarity in attitudes and personality from similarity in background characteristics, but could not.

Finally, what is the relationship between similarity and quality of relationship? Among these couples, similarity on attachment styles was associated with indicators of marital satisfaction, but similarity in attitudes was not. Perhaps we need to revise the adage: "Birds of a feather (attitudinal similarity) may flock, but may not stick, together."

Physical Attractiveness

A great deal of evidence shows that, given a choice of more than one potential partner, individuals will prefer the one who is more physically attractive (Hendrick & Hendrick, 1992). For example, in one study snapshots were taken of college men and women (Berscheid et al., 1971). A dating history of each person was also obtained. Judges then rated the attractiveness of the men and women in the photographs. For the women there was a fairly

Matching phenomenon: The tendency for men and women to choose as partners people who match them, that is, who are similar in attitudes, intelligence, and attractiveness.

strong relationship between attractiveness and popularity. The women judged attractive had had more dates in the last year than the women judged less attractive. There was some relationship between appearance and popularity for men, too, but it was not as marked as it was for women. This phenomenon has even been found in children as young as 3 to 6 years of age, who are more attracted to children with attractive faces (Dion, 1973, 1977).

Physical attractiveness is one aspect of sex appeal, and in fact, young men and women typically rate physical appearance as the most important (Regan, 2004). Other aspects include general body size (measured in various ways) and certain facial features. Much of the research on attractiveness uses data from samples of white persons. One exception is research on the impact of lightness of skin on ratings of attractiveness among African Americans. The National Survey of Black Americans involved interviews conducted by Blacks. At the end of the interview, the interviewer rated the respondent's skin color on a five-category scale from "very dark brown" to "very light brown" and rated the respondent's attractiveness. Skin tone was strongly associated with the attractiveness ratings given female respondents by both male and female interviewers (Hill, 2002). Light skin was rated as more attractive, perhaps reflecting the use of white skin as the standard.

In general, then, we are most attracted to good-looking people. However, this effect depends on gender to some extent. Physical attractiveness is more important to males evaluating females than it is to females evaluating males (Feingold, 1990). Also, our perception of attractiveness or beauty of another person is influenced by our evaluation of their intelligence, liking, and respect (Kniffin & Wilson, 2004). And this phenomenon is somewhat modified by our own feelings of personal worth, as we show in the next section.

The Interpersonal Marketplace

Although this may sound somewhat callous, whom we are attracted to and pair off with depends a lot on how much we think we have to offer and how much we think we can "buy" with it. Generally, the principle seems to be that women's worth is based on their physical beauty, whereas men's worth is based on their success. There is a tendency, then, for beautiful women to be paired with wealthy, successful men.

Data from many studies document this phenomenon. In one study, high school yearbook pictures were rated for attractiveness (Udry & Eckland, 1984). These people were followed up 15 years after graduation, and measures of education, occupational status, and income were obtained. Females who were rated the most attractive in high school were significantly more likely to have husbands who had high incomes and were highly educated (see also Elder, 1969).

In another study, women students were rated on their physical attractiveness (Rubin, 1973, p. 68). They were then asked to complete a questionnaire about what kinds of men they would consider desirable dates. A man's occupation had a big effect on his desirability as a date. Men in high-status occupations—physician, lawyer, chemist—were considered highly desirable dates by virtually all the women. Men in low-status occupations—janitor, bartender—were judged hardly acceptable by most of the women.

A difference emerged between attractive and unattractive women, however, when rating men in middle-status occupations—electrician, bookkeeper, plumber. The attractive women did not feel that these men would be acceptable dates, whereas the unattractive women felt that they would be at least moderately acceptable. Here we see the interpersonal marketplace in action. Men with more status are more desirable. But how desirable a man is judged to be depends on the woman's sense of her own worth. Attractive women are not much interested in middle-status men because they apparently think of themselves as being "worth more." Unattractive women find middle-status men more attractive, presumably because they think such men are reasonably within their "price range."

From the Laboratory to Real Life

The phenomena discussed so far—feelings of attraction to people who are similar to us and who are good looking—have been demonstrated mainly in psychologists' laboratories. Do these phenomena occur in the real world?

A research team did a study to find out whether these results would be obtained in a real-life situation (Byrne et al., 1970). They administered an attitude and personality questionnaire to 420 college students. Then they formed 44 "couples." For half of the couples, both people had made very similar responses on the questionnaire, and for the other half of the couples, the two people had made very different responses. The two people were then introduced and sent to the student union on a brief date. When they returned from the date, an unobtrusive measure of attraction was taken—how close they stood to each other in front of the experimenter's desk. The participants also evaluated their dates on several scales.

The results of the study confirmed those from previous experimental work. The couples who had been matched for similar attitudes were most attracted to each other, and those with dissimilar attitudes were not so attracted to each other. The students had also been rated as to their physical attractiveness both by the experimenter and by their dates, and greater attraction to the better-looking dates was reported. In a follow-up at the end of the semester, those whose dates were similar to them and were physically attractive were more likely to remember the date's name and to express a desire to date the person again in the future. This experiment, which was closer to real life and real dating situations, again demonstrated the importance of similarity and physical appearance.

Attraction Online

Technology has created a new way to meet potential partners—online (Elias, 1997). Some Web sites have tens of thousands of personal ads, and one site claims 500,000 hits per day. Surveys suggest that the people seeking partners online are educated, affluent, 20- to 40-year-olds who don't have the time or the taste for singles bars. "Impatience . . . drives many singles to the . . . digital meat market" (Gottlieb, 2006). Telephone interviews in 2005 with a sample of adults found that 11 percent of Internet users had visited an online dating site.

Users say that one advantage of meeting on the Net is that the technology forces you to focus on the person's interests and values. This focus facilitates finding a person with whom you have a lot in common. Also, in many instances you cannot see the person and so you are not influenced by his or her physical attractiveness or lack thereof. You also do not have access to "body language"—facial expressions, posture, and other cues that provide information. As a result your impressions are heavily influenced by imagination, which can create a powerful attraction to the other (Ben-Ze'ev, 2004).

A major disadvantage is the risk that the other person may not be honest about his or her interests, occupation, or marital status. Chat rooms with names like "Women with Other Men" attract married people. Some of the relationships established in these rooms lead to "Divorce, Internet Style" (Quittner, 1997).

In recent years, online dating sites have enlisted the help of researchers in developing a "scientific" approach to pairing clients (Gottlieb, 2006). The most renowned is eHarmony, thanks to its outgoing founder, Neil Clark Warren. Similar sites include Chemistry.com, whose chief advisor is sociobiologist Helen Fisher, and PerfectMatch.com, whose system was developed by "Dr. Pepper" Schwartz, a sociologist. Each site uses clients' responses to an online questionnaire to match them.

How do they differ? Each site has its matching strategy. eHarmony, following the research on attraction, uses a 436-question survey to assess a broad range of attitude, value, and personality domains. Couples are matched based on relative similarity on each domain. Chemistry.com focuses on pairing adults who will experience a "spark" when they meet. Fisher argues that testosterone, dopamine, oxytocin, and vasopressin are the basis of romance (Gottlieb, 2006). Genes associated with these hormones are associated with traits such as calmness, popularity, rationality, and sympathy. Chemistry.com uses a 146-item survey to measure these traits, and infers the clients' "chemistry."

PerfectMatch.com uses the Duet system, based on 48 questions assessing 8 domains. Schwartz believes that a well-matched couple should be similar on romantic impulsivity, personal energy, outlook, and predictability, and different on flexibility, decision-making style, emotionality, and self-nurturing style. What do you think?

Explaining Our Preferences

The research data are quite consistent in showing that we select as potential partners people who are similar to us in social characteristics—age, race, education—and who share our attitudes and beliefs. Moreover, both men and women prefer physically attractive people, although women place greater emphasis on a man's social status or earning potential (Sprecher et al., 1994). The obvious question is, Why? Two answers are suggested, one drawing on reinforcement theory and one on sociobiology (see Chapter 2 for discussions of these theories).

Reinforcement Theory: Byrne's Law of Attraction

A rather commonsense idea—and one that psychologists agree with—is that we tend to like people who give us rewards and to dislike people who give us punishments. Social psychologist Donn Byrne (1997) has formulated the law of attraction. It says that our attraction to another person is proportionate to the number of reinforcements that person gives us relative to the total number of reinforcements plus punishments the person gives us. Or, simplified even more, we like people who are frequently nice to us and seldom nasty (Figure 11.1).

Figure 11.1   According to Byrne's law of attraction, our liking for a person is influenced by the reinforcements we receive from interacting with them. Shared activities provide the basis for smooth and rewarding interaction.

According to this explanation, we prefer people who are similar because interaction with them is rewarding. People who are similar in age, race, and education are likely to have similar outlooks on life, prefer similar activities, and like the same kinds of people. These shared values and beliefs provide the basis for smooth and rewarding interaction. It will be easy to agree about such things as how important schoolwork is, what TV programs to watch, and what to do on Friday night. Disagreement about such things would cause conflict and hostility, which are definitely not rewards (for most people, anyway). We prefer pretty or handsome partners because we are aware of the high value placed on physical attractiveness in U.S. society, and we believe others will have a higher opinion of us if we have a good-looking partner. Finally, we prefer someone with high social status or earning potential because all the material things that people find rewarding cost money.

These findings have some practical implications (Hatfield & Walster, 1978). If you are trying to get a new relationship going well, make sure you give the other person some positive reinforcement. Also, make sure that you have some good times together, so that you *associate* each other with rewards. Do not spend all your time stripping paint off old furniture or cleaning out the garage. And do not forget to keep the positive reinforcements (or "strokes," if you like that jargon better) going in an old, stable relationship.

A variation of the reinforcement view comes from the implicit egotism perspective (Jones et al., 2004). It states that we are attracted to persons who are similar because they activate our positive views of ourselves. For example, archival research found that men and women are more likely to marry people whose names resemble their own.

Sociobiology: Sexual Strategies Theory

Sociobiologists view sexual behavior within an evolutionary perspective. Historically, the function of mating has been reproduction. Men and women who selected mates according to some preferences were more successful than those who chose them based on other preferences (Allgeier & Wiederman, 1994). The successful ones produced more offspring, who in turn produced more offspring, carrying their mating preferences to the present.

Men and women face different adaptive problems in their efforts to reproduce (Buss & Schmitt, 1993). Since women bear the offspring, men need to identify reproductively valuable women. Other things being equal, younger women are more likely to be fertile than older women, leading to a preference for youth, which results in young men choosing young women (homophily). Also, sociobiologists assert that men want to be certain about the paternity of offspring, and for this reason they want a woman who will be sexually faithful—in other words, a woman who is hard to get, who is not promiscuous.

Other things being equal, a physically attractive person is more likely to be healthy and fertile than someone who isn't, which explains the preference for good-looking partners. If attractiveness is an indicator of health, we would expect it to be more important in societies where chronic diseases are more prevalent. Gangestad and Buss (1993) measured the prevalence of seven pathogens, including those that cause malaria and leprosy, in 29 cultures, and also obtained ratings of the importance of 18 attributes of mates. They found that physical attractiveness was considered more important by residents in societies that had a greater prevalence of pathogens. However, one study found that there was no relationship between rated facial attractiveness (based on a photograph) and a clinical assessment of health in a sample of adolescents. At the same time, the raters ranked more attractive persons as healthier (Kalick et al., 1998).

Women must make a much greater investment than men in order to reproduce. They will be pregnant for nine months, and after the birth they must care for the infant and young child for many years. For these reasons women want to select as mates men who are reproductively valuable, leading to the preference for good-looking mates. They also want mates who are able and willing to invest resources in them and their children. Obviously, men must have resources in order to invest them, so women prefer men with higher incomes and status. Among young people, women will prefer men with greater earning potential and, for this reason, prefer men with greater education and higher occupational aspirations. This matter of resources is more important than the problem of identifying a reproductively valuable male, so women rate income and earning potential as more important than good looks.

Research provides evidence that is consistent with this theory. For example, researchers presented a list of 31 tactics to a sample of undergraduate students and asked them to rate how effective each would be in attracting a long-term mate (Schmitt & Buss, 1996). Tactics communicating sexual exclusivity or faithfulness were judged highly effective in attracting a mate for women. Tactics that displayed resource potential were judged most effective for men.

These two explanations—reinforcement theory and sociobiology—are not inconsistent. We can think about reinforcement in more general terms. Reproduction is a major goal for most adults in every society. Successful reproduction—having a healthy child who develops normally—is very reinforcing. Following the sexual strategies that we have inherited is likely to lead to such reinforcement.

Intimacy

Intimacy is a major component of any close or romantic relationship. Today many people are seeking to increase the intimacy in their relationships. Thus, in this section, we explore intimacy in more detail to try to gain a better understanding of it.

Defining Intimacy

What is intimacy? Psychologists have offered a number of definitions, including the following (Perlman & Fehr, 1987, p. 17):

1. Intimacy's defining features include "openness, honesty, mutual self-disclosure; caring, warmth, protecting, helping; being devoted to each other, mutually attentive, mutually committed; surrendering control, dropping defenses; becoming emotional, feeling distressed when separation occurs."

2. "Emotional intimacy is defined in behavioral terms as mutual self-disclosure and other kinds of verbal sharing, as declarations of liking and loving the other, and as demonstrations of affection."

Notice that the first definition focuses on intimacy as a characteristic of a person and the second as a characteristic of a relationship. One way to think about intimacy is that certain persons have more of a capacity for intimacy or engage in more intimacy-promoting behaviors than others. But we can also think of some relationships as being more intimate than others.

A definition of **intimacy** in romantic relationships is "the level of commitment and positive affective, cognitive and physical closeness one

Intimacy: A quality of relationships characterized by commitment, feelings of closeness and trust, and self-disclosure.

experiences with a partner in a reciprocal (although not necessarily symmetrical) relationship" (Moss & Schwebel, 1993, p. 33). The emphasis in this definition is on closeness or sharing, which has three dimensions: affective (emotional), cognitive, and physical. Note, too, that while intimacy must be reciprocal, it need not be equal. Many people have had the experience of feeling closer to another person than that person seems to feel toward them. Finally, note that while intimacy has a physical dimension, it need not be sexual.

In one study, college students were asked to respond to an open-ended question asking what they thought made a relationship one of intimacy (Roscoe et al., 1987). The qualities that emerged, with great agreement, were sharing, sexual interaction, trust in the partner, and openness. Notice that these qualities are quite similar to the ones listed in the definitions given above.

Intimacy and Self-Disclosure

One of the key characteristics of intimacy, appearing in psychologists' and college students' definitions, is self-disclosure (Derlega, 1984). **Self-disclosure** involves telling your partner some personal things about yourself. It may range from telling your partner about something embarrassing that happened to you at work today, to disclosing a very meaningful event that happened between you and your parents 15 years ago.

Research consistently shows that self-disclosure leads to reciprocity (Berg & Derlega, 1987; Hendrick & Hendrick, 1992). In other words, if one member of the couple self-discloses, this act seems to prompt the other partner to self-disclose also. Self-disclosure by one member of the couple can essentially get the ball rolling.

Why does this occur? Psychologists have proposed a number of reasons (Hendrick & Hendrick, 1992). First, disclosure by our partner may make us like and trust that person more. Second, as social learning theorists would argue, simple modeling and imitation may occur. That is, one partner's self-disclosing serves as a model for the other partner. Norms of equity may also be involved (see Chapter 10 for a discussion of equity theory). After one partner has self-disclosed, the other person may follow suit in order to maintain a sense of balance or equity in the relationship.

Self-disclosure is closely related to satisfaction with the relationship. Research shows that there is a positive correlation between the extent of a couple's self-disclosure and their satisfaction with the relationship. In other words, couples that practice more self-disclosure are more satisfied (Hendrick,

Figure 11.2 Intimacy occurs in a relationship when there is warmth and mutual self-disclosure.

1981). Self-disclosure of sexual likes and dislikes is associated with sexual satisfaction (Byers & Demmons, 1999; Purnine & Carey, 1997).

Patterns of self-disclosure can actually predict whether a couple stays together or breaks up. Research in which couples are followed for periods ranging from two months to four years shows that the greater the self-disclosure, the greater the likelihood that the relationship will continue, and the less the self-disclosure, the greater the likelihood of breakup (Hendrick et al., 1988; Sprecher, 1987).

Self-disclosure promotes intimacy in a relationship and makes us feel close to the other person (Figure 11.2). It also indicates how important it is for the partner to be accepting in response to self-disclosure. If the acceptance is missing, we can feel betrayed or threatened, and we certainly will not feel on more intimate terms with the partner.

A study of naturally occurring interactions examined the relationships between self-disclosure, perceived partner disclosure, and the degree of intimacy experienced (Laurenceau et al., 1998). Young people recorded data about every interaction lasting more than 10 minutes, for 7 or 14 days. Data were analyzed for more than 4,000 two-person interactions recorded by 158 participants. Both self-disclosure and partner disclosure were associated with the participants' rating of the intimacy of the interaction. In addition, self-disclosure of emotion was more closely related to intimacy than was self-disclosure of facts.

Self-disclosure: Telling personal things about yourself.

Self-disclosure and intimacy, then, mutually build on each other. Self-disclosure promotes our feeling that the relationship is intimate, and when we feel that it is, we feel comfortable engaging in further self-disclosure. However, self-disclosure and intimacy don't necessarily increase consistently over time. In some relationships, the pattern may be that an increase in intimacy is followed by a plateau or even a pulling back (Collins & Miller, 1994).

Measuring Intimacy

Psychologists have developed some scales for measuring intimacy, which can give us further insights. One such scale is the Personal Assessment of Intimacy in Relationships (PAIR) Inventory (Schaefer & Olson, 1981). It measures emotional intimacy in a relationship with items such as the following:

1. My partner listens to me when I need someone to talk to.
2. My partner really understands my hurts and joys.

Another scale measuring intimacy in a relationship includes items such as these (Miller & Lefcourt, 1982):

1. How often do you confide very personal information to him or her?
2. How often are you able to understand his or her feelings?
3. How often do you feel close to him or her?
4. How important is your relationship with him or her in your life?

If you are currently in a relationship, answer these questions for yourself and consider what the quality of the intimacy is in your relationship.

In summary, an intimate relationship is characterized by commitment, feelings of closeness and trust, and self-disclosure. We can promote intimacy in our relationships by engaging in self-disclosure (provided, of course, that we trust the person, but it is quite difficult to develop intimacy when there is a lack of trust) and being accepting of the other person's self-disclosures.

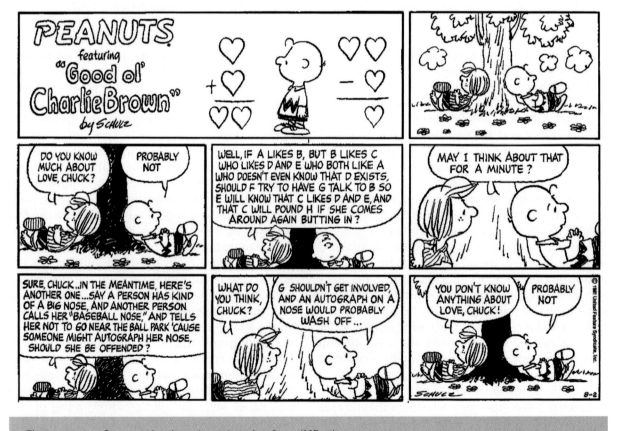

Figure 11.3   Communicating about love is often difficult.

Source: PEANUTS © United Feature Syndicate, Inc.

Love

At the beginning of this chapter, we noted that there is a connection between love and sex in our society. In everyday life and in theories of love, this connection is a continuum (Hendrick & Hendrick, 2004). At one end are "hookups," short-term sexual relationships on a Saturday night, spring break, or a singles cruise, with little romance (Lambert et al., 2003; Maticka-Tyndale et al., 2003; Grello et al., 2006). In theories of love, this is the "love is really sex" view, found, for example, in evolutionary theory. At the other end are romantic love relationships in which sex is nonexistent or incidental, as for example in a nonsexual affair. In theories, this is the view found, for example, in the theory of love as a story. Near the middle is the "sex is really love" view, as in the theory of passionate love. In the center is a relationship that balances sex and love, and theories that recognize both, such as the triangular theory.

In the following sections, we consider four views of love: the triangular theory, the attachment theory, the love-as-a-story perspective, and the passionate love view and its connections to the biology of love.

Triangular Theory of Love

Robert Sternberg (1986) has formulated a triangular theory of the nature of love. According to his theory, love has three fundamental components: intimacy, passion, and decision or commitment.

Three Components of Love

Intimacy. Intimacy is the emotional component of love. It includes our feelings of closeness or bondedness to the other person. The feeling of intimacy usually involves a sense of mutual understanding with the loved one; a sense of sharing one's self; intimate communication with the loved one, involving a sense of having the loved one hear and accept what is shared; and giving and receiving emotional support to and from the loved one.

Intimacy, of course, is present in many relationships besides romantic ones. Intimacy here is definitely *not* a euphemism for sex (as when someone asks, "Have you been intimate with him?"). The kind of emotional closeness involved in intimacy may be found between best friends and between parents and children, just as it is between lovers.

Passion. Passion is the motivational component of love. It includes physical attraction and the drive for sexual expression. Physiological arousal is an important part of passion. Passion is the component that differentiates romantic love from other kinds of love, such as the love of best friends or the love between parents and children. Passion is generally the component of love that is faster to arouse, but in the course of a long-term relationship it is also the component that fades most quickly.

Intimacy and passion are often closely intertwined. In some cases passion comes first, when a couple experience an initial, powerful physical attraction to each other, and emotional intimacy may then follow. In other cases, people know each other only casually, but as emotional intimacy develops, passion follows. Of course, there are also cases where intimacy and passion are completely separate. For example, in cases of casual sex, passion is present but intimacy is not.

Decision or Commitment. The third component is the cognitive component, decision or commitment. This component actually has two aspects. The short-term aspect is the decision that one loves the other person. The long-term aspect is the commitment to maintain that relationship. Commitment is what makes relationships last. Passion comes and goes. All relationships have their better times and their worse times, their ups and their downs. When the words of the traditional marriage service ask whether you promise to love your spouse "for better or for worse," the answer "I do" is the promise of commitment.

The Triangular Theory

Sternberg (1986) calls his theory a *triangular theory of love.* Figure 11.4 shows Sternberg's love

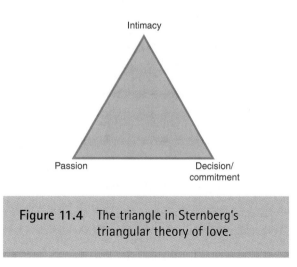

Figure 11.4 The triangle in Sternberg's triangular theory of love.

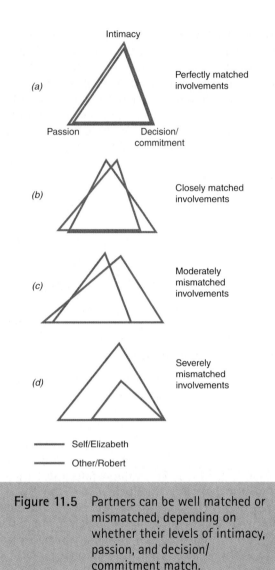

Figure 11.5   Partners can be well matched or mismatched, depending on whether their levels of intimacy, passion, and decision/commitment match.

triangle.[1] The top point of the triangle is intimacy, the left point is passion, and the right point is decision or commitment.

This triangle metaphor allows us to show how the two people in a couple can be well matched or mismatched in the love they feel toward each other. In Figure 11.5(a), Elizabeth feels as much intimacy toward Robert as he does toward her, they both feel equal levels of passion, and they both have the same level of commitment. According to the theory, that is a perfect match. Figure 11.5(b)

shows a situation in which the couple are slightly but not seriously mismatched, and Figure 11.5(c) shows a moderate mismatch. Figure 11.5(d) shows a situation in which there is a severe mismatch. Both partners are equally committed, but Elizabeth feels significantly more intimacy and passion than Robert.

Sternberg's research indicates that when there is a good match between the two partners' love, as shown in Figure 11.5(a) or (b), the partners tend to feel satisfaction with the relationship. When there is a mismatch in the triangles, they feel dissatisfied with the relationship.

Thinking about practical applications of the theory, if a relationship seems to be in trouble, it may be because there is a mismatch of the triangles. We could analyze the love in the relationship in terms of the three components (intimacy, passion, and commitment) to see where the partners are mismatched. It could be that they are well matched for passion, but that one feels and wants more intimacy or commitment than the other does.

Love in Action

Sternberg also argues that each of the three components of love must be translated into action. The intimacy component is expressed in actions such as communicating personal feelings and information, offering emotional (and perhaps financial) support, and expressing empathy for the other. The passion component is expressed in actions such as kissing, touching, and making love. The decision or commitment component is demonstrated by actions such as saying "I love you," getting married, and sticking with a relationship through times when it isn't particularly convenient.

As the great psychoanalyst Erich Fromm wrote in his book *The Art of Loving* (1956), love is something a person *does*, not a state a person is *in*. Fromm believed that loving is an art, something that a person must learn about and practice. And as Sternberg says, "Without expression, even the greatest of loves can die" (1986, p. 132).

Evidence for Sternberg's Triangular Theory of Love

What kind of support is there for Sternberg's theory? Sternberg has developed a questionnaire, the Sternberg Triangular Love Scale (STLS), to measure the three components in his theory. Several studies have been done on the characteristics of the scale itself (e.g., Sternberg, 1987, 1997; Whitley, 1993). The scale provides good measures of the components, especially of passion and commitment. Scores for the same relationship are stable for up to two months.

[1]This terminology should not be confused with the popular use of the term *love triangle,* which refers to a situation in which three people are involved in love, but the love is not reciprocated and so things don't work out quite right. For example, A loves B, B loves C, and C loves A, but A doesn't love C and B doesn't love A. Alas.

Sternberg makes several predictions about how scores ought to change over time. One study recruited 204 adults, ages 18 to 68; 65 percent were married (Acker & Davis, 1992). The average length of the relationship was 9.5 years. As predicted, commitment scores increased as relationships progressed from dating to marriage. Sternberg also expects intimacy to decrease over time as familiarity with the partner increases, and sure enough, behavioral intimacy (sharing inner feelings, trying to understand the partner) decreased as predicted. Contrary to prediction, however, two other measures of intimacy (including Sternberg's) increased.

A study of a sample of German adults assessed the relationship between the three components and sexual activity and satisfaction (Grau & Kimpf, 1993). The theory predicts that the amount of passion should be most closely related to sexual activity, but the results indicated that intimacy was most closely related to sexual behavior and sexual satisfaction.

Attachment Theory of Love

In Chapter 9 we discussed the earliest attachment that humans experience, that between infant and parent. One hypothesis is that the quality of this early attachment—whether secure and pleasant or insecure and unpleasant—profoundly affects us for the rest of our lives, and particularly affects our capacity to form loving attachments to others when we are adults.

The *attachment theory of love* is based on these ideas (Hazan & Shaver, 1987; Simpson, 1990). According to the attachment theory, adults are characterized, in their romantic relationships, by one of three styles. *Secure lovers* are people who find it easy to get close to others and are comfortable having others feel close to them. Mutual dependency in a relationship (depending on the partner and having the partner depend on you) feels right to them. Secure lovers do not fear abandonment.

In contrast, *fearful or avoidant lovers* are uncomfortable feeling close to another person or having that person feel close to them. It is difficult for them to trust or depend on a partner.

The third style, *preoccupied or anxious–ambivalent lovers*, want desperately to get close to a partner but often find the partner does not reciprocate the feeling, perhaps because anxious–ambivalent lovers scare away others. They are insecure in the relationship, worrying that the partner does not really love them.

Research shows that about 53 percent of adults are secure, 26 percent are avoidant, and 20 percent are anxious–ambivalent (Hazan & Shaver, 1987). This research also shows that separation from a parent in childhood—perhaps because of divorce or death—is not related to adult attachment styles. In other words, children of divorced parents are no more or less likely to be secure lovers than are children from intact marriages. (This finding is probably fortunate, given the high divorce rate in the United States.) What did predict adult attachment style? The person's perception of the *quality* of the relationship with each parent was key.

This research has some important implications. First, it helps us understand that adults bring to any particular romantic relationship their own personal history of love and attachment. The forces of that personal history can be strong, and one good and loving partner may not be able to change an avoidant lover into a secure lover. Second, it helps us understand that conflict in some relationships may be caused by a mismatch of attachment styles. A secure lover, who wants a close, intimate relationship, is likely to feel frustrated and dissatisfied with an avoidant lover, who is uncomfortable with feeling close. Attachment theory suggests that the important form of similarity is similarity in attachment style (Latty-Mann & Davis, 1996). Finally, this theory provides some explanation for jealousy, which is most common among anxious–ambivalent lovers (although present among the others) because of their early experience of feeling anxious about their attachment to their parents.

A study of heterosexual couples in serious dating relationships looked at the dynamics of adult attachment styles (Kirkpatrick & Davis, 1994). In over half the couples, both partners had a secure attachment style. About 10 percent consisted of one person with a secure style and one with an avoidant style, and 10 percent consisted of a secure–anxious pairing. As we might expect, there was not a single anxious–anxious or avoidant–avoidant couple. Such couples would be very incompatible.

Partners with a secure style reported the greatest commitment to and satisfaction with their relationships. Relationships in which the woman had an anxious style were rated more negatively by both partners. Men with an avoidant style gave the most negative ratings, not surprisingly, since they are uncomfortable with emotional closeness. These results lend strong support to the attachment theory.

Attachment style affects relationships by affecting the way the partners interact. A study of established couples (average length of relationship

Focus: Milestones in Sex Research
Jealousy

Jealousy—the green-eyed monster—is an unpleasant emotion often associated with romantic and sexual relationships. Intense cases of jealousy may result in violence, including partner abuse, assault, and homicide. As a result, it has been the focus of considerable scholarly work. Several perspectives contribute to our understanding of this emotion.

Jealousy is a cognitive, emotional, and behavioral response to a threat to an interpersonal relationship (Guerrero et al., 2004). The cognitive appraisal perspective suggests that emotions are the result of a cognitive appraisal of a stimulus. In this view, jealousy occurs when an individual *interprets* some stimulus as representing a threat to a valued relationship (Figure 11.6). In reality, there may or may not be a threat to the relationship. A variety of behaviors by the partner may be interpreted as a threat. In one study, individuals in dating relationships said that just having their partner spend time with another person was one of the top three acts of betrayal (Roscoe et al., 1988). In the twenty-first century, interaction with someone via the Internet may elicit a jealous reaction from the partner. Also, behavior or remarks by third parties may elicit jealousy, or circumstances such as coming home late may arouse suspicion.

There are two types of jealousy: emotional and sexual. *Emotional jealousy* occurs when one person believes or knows that the partner is emotionally attached to or in love with another. *Sexual jealousy* occurs when the person believes or knows that the partner wants to engage in or has actually engaged in sexual intimacy with another. The two may occur together or separately.

The evolutionary perspective has hypothesized that there is a gender difference in jealousy. According to this view, men are more upset by a (heterosexual) partner's sexual infidelity, whereas women are more upset by a (heterosexual) partner's emotional infidelity. This hypothesis is based on the argument that the male adaptive problem (or concern) in reproduction is uncertainty about paternity. For this reason, the male, motivated to pass on his genes to the next generation, wants to be sure the children he cares for are his own, so he is highly vigilant about female sexual fidelity. The female adaptive problem is to obtain enough resources to care for herself and her children, so she is highly vigilant about male romantic fidelity. If

her partner fell in love with someone else, he might leave her and she would lose the resources he provides.

Several studies have reported results that support this hypothesis, including a study reporting cross-cultural support using data from the United States, Germany, and the Netherlands (Buunk et al., 1996). However, all of the results supporting the hypothesis are based on a single question that forces men and women to say which would upset them more, emotional or sexual infidelity. Studies asking men and women how upset they would be by each separately report just small or insignificant differences. A careful review of five types of evidence finds little support for this hypothesis (Harris, 2003). A study of both heterosexual and homosexual adults found that men and women were more concerned about emotional infidelity of a partner (Harris, 2002).

Psychologists Gregory White and Paul Mullen (1989) see jealousy as a constellation including thoughts, emotions, and actions. Two situations, according to their research, activate jealousy. One is a situation in which there is a threat to our self-esteem. For example, in a good relationship our romantic partner helps us feel good about ourselves—makes us feel attractive or fun to be with, for example. If a rival appears and our partner shows interest, we may think things like "He finds her more attractive than me" or "She finds him more fun to be with than me." We then feel less attractive or less fun to be with. In other words, our self-esteem is threatened.

The second situation that activates jealousy is a threat to the relationship. If a rival appears on the scene, we may fear that our partner will separate from us and form a new relationship with the rival. Jealousy is activated because of our negative thoughts and feelings about the loss of a relationship that has been good for us and the loss of all the pleasant things that go along with that relationship, such as companionship and sex.

According to White and Mullen, we go through several stages in the jealousy response, sometimes very quickly. The first is cognitive, in which we make an initial appraisal of the situation and find that there is a threat to our self-esteem or to the relationship. Next, we experience an emotional reaction, which in itself has two phases. The first is a rapid stress response, the *jealous flash*. To use the

Figure 11.6 One situation that activates jealousy is a perceived threat to the relationship.

terminology of the two-component theory of love that we discuss in this chapter, this stress response is the physiological component of the jealous emotion. The second phase of emotional response occurs as we reappraise the situation and decide how to cope with it. In the reappraisal stage, we may shift from seeing the situation as a threat to seeing it as a challenge, for example. The intense initial emotions quiet down and may be replaced by feelings of moodiness.

Attempts to cope with jealousy lead to a variety of behaviors. Some of these behaviors are constructive, such as effective communication with the partner (see pp. 303–309 for a discussion of techniques of effective communicators). Such communication may lead to an evaluation of the relationship and attempts to change some of the problematic aspects of it. If the problems seem sufficiently serious, a couple may seek advice from a mediator or therapist.

Other behavioral responses to jealousy are destructive. The threat to a person's self-esteem may lead to depression, substance abuse, or suicide. Aggression may be directed at the partner, the third person, or both, and may result in physical or sexual abuse or even murder.

Research suggests that a person's attachment style may be an important influence on how that person responds to jealousy (Sharpstein & Kirkpatrick, 1997). Undergraduates were asked how they had reacted in the past to jealousy. Those with a secure attachment style reported that they had expressed their anger to the partner and maintained the relationship. Those with an anxious style reported the most intense anger, but they were most likely to say they did not express their anger. People with an avoidant style were more likely to direct their anger toward the third person.

Sources: Fisher (1992); Guerrero et al. (2004); Reiss (1986); White & Mullen (1989).

47 months) assessed attachment style, patterns of accommodation, and satisfaction with the relationship (Scharfe & Bartholomew, 1995). Individuals with a secure attachment reported responding constructively to potentially destructive behavior by the partner, for example, with efforts to discuss and resolve the problem. People who were fearful of attachment to another responded with avoidance or withdrawal.

Bartholomew (1990) proposed a four-group model of attachment. He says that attachment involves working models of self and other, and each may be positive or negative. In combination, these define four attachment styles. In addition to the three discussed above, there is a fourth style, *dismissing*. Persons with this style deny their need for attachment and emphasize self-reliance. Working models of self and other influence cognitive, emotional, and behavioral responses to others (Feeney, 1999). They direct attention to certain aspects of relationships and not others, and they bias memories. They amplify some emotional reactions and minimize others, and they activate behavioral plans.

Love as a Story

When we think of love, our thoughts often turn to the great love stories: Romeo and Juliet, Cinderella and the Prince (Julia Roberts and Richard Gere), King Edward VIII and Wallis Simpson, and *Pygmalion/ My Fair Lady*. According to Sternberg (1998), these stories are much more than entertainment. They shape our beliefs about love and relationships, and our beliefs in turn influence our behavior.

> Zach and Tammy have been married 28 years. Their friends have been predicting divorce since the day they were married. They fight almost constantly. Tammy threatens to leave Zach; he tells her that nothing would make him happier. They lived happily ever after.

> Valerie and Leonard had a perfect marriage. They told each other and all of their friends that they did. Their children say they never fought. Leonard met someone at his office, and left Valerie. They are divorced. (Adapted from Sternberg, 1998)

Wait a minute! Aren't those endings reversed? Zach and Tammy should be divorced, and Valerie and Leonard should be living happily ever after. If love is merely the interaction between two people, how they communicate and behave, you're right—the stories have the wrong endings. But there is more to love than interaction. What matters is how each partner *interprets* the interaction.

Love story: A story about what love should be like, including characters, a plot, and a theme.

To make sense out of what happens in our relationships, we rely on our love stories.

A **love story** is a story about what love should be like, and it has *characters*, a *plot*, and a *theme*. Every love story has two central characters, who play roles that complement each other. The plot details the kinds of events that occur in the relationship. The theme is central, and it provides the meaning of the events that make up the plot and gives direction to the behavior of the principals.

The story guiding Zach and Tammy's relationship is the war story. Each views love as war, and a good relationship involves constant fighting. The two central characters are warriors, doing battle, fighting for what they believe. The plot consists of arguments, fights, threats to leave—in other words, battles. The theme is that love is war. One may win or lose particular battles, but the war continues. Zach and Tammy's relationship endures because they share this view, and because it fits their temperaments. Can you imagine how long a wimp would last in a relationship with either of them?

According to this view, *falling in love* occurs when you meet someone with whom you can create a relationship that fits your love story. Further, we are satisfied with relationships in which we and our partner match the characters in our story (Beall & Sternberg, 1995). Valerie and Leonard's marriage looked great on the surface, but it didn't fit Leonard's love story. He left when he met his "true love"—a woman who could play the complementary role in his primary love story.

Where do our stories come from? Many of them have their origins in the culture, in folk tales, literature, theater, films, and television programs. The cultural context interacts with our personal experience and characteristics to create the stories that each of us has (Sternberg, 1998). As we experience relationships, our stories evolve, taking into account unexpected events. Each person has more than one story, and the stories often form a hierarchy.

One of Leonard's stories was "House and Home," where home was the center of the relationship, and he (in his role of caretaker) showered attention on the house and kids (not on Valerie). But when he met Sharon, with her aloof air, ambiguous past, and dark glasses, he was hooked—she elicited the "Love Is a Mystery" story, which was more salient to Leonard. He could not explain why he left Valerie and the kids, and like most of us, he was not consciously aware of his love stories.

You can see from these examples that love stories derive their power from the fact that they are self-fulfilling. We create events in our relationships according to the plot and then interpret those events according to the theme. Our love relationships are literally social constructions. Because our love stories are self-confirming, they can be very difficult to change.

Sternberg and his colleagues have identified five categories of love stories found in U.S. culture and several specific stories within each category. They have also developed a series of statements that reflect the themes in each story. People who agree with the statements "I think fights actually make a relationship more vital" and "I actually like to fight with my partner" are likely to believe in the war story.

Sternberg and Hojjat (cited in Sternberg, 1998) studied samples of 43 and 55 couples. They found that couples generally believed in similar stories. The more discrepant the stories of the partners, the less happy the couple was. Some stories were associated with high satisfaction—for example, the garden story, in which love is a garden that needs ongoing cultivation. Two stories associated with low satisfaction were the business story (especially the version in which the roles are employer and employee), and the horror story, in which the roles are terrorizer and victim.

The Biology of Love

The three theories considered so far define love as a single phenomenon. A fourth perspective differentiates between two kinds of love: passionate love and companionate love (Berscheid & Hatfield, 1978). **Passionate love** is a state of intense longing for union with the other person and of intense physiological arousal. It has three components: cognitive, emotional, and behavioral (Hatfield & Sprecher, 1986). The cognitive component includes preoccupation with the loved one and idealization of the person or of the relationship. The emotional component includes physiological arousal, sexual attraction, and desire for union. Behavioral elements include taking care of the other and maintaining physical closeness. Passionate love can be overwhelming, obsessive, all-consuming.

By contrast, **companionate love** is a feeling of deep attachment and commitment to a person with whom one has an intimate relationship (Hatfield & Rapson, 1993b). Passionate love is hot, and companionate love is warm.

Passionate love is often the first stage of a romantic relationship. Two people meet, fall wildly in love, and make a commitment to each other. But as the relationship progresses, a gradual shift to companionate love takes place (Cimbalo et al., 1976; Driscoll et al., 1972). The transformation tends to occur when the relationship is between 6 and 30 months old (Hatfield & Walster, 1978).

Some may find this perspective a rather pessimistic commentary on romantic love. But it may actually describe a good way for a relationship to develop. Passionate love may be necessary to hold a relationship together in the early stages, while conflicts are being resolved. But past that point, most of us find that what we really need is a friend—someone who shares our interests, who is happy when we succeed, and who sympathizes when we fail—and that is just what we get with companionate love.

Sexual desire and romantic love may often be independent processes (Diamond, 2003). Sexual desire is a motivational state leading to a search for opportunities for sexual activity. It motivates proximity seeking and contact, and leads to feelings of passion (passionate love). Sexual desire responds to reproductive cues such as physical attractiveness and high status. Romantic love is a motivational state leading to attachment and commitment. It promotes self-disclosure and intimacy leading to long-term relationships (companionate love).

Research involving observation of romantic couples identified distinctive nonverbal displays of affiliation (smiling, leaning toward partner), and of sexual cues (licking the lips, lip puckering) (Gonzaga et al., 2006). Displays of affection were associated with subjective reports of feeling love and of happiness. Displays of sexual cues were associated with subjective reports of sexual arousal and desire.

From an evolutionary perspective, successful reproduction requires mating, and the establishment of a pair-bond to ensure parental care of offspring (see Chapter 2). Fisher and colleagues (2006) propose that there are three internal systems involved in this process: desire to mate, pairing (mating), and parenting. They believe that each system involves reward pathways in the brain and associated hormonal changes. The sex drive motivates a person to seek a partner. Processes of attraction (passionate love?) lead to pairing, a focusing of energies on a specific partner. Processes of attachment (companionate love?) lead to long-term relationships that facilitate parenting.

What causes the complex phenomena of passionate and companionate love? Where does the rush of love at first sight come from? Research suggests that bodily chemistry and neural activity in the brain are the causes. Studies of the prairie vole, a small rodent, have identified specific patterns of neurochemical activity that are associated with mating and pair

SexSource Online
www.mhhe.com/hyde10

"THE DANCE OF LIFE" IN LOVE, INTIMACY, & SEX

Passionate love: A state of intense longing for union with the other person and of intense physiological arousal.
Companionate love: A feeling of deep attachment and commitment to a person with whom one has an intimate relationship.

bonding (preference for a specific partner) (Curtis & Wang, 2003). In female prairie voles, dopamine is released during mating, and in both male and female voles, the dopamine appears to enhance the likelihood of pair bonding. Dopamine is associated with euphoria and craving. A surge of dopamine in the human body can produce increased energy, focused attention, and reduced need for food and sleep, and these are common experiences of people in the early stages of love.

The frequent presence of the loved one, produced initially by passionate love, triggers the production of two other chemicals, prolactin and oxytocin. The levels of prolactin rise following orgasm in humans and are also related to pair bonding in voles.

Oxytocin may contribute to long-term relationships. It has been shown to play an important role in pair bonding in some animals (McEwen, 1997). In humans it is stimulated by touch, including sexual touching and orgasm, and it produces feelings of pleasure and satisfaction. Research indicates that levels of interpersonal trust correlate positively with oxytocin as well (Zak et al., 2003). In an experiment, researchers administered either oxytocin or a placebo through the nose to young men. The men who received the oxytocin were more likely to take social risks, compared to the men who received the placebo (Kosfeld et al., 2005).

The newest research with humans involves the use of magnetic resonance imaging (MRI) to study brain activity related to love. Researchers recruited young men and women who were in love (Bartels & Zeki, 2004). While their brain activity was being measured, each participant was shown photos of the romantic partner and of a close friend. The picture of the partner activated specific areas of the brain. Which ones? The areas rich in dopamine pathways were excited, lending weight to the neurochemical findings that suggest dopamine is important in the experience of love. Furthermore, when measures of levels of brain activity in response to the picture of the lover were correlated with scores on the Passionate Love Scale (which we discuss in the next section), the scores were correlated positively.

Research on Love

So far our discussion has focused on theoretical definitions of various kinds of love. You can see that various theorists—Sternberg, Hazan and Shaver, and Berscheid and

Operational definition: Defining some concept or term by how it is measured, for example, defining intelligence as those abilities that are measured by IQ tests.

Hatfield—mean different things when they use the word *love*. One of the ways psychologists and sociologists define terms is by using an **operational definition,** which defines a concept by the way it is measured. For example, *IQ* is sometimes defined as the kinds of abilities that are measured by IQ tests. We can define *job satisfaction* as a score on a questionnaire that measures a person's attitudes toward his or her job. Operational definitions are very useful because they are precise and help to clarify exactly what a scientist means by a complex term such as *love*.

Measuring Love

We introduced the concept of *passionate love* earlier. Hatfield and Sprecher (1986) developed a paper-and-pencil measure of this concept. For their Passionate Love Scale, they wrote statements intended to measure the cognitive, emotional, and behavioral components of passionate love. The respondent rates each statement on a scale from 1 (not true at all) to 9 (definitely true of him or her).

For example, if you feel that you are in love with someone, think about whether you would agree with each of the following statements, keeping that person in mind.

1. *Cognitive component:*
   Sometimes I feel I can't control my thoughts; they are obsessively on _____.
   For me, _____ is the perfect romantic partner.
2. *Emotional component:*
   I possess a powerful attraction for _____.
   I will love _____ forever.
3. *Behavioral component:*
   I eagerly look for signs indicating _____'s desire for me.
   I feel happy when I am doing things to make _____ happy.

Hatfield and Sprecher administered their questionnaire to students at the University of Wisconsin who were in relationships ranging from casually dating to engaged and living together. The results indicated that scores on the Passionate Love Scale (PLS) were correlated positively with other measures of love and with measures of commitment to and satisfaction with the relationship. These correlations give evidence that the PLS is *valid*—in other words, that it measures what it is supposed to measure. The findings confirm that the scale measures passion. For example, students who got high scores on the PLS reported a stronger desire to be with, held by, and kissed by the partner, and said that they were sexually excited just thinking about their partner. Finally, the passionate love scores increased as the nature of the relationship moved from dating to dating exclusively. Hatfield and Sprecher's research is a good example of how to study an important but complex topic—such as love—scientifically.

Gender Differences

The stereotype is that women are the romantics—they yearn for love, fall in love more easily, cling to love. Do the data support this idea?

In fact, research measuring love in relationships indicates that just the opposite is true. Men hold a more romantic view of male–female relations than women do (Hobart, 1958). They fall in love earlier in a relationship (Kanin et al., 1970; Rubin et al., 1981). Men also cling longer to a dying love affair (Hill et al., 1976; Rubin et al., 1981). Indeed, three times as many men as women commit suicide after a disastrous love affair (Hatfield & Walster, 1978). In a word, it seems that men are the real romantics.

Three decades ago, men and women held very different views of the importance of romantic love in marriage (Simpson et al., 1986). In response to the question "If (someone) had all the other qualities you desired, would you marry this person if you were not in love?" about 30 percent of women said they would refuse to marry, compared with more than 60 percent of men. That is, men were more likely to view love as an essential requirement for marriage. However, these patterns have changed. This survey was repeated in 1976 and again in 1984 (Simpson et al., 1986). By then the gender differences had disappeared, and love was considered more essential to marriage in 1984 than it was in the 1960s. More than 80 percent of both men and women would refuse to marry under the conditions stated in the question.

What does this dramatic shift mean? The researchers interpreted it as a result of great changes in the social roles of men and women. In particular, women are now more likely to hold paid employment and to be more economically independent of men. For this reason, they feel less need to be in a marriage—whether in love or not—in order to be financially supported. Consequently, love can be a necessary requirement for women, too. It is ironic that the sexual revolution—which stressed the right to liberated, even casual, sex—was accompanied by increased, not decreased, emphasis on love.

Love and Adrenaline
Two-Component Theory of Love
Social psychologists Ellen Berscheid and Elaine Walster (1974) propose a **two-component theory of love.** According to their theory, passionate love occurs when two conditions exist simultaneously: (1) the person is in a state of intense *physiological arousal,* and (2) the situation is such that the person applies a particular *label*—"love"—to the sensations being experienced. Their theory is derived from an important theory developed by Stanley Schachter (1964).

Suppose that your heart is pounding, your palms are sweating, and your body is tense. What emotion are you experiencing? Is it love—has reading about passionate love led to obsessive thoughts of another person? Is it fear—are you frantically reading this text because you have an exam tomorrow morning? Is it sexual arousal—are you thinking about physical intimacy later tonight?

It could be any of these, or even anger or embarrassment. A wide variety of emotions are accompanied by the same physiological states: increased blood pressure, a higher heart rate, increased muscular tension, and sweating palms. What differentiates these emotions? The key is the way we interpret or label what we are experiencing.

Schachter's (1964) two-component theory of emotion says just this: An emotion consists of a physiological arousal state plus the label the person assigns to it (for a critical evaluation of this theory, see Reisenzein, 1983). Berscheid and Walster have applied this to the emotion of "love." They suggest that we feel passionate love when we are aroused and when conditions are such that we identify what we are feeling as love.

Evidence for the Two-Component Theory
Several experiments provide evidence for Berscheid and Walster's two-component theory of love. In one study, male research participants exercised vigorously by running in place, and this activity produced the physiological arousal response of pounding heart and sweaty palms (White et al., 1981). Afterward they rated their liking for an attractive woman, who actually was a confederate of the experimenters. Men in the running group said they liked the woman significantly more than did men who were in a control condition and had not exercised.

Two-component theory of love: Berscheid and Walster's theory that two conditions must exist simultaneously for passionate love to occur: physiological arousal and attaching a cognitive label ("love") to the feeling.

Figure 11.7   The misattribution of arousal. If people are physically aroused (e.g., by jogging), they may misattribute this arousal to love or sexual attraction, provided the situation suggests such an interpretation.

This result is consistent with Berscheid and Walster's theory. The effect is called the **misattribution of arousal.** In other words, in a situation like this one, the men misattribute their arousal—which is actually due to exercise—to their liking for the attractive woman. An analysis of 33 experiments found that arousal affects attraction even when the source of the arousal is unambiguous (Foster et al., 1998).

Another study suggests that fear can increase a man's attraction to a woman (Dutton & Aron, 1974; see also Brehm et al., cited in Berscheid & Walster, 1974). An attractive female interviewer approached male passersby either on a fear-arousing suspension bridge or on a non-fear-arousing bridge. The fear-arousing bridge was constructed of boards,

Misattribution of arousal: When a person in a stage of physiological arousal (e.g., from exercising or being in a frightening situation) attributes these feelings to love or attraction to the person present.

attached to cables, and had a tendency to tilt, sway, and wobble. The handrails were low, and there was a 230-foot drop to rocks and shallow rapids below. The control bridge was made of solid cedar. It was firm, and there was only a 10-foot drop to a shallow rivulet below. The interviewer asked subjects to fill out questionnaires that included projective test items. These items were then scored for sexual imagery.

There was more sexual imagery in the questionnaires filled out by the men in the suspension-bridge group, and these men made more attempts to contact the attractive interviewer after the experiment than the men on the control bridge. Intuitively, this result might seem to be peculiar: that men who are in a state of fear are more attracted to a woman than men who are relaxed. But in terms of the Berscheid and Walster two-component theory, it makes perfect sense. The fearful men were physiologically aroused, while the men in the control group were not. And according to this theory, arousal is an important component of love or attraction.[2]

Now, of course, if the men (most of them heterosexuals) had been approached by an elderly man or a child, their responses would probably have been different. In fact, when the interviewer in the experiment was male, the effects discussed above did not occur. Society tells us what the appropriate objects of our love, attraction, or liking are. In other words, we know for what kinds of people it is appropriate to have feelings of love or liking. For these men, feelings toward an attractive woman could reasonably be labeled "love" or "attraction." Such labels would probably not be attached to feelings for an elderly man.

The physical arousal that is important for love need not always be produced by unpleasant or frightening situations. Pleasant stimuli, such as sexual arousal or praise from the other person, may produce arousal and feelings of love. Indeed, Berscheid and Walster's theory does an excellent job of explaining why we seem to have such a strong tendency to associate love and sex. Sexual arousal is one method of producing a state of physiological arousal, and it is one that our culture has taught us to label as "love." Accordingly, both components necessary to feel love are present: arousal and a label. On the other hand, this phenomenon may lead us to confuse love with lust, an all-too-common error.

[2]According to the terminology of Chapter 3, note that the Dutton and Aron study is an example of *experimental* research.

Cross-Cultural Research

In the past two decades, researchers have studied people from various ethnic or cultural groups to see whether attraction, intimacy, and love are experienced in the same way outside the United States. Three topics that have been studied are the impact of culture on how people view love, on whom people fall in love with, and on the importance of love in decisions to marry.

Cultural Values and the Meaning of Love

Cross-cultural psychologists have identified two dimensions on which cultures vary (Hatfield & Rapson, 1993a). The first is individualism–collectivism. *Individualistic cultures,* like those of the United States, Canada, and the western European countries, tend to emphasize individual goals over group and societal goals and interests. *Collectivist cultures,* like those of China, Africa, and the southeast Asian countries, emphasize group and collective goals over personal ones.

Several specific traits have been identified that differentiate these two types of societies (Triandis et al., 1990). In individualistic cultures, behavior is regulated by individual attitudes and cost-benefit considerations, and emotional detachment from the group is accepted. In collectivist cultures, the self is defined by its group membership, behavior is regulated by group norms, and attachment to and harmony within the group are valued.

The two types of cultures have different conceptions of love. American society, for example, emphasizes passionate love as the basis for marriage (Dion & Dion, 1993b). Individuals select mates on the basis of such characteristics as physical attractiveness, similarity (compatibility), and wealth or resources. We look for intimacy in the relationship with our mate. In Chinese society, by contrast, marriages are arranged, and the primary criterion is that the two families be of similar status. The person finds intimacy in relationships with other family members.

The second dimension on which cultures differ is independence–interdependence. Many Western cultures view each person as independent, and value individuality and uniqueness. Many other cultures view the person as interdependent with those around him or her. The self is defined in relation to others. Americans value standing up for one's beliefs. The people of India value conformity and harmony within the group.

In a study of university students in Toronto, representing four ethnocultural groups, students from Asian backgrounds were more likely to view love as companionate, as friendship, in contrast to those

Figure 11.8 Whether a culture is individualistic or collectivistic determines its views on love and marriage. In the United States, an individualistic culture, individuals choose each other and marry for love. In India, a collectivistic culture, marriages are arranged by family members to serve family interests.

from English and Irish backgrounds (Dion & Dion, 1993a). This tendency is consistent with the collectivist orientation of Asian cultures.

In another study, Mexican American students were found to be similar to American students of European background in the emphasis they placed on trust and communication/sharing as components of romantic love, but they placed greater emphasis on mutual respect (Castaneda, 1993). One student wrote, "[In a love relationship] we must respect each other's feelings as we would expect them to show us respect" (p. 265). Such respect allows each partner to express his or her needs to the other.

Cultural Influences on Mate Selection

Buss (1989) conducted a large-scale survey of 10,000 men and women from 37 societies. The sample included people from 4 cultures in Africa, 8 in Asia, and 4 in eastern Europe, in addition to 12 western European and 4 North American ones. Each respondent was given a list of 18 characteristics a person might value in a potential mate and asked to rate how important each was to him or her personally. Regardless of which society they lived in, most respondents—male and female—rated intelligence, kindness, and understanding at the top of the list. Note that these are characteristics of companionate love. Men worldwide placed more weight on cues of reproductive capacity, such as physical attractiveness, and women rated cues of resources as more important. The results clearly support the sociobiological perspective and suggest that there are not large cultural differences in mate selection.

Many people prefer mates who are physically attractive. We often hear that beauty is in the eye of the beholder. This saying suggests that the standards of beauty might vary across cultures. In one study, researchers had students from varying cultural backgrounds rate 45 photographs of women on a scale ranging from very attractive to very unattractive (Cunningham et al., 1995). The photographs portrayed women from many different societies. Overall, Asian, Hispanic, and white students did not differ in their ratings of the individual photographs. However, Asian students' ratings were less influenced by indicators of sexual maturity (such as facial narrowness) and expressivity (such as the vertical distance between the lips when the person smiled).

In a separate study, Black men and white men gave similar ratings to most aspects of female faces, but Black men preferred women with heavier bodies than did white men. Again, the results indicate more similarities than differences across cultures, in this case in standards of physical attractiveness.

Love and Marriage

We noted above that individualistic cultures place a high value on romantic love, while collectivistic cultures emphasize the group. The importance of romantic love in U.S. society was highlighted earlier when we discussed responses to the question "If a man (woman) had all the other qualities you desired,

Table 11.2 "Would You Marry Someone You Didn't Love?"

Cultural Group	Responses (Percent)		
	Yes	Undecided	No
Australia	4.8%	15.2%	80.0%
Brazil	4.3	10.0	85.7
England	7.3	9.1	83.6
Hong Kong	5.8	16.7	77.6
India	49.0	26.9	24.0
Japan	2.3	35.7	62.0
Mexico	10.2	9.3	80.5
Pakistan	50.4	10.4	39.1
Philippines	11.4	25.0	63.6
Thailand	18.8	47.5	33.8
United States	3.5	10.6	85.9

Source: Hatfield (1994).

would you marry this person if you were not in love with him (her)?" Over time, increasing percentages of American men and women answer no.

Levine and his colleagues (1995) asked this question of men and women in 11 different cultures. We would predict that members of individualistic cultures would answer no, whereas those in collectivistic cultures would answer yes. The results are displayed in Table 11.2. Note that, as predicted, many Indians and Pakistanis would marry even though they didn't love the person. In Thailand, which is also collectivistic, a much smaller percentage said yes. In the individualistic cultures of Australia, England, and the United States, few would marry someone they did not love.

The Pattern of the Cross-Cultural Findings

When we look at the findings of the cross-cultural research on love, attraction, and marriage, the pattern that emerges is one of *cross-cultural similarities and cross-cultural differences,* a theme we introduced in Chapter 1. In other words, some phenomena are similar across cultures, for example, valuing intelligence, kindness, and understanding in a mate. Other phenomena differ substantially across cultures, for example, whether love is a prerequisite for marriage.

Communication

Consider the following situation:

Josh and Lauren have been married for about three years. Lauren had had intercourse with only one other person before Josh, and she had never masturbated. Since they have been married, she has had orgasms only twice during intercourse, despite the fact that they make love three or four times per week. She has been reading some magazine articles about female sexuality and is beginning to think that she should be experiencing more sexual satisfaction. As far as she knows, Josh is unaware that there is any problem. Lauren feels lonely and a bit sad.

What should Lauren do? She needs to communicate with Josh. They apparently have not communicated much about sex in the last three years, and they need to begin. In the following sections, we discuss the relationship between sex, communication, and relationships and provide some suggestions on how to communicate effectively.

Communication and Relationships

A good deal of research has looked at differences in communication patterns between nondistressed (happy) married couples and distressed (unhappy, seeking marital counseling) married couples. This research shows, in general, that distressed couples tend to have communication deficits (Gottman, 1994; Markman & Floyd, 1980; Noller, 1984). Research also shows that couples seeking therapy for sex problems have poor communication patterns compared with nondistressed couples (Zimmer, 1983).

Of course, many other factors contribute to marital or relationship conflict or sex problems, but poor communication patterns are certainly among them. The problem with this research is that it is correlational (see Chapter 3 for a discussion of this problem in research methods). In particular, we cannot tell whether poor communication causes unhappy marriages or whether unhappy marriages create poor communication patterns.

An elegant longitudinal study designed to address this problem provides evidence that unrewarding, ineffective communication precedes and predicts later relationship problems (Markman, 1979, 1981). Dating couples who were planning marriage were studied for $5\frac{1}{2}$ years. The more positively couples rated their communication interactions at the beginning of the study, the more satisfaction they reported in their relationship when they were followed up $2\frac{1}{2}$ years later and $5\frac{1}{2}$ years later.

On the basis of this notion that communication deficits cause relationship problems, marriage counselors and marital therapists often work on teaching couples communication skills. Recent research suggests that distressed couples do not differ from nondistressed couples in their communication skills or ability, but rather, some distressed couples use their skills as weapons, to send negative messages (Burleson & Denton, 1997). These results suggest that therapists should focus on the intent of the partners as they communicate with each other, not just on techniques.

But what are these negative messages? Gottman (1994) used audiotape, videotape, and monitoring of physiological arousal to answer this question. He identified four destructive patterns of interaction: criticism, contempt, defensiveness, and withdrawal. *Criticism* refers to attacking a partner's personality or character: "You are so selfish; you never think of anyone else." *Contempt* is intentionally insulting or orally abusing the other person: "How did I get hooked up with such a loser?" *Defensiveness* refers to denying responsibility, making excuses, replying with a complaint of one's own and making other self-protective responses instead of addressing the problem. *Withdrawal* involves such actions as responding to the partner's complaint with silence, turning on the TV, or walking out of the room in anger. You can probably see that these types of communication are likely to lead to an escalation of the hostility rather than a solution to the problem.

Positive communication is important in developing and maintaining intimate relationships. Let's look at some of the skills involved in positive communication.

Being an Effective Communicator

Back to Lauren and Josh. One of the first things to do in a situation like Lauren's is to decide to talk to your partner, admitting that there is a problem. Then the issue is to resolve to communicate and, particularly, to be an *effective* communicator. Suppose Lauren begins by saying,

> You're not giving me any orgasms when we have sex. (Message 1)

Josh gets angry and walks away. Lauren meant to communicate that she wasn't having any orgasms, but Josh thought she meant that he was a lousy lover.

It is important to recognize the distinction between intent and impact in communicating (Gottman et al., 1976; Purnine & Carey, 1997). **Intent** is what you mean. **Impact** is what the other person thinks you mean. A good communicator is one whose impact matches her or his intent. Lauren wasn't an **effective communicator** in this

> **Intent:** What the speaker means.
> **Impact:** What someone else understands the speaker to mean.
> **Effective communicator:** A communicator whose impact matches his or her intent.

Focus: A Sexually Diverse World
Gender Differences in Communication

Linguist Deborah Tannen (1991), author of best-selling books such as *You Just Don't Understand: Women and Men in Conversation*, believes that women and men have radically different verbal communication styles, so different that they essentially belong to different linguistic communities. According to this point of view, communication between women and men is as difficult as cross-cultural communication. These arguments have captured the imagination of the general public and worked their way into corporate training programs. Does the scientific evidence support Tannen's claims? Are there substantial gender differences in communication styles, and if so, what are the implications for sexual interactions?

Research has repeatedly found a number of gender differences in communication. Women are more skilled at reading nonverbal cues than men are. Women are more likely than men to inquire about upsetting situations that another person is in, and to use comforting messages that acknowledge and legitimize the feelings of others. In same-gender pairs, men are more likely to discuss sports, careers, and politics, whereas women are more likely to talk about feelings and relationships. Men interrupt more than women do.

One research finding is that, in conversation, women are more self-disclosing than men are. In other words, women reveal more personal, intimate information about themselves. Yet this pattern is found only with same-gender conversational pairs—men talking with men, and women talking with women. When talking with a woman, men disclose far more than when they talk with a man. In one study, women and men were brought to the laboratory to have a conversation with their best friend of the same gender. They were told to discuss something important and to reveal their thoughts and feelings. No gender differences in self-disclosure occurred. Gender differences in self-disclosure, then, are far from universal, and men are capable of being as self-disclosing as women are.

One claim is that women and men have different goals when they speak. Women use speech to establish and maintain relationships, whereas men use speech to exert control, preserve independence, and enhance their status (Wood, 1994). This pattern is consistent with research findings that indicate that women are more concerned than men are with the quality of the relationship in which sex occurs (see Chapter 12), and that some men use sexual assault to exert power and control over women (see Chapter 15).

A review of dozens of studies of gender differences in communication indicates, however, that the differences, overall, are small (Dindia & Canary, 2006). Research simply does not support the contention that gender differences in communication are so large that it is as if women and men are from different cultures. Another problem with the "two cultures" approach is that it assumes that patterns of gender differences are the same for all ethnic groups and social classes, when almost all the research has been done with middle-class whites.

What are the implications for sexuality? We should not be led astray by flashy claims that men and women have totally different communication styles, making it difficult at best, and impossible at worst, to communicate. Gender differences in communication are small. That is a happy result for sexuality, and particularly for heterosexual interactions.

Good communication is essential for satisfying, mutually pleasurable sex. If men and women could not communicate, it would be a serious problem. Fortunately, the gender differences are small, and, with a little effort, couples should be able to engage in clear, accurate sexual communication.

Sources: Aries (1996); Dindia & Canary (2006); Tannen (1991).

---

example because the impact on Josh was considerably different from her intent. Notice that effectiveness does not depend on the content of the message. A person can be as effective at communicating contempt as communicating praise.

Many people value spontaneity in sex, and this attitude may extend to communicating about sex. It is best to recognize that to be an effective communicator, you may need to plan your strategy. It often takes some thinking to figure out how to make sure your impact will match your intent. Planning also allows you to make sure that the timing is good—that you are not speaking out of anger, or that your partner is not tired or preoccupied with other things.

In the last few decades public communication about sex has become relatively open, but private communication remains difficult (Crawford et al.,

1994). This doesn't mean that Lauren can't communicate. But she shouldn't feel guilty or stupid if it is difficult for her. And she will be better off if she uses some specific communication skills and has some belief that they will work. In the following sections we suggest some skills that are useful in being an effective communicator and how to apply these to sexual relationships.

Good Messages

Every couple has problems. The best way to voice them is to complain rather than to criticize (Gottman, 1994). Complaining involves the use of **"I" language** (e.g., Brenton, 1972). In other words, speak for yourself, not your partner (Miller et al., 1975). By doing this you focus on what you know best—your own thoughts and feelings. "I" language is less likely to make your partner defensive. If Lauren were to use this technique, she might say,

> I feel a bit unhappy because I don't have orgasms very often when we make love. (Message 2)

Notice that she focuses specifically on herself. There is less cause for Josh to get angry than there was in message 1.

One of the best things about "I" language is that it avoids mind reading (Gottman et al., 1976). Suppose Lauren says,

> I know you think women aren't much interested in sex, but I really wish I had more orgasms. (Message 3)

She is engaging in **mind reading.** In other words, she is making certain assumptions about what Josh is thinking. She assumes that Josh believes women aren't interested in sex or having orgasms. Research shows that mind reading is more common among distressed couples than among nondistressed couples (Gottman et al., 1977). Worse, Lauren doesn't *check out* her assumptions with Josh. The problem is that she may be wrong, and Josh may not think that at all. "I" language helps Lauren avoid mind reading by focusing on herself and what she feels rather than on what Josh is doing or failing to do. Another important way to avoid mind reading is by giving and receiving feedback, a technique we discuss in a later section.

Documenting is another important component of giving good messages (Brenton, 1972). In documenting, you give specific examples of the issue. Documenting is not quite so relevant in Lauren's case, because she is talking about a general problem, but even here, specific examples can be helpful. Once Lauren has broached the subject, she might say,

> Last night when we made love, I enjoyed it and felt very aroused, but then I didn't have an orgasm, and I felt disappointed. (Message 4)

Now she has gotten her general complaint down to a specific situation that Josh can remember.

Suppose further that Lauren has some idea of what Josh would need to do to bring her to orgasm: he would have to do more hand stimulation of her clitoris. Then she might do specific documenting, as follows:

> Last night when we made love, I enjoyed it, but I didn't have an orgasm, and then I felt disappointed. I think what I needed was for you to stimulate my clitoris with your hand a bit more. You did it for a while, but it seemed so brief. I think if you had kept doing it for two or three minutes more, I would have had an orgasm. (Message 5)

Now she has not only documented to Josh exactly what the problem was, but she has given a specific suggestion about what could have been done about it, and therefore what could be done in the future.

Another technique in giving good messages is to offer *limited choices* (Langer & Dweck, 1973). Suppose Lauren begins by saying,

> I've been having trouble with orgasms. Could we discuss it? (Message 6)

The trouble with this approach is that a "no" from Josh is not really an acceptable answer to her because she definitely wants to discuss the problem. Yet she set up the question so that he could answer by saying no. To use the technique of limited choices she might say,

> I've been having trouble with orgasms when we make love. Would you like to discuss it now, or would you rather wait until tomorrow night? (Message 7)

Now, either answer he gives will be acceptable to her; she has offered a set of acceptable limited choices.[3] She has also shown some consideration for him by recognizing that he might not be in the mood for such a discussion now and would rather wait.

[3]The technique of limited choices is useful in a number of other situations, including dealing with children. For example, when my (author Janet Hyde) daughter was a 2-year-old and she had finished watching *Sesame Street* and I wanted the TV turned off, I didn't say, "Would you turn the TV off?" (she might say no) but, rather, "Do you want to turn off the TV, or would you like me to?" Of course, sometimes she evaded my efforts and said no anyway, but most of the time it worked.

"I" language: Speaking for yourself, using the word "I"; not mind reading.
Mind reading: Making assumptions about what your partner thinks or feels.
Documenting: Giving specific examples of the issue being discussed.

Figure 11.9

Leveling and Editing

Leveling means telling your partner what you are feeling by stating your thoughts clearly, simply, and honestly (Gottman et al., 1976). This is often the hardest step in communication, especially when the topic is sex. It is especially difficult for adults to reach shared understandings about sex, since there is great secrecy about it in our society (Crawford et al., 1994). In leveling, keep in mind that the purposes are to

1. Make communication clear.
2. Clear up what partners expect of each other.
3. Clear up what is pleasant and what is unpleasant.
4. Clear up what is relevant and what is irrelevant.
5. Notice things that draw you closer or push you apart. (Gottman et al., 1976)

When you begin to level with your partner, you also need to do some editing. **Editing** involves censoring (not saying) things that would be deliberately hurtful to your partner or that would be irrelevant. You must take responsibility for making your communication polite and considerate. Leveling, then, does not mean a "no holds barred" approach. Ironically, research indicates that married people are ruder to each other than they are to strangers (Gottman et al., 1976).

Lauren may be so disgruntled about her lack of orgasms that she's thinking of having an affair to jolt Josh into recognizing her problem, or perhaps in order to see if another man would stimulate her to orgasm. Lauren is probably best advised to edit out this line of thought and concentrate on the specific problem: her lack of orgasms. If she and Josh can solve that problem, she won't need to have an affair.

The trick is to balance leveling and editing. If you edit too much, you may not level at all, and there will be no communication. If you level too much and don't edit, the communication will fail because your partner will respond negatively, and things may get worse rather than better.

Listening

Up to this point, we have concentrated on techniques for you to use in sending messages about sexual relationships. But, of course, communication is a two-way street, and you and your partner will exchange responses. For this reason, it is important for you and your partner to gain some skills in listening and responding constructively to messages.

One of the most important things is that you must really *listen*. Listening means more than just removing the headphones from your ears. It means actively trying to understand what the other person is saying. Often people are so busy trying to think of their next response that they hardly hear what the other person is saying.

Good listening involves positive nonverbal behaviors, such as maintaining eye contact with the speaker and nodding your head when appropriate. Be a *nondefensive listener:* focus on what your partner is saying and feeling, and don't immediately become defensive or counterattack with complaints of your own.

The next step, after you have listened carefully and nondefensively, is to give *feedback*. Feedback often involves brief vocalizations "Uh-huh," "Okay"—nodding your head, or facial movements that indicate you are listening (Gottman et al., 1998). It may involve the technique of **paraphrasing,** that

---

Leveling: Telling your partner what you are feeling by stating your thoughts clearly, simply, and honestly.

Editing: Censoring or not saying things that would be deliberately hurtful to your partner or that are irrelevant.

Paraphrasing: Saying, in your own words, what you thought your partner meant.

(a)

(b)

Figure 11.10   (*a*) A couple with good body language (good eye contact and body position); (*b*) a couple with poor body language (poor eye contact and body position).

is, repeating in your own words what you think your partner meant. Suppose, in response to Lauren's initial statement, "You're not giving me any orgasms when we have sex," Josh hadn't walked away angrily. Instead, he tried to listen and then gave her feedback by paraphrasing. He might have responded,

> I hear you saying that I'm not very skillful at making love to you, and therefore you're not having orgasms. (Message 8)

At that point, Lauren would have had a chance to clear up the confusion she had created with her initial message, because Josh had given her feedback by paraphrasing his understanding of what she said. At that point she could have said, "No, I think you're a good lover, but I'm not having any orgasms, and I don't know why. I thought maybe we could figure it out together." Or perhaps she could have said, "No, I think you're a good lover. I just wish you'd do more of some of the things you do, like rubbing my clitoris."

It's also a good idea to *ask for feedback* from your partner, particularly if you're not sure whether you're communicating clearly.

Body Talk: Nonverbal Communication
Just as it is important to be a good listener to your partner's verbal messages, so too is it important to be good at "reading" your partner's nonverbal messages. Often the precise words we use are not so important as our **nonverbal communication**—the way we say them. Tone of voice, expression on the face, position of the body, whether you touch the other person—all are important in conveying the message (see Figure 11.10).

For example, take the sentence "So you're here." If it is delivered, "So *you're* here" in a hostile tone of voice, the message is that the speaker is very unhappy that you're here. If it is delivered, "So you're *here*" in a pleased voice, the meaning may be that the speaker is glad and surprised to see you here in Wisconsin, having thought you were in Europe. "So you're here" with a smile and arms outstretched for a hug might mean that the speaker has been waiting for you and is delighted to see you.

Suppose that in Lauren and Josh's case, the reason Lauren doesn't have more orgasms is that Josh simply doesn't stimulate her vigorously enough. During sex, Lauren has adopted a very passive, nearly rigid posture for her body. Josh doesn't stimulate her more vigorously because he is afraid that he might hurt her, and he is sure that no lady like his wife would want such a vigorous approach. The response (or rather nonresponse) of her body confirms his assumptions. Her body is saying, "I don't enjoy this. Let's get it over with." And that's exactly what she's getting.

To correct this situation, she might adopt a more active, encouraging approach. She might take his hand and guide it to her clitoris, showing him how firmly she likes to have it rubbed. She might place her hands on his hips and press to indicate how deep and forceful she would like the thrusting of his penis in her vagina to be. She might even take the daring approach of using some verbal communication, perhaps saying "That's good" when he becomes more vigorous.

The point is that in communicating about sex, we need to be sure that our nonverbal signals help to create the impact we intend

Nonverbal communication: Communication not through words, but through the body, e.g., eye contact, tone of voice, touching.

rather than one we don't intend. It is also possible that nonverbal signals are confusing communication and need to be straightened out. *Checking out* is a technique for doing this, which we discuss in a later section.

Interestingly, research shows that distressed couples differ from nondistressed couples more in their nonverbal communication than in their verbal communication (Gottman et al., 1977; Vincent et al., 1979). For example, even when a person from a distressed couple is expressing agreement with his or her spouse, that person is more likely to accompany the verbal expressions of agreement with negative nonverbal behavior. Distressed couples are also more likely to be negative listeners—while listening, the individuals are more likely to display frowning, angry, or disgusted facial expressions, or tense or inattentive body postures. Contempt is often expressed nonverbally, by sneering or rolling the eyes, for example. In contrast, harmonious marriages are characterized by closer physical distances and more relaxed postures than are found in distressed couples (Beier & Sternberg, 1977). Once again, it is not only what we say verbally but how we say it, and how we listen, that makes the difference.

Validating

Another good technique in communication is **validation** (Gottman et al., 1976), which means telling your partner that, given his or her point of view, you can see why he or she thinks a certain way. It doesn't mean that you agree with your partner or that you're giving in. It simply means that you recognize your partner's point of view as legitimate, given his or her set of assumptions, which may be different from yours.

It is important to recognize that all couples will have disagreements. What is important is how you handle these disagreements. If they lead to fights because one partner thinks the other is "wrong," these will likely damage the relationship. It is much better to try to understand the other's viewpoint. In a study of 76 couples, an understanding of the partner's preferences for such things as foreplay, use of erotica, and use of contraception (not agreement with them) was associated with satisfaction with the sexual aspects of the relationship (Purnine & Carey, 1997).

Suppose that Lauren and Josh have gotten into an argument about cunnilingus. She wants him to do it and thinks it would bring her to orgasm. He doesn't want to do it because he finds the idea repulsive and because he believes no real man would do such a thing. If Lauren tried to validate Josh's feelings, she might say,

> I can understand the way you feel about cunnilingus, especially given the way you were brought up to think about sex. (Message 9)

Josh might validate Lauren's feelings by saying,

> I understand how important it is for you to have an orgasm. (Message 10)

Validating hasn't solved their disagreement, but it has left the door open so that they can now make some progress.

Drawing Your Partner Out

Suppose it is Josh who initiates the conversation rather than Lauren. Josh has noticed that Lauren doesn't seem to get a lot of pleasure out of sex, and he would like to find out why and see what they can do about it. He needs to draw her out. He might begin by saying,

> I've noticed lately that you don't seem to be enjoying sex as much as you used to. Am I right about that? (Message 11)

That much is good because he's checking out his assumption. Unfortunately, he's asked a question that leads to a "yes" or "no" answer, and that can stop the communication. So if Lauren replies "yes," Josh had better follow it up with an *open-ended* question like

> Why do you think you aren't enjoying it more? (Message 12)

If she can give a reasonable answer, good communication should be on the way. One of the standard—and best—questions to ask in a situation like this is,

> What can we do to make things better? (Message 13)

Accentuate the Positive

We have been concentrating on negative communications, in other words, communications wherein some problem or complaint needs to be voiced. It is also important to communicate positive things about sex (Miller et al., 1975). If that was a great episode of lovemaking, or the best kiss you've ever experienced, say so. A learning theorist would say that you're giving your partner some positive reinforcement. As we noted earlier, research shows that we tend to like people better who give us positive reinforcements. Recognition of the strengths in a relationship offers the potential for enriching it (e.g., Miller et al., 1975; Otto, 1963). And if you make a habit of positive communications about

Validation: Telling your partner that, given his or her point of view, you can see why he or she thinks a certain way.

sex, it will be easier to initiate the negative ones and they will be better received.

Most communication during sex is limited to muffled groans, or "Mm-m's," or an occasional "Higher, José" or "Did you, Latisha?" It might help your partner greatly if you gave frequent verbal and nonverbal feedback, such as "That was great" or "Let's do that again." This would make the positive communications and the negative ones far easier.

Research shows that nondistressed couples make more positive and fewer negative communications than distressed couples (Billings, 1979; Birchler et al., 1975). In fact, Gottman's (1994) research found that there is a *magic ratio* of positive to negative communication. In stable marriages, there is five times as much positive interaction—verbal and nonverbal, including hugs and kisses—as there is negative. Not only do happy couples make more positive communications, but they are also more likely to respond to a negative communication with something positive (Billings, 1979). Distressed couples, on the other hand, are more likely to respond to negative communication with more negative communication, escalating into conflict. We might all take a cue from the happy couples and make efforts not only to increase our positive communications but even to make them in response to negative comments from our partner.

Fighting Fair

Even if you use all the techniques described above, you may still get into arguments with your partner. Arguments are a natural part of a relationship and are not necessarily bad. Given that there will be arguments in a relationship, it is useful if you and your partner have agreed to a set of rules called **fighting fair** (Bach & Wyden, 1969) so that the arguments may help and won't hurt.

Here are some of the basic rules for fighting fair that may be useful to you (Brenton, 1972; Creighton, 1992):

1. Don't make sarcastic or insulting remarks about your partner's sexual adequacy. This generates resentment, opens you to counterattack, and is just a dirty way to fight.

2. Don't bring up the names of former spouses, lovers, boyfriends, or girlfriends to illustrate how all these problems didn't happen with them. Stick to the issue: your relationship with your partner.

3. Don't play amateur psychologist. Don't say things like "The problem is that you're a compulsive personality" or "You acted that way

Figure 11.11 Arguments are not necessarily bad for a relationship, but it is important to observe the rules for fighting fair.

because you never resolved your Oedipus complex." You really don't have the qualifications (even after reading this book) to do that kind of psychologizing. Even if you did, your partner would not be apt to recognize your expertise in the middle of an argument, thinking, quite rightly, that you're probably biased at the moment.

4. Don't threaten to tell your parents or run home. This involves ganging up on your partner or retreating like a child.

5. If you have children, don't bring them into the argument. It is too stressful emotionally to force them to take sides between you and your partner.

6. Don't engage in dumping. Don't store up gripes for six months and then dump them on your partner all at one time.

7. Don't hit and run. Don't bring up a serious negative issue when there is no opportunity to continue the discussion, such as when you're on the way out the door going to work or when guests are coming for dinner in five minutes.

8. Don't focus on who's to blame. Focus on looking for solutions, not on who's at fault. If you avoid blaming, it lets both you and your partner save face, which helps both of you feel better about the relationship.

Checking Out Sexy Signals

One of the problems with verbal and nonverbal sexual communications

Fighting fair: A set of rules designed to make arguments constructive rather than destructive.

Focus: First Person
How Solid Is Your Relationship?

G ood communication enhances a relationship, and a good relationship facilitates good communication. There are several components of a good relationship. Two of these are love and respect. The following self-test assesses the degree of love and respect in a relationship. If you are in an intimate relationship, answer yes or no to each of the following statements. If you agree or mostly agree, answer yes. If you disagree or mostly disagree, answer no. You can either ask your partner to take the test too or take it a second time yourself, answering the way you think your partner would answer.

1. My partner seeks out my opinion.
   YOU: Yes No YOUR PARTNER: Yes No
2. My partner cares about my feelings.
   YOU: Yes No YOUR PARTNER: Yes No
3. I don't feel ignored very often.
   YOU: Yes No YOUR PARTNER: Yes No
4. We touch each other a lot.
   YOU: Yes No YOUR PARTNER: Yes No
5. We listen to each other.
   YOU: Yes No YOUR PARTNER: Yes No
6. We respect each other's ideas.
   YOU: Yes No YOUR PARTNER: Yes No
7. We are affectionate toward one another.
   YOU: Yes No YOUR PARTNER: Yes No
8. I feel my partner takes good care of me.
   YOU: Yes No YOUR PARTNER: Yes No
9. What I say counts.
   YOU: Yes No YOUR PARTNER: Yes No
10. I am important in our decisions.
    YOU: Yes No YOUR PARTNER: Yes No
11. There's lots of love in our relationship.
    YOU: Yes No YOUR PARTNER: Yes No
12. We are genuinely interested in one another.
    YOU: Yes No YOUR PARTNER: Yes No
13. I love spending time with my partner.
    YOU: Yes No YOUR PARTNER: Yes No
14. We are very good friends.
    YOU: Yes No YOUR PARTNER: Yes No
15. Even during rough times, we can be empathetic.
    YOU: Yes No YOUR PARTNER: Yes No
16. My partner is considerate of my viewpoint.
    YOU: Yes No YOUR PARTNER: Yes No
17. My partner finds me physically attractive.
    YOU: Yes No YOUR PARTNER: Yes No
18. My partner expresses warmth toward me.
    YOU: Yes No YOUR PARTNER: Yes No
19. I feel included in my partner's life.
    YOU: Yes No YOUR PARTNER: Yes No
20. My partner admires me.
    YOU: Yes No YOUR PARTNER: Yes No

Scoring: If you answered yes to fewer than seven items, it is likely that you are not feeling loved and respected in this relationship. You and your partner need to be more active and creative in adding affection to your relationship.

Source: Gottman (1994).

---

is that they are often ambiguous. This problem may occur more often with couples who don't know each other well, but it can cause uncertainty and misunderstanding in long-term couples as well.

Some messages are very direct. Statements like "I want to have sex with you" are not ambiguous at all. Unfortunately, such directness is not common in our society. In a series of studies of tactics people used to promote sexual encounters, college students reported good hygiene, good grooming, and dressing nicely as the actions they most frequently used (Greer & Buss, 1994). These are *very* indirect signals of sexual interest. Consider George, who stands up, stretches, and says "It's time for bed." Does he mean he wants to engage in sexual activity or to go to sleep?

Ambiguous messages can lead to feelings of hurt and rejection, or to unnecessary anger and perhaps complaints to third parties. If George wants to have sex but his partner interprets his behavior as meaning that George is tired, George may go to bed feeling hurt, unattractive, and unloved. A woman who casually puts her arm around the shoulders of a coworker and gives him a hug may find herself explaining to her supervisor that it was a gesture of friendship, not a sexual proposition.

When we confront ambiguous messages, we should check out their meaning. The problem is that most of us are reluctant to do that. Somehow we assume that we ought to know exactly what the other person meant, and that we are dumb or naive if we don't. It is important to recognize that many sexy signals—like putting an arm around someone's shoulders, inviting a date to your apartment for coffee, or french kissing and rubbing your date's (clothed) buttocks—really are ambiguous.

Ideally, each of us should be an effective communicator, making sure our message clearly matches our intent. As recipients of ambiguous messages, we need to make an effort to clear them up. In response to an invitation to a woman's apartment for coffee, a man might reply, "I would like some coffee, but I'm not interested in sex this time." Or he might draw her out with a question: "I'd like some coffee; is that all you have in mind?" Check out sexy signals. Don't make any assumptions about the meaning of ambiguous messages.

SUMMARY

Research indicates that mere repeated exposure to another person facilitates attraction. We tend to be attracted to people who are similar to us socially (age, race or ethnicity, economic status) and psychologically (attitudes, interests). In first impressions, we are most attracted to people who are physically attractive. We also tend to be attracted to people whom we believe to be "within reach" of us, depending on our sense of our own attractiveness or desirability.

According to reinforcement theory, we are attracted to those who give us many reinforcements. Interaction with people who are similar to us is smooth and rewarding; they have similar outlooks and like the same things we do. According to sexual strategies theory, we prefer young, attractive people because they are likely to be healthy and fertile. Men prefer women who are sexually faithful, and women prefer men with resources who will invest in them and their children.

Intimacy is a major component of a romantic relationship. It is defined as a quality of a relationship characterized by commitment, feelings of closeness and trust, and self-disclosure. Disclosure by one person generally leads to disclosure by the other. Self-disclosure is positively associated with relationship satisfaction, and with the longevity of the relationship.

According to the triangular theory, there are three components to love: intimacy, passion, and decision or commitment. Love is a triangle, with each of these components as one of the points. Partners whose love triangles are substantially different are mismatched and are likely to be dissatisfied with their relationship.

According to the attachment theory of love, adults vary in their capacity for love as a result of their love or attachment experiences in infancy. This theory says that there are three types of lovers: secure lovers, avoidant lovers, and anxious–ambivalent lovers.

Love can also be viewed as a story, with characters, a plot, and a theme. People use their love stories to interpret experiences in relationships. Falling in love happens when a person meets someone who can play a compatible role in his or her story.

Love may have a neurochemical component. Passionate love, a state of intense longing and arousal, may be produced by dopamine. Like all chemically induced highs, passionate love eventually comes to an end. It may be replaced by companionate love, a feeling of deep attachment and commitment to the partner. This type of love may be accompanied by elevated levels of prolactin and oxytocin, which may be produced by physical closeness and touch.

Hatfield and Sprecher have constructed a scale to measure passionate love. Such scales make it possible to do scientific research on complex phenomena like love. Scores on this scale were correlated with measures of commitment to and satisfaction with romantic relationships. Research indicates that, in general, men are more romantic than women and fall in love earlier in a relationship.

Berscheid and Walster have hypothesized that there are two basic components of romantic love: being in a state of physiological arousal and attaching the label "love" to the feeling. Several studies report evidence consistent with the hypothesis.

Cross-cultural research indicates that individualistic cultures like that of the United States emphasize love as the basis for marriage and encourage intimacy between partners. Collectivist cultures emphasize intergroup bonds as the basis for marriage, and discourage intimacy between partners. Culture influences the importance of various characteristics in choosing a mate. It also affects our standards of beauty and the likelihood that we would marry someone we don't love.

Research reveals clear differences in communication patterns between happy, nondistressed couples and couples who are unhappy, seeking counseling, or headed for divorce. Destructive patterns of interaction include criticism, contempt, defensiveness, and withdrawal. The key to building a good relationship is reciprocal self-disclosure.

The key to maintaining a good relationship is being a good communicator.

Specific tips for being a good communicator include the following: use "I" language; avoid mind reading; document your points with specific examples; use limited-choice questions; level and edit; be a nondefensive listener; give feedback by paraphrasing; be aware of your nonverbal messages; validate the other's viewpoint; draw your partner out; and engage in positive verbal and nonverbal communication. When you do fight, fight fair. Finally, it is important to check out ambiguous sexy signals to find out what they really mean.

QUESTIONS FOR THOUGHT, DISCUSSION, AND DEBATE

1. If you are currently in love with someone, how would you describe the kind of love you feel, using the various concepts and theories of love discussed in this chapter?

2. Resolved: Selecting mates on the basis of individualistic considerations, such as whether you love the person, contributes to the high rates of divorce and single-parent families.

3. Your best friend has been dating another person exclusively for the past year. One day you ask how the relationship is going. Your friend replies, "I don't know. We get along really well. We like to do the same things, and we can tell each other everything. But I feel like something is missing. How do you know if you are in love?" How would you answer her question?

4. If you are in a long-term relationship, think about the kind of communication pattern you have with your partner. Do you use the methods of communication recommended in this chapter? If not, do you think that there are areas in which you could change and improve? Would your partner cooperate in attempts to improve your communication pattern?

SUGGESTIONS FOR FURTHER READING

Fisher, Helen. (1992). *Anatomy of love.* New York: Fawcett Columbine. Fisher explains sexual anatomy, sexual emotions, mate selection, adultery, and the sexual double standard, among others, using evolutionary perspectives. A provocative book.

Gottman, John. (1994). *Why marriages succeed or fail.* New York: Simon & Schuster. Summarizes the results of 20 years of research on communication in marriage. The book includes self-assessment questions and specific suggestions to help couples enhance their communication.

Hendrick, Susan, and Hendrick, Clyde. (1992). *Liking, loving, and relating.* 2nd ed. Pacific Grove, CA: Brooks/Cole. This textbook explains psychologists' research on interpersonal attraction, love, and the formation and maintenance of relationships.

Sternberg, Robert. (1998). *Love is a story: A new theory of relationships.* Sternberg describes his theory and the 27 love stories he has identified. The book includes items from a scale designed to identify which stories a person holds.

 CHAPTER TWELVE

Gender and Sexuality

The majority of women (happily for them) are not very much troubled with sexual feelings of any kind. What men are habitually, women are only exceptionally.*

I can't mate in captivity.†

*Dr. William Acton. (1857). *The functions and disorders of the reproductive organs.*
†Gloria Steinem, in answer to why she never married.

When a baby is born, what is the first statement made about it? "It's a boy" or "It's a girl," of course. Sociologists tell us that gender is one of the most basic of status characteristics. That is, in terms of both our individual interactions with people and the position we hold in society, gender is exceptionally important. We experience consternation in the rare cases when we are uncertain of a person's gender. We do not know how to interact with such a person, and we feel flustered, not to mention curious, until we can ferret out some clue as to whether the person is a man or a woman. In this chapter we explore gender roles and the impact they may have on sexuality, as well as transsexualism (a disturbance of gender identity).

Gender Roles and Stereotypes

One of the basic ways in which societies codify this emphasis on gender is through gender roles.[1] A **gender role** is a set of norms, or culturally defined expectations, that define how people of one gender ought to behave. A closely related phenomenon is a **stereotype,** which is a generalization about a group of people (e.g., men) that distinguishes those people from others (e.g., women). Research shows that even in modern U.S. society, and even among college students, there is a belief that males and females do differ psychologically in many ways, and these stereotypes have not changed much since 1972 (Bergen & Williams, 1991; DeArmond et al., 2006).

Heterosexuality is an important part of gender roles (Hyde & Jaffee, 2000). The "feminine" woman is expected to be sexually attractive to men and in turn to be attracted to them. Women who violate any part of this role—for example, lesbians—are viewed as violators of

gender roles and are considered masculine (Storms, 1980). Heterosexuality is equally important in the male role.

Gender Roles and Ethnicity

Gender stereotypes vary somewhat among the various ethnic groups of the United States. In one study, data were collected about this very issue (Niemann et al., 1994). College students at the University of Houston—51 percent of whom were European American and the rest of whom were, in decreasing order of frequency, Latino, African American, Asian American, and American Indian—were asked to list 10 adjectives that came to mind when they thought of members of the following groups: Anglo-American males, Anglo-American females, African American males, African American females, Asian American males, Asian American females, Mexican American males, and Mexican American females. The most frequently listed adjectives are shown in Table 12.1.

Two important patterns can be seen in Table 12.1: (1) Within an ethnic group, males and females have some stereotyped traits in common but are also seen as having some traits that differ. For example, both Mexican American males and Mexican American females are stereotyped as pleasant and friendly, but only Mexican American females are stereotyped as overweight. (2) Within a gender, some stereotyped traits are common across ethnic groups, but others differ. For example, females from all ethnic groups are stereotyped as pleasant and friendly. However, Anglo-American and Asian American females are stereotyped as intelligent, whereas African American and Mexican American females are not.

As we consider variations in gender roles across various ethnic groups, it is crucial to understand how these gender roles are a product of *culture.* In the sections that follow, we consider some aspects of the cultures of four ethnic groups and their relevance to gender roles and sexuality.

African Americans

Two factors are especially significant in the cultural heritage of African Americans: the heritage of

Gender role: A set of norms, or culturally defined expectations, that define how people of one gender ought to behave.
Stereotype: A generalization about a group of people (e.g., men) that distinguishes them from others (e.g., women).

[1]The distinction between sex and gender is maintained in this chapter. Male–female roles—and thus gender roles—are discussed here.

Table 12.1	The Interaction of Gender and Ethnicity: Stereotypes of Males and Females from Different Ethnic Groups

Anglo-American Males	Anglo-American Females
Intelligent	Attractive
Egotistical	Intelligent
Upper class	Egotistical
Pleasant/friendly	Pleasant/friendly
Racist	Blond/light hair
Achievement oriented	Sociable

African American Males	African American Females
Athletic	Speak loudly
Antagonistic	Dark skin
Dark skin	Antagonistic
Muscular appearances	Athletic
Criminal activities	Pleasant/friendly
Speak loudly	Unmannerly
	Sociable

Asian American Males	Asian American Females
Intelligent	Intelligent
Short	Speak softly
Achievement oriented	Pleasant/friendly
Speak softly	Short
Hard workers	

Mexican American Males	Mexican American Females
Lower class	Black/brown/dark hair
Hard workers	Attractive
Antagonistic	Pleasant/friendly
Dark skin	Dark skin
Noncollege education	Lower class
Pleasant/friendly	Overweight
Black/brown/dark hair	Baby makers
Ambitionless	

Source: Niemann et al. (1994).

African culture and the experience in America of slavery and subsequent racial oppression (Sudarkasa, 1997). African American culture today, like that of some other ethnic groups but in contrast to European American culture, emphasizes the collective over the individual (Fairchild et al., 2003), in contrast to the "me generation" of contemporary white culture. Mother–child bonds continue to be extremely important in the structure of African American society, and status and honor are accorded to motherhood (Reid & Bing, 2000).

Some say that the central theme for African American men today is pain (Doyle, 1989). Locked in chains during slavery, they are now locked be-

hind bars in prisons. Just walking down the street, Black men observe white women holding their handbags tighter. As one comedian said, "I was born a suspect . . . I asked this white guy for the time and he gave me his watch" (Doyle, 1989, p. 282). In the context of these overwhelmingly negative forces, the courage of the Black men who have not given in and have gone on to forge successful lives for themselves and their families has to be admired.

The provider role is difficult for some African American men because of their high unemployment rate. For example, in 2006 the unemployment rate was 4.0 percent for adult white males; for adult Black males, it was 9.5 percent (U.S. Bureau of Labor Statistics, 2007), more than double the rate for whites. Much of this discrepancy is accounted for by the disappearance of industrial jobs, which had long provided good earnings for Black men. The high unemployment rate creates a gender-role problem because the role of breadwinner or good provider is an important part of the male role in the United States. The inability to fulfill this part of the male role may be expressed in a number of ways. It may turn into antisocial behavior, violence, and crime, reflected in the high crime rate among male African American teenagers. It has been suggested that being in the army becomes an alternative means of fulfilling the male role. Twenty-seven percent of men in the army are African American (U.S. Bureau of the Census, 1997).[2]

The role of husband is closely tied to the breadwinner role. African American men are understandably reluctant to take on the responsibility of marriage when unemployment is such a justified fear. In this context, it is not surprising that African American women expect to hold paying jobs. And, compared with white men, African American men hold more liberal (positive) attitudes about women working, although they are more conservative than white men on many other gender-role issues (Blee & Tickamyer, 1995).

Latinos

Hispanic Americans are now the nation's largest minority, constituting 13 percent of the population (U.S. Bureau of the Census, 2002). When we speak of the cultural heritage of Latinos, we must first understand the concept of **acculturation,** which is the process of incorporating the beliefs

Acculturation: The process of incorporating the beliefs and customs of a new culture.

[2]In trying to update this statistic we found that the Department of Defense no longer reports data on the ethnicity of members of the armed services (U.S. Bureau of the Census, 2003).

Figure 12.1   Fathers and sons at the Millions More Movement March in Washington, D.C., in 2005. Leaders of the march wanted to encourage African American men to take more responsibility for their families and community, and some 1 million men seemed to agree.

and customs of a new culture. The culture of Mexican Americans (Americans of Mexican heritage) is different from both the culture of Mexico and the dominant Anglo culture of the United States. Mexican American culture is based on the Mexican heritage, modified through acculturation to incorporate Anglo components.

The family is the central focus of Hispanic life. Traditional Latinos place a high value on family loyalty and on warm, mutually supportive relationships, so that family and community are highly valued.

As noted in Chapter 1, in traditional Latin American cultures, gender roles are sharply defined (Raffaelli & Ontai, 2004; Salgado de Snyder et al., 2000). Such roles are emphasized early in the socialization process for children (Raffaelli & Ontai, 2004). Boys are given greater freedom, are encour-

aged in sexual exploits, and are not expected to share in household work. Girls are expected to be passive, obedient, virginal, and to stay in the home. One woman described how she and her brother, who was one year older than she, were treated by their mother:

> He had a very much later curfew than I did. He got a car, got to drive a car and then he also got his own car and I never did. . . . I could only go to school-related activities and he could do about anything, he could go any place he wanted. (Raffaelli & Ontai, 2004, p. 290)

These roles are epitomized in the concepts of machismo and marianismo, discussed in Chapter 1. Implicit in the principle of marianismo is a woman's repression of her sexual desires and a view that sex with her husband is an obligation (Reid & Bing, 2000). Young Latinas may feel that they have to choose between being a "good girl" and being a "flirt girl" (Faulkner, 2003).

Asian Americans

Chinese—almost all of them men—were recruited first in the 1840s to come to the United States as laborers in the West and later in the 1860s to work on the transcontinental railroad (for excellent summaries of the cultural heritage of Asian Americans, see Root, 1995, and Tsai & Uemura, 1988). Racist sentiment against the Chinese grew, however, and there was a shift to recruiting first Japanese and Koreans and then Filipinos. Then, in the late 1960s and the 1970s, there was a mass exodus to the United States of refugees from war-torn Southeast Asia. Today, Asian Americans make up 4 percent of the U.S. population.

The cultural values of Asian Americans are in some ways consistent with white middle-class American values but in other ways contradict them. Asian Americans share with the white mid-

dle class an emphasis on achievement and on the importance of education. For example, Asian American women have a higher level of education, on average, than white American women (Humes & McKinnon, 2000). On the other hand, Asian Americans place far more value on family and group interdependence, compared with the white American emphasis on individualism and self-sufficiency. For Asian Americans the family is a great source of emotional nurturance. One has an obligation to the family, and the needs of the family must take precedence over the needs of the individual. For Asian American women, there can be a conflict in cultural values, between the traditional gender roles of Asian culture and those of modern Anglo culture, which increasingly prizes independence and assertiveness in women.

Just as the sexuality of African Americans has been stereotyped, so too has that of Asian Americans. The Asian American man has been stereotyped as asexual (lacking in sexuality), whereas the Asian American woman has been stereotyped as an exotic sex toy (Reid & Bing, 2000; Figure 12.2).

Figure 12.2 Asian American women have often been stereotyped as exotic sex toys. In the film *The World of Suzie Wong*, Nancy Kwan portrayed an alluring prostitute.

Compared with European Americans, Asian Americans tend to hold more conservative sexual attitudes and to experience more anxiety about sex (Brotto et al., 2005). The more acculturated that Asian American women are, the closer their sexual attitudes are to those of European American women (Brotto et al., 2005).

American Indians

At least some Indian tribes, including the Cherokee, Navajo, Iroquois, Hopi, and Zuñi, traditionally had relatively egalitarian gender roles (LaFromboise et al., 1990). That is, their roles were more egalitarian than those of white culture of the same period. The process of acculturation and adaptation to Anglo society seems to have resulted in increased male dominance among American Indians.

Among the more than 200 Native languages spoken in North America, at least two-thirds have a term that refers to a third (or more) gender beyond male and female (Tafoya & Wirth, 1996). Anglo anthropologists labeled this additional category *berdache,* a term rejected by Native peoples, who prefer the term *two-spirit* (Jacobs et al., 1997). These same anthropologists concluded that these people were homosexuals, transsexuals, or transvestites, none of which are accurate from a Native point of view. A man might be married to a two-spirit male, but the marriage would not be considered homosexual because the two were of different genders (Tafoya & Wirth, 1996).

There was also a role of the "manly hearted woman," a role that a woman who was exceptionally independent and aggressive could take on. There was a "warrior woman" role among the Apache, Crow, Cheyenne, Blackfoot, Pawnee, and Navajo tribes (e.g., Buchanan, 1986; House, 1997). In both cases, women could express masculine traits or participate in male-stereotyped activities while continuing to live and dress as women (Figure 12.3).

In summary, research indicates that gender roles in the United States are not uniform. Different ethnic groups define gender roles differently. Let us turn now to some of the processes that create gender stereotypes.

Socialization

Many adult women and men do behave as gender roles say they should. Why does this happen? Psychologists and sociologists believe that it is a result of gender-role socialization. **Socialization** refers to the ways in which society conveys

Socialization: The ways in which society conveys to the individual its norms or expectations for his or her behavior.

Figure 12.3 Some American Indian tribes have three gender roles, the third being known as a "manly hearted woman," or "warrior woman." Chiricahua Tah-des-te was a messenger and warrior in Geronimo's band. She participated in negotiations with several U.S. military leaders and surrendered with Geronimo in 1886.

to the individual its norms or expectations for his or her behavior. Socialization occurs especially in childhood, as children are taught to behave as they will be expected to in adulthood. Socialization may involve several processes. Children may be rewarded for behavior that is appropriate for their gender ("What a brave little man he is") or be punished for behavior that is not appropriate to their gender ("Nice young ladies don't do that"). The adult models they imitate—whether these are parents of the same gender, teachers, or women and men on television—also contribute to their socialization (Figure 12.4). In some cases, simply telling children what is expected of males and females may be sufficient for role learning to take place. Socialization continues in adulthood, as

Figure 12.4   Children are very interested in achieving adult gender roles.

society conveys its norms of appropriate behavior for adult women and men. These norms extend from appropriate jobs to who initiates sexual activity.

Gender socialization comes from multiple sources, including parents, peers, and the media (Leaper & Friedman, 2007). Certainly parents have an early, important influence, from buying dolls for girls and footballs for boys to giving boys more freedom to explore. Research indicates that parents treat girls and boys similarly in many ways, with the exception that parents strongly encourage gender-typed activities (Lytton & Romney, 1991).

Parents are not the only socializing agents, though. The peer group can have a big impact in socializing for gender roles, particularly in adolescence. Other teenagers can be extremely effective in enforcing gender-role standards; for example, they may ridicule or shun a boy whose behavior is effeminate. Thus peers can exert great pressure for gender-role conformity (Maccoby, 1998).

The media are also important socializing agents. Many people assume that things have changed a lot in the last 20 years and that gender stereotypes are a thing of the past. On the contrary, various media—from television to teen magazines—continue to show females and males in stereotyped roles. For example, an analysis of gender stereotyping in children's picture books published from 1980 to 2001 showed no decline over time in the stereotyping (Hamilton et al., 2006). For instance, most of the adults in the books were shown engaged in gender-stereotyped occupations.

An analysis of popular television situation comedies (sitcoms) from the 1950s to the 1990s indicated small trends toward more egalitarian gender roles, but traditional stereotyping was still common (Olson & Douglas, 1997). *The Cosby Show* of the late 1980s earned the highest ratings for equality of gender roles of spouses and equality of gender roles of children (Olson & Douglas, 1997). But the 1990s series *Home Improvement* earned the lowest scores on equality of gender roles— lower even than the *Father Knows Best* series of the 1950s. Traditional gender roles are still alive on prime time.

Dozens of studies show that gender stereotypes shown on television affect children's stereotyped ideas (reviewed by Signorielli, 1990). For example, 3- to 6-year-olds who view more TV have more stereotyped ideas about gender roles than do children who view less. In a naturalistic experiment, children in a town with little availability of television showed fewer gender-stereotyped attitudes than children in a town with great availability of television. Television then became more available in the first town; two years later, the children in that town were as stereotyped in their attitudes as the children in the town that had had great availability of television all along.

But picture books and TV are old-fashioned media. One might expect the new media to be less stereotyped. To the contrary, however, video games show patterns of extreme gender stereotyping, including violence against women. In the Duke Nukem video game, Duke enters a strip club and guns down nearly nude women (Dill et al., 2005). The average eighth- or ninth-grade boy plays computer games 13 hours per week, compared with 5 hours for girls (Gentile et al., 2004). In short, boys' exposure to these games and their gender stereotypes is massive.

Although gender roles themselves are universal (Rosaldo, 1974)—that is, all societies have gender roles—the exact content of these roles varies from one culture to the next, from one ethnic group to another, and from one social class to another. For example, Margaret Mead (1935) studied several cultures in which gender roles were considerably different from those in the United States. One such group is the Mundugumor of New Guinea. In that culture both females and males were extremely aggressive.

Psychological Gender Differences

Gender differences in personality and behavior have been studied extensively by psychologists (e.g., Hyde, 2007). Here we focus on gender differences in two areas that are particularly relevant to gender and sexuality: aggressiveness and communication styles.

Males and females differ in *aggressiveness.* Males are generally more aggressive than females. This is true for virtually all indicators of aggression (physical aggression such as fighting, verbal aggression, and fantasy aggression) (Archer, 2004; Hyde, 1984). It is also true at all ages. As soon as children are old enough to perform aggressive behaviors, boys become more aggressive (Alink et al., 2006), and males dominate the statistics on violent crimes. The gender difference in aggression tends to be largest among preschoolers, but it gets smaller with age, so that gender differences in adults' aggression are small (Hyde, 1984).

Researchers have found that in the United States, men and women differ in their style of communicating, both verbally and nonverbally. This research was reviewed in Chapter 11; see Focus: A Sexually Diverse World, on page 304. Of particular relevance to sexuality, social psychologists have found gender differences in studies of **self-disclosure.** In these studies, people are brought into a laboratory and asked to disclose personal information either to friends or to strangers. Women are more willing to disclose information than men are, at least in situations like these (Dindia & Allen, 1992).

Norms about self-disclosure are changing. Traditional gender roles favored emotional expressiveness for females, but emotional repressiveness and avoidance of self-disclosure for males. There is, however, a contemporary ethic of good communication and openness that demands equal self-disclosure

Self-disclosure: Telling personal information to another person.

from males and females (Rubin et al., 1980). Research with college students who are dating couples confirms the existence of this norm; the majority of both males and females reported that they had disclosed their thoughts and feelings fully to their partners (Rubin et al., 1980). However, women revealed more in some specific areas, particularly their greatest fears. And couples with egalitarian attitudes disclosed more than couples with traditional gender-role attitudes. Thus the traditional expectation that men should not express their feelings seems to be shifting toward an expectation that they be open and communicative.

There are gender differences in people's ability to understand the nonverbal behaviors of others. The technical phrase for this is *decoding nonverbal cues*—that is, the ability to read others' body language correctly. It might be measured, for example, by one's accuracy in interpreting facial expressions. Research shows that women are better than men at decoding such nonverbal cues and discerning others' emotions (Hall, 1998). Certainly this is consistent with the gender-related expectation that women will show greater interpersonal sensitivity.

What are the implications for sexuality of these gender differences in communication styles? For example, if men are unwilling to disclose personal information about themselves, consider whether this might not hamper their ability to communicate their sexual needs to their partners.

Gender Differences in Sexuality

In this section the discussion will focus on areas of sexuality in which there is some evidence of male–female differences. As we will point out, differences do exist, but they are in a rather small number of areas—masturbation, attitudes about casual sex, consistency of orgasm during sex, and sex drive. There is a danger in focusing on these differences to the point of forgetting about gender similarities. Keep in mind that males and females are in many ways quite similar in their sexuality—for example, in the physiology of their sexual responses (Chapter 8)—as you consider the evidence on male–female differences that follows. Also bear in mind that most of the scientific evidence described here is based on North American samples. Only a few cross-cultural surveys are available. The gender differences discussed in the next sections characterize mainstream North American culture.

Gender patterns may be similar or different in other cultures.

Masturbation

In a review of 177 studies of gender differences in sexuality, the authors found that the largest gender difference was the incidence of masturbation (Oliver & Hyde, 1993).

Recall that in the Kinsey data 92 percent of the males had masturbated to orgasm at least once in their lives, as compared with 58 percent of the females. Not only did fewer women masturbate, but, in general, those who did masturbate had begun at a later age than the men. Virtually all men said they had masturbated before age 20 (most began between ages 13 and 15), but substantial numbers of women reported masturbating for the first time at age 25, 30, or 35. This gender difference shows no evidence of diminishing, according to more recent studies. The NHSLS, although it did not collect data on lifetime incidence of masturbation, did ask about masturbation in the last year; 63 percent of the men, compared with 42 percent of the women, reported that they had masturbated (Laumann et al., 1994). The data suggest, then, that there is a substantial gender difference in the incidence of masturbation, with men considerably more likely to have masturbated than women.

Attitudes about Casual Sex

In the review mentioned above, the second-largest gender difference noted was in attitudes toward casual sex—that is, premarital (or nonmarital) intercourse in a situation, such as a "one-night stand," in which there is no emotionally committed relationship between the partners (Oliver & Hyde, 1993; Yost & Zurbriggen, 2006). Men are considerably more approving of such interactions, and women tend to be disapproving. Many women feel that premarital intercourse is ethical or acceptable only in the context of an emotionally committed relationship. For many men, that is a nice context for sex, but it isn't absolutely necessary. As one man said in a *Cosmo* column,

> Being male, I find that sometimes your groin can take over and it's only after the deed is actually done that you regret sleeping with the particular girl. (quoted in Farvid & Braun, 2006, p. 301)

In the NHSLS sample, 76 percent of white women, but only 53 percent of white men, said that they would have sex with someone only if they were in love (Mahay et al., 1999). This gender difference is consistent across other U.S. ethnic groups; the comparable statistics were 77 percent for African American women and 43 percent for African American men, 78 percent for Mexican American women and 57 percent for Mexican American men.

No wonder there is some conflict in relationships between women and men.

Arousal to Erotica

Traditionally in our society most erotic material—sexually arousing pictures, movies, or stories—has been produced for a male audience. The corresponding assumption presumably has been that women are not interested in such things. Does the scientific evidence bear out this notion?

Laboratory research shows that men are more aroused by erotic materials, but the gender difference is not large (Murnen & Stockton, 1997). A classic study by psychologist Julia Heiman (1975; for a similar study with similar results, see Steinman et al., 1981) provides much insight into the responses of males and females to erotic materials. The participants were sexually experienced university students whose responses Heiman studied as they listened to tape recordings of erotic stories. Not only did she obtain the participants' self-ratings of their arousal, as other investigators had done, but she also got objective measures of their physiological levels of arousal. To do this, she used two instruments: a penile strain gauge and a photoplethysmograph (Figure 12.5). The **penile strain gauge** (which our students have dubbed the "peter meter") is used to get a physiological measure of arousal in the male; it is a flexible loop that fits around the base of the penis. The **photoplethysmograph,** or photometer, measures physiological arousal in the female; it is an acrylic cylinder, about the size of a tampon, that is placed just inside the entrance to the vagina. Both instruments measure vasocongestion in the genitals, which is the major physiological response during sexual arousal (see Chapter 8).

Research participants heard one of four kinds of tapes. There is a stereotype that women are more turned on by romance, whereas men are more aroused by "raw sex." The tapes varied according to which of these kinds of content they contained. The first group of tapes was *erotic;* they included excerpts from popular novels giving explicit descriptions of heterosexual sex. The second group of tapes was *romantic;* a couple were heard expressing affection and tenderness for each other, but they did

SexSource Online
www.mhhe.com/hyde10

"THE
PLETHYSMOGRAPH"
IN HISTORY
AND RESEARCH
METHODS

Penile strain gauge: A device used to measure physiological sexual arousal in the male; it is a flexible loop that fits around the base of the penis.

Photoplethysmograph (foh-toh-pleth-ISS-moh-graf): An acrylic cylinder that is placed inside the vagina in order to measure physiological sexual arousal in the female. Also called a *photometer.*

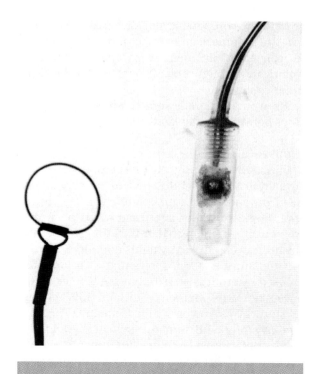

Figure 12.5 Two devices used to measure physiological sexual response in males and females. The penile strain gauge (*left*) consists of a flexible band that fits around the base of the penis. The photoplethysmograph (*right*) is an acrylic cylinder containing a photocell and a light source, which is placed just inside the vagina.

not actually engage in sex. The third group of tapes was *erotic–romantic;* they included erotic elements of explicit sex but also romantic elements. Finally, the fourth group of tapes served as a control; a couple were heard engaging in conversation but nothing else. The plots of the tapes also varied according to whether the man or the woman initiated the activity and whether the description centered on the woman's or the man's physical and psychological responses. Thus the tapes were either male initiated or female initiated and either female centered or male centered. Three important results emerged from the study:

1. Explicit heterosexual sex (the erotic and erotic–romantic tapes) was most arousing, both for women and for men. The great majority of both males and females responded most strongly, both physiologically and in self-ratings, to the erotic and erotic–romantic tapes. Women, in fact, rated the erotic tapes as more arousing than men did. Neither men nor women responded—either physiologically or in self-reports—to the romantic tapes or to the control tapes (except for a couple of men who were aroused by a discussion of the relative merits of an anthropology major versus premed—ah, well).

2. Both men and women found the female-initiated, female-centered tape to be most arousing. Perhaps the female-initiated plot was most arousing because of its somewhat forbidden or taboo nature.

3. Women were sometimes not aware of their own physiological arousal. Generally there was a high correlation between self-ratings of arousal and objective physiological measures of arousal, both for men and for women. When men were physically aroused, they never made an error in reporting this in their self-ratings—it is pretty hard to miss an erection. But when the women were physically aroused, about half of them did not report arousal in their self-ratings (see also Laan et al., 1994). (One might assume that women who were sophisticated enough to volunteer for an experiment of this nature and who were willing to insert a photoplethysmograph into their vagina would not suddenly become bashful about reporting their arousal; that is, it seems likely that these women honestly did not perceive themselves to be aroused.)

In sum, then, Heiman's study indicates that men and women are quite similar in their responses to erotic materials but that women can sometimes be unaware of their own physical arousal.

In statistical terms, Heiman found a low correlation between women's self-reports of arousal and the physiological measures of their arousal. In an interesting follow-up study, one experimental group of women was instructed to attend to their genital signs of sexual arousal ("While rating these slides, I would like you to attend to various changes that may occur in your genital area such as vaginal lubrication, pelvic warmth, and muscular tension"), and a second group was told to attend to nongenital signs of arousal ("While rating these slides, I would like you to attend to various changes that may occur in your body. These are heartrate increase, nipple erection, breast swelling, and muscular tension"), while a control group was given no instructions (Korff & Geer, 1983). Both experimental groups showed high correlations between self-reports and physiological measures of arousal, while the control group showed the same low correlation that Heiman found. This shows that women can be quite accurate in realizing their physical arousal if they are simply told to focus their attention on it. The broader culture, of course, does not give women such instructions but rather tells them to focus on the environment outside themselves—the love, romance, partner—so that many women have not learned to focus on their body. But the experiment described here shows quite clearly that they can.

Orgasm Consistency

Men are more consistent than women at having orgasms during sex. For example, according to the NHSLS, 75 percent of men—but only 29 percent of women—always have an orgasm during sex with their partner (Laumann et al., 1994, p. 116). The gap is narrower for orgasm consistency during masturbation, but even here men seem to be more effective: 80 percent of men, compared with 60 percent of women, report that they usually or always have an orgasm when masturbating (Laumann et al., 1994, p. 84).

Sex Drive

Evidence from a number of sources indicates that men, on average, have a stronger sex drive than women do (Baumeister et al., 2001; Peplau, 2003). Men think about sex more often and have more frequent and varied fantasies than women do. Compared with women, men desire more sexual partners and a greater frequency of intercourse. In a study across 52 nations, the gender difference in the preferred number of partners was found worldwide (Schmitt, 2003). It is important to remember, of course, that these are average differences. For a particular heterosexual couple, it is quite possible that the woman's level of desire would exceed the man's.

Why the Differences?

Four differences in male and female sexuality—the lower percentage of females, compared with males, who masturbate; women's more disapproving attitudes toward casual sex; women's lesser orgasm consistency; and men's greater sex drive—are fairly well documented and in need of explanation. A wide variety of scholars have suggested possible explanations.

Are the Differences Bogus?

One possibility is that many of these gender differences, typically documented by self-report, are not true differences. Instead, it could be that people report what is expected of them, shaped by gender norms. Men are expected to want lots of sex, so they exaggerate their desire in self-reports, or women minimize theirs.

A clever study used the *bogus pipeline method* to investigate this possibility (Alexander & Fisher, 2003). College students were brought to the lab to fill out questionnaires about their sexual attitudes and behaviors. They were randomly assigned to one of three experimental conditions. In the *bogus pipeline condition,* the student was hooked up to a fake polygraph, or lie detector machine, and told that the machine could detect false answers. People should respond very honestly in this condition. In the *anonymous condition,* the student simply filled out the questionnaire anonymously, as is typical of much sex research, and placed the questionnaire in a locked box when finished. In the *exposure threat condition,* respondents were instructed to hand their completed questionnaires directly to the experimenter, who was an undergraduate peer, and the experimenter sat in full view while the respondents completed their questionnaires, serving as a reminder that this other person would easily be able to see their answers. Figure 12.6 shows the results for reports of the number of sexual partners the respondents had had.

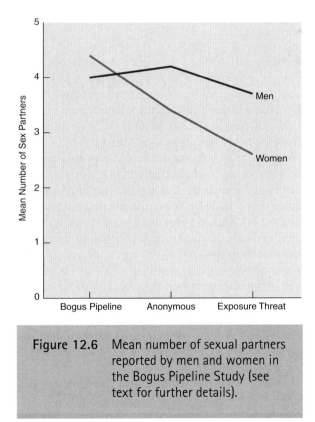

Figure 12.6   Mean number of sexual partners reported by men and women in the Bogus Pipeline Study (see text for further details).

When people were in the bogus pipeline condition and gave the most honest reporting, men's and women's reports of the number of their sexual partners were nearly identical—in fact, women's were slightly higher than men's. In the standard conditions of anonymity used in most sex research, women reported fewer partners than men did, and under a threat that responses would be made public the largest gap between women and men appeared. In the anonymous condition and the exposure threat condition, differences emerged that were consistent with gender roles. Women confirmed the expectation that they have few partners.

What are the implications of this study? Does it mean that all the differences described in the previous section are bogus? Probably not, but it means that findings of gender differences obtained by self-reports are probably exaggerations of the truth. And it is important to note that findings obtained from physiological measures, such as those used in Heiman's study, are not vulnerable to these reporting biases.

Let's assume that the gender differences discussed in the previous section are real, although perhaps not as dramatically large as the research suggests. How then can these differences be explained?

Biological Factors

Gender differences in sexuality might be created, in part, by two biological factors: anatomy and hormones.

Anatomy

The male sexual anatomy is external and visible and has a very obvious response: erection. While the male is nude, he can easily see his sexual organs, either by looking down or by looking in a mirror. The female sexual organs, in contrast, are hidden. The nude female looks down and sees nothing except pubic hair (which really is not very informative); she looks in a full-length mirror and sees the same thing. Only by doing the mirror exercise described in Chapter 4 can she get a good view of her own genitals. To make matters worse, the word *clitoris*—but not *penis*—is often missing from books about sexuality, from parents' talk about sex, and from students' knowledge about sexuality (Ogletree & Ginsburg, 2000). Furthermore, the female's genitals do not have an obvious arousal response like the male's erection. As a result, she may be less aware of her own arousal, a notion that is supported by Heiman's research.

The anatomical explanation, then, is that because the woman's genitals are not in plain view and because their arousal response is less obvious than that of the man's genitals, she is less likely to masturbate and less likely to develop her full sexual potential (Baldwin & Baldwin, 1997). If this explanation is correct, or is at least part of the answer, could steps be taken to help women develop their sexuality? Perhaps parents could tell their daughters about the mirror exercise at an early age and encourage them to become more aware of their own sexual organs. And parents might want to discuss the idea of masturbation with their daughters.

Hormones

The hormonal explanation rests on the finding that testosterone is related to sexual behavior. This evidence was reviewed in Chapter 8. Basically, the evidence comes from studies in which male animals are castrated (and thus lose their natural source of testosterone), with the result that their sexual behavior disappears, presumably reflecting a decrease in sex drive. If replacement injections of testosterone are given, the sexual behavior returns.

Women generally have lower levels of testosterone in their tissues than men have. Human females, for example, have about one-tenth the level of testosterone in their blood that human males have (Janowsky et al., 1998).

The hormonal explanation, then, is that if testosterone is important in activating sexual behavior and if females have only one-tenth as much of it as males have, this might result in a lower level of sexual behavior such as masturbation in women, or a lower sex drive.

There are several problems with this logic. First, it may be that cells in the hypothalamus or the genitals of women are more sensitive to testosterone than the comparable cells in men; thus a little testosterone might go a long way in women's bodies. Second, we must be cautious about making inferences to human males and females from studies done on animals. Although some recent studies have demonstrated the effects of testosterone on sexual interest and behavior in humans, the effects are less consistent and more complex than in other species (Chapter 8).

Cultural Factors

Our culture has traditionally placed tighter restrictions on women's sexuality than it has on men's, and vestiges of these restrictions linger today. It seems likely that these restrictions have acted as a damper on female sexuality, and thus they may help to explain why some women do not masturbate, why some women have difficulty having orgasms, and why some women are wary about casual sex.

One of the clearest reflections of the differences in restrictions on male and female sexuality is the double standard. As we saw in Chapter 9, the double standard says that the same sexual behavior is evaluated differently, depending on whether a male or a female engages in it. The sexual double standard gives men more sexual freedom than women (Crawford & Popp, 2003). An example is premarital sex. Traditionally in our culture, premarital intercourse has been more acceptable for males than for females. Indeed, premarital sexual activity might be a status symbol for a man but a sign of cheapness for a woman. The sexual double standard is alive and well on prime-time television, where negative consequences (e.g., rejection or humiliation) are more common in scenes in which female characters initiate sex than scenes in which male characters initiate (Aubrey, 2004).

Generally there seems to be less of a double standard today than there was in the past. For example, as the data in Chapter 9 indicate, people now approve of premarital intercourse for females about as much as they do for males. This change in attitudes is reflected in behavior. A much higher percentage of women report having engaged in premarital intercourse now than in the 1940s. According to the NHSLS, 70 percent of women and 78 percent of men engaged in sexual intercourse before marriage (Laumann et al., 1994). Thus there is much less of a difference between males and females now than there was a generation or two ago; the vast majority of both males and females are now engaging in premarital intercourse. Premarital intercourse still remains somewhat more common among males, though.

The decline of the double standard may help to explain why some of the gender differences found in older studies of sexual behavior have disappeared in more recent studies. When cultural forces do not make such a distinction between male and female, males and females become more similar in their sexual behavior. Yet vestiges of the double standard remain today in regard to casual sex, which is approved more for men than for women. In the United States, men, but not women, agree with this double standard (Sprecher & Hatfield, 1996).

Gender roles are another cultural force that may contribute to differences in male and female sexuality, as was discussed earlier in this chapter. Gender roles dictate proper behavior for females and males in sexual interactions—that is, they specify the script. For example, there is a stereotype of the male

as the initiator and the female as the passive object of his advances; surely this does not encourage the woman to take active steps to bring about her own orgasms. One study found that women implicitly associate sex with submission, whereas men do not (Sanchez et al., 2006). For the women, the more they associated sex with submission, the greater their difficulty with becoming sexually aroused.

Marital and family roles may play a part. Children can act as a damper on the parents' sexual relationship. The couple lose their privacy when they gain children. They may worry about their children bursting through an unlocked door and witnessing what Freud called "the primal scene" of their parents making love. Or they may be concerned that their children will hear the sounds of lovemaking. Generally, though, the woman is assigned the primary responsibility for child rearing, so she may be more aware of the presence of the children in the house and more concerned about possible harmful effects on them of witnessing their parents engaging in sex. Once again, her worry and anxiety do not contribute to her having a satisfying sexual experience.

Other Factors
A number of other factors, not easily classified as biological or cultural, may also contribute to differences between male and female sexuality.[3]

Women get pregnant and men do not. Particularly in the days before effective contraceptives were available, pregnancy might be a highly undesirable consequence of sexuality for a woman. Thinking that an episode of lovemaking might result in a nine-month pregnancy and another mouth to feed could put a damper on anyone's sexuality. Even today, pregnancy fears can be a force. For example, among sexually active teenage girls, 17 percent used no method of contraception the last time they had sex (Guttmacher Institute, 2006). A woman who is worried about whether she will become pregnant—and, if she is an unmarried teenager, about whether her parents will find out that she has been engaging in sexual activity—is not in a state conducive to the enjoyment of sex, much less the experience of orgasm (although this scarcely explains why more women than men do not masturbate).

Ineffective techniques of stimulating the woman may also be a factor. The commonest techniques of intercourse, with the penis moving in and out of the vagina, may provide good stimulation for the male but not for the female, since she may not be getting

[3]Other possible causes of orgasm problems in women are discussed in Chapter 17.

Focus: A Sexually Diverse World
Male Sexuality

ernie Zibergeld wrote *The New Male Sexuality* on the basis of his experience as a sex therapist and psychotherapist.

He argues that the media have taught us a Fantasy Model of Sex, which is ultimately detrimental to men, and to women as well. He captures this idea in his chapter title "It's Two Feet Long, Hard as Steel, Always Ready, and Will Knock Your Socks Off," describing the Fantasy Model of the erect penis and its power over women. The Fantasy Model of Sex creates unrealistic expectations and performance pressures on men.

Zilbergeld discusses a number of cultural myths based on the Fantasy Model. Here are four of them.

Myth 1. We're liberated folks who are very comfortable with sex. The media teach us that we have completely shed our Victorian heritage and everyone is totally comfortable with sex. The men and women in the movies and on TV never have any concerns or problems with sex. The women don't worry about their ability to orgasm. The men don't worry about the size or hardness of their penises. But if all this is true, why do we have such poor sex education in the United States? Why do parents have such difficulty talking about sex with their children? The truth is that although public manifestations (like the movies) are very open about sex, in our private lives we have all kinds of discomforts and uncertainties about sex.

Myth 2. A real man isn't into sissy stuff like feelings and communicating. Boys are trained into the male role, which discourages the expression of emotions such as tenderness. Communicating about personal feelings becomes difficult if not impossible. As one man said, "What it really comes down to is that I guess I'm not very comfortable with expressing my emotions—I don't think many

men are—but I am pretty comfortable with sex, so I just sort of let sex speak for me" (Zilbergeld, 1999, p. 21). Men are crippled in forming emotional relationships, as a result, and sexual interactions are less satisfying than they might be if there were more communication.

Myth 3. All touching is sexual or should lead to sex. For men, touching is a means to an end: sex. For women, touch more often is a goal in itself, as when women hug each other. Men need to learn that sometimes they just need to be held or stroked, and that that can provide more emotional satisfaction than sexual intercourse.

Myth 6. Sex is centered on a hard penis and what's done with it. Adolescent boys have a fixation on their penis and its erections, and this fascination persists throughout life. It creates heavy performance pressure for an erection—and not just any old erection, but a really big one. As Zilbergeld puts it, "Penises in fantasyland come in only three sizes: large, extra large, and so big you can't get them through the door." Men need to learn that the penis is not the only sexual part of their bodies, and that many very enjoyable forms of sexual behavior require no erection at all. That relieves a lot of performance pressure.

Zilbergeld's books are not based on a survey or laboratory research, but rather on his experiences as a sex therapist. His work with people having problems and seeking therapy may bias his views. But his observations are tremendously insightful, and many people not seeking therapy have benefited from his books.

Sources: Zilbergeld (1999), Farvid & Braun (2006), Taylor (2005).

---

sufficient clitoral stimulation. Perhaps the problem, then, is that women are expected to orgasm as a result of intercourse, when that technique is not very effective for producing orgasms in women.

A relationship probably exists between the evidence that fewer women masturbate than men and gender differences in orgasm consistency. Childhood and adolescent experiences with masturbation are important early sources of learning about sexuality. Through these experiences we learn how our bodies respond to sexual stimulation and what

the most effective techniques are for stimulating our own bodies. This learning is important to our experience of adult, two-person sex. For example, Kinsey's data suggested that women who masturbate to orgasm before marriage are more likely to orgasm in intercourse with their husbands;[4] 31 percent of the

[4]Note that this is in direct contradiction to the old-fashioned advice given in manuals that suggested that "getting hooked" on masturbation might impair later marital sexuality; if anything, just the reverse is true.

women who had never masturbated to orgasm before marriage had not had an orgasm by the end of their first year of marriage, while only 13 to 16 percent of the women who had masturbated had not had orgasms in their first year of marriage (Kinsey et al., 1953, p. 407). One woman spoke of how she discovered masturbation late and how this could be related to her orgasm capacity in heterosexual sex:

> I thought I was frigid, even after three years of marriage, until I read this book and learned how to turn myself on. After I gave myself my first orgasm, I cried for half an hour, I was so relieved. Afterwards, I did it a lot, for many months, and I talked to my doctor and to my husband, and finally I began to make it in intercourse. (Hunt, 1974, pp. 96–97)

Not only may women's relative inexperience with masturbation lead to a lack of sexual learning, but it also may create a kind of "erotic dependency" on men. Typically, boys' earliest sexual experiences are with masturbation, which they learn how to do from other boys. More important, they learn that they can produce their own sexual pleasure. Girls typically have their earliest sexual experiences in heterosexual petting. They therefore learn about sex from boys, and learn that their sexual pleasure is produced by the male. As sex researcher John Gagnon commented,

> Young women may know of masturbation, but not know *how* to masturbate—how to produce pleasure, or even what the pleasures of orgasm might be. . . . Some young women report that they learned how to masturbate after they had orgasm from intercourse and petting, and decided they could do it for themselves. (1977, p. 152)

Once again, such ideas might lead to a recommendation that girls be given information about masturbation.

Numerous factors that may contribute to shaping male and female sexuality have been discussed. Our belief is that a combination of several of these factors produces the differences that do exist. The early differences in experiences with masturbation are very important. Although these differences may result from differences in anatomy, they could be eliminated by giving girls information on masturbation. Women may enter into adult sexual relationships with a lack of experience in the bodily sensations of arousal and orgasm, and they may be unaware of the best techniques for stimulating their own bodies. Put this lack of experience together with various cultural forces, such as the double standard and ineffective techniques of stimulation, and it is not too surprising that there are some gender differences in sexuality.

Beyond the Young Adults

One of the problems with our understanding of gender differences in sexuality is that so much of the research has concentrated on college students or other groups of young adults (as is true of much behavioral research). For example, the 52-nation study of gender differences in preferred number of partners, discussed earlier, tested college students at nearly all sites (Schmitt, 2003). Using this population may provide a very narrow view of male–female differences; they are considered during only a very small part of the life span. In reality, female sexuality and male sexuality change in their nature and focus across the life span. For example, it is a common belief in our culture that men reach their sexual "peak" at around age 19, whereas women do not reach theirs until they are 35 or 40 (Barr et al., 2002). There is some scientific evidence supporting this view. Kinsey (1953) found, for example, that women generally had orgasms more consistently at 40 than they did at 25.

Psychiatrist Helen Singer Kaplan, a specialist in therapy for sexual disorders, advanced an interesting view of differences between male sexuality and female sexuality across the life span (Kaplan & Sager, 1971). According to her analysis, the teenage male's sexuality is very intense and almost exclusively genital in its focus. As the man approaches age 30, he is still highly interested in sex, but not so urgently. He is also satisfied with fewer orgasms, compared with the adolescent male. With age the man's refractory period becomes longer. By age 50, he is typically satisfied with two orgasms a week, and the focus of his sexuality is not so completely genital; sex becomes a more sensuously diffuse experience and has a greater emotional component.

In women, the process is often quite different. Their sexual awakening may occur much later; they may, for example, not begin masturbating until age 30 or 35. While they are in their teens and twenties, their orgasmic response is slow and inconsistent. However, by the time they reach their mid-thirties, their sexual response has become quicker and more intense, and they orgasm more consistently than they did during their teens and twenties. They initiate sex more frequently than they did in the past. Also, the greatest incidence of extramarital sex for women occurs among those in their late thirties. Vaginal lubrication takes place almost instantaneously in women in this age group.

Men, then, seem to begin with an intense, genitally focused sexuality and only later develop an appreciation for the sensuous and emotional aspects of sex. Women have an early awareness of the sensuous and emotional aspects of sex and develop the capacity for intense genital response later. To express this in another way, we might use the terminology suggested by Ira Reiss: **person-centered sex** and **body-centered sex.** Adolescent male sexuality is body centered, and the person-centered aspect is not added until later. Adolescent female sexuality is person centered, and body-centered sex comes later.

It is important to remember, though, that these patterns may be culturally, rather than biologically, produced. In some other cultures—for example, Mangaia in the South Pacific (see Chapter 1)—females have orgasms 100 percent of the time during coitus, even when they are adolescents.

Figure 12.7   A transgender individual.

Transsexualism

Many texts cover transsexualism in the chapter on sexual variations or deviations. However, we have included it in our chapter on gender because it is fundamentally an issue of gender and, more specifically, a problem of gender identity.

A **transsexual** is a person who believes that he or she was born with the body of the other gender. Transsexuals are the candidates for the **gender-reassignment** process (see below) that has received so much publicity. The term *transsexual* can be used to refer to the person both before and after the operation. This condition is also known as **gender dysphoria,** meaning unhappiness or dissatisfaction with one's gender.

The term **transgender** is broader, including transsexuals as well as people whose gender identity does not match their physical gender but who do not seek gender-reassignment surgery and instead prefer only some of the treatments, such as hormones, or may want to leave their body unaltered and think of themselves as falling into the third-gender category of transgender (Figure 12.7). Some also include transvestites, drag queens and kings, and others whose behavior and identity transcend traditional gender boundaries. Other new terms have emerged, including *gender blender, gender bender, gender outlaw,* and *gender-free* (Bockting, 1999).

There are two kinds of transsexuals: those born with male bodies whose identity is female (called **male-to-female transsexuals,** or **MTFs**), and those born with female bodies whose gender identity is male (called **female-to-male transsexuals,** or **FTMs**). Male-to-female transsexuals have been more likely to seek help at clinics and have more often been given gender-reassignment surgery (Olsson & Möller, 2003), in part because the surgery required in such cases is easier. Accordingly, most of the discussion that follows will focus on MTFs.[5]

Keeping in mind the distinction between sex and gender, it is important to understand that transsexualism is a problem not of sexual behavior

Person-centered sex: Sexual expression in which the emphasis is on the relationship and emotions between the two people.

Body-centered sex: Sexual expression in which the emphasis is on the body and physical pleasure.

Transsexual: A person who believes he or she was born with the body of the other gender. See also *transgender.*

Gender reassignment: The process for transsexuals to change their body to the other gender.

Gender dysphoria (dis-FOR-ee-uh): Unhappiness with one's gender; another term for transsexualism.

Transgender: A category including transsexuals, those who think of themselves as a third gender, transvestites, gender benders, and others.

Male-to-female transsexual (MTF): A person who is born with a male body but who has a female identity and wishes to become a female biologically in order to match her identity.

Female-to-male transsexual (FTM): A person born with a female body whose gender identity is male and wishes to undergo gender reassignment.

[5]Because this kind of transgender individual thinks of himself as a female, he prefers to be called "she"; to simplify matters in this discussion, *she* will be used to refer to the transgender individual.

but of gender and gender identity. That is, the transsexual is preoccupied not with some special kind of sexual behavior but rather with wanting to be female when her body is male. For that reason, the term *transgender* has become increasingly popular. References to transsexuals are found in much of recorded history, although of course they are not referred to by that modern, scientific term (Devor, 1997). In the early centuries of Christianity, a number of women transformed themselves into men. One example is Pelagia, a woman who refused to marry and fled, dressing as a man and entering a monastery. She became Pelagius, a man, and was later elected prior of a convent. A woman at the convent became pregnant and accused Pelagius of being the father. Nothing, of course, could have been further from the truth, but he was not in a position to offer his strongest defense. He was expelled from the convent and died in disgrace. When he died, it was discovered that he had a female body.

In addition to the distinction between MTF and FTM transsexuals, we can also make a distinction between *gynephilic* and *androphilic* transgender individuals (Blanchard et al., 1995).[6] Those who are gynephilic are sexually attracted to women, and those who are androphilic are sexually attracted to men. For example, if we think of a female-to-male transsexual, he would be classified as androphilic if he is attracted to men and as gynephilic if he is attracted to women. Androphilic MTFs tend to be shorter and lighter in weight compared with gynephilic MTFs and compared with men in the general population (Blanchard et al., 1995). This may be one reason why androphilic MTFs are more successful in their new gender—they are more convincing as women because they are smaller. Gynephilic MTFs, in contrast, often marry women and have children in young adulthood. They have a history of eroticized cross-dressing in childhood and adolescence. Masculine in appearance, they often make the transition to the new gender after they are 40. Among FTMs, those who are gynephilic are typically more interested in surgery to construct a penis (phalloplasty) compared with those who are androphilic (Chivers & Bailey, 2000). Some transsexuals, too, are bisexual. In one sample of MTFs recruited through the Internet, 32 percent said

they were attracted to men, 31 percent to women, and 28 percent to both (Bockting, 2004).

Psychologically, the transsexual is in an extreme conflict situation. The body says, "I'm a man," but the mind says, "I'm a woman." The person may understandably react with fright and confusion. Particularly in the days before gender-reassignment procedures, or among people who are unaware of it, self-castrations have been reported.

The Gender-Reassignment Process

Gender reassignment, sometimes called *sex change* or, more recently, *gender transition*, is complex and proceeds in several stages (Bockting, 1997; Levine et al., 1998; Peterson & Dickey, 1995). Those in the transsexual community often refer to the process as *crossing*. The first step is very careful counseling and psychological evaluation. It is important to establish that the person is a true transsexual, that is, someone whose gender identity does not match her body type. Some people mistakenly seek gender reassignment; for example, a man who is simply poorly adjusted, unhappy, and not very successful might think that things would go better for him if he were a woman. Sometimes schizophrenics display such confused gender identity that they might be mistaken for transsexuals. It is important to establish that the person is a true transsexual or has a core transgender identity before going ahead with a procedure that is irreversible.

The next step is hormone therapy. The male-to-female transsexual is given estrogen and must remain on it for the rest of her life. The estrogen gradually produces some feminization. The breasts enlarge. The pattern of fat deposits becomes feminine; in particular, the hips become rounded. Balding, if it has begun, stops. Secretions by the prostate diminish, and eventually there is no ejaculate. Erections become less and less frequent, a phenomenon that pleases the transsexual, since they were an unpleasant reminder of the unwanted penis. The female-to-male transsexual is given androgens, which bring about a gradual masculinization. A beard may develop, to varying degrees. The voice deepens. The pattern of fat deposits becomes more masculine. The clitoris enlarges, although not nearly to the size of a penis, and becomes more erectile. The pelvic bone structure cannot be reshaped, and breasts do not disappear except with surgery. New MRI studies suggest that the brain may change as well. In FTMs given androgen treatment, the size of the hypothalamus enlarged from a typical female size to a typical male size (Hulshoff et al., 2006).

---

[6]A heated debate is being waged about the best terminology for these two types. We won't drag you into it. Part of the complexity derives from the issue of, for example, describing an MTF's sexual orientation as "homosexual"—does that refer to same-gender attraction according to the gender before or after surgery? *Gynephilic* and *androphilic* get around this problem.

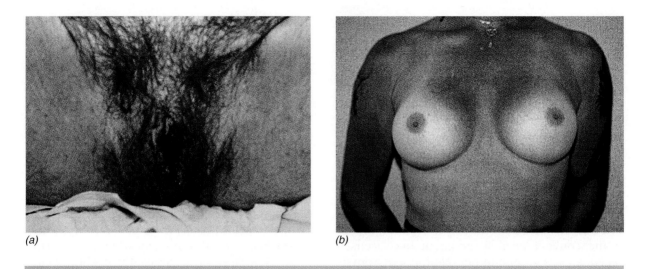

(a)   *(b)*

Figure 12.8   (*a*) The appearance of the genitals following male-to-female transsexual surgery.
(*b*) Breast augmentation for the MTF transsexual. Photos courtesy of Dr. Daniel Greenwald.

Next comes the "real life experience," which is the requirement that the person live as a member of the new gender for a period of one or two years. This is done to ensure that the person will be able to adjust to the role of the new gender; once again, the idea is to be as certain as possible that the person will not regret having had the operation. Some transsexuals, even before consulting a physician, spontaneously enter this cross-dressing stage in their efforts to become women. Problems may arise, though. Cross-dressing is illegal in many cities, and they may be arrested. Most transgender individuals encounter transphobia, sometimes to the point of violence (Lombardi et al., 2001; Monro, 2000).

The final step is the surgery itself, which some transsexuals decide to skip. For the male-to-female transsexual, the penis and testes are removed but without severing the sensory nerves of the penis. The external genitalia are then reconstructed to look as much as possible like a woman's (see Figure 12.8a). The glans of the penis is used to form a clitoris with sexual sensitivity. Next, an artificial vagina—a pouch 15 to 20 centimeters (6 to 8 inches) deep—is constructed. It is lined with the skin of the penis. For about six months afterward, the vagina must be dilated with a plastic device so that it does not reclose. Other cosmetic surgery may also be done, such as reducing the size of the Adam's apple.

The female-to-male change is more complex and generally less successful. A penis and scrotum are constructed from tissues in the genital area and the forearm (see Figure 12.9a). The new penis does not have erectile capacity; in some cases a rigid silicone tube is implanted in the penis so that it can be inserted into a vagina, making coitus possible. Some female-to-male transsexuals choose not to have genital surgery and just go through breast removal and possibly hysterectomy.

An important experience for transsexuals is *passing* (Bockting, 1999). For an MTF, this might mean going into a bank dressed as a woman and having no one notice anything unusual, everyone simply believing she is a woman.

It is important to note that transsexualism as a diagnosis, and the means of treating it (hormones and sex-change surgery), are products of modern European and American culture. As discussed earlier, some other societies simply consider these individuals to be members of a third gender, and they live comfortably in that category. Examples are the two-spirit people among American Indians and the Hijras of India (Jacobs et al., 1997; Nanda, 1997).

What Causes Transsexualism?

Scientists have not found a definite cause of transsexualism. One likely reason is that there may be more than one path to it. As usual, both biological and environmental theories have been proposed.

On the biological side, John Money (1987) argued that the issue is a critical period during prenatal development. Some event, not yet known, may lead to atypical development of some brain structure—possibly the hypothalamus, corpus callosum, or anterior commissure (Devor, 1997). Other theorists,

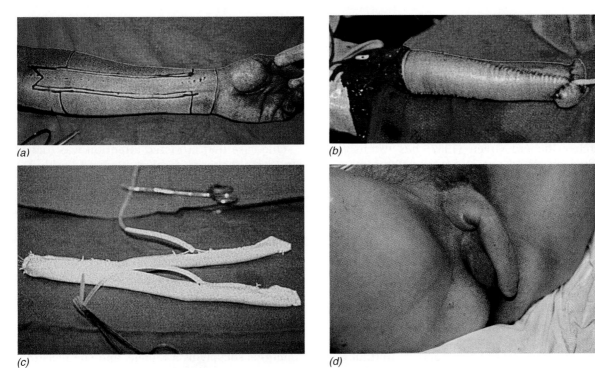

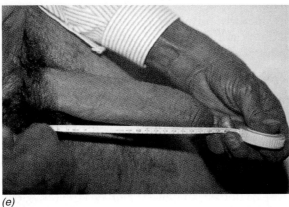

Figure 12.9   Female-to-male transsexual surgery. (*a*) Skin on the forearm marked before transfer to the groin. (*b*) The penis is constructed (blood vessels and nerves shown on the left). (*c*) An inflatable prosthesis, wrapped in Goretex and ready for insertion. (*d*) Penis before insertion of the implant. (*e*) Erect penis. Photos courtesy of Dr. Daniel Greenwald.

following this same line of thinking, have proposed that during prenatal development the fetus, if it is to become a male, must be both defeminized and masculinized (Pillard & Weinrich, 1987). A failure of either process could produce a person with a male body but a female identity. To understand this distinction between defeminization and masculinization, at least for anatomy, recall the discussion in Chapter 5 about the Wolffian and Müllerian ducts. Both are present in all fetuses early in prenatal development. In a normally developing male, the Müllerian ducts degenerate (defeminization) and

the Wolffian ducts thrive (masculinization). If some process failed, though, both might thrive. The same might be true of cells in brain regions having to do with gender identity. Consistent with this view, two studies have found differences between MTFs and typical men, in the bed nucleus of the stria terminalis (BST), which is part of the limbic system (Kruijver et al., 2000; Zhou et al., 1995). As noted in other chapters, the limbic system is important in sexuality.

Again on the biological side, one recent genotyping study showed that MTFs differed from male controls in the gene that creates androgen receptors and in another gene that creates estrogen receptors (Henningsson et al., 2005). This study will need to be repeated, and FTMs will need to be studied as well before we can be certain of these genetic effects, but they may represent one pathway by which people become transsexual.

On the environmental side, noted sex researcher Richard Green (1987) has extensively studied the phenomenon of extreme femininity in boys, which might be a forerunner of either homosexuality or transgenderism. He has found that the parents of these boys basically treat them as if they were girls; for example, they dress them in girls' clothing and then tell them how cute they look. In the case of female-to-male transsexuals, he believes the origins lie in parental practices that include giving the child a gender-ambiguous name and encouraging rough play, and a family constellation in which the mother is unpleasant and emotionally distant (thereby discouraging identification with her) and the father is pleasant and warm (thus encouraging identification with him).

Developmentally, **gender identity disorder (GID)** is found in children as young as 2 or 3 years of age (Zucker, 2000; Zucker et al., 2002) and is characterized by an insistence that he or she is the other gender, a preference for cross-dressing, and an intense desire to participate in stereotypical play of the other gender. If GID persists into adolescence or adulthood, then the person is considered a transsexual. How—or whether—to treat children with GID poses a dilemma (Gender Identity Research and Education Society [GIRES], 2006). In fact, only a minority—23 percent in one study—of children with GID persist in the condition and go on to become transsexual adults (GIRES, 2006). Some argue that children should not even be given a diagnosis of GID because it pathologizes them and the majority go on to lead normal lives (Hill et al., 2007). Other experts note that if GID persists throughout childhood and sex reassignment seems almost certain to be called for, then treatment will be much more effective if the youth does not go through the pubertal processes of his or her original gender (Delemarre-van de Waal & Cohen-Kettenis, 2006).

Male-to-female transsexuals account for the great majority of cases, outnumbering female-to-male transsexuals by a ratio of 2:1 (Bakker et al., 1993; Olsson & Möller, 2003). Several explanations have been offered for this lopsided ratio. Perhaps male prenatal development is more complex and error prone, or perhaps the male role is so restrictive that it does not tolerate variations very well.

Other Issues

The phenomenon of transsexualism raises a number of interesting psychological, legal, and ethical questions for our contemporary society.

One case that attracted attention was that of Dr. Renée Richards, formerly Richard Raskind, a physician who had her gender reassigned. When she was a man, she was a successful tennis player. In 1976 she attempted to enter a women's tennis tournament. The women players protested that she was not a woman, and she protested that she was. Officials subsequently decided to use the **buccal smear** test for gender, which is also the one used in the Olympics, and is a test of genetic gender. Richards protested that this was not the appropriate test to be used on her. Psychologically she is a female, she has female genitals, and she functions socially as a female, and she feels that these are the appropriate criteria. She does, though, have a male pelvic bone structure and other bone structures that are masculine, and these may have important consequences for athletic performance. The important question raised by this case is, What should the criteria be for determining a person's gender? Should it be chromosomal gender (XX or XY) as tested by the buccal smear? Should it be the gender indicated by the external genitals? Should it be psychological gender identity? In 2000, the International Olympic Committee suspended its use of gender verification for female athletes (Genel, 2000). It seemed to be accomplishing nothing, except to embarrass some women who turned out to have genetic anomalies.

Another question that might be raised concerns religious groups that do not permit women to become members of the clergy. Is a male-to-female transsexual, for example, qualified to be a priest before the operation but not after? Is a female-to-male transsexual qualified to be a priest by virtue of having had a sex-change operation?

The transsexual also encounters a number of practical problems when undergoing gender reassignment. Official records, such as the Social Security card, must be changed to show not only the new name but also the new gender. Sometimes an amended birth certificate is issued. If the person was married before the sex change, often—though not always—the spouse is divorced. Changing one's gender is, to say the least, a complicated process.

Transsexuals should be able to give us, through their personal accounts, new insights into the

---

Gender identity disorder (GID): A strong and persistent cross-gender identification.
Buccal smear: A test of genetic sex, in which a small scraping of cells is taken from the inside of the mouth, stained, and examined under a microscope.

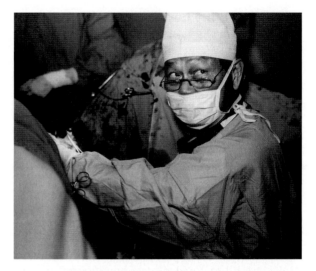

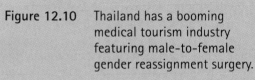

Figure 12.10 Thailand has a booming medical tourism industry featuring male-to-female gender reassignment surgery.

nature of sex and gender. For example, most of us have wondered, at some time, how members of the other gender feel during sexual intercourse. Transgender individuals are in a unique position for giving us information on this question.

Criticisms of Gender-Reassignment Surgery

A number of criticisms of sex-change surgery for transsexuals have been raised. One of these came from a study by Johns Hopkins researcher Jon Meyer (1979). He did a follow-up study of the adjustment of 50 transsexuals, 29 of whom received surgery and 21 of whom did not. His conclusion, much publicized, was that there were no significant differences in the adjustment of the two groups. If that is the case, he claimed, then transsexual surgery is unnecessary and should not be done.

Then criticisms of Meyer's study appeared (e.g., Fleming et al., 1980). Meyer's adjustment scale was somewhat peculiar and involved debatable values. After the Meyer study and the criticisms of it, some clinics ceased doing transsexual surgery, but most continued to do it.

(a)

(b)

Figure 12.11 (a) Actress Hilary Swank as Brandon Teena in the film *Boys Don't Cry,* the true story of a female-to-male transsexual who was murdered because of the ignorance and prejudice of those around him; (b) the real Brandon Teena.

According to more recent research, adjustment of transsexuals is significantly better following surgery (Bodlund & Kullgren, 1996; Green & Fleming, 1990). In one study, 86 percent of MTFs were satisfied with their surgery to create a vagina, and 89 percent of FTMs were satisfied with their surgery to create a penis (De Cuypere et al., 2005). And in a study of 232 MTFs, none expressed regret at having had the surgery (Lawrence, 2003). Yet almost surely we will see more attempts to treat transsexualism with psychotherapy rather than surgery, recognizing that gender does not have to be dichotomous.

SUMMARY

A gender role is a set of norms, or culturally defined expectations, that specify how people of one gender ought to behave. Children are socialized into gender roles first by parents and later by other forces such as peers and the media.

Gender roles are not uniform in the United States. They vary according to ethnic group and other factors. African American women, for example, have traditionally played an important economic role in their families. Among Latinos, gender roles tend to be more sharply defined than they are among Anglos. The sexuality of Asian Americans has been stereotyped, with Asian American men seen as being sexless and Asian American women viewed as exotic sex toys. Some American Indian tribes traditionally had egalitarian gender roles compared with white culture.

Psychological gender differences have been documented in aggressiveness and communication styles.

The two largest male–female differences in sexuality are in the incidence of masturbation (males having the higher incidence) and attitudes toward casual sex (females being more disapproving).

Heiman's study of arousal to erotic materials illustrates how males and females are in some ways similar and in others different in their responses. Males are more consistent at having orgasms, especially during heterosexual intercourse, than females are, and males have a somewhat stronger sex drive.

Three sets of factors have been proposed to explain gender differences in sexuality: biological factors (anatomy, hormones); cultural factors (gender roles, the double standard); and other factors (fear of pregnancy, differences in masturbation patterns creating other gender differences).

Most research on gender and sexuality has been done with college-age samples. There is reason to believe that patterns of gender differences in sexuality change in middle age and beyond.

Transsexuals represent an interesting variation in which gender identity does not match anatomy. Generally, their adjustment is good following the gender-reassignment operation. Transgender is a broader category including those who do not seek surgery or see themselves as being in a third gender category.

QUESTIONS FOR THOUGHT, DISCUSSION, AND DEBATE

1. Do you think that transsexual surgery is the appropriate treatment for transsexuals? Why or why not?

2. Recalling from your childhood, do you think you were socialized in a stereotyped masculine or feminine way? What impact do you think those socialization experiences have had on your current sexual attitudes and behaviors?

3. Do you think there is still a double standard for male and female sexuality today? Explain your answer.

4. Dominic is a strong advocate of equality between men and women, yet his 6-year-old daughter's favorite television program shows both the parents and the children in very stereotyped roles. The mother is a secretary and the father is a physician. The teenage daughter is a cheerleader and thinks of nothing else, while the son plays football. What should Dominic do? Why?

SUGGESTIONS FOR FURTHER READING

Devor, Holly. (1997). *FTM: Female-to-male transsexuals in society.* Bloomington: Indiana University Press. FTMs are the understudied group of transsexuals, and Devor's book fills the gap in an exceptional and fascinating way.

Howey, Noelle. (2002). *Dress codes: Of three girlhoods—my mother's, my father's, and mine.* This is Howey's extraordinary memoir about growing up with a father who proved to be a male-to-female transsexual.

Hyde, Janet S. (2007). *Half the human experience: The psychology of women* (7th ed.). Boston, MA: Houghton-Mifflin. We are not in a very good position to give an objective appraisal of this book, but for what it's worth we think it is an interesting, comprehensive summary of what is known about the psychology of women and gender roles.

Zilbergeld, Bernie. (1999). *The new male sexuality.* New York: Bantam Books. Zilbergeld's original *Male Sexuality* was a great success, and this updated version is every bit as insightful.

CHAPTER THIRTEEN

Sexual Orientation: Gay, Straight, or Bi?

CHAPTER HIGHLIGHTS

Jeffrey and I met when he responded to an online message I posted, seeking gay teenagers willing to discuss their online lives. . . . He made it clear that he could allow no overlap between his online gay life and the life he led in the "real world.". . . He feared that if word of his sexual orientation were to reach his parents, they might refuse to support him or pay for college. From his peers at school he dreaded violence.*

*Egan (2000), p. 113.

One night in June 1969, in response to police harassment, gay men and lesbians rioted in the Stonewall, a gay bar in New York City's Greenwich Village. This may have been the first open group rebellion of homosexual persons in history. Gay liberation was born. Since then, the public has been forced into awareness of an issue—sexual orientation—that it had previously preferred to ignore. Gay liberationists proclaim that gay is good. Meanwhile, many Americans charitably maintain that homosexuals are sick (but can be cured).

Most of us want to know more about sexual orientation. The purpose of this chapter is to try to provide a better understanding of people's sexual orientations, whether homosexual, heterosexual, or bisexual, as well as an understanding of homophobia (the fear and hatred of homosexuals).

Sexual orientation is defined by whom we are sexually attracted to and also have the potential for loving. Thus a **homosexual** is a person whose sexual orientation is toward members of her or his own gender; a **heterosexual** is a person whose sexual orientation is toward members of the other gender; and a **bisexual** is a person whose sexual orientation is toward both genders. The word homosexual is derived from the Greek root *homo*, meaning "same" (not the Latin word *homo*, meaning "man"). The term homosexual may be applied in a general way to homosexuals of both genders or specifically to male homosexuals. The term **lesbian,** which is used to refer to female homosexuals, can be traced to the great Greek poet Sappho, who lived on the island of Lesbos (hence "lesbian") around 600 B.C. She is famous for the love poetry that she wrote to other women. Sappho was married, apparently happily, and had one daughter, but her lesbian feelings were the focus of her life.

Several other terms are also used in conjunction with homosexuality. Gay activists prefer the term **gay** to homosexual because the latter emphasizes the sexual aspects of the lifestyle and can be used as a derogatory label, since there are so many negative connotations to homosexuality. A heterosexual is then referred to as **straight.** The term gay is generally used for male homosexuals, lesbian for female homosexuals. There are, of course, a number of slang terms for gays and lesbians, such as "queer," "fairy," "dyke," and "faggot" or "fag," which are derogatory when used by straight persons to belittle homosexuals. The term *queer* has now been taken back by gay activists and scholars, who use it as a proud term encompassing gays, lesbians, and transgender persons. Queer theory is prominent in lesbian–gay–bisexual (LGB) studies.

In this chapter, we will use the abbreviation LGB for lesbians, gays, and bisexuals, because it is awkward to repeat the phrase gays and lesbians, and even that phrase omits bisexuals.

Attitudes toward Gays and Lesbians

Your sexual orientation has implications for the attitudes people have toward you. First, there is the belief that all people are heterosexual, that heterosexuality is the norm. Furthermore, just as there are stereotypes about other minority groups—for example, the stereotype that all Asian American men are asexual—so there are stereotypes about homosexuals. These stereotypes and negative attitudes lead to discrimination and hate crimes against gays and lesbians. Here we examine some of the scientific data on these negative attitudes.

Attitudes

Many Americans disapprove of homosexuality. For example, as Table 13.1 shows, in a well-sampled 2004 survey of adult Americans, 58 percent expressed the opinion that sexual relations between two adults of the same sex are always wrong.

> **Sexual orientation:** A person's erotic and emotional orientation toward members of his or her own gender or members of the other gender.
>
> **Homosexual:** A person whose sexual orientation is toward members of the same gender.
>
> **Heterosexual:** A person whose sexual orientation is toward members of the other gender.
>
> **Bisexual:** A person whose sexual orientation is toward both men and women.
>
> **Lesbian:** A woman whose sexual orientation is toward other women.
>
> **Gay:** Homosexual; especially male homosexuals.
>
> **Straight:** Heterosexual; that is, a person whose sexual orientation is toward members of the opposite gender.

Table 13.1 Attitudes of Adult Americans toward Homosexuality, 1973 and 2004

Question and Responses	Percentage of Sample	
	1973	2004
1. Are sexual relations between adults of the same sex:		
Always wrong	74	58
Almost always wrong	7	5
Wrong only sometimes	8	7
Not wrong at all	11	31
2. Should an admitted homosexual man be allowed to teach in a college or university?		
Yes	49	80
No	51	20

Source: General Social Survey, 1973, 2004, http://icpsr.umich.edu/

Has the gay liberation movement succeeded in changing the negative attitudes of Americans? The answer seems to be yes, but slowly. Table 13.1 shows that the percentage of people who believe that homosexual behavior is always wrong changed substantially from 1973 to 2004.

Some experts believe that many Americans' attitudes toward homosexuals can best be described as homophobic (Fyfe, 1983; Hudson & Ricketts, 1980). **Homophobia** may be defined as a strong, irrational fear of homosexuals and, more generally, as fixed negative attitudes and reactions to homosexuals. Some scholars dislike the term homophobia because, although certainly some people's feelings are strong enough to be called a phobia, negative attitudes and prejudice are most common. Therefore, some prefer the term **antigay prejudice** or sexual prejudice (Herek, 2000). Another related term is **heterosexism,** which is the belief that everyone is heterosexual and that heterosexuality is the norm; homosexual people and behaviors are denigrated (Berkman & Zinberg, 1997).

The most extreme expressions of antigay prejudice occur in *hate crimes* against LGBs (Cogan & Marcus-Newhall, 2002). One horrifying recent case occurred in Wyoming (Loffreda, 2000). Matthew Shepard, a University of Wyoming freshman, was found tied to a fence, savagely beaten and comatose, on the outskirts of Laramie. He died five days later. Two men, both 21 and high school dropouts, were charged with the murder. Apparently they had led Shepard to believe that they, too, were gay and lured him from a bar to ride in their pickup truck. In the truck, they began beating him with a revolver, then got out and tied him to a fence, beat him more, and left him for dead.

Averaged across 24 different studies of LGBs, the results indicated that 9 percent had been assaulted with a weapon, 17 percent had been physically assaulted, 19 percent had experienced vandalism or other property crimes, 44 percent had been threatened with violence, 13 percent had been spat upon, and 80 percent had been verbally harassed because of their sexual orientation (Berrill, 1992; Cogan, 1996). In a survey of LGB adults, 19 percent of the women and 28 percent of the men had been the victim of a crime because someone had thought they were lesbian, gay, or bisexual (Herek et al., 1999). In a survey of LGB youth between the ages of 15 and 19, 80 percent reported that they had received verbal harassment because of their sexual orientation, 11 percent had been the objects of physical assault, and 9 percent had been the objects of sexual assault (D'Augelli et al., 2006). Males reported more victimization than females did. These studies show that hate crimes against and harassment of gays and lesbians are common—not rare, isolated incidents.

These incidents exact a psychological toll. One high school student said of the verbal harassment, "It's not just name calling. I don't know how schools can isolate it like that. When are they going to see it as a problem? When we're bloody on the ground in front of them?" (Human Rights Watch, 2001).

In 1990, Congress passed the Hate Crimes Statistics Act, in which gays and lesbians were included with ethnic minority persons as having a special status necessitating legal protection from hate-motivated crimes (Morin & Rothblum, 1991). Although this may seem like cold comfort to a person who has already been the victim of such a

Homophobia: A strong, irrational fear of homosexuals; negative attitudes and reactions to homosexuals.
Antigay prejudice: Negative attitudes and behaviors toward gays and lesbians. Also termed *sexual prejudice.*
Heterosexism: The belief that everyone is heterosexual and that heterosexuality is the norm; homosexuality is denigrated.

Figure 13.1 Harvey Milk (left) and George Moscone (right). Harvey Milk, a gay activist, was an elected member of San Francisco's Board of Supervisors, representing a district including many gays. Milk fought for gay rights throughout the state of California and was supported by San Francisco's mayor, George Moscone. On November 17, 1978, Dan White, himself a former police officer and supervisor, entered City Hall and fired shots that killed both Milk and Moscone. White confessed within hours. A jury declined to convict White of first-degree murder, instead finding him guilty of voluntary manslaughter, a lesser offense carrying a reduced jail sentence. The gay community, as well as many sympathetic supporters, were shocked and furious. A protest march and the White Night Riot ensued. The entire incident symbolizes the ambivalent progress achieved by gay liberation: a gay liberationist can be elected to an important public office, but he is then murdered. An observance of these events continues in San Francisco every year.

crime, it is a step in the direction of providing some legal protection.

But we should also recognize the other side of the coin. As we can see from Table 13.1, some Americans are tolerant of or supportive of homosexuals. For example, 80 percent of Americans approve of an overt homosexual teaching in a college or university. Thus Americans are a strange mixture of bigots and supporters on the issue of homosexuality. One woman said,

> I really don't feel that I've ever been oppressed as a lesbian or suffered any abuse. I've been careful who I've told, but those people have been really accepting. (Jay & Young, 1979, p. 716)

Gays and Lesbians as a Minority Group

From the foregoing, it is clear that LGB people are the subject of many negative attitudes, just as other minorities are (Meyer, 2003). Like members of other minority groups, they also suffer from job discrimination. Just as Blacks and women have been denied access to certain jobs, so too have homosexuals. Wage discrimination occurs as well. According to census data, gay men are more educated than straight men, but gay men earn less (Black et al., 2000). Homosexuality has often been grounds for a dishonorable discharge from the armed forces, a fact that became an issue when President Bill Clinton took office in 1993. The result of the controversy was a "Don't ask, don't tell" policy in which gays and lesbians could be members of the armed services as long as they kept their sexual orientation to themselves. Homosexuality has also been grounds for firing a person from federal employment and for denial of a security clearance.[1]

A clever experiment captured discrimination against gays in the workplace (Hebl et al., 2002). Undergraduates who were confederates of the experimenters applied for jobs at local stores in Houston. Half of them wore a baseball cap that said "Gay and Proud" (the experimental group), and the other half wore a cap that said "Texan and Proud" (the control group). A number of measures were collected, including whether the staff person at the store said that a job was available, whether the applicant was given permission to complete a job application, whether they received a callback, and more subtle measures such as the length of the interaction between the applicant and staff.

[1]One gay man commented, "Soldiers who are not afraid of guns, bombs, capture, torture or death say they are afraid of homosexuals. Clearly we should not be used as soldiers, we should be used as weapons."

Measures of formal discrimination, such as being allowed to complete an application, showed no differences between the experimental and control groups. However, measures of subtle discrimination did reveal the effects of wearing the Gay and Proud cap. Conversations between the applicant and the staff person were half as long when the applicant wore the gay cap. Those wearing the gay cap also rated their interactions with the staff person as more negative than those wearing the Texan cap, even though they were kept unaware of which cap they were wearing. This study provides tangible evidence about the kind of discrimination that gays and lesbians encounter in the workplace.

Discrimination goes hand in hand with stereotypes. One such stereotype is that gay men are child molesters. As with many stereotypes, this one is false. Research shows that only 2 to 3 percent of those who sexually abuse children are homosexual (Jenny et al., 1994).

In a spirit of reform in the 1980s, a number of states and cities passed laws prohibiting discrimination on the basis of sexual orientation. For example, in the state of Wisconsin it is illegal to discriminate against gays and lesbians in matters such as employment and housing. Massachusetts, Hawaii, and 17 other states have similar laws (Epstein, 1995). These legal issues are discussed further in Chapter 20.

There is, however, an important way in which homosexuals differ from other minorities. In the case of most other minorities, appearance is a fairly good indicator of minority-group status. It is easy to recognize an African American or a woman, for example, but one cannot tell simply by looking at a person what his or her sexual orientation is. Thus LGBs, unlike other minorities, can hide their status. There are certain advantages to this. It makes it fairly easy to get along in the heterosexual world—to "pass." However, it has the disadvantage of encouraging the person to live a lie and to deny her or his true identity; not only is this dishonest, but it may also be psychologically stressful (Meyer, 2003). A study of gay men (all of whom were uninfected with HIV) indicated that those who concealed their identity had a significantly higher incidence of cancer and infectious diseases than those who did not conceal their identity (Cole et al., 1996). Concealing a stigma—whether it is one's sexual orientation, mental illness, illiteracy, or history of having been raped—exacts a psychological toll (Pachankis, 2007).

We shouldn't leave this discussion of discrimination and prejudice against LGBs without asking a crucial question (Rothblum & Bond, 1996): What can be done to prevent or end this prejudice? Change must occur at the individual, the interpersonal, and the organizational levels (e.g., corporations, educational institutions), as well as society as a whole and its institutions (e.g., the federal government). At the individual level, all of us must examine our own attitudes toward LGBs to see if they are consistent with basic values we hold, such as a commitment to equality and justice. Some people may need to educate themselves or attend antihomophobia workshops to examine their attitudes. These attitudes, though, were formed as we grew up, influenced by our parents, our peers, and the media. Parents must consider the messages they convey to their children about homosexuals. The adolescent peer group is strongly homophobic. What could be done to change it? How can the media change in order not to promote antigay prejudices and stereotypes? At the interpersonal level, people must recognize that LGBs are often a hidden minority. Eric, for example, just told a joke that ridiculed gay men. What he didn't know was that one of his three listeners is gay—just not "out" with him (for obvious reasons). We must examine our interactions with other people, recognizing the extent to which many of us assume that everyone is heterosexual until proven otherwise. At the institutional level, how can education be changed in order to reduce antigay discrimination? A strong program of sexuality education across the grades, with open discussion of sexual orientation, would be a good start (see Looking to the Future: Sexuality Education, at the end of this book). Despite the fact that numerous states have passed laws banning discrimination on the basis of sexual orientation, the U.S. federal government has failed to do so. Such a law would be an important first step.

Life Experiences of LGBs

In understanding lesbian, gay, and bisexual lifestyles, it is important to recognize that there is a wide variety of experiences. One of the most important aspects of this variability is whether the person is covert (in the closet) or overt (out of the closet) about his or her homosexuality. The **covert homosexual** may be heterosexually married, have children, and be a respected professional in the community, spending only a few hours a month engaging in secret same-gender sexual behavior. The **overt homosexual,** on the other hand, may

Covert homosexual: A homosexual who is "in the closet," who keeps his or her sexual orientation a secret.

live almost entirely within an LGB community, particularly if he or she lives in a large city like New York or San Francisco where there is a large gay subculture. There are also various degrees of overtness (being "out") and covertness. Many lesbians and gays are out with trusted friends but not with casual acquaintances. The lifestyle of gay men differs from that of lesbians, as a result of the different roles assigned to males and females in our society and the different ways that males and females are reared. In addition, there is more discrimination against gay men than there is against lesbians. For example, it is considered quite natural for two women to share an apartment, but if two men do so, eyebrows are raised.

The lifestyles of LGBs are thus far from uniform. They vary according to whether one is male or female and overt or covert about the homosexuality and also according to social class, occupation, personality, and a variety of other factors.

Coming Out

In 2002, Esera Tuaolo, a former defensive lineman for the Green Bay Packers, came out (Wilstein, 2002). He lives with his partner, Mitchell, and their twins, Mitchell and Michele, adopted from Tuaolo's native Samoa. While an NFL player, Tuaolo drank himself to sleep and drove crazily at high speeds, while keeping up the pretense that he was straight. Now he feels happy and at peace with himself. He waited to come out until he retired from the NFL, believing that if he revealed that he was gay while playing pro football, he would have been cut and would have been the object of cheap shots on the field. Today he is happy to be able to put a face on the gay football player and help knock down stereotypes. His earlier life, though, reveals the emotional toll of being in the closet.

As we noted earlier, there are significant variations in the gay experience, depending on whether or not one is out of the closet. The process of coming out of the closet, or **coming out,** involves acknowledging to oneself, and then to others, that one is gay or lesbian. The person is psychologically vulnerable during this stage. Whether the person experiences acceptance or rejection from friends and others to whom he or she comes out can be critical to self-esteem.

Following the period of coming out, there is a stage of exploration, in which the person experiments with the new open sexual identity; during this time the person makes contact with the lesbian and gay community and practices new interpersonal skills. Typically, next comes a stage of forming first relationships. These relationships are often short-lived and characterized by jealousy and turbulence, much like many heterosexual dating relationships. Finally, there is the integration stage, in which the person becomes a fully functioning member of society and is capable of maintaining a long-term, committed relationship (Coleman, 1982).

Of course, before the coming-out process can occur, the person must have arrived at a homosexual identity. This identity development typically proceeds in six stages (Cass, 1979; Marszalek et al., 2004):

1. *Identity confusion.* The person most likely began assuming a heterosexual identity because heterosexuality is so normative in our society. As same-gender attractions or behaviors occur, there is confusion. Who am I?

2. *Identity comparison.* The person now thinks, "I may be homosexual." There may be feelings of alienation because the comfortable heterosexual identity has been lost.

3. *Identity tolerance.* At this stage the person thinks, "I probably am homosexual." The person now seeks out homosexuals and makes contact with the gay subculture, hoping for affirmation. The quality of these initial contacts is critical.

4. *Identity acceptance.* The person can now say, "I am homosexual," and accepts rather than tolerates this identity.

5. *Identity pride.* The person dichotomizes the world into homosexuals (who are good and important people) and heterosexuals (who are not). There is a strong identification with the gay group, and an increased coming out of the closet.

6. *Identity synthesis.* The person no longer holds an "us versus them" view of homosexuals and heterosexuals, recognizing that there are some good and supportive heterosexuals. In this final stage, the person is able to synthesize public and private sexual identities.

Although these processes remain largely the same today compared with 20 or 30 years ago, the Internet is having an impact in some crucial aspects (Egan, 2000; McKenna & Bargh, 1998). For a teenage boy who is just realizing that he is gay, the Internet provides boundless information and the

SexSource Online
www.mhhe.com/hyde10

"COREY JOHNSON"
IN SEXUALITY
OVER THE
LIFE-SPAN

Overt homosexual: A homosexual who is "out of the closet," who is open about his or her sexual orientation.

Coming out: The process of acknowledging to oneself, and then to others, that one is gay or lesbian.

opportunity to "chat" with others, while remaining safe in his home and not acknowledging his identity publicly in ways that could be at best embarrassing and at worst dangerous. Interactions with others on the Internet can foster a positive identity and self-acceptance.

Lesbian, Gay, and Bisexual Communities

A loose network of lesbian, gay, and bisexual communities extends around the world (Esterberg, 1996). One woman said,

> I have seen lesbian communities all over the world (e.g., South Africa, Brazil, and Israel) where the lesbians of that nation have more in common with me (i.e., they play the same lesbian records, have read the same books, wear the same lesbian jewelry) than the heterosexual women of that nation have in common with heterosexual women in the U.S. (Rothblum, 2007)

These links have been cemented in the last decade by increases in international travel, globalization, and the international reach of the Internet (Puar, 2001).

Gay and lesbian communities began flourishing in the United States after World War II (D'Augelli & Garnets, 1995). Ironically, in the gender-segregated military, gay men were able to find each other and lesbians find each other in a way that had previously not been possible. Activist groups slowly formed in the 1950s and 1960s, energized particularly by the Stonewall rebellion discussed at the beginning of this chapter. The HIV/AIDS crisis of the 1980s cemented together the gay community as it had never been before. Support networks and activist groups formed rapidly in response to the epidemic.

Today many LGB communities exist in neighborhoods in large cities, with bookstores, restaurants, theaters, and social organizations that are an integral part of the community (D'Augelli & Garnets, 1995). The lesbian community in particular has been involved in creating a lesbian culture, expressed in music and literature and celebrated at festivals and women's sporting events (Dolance, 2005; see Figure 13.2).

Symbols and rituals are important in defining the LGB community. The pink triangle, which the Nazis used to label gay men, has been adopted as a symbol of pride. The Greek letter lambda is another. Lesbian and gay pride marches held in June each year commemorate the Stonewall uprising. The use of slang is another sign of solidarity among LGBs (see Table 13.2).

Gay baths: Clubs where gay men can socialize; features include a swimming pool or whirlpool and access to casual sex.

Figure 13.2   LGB community: Sandy Sachs and Dr. Robin Gans, cofounders of Girl Bar, a 12,000-member nationwide lesbian social club, have entered into a marketing agreement with the WNBA's Los Angeles Sparks.

Gay bars are one aspect of the LGB social life. Drinking, perhaps dancing, socializing, and the possibility of finding a sexual partner or a lover are the important elements. Some gay bars look just like any other bar from the outside, whereas others may have names—for example, The Open Closet—that indicate to the alert who the clientele are. Bars are typically gender segregated—that is, they are either for gay men or for lesbians—although a few are mixed. There are far more bars for gay men than for lesbian women. Typically, the atmosphere is different in the two, the male bars being more for finding sexual partners and the female bars more for talking and socializing. Lest the reader be shocked at the none-too-subtle nature of pickup bars, it is well to remember that there are many bars—singles' bars—that serve precisely the same purpose for heterosexuals.

The **gay baths** are another aspect of some gay men's social and sexual lives. The baths are clubs with many rooms in them, generally including a swimming pool or whirlpool, as well as rooms for dancing, watching television, and socializing; most areas are dimly lit. Once a man has found a sexual

Focus: Milestones in Sex Research
The Ethics of Sex Research: The Tearoom Trade

S ociologist Laud Humphreys's study entitled *Tearoom Trade: Impersonal Sex in Public Places* (1970) is a classic in the field of sex research. In light of concerns on the part of both scientists and the general public about ethical standards in research, however, his methods of data collection are questionable from a contemporary perspective. Important issues are raised about the difficulty of doing good sex research within ethical bounds.

As the title of the book implies, the term tearoom trade refers to impersonal sexual acts in places like public restrooms. Typically, a man enters the restroom and conveys to another man who is already there an interest in having sex. He may do this by making tapping sounds while in one of the stalls, for example. The men generally perform the sexual act in a stall and may not even exchange a word. The activity is typically fellatio, which can be done rapidly and with a minimum of encumbrance.

In the tearoom situation, a third person generally serves as a lookout who watches for police or other intruders while the other two engage in sex. To obtain his data, Humphreys became a lookout. Not only did he observe the behaviors involved in the tearoom trade, but he also wrote down the license-plate numbers of the participants. He traced the numbers through state records and thus was able to get the addresses of the persons involved. He then went to the homes of the people and administered a questionnaire (which included questions on sexual behavior) to them under the pretense of conducting a general survey.

The research provided some important findings, particularly that a large proportion of the men who engaged in the tearoom trade were respectable, heterosexually married men, and many were leaders in their community. This finding provoked quite a controversy over the book; the notion that "heterosexual" men could engage in homosexual behavior was shocking to many. Indeed, many gays find the tearoom trade to be shocking.

In his report of the research, Humphreys maintained the complete anonymity of the participants. However, his work still entails numerous ethical problems. There was no informed consent procedure (this study was carried out before scientific societies and universities instituted such standards). Participants were deceived—a problem made worse by the fact that they were never debriefed and told the true purpose of the research. But these considerations in turn raise the question, Could Humphreys have obtained good data within the bounds of research ethics? The clearly negative aspects of the study have to be weighed against the benefits that knowing more about this form of sexual behavior offers to society.

Source: Humphreys (1970).

---

partner, they go to one of a number of small rooms furnished with beds, where they can engage in sexual activity. The baths feature casual, impersonal sex, since a partner can be found and the act completed without the two even exchanging names, much less making any emotional commitment to each other.

The majority of bathhouses were closed in the 1980s because public health officials feared that they encouraged risky sexual practices and the

Table 13.2	Some Slang Terms from LGB Culture
In the closet	Keeping one's homosexuality hidden, not being open or public
Coming out	Coming out of the closet, or becoming open about one's homosexuality
Queen	An effeminate gay man
Nellie	An effeminate gay man
Closet queen	A homosexual who is covert or in the closet
Drag queen	A gay man who dresses in women's clothing ("drag")
Butch	A masculine gay man or a masculine lesbian
Dyke	A masculine lesbian
Femme	A feminine lesbian
Straight	A heterosexual
Trick	A casual sexual partner
Cruising	Looking for a sexual partner
Tearoom	A public restroom where gay men engage in casual sex

spread of HIV. Bathhouses were resurrected in the 1990s, however, and have created a controversy within the gay community. Some see the baths as an aspect of gay culture that spreads HIV and will continue to do so, killing thousands; they believe the baths must be closed and the destructive practices they encourage should stop (Rotello, 1997; Signorile, 1997). Others celebrate the liberated sexuality fostered by the baths and see it as an essential part of gay men's lifestyle.

Today, of course, a major way for gays to meet each other is through the Internet. Cyberspace is also a place where gays can find community when, geographically, they do not live in a place that has a gay community (Brown et al., 2005). Gay-related websites provide chat rooms and other means for gays to form online relationships and perhaps find partners for casual sex or a long-term relationship (Brown et al., 2005).

Certainly in the last four decades the gay liberation movement has had a tremendous impact on the gay lifestyle and community. In particular, it has encouraged homosexuals to be more overt and to feel less guilty about their behavior. LGB liberation meetings and activities provide a social situation in which gay people can meet and discuss important issues rather than simply play games as a prelude to sex, which tends to be the pattern in the bars. In addition, they provide a political organization that can work to bring about legal change, combat police harassment, and fight cases of job discrimination, as well as do public relations work. The National Gay and Lesbian Task Force[2] is the central clearinghouse for all these groups; it can provide information on local organizations.

There are many places for LGBs to socialize besides bars, including the Metropolitan Community Church (a gay and lesbian church), gay athletic organizations, and gay political organizations.

Among their other accomplishments, members of the gay liberation movement have founded numerous gay newspapers and magazines. These have many of the same features as other newspapers: forums for political opinions, human-interest stories, and fashion news. In addition, the want ads feature advertisements for sexual partners; similar ads for homosexual and heterosexual partners can be found in nonmainstream newspapers in most cities. Probably the best-known LGB magazine is *The Advocate,* published in Los Angeles and circulated throughout the United States. *Lambda Rising*

[2]The National Gay and Lesbian Task Force, 1325 Massachusetts Ave. NW, Washington, DC 20500, (202) 393–8579. See the Appendix at the back of this book for a list of other organizations dealing with various aspects of sexuality.

News, published in Washington, D.C., is an important newspaper. There are also several publications that list all the gay bars and baths by city in the United States, which is handy for the traveler or for those newly arrived on the LGB scene. In 2006, *The Advocate* issued *The Advocate College Guide for LGBT Students,* which lists the 20 most gay-friendly campuses.

Gay and Lesbian Relationships

Contrary to stereotypes, a substantial number of lesbians and gay men form long-term, cohabiting relationships. One such relationship is described in Focus: First Person, on the facing page. Across numerous surveys, between 8 and 21 percent of lesbian couples had been together for 10 or more years, as had between 18 and 28 percent of the gay male couples (Kurdek, 2005). A dramatic testimony to the commitment of many gays and lesbians to long-term relationships occurred in 2004 when gay marriage was legal, briefly, in San Francisco, and became legal in Massachusetts. City halls were

Figure 13.3   A gay male couple. A large percentage of lesbians and gay men report currently being in a steady romantic relationship.

Focus: First Person
A Gay Couple: Lee and Bob

L ee and Bob have been living together as a couple for 10 years. Lee is 30 and Bob is 53; they live in a small town in northern Wisconsin.

Lee feels that he never had a real home while growing up. His father worked in construction, and they moved frequently, living in motel rooms. His parents divorced when he was in kindergarten. His mother remarried soon, but the man turned out to be a wife batterer, so they divorced when Lee was in the fifth grade. His mother, now single, turned to drugs and partying. Home life had no structure and was chaotic, although Lee feels that she loved him. Then his mom was "saved" and joined a repressive, fundamentalist church. She married again, to someone with like beliefs, and is still married to that man.

Lee knew that he liked boys more than girls by the first grade, but he also knew that he shouldn't talk about it. He didn't completely self-label as gay until his first semester in college. At that time he had his first affair, with his boss at Burger King. The affair was tempestuous, and he was heartbroken when it ended badly. His mother sensed that something was up. When he told her that he was gay, she insisted that he go to a psychiatrist to be cured. He agreed to try not to be gay and did try, but of course it didn't work. He and his mother had one more fight about it, and she kicked him out of the house. After two years they reconciled somewhat but not completely, and his stepfather is still rejecting.

Bob, in contrast, had an unremarkable childhood. His parents are still married after 54 years, and he speaks to them every day, although he has never told them that he is gay and they have never asked. Raised as a Catholic in northern Wisconsin, he is nonpracticing today.

Bob began to find boys to be more attractive than girls in high school, but in the 1950s and 1960s no label of "gay" was available. He first acted on his impulses in college and had dated five or six people before meeting Lee.

They met, improbably, in northern Wisconsin when the first gay bar opened in one small town. They dated briefly and quickly settled down as a couple. They have an agreement to be monogamous, which Bob has never breached and Lee has breached only once.

When asked what they liked best about their relationship, Bob said it was the stability of knowing that there's someone to share life with. The relationship seems to him like an investment built up over time. Lee likes being in a relationship because he loves Bob and knows Bob loves him in return. Lee also appreciates the depth of the relationship, which seems to him to be a major accomplishment. They worry a bit about their age gap. Bob is beginning to think about retirement, whereas Lee is getting ready to launch his career and anticipates a major move in the next few years. They also regret their emotional distance from their families.

Today Lee is working on his Ph.D. in clinical psychology, hoping to become a therapist. Bob is a commercial pilot for a major airline.

Source: Based on an interview conducted by Janet Hyde.

---

flooded with same-gender couples seeking marriage licenses (Belluck, 2004).

Beginning in 2000, gay men and lesbians were able to form legal civil unions in Vermont, and we now have an initial round of research on couples entering these unions (Solomon et al., 2004). In the first year of the policy in Vermont, 2,475 civil union certificates were issued. Among those couples, only 21 percent were actually from Vermont; two-thirds of the couples were female. Those seeking civil unions were on average 43–44 years old; lesbians on average had been living together for 9 years, and gay men had been living together for 12 years. Among the lesbian couples, 34 percent had children, 15 percent from the current relationship and 19 percent from a prior relationship. For male couples, 18 percent had children, 8 percent from the current relationship and 11 percent from a prior relationship.

Gay and lesbian couples—like heterosexual couples—must struggle to find a balance that suits both persons. Three aspects of the relationship typically have to be negotiated and can be sources of conflict: money, housework, and sex (Solomon et al., 2005).

In one study, gay couples, lesbian couples, and heterosexual couples were brought to the laboratory and told to discuss a problem (Julien et al., 2003). Each couple's interactions were videotaped and later coded for both positive and negative behaviors by each partner. The results showed no differences between lesbian, gay, and heterosexual couples on any of the interaction measures.

What is striking about all the research on gay and lesbian relationships is how similar they are—in their satisfactions, loves, joys, and conflicts—to heterosexual relationships (Patterson, 2000; Peplau et al., 1996).

Lesbian and Gay Families

Increasingly, gay couples and lesbian couples are creating families that include children (Bowe, 2006). This is a controversial concept to some heterosexual people in the United States, who view a lesbian family or gay family as a damaging setting for children to grow up in. The courts have often assumed that lesbians and gay men are unfit parents, and the same-gender sexual orientation of a parent has been grounds for the other, heterosexual parent to gain custody of children following a divorce. What does the research say about these families and the effects on children in them?

It is important to recognize that these families are diverse along dimensions of race, social class, and gender (Allen & Demo, 1995). In some, the children were born to one of the partners in a previous heterosexual relationship. In others, the children were adopted or, in the case of lesbian couples, born by means of artificial insemination (Figure 13.4). Some have even said that a "lesbian baby boom" is under way (Patterson, 1995). Some are single-parent families, with, for example, a lesbian mother rearing her children from a previous heterosexual marriage.

Three concerns have been raised about how the children fare in these families. First, will they show disturbances in gender identity or sexual identity? Will they become gay or lesbian? Second, will they be less healthy psychologically than children who grow up with two heterosexual parents? Third, will they have difficulties in relationships with their peers, perhaps being stigmatized or teased because of their unusual family situation?

Research on children growing up in lesbian or gay families, compared with those growing up in heterosexual families, dismisses these fears. For example, an overwhelming number of children growing up in lesbian or gay households have a heterosexual orientation (Allen & Burrell, 2002).

The adjustment and mental health of children in lesbian and gay families are no different from those of children in heterosexual families (Golombok et al., 2003; Patterson, 2006).

As for the third concern, about peer relationships, research indicates that children in lesbian or gay families fare about as well in terms of social skills and popularity as children in heterosexual families (Patterson, 1992).

(a)

(b)

Figure 13.4 Gay and lesbian political issues: (*a*) The custody issue—lesbian mothers want the right to keep their children after a divorce; (*b*) the right to adoption—a gay couple with their adopted child.

In conclusion, although concerns have been raised about children growing up in lesbian and gay families, research consistently shows no difference between these children and those in heterosexual families (Allen & Burrell, 2002; Patterson, 2006). One expert in clinical psychology concluded, "It appears that traditional family structures, including father presence and heterosexuality, are not essential for healthy child development. Well-adjusted children of both sexes can be reared in families of varying configurations with the most crucial ingredient appearing to be the presence of at least one supportive, accepting caregiver" (Strickland, 1995).

Recognizing these positive outcomes, in 2002 the American Academy of Pediatrics issued a policy statement supporting adoptions by gay parents (Perrin et al., 2002).

How Many People Are Gay, Straight, or Bi?

Most people believe that homosexuality is rare. What percentages of people in the United States are gay and lesbian? As it turns out, the answer to this question is complex. Basically, it depends on how one defines a homosexual and a heterosexual.

One source of information we have on this question is Kinsey's research (see Chapter 3 for an evaluation of the Kinsey data). Kinsey found that about 37 percent of all males had had at least one homosexual experience to orgasm in adulthood. This is a large percentage. Indeed, it was this statistic, combined with some of the findings on premarital sex, that led

to the furor over the Kinsey report. The comparable figure for females was 13 percent. However, experts agree that, because of problems with sampling, Kinsey's statistics on homosexuality were almost certainly inflated (Pomeroy, 1972).

Today several well-sampled surveys of the U.S. population have given us improved estimates (Savin-Williams, 2006). One of those is the National Survey of Family Growth. Data from that study are shown in Table 13.3 (Mosher et al., 2005). The statistics are complex because much depends on how *homosexual* is defined. Does the definition require someone to have had exclusively same-gender sexual experiences, or just some same-gender experiences, or perhaps just to have experienced sexual attraction to members of his or her own gender without ever acting on it? We will return to this point. What we can say here is that, according to the National Survey of Family Growth, about 2 percent of men and 1 percent of women are exclusively homosexual in their sexual behavior and in their identity. About 10 percent of both men and women have had at least one same-gender sexual experience in adulthood, and about 4 percent of both men and women experience sexual attraction to members of their own gender. Slightly more than 2 percent of men and 1 percent of women have a homosexual identity.

These percentages are considerably smaller than Kinsey's. What accounts for the difference? The National Survey of Family Growth (NSFG) was

Table 13.3	The National Survey of Family Growth Statistics on Same-Gender Behavior, Identity, and Attraction, 2002		

		Percentage	
		Men	Women
Behavior			
Ever had sexual contact with same-gender partner		6.0*	11.0
Same-gender partner, last 12 months		2.9*	4.4
Only same-gender partners, last 12 months		1.6*	1.3
Sexual Identity			
Homosexual		2.3	1.3
Bisexual		1.8	2.8
Something else**		3.9	3.8
Sexual Attraction			
Only or mostly to same gender		2.2	1.5
To both		1.0	1.9
"Mostly" to opposite gender		2.6	2.7

*Different questions were used for males and females, and the male question was narrower, so this percentage is an underestimate.

**The "something else" category may include people identifying as queer, questioning, and so on.

Source: Mosher et al. (2005).

better sampled; it is generally agreed that Kinsey's unsystematic sampling methods led to overestimates of the incidence of homosexuality. But the NSFG may not be perfectly accurate, either. We can expect underreporting on any kind of sensitive topic like homosexuality, and the NSFG asked nonequivalent questions on behavior to males and females, making gender comparisons inaccurate.

The NSFG statistics are comparable to those found in a well-sampled international survey. The results indicated that 6.2, 4.5, and 10.7 percent of males in the United States, United Kingdom, and France, respectively, had engaged in sexual behavior with someone of their own gender in the last five years (Sell et al., 1995). The comparable statistics for women were 3.6, 2.1, and 3.3 percent. These and other surveys confirm that the incidence of homosexuality among men is higher than the incidence among women. Probably twice as many men as women have a homosexual experience to orgasm in adulthood, and the same ratio is probably true for exclusive homosexuality.

After reading these statistics, though, you may still be left wondering how many people are homosexuals. As Kinsey soon realized in trying to answer this question, it depends on how you count. A prevalent notion is that like black and white, homosexual and heterosexual are two quite separate and distinct categories. This is what might be called a typological conceptualization (see Figure 13.5). Kinsey made an important scientific breakthrough when he decided to conceptualize homosexuality and heterosexuality not as two separate categories but as variations on a continuum (Figure 13.5, section 2). The black and white extremes of heterosexuality and homosexuality have a lot of shades of gray in between: people who have had both some heterosexual and some homosexual experience, in various mixtures. To accommodate all this variety, Kinsey constructed a scale running from 0 (exclusively heterosexual) to 6 (exclusively homosexual), with the midpoint of 3 indicating equal amounts of heterosexual and homosexual experience.

Many sex researchers continue to use Kinsey's scale today, but the question remains, When is a person a homosexual? If you have had one homosexual experience, does that make you a homosexual, or do you have to have had substantial homosexual experience (say, a rating of 2 or 3 or higher)? Or do you have to be exclusively homosexual to be a homosexual? Kinsey dealt with this problem in part by devising his scale, but he also made another important point. He argued that we should not talk about homosexuality but rather about homosexual behavior. Homosexuality, as we have seen, is exceedingly difficult to define. Homosexual behavior, on the other hand, can be scientifically defined as a sexual act between two people of the same gender. Therefore, we can talk more precisely about people who have engaged in varying amounts of homosexual behavior or who have had varying amounts of homosexual experience.

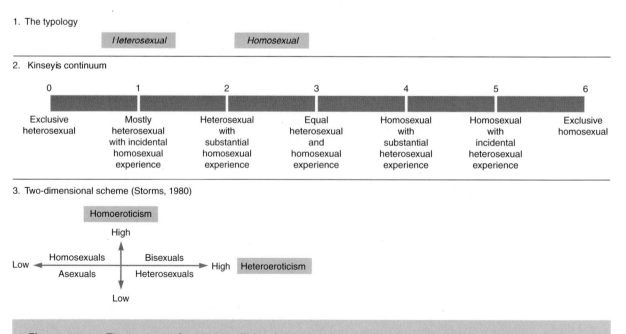

Figure 13.5 Three ways of conceptualizing homosexuality and heterosexuality.

Other theorists have suggested that Kinsey's one-dimensional scale is too simple (Sell, 1997; Storms, 1980). The alternative is to form a two-dimensional scheme. The idea here is to have one scale for heteroeroticism (the extent of one's arousal to members of the opposite gender), ranging from low to high, and another for homoeroticism (the extent of arousal to members of one's own gender), ranging from low to high (see Figure 13.5, section 3). Thus, if one is high on both heteroeroticism and homoeroticism, one is a bisexual; the person high on heteroeroticism and low on homoeroticism is heterosexual; the person high on homoeroticism and low on heteroeroticism is homosexual; and the person low on both scales is asexual. This scheme allows even more complexity in describing homosexuality and heterosexuality than Kinsey's scale does.

The answer to the original question—How many people are homosexual and how many are heterosexual?—is complex. Probably about 90 percent of men and 90 percent of women are exclusively heterosexual. About 10 percent of men and women have had at least one same-gender sexual experience in adulthood. About 2 percent of men and 1 percent of women are exclusively homosexual. These figures are based on the NSFG and the NHSLS, but adjusted somewhat to allow for concealment by some respondents.

Sexual Orientation and Mental Health

Many Americans believe that homosexuality is a kind of mental illness. Is this really true? Do psychologists and psychiatrists agree that homosexuals are poorly adjusted or deviant? What are the implications of sexual orientation for a person's adjustment?

Sin and the Medical Model

The belief that homosexuality is a form of mental illness is actually something of an improvement over previous beliefs about homosexuality. Before the twentieth century, the dominant belief in Europe and the United States was that homosexuality was a sin or a heresy. During the Inquisition, people who were accused of being heretics were also frequently accused of being homosexuals and were burned at the stake. Indeed, in those times, all mental illness was regarded as a sin. In the twentieth century, this view was replaced by the **medical model,** in which mental disturbance, and homosexuality in particular, is viewed as a sickness or

illness (Bullough & Bullough, 1997).[3] This view is now widely held by the general public.

Psychiatrist Thomas Szasz and others are critical of the medical model. In his well-known writing on "the myth of mental illness," Szasz argues that the medical model is obsolete and that we need to develop a more humane and realistic way of dealing with mental disorders and variations from the norm. He has argued the case particularly for homosexuality (Szasz, 1965). LGB activists have joined in, saying that they do not like being called "sick" and that this is just another form of persecution of gays and lesbians.

Research Evidence

What do the scientific data say? Once again, the answers provided by the data are complex and depend on the assumptions of the particular investigator and on the research design used. Basically, four kinds of research designs have been used, representing progressive sophistication and changing assumptions about the nature of homosexuality.

Clinical Studies

The first, and earliest, approach was clinical; homosexuals who were in psychotherapy were studied by the investigator (usually the therapist). He or she looked for disturbances in their current adjustment or in past experiences or home life. The data were then reported in the form of a case history of a single individual or a report of common factors that seemed to emerge in studying a group of homosexuals (e.g., Freud, 1920; reviewed by Rosen, 1974). These clinical studies provided evidence that the homosexual was sick or abnormal; she or he typically was found to be poorly adjusted and neurotic. But the reasoning behind this research was circular. The homosexual was assumed to be mentally ill, and then evidence was found supporting this view.

Studies with Control Groups

The second group of studies made significant improvements over the previous ones by introducing control groups. The question under investigation was rephrased. Rather than Do homosexuals have psychological disturbances? (after all, most of us have some problems), it became Do homosexuals have more psychological disturbances than heterosexuals? The research design

> **Medical model:** A theoretical model in psychology and psychiatry in which mental problems are thought of as sickness or mental illness; the problems in turn are often thought to be due to biological factors.

[3]As one gay comedian quipped, "If homosexuality is an illness, hey, I'm going to call in queer to work tomorrow."

involved comparing a group of homosexuals in therapy with a group of randomly chosen heterosexuals not in therapy. These studies tended to agree with the earlier ones in finding more problems of adjustment among the homosexual group than among the heterosexual group (Rosen, 1974). The homosexuals tended to make more suicide attempts, to be more neurotic, and to have more disturbed family relationships.

Once again, though, it became apparent that there were some problems with this research design. It compared a group of people in therapy with a group of people not in therapy and found, not surprisingly, that the people in therapy had more problems. It was also circular in assuming that homosexuals were abnormal (in therapy) and that heterosexuals were normal (not in therapy) and then finding exactly that.

Nonpatient Research

A major breakthrough came with the third group of studies, which involved nonpatient research. In these studies, a group of homosexuals not in therapy (nonpatients) were compared with a group of heterosexuals not in therapy. The nonpatient homosexuals were generally recruited through LGB organizations, advertisements, or word of mouth. Such nonpatient research generally has found no differences between the groups (Ross et al., 1988; Rothblum, 1994). That is, gays and lesbians seem to be as well adjusted as heterosexuals. This finding is quite remarkable in view of the very negative attitudes that members of the general public tend to hold toward LGBs (Gonsiorek, 1996).

On the basis of these studies, it must be concluded that the evidence does not support the notion that homosexuals are "sick" or poorly adjusted. This position has received official professional recognition by the American Psychiatric Association. Prior to 1973, the APA had listed homosexuality as a disorder under Section V, "Personality Disorders and Certain Other Nonpsychotic Mental Disorders," in its authoritative *Diagnostic and Statistical Manual of Mental Disorders*. In 1973, the APA voted to remove homosexuality from that listing; thus it is no longer considered a psychiatric disorder.

Population Studies

Most recently, a new set of studies has emerged using even better designs that, for example, obtain a random sample of the general population and then compare the homosexuals and heterosexuals in the sample on indexes of mental health (Cochran et al., 2003; Meyer, 2003; Wichstrøm &

Hegna, 2003). These studies find somewhat higher rates of depression among gays and lesbians compared with heterosexuals. And suicide attempts are more common among LGB youth than among heterosexual youth.

However, scientists vigorously debate the meaning of the statistics. One controversy concerns how big or meaningful the differences are. For example, in one study 9.1 percent of LGB adolescents had made a suicide attempt, compared with 3.6 percent for heterosexual adolescents (Wichstrøm & Hegna, 2003). We could focus on the fact that LGB youth were nearly three times as likely to attempt suicide. Alternatively, we could say that it's a gap of less than 6 percentage points and 90.9 percent of the LGBs had not attempted suicide (Savin-Williams, 2001; Savin-Williams & Ream, 2003). Should we view the glass as half full or half empty?

Beyond that, scientists agree that higher rates of depression and suicide among LGBs do not mean that homosexuality per se indicates mental illness. Rather, the higher rates reflect the greater exposure of LGBs to prejudice and hate crimes, and the stress of concealing their true identity (Meyer, 2003).

Can Sexual Orientation Be Changed by Therapy?

Conversion therapy or reparative therapy—treatments designed to change LGBs into heterosexuals—have been around for more than 100 years (Haldeman, 1994; Shidlo et al., 2002). The latest versions come not from trained psychologists but from far-right religious groups. Many earlier techniques were downright inhumane. They included crude behavior therapy that involved giving gay men electrical shocks while they viewed slides of nude men, as well as surgeries ranging from castration to brain surgery. All these treatments rested on the assumption that homosexuality was an illness that could and should be cured.

Investigations of reparative therapies today are revealing the pressures from family and the personal agonies that people experience as they are forced, or perhaps choose, to change their orientation. One man, who is now a psychologist, wrote in his diary,

> I am going to meet with the counselor tomorrow. I don't really know what to think. I feel that I need help but I also feel that I'm trying to do away with a part of myself. I know I should look at it as sinful and ugly, like a wart that needs to be burned off. Is it possible that those emotions are what allow me to be a sensitive caring male? Is it possible that God has allowed this in my life to build certain characteristics? Is it really ugly and sinful that I want to hold and be held by a man and that I want to have

Conversion or reparative therapy: Any one of a number of treatments designed to turn LGBs into heterosexuals.

a relationship with a man that includes sex? It sure sounds ugly on paper. I don't like admitting these things. I really don't. What is it that causes me to think and feel this way? Is it Satanic? Am I possessed? (Ford, 2001, p. 77)

The consequences of reparative therapy can be ugly, because they do not actually change people's sexual orientation but they do make them feel awfully guilty about it. In fact, some psychotherapists have developed a specialty in helping gay and bisexual men recover from conversion therapies (Haldeman, 2001).

Given the evidence discussed earlier in this section supporting the argument that LGBs are not mentally ill, reparative therapies make no sense. Ethical issues are raised as well: Should a person be changed from gay to straight against his or her will? By 2000 the scandals associated with conversion therapies had become so great that the American Psychiatric Association issued an official position statement opposing them (American Psychiatric Association, 2000b).

In sum, it is probably about as easy to change a homosexual person into a happy heterosexual as it is to change a heterosexual person into a happy homosexual—that is, not very.

Why Do People Become Homosexual or Heterosexual?

A fascinating psychological question is, Why do people become homosexual or heterosexual? Several theoretical answers to this question, as well as the relevant evidence, are discussed in this section. You will notice that the older theorists and researchers considered it their task to explain homosexuality; more recent investigators, realizing that heterosexuality needs to be explained as well, are more likely to consider it their task to explain sexual orientation.

Biological Theories

A number of scientists have proposed that homosexuality is caused by biological factors. The likeliest candidates for these biological causes are genetic factors, prenatal factors, differences in brain structure, and an endocrine imbalance.

Genetic Factors

One study recruited gay and bisexual men who had a twin brother or an adopted brother (Bailey & Pillard, 1991). Among the 56 gay men who had an

Figure 13.6 Michael Bailey, Northwestern University, a prominent researcher on the genetics of sexual orientation.

identical twin brother, 52 percent of the cotwins were themselves gay (in the terminology of geneticists, this is a 52 percent concordance rate). Among the 54 gay men who had a nonidentical twin brother, 22 percent of the cotwins were themselves gay. Of the adoptive brothers of gay men, 11 percent were gay. The same research team later repeated the study with lesbians (Bailey et al., 1993). Among the 71 lesbians who had an identical twin, 48 percent of the cotwins were also lesbian. Among the 37 lesbians who had a nonidentical twin sister, 16 percent of the cotwins were lesbian. Of the adoptive sisters of lesbians, 6 percent were lesbian. The statistics for women were therefore quite similar to those for men. Later studies using improved methods have found similar results (Kendler et al., 2000b; Kirk et al., 2000).

The fact that the rate of concordance is substantially higher for identical twins than for nonidentical twins argues in favor of a genetic contribution to sexual orientation. If genetic factors absolutely determined sexual orientation, however, the concordance rate would be 100 percent for the identical twin pairs, and the rates are far from that. The implication is that factors other than genetics also play a role in influencing sexual orientation.

One research group believes that they have discovered a gene, located on the X chromosome, for homosexuality; this research is highly controversial (Hamer et al., 1993; Marshall, 1995). One study, by Hamer, has replicated the finding but others have not (Bailey & Pillard, 1995; Rice et al., 1999).

A milestone came in 2005 with the first full genome scan for sexual orientation in men, using modern genotyping methods (Mustanski et al., 2005). The sample consisted of 456 individuals from 146 different families, all of which had two or more gay brothers. The sample included many heterosexual siblings and parents from those families, as well as the gay siblings. This design is ideal for spotting regions of DNA that are the same for two gay brothers but that differ from the heterosexual siblings or parents. The findings indicated possible influence by three genes, found on chromosomes 7, 8, and 10. It seems likely that multiple genes contribute to sexual orientation. This research is still in its infancy but should yield important findings in the next decade.

Prenatal Factors

Another possible biological cause is that homosexuality develops as a result of factors during the prenatal period. As we saw in Chapter 5, exposure to atypical hormones during fetal development can lead a genetic female to have male genitals, or a genetic male to have female genitals. It has been suggested that a similar process might account for homosexuality (and also for transsexualism—see Chapter 12).

According to one theory, homosexuality is caused by a variation in prenatal development. According to this theory, there is a critical time in fetal development during which the hypothalamus differentiates and sexual orientation is determined (Ellis & Cole-Harding, 2001). Any of several biological variations during this period will produce homosexuality.

One line of research that supports this theory has found evidence that severe stress to a mother during pregnancy tends to produce homosexual offspring. For example, exposing pregnant female rats to stress produces male offspring that assume the female mating posture, although their ejaculatory behavior is normal (Ward et al., 2002). The stress to the mother reduces the amount of testosterone in the fetus, which is thought to produce homosexual rats. Research with humans designed to test the prenatal stress hypothesis reports mixed results. Some studies find effects like those in the rat studies and others do not (Bailey et al., 1991; Ellis & Cole-Harding, 2001).

Another research group has suggested that prenatal exposure to abnormally high levels of estrogen produces human female offspring who are more likely to be lesbian (Meyer-Bahlburg, 1997; Meyer-Bahlburg et al., 1995). To test this hypothesis, they studied adult women who had been exposed to DES before birth. DES, or diethylstilbestrol, is a powerful estrogen that was used to prevent miscarriage until 1971, when its use was discontinued because of harmful side effects. More DES-exposed women than controls were rated as homosexual or bisexual (Kinsey ratings of 2 through 6).

Another research group has studied the birth order of gay men. Their research shows that consistently, across many samples, compared with heterosexual men, gay men are more likely to have a late birth order and to have more older brothers but not more older sisters (Blanchard, 1997; Bogaert, 2003). The researchers find no birth order or sibling effects for lesbians compared with heterosexual women. They believe that they have uncovered a prenatal effect, hypothesizing that with each successive pregnancy with a male fetus, the mother forms more antibodies against an antigen (H-Y antigen) produced by a gene on the Y chromosome (Blanchard, 2001). Because H-Y antigen is known to influence prenatal sexual differentiation, the hypothesis is that the mother's antibodies to this antigen may affect sexual differentiation in the developing fetal brain. These researchers estimate that between 15 and 30 percent of gay men had their sexual orientation created in this manner (Blanchard & Bogaert, 2004; Cantor et al., 2002).

Other researchers have documented an odd, but potentially important, pattern concerning the 2D:4D finger-length ratio. This refers to the ratio of the length of the index finger to the length of the ring finger. In general, men have lower 2D:4D ratios than women; that is, men's index fingers are relatively shorter than their ring fingers, compared with women's. Lesbians have a smaller 2D:4D ratio than heterosexual women; results across studies are inconsistent for comparisons of gay men and heterosexual men (McFadden et al., 2005). Other researchers have found that gays are more likely to be lefthanded than are straights; gay men are about 40 percent more likely than straight men to be lefthanded, and lesbians are nearly twice as likely as heterosexual women to be lefthanded (Lalumière et al., 2000). Both patterns suggest some kind of prenatal hormone effect on the developing brain.

These theories of prenatal influence are intriguing and show much promise for the future.

Brain Factors

Another line of theorizing argues that there are anatomical differences between the brains of gays and straights that produce the differences in sexual orientation. A number of studies have pursued this possibility, all looking at somewhat different regions of the brain (Swaab, 2005). A highly publicized study by neuroscientist Simon LeVay (1991) is an example. LeVay found significant differences between gay men and straight men in certain cells in the anterior portion of the hypothalamus. Anatomically, the hypothalamic cells of the gay men were more similar to those of women than to those of straight men, according to LeVay. However, the study had a number of flaws: (1) The sample size was very small: only 19 gay men, 16 straight men, and 6 straight women were included. This small sample size was necessitated by the fact that the brains had to be dissected in order to examine the hypothalamus, so that the brains of living persons could not be studied. (2) All of the gay men in the sample, but only 6 of the straight men and 1 of the straight women, had died of AIDS. The groups are not comparable, then. Perhaps the brain differences were caused by the neurological effects of AIDS. (3) Lesbian women were omitted from the study, making them invisible in the research—as they often have been in psychological and biological research. (4) The gay men were known to have been gay based on records at the time of death; the others, however, were just presumed to be heterosexual—if there was no record of sexual orientation, the assumption was that the person had been heterosexual, scarcely a sophisticated method of measurement.

It is difficult to know how much confidence to place in LeVay's findings. Other scientists who looked for this effect found no differences in this region of the hypothalamus as a function of the person's sexual orientation (Byne et al., 2000; Swaab, 2005). Yet animal researchers believe that they have identified a similar region in the hypothalamus of the rat, and it does seem to be involved in sexual behavior (Swaab, 2005).

Hormonal Imbalance

Investigating the possibility that an endocrine imbalance is the cause of homosexuality, many researchers have tried to determine whether the testosterone ("male" hormone) levels of male homosexuals differ from those of male heterosexuals. These studies have not found any hormonal differences between the two groups (Banks & Gartrell, 1995; Gooren et al., 1990).

Despite these results, some clinicians have attempted to cure male homosexuality by administering testosterone therapy (Glass & Johnson, 1944). This therapy fails; indeed, it seems to result in even more homosexual behavior than usual. This is not

an unexpected result, since, as we saw in Chapter 8, androgen levels seem to be related to sexual responsiveness. A clinician friend of ours replied to an undergraduate male who was seeking testosterone therapy for his homosexual behavior, "It won't make you heterosexual; it will only make you horny."

In conclusion, of the biological theories, the genetic theory and the prenatal theory have new supporting evidence, but much more research is needed.

Learning Theory

Behaviorists emphasize the importance of learning in the development of sexual orientation. They note the prevalence of bisexual behavior both in other species and in young humans, and they argue that rewards and punishments shape the individual's behavior into predominant homosexuality or predominant heterosexuality. The assumption, then, is that humans have a relatively amorphous, undifferentiated pool of sex drive, which, depending on circumstances (rewards and punishments), may be channeled in any of several directions. In short, people are born sexual, not heterosexual or homosexual. Only through learning does one of these behaviors become more likely than the other. For example, a person who has early heterosexual experiences that are very unpleasant might develop toward homosexuality. Heterosexuality has essentially been punished and therefore becomes less likely. This might occur, for instance, in the case of a girl who is raped at an early age; her first experience with heterosexual sex was extremely unpleasant, so she avoids it and turns to homosexuality. Parents who become upset about their teenagers' heterosexual activities might do well to remember this notion; punishing a young person for engaging in heterosexual behavior may not eliminate the behavior but rather rechannel it in a homosexual direction.

Another possibility, according to a learning-theory approach, is that if early sexual experiences are homosexual and pleasant, the person may become homosexual. Homosexual behavior has essentially been rewarded and therefore becomes more likely.

The learning-theory approach treats homosexuality as a normal form of behavior and recognizes that heterosexuality is not necessarily inborn but must also, like homosexuality, be learned.

The evidence on learning theory's explanation of sexual orientation is mixed. A comprehensive study of the influences on sexual orientation in humans disconfirmed some essential arguments.

The idea that homosexuality results from early unpleasant heterosexual experiences was not supported by the data. Lesbian women, for example, were no more likely to have been raped than heterosexual women (Bell et al., 1981). Yet recent research using an animal model does point to the importance of early learning. Zebra finches are small birds that are monogamous, mate for life, and are almost invariably heterosexual. If the fathers are removed from the cages, though, so that the young birds grow up without adult males or male–female pairs, in adulthood these birds pair with either males or females (Adkins-Regan, 2002). That is, their behavior, which is bisexual, is a result of early experience.

In contrast to the bird research, research with humans indicates that children who grow up with a homosexual parent are not themselves more likely as a result to become gay (Allen & Burrell, 2002; Bailey et al., 1995; Patterson, 2006). In this sense, then, homosexuality is not "learned" from one's parents.

Interactionist Theory

Bem: The Exotic Becomes Erotic

Psychologist Daryl Bem (1996) proposed a theory of the development of sexual orientation that encompasses the interaction of biological factors and experiences with the environment. Bem's theory is diagramed in Figure 13.7.

The theory begins with biological influences, relying on the evidence discussed earlier about biological contributions to sexual orientation (part A in Figure 13.7). However, Bem does not believe that genes and other biological factors directly and magically determine a person's sexual orientation. Rather, he theorizes that biological factors exert their influence on sexual orientation through their influence on temperament in childhood (part A to part B). Psychologists have found abundant evidence that two aspects of temperament have a biological basis: aggression and activity level. Moreover, these two aspects of temperament show reliable gender differences. According to Bem, most children show levels of aggression and activity level that are typical of their gender; boys are generally more aggressive and more active than girls. These tendencies lead children to engage in gender-conforming activities (B to C). Most boys play active, aggressive sports, and most girls prefer quieter play activities. These play patterns also lead children to associate almost exclusively with members of their own gender. The boy playing tackle football is playing in a group that consists

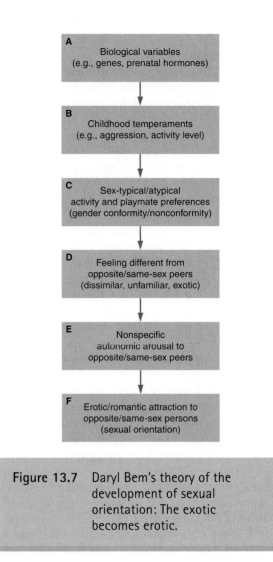

Figure 13.7 Daryl Bem's theory of the development of sexual orientation: The exotic becomes erotic.

either entirely or almost entirely of boys. This chain of events will eventually lead to a heterosexual orientation in adulthood.

A minority of children, however, have temperamental characteristics that are not typical of their gender: Some boys are not particularly active or aggressive and some girls are. These children are then gender-nonconforming in their play patterns. The boys prefer quieter, less active play and have more girls as friends, and the gender-nonconforming girls prefer aggressive sports and have more boys as friends.

These experiences with childhood play and playmates create a feeling in children that certain other children are different from them and therefore are exotic (parts C to D). For the boy who spends most of his time playing active, aggressive sports with other boys, girls are different, mysterious, and exotic. For the gender-nonconforming girl who plays active sports with boys, most girls, too, seem different and exotic to her.

The presence of an exotic other causes a person to feel generalized arousal, whether in childhood, adolescence, or adulthood (parts D to E). Those of you who are heterosexual certainly remember many instances in your past when you felt ill at ease and nervous in the presence of a member of the other gender.

In the final link of the model, this generalized arousal is transformed into erotic/romantic attraction. Essentially, the exotic becomes erotic. This transformation may be a result of processes described in Berscheid and Walster's (1974) two-component theory of attraction, discussed in Chapter 11. Generalized arousal can easily be transformed into sexual arousal and attraction if the conditions are right. For heterosexual persons, the exotic people are members of the other gender, with whom they had less contact in childhood and who have become eroticized. For gays and lesbians, the exotic people are members of their own gender, from whom they felt different in childhood and who have become eroticized.

One well-documented phenomenon is that there are considerably more heterosexuals than homosexuals. The theory deals with this fact by recognizing that U.S. society, like most others, is gender polarized. Gender distinctions are emphasized, and gender roles are strong. For most individuals, then, members of the other gender are exotic. It is only in the minority of cases, those whose childhood temperament leads them to be gender-nonconforming, that members of their own gender are exotic.

Certainly one virtue of the theory is that it is designed to explain sexual orientation (homosexual or heterosexual) rather than homosexuality. That is, the essential process is that the exotic becomes erotic, for both heterosexuals and homosexuals. The difference is that, because of childhood temperament and play activities, members of the other gender seem exotic to heterosexuals, whereas members of their own gender seem exotic to gays and lesbians.

One body of evidence that is consistent with Bem's theory indicates that gay men and lesbians are, on average, more likely than heterosexuals to have had a childhood history of gender nonconformity (Bailey & Zucker, 1995; Cohen, 2002). This pattern has been found cross-culturally as well. For example, in one study of lesbians and heterosexual women in Brazil, Peru, the Philippines, and the United States, the lesbians were, as children, significantly more gender-nonconforming than were the heterosexual women (Whitam & Mathy, 1991). The lesbians were significantly more rejecting of gender-typical activities, such as playing with girls' toys and paying attention to women's fashions, and more involved with gender-atypical activities like playing with boys' toys and being a tomboy. The consistency of these results is particularly striking given how vastly different these four cultures are. Although this evidence is consistent with Bem's theory, it is also consistent with the biological theories.

At the same time, Bem's theory and evidence have been criticized (Peplau et al., 1998; for Bem's response, see Bem, 1998). Two criticisms have been raised: (1) evidence not discussed by Bem contradicts some central propositions of the theory; and (2) the theory reflects male experience and neglects female experience. Regarding the evidence, Bem noted that, in one major study, lesbians (70 percent) were significantly more likely than were heterosexual women (51 percent) to recall feeling somewhat or very different from other girls their age (Bell et al., 1981). The difference is significant, but perhaps more important is the finding that a majority of heterosexual women felt different from other girls. Other girls seemed different or exotic to them. Why didn't they become lesbian, then?

Sociological Theory

Sociologists emphasize the effects of labeling in explaining homosexuality. The label "homosexual" has a big impact in our society. If you are heterosexual, suppose that someone said to you, "I think you are homosexual." How would you react? Your immediate reaction would probably be negative: anger, anxiety, and embarrassment. The label "homosexual" has derogatory connotations and may even be used as an insult, reflecting our society's predominantly negative attitudes toward homosexuality.

But the label "homosexual" may also act as a self-fulfilling prophecy. Suppose that a young boy—possibly because he is slightly effeminate or poor in sports, or for no reason at all—is called a homosexual. He reacts strongly and becomes more and more anxious and worried about his problem. He becomes painfully aware of the slightest homosexual tendency in himself. Finally he convinces himself that he is homosexual. He begins engaging in homosexual behavior and associates with a gay group. In short, a homosexual has been created through labeling.

Recall that in Chapter 2 we discussed Ira Reiss's sociological theory of human sexuality. In his theorizing he addressed the issue of sexual orientation, focusing particularly on gay men. Recognizing the need to explain cross-cultural differences in sexual patterns, he contends that it is male-dominant societies with a great rigidity of gender roles that produce the highest incidence of homosexuality. In such societies there is a rigid male role that must be learned and conformed to, but young boys have little opportunity to learn it from adult men precisely because the gender roles are rigid, so that women take care of children and men have little contact with them. It is therefore difficult to learn the heterosexual component of the male role. In addition, because the male role is rigid, there will be a certain number of males who dislike it and reject its heterosexual component. Cross-cultural studies support his observations (Reiss, 1986). Societies that have a great maternal involvement with infants and low paternal involvement with infants and that have rigid gender roles are precisely those that have the highest incidence of same-gender sexual behavior in males.

This pattern describes the negative pathway to homosexuality. Reiss argues that there is also a positive pathway. It exists in less gender-rigid societies with more permissiveness about sexuality. In such societies, individuals feel freer to experiment with same-gender behavior and may find it satisfying. Examples are provided by several American Indian tribes in which three gender roles have been recognized (see Chapter 12).

The Bottom Line

We have examined a number of theories of sexual orientation and the evidence supporting or refuting them. What is the bottom line? Which theory is correct? The answer is, We don't know yet. We do not know what causes sexual orientation. Several theories have strong evidence supporting them, but no one theory accounts for all cases. We believe that a good lesson can be learned from this somewhat frustrating conclusion.

It has generally been assumed that gays form not only a distinct category (which, we have already seen, is not very accurate) but also a homogeneous category, that is, that all gays are fairly similar. Not so. Probably there are many different kinds or "types" of homosexuals. Indeed, one psychologist, expressing this notion, suggested that we should refer not to homosexuality but rather to the homosexualities (Bell, 1974; Bell & Weinberg, 1978). If this is the case, then one would not expect a single cause of homosexuality but rather many causes, each corresponding to its type. The next step in research, then, should be to identify the various types of homosexuals—not to mention the various types of heterosexuals—and the different pathways of development that lead to each.

Differences between Gay Men and Lesbians

Although gay men and lesbians are commonly lumped together in one category and called homosexuals, evidence from a number of sources indicates that there are some important differences between the two groups that go beyond one group being male and the other female (Lippa, 2007).

Women are more likely to be bisexual, and less likely to be exclusively homosexual, than men are. In the NSFG data set, 2 percent of women and 1 percent of men indicated that they were sexually attracted to both women and men, whereas 1.5 percent of women and 2.2 percent of men rated themselves as being attracted exclusively to members of their own gender (Mosher et al., 2005).

In related research, among both heterosexuals and homosexuals, women show more flexibility or change over time in their sexual orientation (Kinnish et al., 2005). In laboratory research, men are specific in their sexual arousal, whereas women tend not to be (Chivers et al., 2004). That is, heterosexual men tend to be aroused, physiologically, by female stimuli and not male stimuli, and gay men show the reverse pattern. Women, however, whether lesbian or heterosexual, show arousal to both male and female stimuli.

Some of the theories discussed earlier in this chapter seem to work for gay men or for lesbians but not for both. For example, the birth order effect has been found repeatedly; compared with heterosexual men, gays are more likely to have a late birth order and an excess of older brothers. Lesbians, however, are no more or less likely to have a late birth order compared with heterosexual women (Blanchard, 1997; Bogaert, 2003).

We will almost certainly need somewhat different theories to explain the development of sexual orientation in women and in men (Hyde & Jaffee, 2000).

Sexual Orientation in Multicultural Perspective

Just as different cultures around the world hold different views of same-gender sexual behavior (see Focus: A Sexually Diverse World), so do various U.S. ethnic minority groups have different cultural definitions for same-gender behaviors.

It is generally thought that there is less tolerance for homosexuality in the African American community. In one study whites had the lowest

Focus: A Sexually Diverse World
Ritualized Homosexuality in Melanesia

Melanesia is an area of the southwest Pacific that includes the islands of New Guinea and Fiji as well as many others. Anthropologists' research on homosexual behavior in those cultures provides great insight into the ways in which sexual behaviors are the products of the scripts of a culture. This research is rooted in sociological and anthropological theory (see Chapter 2). As such, the analysis focuses on the norms of the society and the symbolic meaning that is attached to sexual behaviors.

Among Melanesians, homosexual behavior has a very different symbolic meaning from the one it has in Western culture. There it is viewed as natural, normal, and indeed necessary. The Melanesian culture actually prescribes the behavior, in contrast to Western cultures, in which it is forbidden or proscribed.

Sociologists and anthropologists believe that most cultures are organized around the dimensions of social class, race, gender, and age. Among Melanesians, age organizes the homosexual behavior. It is not to occur among two men of the same age. Instead, it occurs between an adolescent and a preadolescent, or between an adult man and a pubertal boy. The older partner is always the inserter for the acts of anal intercourse, the younger partner the insertee.

Ritualized homosexual behavior serves several social purposes in these cultures. It is viewed as a means by which a boy at puberty is incorporated into the adult society of men. It is also thought to encourage a boy's growth, so that it helps to "finish off" his growth in puberty. In these societies, semen is viewed as a scarce and valuable commodity. Therefore the homosexual behaviors are viewed as helpful and honorable, a means of passing on strength to younger men and boys. One anthropologist observed,

> Semen is also necessary for young boys to attain full growth to manhood. . . . They need a boost, as it were. When a boy is eleven or twelve years old, he is engaged for several months in homosexual intercourse with a healthy older man chosen by his father. (This is always an in-law or unrelated person, since the same notions of incestuous relations apply to little boys as to marriageable women.) Men point to the rapid growth of adolescent youths, the appearance of peach fuzz beards, and so on, as the favorable results of this child-rearing practice. (Schieffelin, 1976, p. 124)

In all cases, these men are expected later to marry and father children. This points up the contrast between sexual identity and sexual behavior. The sexual behaviors are ones that we would surely term homosexual, yet these cultures are so structured that the boys and men who engage in homosexual behaviors do not form a homosexual identity.

Ritualized homosexual behaviors are declining as these cultures are colonized by Westerners. It is fortunate that anthropologists were able to make their observations over the last several decades to document these interesting and meaningful practices before they disappear.

Source: Herdt (1984).

---

levels of antigay attitudes and Blacks had the highest levels, with Latinos and Asian Americans falling in between (Haslam & Levy, 2006).

The process of sexual identity development and coming out may differ across U.S. ethnic groups. In a study of African American, Latina, and white lesbians, the African Americans and Latinas began wondering if they were lesbian at younger ages (around age 14) than the whites (around age 17). The African American lesbians were considerably less likely to be "out" with nonfamily than the Latinas and whites, perhaps because of the stronger antigay attitudes among African Americans noted earlier.

We should not overemphasize ethnic differences, though. According to one large-scale study of African American lesbians and gay men, respondents typically had partners who were similar in age, education, and income (Peplau et al., 1997). This same pattern has been found in numerous studies of white gays, lesbians, and heterosexuals (see Chapter 11).

It is also true that Black and Latino men are more likely than white men to engage extensively in homosexual behavior while still considering themselves to be heterosexual (Peterson & Marin, 1988; Peterson et al., 1992). A sizable number—we don't know the statistics exactly—of African American men are heterosexually married and present themselves to the world as heterosexual, yet engage in secret sex with other men, a practice called "down low" (Denizet-Lewis, 2003).

An interesting example of these different cultural definitions comes from a study of Mexican and Mexican American men and their same-gender sexual behavior (Magaña & Carrier, 1991). In Mexico, there is a dichotomizing of same-gender sexual behaviors that parallels traditional gender roles. Anal intercourse, because it most resembles penis-in-vagina intercourse, is the preferred behavior, and fellatio is practiced relatively little. A man adopts the role either of receptive partner or inserting partner and does this exclusively. Those who take the receptive role are considered unmanly, feminine, and homosexual. Those who take the inserting role are considered masculine, are not labeled homosexual, and are not stigmatized. This approach differs substantially from that in Anglo culture, where men commonly switch roles, and both are considered gay.

Such different definitions of homosexuality are not limited to Mexican and Mexican American culture. One researcher described the scene in Egypt:

In Egypt, because there was so little sense of homosexuality as an identity, what position you took in bed defined all. Between men, the only sex that counted was anal sex. . . . In the minds of most Egyptians, "gay," if it meant anything at all, signified taking the receptive position in anal sex. On the other hand, a person who took the insertive role—and that seemed to include virtually all Egyptian men, to judge by what my acquaintances told me—was not considered gay. . . . Many of the insults in the Arabic language concern being penetrated anally by another man. (Miller, 1992, p. 76)

As for lesbians, Latinas experience conflicts in the complexities of ethnicity and sexual orientation (Espin, 1987; Gonzalez & Espin, 1996). Although in Latin cultures emotional and physical closeness among women is considered acceptable and desirable, attitudes toward lesbianism are even more restrictive than in Anglo culture (Figure 13.8). The special emphasis on family—defined as mother, father,

Figure 13.8 Ethnicity and sexual orientation. Among Latina women, warmth and physical closeness are very acceptable, but there are strong taboos against female–female sexual relationships.

children, and grandparents—in Latin cultures makes the lesbian even more of an outsider. As a result, Latina lesbians often become part of an Anglo lesbian community while remaining in the closet with their family and among Latinos, creating difficult choices among identities. One Cuban woman responded to a questionnaire, "I identify myself as a lesbian more intensely than as a Cuban/Latin. But it is a very painful question because I feel that I am both, and I don't want to have to choose" (Espin, 1987, p. 47).

Among Chinese Americans, two features of Asian American culture shape attitudes toward homosexuality and its expression: (1) a strong distinction between what may be expressed publicly and what should be kept private; and (2) a stronger value placed on loyalty to one's family and on the performance of family roles than on the expression of one's own desires (Chan, 1995). Sexuality must be expressed only privately, not publicly. And having an identity, much less a sexual identity or a gay lifestyle, apart from one's family is almost incomprehensible to traditional Chinese Americans. As a result, a relatively small proportion of Chinese American LGBs seem to be "out" compared with non-Asians. Chinese American LGBs who are out tend to be more acculturated, that is, influenced by American culture. They echo the sentiments of the Latina lesbian just mentioned, saying that they would prefer not to have to choose between their ethnic identity and their sexual identity but that when forced to make the choice they are more closely tied to the LGB part of their identities (Chan, 1995; Liu & Chan, 1996).

In sum, when we consider sexual orientation from a multicultural perspective, two main points emerge: (1) The very definition of homosexuality is set by culture. In the United States, we would say that a man who is the inserting partner in anal intercourse with another man is engaging in homosexual behavior, but other cultures (such as Mexico and Egypt) would not agree. (2) Some ethnic groups are even more disapproving of homosexuality than are U.S. whites. In those cases, LGBs feel conflicts between their sexual identity and loyalty to their ethnic group.

Bisexuality

Here is a riddle: What is like a bridge that touches both shores but doesn't meet in the middle? The answer: research and theories on sexual orientation. The point is that scientists, as well as lay people, focus on heterosexuals and homosexuals, ignoring all the bisexuals in between.

A bisexual is a person whose sexual orientation is toward both women and men, that is, toward members of the same gender as well as the other gender. A slang term is "ac–dc" (alternating current–direct current).

Bisexuality is not rare; in fact, it is more common than exclusive homosexuality (if a bisexual is defined as a person who has had at least one sexual experience with a male and at least one with a female). About 1.8 percent of men and 2.8 percent of women claim a bisexual identity (Mosher et al., 2005), although there is probably some underreporting.

The proponents of bisexuality argue that it has some strong advantages. It allows more variety in one's sexual and human relationships than does either exclusive heterosexuality or exclusive homosexuality. The bisexual does not rule out any possibilities and is open to the widest variety of experiences and partners.

On the other hand, the bisexual may be viewed with suspicion or downright hostility by the gay community (Rust, 2002). Radical lesbians refer to bisexual women as "fence-sitters," saying that they betray the lesbian cause because they can act straight or lesbian whenever convenient. The term LUGs (lesbians until graduation) is used for women who live a lesbian lifestyle when it is easy in college and then shift to convenient heterosexuality afterward. Some gays even argue that there is no such thing as a true bisexual (Rust, 2002). Heterosexuals, too, can be quite biased against bisexuals (Herek, 2002).

Sexual Identity and Sexual Behavior

A consideration of the phenomenon of bisexuality will illuminate several theoretical points and provide some insights into homosexuality and heterosexuality. First, though, several concepts need to be clarified. A distinction has already been made between sex (sexual behavior) and gender (being male or female) and between gender identity (the psychological sense of maleness or femaleness) and sexual orientation (heterosexual, homosexual, or bisexual). To this, the concept of **sexual identity** should be added; it refers to one's self-label or self-identification as heterosexual, homosexual, or bisexual.

There may be contradictions between people's sexual identity (which is subjective) and their actual choice of sexual partners viewed objectively (Pathela et al., 2006; Weinberg et al., 2001). For example, a woman might identify herself as a lesbian yet occasionally sleep with men. Objectively, her choice of sexual partners is bisexual, but her identity is lesbian. More common are persons who think of themselves as heterosexuals but who engage in both heterosexual and homosexual sex. A good

Sexual identity: One's self-identity as homosexual, heterosexual, or bisexual.

Focus: First Person
Bisexual Tendencies

I am a lesbian with bisexual tendencies. I find myself admitting that I am a bisexual, and then quickly saying, "But I'm involved with a woman." My brief experiences identifying as a single, available bisexual were thrilling, but difficult. During that time I dated a lesbian who decided to stop seeing me partly because she was put off by "that bisexual thing." Similarly, I don't think that the man I saw soon after believed that I wouldn't end up leaving him for a woman. Both of these people also thought that being bisexual means being nonmonogamous. Not for me. One lover is all I can handle.

In my late teens and early twenties I was often in a group of men, one of whom was my lover, arguing about feminism. I wanted a partnership of equals and I just never felt that I could be equal with a man in the eyes of the world.

I began to identify as a lesbian in the late seventies in Ann Arbor. I wanted to be surrounded by women who had the same stake in feminism and leftist politics that I did. Coming out was like dropping backward into a pillow. After several years and a number of relationships with women, I began to admit that I wasn't just interested in feminism or politics, but that I had—and have—strong sexual feelings for women.

Eventually I admitted that I was still attracted to men and had several flirtations. When I did begin to go out with a man again after eight years of love relationships with women, I encountered some surprises. I appreciated the level of understanding of feminist issues I now found in some men.

Then there were my friends' reactions. One said that it was fine if I wanted to see the guy I was dating, but that she didn't ever want to hang out with us together. This is all too familiar to me, having faced the pain of not having my relationships with women accepted, much less welcomed and celebrated, by my family and co-workers. Most of my lesbian friends were supportive, although some appeared concerned. Others revealed that they too had been attracted to men and seemed to take a vicarious pleasure in watching my progress.

At least two otherwise pleasant dinner parties were spoiled by my casual mention of my bisexual tendencies. I brought them up innocent of the inferno of reactions the bi word produces. One lesbian attorney argued quite convincingly that I had no right to call myself a lesbian if I ever have sex with men. At a safe distance, I'm not so sure. I think "lesbian with bisexual tendencies" is fairly descriptive.

Sex, after all, is something to be contained. Sex unties all of the nice packages we use to keep ourselves—and to try to keep one another—from slipping off the edge of the cosmos. Our sexual identities tell us how to live. But I need to remember that I can define my own sexual identity. I take courage from some of the bisexual activists I see around me. As a feminist, I want to see more viable alternatives for women. When I acknowledged my attraction to women and men, the world became exponentially larger. It's a big, big world, full of interesting and attractive people.

Source: Yost (1991).

---

example of this is the tearoom trade discussed earlier—the successful, heterosexually married men in gray flannel suits who occasionally stop off at a public restroom to have another male perform fellatio on them. Once again, the behavior is objectively bisexual, in contradiction to the heterosexual identity. Another example is the group of women who claim to have bisexual identities but who have experienced only heterosexual sex. These women, often as a result of feminist beliefs, claim bisexuality as an ideal they are capable of attaining at some later time. Once again, identity contradicts behavior.

Bisexuals tend to be stereotyped as nonmonogamous (Spalding & Peplau, 1997). Some of those who have a bisexual identity also believe that they have to have regular sexual relations with both women and men (Weinberg et al., 1994). If you have been monogamously heterosexually married for the past five years, how can you think of yourself as bisexual? Monogamy is therefore an issue for bisexuals.

Some bisexuals are heterosexually married. One study examined 26 married couples in which the husband was bisexual (Wolf, 1985; see also Matteson, 1985). The couples had, on average, been married 13 years, and there had been open disclosure of the man's homosexuality for an average of 5.5 years. By and large, the marriages were happy. When asked to rate the quality of the marriage, 42 percent of the men and 32 percent of the women said it was outstanding. The majority of both husbands and wives said that they remained in the marriage because they valued the friendship of the spouse. Nonetheless, there were some conflicts, as in all marriages. Trust was one issue. One woman said, "I feel more suspicious and jealous at times since he lied in the past" (Wolf, 1985, p. 142). Others, however, commented that their trust had deepened. One factor that seemed most related to positive adjustment in these marriages was communication. The couples expressing the most satisfaction with the marriage were the most likely to have very direct styles of communication and to have communicated about the homosexuality early in the marriage or from the beginning of the marriage. In the AIDS era, a different meaning may be attached to a husband's bisexuality; now it is not just an alternative sexual pattern but also a potentially dangerous pattern that could infect the wife with HIV.

Bisexual Development

The available data on bisexual development suggest several important points (see Focus: First Person). Bisexual men and women generally begin to think of themselves as bisexual in their early to mid twenties (Fox, 1995; Weinberg, 1994). There are some gender differences in the sequence of behaviors, though. Bisexual women typically have their first heterosexual attractions and sexual experiences before their first homosexual ones. Bisexual men, in contrast, are more likely to have homosexual experiences first, followed by heterosexual ones. The timing and flexibility of these sequences argue for the importance of late-occurring experiences in the shaping of one's sexual behavior and identity. As already discussed in this chapter, most of the theory and research rest on the assumption that homosexuality is determined by conditions in childhood, or by prenatal or genetic factors. Yet some people have their first heterosexual and then their first homosexual experience in their twenties. It is difficult to believe that these behaviors were determined by some event that occurred before birth.

Deprivation homosexuality, or situational homosexuality, is also a good example of the influence of late-occurring experience. A heterosexual man may engage in homosexual behavior while in prison but return to heterosexuality after his release. Once again, it seems likelier that such a man's homosexual behavior was determined by his circumstances (being in prison) rather than by some problem with prenatal hormone exposure.

Unlike gender identity, which seems to be fixed in the preschool years, sexual identity continues to evolve in adulthood for some people (Diamond, 2003). This contradicts some scientists' assertion that sexual orientation is determined before adolescence (Bell et al., 1981). We think that the point at which sexual orientation is determined is still an open question. For some it may be determined by genetic factors or experiences early in life, but for others it may be determined in adulthood.

Second, a question is raised as to whether heterosexuality is really the "natural" state. The pattern in some theories has been to try to discover the pathological conditions that cause homosexuality (e.g., having a father who is an inadequate role model or a homoseductive mother)—all on the basis of the assumption that heterosexuality is the natural state and that homosexuality must be explained as a deviation from it. As discussed earlier, this approach has failed; there appear to be multiple causes of homosexuality, just as there may be multiple causes of heterosexuality. The important alternative to consider is that bisexuality is the natural state, a point acknowledged by the learning theorists and sociological theorists (Weinberg et al., 1994). This chapter closes, then, with some questions. Psychologically, the real question should concern not the conditions that lead to homosexuality but rather the causes of exclusive homosexuality and exclusive heterosexuality. Why do we eliminate some people as potential sex partners simply on the basis of their gender? Why isn't everyone bisexual?

> **Deprivation homosexuality:** Homosexual activity that occurs in certain situations, such as prisons, when people are deprived of their regular heterosexual activity.

SUMMARY

Sexual orientation is defined as a person's erotic and emotional attraction toward members of his or her own gender, toward members of the other gender, or both.

The majority of Americans believe that homosexuality is wrong. This belief is the basis for much antigay prejudice. In some cases this prejudice is so strong that it results in hate crimes and harassment directed at gays and lesbians.

Lesbian, gay, and bisexual communities can be found around the world. These communities are defined by a common culture and social life and by rituals such as pride marches.

In surveys, the majority of gay men and lesbians report being in a steady romantic relationship. Although concerns have been voiced about the sexual orientation and psychological well-being of children who grow up in lesbian and gay families, these concerns are unfounded, according to the available studies.

The most recent well-sampled surveys indicate (when corrected for some underreporting) that about 2 percent of men and 1 percent of women are exclusively homosexual and that roughly 10 percent of men and 10 percent of women have had at least one same-gender sexual experience in adulthood. Kinsey devised a scale ranging from 0 (exclusively heterosexual) to 6 (exclusively homosexual) to measure this diversity of experience.

Well-conducted research indicates that homosexuality per se is not a sign of poor adjustment. Research does show somewhat elevated rates of depression and suicide among LGBs, which is almost certainly due to exposure to prejudice and hate crimes. Although some groups claim success in reparative therapy to change the sexual orientation of LGBs, there is no scientific evidence that one's sexual orientation can be changed and many indications that these therapies are psychologically harmful. Most therapists believe that it is extremely difficult to change a person's sexual orientation.

In regard to the causes of sexual orientation, biological explanations include genetic factors, hormone imbalance, prenatal factors, and brain factors. The genetic explanation has some support from the data, and there is new evidence of prenatal factors. Learning theorists stress that the sex drive is undifferentiated and is channeled, through experience, into heterosexuality or homosexuality. Bem's interactionist theory proposes that homosexuality results from the influence of biological factors on temperament, which in turn influences whether a child plays with boys or with girls; the less familiar (exotic) gender becomes associated with sexual arousal. Sociologists emphasize the importance of roles and labeling in understanding homosexuality. They also note that gender-rigid, male-dominant societies are likely to produce a higher incidence of gay men. Available data do not point to any single factor as a cause of homosexuality but instead suggest that there may be many types of homosexuality (homosexualities) with corresponding multiple causes.

Gay men and lesbians differ in some important ways. Women are more likely to be bisexual, and some theories that are effective in explaining men's sexual orientation are not supported for women.

Different ethnic groups in the United States, as well as different cultures around the world, hold diverse views of same-gender sexual behaviors.

Bisexuality has been overlooked both by researchers and by the general public. A person's sexual identity may be discordant with his or her actual behavior. Bisexuality may be more "natural" than either exclusive heterosexuality or exclusive homosexuality.

QUESTIONS FOR THOUGHT, DISCUSSION, AND DEBATE

1. Debate the following topic. Resolved: Homosexuals should not be discriminated against in employment, including such occupations as high school teaching.

2. Do you feel that you are homophobic, or do you feel that your attitude toward gays is positive or tolerant? Why do you think your attitudes are the way they are? Are you satisfied with your attitudes, or do you want to change them?

3. Does your college or university, in addition to prohibiting discrimination on the basis of race and sex, also prohibit discrimination on the basis of sexual orientation? Do you think it should?

4. Imagine that you are a gay man employed at a managerial level in an advertising agency in Minneapolis. You and your partner have been together for 11 years and intend to stay that way. It is becoming increasingly awkward for you to pretend that you have no partner and that you are straight when you attend parties for the staff or when people ask you how your weekend was. Should you come out to your colleagues at work? Why or why not?

SUGGESTIONS FOR FURTHER READING

Besen, Wayne R. (2003). *Anything but straight: Unmasking the scandals and lies behind the ex-gay myth*. Binghamton, NY: Harrington Park Press. Besen, a journalist, conducted investigative reporting on conversion therapies for gays that are led by far-right religious groups.

Herek, Gregory M., Kimmel, Douglas C., Amaro, Hortensia, & Melton, Gary B. (1991). Avoiding heterosexist bias in psychological research. *American Psychologist, 46,* 957–963. This stimulating article on research methodology points out ways in which heterosexist bias can enter research and suggests ways to avoid this bias.

Savin-Williams, Ritch C. (2005). *The new gay teenager.* Cambridge, MA: Harvard University Press. Savin-Williams, a leading researcher on sexual orientation, argues that today's teenagers are not caught up in the rigid ideas of previous generations and instead think more flexibly about sexuality. The result—gay teenagers who are thriving!

Windmeyer, Shane L. (2006). *The Advocate college guide for LGBT students*. New York: Alyson Books. This book represents a new kind of college rating guide—one that rates college campuses on the kind of environment they provide for LGB students.

14 CHAPTER FOURTEEN

Variations in Sexual Behavior

CHAPTER HIGHLIGHTS

S ome men love women, some love other men, some love dogs and horses, and occasionally you find one who loves his raincoat.*

*Max Schulman. *I was a teen-age dwarf.*

Most laypeople, as well as most scientists, have a tendency to classify behavior as normal or abnormal. There seems to be a particular tendency to do this with regard to sexual behavior. Many terms are used for abnormal sexual behavior, including *sexual deviance, perversion, sexual variance,* and *paraphilias.* The term *sexual variations* is used in this chapter because it is currently favored in scientific circles.

In Chapter 13 we argued that homosexuality per se is not an abnormal form of sexual behavior. This chapter deals with some behaviors that more people might consider to be abnormal, so it seems advisable at this point to consider exactly when a sexual behavior is abnormal. That is, what is a reasonable set of criteria for deciding what kinds of sexual behavior are abnormal?

When Is Sexual Behavior Abnormal?

Defining *Abnormal*

As we saw in Chapter 1, sexual behavior varies greatly from one culture to the next. There is a corresponding variation across cultures in what is considered to be abnormal sexual behavior. Given this great variability, how can one come up with a reasonable set of criteria for what is abnormal? Perhaps it is best to begin by considering the way others have defined abnormal sexual behavior.

One approach is to use a *statistical definition.* According to this approach, an abnormal sexual behavior is one that is rare, or not practiced by many people. Following this definition, then, standing on one's hands while having intercourse would be considered abnormal because it is rarely done, although it does not seem very abnormal in other ways. This definition, unfortunately, does not give us much insight into the psychological or social functioning of the person who engages in the behavior.

In the *sociological approach,* the problem of culture dependence is explicitly acknowledged. A sociologist might define a deviant sexual behavior as a sexual behavior that violates the norms of society. Thus, if a society says that a particular sexual be-

havior is deviant, it is—at least in that society. This approach recognizes the importance of the individual's interaction with society and of the problems that people must face if their behavior is labeled "deviant" in the culture in which they live.

A *psychological approach* was stated by Arnold Buss in his text entitled *Psychopathology* (1966). He says, "The three criteria of abnormality are discomfort, inefficiency, and bizarreness." The last of these criteria, bizarreness, has the problem of being culturally defined; what seems bizarre in one culture may seem normal in another. However, the first two criteria are good in that they focus on the discomfort and unhappiness felt by the person with a truly abnormal pattern of sexual behavior and also on inefficiency. For example, a male clerk in a Minneapolis supermarket was having intercourse with willing shoppers in their cars several times a day. This apparently compulsive behavior led to his being fired. This is an example of inefficient functioning, a behavior that can reasonably be considered abnormal.

The *medical approach* is exemplified by the definitions included in the *Diagnostic and Statistical Manual of Mental Disorders (DSM-IV-TR)* (American Psychiatric Association, 2000a). It recognizes eight paraphilias: fetishism, transvestic fetishism, sexual sadism, sexual masochism, voyeurism, frotteurism, exhibitionism, and pedophilia. The general definition of **paraphilia** is

> recurrent, intense, sexually arousing fantasies, sexual urges, or behaviors involving non-human objects (Fetishism, Transvestic Fetishism), the suffering or humiliation of oneself or one's partner (Sexual Sadism, Sexual Masochism), children (Pedophilia), or other non-consenting person (Voyeurism, Frotteurism, Exhibitionism). (*DSM-IV-TR*, p. 566)

Additional diagnostic criteria are stated for each of the specific disorders; these generally include that (*a*) the fantasies, urges, or behaviors have occurred over a period of at least six months, and (*b*) they cause "clinically significant distress or impairment in social, occupational, or

Paraphilia (par-uh-FILL-ee-uh): Recurring, unconventional sexual behavior that is obsessive and compulsive.

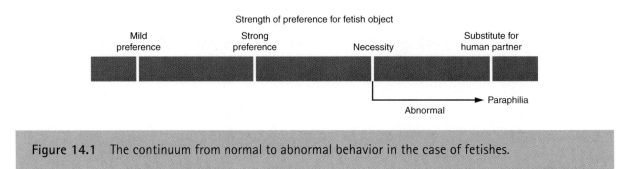

Figure 14.1   The continuum from normal to abnormal behavior in the case of fetishes.

other important areas of functioning." These definitions are very influential, used in many situations to determine who receives treatment and whether medical insurance will cover the cost of treatment.

In this chapter we discuss seven of the paraphilias, all except pedophilia, the sexual abuse of children, which is discussed in Chapter 15. We also discuss several other atypical sexual behaviors, including hypersexuality, asphyxiophilia, compulsive cybersex, and zoophilia.

The Normal–Abnormal Continuum

Each of the approaches just described provides criteria that attempt to distinguish what is normal from what is abnormal. While such distinctions may be made in theory, they are often difficult to make in reality. For example, lingerie is often sexually arousing for both men and women. For a woman who is wearing a low-cut bra and silk thong panties, the sensuous feel of the material against her skin may be arousing; for a man it might be the sight of the woman wearing the lingerie. At the same time, lingerie is a common sexual fetish object. This is an excellent example of the continuum from normal to abnormal sexual behavior. That is, normal sexual behavior and abnormal sexual behavior—like other normal and abnormal behaviors—are not two separate categories but rather gradations on a continuum. Many people have mild fetishes, finding things such as silk underwear arousing, and that is well within the range of normal behavior; only when the fetish becomes extreme is it abnormal. Indeed, in one sample of college men, 42 percent reported that they had engaged in voyeurism and 35 percent had engaged in *frottage* (sexual rubbing against a woman in a crowd) (Templeman & Stinnett, 1991). Unfortunately, the researchers did not ask about fetishes. But the point is that many of these behaviors are common even in normal populations.

This continuum from normal to abnormal behavior might be conceptualized using the scheme shown in Figure 14.1. A mild preference, or even a strong preference, for the fetish object (say, silk panties) is within the normal range of sexual behavior. When the silk panties become a necessity—when the man cannot become aroused and have intercourse unless they are present—we have crossed the boundary into abnormal behavior. When the man becomes obsessed with white silk panties and shoplifts them at every opportunity, so that he will always have them available, the fetish has become a paraphilia. In extreme forms, the silk panties may become a substitute for a human partner, and the man's sexual behavior consists of masturbating with the silk panties present. In these extreme forms, the man may commit burglary or even assault to get the desired fetish object, which would certainly fit our definition of abnormal sexual behavior.

The continuum from normal to abnormal behavior holds for many of the sexual variations discussed in this chapter, such as voyeurism, exhibitionism, and sadism.

Fetishism

Fetishism is characterized by sexual fantasies, urges, or behaviors involving the use of nonliving objects to produce or enhance sexual arousal with or in the absence of a partner, over a period of at least six months and causing significant distress. In extreme cases the person is incapable of becoming aroused and having an orgasm unless the fetish object is present. Typically, the fetish item is something closely associated with the body, such as clothing. Inanimate-object fetishes can be roughly divided into two subcategories: media fetishes and form fetishes.

Media Fetishes and Form Fetishes

In a **media fetish,** the material out of which an object is made is the source of arousal. An example

Fetishism: A person's sexual fixation on some object other than another human being and attachment of great erotic significance to that object.
Media fetish: A fetish whose object is anything made of a particular substance, such as leather.

Focus: First Person
A Case History of a Shoe Fetishist

The following case history is taken directly from the 1886 book *Psychopathia Sexualis,* by Richard von Krafft-Ebing, the great early investigator of sexual deviance. It should give you the flavor of his work.

Case 114. X., aged twenty-four, from a badly tainted family (mother's brother and grandfather insane, one sister epileptic, another sister subject to migraine, parents of excitable temperament). During dentition [teething] he had convulsions. At the age of seven he was taught to masturbate by a servant girl. X. first experienced pleasure in these manipulations when the girl happened to touch his member [penis] with her shoe-clad foot. Thus, in the predisposed boy, an association was established, as a result of which, from that time on, merely the sight of a woman's shoe, and finally, merely the idea of them, sufficed to induce sexual excitement and erection. He now masturbated while looking at women's shoes or while calling them up in imagination. The shoes of the school mistress excited him intensely, and in general he was affected by shoes that were partly concealed by female garments. One day he could not keep from grasping the teacher's shoes—an act that caused him great sexual excitement. In spite of punishment he could not keep from performing this act repeatedly. Finally, it was recognized that there must be an abnormal motive in play, and he was sent to a male teacher. He then revelled in the memory of the shoe scenes with his former school mistress and thus had erections, orgasms, and, after his fourteenth year, ejaculation. At the same time, he masturbated while thinking of a woman's shoes. One day the thought came to him to increase his pleasure by using such a shoe for masturbation. Thereafter he frequently took shoes secretly and used them for that purpose.

Nothing else in a woman could excite him; the thought of coitus filled him with horror. Men did not interest him in any way. At the age of eighteen he opened a shop and, among other things, dealt in ladies' shoes. He was excited sexually by fitting shoes for his female patrons or by manipulating shoes that came for mending. One day while doing this he had an epileptic attack, and, soon after, another while practicing onanism in his customary way. Then he recognized for the first time the injury to health caused by his sexual practices. He tried to overcome his onanism, sold no more shoes, and strove to free himself from the abnormal association between women's shoes and the sexual function. Then frequent pollutions, with erotic dreams about shoes, occurred, and the epileptic attacks continued. Though devoid of the slightest feeling for the female sex, he determined on marriage, which seemed to him to be the only remedy.

He married a pretty young lady. In spite of lively erections when he thought of his wife's shoes, in attempts at cohabitation he was absolutely impotent because his distaste for coitus and for close intercourse in general was far more powerful than the influence of the shoe-idea, which induced sexual excitement. On account of his impotence the patient applied to Dr. Hammond, who treated his epilepsy with bromides and advised him to hang a shoe up over his bed and look at it fixedly during coitus, at the same time imagining his wife to be a shoe. The patient became free from epileptic attacks and potent so that he could have coitus about once a week. His sexual excitation by women's shoes also grew less and less.

Source: Von Krafft-Ebing (1886), p. 288.

would be a leather fetish, in which any leather item is arousing to the person. Media fetishes can be subdivided into hard media fetishes and soft media fetishes. In a hard media fetish the fetish is for a hard substance, such as leather or rubber (Figure 14.2). Hard media fetishes may often be associated with sadomasochism (discussed later in this chapter). In a soft media fetish the substance is soft, such as fur or silk.

In a **form fetish,** it is the object and its shape that are important. An example would be a shoe fetish, in which shoes are highly arousing (see Focus: First Person). Some shoe fetishes require that the shoes

be high heeled; this fetish may be associated with sadomasochism, in which the fetishist derives sexual satisfaction from being walked on by a woman in high heels. Other shoe fetishes require that the shoes be leather boots that have been worn. Other examples of form fetishes are fetishes for nylon stockings, garters, and lingerie.

Why Do People Become Fetishists?
Psychologists are not sure what causes fetishes to develop. Here we consider three theoretical

Form fetish: A fetish whose object is a particular shape, such as high-heeled shoes.

Figure 14.2   A common fetish is for leather, often in association with sexual sadism and masochism. This store caters to clientele interested or involved in those activities.

explanations: learning theory, cognitive theory, and the sexual addiction model. These theories can be applied equally well to explaining many of the other sexual variations in this chapter.

According to learning theory (for example, McGuire et al., 1965), fetishes result from classical conditioning, in which a learned association is built between the fetish object and sexual arousal and orgasm. In some cases a single learning trial might serve to cement the association. For example, one adult male recalled,

> I was home alone and saw my uncle's new penny loafers. I went over and started smelling the fresh new leather scent and kissing and licking them. It turned me on so much that I actually ejaculated my first load into my pants and have been turned on ever since. (Weinberg et al., 1995, p. 22)

Transvestism: The practice of deriving sexual gratification from dressing as a member of the other gender.

In this case, shoes were associated with sexual arousal as the result of an early learning experience. Another example appears to be the shoe fetishist described in Focus: First Person, on page 367. This case clearly exemplifies the *DSM-IV-TR* criteria. The youth/man experienced sexual fantasies and urges associated with women's shoes for years, experienced arousal and ejaculation only when they were present, and experienced significant impairment in his academic and social life as a result. There was even an experiment that demonstrated that males could, in the laboratory, be conditioned to become sexually aroused when viewing pictures of shoes (Rachman, 1966).

A second possible theoretical explanation comes from cognitive psychology, discussed in Chapter 2 (Walen & Roth, 1987). According to cognitive theorists, fetishists (or other paraphiliacs) have a serious cognitive distortion in that they perceive a nonconventional stimulus—such as black leather boots—as erotic. Further, their perception of arousal (link 4 in the model; see Figure 8.5) is distorted. They feel driven to the sexual behavior when aroused, but the arousal may actually be caused by feelings of guilt and self-loathing. Thus there is a chain in which there are initial feelings of guilt at thoughts of the unconventional behavior, which produces arousal, which is misinterpreted as sexual arousal, which leads to a feeling that the fetish ritual must be carried out; it is, and there are orgasm and temporary feelings of relief, but the evaluation of the event is negative, leading to further feelings of guilt and self-loathing, which perpetuates the chain.

A third theory that has been advanced to explain some paraphilias, especially those that seem compulsive, is the theory of sexual addiction, discussed in Focus: Milestones in Sex Research, on page 370.

Whatever the cause, fetishism typically develops early in life. In one sample of foot or shoe fetishists, the mean age at which respondents reported first being sexually aroused by feet or shoes was 12 years (Weinberg et al., 1995).

Transvestism

Transvestism (*trans* [=] "cross"; *vest* [=] "dressing") refers to dressing as a member of the other gender. Cross-dressing may be done by a variety of people for a variety of reasons (see Figure 14.3). Male transsexuals may go through a stage of cross-dressing in the process of becoming women. Some gay men—**drag queens**—dress up as women,

(a)

(b)

Figure 14.3 Two examples of cross-dressing: (*a*) The lead actors in several films have portrayed cross-dressers, for example, the three leads from *To Wong Foo, With Love, Julie Newmar.* (*b*) Men in drag.

and some lesbians dress in masculine clothes (drag kings); these practices, though, are basically caricatures of traditional gender roles. **Female impersonators** are men who dress as women, often as part of their jobs as entertainers. For example, Robin Williams as *Mrs. Doubtfire* and Dustin Hoffman as *Tootsie* won praise from critics and big box office profits for their impersonations of women. Finally, some—perhaps many—adolescent boys cross-dress, usually only once or a few times (Green, 1975). This behavior does not necessarily mean a life of transvestism; it may simply reflect the sexual drives, confusions, and frustrations of adolescence.

In contrast to people who engage in cross-dressing for the reasons discussed earlier, *transvestic fetishism* refers to a heterosexual man who dresses in female clothing to produce or enhance sexual arousal (American Psychiatric Association, 2000a). When this behavior persists for at least six months and causes clinically significant distress, this person is a paraphiliac.[1] The cross-dressing may often be done in private, perhaps by a married man without his wife's knowledge.

Transvestism is almost exclusively a male sexual variation; it is essentially unknown among women. There may be a number of reasons for this difference, including our culture's tolerance of women who wear masculine clothing and intolerance of men who wear feminine clothing. The phenomenon illustrates a more general point, namely, that many sexual variations are defined for, or practiced almost exclusively by, members of one gender; the parallel practice by members of the other gender is often not considered deviant. Most sexual variations are practiced mainly by men.[2]

A survey of a national sample in Sweden asked each participant whether she or he had ever dressed in clothing of the other gender and

[1]A common abbreviation for transvestism, used by both scientists and members of the transvestite subculture, is TV. Therefore, if you see an ad in an underground newspaper placed by a person who is a TV, this is *not* someone who has delusions of broadcasting the six-o'clock news but rather a transvestite.

[2]Several theories have been proposed to explain why there are so many more male than female paraphiliacs (Finkelhor & Russell, 1984). Sociobiologists believe that the difference lies in the evolutionary selection of males to inseminate many partners and to be aroused by sexual stimuli devoid of emotional content (Wilson, 1987). Alternatively, sociologists point to gender-role socialization, which teaches males to be instrumental and to initiate sexual interactions. Females, on the other hand, are taught to be nurturing and to empathize with others, for example, with the vulnerability of children (Traven et al., 1990). Psychoanalytic theory (see Chapter 2) suggests that paraphilias result from *castration anxiety*, which is relieved by a forceful sexual act; since women do not fear castration, they are not subject to paraphilias.

Drag queen: A male homosexual who dresses in women's clothing.
Female impersonator: A man who dresses up as a woman as part of a job in entertainment.

Focus: Milestones in Sex Research
Sexual Addictions?

Patrick Carnes, in his book *The Sexual Addiction*, has advanced the theory that some cases of abnormal sexual behavior are actually a result of an addictive process much like alcoholism. One definition of alcoholism or other drug dependency is that the person has a pathological relationship with the mood-altering substance. In the case of the sexual addiction, the person has a pathological relationship with a sexual event or process, substituting it for a healthy relationship with others.

One common characteristic of alcoholics and sexual addicts alike is that they have a faulty belief system in which there is denial and distortion of reality. For example, the sex addict may deny the possibility of sexually transmitted infection. Sex addicts also engage in self-justification, such as "If I don't have it every few days, the pressure builds up." Like alcoholism, the addiction leads to many self-destructive behaviors. And, like alcoholism, the chief distinguishing feature of the sexual addiction is that the person has lost control of the behavior. Consider these examples:

- George has to take out a secret loan for $2,700 to cover his frequent payments to prostitutes.
- Jeffrey, a respected lawyer, is arrested for the third time for flashing.

According to Carnes's analysis, each episode of the sexually compulsive behavior proceeds through a four-step cycle, which intensifies each time it is repeated.

1. *Preoccupation.* The person can think of nothing other than the sexual act to which he or she is addicted.
2. *Rituals.* The person enacts certain rituals that have become a prelude to the addictive act.
3. *Compulsive sexual behavior.* The sexual behavior is enacted and the person feels that he or she has no control over it.
4. *Despair.* Rather than feeling good after the sexual act is completed, the addict falls into a feeling of hopelessness and despair.

According to Carnes, it is important to understand that not all sexual variations are addictions, and therefore the addiction model will not explain all paraphilias. There are also addictions to some behaviors, such as masturbation, that in and of themselves are perfectly normal. Thus, for example, the man who masturbates while looking at pornographic magazines two times per week is probably not an addict, and the behavior is well within the normal range. However, the man who buys 20 porn magazines a week, masturbates four or five times a day while looking at them, for a total of perhaps two or three hours, and can think of nothing else but where he can buy the next porn magazine and find the next private place to masturbate—that person is addicted. The key is the compulsiveness, the lack of control, the obsession (constant thoughts of the sexual scenario), and the obliviousness to danger or harmful consequences.

Just as our culture celebrates alcohol yet despises the alcoholic, so the culture celebrates sex yet abhors the sex addict. The media glorify alcohol: "You only go around once, so do it with Michelob." Similarly, advertising is filled with sexual messages (see Chapter 16). These sexual sells are difficult reminders for the sex addict who is trying to recover.

According to Carnes, the most effective therapy for the sex addict is the Alcoholics Anonymous program applied to sexual addictions. Several groups have adapted the AA program to sexual addiction, among them Sexaholics Anonymous (SA), Sex Addicts Anonymous (SAA), and Sex and Love Addicts Anonymous (SLAA). These groups can usually be found by calling the local phone number for Alcoholics Anonymous. The first step in the process of recovery is admitting that one is sexually addicted, that the behavior is out of control, and that one's life has become unmanageable. These are hard admissions to make for someone who has spent years denying the existence of a problem. There are frequent meetings with a support group, and there is a strong emphasis on building feelings of self-worth.

There has generally been much praise for Carnes's analysis of sexual addictions. Criticism

experienced sexual arousal (Långström & Zucker, 2005). Almost 3 percent of men and 0.4 percent of women reported at least one such experience. Among men, this behavior was associated with being easily sexually aroused, more frequent masturbation, and same-gender sexual experience.

A common means of studying persons with atypical sexual behavior patterns is to place ads in specialty newsletters and magazines, and to

has come, however, from some gay activists, who feel that the approach is homophobic, that it asserts that gay men are addicted to sex. Surely there are some gay men who are addicted to behaviors such as having impersonal tearoom sex, but the majority of gay men are not sex addicts. The key feature, again, is that the behavior must be out of control and compulsive.

Other criticisms have come from therapists and researchers in the field. The term *addiction,* as to alcohol or heroin, has a very specific definition among professionals, and sexual addictions do not meet the definition in some ways. For example, if one is addicted to alcohol and suddenly stops using it, there is a withdrawal phenomenon that involves striking physical symptoms. If a person abstains from an addictive sexual behavior, there are no physiological withdrawal symptoms. A second criticism is that "addiction" may become an excuse for illegal, destructive behavior. For example, a rapist might say, "I'm sexually addicted to raping and therefore can't stop myself."

There has also been criticism of the application of the AA model to sexual behavior. Applied to alcohol or drugs, the AA model demands that the addict abstain from contact with the substance. This abstinence model cannot be applied to sexuality, because sexual expression is a basic human need.

In order to resolve this debate, some experts recommend that we use the term *compulsive sexual behavior* instead of *sexual addiction* (e.g., Coleman, 1991). **Compulsive sexual behavior (CSB)**

is a disorder in which the individual experiences intense sexually arousing fantasies, urges, and associated sexual behaviors that are intrusive, driven, and repetitive. Individuals with this disorder are (*a*) lacking in impulse control, (*b*) often incur social and legal sanctions, (*c*) cause interference in interpersonal and occupational functioning, and (*d*) create health risks. (Coleman et al., 2001, p. 326)

Note that this perspective differs from the addiction approach in emphasizing that the person may experience social and legal sanctions and take health risks.

Given these theoretical debates, we need empirical research to help resolve them. A scale has been developed to measure CSB (Coleman et al., 2001).

Forty-two items related to sexual control and other aspects included in the definition above were given to three sample groups: 35 pedophiles, 15 persons with CSB who were not paraphiliac, and 42 in a normal control group. Preliminary analyses indicated that 28 of the items were valid. Three factors were identified, which appear to measure *control* (e.g., "How often have you been unable to control your sexual feelings?"), *abuse* (e.g., "Have you been forced to have sex?"), and *violence* (e.g., "Have you ever hit, kicked, or beaten any of your sexual partners?"). The scores on the three scales clearly differentiated between the three groups. Pedophiles had higher scores on abuse and lower scores on violence than the other groups. Thus a measure based on the compulsive sexual behavior model seems to be reliable and to discriminate between groups with different disorders.

Another group of researchers emphasize the out-of-control aspect of problematic sexual behavior (Bancroft & Vukadinovic, 2004). Whereas most people lose interest in sex when anxious or depressed, a minority experience increased sexual interest. When coupled with low sexual inhibition (self-control), the person may engage in compulsive sexual behavior in an attempt to improve/escape from the negative mood. An intensive study of 31 self-defined "sex addicts" provided evidence supporting this perspective.

Several studies have utilized a 10-item Sexual Compulsivity Scale (Kalichman & Rompa, 1995) in research on persons at risk for HIV/AIDS. High scorers on the scale report more sexual partners and more one-time or casual partners (Kalichman & Cain, 2004). A study of several hundred heterosexual college students found the same relationships with high scores in that population (Dodge et al., 2004). In addition, students with high scores were more likely to report unprotected oral, anal, and vaginal intercourse, and that they had engaged in sex in public places.

The availability of measures such as the CSB and the SCS will enable researchers to gather empirical data about these behaviors. That data, in turn, will contribute to refining our understanding and our theories of sexual addictions/compulsive behavior.

Sources: Carnes (1983); Coleman et al. (2001).

solicit participants at meetings and conventions attended by such persons. Using these procedures, researchers gathered survey data from 1,032 cross-dressers (Docter & Prince, 1997). The sample did not include drag queens or female impersonators. The vast majority of the men (87 percent) were heterosexual, 60 percent were married, 65 percent had a college education, and 76 percent reported

Compulsive sexual behavior: A disorder in which the individual experiences intense sexually arousing fantasies, urges, and associated sexual behaviors.

being raised by both parents through age 18. Sixty-six percent reported that their first cross-dressing experience occurred before age 10. Sexual excitement and orgasm were reported by 40 percent as often or almost always associated with cross-dressing. Almost all (93 percent) preferred complete cross-dressing, but only 14 percent frequently went out in public dressed as a woman.

Another survey was conducted by mailing questionnaires to 1,200 members of a national cross-dressing organization (Bullough & Bullough, 1997). There were 372 questionnaires returned. The median age at which the men began to cross-dress was 8.5; 32 percent reported that they first dressed as a female before they were 6. Most of them reported cross-dressing as children, and 56 percent said they were never caught.

How do the wife and children of the transvestite react to his unusual behavior? In one sample of 50 heterosexual transvestites, 60 percent of the wives were accepting of their husband's cross-dressing (Talamini, 1982). Most of these women commented that otherwise he was a good husband. Some of the wives felt fulfilled being supportive of the husband, and some even helped him in dressing and applying makeup. In the same sample, 13 of the couples had told their children about the cross-dressing. They claimed that the relationship with the children was undamaged and that the children were tolerant and understanding.

Transvestism is one of the harmless, victimless sexual variations, particularly when it is done in private. Like other forms of fetishism, it is a problem only when it becomes so extreme that it is the person's only source of erotic gratification, or when it becomes a compulsion the person cannot control and it therefore causes distress in other areas of the person's life.

Sadism and Masochism

Definitions

Sexual sadist: A person who derives sexual satisfaction from inflicting pain, suffering, or humiliation on another person.
Sexual masochist: A person who derives sexual satisfaction from experiencing pain.
Bondage and discipline: The use of physical or psychological restraint to enforce servitude, from which both participants derive sensual pleasure.
Dominance and submission: The use of power consensually given to control the sexual stimulation and behavior of the other person.

A **sexual sadist** is a person who derives sexual satisfaction from inflicting pain, suffering, or humiliation on another person. The term *sadism* derives from the name of the historical character the Marquis de Sade, who lived around the time of the French Revolution. Not only did he practice sadism—several women apparently died from his attentions (Bullough, 1976)—but he also wrote novels about these practices (the best known is *Justine*), thus ensuring his place in history.

A **sexual masochist** is a person who is sexually aroused by fantasies, urges, or behaviors involving being beaten, humiliated, bound, or tortured to enhance or achieve sexual excitement. When this is experienced for at least six months and causes distress or impairment, it is a paraphilia (American Psychiatric Association, 2000a). This variation is named after Leopold von Sacher-Masoch (1836–1895), who was himself a masochist and who wrote novels expressing masochistic fantasies. Notice that the definitions of sadism and masochism make specific their *sexual* nature; the terms are often loosely used to refer to people who are cruel or to people who seem to bring misfortune on themselves, but these are not the meanings used here. These two are often referred to as a pair since the two behaviors or roles (giving and receiving pain) are complementary.

There are two other styles of interaction that are related to sadism-masochism (S-M). These are bondage and discipline (B-D) and dominance and submission (D-S) (Ernulf & Innala, 1995). **Bondage and discipline** refers to the use of physically restraining devices or psychologically restraining commands as a central aspect of sexual interactions. These devices or commands may enforce obedience and servitude without inducing any physical pain. **Dominance and submission** refers to interaction that involves a consensual exchange of power; the dominant partner uses his or her power to control and sexually stimulate the submissive partner. Both B-D and D-S encompass a variety of specific interactions that range from atypical to paraphiliac.

Sadomasochistic Behavior

Sadomasochism (S-M) is a rare form of sexual behavior, although in its milder, nonparaphiliac, forms it is probably more common than many people think. Kinsey found that 26 percent of females and the same percentage of males had experienced definite or frequent erotic responses as a result of being bitten during sexual activity (Kinsey et al., 1953, pp. 677–678). Sadistic or masochistic fantasies appear to be considerably more common than real-life sadomasochistic behavior.

In one study, 178 men who responded to an ad in an S-M magazine or belonged to an S-M support group filled out a questionnaire (Moser & Levitt, 1987). The majority were heterosexual, well educated, and interested in both dominant and submissive roles (switchable). The following are behaviors that the majority of them had both tried and enjoyed: humiliation, bondage, spanking, whipping, fetish behavior, tying up with ropes, and master and slave role playing.

Another study administered questionnaires to 130 males and 52 females who responded to ads placed in S-M magazines; the study focused particularly on the women respondents (Breslow et al., 1985). Thirty-three percent of the males and 28 percent of the females preferred the dominant role; 41 percent of the males and 40 percent of the females preferred the submissive role; and 26 percent of the males and 32 percent of the females were versatile. The majority of these S-M respondents were heterosexual. Men involved in S-M frequently report having been interested in such activity since childhood; women are more likely to report having been introduced to the subculture by someone else (Weinberg, 1994). Women prefer bondage, spanking, oral sex, and master–slave role playing (Levitt et al., 1994).

Thus there is a spectrum of activities that constitute S-M. People who become involved in it often have tried a variety of these behaviors and find only some of them satisfying. They develop a script of activities that they prefer to enact each time they engage in S-M. One group of researchers identified 29 individual sexual behaviors associated with S-M (Santtila et al., 2002). They administered questionnaires to 184 Finnish men and women who were members of S-M clubs. Each participant was asked which of the behaviors he or she had participated in in the preceding year. Four clusters or themes were identified: hypermasculinity (e.g., dildo, enema), administering and receiving pain (e.g., clothespins attached to nipples, caning, hot wax), physical restriction (e.g., handcuffs, straitjackets), and humiliation (e.g., verbal humiliation, face slapping). Further analyses of the participation in the behaviors within each cluster identified a continuum in frequency from very common to very rare, with the order of the behaviors suggesting that this continuum reflects a dimension from least to most intense. For example, the humiliation continuum ranges from flagellation (reported by 81 percent; least intense) to verbal humiliation (70 percent), gagging (53 percent), and face slapping (37 percent) to using knives to make surface wounds (11 percent; most intense). The results suggest that the S-M activities within each cluster are *scripted,* with the less intense behaviors being much more common.

Some observers note that S-M is about play, as in the theater. S-M sexual activities are organized into "scenes"; one "plays" with one's S-M partners.

In addition to the activities such as those discussed above, roles, costumes, and props are important parts of each scene. The roles include slave and master, maid and mistress, and teacher and pupil. The costumes range from simple to elaborate. The props may include tight leather clothing, pins and needles, ropes, whips, and hot wax. In S-M clubs there are often rules governing the social and S-M interaction, particularly the creation and enactment of scenes. According to one Web site, the rules include no touching of another's body without consent, giving players the room they need to enact a scene, and not intruding physically or verbally on a scene in progress; and they may include no sexual penetration.

Interestingly, sexual sadists and masochists do not consistently find experiencing pain and giving pain to be sexually satisfying. For example, the masochist who smashes a finger in a car door will yell and be unhappy just like anyone else. Pain is arousing for such people only when it is part of a carefully scripted ritual. As one woman put it,

> Of course, he doesn't *really* hurt me. I mean quite recently he tied me down ready to receive "punishment," and then by mistake he kicked my heel with his toe as he walked by. I gave a yelp, and he said, "Sorry love—did I hurt you?" (Gosselin & Wilson, 1980, p. 55)

Causes of Sadomasochism

The causes of sadism and masochism are not precisely known. The theories discussed in the section on fetishes can be applied here as well. For example, learning theory points to conditioning as an explanation. A little boy is being spanked over his mother's knee; in the process, his penis rubs against her knee, and he gets an erection. Or a little girl is caught masturbating and is spanked. In both cases, the child has learned to associate pain or spanking with sexual arousal, possibly setting up a lifelong career as a masochist. On the other hand, in one sample of sadomasochists more than 80 percent did *not* recall receiving erotic enjoyment from being punished as a child (Moser, 1979, cited in Weinberg, 1987). Thus forces besides conditioning must be at work.

Another psychological theory has been proposed to explain masochism specifically, although not sadism (Baumeister, 1988a, b). According to the theory, the masochist is motivated by a desire to escape from self-awareness. That is, the masochistic behavior helps the individual escape from being conscious of the self in the same way that drunkenness and some forms of meditation do.

SexSource Online
www.mhhe.com/hyde10

"WHIPSMART"
IN VARIATIONS
IN SEXUAL
BEHAVIOR

In an era dominated by individualism and self-interest, why would anyone want to escape from the self? Probably because high levels of self-awareness can lead to anxiety as a result of a focus on pressures on the self, added responsibilities, the need to keep up a good image in front of others, and so on. Masochistic activity allows the person to escape from being an autonomous, separate individual. Masochism may be an unusually powerful form of escape because of its link to sexual pleasure. This theory can also explain why patterns of masochism seem to be so gender linked (Baumeister, 1988b). According to the theory, the male role is especially burdensome because of the heavy pressures for autonomy, separateness, and individual achievement. Masochism accomplishes an escape from these aspects of the male role, explaining why masochism is more common among males than among females.

Bondage and Discipline

Sexual bondage, the use in sexual behavior of restraining devices that have sexual significance, has been a staple of erotic fiction and art for centuries. Current mainstream and adult films and videos portray this activity. In some communities, individuals interested in B-D have formed clubs (Figure 14.4).

We noted earlier the difficulty of gathering data on participation in variant forms of sexual expression. One innovative study downloaded all the messages about bondage mailed to an international computer discussion group (Ernulf & Innala, 1995). Of the messages in which senders indicated their gender, 75 percent were male. Of

Figure 14.4   Bondage.

those indicating a sexual orientation, most were heterosexual; 18 percent said they were gay, 11 percent lesbian. The messages were coded for discussion of what the person found sexually arousing about B-D. Most frequently mentioned (12 percent) was play: "sex is funny, and sex is lovely, and sex is PLAY." Next was the exchange of power (4 percent): "It is a power trip because the active is responsible for the submissive's pleasure." The next most common themes were intensified sexual pleasure, tactile stimulation associated with the use of ropes and cuffs, and the visual enjoyment experienced by the dominant person.

There is a marked imbalance in preferences for the active ("top") and passive ("bottom") roles. Most men and women, regardless of their sexual orientation, prefer to be "bottom." This may be the reason why there are an estimated 2,500 professional dominatrices in the United States.

Dominance and Submission

Sociologists emphasize that the key to S-M is not pain, but rather dominance and submission (D-S) (Weinberg, 1987). Thus it is not an individual phenomenon but rather a social behavior embedded in a subculture and controlled by elaborate scripts.

Sociologists believe that to understand D-S one must understand the social processes that create and sustain it (Weinberg, 1987). There is a distinct D-S subculture, involving magazines (such as *Corporal*), clubs, and bars. It creates culturally defined meanings for D-S acts. Thus a D-S act is not a wild outbreak of violence but instead a carefully controlled performance with a script (recall the concept of scripts in Chapter 2). One woman reported that

> we got into dominance and submission. Like him giving me orders. Being very rough and pushing me around and giving me orders, calling me a slut, calling me a cunt. Making me crawl around . . . on all fours and beg to suck his cock. Dominance-submission is more important than the pain. I've done lots and lots of scenes that involve no pain. Just a lot of taking orders, being humiliated. (Maurer, 1994, pp. 253, 257)

Within the play, people take on roles such as master, slave, or naughty child. Thus American men can play the submissive role in D-S culture, even though it contradicts the U.S. male role, because it is really not they who are the naughty child, just as an actor can play the part of a murderer and know that he is not a murderer.

One interesting phenomenon, from a sociological point of view, is the social control over risk taking that exists in the D-S subculture (Weinberg, 1987). That is, having allowed oneself to be tied up or restrained and then whipped, one could be seriously injured or even murdered, yet such outcomes are rare. Why? Research shows that complex social arrangements are made in order to reduce the risk (Lee, 1979). First, initial contacts are usually made in protected territories such as bars or meetings, which are inhabited by other D-Sers who play by the same rules. Second, the basic scripts are widely shared, so that everyone understands what will and will not occur. When the participants are strangers, the scenario may be negotiated before it is enacted. Third, as the activity unfolds, very subtle nonverbal signals are used to control the interaction (Weinberg, 1994). By using these signals, the person playing the submissive role can influence what occurs. Thus, as two people enact the master and slave script, the master is not in complete control and the slave not powerless. So it is the *illusion* of control, not actual control, that is central to D-S activity for both the master and the slave.

Voyeurism

There are two types of **voyeur** ("peeping tom").[3] In **scoptophilia,** sexual pleasure is derived from observing sexual acts and the genitals; in *voyeurism,* technically, the sexual pleasure comes from viewing nudes, often while the voyeur is masturbating.

Voyeurism appears to be much more common among men than among women. According to FBI reports, nine men to one woman are arrested on charges of "peeping."

Voyeurism provides another good illustration of the continuum from normal to abnormal behavior. For example, many men and women find it arousing to watch a man or woman undress and "dance"—otherwise, there would be no strip clubs—and this is certainly well within the normal range of behavior. Some women are "crotch watchers," much as men are breast watchers (Friday, 1973, 1975).

The appeal of watching is illustrated by a study of college students that asked whether they would watch an attractive person undress and an attractive couple having sex (Rye & Meaney, 2007). The likelihood of getting caught was specified as 0, 10,

or 25 percent. Two-thirds said they would watch someone undress; 45 percent said they would watch the couple. Likelihood of watching the person undress increased as the risk decreased; likelihood of watching the couple did not vary by risk.

Voyeurism becomes paraphiliac when the fantasies, urges, or behaviors continue for at least six months, and they cause marked distress and interpersonal difficulty (American Psychiatric Association, 2000a).

Peepers typically want the woman they view to be a stranger and do not want her to know what they are doing (Yalom, 1960). The element of risk is also important; while one might think that a nudist camp would be heaven to a peeper, it is not, because the elements of risk and forbiddenness are missing (Sagarin, 1973).

A study of 561 males who sought treatment for paraphilia included 62 voyeurs (Abel & Rouleau, 1990). One-third reported that their first experience occurred before they were 12 years old. One-half said they recognized their interest in peeping prior to age 15. These men estimated that, on average, they had peeped at 470 persons.

In one study of arrested peepers it was found that they were likely to be the youngest child in their family and to have good relationships with their parents but poor ones with their peers (Gebhard et al., 1965). They had few sisters and few female friends. Few were married. These studies, however, point out one of the major problems with the research on sexual variations: Much of it has been done only on people who have been arrested for their behavior or sought treatment. The "respectable paraphiliac" who has the behavior under somewhat better control or who is skilled enough or can pull enough strings not to get caught is not studied in such research. Thus the picture that research provides for us of these variations may be very biased.

Exhibitionism

The complement to voyeurism is exhibitionism ("flashing"), in which the person derives sexual pleasure from exposing his genitals to others in situations where this is clearly inappropriate.[4] The

[3]*Voyeur* comes from the French word *voir,* meaning "to see." "Peeping Tom" comes from the story of Lady Godiva; when she rode through town nude to protest the fact that her husband was raising his tenants' taxes, none of the townspeople looked except one, Tom of Coventry.

[4]Here is a classic limerick on exhibitionism:

There was a young lady of Exeter
So pretty, men craned their necks at her.
  One was even so brave
  As to take out and wave
The distinguishing mark of his sex at her.

Voyeur: A person who becomes sexually aroused from secretly viewing nudes.
Scoptophilia: A sexual variation in which the person becomes sexually aroused by observing others' sexual acts and genitals.

Figure 14.5 Exhibitionism.

According to the benchmark study of males seeking treatment for paraphilia (Abel & Rouleau, 1990), 15 percent of the exhibitionists had exposed themselves at least once by age 12; one-half had done so by age 15. According to other research (Blair & Lanyon, 1981), exhibitionists generally recall their childhoods as being characterized by inconsistent discipline, lack of affection, and little training in appropriate forms of social behavior. An analysis of 10 studies of the social skills of sexual offenders (rapists, molesters, incest offenders, pedophiles, and exhibitionists) found that sexual offenders possess fewer social skills than nonoffenders (Emmers-Sommer et al., 2004).

The exact causes of exhibitionism are not known, but a social learning-theory explanation offers some possibilities (Blair & Lanyon, 1981). According to this view, the parents might have subtly—or perhaps obviously—modeled such behavior to the man when he was a child. In adulthood, there may be reinforcement for the exhibitionistic behavior because the man gets attention when he performs it. In addition, the man may lack the social skills to form an adult relationship, or the sex in his marriage may not be very good, so he receives little reinforcement from normal sex.

The learning-theory approach has been used to devise some programs of therapy that have been successful in treating exhibitionists. For example, in one therapy program exhibitionists were shown photos of scenes in which they typically engaged in exhibitionism; simultaneously, an unpleasant-smelling substance was placed at their nostrils (Maletzky, 1974, 1977, 1980). After 11 to 19 twice-weekly sessions of this conditioning and some self-administered home sessions, all but one of the men passed a temptation test in which they were placed in a naturalistic situation with a volunteer female and managed not to flash at her.

Many women, understandably, are alarmed by exhibitionists. But since the exhibitionist's goal is to produce shock or some other strong emotional response, the woman who becomes extremely upset is gratifying him. Probably the best strategy for a woman to use in this situation is to remain calm and make some remark indicating her coolness, such as suggesting that he should seek professional help for his problem.[5]

A study of 62 female sex offenders in Great Britain identified five women who had exhibited themselves (O'Connor, 1987). One 21-year-old

pronoun "his" is used advisedly, since **exhibitionists** are usually men. The woman who wears a dress that reveals most of her bosom is likely to be thought of as attractive rather than abnormal. When the male exposes himself, however, his behavior is considered offensive (Figure 14.5). Here again, whether a sexual behavior is considered abnormal depends greatly on whether the person doing it is a male or a female. Homosexual exhibitionism is also quite rare, so the prototype we have for exhibitionism is a man exposing himself to a woman. About 30 percent of all arrests for sexual offenses are for exhibitionism (Cox, 1988). According to one survey, 33 percent of college women have been the objects of indecent exposure (Cox, 1988).

When fantasies, urges, or behavior involving surprise exposure of the genitals to a stranger lasts at least six months and causes distress or difficulty, it is paraphilic (American Psychiatric Association, 2000a).

Exhibitionist: A person who derives sexual gratification from exposing his genitals to others in situations in which this is inappropriate.

---

[5]A joke suggests one such reaction: When the man in the overcoat flashed the gate attendant at the airport, she replied, "I want to see your boarding pass, not your stub."

woman stripped off her clothes and masturbated in public on several occasions. A 25-year-old single woman exposed her genitals and invited passersby to have sex with her. A 40-year-old woman entered private residences, took off her clothes, and invited any male present (including one child) to have sex with her. Two women were arrested while urinating in public. All five women had histories of unusual behavior and had been diagnosed with alcohol or psychiatric problems. Their atypical sexual behaviors appear to reflect these problems rather than sexual motivations.

Notice that both voyeurism and exhibitionism are considered problematic behavior when the other person involved is an unwilling participant. A man who derives erotic pleasure from watching his partner undress, or a woman who is aroused by exhibiting her body in new lingerie to her husband, is not engaging in criminal or paraphiliac behavior.

Hypersexuality

We turn now to several variations that are not explicitly listed in the *DSM-IV-TR;* however, each of these may vary from atypical through compulsive to paraphilic, depending on their frequency, duration, and consequences.

Hypersexuality includes nymphomania and satyriasis, conditions in which there is an extraordinarily high level of sexual activity and sex drive; at the extreme, the person is apparently insatiable and sexuality overshadows all other concerns and interests. When it occurs in women, it is called **nymphomania;** in men it is called **satyriasis** (or *Don Juanism*).[6] While this definition seems fairly simple, in practice it is difficult to say when a person has an abnormally high sex drive. As was discussed in Chapters 9 and 10, there is a wide range in the frequencies with which people engage in coitus; therefore, the range we define as "normal" should also be broad. In real life, *nymphomania* or *satyriasis* is often defined by the spouse. Some men, for example, might think that it was unreasonable for a wife to want intercourse once a day or even twice a week, and they would consider such a woman a nymphomaniac.[7] Other men might think

[6]Satyriasis is named for the satyrs, who were part-human, part-animal beasts in Greek mythology. A part of the entourage of Dionysus, the god of wine and fertility, they were jovial and lusty and have become a symbol of the sexually active male.
[7]Someone once defined a nymphomaniac as a woman whom a man can't keep up with.

it would be wonderful to be married to a woman who wanted to make love every day.

Because these two terms are imprecise, some researchers prefer the term *hypersexuality*. **Hypersexuality** refers to an excessive, insatiable sex drive in either a man or a woman. It leads to compulsive sexual behavior in the sense that the person feels driven to it even when there may be very negative consequences (Goldberg, 1987). The person is also never satisfied by the activity, and she or he may not be having orgasms, despite all the sexual activity. Such cases meet the criteria for abnormal behavior discussed at the beginning of this chapter: The compulsiveness of the behavior leads it to become extremely inefficient, with the result that it impairs the functioning in other areas of the person's life.

A study of 100 male patients with paraphilia or related disorders focused on creating an operational definition of hypersexuality (Kafka, 1997). The results supported the use of the criterion of seven or more orgasms per week for a minimum duration of six months. The men reported an average of 7.4/8.0 orgasms per week in the preceding six months; the modal time per day the men spent in unconventional sexual activity was one to two hours. They reported that their hypersexual activity began between the ages of 19 and 21. The most common unconventional behaviors were compulsive masturbation (67 percent of the sample), protracted promiscuity (56 percent), and dependence on pornography (41 percent). The most common paraphilias were exhibitionism (35 percent of those with a paraphilia), voyeurism (27 percent), and pedophilia (25 percent).

This research provides a useful operational definition for men, but note that the suggested criterion should not be applied to women. The criterion is stated as the number of orgasms per week. Some women rarely or never experience orgasms; in fact, their anorgasmia might cause them to engage in compulsive sexual behavior. Another problem is that women who are orgasmic are capable of multiple orgasms during a single session of activity (see Chapter 8). A woman who engages in sexual activity three times a week could experience seven or eight orgasms, which would not be atypical or abnormal. Once again we see that a person's gender is very important in defining abnormality. A valid criterion for hypersexuality in men may thus not be valid for women.

One study of highly sexual women recruited participants from

Nymphomania (nim-foh-MANE-ee-uh): An excessive, insatiable sex drive in a woman.
Satyriasis (sat-ur-EYE-uh-sis): An excessive, insatiable sex drive in a man; also called *Don Juanism.*
Hypersexuality: An excessive, insatiable sex drive in either men or women.

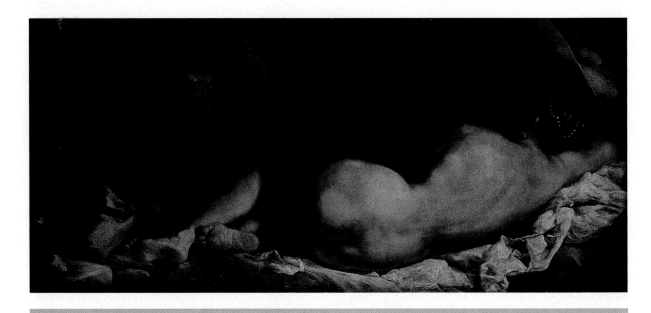

Figure 14.6   Historical painting of a satyr, which gives the name to satyriasis, a sexual variation in which a man has an excessive, insatiable sex drive.

volunteers at presentations about the topic and via newspaper ads in alternative newspapers (Blumberg, 2003). The term *highly sexual* refers to women who desire sexual stimulation to orgasm six or seven times per week, or who think of themselves as highly sexual and their sexuality frequently and strongly affects their lives. Forty-four women were interviewed, ranging in age from 20 to 82, from occupations as diverse as janitor and corporate CEO; 41 of the 44 were white. Twenty-five percent were married, 48 percent separated or divorced. The preferred weekly frequency of sexual episodes—again, not orgasms—ranged from 3 to 70. The women reported that the internal demand for sexual excitement and satisfaction was too strong to be ignored; for many of them, it shaped their daily lives. This demand led to challenges in the areas of their feelings about themselves, their relationships with partners, and their relationships with female friends. Some of the women found it impossible to form a single relationship that could fulfill their needs, leading to multiple partners or the frequent forming of new relationships. The researcher believes that neither the terms *sexual addiction* nor *compulsive sexual behavior* should be applied to this behavior. These women did not feel that their behavior was out of control, and they did not report an increase in frequency of behavior or the impact of it on their lives over time.

Asexuality: Having no sexual attraction to a person of either sex.
Asphyxiophilia: The desire to induce in oneself a state of oxygen deficiency in order to create sexual arousal or to enhance excitement and orgasm.

Asexuality

Little research has been conducted on **asexuality,** defined as having no sexual attraction to a person of either sex. In a survey of a national sample of British residents, 1 percent indicated they were asexual (Bogaert, 2004). These persons reported fewer lifetime sexual partners and less sexual activity. Asexuals were more likely to be women, to attend church frequently, and to be in poor health and of lower socioeconomic status. In another study, a convenience sample of 1,146 persons completed an online survey (Prause & Graham, 2007); 41 persons (3.6 percent) identified as asexual, that is, chose this label to identify themselves. Note that this differs from reporting no desire for sex. These persons reported less desire for partnered sex, but not necessarily no desire.

Asphyxiophilia

Asphyxiophilia is the desire to induce in oneself a state of oxygen deficiency in order to create sexual arousal or to enhance sexual excitement and orgasm (Zaviačič, 1994). A variety of techniques are used, including temporary strangulation by a rope around the neck, a pillow against the face, or a plastic bag over the head or upper body. Obviously,

Figure 14.7 Advertising for partners. Many newspapers and magazines carry such "personal ads."

this is very dangerous behavior; a miscalculation can lead to death. In fact, it is estimated that it causes between 250 and 1,000 deaths per year in the United States (Innala & Ernulf, 1989). The average age of males who die during this activity is 26, leading investigators to suggest that it may be novices who die, due to their inexperience (Lowery & Wetli, 1982).

Little is known about asphyxiophilia. Most of the deaths attributed to the practice involve men. Such cases are often obvious to the trained investigator. Characteristics that distinguish these deaths from intentional suicides include a male who is nude, cross-dressed, or dressed with genitals exposed, and evidence of sexual activity at the time of death (Hucker & Blanchard, 1992). Pornography or other props such as mirrors are often present (Zaviačič, 1994).

Recently, some cases have been identified involving women (Byard et al., 1993). A review of eight fatal cases among women found that only one involved unusual clothing and none involved pornography or props. Two of the cases were initially ruled homicide, one suicide, and five accidental death. The investigators suggest that death due to asphyxiophilia may be much more common among women than we realize, because these deaths are less often recognized for what they are by investigators.

Men and women engage in asphyxiophilia in the belief that arousal and orgasm are intensified by reduced oxygen. There is no way to determine

whether this is true. If the experience is more intense, it may be due to heightened arousal created by the risk rather than by reduced oxygen. Some believe that certain women may experience an orgasm accompanied by urethral ejaculation; this belief has been identified as one reason women engage in asphyxiophilia. Again, there is no evidence.

There is probably a range, from those who try this activity once out of curiosity to those who engage in it repeatedly and compulsively. Obviously, practitioners don't want to kill themselves; most include a self-release mechanism, but these safeguards sometimes fail.

Cybersex Use and Abuse

A major concern in recent years has been whether the use of the Internet to access sexually oriented materials, chat rooms, and bulletin boards can become compulsive, addictive, or paraphilic. Recall that compulsive behavior involves (*a*) a lack of impulse control, (*b*) leading to social and legal sanctions, (*c*) interference in interpersonal and occupational functioning, and (*d*) the creation of health risks. Addictive behavior involves preoccupation, ritual, loss of control, and despair. Paraphilias are behaviors defined as lasting six months or more and causing significant distress. This concern has been raised by therapists and clinicians, who report cases of Internet use leading to job loss, relationship difficulties or divorce, and other adverse consequences (Galbreath et al., 2002).

The Internet is thought to be especially likely to lead to addictive or compulsive behavior because it is characterized by the three A's: anonymity, accessibility, and affordability—if you aren't poor. Unlike face-to-face behaviors such as cruising for a partner or buying or renting X-rated videos, Internet users are anonymous. The Net is available 24/7 and its use is relatively cheap—you can download almost any kind of sexual material for as little as $2.95. The latter enhances its appeal; even if your ideal partner is 5′ 1″, weighs 140 lbs., has red hair and green eyes, and dresses in black leather with an opening exposing the genitals, you can find him or her online.

The research on Internet use has utilized convenience samples of persons who respond to invitations on Web sites and agree to complete an online questionnaire. Obviously, such samples consist of individuals with access to computers who possess basic online skills. Thus these samples may underrepresent lower-income and minority persons. Early research found that almost one-half of the participants spent less than an hour per week in online sexual pursuits (Cooper et al., 1999). Of concern was the 8 percent who reported spending 11 or more hours per week in such activity. A study based on more than 40,000 users assessed the relationship between the frequency and the duration of their Internet use and their mental health. The results indicated that the number of months that had passed since participants first went online was positively associated with a history of mental health problems and treatment as well as with current behavioral difficulties involving alcohol, gambling, food, and sex. The number of hours per week each was online was associated with a history of mental health problems and treatment (Mathy & Cooper, 2003).

A Swedish study focused on cybersex, or online sexual activity (OSA), which is two or more persons engaging in sexual talk for the purpose of sexual pleasure (Daneback et al., 2005). Researchers placed a banner soliciting participation on a Web portal. The banner appeared randomly during a two-week period; 1,835 persons completed the survey. Almost one-third reported cybersex; the most common location was in a chat room. Participants in OSA were

young; homosexual men were four times more likely to report OSA than heterosexual men. Those who reported cybersex spent more time online and reported more offline sex partners.

Research using a sexual compulsivity scale sought to determine what percentage of users were compulsive users (Cooper et al., 2000). The study found that 83 percent of the participants were not problematic users. Eleven percent attained moderate scores on the scale, 4.6 percent were *sexually compulsive,* and 1 percent were *cybersex compulsives;* that is, they attained the highest scores on compulsivity and spent more than 11 hours per week in online sexual pursuits. Persons in the cybersex compulsive group were more likely to be male, to be single and dating, and to report that they were bisexual; they reported spending 15 to 25 hours per week in online sexual pursuits. Twenty-one percent of the respondents reported that their online activities had jeopardized at least one area of their life, the most common being personal relationships. The researchers concluded that bisexuals, and perhaps other sexually marginalized groups, may be especially at risk for online sexual compulsivity.

Other Sexual Variations

The sexual variations discussed below are too rare to have had much research devoted to them; they are nonetheless interesting.

Troilism, or *triolism,* refers to three people having sex together.

Saliromania is a disorder found mainly in men—a desire to damage or soil a woman or her clothes or the image of a woman, such as a painting or statue. The man becomes sexually excited and may ejaculate during the act.

Coprophilia and **urophilia** are both variations having to do with excretion. In coprophilia the feces are important to sexual satisfaction. In urophilia it is the urine that is important. The urophiliac may want to be urinated on as part of the sexual act. Insiders refer to urination as a "golden shower."

Frotteurism is the seventh paraphilia identified by the *DSM-IV-TR.* It is defined as sexual fantasies, urges, or behaviors involving touching or rubbing one's genitals against the body of a nonconsenting person, over a period of at least six months, and causing marked distress or interpersonal difficulty. Milder forms of this activity are common. A man may approach a woman from the

Troilism (TROY-uhl-ism): Three people having sex together.
Saliromania: A desire to damage or soil a woman or her clothes.
Coprophilia (cop-roh-FILL-ee-uh): Deriving sexual satisfaction from contact with feces.
Urophilia (YUR-oh-fill-ee-uh): Deriving sexual satisfaction from contact with urine.
Frotteurism: Deriving sexual satisfaction from fantasies, urges, or behaviors involving touching or rubbing one's genitals against the body of a nonconsenting person.

rear and press his penis against her buttocks, or a woman may approach a man from the side and rub her genitals against his leg or hip. The target may be unaware of it if it occurs in a crowded elevator or subway train or in the crush of a crowd at a sports event or concert. We noted earlier that 35 percent of a sample of college men reported having engaged in this activity.

Necrophilia is sexual contact with a dead person. It is a very rare form of behavior and is considered by experts to be psychotic and extremely deviant. Necrophiliacs derive sexual gratification from viewing a corpse or actually having intercourse with it; the corpse may be mutilated afterward (Thorpe et al., 1961).

Zoophilia is sexual contact with an animal; this behavior is also called *bestiality* or *sodomy*, although the latter term is also used to refer to anal intercourse or even mouth–genital sex between humans. About 8 percent of the males in Kinsey's sample reported having had sexual experiences with animals. Most of this activity was concentrated in adolescence and probably reflected the experimentation and diffuse sexual urges of that period. Not surprisingly, the percentage was considerably higher among boys on farms; 17 percent of boys raised on farms had had animal contacts resulting in orgasm. Kinsey found that only about 3 to 4 percent of all females have had some sexual contact with animals. Contemporary therapists report cases of men and women engaging in sexual activity with household pets. Activities include masturbating the animal, oral–genital contact, and intercourse.

Researchers posted a questionnaire online and recruited participants through a letter to members of a network of people with sexual interests in animals (as we said, you can find anything on the Web—that's accessibility). Those who volunteered were asked to refer others who had interests similar to those assessed by the questionnaire (Williams & Weinberg, 2003). Data were obtained from 114 men, all white, with a median age of 27; 64 percent were single, never married, and 83 percent had at least some college education. These characteristics undoubtedly reflect in part the fact that the sample was obtained via the Web. Ninety-three percent defined themselves as "zoophiles" and said this identity involved a concern for the animal's welfare and an emphasis on consensual sexual activity. They compared themselves favorably with "bestialists," whom they said were not concerned about an animal's welfare. Given a list of possible reasons for sexual interest in animals, the two most common were a desire for affection

and pleasurable sex. The type of sexual contact reported by the men varied by the type of animal. Receiving oral sex and receiving anal intercourse were the most frequent activities with dogs, whereas performing vaginal and anal intercourse were most frequent with horses. Only one man preferred sheep.[8] Many of the men had not had a human partner of either sex in the preceding year. The researchers suggest that a preference for sexual activity with animals can be explained by learning theory in that the rewards offered by sex with animals are immediate, easy, and intense, and thus extremely reinforcing. They suggest that the respondents' choice of animal is explained by their earlier conditioning, most men preferring the type of animal they first had sex with.

Prevention of Sexual Variations

For many of the variations discussed in this chapter, there is a continuum from normal to abnormal. People whose behavior falls at the normal end enjoy these activities at no expense to self or others. People whose behavior falls at the abnormal end are cause for concern.

The misery that many people—for example, the sexually addicted S-Mer—suffer, not to mention the harm they may do to others (e.g., the child molester), is good reason to want to develop programs for preventing sexual variations (Qualls et al., 1978). In preventive medicine, a distinction is made between primary prevention and secondary prevention. Applied to the sexual variations, primary prevention would mean intervening in home life or in other factors during childhood to help prevent problems from developing or trying to teach people how to cope with crises or stress so that problems do not develop. In secondary prevention, the idea is to diagnose and treat the problem as early as possible once it has arisen, so that difficulties are minimized.

It would be highly advantageous to do primary prevention of sexual variations—that is, to head them off before they even develop. Unfortunately, this is proving to be difficult, for a number of reasons. One problem is the diagnostic categories. The categories for the diagnosis of sexual variations are

[8]Giving the lie to the joke, What's the difference between Mick Jagger and a Scotsman?
Mick Jagger sings, "Hey, you, get off of my cloud." The Scotsman says, "Hey, McLeod, get off of my ewe."

Necrophilia: Deriving sexual satisfaction from contact with a dead person.
Zoophilia: Sexual contact with an animal; also called *bestiality* or *sodomy*.

not nearly as clear-cut in real life as they may seem in this chapter, and multiple diagnoses for one person are not uncommon. That is, a given man might have engaged in incest, pedophilia, and exhibitionism. If it is unclear how to diagnose sexual variations, it is going to be rather difficult to figure out how to prevent them. If one is not sure whether there is a difference between chicken pox and measles, it is rather difficult to start giving inoculations.

An alternative approach that seems promising—rather than figuring out ways to prevent each separate variation—is to analyze the *components of sexual development.* Disturbance in one or more of these components in development might lead to different sexual variations. One proposal for these components is as follows (Bancroft, 1978):

1. *Gender identity.* The sense of maleness or femaleness developed in early childhood.
2. *Sexual responsiveness.* Arousal to appropriate stimuli.
3. *Formation of relationships with others.*

It seems clear that different developmental components are disturbed in different variations. For example, in transsexualism it is the first component, gender identity, that is disturbed. In the case of the fetishist, it is the second component, sexual responsiveness to appropriate stimuli, that is disturbed. And in the case of the exhibitionist, it may be that it is the last component, the ability to form relationships, that is disturbed.

The idea would then be to try to ensure that as children grow up their development in each of these three components is healthy. Ideally, sexual variations should not occur then.

Interest in developing preventive programs targeting children has increased as the result of an apparent decline in the age of arrested sex offenders. The number of children or adolescents aged 17 or younger who have been involved in sexual offenses has been increasing steadily since 2001. Some jurisdictions, such as Montgomery County, Texas, have seen a 100 percent increase—from 25 to 49—in the number of 10- to 17-year-olds suspected of committing felony or aggravated sexual assault. One study of adolescents incarcerated for sexual offenses found that 46 percent committed their first offense before the age of 12 (Burton, 2000). Childhood victimization was positively associated with later sexual aggression by the youth, suggesting that social learning can help explain the development of sexual offending.

Space does not permit us to consider what prevention programs might look like for all the different variations (see Bancroft, 1978, for further discussion), so let us consider one example, transsexualism, in some detail (Green, 1978; see Chapter 12 for a discussion of transsexualism).

Suppose that we have a typical case of a very feminine boy, Billy, whose parents bring him in for treatment. Billy prefers to dress in girls' clothes, wants to play with dolls and play house, and dislikes playing with boys because they are too rough. He might be considered a high risk for becoming a transsexual, because virtually all transsexuals recall a sense of being trapped in the wrong body from earliest childhood.

What kind of therapy can be used? Some efforts are made at simple education—making sure Billy understands the anatomical differences between

Figure 14.8 In the twenty-first century some people become celebrities because of their unusual sexual activities. Bob Crane, the star of *Hogan's Heroes,* is the subject of the biopic *Auto Focus;* the film portrays his obsession with documenting on videotape his sexual conquests. His addiction affected both his professional and family life.

boys and girls, and comprehends that one cannot change gender magically. Positive aspects of maleness are emphasized. Male playmates are found who are not rough. Parents are encouraged not to engage in behavior that may reinforce his conflict—for example, commenting that he is cute when dressed up as a girl. The father–son relationship is encouraged, and a male therapist is used so that the boy can identify with him. Finally, intervention may simply involve helping the child accept his own atypical behavior.

Such therapy raises a host of ethical issues. Is it right to make a traditional, stereotyped male out of a boy who might simply be androgynous? Is it right to intervene when one is not sure that he will otherwise become a transsexual? Indeed, in longitudinal follow-up studies of 26 feminine boys, 14 did become transsexuals, transvestites, or homosexuals, but 12 became heterosexuals. Therefore, one cannot be sure about the eventual development of a feminine 5-year-old. And even if superficial masculine behavior is successfully encouraged, what if a host of conflicts continues to simmer below the surface, creating a more seriously disturbed individual? One researcher summarized the complex problems this way:

It may be argued that to induce intervention (which may be prevention) reinforces societal sexism. Regrettably, to a degree it does. But while we have a responsibility to reduce sexism, we have a responsibility to an individual child caught in the cross fire between sex role idealism and the real world in which he is embedded. (Green, 1978, p. 88)

We have a long way to go in preventing sexual variations, to say the least.

Treatment of Sexual Variations

Some of the sexual variations discussed in this chapter, such as the mild fetishes, are well within the normal range of sexual expression. There is no need for treatment. Others, however, fall into the abnormal range, causing personal anguish to the individual and possibly harming unwilling victims. Treatments are needed for this category of variations. Many different treatments have been tried, each based on a different theoretical understanding of the causes of sexual variations. We now look at four categories of treatments: medical treatments, cognitive–behavioral therapies, skills training, and AA-type 12-step programs.

Medical Treatments

Inspired by the notion that sexual variations are caused by biological factors, various medical treatments for sexual variations have been tried over the last century. Some of them look today like nothing other than cruel and unusual punishment. Nonetheless, people would love to have a pill that would cure some of these complex and painful or dangerous paraphilias, so the search for such treatments continues.

Surgical castration was used fairly commonly in the United States in the 1800s as a treatment for various kinds of uncontrollable sexual urges (Bullough, 1976). The idea resurfaced recently in some court cases in which castration was proposed as a treatment for rapists, as discussed in "Sex Offenders—Castration or Incarceration?" in Chapter 8. Such treatments are based on the notion that removing a man's testosterone by removing the testes will lead to a drastic reduction in sex drive, which will in turn erase urges to commit sex offenses. However, as we saw in Chapter 8, a reduction in testosterone levels in humans does not always lead to a reduction in sexual behavior. Surgical castration cannot be recommended as a treatment for sex offenders either on humanitarian grounds or on grounds of effectiveness.

Hormonal treatment involves the use of drugs to reduce sexual desire. Sexual arousability is heavily dependent on maintaining the level of androgen in the bloodstream above a given threshold. Two ways to reduce this level are to administer (1) drugs that reduce the production of androgen in the testes ("chemical castration"), or (2) antiandrogens that bind to androgen receptors in the brain and genitals, blocking the effects of androgen. The use of either should produce a sharp decline in sexual desire. Several drugs have been tried in the past 40 years. The most commonly used in the United States is *medroxyprogesterone acetate* (MPA), which binds to androgen receptors. The drug is given by injection, often weekly. A review of the literature shows that the use of MPA results in reduced sexual interest and a lower level of sexual fantasies, along with decreased erections and ejaculation (Miner & Coleman, 2001). However, "The drop-out rate is extremely high and re-offense rates have been found to exceed 65 percent of those who discontinue antiandrogen treatment" (p. 8).

Recently, clinicians have started using *leuprolide acetate* (LA), a synthetic analog of gonadotropin-releasing hormone (GnRH; see Chapter 5), the continued use of which suppresses androgen production and reduces sexual fantasies and drive. It has fewer side effects than MPA. One paper reports the use of LA with 12 adults with paraphilic or other sexual disorders, with follow-up periods of six months to six years (Krueger & Kaplan, 2001). LA resulted in significant suppression of deviant sexual interests and behavior. A paper reporting its use with six juveniles/young adults states that all six reported a reduction in symptoms (Saleh et al., 2004).

The use of an alternative, *psychopharmacological treatment*, increased dramatically in frequency in the 1990s. Here, psychotropic medications, like antidepressants such as Prozac, are administered to offenders. These medications influence patients' psychological functioning and behavior by their action on the central nervous system. The newness of the drugs being used means there is little research on the effectiveness of this technique. Antidepressants are being used with paraphiliacs who are also diagnosed with obsessive-compulsive disorder or depression. These drugs appear to change the obsessive-compulsive behavior rather than sexual desire (Gijs & Gooren, 1996). There is a great deal of interest in the use of the antidepressants known as selective serotonin reuptake inhibitors (SSRIs). Case reports indicate that SSRIs reduce paraphilic fantasies and urges (Raymond et al., 2002). These drugs have been successfully used to treat compulsive behaviors. Their success with paraphilias suggests that these conditions may be a type of obsessive-compulsive disorder (Miner & Coleman, 2001).

Both hormonal and psychopharmacological treatment should be used as only one element in a complete program of therapy, which would include counseling and treatment for other emotional and social deficits (Saleh & Berlin, 2003). The best results are obtained with men who are highly motivated to change their behavior and therefore comply with the prescribed treatment regimen. If the paraphiliac stops taking the drug or participating in other aspects of treatment, the program will fail. Unfortunately, one of the limitations of research on the effectiveness of these treatments is the dropout rate, which was 46 percent in one study.

Cognitive–Behavioral Therapies

Some treatment programs are based on cognitive–behavioral therapies. Comprehensive programs include (Abel et al., 1992)

1. Behavior therapy to reduce inappropriate sexual arousal and enhance appropriate arousal.
2. Social skills training.
3. Modification of distorted thinking; challenging the rationalizations that the person uses to justify the undesirable behavior.
4. Relapse prevention; helping the person identify and control or avoid whatever triggers the behavior.

Although the media sometimes carry flashy stories about applications of behavior therapy that involve administering electric shocks to a sex offender if he becomes aroused at, say, a picture of a nude child, in fact much milder techniques have been used and are effective. *Covert sensitization* is one such therapy. It involves pairing aversive imagery (thoughts) with fantasies of the target behavior. In the treatment of an exhibitionist, for example, he repeatedly practices a vivid fantasy in which, just as he imagines getting ready to expose himself, he experiences waves of nausea and vomiting. The details, of course, are individualized to the person and his particular problem. Reports indicate that this approach has been effective in cases such as sadism, exhibitionism, and pedophilia (Barlow et al., 1969; Walen & Roth, 1987).

Another approach is *orgasmic reconditioning* (Marquis, 1970; Walen & Roth, 1987). With this method the patient is told to masturbate to his usual paraphiliac fantasies. Then, just at the moment of orgasm, he switches to an acceptable fantasy. After practicing this for some time, he becomes able to orgasm regularly while having an acceptable fantasy. He then is told to move the fantasy progressively to an earlier phase of masturbation. Gradually he becomes conditioned to experiencing sexual arousal in the context of acceptable behavior.

One program designed for female offenders combined cognitive–behavioral with psychodynamic techniques and relied on one-on-one rather than group therapy (Traven et al., 1990). Male offenders typically deny responsibility for their behavior, so the initial stage of treatment may focus on acknowledging one's behavior and its consequences. Women in this program readily acknowledged what they had done and were overwhelmed by guilt and shame, so their initial stage focused on self-esteem. Thus different treatment programs may be needed for male and female paraphiliacs.

Skills Training

According to yet another theoretical understanding, persons with paraphilias engage in their behavior because they have great difficulty forming relationships, and so do not have access to appropriate

Figure 14.9 The centerpiece of 12-step programs such as Sex Addicts Anonymous is group meetings in which participants confront their addiction with the support of other group members.

forms of sexual gratification. This perspective is consistent with data on IQ differences between sex offenders and controls. A meta-analysis included results from 75 reports, involving 236 independent samples and more than 25,000 persons (Cantor et al., 2005). Adult males who committed sex offenses scored significantly lower than nonoffenders, and lower than those who committed nonsexual offenses. Among sex offenders, the younger the age of his/her victims, the lower the IQ score.

Many of these people do not have the skills to initiate and maintain conversation. They may find it difficult to develop intimacy (see Chapter 11) (Keenan & Ward, 2000). Such people may benefit from a treatment program that includes social skills training. Such training may include how to carry on a conversation, how to develop intimacy, how to be appropriately assertive, and identifying irrational fears that are inhibiting the person (Abel et al., 1992). These programs may also include basic sexuality education.

If a person needs to learn and practice sexual interaction skills, one approach would be to have him or her interact with a trained partner. This is the basis for a very controversial practice, the use of *sex surrogates* as part of a treatment program.

The surrogate works with the therapist, interacting socially and sexually with the client to provide opportunities for using the newly acquired information and skills. Some therapists believe that the use of surrogates is ethical, but others see it as a type of prostitution. Just as the definition of *abnormal* depends on one's point of view, so does the definition of *sex therapy.*

AA-Type 12-Step Programs

As we saw in Focus: Milestones in Sex Research, page 370, sexual addiction theory argues that many people who engage in uncontrollable, inappropriate sexual patterns are addicted to their particular sexual practice. The appropriate treatment, according to this approach, is one of the 12-step programs modeled on Alcoholics Anonymous.

Treatment programs based on this approach have become very common in recent years. Some of the programs are run by group members, whereas others are affiliated with professional health care facilities. Twelve-step programs combine cognitive restructuring, obtaining support from other members who have the same or similar problem behaviors, and enhancing spirituality.

This last aspect involves increasing one's awareness of a "higher power" who can be relied on to help one recover. AA-based groups are generally unwilling to cooperate with researchers, believing that to do so would prevent group members from concentrating on recovery. As a result, little research data exist on these programs.

What Works?

What is needed is carefully controlled research on the effectiveness of various approaches to the treatment of sexual variations (Miner & Coleman, 2001). Research to date has tended to apply one method to a heterogeneous group of people. It is likely, however, that each method will be more effective with some paraphilias than with others. Research involving drugs should systematically assess side effects; some drugs have severe side effects on some people, especially if used more than six months. Research should consider the relative likelihood of relapse; some paraphiliacs pose grave danger to themselves (e.g., asphyxiophiliacs) or to others if they resume their problematic behavior.

SUMMARY

It seems reasonable to define *abnormal sexual behavior* as behavior that is uncomfortable for the person, inefficient, bizarre, or physically or psychologically harmful to the person or others. The American Psychiatric Association defines paraphilias as recurrent, intense, sexually arousing fantasies, urges, or behaviors that are obsessive and compulsive.

Four theoretical approaches have been used in understanding the paraphilias: learning theory, cognitive theory, the sexual addiction model, and sociological theory. Several explanations have been proposed for the fact that there are many more male than female paraphiliacs.

A fetishist is a person who becomes erotically attached to some object other than another human being. Most likely, fetishism arises from conditioning, and it provides a good example of the continuum from normal to abnormal behavior.

The transvestite derives sexual satisfaction from dressing as a member of the other gender. Like many other sexual variations, transvestism is much more common among men than among women. Survey data suggest that many men who later become transvestites begin cross-dressing in childhood.

Three styles of sexual interaction involve differences in control over sexual interactions. Dominance and submission involve a consensual exchange of power, and the enacting of scripted performances. Bondage and discipline involve the use of physical restraints or verbal commands by one person to control the other. Both D-S and B-D may occur without genital contact or orgasm. Sadism and masochism involve deriving sexual gratification from giving and receiving pain. Both are recognized as paraphilias if they become compulsive.

The voyeur is sexually aroused by looking at nudes. The exhibitionist displays his or her sex organs to others. Both are generally harmless.

Nymphomania and satyriasis are terms used to describe women and men with an extraordinarily high sex drive. Both terms are ambiguous and subject to misuse. The term *hypersexuality* is potentially more precise, particularly if it is defined behaviorally.

Other sexual variations include asphyxiophilia, zoophilia, and necrophilia. A recent concern is cybersex abuse, which is facilitated by the anonymity, accessibility, and affordability of the Net.

The possibility of programs to prevent sexual variations is being explored. Available programs include medical treatments, cognitive–behavioral therapies, skills training, and AA-type 12-step programs. We need careful research to determine which programs work best in the treatment of given behaviors.

QUESTIONS FOR THOUGHT, DISCUSSION, AND DEBATE

1. What do you think of the idea about preventing sexual variations presented in this chapter? Do you think the schools or some other agency should institute a program to screen children, trying to detect those with characteristics that might indicate they would develop a sexual variation later in life, and then give therapy to those children?

2. Of the sexual variations in this chapter, which seem to you to be the most abnormal? Why? Do the ones you have chosen fit the criteria for abnormality discussed at the beginning of the chapter?

3. A common phenomenon in medical school is for medical students to think they have contracted one of the diseases they are studying. The analogous phenomenon would be for students who read this chapter to think that they have one or more of the paraphilias. Did you notice yourself becoming sexually aroused as you read about one (or more) of the variations? If so, do you think you are abnormal? Why, or why not?

4. Most persons who seek treatment or are arrested for atypical or paraphiliac behaviors are white men. Do you think that this is an accurate picture of our society, or are we just unaware of nonwhites who engage in these behaviors? Based on the data presented and the causes discussed, would you expect Black, Asian, or Hispanic men to engage in these behaviors? Why, or why not?

SUGGESTIONS FOR FURTHER READING

Griffin-Shelley, Eric. (1991). *Sex and love: Addiction, treatment, and recovery.* Westport, CT: Praeger. This book describes the addiction model as it is applied to sex and love. It also describes treatment programs.

Wilson, Glenn D. (Ed.). 1987. *Variant sexuality: Research and theory.* Baltimore: Johns Hopkins University Press. The chapters in this book review different theoretical explanations for sexual variations, from genetics and sociobiology to cross-cultural perspectives.

CHAPTER FIFTEEN

Sexual Coercion

CHAPTER HIGHLIGHTS

E boni's basic education about sex came from what she saw and the direct experiences that she had. When she was 5, she and her brother were wrestling with their uncle. Suddenly her uncle locked her brother out of the room and began taking off Eboni's clothes. He held her down on the bed and began to penetrate her but stopped abruptly. Eboni was frightened of him from then on. She didn't really understand what he intended to do or why he wanted to do it, but she knew that his behavior was unexpected and strange.

. . . Eboni's grandmother and father insisted that she not talk to strangers or take money from them. Eboni understood why—she knew that being molested meant being raped. But strangers were not the predators.*

*Wyatt (1997, pp. 72–73).

This chapter is about sexual activity that involves coercion and is not between consenting adults; specifically, we consider rape, child sexual abuse, and sexual harassment at work and in education. All these topics have been highly publicized in the last 30 years, and much good scientific research on them has appeared.

Rape

Rape is typically defined, following current laws in many states, as "nonconsensual oral, anal, or vaginal penetration, obtained by force, by threat of bodily harm or when the victim is incapable of giving consent" (Koss, 1993, p. 1062). Notice that the definition includes not only forced vaginal intercourse but forced oral sex and anal sex as well. The crucial point is that the activity is nonconsensual— that is, the victim did not consent to it. One type of nonconsent occurs when the victim is incapable of giving consent, perhaps because of being drunk, unconscious, or high on drugs.

Incidence Statistics

In 2005, some 94,000 rapes—completed or attempted—were reported in the United States; this means there were 63 reported rapes for every 100,000 women (FBI, 2006). However, also according to the FBI, forcible rape is one of the most underreported crimes. One study found that only about 1 in 5 (21 percent) of rapes by a stranger had been reported to the police, and only 2 percent of rapes by an acquaintance had been reported (Koss et al., 1988). A well-sampled national study of women college students found that 28 percent had experienced an act that met the legal definition of rape (Koss et al., 1987). In a community sample of women between the ages of 18 and 30 who were studied over a two-year period, 18 percent reported

sexual victimization during that period (Testa et al., 2007). According to the National Violence Against Women Survey, a woman has a 15 percent chance of being raped over her lifetime (Tjaden & Thoennes, 1998). Statistics vary somewhat from one study to another, but most find that a woman's lifetime risk of being raped is between 14 and 25 percent (Koss, 1993). More than half of all rapes of women occur before age 18, and 22 percent occur before age 12 (Centers for Disease Control and Prevention, 2004a).

The Impact of Rape

A large number of studies have investigated the psychological reactions of women following rape (e.g., Frazier et al., 2004; Koss, 1993). This research shows that rape is a time of crisis for a woman and that the effects on many victims' adjustment may persist for a year or more.

Emotional reactions immediately after a rape, in the acute phase, can be severe. The high levels of distress generally reach a peak 3 weeks after the assault and continue at a high level for the next month. There is then gradual improvement beginning 2 or 3 months after the assault (Koss, 1993; Rothbaum et al., 1992). Many differences between raped and nonvictimized women disappear after 3 months, except that raped women continue to report more fear, anxiety, self-esteem problems, and sexual disorders. These effects may persist for 18 months or longer (Koss, 1993). See Focus: First Person, on page 390, for one woman's account of these effects in her life. Sexually victimized women have a somewhat elevated risk of suicidal behavior (Ullman, 2004).

Some women experience self-blame. A woman may spend hours agonizing over what she did to cause the rape or what she might have done to prevent it: "If I hadn't worn that tight sweater . . ."; "If I hadn't been dumb

SexSource Online
www.mhhe.com/hyde10

"BEHIND CLOSED DOORS" IN SEXUAL COERCION

Rape: Nonconsenting oral, anal, or vaginal penetration obtained by force, by threat of bodily harm, or when the victim is incapable of giving consent.

Focus: First Person
A Date-Rape Victim Tells Her Story

During my sophomore year at Northwestern University, I realized I wanted to socialize more. I broke up with my hometown honey, began attending college parties, started drinking, and dated other guys at my school. I was a virgin and didn't want to be anymore. I met my second boyfriend in physics. "G" was a football player and a big, handsome man, the best-looking man I'd ever met. We began to date and at first it was wonderful. He even carried me home once from a party, and I thought, "This is the one." Our first attempt at intercourse was difficult and I began to beg him to stop, but he just kept trying until he was successful and there was blood everywhere. It was awful.

I continued to date G, but he began to act very differently. When he drank, he became extremely violent, and on different occasions I watched him break a vending machine, and pull a toilet out of a wall at a fraternity. He was unhappy with the way he was treated on the football team, and I tried to console him. He became angrier and paranoid. He demanded to know where I was at all times and accused me of cheating on him. I wanted to break up with him, especially since sex was rough and not always consensual, but I was scared of him. I tried avoiding him but he always found me.

One night, G arrived very drunk at a party I was attending. He threatened a guy who was there talking to me. I tried to sneak out of the party. He noticed I left and ran out after me. Another guy slowed me down to try to persuade me to let him drive me home since I had been drinking. G accused me of trying to pick this guy up and threatened the guy, who even volunteered to drive both of us home. But G wouldn't let him and said I would take him home. I didn't want trouble so I drove him to his dorm. He claimed he was too drunk to walk to his dorm, so I tried to help him into his room. When I turned around to leave, he sprang up and locked me in. He attacked me. I tried fighting him, but he wouldn't listen or stop. He hit my head into the wall several times and tried to force me to perform oral sex. I bit him, and that made him more angry. He then tried to force anal sex, and I fought as hard as I could. I finally started crying, and he stopped when he lost his erection. The rest of the night, I felt completely trapped in his dorm room. I lay awake all night and tried to leave, but he would wake up and stop me. I've never forgotten how scared I felt that entire night. He got up that morning and showered and acted as if nothing had happened. He was in all my classes for the rest of my college career.

I began to drink very heavily afterward. I told my roommate, J, and another woman on my floor, D. I never thought to report it, since he was my "boyfriend."

A year and a half later, I began to hear voices. It was a male voice calling me a fucking bitch, whore, and other names. I thought I was going crazy and became very depressed. I decided I must be schizophrenic and decided to kill myself. My attempt was unsuccessful.

Soon after, I was shopping in a bookstore. I saw this title staring right at me, "I Never Called It Rape." I started reading it right there in the store, and I began crying and thinking, "This is what happened to me." I spoke with a faculty member, who arranged for immediate counseling.

The first time I went to see the counselor, I couldn't even speak. I sat in her office and cried for the entire hour. She kept saying, "It's not your fault, it's not your fault." I couldn't believe it. Later we discussed how most of the times G and I had sex had actually been rape, including the first and the last. I participated in a "Take Back the Night March." One fraternity threw bottles at us.

I went through medical school and residency. During my first year of residency, I was assaulted again, this time by a man in a stairwell during a New Year's Eve party at a hotel. I started screaming "You're raping me, you're raping me!" He stopped and I got away! But I didn't go to the ER, I just went home and crawled in bed. My old shame came back. I began to drink heavily again. One night I drank all night and never showed up to work that next morning. I finally rolled into my director's office, depressed, hung over, and still smelling of alcohol, and my boss said I had to stop and straighten up right away or he wouldn't let me back for the next year. So I stopped drinking. I also made two very good friends around the same time. Through their support, I really turned my life around.

Three years later, I moved to Madison, Wisconsin. I was living alone for the first time and had a great deal of anxiety. I joined a Sexual Assault Survivors Support Group. Then in the spring, I was invited to speak at my old university for Career Day for high school students, so I went back there 10 years after the incidents. I was finally successful in my career, had strong, loving relationships with my friends and parents, and was happy. I look back at what happened now and think that I really survived a lot. I feel it helps me to be a better physician because I can empathize with how bad life can be for people.

Source: Based on an interview conducted by Janet Hyde.

Figure 15.1   Rape crisis counseling. Many women experience severe emotional distress after a rape, and it is important that crisis counseling be available to them.

enough to walk on that dark street . . ."; "If I hadn't been stupid enough to trust that guy . . ." This is an example of a tendency on the part of both the victim and others to blame the victim. Self-blame is linked to worse long-term psychological outcomes for victims (Koss & Figueredo, 2004). A subset of rape victims actually increase in risky sexual behavior following the rape, perhaps because it triggered feelings of self-blame and worthlessness (Campbell et al., 2004).

Researchers are finding increased evidence of the damage to women's physical health that may result from rape (Centers for Disease Control and Prevention, 2004a; Heise, 1993; Koss et al., 1991; Koss & Heslet, 1992). Women may suffer physical injuries, such as cuts and bruises, and vaginal pain and bleeding. Women who have been forced to have oral sex may suffer irritation or damage to the throat; rectal bleeding and pain are reported by women forced to have anal intercourse. A raped woman may contract a sexually transmitted infection such as HIV/AIDS or herpes. In about 5 percent of rape cases, pregnancy results (Koss et al., 1991).[1] Women who have been sexually or physically assaulted at some time in the past visit their physician twice as often per year as nonvictimized women (Koss et al., 1991).

Some rape victims who experience severe, long-term psychological symptoms following a rape are actually experiencing **posttraumatic stress disorder (PTSD)** (e.g., Koss, 1993; Ullman et al., 2007). Posttraumatic stress disorder is an official diagnosis that was originally developed to describe the long-term psychological distress suffered by war veterans, most of whom are men. Symptoms can include persistently reexperiencing the traumatic event (flashbacks, nightmares), avoiding stimuli associated with it (avoiding certain locations or activities), and hyperarousal (sleep difficulties, difficulty concentrating, irritability). According to a cognitive–behavioral view of PTSD, people who have experienced a terrifying event form a memory schema that involves information about the situation and their responses to it (Foa et al., 1989). Because the schema is large, many cues can trigger it and therefore evoke the feelings of terror that occurred at

Posttraumatic stress disorder (PTSD): Long-term psychological distress suffered by someone who has experienced a terrifying event.

[1]Tests for sexually transmitted infections should routinely be done as part of the hospital treatment of rape victims. Pregnancy tests can be done if the woman's period is late. If pregnancy seems likely, emergency contraception can be used (see Chapter 7).

Focus: First Person
How Can Friends Help a Rape Victim?

What the Victim Needs to Do

Obtain medical assistance.

Feel safe. Rape is a traumatic violation of the person. Especially in the beginning, it is often difficult for victims to be alone.

Be believed. With date rape especially, victims need to be believed that what occurred was, in fact, a rape.

Know it was not her fault. Most rape victims feel guilty and feel that the attack was somehow their fault.

Take control of her life. When a person is raped, she may feel completely out of control of what is happening to her. A significant step on the road to recovery is to regain a sense of control in little, as well as big, things.

Things You Can Do to Help

Listen, do not judge. Accept her version of the facts and be supportive.

Offer shelter. If possible, stay with her at her place or let her spend at least one night at your place. This is not the time for her to be alone.

Be available. She may need to talk at odd hours, or a great deal in the beginning. Also encourage her to call a hotline or go for counseling. Be available even months later.

Give comfort. She needs to be nurtured.

Let her know she is not to blame.

Encourage action. For example, suggest she call a hotline, go to a hospital, and/or call the police. Respect her decision if she decides not to file charges. Do not make her decisions for her, because she needs to regain a sense of control of her life.

Put aside your feelings and deal with them somewhere else. Although it is supportive for a rape survivor to know that others are equally upset with what happened, it does her no good if she also has to deal with, for example, your feelings of rage. If you have strong feelings, talk to another friend or to a local hotline.

Source: Condensed from Hughes & Sandler (1987). Used with permission.

---

the time; the schema is probably activated at some level all the time. Schemas also affect how we interpret new events, so that the consequences are far-reaching and long-lasting. The strongest predictors of which rape survivors develop PTSD are (1) negative reactions and lack of support from others, and (2) avoidance coping, that is, avoiding thinking about and resolving the issue (Ullman et al., 2007).

Rape affects many people besides the victim. Most women routinely do a number of things that stem from rape fears. For example, a single woman is not supposed to list her full first name, but rather her first initial or a man's name, in the telephone book, so as not to reveal that she lives alone. Many women, when getting into their car at night, almost reflexively check the backseat to make sure no one is hiding there. Most college women avoid walking alone through dark parts of the campus at night. At least once in their lives, most women have been afraid of spending the night alone. If you are a woman, you can probably extend this list from your own experience. The point is that

> **Posttraumatic growth:** Positive life changes and psychological development following exposure to trauma.

most women experience the fear of rape, if not rape itself (Burt & Estep, 1981; Warr, 1985), and this fear restricts their activities.

Spouses or partners of victims may also be profoundly affected. At the same time, they can provide important support for the woman as she recovers (see Focus: First Person, above).

New research in psychology indicates that not everyone who experiences a serious traumatic event develops PTSD. Some, in fact, display **posttraumatic growth,** that is, positive life changes and psychological development following exposure to trauma (Tedeschi et al., 1998). Research with rape victims—or, more accurately, rape survivors—confirms that some of them do report positive life changes, such as an increased ability to take care of themselves, a greater sense of purpose in life, and greater concern for others in similar situations (Frazier et al., 2004).

Date Rape
In Mary Koss's pathbreaking national study of college women, among those who had experienced an act that met the legal definition of rape, 57 percent

of the rapes involved a date, often a steady dating partner (Koss et al., 1988; Koss & Cook, 1994). Date rape is one of the most common forms of rape, especially on college campuses. High school students are not exempt either; a well-sampled study of high school seniors found that 6 percent of the girls had been victims of date rape (Ackard & Neumark-Sztainer, 2002).

In some cases, date rape seems to result from male–female miscommunication. Men's traditional view in dating relationships has been that a woman who says no really means yes (Osman, 2003). Men need to learn that no means no. Consider this example of miscommunication and different perceptions in a case of date rape:

> Bob: Patty and I were in the same statistics class together. She usually sat near me and was always very friendly. I liked her and thought maybe she liked me, too. Last Thursday I decided to find out. After class I suggested that she come to my place to study for midterms together. She agreed immediately, which was a good sign. That night everything seemed to go perfectly. We studied for a while and then took a break. I could tell that she liked me, and I was attracted to her. I was getting excited. I started kissing her. I could tell that she really liked it. We started touching each other and it felt really good. All of a sudden she pulled away and said "Stop." I figured she didn't want me to think that she was "easy" or "loose." A lot of girls think they have to say no at first. I knew once I showed her what a good time she could have, and that I would respect her in the morning, it would be OK. I just ignored her protests and eventually she stopped struggling. I think she liked it but afterwards she acted bummed out and cold. Who knows what her problem was?

> Patty: I knew Bob from my statistics class. He's cute and we are both good at statistics, so when a tough midterm was scheduled, I was glad that he suggested we study together. It never occurred to me that it was anything except a study date. That night everything went fine at first, we got a lot of studying done in a short amount of time, so when he suggested we take a break I thought we deserved it. Well, all of a sudden he started acting really romantic and starting kissing me. I liked the kissing but then he started touching me below the waist. I pulled away and tried to stop him but he didn't listen. After a while I stopped struggling; he was hurting me and I was scared. He was so much bigger and stronger than me. I couldn't believe it was happening to me. I didn't know what to do. He actually forced me to have sex with him. I guess looking back on it I should have screamed or done something besides trying to reason with him but it was so unexpected. I couldn't believe it was

happening. I still can't believe it did. (Hughes & Sandler, 1987, p. 1)

Several explanations have been proposed for why sexually aggressive men misperceive women's communications. The first proposes that aggressors lack competence in reading women's negative emotions; they just don't get it when she's "bummed out." The second suggests that sexually aggressive men fail to make subtle distinctions between women's friendliness and seductiveness. The third proposes that they have a "suspicious schema" and automatically doubt that women are communicating truthfully and accurately. Research testing these explanations supports the third explanation—sexually aggressive men generally believe that women do not communicate honestly, particularly when the woman communicates clearly and assertively that she is rejecting an advance (Malamuth & Brown, 1994). These findings have important implications for prevention and treatment programs for sexual aggressors. They suggest that simple skills training—to read women's emotions or distinguish between friendly and seductive behavior—may not be the key. Cognitive therapy using cognitive restructuring may be the most effective, the goal being to get the man to change his suspicious schema. Such programs might be used with incarcerated rapists, but they might also be used in prevention programs with high school or college men who have been identified as being rape prone.

One of the most frightening problems today is the emergence of the so-called date-rape drug, rohypnol (row-HiP-nawl, "roofie," drug name flunitrozepam). Numerous cases have been reported of men who slipped the drug into a woman's drink. The drug causes drowsiness or sleep, and the man rapes the woman while she is asleep. The drug also causes the woman not to remember the event the next day. Several strategies for avoiding this situation have been suggested, including, especially, not accepting a drink from a stranger, and never leaving your drink unattended.

Marital Rape

How common is **marital rape,** that is, rape by a current or former spouse? In a random sample of San Francisco women, 14 percent of those who had ever been married had been raped by a husband or ex-husband (Russell, 1983). A national probability sample showed that 13 percent of married women had been raped by their current husband (Basile, 2002).

> **Marital rape:** The rape of a person by her or his current or former spouse.

One phenomenon that emerges from the research is an association between marital violence and marital rape—that is, the man who batters his wife is also likely to rape her (Centers for Disease Control and Prevention, 2004b).

A man might rape his wife for many motives, including anger, power and domination, sadism, or a desire for sex regardless of whether his wife is willing (Russell, 1990). In some cases the husband is extremely angry, perhaps in the middle of a family argument, and he expresses his anger toward his wife by raping her. In other cases, power and domination of the wife seem to be the motive; for example, the wife may be threatening to leave him, and he forces or dominates her into staying by raping her. Finally, some rapes appear to occur because the husband is sadistic—enjoys inflicting pain—and is psychiatrically disturbed.

Causes of Rape

To provide a perspective for the discussion that follows, we can distinguish among four major theoretical views of the nature of rape (Albin, 1977; Baron & Straus, 1989):

1. **Victim-precipitated rape.** This view holds that a rape is always caused by a woman "asking for it." Rape, then, is considered basically the woman's fault. This view represents the tendency to blame the victim.
2. *Psychopathology of rapists.* This theoretical view holds that rape is an act committed by a psychologically disturbed man. His deviance is responsible for the crime occurring.
3. *Feminist.* Feminist theorists view rapists as the product of gender-role socialization in our culture. They have theorized about the complex links between sex and power: In some rapes, men use sex to demonstrate their power over women; in other rapes, men use their power over women to get sex. Feminists also point to the eroticization of violence in our society. Gender inequality is both the cause and the result of rape in this view.
4. *Social disorganization.* Sociologists believe that crime rates, including rape rates, increase when the social organization of a community is disrupted. Under such conditions the community cannot enforce its norms against crime.

You personally may subscribe to one or more of these views. It is also true that researchers in this area have generally based their work on one of these theoretical models, which may influence their research. You should keep these models in mind as you read the rest of this chapter.

What do the data say? Research indicates that a number of factors contribute to rape, ranging from forces at the cultural level to factors at the individual level, including the following: cultural values; sexual scripts; early family influences; peer-group influences; characteristics of the situation; miscommunication; sex and power motives; and masculinity norms and men's attitudes. The data on each of these factors are considered below.

Cultural values can serve to support rape. Cross-culturally, in preliterate societies, rape is significantly more common in cultures that are characterized by male dominance, a high degree of general violence, and an ideology of male toughness (Sanday, 1981).

Two sociologists, experts in violence research, did an extensive study to test the last two theories, feminist theory and social disorganization theory (Baron & Straus, 1989). Both theories deal with rape as a result of cultural context. Baron and Straus collected extensive data on each of the 50 states in the United States, seeing them as representing variations in cultural context (think, for example, of the different cultures of Louisiana, New York, and North Dakota). To test feminist theory, they collected data on the extent of gender inequality in each state (for example, the gap between men's and women's wages); they also examined the feminist hypothesis that use of pornography encourages rape, by collecting data on the circulation of pornographic magazines in each state. They also obtained measures of social disorganization, such as the number of people moving into or out of the state, the divorce rate, and even the number of tourists flowing into the state. Their data gave strong support to three conclusions: (1) Gender inequality is related to rape—the states with the greatest gender inequality had the highest rape rates; (2) pornography provides ideological support for rape—the states with the highest circulation of pornographic magazines tended to have the highest rape rates; and (3) social disorganization contributes to rape—the states with the greatest social disorganization tended to have the highest rape rates. This research emphasizes how important cultural context is in creating a social climate that encourages or discourages rape.

Sexual scripts play a role in rape as well (Byers, 1996; Carroll & Clark, 2006). Adolescents quickly learn society's expectations about dating and sex through culturally transmitted sexual scripts. These

Victim-precipitated rape: The view that rape is a result of a woman "asking for it."

Focus: Milestones in Sex Research
Fraternity Gang Rape

Anthropologist Peggy Sanday (1990) investigated a widely publicized case of gang rape in a fraternity at a particular university, as well as many other similar cases documented at other universities.

Men join fraternities for many possible reasons. Some may anticipate establishing networks of friendships that will help them in their future careers. But often freshmen, insecure in a complex new environment, join the fraternity to find security. According to Sanday's analysis, the initiation rituals of many fraternities follow a sequence of creating high levels of anxiety in the new members, followed by a male bonding ritual that makes them "brothers." Essentially the young man's identity as an individual is undermined while loyalty to the group is prized, indeed enforced.

In the case investigated by Sanday, the XYZ fraternity (she used this name to guard the anonymity of the population being studied, as required by the ethical standards for anthropologists) had a practice called the "XYZ express," referring to an express train. It involved a gang rape in which a woman, typically drunk or surreptitiously drugged so that she was barely conscious, was raped successively by a series of brothers who stood in line to take their turn, just as cars in a train are in a line.

Often this occurred toward the end of a party, when the brothers themselves were drunk.

Sanday pointed out how this practice has two consequences: It establishes dominance over a woman, and it promotes strong bonds among the fraternity brothers. The practice, of course, fits the definition of rape and is illegal. Yet many of the brothers, when the case was brought to court, said that they had no idea that their activities were wrong or illegal. The culture of the fraternity had dulled their capacity to make a rational judgment. The judge who heard the case was astounded that universities would tolerate, indeed support, institutions that created an environment in which such acts could occur.

Sanday noted anthropologists' findings that, cross-culturally, some societies are free of sexual assault whereas others are rape prone. She concluded, "Social ideologies, not human nature, prepare men to abuse women" (p. 192). The XYZ fraternity and others like it are essentially a subculture that socializes men to have sexist attitudes toward women and creates an environment in which gang rape is likely to occur.

Source: Sanday (1990).

---

scripts support rape when they convey the message that the man is supposed to be oversexed and the sexual aggressor. By adolescence, both girls and boys endorse scripts that justify rape (Koss et al., 1994). A study of 1,700 middle school students revealed that approximately 25 percent of the boys said that it was acceptable for a man to force sex on a woman if he had spent money on her (Koss et al., 1994). These findings have been replicated in a number of studies of high school and college students (e.g., Goodchilds & Zellman, 1984; Muehlenhard, 1988).

Early family influences may play a role in shaping a man into becoming a sexual aggressor. Specifically, young men who are sexual aggressors are likely to have been sexually abused themselves in childhood (Friedrich et al., 1988; Koss et al., 1994).

The peer group can have a powerful influence, encouraging men to rape. For an example, see Focus: Milestones in Sex Research, above, which describes the ways in which the peer group in a

fraternity created a climate that encouraged its members to rape.

Characteristics of the situation play a role. Secluded places foster rape, as do parties in which excessive alcohol use is involved (Koss et al., 1994). Another situational factor is social disorganization, as noted earlier. An extreme example is war, in which rape of women is common (Brownmiller, 1975; Gottschall, 2004; Sackellares, 2005). In the 1990s we saw graphic examples of this in the war in the former Yugoslavia. Bosnian women—Croats and Muslims—were frequently raped by the attacking Serbs.

Miscommunication between women and men is a factor. In the section on date rape we saw a case in which the man and the woman had totally different understandings of what had occurred. Because many people in the United States are reluctant to discuss sex directly, they try to infer sexual interest from subtle nonverbal cues, a process that is highly prone to errors (Abbey, 1991). Specifically, some men have a predisposition to interpret a woman's friendly behavior or sexy clothing as carrying a sexual message that she did not intend (Abbey, 1991; Farris et al., 2006).

Sex and power motives are involved in rape. Feminists have stressed that rape is an expression of power and dominance by men over women (Brownmiller, 1975). Current theory emphasizes that both sexual motives and power motives are involved and interact with each other. A number of processes may be involved (Barbaree & Marshall, 1991). For example, rapists may differ from non-rapists in their ability to suppress sexual arousal when it occurs under inappropriate circumstances. Rapists may be capable of experiencing sexual arousal and hostile aggression simultaneously, whereas other men find that hostile aggression inhibits sexual arousal.

Finally, masculinity norms and men's attitudes are another factor (Abrams et al., 2003; Koss et al., 1994), as we discuss in the next section. Supporting the feminist theoretical view, research shows that hypermasculine attitudes are correlated with men's history of sexual aggression (Murnen et al., 2002). The very commonness of rape, especially date rape, argues against the psychopathology of rapists. Hypermasculinity is a far more common cause than psychopathology.

Rapists

What is the profile of the typical rapist? The basic answer is that there is no typical rapist. Rapists vary tremendously in occupation, education, marital status, previous criminal record, and motivation for committing rape.

One thing we do know about rapists is that they tend to be repeat offenders. In one study of undetected rapists—men who admitted to rape on a survey but had never been prosecuted—the majority had committed the crime more than once (Lisak & Miller, 2002). Those who were repeat offenders averaged about six rapes each. Persistent rapists have especially high scores on hostility toward women and have a history of delinquency, as explained below (Abbey & McAuslan, 2004; Hall et al., 2006).

A massive program of research by Neil Malamuth, Mary Koss, and their colleagues identified four factors that predispose men to engage in sexual coercion of women (Malamuth, 1998; Malamuth et al., 1991; see also Hall et al., 2005, 2006):

1. *A violent home environment.* A boy who grows up in a hostile home environment has a higher likelihood of engaging in sexual aggression against women. Factors that create a hostile home environment include violence between the parents or abuse directed toward the child, whether battering or sexual abuse.

2. *Delinquency.* Being involved in delinquency is itself made more likely by coming from a hostile home. But the delinquency in turn increases the likelihood of engaging in sexual coercion—the boy associates with delinquent peers who, for example, encourage hostile attitudes and rationalizations for committing illegal acts and reward a tough, aggressive image.

3. *Sexual promiscuity.* The male, often in the context of the delinquent peer group, develops a heavy emphasis on sexual conquests to bring him self-esteem and status with the peer group. Coercion may seem to him a reasonable way of making conquests.

4. *A hostile masculine personality.* This personality constellation involves deep-seated hostility toward women together with negatively defined, exaggerated masculinity—masculinity defined as rejecting anything feminine such as nurturance, and emphasizing power, control, and macho characteristics.

Perhaps surprisingly, this research was not based on convicted rapists but rather on a national representative sample of male college students. The factors that contribute to sexual aggression against women can be present even in such apparently benevolent populations.

One factor seems to attenuate or reduce a man's likelihood of raping: empathy. That is, a man who has several of the risk factors listed earlier, but who also is sensitive to others' feelings and needs and is not self-centered, is not likely to rape, compared with a man who has the risk factors and lacks empathy and is self-centered (Baumeister et al., 2002). These research findings have important implications for programs of therapy for convicted rapists. Empathy training should be emphasized, as it is in the most modern programs (Marshall, 1993; Pithers, 1993).

Men as Victims of Rape

Women are far more likely than men to be the victims of rape; according to the NHSLS, 22 percent of women had been the objects of forced sex with a man, whereas only about 1 percent of men had been the objects of forced sex with a woman (Laumann et al., 1994). In fact, it is more common for a man to have been forced to have sex by another man (1.9 percent of men) than by a woman (1.3 percent of men).

Nonetheless, it is possible for a woman to rape a man; research shows that men may respond with an erection in emotional states such as anger and terror. In a study of 115 men who had been sexually assaulted, 7 percent had been assaulted by a woman or group of women and an additional 6 percent by both a man and a woman (King & Woollett, 1997). Forced vaginal intercourse occurred in only two of the cases. Research shows that men who have been raped experience symptoms of PTSD, as women do. Men who have been raped by other men also experience very negative psychological consequences (Walker et al., 2005). It is important for counselors and others in the helping professions to recognize this possibility of male rape victims.

In a study of sexual coercion in a sample of college students, 78 percent of the women and 58 percent of the men reported being the objects of sexual persistence after they had refused (Struckman-Johnson et al., 2003). The sexual persistence included such tactics as persistent kissing and touching, the perpetrator taking off his or her own clothes, telling lies, and using physical restraints. One man said,

> At a party, she came up and began talking to me. I was already drinking some at the time. While playing cards, she talked me into finishing several of her drinks and beers. She said there was another party and convinced me to go. I was too drunk to drive, so she drove us. The "party" seemed to lack other people. After about ½ hour of kissing/making out, I was tired and wanted to go home. She said no and told me she wanted to have sex. I said no, but she continued to kiss me and try to talk me into it. When she produced a condom, I gave in. . . . (Struckman-Johnson et al., 2003, p. 83)

Some of these incidents would fit the legal definition of rape and others would not, but they do indicate the ways in which men, too, can be coerced into sexual activity.

Prison Rape

According to a study of 516 men and women prisoners in a state prison system, 22 percent of the men and 7 percent of the women had been the objects of sexual coercion (Struckman-Johnson et al., 1996). Prison staff were the perpetrators in 18 percent of the cases, fellow prisoners in the remainder. Among the male victims, 53 percent had been forced to have receptive anal sex, sometimes with multiple male perpetrators, and 8 percent were forced to have receptive oral sex. The men reported severe emotional consequences. Inmates offered a number of suggestions for ending prison sexual

violence. The most frequent was to segregate the most vulnerable: those who are young, nonviolent, new in prison, white. Many also favored allowing conjugal visits.

Prison rape is a particularly clear example of the way in which rape is an expression of power and aggression; prisoners use it as a means of establishing a dominance hierarchy.

Ethnicity and Rape

We have seen how cultural context can promote or inhibit rape and affect the meaning people attach to rape. The cultural heritages of the various ethnic groups in the United States provide different cultural contexts for people of those groups, so it is important to consider patterns of rape in U.S. ethnic groups.

Rape has a highly charged meaning in the history of African Americans (Wyatt, 1992). In the period following the Civil War, an African American man convicted of rape or attempted rape of a white woman was typically castrated or lynched. In sharp contrast, there was no penalty for a white man who raped a Black woman (Figure 15.2). Moreover, stereotypes originating at that time and continuing to the present portray both African American men and African American women as being highly sexual. Black women are so highly sexual, the reasoning goes, that they cannot be raped (Neville et al., 2004). The result is that African American women have a long history of nondisclosure of rape, a pattern that exceeds even that of white women. Many African American women think that no one will believe they can be raped and that they will have no credibility as rape victims.

Research on a random sample of women in Los Angeles indicates that the rate of attempted or completed rape incidents was nearly the same for the two groups—25 percent for African American women and 20 percent for white women (Wyatt, 1992). However, only 23 percent of the Black women reported the incident to the police or a rape crisis center, compared with 31 percent of the white women. Black women and white women were similar in their experience of the effects of the rape, such as its negative impact on their later sexual functioning.

Another study of Black and white female rape survivors found that they were similar in many ways, such as their self-esteem and coping after the rape (Neville et al., 2004). The Black women's responses, though, were linked to the Jezebel stereotype that Black women are sexually "loose," and therefore cannot be raped. Many of the Black

Figure 15.2 Ethnicity and rape. Rape has a highly charged meaning in the history of African Americans. In the time of slavery, although there was no penalty for a white man who raped a Black woman, a Black man convicted of raping a white woman was typically castrated or put to death.

women believed that the Jezebel stereotype was one of the reasons they were raped, and women who endorsed this attribution more strongly showed lower self-esteem.

Another survey of a random sample of Los Angeles women compared the rape experiences of Anglo and Latina women (Sorenson & Siegel, 1992). The results indicated that the Latinas were considerably less likely to have been the victims of a sexual assault—8.1 percent of Latinas compared with 19.9 percent of Anglos. The researchers interpreted this difference as being due to values in Latino culture, particularly among those born in Mexico, who place strong emphasis on the family and uphold patriarchal attitudes that insist that men should protect women.

Sometimes ethnicity can help. In Asian cultures, saving face is very important. For Asian American men, the potential for loss of face by raping is a deterrent to such activity (Hall et al., 2005).

Preventing Rape

Strategies for preventing rape fall into three categories: (1) avoiding situations in which there is a high risk of rape; (2) if the first strategy has failed, knowing some self-defense techniques in case a rape attempt is made; and (3) changing attitudes that contribute to rape.

The first strategy, of course, is to be alert to situations in which there is a high risk of rape and to avoid them. The Association of American Colleges, for example, recommends the following to avoid date-rape situations (Hughes & Sandler, 1987, p. 3):

Set sexual limits. No one has a right to force you to do something with your body that you don't want to do. If you don't want to be touched, for example, you have a right to say, "Don't touch me," and to leave if your wishes are not respected.

Decide early if you would like to have intercourse. The sooner you communicate your intentions firmly and clearly, the easier it will be for your partner to understand and accept your decision.

Do not give mixed messages; be clear. Say yes when you mean yes and no only when you mean no.

Be forceful and firm. Do not worry about being polite if your wishes are being ignored.

Do not do anything you do not want to do just to avoid a scene or unpleasantness. Do not be raped because you are too polite to get out of a dangerous situation or because you are worried about

Figure 15.3 Self-defense classes for women. Many experts believe that all women should take such classes to gain the skills necessary to defend themselves in the case of an attempted rape.

hurting your date's feelings. If things get out of hand, be loud in protesting; leave, and go for help.

Be aware that alcohol and drugs are often related to date rape. They compromise your ability—and that of your date—to make responsible decisions.

Trust your gut-level feelings. If the situation feels risky to you, or if you feel you are being pressured, trust your feelings. Leave the situation or confront the person immediately. Be careful when you invite someone to your home or you are invited to your date's home. These are the most likely places for date rapes to occur.

If this first set of strategies—avoiding rape situations—does not work, self-defense strategies are needed. Always remember that the goal is to get away from the attacker and run for help.

Many universities and other organizations offer self-defense classes for women, and we believe that every woman should take at least one such course. Many techniques are available. Judo (and aikido, which is similar) emphasizes throwing and wrestling. Tae kwon do (Korean karate) emphasizes kicking. Jujitsu uses combinations of these strate-

gies. The exact method the woman chooses is probably not important, as long as she does know some techniques (Figure 15.3). Related to this is the importance of getting exercise and keeping in shape; this gives a woman the strength to fight back and the speed to run fast. Research shows that fighting back—fighting, yelling, fleeing—increases a woman's likelihood of thwarting a rape attempt (Brecklin & Ullman, 2005; Zoucha-Jensen & Coyne, 1993).

Self-defense, though, is useful to the woman only in defending herself once an attack has been made. It would be better if rape could be rooted out at a far earlier stage so that attacks never occur. To do this, our society would need to make a radical change in the way it socializes males (Hall & Barongan, 1997). If little boys were not so pressed to be aggressive and tough, perhaps rapists would never develop. If adolescent boys did not have to demonstrate that they are hypersexual, perhaps there would be no rapists. As we noted earlier, rape is unheard of in some societies where males are socialized to be nurturant rather than aggressive.

Rape prevention programs have been attempted over the past several decades. Often they are designed for a mixed-gender audience of first-year college students. Sadly and frustratingly, evaluations of these programs typically show only small changes in attitudes that do not last long and no changes in actual rape rates (Breitenbecher, 2000; Rozée & Koss, 2001). Experts in the field are developing much better ideas for creating effective prevention programs for both women and men; we need to put our best energies into these efforts (Lonsway & Kothari, 2000; Rozée & Koss, 2001).

Child Sexual Abuse

In this section we discuss the sexual coercion of children, including the broad category of child sexual abuse and one specific subcategory, incest, when the sexual abuse occurs within the family.

Patterns of Child Sexual Abuse

How common is child sexual abuse? According to the NHSLS, 17 percent of women and 12 percent of men had had sexual contact, as a child, with an adolescent (aged 14 to 17) or an adult (Laumann et al., 1994). Worldwide, roughly 20 percent of women and 5 to 10 percent of men report sexual contact with an adult when they were a child (Freyd et al., 2005). It seems clear that child sexual abuse is not rare and that girls, more often than boys, are its victims.

Most cases are never reported. In the NHSLS, only 22 percent of victims said that they had told anyone.

The great majority of perpetrators of child sexual abuse are men. According to the NHSLS, for girls almost all the cases involved sexual contact with men; for boys, some cases involved men and some women, although cases involving men were considerably more common. In another study, 94 percent of all perpetrators were men (Finkelhor, 1984). A number of factors probably account for this great imbalance. Men in our culture are socialized more toward seeing sexuality as focused on sexual acts rather than as part of an emotional relationship. The sexual script for men involves partners who are smaller and younger than themselves, whereas women's sexual script involves partners who are larger and older than they are.

little hearts, big hurts

Child abuse is everyone's business. Call us to find out how you can help.

THE NATIONAL CENTER FOR
Victims of Crime
1.800.FYI.CALL   www.ncvc.org

Figure 15.4   Child sexual abuse has become a major concern, as exemplified by this educational poster.

In the great majority of cases, both for boys and girls, the sexual activity involved only touching of the genitals (Laumann et al., 1994). However, for girls, 10 percent of cases involved forced oral sex, 14 percent of cases involved forced vaginal intercourse, and 1 percent involved forced anal sex. For boys, 30 percent of cases involved forced oral sex and 18 percent involved forced anal sex.

Sexual abuse may occur at astoundingly young ages. For example, for girls, 33 percent of cases occurred when they were under 7 years of age, and an additional 40 percent occurred among girls between 7 and 10 years of age (Laumann et al., 1994).

Table 15.1 shows the relationship between adults who committed child sexual abuse and their victims, according to the NHSLS. Notice that sexual abuse by strangers is not common. Most abusers are family friends and relatives.

Patterns of Incest

Incest is typically defined as sexual contact between blood relatives, although the definition is

Incest: Sexual activity between relatives.

Table 15.1 Categories of People Who Sexually Abuse Children, as Reported by Adults Recalling Incidents of Sexual Abuse in Their Childhood

	Percentage of Adults Abused as Children*	
Perpetrators	Women	Men
Stranger	7%	4%
Teacher	3	4
Family friend	29	40
Older friend of respondent	1	4
Older brother	9	4
Stepfather or mother's boyfriend	9	2
Father	7	1
Other relative	29	13
Other	19	17

*Percentages do not total 100 because some respondents reported on multiple categories of abuse.

Source: Laumann et al. (1994), adapted from Table 9.14, p. 343.

often extended to include sex between nonblood relatives—for example, between stepfather and stepdaughter.

Fifty years ago, incest was widely believed to be a rare and bizarre occurrence. Early research confirmed this notion, indicating that the incidence of incest cases prosecuted by the police was only about one or two people per million per year in the United States (Weinberg, 1955). The catch, though, is that the overwhelming majority of cases were (and still are) going unreported to authorities and unprosecuted. The NHSLS data (Table 15.1) show what a large percentage of child sexual abuse cases are perpetrated by adults within the family. However, because it specified that the sexual contact had to be with an adult or an adolescent aged 14 or older, the NHSLS missed one category of incest, namely, sibling incest. In a general survey of undergraduates, 15 percent of the females and 10 percent of the males said that they had had a sexual experience with a sibling (Finkelhor, 1980). It is likely that sibling incest is the most common form of incest.

Impact on the Victim

Many therapists who are experienced with cases of child sexual abuse believe that the effects on the victim can be serious and long lasting (Herman, 1981). Consider the following case:

A 25-year-old office worker was seen in the emergency room with an acute anxiety attack. She was pacing, agitated, unable to eat or sleep, and had a feeling of impending doom. She related a vivid fantasy of being pursued by a man with a knife. The previous day she had been cornered in the office by her boss, who aggressively propositioned her. She needed the job badly and did not want to lose it, but she dreaded the thought of returning to work. It later emerged in psychotherapy that this episode of sexual harassment had reawakened previously repressed memories of sexual assaults by her father. From the age of 6 until midadolescence, her father had repeatedly exhibited himself to her and insisted that she masturbate him. The experience of being entrapped at work had recalled her childhood feelings of helplessness and fear. (Herman, 1981, p. 8)

In a major review of studies of children who were sexually abused (either by family members or by nonrelatives), the researchers concluded that there is strong evidence of a number of negative effects on these children, compared with control groups of nonabused children (Kendall-Tackett et al., 1993; but see Rind et al., 1998). Sexually abused children are significantly more likely to have symptoms of anxiety, posttraumatic stress disorder, depression, poor self-esteem, health complaints, aggressive and antisocial behavior, inappropriate sexual behavior, school problems, and behavior problems such as hyperactivity. Victims had more severe symptoms when (1) the perpetrator was a member of the family; (2) the sexual contact was frequent or occurred over a long period of time; and (3) the sexual activity involved penetration (vaginal, oral, or anal). The child's gender did not seem to be a factor; that is, there were no differences in symptoms between boys and girls. However, the researchers noted that gender was not investigated in many studies, probably because so few boys appeared in most samples.

If a case is reported and prosecuted, the child may be as traumatized by testifying in court as by the abuse itself. Repeatedly testifying about severe abuse is associated with worse mental health outcomes (Quas et al., 2005). Interestingly, the perpetrator receiving a light sentence is also associated with worse mental health outcomes.

Adults who were sexually abused as children display more depression, anxiety, eating disorders, alcohol and drug dependence, negative feelings about sex, and difficulty forming stable, safe romantic relationships, compared with controls (Bulik et al., 2001; Kendler et al., 2000a; Testa et al., 2005). The risk of these difficulties is greater if attempted or completed intercourse occurred, if the abuse was by a relative, and if the victim told someone and received a negative response from that person. Adult survivors of child sexual abuse are also more likely to experience sexual disorders such as fears of sex (sexual aversion), lack of sexual desire, and lack of arousal (Leonard & Follette, 2002; Loeb et al., 2002; Meston et al., 2006; Najman et al., 2005). Women who were sexually abused as children are also more likely to be preoccupied with sex, younger at the time of their first voluntary intercourse, and more likely to be teen mothers (Noll et al., 2003). Their sexuality is ambivalent—they experience both sexual aversion and a preoccupation with sex.

Child sexual abuse (CSA) has effects not only on mental health, but on physical health as well. Adults who were victims of CSA are one and a half times as likely as those who weren't abused to have had health problems in the past year (Sachs-Ericsson et al., 2005).

One study, however, reached different conclusions. In a general survey of 526 undergraduates, 17 percent of the students reported having had a sibling sexual encounter in childhood (Greenwald & Leitenberg, 1989; see also Finkelhor, 1980). There were no differences between this group and those who had had no such encounters, on a variety of measures of sexual behavior and adjustment, including incidence of premarital intercourse, age at first intercourse, number of sexual partners, sexual satisfaction, and sexual disorders. The researchers concluded that childhood sexual experiences with a sibling close in age have no effect—positive or negative—on adult sexual adjustment, on average.

What, then, are the psychological consequences of incest or other childhood sexual abuse for the victim? Childhood sexual abuse may not be damaging to the victim in some cases, particularly if it is brother–sister incest when the two are close in age and it is consensual. However, in most cases childhood sexual abuse is psychologically damaging, and may lead to symptoms such as depression and PTSD. The evidence indicates that the extent of distress is associated with a number of factors, including, especially, the severity of the abuse (Kallstrom-Fuqua et al., 2004). Patterns of sexual abuse can range from five minutes of fondling by a distant cousin to repeated forced intercourse by a father or stepfather over a period of several years. The effects of sexual abuse are the most severe when it involved intercourse, occurred repeatedly over years, and was committed by a father or stepfather (Fleming et al., 1999; Kendler et al., 2000a).

In contrast, some women who were the objects of child sexual abuse perceive some benefit from this adverse life experience. They believe that it made them better at protecting their own children from abuse and made them stronger people (McMillen et al., 1995). This is another example of posttraumatic growth.

Treatments such as cognitive–behavioral therapy are available and effective in treating adults with PTSD following child sexual abuse (McDonagh et al., 2005).

The Offenders

In 1994, Leroy Hendricks was released from prison in Kansas, having served a 10-year term for molesting two 13-year-old boys (Davey & Goodnough, 2007). Rather than walking free, however, he was immediately transferred to a correctional mental health facility where he might remain for the rest of his life. A 1994 Kansas law, the Sexually Violent Predator Act, allowed him to be put away for life, on the grounds that his mental problems made him likely to attack again. In fact, the 1994 conviction was his fifth over a span of about 30 years. Hendricks challenged the constitutionality of the law, but the Supreme Court, in 1997, upheld the law and his treatment under it. Today he remains in the facility, at a cost to taxpayers of $185,000 per year.

What do the data say about child sexual abusers? Are they likely to repeat the offense? Are there effective treatments for them?

Pedophilia (child molesting) involves an adult having sexual activity with a prepubescent child, generally age 13 or younger (American Psychiatric Association, 2000a). To meet the official criteria for diagnosis, the person must have intense sexually arousing fantasies, sexual urges, or behaviors, over a period of at least six months, that involve sexual activity with a prepubescent child. Pedophilia is a paraphilia, to use the terminology introduced in Chapter 14.

Pedophiles fall into a number of categories, depending on the gender of the children they are attracted to and other factors. In one study of 678 pedophiles, all of them men, 27 percent were attracted to boys, 47 percent to girls, and 25 percent to both (Blanchard et al., 1999). Child molesters also differ in whether they are incest offenders, pseudo-incest offenders (sex with a stepchild), molesters of familiar children, or molesters of unfamiliar children (Guay et al., 2001). Pedophiles tend to be repeat offenders, and their patterns of preference tend to be stable over time.

Child molesters score low on measures of heterosocial competence (Dreznick, 2003). That is, they lack the interpersonal skills to function well in adult heterosexual relationships. Pedophiles are more likely than controls to have had accidents involving head injury and unconsciousness before the age of 6 (Blanchard et al., 2002). This suggests that some injury to the developing brain may create this disorder in some cases.

Researchers are very interested in developing measures that might identify pedophiles who have not been arrested, and perhaps have not even offended yet (Seto, 2004). Sophisticated cognitive tests using reaction times indicate that pedophiles have a strong mental association between children and sex, whereas nonpedophiles have an association between adults and sex (Gray et al., 2005). Phallometric measures, such as those discussed in Chapter 12, indicate that men who are attracted to child pornography show greater arousal to child photos than to adult photos, and their arousal to child photos is even greater than the arousal of men who have actually sexually offended against children (Seto et al., 2006). Possession of child pornorgraphy itself might be an indicator (Seto, 2004). Measures such as these may provide ways to identify men who are likely to offend even before they commit their crime.

A U.S. Department of Justice study attempted to answer the question of recidivism (repeat offending) by following for three years a large sample of sex offenders released from prison in 1994 (Langan et al., 2003). Among child molesters, only 3.3 percent were rearrested for a sex crime with a child in the three years following release. The problem with this statistic is that it is without doubt a serious underestimate of the actual rates of reoffending, because so much child sexual abuse goes unreported (Hanson, 2000). Moreover, among those who had an additional prior arrest for child molesting, the recidivism rate was three times that for first offenders. Another study found recidivism rates of 13 percent for child molesters within four to five years of the offense, but this is again likely to be an underestimate (Hanson & Brussiere, 1998). According to this same study, certain subgroups of child molesters had much higher rates of recidivism. Recidivism was higher among those who had committed previous sexual offenses, had begun sexual offending at an early age, and had targeted male victims. The strongest predictor of recidivism was phallometric measures of sexual deviance (recall the penile strain gauge discussed in Chapter 12). Offenders are shown slides of children and their arousal (erection) is measured. Those who show the strongest sexual arousal to pictures of children have the highest recidivism rates. Therefore, depending on the particular case, there may be a very low or very high risk of repeating the offense, and we know some of the factors that predict which category a particular offender might belong in. It is also true that, in the studies that were reviewed, many of the offenders had been given some treatment. The low recidivism rate might therefore tell us more about the success of the treatment programs than about natural rates of recidivism among those who have not been given some rehabilitation.

A number of treatments for child sexual abusers are in use: surgical castration, antiandrogen drugs, hormones, SSRIs (explained below), and cognitive–behavioral therapy (Abracen & Looman, 2004; Bradford & Greenberg, 1996; Hall, 1995). As discussed in Chapter 5, the idea behind surgical castration is that removal of a man's testes sharply reduces his levels of testosterone, with the hope that his sexual and aggressive behavior will also be reduced sharply. Cyproterone acetate (CPA) is an antiandrogen drug—that is, it reduces the action of testosterone in the body and is therefore a kind of chemical castration—that has been used in the treatment of child sexual abusers. Research indicates that

Pedophilia: Child molesting; an adult having sexual activity with a prepubescent child.

Focus: Milestones in Sex Research
False Memory Syndrome? Recovered Memory?

One of the nastiest professional controversies today concerns the issue of what some call recovered memory and what others call false memory syndrome. The issue is sexual abuse or other severe trauma in childhood and whether the child victim can forget (suppress) the memory of the event and later recover that memory.

On one side of the argument, the recovered memory side, psychotherapists see adult clients who display serious symptoms of prior trauma, such as severe depression and anxiety. Sometimes these clients have clear memories of being sexually abused in childhood and have always remembered the events but have never told anyone until the therapist. In other cases, the client doesn't remember that any abuse occurred, but during the process of therapy, or sometimes spontaneously before therapy, something triggers the memory and the client then recalls the sexual abuse. Psychotherapists are understandably outraged about the psychological trauma that results from childhood sexual abuse.

On the other side, some psychologists believe that these memories for events that had been forgotten and then are remembered are actually false memories—that is, the events never occurred. They argue that unscrupulous or overzealous therapists may induce these memories by hypnotizing clients or strongly suggesting to clients that they had been abused in childhood.

What do the data say? First, there is evidence from laboratory studies that information associated with unpleasant emotions is more likely to be forgotten (e.g., Bootzin & Natzoulas, 1965). Research directly on the issue of child sexual abuse also provides support for the idea that forgetting does occur in some cases. In one study, 129 women who were known to have been sexually abused as children—they had been brought to a hospital for treatment at the time and the abuse had been medically verified—were interviewed 17 years later; 38 percent did not remember their prior abuse (Williams, 1994). The possible flaw in this study is that some of the respondents may have remembered but not have reported it to the interviewer. However, they were reporting many other intimate sexual experiences, so it seems likely that they would report accurately about this one, too. In a study of adult women who reported to a researcher that they had been victims of child sexual abuse, 30 percent said that they had completely blocked out any memory of the abuse for a full year or more (Gold et al., 1994). In another, similar study, 19 percent of adult women who reported child sexual abuse said that they forgot the abuse for a period of time (Loftus et al., 1994). In a national survey of a sample of psychologists, 24 percent reported being the victims of child sexual abuse; of those, 40 percent reported a period of forgetting (Feldman-Summers & Pope, 1994).

Abuse was more likely to have been forgotten when it was more severe. Therefore, the evidence seems to indicate that, in 19 to 40 percent of

CPA greatly reduces pedophiles' sexual arousal to children (Bradford & Greenberg, 1996). Results with a new anti-GnRH drug are quite promising (Rosler & Witztum, 1998). By blocking the action of GnRH, pituitary and gonadal functioning is inhibited, again reducing levels of testosterone. One class of antidepressants (the SSRIs, which include Prozac and Zoloft) is also proving to be successful in the treatment of sex offenders (Bradford & Greenberg, 1996). Its use is based on the assumption that sex offending can be a particular kind of obsessive–compulsive disorder, and such disorders generally respond well to these antidepressants. Cognitive–behavioral therapy makes use of a number of techniques, including cognitive restructuring, masturbation reconditioning (the man learns to experience arousal to appropriate persons [adults] rather than inappropriate persons [children]), role playing, desensitization, and stress management (Abracen & Loomis, 2004).

In a follow-up of high-risk sex offenders (high risk because they had a history of multiple offenses or violent offenses), the recidivism rate was 52 percent for untreated sex offenders and 24 percent for treated sex offenders, a significant improvement with treatment (Abracen & Loomis, 2004). The treatment was cognitive–behavioral therapy. One of its advantages, compared with drug treatment, is that a large proportion of offenders refuse hormone treatment or discontinue it.

cases, memories of childhood sexual abuse are forgotten for a period of time and then remembered again. In fact, it has been theorized that amnesia for traumatic events of this kind, particularly when the child has been betrayed by someone like a parent, is an adaptive response that helps the child survive in a terribly distressed family situation (Freyd, 1996).

The other question is, Can memories of events that did not occur be "implanted" in someone? In one study, the researcher was able to create false memories of childhood events in 25 percent of the adults given the treatment (Loftus, 1993). Certain conditions seem to increase the chances that people will think they remember things that did not actually occur, including suggestion by an authority figure and suggestion under hypnosis.

Two recent studies shed additional light on this debate. One was a study of women admitted to a hospital unit specializing in the treatment of trauma-related psychological disorders (Chu et al., 1999). Among those reporting childhood sexual abuse, 26 percent had partial amnesia for it and 27 percent had complete amnesia for a period of time before recalling it. These patients also displayed dissociative symptoms. Dissociative amnesia is an inability to recall important personal information, usually of a traumatic nature (American Psychiatric Association, 2000a). The great majority of those who suffered child sexual abuse had been able to corroborate the occurrences by some method such as medical records. And, very important, most of them first remembered the abuse while at home, and about half were not involved in any kind of treatment or counseling at the time they remembered, ruling out the possibility of suggestion by a therapist.

In another study, normal participants' brains were scanned using fMRI (functional magnetic resonance imaging) while they were suppressing unwanted memories (Anderson et al., 2004). Neural systems underlying suppression were clearly identified and included a region in the prefrontal cortex and the hippocampus. From this study we can see that suppression of memories is not just hocus-pocus but has a real basis in the brain.

What is the bottom line? There is evidence that some people do forget childhood sexual abuse and remember it later. There is also evidence that some people can form false memories based on suggestions made by another person. It seems likely that most of the cases of recovered memory of child sexual abuse are true, but that a few are false and the product of suggestion. To put the matter in perspective, each year thousands of children are sexually abused; the vast majority of these cases go unreported and the perpetrators go unpunished. It is also probably true that false accusations of past child abuse are made, often by a well-intentioned "victim" who is highly suggestible to media reports of other cases or who has been misled by an overzealous therapist. As a result, an accused person who is innocent may be arrested. Errors of justice occur on both sides. Nonetheless, there are many more cases of unreported and unpunished perpetrators than of falsely convicted persons.

Sources: Anderson et al., 2004; Bootzin & Natzoulas (1965); Chu et al., 1999; Feldman-Summers & Pope (1994); Freyd (1996); Gold et al. (1994); Loftus (1993); Loftus et al. (1994); Williams (1994).

Sexual Harassment

The issue of sexual harassment exploded into public awareness during the dramatic and widely televised hearings involving Anita Hill and Clarence Thomas during Thomas's confirmation to the Supreme Court in 1992 (Figure 15.5). The issue is a powerful one—it can force a victim out of a job, but it also might force a perpetrator from a job.

The official definition of sexual harassment, given by the U.S. Equal Employment Opportunity Commission (EEOC, 1993), is as follows:

Unwelcome sexual advances, requests for sexual favors, and other verbal or physical conduct of a sexual nature constitute sexual harassment when

A. Submission to such conduct is made either explicitly or implicitly a term or condition of an individual's employment or academic advancement,

B. Submission to or rejection of such conduct by an individual is used as the basis for academic or employment decisions affecting that individual, or

C. Such conduct has the purpose or effect of unreasonably interfering with an individual's work or academic performance or creating an intimidating, hostile, or offensive working or educational environment.

The key ingredients for sexual harassment, then, are that the sexual advances are unwelcome and are coercive in the sense that the victim's job or grade is at stake. This is termed *quid pro quo harassment* (quid pro quo meaning "I'll do

(a)   (b)

Figure 15.5   In 1992, the testimony of Anita Hill (*a*) in the televised confirmation hearings of Supreme Court nominee Clarence Thomas (*b*) captured the nation's attention and sparked much debate over sexual harassment.

something for you if you'll do something for me"). Point C of the definition specifies that a hostile environment also constitutes harassment—that is, a work environment that is so hostile (constant lewd innuendoes, verbal intimidation, and so on) that an employee cannot work effectively fits the definition of harassment, even if no explicit sexual proposition has been directed to the employee.

The EEOC definition addresses sexual harassment at work and in education. Sexual harassment may occur in other contexts as well, such as in psychotherapy or on the street.

Sexual Harassment at Work

Sexual harassment at work may take a number of different forms. A prospective employer may make it clear that sexual activity is a prerequisite to being hired. Stories of such incidents are rampant among actresses, for example. Once on the job, sexual activity may be made a condition for continued employment, for a promotion, or for other benefits such as a raise. Here is one case:

I work at a family-owned restaurant. Because I am a bartender, it is often just me behind the bar. On numerous occasions, I have caught one of the owners staring at my backside as I am getting things out of the refrigerator behind the bar. He has also blatantly stared at my legs, if I am wearing a skirt, while I am trying to speak with him. This owner also enjoys standing at the end of the counter so he partially obstructs the walkway that allows me to move from behind the bar. When I try to get out and say "Excuse me," he leans forward on the counter so I have to squeeze between him and the wine rack. He has also shown me how to clean the nozzle used to foam milk for coffee drinks, but does so in a fashion that looks much like someone manually stimulating a certain piece of the male anatomy, and then looks at me with a grin on his face. There have been times when the dishwasher wasn't working and he made comments to the male bartender, as I was standing right there, such as, "Be gentle with her . . . you have to go slowly so you don't hurt it . . . it needs lubrication." He has walked up behind me and blown on my neck.

All of the comments and actions are very unnerving. (From a student essay)

Figure 15.6 Sexual harassment at work: This man is engaging in inappropriate touching, but if he is her supervisor, she may be hesitant to protest.

This situation fits the definition of hostile environment harassment given earlier. It is clear how psychologically damaging such environments are to the victim.

Surveys indicate that sexual harassment at work is far more common than many people realize. In a survey of federal employees, 33 percent had been sexually harassed (Jackson & Newman, 2004). Averaged over many studies, between 25 and 50 percent of women have been sexually harassed at work, counting harassment both by supervisors and by coworkers (Ilies et al., 2003; Welsh, 1999).

Both female and male victims report that harassment has negative effects on their emotional and physical condition, their ability to work with others on the job, and their feelings about work (Sbraga & O'Donohue, 2000). However, men are more likely to feel that the overtures from women ended up being reciprocal and mutually enjoyable. Women, in contrast, are more likely to report damaging consequences, including being fired or quitting their job (Gutek, 1985). There is evidence linking the experience of sexual harassment to depression, anxiety, and PTSD (Rederstorff et al., 2007). Even subtle sexual harassment, such as asking, "Do you have a boyfriend?" in a job interview can damage women's performance in the interview (Woodzicka & LaFrance, 2005).

Men who are sexual harassers tend to be repeat offenders (Lucero et al., 2006). Therefore, unless they are disciplined, they will simply move on to another victim.

Why does sexual harassment at work occur? According to one theory, it results from a combination of gender stereotyping and men's ambivalent motives (Fiske & Glick, 1995). Stereotypes of women in U.S. culture are complex and include three distinct clusters: sexy, nontraditional (e.g., feminist), and traditional (e.g., mother). Many men have ambivalent motives in their interactions with women because they desire both dominance and intimacy. The researchers argue that there are four types of harassment. With the first, *earnest harassment*, the man is truly motivated by a desire for sexual intimacy, but he won't take no for an answer and persists with unwelcome sexual advances. He stereotypes women as sexy. With the second type, *hostile harassment*, the man's motivation is domination of the woman, often because he perceives her as being competitive with him in the workplace. He holds the stereotype of women as nontraditional and therefore competitive with him. His response to rejection by a woman is increased harassment. The third and fourth types of harassment involve ambivalent combinations of the two basic motives, dominance and a desire for intimacy. In the third type, *paternalistic–ambivalent harassment*, the man is motivated by a desire for sexual intimacy but also by a paternalistic desire to be like a father to the woman. This type of harassment may be particularly insidious because the man thinks of himself as acting benevolently toward the woman. Finally, the fourth type, *competitive–ambivalent harassment*, mixes real sexual attraction and a stereotype of women as sexy with the man's hostile desire to dominate the woman, which is based on his belief that she is nontraditional and competitive with him. This theory gives us an excellent view of the complex motives that underlie men's sexual harassment of women.

Social psychologists have developed a clever method for studying sexual harassment experimentally in the laboratory, the Computer Harassment Paradigm (Maass et al., 2003). In one study, college men were first exposed to a female confederate of the experimenters, who expressed either strong feminist beliefs (intentions to get a high-level career in an area usually reserved for men, and involvement in an organization for women's rights) or traditional beliefs. The men then had the opportunity to harass the woman by sending her pornographic material on a computer (she did not actually receive it). The men exposed to the feminist sent significantly more pornography to her than did men in the control group. However, not all men in the feminist-threat condition responded with harassment; those who did so were mainly men who identified strongly with the male role. The findings of this experiment are consistent with the type of harassment known as hostile environment harassment.

Sexual harassment at work is more than just an annoyance. Particularly for women, because they are more likely to be harassed by supervisors, it can make a critical difference in career advancement. For the working-class woman who supports her family, being fired for sexual noncompliance is a catastrophe. The power of coercion is enormous.

Sexual Harassment in Education: An A for a Lay

Sexual harassment in education was brought to public attention when, in 1977, women students sued Yale University, complaining of sexual harassment, in the important case *Alexander v. Yale*. The case recognized that sexual harassment of women in education was a violation of Title IX of the Civil Rights Act.

The data indicate that about 50 percent of female students have been harassed by professors, with acts ranging from insults and come-ons to sexual assault (Fitzgerald, 1993). In a survey of medical students, 37 percent reported experiencing sexual harassment during their medical training (Witte et al., 2006). Women report dropping courses, changing majors, or dropping out of higher education as a result of sexual harassment (Fitzgerald, 1993).

In the wake of the Yale case and others, most universities have set up reporting and grievance procedures for sexual harassment cases.

Sexual harassment is not confined to college or to teachers harassing students. One survey of 14- and 15-year-olds in the Netherlands found that 24 percent of the girls and 11 percent of the boys had been the objects of sexual harassment (Timmerman, 2003). Of those cases, 73 percent represented harassment by peers and 27 percent harassment by teachers (or other school-related

adults such as a tutor or principal). Of the teachers who were harassers, 90 percent were men. The psychological consequences were more severe when the harasser was a teacher than when this person was a peer. A U.S. study found that 79 percent of boys and 83 percent of girls experienced peer sexual harassment in high school (AAUW, 2001).

Psychotherapist–Client Sex

Legal definitions of sexual harassment focus on these problems in the workplace or in education. However, there is another category of coercive and potentially damaging sexual encounters—those between a psychotherapist and client, or between other professionals, such as physicians, and patients. Professional societies such as the American Psychological Association state clearly in their codes that such behaviors are unethical. Nonetheless, they occur and can be damaging.

One survey of a sample of licensed Ph.D. psychologists found that 5.5 percent of the male and 0.6 percent of the female psychologists admitted having engaged in sexual intercourse with a client during the time the patient was in therapy, and an additional 2.6 percent of male and 0.3 percent of female therapists had intercourse with clients within three months of the termination of therapy (Holroyd & Brodsky, 1977). These are probably best regarded as minimum figures because they are based on the self-reports of the therapists and some might not be willing to admit such activity even though the questionnaire was anonymous. Of the therapists who had intercourse with clients, 80 percent repeated the activity with other clients.

Experts regard this kind of situation as having the potential for serious emotional damage to the client (Pope, 2001). Like the cases of sexual harassment discussed earlier, it is a situation of unequal power, in which the more powerful person—the therapist—imposes sexual activity on the less powerful person, the client. The situation is regarded as particularly serious because people in psychotherapy have opened themselves up emotionally to the therapist and therefore are extremely vulnerable emotionally.

SUMMARY

Rape is defined as nonconsensual oral, anal, or vaginal penetration obtained by force, by threat of bodily harm, or when the victim is incapable of giving consent. A woman's lifetime risk of being raped is between 14 and 25 percent. Victims may experience posttraumatic stress disorder (PTSD) as a result of the assault. Date rape and marital rape are more common than many people realize. There are four major theoretical views of rape: victim precipitated, psychopathology of rapists, feminist, and social disorganization. Rape has particularly charged meanings for some ethnic groups within the United States.

Approximately 17 percent of women and 12 percent of men report that, when they were children, they had sexual contact with an adult or adolescent over 14 years of age. Most sexual abuse of children is committed by a relative or a family friend. Sexually abused children are more likely than other children to have symptoms such as anxiety, PTSD, depression, and health complaints. More severe psychological consequences are likely to occur when the perpetrator is a close family member who is an adult (sibling incest seems less harmful) and when the sexual contact is extensive and involves penetration. Pedophiles are more likely to be attracted to girls than to boys. Some types of child molesters have a low rate of recidivism, but certain types are highly likely to repeat their offense. Drugs such as MPA and CPA are effective treatments for sex offenders, as is cognitive–behavioral therapy.

There is controversy among professionals over whether adults can recover memories of child sexual abuse that they had forgotten (recovered memory), or whether these are cases of false memory syndrome, in which the supposedly remembered incidents never actually occurred.

Sexual harassment, whether on the job or in education, involves unwelcome sexual advances when there is some coercion involved, such as making the sexual contact a condition of being hired or receiving an A grade in a course. In another form of sexual harassment, the work or educational environment is made so hostile, on a sexual and gender basis, that the employee cannot work effectively. Surveys show that sexual harassment at work is fairly common. In severe cases it can lead to damaging psychological consequences such as PTSD for the victim. In education, the data indicate that about 50 percent of female students have been harassed by professors. This abuse can lead to negative consequences for the student, such as being forced to change majors or drop out of school. Sex between psychotherapist and client also carries the potential for psychological damage to the client.

QUESTIONS FOR THOUGHT, DISCUSSION, AND DEBATE

1. On your campus, what services are available for rape victims? Do these services seem adequate, given what you have read in this chapter about victim responses to rape? What could be done to improve the services?

2. Find out what procedures are available on your campus to deal with incidents of sexual harassment of a student by a professor.

3. Apply the four theoretical views of rape to child sexual abuse.

4. Angie was raped last night at a party, by a man she had met previously in one of her classes. Should she report it to the police?

5. In this chapter we have discussed sexual harassment, which involves repeated unwelcome sexual advances, or a requirement of sex in return for something like being hired or getting a raise, or an environment that is so sexually hostile that the person has difficulty working. Do you think there is a racial parallel to sexual harassment? That is, do you think that racial harassment exists? If yes, how would you define it, and do you think it should be illegal? If not, why not?

SUGGESTIONS FOR FURTHER READING

Antilla, Susan (2002). *Tales from the boom-boom room: Women vs. Wall Street.* Princeton, NJ: Bloomberg Press. The author chronicles sexual harassment against women in the financial industry.

Brady, Katherine. (1979). *Father's days.* New York: Dell paperback. This autobiography of an incest victim is both moving and insightful.

Raine, Nancy V. (1998). *After silence: Rape and my journey back.* New York: Crown. Raine, a professional writer, provides an intense account of the aftermath of being raped.

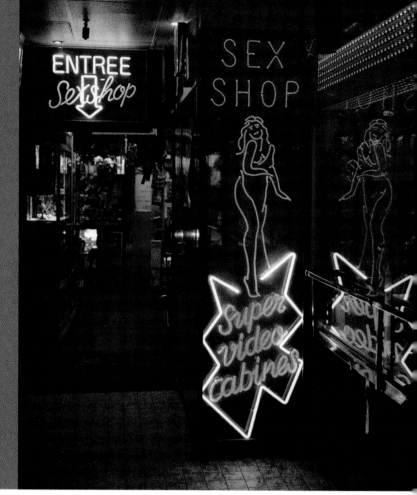

CHAPTER SIXTEEN

Sex for Sale

CHAPTER HIGHLIGHTS

Pornography is an expression not of human erotic feeling and desire, and not a love of the life of the body, but of a fear of bodily knowledge, and a desire to silence eros.*

*Griffin (1981).

The exchange of sexual gratification for money is a prominent feature of many contemporary societies. It involves at least $20 billion a year in economic activity (The Sex Industry, 1998). In this chapter, we consider two ways in which sex can be bought and sold: prostitution and pornography. Both involve complex legal issues and public controversy, but also attract a steady stream of eager customers.

Prostitution

Prostitutes or **commercial sex workers** ("hookers") engage in partnered sexual activity or interactions in return for money, material gifts, or some other form of payment such as drugs. As social critics have pointed out, some dating and living arrangements and long-term relationships, including certain marriages, also fall in this category.

Venues for Sex Work

There are a number of settings or venues in which commercial sexual activity occurs. The nature of the venue or social/sexual context influences the type of sex worker and client found there (e.g., race, social class), the activity that occurs, and its associated risks. The following discussion focuses on female workers and their male clients, but keep in mind that there are male, female, gay, lesbian, bisexual, and transgender sex workers and clients.

The **call girl**—notice the diminutive "girl"—works out of her own residence, making appointments with clients by a landline or cell phone. She is often from a middle-class background and may be a college graduate. She dresses expensively and lives in an upscale neighborhood. A call girl in a medium-size city may charge a minimum of $100 per hour and more if she engages in atypical activities; call girls in major metropolitan areas charge $200 or more per hour. A call girl can earn a great deal of money. But she also has heavy business expenses: an expensive residence, an extensive wardrobe, bills for makeup and hairdressers, high medical bills for maintaining her health, and tips for doormen and landlords.

A call girl may have a number of regular customers and may accept new clients only on referral. Because she makes dates by telephone, she can exercise close control over whom she sees and over her schedule. She usually sees clients in her residence, which allows her also to control the setting in which she works. In addition to sexual gratification, she may provide other services, such as accompanying clients to business and social gatherings. Call girls have considerable autonomy, and their physical and health risks are reduced by the setting in which they work.

Another venue for commercial sex work is the **brothel.** In the 1800s and early 1900s there were many successful brothels in the United States. They varied from storefront clipjoints, where the customer's money was stolen while he was sexually occupied, to elegant mansions where the customer was treated like a distinguished dinner guest. Brothels declined in number after World War II. A few remain in places like Nevada, where prostitution is legal in five counties. In the past 20 years, most have been replaced by **in-call services,** which employ women working regular shifts in an apartment or condo, servicing clients who come to the apartment. These services provide sexual gratification; charges are on an hourly basis. In major cities the charge is $150 or $200 per hour; in exchange, the client can participate in standard sexual activity including fellatio, cunnilingus, and vaginal intercourse. Many in-call services require initial contact by telephone, although others advertise their location in specialized media or even telephone books. A sex worker in this setting generally has less autonomy than a call girl; there is usually a manager or madam (see below) who determines the conditions of work and the fees to be charged and who collects a substantial percentage of each fee. In-call workers have less choice of clients and may be expected to service several per shift.

Another contemporary setting for commercial sex is the **massage parlor.** Some massage parlors

Prostitutes/commercial sex workers: A person who engages in sexual acts in return for money or drugs and does so in a promiscuous, fairly nondiscriminating fashion.
Call girl: The most expensive and exclusive category of prostitutes.
Brothel (BRAH-thul): A house of prostitution where prostitutes and customers meet for sexual activity.
In-call service: A residence in which prostitutes work regular shifts, selling sexual services on an hourly basis.
Massage parlor: A place where massages, as well as sexual services, can generally be purchased.

Figure 16.1   Sex for sale.

provide legitimate massage therapy. In others, the employees sell sexual services; these often advertise "sensual massage" or "stripassage," making it pretty clear which type of parlor they are. Some parlors offer a standard list of services and prices; others allow the masseuse or masseur to decide what she or he will do with a particular client and possibly how much of a "tip" is required for that activity. Massage parlors vary greatly in decor and price. Some are located in "professional" buildings, expensively decorated, and provide food and drinks in addition to sexual gratification. Charges may range from $100 to $300 or more. Such parlors may accept charge cards, with the business listed on the monthly statement as a restaurant. At the other end of the scale, storefront parlors, often located in "commercial sex districts," offer no amenities and charge rates of $40 to $100.

Another venue for a sex business is the *escort service*. These services have revealing names such as Alternative Lifestyle Services, First Affair, All Yours, Versatile Entertainment,

and Hubbies for Hire. Most escort services employ both men and women who will engage in sexual activity; like massage parlors, the service may have a standard menu, or the escort may have the autonomy to decide what activities he or she will do with a client. Prostitution in this setting is referred to as an **out-call service,** since the escorts go to the clients. This is obviously a more risky business in that the escort cannot control the setting in which the services are provided. Escorts are usually required to telephone the service when they arrive and when they leave the client's location. This not only contributes to their safety but allows the service to monitor how long the escort spent with the clients, and therefore the amount owed the service.

In most communities, the most visible sex worker is the **streetwalker.** She sells her wares on the streets of cities. She is generally less attractive and less fashionably dressed than the call girl, and she charges correspondingly less for services, perhaps as little as $20 for a "quickie." She is more likely to impose strict time constraints on the customer. Because her mode of operation is obvious, she is likely to be arrested.

Out-call service: A service that sends a prostitute or sex worker to a location specified by the client to provide sexual services.

Streetwalker: A lower-status prostitute or sex worker who walks the streets selling sexual services.

In some large cities, most women who are arrested and charged with prostitution are streetwalkers and are often members of racial or ethnic minority groups. In part this reflects the limited employment prospects for women of color in U.S. society; in some cases it also reflects a bias on the part of police, who arrest minority women but not white women who work on the streets. Because streetwalkers have relatively little control over the conditions in which they work, they are at greater risk of disease and violence at the hands of their customers, pimps (see below), and even police officers.

Studies of commercial sex workers find that the same person may work in several different venues over time (Lewis et al., 2004). For example, in areas with cold winters, people who work on the streets in the summer and fall may work in in-call services or bars during the winter. Women may also move back and forth between an escort service and working as a call girl.

The Role of Third Parties

Many people associate prostitutes with a **pimp** ("The Man"), portrayed as her companion–master. If she has a pimp, she supports him with her earnings, and in return he may provide her with companionship and sex, bail her out of jail, and provide her with food, shelter, clothing, and drugs. If he keeps an eye on her when she is working, he may provide some protection against theft and violence, because a prostitute is scarcely in a position to go to the police if she is robbed by a customer. But the pimp may also exercise considerable control over her and engage in verbal, physical, and sexual abuse toward her if she fails to obey him.

Another third party in commercial sex work is the **madam,** a woman who manages or owns an in-call service, an out-call service, a brothel, or an escort service. A madam is usually experienced and skilled at managing sex workers and businesses. Sometimes she is socially skilled also, with a network of contacts in the community.

In other venues there may be other third parties. Massage parlors employ managers who are on the premises at all times and may exercise close control of their employees. The importance of these third parties is that they reduce the autonomy of the sex workers they supervise and may coerce them to perform activities or work with clients that they object to. There is sharp disagreement among observers over the extent to which a sex worker can exercise choice with regard to his or her activities. Some argue workers choose who they serve and what acts they perform; others argue they have

little choice if they need money. The reality depends, in part, on the involvement of the third parties in the worker's daily life.

Although there is disagreement about whether call girls, in-call workers, and streetwalkers have autonomy or are coerced to participate, everyone agrees that the girls and women caught up in sex trafficking are forced to engage in it. **Sex trafficking** refers to the recruitment and control of persons, by threat or use of force or deception, for purposes of sexual exploitation (Hynes & Raymond, 2002). Typically, girls and young women are recruited in third-world or developing countries, by ads or people who promise them a good job (as a dancer, nanny, secretary), education, or a husband in a developed country. Recruiters may even supply forged travel documents, often for a price. When the women arrive in the destination country, they find themselves captive; often their travel documents are taken away, the money earned by their activity goes to those who control them, and their controllers threaten physical harm to the women or their families if they disobey or run away. The women often work in bars, brothels, and massage parlors and may be moved every few weeks. One woman interviewed in the United States reported having 10 to 30 customers per day. An estimated 45,000 to 50,000 girls and women are trafficked into the United States each year, many for the sex industry. One case began with the discovery of 8 girls ages 15 and 16 working in a brothel in Atlanta in 1998; follow-up investigation revealed that this brothel was part of a network operating in 14 states and that at least 500 girls and women had passed through the Atlanta house alone, most of them being from Asian countries (Ellison, 1999). Clearly, these women are being exploited, because third parties control every detail of their lives.

The Career of a Sex Worker

The first step in a prostitute's career is entry. Women enter prostitution for a variety of reasons (Vanwesenbeeck, 2001). For sex workers in the West, the most important one is economics. Some women are motivated by a desire for money, material goods, and an exciting lifestyle. These women are attracted by the image of the call girl, a status some of them are fortunate enough to attain. For some women—for example, a poor but attractive woman—prostitution can be a means of upward economic mobility. Other women enter out of economic necessity, in order to survive. A poorly educated single mother may have no alternative

Pimp: A prostitute's companion, protector, and master.
Madam: A woman who manages a brothel, in-call, out-call, or escort service.
Sex trafficking: The recruitment and control of persons for sexual exploitation.

means of earning a living. Some women become prostitutes in order to support a drug addiction.

Force or coercion is another factor. Some women report being coerced physically or psychologically by a husband or lover into selling sex for money. As noted above, coercion is a major factor in sex trafficking. Young women in Slavic and Asian countries answer ads in local papers promising wealth and glamour; they are taken to countries such as Israel and Thailand expecting to work in restaurants or hotels but instead are forced into prostitution (Specter, 1998). The "employer" may destroy the woman's passport and threaten her with deportation if she does not comply with his demands.

Another category of reasons involves gaining power. For example, a woman who serves as a call girl to famous politicians may think of herself as having access to real political power. Some women become involved in prostitution through a family member or friend who is already a sex worker and can teach them the ropes (Miller, 1986).

On entering prostitution, most women go through an apprenticeship in which they learn the skills of the profession. The apprentice learns sexual techniques, especially fellatio, since many customers want oral sex. She learns how to hustle, to successfully negotiate her services and pricing with potential customers. She learns how to maintain control over the interaction so that she can protect herself from being hurt or robbed by clients. She learns values, like "the customer is always right," and fairness to other "working girls."[1] Women who are recruited into the life by a pimp may be trained by one of his more experienced "wives." Some women are trained by an experienced madam, in exchange for a large percentage of their fees.

There has been relatively little research on the "midcareer" sex worker. We have noted that a sex worker may work in several different venues over time. A woman might move from in-call to out-call as she becomes more experienced at managing clients. She might move from the street into work in bars or at truck stops in response to changes in the weather or her health. Sex workers who are addicted to drugs may be forced to work long hours and service many customers in more than one venue in order to support their habit. Again, some of these changes may result from coercion or exploitation by a pimp or a sex trafficker.

"Squaring up" or "leaving the life" refers to giving up prostitution. Financially it is a difficult thing to

do, particularly for the woman with no job skills; recognizing this, analysts call for comprehensive programs that provide education and job training, shelters, medical care, and counseling for women (and men) who want to leave commercial sex work (Hynes & Raymond, 2002). A former sex worker, Norma Hotaling, founded one such program in 1992—SAGE, Standing Against Global Exploitation.

The married prostitute may go back to being a housewife. The unmarried woman may leave through marriage, since she may get proposals from her regular customers.

Other reasons for leaving include arrest and the threat of a long-term jail sentence, government agencies' insistence that she give up her children, and the knowledge that a friend was the victim of violence while working as a prostitute. Violence is a major hazard associated with being a prostitute: 81 percent of women who work outdoors, and 48 percent of women who work indoors, reported being kicked, slapped, or punched by a client (Church et al., 2001).

Sex Workers' Well-Being

There are a variety of images of the contemporary prostitute: young, attractive, autonomous, healthy, "the happy hooker"; young, brazen, aggressive, the "tough chick"; not-so-young, bruised emotionally and physically, a victim. Which one is valid?

According to a landmark study (Vanwesenbeeck, 1994), all these images are accurate. In the first phase, researchers recruited 90 prostitutes and former prostitutes in the Netherlands and conducted extended interviews with them about their daily lives. Two years later, 100 women who had been working for at least one year were recruited for a study of "sex and health"; these women were interviewed and completed several measures of coping style and well-being. The samples included women who worked on the street, in windows, in clubs and brothels, for escort services, and in their own homes. The results indicated that one-fourth of the women were doing well. They had few physical or psychosocial complaints, used problem-focused coping strategies, and were satisfied with their lives. Another quarter were at the opposite end. They complained of headaches, backaches, anxiety, and depression; their coping strategies involved dissociation (seeing problems as unrelated to the self) and denial, and they were dissatisfied with prostitution. The remaining women were in the middle.

The risks to a woman and thus her well-being varied according to the venue in which she

---

[1]A 1986 film entitled *Working Girls* provides a realistic look at an in-call service.

worked. In the Netherlands, where sex work has been legalized, women who worked in windows and on the streets were at greater risk. Working the streets was associated with greater risk of arrest and of violence by clients, which obviously influences physical and mental health. Women who worked in windows or on the streets worked faster, had more clients, and earned less per customer than those working in in-call and out-call services. In a more recent study of indoor sex workers in the Netherlands, workers reported having an average 9-hour workday; more than one-third worked in excess of 40 hours per week, and half had taken no holidays in the past year (Venicz & Vanwesenbeeck, 2000). Scores of indoor sex workers on measures of burnout—depersonalization and emotional exhaustion—were compared with scores of female health care workers and persons in treatment for work-related problems. Sex workers scored significantly higher on depersonalization, which was mainly explained by contextual factors—working due to coercion, experiences of violence, and lack of control in interaction with clients (Vanwesenbeeck, 2005). An important caveat in interpreting these studies is that they were conducted in the context of legalized prostitution in the Netherlands. Doubtless the health outcomes would be worse in countries in which prostitution was illegal and therefore prostitutes have little recourse if, for example, they are assaulted.

Risks are especially high for women who are being trafficked, because they are at risk of suffering abuse and injury by both clients and masters, undergoing illness and infection, and facing medical neglect (Hynes & Raymond, 2002).

There is also the risk of exposure to sexually transmitted diseases, especially HIV/AIDS. Prostitutes infected with HIV are often workers who are also injecting drugs, with research indicating that it is the injecting that is the risk. In the Western world, studies show that the sex worker's risk of HIV infection is greater in his or her private sex life than in their sex work. In other parts of the world, the risk varies greatly, with high rates of HIV/AIDS in some cities and countries but low rates in others (Vanwesenbeeck, 2001).

It has been suggested that the high levels of violence and of psychological distress found among sex workers are not due to the nature of the sex work per se but instead reflect the stigma associated with the work itself (Vanwesenbeeck, 2001). Prostitutes are at risk of rape because of attitudes such as the view that you can't rape a prostitute but no harm is done if you do (Miller & Schwartz, 1995). The risk of arrest and mistreatment by law-enforcement personnel, and the resulting anxiety and distress, reflect the fact that sex work is illegal.

Sex workers use a variety of cognitive and behavioral strategies to cope with the risks of their work. Some use drugs and alcohol to increase their confidence and decrease guilt. Others use a strategy of shutting down their feelings and focusing narrowly on the task. The consequences of this distancing are often referred to as depersonalization (not, of course, an experience unique to sex work). Some emphasize the rewarding aspects of the work, as perhaps that it supports their children. Many sex workers use as a coping technique the careful management of time and place, locating their sex work in a specific physical and temporal place separated from their private sexual and familial relationships (also not unique to sex work). Sex workers may also use a network of contacts with other sex workers as a source of support; in one such case, workers on one "stroll" worked together to protect a pregnant colleague by giving her all the customers who wanted a "blow job" and protecting her from clients known to be rough (Anderson, 2004).

Thus, sex workers face risks due to discrimination, criminalization, and exploitation, and perhaps due to violence, disease, and drug use. There are promising approaches available that can reduce harm, including education (especially job training), empowerment, preventive health care, and improved occupational and safety conditions. There are also interventions that have been shown to work, including peer education, training in safe sex negotiating skills, and provision of condoms (Rekart, 2005). Unfortunately, in the United States federal regulations prohibit any organization receiving federal funds from providing any of these services (Cohen, 2005).

The Role of Early Abuse

The study of women working in the Netherlands found that, in addition to their work venue, having a history of victimization and trauma as children or adolescents, before they entered prostitution, was associated with poorer well-being (Vanwesenbeeck, 1994). Much of the research literature prior to 1990 reported that a high percentage of prostitutes had been physically or sexually abused as children, which was then often taken as the cause of their entry into sex work (Vanwesenbeeck, 2001). It was often suggested that their childhood abuse led to feelings of stigmatization, which in turn resulted in their early sexual activity and/or drug use, running away from home, and a drift into sex work. There is no doubt that some men and women do enter commercial sex work via this path. But the research on which this is based used samples of streetwalkers, women in jail, or former prostitutes located through social service agencies. These respondents are not representative of all sex workers, so these results cannot be generalized. We don't in fact know how important a history of abuse might be in any one person's entry into sex work. Clearly, any adult who has experienced childhood victimization may have poor well-being.

Coercive sexual activity in adolescence or young adulthood is associated with a variety of adverse health and social outcomes (Ganju et al., 2004). Early coercion is associated with subsequent nonconsensual sex (e.g., trafficking), unintended pregnancy, and abortion. Adverse mental health outcomes include low self-esteem as well as substance abuse.

Customers

At the time of the Kinsey research, about 69 percent of all white males had had some experience with prostitutes (Kinsey et al., 1948). In 1992 the NHSLS asked all respondents whether they had had sex with someone they paid or who paid them (Laumann et al., 1994). Only 17 percent of men and 2 percent of women reported that they had had sex with such a partner since age 18. Thus, the use of prostitutes has declined dramatically in the past 50 years. This reflects the increased frequency of nonmarital and casual sexual activity during this same period (see Chapters 9 and 10).

Prostitutes refer to their customers as "johns." About 50 percent of the clients are occasional johns; they may be respectable businessmen who seek only occasional contacts with prostitutes, perhaps while on business trips. Nearly 50 percent are repeat clients who seek a regular relationship with one particular prostitute or a small group of them (Freund et al., 1991). The remainder are compulsive johns, who use prostitutes for their major sexual outlet. They are driven to them and cannot stay away (see Chapter 14). Some of these men are able to function sexually only with prostitutes (Bess & Janus, 1976). About 40 percent of these men are married (Freund et al., 1991).

A study of the clients of male and female prostitutes in Atlanta found that the two groups of men were very similar. On the average, they were 35 years old and had completed 1 or 2 years of college. Fifty-four percent were white, the rest Black. The men reported having had an average of four sexual partners during the preceding month, of whom 2.5 were paid. The clients of male prostitutes had been using prostitutes for 6 years, the clients of female prostitutes for 7.5 years (Boles & Ellifson, 1994). The participants were recruited through newspaper ads, so they are probably not a representative sample.

Men use the services of prostitutes for a variety of reasons. A survey of visitors to a commercial sex event in Australia found that 23 percent of men had paid for sex at least once. These men reported that the main reasons were to satisfy sexual needs, that it was easy, and that it would be entertaining (Pitts et al., 2004). Some married men want sex more frequently than their wives do or want to engage in practices—such as fellatio (Monto, 2001)—that they think their wives would not be willing to do (McKeganey, 1994). Some use prostitutes to satisfy their exotic sexual needs, such as being whipped or having sex with a woman who pretends to be a corpse. Others, particularly adolescents, may have sex with prostitutes to prove their manhood or gain sexual experience. Finally, some men enjoy sex with prostitutes simply because it is "forbidden."

Commercial sex work is common in locations where there are large numbers of men separated from their usual social contacts, such as military bases. In the twenty-first century, the provision of sex workers near bases often involves women who have been trafficked, especially in places like South Korea. In 2004, the U.S. Defense Department proposed making contact with a sex worker a military offense, to aid in the fight against sex trafficking. Interviews with a random sample of Hispanic men in North Carolina, where men outnumber Hispanic women 2.3 to 1, found that 28 percent had visited a commercial sex worker in the preceding year. Forty-six percent of single men and 40 percent of married men not living with their wives reported using a sex worker. The men reported an average of five or more visits in the preceding year (Parrado et al., 2004).

Male Sex Workers

Some male prostitutes serve a heterosexual clientele, selling their services to women. These prostitutes work in three settings. Some of them work for escort services and provide companionship and sexual gratification on an out-call basis. Working in such a setting is much less risky for male prostitutes than for female prostitutes. Some men work in massage parlors, under the same conditions as female employees. These male prostitutes virtually never work the street, in contrast to female streetwalkers and male *hustlers* (see below). This reflects gender-role socialization; female clients are unlikely to cruise the streets and pick up a prostitute, because they have been taught to let the male take the initiative.

A third type is the **gigolo** (in French, "one who dances"), a man who provides companionship and sexual gratification on a continuing basis to a woman in exchange for money. A gigolo often, though not always, has only one client at a time. There are several types, including the "Golden Boy," the pampered playboy kept by a very wealthy woman; the "Lap Dog," who enters into a series of marriages of convenience; and the "Toy Boy," or stud, who works as a companion on a limited-term basis (Nelson & Robinson, 1994). The demand for gigolos reflects the fact that women, like men, desire sexual gratification on a continuing basis and will pay for it when circumstances require or allow them to do so. On the other hand, women, unlike men, often prefer their sexual activity to be part of an ongoing relationship that involves love.

Hustlers are male sex workers who cater to a homosexual clientele. Interestingly, some of them consider themselves to be heterosexual, not homosexual. They may have strict rules for their customers to follow, such as only permitting the customer to perform fellatio on them. To indicate their masculinity, they may wear leather jackets and tight jeans. There is some market for "chickens" (young boys) as prostitutes.

Parallel to patterns of heterosexual prostitution, there are male homosexual escort services for a more upscale clientele (Salamon, 1989).

Male hustlers seem to fall into four categories (Allen, 1980). First are the full-time street and bar hustlers, who operate much as female streetwalkers do. Second are full-time call boys or kept boys. They tend to have a more exclusive clientele and to be more attractive and more sexually versatile than the streetwalkers. Surprisingly, by far the largest group is the third: part-time hustlers, who are typically students or individuals employed in another occupation. They generally work at prostitution only when they need money. The part-time hustlers are notable because, unlike those in the other groups, they are less likely to come from inadequate families. They also have the best long-term chance for acquiring an education and a stable job and achieving a good social adjustment. A fourth group is made up of delinquents who use prostitution as an extension of other criminal activities, such as assault and robbery. They are taught by older gang members how to pick up homosexuals and then threaten, blackmail, or assault them.

In one study of adolescent male prostitutes in San Francisco, the main reason for engaging in prostitution—stated by 87 percent—was money (Weisberg, 1985). Most often they had left home because of conflict in the family, typically leaving when they were 15 or 16 years old, although some had left when they were 11 or 12. The majority (72 percent) reported using drugs while engaging in acts of prostitution. The reason most often cited was the enjoyment of being high. Drugs were also used to reduce feelings of anxiety or fear stemming from the scary nature of the work.

Sex Tourism

An increasingly important type of commercial sex is **sex tourism,** which refers to varieties of leisure travel that have as their purpose the purchase of sexual services (Wonders & Michalowski, 2001). Sex tourism is made possible by three large-scale social forces: the migration of men and women from less developed nations, or from rural to urban areas, in search of jobs; the *commodification* of sexual intimacy, making all types of sex a commodity or service for sale; and increased travel for recreational purposes. All three of these forces are tied to increasing *globalization*, the movement of information and people freely across national boundaries.

The migration of people in search of economic opportunities provides a large group of young men and women in search of work. In some locales they are aggressively recruited into sex work by pimps or persons with ties to sex trafficking. In other places, they enter into the life more or less voluntarily, often because there are few other opportunities for persons of their racial or ethnic background. In Amsterdam, where the attitude toward sex work can be described as *regulated tolerance,* a few individuals control much of the commercial sex work, recruiting foreign migrants to work in windows and brothels. In Havana, Cuba, commercial sex work is decentralized, with many men and women working independently. They contact potential clients in hotels, bars, and on the street, hoping to connect with someone who will employ them for several days. In some countries, sex tourism is the most rapidly growing economic sector and a major source of hard currency; in such places, governments have little incentive to attempt to reduce or eliminate it.

Gigolo (JIG-uh-loh): A male who provides companionship and sexual gratification on a continuing basis to a woman in exchange for money.
Hustler: A male sex worker who sells his services to men.
Sex tourism: Leisure travel with the purpose of purchasing sexual services.

One estimate places the value of the global sex industry at $20 billion per year.

The tourists who can purchase sexual services are obviously wealthy enough to travel, which in turn often means they are citizens of developed countries and members of the middle and upper classes in their home societies. The sex workers are often from a different national and ethnic background. One of the attractions for the tourist is sex with this "dark-skinned other," perhaps someone from a group stereotyped as sexually free and uninhibited. The encounter is appealing because it is a sharp contrast to the tourist's usual sexual experience (Frank, 2003). Unfortunately, one such appeal for men is sex with a young girl, and in some Asian cities girls as young as 12 and 13 are available in brothels tightly controlled by their managers.

Pornography

A debate over pornography has been raging for more than five decades. Religious fundamentalists and some feminists (strange bedfellows, indeed!) agree that some kinds of pornography should be made illegal, while civil liberties groups and some other feminists argue that freedom of expression, guaranteed in the Constitution, must be preserved and therefore pornography should not be restricted by law. Meanwhile, Joe Brown stops at his local video store, buys *Wall to Wall Sex, v. 46,* and drives home for a pleasurable evening's entertainment. Here we examine what the issues are, paying particular attention to social scientists' research on the effects of pornography on people who are exposed to it. First, we need to clarify some terminology.

Terms

We can distinguish between pornography, obscenity, and erotica. The term *pornography* comes from the Greek word *porneia,* which means, quite simply, "prostitution," and *graphos,* which means "writing." In general usage today, **pornography** refers to literature, films, and so on, that are intended to be sexually arousing (Malamuth, 1998).

In legal terminology the word used is *obscenity,* not pornography. **Obscenity** refers to that which is foul, disgusting, or lewd. It is used as a legal term for that which is offensive to the authorities or to

Pornography: Sexually arousing art, literature, or films.
Obscenity: Something that is offensive according to accepted standards of decency; the legal term for pornography.
Erotica: Sexually arousing material that is not degrading or demeaning to women, men, or children.

society (Wilson, 1973). The U.S. Supreme Court has had a rather hard time defining exactly what is obscene and what can be regulated legally, a point discussed in more detail in Chapter 20.

In the debate over pornography, some make the distinction between pornography (which is unacceptable to them) and erotica (which is acceptable). For example, a noted sociologist defines pornography as "explicit representations of sexual behavior, verbal or pictorial, that have as a distinguishing characteristic the degrading or demeaning portrayal of human beings, especially women" (Russell, 1980, p. 218). In contrast, **erotica** is defined as differing from pornography "by virtue of not degrading or demeaning women, men, or children" (Russell, 1980, p. 218). According to this distinction, a movie of a woman being raped would be pornography, whereas a movie of two mutually consenting adults who are both enjoying having sexual intercourse together would be considered erotica.

Beyond these definitions given by scholars in the area, it is interesting to see how typical Americans define pornography. Research shows that there is great diversity in what people consider pornography. A *Time* magazine well-sampled survey on this topic (July 21, 1986) showed that 56 percent of Americans consider books describing sex acts to be pornographic; this means that about half of Americans consider such books to be pornographic, but half do not. There are also substantial gender differences. Fifty-two percent of the women polled consider nude photos in magazines to be pornographic, whereas only 39 percent of men hold this view. There is not a clear consensus on what is pornographic, a difficult problem when the topic under debate is what laws we should or should not have on this issue. This same poll also showed that the majority of Americans have been exposed to various kinds of sexually explicit materials.

Types of Pornography

Pornography is a multibillion-dollar business in the United States. Included in this business are a number of products: magazines directed to various audiences, films, X-rated videos and DVDs, live sex shows, telephone sex, computer porn, and kiddie porn. Some of this activity is legal (e.g., publishing *Penthouse*); some of it is illegal (e.g., producing films featuring children engaged in sex); and the legality of the rest is hotly debated. It is impossible to obtain precise data on the economics of pornography. According to a report by *Forbes* magazine (2001), it is a $4 billion per year industry, while *ABC News* (2004) puts the estimate at $10 billion per year.

Magazines

A large chunk of the pornography market consists of magazines, ranging from *Playboy* and *Penthouse*—soft core—to *Hustler* and hundreds of other hard-core magazines with less well-known names (Figure 16.2). The soft-core magazines mushroomed in the 1970s. In the 1990s the market was large, including both general magazines and those catering to specialized tastes. *Playboy* has reported a circulation of 3.2 million copies per issue, *Penthouse* a circulation of 980,000, and *Hustler* a circulation of 1 million (Ulrich's, 2001).

Much pornography is designed for the heterosexual male reader. *Playgirl*, however, features "beefcake" in an attempt to attract heterosexual women. The magazine now has a circulation of 575,000 copies per month. There is also a large variety of printed material designed for gay men, lesbians, people interested in interracial sex, swingers, and other groups.

Hard-core magazines have a no-holds-barred approach to what they present. Photographs may include everything from vaginal intercourse to anal intercourse, sadomasochism, bondage, and sex with animals. A study of the titles of magazines and books found in "adult" bookstores revealed that 17 percent were about a paraphilia or sexual variation (Lebeque, 1991). Of those, 50 percent featured sadomasochism. An additional 21 percent dealt with incest.

The profit on magazines is high. The markups may be as great as 600 percent, and it is estimated that there are approximately 20,000 outlets in the United States selling hard-core magazines. Repeat, frequent customers account for a large part of sales in stores. Yet more profit comes from customers who have regular subscriptions for pornographic magazines by mail.

Films, Videos, and DVDs

Although sexually explicit movies were made as early as 1915, only in the last four decades have these films been slick and well produced. The *hardcore film* industry began to emerge in a big way around 1970. Two films were especially important in this breakthrough. *I Am Curious, Yellow,* appearing in 1970, showed sexual intercourse explicitly. In part because it was a foreign film with an intellectual tone, it became fashionable for people, including married couples, to see it. The other important early film was *Deep Throat,* appearing in 1973. With its humor and creative plot, it was respectable and

Figure 16.2 Porn magazines designed for a male audience. They run the gamut from the relatively tame *Playboy* to the raunchier and more sexually explicit *Hustler.*

popular among the middle class. Linda Lovelace, the female star, gained national recognition and later appeared on the cover of *Esquire.*

After the success of *Deep Throat,* many more full-length, technically well-done hard-core films soon appeared. *Deep Throat* had made it clear that there were big profits to be made. It cost $24,000 to make, yet by 1982 it had yielded $25 million in profits.

Loops are short (10-minute) hard-core films. They are set up in coin-operated computers in private booths, usually in adult bookstores. The patron can enter and view the film in privacy and perhaps masturbate while doing so.

In the early 1980s, X-rated *videocassettes* for home viewing began to replace porn theaters. For example, *Deep Throat* became available on videocassette in 1977 and, by 1982, had sold 300,000 copies (Cohn, 1983). Cable television has also entered the arena, with porn channels thriving in some areas of the country. The latest advance is the DVD.

Many hard-core films and X-rated videocassettes and DVDs are made for a heterosexual audience. According to the General Social Survey data, 24 percent of U.S. adults reported seeing an X-rated movie in 1997 (GSS, nd). Nationally, "adult videos" earn $4 billion per year and account for more than 700 million video rentals annually (Rich, 2001). They portray couples engaging in both male-active and female-active oral sex, and vaginal and anal intercourse in various settings and body positions. Less often, films and videos show sexual activity involving three or more people, or two women (Davis & Bauserman, 1993).

Focus: First Person
Behind the Scenes: Making X-Rated Videos

Dave Cummings bounces out of bed. He's working today, so he goes through his routine; he showers, shaves extremely close to get a smooth face, trims his fingernails and his pubic hair, applies lotion to his groin, and finishes with hand lotion. He dresses casually and drives to a large, expensive home in Beverly Hills, rented for the shoot. When he arrives, he greets the other performers, mostly young women and men in their twenties and thirties. In this group, Dave is the odd man out. He is 67 years old, balding, and looks like your doctor, not the typical male performer in an X-rated video. He represents the "greying of porn." It is that appearance that gets him work. Dave provides the realism in the video; he is believable as a doctor, lawyer, judge, or schoolteacher, in roles where a hard-bodied, bronzed guy in his twenties is not credible. It is Dave's appearance that got him into the industry; that and one other characteristic: his sexual stamina. In his own words, he can "get it up, keep it up, not come before [I am] told to, and can climax on cue" (Kikuras, 2004).

Dave points to one of the most important qualifications for a male actor in the world of X-rated videos: the ability to perform sexually. Many videos are budgeted to be shot in three days. The script calls for six to nine episodes of sex, each requiring one or more erect penises; the majority are to end with visible ejaculation. In other words, these videos place a premium on male sexual performance, perhaps not surprising in a performance-oriented culture. It costs money and frustrates everyone involved if a male actor has a long refractory period (see Chapter 8). To make it in the industry, a man has to demonstrate that he is up to the demands. Dave is lucky; he has good genes and stamina. In years past, a man without Dave's talents would not last in this line of work. But a pharmaceutical breakthrough—Viagra—has changed all that. Many male porn actors routinely use Viagra, which enables them to get it up and keep it up. (Some actors inject the drug directly into the penis; the resulting needle marks really turn off some of the female performers.) As a result, hundreds of men are competing for the available jobs.

One consequence of this competition is pressure to perform acts and take risks that the actor might prefer to avoid. Even in this era of widespread knowledge of HIV infection and AIDS, condom use is rare in the porn industry, some viewers don't like to see them, some directors and producers don't allow them, and some actors and actresses don't like the resulting hassle or change in sensation. The risk became very real in May 2004 when it was announced that five performers had positive HIV tests. Another consequence of the competition is low pay. Men may be paid as little as $500 for a video. The industry is built primarily around women. It is the females who achieve a kind of stardom, whose names appear in the publicity and on the video boxes, and whose bodies are featured in the videos. Relatively new performers may be paid $350 to $1,000 for a film featuring conventional sex. Engaging in unconventional or rough sex brings a higher fee. Needless to say, no royalties are paid to the performers. The typical film is budgeted at $5,000 to $35,000 (Huffstutter & Frammolino, 2001). A typical release sells 1,000 to 2,000 copies; it is only the rare hit that brings in $1 million (*Forbes*, 2001). Thus there is constant pressure to keep costs at a minimum.

A rapidly expanding part of the porn industry is the "amateur" video. The development of the home-video camera has enabled anybody with a willing partner, friends, or neighbors to produce homemade porn. Such videos cost virtually nothing to make, and distributors are eager to purchase them. These films account for at least 20 percent of all adult videos made in the United States (The Sex Industry, 1998). In 2005, the first "Hump!" festival was held in Seattle, featuring homemade erotic videos. In 2006, there were 40 entries and 14 sold-out screenings.

In the 1990s, a number of companies began marketing videos designed to educate people about various aspects of human sexuality. With names like the "Better Sex" video series, these include explicit portrayals of a wide variety of consenting heterosexual activities. As such, these are erotica, not pornography. They often include commentary by a psychologist or sex therapist reassuring viewers that the activities portrayed are normal. These series are advertised in national magazines and some daily newspapers.

The continuum noted in magazines from the subtle to the explicit also exists in video. The subtle end is found in *music videos*. The sexual content of many videos shown on MTV is unmistakable

Figure 16.3 The greying of pornography: as baby boomers get older, the demand for older performers is increasing. Here, De'Bella, 50, waits for the director's call for her close-ups; her male co-stars are usually in their twenties.

We noted that there are a variety of pathways into commercial sex work. Dave Cummings voluntarily entered the industry at age 54. Once he had demonstrated his prowess, he found himself in continuing demand. In fact, he is now producing his own line of videos. Cummings says he does it because he enjoys sex and for the opportunity to have sex with lots of attractive young women. A 21-year-old starlet, Sienna drifted into performing in adult videos. She had worked in a fast-food outlet and bagel shop; she saw an ad in the newspaper for "nude modeling" and tried it. For the first year she did still photo shoots, $350 to $400 for a few hours. Then she moved to working for an Internet company, engaging in masturbation while clients watched her via the Net. After a few months she thought, "If I'm gonna do this, I might as well do porn and make more money." Sienna says she may leave the industry soon; "I've just been pounded so much in these movies that I'm starting to get tired" (Petkovich, 2004). Some performers report being coerced into performing for stills or movies through the use of alcohol or drugs or through the use of physical force by others on camera.

The X-rated video industry in the United States reflects our society. Demand for the videos is created by an abstinence-only approach to sexuality education and taboos on portrayals of sexual activities and relationships in other media. The production of an estimated 11,000 of them per year (ABC, 2004) reflects the development of video technology, enabling both the producer to produce and the purchaser to buy them cheaply. The emphasis on sexual performance reflects the larger culture, and it is often chemically enhanced as are many other performances in the contemporary world. The distribution and sale of the videos reflects the commercialization of sex, turning access to sexual images and sexual gratification into a commodity to be sold for cash or credit.

(Figure 16.4). Men are portrayed as dominant and aggressive, with prominent posturing and a clear characterization that they are wanted by and have sex with attractive women (Ward et al., 2005). Women are portrayed in a condescending manner and are valued almost exclusively for their physical appearance and sex appeal.

Live Entertainment

Shows providing live, sexualized entertainment are yet another part of the sex industry. Burlesque, which featured women seductively undressing on a stage in a theater, has been transformed into strip clubs. These provide semi-nude (pasties and a g-string) or nude dancing in a lounge setting; often dancers circulate among the patrons when not onstage. These clubs range in style from converted neighborhood bars to upscale gentlemen's clubs. Participant-observation research, supplemented by interviews, indicates that many of the customers are regulars; they come, not for sexual release, but for the opportunity to interact with attractive young women, and the pleasure of a sexualized interaction without the need to "perform" sexually (Frank, 2005). Male strippers catering to a female audience are less common but perform periodically in many communities. In the commercial sex districts of large cities, there are also live

Figure 16.4 The sexual content of many music videos played on MTV is unmistakable.

sex shows featuring couples or groups engaging in sexual acts onstage. These shows are "second cousins" to the elaborately staged reviews in major casinos and hotels that often feature nudity and simulated sexual activity in a lavish setting.

The Business of Sex

Wanted: Legitimacy. That's the imaginary marquee outside the building that houses the Sin City Chamber of Commerce. The chamber is located—where else?—in the city that advertises "What happens here, stays here"™: Las Vegas, Nevada. Sex-oriented businesses have big profits, celebrity starlets and studs, publicity, and paparazzi. Now they want legitimacy. When the Las Vegas Chamber of Commerce seemingly gave the cold shoulder to the efforts of these businesses to join, Loretta Holt, former chamber employee and grandmother of 19, decided to provide an alternative. Membership fees range from $250 up. In February 2007, the Sin City Chamber listed 450 member businesses, not all of them sex-related. The major benefits are social gatherings and a link on the chamber's Web site.

Telephone Sex

Telephone sex provides another example of enlisting technology to sell sexual titillation. Initially, "dial-a-porn" was available through 900-number services, but after the Federal Communications Commission tightened the regulation of such services in 1991, most telephone sex moved to 800-number or regular long-distance services (Glascock & LaRose, 1993).

A study of a sample of prerecorded messages identified several patterns (Glascock & LaRose, 1993). The typical recording was of a female voice describing a series of sexual activities in which the caller was a participant. Callers to 800 and long-distance numbers were likely to hear fantasies involving masturbation, vaginal intercourse, and oral sex. Few of the descriptions included violence or rape. More frequent were descriptions of activities in which the woman dominated and degraded the man.

There are also phone sex services that provide live conversation. In some cases, large numbers of workers may be in the same location talking to callers. In other cases, the phone sex worker takes calls at his or her home. A male described one conversation:

I say, "When you give a guy a blow job, what's your favorite way to do it?" She says, "Well, I love being on my knees, 'cause being on my knees with him standing is so submissive." I said, "Do you like looking at his cock in his pants, does that really turn you on?" She says, "I love that." I say, "I would love to be standing in front of you." She says, "Oh, that would really turn me on." "Do you like having your breasts played with when you're giving a blow job?" "Yes, I like it very much. I also like to be fingered." "How many fingers do you like inside you?" "I love two fingers." "And why do you like blowing a guy so much?" "Because I'm getting him excited and I know I can't wait for him to fuck me." "Do you like to fuck for a long time?" "Yes, I get lost in it." So then I said, "Well, I've really been thinking about you on top of me, and while you're riding me, I'll be spanking you." She said, "Oh God, I love that." I was masturbating and I came. It was great. (Maurer, 1994, pp. 349–350)

Computer Porn

In the past 15 years the World Wide Web and Internet have made available a wide variety of sex-related services for every computer installed with a modem or dsl line, whether at work, at school, or at home. An analysis of random samples of 50,000 Web sites from the Google index and 1 million sites from the MSN index found that 1.1 percent of the sites on both were sexually explicit adult entertainment sites (Stark, 2006). The samples were drawn in late 2005 and early 2006. The services include online chats or conversations; exchanging messages with like-minded persons via discussion groups; access to sexually arousing stories, photographs, videos, and films; and access to a broad array of goods and services via specialized Web sites.

Chat Rooms. *Chat rooms,* or Internet relay chat groups, provide a location where individuals can meet and carry on conversations electronically. These rooms are often oriented toward persons with particular sexual interests, often captured by their names. An Internet resource guide had links to 147 sex-oriented chat rooms in February 2007. The conversations often involve graphic descriptions of sexual activities or fantasies. The phone sex conversation reproduced above could have taken place electronically, with the words displayed on a computer screen instead of spoken over a phone line. Some people have left relationships, including marriages, for someone they knew only through electronic conversation. In this context, an interesting feature of these chats is that the other person cannot see you. This allows you to present yourself in any way you desire, to rehearse or try out a broad range of identities.

Doug is a midwestern college junior. He plays four characters. . . . One is a seductive woman. One is a macho, cowboy type whose self-description stresses that he is a "Marlboros-rolled-in-the-T-shirt sleeve

Table 16.1	Total Surveyed "Adult" Usenet Files and Downloads by Classification	

Classification	Total Files	Total Downloads
Hard core	133,180 (45.6%)	2,102,329 (37.9%)
Soft core	75,659 (25.9)	760,009 (13.7)
Paraphilia	63,232 (21.6)	1,821,444 (32.8)
Pedophilia	20,043 (6.9)	864,333 (15.6)

Source: Rimm (1995), Table 5, p. 1891.

kind of guy." The third is a rabbit of unspecified gender . . . a character he calls Carrot. (Turkle, 1995, p. 13)

Doug would not describe the fourth character, beyond saying it was furry. Remember that the character you are chatting with may not be who she or he seems to be.

News Groups. People can also log on to sex-oriented news or discussion groups, read messages posted by others, and post messages themselves. The messages may include personal information, or they may be a story or a file containing pornographic pictures in digital format. Stories can be printed by the user; picture files can be downloaded and viewed through a "plug-in." Often, the messages are simply advertisements for or links to sex-oriented Web sites that sell pornographic material. The resource guide mentioned previously had links to 677 sex-oriented news groups.

Commercial Bulletin Boards. There are numerous commercial bulletin boards that contain sexually explicit photographs in digital form. The aforementioned Internet resource guide listed 35 sex-oriented bulletin boards. Users may log on to these bulletin boards and download images for a fee. Each image is listed in an electronic catalog with a short description. Table 16.1 shows the results of a large-scale analysis of images on bulletin boards. Hard-core images (sample description: "Girl with big tits gets fucked by guy") made up 38 percent of the downloaded images. Another 33 percent were images of paraphilias ("Girl with big tits gets fucked by horse"). Of particular concern is the popularity of pedophilic images, which accounted for 15.6 percent of the downloaded images. Such images are illegal and not readily available elsewhere. The researchers concluded, "The 'adult' BBS market is driven largely by the demand for paraphiliac and pedophilic imagery. The availability of, and the demand for, vaginal sex imagery is relatively small"

SexSource Online
www.mhhe.com/hyde10

"TECHNOLOGY AND SEXUAL FANTASY" IN SEX AND THE LAW

Figure 16.5   The newest innovation in the porn business is computer porn.

(Rimm, 1995, p. 1890). The U.S. Congress and various governmental agencies continue to debate what, if anything, can be done to regulate the flow of these materials on computer networks.

Adult Web Sites.   Adult Web sites sell a variety of pornographic services and sexual materials. The Internet resource guide had links to 768 such sites, with names like Amateur Yearbook, Asian Pleasures, Cheerleader Ezine, Lydia Lashes, Pantyhose Ezine, and Sorority Girls. Each site typically includes thousands of photos organized by content, pornographic videos that can be viewed on your computer screen, stories, links to live sex shows, and links to live video cameras in places such as men's and women's locker rooms. Some also sell videos, CD-ROMs, sex aids such as dildos, and other sexual devices and costumes. Some also include interactive sex shows, where the viewer can request that the actors perform specific acts. Many of these sites specialize, featuring "teenagers" (if the actors are under 18, the material violates the law), Black, Asian, or Hispanic women, gays, lesbians, pregnant women, and on

and on. Each site charges a daily, weekly, or monthly "membership fee" for access; the fee can usually be paid by supplying a valid credit card number.

Computer porn is cause for concern, for several reasons. One is that the large and ever-increasing number of chat rooms, news groups, and Web sites facilitate a person becoming dependent on or addicted to (see Chapter 14) this type of sexual content (Yellowlees & Marks, 2007). None of these involve face-to-face social interaction, which is central to most sexual relationships; the risk is that they become a substitute. There is also a great deal of concern that children will access these materials. All sites include a printed notice that one must be over 18 to access the site, and that one who is offended by sexually explicit material should not enter the site. This "honor system" is not an effective control. It is true that to access a Web site or download photographs from bulletin boards, the user must supply a valid credit card number, but this is not a major deterrent for many adolescents. We discuss the regulation of Internet access by the law in Chapter 20.

Focus: First Person
Ernie: A Pedophile and Child Pornographer

In a study of child sexual abuse and child pornography, the investigators reported the following description of one offender:

Contact was made with Ernie, a northern Indiana man, and arrangements were made to meet with him to share child pornography collections. Ernie arrived at a motel room carrying a small suitcase containing approximately 75 magazines and a metal file box containing 12 super-8mm movies. The metal box was also filled with numerous photographs. Ernie then began to discuss his collection. He described himself as a pedophile and showed a series of instant photographs he had taken of his 7-year-old niece while she slept. The pictures revealed Ernie's middle finger inserted into the young girl's uncovered genitals, and he described how he had worked his finger up into her. Other photographs featured the girl being molested in various ways by Ernie while she remained asleep.

Despite the fact that he had engaged in numerous incidents of child molestation, Ernie had not been discovered because his victims remained asleep. He had molested and exploited both males and females, his own children, grandchildren, and neighborhood children. In order to photograph the uncovered genitals of his sleeping victims, Ernie had devised a string and hook mechanism. The hook was attached to the crotch of the panties, and he would uncover his sleeping victims' genitals as he photographed them with an instant-developing camera.

Ernie displayed his collection with the pride of a hobbyist. He exhibited photographs he had reproduced from magazines; he had reproduced these same photographs repeatedly and had engaged in a child pornography business from his residence.

While displaying his magazines and films, Ernie was arrested. A search warrant was obtained for his residence, and material seized from his one-bedroom apartment filled two pickup trucks. Numerous sexually explicit films, photographs, magazines, advertisements, and children's soiled underwear were confiscated. The panties had been encased in plastic, the child's school photograph featured with the panties. Also confiscated were nine cameras and a projector.

Several months passed before investigators found proof that Ernie had processed, through a central Indiana photographic lab, approximately 1,500 photographs per week. It is believed that Ernie sold these pictures at $2 each, grossing an estimated $3,000 per week.

Source: Burgess (1984), pp. 26–27.

Kiddie Porn

Kiddie porn features photographs or films of sexual acts involving children. It is viewed as the most reprehensible part of the porn industry because it produces such an obvious victim, the child model. Children, by virtue of their developmental level, cannot give truly informed consent to participation in such activities, and the potential for doing psychological and physical damage to them is great. Many states have moved to outlaw kiddie porn, making it illegal to photograph or sell such material. As of 1994, 38 states prohibited possession of child pornography (Posner & Silbaugh, 1996).

Again, the profit motives are strong. An advertisement in the magazine *Screw* offered $200 for little girls to appear in porn films, and dozens of parents responded. A reporter covering the scene said,

Some parents appeared in the movie with their children; others merely allowed their children to have sex. One little girl, age 11, who ran crying from the bedroom after being told to have sex with a man of 40, protested, "Mommy I can't do it." "You have to do it," her mother answered. "We need the money." And of course the little girl did. (Anson, 1977)

Some major, well-known films could easily be classified as kiddie porn. *Taxi Driver* featured Jodie Foster as a 12-year-old prostitute. And *Pretty Baby* launched the career of Brooke Shields, playing the role of a 12-year-old brothel prostitute in New Orleans. Shields herself was 12 years old when the film was made.

A study involving interviews with a national sample of law-enforcement personnel identified 2,500 arrests in 2001 for Internet sex crimes involving minors. Thirty-six percent involved possession, distribution, or trade of child pornography. More than 90 percent of the offenders were white men over 26; 97 percent acted alone (Wolak et al., 2003).

Kiddie porn: Pictures or films of sexual acts involving children.

Figure 16.6 Sex in advertising. Many advertisers, including Calvin Klein, use sexual images to sell products.

Advertising

Let's close our discussion of pornography by considering a mating of sex and money that all of us encounter every day—*sex in advertising.* Both subtle and obvious sexual promises are used to sell a wide variety of products. A muscular young man wearing low-slung jeans and no shirt sells Calvin Kleins. Abercrombie & Fitch catalogs feature photos of nude young people in bed or in pools. Perfumes promise that they will make women instantly sexually attractive. One brand of coffee seems to guarantee a warm, romantic, sensuous evening for the couple who drink it.

How much sexual content is there in advertising? One study analyzed the sexual content of magazine advertising in 1983 and 2003 (Reichert & Carpenter, 2004). Sexual clothing as well as portrayals of intimate contact became more frequent from 1983 to 2003. In 2003, for example, 78 percent of women in

ads in men's magazines were attired in sexually suggestive clothing. Sexually provocative behavior is another aspect of sex found in magazine advertising; in ads portraying heterosexual couples, 53 percent engaged in sexual contact (passionate kissing; simulated intercourse) (Reichert, 2002).

Television advertising uses not only bodily display or nudity and sexually suggestive interaction but also context (a Caribbean beach; a bed or bedroom) and language including double entendre (a message with two meanings, one being sexual) and talk about sexual activity. Some advertisers, such as Victoria's Secret and Calvin Klein, cultivate a sexually suggestive image. A study of prime-time commercials broadcast on NBC found that 12 percent of the female models and 2 percent of the male ones were dressed to be sexually suggestive. Network promotional ads were more likely to include sexual content. Sexual contact increased from 12 percent in 1990 to 21 percent in 1998. A review of the research on the effects of advertising concludes that sexual information attracts attention, and viewers are more likely to remember the sexual image; paradoxically, however, they are less likely to remember the brand name (Reichert, 2002).

Beyond the effects of ads on brand images and purchasing, there is concern that continuing exposure to ads that contain gender-stereotyped ideas and images—such as thin, attractive females and taut, buff males—may affect attitudes toward one's body. Male and female college students were shown 20 sexist ads, 15 sexist and 5 neutral, or no ads. The results indicated that exposure to the sexist ads was associated with dissatisfaction with one's body among *both* men and women (Lavine et al., 1999).

The Customers

What is known about the consumer of pornography? Studies consistently find that the typical customer in an X-rated bookstore is an educated, middle-class male between the ages of 22 and 34 (Mahoney, 1983). That is, the use of the materials sold in such stores is "typical" or "normal" (in the statistical sense) among males. But the range is wide. The manager of one store said,

> We get everyone in here from millionaires to scum of the earth. The blue-collar and white-collar men come for the tapes. Married couples come in for things to help their sex life. The gay crowd cruises the booths in back. Groups of women come in for gag items. (Moore, 1994)

Women purchase and watch pornographic videos. Research conducted in Australia in 1999 reported that 65 percent of X-rated videos were

Figure 16.7   Not all producers of porn are men. Women are increasingly involved in the production of sexually explicit video and Internet materials.

purchased by a woman or a heterosexual couple. In data from 280 women, 20 percent said they selected the video, 50 percent said both selected it, 18 percent said the partner selected it with both their preferences in mind, and 9 percent said the partner selected it (Contessini, 2003). Female interest in erotica was recognized 20 years ago by Candida Royale, then a film star, who became a producer and director who has made more than a dozen films directed toward women. A growing number of men and women are attempting to market to women, producing what is called *female-empowered* adult entertainment, including films, cable TV programs, sex toy stores, and Web sites.

Surveys also suggest that many students use sexually explicit materials. In one survey, 59 percent of white male college students and 36 percent of white female students said they went to X-rated movies or read pornographic books (Houston, 1981). More than 5 percent of the females and 9 percent of the males said they did so frequently or very frequently.

Repeat customers are a crucial part of the success of the porn business. "There are people who

come in here three to five times a day for their fix. Before work. At lunch. After work. Late at night. Their addiction isn't to the perversion of it, just the pornography" (Moore, 1994). It is estimated that millions of persons patronize adult retail stores annually in the United States. This makes them potentially important as sources of sexual health information and products (Reece et al., 2004). A survey of employees of 80 stores found that most sold condoms and lubricants, and up to one-half provided written health information. Partnerships with sexual health professionals and training for employees could exploit this potential.

Computer porn attracts a more varied clientele. Chat rooms and news groups attract both men and women of diverse ages (assuming that those who describe themselves are doing so accurately). Some of these people are married. There have been reports of a man or woman leaving a spouse or partner in order to live with someone he or she met via the Internet. Depending on the focus of the room or group, participants may be from diverse racial or ethnic backgrounds. Bulletin boards and

Table 16.2   Do you use porn? A survey by the Kinsey Institute (N = 10,453)

Sex		
	Male	80%
	Female	17%
Age		
	18 to 20	11%
	21 to 30	31%
	31 to 40	29%
	41 to 50	15%
	51 to 60	7%
	61 to 70	2%
	71 or older	1%
Viewed sexual images in the past month?		
	Never have viewed them	3%
	Not once, but I have in the past	20%
	One or two times	16%
	Once a week	10%
	A few times a week	27%
	Once a day	9%
	Several times a day	10%
How much time per week in the past month?		
	I did not use porn in the past month	11%
	Less than one hour	18%
	1 to 5 hours	37%
	6 to 15 hours	16%
	16 to 25 hours	6%
	26 to 50 hours	3%
	More than 50 hours	3%
Why do you use porn? (Top 5 answers)		
	To masturbate / for physical release	72%
	To sexually arouse myself and / or others	69%
	Out of curiosity	54%
	To fantasize about things I would not necessarily want in real life	43%
	To distract myself	38%

Source: An online survey conducted in association with Public Broadcasting System. Results at http://www.pbs.org/wgbh/pages/frontline/shows/porn/etc/surveyres.html.

adult Web sites probably attract the same types of clients as adult bookstores—middle-aged, middle-class, white men—although some emphasize materials oriented toward other clienteles. Table 16.2 presents results from an online survey that assessed the number of times and number of hours per month that users view sexual materials.

Feminist Objections to Pornography

Some, though not all, feminists are very critical of pornography (e.g., Griffin, 1981; Lederer, 1980; Morgan, 1978). Why would feminists, who prize sexual liberation, be opposed to pornography?

There are three basic reasons some feminists object to pornography. First, they argue that pornography debases women. In the milder, soft-core versions it portrays women as sex objects whose breasts, legs, and buttocks can be purchased and then ogled. In the hard-core versions women may be shown being urinated upon or being chained. To what extent does mainstream pornography objectify women? The answer depends in part on how one defines the term, and there is controversy over that. Defining objectification as including treating another person as an object, one partner dominating another, and penis worship, one researcher performed a content analysis of the 50 best-selling pornographic videos in Australia (McKee, 2005). Many of the videos were imports from the United States and Europe. Seven measures allowed direct comparison of portrayals of men and portrayals of women. On one, not having an orgasm, women were significantly higher than men. On three, less time spent looking at the camera, less time spent talking to the camera, and less likely to initiate sex, men were significantly higher than women. On three measures, having a name, being a central character, and time spent talking, there were no significant differences.

Second, pornography associates sex with violence toward women. As such, it contributes to rape and other forms of violence against women and girls. One feminist writer has put it bluntly: "pornography is the theory and rape is the practice" (Morgan, 1980, p. 139). This is a point that can be tested with scientific data, producing evidence that is covered in the next section.

Third, pornography shows—indeed, glamorizes—unequal power relationships between women and men. A common theme in pornography is men forcing women to have sex, so the power of men and subordination of women are emphasized. Consistent with this point, feminists do not object to sexual materials that portray women and men in equal, humanized relationships—what we have termed *erotica*.

Feminists also note the intimate relationship between pornography and traditional gender roles. Pornography is enmeshed as both cause and effect. That is, pornography in part results from traditional gender roles that make it socially acceptable for men to use and require hypersexuality and aggressiveness as part of the male role. In turn, pornography may serve to perpetuate traditional gender roles. By seeing or reading about dominant males and submissive, dehumanized females, each new generation of adolescent boys is socialized to accept these roles.

The Effects of Pornography[2]

Some of the assertions summarized above—for example, that using violent pornography may predispose men toward committing violent crimes against women—can be tested using the methods of social science. A number of social psychologists have been collecting data for 35 years to test such assertions.

Four questions can be asked about the effects of using pornography. First, does it produce sexual arousal? Second, does it affect users' attitudes, particularly about aggression toward women and rape? Third, does it affect the sexual behavior of users? Fourth, does it affect the aggressive or criminal behavior of users, particularly aggressive behavior toward women?

More than 40 studies have examined the effect of sexually explicit material on sexual arousal. This research consistently finds that exposure to *material*

that the viewer finds acceptable does produce arousal (Davis & Bauserman, 1993). Exposure to portrayals that the viewer finds objectionable produces a negative reaction. Most people disapprove of paraphiliac behaviors (see Chapter 14), rape, and sexual activity involving children, so they react negatively to hard-core and kiddie porn. The one exception is that men who report, before they view pornography, that they would commit rape under some circumstances are aroused by portrayals of rape.

There are gender differences in self-reports of response to sexually explicit materials. Men report higher levels of arousal to such portrayals than do women (Malamuth, 1998). The differences are larger in response to pornography than to erotica, and the difference is much larger among college students than among older persons (Murnen & Stockton, 1997). This difference between men and women is often attributed to the fact that most erotica and pornography is male oriented. The focus is almost exclusively on sexual behavior, with little character development or concern for relationships. There is limited foreplay and afterplay; the male typically ejaculates on some part of the woman's body (the "cum shot") rather than inside her. As noted earlier, former porn film star Candida Royale produces videos made for women. An experiment found that male college students responded positively to and were aroused by videos made for men and for women; females reported negative responses to the videos intended for males and positive responses and sexual arousal to the videos designed for women (Mosher & MacIan, 1994).

What about the effect of pornography on attitudes? The research indicates that a single exposure to stories, photographs, or videos has little or no effect. Massive exposure, such as viewing videos for five hours, does lead to more permissive attitudes. In this situation, viewers become more tolerant of the behavior observed and less in favor of restrictions on it (Davis & Bauserman, 1993). What about attitudes toward aggression against women? Some studies show that exposure to portrayals of rape lead men to be more tolerant of sexual assault, but other studies do not find a relationship between exposure and attitudes (Fisher & Grenier, 1994). Men exposed to portrayals of sexual aggression against women do not report a greater willingness to rape a woman (Davis & Bauserman, 1993).

With regard to sexual behavior, the research shows that, in response to erotic portrayals of consenting heterosexual activity, both men and women may report an increase in sexual thoughts and fantasies and in behaviors such as masturbation and intercourse. Exposure to portrayals of

[2]Note that this discussion refers to violent pornography. There are many other sexual images that are not of concern.

Figure 16.8   While there are differences between men and women in their response to pornography, some women enjoy watching a stripper as much as some men do. The final scenes of *The Full Monty* portray the pleasure both the male performers and the female audience experience.

behavior the person has not personally engaged in does *not* lead to an increase in these behaviors (Davis & Bauserman, 1993).

Finally, there has been great interest in whether exposure to portrayals of sexual aggression (which almost always involve men behaving aggressively toward women) increases aggressive behavior. In laboratory studies, males who are insulted or provoked by a woman will respond aggressively toward her if given the opportunity. Males who have been exposed to violent pornography are significantly more aggressive toward a woman in this situation, compared with men exposed to sexually explicit but nonviolent material. If the comparison group is men exposed to nonsexual violent films, many studies find no differences between the two, but some find that the exposure to sexual violence increases aggression toward a woman more than exposure just to violence (Davis & Bauserman, 1993).

In sum, then, we can conclude that exposure to sexually explicit material that the viewer finds acceptable is arousing to both men and women. Exposure to aggressive pornography does increase males' aggression toward women and may affect males' attitudes, making them more accepting of violence against women.

What Is the Solution?

These are disturbing conclusions. What is the solution? Should pornography be censored or made illegal? Or would this only make it forbidden and therefore more attractive, and still available on the black market? Or should all forms of pornography be legal and readily available, and should we rely on other methods—such as education of parents and students through the school system—to abolish its use? Or should we adopt some in-between strategy, making some forms of pornography—say, kiddie porn and violent porn—illegal, while allowing free access to erotica?

Our own opinion is that legal restrictions—known less politely as censorship—are probably

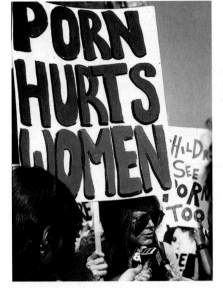

(a)

(b)

Figure 16.9   The controversy over pornography has put some members of the political left wing on the same side as some from the right wing. (*a*) Feminist Gloria Steinem protests pornography. (*b*) Conservatives have encouraged citizens to picket "adult" businesses located in or near residential neighborhoods.

not the solution. We agree with the view put forth by a group of researchers that a better solution is education (Donnerstein et al., 1987; Linz et al., 1987). In their experiments, they have debriefed male participants at the conclusion of the procedures. They then convey to the participants that media depictions are unreal and that the portrayal of women enjoying forced sex is fictitious. They dispel common rape myths, especially any that were shown in the film used in the experiment. Participants who have been debriefed in this way show less acceptance of rape myths and more sensitivity to rape victims than participants shown a neutral film (Donnerstein et al., 1987).

Subsequently, some researchers introduced *prebriefing* of participants in research involving exposure to sexually explicit materials. The typical briefing—pre or post—consists of a short audiotape or a printed handout pointing out that the material is fictional. It reminds participants that women do not enjoy forced sex and that rape is a serious crime. Researchers identified 10 studies that included prebriefing or debriefing, and measures of the effects of exposure to the material. All 10 found that there were no negative effects of exposure accompanied by an educational briefing. In 6 of the studies, participants were less accepting of rape myths at the conclusion of the study than at the beginning (Allen et al., 1996). This research provides solid evidence that education can eliminate at least negative effects on attitudes.

SUMMARY

Commercial sex is a major industry in the United States and increasingly around the world. Two prominent aspects of it are prostitution and pornography.

Commercial sex workers engage in partnered sexual activity in return for payment, such as money, gifts, or drugs. There are several venues in which they work in the United States, including their own homes, in-call services, out-call services, and massage parlors. The working conditions, risks, and income of a sex worker depend on the setting. Third parties who may be involved include a pimp, madam, or manager; the involvement of these people generally limits a worker's autonomy. Sex trafficking involves exploitation and is a major problem.

Research suggests that a sex worker's well-being depends on the risk level of the setting in which she works, the reasons she entered sex work, and whether she experienced victimization as a child or adolescent.

Data indicate that the use of prostitutes has declined substantially in the United States in the past 50 years. About one-half of the clients of female workers are occasional johns; the other 50 percent are repeat clients. Some men rely on sex workers for their sexual outlet.

Some male sex workers serve a female clientele. They may work as escorts, employees of massage parlors, or gigolos. Hustlers cater to a male homosexual clientele.

Distinctions are made among pornography (sexually arousing art, literature, or film), obscenity (material offensive to authorities or society), and erotica (sexual material that shows men and women in equal, humane relationships). Pornographic magazines, films, and videocassettes, both soft core (erotica) and hard core, are a multibillion-dollar business. Computer porn has mushroomed in the past 20 years; people can discuss explicit sexual activity online, read sexually arousing stories, download sexually explicit images, or purchase a variety of goods and services at adult Web sites. Children, often runaways, are the star victims in kiddie porn.

Some feminists object to pornography on the grounds that it debases women, encourages violence against women, and portrays unequal relationships between men and women.

Social–psychological research indicates that exposure to portrayals that the viewer finds acceptable is arousing to both men and women. Men are more likely to report arousal than women. Massive exposure leads to more favorable attitudes toward the behavior observed. Some studies find that exposure to violent pornography creates more tolerant attitudes toward violence against women, but others find no such effect. Exposure to portrayals of consenting heterosexual activity leads to an increase in sexual thoughts and behavior. Exposure to portrayals of sexual or nonsexual violence toward women increases men's aggression against women. Education about the effects of pornography is probably the best solution to the problems created by pornography.

QUESTIONS FOR THOUGHT, DISCUSSION, AND DEBATE

1. What is your position on the issue of censoring pornography? Do you think that all pornography should be illegal? Or should all pornography be legal? Or should some kinds—such as kiddie porn and violent porn—be illegal, but not other kinds? What reasoning led you to your position?

2. Prostitution is becoming more visible in your community. Some people are demanding stricter laws and longer sentences for women who exchange sex for money. They claim this will deter women from entering prostitution. Based on what you know about why women enter prostitution, their varied lifestyles, and the risks these women face, is this claim plausible? If not, what alternative approach would you suggest?

3. Many of the streetwalkers in major cities are black or Asian women. Adult Web sites often prominently display photographs, stories, and videos about "interracial sex." Yet most of the customers of both prostitutes and adult Web sites are white males. Why are white men attracted by materials featuring women from other ethnic groups? Why aren't more Black men among the customers for sexual services?

SUGGESTIONS FOR FURTHER READING

Albert, Alexa. (2001). *Brothel: Mustang Ranch and its women.* New York: Random House. This book is based on a qualitative study of Mustang Ranch. It includes the stories of some of the women who work there, their attitudes, their circumstances, and their sense of professionalism.

Bullough, Vern, & Bullough, Bonnie. (1987). *Women and prostitution: A social history.* Buffalo, NY: Prometheus Books. A fascinating history of the oldest profession, from ancient Greece and Rome through medieval times, India, and China, to the present.

Vanwesenbeeck, Ine. (1994). *Prostitutes' well-being and risk.* Amsterdam: VU University Press. An excellent empirical study of the determinants of psychological well-being among prostitutes.

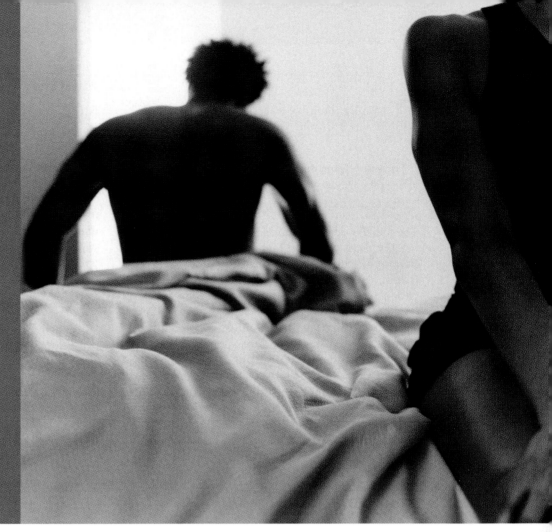

CHAPTER SEVENTEEN

Sexual Disorders and Sex Therapy

CHAPTER HIGHLIGHTS

The only thing we have to fear is fear itself.*

*Franklin Delano Roosevelt, First Inaugural Address, March 4, 1933.

Sexual disorders—such as premature (early) ejaculation in men and an inability to have orgasms in women—cause a great deal of psychological distress to the individuals troubled by them and to their partners. Until the 1960s, the only available treatment was long-term psychoanalysis, which is costly and inaccessible for most people. Masters and Johnson ushered in a new era in understanding and treatment with the publication, in 1970, of *Human Sexual Inadequacy*. This book reported on the team's research on sexual disorders, as well as on their rapid-treatment program of behavioral therapy. Since then, many additional developments have taken place in the field, including cognitive–behavior therapy and medical (drug) treatments. Sex disorders and treatments for them are the topics of this chapter.

A **sexual disorder** is a problem with sexual response that causes a person mental distress. The term *sexual dysfunction* is also used. Examples are a man's inability to get an erection and a woman's inability to orgasm. This definition seems fairly simple; however, in practice it can be difficult to determine exactly when something is a sexual disorder. In addition, there is a tendency to think in terms of only two categories, people with a sexual disorder and "normal" people. In fact, there is a continuum, much like the Kinsey scale for gradations in sexual orientation that we discussed in Chapter 13. Most of us have had, at one time or another, a sex problem that went away in a day or a few months without treatment. These cases represent the shades of gray that lie between absolutely great sexual functioning and long-term difficulties that require sex therapy.

Sexual disorders can be further classified. A **lifelong sexual disorder** is one that has been present ever since the person became sexual; an **acquired sexual disorder** is a dysfunction that develops after a period of normal functioning.

First we consider the kinds of sexual disorders, then review the causes of these disorders and the treatments for them.

Sexual disorder: A problem with sexual response that causes a person mental distress.
Lifelong sexual disorder: A sexual disorder that has been present ever since the person began sexual functioning.
Acquired sexual disorder: A sexual disorder that develops after a period of normal functioning.
Hypoactive sexual desire (HSD): A sexual disorder in which there is a lack of interest in sexual activity; also termed *inhibited sexual desire* or *low sexual desire.*

Kinds of Sexual Disorders

In this section we discuss the four categories of sexual disorders: desire disorders (hypoactive sexual desire, sexual aversion disorder), arousal disorders (female sexual arousal disorder, erectile disorder), orgasmic disorders (female orgasmic disorder, male orgasmic disorder, premature ejaculation), and sexual pain disorders (dyspareunia, vaginismus). Notice that the first three categories correspond to components of the sexual response cycle, discussed in Chapter 8.

Desire Disorders
Hypoactive Sexual Desire
Sexual desire, or *libido,* refers to an interest in sexual activity, leading the individual to seek out sexual activity or to be pleasurably receptive to it. When sexual desire is very low, so that the individual is not interested in sexual activity, this is a disorder termed **hypoactive sexual desire (HSD;** the prefix *hypo-* means "low") (Basson, 2004). It is also sometimes termed *inhibited sexual desire* or *low sexual desire.* This disorder is found in both women and men. The defining characteristics are lack of interest in sex or sharply reduced interest, or a lack of responsive desire (Basson, 2007). Many people's desire occurs before sexual activity begins and leads them to initiate sex, whereas in other cases they begin to feel desire as sexual activity starts; this latter pattern is called *responsive desire.*

People with HSD typically avoid situations that will evoke sexual feelings. If, despite their best efforts, they find themselves in an arousing situation, they experience a rapid "turn-off" so that they feel nothing. The turn-off may be so intense that they report negative, unpleasant feelings; they may even report *sexual anesthesia,* that is, no feeling at all, even though they may respond to the point of having an orgasm.

Surveys of the general population indicate that lack of interest in sex is common. Too little sexual desire is the most common sexual issue reported by women (Basson, 2006). Roughly 10 to 15 percent of women report no sexual desire, with the percentage increasing as women age (West et al., 2004). About half as many men as women experience desire problems, but men definitely can experience them (Laumann et al., 1999; Maurice, 2007).

Like other sexual disorders, HSD poses complex problems of definition. There are many circumstances when it is perfectly normal for a person's desire to be inhibited. For example, one cannot be expected to be turned on by every potential partner.

It is also often true that the problem is not the individual's absolute level of sexual desire but a discrepancy between the partners' levels (Zilbergeld & Ellison, 1980). That is, if one partner wants sex considerably less frequently than the other does, there is a conflict. This problem is termed **discrepancy of sexual desire.**

Sexual Aversion Disorder

In sexual aversion disorder, the person has a strong aversion involving anxiety, fear, or disgust to sexual interaction and actively avoids any kind of genital contact with a partner (American Psychiatric Association, 2000a). This problem causes great difficulty in the person's relationships. The prevalence of this disorder in the general population has not been documented in well-sampled studies, but experts believe that it is rare (Heiman, 2002a). It is fairly common, though, in persons who have panic disorder (Figueira et al., 2001).

Arousal Disorders

Female Sexual Arousal Disorder

Female sexual arousal disorder (FSAD) refers to a lack of response to sexual stimulation, including a lack of lubrication (American Psychiatric Association, 2000a). The disorder involves both a subjective, psychological component and a physiological element (Basson et al., 2004). Some cases are defined by the woman's own subjective sense that she does not feel aroused despite adequate stimulation, and others are defined by difficulties with vaginal lubrication.

Difficulties with lubrication are common, reported by 19 percent of the women in the NHSLS (Laumann et al., 1999). These problems become particularly frequent among women during and after menopause: As estrogen levels decline, vaginal lubrication decreases. The use of sterile lubricants is an easy way to deal with this problem. The absence of subjective feelings of arousal is more complex to treat.

Erectile Disorder

Erectile disorder is the inability to have an erection or maintain one. Other terms for it are *erectile dysfunction, inhibited sexual excitement,* and *impotence,* the term used by laypersons. One result of erectile disorder is that the man cannot engage in sexual intercourse. Using terminology discussed earlier, a case of erectile disorder may be either lifelong or acquired. In **lifelong erectile disorder,** the man has never been able to have an erection that is satisfactory for intercourse. In **acquired erectile disorder,** the man has difficulty getting or maintaining an erection but has had erections sufficient for intercourse at other times.

According to the NHSLS, about 10 percent of men have experienced an erection problem within the last 12 months (Laumann et al., 1999). This statistic varies greatly by age: It is only 7 percent for 18- to 29-year-olds, but 18 percent for 50- to 59-year-olds. Another national survey found rates of 19 percent in men aged 50 to 59 and 39 percent in men 60 and older (Carson et al., 2002). Studies in Germany and France have found similar rates (Braun et al., 2000; Giuliano et al., 2002). Erectile disorder is the most common of the disorders among men who seek sex therapy, particularly since the introduction of Viagra.

Psychological reactions to erectile disorder may be severe. For many men, it is one of the most embarrassing things they can imagine. Depression may follow from repeated episodes. It may also cause embarrassment or worry to the man's partner.

The causes of erectile disorder and its treatment will be discussed later in this chapter.

Orgasmic Disorders

Premature Ejaculation

Premature ejaculation (PE) occurs when a man has an orgasm and ejaculates too soon. In extreme cases, ejaculation may take place so soon after erection that it occurs before intercourse can even begin. In other cases, the man is able to delay the orgasm to some extent, but not as long as he would like or not long enough to meet his partner's preferences. Some experts prefer the terms *early ejaculation* or *rapid ejaculation* as having fewer negative connotations (Grenier & Byers, 2001; Lewis et al., 2004).

Although the definition given above—having an orgasm and ejaculating too soon—seems simple enough, in practice it is difficult to specify when a man is a premature ejaculator (Grenier & Byers, 1995; Metz et al., 1997). What should the precise criterion for "too soon" be? Should the man be required to last for at least 30 seconds after erection? For 12 minutes? For 2 minutes after insertion of the penis into the vagina? The definitions used by authorities in the field vary widely. One source defines "prematurity"

Discrepancy of sexual desire: A sexual disorder in which the partners have considerably different levels of sexual desire.

Female sexual arousal disorder (FSAD): A sexual disorder in which there is a lack of response to sexual stimulation.

Erectile (eh-REK-tile) disorder: The inability to have or maintain an erection.

Lifelong erectile disorder: Cases of erectile disorder in which the man has never had an erection sufficient to have intercourse.

Acquired erectile disorder: Cases of erectile disorder in which the man at one time was able to have satisfactory erections but can no longer do so.

Premature (early) ejaculation: A sexual disorder in which the man ejaculates too soon and thinks he cannot control when he ejaculates. Also called *rapid ejaculation.*

as the occurrence of orgasm less than 30 seconds after the penis has been inserted into the vagina. Another group has extended this to 90 seconds; for a third, the criterion is ejaculation before there have been 10 pelvic thrusts. Masters and Johnson defined premature ejaculation as the inability to delay ejaculation long enough for the woman to have an orgasm at least 50 percent of the time. This last definition has merit because it stresses the importance of the interaction between the two partners; however, it carries with it the question of how easily the woman is stimulated to orgasm. Psychiatrist and sex therapist Helen Singer Kaplan believed that the key to defining the premature ejaculator is the absence of voluntary control of orgasm; that is, the real problem is that the premature ejaculator has little control over when he orgasms (Kaplan, 1974; see also Grenier & Byers, 2001). Another good definition is self-definition: if a man finds that he has become greatly concerned about his lack of ejaculatory control or that it is interfering with his ability to form intimate relationships, or if a couple agree that it is a problem in their relationship, then it may reasonably be called premature ejaculation.

Premature ejaculation is a common problem in the general male population (Bancroft et al., 2005). In the NHSLS, 29 percent of the men reported having problems in the last 12 months with climaxing too early (Laumann et al., 1999). The great majority of men probably never seek therapy for the problem, either because it goes away by itself or because they are too embarrassed.

Like erectile disorders, premature ejaculation may create a web of related psychological problems. Because the ability to postpone ejaculation and "satisfy" a partner is so important in our concept of a man who is a competent lover, rapid ejaculation can cause a man to become anxious about his sexual competence. Furthermore, the partner may become frustrated because she or he is not having a satisfying sexual experience either. So the condition may create friction in the relationship.

The negative psychological effects of early ejaculation are illustrated by a young man in one of our sexuality classes who handed in an anonymous question. He described himself as a premature ejaculator and said that after several humiliating experiences during intercourse with dates, he was now convinced that no woman would want him in that condition. He no longer had the courage to ask women out, so he had stopped dating. He wanted to know how the women in the class would react to a man with such a problem. The question was discussed in class, and most of the women agreed that their reaction to his problem would depend a great deal on the quality of the relationship they had with him. If they cared deeply for him, they would be sympathetic and patient and help him overcome the difficulty. The point is, though, that the early ejaculation had created problems so severe that the young man not only had stopped having sex but also had stopped dating.

Male Orgasmic Disorder

Male orgasmic disorder, sometimes called *retarded ejaculation*, is the opposite of premature ejaculation. The man is unable to have an orgasm, or it is greatly delayed, even though he has a solid erection and has had more than adequate stimulation (Apfelbaum, 2000; Perelman & Rowland, 2006). The severity of the problem may range from only occasional problems with orgasming to a history of never having experienced an orgasm. In the most common version, the man is incapable of orgasm during intercourse but may be able to orgasm as a result of hand or mouth stimulation. Fortunately, these problems are rare.

Male orgasmic disorder is far less common than premature ejaculation. In the NHSLS, 8 percent of the male respondents had had a problem in the last 12 months with being unable to orgasm (Laumann et al., 1999). The incidence varies only slightly as a function of age: it was 7 percent for 18- to 29-year-olds and 9 percent for 50- to 59-year-olds. It also varies somewhat as a function of ethnicity, being more common among Asian Americans (19 percent) than whites or Blacks.

Male orgasmic disorder is, to say the least, a frustrating experience for the man. One would think that any woman would be delighted to have intercourse with a man who has a long-lasting erection that is not terminated by orgasm. In fact, though, some women react negatively to this condition, seeing their partner's inability to have an orgasm as a personal rejection. Some men, anticipating these negative reactions, have adopted the practice of faking orgasm. In some cases, too, the man's orgasmic disorder can create painful intercourse in the woman because intercourse simply goes on too long.

Female Orgasmic Disorder

Female orgasmic disorder is the inability to have an orgasm. This condition goes by a variety of other terms, including *orgasmic dysfunction, anorgasmia,* and *inhibited female orgasm.* Laypersons may call it *frigidity,* but sex therapists reject this

Male orgasmic disorder: A sexual disorder in which the man cannot have an orgasm, even though he is highly aroused and has had a great deal of sexual stimulation.
Female orgasmic disorder: A sexual disorder in which the woman is unable to have an orgasm.

term because it has derogatory connotations and is imprecise. *Frigidity* may refer to a variety of conditions ranging from total lack of sexual arousal to arousal without orgasm. Therefore, the term *female orgasmic disorder* is preferred.

Like the other sexual disorders, cases of female orgasmic disorder may be classified into lifelong and acquired. **Lifelong orgasmic disorder** refers to cases in which the woman has never in her life experienced an orgasm (American Psychiatric Association, 2000a). **Acquired orgasmic disorder** refers to cases in which the woman had orgasms at some time in her life but no longer does so. A common pattern is **situational orgasmic disorder,** in which the woman has orgasms in some situations but not others. For example, she may be able to have orgasms while masturbating but not while having sexual intercourse. Orgasmic disorders are common among women (Heiman, 2007). Roughly 20 percent of women report difficulties with anorgasmia (West et al., 2004).

Once again, though, these definitions become more complicated in practice than in theory. Consider the case of the woman who has orgasms as a result of masturbation or hand or mouth stimulation by a partner but who does not orgasm in vaginal intercourse. Is this really a sexual disorder? The notion that it is a disorder can be traced to sexual scripts and beliefs that there is a "right" way to have sex—with the penis inside the vagina—and a corresponding "right" way to have orgasms. Because this pattern of situational orgasmic disorder is so common, some experts consider it to be well within the normal range of female sexual response. Perhaps the woman who orgasms as a result of hand or mouth stimulation, but not penile thrusting, is simply having orgasms when she is adequately stimulated and is not having them when she is inadequately stimulated.

Nonetheless, there should be room for self-definition of disorders. If a woman has situational orgasmic disorder, is truly distressed that she is not able to have orgasms during vaginal intercourse, and wants therapy, then it may be appropriate to classify her condition as a disorder and provide therapy. The therapist, however, should be careful to explain to her the problems of definition raised above, in order to be sure that her request for therapy stems from her own dissatisfaction with her sexual responding rather than from an overly idealistic sexual script. Therapy in such cases is probably best viewed as an effort to enrich the client's experience rather than to fix a problem.

Pain Disorders

Painful Intercourse

Painful intercourse, or **dyspareunia,** refers to genital pain experienced during intercourse (American Psychiatric Association, 2000a). It is usually thought of as a female sexual disorder, but males occasionally experience it as well. In the NHSLS, 14 percent of the women reported pain during sex, compared with 3 percent of the men (Laumann et al., 1994). While complaints of occasional pain during intercourse are fairly common among women, persistent dyspareunia is not very common. In women, the pain may be felt in the vagina, around the vaginal entrance and clitoris, or deep in the pelvis. In men, the pain is felt in the penis or testes. To put it mildly, dyspareunia decreases one's enjoyment of the sexual experience and may even lead one to abstain from sexual activity.

According to another perspective, this disorder is really about pain that happens to occur in the genitals; that is, it is fundamentally about pain, not about sex (Binik et al., 2007). Many people, the reasoning goes, have back pain, some of them because of work-related injuries and others because of sports-related injuries. Yet we don't refer to work-induced back pain and sports-induced back pain but rather focus on the back pain itself. Similarly, with painful intercourse the focus should be on the genital pain suffered by those with this disorder.

Painful intercourse may be related to a variety of physical factors, to be discussed later.

Vaginismus

Vaginismus (the suffix *-ismus* means "spasm") is a spastic contraction of the outer third of the vagina (see Figure 17.1); in some cases it is so severe that the entrance to the vagina is closed and the woman cannot have intercourse (Leiblum, 2000). Vaginismus and dyspareunia are often associated (Binik et al., 2007). That is, if intercourse is painful, one result may be spasms that close off the entrance to the vagina.

Vaginismus is not a very common sexual disorder in the general population. Women may be more likely to seek treatment for it than for other disorders because it can make intercourse impossible, creating enormous difficulties in a couple's relationship.

Lifelong orgasmic disorder: A case of female orgasmic disorder in which the woman has never in her life had an orgasm.
Acquired orgasmic disorder: A case of female orgasmic disorder in which the woman had orgasms at some time in her life but no longer does so.
Situational orgasmic disorder: A case of orgasmic disorder in which the woman is able to have an orgasm in some situations (e.g., while masturbating) but not in others (e.g., while having sexual intercourse).
Dyspareunia (dis-pah-ROO-nee-uh): Painful intercourse.
Vaginismus (vaj-in-IS-mus): A sexual disorder in which there is a spastic contraction of the muscles surrounding the entrance to the vagina, in some cases so severe that intercourse is impossible.

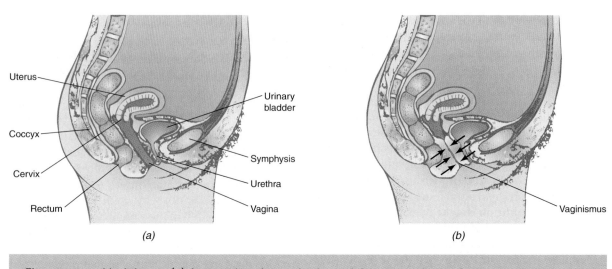

Uterus
Coccyx
Cervix
Rectum
Urinary bladder
Symphysis
Urethra
Vagina

(a)

Vaginismus

(b)

Figure 17.1   Vaginismus. (*a*) A normal vagina and other pelvic organs, viewed from the side, and (*b*) vaginismus, or involuntary constriction of the outer third of the vagina.

What Causes Sexual Disorders?

There are many causes of sexual disorders, varying from person to person and from one disorder to another. Several categories of factors may be related to sexual disorders: physical factors (organic factors and drugs), individual psychological factors, combined cognitive and physiological factors, and interpersonal factors. Each of these categories is discussed here.

Physical Causes

Physical factors that cause sexual disorders include **organic factors** (such as diseases or injuries) and drugs. Organic factors that have been implicated in various disorders are discussed first, followed by a discussion of the effects of drugs.

Erectile Disorder

Perhaps 50 percent or more of cases of erectile disorder (ED) may be due to organic factors or to a combination of organic and other factors (Buvat et al., 1990; Richardson, 1991).

Diseases associated with the heart and the circulatory system are particularly likely to be associated with the condition, since erection itself depends on the circulatory system (Rosen, 2007). Any kind of vascular pathology (problems in the blood vessels supplying the penis) can produce erection problems. Erection depends

Organic factors of sexual disorders: Physical factors, such as disease or injury, that cause sexual disorders.

on having a great deal of blood flowing into the penis via the arteries, with simultaneous constricting of the veins so that the blood cannot flow out as rapidly as it is coming in. Thus damage to either these arteries or the veins may produce erectile disorder.

Erectile disorder is associated with diabetes mellitus. Several aspects of diabetes are involved, including circulation problems and peripheral nerve damage (Sáenz de Tejada et al., 2004). In fact, erectile disorder may in some cases be the earliest symptom of a developing case of diabetes. Of course, not all diabetic men have erectile disorders; indeed, the majority do not. One estimate is that 28 percent of men with diabetes have an erectile disorder (Sáenz de Tejada et al., 2004).

Hypogonadism—an underfunctioning of the testes so that testosterone levels are very low—is associated with ED (Morales & Heaton, 2001). ED is also associated with a condition called hyperprolactinemia, in which there is excessive production of prolactin (Johri et al., 2001).

Any disease or injury that damages the lower part of the spinal cord may cause erectile disorder, since that is the location of the erection reflex center (see Chapter 8). Erectile disorder may also result from severe stress or fatigue. Finally, some, though not all, kinds of prostate surgery may cause the condition (Burnett, 2005).

With erectile disorders, as with most sexual disorders, it is important to recognize that the distinction between organic causes and psychological causes is too simple. Many sexual disorders result from a complex interplay of the two causes (Rosen, 2007). For example, a man who has circulatory problems that initially cause him to have erection problems is likely to develop anxieties about erection, which in turn may create further difficulties. This notion of dual causes has important implications for therapy. Many people with such disorders require both medical treatment and psychotherapy.

Premature Ejaculation

Rapid ejaculation is more often caused by psychological than physical factors. In cases of acquired disorder, though, in which the man at one time had ejaculatory control but later lost it, physical factors may be involved. A local infection such as prostatitis may be the cause, as may degeneration in the related parts of the nervous system, which may occur in neural disorders such as multiple sclerosis.

An intriguing explanation for early ejaculation comes from the sociobiologists (Hong, 1984). Their idea is that rapid ejaculation has been selected for in the process of evolution, what we might call "survival of the fastest." In monkeys and apes, the argument goes, copulating and ejaculating rapidly would be advantageous in that the female would be less likely to get away and the male would be less likely to be attacked by other sexually aroused males while he was copulating. Thus males who ejaculated quickly were more likely to survive and to reproduce. Interestingly, among chimpanzees, which some see as our nearest evolutionary relatives, the average time from intromission (insertion of the penis into the vagina) to ejaculation is 7 seconds (Tutin & McGinnis, 1981). In modern U.S. society, of course, rapid ejaculation is not particularly advantageous and might even lead a man to have difficulty finding partners. Nonetheless, according to the sociobiologists, plenty of genes for rapid ejaculation are still hanging around from the natural selection that occurred thousands of years ago. (For a critique of this hypothesis, see Bixler, 1986.)

Male Orgasmic Disorder

Male orgasmic disorder, or retarded ejaculation, may be associated with a variety of medical or surgical conditions, such as multiple sclerosis, spinal cord injury, and prostate surgery (McMahon et al., 2004). Most commonly, though, it is associated with psychological factors.

Female Orgasmic Disorder

Orgasmic disorder in women may be caused by severe illness, general ill health, or extreme fatigue. Injury to the spinal cord can cause orgasm problems

(Sipski et al., 2001). However, most cases are caused by psychological factors.

Painful Intercourse

Dyspareunia in women is often caused by organic factors, including the following:

1. *Disorders of the vaginal entrance.* Irritated remnants of the hymen; painful scars, perhaps from an episiotomy or sexual assault; or infection of the Bartholin glands.
2. *Disorders of the vagina.* Vaginal infections; allergic reactions to spermicidal creams or the latex in condoms or diaphragms; a thinning of the vaginal walls, which occurs naturally with age; or scarring of the roof of the vagina, which can occur after a hysterectomy.
3. *Pelvic disorders.* Pelvic infection such as pelvic inflammatory disease, endometriosis, tumors, cysts, or a tearing of the ligaments supporting the uterus.

Painful intercourse in men can also be caused by a variety of organic factors. For an uncircumcised man, poor hygiene may be a cause; if the penis is not washed thoroughly with the foreskin retracted, material may collect under the foreskin, causing infection. Phimosis, a condition in which the foreskin cannot be pulled back, can also cause painful intercourse. An allergic reaction to spermicidal creams or to the latex in condoms may also be involved. Finally, various prostate problems may cause pain on ejaculation.

Vaginismus

Vaginismus is sometimes caused by painful intercourse, and therefore by organic factors that cause that condition (Binik et al., 2007). More frequently, though, it is caused by individual psychological factors or interpersonal factors (Rosen & Leiblum, 1995b).

Drugs

Some drugs may have side effects that cause sexual disorders (Segraves & Balon, 2003). For example, some drugs used to treat high blood pressure increase problems with erection in men and with decreased sexual desire in both men and women. Although it would be impossible to list every drug effect on every aspect of sexual functioning, some of the major drugs that may cause sexual disorders are listed in Table 17.1. Here we consider the effects of alcohol, illicit drugs, and prescription drugs.

Table 17.1   Drugs That May Impair—or Improve—Sexual Response

Drug	How It Affects Sexual Functioning	Common Medical Uses
1. Psychoactive Drugs		
Antianxiety drugs/tranquilizers		Anxiety, panic disorders
Buspirone	Enhanced desire, orgasm	
Benzodiazepines (Librium, Valium, Ativan)	Decreases hypoactive desire, improves premature ejaculation	
Antidepressants I: Tricyclics	Desire disorders, erection problems, orgasm problems, ejaculation problems May treat hypersexuality, premature ejaculation	Depression
Antidepressants II: Serotonin reuptake inhibitors (Paxil, Prozac, Zoloft)	Desire disorders, erection problems, orgasm problems	Depression, obsessive-compulsive disorder, panic disorders
Lithium	Desire disorders, erection problems	Bipolar disorder
Antipsychotics Thorazine, Haldol	Desire disorders, erection problems, orgasm problems, ejaculation problems	Schizophrenia
2. Antihypertensives		High blood pressure
Reserpine, Methyldopa	Desire disorders, erection difficulties, orgasm delayed or blocked	
Ace inhibitors (Vasotec)	Erection difficulties	
3. Substance Use and Abuse		
Alcohol	At low doses, increases desire At high doses, decreases erection, arousal, orgasm Alcoholism creates many disorders and atrophied testicles, infertility	
Nicotine	Decreases blood flow to penis, creates erectile disorder	
Opiods		
Endogenous: Endorphines	Sense of well-being and relaxation	
Heroin	Decrease in desire, orgasm, ejaculation, replaces sex	
Marijuana	Enhances sexual pleasure but not actual performance; chronic use decreases desire	

Sources: Ashton (2007); Meston et al. (2004); Segraves & Balon (2003).

Alcohol

The effects of alcohol on sexual responding vary considerably. We can think of these effects as falling into three categories: (1) short-term pharmacological effects, (2) expectancy effects, and (3) long-term effects of chronic alcohol abuse. In regard to the last category, alcoholics, particularly in the later stages of alcoholism, frequently have sexual disorders, typically including erectile disorder, orgasmic disorder, and loss of desire (Segraves & Balon, 2003). These sex problems may be the result of any of a number of organic effects of long-term alcoholism. For example, chronic alcoholism in men may cause disturbances in sex hormone production because of atrophy of the testes. Chronic alcohol abuse, too, generally has negative effects on the person's interpersonal relationships, which may contribute to sexual disorders.

What about the person who is not an alcoholic but rather has had one or many drinks on a particular evening and then proceeds to a sexual interaction? As noted earlier, there is an interplay of two effects: expectancy effects and actual pharmacological effects (George & Stoner, 2000; George et al., 2006). Many people have the expectation that alcohol will loosen them up, making them more sociable and sexually uninhibited. These expectancy effects in themselves produce increased physiological arousal and subjective feelings of arousal. Expectancy effects, though, interact with the pharmacological effects and work mainly at low doses, that is, when only a little alcohol has been consumed. At high dosage levels, alcohol acts as a depressant and sexual arousal is markedly suppressed, in both men and women.[1]

[1]Some refer to the resulting erection problems as "whiskey dick."

(a)   *(b)*

Figure 17.2   Alcohol and cocaine are popular recreational drugs that many people believe enhance sexual experience. Research shows, though, that high levels of alcohol suppress sexual arousal, and repeated use of cocaine is associated with loss of sexual desire, orgasm disorders, and erection problems.

Illicit or Recreational Drugs

There is a widespread belief that *marijuana* has aphrodisiac properties. Little scientific research has been done on its actual effects, and most of what has been done is old and based on small samples. Therefore we can provide only tentative ideas about the effects of marijuana on sexual functioning. In surveys of users, many respondents report that it increases sexual desire and makes sexual interactions more pleasurable (McKay, 2005). In regard to potential negative effects, there is concern that marijuana use contributes to risky sexual behavior such as unprotected sex (Collins et al., 2005). Chronic users report decreased sexual desire (Segraves & Balon, 2003). In studies of the general population, marijuana use has been associated with orgasmic disorder (Johnson et al., 2004).

Among drug users, *cocaine* is reported to be the drug of choice for enhancing sexual experiences. It is said to increase sexual desire, enhance sensuality, and delay orgasm. Chronic use of cocaine, however, is associated with loss of sexual desire, orgasmic disorders, and erectile disorders (Segraves & Balon, 2003). The effects also depend on the means of administration—whether the cocaine is inhaled, smoked, or injected. The most negative effects on sexual functioning occur among those who regularly inject the drug. Crack cocaine is highly addictive, and the crack epidemic, especially in the inner city, often involves the exchange of sex for drugs (Green et al., 2005).

Stimulant drugs, notably *amphetamines,* are associated with increased sexual desire and better control of orgasm in some studies (Segraves & Balon, 2003). Injection of amphetamines itself causes a physical sensation that is described by some as a total-body orgasm. In some cases, though, orgasm becomes difficult or impossible when using amphetamines.

Crystal methamphetamine ("ice") is a recreational drug that is of particular concern because, while high on it, people have a tendency to engage in risky sexual behaviors (Semple et al., 2004; Urbina & Jones, 2004; Wohl et al., 2002). One study of heterosexual, HIV-negative adults using meth indicated that, over a two-month period, they averaged 22 acts of unprotected vaginal sex and 9 different sex partners (Semple et al., 2004). Crystal meth can also lead to paranoia, hallucinations, and violent behavior (Brecht et al., 2004). We cannot recommend it.

The *opiates* or narcotics, such as morphine, heroin, and methadone, have strong suppression effects on sexual desire and response (Segraves & Balon, 2003). Long-term use of heroin, in particular, leads to decreased testosterone levels in males.

Prescription Drugs

Table 17.1 provides a partial list of prescription drugs that can affect sexual responding.

Some *psychiatric drugs*—that is, drugs used in the treatment of psychological disorders—may affect sexual functioning (Segraves & Balon, 2003). In general, these drugs have their beneficial psychological effects because they alter neurotransmitter levels and the functioning of the central nervous system. But these CNS alterations in turn affect sexual functioning. For example, the drugs used to treat schizophrenia may cause delayed orgasm or "dry orgasm" in men—that is, orgasm with no ejaculation. Tranquilizers and antidepressants often improve sexual responding as a result of improvement of the person's mental state. However, there may also be negative effects. Some of the antidepressants, for example, are associated with problems of both arousal and delayed orgasm in men as well as women. A few antidepressants—most notably, bupropion (Wellbutrin)—have few sexual side effects and are becoming popular for that very reason.

The list of other prescription drugs that can affect sexual functioning is long, so we will mention just two examples. Antihistamines can reduce vaginal lubrication. Some of the antihypertensive drugs (used to treat high blood pressure) can cause erection problems in men (Segraves & Balon, 2003). Most of the research on antihypertensive drug effects has been done with men, so we have less knowledge of these effects on women, although sexual problems have been reported among women using antihypertensive drugs. Some of the drugs used to treat epilepsy appear to cause erection problems and decreased sexual desire, although epilepsy by itself also seems to be associated with sexual disorders.

Psychological Causes

Immediate Psychological Causes

The psychological sources of sexual disorders include immediate causes and prior learning. **Prior learning** refers to the things that people have learned earlier—for example, in childhood—that now inhibit their sexual response. **Immediate causes** are various things that happen in the act of lovemaking itself that inhibit the sexual response.

The following four factors have been identified as immediate psychological causes of sexual disorder: (1) anxieties such as fear of failure, (2) cognitive interference, (3) failure of the partners to communicate, and (4) failure to engage in effective, sexually stimulating behavior.

Masters and Johnson theorized that *anxiety* during intercourse can be a source of sexual disorders. Anxiety may be caused by fear of failure—that is, fear of being unable to perform. But anxiety itself can block sexual response in some people. Often anxiety can create a vicious cycle of self-fulfilling prophecy in which fear of failure produces a failure, which produces more fear, which produces another failure, and so on. For example, a man may have one episode of erectile dysfunction, perhaps after drinking too much at a party. The next time he has sex, he anxiously wonders whether he will "fail" again. His anxiety is so great that he cannot get an erection. At this point he is convinced that the condition is permanent, and all future sexual activity is marked by such intense fear of failure that erectile disorder results. The prophecy is fulfilled.

Cognitive interference is a second immediate cause of sexual disorders. It refers to thoughts that distract the person from focusing on the erotic experience. The problem is basically one of attention and of whether the person is focusing his or her attention on erotic thoughts or on distracting thoughts (Will my technique be good enough to please her? Will my body be beautiful enough to arouse him?). **Spectatoring,** a term coined by Masters and Johnson, is one kind of cognitive interference. The person behaves like a spectator or judge of his or her own sexual "performance." People who do this are constantly (mentally) stepping outside the sexual act in which they are engaged, to evaluate how they are doing, mentally commenting, "Good job," or "Lousy," or "Could stand improvement." Today, both men and women experience performance-related distractions, but men experience more performance-related distractions

---

Prior learning: Things that people have learned earlier—for example, in childhood—that now affect their sexual response.

Immediate causes: Various factors that occur in the act of lovemaking that inhibit sexual response.

Cognitive interference: Negative thoughts that distract a person from focusing on the erotic experience.

Spectatoring: Masters and Johnson's term for acting as an observer or judge of one's own sexual performance; thought to contribute to sexual disorders.

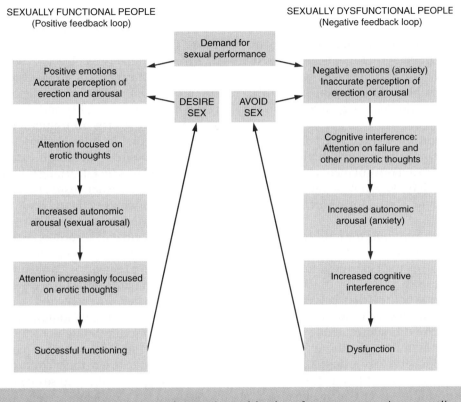

SEXUALLY FUNCTIONAL PEOPLE
(Positive feedback loop)

SEXUALLY DYSFUNCTIONAL PEOPLE
(Negative feedback loop)

Demand for
sexual performance

Positive emotions
Accurate perception of
erection and arousal

DESIRE
SEX

AVOID
SEX

Negative emotions (anxiety)
Inaccurate perception of
erection or arousal

Attention focused on
erotic thoughts

Cognitive interference:
Attention on failure and
other nonerotic thoughts

Increased autonomic
arousal (sexual arousal)

Increased autonomic
arousal (anxiety)

Attention increasingly focused
on erotic thoughts

Increased cognitive
interference

Successful functioning

Dysfunction

Figure 17.3   This model shows how anxiety and cognitive interference can produce erectile dysfunction and other sexual disorders (Barlow, 1986).

and women experience more appearance-related distractions (Meana & Nunnink, 2006; Purdon & Holdaway, 2006). These ideas on the importance of cognition in sexual disorder derive from the cognitive theories of sexual responding discussed in Chapters 2 and 8.

Sex researcher David Barlow (1986) ran an elegant series of experiments to test the ways in which anxiety and cognitive interference affect sexual functioning. He studied men who were functioning well sexually and men with sexual disorders, particularly erectile disorder. We will call these two groups the *functionals* and the *dysfunctionals*. He found that functionals and dysfunctionals respond very differently to stimuli in sexual situations. For example, anxiety (induced by the threat of being shocked) *increases* the arousal of functional men, but *decreases* the arousal of dysfunctional men while watching erotic films. Demands for performance (e.g., the experimenter says the research participant must have an erection or he will be shocked) increase the arousal of functionals but are distracting to (create cognitive interference in) and decrease the arousal of dysfunctionals. When

both self-reports of arousal and physiological measures of arousal (the penile strain gauge) are used, dysfunctional men consistently underestimate their physical arousal, whereas functional men are accurate in their reporting.

From these laboratory findings, Barlow constructed a model that describes how anxiety and cognitive interference act together to produce sexual disorders such as erectile disorder (see Figure 17.3). When dysfunctionals are in a sexual situation, there is a performance demand. This causes them to feel negative emotions such as anxiety. They then experience cognitive interference and focus their attention on nonerotic thoughts, such as thinking about how awful it will be when they don't have an erection. This increases arousal of their autonomic nervous system. To them, that feels like anxiety, whereas a functional person would experience it as sexual arousal. For the dysfunctionals, the anxiety creates further cognitive interference, and eventually the sexual performance is dysfunctional—they don't manage to get an erection. This leads them to avoid future sexual encounters or, when they are in one, to experience negative feelings, and the vicious cycle repeats itself.

This analysis is insightful and is backed by numerous well-controlled experiments. It fails to tell us, however, how the dysfunctionals got into this pattern in the first place. That explanation probably has to do with prior learning, discussed in the next section.

It is also important to note that anxiety produces sex problems only in some men—the dysfunctionals. For the majority of men, who function well sexually, anxiety does not impair sexual responding. The same is true for women (Elliott & O'Donohue, 1997).

Third, *failure to communicate* is one of the most important immediate causes of sexual disorders. Many people expect their partners to have ESP concerning their own sexual needs. You are the leading expert in the field of what feels good to you, and your partner will never know what turns you on unless you make this known, either verbally or nonverbally. But many people do not communicate their sexual desires. For example, a woman who needs a great deal of clitoral stimulation to have an orgasm may never tell her partner this; as a result, she does not get the stimulation she needs and consequently does not orgasm.

A fourth immediate cause of sexual disorders is a *failure to engage in effective sexually stimulating behavior.* Often this is a result of simple ignorance. For example, some couples may seek sex therapy because of the wife's failure to have orgasms; the therapist soon discovers that neither the husband nor wife is aware of the location of the clitoris, much less of its fantastic erotic potential. Often such cases can be cleared up by simple educational techniques.

Prior Learning

Another major category of psychological sources of sexual disorders is *prior learning.* This category includes various things that were learned or experienced in childhood, adolescence, or even adulthood.

In some cases of sexual disorders, the person's first sexual act was traumatic. An example would be a young man who could not get an erection the first time he attempted intercourse and was laughed at by his partner. Such an experience sets the stage for future erectile disorder.

Seductive behavior by parents and child sexual abuse by parents or other adults are the more serious of the traumatic early experiences that lead to later sexual disorders (Najman et al., 2005). A history of sexual abuse is frequently reported by

women seeking therapy for problems with sexual desire, arousal, or aversion (Leonard & Follette, 2002). The findings are similar for men with desire or arousal problems (Loeb et al., 2002).

In some other cases of sexual disorders, the person grew up in a very strict, religious family and was taught that sex is dirty and sinful. Such a person may have grown up thinking that sex is not pleasurable, that it should be gotten over with as quickly as possible, and that it is for purposes of procreation only. Such learning inhibits the enjoyment of a full sexual response; in fact, to use Byrne's terminology (Chapter 8), it may create an erotophobic personality.

Another source of disorders originating in the family occurs when parents punish children severely for sexual activity such as masturbation. An example is the little girl who is caught masturbating, is punished severely, and is told never to "touch herself" again; in adulthood she finds that she cannot orgasm through masturbation or as a result of hand stimulation by her partner.

Parents who teach their children the double standard may contribute to sexual disorders, particularly in their daughters. Many women whose sexual response is inhibited in adulthood were taught as children that no nice lady is interested in sex or enjoys it.

Emotional Factors

Although researchers and therapists have focused mainly on cognitions such as negative or distracting thoughts as psychological sources of sexual disorders, emotions can play a role as well and are now being investigated. Depression, for example, is associated with erectile disorder and other sexual disorders (Araujo et al., 1998; Frohlich & Meston, 2002). Emotions such as anger and sadness can interfere with sexual responding (Araujo et al., 2000). And as we saw earlier, anxiety can be a powerful impediment to sexual functioning.

Behavioral or Lifestyle Factors

Smoking, alcohol consumption, and obesity are all associated with higher rates of sexual disorders, and all involve behavior (Derby et al., 2000; Segraves & Balon, 2003). As such, they are quite modifiable. A study of obese men between the ages of 35 and 55 showed that regular physical exercise reduced their body mass index (BMI) and the incidence of erectile disorder (Esposito et al., 2004).

Combined Cognitive and Physiological Factors

In Chapter 11 we discussed the two-component theory of love, which holds that we experience love when two conditions are present: physiological arousal and a cognitive label of "love" attached to it (Berscheid & Walster, 1974). An analogous cognitive–physiological model of sexual functioning and dysfunction has also been proposed (Palace, 1995a, 1995b). According to this model, we function well sexually when we are physiologically aroused and interpret that as sexual arousal (rather than something else, like nervousness). As we've seen from Barlow's research, people with sexual disorders tend to interpret that arousal as anxiety. In addition, the physiological processes and cognitive interpretations form a feedback loop (see discussion of cognitive theories in Chapter 2). That is, interpreting arousal as sexual arousal increases one's arousal further.

In a clever experiment based on this model, women with sexual disorders were exposed, in a laboratory setting, to a frightening movie, which increased their general autonomic arousal (Palace, 1995b). The women were then shown a brief erotic video and given feedback (actually false) that their genitals had shown a strong arousal response to it. This feedback created a cognitive interpretation for the way they were feeling. The combination of general autonomic arousal and the belief that they were responding with strong sexual arousal led these women, compared with the controls, to greater vaginal arousal responses and subjective reports of arousal in subsequent sessions. This demonstration of the effectiveness of combined physiological and cognitive factors is particularly striking because the women began with problems in sexual responding.

Following from these ideas, many experts today recommend a combination of medical and psychological treatments for sexual disorders, as discussed later in this chapter (Rosen, 2007).

Interpersonal Factors

Disturbances in a couple's relationship are another leading cause of sexual disorders (Althof et al., 2004). Anger or resentment toward one's partner does not create an optimal environment for sexual enjoyment. Sex can also be used as a weapon to hurt a partner; for example, a woman can hurt her husband by refusing to engage in a sexual behavior that he wants. Conflicts over power may contribute to sex problems.

Intimacy problems in a relationship can be a factor in sexual disorders. These problems typically represent a combination of individual psychological factors and relationship problems. Some individuals have a fear of intimacy—that is, of deep emotional closeness to another person (Kaplan, 1979). Indeed, some people seem to like sex but fear intimacy. They would prefer to watch TV or talk about the weather or have sex than to engage in a truly intimate, emotionally vulnerable, trusting conversation with another person. They typically progress in a dating relationship to a certain degree of closeness and then lose interest. This pattern is repeated with successive partners. The fear of intimacy may be a result of negative or disappointing intimate relationships, particularly with parents, in early childhood. The fear of intimacy causes a person to draw back from a sexual relationship before it becomes truly fulfilling.

A New View of Women's Sexual Problems and Their Causes

Over the past decade, a group of sex therapists specializing in treating women's sex problems worked together to formulate what they call a New View of the nature of women's sexual problems and their causes (Tiefer, 2001). This new view is critical of the categories of disorders formulated by the American Psychiatric Association in the *DSM* and listed earlier in this chapter. It argues that these diagnostic categories have three flaws: (1) they treat male sexuality and female sexuality as totally equivalent, when they differ in some important ways; (2) they ignore the relational context of sexuality and desires for emotional intimacy; and (3) they ignore differences among women and naturally occurring variations in women's sexuality.

These experts proposed new categories of sexual disorders for women, as described below.

Sexual Problems Due to Sociocultural, Political, or Economic Factors

This category includes problems due to (1) ignorance and anxiety due to inadequate sexuality education, lack of access to health services, or other social constraints; (2) sexual avoidance or distress due to perceived inability to meet cultural norms regarding ideal sexuality (e.g., anxiety about one's body or about sexual orientation); (3) inhibitions due to conflict between the norms of one's culture of origin and those of the dominant culture; and (4) lack of interest or fatigue due to family and work obligations.

Sexual Problems Relating to Partner and Relationship

Problems in this category involve (1) sexual inhibition or distress arising from betrayal or fear of the partner because of abuse; (2) discrepancies in desire or preferences for sexual activities; (3) ignorance or inhibition about sexual communications; (4) loss of sexual interest as a result of conflicts over issues such as money, or resulting from traumatic experiences such as infertility; and (5) loss of arousal due to partner's health or sexual problems.

Sexual Problems Due to Psychological Factors

This category includes the following problems: (1) sexual aversion or inhibition of sexual pleasure due to past experiences of physical, sexual, or emotional abuse; personality problems with attachment or rejection; or depression or anxiety; and (2) sexual inhibition due to fear of sexual acts or their possible consequences, such as pain during intercourse or fear of pregnancy or STIs.

Sexual Problems Due to Medical Factors

When sexual problems arise despite a supportive interpersonal situation, adequate sexual knowledge, and positive attitudes, they may be a result of (1) any number of medical conditions that affect neurological, circulatory, endocrine, or other systems of the body; (2) pregnancy or STIs; (3) side effects of medications.

As you can see, this way of thinking about sexual disorders and their causes in women is considerably different from the dominant ways of thinking and the categories listed in the DSM. Do you think these categories of disorders and their causes would apply equally well to men?

Therapies for Sexual Disorders

A variety of therapies for sexual disorders are available, each relying on a different theoretical understanding of what causes sexual disorders. Here we examine four major categories of therapies: behavior therapy, cognitive–behavioral therapy, couple therapy, and biomedical therapies.

Behavior Therapy

Behavior therapy has its roots in behaviorism and learning theory. The basic assumption is that sex problems are the result of prior learning (as discussed earlier) and that they are maintained by ongoing reinforcements and punishments (immediate causes). It follows that these problem behaviors can be unlearned by new conditioning. One of the key techniques is systematic

> **Behavior therapy:** A system of therapy based on learning theory, in which the focus is on the problem behavior and how it can be modified or changed.
>
> **Sensate focus exercise:** A part of the sex therapy developed by Masters and Johnson in which one partner caresses the other, the other communicates what is pleasurable, and there are no performance demands.

desensitization, in which the client is gradually led through exercises that reduce anxiety.

In 1970, Masters and Johnson reported on their development of a set of techniques for sex therapy and ushered in a new era of sex therapy. They operated from a behavior therapy model because they saw sexual disorders as learned behaviors rather than as symptoms of psychiatric illness. If sexual disorders are the result of learning, they can be unlearned. Masters and Johnson used a rapid two-week program of intensive therapy that consisted mainly of education and specific behavioral exercises, or "homework assignments."

One of the basic goals of Masters and Johnson's therapy was to eliminate goal-oriented sexual performance. Many clients believe that in sex they must perform and achieve certain things. If sex is an achievement situation, it can also become the scene of failure, and perceived failures lead people to believe that they have a sexual problem. The form of cognitive interference known as *spectatoring* (discussed earlier) contributes to this problem because it generates anxiety and other unpleasant feelings. The idea is to use therapy techniques to reduce anxiety.

In one technique used in behavior therapy to eliminate a goal-oriented attitude toward sex, the couple is forbidden to have sexual intercourse until they are specifically permitted to by the therapists. They are assigned **sensate focus exercises** that reduce the demands on them. As the couple successfully complete each of these exercises, the sexual component of subsequent exercises is gradually increased. The couple chalk up a series of successes until eventually they are having intercourse and the disorder has disappeared.

Sensate focus exercises are based on the notion that touching and being touched are important forms of sexual expression and that touching is also an important form of communication; for example, a touch can express affection, desire, understanding, or a lack of caring. In the exercises, one member of the couple plays the "giving" role (touches and strokes the other), while the other person plays the "getting" role (is touched by the other). The giving partner is instructed to massage or fondle the other, while the getting partner is instructed to communicate to the giver what is most pleasurable. Thus the exercise fosters communication. The partners switch roles after a certain period of time. In the first exercises, the giver is not to stroke the genitals or breasts but may touch any other area. As the couple progress through the exercises, they are instructed to begin touching the genitals and breasts. These exercises also

Focus: First Person
A Case of Low Sexual Desire

Sarah, age 27, was referred to a sex therapist by an endocrinologist, to be considered for testosterone treatment for her complaints of low sexual desire. Sarah had no ovarian tissue. One ovary that had a large cyst had been removed when she was 13, and her other ovary had undergone torsion (twisting that cut off the blood supply) and had to be removed when she was 16. She had been given estrogen and progesterone replacement immediately so that her menstrual periods never stopped.

When Sara met with the therapist, she explained that sex with her partner Carl was enjoyable. They had been together 4 years and were sexual approximately once a week. Carl would have preferred to be sexual every day, but Sarah resisted. She said that even though sex was enjoyable and satisfying, if she never had sex again, it would be fine with her. She reported that both Carl and her endocrinologist thought that she was very abnormal.

Sarah had very few sexual thoughts about arousal or anticipating sexual activity. Her sexual thoughts were instead troubling and focused on her guilt that their sexual interactions were infrequent and that she was abnormal. During sexual interactions with Carl, she was aroused, she enjoyed the experience, and had orgasms. She found arousing Carl to be pleasurable and arousing for her.

Using the New View of Women's Sexual Problems, the therapist explained to Sarah that her experience was within normal limits. In a meeting with Carl, the therapist described the range of women's sexual experiences. The next question was whether some factors were causing Sarah's behavior to be toward the end of the spectrum. Both biological and psychological factors seemed to be involved. Because of the removal of her ovaries, she was manufacturing no testosterone, although androgens manufactured by the adrenal gland were present. Sarah's life history also gave clues regarding possible psychological factors. Sarah grew up with an alcoholic father who was prone to shouting, arguing, and engaging in emotional abuse; Sarah coped by retreating to her bedroom. She suppressed her feelings of anger and did not rebel even when she was a teenager. This coping style worked well at the time. However, as an adult, she was probably still in the habit of suppressing emotions generally. Sarah agreed about this and understood that her sexual emotions were probably also suppressed.

The therapist decided against testosterone treatment and instead focused on encouraging Sarah to deliberately attempt to feel more nonsexual emotion throughout the day. In addition, she was to deliberately allow more sexual stimuli in her life, such as music, movies, dancing, and erotic conversations.

The therapist met with Carl to explain the situation and assess his own family history. His parents had a bitter divorce when he was just 10. He felt that neither parent had really loved him. For Carl, having sex with his partner was a sign that he was loved. Carl was able to realize that pressuring Sarah did not help the situation, and he ceased doing so, which Sarah appreciated. In addition, when Sarah realized the origins and extent of Carl's need to feel loved, she became strongly motivated to find the triggers that were able to make her feel more sexual. Salsa dancing proved to be one of those triggers, combined with encouraging Carl to flirt with her more often. Sarah's sexual self-image increased markedly, as did her sexual desire.

Source: Basson (2007, pp. 42–43).

---

encourage the partners to focus their attention or concentrate on the sensuous pleasures they are receiving. Many people's sexual response is dulled because they are distracted; they are thinking about how to solve a family financial problem or are spectatoring their own performance. They are victims of cognitive interference. The sensate focus exercises train people to concentrate only on their sexual experience, thereby increasing the pleasure of it.

In addition to these exercises, behavior therapists supply simple education. The couple is given thorough instruction in the anatomy and physiology of the male and female sexual organs. Some couples, for example, have no idea what or where the clitoris is. These instructions may also clear up misunderstandings that either member of the couple may have had since childhood. For example, a man with an erectile disorder may have been told as a child that men can have only a fixed number of orgasms in their lifetime. As he approaches middle age, he starts to worry about whether he may have used up almost all of his orgasms, which creates the erectile disorder. It is important for such men to learn that nature has imposed no quota on them.

Masters and Johnson collected data on the success and failure rates of their therapy. In their book *Human Sexual Inadequacy* they reported on the treatment of 790 persons. Of these, 142 still had a disorder at the end of the two-week therapy program. This translates to a failure rate of 18 percent, or a *success rate of 82 percent*. While the failure rate ran around 18 percent for most disorders, there were two exceptions: Therapy for premature ejaculation had a very low failure rate (2.2 percent), and therapy for primary erectile disorder had a high failure rate (40.6 percent). That is, premature ejaculation was quite easy to cure, primary erectile disorder very difficult. Masters and Johnson's success rate is impressive, although their results have been called into question, as we shall see later in this chapter.

In Masters and Johnson's initial development of their therapy techniques, all of the couples were heterosexual. They later used the same techniques in treating sexual disorders in gay and lesbian couples, with a comparable success rate (Masters & Johnson, 1979).

Cognitive–Behavioral Therapy

As we discussed in Chapter 2, cognitive theories are increasingly important in psychology. Paralleling this increased importance in theory, cognitive approaches in psychotherapy are also becoming important. Today, many sex therapists use a combination of the behavioral exercises pioneered by Masters and Johnson and cognitive therapy (Heiman, 2002b). This is termed **cognitive–behavioral therapy.**

Cognitive restructuring is an important technique in a cognitive approach to sex therapy (Wincze & Carey, 1991). In cognitive restructuring, the therapist essentially helps the client restructure his or her thought patterns, helping them to become more positive (for an example, see Focus: First Person, on page 447). In one form of cognitive restructuring, the therapist challenges the client's negative attitudes. These attitudes may be as general as a woman's

distrusting attitudes toward all men, or as specific as a man's negative attitudes toward masturbation. The client is helped to reshape these attitudes into more positive ones.

Earlier in this chapter we noted that cognitive interference is one of the immediate causes of sexual disorders. That is exactly the kind of issue that a cognitive–behavioral therapist likes to address. The general idea is to reduce the presence of interfering thoughts during sex. First the therapist must help the client identify the presence of such thoughts. The therapist then suggests techniques for reducing these thoughts, generally by replacing them with erotic thoughts—perhaps focusing attention on a particular part of one's body and how it is responding with arousal, or perhaps having an erotic fantasy. Out go the bad thoughts, in come the good thoughts.

Couple Therapy

As we noted earlier, a significant cause of sexual disorders is interpersonal difficulties. Accordingly, some sex therapists use couple therapy as part of the treatment. This approach rests on the assumption that there is a reciprocal relationship between interpersonal conflict and sex problems. Sex problems can cause conflicts, and conflicts can cause sex problems. In couple therapy, the relationship itself is treated, with the goal of reducing antagonisms and tensions between the partners. As the relationship improves, the sex problem should be reduced.

For certain disorders and certain couples, therapists may use a combination of cognitive–behavioral and couple therapy. For example, sex therapists Raymond Rosen, Sandra Leiblum, and Ilana Spector (1994) use a five-part model in treating men with erectile disorder:

1. *Sexual and performance anxiety reduction.* Men with erectile disorder often have a great deal of performance anxiety. This can be treated using such techniques as the sensate focus exercises discussed earlier in this chapter.

2. *Education and cognitive intervention.* Men with erectile disorder often lack sexual information and have unrealistic expectations about sexual performance and satisfaction. For example, older men may not be aware of the natural effects of aging on male sexual response. Cognitive interventions may help the man to overcome "all or nothing" thinking—that is, the belief that if any aspect

Cognitive–behavioral therapy: A form of therapy that combines behavior therapy and restructuring of negative thought patterns.

of his sexual performance is not perfect, the whole interaction is a disaster. An example is the belief "I failed sexually because my erection was not 100 percent rigid."

3. *Script assessment and modification.* The man with erectile disorder and his partner have a sexual script that they enact together. People with sexual disorders typically have a restricted, repetitive, and inflexible script, using a small number of techniques that they never change. Novelty is one of the greatest turn-ons, so therapy is designed to help the couple break out of their restricted script.

4. *Conflict resolution and relationship enhancement.* As we have discussed, conflicts in a couple's relationship can lead to sexual disorders. In therapy, these conflicts are identified and the couple can work to resolve them.

5. *Relapse prevention training.* Sometimes a relapse—a return of the disorder—occurs following therapy. Therapists have developed techniques to help couples avoid or deal with such relapses. For example, they are told to engage in sensate focus sessions at least once a month.

Notice that part 1 represents the behavior therapy techniques pioneered by Masters and Johnson; parts 2 and 3 are cognitive therapy techniques; and part 4 is couple therapy. Most skilled sex therapists today use combined or integrated techniques such as these, tailored to the specific disorder and situation of the couple.

Sex Therapy Online
Dr. Patti Britton is a trained, board-certified sex therapist who runs a successful sex therapy Web site (Britton, 2004). It is difficult to find such legitimate sites because searching for terms such as "sex therapy" leads to a deluge of porn sites (as of this writing, Britton's URL is www.yoursexcoach.com). Her site includes a chat room where people can talk with others about their sexual experiences and problems. You can book an appointment with Britton on the site, for a live online or telephone session. She is also one of the sexuality experts at iVillage.com in the relationships channel, a site devoted to women's issues, which serves 18 million women and some men.

Is sex therapy online the wave of the future? What are its advantages and disadvantages? Proponents argue that it is more affordable than traditional in-person therapy and that its anonymity is a major advantage. People who are too shy or em-

barrassed to tell their story to a sex therapist can log on and type their questions anonymously. A person could easily obtain help without even their partner knowing about it. The advice columns at these sites can provide accurate, explicit, and nonjudgmental information. Interactions with a therapist online can break the wall of isolation surrounding a person with a sexual disorder. Specialized message boards and chat rooms for people who share a common theme (e.g., bisexuals, persons with disabilities) can help to create a sense of community, especially for those who are geographically isolated. Because the Web is international, people in countries in which sex therapy is unknown can obtain helpful information that would otherwise be unavailable.

There are disadvantages, too. Currently there is no system for licensing online sex therapists, so unqualified and perhaps unethical persons could easily present themselves as therapists. Moreover, online sex therapists probably will not be able to give true intensive therapy of the kind one would get in multiple in-person sessions with a therapist. What online therapists can do is provide permission and positive encouragement as well as accurate information, and that is enough to solve many people's problems.

Specific Treatments for Specific Problems
Some very specific techniques have been developed for the treatment of certain sexual disorders.

The Stop-Start Technique
The stop-start technique is used in the treatment of premature ejaculation (see Figure 17.4). The woman uses her hand to stimulate the man to erection. Then she stops the stimulation. Gradually he loses his erection. She resumes stimulation, he gets another erection, she stops, and so on. The man learns that he can have an erection and be highly aroused without having an orgasm. Using this technique, the couple may extend their sex play to 15 or 20 minutes, and the man gains control over his orgasm. Another version of this method is the squeeze technique, in which the woman adds a squeeze around the coronal ridge, which also stops orgasm.

Masturbation
The most effective form of therapy for women with primary orgasmic disorder is a program of directed masturbation (LoPiccolo & Stock, 1986; Meston et al., 2004). The data indicate that masturbation is the technique most likely to produce orgasm in

Figure 17.4 The stop-start technique for treating premature ejaculation and the position of the couple while using the stop-start technique.

women; it is therefore a logical treatment for women who have problems with having orgasms, many of whom have never masturbated. Masturbation is sometimes recommended as therapy for men as well.

Kegel Exercises

One technique that is used with women is the **Kegel exercises,** named for the physician who devised them (Kegel, 1952). They are designed to exercise and strengthen the *pubococcygeal muscle,* or PC muscle, which runs along the sides of the entrance of the vagina (see Figure 4.8 in Chapter 4). The exercises are particularly helpful for women who have had this muscle stretched in childbirth and for those who simply have poor tone in the muscle. The woman is instructed first to find her PC muscle by sitting on a toilet with her legs spread apart, beginning to urinate, and stopping the flow of urine voluntarily. The muscle that stops the flow is the PC muscle. After that, the woman is told to contract the muscle 10 times during each of six sessions per day. Gradually she can work up to

more.[2] These exercises seem to enhance arousal and facilitate orgasm, perhaps by increasing women's awareness of and comfort with their genitals (Heiman, 2007). They also permit the woman to stimulate her partner more because her vagina can grip his penis more tightly, and they are a cure for women who have problems with involuntarily urinating as they orgasm. Kegel exercises are sometimes also used in treating men.

Bibliotherapy

Bibliotherapy refers simply to the use of a self-help book to treat a disorder. Research shows that bibliotherapy is effective for orgasmic disorders in women (Van Lankveld, 1998). Julia Heiman et al.'s *Becoming Orgasmic: A Sexual Growth Program for Women* (1976) has been used extensively for this purpose. Bibliotherapy has also been shown to be effective for couples with a mixture of sexual disorders, both in men and in women (Van Lankveld et al., 2001).

[2]Students should recognize the exciting possibilities for doing these exercises. For example, they are a good way to amuse yourself in the middle of a boring lecture, and no one will ever know you are doing them.

Kegel (KAY-gul) exercises: A part of sex therapy for women with orgasmic disorder, in which the woman exercises the muscles surrounding the vagina; also called *pubococcygeal* or *PC muscle exercises.*

Bibliotherapy: The use of a self-help book to treat a disorder.

Biomedical Therapies

In the last decade, there has been increased recognition of the biological bases of some sexual disorders. Consistent with this emphasis, many developments in medical and drug treatments and even surgical treatment have occurred.

Drug Treatments

Many promising advances have been made in the identification of drugs that cure sexual disorders or work well when used together with cognitive–behavioral therapy or other psychological forms of sex therapy (Ashton, 2007; Rosen, 2007; Rowland & Burnett, 2000). Some are drugs that have direct sexual effects, whereas others are psychotherapeutic drugs such as antidepressants that work by improving the person's mood.

Certainly the most widely publicized breakthrough among these treatments was the release, in 1998, of **Viagra** (sildenafil) for the treatment of erectile disorder (Figure 17.5). Earlier biomedical treatments were unsatisfactory for various reasons. For example, intracavernosal injections (discussed in the following section) are not exactly

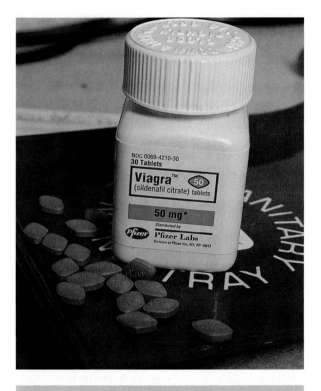

Figure 17.5 Viagra, one of the prescription drugs available for treating erectile disorder.

romantic. Viagra is taken by mouth approximately one hour before anticipated sexual activity. It does not, by itself, produce an erection. Rather, when the man is stimulated sexually after taking Viagra, the drug facilitates the physiological processes that produce erection. Specifically, it relaxes the smooth muscles in the corpora cavernosa, allowing blood to flow in and create an erection. Averaged over 27 clinical trials, about 57 percent of men respond successfully to Viagra—compared with 21 percent responding to the placebo (Fink et al., 2002). Men have generally been quite satisfied with Viagra. Side effects are not common; they include headache, flushing, and vision disturbances (Ashton, 2007).

On balance, Viagra seems to be quite safe (Morales et al., 1998; Rosen & McKenna, 2002). It does not seem to cause priapism (an erection that just won't go away). Yet the very ease of its use may lead physicians to overprescribe it and men to demand it in inappropriate circumstances. Today it is easily available on the Internet. If the erection difficulties are due to a relationship problem, Viagra will provide at most a temporary solution. It is not helpful for sexual disorders other than erectile disorder. And there is no evidence that it enhances sexual performance in men who function sexually within the normal range (Mondaini et al., 2003). Its recreational or high-performance use are causes for concern.

Viagra was such a success, financially and otherwise, that drug companies immediately sought successors—drugs that would be more convenient or work in cases that were not effectively treated with Viagra. One of these is Cialis (tadalafil), which is very much like Viagra in that it relaxes the smooth muscle surrounding the arteries to the penis, facilitating engorgement (Brock et al., 2002; Montorsi et al., 2004; Padma-Nathan et al., 2001). Whereas Viagra lasts only a few hours, Cialis is effective for as long as 24 to 36 hours. Someone at the drug company apparently decided that planning to have sex, as one does with Viagra, is not a good idea. Drugs such as Cialis have been shown to have no negative effects on sperm production or sex hormone production (Hellstrom et al., 2003a).

Levitra (vardenafil) is another drug that works much like Viagra but has a slightly different formulation and is somewhat more potent (Hatzichristou et al., 2004; Hellstrom et al., 2003b; Rosen & McKenna, 2002). A particularly important success story is that these drugs are effective in treating erectile dysfunction that results from complete surgical removal of the prostate (Brock et al., 2003).

Viagra: A drug used in the treatment of erectile disorder; sildenafil.

Figure 17.6   At the time Viagra was released, the media were full of jokes about this "delicate" subject.

Both Viagra and Cialis act peripherally; that is, they act on sites in the penis. Another alternative is centrally acting drugs, meaning drugs that act on regions of the brain involved in arousal. One of these is Uprima (apomorphine SL[3]; Heaton, 2001). It acts in about 20 minutes and, like the other drugs, does not produce a spontaneous erection. Rather, it has to be accompanied by sexual stimulation. Uprima acts by boosting levels of the neurotransmitter dopamine in the brain, particularly in the hypothalamus, and is effective in about 55 percent of cases (Heaton, 2001; Montorsi et al., 2003a, 2003b).

And how about a Viagra for women? The drug company Pfizer, as well as many scientists, hoped that Viagra would also work for women—that is, that it would cure their orgasm problems. The problem is that Viagra works by increasing vasocongestion, and insufficient vasocongestion is probably not what causes most women's orgasm difficulties. After many failed clinical trials, Pfizer announced in 2004 that it would give up on testing Viagra for women (Harris, 2004).

Women's sexual problems most commonly involve orgasm difficulties and low sexual desire, the latter being a problem particularly as women age and their ovaries decline in production of testosterone. The most promising lead at the moment in drug treatment is administration of testosterone or some other androgen (Baulieu et al., 2000). As of this writing, Procter & Gamble is conducting clinical trials of Intrinsa, a testosterone patch designed for postmenopausal women experiencing low sexual desire.

The other issue concerning women and Viagra involves the wives or partners of men with newfound Viagra-aided erections. Not all women, some of whom had adjusted to a relationship without intercourse, welcome their husbands' new capacity, an issue that has been ignored in the medical "fix" approach (Potts et al., 2003; Rosen & McKenna, 2002). Often it is important to combine couple therapy with drug therapy. Some women, of course, are absolutely delighted with the Viagra results (Montorsi & Althof, 2004).

[3]The SL means *sublingual;* that is, you take it by putting it under your tongue and letting it dissolve rather than by swallowing it. It gets to the brain more efficiently that way. Previously, apomorphine had been used to treat Parkinson's disease.

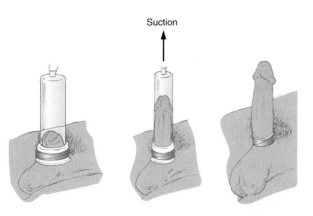

Suction

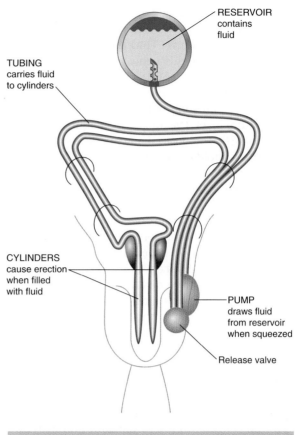

RESERVOIR
contains
fluid

TUBING
carries fluid
to cylinders

CYLINDERS
cause erection
when filled
with fluid

PUMP
draws fluid
from reservoir
when squeezed

Release valve

Figure 17.7 A treatment for erectile disorder. An external tube, with a rubberband around it, is placed over the lubricated penis. Suction applied to the tube produces erection, which is maintained by the constricting action of the rubberband once the plastic tube has been removed.

Figure 17.8 A surgically implanted prosthesis can be used in treating erectile dysfunction, although it should be regarded as a treatment of last resort.

Intracavernosal Injection

Intracavernosal injection (ICI) is a treatment for erectile disorders (Levitt & Mulcahy, 1995; Shabsigh et al., 2000). It involves injecting a drug (such as alprostadil, or Edex) into the corpora cavernosa of the penis. The drugs used are vasodilators—that is, they dilate the blood vessels in the penis so that much more blood can accumulate there, producing an erection.

Since the introduction of Viagra, ICI is now used mainly in cases in which the erection problem is organic and the man does not respond to Viagra or its successors (Shabsigh et al., 2000). It can also be used in conjunction with cognitive–behavioral therapy in cases that have combined organic and psychological causes. Like Viagra, ICI can have positive psychological effects, because it restores the man's confidence in his ability to get erections and it reduces his performance anxiety since he is able to engage in intercourse successfully. Some men experience penile pain from this treatment. There are also potential abuses. Men who have normal erections should not use ICI in an attempt to produce a "super erection."

Alprostadil is also available as a suppository to place inside the urethra or as a cream to rub on, eliminating the need for the needle.

Suction Devices

Suction devices are another treatment for erectile disorders (Rosen, 2007). Essentially, they pump you up! A tube is placed over the penis (see Figure 17.7). With some devices, the mouth can produce enough suction; with others, a small hand pump is used. Once a reasonably firm erection is present, the tube is removed and a rubber ring is placed around the base of the penis to maintain the engorgement with blood. These devices have been used successfully with, for example, diabetic men. They can also be helpful in combination with cognitive–behavioral couple therapy for cases of erectile dysfunction that are mainly psychological in origin (Wylie et al., 2003).

Surgical Therapy: The Inflatable Penis

For severe cases of erectile disorder, surgical therapy is possible. The surgery involves implanting a **penile prosthesis** (see Figure 17.8) (Hellstrom, 2003; Kabalin & Kuo, 1997). A sac or bladder of water is implanted in the

Penile prosthesis (prahs-THEE-sis): A surgical treatment for erectile dysfunction, in which inflatable tubes are inserted into the penis.

lower abdomen, connected to two inflatable tubes running the length of the corpus spongiosum, with a pump in the scrotum. Thus the man can literally pump up or inflate his penis so that he has a full erection.

The surgery takes approximately one and a half hours and requires only one incision, where the penis and scrotum meet. The total cost is about $10,000.

It should be emphasized that this is a radical treatment that should be reserved only for those cases that have not been cured by sex therapy or drug therapy. Typically it should be a case of primary erectile disorder that is the result of organic factors such as diabetes. The patient must understand that the surgery itself destroys some portions of the penis, so that a natural erection will never again be possible. Research shows that about one-fourth of men who have had this treatment are dissatisfied afterward. Reasons for dissatisfaction include the penis being smaller when erect than it was presurgery, different sensations during arousal, and different sensations during ejaculation (Steege et al., 1986). Although the treatment is radical and should be used conservatively, it is a godsend for some men who have been incapable of erection because of organic difficulties. Indeed, more than a dozen children have been born as a result of this surgery, to women whose partners were previously incapable of intercourse.

In another version of a surgical approach, a semirigid, silicone-like rod is implanted into the penis (Melman & Tiefer, 1992; Shandera & Thompson, 1994). This noninflatable device is less costly than the inflatable version and has a lower rate of complications (Rosen & Leiblum, 1995b).

Critiques of Sex Therapy

One of the most basic questions we must ask about sex therapy is, Is it effective?

Psychologists Bernie Zilbergeld and Michael Evans (1980) did an extensive critique of the research methods used by Masters and Johnson in evaluating the success of their sex therapy. Zilbergeld and Evans concluded that there were a number of substantial problems. In brief, the criticisms suggest that we really do not know what the success rate of Masters and Johnson's therapy is, and it is almost surely lower than the 80 percent they claimed. A discussion of the specific criticisms follows. These points are important to bear in mind when evaluating any type of sex therapy.

First, Masters and Johnson never actually reported a *success* rate for the therapy. Instead, they reported a *failure* rate of about 20 percent. Thus, most people have concluded, as we did earlier in this chapter (and you probably thought it was logical as you read it), that this implies a success rate of about 80 percent. But Masters and Johnson responded that this was not the case. That is, the 80 percent apparently included a mixture of clear successes and cases that were ambiguous as to whether they were successes or failures—in short, they had 80 percent nonfailures, but that does not mean 80 percent successes.

Furthermore, Masters and Johnson never defined what they meant by a "success" in therapy. This is an important issue. How improved does a person have to be to be counted as a success? Suppose a woman seeks help for anorgasmia; she has never had an orgasm. By the end of therapy, she is able to orgasm from a vibrator, but not from hand stimulation or mouth stimulation by her partner, nor by intercourse. Is this case a success? How would Masters and Johnson have classified her? We cannot tell from their book.

Zilbergeld and Evans initiated their critical appraisal after finding that they and other sex therapists were unable to obtain success rates as dramatic as the ones Masters and Johnson reported. The obvious possibility is that other sex therapists have been using definitions of therapy success that are much stricter and more precise than the definition used by Masters and Johnson.

Masters and Johnson did not report clearly how their initial population of clients for therapy was chosen. They said that they rejected some people from therapy, but they did not specify who made the decision, how the decision was made, and how many people were thus rejected. It seems quite possible that Masters and Johnson weeded out the most difficult cases, leaving themselves with the easier ones and consequently a high success rate.

With their five-year follow-up of patients, Masters and Johnson reported an amazingly low relapse rate of 7 percent, but other sex therapists find much higher relapse rates. Once again, Masters and Johnson did not specify their exact criterion for relapse, so it is hard to evaluate or replicate the 7 percent figure.

Finally, Masters and Johnson never discussed the possible harmful effects of their therapy. They made fleeting references to a couple of cases in which the therapy apparently ended in divorce, but they made no systematic attempt to assess problems of this sort. Their five-year follow-up was of "successes" only, not failures. It seems likely that the failures were precisely those who might have been harmed, yet no information on them was provided.

A broader critique pointed out that a major shortcoming of the field of sex therapy is the lack of carefully controlled studies that (1) investigate the success of various therapies compared with other therapies and with untreated controls; and (2) examine what aspect of a particular therapy or combination of therapies seems to provide the beneficial effect (Rosen & Leiblum, 1995b).

Nonetheless, there is sufficient evidence evaluating certain treatments for certain disorders to reach the following conclusions (Heiman & Meston, 1997; Heiman, 2002b):

- Primary orgasmic dysfunction in women is successfully treated with directed masturbation, and the treatment can be enhanced with sensate focus exercises.
- Treatments for secondary orgasmic dysfunction are somewhat less successful. Therapy that combines some or all of the following components seems to be most effective: sex education, sexual skills training, communication skills training, and body image therapy. The problem here, most likely, is that there are many different patterns of secondary anorgasmia, with a need to match treatment to the pattern of the disorder, something that research has not been able to untangle.
- Vaginismus is successfully treated with progressive vaginal dilators; relaxation and Kegel exercises may also be helpful, but the evidence is not as strong.
- The squeeze technique is effective for treating premature ejaculation. Drugs, specifically some antidepressants (serotonin reuptake inhibitors), may also be effective.
- For some disorders—sexual desire disorders, dyspareunia, and delayed orgasm in men—research is insufficient to conclude that there is an effective treatment.

Another critique points out the *medicalization* of sexual disorders, particularly male erectile problems (Tiefer, 1994, 2000). Research has increasingly identified organic sources of sexual disorders, with advances that have brought attempts to identify drugs and surgeries, rather than psychotherapies, to treat problems. In part, political issues are involved, as physicians try to seize the treatment of sexual disorders from psychologists. But there is also a cost to the patient, as the disorder may be given a quick fix with drugs while the patient's anxieties and relationship problems are ignored. The New View of women's sexual problems, discussed earlier in the chapter, was proposed in part as an alternative to medicalization.

In contrast to these scientific criticisms is the criticism by psychiatrist Thomas Szasz. In his book *Sex by Prescription* (1980) he criticized the philosophical basis of sex therapy. Szasz has long been an outspoken critic of psychotherapy. He is particularly critical of the medical model in dealing with psychological problems (see, for example, his classic *The Myth of Mental Illness*). His essential argument is that psychologists and psychiatrists take people who have problems in living, or perhaps have freely chosen lifestyles, and classify them as "sick" or "mentally ill" (the medical model) and in need of therapy. Although the professionals may think they are being helpful, they may do more harm than good. For example, once persons are classified as "sick," the implication is that they need a psychologist or physician to fix them up; whereas in fact, Szasz maintains, it might be better for them to make active efforts to solve their own problems.

Applying this thinking to the sex therapy field, Szasz argued that the sex therapists have essentially created a lot of illnesses by creating the (somewhat arbitrary) diagnostic categories of the sexual disorders. For example, the man who cannot have intercourse because he cannot manage an erection is said to have "erectile dysfunction," yet the man who cannot bring himself to perform cunnilingus is not regarded as having any dysfunction. Why should the first problem be an illness and the second one not? A man who ejaculates rapidly is termed a "premature ejaculator" and considered in need of therapy, but what exactly is wrong with ejaculating rapidly?

Szasz summarized his arguments as follows:

I do not deny that sexual problems exist or are real. . . . I maintain only that such problems—including sexual problems—are integral parts of people's lives. . . .

As some of the examples cited in the book illustrate, one medical epoch's or person's sexual problem may be another epoch's or person's sexual remedy. Today, it is dogmatically asserted—by the medical profession and the official opinion-makers of our society—that it is healthy or normal for people to enjoy sex, that the lack of such enjoyment is the symptom of a sexual disorder, that such disorders can be relieved by appropriate medical (sex-therapeutic) interventions, and that they ought, whenever possible, to be so treated. This view, though it pretends to be scientific, is, in fact, moral or religious: it is an expression of the medical ideology we have substituted for traditional religious creeds. (1980, pp. 164–165)

In summary, a number of criticisms have been raised about the field of sex therapy. The research methods used by Masters and Johnson to evaluate the success of their therapy had a number of problems and, as a result, their implied success rate of 80 percent is probably unrealistically high. Despite more than three decades of rapid advances in both psychological and medical treatments of sexual disorders, adequate research has not yet been done on the effectiveness of many of these treatments. There is a trend to medicalize sexual disorders, particularly erectile disorder, which may lead to the neglect of needs for psychological treatment. Finally, Szasz questions the whole notion of sexual disorders as such.

Where do these criticisms leave us? In our opinion, they do not invalidate the work of sex therapists. Rather, they urge us to be cautious. Most sexual disorders will not have cure rates of 80 percent, but they may well turn out to have cure rates of 60 percent or more (Kaplan, 1979). A single method of therapy, such as behavior therapy, will not be effective with every disorder. Finally, we must be sensitive to the values expressed in labeling something as being, or someone as having, a "disorder."

Some Practical Advice

Avoiding Sexual Disorders

The old motto "Prevention is better than cure" could well be applied to sexual disorders. That is, people could use some of the principles that emerge from sex therapists' work to avoid having sexual disorders in the first place. In Chapter 1 we introduced the concept of sexual health. The following are some principles of good sexual mental health:

1. *Communicate with your partner.* Don't expect him or her to be a mind reader concerning what is pleasurable to you. One way to do this is to make it a habit to talk to your partner while you are having sex; verbal communication then does not come as a shock. Some people, though, feel uncomfortable talking at such times; nonverbal communication, such as placing your hand on top of your partner's and moving it where you want it, works well too (see Chapter 11 for more detail).

2. *Don't be a spectator.* Don't feel like you are putting on a sexual performance that you constantly need to evaluate. Concentrate as much as possible on the giving and receiving of sensual pleasures, not on how well you are doing.

3. *Don't set up goals of sexual performance.* If you have a goal, you can fail, and failure can produce disorders. Don't set your heart on having simultaneous orgasms or, if you are a woman, on having five orgasms before your partner has one. Just relax and enjoy yourself.

4. *Be choosy about the situations in which you have sex.* Don't have sex when you are in a terrific hurry or are afraid you will be disturbed. Also be choosy about who your partner is. Trusting your partner is essential to good sexual functioning; similarly, a partner who really cares for you will be understanding if things don't go well and will not laugh or be sarcastic.

5. *"Failures" will occur.* They do in any sexual relationship. What is important is how you deal with them. Don't let them ruin the relationship. Instead, try to think, How can we make this turn out well anyhow?

Choosing a Sex Therapist

Unfortunately, most states do not have licensing requirements for sex therapists, though most do have requirements for marriage counselors and psychologists. Particularly with the popularizing of Masters and Johnson's work, quite a few quacks have hung out shingles saying "Sex Therapist," and many states have made no attempt to regulate this. Some of these "therapists" have no more qualifications than having had a few orgasms themselves.

How do you go about finding a good, qualified sex therapist? Your local medical or psychological association can provide a list of psychiatrists or psychologists and may be able to tell you which ones have special training in sex therapy. There are also professional organizations of sex therapists. The American Association of Sex Educators, Counselors, and Therapists certifies sex therapists (see Appendix A for complete information on this organization and many other useful ones). Choose a therapist or clinic that offers an *integrated approach* that recognizes the potential biological, cognitive–behavioral, and relationship influences on any sexual disorder and is prepared to address all of these.

SUMMARY

Sexual disorders fall into four categories: desire disorders (hypoactive sexual desire, discrepancy of sexual desire, sexual aversion), arousal disorders (female sexual arousal disorder, erectile disorder), orgasmic disorders (premature ejaculation, male orgasmic disorder, female orgasmic disorder), and sexual pain disorders (dyspareunia, vaginismus).

Sexual disorders may be caused by physical factors, individual psychological factors, and interpersonal factors. Organic causes include some illnesses, infections, and damage to the spinal cord. Certain drugs may also create problems with sexual functioning. Individual psychological causes are categorized into immediate causes, such as anxiety or cognitive interference; prior learning; emotional factors; and behavioral or lifestyle factors. Interpersonal factors include conflict in the couple's relationship and intimacy problems. The New View of women's sexual problems conceptualizes the issues differently and focuses on different categories of causes, such as inadequate sexuality education, distress about not being able to meet cultural norms regarding ideal sexuality, and sexual inhibition due to fear of abuse by one's partner.

Therapies for sexual disorders include behavior therapy (pioneered by Masters and Johnson) based on learning theory, cognitive–behavioral therapy, couple therapy, specific treatments for specific problems (e.g., stop-start for premature ejaculation), and a variety of biomedical treatments, which include drug treatments (e.g., Viagra).

A number of criticisms of sex therapy have been raised, including concerns about the research methods used to evaluate the success of Masters and Johnson's therapy, the lack of evaluation research on recently developed therapies, the medicalization of sexual disorders, and the entire enterprise of identifying and labeling sexual disorders.

QUESTIONS FOR THOUGHT, DISCUSSION, AND DEBATE

1. When (or if) you engage in sexual activity with a partner, do you feel that you are under pressure to perform and that you engage in spectatoring? If so, what might you do to change this pattern?

2. Considering the prior learning causes of sexual disorders, what are the implications for parents who want to raise sexually healthy children? Could parents do certain things that would avoid or prevent sexual disorders in their children?

3. Your best friend, Steve, who is 22, discloses to you a long history of premature ejaculation, which has been very embarrassing and frustrating for him. He has heard about Viagra and, knowing that you are taking a human sexuality course, comes to you for advice about whether he should go to a doctor to get a prescription for it. What advice would you give him?

4. Hypoactive sexual desire is a common sexual disorder in the United States today. Given what you know about this disorder and its causes, do you think it is also common in other cultures? Think about Britain, China, India, and Mexico as examples. (For further information, see Bhurga & de Silva, 1993.)

SUGGESTIONS FOR FURTHER READING

Barbach, Lonnie G. (1975). *For yourself: The fulfillment of female sexuality.* Garden City, NY: Doubleday. Provides good information for women with orgasmic disorders, based on the author's experiences as a sex therapist. Still the classic in the field.

Barbach, Lonnie G. (1983). *For each other: Sharing sexual intimacy.* Garden City, NY: Anchor Books. Barbach's sequel to *For Yourself* (see above); this volume is designed for couples.

McCarthy, Barry, & McCarthy, Emily. (2002). *Sexual awareness: Couple sexuality for the twenty-first century.* New York: Carroll & Graf Publishers. Another good sex therapy book.

Tiefer, Leonore. (2004). *Sex is not a natural act, and other essays,* 2nd ed. Boulder, CO: Westview. Tiefer is a brilliant and entertaining writer, and her criticisms of sex therapy are insightful.

18 CHAPTER EIGHTEEN

Sexually Transmitted Infections

CHAPTER HIGHLIGHTS

M aria and Luis get home after an evening on the town and enter the house hungry for passion. The two embrace, clinging to each other, longing for each other. Luis slowly undresses Maria, hungry for the silky flesh he feels beneath him. As their passion grows, she begins reaching for him, ripping his clothes off as she explores his body with her tongue. As Luis gets more and more excited, Maria rips a condom package open with her teeth and slowly slides the condom over Luis's erect penis. After an hour of incredible lovemaking, Luis, exhausted with pleasure, turns to Maria and says, "You were right, the BEST sex is SAFE sex with LATEX!"*

*From a student essay.

The sexual scene is not the same as it was 30 years ago. AIDS poses a real threat. We need to do many things to combat such dangers. One is that we must rewrite our sexual scripts, as the quotation above illustrates. We also need to inform ourselves, and the goal of this chapter is to provide you with the important information you need to make decisions about your sexual activity.

Your health is very important, and a good way to ruin it or cause yourself a lot of suffering is to have an untreated case of a *sexually transmitted disease* (STD), also called a *sexually transmitted infection,* or STI. Consequently, it is very important to know the symptoms of the various kinds of STIs so that you can seek treatment if you develop any of them. Also, there are some ways to prevent STIs or at least reduce your chances of getting them, and these are certainly worth knowing about. Finally, after you have read some of the statistics on how many people contract STIs every year and on your chances of getting one, you may want to modify your sexual behavior somewhat. If you love, love wisely.

One of the most disturbing things about the STI epidemic in the United States is that it disproportionately affects teens and young adults. Approximately 19 million new cases of STIs occur each year in the United States, and of those, approximately 9 million (48 percent) are among people between the ages of 15 and 24 (Weinstock et al., 2004). For people in this age group, three infections— human papillomavirus (HPV), trichomoniasis, and chlamydia—account for the great majority of cases. Worldwide, of the 60 million people who have been infected with HIV, about half became infected between the ages of 15 and 24 (Kiragu et al., 2001). It is clear that prevention efforts, including sexuality education for youth, must have a higher priority than they have had in the past.

The STIs are presented in this chapter in the following order. First we look at a group of three diseases—chlamydia, HPV (genital warts), and herpes—that are all frequent among college students. After that is a discussion of HIV infection and AIDS, which is less common among college students but is one of the world's major public-health problems and is generating an enormous amount of research. Next we discuss gonorrhea, syphilis, viral hepatitis, and trichomoniasis. Then comes not an infection but a bug, the pubic louse. After a practical section for you on preventing STIs, the chapter ends with a section about various other genital infections that, for the most part, are not sexually transmitted.

Many statistics throughout this chapter are taken from the Centers for Disease Control and Prevention (CDC) Web site www.cdc.gov/std. The CDC is in Atlanta, Georgia. It is the federal agency that monitors diseases in the United States and conducts research and prevention programs. Data from the CDC are used so frequently throughout the chapter that we do not provide a citation every time. Information on STIs changes quickly, so to get the most up-to-date information, check the Web site.

Some STIs are caused by *bacteria,* some are caused by *viruses,* and a few are caused by other organisms. The distinction between bacterial infections and viral infections is important because bacterial infections can be cured using antibiotics. Viral infections cannot be cured, but they can be treated to reduce symptoms. Chlamydia, gonorrhea, and syphilis are all caused by bacteria. Herpes, AIDS, genital warts, and hepatitis B are caused by viruses.

One final note before we proceed: A lot of illustrations in this chapter show the symptoms of various STIs, and some of the photos may make you say "Nasty!" These illustrations are not meant to scare you but rather to help you recognize the symptoms of STIs. You should know what herpes blisters, for example, look like, in case you spot them on a prospective sexual partner and in case they appear on you.

Chlamydia

Chlamydia trachomatis is a bacterium that is spread by sexual contact and infects the genital organs of both males and females.

Statistics indicate that **chlamydia** has become one of the major sexually transmitted infections in the United States. Approximately 975,000 new cases of chlamydia are reported each year in this country, compared with 300,000 cases of gonorrhea (CDC, 2006c). Adolescent girls have a particularly high rate of infection. When a man consults a physician because of a urethral discharge, his chances of having chlamydia are greater than his chances of having gonorrhea. It is important that the correct diagnosis be made because chlamydia does not respond to the drugs used to cure gonorrhea.

Symptoms

The main symptoms in men are a thin, usually clear discharge and mild discomfort on urination appearing 7 to 14 days after infection. The symptoms are somewhat similar to the symptoms of gonorrhea in the male. However, gonorrhea tends to produce more painful urination and a more profuse, puslike discharge. Diagnosis is made from a urine sample in men and from a sample of cells from the cervix (or urine sample) in women. Tests are then used to detect the bacterium. Unfortunately, 75 percent of the cases of chlamydia infection are **asymptomatic** in women. This means that the woman never goes to a clinic for treatment, and she goes undiagnosed and untreated. The consequences of untreated chlamydia in women are discussed in the next section. Even among men, 50 percent of the cases are asymptomatic.

Treatment

Chlamydia is quite curable. It is treated with azithromycin or doxycycline; it does not respond to penicillin. Poorly treated or undiagnosed cases may lead to a number of complications: urethral damage, epididymitis (infection of the epididymis), Reiter's syndrome,[1] and proctitis in men who have had anal intercourse. Women with untreated or undiagnosed chlamydia may experience serious complications if not treated:

Chlamydia (klah-MIH-dee-uh): An organism causing a sexually transmitted infection; the symptoms in males are a thin, clear discharge and mild pain on urination; females are frequently asymptomatic.

Asymptomatic (ay-simp-toh-MAT-ik): Having no symptoms.

Pelvic inflammatory disease (PID): An infection and inflammation of the pelvic organs, such as the fallopian tubes and the uterus, in the female.

HPV: Human papillomavirus, the organism that causes genital warts.

Genital warts: A sexually transmitted infection causing warts on the genitals.

[1]Reiter's syndrome involves the following symptoms: urethritis, eye inflammations, and arthritis.

pelvic inflammatory disease (PID), and possibly infertility due to scarring of the fallopian tubes. A baby born to an infected mother may develop pneumonia or an eye infection.

Prevention?

Scientists doing research on chlamydia have a major goal of developing a vaccine that would prevent infection (Berry et al., 2004). Vaccines have been developed that are effective in mice, but technical obstacles prevent their use with humans. An effective vaccine for humans should be available in the next decade.

Until a vaccine is available, one of the most effective tools for prevention is screening. The problem with chlamydia is that so many infected people are asymptomatic and spread the disease unknowingly. In screening programs, asymptomatic carriers are identified, treated, and cured so that they do not continue to spread the disease. The CDC has conducted several demonstration projects that have yielded impressive results. In one, screening was conducted in family planning clinics in Alaska, Idaho, Oregon, and Washington. In the first eight years of the program, from 1988 to 1995, a 65 percent decline occurred in the rate of infection.

In an innovative program, high school girls attending a school health clinic (not necessarily for STIs) collected vaginal swabs themselves, and the swabs were then subjected to laboratory tests (Wiesenfeld et al., 2001). Overall, 18 percent of the girls were infected with something: 10 percent had trichomoniasis, 8 percent had chlamydia, and 2 percent had gonorrhea. None had symptoms, so these cases would have gone undetected. About half said that they would never have had a gynecological exam to get a test—yet they agreed to self-collection of vaginal swabs. This method is promising for screening teens.

On an individual level, the best method of prevention is the consistent use of a condom.

HPV

HPV stands for human papillomavirus, which causes genital warts. **Genital warts** are cauliflower-like warts appearing on the genitals, usually around the urethral opening of the penis, the shaft of the penis, or the scrotum in the male, and on the vulva, the walls of the vagina, or the cervix in the female (see Figure 18.1). Warts may also occur on the anus. Typically they appear three to eight

year in the United States (CDC, 2001). In a large, well-sampled study of women in the United States between the ages of 14 and 59, 27 percent were infected (Dunne et al., 2007). Even among 14- to 19-year-olds, the prevalence was 25 percent.

HPV infection is the single most important risk factor for cervical cancer (CDC, 2001). In fact, there are 30 distinct types of HPV that are sexually transmitted. Some types cause genital warts and are called "low risk" because they do not cause cancer. Other types sharply increase the risk of cervical cancer and are called high-risk types. HPV 16 and 18 account for 70 percent of the cases of cervical cancer (Dailard, 2006a). HPV infection is also associated with cancer of the penis and anus.

New research shows that oral sex can transmit HPV. Individuals infected this way have an increased risk of oral cancers, that is, cancer of the mouth or throat (Herrero et al., 2003; Kreimer et al., 2004).

Diagnosis

Diagnosis can sometimes be made simply by inspecting the warts, because their appearance is distinctive. However, some strains of warts are flat and less obvious. Also, the warts may grow inside the vagina and may not be detected there. And high-risk types do not produce warts. One test involves analysis of the DNA from a sample of cells taken from the cervix, vagina, or other area of suspected infection and tests directly for the presence of the HPV virus.

Treatment

Several treatments for genital warts are available. Chemicals such as podophyllin or bichloroacetic acid (BCA) can be applied directly to the warts. Typically these treatments have to be repeated several times, and the warts then fall off. With cryotherapy (often using liquid nitrogen), the warts are frozen off; again, it is typically necessary to apply more than one treatment. Laser therapy can also be used to destroy the warts. Many cases of HPV infection go away on their own, but others persist for long periods. In one study of college women, HPV infection lasted, on average, only eight months (Ho et al., 1998). The duration of infection was longer with older women, and the risk of cervical cancer increases with longer infections.

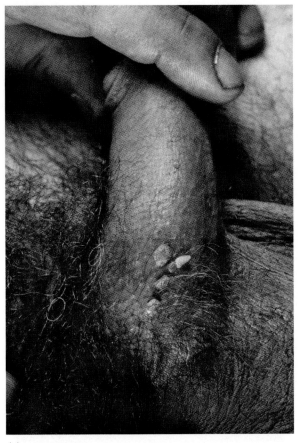

(a)

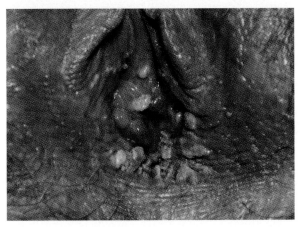

(b)

Figure 18.1 Genital warts (a) on the penis and (b) on the vulva.

months after intercourse with an infected person. The majority of people infected with HPV, however, are asymptomatic.

Infection with HPV is widespread. An estimated 5.5 million people become infected with HPV each

Vaccine

As noted, almost all cases of cervical cancer are linked to HPV infection. Therefore, a vaccine against HPV would prevent most cases of cervical cancer. Such a vaccine was introduced in the

CHAPTER 18 • SEXUALLY TRANSMITTED INFECTIONS

United States in 2006 (Dailard, 2006b). The vaccine is called Gardasil and must be administered in 3 shots over a 6-month period. The idea would be to administer it to girls around ages 11 to 12, before sexual activity would have started, but it might be given as early as 9 years of age. The vaccine protects against HPV types 16 and 18, the ones associated with cervical cancer, as well as two other types that cause most cases of genital warts, which would also be good to avoid. Randomized controlled trials show the vaccine to be highly effective (Villa et al., 2006). We recommend that all girls be given this vaccination against cervical cancer.

Genital Herpes

Genital herpes is a disease of the genital organs caused by the herpes simplex virus (HSV). Two strains of HSV are circulating: HSV-1 and HSV-2. In simpler times, HSV-2 caused genital herpes and HSV-1 caused cold sores around the mouth. Today, however, there is more crossing over. Genital herpes, then, can be caused by either HSV-1 or HSV-2. Genital herpes is transmitted by sexual intercourse and by oral–genital sex.

According to well-sampled studies, 17 percent of Americans are infected with HSV-2 and 58 percent are infected with HSV-1 (Xu et al., 2006). Of those who test positive for HSV-2 in their blood, only 14 percent report having been diagnosed with herpes; the great majority are asymptomatic and do not know they are infected. These persons transmit the disease to others unknowingly. Of those with HSV-1 in their blood but not HSV-2, 2 percent report having been diagnosed with genital herpes.

Symptoms

SexSource Online
www.mhhe.com/hyde10

"HERPES"
IN SEXUALLY
TRANSMITTED
DISEASES

The symptoms of genital herpes caused by HSV-2 are small, painful bumps or blisters on the genitals (see Figure 18.2). In women, they are usually found on the vaginal lips; in men, they usually occur on the penis. They may be found around the anus if the person has had anal intercourse. The blisters burst and can be quite painful. Fever, painful urination, and headaches may occur. The blisters heal on their own in about 3 weeks in the first episode of infection. The virus continues to live in the body, however. It may remain dormant for the rest of the person's life. But the symptoms may recur unpredictably, so that the person repeatedly undergoes 7- to 14-day periods of sores. HSV-1 infections tend to be less severe.

Genital herpes (HER-pees): A sexually transmitted infection, the symptoms of which are small, painful bumps or blisters on the genitals.

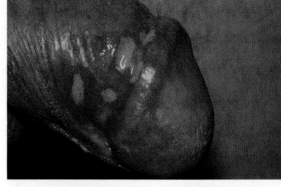

(a)

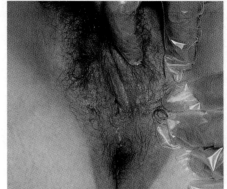

(b)

Figure 18.2 (*a*) Herpes blisters on the penis. (*b*) Herpes infection of the vulva.

People with herpes are most infectious when they are having an active outbreak. However, people are infectious even when there is no outbreak or if they have never been symptomatic. Therefore, there is no safe period.

Treatment

Unfortunately, there is no known drug that kills the virus; that is, there is no cure. Researchers are pursuing two solutions: drugs that would treat symptoms in someone who is already infected, and vaccinations that would prevent herpes. The drug acyclovir prevents or reduces the recurring symptoms, although it does not actually cure the disease.

Valacyclovir and famciclovir are newer drugs that are even more effective at shortening outbreaks and suppressing recurrences (Corey et al., 2004; Wald et al., 2006). They also reduce rates of transmission from an infected partner to an uninfected one.

Scientists are actively working to create a method for immunization against herpes (Augustinova et al., 2004; Meseda et al., 2004; Milligan et al., 2004).

Long-Term Consequences

Either men or women with recurrent herpes may develop complications such as meningitis or narrowing of the urethra due to scarring, leading to difficulties with urination. However, such complications do not affect the majority of those with herpes. There are two more serious long-term consequences. One is that having a herpes infection increases one's risk of becoming infected with HIV, probably because the open blisters during an outbreak make it easy for HIV to enter the body. Therefore, people who have herpes should be especially careful to use safer sex practices.

The other serious risk involves the transfer of the virus from mother to infant in childbirth, which in some cases leads to serious illness or death in the baby (Brown et al., 2005). The risk of transmission to the infant is highest in women who have recently been infected and are having their first outbreak. The risk is less with women who have had the disease longer, and is low if the woman is not having an outbreak. C-sections are therefore usually performed on women with an outbreak, but vaginal delivery is possible if there is not an outbreak.

Psychological Aspects: Coping with Herpes

The psychological consequences of herpes need to be taken as seriously as the medical consequences. The range of psychological responses is enormous. At one end of the spectrum are persons with asymptomatic herpes, who are not aware that they have the disease and are happily sexually active— and at the same time unknowingly spreading the disease to others. At the other end of the spectrum are persons who experience frequent, severe, painful recurrences, who feel stigmatized because of their disease, and who believe that they should abstain from sex in order to avoid infecting others. These difficulties are aggravated by the fact that outbreaks are often unpredictable, and current scientific evidence indicates that people are somewhat infectious even when they are not having an active outbreak. On the other hand, many people with herpes are able to cope.

Psychologists are exploring therapies for herpes patients. One highly effective treatment program consists of a combination of information on herpes, relaxation training, instruction in stress management, and instruction in an imagery technique in which the patient envisions the genitals free of lesions and imagines that he or she is highly resistant to the virus (Longo et al., 1988). (See Ebel & Wald, 2002, for an excellent book on living with herpes.)

HIV Infection and AIDS

In 1981, a physician in Los Angeles reported a mysterious and frightening new disease identified in several gay men. Within two years, the number of cases had escalated sharply and the gay community had become both frightened and outraged; within a few more years, the federal government had funded a major public health effort aimed at understanding and eradicating the disease. The disease was named **AIDS,** an abbreviation for **acquired immune deficiency syndrome.**

A major breakthrough came in 1984 when Robert Gallo, of the National Institutes of Health (NIH), announced that he had identified the virus causing AIDS. A French team, headed by Luc Montagnier of the Pasteur Institute, simultaneously announced the same discovery. The virus is called **HIV,** for human immune deficiency virus. Another strain of the virus, HIV-2, has been identified; it is found almost exclusively in Africa. HIV-1 accounts for almost all infections in North America.

As the name implies, HIV destroys the body's natural system of immunity to diseases. Once HIV has damaged an individual's immune system, opportunistic diseases may take over, and the person usually dies within a few months to a few years.

An Epidemic?

By the end of 2005, roughly 1 million persons in the United States had been diagnosed as having AIDS, and 550,000 of them had died from it. However, public health officials warn that these statistics represent only the tip of the iceberg, for they do not count persons who are just infected with HIV and do not yet have symptoms of full-blown AIDS; nor do they count persons who have mild symptoms of the disease but whose symptoms are not severe enough to be classified as AIDS. Experts estimate that 40 million persons worldwide are infected with HIV, although the majority of them show no symptoms yet and are unaware that they are infected (Simon et al., 2006). In 2005 alone, HIV infection caused approximately 2.8 million deaths worldwide. Thus the terms *global epidemic* and *pandemic* (a widespread epidemic) have been used, with reason.

AIDS (acquired immune deficiency syndrome): A sexually transmitted disease that destroys the body's natural immunity to infection so that the person is susceptible to and may die from a disease such as pneumonia or cancer.
HIV: Human immunodeficiency virus; the virus that causes AIDS.

Focus: A Sexually Diverse World
AIDS in Thailand

G lobally, HIV is pandemic; that is, it is an epidemic that has spread around the world. The World Health Organization estimates that 40 million persons are infected worldwide, of whom 90 percent are in developing nations. This pandemic is producing serious social and economic strains on many countries, as well as the suffering of individuals.

Asia has generally lagged behind other regions in the spread of HIV. Thailand is a notable exception to the pattern: an epidemic is raging there. In the early 1990s, depending on the region of the country, 40 to 50 percent of injection drug users were infected, as were 20 to 45 percent of brothel prostitutes. Approximately 1 million of the 60 million people of Thailand are believed to have been infected.

Sociocultural context is the key to understanding why AIDS struck Thailand. Two closely linked factors are Thailand's commercial sex industry and its booming tourism. A large commercial sex industry flourishes in Thailand. It is estimated that approximately half a million young women there work as prostitutes, most of those being in the 16 to 24 age group. A wide variety of forms of prostitution exist, catering to every budget, ranging from call girl agencies, executive clubs, and go-go bars to massage parlors, brothels, streetwalkers, and even mobile operations that go out to rural areas.

Why is there such a large commercial sex industry in Thailand? The major factor is economics. Social and income gaps in Thailand are enormous, ranging from rural areas characterized by great poverty to the conspicuous wealth of Bangkok. A young rural girl may go to the city and enter prostitution in order to pay off family debts, for example. Prostitution is very lucrative; it has been estimated that commercial sex workers can earn 25 times as much as young women who work as maids and in other jobs available to them. Another factor is a cultural belief that women are of only two types: virtuous women who are virgins until marriage, and prostitutes. Thailand is also a country that historically practiced polygamy and concubinage. And a man who does not use prostitutes is considered something less than a real man. These cultural factors combine to create great demand for prostitutes. Finally, beginning around the time of the Vietnam War, Thailand became a sex playground for foreign tourists and remains so to the present day.

Tourism provides more clients for prostitutes and therefore provides the incentive for more women to enter prostitution. But tourism also plays a major role in the international spread of HIV, bringing it into Thailand and in turn spreading it to the home countries of the tourists.

Today, Thailand is regarded as a major success story. In 1990 AIDS education was introduced into the schools. In 1991 a "100 percent condom program" was instituted with the help of the owners of sex parlors and sex workers, encouraging all clients to use condoms. The government supplied 60 million condoms a year to the effort. Research shows that the incidence of extramarital sex and sex with commercial sex workers decreased from 22 percent in 1990 to 10 percent in 1997 (Phoolcharoen, 1998). Officials estimate that, without the condom campaign, 10 percent of adult Thais would have been infected by 2000, whereas only 2 percent were, and the rate is not increasing.

Despite the success of these efforts, the epidemic is still serious. Thai officials, working with researchers in the United States, are therefore considering more daring strategies.

Promising vaccines against HIV have been developed in the United States, but U.S. officials have decided not to move them into trials in this country. Thai officials, facing a much more desperate situation, are negotiating to conduct the trials there. Ironically, the political complications of the democratic process in the United States, combined with a great concern for safety, slow down developments in the United States—whereas in Thailand, if officials decide to do it, it happens. The strategy would be to vaccinate uninfected volunteers whose sex partners are HIV positive. Thus it is possible that Thailand's tragedy will lead to the identification of an effective vaccine that can be used worldwide in stemming the pandemic.

Sources: Balter (1998); Cohen (2003); Ford & Koetsawang (1991); Phoolcharoen (1998); Simon et al. (2006); Stoneburner et al. (1994).

Transmission

HIV is transmitted by exchange of body fluids: semen, blood, and possibly secretions of the cervix and vagina. HIV is spread in four ways: (1) by sexual intercourse (either penis-in-vagina intercourse or anal intercourse[2]); (2) by contaminated blood (a risk for people who receive a blood transfusion if the blood has not been screened); (3) by contaminated hypodermic needles (a risk for those who inject drugs or for health care workers who receive accidental sticks); and (4) from an infected woman to her baby during pregnancy or childbirth.

Supporting these assertions, statistics for adult and adolescent cases of AIDS in the United States indicate that infected men are from the following exposure categories: (1) men who have sex with men (65 percent); (2) heterosexual contact (16 percent); (3) injection drug use (14 percent); (4) multiple sources (5 percent); and (5) other, including recipients of contaminated blood transfusions (less than 1 percent) (CDC, 2006d). In the United States in the early years of the epidemic, men who have sex with men accounted for the majority of cases. Today, however, women are the fastest-growing group for new HIV infection, accounting for 27 percent of new cases (CDC, 2006d). Among women, the leading categories of exposure are heterosexual contact (78 percent) and injection drug use (20 percent). Worldwide, the majority of cases result from heterosexual transmission.

How great is your risk of becoming infected with HIV? In essence, it depends on what your sexual practices are (leaving aside the issues of injection drug use, which are beyond the scope of this book) (Varghese et al., 2002). *The sexual behavior most likely to spread AIDS is anal intercourse, and being the receiving partner puts one most at risk.* This is true for heterosexuals as well as gays. Whether you are gay or straight, *the greater your number of sexual partners, the greater your risk of getting infected with HIV.* You may have heard the saying "six degrees of separation." It turns out that it is true for HIV as well. One study found that most people are just a few degrees of sexual separation from someone who is HIV infected (Liljeros et al., 2001). The greater your number of partners, the greater your chances of connecting with that HIV-positive person.

Table 18.1	Risk of Being Infected with an STI as a Result of One Act of Sexual Intercourse with an Infected Person, Using No Condom

	Percent Risk of Transmission from	
	Male to Female	*Female to Male*
Gonorrhea	50 to 90%	20%
Genital herpes	0.2%	0.05%
HIV	0.1 to 20%	0.01 to 10%

Source: Stone (1994), pp. 203–212.

Heterosexual, penis-in-vagina intercourse spreads HIV as well. The risk varies considerably depending on who you have sex with and whether you use a condom. *Sexual intercourse is riskier if it is with a person who is infected with HIV (seropositive), if the person is in a high-risk group (gay, injection drug user), or if condoms are not used.* Table 18.1 shows the relative risk of becoming infected from a single act of intercourse with an infected person, using no condom. A study of heterosexual transmission of HIV among 415 Ugandan couples in which one partner was infected at the beginning and one was not indicated that 22 percent of the uninfected became infected over a two-year period (Quinn et al., 2000). The male-to-female transmission rates and female-to-male rates were about equal. The higher the viral count in the infected person, the greater the rate of transmission. None of the circumcised men became infected.

Most important, condoms are 87 percent effective in protecting against HIV transmission during heterosexual intercourse (Davis & Weller, 1999). This isn't perfect protection, but it's darned good and far better than no protection. Far-right religious groups have tried to convince the public—especially schoolchildren—that condoms are totally ineffective, but the scientific studies say otherwise.

The Virus

HIV is one of a group of retroviruses. Retroviruses reproduce only in living cells of the host species, in this case humans. They invade a host cell, and each time the host cell divides, copies of the virus are produced along with more host cells, each containing the genetic code of the virus. Current

[2]There is also a chance that mouth–genital sex can spread HIV, particularly if there is ejaculation by an infected person into the mouth.

Figure 18.3   Experts agree that, in the absence of a cure or vaccine for AIDS, the best weapon that we have is education.

research is aimed at finding drugs that will prevent the virus from infecting new cells. At least two strains of HIV are found in the United States today, HIV-1 and HIV-2, and there are several subgroups of HIV-1 that differ genetically (Simon et al., 2006).

HIV invades a specific group of white blood cells (lymphocytes) called CD4+ T-lymphocytes. We'll just call them T cells. These cells are critical to the body's immune response in fighting off infections. When HIV reproduces, it destroys the infected T cell. Eventually the HIV-positive person's number of T cells is so reduced that infections cannot be fought off.

Scientists have pressed hard to understand the functioning of HIV. They have identified two *coreceptors* for HIV, CCR5 and CXCR4, which allow HIV to enter T cells (Simon et al., 2006). CCR5 seems to be the important coreceptor in the early stages of the disease and CXCR4 in the later stages. This discovery may lead to advances in treatment if drugs can be used that block these coreceptors.

The Disease

The Centers for Disease Control and Prevention established the following categorization for broad classes of HIV infection and progression of the disease:

1. *Early stage.* This stage begins with initial infection and development of antibodies to the virus over the next two to eight weeks. This stage lasts as long as the person keeps feeling well and the T4 cell count stays around 1,000. A normal count is approximately 1,000 cells per cubic millimeter of blood. People in this stage are asymptomatic carriers. That is, they have no symptoms and may be unaware that they are infected, yet they can infect other persons, which is a dangerous situation.

2. *Middle stage.* The T4 cell count drops by half, to around 500, but the person still may have no outward symptoms. The immune system is silently failing, however. In this stage, many infected persons develop symptoms that are

not immediately life threatening: swollen lymph nodes, night sweats, fever, diarrhea, persistent yeast infections in the throat or vagina, shingles, fatigue, or abnormal or cancerous cells in the cervix. Treatment with AZT, DDI, and other drugs may begin at this time; there is some evidence that these drug treatments (discussed later) are more effective if begun early.

3. *AIDS.* According to the CDC guidelines, the diagnosis of AIDS should be applied when the person tests positive for HIV and meets any of a number of criteria: (a) the person is affected by life-threatening opportunistic infections (infections that occur only in people with severely reduced immunity), such as *Pneumocystis carinii* pneumonia (PCP) and Kaposi's sarcoma (KS), a rare form of skin cancer; (b) the person's T cell count falls below 200; (c) the person is affected by other infections such as tuberculosis or recurrent pneumonia; or (d) the person has invasive cervical cancer. Because the virus can infect the cells of the brain, symptoms may include seizures and mental problems.

Diagnosis

The blood test that detects the presence of antibodies to HIV uses the ELISA (for enzyme-linked immunosorbent assay) technique, which is easy and cheap to perform. It can be used in two important ways: (1) to screen donated blood; all donated blood in the United States is now screened with ELISA, so that infections because of transfusions should rarely occur, although some did occur before ELISA was developed and a tiny risk remains even with ELISA;[3] and (2) to help people determine whether they are infected (HIV positive) but are asymptomatic carriers. The latter use is important because if people suspect that they are infected and find through the blood test that they are, they should either abstain from sexual activity or, at the very least, use a condom consistently, in order not to spread the disease to others. Only by responsible behavior of this kind can the epidemic be brought under control.

ELISA is a very sensitive test; that is, it is highly accurate in detecting HIV antibodies (it has a very

[3]The risk that ELISA will miss occasional cases of infected blood results from the fact that it detects antibodies to HIV, not HIV itself. It takes six to eight weeks for antibodies to form. Thus if a person donates blood within a few weeks of becoming infected and before antibodies form, ELISA will not detect the infection. Usually ELISA is positive within three months of infection.

low rate of false negatives, in statistical language). However, it does produce a substantial number of false positives—the test saying HIV antibodies are present when they really are not. Thus positive results on ELISA should always be confirmed by a second, more specific test.

The other major test, using the Western blot or immunoblot method, provides such confirmation. It is more expensive and difficult to perform, so it is not practical for mass screening of blood, as is ELISA. However, it is highly accurate (false positives are rare) and thus very useful in confirming or disconfirming a positive test from ELISA.

It should be emphasized that both tests detect only the presence of HIV antibodies. They do not predict whether the person will develop symptoms or will progress to the AIDS classification.

One of the drawbacks to the ELISA test is that it involves a long waiting period—more than a week—before test results are known. Two important developments were the approval by the FDA of the OraQuick rapid HIV test for blood in 2002 and the OraQuick rapid HIV test for oral fluid in 2004. Both must be done in clinics. The blood test involves a finger stick and detects antibodies to both HIV-1 and HIV-2. The mouth-fluid test detects antibodies to HIV-1. In both cases, results are available in 20 to 30 minutes.

Treatment

There is not yet any cure for AIDS. However, some progress is being made in developing treatments to control the disease. One antiviral drug, **AZT** (azidothymidine, also called *zidovudine* or *ZDV*), has been used widely. It can stop the virus from multiplying, but it cannot repair the person's damaged immune system. Unfortunately, AZT has many side effects and cannot be used by some patients, or can be used only for limited periods of time. Therefore a concerted effort is being made to find new drugs that will slow or stop the progression of the disease.

DDI (dideoxyinosine or didanosine) is one such drug. Like AZT, DDI slows the progression of the disease by preventing replication of the virus. DDC (dideoxycytidine), a drug developed in tandem with DDI, also stops the AIDS virus from replicating. D4T is yet another, similar drug. Collectively, these drugs are called ART for antiretroviral therapy.

A major breakthrough came in 1996 with the availability of the category of drugs known as *protease inhibitors* (Kempf et al., 1995). Protease inhibitors attack the viral enzyme protease, which is

AZT: A drug used to treat HIV-infected persons; also called *ZDV.*

necessary for HIV to make copies of itself and multiply. Another breakthrough came in 2006 with the introduction of darunavir, a drug that acts on viruses that are resistant to the protease inhibitors (Simon et al., 2006).

Today patients take a "drug cocktail" of one of the protease inhibitors combined with AZT and one other anti-HIV drug. This combination is called *HAART,* for highly active antiretroviral therapy. Within a year of the introduction of HAART, thrilling reports emerged that the HIV count had become undetectable in the blood of persons taking the drug cocktail (Cohen, 1997). Some people believed that the cure had been found. The number of deaths from AIDS declined for the first year since the disease had been identified.

HIV research, unfortunately, is much like a roller-coaster ride, with elated highs followed by plunges to the depths. HIV mutated to drug-resistant forms. And, although HIV had become undetectable in the blood of persons treated with the drug cocktail, it was hiding out in T cells and the lymph nodes and in organs such as the brain, eyes, and testes (Cohen, 1998; Finzi et al., 1997; Wong et al., 1997). In short, it is not eradicated by the drug cocktail treatment.

Today, HAART is making HIV infection a manageable disease for many persons, who are surviving for much longer than they would have without this treatment. For others, long-term HAART treatment causes serious side effects, such as diabetes-like problems, brittle bones, and heart disease, which means the patient must stop the treatment or switch to another one (Cohen, 2002). Others simply stop responding to the HAART regimen, and there is concern about the emergence of resistant strains.

On another front, progress is also being made with drugs that prevent the opportunistic infections that strike people with AIDS. The drug pentamidine, for example, in aerosol form, is a standard treatment to prevent *Pneumocystis carinii* pneumonia.

Women, Children, Ethnic Minorities, and AIDS

In the early days of the AIDS epidemic, men accounted for most cases in the United States, but the picture has since changed considerably. Whereas in 1985 women were only 7 percent of AIDS cases, today they are 27 percent (CDC, 2006d). HIV/AIDS is now the fifth-leading cause of death for U.S. women between the ages of 25 and 44 and is the leading cause of death for African American women between the ages of 25 and 34. The urgency of addressing the needs of women with HIV infection is thus increasing.

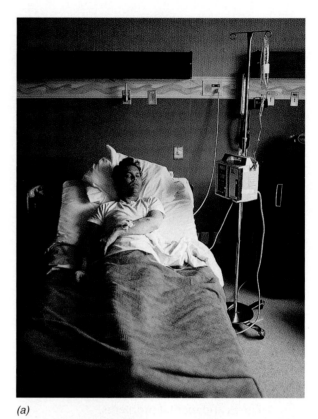

(a)

(b)

Figure 18.4   AIDS is a multicultural disease. (*a*) An American man with AIDS. (*b*) An African woman with AIDS.

As of 2006, new cases of women with HIV infection were most likely to be the result of heterosexual contact (78 percent) and injection drug use (20 percent) (CDC, 2006d).

Women need far more recognition in AIDS research. For example, intervention programs

Focus: First Person
An HIV-Positive Man Tells His Story

Tim Lapp, 44, is a retired chiropractor, retired because he lost his practice when he became too sick with HIV infection to be able to see his patients.

Tim was infected in 1992. Before that, he had been in two long-term relationships and he and his partners got tested regularly for HIV. On a Halloween trip to San Francisco, however, he had sex with a man and they practiced safe sex, but the condom broke. He is certain that this incident was the source of his infection. He never saw that man again. He does not blame him, because they conscientiously practiced safe sex and the other person did not lie to him.

Tim went on, keeping his infection a secret for many reasons, including the fact that in Wisconsin, he would lose his license as a chiropractor if it were known that he was HIV infected. He did not receive early treatment because he was on a new insurance plan and the insurer would have declared the HIV infection a preexisting condition and therefore would not have paid for treatment.

In 1998 he went on a dream trip to Russia. Not realizing that dairy products there are not pasteurized, he ate them and, with his compromised immune system, contracted typhoid fever. He became very sick and was hospitalized. The typhoid fever was cured, but he had a series of serious GI infections over the next year. It was in the midst of all this debilitating illness that he gave up his practice.

Today, Tim is receiving the best treatment available. His T cell count is 150, the highest in years (it has been as low as 18), and he feels healthy. Protease inhibitors, unfortunately, make him sick, so he is not able to take them. Therefore, he is on a drug cocktail minus the protease inhibitors. His current drug combination has worked well for him for two years but just recently has become ineffective, so he will have to switch to different drugs soon. Taking the drugs is not without its problems; about twice a week he vomits four or five times in the morning, but he has learned to accept that.

Tim is in a five-year-long relationship with a man who is an accountant. His partner is HIV negative, they practice safe sex, and his partner has not become infected. Asked why he has a partner who is uninfected and whether he worries about infecting him, Tim said that it is too difficult to find someone whom you love and are compatible with to put up barriers like each other's HIV status. Tim feels that the support he receives from his partner is a large part of the reason he is so healthy now. Tim does extensive volunteer work, especially with the local AIDS support network, serving on the board and coordinating special events.

When I asked Tim what he would say to people reading this book, he replied that he wanted them to know how easy it is to contract the disease. People must use condoms every time they have sex, or all their dreams could go down the drain. He worries that only gay men are careful because they are more aware of the risk and that others are not careful. Yet he also conveyed a message of hope, because treatments have improved dramatically, and, for many, the disease is roughly equivalent to diabetes in that it can be managed. Tim believes today that he can actually look forward to a future.

Source: Based on an interview conducted by Janet Hyde.

---

tailored to the needs of women should be developed. Such programs should include sexual assertiveness training, in which women are empowered to insist that their sex partners use condoms. Women also need to be included in clinical trials of drug treatments.

Some of the saddest cases are children with AIDS; these cases are known as pediatric AIDS. Children become HIV infected either at birth from an infected mother (89 percent of cases) or because of hemophilia (4 percent) or transfusions with contaminated blood (6 percent). Babies born to infected mothers are often, but not always, infected. One bright spot is the finding that using AZT to treat infected women during pregnancy can substantially reduce the rate of infection in their babies to as low as 5 percent (Harris et al., 2002). In the United States, AIDS in infants has nearly been eliminated through helping pregnant women know their HIV status and having those who are infected use AZT (Santora, 2005).

People of color in the United States—and worldwide—have borne a disproportionate burden of the cases of AIDS. African Americans constitute just 12 percent of the U.S. population, but they account for 50 percent of persons with AIDS (CDC, 2006d). Hispanics are also overrepresented; they are 13 percent of the U.S. population, but 18 percent of the cases of AIDS. The incidence of AIDS is low among Asian Americans (less than 1 percent of cases) and Native Americans (also less than 1 percent of cases).

In understanding the impact of AIDS on ethnic minorities in the United States, it is important to recognize that some minority groups, particularly African Americans, hold a very different view of AIDS from the white majority (Aragon et al., 2001). Some African Americans see AIDS as a planned strategy to kill African Americans. These beliefs must be understood in cultural context. Most African Americans are well aware of the Tuskegee Syphilis Study, in which Black men in Alabama who had syphilis were purposely left untreated for decades in order to see what the long-term consequences of the disease would be. That study was appallingly cruel and unethical; no research ethics committee would approve it today. In the wake of that study, African Americans find it hard to trust the white-dominated medical community, or white Americans in general, in matters having to do with sexually transmitted infections.

There is an urgent need to develop education and prevention programs for the Black and Latino communities like those that have been launched in the gay community. These programs must be culturally sensitive and should focus on the elimination of needle sharing and unsafe sexual practices.

Psychological Considerations in AIDS

Psychological issues for those infected with HIV and for AIDS patients are profound. A personal view of the psychological struggles of such a person is presented in Focus: First Person, on page 469. There are some analogies to people who receive a diagnosis of an incurable cancer, for AIDS is, at least at present, incurable. Many patients experience the typical reactions for such situations, including a denial of the reality, followed by anger, depression, or both. However, the analogy to cancer patients is not perfect, for AIDS is a socially stigmatized disease in a way that cancer is not. Thus the revelation that one has AIDS must often be accompanied by the announcement that one is gay or drug addicted. Also, as the patient becomes sicker, he or she is unlikely to be able to hold a job, and financial worries become an additional strain.

There is a great need to be sensitive to the psychological needs of AIDS patients. In most cities, support groups for AIDS patients and their families have formed. Social and psychological support from others is essential as people weather this crisis (Gonzalez et al., 2004).

Cognitive–behavioral therapy combined with stress-management therapy has been shown to be effective in improving quality of life and decreasing anxiety and depression in HIV-infected people (Cruess et al., 2002; Lechner et al., 2003). The effectiveness of this therapy is important for two reasons. First, it improves the quality of life of affected people. Second, research shows that HIV-positive people who do not have symptoms but are depressed die earlier than similar people who are not depressed (Burack et al., 1993). Psychotherapy is therefore likely to have a positive impact on both mental health and physical health.

In Chapter 15 we discussed the phenomenon of *posttraumatic growth* following rape. Between 60 and 80 percent of people with HIV infection report positive psychological growth following diagnosis; people who experience posttraumatic growth and are optimistic tend to have higher T cell counts, helping them to fight disease progression (Milam, 2006).

Recent Progress in AIDS Research

As this discussion makes clear, much more research on AIDS is needed. We need better treatments to control this disease, we need a cure for it, and we need a vaccine against it. Those are tall orders, and it is unlikely that any of them will appear in the next few years.

Vaccine

Researchers have been working hard to develop a vaccine against HIV, but the job has turned out to be much more difficult than expected. The problem is that HIV has many forms, and, even worse, it mutates rapidly and recombines, creating more forms. In effect, the virus doesn't hold still long enough for a vaccine to take effective aim at it.

One strategy in developing a vaccine is to first develop a vaccine that works with monkeys, which can be infected by an analog to HIV called SIV (simian immunodeficiency virus). Progress has been made toward developing vaccines that protect monkeys from infection with SIV (Amara et al., 2001; Casimiro et al., 2003).

Yet another strategy involves the development of a vaccine to be administered to people recently infected with HIV. The goal is to boost their immune function so that they can fight off the virus. Vaccines of this type are being developed (Barouch et al., 2000; Rosenberg et al., 2000; Schooley et al., 2000).

Two other strategies involve developing a vaccine that stimulates the body to form resistance (i.e., antibodies) to HIV, or a vaccine that acts at the cellular level by stimulating the production of specialized T cells that are toxic to HIV (Luzuriaga et al., 2006). Another possibility is a vaccine that combines both. Yet another possibility is to develop a vaccine to be administered to infants, which would prevent transmission through breast milk, as well as later infection when they become sexually active. Several of these vaccines have moved into clinical trials with humans.

Research on Nonprogressors

Some specific groups of people are being studied for clues to breakthroughs in the war against AIDS. One such group is *nonprogressors*. Approximately 5 percent of HIV-infected people go for 10 years or more without symptoms and with no deterioration of their immune system (see Figure 18.5). Their T cell count remains higher than 500. Nonprogressors turn out to have less HIV in their bodies, even though they have been infected for over a decade. Why? One possibility is that these people have unusually strong immune systems that have essentially managed to contain the virus. Another is that they were infected with a weak strain of the virus. Some individuals were infected with a genetically defective strain of HIV that does not replicate; this situation is intriguing because it might be useful in producing a vaccine. Nonprogressors also have particularly high levels of defensins, chemicals secreted by white blood cells (Ganz, 2002). Defensins are known to contribute to the killing of microbes such as HIV.

Chemokines

Another major scientific advance is the discovery of HIV-suppressor factors or *chemokines* (Balter, 1995; Cocchi et al., 1995; Cohen, 1997). Certain lymphocytes (CD8+ T cells) battle against HIV in the body. They do so by secreting three chemokines (which are molecules), named RANTES, MIP-1a, and MIP-1b. HIV-infected persons who are nonprogressors have high levels of CD8 cells and high levels of chemokines compared with rapid progressors (Haynes et al., 1996). The chemokines can bind to the coreceptor CCR5, blocking HIV from entering cells. Scientists hope that these discoveries may lead to improved treatments for HIV-infected persons and possibly to vaccines that boost the level of chemokines and therefore boost the body's resistance to HIV infection.

Figure 18.5   One promising strategy in the search for a cure for AIDS is to study the rare individuals who have been HIV infected for 10 years or more but have not died or even developed AIDS. Artist Robert Anderson has had HIV for 15 years and is still healthy.

Genetic Resistance

Scientists have discovered a mutation of a gene and the mutation creates strong resistance to HIV infection (Galvani & Slatkin, 2003; Novembre et al., 2005). The gene is called CCR5 because it is the gene for the CCR5 receptor that, as discussed earlier, allows HIV to enter cells. The mutation occurred some time in history as humans spread out of Africa. The evidence indicates that the mutation was strongly selected for during the bubonic plague or smallpox plagues that occurred in Europe, and the mutation is much more common there than in other parts of the world. People with

2 copies of the mutation (homozygotes) are resistant to infection, whereas people with 1 copy (heterozygotes) may become infected but show much slower disease progression.

Researchers are also pursuing *gene therapy* for HIV and many other diseases (Strachan & Read, 2004). This would involve injecting the patient with genetic material created to wreak havoc on HIV in any number of ways—for example, by preventing it from replicating or by inactivating proteins that HIV needs to complete its life cycle and go on infecting more lymphocytes. With all the progress made by the Human Genome Project, this approach seems quite promising.

Microbicides

Microbicides are substances, usually in ointment form, that kill microbes such as HIV. These ointments could be put into the vagina or anus or spread on the penis to battle HIV transmission. The old standby nonoxynol-9 was thought to be effective in killing HIV some years ago, but today we know that it is not only ineffective but actually makes women more vulnerable to infection by irritating the lining of the vagina (Van Damme et al., 2002). Much effort is now going into developing effective microbicides that will attack HIV as well as other sexually transmitted viruses. Some are already in clinical trials, including PRO 2000 Gel and BufferGel (Upadhyay et al., 2005). BufferGel is a vaginal defense enhancer, meaning that it boosts the vagina's natural resistance to infection; it should provide protection against HIV, chlamydia, herpes, and HPV, as well as pregnancy. PRO 2000 is an entry and fusion inhibitor, which means that it binds to viruses and bacteria so that they don't infect healthy cells; it is aimed at protecting against HIV, gonorrhea, and herpes, as well as pregnancy.

Behavioral Prevention

In the last analysis, prevention is better than cure. Until we have an effective vaccine, our best hope is interventions that aim to change people's behavior, because it is behavior—sexual activity, injection drug use—that spreads HIV. The big success story in behavioral prevention is in Uganda. In 1991, screening of pregnant women there indicated that 21 percent were infected; by 1998, this figure had dropped to 10 percent (Stoneburner & Low-Beer, 2004). In the early 1990s, the Ugandan government launched a bold and forceful program called ABC, for Abstinence, Be faithful, and use Condoms. It blanketed the country with advertising about the program, which urged unmarried persons to abstain from sex, married people to be faithful, and everyone to use condoms. The whole emphasis was on behavior change, with no need for the costly drugs that Uganda couldn't afford. It isn't completely clear which of the three components of the program had the most effect, but in any case the program worked, and the epidemic is under control in that country. Scientists have estimated that this intervention had an effect equivalent to a vaccine with 80 percent effectiveness (Stoneburner & Low-Beer, 2004).

Gonorrhea

Historical records indicate that **gonorrhea** ("the clap," "the drip") is the oldest of the sexual diseases. Its symptoms are described in the Old Testament, in Leviticus 15 (about 3,500 years ago). The Greek physician Hippocrates, some 2,400 years ago, believed that gonorrhea resulted from "excessive indulgence in the pleasures of Venus," the goddess of love (hence the term *venereal* disease). Albert Neisser identified the bacterium that causes it, the gonococcus *Neisseria gonorrhoeae,* in 1879.

Gonorrhea has always been a particular problem in wartime, when it spreads rapidly among the soldiers and the prostitutes they patronize. In the twentieth century, a gonorrhea epidemic occurred during World War I, and gonorrhea was also a serious problem during World War II. Then, with the discovery of penicillin and its use in curing gonorrhea, the disease became much less prevalent in the 1950s; indeed, public health officials thought that it would be virtually eliminated.

Then there was a resurgence of gonorrhea, with about 1 million cases per year reported in the 1970s (CDC, 2003a). It is clear that one of the reasons for the resurgence was the shift in contraceptive practices to the use of the pill, which (unlike the condom) provides no protection from gonorrhea and actually increases a woman's susceptibility. Today there are about 300,000 cases per year, the decline due mainly to increased use of condoms.

Symptoms

Most cases of gonorrhea result from penis-in-vagina intercourse. In the male, the gonococcus invades the urethra, producing urethritis (inflammation of the urethra). White blood cells rush to

---

Gonorrhea (gon-uh-REE-uh): A sexually transmitted infection that usually causes symptoms of a puslike discharge and painful, burning urination in the male but is frequently asymptomatic in the female.

Focus: First Person
Safer Sex in the AIDS Era

In this age of AIDS, everyone needs to think about positive health practices that will prevent, or at least reduce the chances of, infection. Technically, these practices are called *safer sex*, there being no true safe sex except no sex. What choices are available? Health experts agree that the following practices will make sex safer:

1. If you choose to be sexually active (and abstinence is one alternative to consider), have sex only in a stable, faithful, monogamous relationship with an uninfected partner whom you know is uninfected because you both have been tested.

2. If you are sexually active with more than one partner, always use latex condoms. They have a good track record in preventing many sexually transmitted infections. Laboratory tests indicate that latex condoms are effective protection against HIV. Condoms have a failure rate in preventing disease just as they do in preventing pregnancy, but they are still much better than nothing.

3. If there is any risk that you are infected or that your partner is, abstain from sex, always use condoms, or consider alternative forms of sexual expression such as hand–genital stimulation.

4. Do not have sexual intercourse with someone who has had many previous partners.

5. Do not engage in anal intercourse if there is even the slightest risk that your partner is infected.

6. Remember that both vaginal intercourse and anal intercourse transmit HIV. Mouth–genital sex may also transmit HIV, particularly if semen enters the mouth.

Figure 18.6 Quality control of condoms.

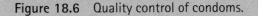

7. If you think that you may be infected, have a blood test to find out. If you learn that you are infected, at the very least use a condom every time you engage in anal or vaginal intercourse, or, preferably, abstain from these behaviors.

8. If you are a woman and you think that you might be infected, think carefully before getting pregnant, because of the risk of transmitting the disease to the baby during pregnancy and childbirth.

9. Consider "outercourse" as an alternative to intercourse. Outercourse involves activities like mutual masturbation and erotic massage, which don't transmit diseases.

the area and attempt to destroy the bacteria, but the bacteria soon win the battle. In most cases, symptoms appear two to five days after infection, although they may appear as early as the first day or as late as two weeks after infection. Initially a thin, clear mucous discharge seeps out of the meatus (the opening at the tip of the penis). Within a day or so it becomes thick and creamy and may be white, yellowish, or yellow-green (see Figure 18.7). This is often referred to as a *purulent* (puslike) discharge. The area around the meatus may become swollen. About half of infected men experience a painful burning sensation when urinating. The urine may contain pus or blood, and in some cases the lymph glands of the groin become enlarged and tender.

Because the early symptoms of gonorrhea in men are obvious and often painful, most men seek treatment immediately and are cured. If the disease is not treated, however, the urethritis spreads up the urethra, causing inflammations in the prostate (prostatitis), seminal vesicles (seminal

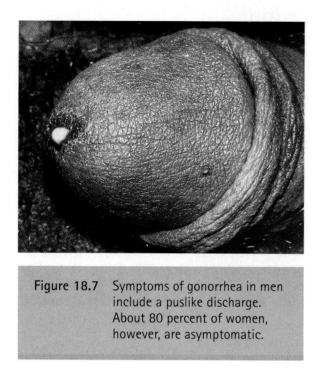

Figure 18.7 Symptoms of gonorrhea in men include a puslike discharge. About 80 percent of women, however, are asymptomatic.

vesiculitis), urinary bladder (cystitis), and epididymis (epididymitis). Pain on urination becomes worse and is felt in the whole penis. Then these early symptoms may disappear as the disease spreads to the other organs. If the epididymitis is left untreated, it may spread to the testicles and the resulting scar tissue may cause sterility.

Asymptomatic gonorrhea (gonorrhea with no symptoms) does occur in males, but its incidence is low. In contrast, about 60 to 80 percent of women infected with gonorrhea are asymptomatic during the early stages of the disease. Many women are unaware of their infection unless they are told by a male partner. Therefore, it is extremely important for any male who is infected to inform all his contacts.

The gonorrheal infection in the woman invades the cervix. Pus is discharged, but the amount may be so slight that it is not noticed. When present, it is yellow-green and irritating to the vulva, but it is generally not heavy (it is not to be confused with normal cervical mucus, which is clear or white and nonirritating, or with discharges resulting from the various kinds of vaginitis—discussed in this chapter—that are irritating but white). Although the cervix is the primary site of infection, the inflammation may also spread to the urethra, causing burning pain on urination (not to be confused with cystitis).

If the infection is not treated, the Bartholin glands may become infected and, in rare cases, swell and produce pus. The infection may also be spread to the anus and rectum, either by a heavy cervical discharge or by the menstrual discharge.

Because so many women are asymptomatic in the early stages of gonorrhea, many receive no treatment, and thus there is a high risk of serious complications. In about 20 percent of women who go untreated, the gonococcus moves up into the uterus. From there it infects the fallopian tubes. The tissues become swollen and inflamed, and thus the condition is called pelvic inflammatory disease (PID)—although PID can be caused by diseases other than gonorrhea. The major symptom is pelvic pain and, in some cases, irregular or painful menstruation. If the PID is not treated, scar tissue may form, blocking the tubes and leaving the woman sterile. Indeed, untreated gonorrhea is one of the most common causes of infertility in women. If the tubes are partially blocked, so that sperm can get up them but eggs cannot move down, ectopic pregnancy can result, because the fertilized egg is trapped in the tube.

There are three other major sites for nongenital gonorrhea infection: the mouth and throat, the anus and rectum, and the eyes. If fellatio is performed on an infected man, the gonococcus may invade the throat. (Cunnilingus is less likely to spread gonorrhea, and mouth-to-mouth kissing rarely does.) Such an infection is often asymptomatic; the typical symptom, if there is one, is a sore throat. Rectal gonorrhea is contracted through anal intercourse and thus affects both women in heterosexual relations and, more commonly, men who have sex with men. Symptoms include some discharge from the rectum and itching, but many cases are asymptomatic. Gonorrhea may also invade the eyes. This occurs only rarely in adults, when they touch the genitals and then transfer the bacteria-containing pus to their eyes by touching them. This eye infection is much more common in newborn infants. The infection is transferred from the mother's cervix to the infant's eyes during birth. For this reason, most states require that silver nitrate, or erythromycin or some other antibiotic, be put in every newborn's eyes to prevent any such infection. If left untreated, the eyes become swollen and painful within a few days, and there is a discharge of pus. Blindness was a common result in the preantibiotic era.

Diagnosis

A urine test is available for men. If gonorrhea in the throat is suspected, a swab should be taken and cultured. People who suspect that they may have rectal gonorrhea should request that a swab be taken from the rectum, since many physicians will not automatically think to do this.

In females, a sample of the cervical discharge is taken from the cervix and tested. A pelvic examination should also be performed. Pain during this exam may indicate PID. Women who suspect throat or rectal infection should request that samples be taken from those sites as well.

Treatment

The traditional treatment for gonorrhea was a large dose of penicillin, or tetracycline for those who were allergic to penicillin. However, strains of the gonococcus that are resistant to penicillin and tetracycline become so common that the newer antibiotic Cipro had to be used. In 2007 the CDC announced that cases that were resistant to Cipro had become so common that doctors should stop using it and switch to Ceftriaxone. The worry is that if resistance develops to it, there will be no remaining antibiotics for treatment.

Syphilis

There has been considerable debate over the exact origins of **syphilis.** The disease, called "the Great Pox," was present in Europe during the 1400s and became a pandemic by 1500.

The bacterium that causes syphilis is called *Treponema pallidum.* It is spiral shaped and is thus often called a *spirochete.* In 1906, Wassermann, Neisser, and Bruck described a test for diagnosing syphilis, which became known as the *Wassermann test* or *Wassermann reaction.* This test has been replaced by more modern blood tests, but the Wassermann label hangs on.

The incidence of syphilis is much less than that of gonorrhea or chlamydia. There were 8,700 reported new cases in 2005, a sharp decline from the early 1990s (CDC, 2006c). The rates now are the lowest since reporting began in 1941. The CDC, seizing the opportunity, has launched a National Plan to Eliminate Syphilis in the United States.

Although syphilis is not nearly as common as chlamydia or gonorrhea, its effects are much more serious if left untreated. In most cases, chlamydia or gonorrhea cause only discomfort and, sometimes, sterility; syphilis, if left untreated, can damage the nervous system and even cause death. There are many cases today of coinfection, in which the person is infected with both syphilis and HIV. Syphilis infection makes one more vulnerable to HIV and vice versa.

Symptoms

The major early symptom of syphilis is the **chancre**—a round, ulcerlike lesion with a hard, raised edge, resembling a crater. One of the distinctive things about the chancre is that although it looks terrible, it is painless. It appears about 3 weeks (as early as 10 days or as late as 3 months) after intercourse with an infected person. The chancre appears at the point where the bacteria entered the body. Typically, the bacteria enter through the mucous membranes of the genitals as a result of intercourse with an infected person. Thus in men the chancre often appears on the penis or scrotum. In women, the chancre often appears on the cervix, and thus the woman does not notice it and is unaware that she is infected (this is one good reason for a woman to do the pelvic self-exam with a speculum as described in Chapter 4). The chancre may also appear on the vaginal walls or, externally, on the vulva (see Figure 18.8).

If oral sex or anal intercourse with an infected person occurs, the bacteria can also invade the mucous membranes of the mouth or rectum. Thus the chancre may appear on the lips, tongue, or tonsils or around the anus. In addition, the bacteria may enter through a cut in the skin anywhere on the body. Thus it is possible (though rare) to get syphilis by touching the chancre of an infected person. The chancre would then appear on the hand at the point where the bacteria entered through the break in the skin.

The progress of the disease once the person has been infected is generally divided into four stages: primary-stage syphilis, secondary-stage syphilis, latent syphilis, and late syphilis. The phase described earlier, in which the chancre forms, is **primary-stage syphilis.** If left untreated, the chancre goes away by itself within 1 to 5 weeks after it appears. This marks the end of the primary stage. However, the disease has not gone away just because the chancre has healed; it has only gone underground.

Beginning a few months after the original appearance of the chancre, a generalized body rash develops, marking the beginning of **secondary-stage syphilis.** The rash is variable in its appearance, the most distinctive feature being that it does not itch or hurt. Hair loss may also occur during the secondary stage. Usually the symptoms are troublesome enough to cause the person to seek medical help. With appropriate treatment at this

Syphilis (SIFF-ih-lis): A sexually transmitted infection that causes a chancre to appear in the primary stage.
Chancre (SHANK-er): A painless, ulcerlike lesion with a hard, raised edge that is a symptom of syphilis.
Primary-stage syphilis: The first few weeks of a syphilis infection during which the chancre is present.
Secondary-stage syphilis: The second stage of syphilis, occurring several months after infection, during which the chancre has disappeared and a generalized body rash appears.

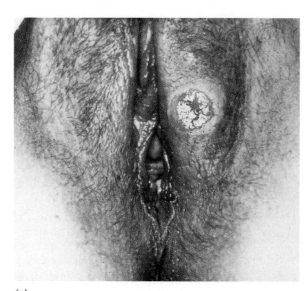

(a)

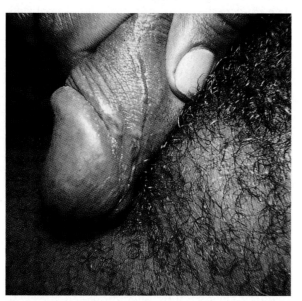

(b)

Figure 18.8 The chancre characteristic of primary stage syphilis (*a*) on the labia majora and (*b*) on the penis.

Latent (LAY-tent) syphilis: The third stage of syphilis, which may last for years, during which symptoms disappear although the person is still infected.
Late syphilis: The fourth and final stage of syphilis, during which the disease does damage to major organs of the body such as the lungs, heart, or brain.
Congenital (kun-JEN-ih-tul) syphilis: A syphilis infection in a newborn baby resulting from transmission from an infected mother.

stage, the disease can still be cured and there will be no permanent effects.

Even without treatment, the secondary-stage symptoms go away in a few weeks, leading people to believe mistakenly that the disease has gone away. Instead, it has entered a more dangerous stage.

After the symptoms of the secondary stage have disappeared, the disease is in the latent stage; **latent syphilis** may last for years. Although there are no symptoms in this stage, *Treponema pallidum* is busily burrowing into the tissues of the body, especially the blood vessels, central nervous system (brain and spinal cord), and bones. After the first year or so of the latent stage, the disease is no longer infectious, except that a pregnant woman can still pass it on to the fetus.

About half of the people who enter the latent stage remain in it permanently, living out the rest of their lives without further complications. The other half, however, move into the dangerous **late syphilis.** In *cardiovascular late syphilis* the heart and major blood vessels are attacked; this occurs 10 to 40 years after the initial infection. Cardiovascular syphilis can lead to death. In *neurosyphilis* the brain and spinal cord are attacked, leading to insanity and paralysis, which appear 10 to 20 years after infection. Neurosyphilis may be fatal.

If a pregnant woman has syphilis, the fetus may be infected when the bacteria cross the placental barrier, and the child gets **congenital** (meaning present from birth) **syphilis.** The infection may cause early death of the fetus (spontaneous abortion) or severe illness at or shortly after birth. It may also lead to late complications that show up only at 10 or 20 years of age. Women are most infectious to their baby when they have primary- or secondary-stage syphilis, but they may transmit the infection to the fetus as long as 8 years after the mother's initial infection. If the disease is diagnosed and treated before the fourth month of pregnancy, the fetus will not develop the disease. For this reason, a syphilis test is done as a routine part of the blood analysis in a pregnancy test.

Diagnosis

Syphilis is somewhat difficult to diagnose from symptoms because, as noted earlier, its symptoms are like those of many other diseases.

The physical exam should include inspection not only of the genitals but also of the entire body surface. Women should have a pelvic exam so that the vagina and the cervix can be checked for chancres. If the patient has had anal intercourse, a rectal exam should also be performed.

If a chancre is present, some of its fluid is taken and placed on a slide for inspection under a darkfield microscope. If the person has syphilis, *Treponema pallidum* should be present.

The most common tests for syphilis are blood tests, all of which are based on antibody reactions. The VDRL (named for the Venereal Disease Research

Laboratory of the U.S. Public Health Service, where the test was developed) is one of these blood tests. It is fairly accurate, cheap, and easy to perform.

Treatment

The treatment of choice for syphilis is penicillin. *Treponema pallidum* is actually rather fragile, so large doses are not necessary in treatment. The recommended dose is two shots of benzathine penicillin, one in each of the buttocks. Latent, later, and congenital syphilis require larger doses. For those allergic to penicillin, the recommended treatment is tetracycline or doxycycline, but it should not be given to pregnant women.

Elimination of Syphilis?

In 1998 the U.S. Public Health Service announced that it was targeting syphilis for complete elimination in the United States (St. Louis & Wasserheit, 1998). On the surface, the goal may seem odd, given that syphilis is relatively rare compared with other STIs. But syphilis infection makes a person much more vulnerable to HIV infection because of the open sores produced by syphilis, and a person who is HIV infected and then contracts syphilis may experience immediately life-threatening conditions. For these reasons, syphilis is more serious than the small rate of infection indicates. Moreover, syphilis is completely curable with a single dose of penicillin, it is easily detectable with inexpensive laboratory tests, and it has not developed resistant strains. Experience since World War II indicates that, even when syphilis is effectively treated and brought to a low incidence, it still resurges periodically in epidemics. Therefore, total elimination is the best goal, and it seems feasible.

Viral Hepatitis

Viral hepatitis is a disease of the liver. One symptom is an enlarged liver that is somewhat tender. The disease can vary greatly in severity from asymptomatic cases to ones in which there is fever, fatigue, jaundice (yellowish skin), and vomiting, much as one might experience with a serious case of the flu. There are five types of viral hepatitis: hepatitis A, B, C, D, and E. The one that is of most interest in a discussion of sexually transmitted infections is hepatitis B. Hepatitis C and D (or delta) can also be transmitted sexually, but they are rare compared with B.

The virus for hepatitis B (HBV) can be transmitted through blood, saliva, semen, vaginal secretions, and other body fluids. The behaviors that spread it include needle sharing by people who inject drugs, vaginal and anal intercourse, and oral–anal sex. The disease is found among men who have sex with men and among heterosexuals. It has many similarities to AIDS, although hepatitis B is more contagious. People who have had the disease continue to have a positive blood test for it for the rest of their lives.

Many adults infected with HBV are asymptomatic; their bodies fight off the virus and they are left uninfected, with permanent immunity. Others develop an early, acute (short-term) illness and display a variety of symptoms but recover from the illness. A third group develops chronic (long-term) hepatitis B. They continue to be infectious and may develop serious liver disease involving cirrhosis or cancer. Fortunately, antiviral treatments are now available for those with chronic hepatitis B (Fung & Lok, 2004; Hom et al., 2004; Saltik-Temizel et al., 2004).

The good news is that there is a vaccine against hepatitis B. The current recommendation is that all teenagers and infants be vaccinated. We urge you to be vaccinated if you are a gay man or a heterosexual man or woman who has had a number of partners. If there is even a hint that you have been exposed, you should be tested.

Trichomoniasis

Trichomoniasis ("trich") is caused by the protozoan *Trichomonas vaginalis* (Swygard et al., 2004). The organism can survive for a time on toilet seats and other objects, so it is occasionally transmitted nonsexually; but it is transmitted mainly through sexual intercourse.

For women, the symptom is an abundant, frothy, white or yellow vaginal discharge that irritates the vulva and has an unpleasant smell. In men, there may be irritation of the urethra and a discharge from the penis, but some men are asymptomatic. It is important that accurate diagnosis be made, because the drugs used to treat trichomoniasis are different from those used to treat other STIs that have similar symptoms, and the long-term effects of untreated trichomoniasis can be serious.

The treatment of choice is metronidazole (Flagyl) taken orally. If left untreated, trich can lead to pelvic inflammatory disease and problems with birth (Swygard et al., 2004). It also increases susceptibility to HIV infection.

Trichomoniasis (trick–oh–moh–NY–us–is): A form of vaginitis causing a frothy white or yellow discharge with an unpleasant odor.

Pubic Lice

Pubic lice ("crabs" or *pediculosis pubis*) are tiny lice that attach themselves to the base of pubic hairs and there feed on blood from their human host. They are about the size of a pinhead and, under magnification, resemble a crab (see Figure 18.9). They lay eggs frequently and live for about 30 days, but they die within 24 hours if they are taken off a human host. Crabs are transmitted by sexual contact, but they may also be picked up from sheets, towels, sleeping bags, or toilet seats. (Yes, there are some things you can catch from toilet seats.)

The major symptom of pubic lice is fierce itching in the region of the pubic hair. Diagnosis is made by finding the lice or the eggs attached to the hairs.

Pubic lice are treated with the drugs Nix and Rid, which are available without prescription. Both kill the lice. After treatment, the person should put on clean clothing. Since the lice die within 24 hours, it is not necessary to disinfect clothing that has not been used for longer than 24 hours. However, the eggs can live for up to 6 days, and in difficult cases it may be necessary to boil or dry-clean one's clothing or use a spray such as R and C.

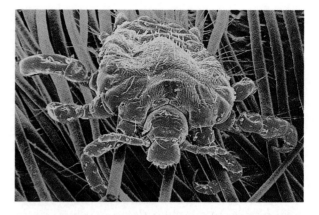

Figure 18.9 A pubic louse, enlarged. The actual size is about the same as the head of a pin.

Preventing STIs

While most of the literature one reads concentrates on the rapid diagnosis and treatment of STIs, prevention would be much better than cure, and there are some ways in which one can avoid getting STIs, or at least reduce one's chances of doing so. The most obvious ways, of course, are to limit yourself to a monogamous relationship with an uninfected person or to abstain from sexual activity. If these strategies are unacceptable to you, other techniques are available.

The latex condom, in addition to being a decent contraceptive, gives good (though not perfect) protection against HIV, HPV, gonorrhea, chlamydia, herpes, syphilis, and other STIs (Baldwin et al., 2004; Steiner & Cates, 2006; Wald et al., 2005; Winer et al., 2006). With the rise of the STI epidemic, the condom is again becoming popular. The key is to eroticize condom use. The diaphragm also provides some protection for women, as does the female condom. Table 18.2 presents a possible dialogue to overcoming a partner's objections to condom use.

Some simple health precautions are also helpful. Successful prostitutes, who need to be careful about STIs, take such precautions. Washing the genitals before intercourse helps remove bacteria. This may not sound like a romantic prelude to lovemaking, but prostitutes make a sensuous game out of soaping the man's genitals. You can do this as part of taking a shower or bath with your partner. The other important technique is inspecting your partner's genitals. If you see a chancre, a wart, a herpes blister, or a discharge, put on your clothes and leave or, at the very least, immediately start a conversation about STI status (do not fall for the "it's only a pimple" routine). This technique may sound a little crude or embarrassing, but if you are intimate enough with someone to make love with that person, you ought to be intimate enough to look at her or his genitals. Once again, if you are cool about it, you can make this an erotic part of foreplay.

However, just because a partner has no obvious symptoms like herpes blisters or warts, don't assume that the person is uninfected. We have seen in this chapter how many of these diseases—for example, chlamydia, herpes, and warts—can be asymptomatic. The only way to really know is to have a complete battery of tests for STIs, a choice more and more people are making. Not every disease is tested in the standard battery—for example, herpes and HPV usually are not—but it will catch most infections.

Urinating both before and after intercourse helps to keep bacteria out of the urethra.

Finally, each person needs to recognize that it is his or her ethical responsibility to seek out early diagnosis and treatment. Probably the most important responsibility is that of informing prospective partners if you have an STI and of informing past partners as soon as you discover that you have one. For example, because so many women are asymptomatic for chlamydia, it is particularly important

SexSource Online
www.mhhe.com/hyde10

"JUST LIKE ME"
IN SEXUALLY
TRANSMITTED
DISEASES

Pubic lice: Tiny lice that attach themselves to the base of pubic hairs and cause itching; also called *crabs* or *pediculosis pubis*.

Focus: First Person
Cool Lines about Safer Sex

Partner	*You*
What's that?	A condom, baby.
What for?	To use when we're making love.
I don't like using them.	Why not?
It doesn't feel as good with a rubber.	I'll feel more relaxed. If I'm more relaxed, I can make it feel better for you.
But we've never used a condom before.	I don't want to take any more risks.
Rubbers are gross.	Being pregnant when I don't want to be is worse. So is getting AIDS.
Don't you trust me?	Trust isn't the point. People carry sexually transmitted infections without knowing it.
I'll pull out in time.	Women can get pregnant from precum. It can also carry sexually transmitted infections.
I thought you said using condoms made you feel cheap.	I decided to face facts. I like having sex, and I want to stay healthy and happy.
Rubbers aren't romantic.	Making love and protecting each other's health sounds romantic enough to me.
Making love with a rubber on is like taking a shower with a raincoat on.	Doing it without a rubber is playing Russian roulette.
It just isn't as sensitive.	With a condom you might last even longer, and that'll make up for it.
I don't stay hard when I put on a condom.	I can do something about that.
Putting it on interrupts everything.	Not if I help put it on.
I'll try, but it might not work.	Practice makes perfect.
But I love you.	Then you'll help me protect myself.
I guess you don't really love me.	I'm not going to prove my love by risking my life.
I'm not using a rubber, no matter what.	Well, then I guess we're not having sex.
Just this once without it.	It only takes once to get pregnant. It only takes once to get AIDS.
It won't fit.	Condoms come in all different sizes.

Source: www.teenwire.com, June 22, 2004.

for men to take the responsibility of informing their female partners if they find that they have the disease. It is important to take care of your own health, but it is equally important to take care of your partner's health.

Other Genital Infections

Vaginitis (vaginal inflammation or irritation) is very common among women and is endemic in college populations. Two kinds of vaginitis, as well as cystitis (inflammation of the urinary bladder) and prostatitis, are considered here. None of these infections are STIs, because they are not transmitted by sexual contact; they are, however, common infections of the sex organs.

A few simple steps can help prevent vaginitis. Every time you shower or take a bath, wash the vulva carefully and dry it thoroughly. Do not use feminine hygiene deodorant sprays; they are unnecessary and can irritate the vagina. Wear cotton underpants; nylon and other synthetics retain moisture, and vaginitis-producing organisms thrive on moisture. Avoid wearing pants that are too tight in

Vaginitis (vaj–in–ITE–is): An irritation or inflammation of the vagina, usually causing a discharge.

the crotch; they increase moisture and may irritate the vulva. Wipe the anus from front to back so that bacteria from the anus do not get into the vagina. For the same reason, never go immediately from anal intercourse to vaginal intercourse. Finally, if an attack of vaginitis seems to be coming on, placing some yogurt with active cultures into the vagina can help restore the good bacteria.

Monilia

Monilia (also called *candida, yeast infection, fungus,* and *moniliasis*) is a form of vaginitis caused by the yeast fungus *Candida. Candida* is normally present in the vagina, but if the delicate environmental balance there is disturbed (e.g., if the pH is changed), the growth of *Candida* can get out of hand. Conditions that encourage the growth of *Candida* include long-term use of birth control pills, menstruation, diabetes or a prediabetic condition, pregnancy, and long-term use of antibiotics such as tetracycline. It is not a sexually transmitted infection, but intercourse may aggravate it.

The major symptom is a thick, white, curdlike vaginal discharge, found on the vaginal lips and the walls of the vagina. The discharge can cause extreme itching, to the point where the woman is not interested in having intercourse.

Treatment is by the drugs miconazole or clotelnazole, both available over the counter. Fluconazole, a single-dose treatment, is available by prescription.

If a woman has monilia while she is pregnant, she can transmit it to her baby during birth. The baby gets the yeast in its digestive system, a condition known as *thrush.* Thrush can also result from oral–genital sex.

Bacterial vaginosis is another vaginal infection that produces a similar discharge. The distinctive feature is that the discharge has a foul odor.

Monilia (Moh–NILL–ee–uh): A form of vaginitis causing a thick, white discharge; also called candida or yeast infection.

Cystitis (sis–TY–tis): An infection of the urinary bladder in women, causing painful, burning urination.

Prostatitis (pros–tuh–TY–tis): An infection or inflammation of the prostate gland.

Cystitis

Cystitis is an infection of the urinary bladder that occurs almost exclusively in women. In many cases it is caused by the bacterium *Escherichia coli.* The bacteria are normally present in the body (in the intestine), and in some cases, for unknown reasons, they get into the urethra and the bladder. Sometimes frequent, vigorous sexual intercourse will irritate the urethral opening, permitting the bacteria to get in.

The symptoms are a desire to urinate every few minutes, with a burning pain on urination. The urine may be hazy or even tinged with red; this is caused by pus and blood from the infected bladder. There may also be backache. Diagnosis can usually be made simply on the basis of these symptoms. A urine sample should be taken and analyzed, though, for confirmation.

Treatment is usually with Bactrim or another antibiotic. The drug may include a dye that helps relieve the burning sensation on urination; the dye turns the urine bright orange-red.

To prevent cystitis or prevent recurring bouts of it, drink lots of water and urinate frequently, especially just before and after intercourse. This will help flush out any bacteria from the bladder and urethra.

Prostatitis

Prostatitis is an inflammation of the prostate gland. As with cystitis in women, the infection is often caused by the bacterium *E. coli.* It can also be caused by gonorrhea or chlamydia. The symptoms are fever, chills, pain around the anus and rectum, and a need for frequent urination. It may produce sexual dysfunction, typically painful ejaculation. In some cases, prostatitis may be chronic (long-lasting) and may have no symptoms, or only lower-back pain. Antibiotics are used in treatment.

SUMMARY

Sexually transmitted infections (STIs) are at epidemic levels in the United States and worldwide. Three common STIs among college students are chlamydia, HPV, and herpes.

Chlamydia is often asymptomatic, especially in women. In men, it produces a thin discharge from the penis and mild pain on urination. It is quite curable with antibiotics. If left untreated in women, the possible complications include pelvic inflammatory disease and possibly infertility.

HPV (human papillomavirus) causes genital warts. Sometimes the warts are obvious, but in other cases they are small and may not be visible. HPV infection increases women's risk of cervical cancer, and a vaccine is now available.

Genital herpes, caused by the HSV virus, produces bouts of painful blisters on the genitals. These episodes may recur for the rest of the person's life, although some infected persons experience no or only a few outbreaks. Currently there is no cure, although the drug acyclovir minimizes the symptoms. Herpes infection increases one's risk of HIV infection.

The virus HIV destroys the body's natural immune system and leaves the person vulnerable to certain kinds of infections and cancers that lead to death. Most HIV-positive people come from three risk groups: men who have sex with men, injection drug users, and heterosexual partners of infected persons. Drugs such as AZT and ritonavir (a protease inhibitor) are used to slow the progression of the disease. More attention needs to focus on the special concerns of HIV-infected women and ethnic minorities. Several strategies for producing a vaccine are being pursued.

The primary symptoms of gonorrhea in the male, appearing two to five days after infection, are a white or yellow discharge from the penis and a burning pain on urination. The majority of women with gonorrhea are asymptomatic. Gonorrhea is caused by a bacterium, the gonococcus, and is cured with antibiotics. If left untreated, it may lead to infertility.

Syphilis is caused by the bacterium *Treponema pallidum*. The first symptom is a chancre. Penicillin is effective as a cure. If left untreated, the disease progresses through several stages that may lead to death.

Hepatitis B, caused by the virus HBV, is transmitted sexually as well as by needle sharing. Antiviral drugs are available to treat chronic cases. A vaccine is now available and administered widely.

Pubic lice are tiny lice that attach to the pubic hair. They are spread through sexual and other types of physical contact. Shampoos are available for treatment.

Techniques for preventing STIs include thorough washing of both partners' genitals before intercourse; urination both before and after intercourse; inspecting the partner's genitals for symptoms like a wart or urethral discharge; and the use of a condom.

Other vaginal infections include monilia, trichomoniasis, and bacterial vaginosis. Cystitis is an infection of the urinary bladder in women, leading to frequent, burning urination. Prostatitis is inflammation of the prostate gland.

QUESTIONS FOR THOUGHT, DISCUSSION, AND DEBATE

1. Contact the student health service on your campus and see whether they might be willing to share with you the number of cases of chlamydia, gonorrhea, genital warts, and herpes they diagnose per year; then share the information with your class.

2. Design a program to reduce the number of cases of sexually transmitted infection on your campus.

3. Michael has had a monogamous relationship with Heather for six months. At her annual pelvic exam, Sonya discovers that she has chlamydia and blows up at Michael for giving it to her. Michael has never been tested for anything. What should Michael and Heather discuss with each other, what other information do they need, and what should they do?

4. If you were designing an intervention for Latino teenagers to reduce the spread of HIV, how would you make that intervention culturally sensitive? Would the approach be different for women and for men? If you think that you don't know enough about Latino culture, interview some Latino students or community members to find out more.

SUGGESTIONS FOR FURTHER READING

Ebel, Charles, & Wald, Anna. (2002). *Managing herpes: How to live and love with a chronic STD.* Research Triangle Park, NC: American Social Health Association. People say this is the best herpes book ever.

Gallo, Roe, & McIvenna, Ted. (2003). *Sexual strategies for pleasure and safety.* Specific Press. An excellent guide to creating a safer sex life.

Jones, James H. (1981). *Bad blood: The Tuskegee syphilis experiment.* New York: Free Press. The shocking story of the study in which Black men with syphilis were left untreated so that the course of the disease could be observed.

CHAPTER NINETEEN

Ethics, Religion, and Sexuality

Aviable sexual theology for our time will affirm that sexuality is always much more than genital expression. Sexuality expresses the mystery of our creation as those who need to reach out for the physical and spiritual embrace of others. It expresses God's intention that we find our authentic humanness not in isolation but in relationship.*

*Nelson (1992).

A high school student is in love with her boyfriend and wonders whether they ought to begin sleeping together. A corporation executive hears rumors that one of his employees is gay, and he tries to decide what to do about it. A minister is asked to counsel a husband and wife, one of whom is involved in an affair. A presidential candidate is confronted by a right-to-life group demanding support for a constitutional amendment to ban abortion. All these people, facing the need to make decisions that involve sexuality, find that issues of values make the decisions difficult. The two principal conceptual frameworks for dealing with questions of values are religion and ethics, which are the topics of this chapter.

Two concerns give force to our consideration of the religious and ethical aspects of human sexuality. First, there is the scientific concern to explain sexual phenomena. Because religion and ethics are important influences on people's behaviors, especially in matters of sex, one cannot fully appreciate why people do what they do without looking at these influences. Second, there is also a personal side to this coin. We are all ethical decision makers; we all have a personal system of values. Each of us must make decisions with respect to our own sexuality. Therefore, we would do well to consider how such decisions are made.

Ethics refers to a system of moral principles, a way of deciding what is right and wrong. We use ethics when there is a conflict between things we prize or desire highly. Sexual pleasure may be an important value for one person but something to be avoided for another. However, regardless of the importance we attach to sex, we need a way of integrating our sexuality into our patterns of decision making. To do this we use such categories as right or wrong, good or bad, appropriate or inappropriate, and moral or immoral. These are the kinds of distinctions made in the field of ethics; since we use them every day, we are all practical ethicists.

Religion enters the picture as a source of values, attitudes, and ethics. For believers, religion sets forth an ethical code and provides sanctions (rewards and punishments) that motivate them to

obey the rules. When a particular religion is practiced by many people in a society, it helps create culture, which then influences even those who do not accept the religion. Therefore, it is important to study the relationship of religion to sexuality, for two reasons. First, it is a powerful influence on the sexual attitudes of many individuals. And second, as a creator of culture, it often forms a whole society's orientation toward human sexuality.

Let us begin by defining some terms that are useful in discussing ethics, religion, and sexuality. **Hedonism** and **asceticism** have to do with one's approach to the physical and material aspects of life in general and to sexuality in particular. The word *hedonism* comes from the Greek word meaning "pleasure" and refers to the belief that the ultimate goal of human life is the pursuit of pleasure, the avoidance of pain, and the fulfillment of physical needs and desires: "Eat, drink, and be merry, for tomorrow we die." Asceticism, in contrast, holds that there is more to life than its material aspects, which must be transcended to achieve true humanity. Ascetics are likely to view sexuality as neutral at best and evil at worst; they prize self-discipline, the avoidance of physical gratification, and the cultivation of spiritual values. Orders of monks and nuns, found in Eastern religions as well as in Christianity, are good examples of institutionalized asceticism, with their affirmations of celibacy, virginity, and poverty.

The terms **legalism** and **situationism** refer to methods of ethical decision making. As an approach to ethics, legalism is concerned with following a moral law, or set of principles, which comes from a source outside the individual, such as religion. Legalistic ethics are focused on the rightness or wrongness of specific acts and set forth a series of rules—"Do this" and "Don't do that"—that persons are to follow. The term *situationism* has been used since it was coined by Joseph Fletcher in his 1966 book *Situation Ethics.*

Ethics: A system of moral principles; a way of determining right and wrong.
Hedonism: A moral system based on maximizing pleasure and avoiding pain.
Asceticism: An approach to life emphasizing discipline and impulse control.
Legalism: Ethics based on the assumption that there are rules for human conduct and that morality consists of knowing the rules and obeying them.
Situationism: Ethics based on the assumption that there are no absolute rules, or at least very few, and that each situation must be judged individually.

Also called *contextual ethics,* this approach suggests that although there may be broad general guidelines for ethical behavior, each ethical decision should be made according to the individuals and situations involved. Situationism is based in human experience and, in matters of sexual morality, tends to focus on relationships rather than rules. Whereas legalism deals in universal laws, situationism decides matters on a case-by-case basis, informed by certain guiding principles, such as love. Traditional religious ethical systems (which we might call the *Old Morality*) have tended to be quite legalistic, and many continue to be so today (e.g., Orthodox Judaism, Roman Catholicism, and fundamentalist Protestantism). However, with the advent of the modern scientific worldview, the situationist approach (the *New Morality*) has attracted many adherents (Nelson, 1978). Of course, few ethical systems are purely hedonistic or ascetic or entirely legalistic or situationist; most lie between these extremes.

Sexuality in Great Ethical Traditions

With these ways of looking at sexual ethics as background, let us examine certain great ethical traditions to see how they deal with norms for sexual behavior. Although some attention is given to non-Western sexual ethics, the focus of this section is on ethical traditions of Western culture, primarily because this is a text for U.S. undergraduates, who are part of that culture. This culture can, at the risk of oversimplification, be seen as originating in the confrontation of Greek culture, preserved and developed by the Romans, and Jewish tradition, extended by Christianity. From that point on until rather recently, Western culture was Christian, at least officially. Even self-conscious revolts against Christian culture in the West are part of that tradition because of their roots.

Classical Greek Philosophy

During the Golden Age of Greek culture, covering roughly the fifth and fourth centuries B.C.E.,[1] brilliant philosophers such as Socrates, Plato, and Aristotle pondered most of the great ethical questions. They regarded the beautiful and the good as the chief goal of life, and they admired the figure of the warrior–intellectual, who embodied the virtues of wisdom, courage, temperance, justice, and piety.

While nothing in Greek culture rejected sex as evil—the gods and goddesses of Greek mythology are often pictured enjoying it—the great philosophers did develop a kind of asceticism that assumed an important place in Western thought. They thought that virtue resulted from wisdom, and they believed that people would do right if they could, failing to live morally only through ignorance. To achieve wisdom and cultivate virtue, violent passions must be avoided, and these might well include sex. Plato believed that love led toward immortality and was therefore a good thing. However, since this kind of love was rather intellectual and more like friendship than sexuality, the term *platonic love* has come to mean sexless affection. There was also, especially among the warrior class, approval of **pederasty** (a sexual relationship between an older man and a younger one). The older man was to serve as the younger one's teacher and model of courage and virtue. An army of male couples was thought to be especially fierce because of the desire of each to protect his beloved (Crompton, 2003).

Figure 19.1   The ancient Greeks not only approved of, but idealized, pederasty.

Pederasty: Sex between an older man and a younger man, or a boy; sometimes called *boy love.*

[1] Before the Common Era; today it is preferred over the Christian-centered Before Christ (B.C.).

Later, Greek philosophy became even more ascetic than in the Golden Age. Epicurus (341–270 B.C.E.) taught that the goal of life was *ataraxia,* a tranquil state between pleasure and pain in which the mind is unaffected by emotion. He, like other Stoics of the same period, valued detachment from worldly anxieties and pleasures and, indeed, a total indifference to either life or death. Sex was seen not necessarily as evil but as less important than wisdom and virtue, something to be transcended to achieve the beautiful and good.

Judaism

The basic source of the Judeo–Christian tradition, which is the religious foundation of Western culture, is the Hebrew scriptures or the Old Testament of the Bible, the basis for Judaism and a major source for Christianity as well. Written between approximately 800 and 200 B.C.E., the Old Testament has a great deal to say about the place of sexuality in human life and society, always seen in religious terms.

The view of sexuality in the Hebrew scriptures (what Christians call the Old Testament) is fundamentally positive. In the Genesis myth of creation we read, "So God created man in his own image, in the image of God he created him; male and female he created them" (Genesis 1:27). Human sexual differentiation is not an afterthought or an aberration; it is an integral part of creation, which God calls "good." Judaism sees sexuality as a gift to be used responsibly and in obedience to God's will, never as something evil in itself. The command to marry and to procreate within marriage is clear (Farley, 1994). Looking at the Hebrew scriptures as a whole, we can find three themes in this view of sexuality.

First, sex is seen not as just another biological function but as a deep and intimate part of a *relationship* between two people. The very ancient story of Adam and Eve states that "a man leaves his father and cleaves to his wife and the two become one flesh" (Genesis 2:24). Frequently, biblical Hebrew uses the verb *to know* to mean sexual intercourse (as in "Adam knew Eve and she conceived a child"). It also uses the word *knowledge,* with this suggestion of deep intimacy, to describe the relationship between God and his people.[2] The use of sexual imagery in describing both marital and divine–human relationships testifies to the positive view of the Old Testament toward sex.

Second, in the Hebrew scriptures, sexuality could never be separated from its *social consequences.* Historically, Israel began as a small group of nomadic tribes fighting to stay alive in the near-desert of the Arabian peninsula. Sheer survival demanded that there be plenty of children, especially boys, so that there would be enough herdsmen and warriors.[3] Thus nonprocreative sex could not be allowed. Furthermore, because the tribes were small and close-knit, sex had to be regulated to prevent jealousy over sexual partners, which could have divided and destroyed the group. It is not surprising, then, that so much of the Old Testament is concerned with laws regarding people living together in society and that these laws often include the regulation of sexual practices.

Finally, the Hebrew scriptures see sexual behavior as an aspect of *national and religious loyalty.* When the Israelites settled in what is now the state of Israel, about 1200 to 1000 B.C.E., they came into contact with the original inhabitants, whom they called Canaanites. Like many agricultural peoples of the time, the Canaanites sought to encourage the growth of their crops through their religion. In this **fertility cult** Baal, the Sky Father, was encouraged to mate with Asherah (Astarte or Ishtar), the Earth Mother, so that crops would grow. This mating was encouraged by ritual sex, and temple prostitutes (male and female) were a central part of Canaanite religion. Hebrew religious leaders saw in the fertility cult a threat to their religion, and many sexual practices are forbidden in the Hebrew scriptures because they were found among the Canaanites and might lead to infidelity to Israel's God.

The many sexual regulations of the Old Testament need to be seen both in the context of the times and against this historical background. From Israel's struggle for survival during the nomadic period came institutions such as polygyny (many wives) and concubinage (slaves kept for childbearing purposes) designed to produce children in the case of a childless marriage (Farley, 1994), and also laws against illegitimacy and nonprocreative sex. From the confrontation with the fertility cult, Israel derived prohibitions against nakedness, cultic prostitution, and other such typically Canaanite practices. Both themes are present in this passage from Leviticus 20:10–19:

[2]See, for example, Hosea, the Song of Solomon, and, in the New Testament, Revelation.

[3]Note that the heart of God's promise to the patriarch Abraham was descendants as numberless as the grains of sand or the stars in the sky (Genesis 13:14–17, among many places).

Fertility cult: A form of nature religion in which the fertility of the soil is encouraged through various forms of ritual magic, often including ritual sexual intercourse.

If a man commits adultery with his neighbor's wife, both adulterer and adulteress shall be put to death. The man who has intercourse with his father's wife has brought shame on his father. They shall both be put to death; their blood shall be on their own heads. . . . A man who has intercourse with any beast shall be put to death, and you shall kill the beast. . . . If a man takes his sister, his father's daughter or his mother's daughter, and they see one another naked, it is a scandalous disgrace. They shall be cut off in the presence of their people. . . . If a man lies with a woman during her monthly period and brings shame upon her, he has exposed her discharge and she has uncovered the source of her discharge; they shall both be cut off from their people.

Adultery and incest are threats to the harmony of the group. Bestiality is not only "unnatural" but also nonprocreative and may have been a feature of Canaanite religion. The menstrual taboo is typical of many societies (see Chapter 5).

It should be noted that all societies have had laws regulating sex (Chapter 1) and that these laws, however exotic they may seem to us, made sense in their historical context and were, for the most part, remarkably humane for the time. The Hebrew scriptures are characterized by a great regard for married love, affection, and sexuality; this is in marked contrast to, for example, the Greek view of marriage as an institution for breeding and housekeeping. The Judaism of the time was highly legalistic but not particularly ascetic, displaying high regard for responsible sexuality as a good and integral part of human life.

Christianity

As our discussion turns to Christianity, which grew in three centuries from an obscure Jewish sect to the dominant religion in the West, the complex conditions of the Mediterranean world between 100 B.C.E. and 100 C.E.[4] must be noted. The world in which Christianity developed was one of tremendous ferment in the spheres of philosophy, religion, and morals. There were many strange cults, often characterized by some sort of **dualism.** This was the notion that body and spirit were unalterably separate and opposed to each other and that the goal of life was to become purely spiritual by transcending the physical and material side of life. Public morals were notably decadent, and even ethical pagans were shocked by a society

Dualism: A religious or philosophical belief that body and spirit are separate and opposed to each other and that the goal of life is to free the spirit from the bondage of the body; thus a depreciation of the material world and the physical aspect of humanity.

[4] The Common Era, an alternative to Anno Domini (A.D.).

in which people—or at least those who could afford it—prized pleasure above all things.

Revulsion at the excesses of Roman life affected Judaism, which became markedly more dualistic and antisex by the time of Jesus' birth and the growth of the Christian Church. That church's ethical tradition is rooted in Old Testament Judaism and was given its direction by the teachings of Jesus, the writings of St. Paul, and the theology of the fathers of early Christianity. From these beginnings, Christian ethics have evolved and developed over 2,000 years in many and various ways. This makes oversimplification a real danger, yet it is possible to speak in general terms of a Christian tradition of sexual ethics and morality.

Christianity is distinctive among the major world religions in insisting on monogamy (Parrinder, 1996). Most other religions permit polygyny, or a man's having several wives. The Christian standard of monogamy, which may seem strict by today's standards, may be viewed in another light as a major step toward equality between women and men. Men were no longer permitted to have many wives as "possessions." Similarly, Jesus opposed divorce, which again may seem strict. However, it reversed the traditional Hebrew rule—and the practice in many other cultures—that a man could divorce his wife simply at will, yet a wife had no similar power.

The New Testament

At the heart of the Christian scriptures are the Gospels, which describe the life and teachings of Jesus. Because Jesus said almost nothing on the subject of sex, it is difficult to derive a sexual ethic from the Gospels alone. Jesus' ethical teaching was based on the tradition of the Hebrew prophets, and his view of sexuality follows in that tradition. He urged his followers to strive for ethical perfection, and he spoke strongly against pride, hypocrisy, injustice, and the misuse of wealth. Toward penitent sinners, including those whose sins were sexual, the Gospels show Jesus as compassionate and forgiving (see, for example, his dealings with "fallen women" in John 4:1–30, John 8:53–9:11, and Luke 7:36–50). He did not put any particular emphasis on sexual conduct, apparently regarding it as a part of a whole moral life based on the love of God and neighbor.

The task of first applying the principles of Jesus in concrete situations fell to St. Paul, documented in his letters. Paul's view of sexuality and women was ambivalent, deriving both from the immorality of much Greco-Roman culture and from his expectation that Jesus would return within the next few weeks or years, bringing the world to an end (Parrinder, 1996). Paul advocated celibacy, not

Figure 19.2 The most notable of the Western Fathers was St. Augustine (354–430 C.E.), who had had a promiscuous youth and overreacted after his conversion to Christianity. For Augustine, sexuality was a consequence of the Fall, and every sexual act was tainted by concupiscence (from the Latin word *concupiscentia,* meaning "lust" or "evil desire of the flesh"). Even sex in marriage was sinful, and in *The City of God,* he wrote that "children could not have been begotten in any other way than they know them to be begotten now, i.e., by lust, at which even honorable marriage blushes" (1950 ed., Article 21). The stature of Augustine meant that his negative view of sexuality was perpetuated in subsequent Christian theology.

necessarily because he was opposed to sex but because marriage might prove a distraction from prayer, worship, and proclaiming the Gospel before the world came to an end. As a Jew, Paul opposed all sexual expression outside marriage and judged sexual immorality harshly. However, he did not single out sexual sin. He condemned the "sins of the flesh," but by this he meant all aspects, such as "immorality, impurity, sorcery, enmity, strife, jealousy, anger, selfishness, party spirit, envy, drunkenness, carousing and the like" (Galatians 5:19–21). Later Christian theologians tended to understand the "sins of the flesh" primarily in sexual terms, giving Christianity a bias against sexuality beyond what Paul probably intended. Given the times, it is not surprising that the New Testament is ambivalent about sexuality, probably more so than the Old Testament.

The Early Christian Church

The "Fathers of the Church," such as St. Augustine (Figure 19.2), wrote roughly between 150 and 600 C.E. and completed the basic theological shape of the Christian faith. During this time, Christian ethics became increasingly ascetic, for several reasons including the assimilation of often dualistic Greek philosophy (especially Stoicism), the decadence of Roman society, and the conversion of the Roman Emperor Constantine in 325. As the Church became the official religion of the Roman Empire, much of its original fervor was lost and it began to grow corrupt and worldly.

Serious Christians revolted against this situation by moving to the desert to become monks and hermits, to fast, to pray, and to practice all sorts of self-denial, including **celibacy.** From this point on, monks and monasticism became a permanent reform movement within the Church, a vanguard of ascetics calling Christians to greater rigor. Their success can be seen in the twelfth-century requirement that all clergy in the West be celibate, a departure from early Church practice.[5] The Fathers of the Church, almost all of whom were celibates, allowed that marriage was good and honorable but thought virginity to be a much superior state.

The Middle Ages

During the Middle Ages, these basic principles continued to be elaborated and extended. The most important figure of the period, and even

---

[5] The First Epistle of Timothy, Chapter 3, shows the clear expectation that clergy will be married and father children.

Celibacy: The practice of remaining celibate. Sometimes used to refer to abstaining from sexual intercourse, the correct term for which is *chastity.* A *celibate* is a person who remains unmarried, usually for religious reasons.

Figure 19.3   The Virgin Mary. During the Middle Ages, a great devotion to the mother of Jesus developed, emphasizing her perpetual virginity, purity, and freedom from all sin. That devotion lives on in most Latin American countries today.

today the basic source of Catholic moral theology, was St. Thomas Aquinas (1225–1274). His great achievement was the *Summa Theologica,* which answered virtually any question a Christian might have on any topic. Thomas's "natural law" approach to ethics was normative in Western Christianity for many centuries and remains so for Roman Catholicism. His argument was that whatever was natural was good, *natural* being defined by the science of 1267 C.E. Anything that was not natural was sinful.

Thomas believed that sex was obviously intended for procreation and that, therefore, all nonprocreative sex violated the natural law and was sinful, being opposed to both human nature and the will of God. In the *Summa,* Thomas devoted a chapter to various sorts of lust and condemned as grave sin such things as fornication (premarital intercourse), nocturnal emissions, seduction, rape, adultery, incest, and "unnatural vice," which included masturbation, bestiality, and homosexuality.

The theology of Aquinas was communicated to the ordinary Christian through the Church's canon law, which determined when intercourse was or was not sinful. All sex outside marriage was, by definition, a sin. Even within marriage the Church forbade intercourse during certain times in a woman's reproductive cycle (during menstruation, pregnancy, and up to 40 days postpartum) as well as on certain holy days, fast days (such as Fridays), and even during whole liturgical seasons (such as Advent and Lent). These rules were "enforced" through the *Penitentials,* guidebooks for priests hearing confessions, which instructed them on how to judge certain sins and what penances to assign for them. All of this communicated to the ordinary person that the Church regarded sex as basically evil, for procreation only, and probably not something one should enjoy.

The Protestants

The Protestant Reformation in the sixteenth century destroyed the Christian unity of Europe and shook the theological foundations of the Catholic Church. However, in matters of sexual ethics there were few changes. The Protestant churches abandoned clerical celibacy, regarding it as unnatural and the source of many abuses, and placed a higher value on marriage and family life. Reformers nonetheless feared illegitimacy and approved of sexuality only in the confines of matrimony. Even then, they were often ambivalent. For example, Martin Luther, the founder of the Reformation and happily married to a former nun, called marriage "a hospital for the sick" and saw its purpose as being to "aid human infirmity and prevent unchastity" (quoted in Thielicke, 1964, p. 136)—scarcely an enthusiastic approach.

A significant contribution of Reformation Protestantism to Christianity was a renewed emphasis on the individual conscience in matters such as the interpretation of the Bible and ethical decision making. Such an emphasis on freedom and individual responsibility has led to the serious questioning of legalistic ethics and, in part, to today's ethical debates.

The Reformation also gave rise to Puritanism. The Puritans followed Augustine in emphasizing the doctrine of "original sin" and the "total depravity" of fallen humanity. This led them to use civil law to try to regulate human behavior in an attempt to suppress immorality. As we discuss in the next chapter, this urge to make people good by law has many sexual applications, although the Puritans were probably no more sexually repressive than other Christians of the time. What we often think of as "Puritan" sexual rigidity is probably more properly referred to as "Victorian." During the 60-year reign of Queen Victoria (1819–1901), English society held sexual expression in exaggerated disgust and probably overemphasized its importance. While strict public standards of decency and purity were enforced, many Victorians indulged in private vices of pornography and prostitution. It is against this typically Victorian combination of repressiveness and hypocrisy that many people of the twentieth century revolted, wrongly thinking the Victorian period representative of the whole Christian ethical tradition.

Current Trends

Across Western history there has been a fairly stable consensus on the fundamentals of sexual ethics, which some call the Old Morality. Sex has been understood as a good part of divine creation but also as a source of temptation that needs to be controlled. Although at various times chastity has been exalted, marriage and the family have always been held in esteem and sex outside marriage condemned, in theory if not always in practice. The only approved purpose for sex has been procreation, with nonprocreative sex having been regarded as unnatural and sinful. However, this consensus largely broke down in the twentieth century, and sexual ethics is now a topic of heated debate. Several factors, both within the religious community and outside it, have contributed to this ferment.

The rise of historical–critical methods in biblical scholarship led to a questioning of the absoluteness of scriptural norms. Many scholars now see them as shaped by the time and culture in which they were written and not necessarily binding today. Furthermore, traditional understandings of biblical statements about sexuality have been questioned as more is learned about the original historical context. The Reformation emphasis on the Bible and individual conscience called into question the natural-law approach. The religious community has also been influenced by the behavioral sciences, which suggest that sexuality is much more complex than had been thought and question older assumptions about what is "natural" or "normal." Technology has made it possible, for the first time in human history, to prevent conception reliably and to terminate pregnancy safely, which, among other things, blunts the force of arguments against premarital intercourse on the basis of the disapproval of illegitimacy. Indeed, technology

itself has raised a host of ethical issues as humans gain more and more control over what had once been a matter of "doing what comes naturally."

All this has led religious groups into serious debate and even conflict. Within Judaism, the Orthodox who still live by the rabbinic interpretation of the Bible may be in serious conflict with the Conservative and Reformed groups. Protestants are deeply divided among conservatives who hold to the Old Morality, liberals inclined to the New Morality, and others who come out somewhere in between. Perhaps no single religious community has experienced as much tension over sexual morality as the Roman Catholic Church in the United States (see Focus: A Sexually Diverse World, p. 490).

Humanism

It would be misleading to suggest that within Western culture, at least since the Renaissance, all ethical thinking has been religious in origin. Many ethicists have quite consciously tried to find a framework for moral behavior that does not rely on divine revelation or any direction from a source outside human intellect. Nonreligious ethics covers a broad spectrum; however, we can look at a fairly broad mainstream called **humanism.**

Humanistic ethics accepts no supernatural source for direction and insists that values can be found only in human experience in this world, as observed by the philosopher or social scientist. Most humanists would hold that the basic goals of human life are happiness, self-awareness, the avoidance of pain and suffering, and the fulfillment of human needs. Of course, the individual pursuit of these ends must be tempered by the fact that no one lives in the world alone and that some limitation of individual happiness may be required for the common good. Another important humanistic principle is that the individual must make his or her own decisions and accept responsibility for them and their consequences, without appeal to some higher authority, such as God.

In the area of human sexuality, humanism demands a realistic approach to behavior: one that does not create arbitrary or unreasonable standards and expectations. Humanism is very distrustful of the legalistic approach. It seeks real intimacy between persons and condemns impersonal and exploitative relationships, though probably not with the vigor that marks religious ethics. It tends to be tolerant, compassionate, and skeptical of claims of absolute right or wrong.

> **Humanism:** A philosophical system that denies a divine origin for morality and holds that ethical judgments must be made on the basis of human experience and human reason.

Focus: A Sexually Diverse World
Dissent over Sexual Ethics in the Roman Catholic Church

D iverse views about sexual ethics exist not only across religions but also within a single religious tradition. Beginning in the 1980s the Roman Catholic Church in the United States experienced a number of serious controversies, many of them in the area of sexual ethics. The Church's traditional teaching on sexuality was vigorously reasserted by Pope John Paul II in the face of calls for a less legalistic and strict approach. John Paul repeatedly condemned all sexual activity outside marriage and all nonprocreative sex, such as masturbation. In 1983, for example, the Vatican issued *Educational Guidance in Human Love*, a pamphlet for parents and teachers. In this document procreation is seen as the essential purpose of marital sex; masturbation, extramarital sex, and homosexuality are all described as "grave moral disorders." However, such teaching has not always been welcomed by either Catholic ethicists or ordinary Catholic laypeople. Thus the debate within U.S. Catholicism mirrors the controversy that has been going on in the society at large. At issue are such topics as contraception, abortion, homosexuality, reproductive technologies, and sexual abuse.

Contraception
Although the Vatican and the U.S. Roman Catholic hierarchy have not moved from condemning "artificial" birth control as set forth in Pope Paul VI's encyclical *Humanae Vitae* of 1968, there is evidence that many American Catholics ignore the condemnation and use contraceptives, often with the tacit approval of their priests. For example, a 1993 *Newsweek* poll asked U.S. Catholics, "Do you or do other Catholics you know personally use artificial birth control?" and 63 percent responded yes. Moreover, since *Humanae Vitae* was not an infallible teaching, some Catholic ethicists still treat contraception as an open question. Interestingly, the current pope, Benedict XVI, in his first encyclical, did not mention abortion, homosexuality, or contraception, but rather titled it "God Is Love," focusing on the centrality of love to Christianity and perhaps signaling a desire to turn away from uniformly negative views of sexuality (Fisher, 2006).

Abortion
There is sharp division among U.S. Catholics on the issue of abortion. A large segment of Catholics actively or passively support the antiabortion, or right-to-life, movement, yet there are many dissenters. The *Newsweek* poll asked, "Is the Catholic Church's position on abortion too conservative, too liberal, or about right?" Forty-one percent thought it was too conservative, and 43 percent thought it was about right, showing a nearly even division of opinion.

Homosexuality
In 1976, Jesuit priest and psychotherapist John J. McNeill published *The Church and the Homosexual,* in which he questioned the Church's traditional teaching on homosexuality and its scriptural and theological bases. At the time, Father McNeill was forbidden by his Jesuit superiors to speak or write further on the subject. He obeyed the order for 10 years, until his superiors ordered him to cease all ministry to the gay community, at which point he left the Jesuits and the priesthood. Other Catholic thinkers, such as Daniel Helminiak (2006) are also trying to help the Church rethink its approach to gays and lesbians.

Reproductive Technologies
In 1987, the Congregation for the Doctrine of the Faith issued a document called "Instruction for Human Life in Its Origins and on the Dignity of Procreation," which condemned in vitro fertilization, surrogate motherhood, artificial insemination, and other new reproductive technologies. The document was severely criticized by many U.S. Catholic ethicists, who found it too rigid and ill informed.

Condoms
Today, condoms pose a dilemma for the Catholic Church. To date it has uniformly prohibited them as a means of birth control. In the AIDS era, however, they represent a method for preventing disease and actually preserving life, a principle to which the Catholic Church is firmly committed. Essentially the argument is that, between condoms and AIDS, condoms are the lesser of two evils. In 2006 Pope Benedict authorized a study of condoms, a move that would have been unthinkable even 20 years ago.

Sexual Abuse by Clergy
Perhaps the most difficult sexual issue that faces the Catholic Church today is that of sexual abuse of children by Catholic priests. One of the most publicized cases was that of Father Paul Shanley of the Boston archdiocese. As early as 1961, just a year after his ordination, he had been reported to the police by the father of an 11-year-old boy whom he

Figure 19.4 Some nuns and other Catholic women challenge teachings of the Church.

had molested. He was finally arrested in 2002 at the age of 71, for raping a 6-year-old boy in 1983. In the process, more than 30 men came forward with allegations of abuse by him spanning more than three decades. He was described as a contradictory combination of protector and predator: a wonderful priest to some, a sexual predator to others. Shanley says that he himself was abused by a priest when he was a child.

As of 2004 approximately 4 percent (4,392) of U.S. priests had been accused of sexually abusing minors (U.S. Conference of Catholic Bishops, 2004; reported by Goodstein, 2004). Of the alleged victims, 81 percent are male. Most frequently, they were molested beginning around 12 to 14 years of age.

What is perhaps most distressing to some is that the hierarchy of the Catholic Church covered up these scandals and continued to assign priests like Shanley to other churches and even to youth work. The mother of the boy molested in 1961 wrote to Boston's Cardinal Richard Cushing, but no investigation resulted. In 1990 Cardinal Bernard F. Law allowed Shanley to go on sick leave to Southern California but never told the local bishop about Shanley's problem, so he continued to serve as a priest. Essentially, bishops allowed priests to

continue abusing children. Some even trace the responsibility to Pope John Paul II, who led a conservative backlash against the liberalization of the Catholic Church (which occurred in the 1960s) and insisted on the imperial authority of parish priests (Berry & Renner, 2004).

This scandal has caused an enormous shift in Catholics' views of priests; they were once regarded as holy because of their renunciation of all sexual activity, but now are revealed to be capable of grave sexual sins. The crisis has led some to question the church's rule of priestly celibacy, the suggestion being that perhaps if priests were allowed to live normal, married lives, these problems would not occur. The scandal has caused a profound shift in authority within the Catholic Church, which once dictated sexual morals for laypeople but now finds itself defending some of its priests on charges of truly serious sexual immorality.

Sources: Berry & Renner (2004); Butterfield (2002); Curran (1988); Fisher (2006); Grammick (1986); Investigative Staff of the *Boston Globe* (2002); Helminiak (2006); Jenkins (1996); Maguire (2001); McNeill (1987); *Newsweek* (1993); Reuther (1985); Sipe (1995).

Sexuality in Other Major Religions

The discussion so far has been mostly concerned with Western culture and the Judeo–Christian tradition. It will broaden our outlook if we consider human sexuality in religious traditions outside dominant U.S. culture. Obviously, this could be the topic for a very large book itself; here we provide only a brief look at the three non-Western religions with the largest number of adherents: Islam, Hinduism, and Buddhism.

Islam

Geographically, and in terms of its roots, Islam is the closest faith to the Judeo–Christian heritage. It was founded by the Prophet Muhammad, who lived from 570 to 632 C.E. in what is now Saudi Arabia. Its followers are called *Muslims,* and its sacred scripture is the Koran (Qur'an). Classical Islam values sexuality very positively, and Muhammad saw intercourse in marriage as the highest good of human life. Islam sanctions both polygyny and concubinage, and the Prophet had several wives. Sex outside marriage or concubinage, however, is viewed as a sin. In reality a double standard prevails, in which men's extramari-

tal affairs are tolerated. An adulterous wife, however, may be the object of an *honor killing* in which she is murdered for her transgression (Ilkkaracan, 2001). The Prophet opposed celibacy, and Islam has very little ascetic tradition. A male-dominated faith, Islam has a strong double standard but recognizes a number of rights and prerogatives for women.

Because Islam does not have a single, central source of authority like the Pope, it is not a monolithic faith, and there is great variety in the ways in which the laws of the Koran are carried out in societies throughout the Muslim world (Boonstra, 2001; Ilkkaracan, 2001). Some Muslim states (e.g., Iran) are theocracies in which religious law is enacted in civil law. In these nations sexual offenses are likely to be more stringently punished, and women have less freedom. Other Islamic countries (such as Egypt and Syria) are secular states in which Western values have been adopted to some extent. In these, women have more rights, and sexual mores are more pluralistic. Moreover, there is considerable variation in the interpretation of the Koran, especially between Sunnis and Shi'ites, the two principal Islamic "denominations."

Although Islam accepts the Hebrew scriptures as sacred, it does not interpret the Adam and Eve

Figure 19.5 Contraception is not only permitted but encouraged by Islamic law.

story to mean that humans are tainted by original sin (Ahmadi, 2003). Striving for worldly pleasures is therefore acceptable, and sexuality is regarded primarily as a source of pleasure and only secondarily as a means of reproduction.

Contraception is not only permitted but encouraged by Islamic law (Boonstra, 2001; Maguire, 2001). Muhammad himself encouraged the practice of *al'azl* (withdrawal, or *coitus interruptus*). Even the strict state of Iran today has an extensive family planning program, and 73 percent of married women use contraceptives.

Hinduism

Hinduism is an inclusive term that refers to a highly varied complex of mythology and religious practice founded on the Indian subcontinent. Here can be found virtually every approach to sexuality that humans have yet invented. However, certain themes can be identified. In Hinduism, four possible approaches to life are acceptable: Kama, the pursuit of pleasure; Artha, the pursuit of success and material wealth; Dharma, the pursuit of the moral life; and Moksha, the pursuit of liberation

through the negation of the self in a state of being that is known as nirvana. Kama is notable because it has produced an extensive literature on the achievement of sexual pleasure, notably the *Kama Sutra* of Vatsyayana, a masterpiece of erotic hedonism. This book testifies to the highly positive view of sexuality to be found in Hinduism.

In contrast, the ways of Dharma and Moksha can be as rigorously ascetic as anything in Christianity. By avoiding all passions, including sex, the follower seeks to pass out of the cycle of continual rebirth to absorption into the godhead. Part of this is *brahmacharya,* or celibacy, which is to be cultivated at the beginning of life (for the purposes of education and discipline) and at the end of life (for the purpose of finding peace). It is interesting to note that in between it is permissible to marry and raise a family, and thus this form of Hinduism makes active sexuality and asceticism possible in the same lifetime (Noss, 1963).

Buddhism

Buddhism developed out of Hinduism; it originated in the life and thought of Gautama (560–480 B.C.E.),

Figure 19.6 Buddhism encourages men to live celibate lives as monks.

the Buddha, and has been elaborated in many forms since then. There is little discussion of sex in the teachings of the Buddha; his way is generally ascetic and concentrates on the achievement of enlightenment and on escape from the suffering of the world. Two main traditions, Theravada and Mahayana, both found in contemporary Buddhism, differ greatly. The ethics of Theravada include the strict nonindulgence of the desires that bring joy; understanding, morals, and discipline are emphasized. The ethics of Mahayana are more active and directed toward love of others. Both encourage men to live celibate lives as monks. Originally, Buddha sought a "middle way" of moderation between extreme asceticism and extreme hedonism (Maguire, 2001). Today, though, the situation is rather like that of medieval Christianity: The masses live ordinary—and usually married—lives while the monks cultivate ascetic wisdom.

Tantric Buddhism, found particularly in Tibet and India, is a form of Buddhism that is of particular interest. It teaches that sexual union epitomizes the essential unity of all things by the joining of female energy (shakti) and male energy (shiva) (Lorius, 1999). In the context of honoring one's partner and the relationship, sexual expression can therefore lead to spiritual enlightenment. This sexual mysticism is by no means common, but it is one of the various forms that Eastern religion may take (Parrinder, 1980).

Contemporary Issues in Sexual Ethics

Human sexuality is heavily value laden and therefore is likely to be the subject of strongly and emotionally held convictions. It is also likely to be the focal point of conflicts in society, if there is no broad consensus on the norms of sexual behavior. This is clearly the case in contemporary American society. The "sexual revolution" is perceived by many people as a threat to all they hold dear; not surprisingly, they respond with fear and anger. The backlash against the more liberal view of sexuality and the greater freedom of sexual behavior that has come about in the last 40 years, accelerated by the spread of AIDS and other STIs, has resulted in explosive public debate, organized attempts at legislating the Old Morality back into force, and a reassertion of a highly legalistic view of the Judeo–Christian

Moralism: A religious or philosophical attitude that emphasizes moral behavior, usually according to strict standards, as the highest goal of human life. Moralists tend to favor strict regulation of human conduct to help make people good.
Pluralism: A philosophical or political attitude that affirms the value of many competing opinions and believes that the truth is discovered in the clash of diverse perspectives. Pluralists, therefore, believe in the maximum human freedom possible.

ethic. The debate promises to continue for some time and to generate much heat.

This debate over the limits, if any, of individual sexual freedom can be seen as a clash between the New Morality and the Old Morality, but let us propose a more helpful model. The Old Morality is, to a great extent, supported by people who believe that there are clearly and objectively defined standards of right and wrong and that a society has a right to insist that all its members conform to them. This view is termed **moralism;** it has many proponents in the religious community who see the objective standard of morality as deriving from divine law. Opposed to this view are the proponents of **pluralism,** who see the question of public morality as being much more complex. Pluralists deny that standards of morality are objective and unchanging, and they contend that truth is to be discovered in the clash of differing opinions and convictions. According to this view, society is wise to allow many points of view to be advocated and expressed. The conscience and rights of the individual are to be stressed over society's needs for order and uniformity. Pluralists are much less likely than moralists to appeal to either law or religion for the enforcement of their views, and they are more likely to allow freedom to individuals. The debate between moralist and pluralist has been going on for a very long time, both in the religious community itself and throughout American history. It will not be settled any time soon.

An illustration of the moralistic view can be found in the "pro-family" position that is rooted in religious conservatism and makes strong attempts to influence legislation. Pro-family activists are in favor of an absolute constitutional ban on abortion, against any kind of legal tolerance of the cohabitation of unmarried persons, and in favor of legal discrimination against homosexuals in such areas as housing, child custody, and employment.

This position is essentially that of the New Religious Right, a coalition of conservative religious and political groups. Members of this movement, largely but not exclusively fundamentalist Protestants, argue that the New Morality has sapped the moral vigor of U.S. society, leaving the country open to inner decay and divine judgment. Their efforts to enforce their religious convictions by legislation have created one of the most intense church–state controversies of the late twentieth and early twenty-first centuries (see Chapter 20). Their position is odious to pluralists and to those who have benefited by the liberalization of laws and attitudes concerning sexuality. These persons fight to keep what they consider to be gains, while pro-family and New Right activists seek to turn the clock back to what they perceive to have been a healthier and more moral time.

This conflict can be found within most religious communities today. Even liberal mainline Protestant groups, which have tended to accommodate at least some of the New Morality, have been under attack from portions of their own membership on such issues as abortion, premarital sex, and homosexuality. Reports in the press of national gatherings of U.S. religious groups reveal a remarkable number of debates related to human sexuality, debates that parallel those in society at large. Here we illustrate this ferment by discussing the ethical issues posed by sex outside marriage, contraception, abortion, homosexuality, AIDS, and reproductive technologies.

Sex Outside Marriage

The biblical tradition underlying Western ethics has almost always seen sexual intercourse as legitimate only in marriage. This view is rooted in a religious understanding of marriage as God's will for most men and women, the way in which sin is avoided and children are cared for. Thus, the tradition has condemned both sex before marriage (which the Bible calls **fornication**) and sex by persons married to others (**adultery**). Today, this position continues to be held by theological conservatives among Jews, Protestants, and Roman Catholics. A Roman Catholic statement on the subject is typical of this position:

> Today there are many who vindicate the right to sexual union before marriage, at least in those cases where a firm intention to marry and an affection which is already in some way conjugal in the psychology of the subjects require this completion which they judge to be connatural. . . . This option is contrary to Christian doctrine, which states that every genital act must be within the framework of marriage. (Sacred Congregation for the Doctrine of the Faith, 1976, p. 11)

However, trends in society have caused many ethicists to reopen the question and to take less dogmatic positions. Among these are the development of safe and reliable contraception, later age at first marriage, the fact that many people experience the singleness of divorce and widowhood, and empirical evidence indicating widespread sexual activity among adolescents. These ethicists are concerned that people be given more helpful guidance than "thou shalt not" and "just say no." For them, the quality of the relationship is more important ethically than its legal status.

Criteria for judging the morality of nonmarital sexual acts could include the following (Countryman, 1994). First, is there a genuine respect for the personhood of all involved? Virtually all ethicists would agree that sexual exploitation of one person by another (whether married or not)—the use of other human beings merely for one's pleasure—is wrong. Furthermore, most would require genuine affection and serious commitment from both parties. This commitment would be manifested in responsible behavior such as using contraceptives if the couple were not willing or able to have children and taking precautions against STIs. Finally, many ethicists would insist that moral sexual behavior must include genuine openness and honesty between the partners. Public and private institutions, in this view, should be involved in helping people to make good ethical choices about sexual behavior in a culture that tends to glorify and exploit sex (Lebacqz, 1987; Moore, 1987).[6]

Extramarital sex (adultery) has always been regarded as a grave matter in the Judeo–Christian tradition. In the Hebrew scriptures, the penalty for it was to be stoned to death; in the New Testament, it is the only grounds for divorce allowed by Jesus (Matthew 6:21–22). Adultery has been understood as a serious breach of trust by a spouse, as well as an act of unfaithfulness to God (a violation of religiously significant promises). Few contemporary ethicists seek to modify this position, but many would argue for a less judgmental, more humane approach to those involved. In this view, people in extramarital relationships should be helped to find the root causes of their infidelity and to move toward a reconciliation with their spouses based on forgiveness and love. This approach suggests that counseling is more helpful than condemnation. Above all, some argue, religious organizations need to assist people in establishing and maintaining good marriages based on mutual respect, communication, and commitment.

Contraception

Roman Catholics and Orthodox Jews oppose any "artificial" means of contraception; other Jews and most Protestants favor responsible family planning by married couples. Moreover, most ethicists would suggest that unmarried persons who are sexually active ought to be using birth control.

[6]A fine discussion of these issues from different perspectives (liberal Protestant and Roman Catholic, respectively) can be found in Nelson (1978) and Genovesi (1987).

Fornication: The biblical term for sex by unmarried persons and, more generally, all immoral sexual behavior.
Adultery: Voluntary sexual intercourse by a husband or wife with someone other than one's spouse; thus, betrayal of one's marriage vows.

Those who oppose birth control for religious reasons see it as being contrary to the will of God, against the natural law, or both. Orthodox Judaism cites the biblical command to "be fruitful and multiply" (Genesis 1:26), not to be disobeyed in any way. Furthermore, some members of other Jewish communities warn that limiting family size threatens the future existence of the Jewish people, and they call for a return to the traditionally large Jewish family.

The Roman Catholic position is best articulated in Pope Paul VI's 1968 encyclical, *Humanae Vitae:*

> Marriage and conjugal love are by their nature ordained toward the begetting and educating of children. . . . In the task of transmitting life, therefore, they are not free to proceed completely at will, as if they could determine in a wholly autonomous way the honest path to follow, but they must conform their activity to the creative intention of God, expressed in the very nature of marriage and by its acts, and manifested by the constant teaching of the Church. (p. 20)

The encyclical continued the Church's approval of "natural family planning," that is, abstinence during fertile periods, popularly known as the "rhythm method" or "Vatican roulette." *Humanae Vitae* was not enthusiastically accepted by all Catholics and the evidence indicates that many Catholic couples, often with the encouragement or tacit approval of their priest, ignore these teachings and use contraceptives anyway.

Those in the religious community who favor the use of contraceptives do so for a variety of reasons. Many express a concern that all children who are born should be "wanted," and they see family planning as a means to this end. Others, emphasizing the dangers that overpopulation poses to the quality and future of human life, the need for a more equitable distribution and conservation of natural resources, and the needs of the emerging nations, call for family planning as a matter of justice. Another point of view regards the use of contraceptives as part of the responsible use of freedom. In this view, any couple who are unwilling or unready to assume the responsibility of children have a duty to use contraceptives. For these groups, the decision to use contraceptives is a highly individual one, and the government must allow each individual the free exercise of his or her conscience (Curran, 1988). Others argue that Thomas Aquinas's natural law, which was based on the science of the Middle Ages, should be updated to a natural law based on current biological and social science, which would lead to very different conclusions about contraception

and many other issues, including homosexuality (Helminiak, 2001a, 2001b, 2004).

Abortion

One of the most convulsive debates of our time continues to be waged over the issue of abortion. Pro-life and pro-choice activists are well organized and deeply convinced of the rightness of their positions. The conflict is a clash of religious belief, political conviction, and worldview in the realm of public policy, one that allows for no easy solutions.[7]

Two distinctions should be made at the outset. First, there is no consensus on the relation between abortion and contraception. For the Roman Catholic Church and others within the pro-life movement, the two are the same in intention; indeed, many pro-life activists wish to ban all contraception except natural family planning. In the other camp, there are some pro-choice advocates who also regard abortion as a variety of contraception—less desirable, perhaps, but better than unwanted pregnancy. However, most centrist ethicists do distinguish between abortion and contraception, typically favoring the latter while raising ethical questions about the former. Second, a distinction is frequently made between therapeutic abortion and elective abortion. Therapeutic abortion is a termination of pregnancy when the life or mental health of the woman is threatened or when there is trauma, such as in cases of rape or incest. Many ethical theorists are willing to endorse therapeutic abortion as the lesser of two evils but do not sanction elective abortion—that is, abortion whenever requested by a woman for any reason.

The leadership of the antiabortion movement clearly comes from the Roman Catholic Church, for which putting an end to abortion is a major policy goal. For many Catholics, opposition to abortion is seen as part of an overall commitment to respect for life, which Joseph Cardinal Bernardin called the "seamless garment" that includes opposition to capital punishment, euthanasia (mercy killing), and social injustice, and a very positive stance toward peace (Cahill, 1985). Pope John Paul II reaffirmed this position in his 1995 encyclical *Evangelium Vitae* (Gospel of Life), saying, "I declare that direct abortion, that is, abortion willed as an ends and a means, always

[7] For a thorough and careful study of what pro-life and pro-choice activists believe they have at stake, see Ginsburg (1989).

(a)

(b)

Figure 19.7 The abortion controversy. Pro-life and pro-choice advocates are both adamant about their positions. (*a*) On August 25, 2004, 1 million pro-choice advocates marched on Washington to protest trends toward limiting access to abortion. (*b*) Some counter-protestors also appeared.

constitutes a grave moral disorder, since it is the deliberate killing of an innocent human being." He went on to condemn capital punishment and euthanasia. The underlying principle of this position is that all life is a gift from God that human beings are not permitted to take. It is the position of the pro-life movement that human life begins at the moment of conception and that the fetus is, from that beginning, entitled to full rights and protections. The Roman Catholic position is shared by Orthodox Jews, Eastern Orthodox Christians, and many conservative, or fundamentalist, Protestants (see Focus: A Sexually Diverse World, p. 498). An end to legalized abortion is at the top of the political agenda of many theologically conservative groups and has been a major issue in presidential and congressional elections and Supreme Court appointments for the past 30 years.

Nonetheless, there has been some significant dissent from this position even within the Catholic Church. Pro-choice Catholics point out that for most of its history the Church accepted Aristotle's teaching, reaffirmed by St. Thomas Aquinas, that "ensoulment," that is, the entry into the fetus of its distinctively human soul, takes place roughly three months after conception (Maguire, 2001). Theoretically, this permits at least first-trimester abortion. It was not until 1869 that Pope Pius IX eliminated the concept of ensoulment, holding that life begins at conception and that all abortion is therefore murder (Luker, 1984). Though regularly denounced by the Vatican and the U.S. Church's hierarchy, some Catholic ethicists insist that the Church's position is not unchangeable and argue that the concerns and needs of women should be more carefully considered (Kolbenschlag, 1985; Maguire, 2001; Reuther, 1985).

The pro-choice position takes at least two forms: absolute and modified. The absolute position argues that pregnancy is solely the concern of a woman and that she should have the absolute right to control her own body and determine whether to carry a fetus to term. Ethically, this position is based on the conviction that the individual must be free and autonomous in all personal decisions. It is also inspired by feminism, which regards such autonomy as necessary if women are to be truly equal to men. Feminists also observe that, historically, the rules about abortion were made by men, who do not become pregnant, and thus are deeply suspect. Indeed, for many feminists complete access to abortion is an absolute principle for women's liberation. Concerns for autonomy and individualism have formed a significant part of

Focus: A Sexually Diverse World
Religious Position Statements on Abortion:
Pro-life versus Pro-choice

The following statements come from a variety of major religious organizations. They reflect the nature of the arguments and the rhetoric of the abortion debate. Consider these statements in relation to the Gallup poll (Table 19.1) that shows a wide diversity of opinion among the American public.

Pro-life Statements

[The] Church has always rejected abortion as a grave moral evil. It has always seen that the child's helplessness, both before and after birth, far from diminishing his or her right to life, increases our moral obligation to respect and to protect that right. . . . The Church also realizes that a society which tolerates the direct destruction of innocent life, as in the current practice of abortion, is in danger of losing its respect for life in all other contexts. (National Conference of Catholic Bishops, 1985)

All human beings ought to value every person for his or her uniqueness as a creature of God, called to be a brother or sister of Christ by reason of the incarnation and universal redemption. For us, the sacredness of human life is based on these premises. And it is on the same premises that there is based our celebration of human life—all human life. This explains our efforts to defend human life against every influence or action that threatens or weakens

	Percentage		
	1975	1992	2006
Abortion should be:			
Legal under any circumstances	21%	31%	30%
Legal under only certain circumstances	54	53	53
Illegal under all circumstances	22	14	15
No opinion	3	2	2

Table 19.1 Gallup Poll Findings on Americans' Attitudes toward Abortion

Source: http://www.galluppoll.com

it, as well as our endeavors to make every life more human in all its aspects. (Pope John Paul II, 1979)

Orthodox Christians have always viewed the willful abortion of unborn children as a heinous act of evil. The Church's canonical tradition identifies any action intended to destroy a fetus as the crime of murder. (Orthodox Church in America, 1992)

Abortion is not a moral option, except as a tragically unavoidable by-product of medical procedures

Western ethics and American social theory for more than two centuries.

For those who hold the modified pro-choice position—which includes most liberal Protestants and Jews—the issue is more complex and means balancing several goods against one another. They affirm that human life is good and ought to be preserved but also argue that the quality of life is important. They argue that an unborn child may have a right to life, but ask if the child does not also have the right to be wanted and cared for. In high-risk situations, might not the danger to the well-being of a woman already alive take precedence over the well-being of an unborn fetus? Few in this camp regard abortion as a good thing, but most suggest that there may be many situations in which it is the least bad choice. Moreover, these ethicists tend to observe that since there is no real consensus in society over the morality of abortion, the government

ought to keep out and let the individual woman make up her own mind.

The pro-life position is, as is typical with moralism, much more absolute and apparently simple, while the pluralist pro-choice position is complex. Both positions agree on the value and dignity of human life but are sharply divided on when life begins, how various conflicting interests are to be balanced, and how human life is best preserved and enhanced. Several factors ensure that the debate will continue for some time. Advances in neonatal medicine are pushing back the threshold of "viability" (the survival of premature infants), which may affect the ethical acceptability of second-trimester abortions for some people (Callahan, 1986). The politicalization of the issue will keep it in the public consciousness, and legal challenges will undoubtedly continue (see Chapter 20). Certainly, the intensity is not likely to diminish, as it is

necessary to prevent the death of another human being, viz., the mother. (Lutheran Church—Missouri Synod, 1979)

[W]e do affirm our opposition to legalized abortion and our support of appropriate federal and state legislation and/or constitutional amendment which will prohibit abortion except to prevent the imminent death of the mother. (Southern Baptist Convention, 1989)

Pro-choice Statements

The United Church of Christ has affirmed and reaffirmed since 1971 that access to safe and legal abortion is consistent with a woman's right to follow the dictates of her own faith and beliefs in determining when and if she should have children, and has supported comprehensive sexuality education as one measure to prevent unwanted or unplanned pregnancies. (United Church of Christ, 2004)

Abortion is an extremely difficult choice faced by a woman. In all circumstances, it should be her decision whether or not to terminate a pregnancy, backed up by those whom she trusts (physician, therapist, partner, etc.). This decision should not be taken lightly (abortion should never be used for birth control purposes) and can have life-long ramifications. However, any decision should be left up to the woman within whose body the fetus is growing. (Union for Reform Judaism, 2004)

Our belief in the sanctity of unborn human life makes us reluctant to approve abortion. But we are equally bound to respect the sacredness of the life and well-being of the mother, for whom

devastating damage may result from an unacceptable pregnancy. In continuity with past Christian teaching, we recognize tragic conflicts of life with life that may justify abortion, and in such cases we support the legal option of abortion under proper medical procedures. We cannot affirm abortion as an acceptable means of birth control, and we unconditionally reject it as a means of gender selection. (United Methodist Church, 2000)

We believe that legislation concerning abortions will not address the root of the problem. We therefore express our deep conviction that any proposed legislation on the part of national or state governments regarding abortions must take special care to see that individual conscience is respected and that the responsibility of individuals to reach informed decisions in this matter is acknowledged and honored. (Episcopal Church, 1994)

Judaism does not believe that personhood and human rights begin with conception. The premise that personhood begins with conception is founded on a religious position which is not identical with Jewish tradition. Therefore, under special circumstances, Judaism chooses and requires abortion as an act which affirms and protects the life, well being and health of the mother. To deny a Jewish woman and her family the ability to obtain a safe, legal abortion when so mandated by Jewish tradition, is to deprive Jews of their fundamental right of religious freedom. (United Synagogue of Conservative Judaism, 1989)

Sources: National Right to Life; Religious Coalition for Reproductive Choice (2004).

a clash about life, law, freedom, and values, and few people are neutral on these issues.

Homosexuality

Mirroring society as a whole, religious communities have been engaged in a vigorous debate on the subject of homosexuality. Until recently it was assumed that all homosexual acts and persons were condemned by the Judeo–Christian tradition. However, many contemporary ethicists, and some religious bodies, have started reexamining their attitudes toward homosexuality (Siker, 1994; White, 2001). This change has occurred in part because some recent scholarship suggests that the traditional interpretation of the Bible passages on this topic is not accurate, and in part because the impact of social science has led many ethicists to question whether homosexuality is truly abnormal and unnatural and therefore against the will of God. There are three positions, broadly speaking,

on the issue: rejection, love the sinner but hate the sin, and full acceptance.

Rejectionism

Regarding the *rejectionist position,* it has generally been presumed that the weight of the Judeo–Christian tradition absolutely opposes any sexual acts between persons of the same gender and regards those committing such acts as dreadful sinners, utterly condemned by God. Although there are few references in the Bible, all are negative, the most famous being the passage about the destruction of Sodom (see Figure 19.8).[8]

In the Hebrew scriptures, homosexual practices are included on lists of offenses against God. Jesus made no comment on the subject, but St. Paul was unambiguously against homosexual acts, seeing

[8]Other relevant biblical passages include Leviticus 18:22 and 20:13; Genesis 19; Romans 1:26; and I Corinthians 6:9.

Figure 19.8 In this Dürer painting, Lot and his family flee as the city of Sodom burns. In Genesis 19:4–11, God sends two angels to the city of Sodom to investigate its alleged immorality. The angels are granted hospitality by Lot, but his house is surrounded by a crowd of men demanding that he send the angels out, "that we may know them." Lot offers his virgin daughters instead, but the men of Sodom insist, the angels strike them blind, and God destroys the city. This story has been understood to condemn all homosexual acts. However, some modern scholars question this interpretation, noting that at most it condemns homosexual rape. Moreover, scholars point out that in other portions of the Bible and in Jewish history, the sin of Sodom is never seen as homosexuality but rather as general immorality and lack of hospitality, a serious offense in the ancient Near East (Helminiak, 2000).

them as perverse behavior by fundamentally heterosexual persons. Thus he included them in lists of sexual sins, along with adultery and fornication, that are in opposition to the will of God and symptomatic of human depravity. However, Paul did not seem to have found homosexuality any more dreadful than other sexual sins.

Homosexuality was not uncommon in the Mediterranean world of the early Church, and the Church condemned it as part of the immoral world in which it found itself. The Church saw it as a crime against nature that might bring down the wrath of God upon the whole community (Kosnick, 1977). In the Middle Ages, Thomas Aquinas stated that "unnatural vice . . . flouts nature by transgressing its basic principle of sexuality and is in this matter the gravest of sin" (1968 ed., II-II, q. 154, a. 12).

The rejectionist position continues to be held by many members of the religious community who condemn homosexual acts and reject homosexual persons unless they repent and become heterosexual. An example of this stance is a 1987 resolution of the Southern Baptist Convention, which stated that "homosexuality is a perversion of divine standards and a violation of nature and of natural affections. . . . [While] God loves the homosexual and offers salvation, homosexuality is not a normal lifestyle and is an abomination in the eyes of God."

Love the Sinner but Hate the Sin

Many religious groups would modify this position somewhat, through a distinction between homosexual orientation and behavior. In essence this stance regards a person's homosexual orientation—assuming that it cannot be changed—as morally neutral but rejects homosexual behaviors. Thus an ethical homosexual person may be fully obedient to the will of God, as long as she or he remains abstinent. This is the official position of the Roman Catholic Church, reiterated in a Vatican directive entitled "The Pastoral Care of Homosexual Persons," which states in part,

Although the particular inclination of the homosexual person is not a sin, it is a more or less strong tendency ordered toward an intrinsic moral evil and thus the inclination itself must be seen as an objective disorder. Therefore special concern and pastoral attention should be directed toward those who have this condition, lest they be led to believe that the living out of this orientation in homosexual activity is a morally acceptable option. It is not. (Congregation for the Doctrine of the Faith, 1986, p. 379. This position was reiterated in 2003. Documents such as this can now be found online at http://www.vatican.va/roman_curia/congrega-tions/cfaith/index.htm)

As a result of this instruction, many chapters of Dignity, an organization of lesbian and gay Catholics, were denied the use of church facilities by American bishops. Various Protestant groups have taken the same stance—that is, being gay per se may not be sinful, but homosexual acts are.

Full Acceptance

At the other end of the spectrum are those in the religious community who favor *full acceptance* of lesbian and gay persons, usually basing this on a revisionist view of the Bible and church tradition. Some scholars question whether the apparent condemnation in the scriptures is really relevant to homosexuality as it is generally understood today (Furnish, 1994). New Testament scholar Robin Scroggs, for example, says that the only form of same-gender behavior known to the world of the New Testament involved older men and youths (often prostitutes or slaves), and he concluded that "what the New Testament was against was the image of homosexuality as pederasty and primarily here its more sordid and dehumanizing dimensions" (1983, p. 126). Yale historian John Boswell's detailed research into early and medieval Christianity led him to conclude that up until about the thirteenth century the Christian Church was relatively neutral toward homosexuality and, when it did see homosexual behavior as sinful, did not regard it as any worse than heterosexual transgressions (Boswell, 1980). Boswell found a gay subculture that flourished throughout this period and argues that it was known to the Church, that clergy and church officials were often part of it, that it was not infrequently tolerated by religious and civil authorities alike, and that in it same-gender marriages or "unions" occurred. This sort of reinterpretation has led some theologians, such as Roman Catholic John McNeill and Anglican Norman Pittenger, to question whether the tradition has been understood properly and to conclude that sexual relationships that are characterized by mutual respect, concern, and commitment—by love in its fullest sense—are to be valued and affirmed, whatever the gender of the partners (Pittenger, 1970; McNeill, 1987). The revisionist view seems to be gaining adherents over time.

Different religious bodies have moved toward acceptance in varied ways. For example, in 1985 the Episcopal Church's General Convention committed itself

to find an effective way to foster a better understanding of homosexual persons, to dispel myths and prejudices about homosexuality, to provide pastoral support, and to give life to the claim of homosexual persons upon the love, acceptance, and pastoral care and concern of the Church. (*Journal of the General Convention,* 1985, p. 505)

The Episcopal Church stands, with many other religious groups, for full civil rights and liberties for homosexual persons.

In 1963 a group of English Friends challenged traditional thinking about sexuality, including homosexuality, in *Toward a Quaker View of Sex.* Since that time, Quakers and Unitarians have been notable for their acceptance not only of the homosexual person but also of her or his sexual behavior, as long as it is conscientious.

Within virtually all the mainline churches, gay caucuses and organizations have been formed in an effort to move fellow believers toward greater understanding and tolerance. A considerable number of lesbians and gays have simply left the established religious organizations and founded their own churches, synagogues, temples, and other groups, of which the largest is the Metropolitan Community Church (see Figure 19.9). On the other hand, many homosexual persons reject all forms of religion as oppressive and invalid, making religion as controversial within the gay community as homosexuality is within religious bodies.

Two issues in particular seem to provoke the most debate: ordination and the marriage of homosexual people. Beginning in the 1970s, most major American Protestant denominations debated the appropriateness of ordaining lesbians and gays to the ministry. The debates were emotional and explosive, and nearly all resulted in legislation forbidding homosexual ordination. The debate in 2004 at the General Conference of the United Methodist Church was typical. In a highly charged atmosphere including demonstrations, the group voted, by a 2 to 1 margin, that "practicing homosexuals" cannot be ordained and that Methodist ministers may not bless same-sex unions (Bloom, 2004). The largest branch of Lutherans in the United States, the Evangelical Lutheran Church in America (ELCA), in 2005 retained its policy against blessing same-sex unions and ordaining gays, but at the same time said that it would not punish pastors or congregations that chose to do so (Banerjee, 2005). Talk about a compromise! At present only the Unitarian–Universalist Association, the United Church of Christ (Congregationalists), and both Reform and Orthodox Jews are willing to ordain gay and lesbian people

Figure 19.9 The Reverend Troy Perry founded the Universal Fellowship of Metropolitan Community Churches in 1968 as part of his coming out—the story of which is told in his book *The Lord Is My Shepherd and He Knows I'm Gay.* Providing a home for more than 30,000 members, in 1983 the UFMCC applied for membership in the National Council of Churches, the major U.S. organization of Christian bodies. After much debate, its application was placed on permanent hold (Glaser, 1994).

openly, and the lines are pretty clearly drawn in other religious groups. In 2003 the Episcopal Church, amid much controversy, approved the consecration as bishop of an openly gay priest (Davey, 2003a).

Many who favor full acceptance of homosexual persons have argued for formal recognition of committed relationships along the lines of marriage. In 2000, American Reform Jewish rabbis approved of such unions and authorized the development of an appropriate ceremony (Hames, 2000). The United Church of Christ blesses same-sex unions. Several other mainline Protestant groups,

such as the Episcopalians, Presbyterians, and ELCA Lutherans, are actively debating and studying the question (Davey, 2003b; Evangelical Lutheran Church in America, 2003).

AIDS

AIDS has raised a host of complex and difficult ethical issues for individuals, religious communities, and society as a whole. These issues are often debated in an atmosphere of fear, anger, and ignorance, which is focused on the fatality of the disease and the fact that the majority of sufferers in the United States are either homosexual men or injection drug users, two populations about which the society has profound ambivalence. Religious groups, like the rest of society, have struggled to develop effective ways of ministering to persons with HIV infection or AIDS (Jantzen, 1994). Responses have ranged from declaring AIDS to be God's punishment on sinners to actively organizing to minister to persons with AIDS and seeking to educate members of churches and synagogues about the disease and how they can respond compassionately (Countryman, 1987; Godges, 1986; Jantzen, 1994).

Broadly speaking, the major ethical conflicts center on the dignity and autonomy of the person, on the one hand, and the welfare of society on the other. This issue has both personal and public aspects. For the person who has AIDS or who is HIV positive, a primary issue is confidentiality. Given that disclosure can lead to the loss of one's job, housing, friends, and family, such persons may well wonder if anyone has a right to know about their condition. However, many people argue that the public, or at least certain groups within society, have a right to know who is infected in order to be protected from them.

It has been proposed that children with HIV infection not be allowed to attend public schools and that infected persons be registered for the protection of emergency medical personnel, health care workers, coroners, and morticians. Several large populations, including military personnel, would-be immigrants, and some prisoners, have been required to undergo mandatory testing for HIV. Many public health officials and AIDS researchers oppose such measures because they fear that persons at risk would be driven underground. They argue that the public health is best protected by voluntary testing and the fairly stringent protection of confidentiality (Levine & Bermel, 1985, 1986).

Ethically, a solid middle position would encourage persons in high-risk categories to take responsibility for themselves by undergoing voluntary testing and practicing safer sex. This position would argue that infected persons have a right to confidentiality but should voluntarily disclose their status to anyone put at risk by it—notably health care personnel and sexual partners. For health care workers, there is the personal ethical problem of whether to treat persons who are HIV positive. It is probable that there is an ethical obligation to treat, but that there is also an obligation to take appropriate precautions (Zuger, 1987).

Many of the ethical issues of public policy revolve around the very high cost of AIDS, both for treating its victims and in seeking a medical solution. Who should pay this cost? Insurance companies have sought ways in which to deny health coverage to persons in high-risk groups. People with AIDS often cannot work and so lose job-related insurance benefits. Who should pay for their care—hospitals, cities, states, the federal government? Specialized services and facilities—such as home care and hospices—are needed. Who is responsible for providing them? Given the limited funds available for research, what should the focus of that research be? Should resources be concentrated on prevention through a vaccine or on treatment of those who already have the disease? Who should develop treatments, public agencies or private drug companies? And again, who will pay?

Public education for prevention, generally regarded as the only really effective response at present, raises some ethical problems. What kind of education is appropriate? At what age should it begin? How explicit should it be? Does government advocacy of "safer sex" mean endorsement of sexual practices abhorrent to some Americans? Because of its stand on birth control, the Roman Catholic Church absolutely opposes the use of condoms. Should Catholics have to support government programs to make them generally available? Some public health officials, alarmed by the rapid spread of AIDS among injection drug users, suggest the reversal of a longtime policy of fighting drug abuse by restricting the availability of syringes. They argue that if addicts could readily obtain clean needles, they would not have to share and risk infection. However, this strategy outrages the sensibilities of those who believe that drug addiction is a moral and social evil.

Most of the choices that must be made in dealing with AIDS are unappealing, expensive, or both. American society is being challenged to maintain its own values and to deal compassionately and effectively with what many have described as the greatest health crisis since the bubonic plague.

Technology and Sexual Ethics

A major challenge to ethicists today is the rapid development of technologies that raise new moral issues before the old ones have been resolved. We have already discussed several issues in which technology has played a major role. Although sex outside marriage is hardly a problem unique to our time, the availability of reliable birth control techniques has probably increased the incidence of premarital and extramarital sex. The fact that millions of people can enjoy vigorous sex lives without conceiving children unless they choose to has markedly changed the basic moral climate.

The issue of abortion has also been intensified by the technological advances of the past few decades and will only get more complicated in the future. The developing medical science of neonatology means that fetuses are viable outside the uterus earlier and earlier. Some late-pregnancy abortions produce a fetus that could be kept alive, confronting hospital staffs with agonizing questions about what should be done in such cases. Traditional ethics suggest that such unwanted children be kept alive, yet this can be incredibly costly and the children are often severely handicapped. Hospitals may limit, or even forbid, second-trimester abortions to deal with this issue (Callahan, 1986).

Another complex of ethical issues arises out of the host of new reproductive technologies that enable people to conceive children outside the "normal" process of sexual intercourse. These include artificial insemination, either by husband or donor (AIH or AID), in vitro fertilization (IVF), embryo transfer, and surrogate motherhood.

For many ethicists these technologies can be tentatively approved, because they enable otherwise infertile people to have children with at least one partner's genes (Strong, 1997). Certainly, having children of one's own has had a very high value for most people throughout history, and barrenness has been seen as a curse in most cultures.

These technologies bring with them a number of ethical problems, too, chief among which is that they involve "playing God." That is, they give human beings control over things that are, it is argued, best left up to nature and raise serious problems of who will decide how they are to be used. It is also argued that separating conception from marital intercourse may confuse the parenthood of children and have a negative effect on the family. Another concern is the possibility of exploiting others, particularly in the case of surrogacy.

Some ethicists fear that rich couples will "rent wombs" or "buy babies" from low-income women. Many question the morality of conceiving and/or carrying a child one never intends to raise. Others worry that AID and IVF will be used to select the sex of a child or predetermine other characteristics, ushering in a "Brave New World" that is less than human (Boyd et al., 1986; Krimmel, 1983; McDowell, 1983; Schneider, 1985).

Now that technologies such as in vitro fertilization are commonplace, new issues are emerging. Often more than one embryo is implanted, the goal being to maximize the chances of a successful pregnancy. The result in some cases is multiple births of six or more babies, born long before 9 months of gestation. One study of children born at 25 weeks of gestation or earlier—not necessarily as part of a multiple birth—found that 49 percent had a disability and 23 percent had a severe disability (Wood et al., 2000). Is it ethical to use procedures that pose such serious risks to the baby?

Two religious communities have condemned most or all of these technologies, though on somewhat different grounds. Orthodox Judaism might permit the use of techniques that would allow an otherwise infertile couple to have a child if both egg and sperm come from the couple—for example, in AIH or IVF with implantation in the wife's uterus. Any technique involving a third party is condemned as being de facto adultery and confusing the parentage of the child (Green, 1984; Rosner, 1983). The Roman Catholic position was stated clearly in a 1987 statement issued by the Vatican, "Instruction on Respect for Human Life in Its Origin and on the Dignity of Procreation." The statement admitted as an open moral question fertility techniques that remained within the woman's body using her husband's sperm not collected by masturbation. Otherwise, all techniques such as AID, IVF, and surrogacy were unequivocally condemned as an assault on the dignity of the embryo (in Catholic theology a human person) and on the sanctity of marriage as the only licit means of procreation (Congregation for the Doctrine of the Faith, 1987).

A centrist position on new reproductive technologies might approve their use in many cases, such as AIH in which a married couple use their own egg and sperm and the woman's uterus and simply accomplish fertilization and implantation by artificial means, perhaps because the wife's fallopian tubes are blocked. At the same time, this centrist position might forbid other practices, such as the use of a stranger for her egg and gestation with only the husband's sperm contributed by the "parental" couple. One question then would be whether technological conception should be regulated according to the mother's age. Rosanna Dalla Corte, a 62-year-old Italian woman, created headlines when she gave birth, having used an ovum donation because she was postmenopausal (Strong, 1997). She would be 80 at the time of her son's high school graduation.

The announcement, in 1997, that Scottish scientists had successfully cloned a sheep, Dolly, confronted the public with the possibility of human cloning and its ethical issues when most had thought that cloning was largely a science-fiction fantasy (see Figure 19.10). The technique itself, called **somatic cell nuclear transfer,** involves substituting the genetic material from an adult's cell for the nucleus in an egg (Shapiro, 1997). President Clinton swiftly asked the National Bioethics Advisory Commission to report on the ethical and legal issues surrounding human cloning. The group considered a number of ethical perspectives (Shapiro, 1997). A child born through cloning might have a diminished sense of individuality and personal autonomy, being genetically identical, for

Somatic cell nuclear transfer: A cloning technique that involves substituting genetic material from an adult's cell for the nucleus of an egg.

Figure 19.10 The successful cloning of Dolly, the sheep, was a technological breakthrough that also raised a series of ethical questions.

example, to her mother. The practice might open the door to a eugenics movement in which many copies of genetically "desirable" individuals were created while others were not permitted to reproduce. Yet these concerns must be balanced against important principles such as the right to privacy and to personal freedom, as well as the need to pursue scientific research. The commission concluded that, at this time, it would be morally unacceptable for anyone to create a human child using somatic cell nuclear transfer cloning, in part because the evidence indicates that the technique, at this time, is not safe and could introduce serious, unknown risks to a fetus. At the same time, the commission concluded that various religious bodies held divergent views on cloning and that widespread public debate needed to occur in order to refine and reach consensus on these ethical issues.

The newest development is **therapeutic cloning,** which refers to creating tissues or cells that are genetically identical to those of a patient, who needs them to treat any of a number of diseases (Pollack, 2004). Therapeutic cloning is therefore distinct from reproductive cloning to create another individual, like Dolly. As the cloned embryo develops, *stem cells* can be extracted from it, which hold great promise for treating various neurological diseases such as Alzheimer's. Currently this research is banned in the United States but is being carried out in other countries. Meanwhile, ethicists debate the morality of stem-cell research, which may involve the destruction of embryos.

There is no way to stop the development of technology, or to slow its speed. Nonetheless, it is important to recognize that decisions about human life and reproduction should not be made on purely scientific grounds. By definition, they have the deepest moral implications, which must be adequately addressed if essential human values are to be preserved.

Toward an Ethics of *Human* Sexuality

The combined forces of the sexual revolution and the New Morality have attacked the traditional Judeo–Christian sexual ethic as narrow and repressive. This may be true, but it has not yet been proven to everyone's satisfaction that the alternatives proposed are a real improvement over the Old Morality. Whether the debate will be resolved, and how, remains to be seen. Some of the arguments and possibilities follow.

The Old Morality tends to be ascetic and legalistic and, at its worst, reduces ethical behavior to following a series of rules. Its asceticism may downgrade the goodness of human sexuality and negate the very real joys of physical pleasure. A healthy personality needs to integrate the physical side of life and affirm it, and this kind of self-acceptance may be made more difficult by the Old Morality. Furthermore, if morality is simply a matter of applying universal rules, there is no real choice and human freedom is undermined. In short, opponents of the Old Morality might argue, this approach diminishes the full nature of humanity and impoverishes human life.

However, the traditional approach deserves a few kind words as well. For one thing, with the traditional morality people almost always know where they stand. Right and wrong and good and bad are clearly, if somewhat inflexibly, spelled out. Moreover, asceticism does bear witness to the fact that the human is more than merely the body.

The New Morality, with its situational approach and tendencies toward hedonism, has its own share of pluses and minuses. It affirms quite positively the physical and sexual side of human nature as an integral part of the individual. This is helpful, but if it is pushed too far it can leave people under no control and thus less than fully human. Situation ethics calls for an evaluation of every ethical decision on the basis of the concrete aspects of the persons involved and the context of the decision. Its broad principles of love, respect, and interpersonal responsibility are sound, but it can be argued that situationism does not take sufficiently into account the problem of human selfishness. Dishonesty about our real motives may blind us to the actual effects of our actions, however sincere we profess to be. Furthermore, situationism is a much less certain guide than the older approach, since so many situations are ambiguous.

There is a middle way between these two extremes, one that may prove to be the synthesis that sexual ethics seems to be searching for. This approach would use the traditional principles (laws) as guidelines for actions while insisting that they must occasionally be reworked in view of certain specific situations. This approach differs from the Old Morality by stating that ethical principles must be flexible and from the New Morality by holding that departures from tradition must be based on very strong evidence that the old rules do not apply.

In the specific case of sexual ethics, such a middle-of-the-road approach would affirm the goodness of human sexuality but insist that sexual behavior needs to be responsible and based

Therapeutic cloning: Creating tissues or cells that are genetically identical to those of a patient, to treat a disease.

on reason, experience, and conscience. It would accept sexuality as a vital part of human personality but not the sum total of who we are. If, as is sometimes claimed, the sexual revolution is over and there is a movement toward relationship and commitment, this might prove to be just the sexual morality that people in our time are looking for.

SUMMARY

It is important to study religion and ethics in conjunction with human sexuality because they frequently provide the framework within which people judge the rightness or wrongness of sexual activity. They give rise to attitudes that influence the way members of a society regard sexuality, and they are therefore powerful influences on behavior. Religion and ethics may be hedonistic (pleasure oriented) or ascetic (emphasizing self-discipline). They may be legalistic (operating by rules) or situational (making decisions in concrete situations, with few rules).

In the great ethical traditions, ancient Judaism had a positive, though legalistic, view of sexuality. Christian sources are ambivalent about sexuality, with Jesus saying little on the subject, and with St. Paul, influenced by the immorality of Roman culture and his expectation of the end of the world, being somewhat negative. Later, Christianity became much more ascetic, as reflected in the writings of Augustine and Thomas Aquinas, who placed Catholic moral theology in the natural-law mold. The Protestant Reformation abolished clerical celibacy and opened the door to greater individual freedom in ethics. Today, new biblical scholarship has lcd to a wide variety of positions on issues of sexual ethics.

Humanistic ethics rejects external authority, replacing it with a person-centered approach to ethics. A variety of approaches to sexuality can be found in Islam, Hinduism, and Buddhism.

Six ethical issues involving human sexuality have provoked lively debate recently. Although the Western ethical tradition opposes sex outside marriage, some liberals are open to sex among the unmarried, under certain conditions. Contraception is opposed by Roman Catholicism and Orthodox Judaism on scriptural and natural-law grounds, but it is valued positively by other groups. Abortion provokes a very emotional argument, with positions ranging from condemnation on the grounds that it is murder to a view that asserts the moral right of women to control their own bodies. Although the traditional view condemns homosexuality absolutely, there is some movement toward either a qualified approval of at least civil rights for gay people or a more complete acceptance of their lifestyle. The spread of AIDS poses serious ethical problems, which involve a balancing of individual needs with the welfare of society. Developments in the technology of human reproduction are creating complex ethical issues with few clear norms.

A possible resolution of the conflict between the Old Morality and the New Morality involves an ethics of *human* sexuality, neither hedonistic nor rigidly ascetic, that takes seriously the historical tradition of ethical thinking while insisting that decisions be made on the basis of the specific situation.

QUESTIONS FOR THOUGHT, DISCUSSION, AND DEBATE

1. If you are a member of a religious group, investigate your group's beliefs on the issues discussed in this chapter (sex outside marriage, contraception, abortion, homosexuality, AIDS, and reproductive technology). Do you agree with those positions? If you are not a member of a religious group, see if you can formulate a statement of sexual ethics that is consistent with your philosophy of life.

2. Seek out a person, group, or written material which takes the opposite of your position on abortion and carefully consider those arguments. What effect does this have on your views?

3. Ruth Greenberg is the judge in an unusual custody case. Chad and Michele are a married couple with an infertility problem. Medical testing revealed that Chad had an extremely

low sperm count that was unlikely to produce successful fertilization. To make matters worse, Michele had a small, undeveloped uterus and probably would always miscarry early in a pregnancy. Yet they desperately wanted children. They contracted with a surrogate, Mary, to provide an egg and gestation, and used sperm from a sperm bank for the fertilization. The baby, a little girl, has been born, but Mary has now decided that she wants to keep her. The court battle is between Chad and Michele on the one hand and Mary on the other as to who should get the baby. What should Judge Greenberg do?

SUGGESTIONS FOR FURTHER READING

Biale, David. (1997). *Eros and the Jews.* Berkeley, CA: University of California Press. A history of sex and the Jewish people.

Genovesi, Vincent J. (1987). *In pursuit of love: Catholic morality and human sexuality.* Wilmington, DE: Michael Glazier. Well-written, scholarly work treating the whole field from the mainline Roman Catholic point of view.

Helminiak, Daniel A. (2000). *What the Bible* really *says about homosexuality.* Millennium edition. New Mexico: Alamo Square Press. The author, a Roman Catholic priest and professor of psychology, questions traditional interpretations of biblical passages about homosexuality, arguing that they have been misinterpreted and do not in fact condemn it. See also his *Sex and the sacred; gay identity and spiritual growth* (2006).

Jung, Patricia B., Hunt, Mary E., & Balakrishnan, Radhika (Eds.). (2001). *Good sex: Feminist perspectives from the world's religions.* New Brunswick, NJ: Rutgers University Press. This book examines the possibilities for women's sexuality in contemporary Islam, Buddhism, Judaism, and Christianity.

Lorius, Cassandra. (1999). *Tantric sex: Making love last.* London: Thorsons/HarperCollins. This books explains Tantra and its connection to better sex.

Maguire, Daniel C. (2001). *Sacred choices: The right to contraception and abortion in ten world religions.* Minneapolis: Fortress Press. Maguire, a Catholic theologian, finds much authority for contraception and even abortion in the world's religions, including Roman Catholicism.

Moore, Thomas. (1999). *The soul of sex: Cultivating life as an act of love.* New York: HarperCollins. Moore argues that the link between the soul and sex, between spirituality and sexuality, is valuable for everyone.

Parrinder, Geoffrey. (1996). *Sexual morality in the world's religions.* New York: Oxford University Press. A superb, concise treatment of the variety of religious approaches to human sexuality. The best short book in the field.

CHAPTER TWENTY

Sex and the Law

CHAPTER HIGHLIGHTS

S ex, although considered by many in our culture the quintessential private activity, is blanketed by a staggering number and variety of laws. Such a crazy quilt of state laws means that a perfectly legitimate sexual practice in one state may be a felony in another. By crossing a state boundary one may be stepping into a different moral universe.*

*Posner & Silbaugh (1996).

Every day, millions of people in the United States engage in sexual behaviors that are illegal. This may surprise you, since arrests for criminal sexual conduct are rare (Posner, 1992). But in many states or cities, sexual activity with someone under 18 (statutory rape), sexual activity accomplished through use or threat of force (sexual assault), and sex with someone who is legally married to someone else (adultery) are crimes. In fact, there are numerous laws telling people, in effect, what they can do and how, where, and with whom they can do it. This chapter considers why such laws exist, what sorts of behaviors are affected, how these laws are enforced, how they are changing, and what the future prospects for sex-law reform might be.

Why Are There Sex Laws?

To begin, we might well ask why there are laws regulating sexual conduct in the first place. This is a very modern question, for throughout most of Western history the regulation of sexual conduct was taken for granted. Sexual legislation is quite ancient, dating back certainly to the time of the Old Testament (see Chapter 19). Since then, in countries where the Judeo–Christian tradition has been influential, attempts to regulate morals have been the rule. Today we are likely to regard sex as a private matter, of concern only to those involved. However, historically it has been seen as a matter that very much affects society and therefore is a fit subject for law. Most societies regulate sexual behavior, both by custom and by law.

Even today, certain kinds of sex laws are probably legitimate and necessary. One scholar has argued that the following might be rationally included in law: protection "against force and equivalent means of coercion to secure sexual gratification," "protection of the immature against sexual exploitation," and (a somewhat problematic category) "the prevention of conduct that gives offense or is likely to give offense to innocent bystanders" (Packer, 1968, p. 306). It seems obvious that people ought to be free from sexual assault and coercion and that children should not be sexually exploited; individual rights and the interests of society are here in agreement.

However, sex laws have also been designed for other purposes that may be open to debate. Historically, one rationale was to preserve the family as the principal unit of the social order by protecting its integrity from, for example, adultery or desertion of a spouse. Sex laws also seek to ensure that children have a supportive family by prohibiting conduct such as **fornication,** which is likely to result in out-of-wedlock births. Changing social conditions may call for revision of these statutes, but the principles behind them are understandable.

There is yet another realm of motivation behind sex laws that is highly problematic: the protection of society's morals. The concern for public morality results in laws against nonprocreative sex, for reasons outlined in Chapter 19. Thus there have been laws against homosexual acts, bestiality, and contraception. Religious beliefs as to what is "unnatural," "immoral," or "sinful" have found expression in law, as it was often held that the state had a duty to uphold religion as a pillar of civilized society, using the law to make people good. The example of England is instructive, since U.S. law derives so extensively from English law. Church and state in England have historically been seen as identical, and the state had an obligation to protect the interests of the church. A secular government not tied to the church, such as the United States, was unthinkable, and an individual's morals were a matter of public concern.

In the United States, in contrast, the Constitution separates church and state in order to prevent one religious group from imposing its beliefs on others. To the extent that today's laws are derived from the Judeo–Christian (or any other) religious tradition, they violate this principle. Moreover, we have witnessed increasing heterogeneity of moral beliefs in recent decades (Posner & Silbaugh, 1996). Even if we accept the use of law to regulate morality, there is no longer—if there ever was—a consensus about which morals should be codified into law.

Fornication: Sex between two unmarried persons.

It can be argued that another principal source of sex laws is *sexism*, which is deeply rooted in Western culture. One scholar has suggested that the history of the regulation of sexual activity could as well be called the history of the double standard. He went on to note,

> The law of marriage and the law controlling sexual expression are really the same question looked at from different angles. Women have always been looked upon as the property of men—whether fathers or husbands. Marriage has frequently in history been a commercial transaction or a way in which the fabric of society could be maintained. The male insistence on chastity was simply an attempt to regulate social relations, to cement dynasties, to ensure the orderly succession of property (particularly real property) and to perpetuate male domination. (Parker, 1983, p. 190)

It is probably not coincidental that the movement for sex-law reform has gone hand in hand with the movement for the liberation of women.

The American tradition of moralism in politics, the prudery of the Victorian period (during which much of the U.S. legal system came into being), and the zealousness of such individuals as Anthony Comstock (see Focus: First Person, p. 511) have combined to provide the United States with an enormous amount of sexual legislation. This legislation reflects a great deal of conflict in our attitudes toward sex, which is perhaps unsurprising in such a pluralistic society. According to one authority, "The United States criminalizes more sexual conduct than other developed countries do and punishes the sexual conduct that it criminalizes in common with those countries more severely" (Posner, 1992, p. 78). Table 20.1 lists the maximum punishment (years in prison) allowed by the laws of six countries for three sex crimes and three property crimes. For the three sex crimes, the allowable punishment in the United States is among the more severe, whereas the punishment for the three property crimes in the United States is about average for the six countries. Persons convicted of a crime in the United States actually spend much less time in jail, but these maximum sentences tell us which crimes legislators think are most serious.

The conflict in our attitudes toward many kinds of sexual activity resulted in the **Victorian compromise;** typically, the law does not criminalize behavior per se but does criminalize conduct that is visible to the outside world (Silbaugh, 2002). Thus laws in many jurisdictions do not criminalize commercial sexual intercourse but do penalize *soliciting* sexual activity in exchange for goods and services. In another example, state laws may criminalize "open and notorious" adultery but not the act of having sex with someone who is married. To some observers, this may appear to be hypocrisy. The rationale is that some (many?) people are offended by visible sexual misconduct and that it therefore harms the community. Also, persons who favor maintaining the status quo, as in for instance preserving heterosexual marriage, do not want to be presented with public examples of alternative forms of conduct that might lead others to adopt these alternative behaviors or lifestyles. And it is true that many people become more open in expressing nontraditional behavior when they learn that others share their interest or preference. This is one of the effects of widespread access to the Internet.

The U.S. legal tradition assumes both the right of the state to enforce morals and a consensus in society as to which morals are to be enforced. However, some citizens have come to question the legitimacy of government interference in what

Victorian compromise: The decision not to criminalize behavior per se and instead criminalize conduct that is visible to the outside world.

Table 20.1	Severity of Punishment for Three Sex Crimes and Three Property Crimes, Selected Countries					
	Maximum Prison Sentence (years) in					
Crime	*England*	*France*	*Italy*	*Japan*	*Sweden*	*United States*
Rape	30	20	10	15	6	18
Statutory rape	16	10	10	15	4	16
Incest	7	20	6.5	NA	2	10
Arson	30	30	7	15	8	14
Robbery	30	30	10	15	6	14
Larceny	10	10	3	10	2	8

Source: Adapted and reprinted by permission of the publisher from *Sex and Reason* by Richard A. Posner, pp. 75–76, Cambridge, Mass.: Harvard University Press, Copyright © 1992 by the President and Fellows of Harvard College.

Focus: First Person
Anthony Comstock: Crusader against Vice

In any discussion of laws regulating sexual behavior, the name Anthony Comstock looms large. His zeal for moral reform is reflected in the use of the term *Comstock laws* for the kinds of restrictive statutes considered here.

Comstock was born in Connecticut in 1844 and was reared as a strict Puritan Congregationalist; he had a well-developed sense of his own sinfulness—and of others' as well. He served in the Union Army during the Civil War and worked as a dry-goods salesperson. While still a young man, he became very active in the Young Men's Christian Association, seeking the arrest and conviction of dealers in pornography. He helped found the Committee for the Suppression of Vice within the YMCA. This later became an independent society as his efforts gained him national attention.

Comstock's most noteworthy success was probably a comprehensive antiobscenity bill that passed Congress in 1873. The law prohibited the mailing of obscene matter within the United States, as well as advertisements for obscenity, which included matter "for the prevention of conception." Comstock initiated the passage of a similar law in New York, making it illegal to give contraceptive information verbally, and many other states followed suit. At the same time, Comstock received an appointment as a special agent of the U.S. Post Office, which gave him the personal authority to enforce the Comstock Law. He did so with a vengeance, claiming at the end of his career to have been personally responsible for the jailing of over 3,600 offenders against public decency.

Comstock's energies were directed not only against pornography but also against abortionists, fraudulent advertisers and sellers of quack medicines, lotteries, saloonkeepers, artists who painted nude subjects, and advocates of free love. Among the objects of his wrath were many of the most famous advocates of unpopular opinions of his day. He carried on a crusade against women's movement pioneers Victoria Woodhull and her sister Tennessee Claflin; he helped jail William Sanger, husband of Margaret Sanger, the birth control crusader; he attacked Robert Ingersoll, a noted atheist; and he tried to prevent the New York production of George Bernard Shaw's play about a prostitute, *Mrs. Warren's Profession*. For the last of these efforts Shaw rewarded him by coining the word *Comstockery*.

Anthony Comstock was a controversial figure during his own lifetime and has often been blamed for all legislation reflecting his views. However, it is important to understand that he had a great deal of support from the public, without which he could not have jailed his 3,600 miscreants. He will probably go down in history as a symbol of the effort to make people moral by legislation. He died in 1915 shortly after representing the United States at an International Purity Congress.

Anthony Comstock may be long dead, but Comstockery has always been a feature of American society and seems to have made a comeback in the 2000s. He might very well be a patron saint for the Christian Far Right.

Source: Broun & Leech (1927).

---

they regard as their private affairs. This tension has led to a widespread demand for a radical overhaul of laws that regulate sexual conduct. It all makes for a fascinating, if frustrating, field of study, for law has a way of reflecting the ambiguities and conflicts of society.

What Kinds of Sex Laws Are There?

Cataloging the laws pertaining to sexual conduct would be a difficult project. It is possible that no one really knows how many such laws there are,

given the large number of jurisdictions in the U.S. legal system. When one considers the range of federal law, the Uniform Code of Military Justice, state laws, municipal codes, county ordinances, and so on, the magnitude of the problem becomes clear. In addition to *criminal law*, portions of civil law that may penalize certain sexual behaviors—such as licensing for professions, personnel rules for government employees, and immigration regulations—must also be considered. Furthermore, these laws are changing all the time, so any list would become obsolete before it went to press. Therefore, what is offered here is not so much a statistical summary of specific sex laws as a look at the *kinds* of laws that are, or have been, on the statute books.[1] The subheadings, all of which contain the word *crime,* have been chosen with care, as a reminder that we are discussing legal offenses that can carry with them the penalty of going to jail, loss of reputation, monetary fines, or all of these. However quaint and amusing some of these laws may seem, they are a serious matter.

Crimes of Exploitation and Force

Recalling our earlier discussion about the kinds of sex laws that seem to make sense in a pluralistic society, let us begin with those seeking to prevent the use of force or exploitation in sexual relations— chiefly laws against rape and sexual relations with children. In the past two decades, there has been a movement toward seeing such crimes not so much as sex crimes but as crimes of violence and victimization, with laws being revised to accommodate this different understanding and to protect the victims (see Chapter 15).

Rape is typically defined, following current laws in many states, as "nonconsensual oral, anal, or vaginal penetration, obtained by force, by threat of bodily harm, or when the victim is incapable of giving consent" (Koss, 1993, p. 1062). A victim might be incapable of giving consent because of being unconscious or drunk.

Rape of a spouse is a crime in all 50 states and the District of Columbia (National Center for Victims of Crime, 2004). However, in some jurisdictions there are additional legal hurdles that must be overcome in order to prosecute the case. One is a shorter time limit for reporting the rape to authorities. A second hurdle is that the act must be accomplished by force or threat of force; in nonspousal cases, lack of consent is often sufficient to bring charges.

Laws that seek to prevent the sexual exploitation of children and young people are complicated by the issues of consent, coercion, and immaturity, all of which are rather difficult to define. Most states have laws against *statutory rape,* or carnal knowledge of a juvenile. These laws presume that all intercourse by an adult male (normally one over 17 or 18) with any female under a certain age is, by definition, illicit because she cannot give genuine consent. The age of consent varies from state to state, ranging from

14 to 18; in most states, it is 15 or 16 (Posner & Silbaugh, 1996).[2] Many states have laws that also include a reference to the difference in ages between the male and the female, on the assumption that there is a difference in criminality between a 16-year-old girl having intercourse with her 18-year-old boyfriend and with a man in his thirties or forties (MacNamara & Sagarin, 1977; Mueller, 1980).

There is a great variety of laws against the *sexual abuse of children,* called variously child molestation, carnal abuse of a child, or impairing the morals of a child. These general terms usually cover all sexual contact between adult and child, regardless of gender, and can include the use of sexual language, exhibitionism, showing pornography to a child, having a child witness intercourse, or taking a child to a brothel or gay bar (MacNamara & Sagarin, 1977). Such statutes attempt to protect children, a reasonable goal, but some are so vague as either to be ineffective or to criminalize innocuous behavior. In order to prevent misuse of these laws, it is important to develop more precise ones.

Finally, every state includes laws against **incest** in its penal code. These laws prohibit sexual relations between children and "biological parents, ancestors, or other siblings"; some also prohibit activity involving step- and adoptive parents (Posner & Silbaugh, 1996). Most prosecutions are cases involving children and adult relatives. The nearly universal taboo against incest seems to have as its purpose the guarantee to children that the home will be a place where they can be free from sexual pressure. In many states, the closer the relationship, the more severe the penalties against incest (Mueller, 1980). Incest laws also seek to prevent the alleged genetic problems of inbreeding.

Criminal Consensual Acts

Although it is not hard to see the logic of laws against force and exploitation of the young, many people are amazed to discover the number of sexual acts that are legally forbidden to consenting adults. These laws have been justified on the grounds of the prevention of illegitimacy, the preservation of the family, the promotion of public

---

Rape: Nonconsensual oral, anal, or vaginal penetration, obtained by force, by threat of bodily harm, or when the victim is incapable of giving consent.
Incest: Sexual relations between persons closely related to each other.

[1] A general discussion of the kinds of laws may be found in MacNamara & Sagarin (1977). State-by-state listings appear in Bernard et al. (1985), Hunter et al. (1992), and Posner & Silbaugh (1996).

[2] Statutory rape laws are the subject of many jokes. One that reflects respect for such laws: A police officer patrolling Lover's Lane shortly before midnight noticed a parked car with its interior light on and two people sitting in the front seat. He decided to investigate. As he approached the car, he saw a young man in the driver's seat reading a book, and a young woman in the passenger's seat knitting. He tapped on the driver's window, and the young man opened it. "How old are you two?" the officer asked brusquely. The young man replied, "I'm 19, and in 11 minutes she'll be 18."

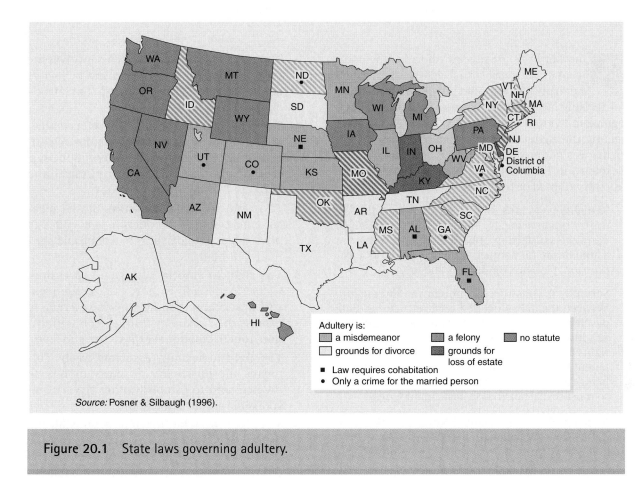

Adultery is:

- ▨ a misdemeanor
- ▨ a felony
- ▨ no statute
- ☐ grounds for divorce
- ▨ grounds for loss of estate
- ■ Law requires cohabitation
- ● Only a crime for the married person

Source: Posner & Silbaugh (1996).

Figure 20.1 State laws governing adultery.

health, and the enforcement of morality (Bernard et al., 1985). There are a number of laws against fornication, **cohabitation,** and adultery. As of 2002, fornication was illegal in 11 states and the District of Columbia. As of 2005, cohabitation was outlawed in 7 states (www.unmarriedamerica.org).

Adultery, intercourse involving persons at least one of whom is married to someone else, is a crime in 24 states and the District of Columbia. It is grounds for divorce in almost every state (see Figure 20.1). Two issues arise in defining adultery. The first is whether both parties or only the married person is guilty of a crime; in 1 state only the married participant can be charged. The other is what constitutes adultery, a single incident (42 states) or habitual or open conduct (10 states) (recall the discussions of the Victorian compromise).

Besides specifying with whom one may have sex, laws have attempted to regulate what acts are permissible, even in the case of a legally married couple. In 1986, 24 states had laws prohibiting **sodomy;** in some states, the law defined *sodomy* very broadly, as "crimes against nature" or "deviate sexual intercourse," while in other states the law was

very specific—for example, "contact between the penis and anus, the mouth and the penis, or the mouth and the vulva." In the 1990s, the laws in several states were ruled unconstitutional by state and appeal courts. In 1998 John Geddes Lawrence and Tyron Garner were arrested in Texas after police found them engaging in consensual activity in Lawrence's apartment. They were charged under the state's Homosexual Conduct Law, which prohibited same-sex intercourse; each pleaded no contest and was fined $200. When the case was appealed, the U.S. Supreme Court, in 2003, ruled 6 to 3 that such laws are an unconstitutional invasion of privacy (*Lawrence et al. v. Texas,* 539 U.S. 102, 2003). This decision invalidated the sodomy laws that remained in the legal codes in 13 states. The majority opinion included reference to a decision by the European Court of Human Rights supporting gay rights; this is an outstanding example of the impact of the burgeoning human rights—including sexual rights—movement (see Focus: A Sexually Diverse World, p. 514).

Cohabitation: Unmarried persons living together (with sexual relations assumed).
Adultery: Intercourse involving persons at least one of whom is married to someone else.
Sodomy: Originally "crimes against nature"; in contemporary laws, oral and anal intercourse.

Focus: A Sexually Diverse World
Universal Sexual Rights

A nother basis for sex-law reform is the concept of universal sexual rights. Adoption of such principles would provide a foundation for revising laws in every country so that they recognize individual freedom and dignity while protecting the rights of others. A statement of these rights was adopted at the 14th World Congress of Sexology, in Hong Kong in 1999, and was subsequently adopted by the World Health Organization.

Sexuality is an integral part of the personality of every human being. Its full development depends upon the satisfaction of basic human needs such as the desire for contact, intimacy, emotional expression, pleasure, tenderness and love.

Sexuality is constructed through the interaction between the individual and social structures. Full development of sexuality is essential for individual, interpersonal, and societal well being. Sexual rights are universal human rights based on the inherent freedom, dignity, and equality of all human beings. Since health is a fundamental human right, so must sexual health be a basic human right.

In order to ensure that human beings and societies develop healthy sexuality, the following sexual rights must be recognized, promoted, respected, and defended by all societies through all means. Sexual health is the result of an environment that recognizes, respects, and exercises these sexual rights.

1. **The right to sexual freedom.** Sexual freedom encompasses the possibility for individuals to express their full sexual potential. However, this excludes all forms of sexual coercion, exploitation and abuse at any time and situations in life.

2. **The right to sexual autonomy, sexual integrity, and safety of the sexual body.** This right involves the ability to make autonomous decisions about one's sexual life within a context of one's own personal and social ethics. It also encompasses control and enjoyment of our own bodies free from torture, mutilation, and violence of any sort.

3. **The right to sexual privacy.** This involves the right for individual decisions and behaviors about intimacy as long as they do not intrude on the sexual rights of others.

4. **The right to sexual equity.** This refers to freedom from all forms of discrimination regardless of sex, gender, sexual orientation, age, race, social class, religion, or physical and emotional disability.

5. **The right to sexual pleasure.** Sexual pleasure, including autoeroticism, is a source of physical, psychological, intellectual and spiritual well-being.

6. **The right to emotional sexual expression.** Sexual expression is more than erotic pleasure or sexual acts. Individuals have a right to express their sexuality through communication, touch, emotional expression, and love.

7. **The right to sexually associate freely.** This means the possibility to marry or not, to divorce, and to establish other types of responsible sexual associations.

8. **The right to make free and responsible reproductive choices.** This encompasses the right to decide whether or not to have children, the number and spacing of children, and the right to full access to the means of fertility regulation.

9. **The right to sexual information based upon scientific inquiry.** This right implies that sexual information should be generated through the process of unencumbered and yet scientifically ethical inquiry, and disseminated in appropriate ways at all societal levels.

10. **The right to comprehensive sexuality education.** This is a lifelong process from birth throughout the life cycle and should involve all social institutions.

11. **The right to sexual health care.** Sexual health care should be available for prevention and treatment of all sexual concerns, problems, and disorders.

Gay, lesbian, bisexual, and transgender persons continue to face discrimination based on a range of local, state, and federal laws and regulations, although the discriminatory practices and the regulations they are based on are under attack. In many places, such persons may be denied private employment. However, the federal civil service regulations forbid such discrimination in public employment, and some state governors and mayors have issued executive orders forbidding discrimination based on sexual orientation. Many professional and occupational licensing requirements nevertheless have "good character" or morality clauses that may be used as a basis for discrimination. For example, a number of public school teachers have been dismissed or reassigned when their homosexuality or transgender status has become known. At least 17 states, some counties, and 157 municipalities have laws or policies prohibiting discrimination on the basis of sexual orientation, notably in housing and employment (Epstein, 1995). These laws have withstood court tests but are often unpopular and remain subject to repeal by referendum. The law in Dade County, Florida, enacted in 1998, was challenged by a large, well-financed campaign in 2002, with the effort to repeal it defeated by just 6 percent.

Gays and lesbians have an ambiguous status with regard to service in the United States military. For many years they could be refused entry to or dismissed from military service. And in 1990, the U.S. Supreme Court upheld the military's right to ban gays and lesbians. Lower-court cases make an effort to distinguish between statements of orientation and actual behavior, acting to protect the latter (*Meinhold v. U.S.* 34 F 3d 1469, 1994). In 1994 the Clinton administration adopted a "Don't ask, don't tell" policy: Military authorities henceforth cannot ask a person about his or her sexual orientation, and nonheterosexuals are not to make their orientation public—that Victorian compromise again (Figure 20.2).

Every year, hundreds of men and women are dismissed from the armed services, in most cases for disclosing their orientation. In 1999, in response to several widely publicized cases of assault or murder of military personnel related to sexual orientation issues, the military announced a policy of requiring antigay harassment training throughout one's military career. Article 125 of the *Uniform Code of Military Justice* prohibits consensual sodomy. Military personnel convicted of violating this article are ap-

Figure 20.2   In 1994, President Bill Clinton, together with then-General Colin Powell, announced the new "Don't ask, don't tell" policy for gays and lesbians in the military. The policy has been upheld by several court decisions.

pealing their convictions, some of which involve heterosexual sodomy. Based on the U.S. Supreme Court ruling in *Lawrence et al. v. Texas,* a coalition of civil rights groups has petitioned the top military court to strike Article 125. The number of persons discharged from military service for homosexuality increased from 1,000 in 1997 to 1,227 in 2001. The number has steadily declined since, to 601 in 2006. The decline occurred during the Iraq and Afghanistan conflicts, leading some to charge that the armed services are retaining gay and lesbian troops because it needs them to fight (Tyson, 2007).

Beyond discrimination in employment and the military, distinctions are drawn in other areas as well. At least until 2004, gay and lesbian relationships had very little legal support. This means that the partner of a gay man or a lesbian is not entitled to health insurance coverage or Social Security benefits, although polls indicate that a majority of Americans support such entitlements (see Table 20.2). Same-sex couples cannot automatically inherit each other's property. With few exceptions, children of same-gender parents face economic and legal discrimination or hardship because their bonds to their parents are not recognized (Pawelski et al., 2006; Herek, 2006). The homosexuality or transgendered status of a parent may be a serious disadvantage in child custody proceedings. One strategy being pursued is to gain recognition of the "domestic partner" status, which would provide access for the partner to some or all of the benefits of a spouse. Some cities, public agencies such as universities, and corporations have recognized such persons and extended benefits to them. A law adopted in Vermont in 2000 established "civil unions," which provide couples with the rights and benefits of marriage.

An alternative strategy is to gain approval for and recognition of marriages involving nonheterosexual

Figure 20.3 The issue of laws governing marriage between same-sex couples has stirred heated debate.

couples. In 2002, the Ontario Superior Court ruled that denying legal recognition to same-sex marriages violated the Canadian Charter of Rights and Freedoms. In 2003, the Massachusetts Supreme Court ruled, 4 to 3, that same-sex couples are entitled to marry (*Goodridge v. Department of Public Health,* SJC-08860, November 18, 2003). Writing for the majority, Chief Justice Margaret H. Marshall wrote,

Table 20.2 Americans' Attitudes toward Gay Rights

	Percentage Who Said		
	Should	*Should Not*	*Don't Know*
Do you think there should or should not be			
Laws to protect gays and lesbians from prejudice and discrimination in jobs? (2005)	64	30	5
Equal rights in terms of housing? (2000)	78	15	7
Health insurance and other employee benefits for gay spouses? (2000)	58	34	8
Social Security benefits for gay spouses? (2000)	54	38	8
Legally sanctioned gay and lesbian unions or partnerships? (2004)	40	51	8
Adoption rights for gay spouses? (2000)	39	50	11
Homosexuals hired to serve in the armed forces? (2005)	76	22	2

Source: Telephone polls conducted by Princeton Survey Research Associates; the year the question was asked is indicated in parentheses.

Without the right to marry—or more properly, the right to choose to marry—one is excluded from the full range of human experience and denied full protection of the laws for one's "avowed commitment to an intimate and lasting human relationship."

The court gave the Massachusetts state legislature 180 days to enact appropriate laws. When it did not, "gay marriage" became legal in Massachusetts, on May 17, 2004. City officials in Boston immediately began recognizing civil and religious marriages involving same-sex couples.

On February 12, 2004, in a direct challenge to state law, San Francisco Mayor Gavin Newsom directed city officials to start issuing licenses for same-sex marriages. More than 4,000 were issued before the California Supreme Court ordered Newsom to stop. The legal challenges to both the law and the validity of the licenses have been consolidated into one case that is to be heard in San Francisco Superior Court.

Most observers expect the case to be appealed to the California Supreme Court, which may take several years. In the meantime, the status of the "marriages" performed in San Francisco is ambiguous.

These moves toward recognition of gay marriage have predictably stimulated opposition. In February 2004 President George W. Bush joined many politicians and religious leaders in calling for an amendment to the U.S. Constitution that would restrict marriage to two people of the opposite sex. As precedent, Bush pointed to the federal Defense of Marriage Act (DOMA) passed in 1996 and signed by President Clinton. Forty-one states have laws that prohibit gay and lesbian couples from marrying, many of them modeled on the DOMA (Lambda Legal, 2007).

In November 2004, voters in 11 states approved amendments to their state constitutions making marriage exclusively heterosexual. The margin of

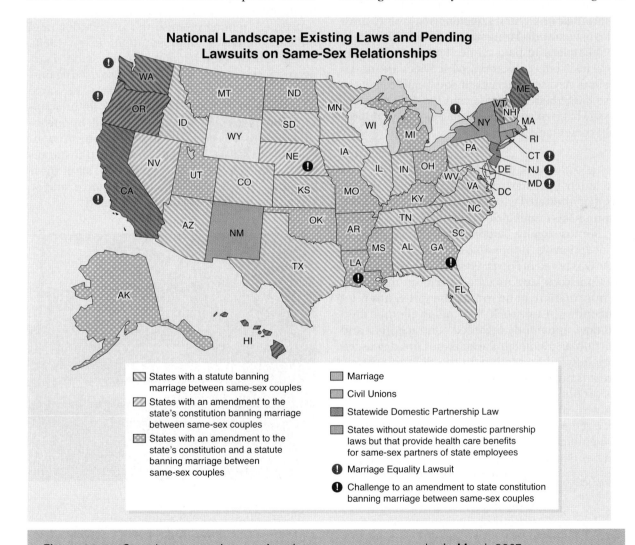

National Landscape: Existing Laws and Pending Lawsuits on Same-Sex Relationships

Legend:
- States with a statute banning marriage between same-sex couples
- States with an amendment to the state's constitution banning marriage between same-sex couples
- States with an amendment to the state's constitution and a statute banning marriage between same-sex couples
- Marriage
- Civil Unions
- Statewide Domestic Partnership Law
- States without statewide domestic partnership laws but that provide health care benefits for same-sex partners of state employees
- ❗ Marriage Equality Lawsuit
- ❗ Challenge to an amendment to state constitution banning marriage between same-sex couples

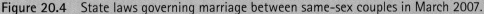

Figure 20.4 State laws governing marriage between same-sex couples in March 2007.

Source: Lamda Legal, 2007.

victory ranged from 7 to 5 in Oregon to 6 to 1 in Mississippi (see Figure 20.4). Clearly, gay marriage is a contentious issue. A Gallup poll taken in May 2004 found the public almost evenly split, 51 percent in favor of a constitutional amendment and 45 percent opposed (Roper Center, 2004). In November 2006, voters in 7 additional states banned same-sex marriage, by majorities of 52 to 81 percent. Only voters in Arizona rejected the proposed ban, 51 to 49 percent.

Crimes against Good Taste

Another broad category of sex offenses can be viewed as crimes against community standards of good taste and delicacy. In this area we find laws against **exhibitionism, voyeurism,** solicitation, disorderly conduct, being a public nuisance, and "general lewdness." These statutes are by and large quite vague and punish acts that are offensive, or *likely* to be offensive, to someone. Forty states have laws prohibiting intentional public nudity and exhibitionism. Twenty-three states have laws declaring sexual contact or activity in a public place to be a crime (Posner & Silbaugh, 1996). In all but two states these activities are misdemeanors. As discussed later, unequal enforcement of these laws, their vagueness, and the difference between what is offensive and what is actually criminal make these statutes suspect.

Crimes against Reproduction

The Judeo–Christian tradition considered behaviors that interfered with reproduction sins. English common law criminalized these behaviors, including homosexuality, sodomy, and birth control. (Conception was impossible with these behaviors.)

As was noted in Focus: First Person on page 511, the Comstock laws included a ban on the giving of information concerning the prevention of conception. Comstock, like many people then and now, apparently regarded contraception and abortion as identical. These issues are discussed more fully in the section on the right to privacy; here it is mentioned only that until 1973 abortion was prohibited or severely limited in many jurisdictions, and contraception was prohibited in some. These laws are clear examples of the enshrinement in the statute books of the values of another day. They arise from an understanding of reproduction as the only legitimate purpose of sex and a belief in the necessity of vigorous propagation of the species. Such laws were overturned by Supreme Court action, but continuing agitation, at least in the case of abortion, ensures that public debate will endure for some time.

Criminal Commercial Sex

The law has also deemed it illegal to make money from sex, at least in certain circumstances. It is not illegal to sell products with subtle promises of sexual fulfillment, but it is illegal to provide such fulfillment, either in direct form (that is, prostitution) or on paper or electronically, as in pornography. We treat both in greater detail later; first, however, let us examine the kinds of laws on these subjects.

Prostitution is the exchange of sex for money or other payment such as drugs. Except in Nevada, where five counties allow it, prostitution is illegal in every jurisdiction in the United States, though it is legal in many other countries. In most states, prostitution is a misdemeanor, punishable by a fine or jail sentence. The law also forbids activities related to it, such as solicitation, pandering (pimping, procuring), renting premises for prostitution, and enticing minors into prostitution (Perry, 1980). These activities are felonies in most states. Laws against vagrancy and loitering are also used against prostitutes. Many state laws provide the same penalty for patronizing a prostitute as for prostitution. However, clients are rarely charged. By one estimate, only 10 percent of the 100,000 prostitution-related arrests per year are of clients (Prostitutes Education Network, 1998). In general, all of these laws have proved very difficult to enforce, and so the "oldest profession" goes on unabated.

Figure 20.5 The oldest profession. A prostitute solicits a potential customer.

Exhibitionism: Showing one's genitals in a public place, to passersby; indecent exposure.
Voyeurism: Secretly watching people who are nude.
Prostitution: The exchange of sex for money or other payment such as drugs.

Obscenity is discussed in more detail in a later section. Suffice it to say here that in most jurisdictions it is a crime to sell material or to present a play, film, or other live performance that is "obscene." That much is fairly simple. The real problem comes in deciding *what* exactly is obscene and how that will be determined without doing violence to the First Amendment's guarantee of freedom of the press. So far, no satisfactory answer has been found. Obscenity laws seem to have a twofold basis. First, they attempt to prevent the corruption of morals by materials that incite sexual thoughts and desires. Second, they attempt to ensure that no one will profit by the production and distribution of such materials. Whether either can be done, or is worth doing, is a question that we take up later in this chapter.

Sex-Law Enforcement

From the foregoing, it is clear that the law has intruded into areas that the reader may well have thought were his or her own business. We can now ask, How are sex laws enforced? The answer is simple: with *great* inconsistency. One authority estimated that "the enforcement rate of private consensual sex offenders must show incredibly heavy odds against arrest—perhaps one in ten million" (Packer, 1968, p. 304); little has changed since 1968. The contrast between the number and severity of the laws themselves and the infrequency and capriciousness of their enforcement reflects society's ambivalence toward the whole subject.

This contrast leads to serious abuses and to demands for radical reform of sex laws. A summary of the arguments for reform will be presented in the next section. First, however, it should be noted that as long as the laws are on the books, the *threat* of prosecution, or even of arrest, can exact a great penalty from the "offender." Loss of job, reputation, friendship, family, and so on can and does in some cases result from the sporadic enforcement of sex laws. For persons engaging in the prohibited acts, the threat of blackmail is ever present. Of course, for those actually convicted on "morals charges," the situation is even worse. That individuals should be subjected to such punishments for private acts is questionable.

Second, the uneven enforcement of sex laws may have a very bad effect on law enforcement in general. It invites arbitrary and unfair behavior and abuse of authority by police and prosecutors. With regard to commercial sex workers, arrest practices seem highly discriminatory. First, 90 percent of all arrests are of workers (not clients). Of these, 50 to 80 percent are of minority women, even though most prostitutes are white. Finally, a large minority of those sentenced to jail are women of color; white women are more likely to be fined (Prostitutes Education Network, 1998). Another serious abuse is entrapment, in which an undercover police agent, posing, for example, as a potential client, actually solicits the commission of a crime. Because a sexual act between consenting parties means that there is no one to report the act to the authorities, undercover agents must create the crime in order to achieve an arrest for it. Such entrapment hardly leads to respect for the law. Moreover, the knowledge that sex laws are violated with impunity creates a general disrespect for the law, particularly among those who know that they are, strictly speaking, "criminals" under it. If nothing else, the failure of Prohibition ought to demonstrate that outlawing activities of which a substantial proportion of the population approves is bad public policy. It may well be said that more violations of the public good result from the enforcement of sex laws than from the acts they seek to prevent.[3] Keeping this in mind, let us turn to the prospects for the future.

Trends in Sex-Law Reform

It is difficult to specify the number and details of sex laws. Our distaste for these attempts to regulate human behavior leads us to call attempts to change them *reform,* although many in our society would contend that the change is often for the worse. Sex being a topic heavily laden with values, such reform is not likely to be accomplished without a good deal of conflict. This makes it difficult to predict either the precise directions of change or its speed. However, some important legal principles are used to bring about changes in sex laws.

Efforts at Sex-Law Reform
Following a thorough review of legal practices in the United States, the American Law Institute's Model Penal Code recommended **decriminalization** of many kinds of sexual behavior previously outlawed. Under the section dealing with sexual offenses, it includes as reasonable for the law to regulate only rape,

> **Obscenity:** That which is offensive to decency or modesty, or calculated to arouse sexual excitement or lust.
>
> **Decriminalization:** Removing an act from those prohibited by law, ceasing to define it as a crime.

[3]For a good discussion of these and other arguments, see Packer (1968, pp. 301–306).

deviate sexual intercourse by force or imposition, corruption and seduction of minors, sexual assault, and indecent exposure (American Law Institute, 1962, Article 213). With the notable exception of commercial sex work, which it still makes illegal, the American Law Institute follows the principle that private sexual behavior between consenting adults is not really the law's business. The recommendation of the Model Penal Code has been followed by nearly half the states.

While there are exceptions, a state is more likely to reform its sex laws as part of a complete overhaul of its criminal code than to make specific repeal of such laws. The reason for this is political and is grounded in the distinction between legalization and decriminalization. If legislators "legalize" unconventional sexual practices, people are likely to become upset and accuse the state of "condoning" them. It is therefore important to note that what is advocated is decriminalization; that is, ceasing to define certain acts as criminal or removing the penalties attached to them. Decriminalization is morally neutral; it neither approves nor disapproves, but simply revises the definitions.

Right to Privacy

SexSource Online
www.mhhe.com/hyde10

"THE RIGHT TO
PRIVACY" IN
SEX AND
THE LAW

A legal principle that has been very important in sex-law reform is the right to privacy. This has come into play chiefly in attacks on sex laws through the courts. Interestingly enough, although the right to privacy is invoked in connection with an amazing variety of matters—criminal records, credit bureaus and banks, school records, medical information, government files, wiretapping, and the 1974 amendment to the Freedom of Information Act (known as the Privacy Act), to name a few— the definitive articulation of the constitutional principle came in a sex-related case (Brent, 1976).

In 1965 the Supreme Court decided the case of *Griswold v. Connecticut*, invalidating a state law under which a physician was prosecuted for providing a married couple with information and medical advice concerning contraception. Justice William Douglas stated flatly that "we deal with a right of privacy older than the Bill of Rights, older than our political parties, older than our school system" (*Griswold v. Connecticut*, 1965, p. 486). The problem that Douglas, and the six justices who voted with him, faced was finding the specific provisions of the Constitution that guaranteed this right. Douglas found it not in any actual article of the Bill of Rights but in "penumbras, formed by emanations from those guarantees that help give them life and substance" (*Griswold v. Connecticut*, 1965, p. 484). Critics have found this a splendid example of con-stitutional double-talk, and the debate over the application of the right to privacy continues. Nonetheless, in invalidating the Connecticut law, the Court defined a right to privacy that was, in this instance, abridged when a married couple was denied access to information on contraception.

While the decision in the Griswold case declared the marriage bed an area of privacy, in the 1972 case of *Eisenstadt v. Baird*, the Court invalidated a Massachusetts law forbidding the dissemination of contraception information to the unmarried. In doing so the Court stated that "if the right of privacy means anything, it is the right of the individual, married or single, to be free from unwarranted governmental intrusion into matters as fundamentally affecting a person as the decision whether to bear or beget a child" (*Eisenstadt v. Baird*, 1972, p. 453). Other decisions have established one's home as a protected sphere of privacy that the law cannot invade (Brent, 1976).

The right to privacy was also invoked by the Court in 1973 in one of its most controversial cases, *Roe v. Wade*, which invalidated laws prohibiting abortion. Suing under the assumed name of Jane Roe, a Texas resident argued that her state's law against abortion denied her a constitutional right. The Court agreed that "the right of personal privacy includes the abortion decision" (*Roe v. Wade*, 1973, p. 113). However, it held that such a right is not absolute and that the state has certain legitimate interests that it may preserve through law, such as the protection of a viable fetus. Nonetheless, the Court declared that a fetus is not a person and therefore is not entitled to constitutional protection. The effect of the *Roe* case, and of related litigation, was to invalidate most state laws against abortion. The Court limited second- and third-trimester abortions to reasons of maternal health but made a woman's right to a first-trimester abortion nearly absolute. However, the 1989 decision in *Webster v. Reproductive Health Services* and the 1992 decision in *Planned Parenthood v. Casey* changed the shape of abortion laws, as discussed later in this chapter.

The Supreme Court further extended the right to privacy in *Lawrence et al. v. Texas*. The majority opinion noted the effects of the Texas statute prohibiting same-sex intercourse and similar laws: "Their penalties and purposes have more far-reaching consequences, touching upon the most private human conduct, sexual behavior, and in the most private of places, the home" (539 U.S. 103, 2003, pp.1–2). This is the strongest statement yet with regard to the protected nature of consensual sexual conduct in one's home.

Even vibrators and dildos have been part of the legal action. In the case of *Williams, et al. v. Pryor* (Alabama) (CV-98-S1938-NE), a U.S. District Court ruled unconstitutional the Alabama law that prohibited distribution of "any device . . . for the stimulation of human genitals." The court stated that the plaintiffs had shown that "the right of sexual privacy" protected the use of such devices.

Equal Protection

Another important legal principle is the right to equal protection of the law. This right is guaranteed by the U.S. Constitution, in the Fifth and Fourteenth Amendments. If law or government action results in disadvantage to some group, that group can seek relief, typically through court action.

Challenges to laws or policies that discriminate against gays, lesbians, commercial sex workers, and other groups distinguished by sexual conduct have been based on this principle. A series of cases have been brought by gays and lesbians against actions by or policies of the U.S. military, such as policies requiring the discharge of lesbians or gays from the armed forces. Some of these cases have been decided in favor of the plaintiffs, others not.

Discrimination against gays and lesbians in employment and other arenas has also been challenged in court. The most celebrated case is *Evans v. Romer*. In 1992, Amendment 2 to the Constitution of the state of Colorado was put on the ballot, prohibiting the enactment of antidiscrimination laws or policies favoring homosexuals. In November 1992, the amendment was adopted with 54 percent of the votes cast. In 1996, the Supreme Court declared Amendment 2 unconstitutional (517 U.S. 620); that is, states may not prohibit antidiscrimination laws. The equal protection clause is the basis for the decision by the Massachusetts Supreme Court invalidating prohibitions on same-sex marriage, as noted above.

Victimless Crimes

In the past four decades, much legislative change has taken place involving the principle of *victimless crimes*—a concept that has broad applicability beyond sexual behavior. The argument is that when an act does no legal harm to anyone or does not provide a demonstrable victim, it cannot reasonably be defined as a crime. The thrust of the argument has been well articulated by Norval Morris, the former dean of the University of Chicago Law School:

> Most of our legislation concerning drunkenness, narcotics, gambling and sexual behavior is wholly misguided. It is based on an exaggerated conception of the capacity of the criminal law to influence men and, ironically, on a simultaneous belief in the limited capacity of men to govern themselves. We incur enormous collateral costs for that exaggeration and we overload our criminal justice system to a degree that renders it grossly defective where we really need protection—from violence and depredations on our property. But in attempting to remedy this situation, we should not substitute a mindless "legalization" of what we now proscribe as crime. Instead, regulatory programs, backed up by criminal sanctions, must take the place of our present unenforceable, crime-breeding and corrupting prohibitions. (1973, p. 11)

The victimless-crime argument should appeal to the public's sense of privacy and to its pocketbooks. Crimes in which there is no readily identifiable victim account for over half the cases handled by U.S. courts (Boruchowitz, 1973). If the court dockets could be cleared and law enforcement officers reassigned, protection against violent crimes would be rendered more efficient and less expensive.

"Be right with you, maám, soon as I've brought these lawbreakers to justice."

Figure 20.6 A cartoonist's view of victimless crime.

The application of this principle to some of the issues discussed earlier should be obvious. A sexual act performed by consenting adults produces no legal harm, and neither of the participants are victims. The only conceivable end served by criminalizing such an act is the protection of "public morals," which, in a society with diverse values, seems an end not worth the cost, if it is even achievable.

Applying this principle, in 2005 the Supreme Court of Canada overturned the conviction of Jean-Paul Lebaye for keeping a common bawdy house. LeBaye operated a club in Montreal that allowed members and their guests admission for the purpose of meeting others, and in some cases engaging in group sex in two private rooms. Prospective members were screened, and participation was voluntary. The majority ruled that the conduct did not cause harm or present a risk of harm to individuals or society *(R. v. Lebaye, 3 S.C.R. 728)*. In 2007, "sex clubs" in Denver, Phoenix, and Washington, D.C., faced a variety of legal challenges.

The most common reference to the decriminalization of victimless acts is with respect to prostitution. Police efforts at curbing the "oldest profession" seem to be ineffective, open to corruption and questionable practices, and tremendously expensive. Since prosecution is normally of the worker and not her customer, there seems to be a clear pattern of discrimination against women that violates the constitutional principle of equal protection. Finally, as all manner of adult consensual behavior comes to be decriminalized, the legitimacy of distinguishing between commercial and noncommercial consensual sex has been questioned (Parnas, 1981). It has been suggested that much of the demonstrable harm associated with commercial sex work, such as the committing of robbery and other crimes by workers and pimps and the connections with organized crime, has resulted *because* the practice is illegal (Caughey, 1974). Thus it has been argued that if it were no longer defined as a crime, all would benefit—the worker, the client, the police, and society at large (Parnas, 1981; Rosenbleet & Pariente, 1973).

San Francisco has a long tradition of prostitution, dating back to the 1860s. It also has thousands of people employed in commercial sexual activity. In 1994, the board of supervisors created a Task Force on Prostitution. After 18 months of hearings and study, the Task Force concluded that

> not only are the current responses ineffective, they are also harmful. They marginalize and victimize prostitutes, making it more difficult for those who want to get out of the industry and more difficult

for those who remain in prostitution to claim their civil and human rights. (San Francisco Task Force on Prostitution, 1996)

The Task Force therefore recommended

> that the City departments stop enforcing and prosecuting prostitution crimes. It further recommends that the departments instead focus on the quality of life infractions about which the neighborhoods complain and redirect funds from prosecution, public defense, court time, legal system overhead, and incarceration towards services and alternatives for needy constituencies.

The argument against the criminalization of prostitution assumes that if it were legal it could be regulated and the problems of crime, public offense, and the spread of sexually transmitted infections associated with it might be avoided. In this case, then, there would be no victims and no societal need to ban the practice. However, this argument can be countered by suggestions that commercial sex work may indeed have victims.

As we noted in Chapter 16, some workers, such as those involved in sex trafficking, are forced to

Figure 20.7   The "Big Boss" of a sex-oriented business in Macau, Malaysia, inspects one of the hostesses. There is heated disagreement over whether we can say that sex workers such as this woman consent to the sexual activity their work requires. What do you think?

engage in sexual activity and may have no opportunity to escape from it. Some workers are forced by a pimp or madam, or perhaps by physical abuse, to stay "in the life." Some young men and women enter commercial sex work because they have few other marketable skills and are lured by the promise of a big income. These cases suggest that there is a continuum of consent, ranging from none through coerced through lack of options to more or less voluntary participation. This continuum probably characterizes not only workers who sell sexual gratification but also those employed in the porn industry. At what point does such activity become consensual? Second, a feminist analysis of prostitution suggests that commercial sex work of all kinds is inherently degrading and contributes to the objectification of women and their bodies, thus harming all women. Third, other activities involving consenting adults can harm other persons. Adultery may damage one or two marriages, harming the spouses and children of the participants, leading at the extreme to divorce and the disruption of a family. Finally, we should consider the possibility that some consensual activities may result in moral, religious, or ethical harm (Silbaugh, 2002).

The Problem of Obscenity and Pornography

Among the most controversial topics in the area of sexual regulation is obscenity and pornography. A substantial portion of the U.S. populace (38 percent in 2004 according to the General Social Survey) finds pornography offensive and wishes it suppressed. Many others do not share this view and find any form of censorship outrageous and unconstitutional. Antivice crusaders consider "smut" dangerous to the average citizen. Legislators are swamped with demands that something be done, while the courts have labored unsuccessfully for years to balance the First Amendment right of freedom of speech with the desire of some to outlaw, or at least regulate, pornography.

To begin with, we have a problem of definition. Here it is helpful to distinguish between *pornography* as a popular term and *obscenity* as a legal concept. *Pornography* comes from the Greek word *porneia*, which means, quite simply, "prostitution," and *graphos*, which means "writing." In general usage today, pornography refers to literature, art, films, speech, and so on that are intended to be sexually arousing, or presumed to be arousing, in nature. Pornography may be *soft-core* (suggestive) or *hard-core*, which usually means it involves an explicit depiction of some sort of sexual activity and genitalia. Pornography, as such, has never

been illegal, but obscenity is. The word *obscene* refers to that which is foul, disgusting, or lewd, and is used as a legal term for that which is offensive to the authorities or to society (Wilson, 1973).

Obscenity has been a legal issue ever since the Supreme Court decided the *Roth* case in 1957. In it the Court explicitly stated that obscenity was not protected by the First Amendment—which guarantees freedom of speech and the press and which, by long-recognized extensions, includes films, pictures, literature, and other forms of artistic expression. However, it also ruled that not all sexual expression is obscene, defining obscenity as material "which deals with sex in a manner appealing to prurient interest" (*U.S. v. Roth*, 1957, p. 487). The *Roth* decision evoked much controversy, both from those who thought the Court had opened the floodgates of pornography and from civil libertarians who found the definition too restrictive. The Court continued to try to refine the test for obscenity. In the 1966 *Memoirs* case, obscenity was additionally defined as that which is "utterly without redeeming social value." In the *Ginzburg* decision the same year, the Court upheld the obscenity conviction of a publisher for "pandering" in his advertising; that is, flagrantly exploiting the sexually arousing nature of his publication. However, none of these tests was persuasive to more than five members of the Court, much less to the public at large.[4]

The current standard definition of obscenity by the Supreme Court came in the 1973 case of *Miller v. California*. Rejecting the "utterly without redeeming social value" test, Chief Justice Burger and the four justices concurring with him proposed the following definition:

> (a) whether "the average person, applying contemporary community standards," would find that the work, taken as a whole, appeals to the prurient interest, (b) whether the work depicts or describes, in a patently offensive way, sexual conduct specifically defined by the applicable state law, and (c) whether the work, taken as a whole, lacks serious literary, artistic, political or scientific value. (*Miller v. California*, 1973, p. 24)

The goals of this decision seem to be to define as obscenity "hard-core pornography" in the popular sense, to require from state statutes precise descriptions of what is to be outlawed, and to give governments more power to regulate it (Gruntz,

---

[4]The frustration of defining obscenity was perhaps best expressed by Justice Potter Stewart in *Jacobelis v. Ohio* (1964): "I shall not further attempt to define [hard-core pornography], and perhaps I could not ever succeed in intelligibly doing so. But I know it when I see it" (378 U.S. 197).

1974). The notable problem with the *Miller* test, at least for civil libertarians, is the "contemporary community standards" provision. This allows the local community to determine what is obscene, rather than using national norms, making it impossible to predict what a given jury in a particular town might find obscene.

One important factor that has affected the law on pornography is the extent to which legislators, law-enforcement officers, and courts believe that it causes harm to the general population. For evidence, they have often turned to social science and found a mixture of data and conclusions. The Commission on Pornography appointed by Attorney General Edwin Meese, in its 1986 *Final Report,* concluded, using personal testimony and scientific studies, that pornography is harmful and linked to the abuse of children and women. The commission's controversial recommendations affirmed the existing antiobscenity statutes and urged their vigorous enforcement. It also seemed to approve other strategies for combating pornography (U.S. Department of Justice, 1986).

The least controversial of these strategies is concerned with the problem of child pornography, depictions of sexual activities involving children, even where real children are not used, which is widespread and damaging to the young people involved in it (Burgess, 1984). In the 1982 case of *New York v. Ferber,* the U.S. Supreme Court ruled unanimously that child pornography, whether or not it is obscene under the prevailing legal standards, is not protected by the Constitution. This decision gave states broader latitude in legislation, based on the government's obligation to protect children from abuse (Shewaga, 1983). The Court required states to be precise about whether they were prohibiting the production, processing, or distribution of child pornography, and to develop clear definitions of what was to be outlawed. This has proved difficult, but efforts continue. Another approach to the problem is to make tougher and more precise laws against child sexual abuse, without which "kiddie porn" could not be made. This approach would criminalize the very production of such material and sidestep the more complicated constitutional issue of distribution and sale (Shouvlin, 1981).

A more fruitful approach for those who oppose pornography has been the attempt to regulate, or eliminate, its sale through zoning. In an effort to keep adult movie theaters out of the community, the city of Renton, Washington, passed an ordinance forbidding adult film theaters within 1,000 feet of any residential zone, single- or multiple-family dwelling, church, park, or school. Citing precedents and a municipality's right to prevent crime and protect property values, the Supreme Court upheld the Renton ordinance in 1986. Such zoning laws are content neutral and thus can avoid First Amendment issues. National City, California, later enacted a very restrictive zoning ordinance, which has been upheld by the California Supreme Court (Ragona, 1993).

In 2001 the city of Spokane, Washington, adopted a zoning ordinance that prohibited locating sex-oriented businesses within 750 feet of a public park, library, school, day care center, church, home, apartment building, or farm. At the same time, the city established zones where such businesses could be located and gave nonconforming businesses one year to relocate to those zones. World Wide Video, an owner of adult businesses in Spokane, chose not to relocate its nonconforming stores and filed a lawsuit challenging the ordinance. World Wide alleged that the City had not proven that sex-oriented businesses negatively affect a community and argued that one year was not a reasonable period for it to relocate or change its retail operation. In 2004 the 9th U.S. Circuit Court of Appeals upheld the ordinance (*World Wide Video v. City of Spokane,* CV-02-00074-AAM, May 27, 2004). The Court ruled that the City did not have to conduct research to prove the existence of negative effects. A provocative counter to the use of zoning ordinances is that the effect of them is to separate and distance middle- and upper-class women from pornography, so that they can easily ignore it (Lasker, 2002). At the same time, zoning often results in sex-oriented businesses being located near lower-class and minority communities, forcing residents to confront it on a daily basis; furthermore, this prevents middle- and upper-class women from engaging pornographic discourse and challenging the stereotypes in it.

The Supreme Court has not abandoned the *Miller* "community standards" test, but it seems likely that attempts will continue to be made to reduce or eliminate the availability of what some see as harmful pornography. The complexity of the legal issues and the continuing debate over what is appropriate for Americans to read and view will undoubtedly keep the matter of pornography, obscenity, and erotica controversial for some time to come. While it is difficult to define obscenity, the courts have consistently ruled that states and local communities have the right to regulate public conduct and public artistic expression (Leonard, 1993).

Owners of adult businesses are fighting back. In Ohio, prior to the election in 2006, many adult establishments handed out voter registration forms and encouraged patrons to register and vote. We noted in Chapter 16 that adult-oriented businesses in Las Vegas have formed their own Chamber of Commerce; like their traditional sibling, the Chamber lobbies against laws that would harm members' business.

Contemporary controversy about pornography is centered on the Internet. We described in Chapter 16 the various sex-oriented goods and services available online to anyone with a computer and Internet access. In the past, a potential user of X-rated books, photographs, videos, or CD-ROMs had to purchase them through a retail store or a mail-order firm. These businesses could, at least in theory, control who purchased these items. Specifically, they could require proof of age, thereby preventing minors from gaining access to such material. No one serves as a gatekeeper and controls access to these items on the Internet.

Existing laws governing the production, distribution, sale, and possession of kiddie porn apply to the Internet, and some law-enforcement agencies do in fact seek out and arrest offenders. More problematic are materials featuring persons over 18. While adult Web sites require users to click on a statement certifying that they are 18 or older in order to gain access, there is no practical way to enforce this restriction. Once the user gains access, many adult Web sites provide free viewing of X-rated photos and stories; users may download the photographs and print the stories. In response to this situation, in 1996 the U.S. Congress passed the Communications Decency Act, which made it illegal to distribute via the Internet "indecent material" a child could access. Several groups immediately challenged the constitutionality of the act, claiming that it violated individuals' First Amendment rights. The U.S. Supreme Court declared the law unconstitutional in 1997.

In a new effort, Congress passed the Children's Online Privacy Protection Act in 1998. It declared criminal any communication for commercial purposes via the Web if it "includes any material that is harmful to minors" (47 U.S.C. 231). A coalition of groups successfully challenged the law, which the U.S. Supreme Court declared unconstitutional, by a vote of 6 to 3, in 2002 (Ashcroft v. Free Speech Coalition, 00-795). The majority opinion declared the law overly broad, saying that it would ban images that are not obscene as the Court defines the term.

At least three states have passed laws banning all state employees—including those who teach and do research in human sexuality—from using government computers to access sexually explicit

materials. A number of corporations and many school districts have adopted similar policies.

The Controversy over Reproductive Freedom

An even more convulsive controversy is to be found in the matter of abortion. Although the Supreme Court's decision in the *Roe* case was quite clear, it has been under continuous attack since it was handed down in 1973. Opposition comes from a broad coalition of antiabortion groups that prefer to call themselves *pro-life* and include the Roman Catholic Church, evangelical Protestants, various "New Right" organizations, and the Republican party. The controversy has been carried on in recent elections, in the courts, in state legislatures, and in Congress. The pro-life movement is well organized and well financed and has proved to be an effective lobbying force, instrumental in the defeat of a number of legislators who have not supported the antiabortion cause. Those seeking to preserve the right of women to legal abortions, who call themselves *pro-choice,* have also organized and been effective as well. Beginning in the 1980s and continuing to the present, the pro-life movement has used five basic strategies to eliminate or reduce abortions: (1) funding restrictions; (2) parental consent, spousal notification, and procedural requirements; (3) the Human Life Amendment; (4) a ban on partial birth abortions; and (5) disruptive action against abortion providers.

The most notable example of funding restrictions is the Hyde Amendment, annually proposed by former Congressman Henry Hyde (no relation to the coauthor of this text). This is a rider to the appropriations bills forbidding the expenditure of any federal money for abortions under most circumstances. In various years this restriction has been applied to the departments of Health and Human Services, Defense, Justice, and the Treasury (Wilcox et al., 1998). This approach was ruled constitutional in the 1980 case of *Harris v. McRae* (440 U.S. 297, 1980), and poor women have subsequently been denied this means of obtaining abortions (Milbauer, 1983). Various states have introduced similar restrictions on state money that has been used to cover the gap in federal funding for abortions. Another strategy involves regulations in Title X of the Public Health Act denying funds to organizations, such as family planning agencies, that make referrals for abortions and granting funds to organizations that oppose abortions (Paul & Klassel, 1987).

The second strategy to make abortion more difficult to obtain has been to restrict abortion by requiring *parental consent* for a minor to have an abortion or *notification* of the husband of a married woman seeking an abortion. In the 1992 case of *Planned Parenthood v. Casey* (112 S. Ct. 2791, 120 L. Ed. 674), the Supreme Court ruled that states could require parental consent for unmarried girls under 18 seeking abortions. However, it struck down the requirement that married women must notify their husbands. In 2007, 34 states required parental involvement, 21 required consent, and 13 required notification (Donohoe, 2007). There is no evidence that parental notification requirements lead to a drop in teen abortion rates (Lehren & Leland, 2006). These requirements are opposed by the American Medical Association, the American Academy of Pediatrics, the American Academy of Obstetrics and Gynecology, and other groups.

Another effort to restrict abortion by making it more difficult or unpleasant is to require that women seeking an abortion be given certain information—for example, that they be informed about fetal development or the medical or psychological consequences of abortion. Some laws along these lines have specified information that is reasonably accurate scientifically, whereas others specify information that is propaganda with little scientific basis. In 1983 the Supreme Court struck down an Akron, Ohio, ordinance that required information of the propaganda variety (Fox, 1983). However, in the 1992 *Planned Parenthood v. Casey* decision the Supreme Court upheld Pennsylvania's requirement that women seeking abortion be informed about fetal development during the three trimesters of pregnancy and the possible viability of fetuses during the third trimester. A review of the materials used in 22 states, often written by state health department employees, finds that the information is often outdated, biased, or both. In some cases the information is patently wrong—for example, claims that receiving an abortion is linked to breast cancer, or that it is followed by adverse outcomes such as depression (Richardson & Nash, 2006).

The waning of the Supreme Court majority recognizing a woman's right to an abortion became clear in the important 1989 decision *Webster v. Reproductive Health Services*. The case concerned a Missouri law that (*a*) prohibited state employees from assisting in abortions and prohibited abortions from being performed in state-owned hospitals and (*b*) banned abortions of "viable" fetuses. The Court upheld the Missouri law. Thus it essentially said that states may pass certain kinds of laws regulating abortions. For example, states may require doctors to perform a viability test on any fetus if a woman is believed to be 20 weeks or more pregnant

and may make it illegal to perform an abortion if the test shows that the fetus could live (such tests are not 100 percent accurate). Ironically, abortions of genetically defective fetuses might be prevented by this ruling because amniocentesis does not provide results until the eighteenth or nineteenth week of pregnancy. The broader effect of the Court's decision, however, is to throw the hot potato back to the state legislatures.

By 1992 the membership of the Supreme Court had shifted to a majority of conservatives as a result of appointments made during the Ronald Reagan and George H. W. Bush administrations. As mentioned, the *Planned Parenthood v. Casey* case concerned a Pennsylvania law that placed many procedural obstacles in the way of a woman seeking abortion. She had to be given information about fetal development and then wait 24 hours before the abortion could be performed. Unmarried girls under 18 had to gain the consent of at least one parent, or a state judge had to rule that she was mature enough to make the decision herself (called a *judicial bypass*). Married women had to notify their husbands before obtaining an abortion. The Court's decision was complex. It did not overturn *Roe v. Wade*, as many had expected. Instead, it reaffirmed a woman's constitutional right to an abortion before the fetus is viable. On the other hand, it upheld all the restrictions in the Pennsylvania law except the one requiring a married woman to notify her husband. The Court was again ruling that states could pass laws placing restrictions on abortion, although abortion itself could not be outlawed, and the laws could not place an "undue burden" on a woman seeking an abortion.

In summary, then, *Roe v. Wade* (1973) decriminalized abortion and said that states could not restrict access to first-trimester abortion. Two decisions have since chipped away at *Roe v. Wade*, without overturning it completely. In *Webster v. Reproductive Health Services* (1989) the Court said that states could restrict abortion in some ways, namely, by forbidding it in state-owned hospitals and by banning abortion of viable fetuses. In *Planned Parenthood v. Casey* (1992) the Court again upheld a state law placing restrictions on abortion, involving parental consent, information, and a waiting period. However, requiring a woman to notify her husband was going too far, according to the decision, which said the laws could not place an undue burden on women seeking an abortion.

A third strategy used by opponents of abortion has been to champion the Human Life Amendment to the Constitution, which would prohibit all abortions. This amendment or similar legislation has been introduced in every session of Congress since 1983, but no serious effort has been made to bring it to a vote (Wilcox et al., 1998).

A fourth strategy to reduce access to abortion is an ongoing effort to ban partial birth abortions, or other broadly defined procedures. Partial birth abortion is not a recognized medical procedure; some bills banning it have not included a description of what is being banned, and others provide only a vague description. The bills' lack of specificity raises the concern that the backers' intent is to have the law enacted, then use it to challenge a broad range of procedures. Between 1995 and 2004, 31 states enacted laws that prohibit partial birth abortion procedures (American Civil Liberties Union, 2004). In 18 of these states the laws have been challenged and declared unconstitutional; in 8 states the laws have not been challenged (Alan Guttmacher Institute, 2004b). In the laws in 4 states the banned procedures are narrowly defined, allow for exceptions, and have been ruled constitutional. The accession of George W. Bush to the presidency in 2001 and the Republican control of Congress enabled the passage of a federal ban on partial birth abortion in 2003. Planned Parenthood of America immediately challenged the Partial Birth Abortion Ban Act in the federal courts, and in June 2004 a federal judge ruled the law unconstitutional (*Planned Parenthood Federation of America v. Ashcroft*, 03-8695 RCC). The judge ruled that the language was so vague it could be used to outlaw all or most abortions. On April 18, 2007, the Supreme Court ruled in a 5 to 4 decision that the law was not unconstitutional (*Gonzales v. Carhart et al.* 05-380).

A fifth strategy adopted by members of Operation Rescue and other pro-life activists involves disruption, such as picketing and engaging in acts of civil disobedience outside abortion clinics, Planned Parenthood facilities, or the homes of physicians who perform abortions. Some individuals, including members of Defensive Action and the Army of God, have engaged in arson and bombings of clinics where abortions are performed. The Army of God has published a handbook on how to conduct violent protests. In response to these incidents, in 1994 the U.S. Congress passed the Freedom of Access to Clinic Entrances Act. This law makes it a federal crime to use violence or the threat of violence to interfere with access to a reproductive services provider. In October 1995, the Supreme Court ruled that the act is constitutional.

Incidents of violence against abortion clinics and providers—for example, murder, bombings, arson, invasion, and vandalism—peaked in 2001, at 795 across the United States and in Canada. The number of such incidents declined to 143 in 2003 (National Abortion Federation, 2007). The decline was due in part to the vigorous prosecution and long sentences given to perpetrators of such acts. James Charles Kopp was convicted in 2003 of the murder of Dr. Barnett Slepian (a physician who performed abortions) in 1998; Kopp was sentenced to 25 years to life. In 2005 there were 761 incidents, and in 2006 there were 473. Much of the fluctuation from year to year is variation in the number of trespassing incidents. On the other hand, incidents of disruption—for example, hate mail, Internet/e-mail harassment, bomb threats, and picketing—reached their highest level in 2005, at 14,034. Though small, groups of picketers are sometimes successful in blocking access to clinics by physically blocking entrances and driveways.

Ethnicity and Sex Laws

Although the Constitution promises equal protection to people of all races, in practice people of color and low-income people are often at a disadvantage, and this is no less true in the area of sexuality than elsewhere. Here we will consider abortion as an example (Nsiah-Jefferson, 1989; Roberts, 1993).

Little information exists on the abortion or reproduction-related needs of women of color. Until 1990, abortion statistics were published for only two categories of U.S. women: white and Black. Data are now available on Hispanic women, but not on American Indian or Asian American women. Given the different cultural heritages of these ethnic groups, abortion undoubtedly has different meanings for women in these groups, yet we lack data on the specifics.

Although for decades white women have had some control over their reproduction, for many women of color this is a new step. They may be wary because of the history of negative experiences of women of color in this area, such as the experimental work on the introduction of the birth control pill, which was done with poor women in Puerto Rico. Therefore, women of color need far more access to information and education, and it is critical that this information be sensitive to their cultural heritage.

Women of color are more likely to have abortions than are white women. Of the reported abortions performed in 2000, 39 percent were for white women (who make up 69 percent of the population of women), 36 percent for Black women (12 percent of the population), and 17 percent for Hispanic women (13 percent; Centers for Disease Control and Prevention, 2003c). A significantly higher percentage of women of color obtain abortions after the first trimester than do white women. Data indicate that 9 percent of all abortions obtained by white women were performed after the first trimester (that is, 91 percent were done in the first trimester). By comparison, 14 percent of all abortions obtained by Black women, and 12 percent of all abortions for Hispanic women, were performed after the first trimester.

It seems clear that the Hyde Amendment, which prohibits the use of federal Medicaid funds to pay for abortions for low-income women, is a key factor in this difference. Women of color, who are disproportionately represented in the low-income group, must often spend a good deal of time raising the funds for an abortion because Medicaid is denied them, and this process of raising funds delays the abortion until the second trimester.

In some cases, women of color may have significantly less access to abortion (Nsiah-Jefferson, 1989). For example, American Indian women living on reservations are denied federal funding for abortions, and, to make matters worse, no Indian Health Service clinics or hospitals may perform abortions even when paid for with private funds. American Indian women can therefore be literally hundreds of miles away from access to an abortion.

The number of abortion providers in the United States has been slowly declining since 1982 (Henshaw & Van Vort, 1994). Eighty-six percent of U.S. counties have no known provider, and 31 percent of metropolitan areas have no provider (Henshaw & Finer, 2003). This means that, for millions of women, access to an abortion requires travel to another city, county, or state. Poor women, who are disproportionately women of color, are less likely to be able to afford such travel.

Abortion is only one example of ways in which people of color are disadvantaged under the present system of sex laws. This example illustrates clearly that efforts at sex-law reform need to include a consideration of the laws' impact on people of color (Figure 20.8).

Figure 20.8 It is important that women of color have the same access to abortion as middle-class white women.

Sex and the Law in the Future

Nothing seems riskier than to try to predict with any degree of confidence how society's views of sex, and the laws that express those views, will develop and change. Thus any look ahead is at best a guess about what might happen, based on what has happened. Unforeseen events have a way of upsetting our calculations and introducing new variables into the mix. For example, in 1978 the first edition of this text predicted that sex-law reform would go on as it had in the 1970s, with the extension of the right to privacy and wide use of the victimless-crime argument for decriminalization of various sexual practices. The election of 1980 in which Ronald Reagan became president, the rise of the New Right, and the increasing appeal of its "social agenda" rendered that prophecy wrong. Likewise, the third edition of this text (1986) was written without attending to the complex legal issues posed by AIDS and the new reproductive technologies. As we now focus on these issues, you might well speculate on what will need to be included in the next edition.

Sex-Law Reform and Backlash

The movement toward more permissive sex laws, which probably had its roots in the civil rights movement, the sexual revolution, and feminism, has achieved virtually all the gains it is likely to for the time being. The decriminalization of sex offenses essentially ceased by 1980. New strategies for combating pornography have been tried, and some have succeeded. The New Right and its allies in the conservative evangelical sector of the religious community have, it would seem, taken the initiative away from those who favor less restrictive sex laws. The latter now find themselves seeking to defend and preserve the gains already made rather than extending them. During George W. Bush's presidency, Congress and state legislators have passed restrictive laws in several areas, and opponents have been forced to challenge them in the courts. So far, the courts have struck down most of this legislation.

While the pro-family coalition has by no means attained all its goals, it has certainly stopped sex-law reform and may be on the way to reversing it. On the other hand, the highly publicized case of Rev. Ted Haggard slowed the momentum of the religious right in 2007. Haggard had been one of the most vocal in condemning homosexuality and opposing rights for gays and lesbians. Revelations in November 2006 that Haggard, head of the 30-million-member National Association of Evangelicals, visited a male commercial sex worker, led to his resignation as head of NAE. He was also stripped of his ministry at New Life church by its board.

Above all, fear of AIDS may be the motivating force behind increasingly restrictive laws regulating sexual behavior. This would be very much in the tradition of the U.S. legal system, which has always tended to reflect both the dominant values and the conflicts of the society.

The Legal Challenge of New Reproductive Technologies

Very complex legal questions are being raised by the proliferation of techniques enabling previously infertile people, and others, to have children. These include artificial insemination, in vitro fertilization (IVF), surrogate motherhood, and various kinds of embryo fertilization and transfer.

There are few state laws on the subject. There are, however, in all jurisdictions, laws prohibiting trafficking in children ("baby buying"); some argue that these laws prohibit surrogacy. Twenty-seven states have laws regulating artificial insemination. Thirteen states have laws that prohibit cloning for reproductive purposes; six of these states also prohibit therapeutic cloning, or cloning for research purposes (National Conference of State Legislatures, 2006). There are few federal standards. In March 2004 the President's Council on Bioethics issued a report whose General Conclusion states that "**there is no uniform, comprehensive, and enforceable system of data collection, monitoring, or oversight for the biotechnologies affecting human reproduction** [emphasis in original]. The present system is a patchwork of federal, state, and professional self-regulation." One result of the lack of such a system is a number of contentious, highly publicized lawsuits. The fact that these cases are controversial reflects the deep emotions many people feel about reproduction, especially those who have struggled to overcome infertility.

A fundamental difficulty is that these technologies bring a very public quality to what has always been one of the most private of all human activities, the conception of children. Some of them involve a third party—as a donor of sperm, egg, embryo, or uterus—in what had been a matter solely between a man and a woman. Even the nomenclature is complicated. In this section we adopt the convention of designating as *parent(s)* the person(s) who rear the child and accept legal responsibility for her or him. Those who provide some necessary aspect of the process we call *donors,* or in the special case of women in whose wombs embryos are implanted, *surrogates.* In the absence of clear legislation or case law, we are mostly able to point to the questions raised.

Perhaps the foremost question is whether there is a fundamental right to reproduce (Strong, 1997). If there is, it is hard to argue against the use of any appropriate technique to achieve that end, including third-party participation, or what some call *collaborative conception.* On the other hand, if there is no such fundamental right, it may be reasonable to limit or even prohibit the use of such technology. There is a well-established right *not* to conceive under the right to privacy. A Washington State appeals court, in a case involving custody of *pre-embryos,* ruled that there is no right to procreate, but there is a right not to procreate.

Closely related is the question of the legal status of an embryo, since in several of these techniques fertilization and conception take place outside the uterus. Is the embryo a *person* or a *property* (Cunningham, nd)? Those who assert that life begins at conception would accord full personhood and legal rights to the embryo from the first cell division. Some states have enacted laws aimed at protecting embryos. For example, a Louisiana law specifies

Focus: Milestones in Sex Research
AIDS and the Law

The spread of AIDS (see Chapter 18) has created some challenging legal issues. None of the choices facing legislators and judges is easy. Any reflection on AIDS and the law must take into account two factors, both of which render the issue more complex and emotional. First, AIDS is identified, both statistically and in the popular mind, with outsiders, persons who are already disliked, feared, and discriminated against: gay men and intravenous drug users. Second, at this writing no vaccine or cure for AIDS exists. This combination of factors has led some commentators to write of the two epidemics: the social epidemic of fear of AIDS and the medical epidemic of the disease.

The existence of the two epidemics makes the legal balancing act even more difficult. Government has two very important responsibilities with respect to HIV infection and those who suffer from it. On the one hand, the state is obligated to protect individual rights and defend its citizens from discrimination and injustice. On the other hand, it is equally obligated to protect the health and welfare of the population. AIDS is a tragic case in which these two obligations are in severe conflict. This may be why the federal government has failed to develop comprehensive plans for research and treatment of HIV and AIDS. It is difficult to predict how government will resolve this tension, although history suggests that it is more likely to emphasize the general welfare than individual rights, especially in view of the epidemic of fear.

There is significant case law, much of it from the early twentieth century, when cities were swept with epidemics of tuberculosis and other infectious diseases, affirming the right and the responsibility of the state to protect its populace. As one scholar notes, "Courts have traditionally deferred to public health authorities in their struggle to control epidemics, even when these efforts infringed on the constitutional rights of individual citizens" (Nanula, 1987, p. 330). Measures approved include the reporting of cases to local public health officials, mass vaccination programs, quarantine, and other restrictions on known or suspected disease carriers. At the same time, public health officials must demonstrate that any measure is directly aimed at the disease in question and is not arbitrary, capricious, or oppressive (Lazzo & McElgunn, 1986).

There has been much debate about the mandatory testing of certain populations. Testing identifies those who are infected and is the gateway to treatment. So far, testing is legally required of all military recruits, Job Corps entrants, would-be immigrants, and, in some states, prison inmates. None of these requirements have been invalidated by the courts. There are proposals to test other high-risk groups, such as people with STIs or all pregnant women. The issue is especially important in the case of pregnant women, because the baby of an HIV-positive woman has a 33 percent probability of being born infected. There is now a treatment regimen that, if started early enough in pregnancy, reduces the infant's risk by two-thirds. However, some fear that widespread mandatory testing—of, for example, all fertile women or all who seek treatment for other STIs—will only serve to keep away those who most need testing and treatment, or drive them underground (Nanula, 1987).

Public health authorities in some cities have closed gay bathhouses and bars where sexual activity was reportedly occurring. Some of these closings have been very unpopular in the gay community. Many other traditional public health measures, such as mass testing in public places and the quarantine of infected persons, are rendered suspect by the number of persons thought to be infected (1 million to 2 million in the United States) and by the relatively restricted ways in which the virus is transmitted.

Protection of individual rights poses a thorny problem. To have AIDS, or even to be thought to have the disease, has caused many individuals to be fired from their jobs, divorced parents to lose custody or visitation rights, people to lose health insurance coverage or even to be deprived of medical care, and children to be barred from attending school; these people have also endured all sorts of informal harassment and discrimination. However, federal regulations, laws in some states, and ordinances in some counties and municipalities prohibit discrimination against those who have or are thought to have AIDS.

A major issue concerning AIDS is the confidentiality of test results and medical records. Most states have passed laws protecting the confidentiality of antibody test records. Persons with positive tests have a reasonable fear of losing their jobs, and some insurance companies have made efforts to find ways of denying coverage to individuals who are thought to carry the virus, and even to all members of high-risk groups (Schatz, 1987). Some legal scholars argue that the constitutional right to privacy should afford protection to individuals infected with HIV. Still, positive test results need to be disclosed to medical care providers so that they

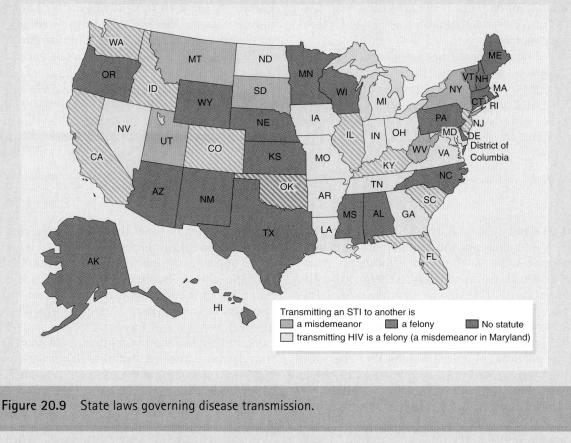

Transmitting an STI to another is
- a misdemeanor
- a felony
- No statute
- transmitting HIV is a felony (a misdemeanor in Maryland)

Figure 20.9 State laws governing disease transmission.

Source: Posner & Silbaugh (1996); HIV CLAPP (2004).

can provide the necessary treatment. In one-half of the states, physicians have the discretion to notify sexual partners of those who test positive for HIV (Burris, 1993). Such contact tracing and partner notification have been important public health tools in dealing with other STIs. Laws in all 50 states require that names of persons with AIDS be reported to local or state health authorities (HIV CLAPP, 2004).

Individuals who experience discrimination because they are HIV positive or have AIDS can seek protection under several federal laws. The Vocational Rehabilitation Act of 1973 (29 U.S.C.S., 701, *et seq*) prohibits discrimination against disabled persons in employment, transportation, and access to public and health services. The Fair Housing Act of 1988 (42 U.S.C.S., 3601, *et seq*) prohibits discrimination in housing practices against disabled individuals and their families. The Americans with Disabilities Act of 1990 (42 U.S.C.S., 12101, *et seq*) prohibits discrimination in employment and places of public accommodation on the basis of disability. In 1998 the U.S. Supreme Court ruled that HIV infection is a disability covered by these statutes, even if the person is asymptomatic.

The laws of the 50 states governing HIV transmission are portrayed in Figure 20.9. A thorough search by the HIV Criminal Law and Public Policy

Project for the period 1986–2001 identified 316 cases in which a person was prosecuted for transmission of HIV. The number of prosecutions peaked in 1998–1999 at more than 50. About 25 percent of the cases involved exposure via consensual sex, in which the infected person did not inform his or her partner of his or her HIV status. For example, in Tennessee, 30-year-old Pamela Wiser was arrested for having unprotected sex with men without informing them that she was HIV positive. She initially claimed that she had unprotected sex with 50 men but later said the number was only 5. She was ultimately charged with 22 counts of criminal exposure to HIV, a felony under state law. She was convicted and sentenced to 26½ years in prison. She appealed, claiming that the sentence was not reasonably related to the severity of her offenses. An appeals court upheld her sentencing (*State of Tennessee v. Pamela Denise Wiser*, M1999-02500-CCA-R3-CD, 2000).

In one qualitative study, one-third of gay men reported lying about their HIV status (Klitzman & Bayer, 2003); often people are frightened that they will be rejected or even assaulted if they disclose their status. Returning to the data on prosecutions, 70 percent of the cases involved spitting, biting, or scratching that was intended to transmit HIV. The outcomes of 228 of the 316 cases were determined;

in more than 80 percent the defendant was convicted or received an enhanced sentence for a related criminal act.

In the future, legislatures and courts will struggle to resolve a host of questions, including, Who has a right to know that a person has tested positive for HIV? Should there be registries of infected persons, and who should have access to such registries? Should people be held legally liable if they knowingly (or even unknowingly) infect another person with the disease? Who is going to pay the enormous costs of this disease? How are the rights of the public and of individuals to be balanced and protected?

Sources: Burris (1993); Dalton (1993); Dalton & Burris (1987); Dennis (1993); HIV CLAPP (2004); Nanula (1987); Schatz (1987).

that an embryo, even outside anyone's body, is a person and shall not intentionally be destroyed (Andrews, 1989). At the other extreme are those who regard an embryo merely as tissue, to be disposed of at will. This view puts no limits on reproductive technologies. A moderate view sees the embryo as less than a person but more than mere tissue and argues that it should be treated with the respect due potential human life. This view would seem to lead to some regulation of reproductive technology short of prohibition (Robertson, 1986). The question of what can be done with embryos not implanted also arises and is related. An embryo's status—even in the maternal womb, much less outside it—is a question the Supreme Court has explicitly avoided considering in its abortion decisions.

Another complex of questions is to be found in the matter of kinship, parental rights, and responsibilities. When a child is born as a result of these techniques, who exactly are the parents?

One commentator notes that there can be five: an egg donor, a sperm donor, the donor of a uterus for all or part of the gestation, and the couple who rear the child (Shapiro, 1986, p. 54). Issues of parental rights and responsibilities are especially complex in cases where a couple (regardless of gender) arrange and pay for assisted reproduction, and subsequently separate or divorce. Custody battles, contested visitation rights, and financial responsibility for the child have generated many court cases, involving not only the couple but donors and surrogate as well. It is likely that they will continue to do so (Schwartz, 2003).

Surrogacy and surrogacy contracts raise particularly complex issues, especially if the woman has contributed not only her uterus but an egg as well. A man who donates his sperm to a sperm bank renounces any right to further contact with children who may be conceived; however, no equivalent principles have been established for women who donate eggs or a uterus. Some argue that state laws

Figure 20.10 The law has not yet dealt adequately with the consequences of new reproductive technologies, as this cartoon indicates.

Source: Signe Wilkinson. Reprinted by permission of Cartoonists & Writers Syndicate.

against trafficking in children make surrogacy contracts, especially surrogacy for pay, illegal. Others have raised the concern that commercializing reproduction is inherently corrupting and should be prohibited because it turns children into commodities. Some are concerned that surrogacy may lead to the exploitation of low-income women, who will "rent" their wombs because they need the money, despite the possible psychological stresses and health risks of surrogate motherhood (Andrews, 1989; O'Brien, 1986; Taub, 1987).

Taking a broad perspective, there are a number of alternatives for legal approaches to the issue of surrogacy (Andrews, 1989). The most restrictive one is to outlaw all surrogacy contracts for pay, as Michigan did in 1988. A second alternative would be to have courts scrutinize all surrogacy contracts to ensure, for example, that the woman has not been coerced. Some proposed laws require that a mental health professional interview all participants—surrogate, egg donor, sperm donor, potential rearing parents—to be sure that all are truly giving informed consent. Another alternative, to address the concern that the surrogate may be exploited, is to require that surrogates have their own legal counsel when they enter into a contract. Some suggest that all surrogacy arrangements and contracts should be handled by nonprofit agencies, as adoptions are, to discourage profit making. Another possibility is to declare surrogacy to be a special case of adoption. That is, the surrogate is treated the same as any other birth mother who arranges to give her child up for adoption. This ensures that she has a period of six weeks or so after the birth to decide whether she wants to keep the baby, and it clearly establishes whose baby it is.

A final possibility, at the other end of the spectrum, is that the government stay out of this matter entirely, on the grounds that this is a private matter between the people involved. We don't see this as a viable option, because contested surrogacy cases have been reaching the courts and the government is already involved. It would be far better to have well-thought-out legislation on this matter to provide guidance and reduce the number of painful contested cases.

Finally, there are a host of procedural issues that will inevitably arise if any of these reproductive techniques become legally permitted and regulated. What will the standards of confidentiality be, especially with regard to the identity of nonparent donors? If something goes wrong during one of these procedures—and they are risky—who is liable? Who will take responsibility for a defective child born through one of these techniques? Who will bear the expense? Must insurance companies pay for artificial insemination, IVF, embryo transfer, or even surrogacy? Should such procedures be covered under Medicaid for the poor? Many more such questions will develop in the future.

Underlying all these issues are the following root questions: What is the government's interest, if any, in human reproduction, and how should it be expressed? What procedures shall be used to put into law society's concerns, if this is not deemed to be a strictly private matter? And, above all, who is to decide these issues? The legislatures and courts have shown a marked disinclination to enter this field, but evasion cannot remain a viable strategy much longer.[5]

In 1996 a group of medical and social scientists and legal scholars presented a report to the European Commission that discussed many of these issues (Evans & Evans, 1996). The group agreed that there should be a uniform, *minimum* threshold of laws and regulations governing artificial procreation. The participants reached consensus on a number of issues, including the following:

1. Artificial procreation services should be noncommercial.
2. A licensing system should be created to ensure the quality of clinical services offered to the public.
3. Clinics should obtain advance directives from donors regarding the use or disposal of sperm, ova, and embryos.
4. Time limits should be agreed upon by all parties in advance regarding cryopreservation of gametes and embryos.
5. Access to services should be available to all married or cohabiting couples.
6. Cloning and related technologies should be prohibited.

On a number of other issues there was no consensus, including the following:

1. Access to services for single women and lesbians.
2. The cryopreservation of human embryos.
3. Allowing children produced by assisted reproduction access to information about their conception and parentage.
4. The permissibility of experimentation with human embryos.

---

[5]For more of these issues, see Cohen & Taub (1989).

Ideally legislatures and policy makers should use this report as a basis for constructing the minimum threshold described in the report. Unfortunately, our survey of laws in this section and the Report of the President's Commission indicate that, so far, they have not.

SUMMARY

Laws to protect adults from coercion, children from sexual exploitation, and the public from offensive behavior are justifiable. However, many laws against sexual conduct originated in a desire to promote public morality and perpetuate sexism, and it is hard to justify them.

The laws governing sexual conduct include laws against crimes of exploitation and force (such as rape, carnal knowledge of a juvenile, and child molestation), against various consensual acts (such as fornication and adultery), against gays and lesbians, against offending public taste (exhibitionism, voyeurism, solicitation, disorderly conduct, lewdness, and the like), against behaviors involved in reproduction (contraception and abortion), and against criminal commercial sex (notably prostitution and obscenity). These laws are often capriciously enforced, and this unequal enforcement has high social costs that may require reform.

Certain trends can be discerned in the reform of such sex laws. The American Model Penal Code included proposals to decriminalize consensual sexual behavior. The legal principle that has accounted for much court action to reform laws against contraception and abortion is the right to privacy. The constitutional principle of equal protection has been used to combat discrimination against groups identified by their sexual conduct, including gays, lesbians, and commercial sex workers. Legislators have been influenced by the movement for the decriminalization of victimless crimes; recently, however, critics have challenged the argument that no one is harmed by prostitution or adultery. The issue of pornography and obscenity, which includes such problems as definition, conflicting societal values, and actual demonstration of effects, is a confusing one. The latest controversy is over the availability of X-rated goods and services on the Internet. Abortion remains a volatile and highly controversial matter.

Sex-law reform moved more slowly in the 1990s and early twenty-first century than it did in the previous decades, and there are signs of a conservative backlash. In the future, the law will need to balance individual rights and the public interest when it comes to issues such as AIDS and new reproductive technologies.

QUESTIONS FOR THOUGHT, DISCUSSION, AND DEBATE

1. Find out what sorts of laws relate to sexual activity in the state in which you live or go to school. Are there any moves to change those laws?
2. What aspects of human sexuality do you think it is reasonable for the law to regulate?
3. How do you think young children can best be protected from sexual abuse and exploitation?
4. If you were a state legislator, what kinds of laws would you favor regarding AIDS and surrogate parenthood?

SUGGESTIONS FOR FURTHER READING

Burris, Scott, Dalton, Harlon L., & Miller, Judith (Eds.). (1993). *AIDS law today.* New Haven, CT: Yale University Press. Produced by the Yale AIDS Law Project, this excellent book discusses the legal issues regarding AIDS.

Hunter, Nan, Michaelson, Sherryl, & Stoddard, Thomas. (1992). *The rights of lesbians and gay men: The basic ACLU guide to a gay person's rights.* Carbondale, IL: Southern Illinois University. Prepared by the American Civil Liberties

Union, this guide covers most laws relevant to gays and lesbians.

Messer, Ellen, & May, Kathryn E. (1988). *Backrooms: Voices from the illegal abortion era.* New York: St. Martin's Press. This book is based on interviews with 24 women, all of whom had unwanted pregnancies before *Roe v. Wade.* The women tell the stories of their illegal abortions and the consequences. It is important reading, especially for those who have grown up in the era of legal abortions.

Tribe, Laurence H. (1990). *Abortion: The clash of absolutes.* New York: Norton. Constitutional scholar Tribe analyzes the arguments on the two sides of the abortion debate and explains why no progress toward a compromise on this issue has been made.

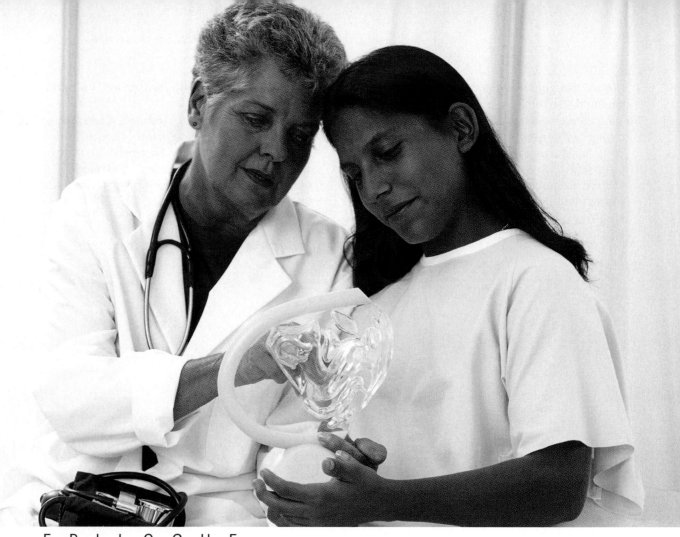

Looking to the Future: Sexuality Education

As we look to the future, a top priority for society has to be sexuality education. If you have studied this textbook, you should be prepared to be a good sexuality educator for your own children. You should also be a well-informed citizen who can make thoughtful decisions about sexuality education in the schools. Sexuality education, of course, can occur in many settings: home, school, church or synagogue, youth programs, relationships, or via information found on the Internet.

In the Home, in the School, or Somewhere Else?

When parents of children and teenagers get together to urge their school system to adopt a sexuality education curriculum, invariably some citizens of the community raise a protest. They might say that sexuality education promotes promiscuity, teenage pregnancy, or AIDS, and they are sure that

Table E.1	Sources of Information about Sex		
		Percentage Saying "A Lot"	
		Children 10–12	Teens 13–15
How much do children your age find out about sex from:			
Mothers		38%	38%
TV, movies, other entertainment		38	61
Schools and teachers		38	44
Fathers		34	—
Friends		31	64
The Internet		—	40

Source: From the Nickelodeon/Talking with Kids: "Talking with Kids about Tough Issues: A National Survey of Parents and Kids," 2001. Used with permission from the Kaiser Family Foundation.

it should take place only in the home (or possibly the church), but certainly not in the schools.

What these citizens overlook is the realistic alternative to sexuality education in the schools. Among children aged 10 to 12, at least one-third do get information about sex from their parents (see Table E.1). Notice that two frequently mentioned sources in both age groups are TV and magazines; among teens, friends are also an important source. In many cases the information provided about sexuality on TV is sensationalized and unrealistic (see Focus on page 240). Relying on friends for information is a classic case of the blind leading the blind. Interestingly, young people would like to hear about sex from their parents (Sanders & Mullis, 1988). The fact is that many children are given no sexuality education in the home. Rather, they learn about sex from TV and peers, and the result is a massive amount of misinformation. Thus, people who say that sexuality education should be carried out in the home, not in the school, are not making a sensible argument.

There are two reasons why parents do not provide much explicit education to their children. First, many people are embarrassed about discussing sexuality. We see few models of how to have an explicit, matter-of-fact discussion; we are much more likely to see people discussing sex indirectly, with euphemisms and innuendo, or telling dirty jokes. Second, there are a number of things about sexuality that many adults do not know. Many did not have good sexuality education themselves, and they may be painfully aware of their ignorance.

Surveys consistently find that a large majority of adults in the United States and Canada favor sexuality education in the schools. For example, a telephone survey of a nationally representative sample in the United States in 2003 found that 93 percent of the parents of seventh and eighth graders and 91 percent of parents of ninth through twelfth graders said it is "very important" or "important" that sexuality education be part of the school curriculum (Kaiser Family Foundation, 2004a). A survey of parents of seventh through twelfth graders found that the great majority favored teaching children about AIDS and other sexually transmitted infections, premarital sex, birth control, abortion, and homosexuality (Kaiser Family Foundation, 2000). Many adults believe that school health clinics should make birth control information available, although only a minority believe that the clinics should provide contraceptives. The point is that there is strong support for detailed sexuality education in the schools, beginning at least when children are 12 years old or in sixth or seventh grade. In spite of this high level of public support, a minority continue to try to push sexuality education out of the schools (Fields & Tolman, 2006).

You may be surprised to learn that most adults favor sexuality education. The media regularly publicize controversies, cases in which parents are protesting sexuality education in the schools. There are three things to keep in mind about such cases. First, they are rare. The vast majority of schools with sexuality education programs have not experienced such conflict (Kaiser Family Foundation, 2004b). Second, the protestors are usually in a minority. In a case in Wisconsin, protestors packed a school board meeting and the board voted to delay implementation of a program. A subsequent survey of all the parents in the district found that 71 percent approved and only 18 percent disapproved of the program. Third, the controversy is often not over whether there should be a program, but over the use of a particular curriculum, book, or video.

Sexuality education in the schools is not "instead of" education in the home. In a 2003 Kaiser Family Foundation survey, 88 percent of the parents of seventh and eighth graders and 80 percent of the parents of ninth through twelfth graders agreed that having a program in the school makes it easier to talk to their children about sexual issues (Kaiser Family Foundation, 2004a). Some sexuality education programs actively involve parents by including homework to be done jointly by parent and child. The evaluation of one program of this type found that students receiving classroom instruction plus homework felt more able to refuse high-risk behaviors and more often intended to delay the initiation of intercourse compared to students receiving only classroom instruction (Blake et al., 2001). The homework assignments, which appeared to reinforce the school-based program, resulted in greater parent-child communication about sex.

Purposes of Sexuality Education

The Sexuality Information and Education Council of the United States (**SIECUS**) has been one of the most active groups promoting high-quality sexuality education. According to SIECUS, the goals of sexuality education should be as follows:

1. *Information.* To provide accurate information about human sexuality including growth and development, human reproduction, anatomy, physiology, masturbation, family life, pregnancy, childbirth, parenthood, sexual response, sexual orientation, gender identity, contraception, abortion, sexual abuse, HIV/AIDS, and other sexually transmitted diseases.
2. *Attitudes, values, and insights.* To provide an opportunity for young people to question, explore, and assess their sexual attitudes in order to understand their family's values, develop their own values, improve critical-thinking skills, increase self-esteem, develop insights concerning relationships with family and individuals of all genders, and understand their obligations and responsibilities to their families and society.
3. *Relationships and interpersonal skills.* To help young people develop interpersonal skills, including communication, decision-making, assertiveness, and peer refusal skills, as well as the ability to create reciprocal and satisfying relationships. Sexuality education programs should prepare students to understand their sexuality effectively and creatively in adult roles. This includes helping young people develop the capacity for caring, supportive, noncoercive, and mutually pleasurable intimate and sexual relationships.
4. *Responsibility.* To help young people exercise responsibility regarding sexual relationships by addressing such issues as abstinence, how to resist pressures to become involved in unwanted or early sexual intercourse, and the use of contraception and other sexual health measures (SIECUS, 2004).

What to Teach at Different Ages

Sexuality education is not something that can be carried out in one week during fifth grade. Like teaching math, it is a process that must begin when children are young. They should learn simple concepts first, progressing to more difficult ones as they grow older. What is taught at any particular age depends on the child's sexual behavior (see Chapter 9), sexual knowledge, and sexual interests at that age. This section will concentrate on theories and research that provide information on the last two points.

Children's Sexual Knowledge

A few researchers have investigated what children know about sex and reproduction at various ages. For example, children begin to develop an understanding of pregnancy and birth at a very early age. Very young children may believe that a baby has always existed: that it existed somewhere else before it got inside the mother. The following dialogue demonstrates this:

> (How did the baby happen to be in your Mommy's tummy?) It just grows inside. (How did it get there?) It's there all the time. Mommy doesn't have to do anything. She waits until she feels it. (You said that the baby wasn't in there when you were there.) Yeah, then he was in the other place . . . in America. (In America?) Yeah, in somebody else's tummy. (Bernstein & Cowan, 1975, p. 86)

By age 7 or 8, children have a more sophisticated understanding of reproduction. They may know that three things are involved in making a baby: a social relationship between two people, such as love or marriage; sexual intercourse; and the union of sperm and egg. At age 12, some children can give a good physiological explanation of reproduction that includes the idea that the embryo

Table E.2 Responses of 9-Year-Olds in Four Cultures in the Goldman Study

Concept	Percentage of Correct Answers Among			
	Australians	*British*	*North Americans*	*Swedish*
Knowing physical sex differences of newborn babies	60	35	23	40
Knowing correct terms for the genitals	50	33	20	—*
Knowing length of gestation is 8 to 10 months	45	32	30	67
Knowing that one purpose of coitus is enjoyment	6	10	4	60
Knowing the meaning of the term "uterus"	0	0	0	23

*Owing to the difficulties of translating from the Swedish language, this percentage is not available.

Source: Goldman & Goldman (1982), pp. 197, 213, 240, 263, 354.

begins its biological existence at the moment of conception and is the product of genetic material from both parents. As one preteen explained,

The sperm encounters one ovum, and one sperm breaks into the ovum which produces, the sperm makes like a cell, and the cell separates and divides. And so it's dividing, and the ovum goes through a tube and embeds itself in the wall of the, I think it's the fetus of the woman. (Bernstein & Cowan, 1975, p. 89)

These findings have important implications for sexuality education. Educators need to be aware of the level of the child's understanding and should not inundate him or her with information inappropriate for his or her age. Instead, the educator should attempt to clarify misunderstandings in the child's beliefs. For example, if a child believes a baby has always existed, the educator might say, "To make a baby, you need two grown-ups: a man and a woman."

Probably the most comprehensive study of children's sexual knowledge was conducted by Ronald and Juliette Goldman (1982), who did a massive cross-cultural study of children's understanding of sexual matters. From their results, they concluded that American children are sexual illiterates! The Goldmans did face-to-face interviews with children aged 5, 7, 9, 11, 13, and 15 in four cultures: Australia, England, North America, and Sweden. The Swedish sample is particularly interesting because there is compulsory sexuality education for all children in Swedish schools, beginning at age 8. The Goldmans questioned children only about sexual concepts, not about their own sexual behavior.

A comparison of the results from the North American children with those from children in the other three cultures led the Goldmans to conclude that American children are strikingly lacking in

sexual information. Some of the results are shown in Table E.2. Notice, for example, that only 23 percent of North American 9-year-olds, but 60 percent of Australian 9-year-olds, knew the genital differences between newborn baby boys and girls. The Swedish children were consistently more knowledgeable than the American children, indicating the positive effects of sexuality education.

Some of the children's responses can only be classified as amusing. In response to the question "How can anyone know a newborn baby is a boy or a girl?" an 11-year-old English boy said, "If it's got a penis or not. If it has it's a boy. Girls have a virginia." And in all cultures there seems to be a lot of confusion about contraception. Here are some responses:

The pill goes down the stomach and dissolves the baby and it goes out in the bowels. You should take three pills a day. (American boy, 7 years old)

If you don't want to start one, you don't get married. There's no other way. (English girl, 7 years old)

The tubes are tied, the vocal cords. (Australian girl, 15 years old)

If the Goldmans' conclusion is right, that American children are sexual illiterates, the remedy seems to be a massive program of sexuality education in the United States.

Children's Sexual Interests
Children's knowledge of and interest in sex are reflected in the questions they ask. At age 5, kids may be asking where babies come from. At age 9, a boy or girl may ask about sexual behaviors, as for instance, "What's oral sex?" Such questions are often stimulated by hearing the term in conversation or in the media. A 10-year-old may be interested in bodily processes and ask, "What's a period?" By age 11, many children are asking questions related to puberty, such as, "When will I get breasts?" or

"When will I grow taller?" Such questions typically reflect an awareness that other youth are experiencing such growth. At age 13 or 14, many youth have specific questions about sexual activity. One boy asked, "Do girls move a lot when they have sex?" (Blake, 2004). It is important that the sexuality education curriculum for a particular age group address the questions of that age group, rather than questions members of that age group haven't thought of yet or questions they thought about but answered long ago.

High school students agree that sexuality education should begin in early elementary school and progress from the simple to the complex (Eisenberg et al., 1997). They believe that the ideal class should cover a wide range of topics, including reproduction, pregnancy, abortion, birth control options, disease prevention, sexual violence, relationships and gender roles, and values. They would like all these topics presented by eighth grade.

The Curriculum

The term *sexuality education* has been used to refer to a wide variety of programs. At one end of the continuum are programs that involve showing youngsters one or two videos and distributing some brochures. At the other end are well-developed curricula that include lectures, books, videos, and classroom discussion presented over four to six weeks. We will focus on the more substantial programs.

Abstinence-Only Programs

Abstinence-only programs developed out of opposition to sexuality education in the schools. The concerns led to passage by the U.S. Congress of the Adolescent Family Life Act in 1981; the AFLA limited the use of federal funds to **abstinence-only programs,** programs that "promoted sexual abstinence as the sole means of preventing pregnancy and exposure to sexually transmitted diseases" (Wilcox & Wyatt, 1997, p. 4). Hundreds of millions of dollars have been spent by state and federal governments to support the development and widespread use of these programs. In 1994 Congress attempted to mandate that all sexuality education in the United States be abstinence-only; this effort failed because at least four federal laws prohibit the federal government from prescribing local curricular standards (Advocates for Youth, 2004a).

The U.S. Congress discovered that, while it could not mandate abstinence-only programs, it could restrict the funding available to the states and schools to support sexuality education. Accordingly, Congress included in the Personal Responsibility and Work Opportunity Act (PRWOA) of 1996 (welfare reform) a provision that made available $50 million per year to states to support the cost of abstinence-only programs. Via the AFLA, the PRWOA, and a third program, a total of $899 million was spent nationally on these programs between 1998 and 2003 (SIECUS, 2004b).

There are a number of well-developed abstinence-only curricula. The two most widely known are *Sex Respect* and *Teen Aid. Sex Respect* represents a politically conservative approach to sexuality education. Federally funded, it is targeted at middle-school students. The major goal of this curriculum is to teach that abstinence is the only approach that is moral and safe. The curriculum uses cartoons and other attention-grabbing techniques. There are catchy slogans for children to chant in class, such as

> Don't be a louse, wait for your spouse!
> Do the right thing, wait for the ring!
> Pet your dog, not your date!

All students take a "chastity pledge," and the curriculum includes a chart of physical intimacy in which a prolonged kiss is characterized as the "beginning of danger." The curriculum teaches that condoms can be the road to ruin because many fail, resulting in pregnancy.

Sex Respect throws in a lot of gender-role stereotypes as well, characterizing boys as "sexual aggressors" and girls as "virginity protectors." It presents the two-parent, heterosexual couple as "the sole model of a healthy, real family."

On behalf of parents who objected to the curriculum, Wisconsin's chapter of the American Civil Liberties Union (ACLU) demanded that it be removed from all public schools using it. The ACLU argued that the curriculum amounts to discrimination based on gender, marital status, sexual orientation, and religion, all of which are illegal under Wisconsin laws.

In fairness to *Sex Respect*, it may have some good points in that it teaches students skills in resisting peer pressure. On the other hand, it includes a lot of "facts" that are really misinformation (for example, it says that condoms frequently fail, but they actually have a very low failure rate), and it seems out of touch with today's teenagers. The widespread adoption of this curriculum points out how important it is for parents to examine the sexuality education materials being presented to their children.

How effective are these curricula? Researchers who assessed the content of *Sex Respect* concluded that it omits a number of important topics, including sexual anatomy (!), sexual physiology, sexual response, contraception, and abortion (Goodson & Edmundson, 1994). We noted earlier that high school students say that all of these topics should be included in an ideal class. As a result of their widespread use, there have been many evaluations of these programs' effects on student attitudes and behavior. A review of 52 evaluations that meet minimal methodological standards concluded that "none of the best studies [by methodological criteria] found positive changes . . . in age of onset of sexual activity, rates of sexual activity, pregnancies, or STIs" (Wilcox & Wyatt, 1997, p. 13). A review of published randomized controlled trials (the "gold standard") of programs in high schools identified 16 such projects (Bennett & Assefi, 2005). The results were consistent with those reported by Wilcox and Wyatt a decade earlier: abstinence-only education was ineffective.

The Politics of Sexuality Education

The 1996 PRWOA legislation contains the requirement that abstinence-only programs funded under it be evaluated. To examine the possible effects of abstinence-only sex education, the Department of Health and Human Services assembled a panel of nationally recognized researchers and educators for an exhaustive review of the data available through 2001. At that time the results of more than 50 evaluations were available. The panel concluded that there was no evidence that abstinence-only sexuality education programs either delay intercourse or reduce rates of teenage pregnancy (Technical Working Group, 2002).

Many educators, social scientists, relevant professional organizations, and citizens have concluded that abstinence-only programs do not work and that the hundreds of millions of dollars being spent on them are a gross misuse of federal, state, and local funds. Advocates for Youth, joined by more than 77 national organizations, sent an open letter to President George W. Bush in 2002 asking him to end his support for, and requests to increase, funding for such programs. The American Civil Liberties Union petitioned Congress in March 2004 to oppose new funding for such programs. The American Psychological Association adopted a resolution in 2004 opposing reliance on such programs to provide sexuality education to youth. Finally, the results of a national poll of 1,050 adults found that 70 percent oppose the laws that restrict federal funds to abstinence-only programs (Advocates for Youth, 2004b). As of this writing, President Bush and his appointees have ignored these requests and the scientific and other evidence on which they are based. One White House insider, when asked how the president could ask for an additional $33 million for abstinence-only sexuality education when it is clear that it doesn't work, replied, "Values trump data" (Wingert, 2002).

In March 2007, three members of Congress introduced the Responsible Education About Life (REAL) Act. The bill would provide federal funds for comprehensive sexuality education that is age appropriate, is medically accurate, and stresses abstinence while providing education about contraception.

HIV and AIDS Risk Education

In the 1990s the focus of sexuality education shifted from pregnancy prevention to AIDS and other STI prevention. A strong case has been made for education about HIV and AIDS in the schools (National Commission on AIDS, 1994). In 2007, 35 states and the District of Columbia required such educational programs (Guttmacher Institute, 2007). (In contrast, only 19 states and the District of Columbia require that sexuality education be taught.) A 2003 Kaiser Family Foundation survey found that 99 percent of parents of seventh and eighth graders and 97 percent of the parents of high school students believe that such instruction is appropriate in the schools. HIV instruction may be presented alone, or in combination with either abstinence-only or comprehensive sexuality education programs.

Programs of this type are often sharply focused on disease prevention. They have a variety of goals, including challenging myths about AIDS and other STIs, encouraging delay of sexual intercourse, and supporting condom use or abstinence from unprotected intercourse. These programs are usually short, lasting as few as five class periods.

A review of the effectiveness of these programs found that they improved knowledge significantly (Kim et al., 1997). In addition, many studies reported positive changes in respondents' intention to use condoms.

Recent national surveys indicate that teenagers are very well informed about HIV transmission. Most know that condoms prevent transmission of AIDS and other STIs. School-based HIV education programs may have contributed to these outcomes.

Focus

A Sampling from a Comprehensive Sexuality Education Curriculum

A n authoritative set of curriculum guidelines for sexuality education, developed by SIECUS, is based on teaching about six key concepts, and teaching about each concept at each age level, with age-appropriate material. The age levels are as follows:

Level 1: ages 5 to 8; early elementary school.

Level 2: ages 9 to 12; upper elementary school.

Level 3: ages 12 to 15; middle school or junior high.

Level 4: ages 15 to 18; high school.

The following is a sampling of the material recommended by the guidelines:

Key Concept 1: Human Development

Topic 1: Reproductive Anatomy and Physiology

Level 1: Each body part has a correct name and a specific function. A person's genitals, reproductive organs, and genes determine whether the person is male or female. A boy/man has nipples, a penis, scrotum, and testicles. A girl/woman has breasts, nipples, a vulva, a clitoris, a vagina, a uterus, and ovaries. Some sexual or reproductive organs, such as penises and vulvas, are outside the body, while others, such as ovaries and testes, are inside the body. Both girls and boys have body parts that feel good when touched.

Topic 2: Puberty

Level 2: Puberty begins and ends at different ages for different people. Everybody's body changes at its own pace. Some people will not complete puberty until their middle or late teens. Girls often begin pubertal changes before boys. Most changes in puberty, such as growth of body hair and an increase in body odor, are similar for boys and girls. The sexual and reproductive systems mature during puberty. During puberty, girls begin to ovulate and menstruate, and boys begin to produce sperm and ejaculate. Once this occurs, girls are physically capable of becoming pregnant and boys of getting a female pregnant. During puberty, many people begin to develop sexual and romantic feelings. Young teenagers sometimes feel uncomfortable, clumsy, and/or self-conscious because of the rapid changes in their bodies.

Topic 3: Reproduction

Level 1: Men and women have reproductive organs that enable them to have a child. Men and women have specific cells in their bodies (sperm cells and egg cells) that enable them to reproduce. Reproduction requires that a sperm and egg join. Vaginal intercourse—when a penis is placed inside a vagina—is the most common way for a sperm and egg to join. When a woman is pregnant, the fetus grows inside her body in her uterus. A woman can

---

Comprehensive, Theoretically Based Programs

The newest programs are comprehensive and are explicitly based on social science theories of health promotion, including the Health Belief Model, social inoculation theory, and social learning theory. The curriculum described in the Focus box is of this type. The best known of these curricula are *Postponing Sexual Involvement* and *Reducing the Risk.* These programs include discussion of the social pressures to engage in sex, and ways to resist these influences (based on inoculation theory). Social learning theory emphasizes the importance of practicing new skills, so these curricula include rehearsal and role-playing activities.

In light of the continuing high levels of teenage pregnancy, the sharp increases in rates of STIs among persons 15 to 24 years of age, and the increasing rate of HIV infection in adolescents, it is imperative that we identify sexuality education programs that are effective in reducing risky sexual behavior. At the request of the U.S. Centers for Disease Control and Prevention, a number of researchers undertook a thorough review of the research on the effectiveness of school-based programs (Kirby et al., 1994). They identified six characteristics that, according to the scientific evidence, are associated with delaying the initiation of intercourse, reducing the frequency of intercourse, reducing the number of sexual partners, and increasing the use of condoms and other contraceptives. In general, these are characteristic of the comprehensive programs.

be pregnant with more than one fetus at a time. Babies usually come out of a woman's body through an opening called a vagina. Some babies are born by an operation called a Cesarian Section. A woman's breasts can provide milk for a baby. Not all men and women decide to have children. People who cannot have children may choose to adopt.

Level 3: People should use contraception during vaginal intercourse unless they want to have a child. Conception can occur once a woman has ovulated (released an egg). Ovulation is most likely to occur two weeks before a woman's menstrual period. Predicting ovulation accurately can be difficult. A common sign of pregnancy is a missed menstrual period. Sexual intercourse during pregnancy usually will not harm the developing fetus.

Topic 4: Body Image

Level 1: Individual bodies are different sizes, shapes, and colors. All bodies are equally special, including those that are disabled. Differences make us unique. Good health habits, such as eating well and exercise, can improve the way a person feels about his or her body. Each person can be proud of his/her body.

Level 3: The size and shape of penises, breasts, and vulvas can vary significantly. The size and shape of sexual organs does not affect a person's ability to reproduce or experience sexual pleasure. The size and shape of a person's body may affect how others feel about and behave toward that person. Some people may develop disordered eating as a result of how they feel about their bodies. The media portrays beauty as a narrow and limited idea, but beautiful people come in all shapes, sizes, colors, and abilities. Although people stop growing once they reach adulthood, bodies change shape and size throughout life.

Topic 5: Sexual Orientation

Level 1: Human beings can love people of the same gender and people of another gender. Some people are heterosexual, which means they can be attracted to and fall in love with someone of the other gender. Some people are homosexual, which means they can be attracted to and fall in love with someone of the same gender. Homosexual men and women are also known as gay men and lesbians. People deserve respect regardless of who they are attracted to. Making fun of people by calling them gay (e.g., "homo," "fag," "queer") is disrespectful and hurtful.

Level 4: Sexual orientation is determined by a combination of a person's attractions, fantasies, and sexual behaviors. The understanding and identification of one's sexual orientation may change over the course of his/her lifetime. Many states ban discrimination against people based on their sexual orientation. If an individual is being intimidated, harassed, or harmed because of a real or perceived sexual orientation, it is important to tell a trusted adult, school official, or law enforcement official.

The curriculum guidelines continue with equally detailed content for the remaining five key concepts: Key Concept 2: Relationships; Key Concept 3: Personal Skills; Key Concept 4: Sexual Behavior; Key Concept 5: Sexual Health; Key Concept 6: Society and Culture. Space does not permit us to list all the details under each of these concepts, so interested readers may want to consult the source listed below.

SIECUS. (2004). *Guidelines for comprehensive sexuality education, 3rd ed.* New York: SIECUS. Online at http://www.siecus.org/pubs/guidelines/guidelines.pdf

---

Effective programs focus on reducing risk-taking behavior. Such programs have a small number of specific goals. They do not emphasize general issues such as gender equality and dating.

Effective programs are based on theories of social learning. Programs that utilize theory in designing the curriculum are more effective than nontheoretical programs. The theories suggest that, to be effective, the program must increase knowledge, elicit or increase motivation to protect oneself, demonstrate that specific behaviors will protect the person, and teach the person how to use those behaviors effectively.

Effective programs teach through experiential activities that personalize the messages. Such programs avoid lectures and videos; instead, they use small group discussions, simulation and games, role playing, rehearsal, and similar educational techniques. Some of these programs rely on peer educators.

Effective programs address media and other social influences that encourage sexual risk-taking behaviors. Some programs look at how the media use sex to sell products. All the effective programs analyze the "lines" that young people use to try to get someone else to engage in sex, and teach ways of responding to these approaches.

Effective programs reinforce clear and appropriate values. These programs are not value-free.

They emphasize the values of postponing sex and avoiding unprotected sex and high-risk partners. The values and norms must be tailored to the target population. Different programs are needed for middle school students, for white middle-class high school students, and for ethnic minority high school students.

Effective programs enhance communication skills. Such programs provide models of good communication and opportunities for practice and skill rehearsal.

Effective sexuality education is cost effective. A school-based program that prevents HIV infection, STIs, and unintended pregnancy among high school students can actually save money. Data from sexually active high school students in California and Texas found that the program Safer Choices resulted in a 15 percent increase in condom use and an 11 percent increase in the use of other contraceptives. Using a statistical model, researchers then estimated that the program prevented 0.12 cases of HIV infection, 24 cases of chlamydia, 2.8 cases of gonorrhea, 5.9 cases of pelvic inflammatory disease, and 18 pregnancies. The researchers concluded that the program saved $2.65 in medical and social costs for every dollar spent on the program (Wang et al., 2000). Using these estimates of the prevention accomplished by the $105,000 cost of the program, we can estimate the consequences if federal funds spent on abstinence-only programs were spent on effective, comprehensive sexuality education. If the $899 million spent between 1998 and 2003 to support abstinence-only education had been spent on effective sexuality education, it could have prevented 1,027 cases of HIV infection, 208,000 cases of chlamydia, 23,974 cases of gonorrhea, one-half million cases of PID, and 158,397 cases of unwanted pregnancy among teens (about 18 percent of teen pregnancies). The overall net savings would have been $2.3 billion.

The Teacher

Suppose you have decided to start a program of sexuality education. You have found a curriculum that is consistent with your objectives, whether those are to promote premarital abstinence or condom use with every act of sexual intercourse. Wherever the program is to be carried out—in the home, the school, the place of worship, or someplace else—the next resource you need is a teacher. There are two essential qualifications: The person must be educated about sexuality, and he or she must be comfortable interacting with your learners about sexual topics. High school students in Minneapolis–St. Paul participating in focus groups agreed that these two qualifications are essential (Eisenberg et al., 1997). They also cited as important the ability of the teacher to relate the material to their lives.

A good teacher is also a good listener who can assess what the learner knows from the questions asked and who can understand what a child really wants to know when she or he asks a question. As one joke had it, little Billy ran into the kitchen one day after kindergarten and asked his mother where he had come from; she gritted her teeth, realized the time had come, and proceeded with a 15-minute discussion of intercourse, conception, and birth, blushing the whole time. Billy listened, but at the end he appeared somewhat confused and walked away shaking his head, saying, "That's funny. Jimmy says he came from Illinois."

Condom Distribution

One visible conflict has been over whether condoms should be distributed by schools to students. In 1998–1999 there were 1,135 school-based health centers across the United States, located in 45 states and the District of Columbia (Alan Guttmacher Institute, 2000). Only 23 percent of these centers were allowed to distribute birth control on-site.

In some schools, condoms are available through the sexuality education program. In others, clinics providing health care services to adolescents dispense birth control, including condoms. In still other schools, condoms are sold in vending machines. Again, data indicate widespread support for the distribution of condoms in the schools. In New York City, where condoms are available in all public high schools, a survey found that 69 percent of the parents of high school students supported the program, although half also felt that they should be able to prevent their child from receiving condoms (Guttmacher et al., 1995). Fifty-five percent of Americans believe it is appropriate for schools to distribute condoms to students (SIECUS, 2004a).

The most visible opposition to condom distribution programs is by the Roman Catholic Church.

Church officials oppose such programs because of their religion's ban on all artificial forms of contraception. Others oppose such programs on the grounds that they will encourage sexual intercourse outside of marriage. As one critic put it,

> Instead of amoral, secular humanistic sex education and condom distribution in the schools, families, churches, schools, social organizations, and the business community must re-emphasize the teaching, learning, and practice of virtues like courtesy, kindness, honesty, decency, moral courage, integrity, justice, fair play, self-respect, respect for others, and the Golden Rule. (Gow, 1994, p. 184)

In January 1996, the U.S. Supreme Court rejected a challenge to a condom distribution program in the Falmouth, Massachusetts, public schools.

Condoms are available in all 15 high schools in Seattle (Brown et al., 1997). Forty-eight percent of the students who reported having intercourse during the two years prior to a survey said they had obtained condoms from school. In focus groups, students said that the availability of condoms had not led to an increase in their rates of sexual activity. Students preferred that condoms be available in private locations (nurse's office) rather than public ones (vending machines). Students also wanted comprehensive sexuality education programs in conjunction with condoms.

Research indicates that condom distribution programs are associated with a reduction in the incidence and frequency of sexual intercourse among high school students. Researchers identified high schools in Massachusetts that had condom availability programs. They then drew a representative sample of students at schools that did and schools that did not have such programs. Students in schools with condoms available were less likely to report ever having had intercourse and less likely to report recent intercourse (Blake et al., 2003). Sexually active students in schools that made condoms available were twice as likely to use condoms.

In a number of schools, condom availability programs are the result of efforts by students. In Thorndike, Maine, after 20 percent of the senior girls became pregnant in 2000, two junior girls developed a campaign to make condoms available in schools. They conducted research involving students and staff, and compiled statistics. Based on a presentation they made, the school board voted 8 to 2 to allow distribution of condoms. Schools in California and Missouri now have such programs, thanks also to student initiatives.

Effective Multicultural Sexuality Education

Much of the discussion in this chapter has assumed that the participants in a sexuality education program are homogeneous, that they are all from the same culture. In some situations that assumption is valid, but in other settings the learners may be from diverse cultural backgrounds.

Cultures vary in a number of ways that are directly related to the success or failure of a sexuality education program (Irvine, 1995). Cultural differences exist in sexual practices; some of these were discussed in Chapters 1 and 9. The acceptability of explicit sexual language or of particular types of language, such as street slang, varies from one culture to another. Cultures vary in the meaning they attach to sexuality. White, Euro-American cultures have emphasized sex for the purpose of reproduction and thus tend to regard vaginal intercourse as the norm (see Chapter 19). Other cultures place greater emphasis on the pleasure that can be derived from sexual stimulation. Finally, cultures vary in the definition of, and the roles expected within, the family.

Of necessity, sexuality education programs rely on language. Street slang might enhance rapport with Black urban youth but deeply offend Latinas. Curriculum development and teachers base their programs on assumptions about the prevalence of specific sexual practices, such as vaginal and anal intercourse. They implicitly or explicitly identify some practices as desirable, as for example condom use. They reflect assumptions about the purposes of sexual intimacy; for instance, abstinence-based programs assume that sexual intercourse is most meaningful only within marriage.

If sexuality education is to be successful, it must reflect, or at least accept, the cultures of the participants. The educator must assess the audience, the intended messages, and the context, then target the program accordingly (Irvine, 1995). Educators must recognize their own sexual culture, learn about the sexual culture(s) of the students, and be aware of the power differences between groups in our society. In the classroom they should use this knowledge to enhance the effectiveness of the presentation. The use of communication styles and media common to the cultures of the participants— for example, certain rap songs that appeal to young urban African Americans—can be a valuable tool. Finally, it is important that the program not advocate beliefs and practices that are incompatible with the participants' cultures. Such programs are doomed to failure.

One attempt to develop a curriculum for African American adolescents is the *Let the Circle Be Unbroken: Rites of Passage* program (Okwumabua et al., 1998). This program is based on the premise that a successful transition into adolescence requires preparation and celebration. It is presented to 10- to 14-year-olds, lasts four to six months, and involves youth, parents, and friends. Staff are specially trained during an "orientation phase." During the "passage phase," there are weekly programs lasting 60 to 90 minutes; these programs focus on preparation for adult roles, including the making of sexual decisions and deciding on appropriate behavior. The last four weeks make up the "culminating phase," in which everyone plans for the final celebration, the *rite de passage.* Programs like this one respond to the call for sexuality education that incorporates the family and community context in which our sexuality is grounded (Maddock, 1997; Young, 1996).

Another group that needs to have sexuality education tailored to its needs is the developmentally disabled. The American Academy of Pediatrics (Committee on Children with Disabilities, 1996) addressed the special circumstances of children and adolescents with developmental disabilities in a policy statement. The statement points out that we cannot assume that curricula designed for sixth graders can be presented to 12-year-olds with these disabilities. Instead, programs need to assess the cognitive and emotional abilities of each child and adolescent, then present developmentally appropriate materials. Information about forms of romantic and sexual expression may have to emphasize social norms about what is appropriate and discourage inappropriate behaviors in public. Also, programs for persons with disabilities must recognize their vulnerability to exploitation and make special efforts to teach them self-protection skills.

An institute in Mexico has been involved in a long-term project to develop sexuality education programs appropriate for that culture (Pick et al., 2003). In that cultural context, programs must take into account strong, traditional gender roles. Men who have many sex partners are widely admired; women are to be modest and not display pleasure in sexuality. Decisions regarding sexuality and reproduction are made by the man, with the woman playing a passive role. Ninety-five percent of the population is Roman Catholic, so the traditions of that religion must be considered. Taking into account all these factors, the educational programs that the institute developed emphasize a participatory learning style, concrete knowledge about not only sexuality but gender roles and expectations, and communication skills, especially those for communicating with parents.

As we increasingly recognize diversity within the United States and around the world, the creation of developmentally and culturally effective sexuality education programs should be an important priority.

Bibliography

AARP. (1999). *American Association of Retired Persons/Modern Maturity sexuality study*. Washington, DC: AARP.

AAUW. (2001). *Hostile hallways: Bullying, teasing, and sexual harassment in school*. Washington, DC: American Association of University Women.

Abbey, Antonia. (1991). Misperception as an antecedent of acquaintance rape: A consequence of ambiguity in communication between men and women. In A. Parrott & L. Bechhofer (Eds.), *Acquaintance rape: The hidden crime*. New York: Wiley.

Abbey, Antonia, Andrews, Frank M., & Halman, L. Jill. (1992). Infertility and subjective well-being: The mediating roles of self-esteem, internal control, and interpersonal conflict. *Journal of Marriage and the Family, 54,* 408–417.

Abbey, Antonia, & McAuslan, Pam. (2004). A longitudinal examination of male college students' perpetration of sexual assault. *Journal of Consulting and Clinical Psychology, 72,* 747–756.

ABC. (2004, May 27). American porn: Corporate America is profiting from porn—quietly. *ABCNews,* www.abcnews.go.com/sections/primetime/entertainment/porn_business.

Abel, Ernest L. (1980). Fetal alcohol syndrome. *Psychological Bulletin, 87,* 29–50.

Abel, Ernest L. (1984). *Fetal alcohol syndrome and fetal alcohol effects*. New York: Plenum.

Abel, Gene G., et al. (1992). Current treatments of paraphiliacs. *Annual Review of Sex Research, 3,* 255–290.

Abel, Gene, & Rouleau, Joanne-L. (1990). The nature and extent of sexual assault. In W. L. Marshall, D. R. Laws, & H. E. Bartarce (Eds.), *Handbook of sexual assault* (pp. 9–21). New York: Plenum.

Abracen, Jeffrey, & Looman, Jan. (2004). Issues in the treatment of sexual offenders: Recent development and directions for future research. *Aggression and Violent Behavior, 9,* 229–246.

Abramowitz, Stephen I. (1986). Psychosocial outcomes of sex reassignment surgery. *Journal of Consulting and Clinical Psychology, 54,* 183–189.

Abrams, Dominic, et al. (2003). Perceptions of stranger and acquaintance rape: The role of benevolent and hostile sexism in victim blame and rape proclivity. *Journal of Personality and Social Psychology, 84,* 111–125.

Ackard, Diann M., & Neumark-Sztainer, Dianne. (2002). Date violence and date rape among adolescents: Associations with disordered eating behaviors and psychological health. *Child Abuse and Neglect, 26,* 455–473.

Acker, Michele, & Davis, Mark. (1992). Intimacy, passion and commitment in adult romantic relationships: A test of the triangular theory of love. *Journal of Social and Personal Relationships, 9,* 21–50.

ACSF Investigators. (1992). AIDS and sexual behaviour in France. *Nature, 360,* 407–409.

Adam & Eve. (2004). *Sex Stat: Sexy Internet sites gain in popularity*. Atlanta: Adam & Eve.

Adams, M. A., et al. (1997). Vascular control mechanisms in penile erection: Phylogeny and the inevitability of multiple and overlapping systems. *International Journal of Impotence Research, 9,* 85–91.

Addiego, Frank, et al. (1981). Female ejaculation: A case study. *Journal of Sex Research, 17,* 13–21.

Adeoya-Osiguwa, S. A., et al. (2003). 17B-estradiol and environmental estrogens significantly affect mammalian sperm function. *Human Reproduction, 18,* 101–107.

Adkins-Regan, Elizabeth. (2002). Development of sexual partner preference in the zebra finch: A socially monogamous, pair-bonding animal. *Archives of Sexual Behavior, 31,* 27–34.

Advocates for Youth. (2004a). Abstinence-only-until-marriage programs: History of government funding. www.advocatesforyouth.org/rrr/history.htm.

Advocates for Youth. (2004b). Americans support sexuality education. www.advocatesforyouth.org/rrr/history.htm.

Afriat, Cydney. (1995). Antepartum care. In Donald R. Coustan, Ray V. Hunning, Jr., & Don Singer (Eds.), *Human reproduction: Growth and development* (pp. 213–234). Boston: Little, Brown & Co.

Ahluwalia, I. B., et al. (2001). Multiple lifestyle and psychosocial risks and delivery of small for gestational age infants. *Obstetrics and Gynecology, 97,* 649–656.

Ahmadi, Nader. (2003). Rocking sexualities: Iranian migrants' views on sexuality. *Archives of Sexual Behavior, 32,* 317–326.

Ainsworth, Claire. (2005). The secret life of sperm. *Nature, 436,* 770–771.

Alan Guttmacher Institute. (2000). School-based health centers and the birth control debate. *The Guttmacher Report, 3* (5).

Alan Guttmacher Institute. (2001). U.S. teenage pregnancy statistics. New York: Alan Guttmacher Institute. www.agi-usa.org.

Alan Guttmacher Institute. (2004a). *U.S. teenage pregnancy statistics*. New York: Alan Guttmacher Institute. http://www.guttmacher.org.

Alan Guttmacher Institute. (2004b). State policies in brief: Bans on "partial birth" abortion (as of June 1, 2004).

Alan Guttmacher Institute. (2004c). State policies in brief: Sex and STD/HIV education. New York: Alan Guttmacher Institute.

Alan Guttmacher Institute. (2006). *Facts on American teens' sexual and reproductive health*. New York: Alan Guttmacher Institute.

Albert, Alexa. (2001). *Brothel: Mustang Ranch and its women*. New York: Random House.

Albert, B., Brown, S., & Flanigan, C. (Eds.). (2003). *14 and younger: The sexual behavior of young adolescents (Summary)*. Washington, DC: National Campaign to Prevent Teen Pregnancy.

Albin, Rochelle S. (1977). Psychological studies of rape. *Signs, 3,* 423–435.

Alexander, Kristen W., et al. (2005). Traumatic impact predicts long-term memory for documented child sexual abuse. *Psychological Science, 16*, 33–40.

Alexander, Michele G., & Fisher, Terri D. (2003). Truth and consequences: Using the bogus pipeline to examine sex differences in self-reported sexuality. *Journal of Sex Research, 40*, 27–35.

Alink, Lenneke, et al. (2006). The early child aggression curve: Development of physical aggression in 10- to 50-month-old children. *Child Development, 77*, 954–966.

Alkhatib, G., et al. (1996). CC CKR5: A RANTES, MIP1a, MIP1b receptor as a fusion cofactor for macrophage-tropic HIV-1. *Science, 272*, 1955.

Allen, Donald M. (1980). Young male prostitutes: A psychological study. *Archives of Sexual Behavior, 9*, 399–426.

Allen, Katherine R., & Demo, David H. (1995). The families of lesbians and gay men: A new frontier in family research. *Journal of Marriage and the Family, 57*, 111–127.

Allen, Mike, & Burrell, Nancy A. (2002). Sexual orientation of the parent: The impact on the child. In M. Allen et al. (Eds.), *Interpersonal communication research: Advances through meta-analysis* (pp. 125–143). Mahwah, NJ: Erlbaum.

Allen, Mike, et al. (1996). The role of educational briefings in mitigating effects of experimental exposure to violent sexually explicit material. *Journal of Sex Research, 33*, 135–141.

Allgeier, Elizabeth, & Wiederman, Michael W. (1994). How useful is evolutionary psychology for understanding contemporary human sexual behavior? *Annual Review of Sex Research, 5*, 218–256.

Almroth, Lars, et al. (2001). Male complications of female genital mutilation. *Social Science and Medicine, 53*, 1455–1460.

Almroth, Lars, et al. (2005). Primary infertility after genital mutilation in girlhood in Sudan: A case-control study. *The Lancet, 366*, 385–391.

Althof, Stanley E., et al. (2004). Psychological and interpersonal dimensions of sexual function and dysfunction. In T. F. Lue et al. (Eds.), *Sexual medicine: Sexual dysfunctions in men and women* (pp. 73–115). Paris: Editions 21.

Althof, Stanley E. (2007). Treatment of rapid ejaculation: Psychotherapy, pharmacotherapy, and combined therapy. In S. Leiblum (Ed.), *Principles and practice of sex therapy* (4th ed., pp. 212–240). New York: Guilford.

Amara, Rama R., et al. (2001). Control of a mucosal challenge and prevention of AIDS by a multiprotein DNA/MVA vaccine. *Science, 292*, 69–74.

Ambrosone, Christine B., et al. (1996). Cigarette smoking, N-Acetyltransferase 2 genetic polymorphisms, and breast cancer risk. *Journal of the American Medical Association, 276*, 1494–1501.

American Academy of Pediatrics. (1997). Breastfeeding and the use of human milk. *Pediatrics, 100* (6), 1035–1039.

American Academy of Pediatrics. (1999). Circumcision policy statement. *Pediatrics, 103*, 686.

American Academy of Pediatrics Committee on Genetics. (2000). Evaluation of the newborn with developmental anomalies of the external genitalia. *Pediatrics, 106*, 138–142.

American Cancer Society. (1995). *Cancer facts and figures—1995*. Atlanta: American Cancer Society.

American Cancer Society. (2004). *Cancer facts and figures 2004*. Atlanta: American Cancer Society. www.cancer.org.

American Cancer Society. (2007). *Cancer facts & figures 2007*. Atlanta, GA: American Cancer Society. www.cancer.org.

American Civil Liberties Union. (2004). Abortion bans: In the states. www.aclu.org.

American Law Institute. (1962). *Model penal code: Proposed official draft*. Philadelphia: ALI.

American Psychiatric Association. (2000a). *Diagnostic and statistical manual of mental disorders* (4th ed.). Text Revision (*DSM-IV-TR*). Washington, DC: American Psychiatric Association.

American Psychiatric Association. (2000b). Position statement on therapies focused on attempts to change sexual orientation (reparative or conversion therapies). *American Journal of Psychiatry, 157*, 1719–1721. www.psych.org.

American Psychological Association, Task Force on the Sexualization of Girls. (2007). *Report of the APA Task Force on the Sexualization of Girls*. Washington, DC: American Psychological Association. www.apa.org/pi/wpo/sexualization.html.

Ames, Thomas-Robert. (1991). Guidelines for providing sexuality-related services to severely and profoundly retarded individuals: The challenge for the 1990s. *Sexuality and Disability, 9*, 113–122.

Anderson, E. (1989). Sex codes and family life among poor inner-city youths. *Annals of the American Academy of Political and Social Science, 501*, 59–78.

Anderson, J. E., Santelli, J. S., & Morrow, B. (2006). Trends in adolescent contraceptive use, unprotected and poorly protected sex, 1991–2003. *Journal of Adolescent Health, 38*, 734–739.

Anderson, Kermyt, Kaplan, Hillard, & Lancaster, Jane. (2001). *Men's financial expenditures on genetic children and stepchildren from current and former relationships*. Ann Arbor, MI: Population Studies Center, Report No. 01–484.

Anderson, M. (2004). *Personal communication*.

Anderson, Michael C., et al. (2004). Neural systems underlying the suppression of unwanted memories. *Science, 303*, 232–235.

Andrews, Lori B. (1989). Alternative modes of reproduction. In S. Cohen & N. Taub (Eds.), *Reproductive laws for the 1990s* (pp. 361–404). Clifton, NJ: Humana Press.

Angelone, D. J., et al. (2005). The influence of peer interactions on sexually oriented joke telling. *Sex Roles, 52*, 187–200.

Anson, Robert S. (1977, October 25). *San Francisco Chronicle*.

Antilla, Susan. (2002). *Tales from the boom-boom room: Women vs. Wall Street*. Princeton, NJ: Bloomberg Press.

Antle, Katharyn. (1978). Active involvement of expectant fathers in pregnancy: Some further considerations. *Journal of Obstetric, Gynecologic and Neonatal Nursing, 7* (2), 7–12.

Antoni, Michael H., et al. (2001). Cognitive-behavioral stress management intervention decreases the prevalence of depression and enhances benefit finding among women under treatment for early-stage breast cancer. *Health Psychology, 20*, 20–32.

AOL Search. (2006). *Year in review 2006*. Retrieved December 30, 2006, from http://about-search.aol.com/hotsearches2006/index.html.

Apfelbaum, Bernard. (2000). Retarded ejaculation: A much misunderstood syndrome. In S. Leiblum & R. Rosen (Eds.), *Principles and practice of sex therapy* (3rd ed., pp. 205–241). New York: Guilford.

Arafat, Ibtihaj S., & Cotton, Wayne L. (1974). Masturbation practices of males and females. *Journal of Sex Research, 10*, 293–307.

Aragon, Regina, et al. (2001). *African Americans' views of the HIV/AIDS epidemic at 20 years*. Menlo Park, CA: The Henry J. Kaiser Family Foundation. www.kff.org.

Araujo, A., et al. (1998). The relationship between depressive symptoms and male erectile dysfunction: Cross-sectional results from the Massachusetts Male Aging Study. *Psychosomatic Medicine, 60*, 458–465.

Araujo, A., et al. (2000). Relation between psychosocial risk factors and incident erectile dysfunction: Prospective results from the Massachusetts Male Aging Study. *American Journal of Epidemiology, 152*, 533–541.

Archer, John. (2004). Sex differences in aggression in real-world setting: A meta-analytic review. *Review of General Psychology, 8*, 291–322.

Arévalo, Marcos, Jennings, Victoria, & Sinai, Irit. (2002). Efficacy of a new method of family planning: The Standard Days Method. *Contraception, 65*, 333–338.

Aries, Elizabeth. (1996). *Men and women in interaction: Reconsidering the differences*. New York: Oxford University Press.

Arnold, Arthur P. (2003). The gender of the voice within: The neural origin of sex differences in the brain. *Current Opinion in Neurobiology, 13*, 759–764.

Arnow, Bruce A., et al. (2002). Brain activation and sexual arousal in healthy, heterosexual males. *Brain, 125*, 1014–1023.

Arthur, Lisa, & Driscoll, Amy. (2002, May 16). Castration or life term? Judge to rule. *Miami Herald*.

Ascensio, Marysol. (2002). *Sex and sexuality among New York's Puerto Rican youth*. Boulder, CO: Lynne Rienner.

Ashton, Adam K. (2007). The new sexual pharmacology: A guide for the clinician. In S. Leiblum (Ed.), *Principles and practice of sex therapy* (4th ed., pp. 509–542). New York: Guilford.

Associated Press. (1984, March 25). Baby girl is born from transferred embryo. *The New York Times.*

Atkins, David, Yi, J., Baucom, D., & Christensen, A. (2005). Infidelity in couples seeking marital therapy. *Journal of Family Psychology, 19,* 470–473.

Aubrey, Jennifer S. (2004). Sex and punishment: An examination of sexual consequences and the sexual double standard in teen programming. *Sex Roles, 50,* 505–514.

Aubrey, Jennifer S., & Harrison, Kristen. (2004). The gender-role content of children's favorite television programs and its links to their gender-related perceptions. *Media Psychology, 6,* 111–146.

Audet, M. C., et al. (2001). Evaluation of contraceptive efficacy and cycle control of a transdermal contraceptive patch vs. an oral contraceptive: A randomized controlled trial. *Journal of the American Medical Association, 285,* 2347–2354.

Augustinova, H., Hoeller, D., & Yao, F. (2004). The dominant-negative herpes simplex virus type 1 (HSV-1) recombinant CJ83193 can serve as an effective vaccine against wild-type HSV-1 infection in mice. *Journal of Virology, 78,* 5756–5765.

Autry, Amy M., et al. (2002). A comparison of medical induction and dilation and evacuation for second-trimester abortion. *American Journal of Obstetrics and Gynecology, 187,* 393–397.

Avis, Nancy E., & McKinlay, Sonja M. (1995, March–April). The Massachusetts Women's Health Study: An epidemiological investigation of the menopause. *Journal of the American Medical Women's Association, 50,* 45–63.

Avis, Nancy E., et al. (2005). Correlates of sexual function among multi-ethnic middle-aged women: Results from the Study of Women's Health Across the Nation (SWAN). *Menopause, 12,* 385–398.

Azimi, Negar. (2006, December 3). Prisoners of sex. *New York Times Magazine,* pp. 64–67.

Bach, G., & Wyden, P. (1969). *The intimate enemy: How to fight fair in love and marriage.* New York: Morrow.

Bachmann, G. A., & Leiblum, S. R. (1991). Sexuality in sexagenarian women. *Maturitas, 13,* 43–50.

Bagemihl, Bruce. (1999). *Biological exuberance: Animal homosexuality and natural diversity.* New York: St. Martin's Press.

Bailey, J. Michael, & Pillard, Richard C. (1991). A genetic study of male sexual orientation. *Archives of General Psychiatry, 48,* 1089–1096.

Bailey, J. Michael, & Pillard, Richard C. (1995). Genetics of human sexual orientation. *Annual Review of Sex Research, 6,* 126–150.

Bailey, J. Michael, & Zucker, Kenneth J. (1995). Childhood sex-typed behavior and sexual orientation. *Developmental Psychology, 31,* 43–55.

Bailey, J. Michael, et al. (1993). Heritable factors influence sexual orientation in women. *Archives of General Psychiatry, 50,* 217–223.

Bailey, J. Michael, et al. (1995). Sexual orientation of adult sons of gay fathers. *Developmental Psychology, 31,* 124–129.

Bailey, J. Michael, Willerman, L., & Parks, C. (1991). A test of the maternal stress theory of human male homosexuality. *Archives of Sexual Behavior, 20,* 277–294.

Baker, Christina N. (2005). Images of women's sexuality in advertisements: A content analysis of Black and white oriented women's and men's magazines. *Sex Roles, 52,* 13–28.

Baker, F. C., et al. (2002). Acetaminophen does not affect 24-h body temperature or sleep in the luteal phase of the menstrual cycle. *Journal of Applied Physiology, 92,* 1684–1691.

Baker, Robin. (1996). *Sperm wars: The evolutionary logic of love and lust.* New York: Basic Books.

Bakker, A., et al. (1993). The prevalence of transsexualism in the Netherlands. *Acta Psychiatrica Scandinavica, 87,* 237–238.

Baladerian, Nora J. (1991). Sexual abuse of people with developmental disabilities. *Sexuality and Disability, 9,* 323–335.

Baldwin, John D., & Baldwin, Janice I. (1989). The socialization of homosexuality and heterosexuality in a non-Western society. *Archives of Sexual Behavior, 18,* 13–30.

Baldwin, John D., & Baldwin, Janice I. (1997). Gender differences in sexual interest. *Archives of Sexual Behavior, 26,* 181–210.

Baldwin, Susie B., et al. (2004). Condom use and other factors affecting penile human papillomavirus detection in men attending a sexually transmitted disease clinic. *Sexually Transmitted Diseases, 31,* 601–607.

Balsam, Kimberly F. (2005). Victimization over the life span: A comparison of lesbian, gay, bisexual, and heterosexual siblings. *Journal of Consulting and Clinical Psychology, 73,* 477–487.

Balsam, Kimberly F., et al. (2005). Mental health of lesbian, gay, bisexual, and heterosexual siblings: Effects of gender, sexual orientation, and family. *Journal of Abnormal Psychology, 114,* 471–476.

Balter, Michael. (1995). Elusive HIV-suppressor factors found. *Science, 270,* 1560–1561.

Balter, Michael. (1996). A second coreceptor for HIV in early stages of infection. *Science, 272,* 1740.

Balter, Michael. (1998). Impending AIDS vaccine trial opens old wounds. *Science, 279,* 650.

Bancroft, J. (1997). Sexual problems. In D. Clark & C. Fairburn (Eds.), *Science and practice of cognitive behaviour therapy* (pp. 243–257). London: Oxford University Press.

Bancroft, John. (1978). The prevention of sexual offenses. In C. B. Qualls et al. (Eds.), *The prevention of sexual disorders* (pp. 95–116). New York: Plenum.

Bancroft, John. (2004). Alfred C. Kinsey and the politics of sex research. *Annual Review of Sex Research, 15,* 1–39.

Bancroft, John, & Gutierrez, P. (1996). Erectile dysfunction in men with and without diabetes mellitus. *Diabetic Medicine, 13,* 84–89.

Bancroft, John, Herbenick, Debra, & Reynolds, Meredith. (2003). Masturbation as a marker of sexual development. In John Bancroft (Ed.), *Sexual development.* Bloomington: Indiana University Press.

Bancroft, John, Janssen, E., et al. (2004). Sexual activity and risk taking in young heterosexual men: The relevance of sexual arousability, mood, and sensation seeking. *Journal of Sex Research, 41,* 181–192.

Bancroft, John, & Vukadinovic, Zoran. (2004). Sexual addiction, sexual compulsivity, sexual impulsivity, or what? Toward a theoretical model. *Journal of Sex Research, 41,* 225–234.

Bancroft, John, et al. (2005). Erectile and ejaculatory problems in gay and heterosexual men. *Archives of Sexual Behavior, 34,* 285–297.

Bandura, Albert. (1977). *Social learning theory.* Englewood Cliffs, NJ: Prentice-Hall.

Bandura, Albert. (1982). Self-efficacy mechanism in human agency. *American Psychologist, 37,* 122–147.

Bandura, Albert. (1986). *Social foundations of thought and action: A social cognitive theory.* Englewood Cliffs, NJ: Prentice-Hall.

Bandura, Albert, & Walters, Richard H. (1963). *Social learning and personality development.* New York: Holt.

Banerjee, Neela. (2005, January 14). Lutherans recommend tolerance on gay policy. *New York Times.*

Bang, A. K., et al. (2005). A study of finger lengths, semen quality and sex hormones in 360 young men from the general Danish population. *Human Reproduction, 20,* 3109–3113.

Banks, Amy, & Gartrell, Nanette K. (1995). Hormones and sexual orientation: A questionable link. *Journal of Homosexuality, 28,* 247–268.

Barash, David P. (1982). *Sociobiology and behavior* (2nd ed.). New York: Elsevier.

Barbach, Lonnie G. (1975). *For yourself: The fulfillment of female sexuality.* Garden City, NY: Doubleday.

Barbach, Lonnie G. (1983). *For each other: Sharing sexual intimacy.* Garden City, NY: Anchor Books.

Barbach, Lonnie G. (1993). *The pause: Positive approaches to menopause.* New York: Dutton.

Barbaree, H. E., & Marshall, W. L. (1991). The role of male sexual arousal in rape: Six models. *Journal of Consulting and Clinical Psychology, 59,* 621–630.

Barclay, Laurie. (2003). USPSTF issues first recommendation to promote breast-feeding. *Medscape Medical News,* article 459383.

Barlow, David H. (1986). Causes of sexual dysfunction: The role of cognitive interference. *Journal of Consulting and Clinical Psychology, 54,* 140–148.

Barlow, David H., Leitenberg, H., & Agras, W. S. (1969). Experimental control of sexual deviation through manipulation of noxious scenes in covert sensitization. *Journal of Abnormal Psychology, 74,* 596–601.

Baron, Larry, & Straus, Murray A. (1989). *Four theories of rape in American society.* New Haven, CT: Yale University Press.

Barouch, Dan H., et al. (2000). Control of viremia and prevention of clinical AIDS in rhesus monkeys by cytokine-augmented DNA vaccination. *Science, 290*, 486–492.

Barr, A., Bryan, A., & Kenrick, D. (2002). Sexual peak: Socially shared cognitions about desire, frequency, and satisfaction in men and women. *Personal Relationships, 9*, 287–299.

Barr, Helen M., et al. (1990). Prenatal exposure to alcohol, caffeine, tobacco and aspirin: Effects on fine and gross motor performance in 4-year-old children. *Developmental Psychology, 26*, 339–348.

Bartell, Gilbert D. (1970). Group sex among the mid-Americans. *Journal of Sex Research, 6*, 113–130.

Bartels, A., & Zeki, S. (2004). The neural correlates of maternal and romantic love. *NeuroImage, 21*, 1155–1166.

Bartholomew, K. (1990). Avoidance of intimacy: An attachment perspective. *Journal of Personal and Social Relationships, 7*, 147–178.

Basile, Kathleen C. (2002). Prevalence of wife rape and other intimate partner sexual coercion in a nationally representative sample of women. *Violence and Victims, 17*, 511–524.

Basson, Renée. (2004). Summary of the recommendations on women's sexual dysfunctions. In T. F. Lue et al. (Eds.), *Sexual medicine: Sexual dysfunctions in men and women* (pp. 975–990). Paris: Editions 21.

Basson, Rosemary. (2006). Sexual desire and arousal disorders in women. *New England Journal of Medicine, 354*, 1497–1506.

Basson, Rosemary. (2007). Sexual desire/arousal disorders in women. In S. Leiblum (Ed.), *Principles and practice of sex therapy* (4th ed., pp. 25–53). New York: Guilford.

Bauer, Charles, et al. (2002). The maternal lifestyle study: Drug exposure during pregnancy and short-term maternal outcomes. *American Journal of Obstetrics and Gynecology, 186*, 487–495.

Bauer, Greta R., & Wayne, Linda D. (2005). Cultural sensitivity and research involving sexual minorities. *Perspectives on Sexual and Reproductive Health, 37*, 45–47.

Baulieu, E. E., et al. (2000). Dehydroepiandrosterone (DHEA), DHEA sulfate, and aging: Contributions of the DHEAge Study to a sociobiomedical issue. *Proceedings of the National Academy of Sciences—USA, 97*, 4279–4284.

Baumeister, Roy F. (1988a). Masochism as escape from the self. *Journal of Sex Research, 25*, 28–59.

Baumeister, Roy F. (1988b). Gender differences in masochistic scripts. *Journal of Sex Research, 25*, 478–499.

Baumeister, Roy F., Catanese, K., & Vohs, K. (2001). Is there a gender difference in strength of sex drive? Theoretical views, conceptual distinctions, and a review of relevant evidence. *Personality and Social Psychology Review, 5*, 242–273.

Baumeister, Roy F., Catanese, Kathleen, & Wallace, Harry. (2002). Conquest by force: A narcissistic reactance theory of rape and sexual coercion. *Review of General Psychology, 6*, 92–135.

Bazelon, Emily. (2007, January 21). Is there a post-abortion syndrome? *New York Times Magazine.*

Beach, Frank A. (1947). Evolutionary changes in the physiological control of mating behavior in mammals. *Psychological Review, 54*, 297–315.

Beach, Frank A. (Ed.). (1976). *Human sexuality in four perspectives.* Baltimore: Johns Hopkins University Press.

Beach, Frank, & Merari, A. (1970). Coital behavior in dogs. V. Effects of estrogen and progesterone on mating and other forms of social behavior in the bitch. *Journal of Comparative and Physiological Psychology Monograph, 70* (1), Part 2, 1–22.

Beall, Anne, & Sternberg, Robert. (1995). The social construction of love. *Journal of Social and Personal Relationships, 12*, 417–438.

Bearman, Peter, & Bruckner, Hannah. (2001). Promising the future: Virginity pledges and the transition to first intercourse. *American Journal of Sociology, 106*, 859–912.

Beck, J. Gayle. (1995). Hypoactive sexual desire disorder: An overview. *Journal of Consulting and Clinical Psychology, 63*, 919–927.

Beier, E. G., & Sternberg, D. P. (1977). Marital communication. *Journal of Communication, 27*, 92–103.

Bell, Alan P. (1974). Homosexualities: Their range and character. In *Nebraska symposium on motivation 1973.* Lincoln: University of Nebraska Press.

Bell, Alan P., & Weinberg, Martin S. (1978). *Homosexualities.* New York: Simon & Schuster.

Bell, Alan P., Weinberg, Martin S., & Hammersmith, Sue K. (1981). *Sexual preference.* Bloomington: Indiana University Press.

Belluck, Pam. (2004, May 17). Gay couples apply for marriage licenses in Massachusetts. *New York Times.*

Belzer, E. G. (1981). Orgasmic expulsions of women: A review and heuristic inquiry. *Journal of Sex Research, 17*, 1–12.

Bem, Daryl J. (1996). Exotic becomes erotic: A developmental theory of sexual orientation. *Psychological Review, 103*, 320–335.

Bem, Daryl J. (1998). Is EBE theory supported by the evidence? Is it androcentric? A reply to Peplau et al. (1998). *Psychological Review, 105*, 395–398.

Bem, Sandra L. (1981). Gender schema theory: A cognitive account of sex typing. *Psychological Review, 88*, 354–364.

Bem, Sandra L. (1989). Genital knowledge and gender consistency in preschool children. *Child Development, 60*, 649–662.

Benedetti, Jacqueline, Corey, Lawrence, & Ashley, Rhoda. (1994). Recurrence rates in genital herpes after symptomatic first-episode infection. *Annals of Internal Medicine, 121*, 847–854.

Bennett, Sylvana, & Assefi, Nassim. (2005). School-based teenage pregnancy prevention programs: A systematic review of randomized controlled trials. *Journal of Adolescent Health, 36*, 72–81.

Ben-Ze'ev, A. (2004). *Love online: Emotions on the Internet.* Cambridge, UK: Cambridge University Press.

Bérard, E. J. J. (1989). The sexuality of spinal cord injured women: Physiology and pathophysiology: A review. *Paraplegia, 27*, 99–112.

Berenbaum, Sheri A. (2006). Psychological outcome in children with disorders of sex development: Implications for understanding typical development. *Annual Review of Sex Research, 17*, 1–38.

Beretta, G., Chelo, E., & Zanollo, A. (1989). Reproductive aspects in spinal cord injured males. *Paraplegia, 27*, 113–118.

Berg, J. H., & Derlega, V. J. (1987). Themes in the study of self-disclosure. In V. J. Derlega & J. H. Berg (Eds.), *Self-disclosure: Theory, research and therapy* (pp. 1–8). New York: Plenum.

Bergen, D. J., & Williams, J. E. (1991). Sex stereotypes in the United States revisited: 1972–1988. *Sex Roles, 24*, 413–423.

Berglund, Hans, et al. (2006). Brain response to putative pheromones in lesbian women. *PNAS, 103*, 8269–8274.

Bergman, K. M., Sarkar, P., O'Connor, T. G., Modi, N., & Glover, V. (2007). Prenatal stressful life events predict child cognitive outcomes. *Early Human Development, 83*, 136.

Berkley, Karen J., Rapkin, A., & Papka, R. (2005). The pains of endometriosis. *Science, 308*, 1587–1589.

Berkman, C. S., & Zinberg, G. (1997). Homophobia and heterosexism in social workers. *Social Work, 42*, 319–332.

Berliner, David L., Jennings-White, Clive, & Lavker, Robert M. (1991). The human skin: Fragrances and pheromones. *Journal of Steroid Biochemistry and Molecular Biology, 39*, 671–679.

Berman, Jennifer R., Adhikari, S., & Goldstein, I. (2000). Anatomy and physiology of female sexual function and dysfunction. *European Urology, 38*, 20–29.

Bermant, Gordon, & Davidson, Julian M. (1974). *Biological bases of sexual behavior.* New York: Harper & Row.

Bernard, M., et al. (1985). *The rights of single people.* New York: Bantam Books.

Berne, Eric. (1970). *Sex in human loving.* New York: Simon & Schuster.

Bernstein, Anne C., & Cowan, Philip A. (1975). Children's concepts of how people get babies. *Child Development, 46*, 77–92.

Berrill, K. T. (1992). Antigay violence and victimization in the United States. In G. M. Herek & K. T. Berrill (Eds.), *Hate crimes: Confronting violence against lesbians and gay men* (pp. 259–269). Newbury Park, CA: Sage.

Berry, Jason, & Renner, Gerald. (2004). *Vows of silence: The abuse of power in the papacy of John Paul II.* New York: Free Press.

Berry, L. J., et al. (2004). Transcutaneous immunization with combined cholera toxin and CpG adjuvant protects against *Chlamydia muridarum* genital tract infection. *Infection and Immunity, 72*, 1019–1028.

Berscheid, Ellen, & Hatfield, Elaine. (1978). *Interpersonal attraction* (2nd ed.). Reading, MA: Addison-Wesley.

Berscheid, Ellen, & Walster, Elaine. (1974). A little bit about love. In T. L. Huston (Ed.), *Foundations of interpersonal attraction.* New York: Academic.

Berscheid, Ellen, et al. (1971). Physical attractiveness and dating choice: A test of the matching hypothesis. *Journal of Experimental Social Psychology, 7,* 173–189.

Besen, Wayne. (2003). *Anything but straight: Unmasking the scandals and lies behind the "ex-gay" myth.* Binghamton, NY: Harrington Park Press.

Bess, Barbara E., & Janus, Samuel S. (1976). Prostitution. In B. J. Sadock et al. (Eds.), *The sexual experience.* Baltimore: Williams & Wilkins.

Bhurga, Dinesh, & de Silva, Padmal. (1993). Sexual dysfunction across cultures. *International Review of Psychiatry, 5,* 243–252.

Bieber, Irving. (1976). A discussion of "Homosexuality: The ethical challenge." *Journal of Consulting and Clinical Psychology, 47,* 368–376.

Bieber, Irving, Dain, H. J., & Dince, P. R. (1962). *Homosexuality: A psychoanalytic study.* New York: Basic Books.

Biller, Henry, & Meredith, D. (1975). *Father power.* New York: Anchor Books.

Billings, Andrew. (1979). Conflict resolution in distressed and non-distressed married couples. *Journal of Consulting and Clinical Psychology, 47,* 368–376.

Billy, J. O. G., et al. (1993). The sexual behavior of men in the United States. *Family Planning Perspectives, 25* (2), 52–60.

Binik, Yitzchak M. (2005). Should dyspareunia be retained as a sexual dysfunction in DSM-V? A painful classification decision. *Archives of Sexual Behavior, 34,* 11–22.

Binik, Yitzchak M., et al. (2002). The female sexual pain disorders: Genital pain or sexual dysfunction? *Archives of Sexual Behavior, 31,* 425–430.

Binik, Yitzchak M., et al. (2007). Dyspareunia and vaginismus: So-called sexual pain. In S. Leiblum (Ed.), *Principles and practice of sex therapy* (4th ed., pp. 124–156). New York: Guilford.

Birchler, Gary R., Weiss, R. L., & Vincent, J. P. (1975). Multimethod analysis of social reinforcement exchange between maritally distressed and nondistressed spouse and stranger dyads. *Journal of Personality and Social Psychology, 31,* 349–360.

Bird, S. Elizabeth. (1999, Summer). Gendered construction of the American Indian in popular media. *Journal of Communication,* 61–83.

Birnbaum, Gurit E., & Reis, Harry T. (2006). Women's sexual working models: An evolutionary-attachment perspective. *Journal of Sex Research, 43,* 328–342.

Bixler, Ray H. (1986). Of apes and men (including females). *Journal of Sex Research, 22,* 255–267.

Black, Dan, et al. (2000). Demographics of the gay and lesbian population in the United States: Evidence from available systematic data sources. *Demography, 37,* 139–154.

Blackless, Melanie, et al. (2000). How sexually dimorphic are we? Review and synthesis. *American Journal of Human Biology, 12,* 151–166.

Blair, C. David, & Lanyon, Richard I. (1981). Exhibitionism: Etiology and treatment. *Psychological Bulletin, 89,* 439–463.

Blake, Jeanne. (2004). *Words can work: When talking with kids about sexual health.* Gloucester, MA: Blake Works, Inc.

Blake, S. M., Simkin, L., Ledsky, R. Perkins, C., & Calabrese, J. M. (2001). Effect of a parent-child communications intervention on young adolescents' risk of early onset of sexual intercourse. *Family Planning Perspectives, 33,* 52–61.

Blake, Susan, et al. (2003). Condom availability programs in Massachusetts high schools: Relationships with condom use and sexual behavior. *American Journal of Public Health, 93,* 955–962.

Blanchard, Ray. (1997). Birth order and sibling sex ratio in homosexual versus heterosexual males and females. *Annual Review of Sex Research, 8,* 27–67.

Blanchard, Ray. (2001). Fraternal birth order and the maternal immune hypothesis of male homosexuality. *Hormones and Behavior, 40,* 105–114.

Blanchard, Ray, & Bogaert, A. (2004). Proportion of homosexual men who owe their sexual orientation to fraternal birth order: An estimate based on two national probability samples. *American Journal of Human Biology, 16,* 151–157.

Blanchard, Ray, Dickey, R., & Jones, C. (1995). Comparison of height and weight in homosexual versus nonhomosexual gender dysphorics. *Archives of Sexual Behavior, 24,* 543–554.

Blanchard, Ray, et al. (1999). Pedophiles: Mental retardation, maternal age, and sexual orientation. *Archives of Sexual Behavior, 28,* 111–127.

Blanchard, Ray, et al. (2002). Retrospective self-reports of childhood accidents causing unconsciousness in phallometrically diagnosed pedophiles. *Archives of Sexual Behavior, 31,* 511–526.

Blechman, Elaine A., et al. (1988). The premenstrual experience. In E. Blechman & K. Brownell (Eds.), *Handbook of behavioral medicine for women* (pp. 80–91). New York: Pergamon.

Blee, Kathleen M., & Tickamyer, Ann R. (1995). Racial differences in men's attitudes about women's gender roles. *Journal of Marriage and the Family, 57,* 21–30.

Bloom, Linda. (2004, May 4). Delegates retain stance on homosexual issues while demonstrators express beliefs. www.umc.org/interior?ptid=16&mid=4559.

Blumberg, Eric. (2003). The lives and voices of highly sexual women. *Journal of Sex Research, 40,* 146–157.

Blumstein, Philip W., & Schwartz, Pepper. (1983). *American couples.* New York: Morrow.

Boardman, Jason, et al. (nd). *Low birth weight, social factors, and developmental outcomes among children in the United States.* Austin, TX: Population Research Center, No. 01-02-05.

Bockting, Walter O. (1997). The assessment and treatment of gender dysphoria. *Directions in Clinical and Counseling Psychology, 7,* 11-1-11-22.

Bockting, Walter O. (1999, October–November). From construction to context: Gender through the eyes of the transgendered. *SIECUS Report,* 3–7.

Bockting, Walter O. (2004). Plastic and reconstructive surgery for transgender and transsexual patients. In D. B. Sarwer et al. (Eds.), *Psychological aspects of plastic surgery.* Philadelphia: Lippincott Williams & Wilkins.

Bodlund, Owe, & Kullgren, Gunnar. (1996). Transsexualism—General outcome and prognostic factors: A five-year follow-up study of 19 transsexuals in the process of changing sex. *Archives of Sexual Behavior, 25,* 303–316.

Bodnar, L. M., et al. (2004). Prepregnancy body mass index and the risk of preeclampsia [Abstract]. *Federation of American Societies for Experimental Biology Journal, 18* (5), A928.

Bogaert, Anthony F. (2003). Number of older brothers and sexual orientation: New tests and the attraction/behavior distinction in two national probability samples. *Journal of Personality and Social Psychology, 84,* 644–652.

Bogaert, Anthony E. (2006). Asexuality: Prevalence and associated factors in a national probability sample. *Journal of Sex Research, 41,* 279–287.

Bogren, Lennart Y. (1991). Changes in sexuality in women and men during pregnancy. *Archives of Sexual Behavior, 20,* 35–45.

Boles, J., & Ellifson, K. (1994). *Risk factors associated with HIV seropositivity in clients of male and female prostitutes.* Presented at the Annual Meeting, Society for the Scientific Study of Sexuality, Miami, FL.

Boonstra, Heather. (2001). Islam, women and family planning: A primer. *Guttmacher Report on Public Policy.*

Booth, Cathryn L., & Meltzoff, Andrew N. (1984). Expected and actual experience in labour and delivery and their relationship to maternal attachment. *Journal of Reproductive and Infant Psychology, 2,* 79–91.

Bootzin, R. R., & Natzoulas, T. (1965). Evidence for perceptual defense uncontaminated by response bias. *Journal of Personality and Social Psychology, 1,* 461–468.

Bornstein, Robert F. (1989). Exposure and affect: Overview and meta-analysis of research, 1968–1987. *Psychological Bulletin, 106,* 265–289.

Boruchowitz, Robert C. (1973). Victimless crimes: A proposal to free the courts. *Judicature, 57,* 69–78.

Bosch, F. X., et al. (1995). Prevalence of human papillomavirus in cervical cancer: A worldwide perspective. *Journal of the National Cancer Institute, 87,* 796–802.

Boston Women's Health Book Collective. (1996). *The new our bodies, ourselves.* New York: Simon & Schuster.

Boston Women's Health Book Collective. (1998). *Our bodies, ourselves for the new century.* New York: Simon & Schuster.

Boston Women's Health Book Collective. (2005). *Our bodies, ourselves.* New York: Simon & Schuster, Touchstone Books.

Boswell, John. (1980). *Christianity, social tolerance, and homosexuality.* Chicago: University of Chicago Press.

Bouyer, J., et al. (2003). Risk factors for ectopic pregnancy: A comprehensive analysis based on a large case-control, population-based study in France. *American Journal of Epidemiology, 157,* 185–194.

Bowe, John. (2006, November 19). Gay donor or gay dad? *New York Times Magazine,* pp. 66–73.

Bowen, Anne. (2005). Internet sexuality research with rural men who have sex with men: Can we recruit and retain them? *Journal of Sex Research, 42,* 317–323.

Bowleg, Lisa, Craig, Melynda L., & Burkholder, Gary. (2004). Rising and surviving: A conceptual model of active coping among Black lesbians. *Cultural Diversity & Ethnic Minority Psychology, 10,* 229–240.

Boyd, K., Callaghan, B., & Shotter, E. (1986). *Life before birth.* London: SPCK.

Bradford, John M. W., & Greenberg, D. M. (1996). Pharmacological treatment of deviant sexual behaviour. *Annual Review of Sex Research, 7,* 283–306.

Brady, Katherine. (1978). *Father's days.* New York: Dell.

Braun, M., et al. (2000). Epidemiology of erectile dysfunction: Results of the "Cologne Male Survey." *International Journal of Impotence Research, 12,* 305–311.

Braun, Stephen. (1996). New experiments underscore warnings on maternal drinking. *Science, 273,* 738–739.

Braun, Virginia, & Kitzinger, Celia. (2001). "Snatch," "hole," or "honey-pot"? Semantic categories and the problem of nonspecificity in female genital slang. *Journal of Sex Research, 38,* 146–158.

Brecher, Edward M. (1984). *Love, sex, and aging.* Mount Vernon, NY: Consumers Union.

Brecher, Ruth, & Brecher, Edward (Eds.). (1966). *An analysis of Human Sexual Response.* New York: Signet Books, New American Library.

Brecht, M. L., et al. (2004). Methamphetamine use behaviors and gender differences. *Addictive Behaviors, 29,* 89–106.

Brecklin, Leanne R., & Ullman, Sarah E. (2005). Self-defense or assertiveness training and women's responses to sexual attacks. *Journal of Interpersonal Violence, 20,* 738–762.

Breitenbecher, K. H. (2000). Sexual assault on college campuses: Is an ounce of prevention enough? *Applied and Preventive Psychology, 9,* 23–52.

Brennan, Peter A., & Kendrick, Keith M. (2006). Mammalian social odours: Attraction and individual recognition. *Philosophical Transactions of the Royal Society B, 361,* 2061–2078.

Brent, Jonathan. (1976). A general introduction to privacy. *Massachusetts Law Quarterly, 61,* 10–18.

Brenton, Myron. (1972). *Sex talk.* New York: Stein and Day.

Breslow, N., Evans, I., & Langley, J. (1985). On the prevalence and roles of females in the sadomasochistic subculture: Report of an empirical study. *Archives of Sexual Behavior, 14,* 303–318.

Breton, Sylvie, et al. (1996). Acidification of the male reproductive tract by a proton pumping (H^+)-ATPase. *Nature Medicine, 2,* 470–472.

Bretschneider, Judy G., & McCoy, Norma L. (1988). Sexual interest and behavior in healthy 80- and 102-year-olds. *Archives of Sexual Behavior, 17,* 109–130.

Brewster, Karin. (1994). Race differences in sexual activity among adolescent women: The role of neighborhood characteristics. *American Sociological Review, 59,* 408–424.

Brim, Orville G. (1992). *Ambition.* New York: Basic Books.

Brinton, Louise A., & Schairer, Catherine. (1997). Postmenopausal hormone-replacement therapy—Time for a reappraisal? *New England Journal of Medicine, 336,* 1821–1822.

Brock, G., et al. (2002). Efficacy and safety of tadalafil in men with erectile dysfunction: An integrated analysis of registration trials. *Journal of Urology, 167,* 178 Suppl. S.

Brock, G., et al. (2003). Safety and efficacy of vardenafil for the treatment of men with erectile dysfunction after radical retropubic prostatectomy. *Journal of Urology, 170,* 1278–1283.

Broderick, Carlfred B. (1966a). Sexual behavior among preadolescents. *Journal of Social Issues, 22* (2), 6–21.

Broderick, Carlfred B. (1966b). Socio-sexual development in a suburban community. *Journal of Sex Research, 2,* 1–24.

Brosius, Hans-Berad, Weaver, James B., III, & Staab, Joachim. (1993). Exploring the social and sexual "reality" of contemporary pornography. *Journal of Sex Research, 30,* 161–170.

Brotman, Harris. (1984, January 8). Human embryo transplants. *New York Times Magazine,* p. 42ff.

Brotto, Lori, et al. (2005). Acculturation and sexual function in Asian women. *Archives of Sexual Behavior, 34,* 595–612.

Broun, Heywood, & Leech, Margaret. (1927). *Anthony Comstock: Roundsman of the Lord.* New York: Boni.

Brown, Graham, Maycock, B., & Burns, S. (2005). Your picture is your bait: Use and meaning of cyberspace among gay men. *Journal of Sex Research, 42,* 63–73.

Brown, Jane D. (2002). Mass media influences on sexuality. *Journal of Sex Research, 39,* 42–45.

Brown, Jane, & Steele, Jeanne R. (1996). Sexuality and the mass media: An overview. *SIECUS Report, 24* (4), 3–9.

Brown, Nancy L., Pennylegion, Michelle, & Hillard, Pamela. (1997). A process evaluation of condom availability in the Seattle, Washington public schools. *Journal of School Health, 67,* 336–340.

Brown, Zane A., et al. (2005). Genital herpes complicating pregnancy. *Obstetrics & Gynecology, 106,* 845–856.

Brownmiller, Susan. (1975). *Against our will: Men, women, and rape.* New York: Simon & Schuster.

Brückner, Hannah, Martin, Anne, & Bearman, Peter S. (2004). Ambivalence and pregnancy: Adolescents' attitudes, contraceptive use and pregnancy. *Perspectives on Sexual and Reproductive Health, 36,* 248–257.

Bryant, J., & Rockwell, S. C. (1994). Effects of massive exposure to sexually oriented prime-time television programming on adolescents' moral judgment. In D. Zillman, J. Bryant, and A. C. Houston (Eds.), *Media, children, and the family: Social, scientific, psychodynamic, and clinical perspectives* (pp. 183–195). Hillsdale, NJ: Lawrence Erlbaum.

Buchanan, K. M. (1986). *Apache women warriors.* El Paso: Texas Western Press.

Buchbinder, Susan P., et al. (1994). Long-term HIV-1 infection without immunologic progression. *AIDS, 8,* 1123–1128.

Buffet, N. Chabbert, et al. (1998). Regulation of the human menstrual cycle. *Frontiers in Neuroendocrinology, 19,* 151–186.

Bulik, C., Prescott, C., & Kendler, K. (2001). Features of childhood sexual abuse and the development of psychiatric and substance use disorders. *British Journal of Psychiatry, 179,* 444–449.

Bullivant, Susan B., et al. (2004). Women's sexual experience during the menstrual cycle: Identification of the sexual phase by non-invasive measurement of luteinizing hormone. *Journal of Sex Research, 41,* 82–93.

Bullough, Bonnie, & Bullough, Vern. (1997). Are transvestites necessarily heterosexual? *Archives of Sexual Behavior, 26,* 1–12.

Bullough, Vern L. (1976). *Sexual variance in society and history.* New York: Wiley.

Bullough, Vern L. (1994). *Science in the bedroom: A history of sex research.* New York: Basic Books.

Bullough, Vern, & Bullough, Bonnie. (1987). *Women and prostitution: A social history.* Buffalo, NY: Prometheus Books.

Bumpass, Larry L., Sweet, James A., & Cherlin, Andrew. (1991). The role of cohabitation in declining rates of marriage. *Journal of Marriage and the Family, 53,* 913–927.

Burack, J. H., et al. (1993). Depressive symptoms and CD4 lymphocyte decline among HIV-infected men. *Journal of the American Medical Association, 270,* 2568–2573.

Burger, H. G. (1993). Evidence for a negative feedback role of inhibin in follicle stimulating hormone regulation in women. *Human Reproduction, 8,* Suppl. 2, 129–132.

Burgess, Ann W. (1984). *Child pornography and sex rings.* Lexington, MA: Lexington Books (D.C. Heath).

Burgess, Ann W., & Holmstrom, Lynda L. (1974a). Rape trauma syndrome. *American Journal of Psychiatry, 131,* 981–986.

Burgess, Ann W., & Holmstrom, Lynda L. (1974b). *Rape: Victims of crisis.* Bowie, MD: Robert J. Brady.

Burleson, Brant, & Denton, Wayne. (1997). The relationship between communication skill and marital satisfaction: Some moderating effects. *Journal of Marriage and the Family, 59,* 884–902.

Burnett, Arthur L. (2005). Erectile dysfunction following radical prostatectomy. *Journal of the American Medical Association, 293,* 2648–2653.

Burris, Scott. (1993). Testing, disclosure, and the right to privacy. In S. Burris, H. L. Dalton, & J. L. Miller (Eds.), *AIDS law today* (pp. 115–149). New Haven, CT: Yale University Press.

Burris, Scott, Dalton, Harlon L., and Miller, Judith (Eds.). (1993). *AIDS law today.* New Haven, CT: Yale University Press.

Burt, Martha R., & Estep, Rhoda E. (1981). Apprehension and fear: Learning a sense of sexual vulnerability. *Sex Roles, 7,* 511–522.

Burton, D. L. (2000). Were adolescent sexual offenders children with sexual behavior problems? *Sex Abuse, 12,* 37–48.

Burton, Frances D. (1970). Sexual climax in Macaca Mulatta. *Proceedings of the Third International Congress on Primatology, 3,* 180–191.

Buss, Arnold. (1966). *Psychopathology.* New York: Wiley.

Buss, David M. (1988). The evolution of human intra-sexual competition: Tactics of mate attraction. *Journal of Personality and Social Psychology, 54,* 616–628.

Buss, David M. (1989). Sex differences in human mate preferences: Evolutionary hypotheses tested in 37 cultures. *Behavioral and Brain Sciences, 12,* 1–49.

Buss, David M. (1991). Evolutionary personality psychology. *Annual Review of Psychology, 42,* 459–491.

Buss, David M. (1994). *The evolution of desire: Strategies of human mating.* New York: Basic Books.

Buss, David M. (2000). *The dangerous passion: Why jealousy is as necessary as love and sex.* New York: Free Press.

Buss, David M., & Schmitt, David P. (1993). Sexual strategies theory: An evolutionary perspective on human mating. *Psychological Review, 100,* 204–232.

Buss, David, & Shackelford, Todd. (1997a). From vigilance to violence: Mate retention tactics in married couples. *Journal of Personality and Social Psychology, 72,* 346–361.

Buss, David, & Shackelford, Todd. (1997b). Susceptibility to infidelity in the first year of marriage. *Journal of Research in Personality, 31,* 193–221.

Butterfield, Fox. (2002, May 19). A priest's two faces: Protector, predator. *New York Times.*

Buunk, Bram, et al. (1996). Sex differences in jealousy in evolutionary and cultural perspective: Tests from the Netherlands, Germany, and the United States. *Psychological Science, 7,* 359–363.

Buvat, Jacques, et al. (1990). Recent developments in the clinical assessment and diagnosis of erectile dysfunction. *Annual Review of Sex Research, 1,* 265–308.

Byard, Roger, Hucker, Stephen, & Hazelwood, Robert. (1993). Fatal and near-fatal autoerotic asphyxial episodes in women. *American Journal of Forensic Medicine and Pathology, 14,* 70–73.

Byers, E. Sandra. (1996). How well does the traditional sexual script explain sexual coercion? Review of a program of research. *Journal of Psychology and Human Sexuality, 8,* 7–25.

Byers, E. Sandra, & Demmons, Stephanie. (1999). Sexual satisfaction and sexual self-disclosure within dating relationships. *Journal of Sex Research, 36,* 180–189.

Byers, E. Sandra, Purdon, Christine, & Clark, David. (1998). Sexually intrusive thoughts of college students. *Journal of Sex Research, 35,* 359–369.

Byler, Ruth V. (1969). *Teach us what we want to know.* New York: Mental Health Materials Center (for the Connecticut State Board of Education).

Byne, William, et al. (2000). The interstitial nuclei of the human anterior hypothalamus: Assessment for sexual variation in volume and neuronal size, density, and number. *Brain Research, 856,* 254–258.

Byrne, Donn. (1971). *The attraction paradigm.* New York: Academic.

Byrne, Donn. (1983). Sex without contraception. In D. Byrne & W. A. Fisher (Eds.), *Adolescents, sex, and contraception.* Hillsdale, NJ: Lawrence Erlbaum.

Byrne, Donn. (1997). An overview (and underview) of research and theory within the attraction paradigm. *Journal of Social and Personal Relationships, 14,* 417–431.

Byrne, Donn, Ervin, C. E., & Lamberth, J. (1970). Continuity between the experimental study of attraction and real-life computer dating. *Journal of Personality and Social Psychology, 16,* 157–165.

Cado, Suzanne, & Leitenberg, Harold. (1990). Guilt reactions to sexual fantasies during intercourse. *Archives of Sexual Behavior, 19,* 49–64.

Cahill, Larry. (2005). His brain, her brain. *Scientific American, 292* (5), 40–47.

Cahill, Lisa Sowle. (1985). The "seamless garment": Life in its beginnings. *Theological Studies, 46,* 64–80.

Calderwood, Deryck. (1987, May). The male rape victim. *Medical Aspects of Human Sexuality,* 53–55.

Call, Vaughn, Sprecher, Susan, & Schwartz, Pepper. (1995). The incidence and frequency of marital sex in a national sample. *Journal of Marriage and the Family, 57,* 639–652.

Callahan, Daniel. (1986, February). How technology is reframing the abortion debate. *Hastings Center Report,* 33–42.

Callan, Joanne E. (2001). Gender development: Psychoanalytic perspectives. In J. Worell, (Ed.), *Encyclopedia of women and gender* (pp. 523–535). San Diego, CA: Aca-demic Press.

Campbell, Rebecca, Sefl, Tracy, & Ahrens, Courtney E. (2004). The impact of rape on women's sexual health risk behaviors. *Health Psychology, 23,* 67–74.

Canary, Daniel J., & Dindia, Kathryn (Eds.). (1998). *Sex differences and similarities in communication.* Mahwah, NJ: Erlbaum.

Canary, Daniel J., & Hause, Kimberley S. (1993). Is there any reason to research sex differences in communication? *Communication Quarterly, 41,* 129–144.

Cantor, James M., Blanchard, R., Robichaud, L., & Christensen, B. (2005). Quantitative reanalysis of aggregate data on IQ in sexual offenders. *Psychological Bulletin, 131,* 555–568.

Cantor, James M., et al. (2002). How many gay men owe their sexual orientation to fraternal birth order? *Archives of Sexual Behavior, 31,* 63–72.

Caplan, Paula. (1995). *How do they decide who is normal?* Reading, MA: Addison-Wesley.

Carani, Cesare, et al. (1990). Effects of androgen treatment in impotent men with normal and low levels of free testosterone. *Archives of Sexual Behavior, 19,* 223–234.

Carnes, Patrick. (1983). *The sexual addiction.* Minneapolis: Comp-Care Publications.

Carpenter, Laura M. (2001). The ambiguity of "having sex": The subjective experience of virginity loss in the United States. *Journal of Sex Research, 38,* 127–139.

Carpentier, Melissa Y., Silovsky, Jane, & Chaffin, Mark. (2006). Randomized trial of treatment for children with sexual behavior problems: Ten-year follow-up. *Journal of Consulting and Clinical Psychology, 74,* 482–488.

Carroll, Janell, Volk, K., & Hyde, J. S. (1985). Differences between males and females in motives for engaging in sexual intercourse. *Archives of Sexual Behavior, 14,* 131–139.

Carroll, Marjorie H., & Clark, M. Diane. (2006). Men's acquaintance rape scripts; A comparison between a regional university and a military academy. *Sex Roles, 55,* 469–480.

Carson, Culley C., et al. (2002). Prevalence and correlates of erectile dysfunction in a United States nationwide population-based sample: Phase I results. *Journal of Urology, 167,* S29–30.

Carter, C. Sue. (1992). Hormonal influences on human sexual behavior. In J. B. Becker et al. (Eds.), *Behavioral endocrinology* (pp. 131–142). Cambridge, MA: MIT Press.

Carver, Priscilla, Egan, Susan, & Perry, David. (2004). Children who question their heterosexuality. *Developmental Psychology, 40,* 43–53.

Casimiro, D. R., et al. (2003). Vaccine-induced immunity in baboons by using DNA and replication-incompetent adenovirus type 5 vectors expressing a human immuno-deficiency virus type 1 gag gene. *Journal of Virology, 77,* 7663–7668.

Cass, Vivienne C. (1979). Homosexual identity formation: A theoretical model. *Journal of Homosexuality, 4,* 219–235.

Castaneda, Donna. (1993). The meaning of romantic love among Mexican-Americans. *Journal of Social Behavior and Personality, 8,* 257–272.

Castellsagué, Xavier, et al. (2002). Male circumcision, penile human papillomavirus infection, and cervical cancer in female partners. *New England Journal of Medicine, 346,* 1105–1112.

Catania, J. A., et al. (2001). National trends in condom use among at-risk heterosexuals in the United States. *Journal of Acquired Immune Deficiency Syndrome, 27,* 176–182.

Catania, Joseph A., et al. (1990). Response bias in assessing sexual behaviors relevant to HIV transmission. *Evaluation and Program Planning, 13,* 19–29.

Catania, Joseph A., et al. (1995). Methodological research on sexual behavior in the AIDS era. *Annual Review of Sex Research, 6,* 77–125.

Cates, Willard. (2001). The NIH condom report: The glass is 90% full. *Family Planning Perspectives, 33,* 231–233.

Caughey, Madeline S. (1974). The principle of harm and its application to laws criminalizing prostitution. *Denver Law Journal, 51,* 235–262.

Cave, Damien. (2006, November 7). New York plans to make gender personal choice. *New York Times.*

Centers for Disease Control and Prevention. (1997). Abortion surveillance: Preliminary analysis—United States, 1995. *Morbidity and Mortality Weekly Report, 46,* 1133–1137.

Centers for Disease Control and Prevention. (2000a). HIV/AIDS surveillance, 1999.

Centers for Disease Control and Prevention. (2000b). Youth risk behavior surveillance—United States, 1999. *Morbidity and Mortality Weekly Report, 49,* SS-5.

Centers for Disease Control and Prevention. (2001). *Tracking the hidden epidemics: Trends in STDs in the United States, 2000.* Atlanta: CDC. www.cdc.gov/nchstp/dstd.

Centers for Disease Control and Prevention. (2002). Alcohol use and pregnancy: Fact sheet. www.cdc.gov/ncbddd/factsheets/alcoholuse.pdf.

Centers for Disease Control and Prevention. (2003a). STD surveillance 2002. www.cdc.gov/std.

Centers for Disease Control and Prevention. (2003b). Surveillance and epidemiology, AIDS surveillance (Table 53). Health, United States. Centers for Disease Control and Prevention.

Centers for Disease Control and Prevention. (2003c). Abortion surveillance—United States, 2000. *Morbidity and Mortality Weekly Report, 52* (SS12), 1–32.

Centers for Disease Control and Prevention. (2004a). Sexual violence: Fact sheet. Retrieved June 1, 2004, from www.cdc.gov/ncipc/factsheets/svfacts.htm.

Centers for Disease Control and Prevention. (2004b). Intimate partner violence: Fact sheet. Retrieved June 1, 2004, from www.cdc.gov/ncipc/factsheets/ipvfacts.htm.

Centers for Disease Control. (2006a). Abortion surveillance—United States, 2003. *Morbidity and Mortality Weekly Report, 55,* SS-11.

Centers for Disease Control. (2006b). *Morbidity and Mortality Weekly Report, 55,* 722–740.

Centers for Disease Control. (2006c). *Sexually transmitted disease surveillance 2005.* Atlanta: CDC. www.cdc.gov/std/.

Centers for Disease Control. (2006d). *A glance at the HIV/AIDS epidemic.* http://www.cdc.gov/hiv.

Centers for Disease Control and Prevention. (2007). Cases of HIV infection and AIDS in the United States and depen-dent areas, 2005. *HIV/AIDS Surveillance Report, 17,* Table 5a.

Chalker, Rebecca. (1995, November/December). Sexual pleasure unscripted. *Ms,* 49–52.

Chan, Connie S. (1995). Issues of sexual identity in an ethnic minority: The case of Chinese American lesbians, gay men, and bisexual people. In A. R. D'Augelli & C. J. Patterson (Eds.), *Lesbian, gay, and bisexual identities over the lifespan* (pp. 87–101). New York: Oxford University Press.

Chapman, Audrey. (1997). The Black search for love and devotion: Facing the future against all odds. In H. P. McAdoo (Ed.), *Black families* (3rd ed.). Thousand Oaks, CA: Sage.

Chapman, Heather, Hobfoll, Stevan, & Ritter, Christian. (1997). Partners' stress underestimations lead to women's distress: A study of pregnant inner-city women. *Journal of Personality and Social Psychology, 73,* 418–425.

Charon, Joel. (1995). *Symbolic interactionism: An introduction, interpretation, and integration* (5th ed). Englewood Cliffs, NJ: Prentice-Hall.

Check, Erika. (2005). Trial aims to measure social effects of choosing babies' sex. *Nature, 437,* 1214–1215.

Chen, C. L., et al. (2002). Hormone replacement therapy in relation to breast cancer. *Journal of the American Medical Association, 287,* 734–741.

Cheng, Jeani, et al. (2003, February 21). Pregnancy-related mortality surveillance—United States, 1991–1999. *Morbidity and Mortality Weekly Report, 52,* 1–8.

Cheng, Mariah M., & Udry, J. Richard. (2003). How much do mentally disabled adolescents know about sex and birth control? *Adolescent and Family Health, 3,* 28–38.

Cherry, Kittredge, & Mitulski, James. (1988). We are the church alive, the church with AIDS. *Christian Century, 105,* 85–88.

Cherukuri, R., et al. (1988). A cohort study of alkaloidal cocaine ("crack") in pregnancy. *Obstetrics and Gynecology, 72,* 147–151.

Chesler, Ellen. (1992). *Woman of valor: Margaret Sanger and the birth control movement.* New York: Simon & Schuster.

Chivers, Meredith L., et al. (2004). A sex difference in the specificity of sexual arousal. *Psychological Science, 15,* 736–744.

Chivers, Meredith, & Bailey, J. M. (2000). Sexual orientation of female-to-male transsexuals: A comparison of homosexual and nonhomosexual types. *Archives of Sexual Behavior, 29,* 259–278.

Choi, E. J., et al. (2001). Low-density DNA array-coupled to PCR differential display identifies new estrogen-responsive genes during the postnatal differentiation of the rat hypothalamus. *Molecular Brain Research, 97,* 115–128.

Chow, J. M., et al. (1990). The association between chlamydia trachomatis and ectopic pregnancy: A matched-pair, case-control study. *Journal of the American Medical Association, 263,* 3164.

Chow, Yung-Kang, et al. (1993). Use of evolutionary limitations of HIV-1 multidrug resistance to optimize therapy. *Nature, 361,* 650–654.

Chrisler, Joan C., et al. (2006). The PMS illusion: Social cognition maintains social construction. *Sex Roles, 54,* 371–376.

Christensen, Cornelia V. (1971). *Kinsey: A biography.* Bloomington: Indiana University Press.

Christopher, F. Scott, & Sprecher, Susan. (2000). Sexuality in marriage, dating, and other relationships: A decade review. *Journal of Marriage and the Family, 62,* 999–1017.

Chu, James A., et al. (1999). Memories of childhood abuse: Dissociation amnesia, and corroboration. *American Journal of Psychiatry, 156,* 749–755.

Chumlea, William C., et al. (2003). Age at menarche and racial comparison in US girls. *Pediatrics, 111,* 110–113.

Church, Stephanie, et al. (2001). Violence by clients towards female prostitutes in different work settings: Questionnaire survey. *British Medical Journal, 322,* 524–525.

Cimbalo, R. S., Faling, B., & Mousaw, P. (1976). The course of love: A cross-sectional design. *Psychological Reports, 38,* 1292–1294.

Clark, Jacquelyn L., Taum, Nancy O., & Noble, Sara L. (1995). Management of genital herpes. *American Family Physician, 51,* 175–182.

Clark, Jocalyn. (2003). Furor erupts over NIH "hit list." *British Medical Journal, 327,* 1065.

Clemente, Carmine D. (1987). *Anatomy: A regional atlas of the human body* (3rd ed.). Baltimore: Urban & Schwarzenberg.

Cocchi, Fiorenzo, et al. (1995). Identification of RANTES, MIP-1a, and MIP-1b as the major HIV-suppressive factors produced by $CD8^+$ T cells. *Science, 270,* 1811–1815.

Cochran, Susan D., & Peplau, L. Anne. (1985). Value orientations in heterosexual relationships. *Psychology of Women Quarterly, 9,* 477–488.

Cochran, Susan, Sullivan, J. G., & Mays, V. (2003). Prevalence of mental disorders, psychological distress, and mental health services use among lesbian, gay, and bisexual adults in the United States. *Journal of Consulting and Clinical Psychology, 71,* 53–61.

Cochran, W. G., Mosteller, F., & Tukey, J. W. (1953). Statistical problems of the Kinsey report. *Journal of the American Statistical Association, 48,* 673–716.

Cogan, Jeanine C. (1996). The prevention of anti-lesbian/gay hate crimes through social change and empowerment. In E. Rothblum & L. A. Bond (Eds.), *Preventing heterosexism and homophobia* (pp. 219–238). Thousand Oaks, CA: Sage.

Cogan, Jeanine C., & Marcus-Newhall, Amy. (2002). Hate crimes: Research, policy, and action. *American Behavioral Scientist, 45* (12), special issue.

Cohen, I., et al. (1990). Improved pregnancy outcome following successful treatment of chlamydial infection. *Journal of the American Medical Association, 263*, 3160.

Cohen, Jon. (1997). Exploiting the HIV-chemokine nexus. *Science, 275*, 1261–1264.

Cohen, Jon. (1998). Exploring how to get at—and eradicate—hidden HIV. *Science, 279*, 1854–1855.

Cohen, Jon. (2001). AIDS vaccines show promise after years of frustration. *Science, 291*, 1686–1688.

Cohen, Jon. (2002). Confronting the limits of success. *Science, 296*, 2320–2326.

Cohen, Jon. (2003). Thailand and Cambodia: Two hard-hit countries offer rare success stories. *Science, 301*, 1658–1663.

Cohen, Kenneth M. (2002). Relationships among childhood sex-atypical behavior, spatial ability, handedness, and sexual orientation in men. *Archives of Sexual Behavior, 31*, 129–144.

Cohen, Sherrill, & Taub, Nadine. (1989). *Reproductive laws for the 1990s.* Clifton, NJ: Humana Press.

Cohen, Susan. (2005). Ominous convergence: Sex trafficking, prostitution, and international family planning. *The Guttmacher Report of Family Planning,* February, 12–14.

Cohen-Kettenis, Peggy T. (2005). Gender change in 46, XY persons with 5α-reductase-2 deficiency and 17β-hydroxysteroid dehydrogenase-3 deficiency. *Archives of Sexual Behavior, 34*, 399–410.

Cohn, Lawrence. (1983, November 16). Pix less able but porn is stable. *Variety, 313* (3), 1–2.

Cole, Elizabeth R., & Zucker, Alyssa N. (2007). Black and white women's perspectives on femininity. *Cultural Diversity and Ethnic Minority Psychology, 13*, 1–9.

Cole, Laurence, Khantian, S., Sutton, J., Davies, S., & Rayburn, W. (2004). Accuracy of home pregnancy tests at the time of missed menses. *American Journal of Obstetrics and Gynecology, 190*, 100–105.

Cole, Steve W., et al. (1996). Elevated physical health risk among gay men who conceal their homosexual identity. *Health Psychology, 15*, 243–251.

Cole, Theodore M., & Cole, S. (1978). The handicapped and sexual health. In A. Comfort (Ed.), *Sexual consequences of disability.* Philadelphia: G. F. Stickley.

Coleman, Eli. (1982). Developmental stages of the coming-out process. In W. Paul et al. (Eds.), *Homosexuality: Social, psychological, and biological issues.* Beverly Hills, CA: Sage.

Coleman, Eli. (1991). Compulsive sexual behavior: New concepts and treatments. *Journal of Psychology and Human Sexuality, 4* (2), 37–51.

Coleman, Eli, et al. (2001). Compulsive Sexual Behavior Inventory: A preliminary study of reliability and validity. *Journal of Sex and Marital Therapy, 27*, 325–332.

Coley, Rebekah & Chase-Lansdale, P. Lindsay. (1998). Adolescent pregnancy and parenthood: Recent evidence and future directions. *American Psychologist, 53*, 152–166.

Collaborative Group on Hormonal Factors in Breast Cancer. (2002). Breast cancer and breast-feeding. *Lancet, 360*, 187–195.

Collaer, Marcia L., & Hines, Melissa. (1995). Human behavioral sex differences: A role for gonadal hormones during early development? *Psychological Bulletin, 118*, 55–107.

Collins, James. (1997, July 7). Throwing away the key. *Time,* p. 29.

Collins, Nancy L., & Miller, Lynn C. (1994). Self-disclosure and liking: A meta-analytic review. *Psychological Bulletin, 116*, 457–475.

Collins, R. L., et al. (2004). Watching sex on television predicts adolescent initiation of sexual behavior. *Pediatrics, 114*, e280–e289.

Collins, Rebecca L., et al. (2005). Isolating the nexus of substance use, violence and sexual risk for HIV infection among young adults in the United States. *AIDS and Behavior, 9*, 73–87.

Comas-Diaz, Lillian. (1987). Feminist therapy with mainland Puerto Rican women. *Psychology of Women Quarterly, 11*, 461–474.

COMET (Comparative Obstetric Mobile Epidural Trial) Study Group. (2001). Effect of low-dose mobile versus traditional epidural techniques on mode of delivery: A randomised controlled trial. *Lancet, 358*, 19–23.

Comfort, Alex. (1991). *The new joy of sex: A gourmet guide to lovemaking for the nineties.* New York: Crown.

Committee on Children with Disabilities. (1996). Sexuality education of children and adolescents with developmental disabilities. *Pediatrics, 97*, 275–278.

Compas, Bruce E., & Luecken, Linda. (2002). Psychological adjustment to breast cancer. *Current Directions in Psychological Science, 11*, 111–114.

Comstock, George. (1991). *Television and one American child.* San Diego, CA: Academic Press.

Congregation for the Doctrine of the Faith. (1986). The pastoral care of homosexual persons. *Origins, 26*, 378–382.

Congregation for the Doctrine of the Faith. (1987). Instruction on respect for human life in its origin and on the dignity of procreation. *Origins, 16*, 198–211.

Connolly, Jennifer, et al. (2004). Mixed-gender groups, dating, and romantic relationships in early adolescence. *Journal of Research on Adolescence, 14*, 185–207.

Consolacion, Theodora, Russell, Stephen T., & Sue, Stanley. (2004). Sex, race/ethnicity, and romantic attractions: Multiple minority status adolescents and mental health. *Cultural Diversity & Ethnic Minority Psychology, 10*, 200–214.

Consumer Reports Staff. (1995, May). How reliable are condoms? *Consumer Reports,* 320–324.

Consumer Reports Staff. (1999, June). Condoms get better. *Consumer Reports.*

Contessini, Claudia. (2003). Personal communication.

Cook, Karen, & Rice, Eric. (2004). Social exchange theory. In J. DeLamater (Ed.), *The handbook of social psychology* (pp. 53–76). New York: Kluwer-Plenum.

Coombs, N. R. (1974). Male prostitution: A psychosocial view of behavior. *American Journal of Orthopsychiatry, 44*, 782.

Cooper, Al, Delmonico, David, & Burg, Ron. (2000). Cybersex users, abusers and compulsives: New findings and implications. *Sexual Addiction and Compulsivity, 7*, 5–29.

Cooper, Al, et al. (1999). Sexuality on the Internet: From sexual exploration to pathological expression. *Professional Psychology Research and Practice, 30*, 154–164.

Cooper, M. Lynne. (2006). Does drinking promote risky sexual behavior? *Current Directions in Psychological Science, 15*, 19–23.

Cordova, Matthew J., et al. (2001). Posttraumatic growth following breast cancer: A controlled comparison study. *Health Psychology, 20*, 176–185.

Corey, Lawrence. (1990). Genital herpes. In K. Holmes et al. (Eds.), *Sexually transmitted diseases* (pp. 391–414). New York: McGraw-Hill.

Corey, Lawrence, & Wald, Anna. (1999). Genital herpes. In K. Holmes et al. (Eds.), *Sexually transmitted diseases* (3rd ed.). New York: McGraw-Hill.

Corey, Lawrence, et al. (2004). Once-daily valacyclovir to reduce the risk of transmission of genital herpes. *New England Journal of Medicine, 350*, 11–20.

Council on Scientific Affairs. (1995). Female genital mutilation. *Journal of the American Medical Association, 274*, 1714–1716.

Countryman, L. William. (1987). The AIDS crisis: Theological and ethical reflections. *Anglican Theological Review, 69*, 125–134.

Countryman, L. William. (1994). New Testament sexual ethics and today's world. In J. B. Nelson & S. P. Longfellow (Eds.), *Sexuality and the sacred* (pp. 28–53). Louisville, KY: Westminster/John Knox Press.

Coustan, Donald. (1995). Obstetric analgesia and anesthesia. In D. R. Coustan et al. (Eds.), *Human reproduction: Growth and development* (pp. 327–340). Boston: Little, Brown.

Coustan, Donald, & Angelini, Diane. (1995). The puerperium. In D. R. Coustan et al. (Eds.), *Human reproduction: Growth and development* (pp. 341–358). Boston: Little, Brown.

Couzin, Jennifer. (2003). The twists and turns in BRCA's path. *Science, 302*, 591–593.

Couzinet, Beatrice, et al. (1986). Termination of early pregnancy by the progesterone antagonist RU486 (mifepristone). *New England Journal of Medicine, 315*, 1565–1569.

Cowley, J. J., & Brooksbank, B. W. L. (1991). Human exposure to putative pheromones and changes in aspects of social behavior. *Journal of Steroid Biochemistry and Molecular Biology, 39,* 647–659.

Cox, Daniel J. (1988). Incidence and nature of male genital exposure behavior as reported by college women. *Journal of Sex Research, 24,* 227–234.

Coxon, Anthony P. M. (1996). *Between the sheets: Sexual diaries and gay men's sex in the era of AIDS.* London: Cassell.

Coyle, Catherine T., & Enright, Robert D. (1997). Forgiveness intervention with postabortion men. *Journal of Consulting and Clinical Psychology, 65,* 1042–1046.

Coyne, Jerry A., & Berry, Andrew. (2000). Rape as an adaptation. *Nature, 404,* 121–122.

Crawford, June, Kippax, Susan, & Waldby, Catherine. (1994). Women's sex talk and men's sex talk: Different worlds. *Feminism and Psychology, 4,* 571–587.

Crawford, Mary, & Popp, Danielle. (2003). Sexual double standards: A review and methodological critique of two decades of research. *Journal of Sex Research, 40,* 13–26.

Creighton, James. (1992). *Don't go away mad.* New York: Doubleday.

Creighton, Sarah, & Minto, Catherine. (2001). Managing intersex: Most vaginal surgery in childhood should be deferred. *British Medical Journal, 323,* 1264–1265.

Creighton, Sarah M., Minto, C., & Steele, S. (2001). Objective cosmetic and anatomical outcomes at adolescence of feminising surgery for ambiguous genitalia done in childhood. *Lancet, 358,* 124–125.

Crenshaw, Theresa L., & Goldberg, James P. (1996). *Sexual pharmacology: Drugs that affect sexual function.* New York: Norton.

Crompton, Louis. (2003). *Homosexuality and civilization.* Cambridge, MA: Harvard University Press.

Cruess, Stacy, et al. (2002). Changes in mood and depressive symptoms and related change processes during cognitive-behavioral stress management in HIV-infected men. *Cognitive Therapy and Research, 26,* 373–392.

Cunningham, F. Gary, et al. (1993). *Williams obstetrics* (19th ed.). Norwalk, CT: Appleton and Lange.

Cunningham, F. Gary, MacDonald, Paul C., & Gant, Norman F. (1989). *Williams obstetrics* (18th ed.). Norwalk, CT: Appleton and Lange.

Cunningham, M. R., Barbee, A. P., & Druen, P. B. (1996). Social allergens and the reactions that they produce: Escalation of annoyance and disgust in love and work. In R. M. Kowalski (Ed.), *Aversive interpersonal behaviors* (pp. 189–214). New York: Plenum.

Cunningham, Michael, et al. (1995). "Their ideas of beauty are, on the whole, the same as ours": Consistency and variability in the cross-cultural perception of female physical attractiveness. *Journal of Personality and Social Psychology, 68,* 261–279.

Cunningham, Paige. (nd). Embryo adoption or embryo donation? The distinction and its implications. Center for Bioethics and Human Dignity. www.cbhd.org.

Curran, Charles E. (1988). Roman Catholic sexual ethics: A dissenting view. *Christian Century, 105,* 1139–1142.

Curtis, J. T., & Wang, Z. X. (2003). The neurochemistry of pair bonding. *Current Directions in Psychological Science, 12,* 49–53.

Cutler, Winnifred B. (1999). Human sex-attractant hormones. *Psychiatric Annals, 29,* 54–59.

Cyberatlas. (2004). Top searches of 2003. Retrieved January 25, 2004, from http://cyberatlas.internet.com.

D'Augelli, Anthony R. (1992). Lesbian and gay male undergraduates' experiences of harassment and fear on campus. *Journal of Interpersonal Violence, 7,* 383–395.

D'Augelli, Anthony R., & Garnets, Linda D. (1995). Lesbian, gay, and bisexual communities. In A. D'Augelli & C. Patterson (Eds.), *Lesbian, gay, and bisexual identities over the lifespan* (pp. 293–320). New York: Oxford University Press.

D'Augelli, Anthony R., Grossman, Arnold H., & Starks, Michael T. (2006). Childhood gender atypicality, victimization, and PTSD among lesbian, gay, and bisexual youth. *Journal of Interpersonal Violence, 21,* 1462–1482.

Dailard, Cynthia. (2006a). The public health promise and potential pitfalls of the world's first cervical cancer vaccine. *Guttmacher Policy Review, 9* (1), 6–9.

Dailard, Cynthia. (2006b). The cervical cancer vaccine; Coming soon to a doctor's office near you. *Guttmacher Policy Review, 9* (3), 18.

Dalton, Harlon. (1993). Communal law. In S. Burris, H. L. Dalton, & J. L. Miller (Eds.), *AIDS law today* (pp. 242–262). New Haven, CT: Yale University Press.

Dalton, Harlon L., & Burris, Scott (Eds.). (1987). *AIDS and the law: A guide for the public.* New Haven, CT: Yale University Press.

Damgaard, Ida, Jensen, T., the Nordic Cryptorchidism Study Group, et al. (2006). Cryptorchidism and maternal alcohol consumption during pregnancy. *Environmental Health Perspectives,* doi:10.1289/ehp.9608 (available at http://dx.doi.org/).

Daneback, Kristian, Cooper, A., & Månsson, S. (2005). An Internet study of cybersex participants. *Archives of Sexual Behavior, 34,* 321–329.

Daneback, Kristian, Cooper, Al, & Mansson, Sven-Axel. (2004). *An investigation of cybersex: Who participates, reasons that they do, and resulting consequences.* Unpublished manuscript.

Dansky, B. S., & Kilpatrick, D. G. (1997). Effects of sexual harassment. In W. O'Donohue (Ed.), *Sexual harassment: Theory, research, and treatment* (pp. 151–174). Boston: Allyn & Bacon.

Darling, Carol A., Davidson, J. K., & Conway-Welch, C. (1990). Female ejaculation: Perceived origins, the Gräfenberg spot/area, and sexual responsiveness. *Archives of Sexual Behavior, 19,* 29–48.

Darling, Carol A., Davidson, J. Kenneth, & Jennings, Donna A. (1991). The female sexual response revisited: Understanding the multiorgasmic experience in women. *Archives of Sexual Behavior, 20,* 527–540.

Darroch, Jacqueline, et al. (2001). Differences in teenage pregnancy rates among five developed countries: The role of sexual activity and contraceptive use. *Family Planning Perspectives, 2001, 33,* 244–250, 281.

Darroch, Jacqueline, Landry, David, & Singh, Susheela. (2000). Changing emphases in sexuality education in U.S. public secondary schools. *Family Planning Perspectives, 32,* 204–211, 265.

Davey, Monica. (2003a, August 4). Episcopalians give first nod for gay bishop. *New York Times.*

Davey, Monica. (2003b, August 7). Episcopal leaders reject proposal for same-sex union liturgy. *New York Times.*

Davey, Monica, & Goodnough, Abby (2007, March 4). Doubts rise as states hold sex offender after prison. *New York Times.*

David, Henry P., Dytrych, Zdenek, & Matejcek, Zdenek. (2003). Born unwanted: Observations from the Prague study. *American Psychologist, 58,* 224–229.

Davidson, J. Kenneth, & Darling, Carol A. (1988). The stereotype of single women revisited: Sexual practices and sexual satisfaction among professional women. *Health Care for Women International, 9,* 317–336.

Davies, Michelle. (2004). Correlates of negative attitudes toward gay men: Sexism, male role norms, and male sexuality. *Journal of Sex Research, 41,* 259–266.

Davis, Anne R., & Castaño, Paula M. (2004). Oral contraceptives and libido in women. *Annual Review of Sex Research, 15,* 297–320.

Davis, Clive M., & Bauserman, R. (1993). Exposure to sexually explicit materials: An attitude change perspective. *Annual Review of Sex Research, 4,* 121–210.

Davis, J. A., & Smith, T. (1991). *General social surveys, 1972–1991.* Storrs: University of Connecticut, Roper Center for Public Opinion Research.

Davis, Karen R., & Weller, Susan C. (1999). The effectiveness of condoms in reducing heterosexual transmission of HIV. *Family Planning Perspectives, 31* (6), 272–279.

Davis, Susan R., et al. (2005). Circulating androgen levels and self-reported sexual function in women. *Journal of the American Medical Association, 294,* 91–96.

Day, Nancy L., & Richardson, Gale. (1994). Comparative teratogenicity of alcohol and other drugs. *Alcohol Health and Research World, 18,* 42–48.

Day, Randal. (1992). The transition to first intercourse among racially and culturally diverse youth. *Journal of Marriage and the Family, 54,* 749–762.

De Cuypere, Griet, et al. (2005). Sexual and physical health after sex reassignment surgery. *Archives of Sexual Behavior, 34,* 679–690.

de Gaston, Jacqueline F., et al. (1994). Teacher philosophy and program implementation and the impact of sex education outcomes. *Journal of Research and Development in Education, 27,* 265–270.

De Graaf, Ron, et al. (2006). Suicidality and sexual orientation: Differences between men and women in a general population-based sample from the Netherlands. *Archives of Sexual Behavior, 35,* 253–262.

de Waal, Frans. (2002). Evolutionary psychology: The wheat and the chaff. *Current Directions in Psychological Science, 11,* 187–191.

Dean, Karol E., & Malamuth, Neil M. (1997). Characteristics of men who aggress sexually and of men who imagine aggressing: Risk and moderating variables. *Journal of Personality and Social Psychology, 72,* 449–455.

DeArmond, Sarah, et al. (2006). Age and gender stereotypes: New challenges in a changing workplace and workforce. *Journal of Applied Social Psychology, 36,* 2184–2214.

Declercq, E., Menacker, F., & Macdorman, M. (2006). Maternal risk profiles and primary cesarean rate in the United States, 1991–2002. *American Journal of Public Health, 96* (5), 867–872.

DeLamater, John. (1987). A sociological perspective. In J. H. Geer & W. T. O'Donohue (Eds.), *Theories of human sexuality* (pp. 237–256). New York: Plenum.

DeLamater, John. (2003). Discussion paper. In John Bancroft (Ed.), *Sexual development* (pp. 186–191). Bloomington, Indiana University Press.

DeLamater, John, & MacCorquodale, Patricia. (1979). *Premarital sexuality: Attitudes, relationships, behavior.* Madison: University of Wisconsin Press.

DeLamater, John, & Moorman, Sava. (2007). Sexual behavior in later life. *Journal of Aging and Health, 19,* in press.

DeLamater, John, Wagstaff, David A., & Havens, Kayt Klein. (2000). The impact of a culturally appropriate STD/AIDS education intervention on Black male adolescents' sexual and condom use behavior. *Health Education and Behavior, 27,* 454–470.

Delemarre-van de Waal, Henriette, & Cohen-Kettenis, Peggy. (2006). Clinical management of gender identity disorder in adolescents: A protocol on psychological and paediatric endocrinology aspects. *European Journal of Endocrinology, 155,* S131–S137.

Deligeoroglou, E. (2000). Dysmenorrhea. *Annals of the New York Academy of Sciences, 900,* 237–244.

Delmas, Pierre D., et al. (1997). Effects of raloxifene on bone mineral density, serum cholesterol concentrations, and uterine endometrium in postmenopausal women. *New England Journal of Medicine, 337,* 1641–1647.

Denizet-Lewis, Benoit. (2003, August 3). Double lives on the down low. *New York Times Magazine.*

Denizet-Lewis, Benoit. (2004, May 30). Friends, friends with benefits, and the benefits of the local mall. *New York Times Magazine,* 30–35ff.

Dennerstein, Lorraine, Alexander, Jeanne L., & Kotz, Krista. (2003). The menopause and sexual functioning: A review of the population-based studies. *Annual Review of Sex Research, 14,* 64–82.

Dennis, Cindy-Lee. (2005). Psychosocial and psychological interventions for prevention of post-natal depression: Systematic review. *British Medical Journal, 331,* 15.

Dennis, Donna. (1993). HIV screening and discrimination: The federal example. In S. Burris, H. L. Dalton, & J. L. Miller (Eds.), *AIDS law today* (pp. 187–215). New Haven, CT: Yale University Press.

Derby, C., et al. (2000). Modifiable risk factors and erectile dysfunction: Can lifestyle changes modify risk? *Urology, 56,* 302–306.

Deren, Sherry, Tortu, Stephanie, & Davis, W. Rees. (1993). An AIDS risk reduction project with inner-city women. In C. Squire (Ed.), *Women and AIDS: Psychological perspectives* (pp. 73–89). London: Sage.

Derlega, Valerian J. (Ed.). (1984). *Communication, intimacy, and close relationships.* New York: Academic.

Dessens, Arianne, Slijper, F., & Drop, S. (2005). Gender dysphoria and gender change in chromosomal females with congenital adrenal hyperplasia. *Archives of Sexual Behavior, 34,* 289–298.

Devor, Holly. (1997). *FTM: Female-to-male transsexuals in society.* Bloomington: Indiana University Press.

Dew, P. C., Guillory, J., Okah, F. A., Cai, J., & Hoff, G. L. (2007). The effect of health compromising behaviors on preterm births. *Maternal and Child Health, 11,* 227–233.

Dialani, Vandana, & Levine, Deborah. (2004). Ectopic pregnancy: A review. *Ultrasound Quarterly, 20,* 105–117.

Diamond, Lisa M. (2003). Was it a phase? Young women's relinquishment of lesbian/bisexual identities over a 5-year period. *Journal of Personality and Social Psychology, 84,* 352–364.

Diamond, Lisa. (2003). What does sexual orientation orient? A biobehavioral model distinguishing romantic love and sexual desire. *Psychological Review, 110,* 173–192.

Diamond, Lisa M. (2005). A new view of lesbian subtypes: Stable versus fluid identity trajectories over an 8-year period. *Psychology of Women Quarterly, 29,* 119–128.

Diamond, Milton. (1996). Prenatal predisposition and the clinical management of some pediatric conditions. *Journal of Sex and Marital Therapy, 22,* 139–147.

Diamond, Milton. (1999). Pediatric management of ambiguous and traumatized genitalia. *Journal of Urology, 162,* 1021–1028.

Diamond, Milton, & Sigmundson, H. Keith. (1997). Sex reassignment at birth: Long-term review and clinical implications. *Archives of Pediatric and Adolescent Medicine, 151,* 298–304.

Dickinson, Robert L. (1949). *Atlas of human sex anatomy.* Baltimore: Williams & Wilkins.

Dickson, N., Paul, C., & Herbison, P. (2003). Same-sex attraction in a birth cohort: Prevalence and persistence in early adulthood. *Social Science & Medicine, 56,* 1607–1615.

Dieben, Thom, Roumen, Frans, & Apter, Dan. (2002). Efficacy, cycle control, and user acceptability of a novel combined contraceptive vaginal ring. *Obstetrics and Gynecology, 100,* 585–593.

Dill, Karen E., et al. (2005). Violence, sex, race, and age in popular video games: A content analysis. In E. Cole & J. H. Daniel (Eds.), *Featuring females: Feminist analyses of media* (pp. 1115–1130). Washington, DC: American Psychological Association.

Dindia, Kathryn, & Allen, Michael. (1992). Sex differences in self-disclosure: A meta-analysis. *Psychological Bulletin, 112,* 106–124.

Dindia, Kathryn, & Canary, Daniel. (2006). *Sex differences and similarities in communication.* Mahwah, NJ: Lawrence Erlbaum Associates.

Dion, Karen K. (1973). Young children's stereotyping of facial attractiveness. *Developmental Psychology, 9,* 183–188.

Dion, Karen K., & Dion, Kenneth L. (1993b). Individualistic and collectivistic perspectives on gender and the cultural content of love and intimacy. *Journal of Social Issues, 49,* 53–69.

Dion, Kenneth. (1977). The incentive value of physical attractiveness for young children. *Personality and Social Psychology Bulletin, 3,* 67–70.

Dion, Kenneth L., & Dion, Karen K. (1993a). Gender and ethnocultural comparisons in styles of love. *Psychology of Women Quarterly, 17,* 463–474.

Dixson, Alan F. (1990). The neuroendocrine regulation of sexual behavior in female primates. *Annual Review of Sex Research, 1,* 197–226.

Docter, Richard F., & Prince, Virginia. (1997). Transvestism: A survey of 1032 cross-dressers. *Archives of Sexual Behavior, 26,* 589–606.

Dodge, Brian, Reece, M., Cole, S., & Sandfort, T. (2004). Sexual compulsivity among heterosexual college students. *Journal of Sex Research, 41,* 343–350.

Dodson, Betty. (1987). *Sex for one: The joy of self-loving.* New York: Harmony Books (Crown).

Dolance, Susannah. (2005). "A whole stadium full": Lesbian community at Women's National Basketball Association games. *Journal of Sex Research, 42,* 74–83.

Donahey, Karen M., & Carroll, Richard A. (1993). Gender differences in factors associated with hypoactive sexual desire. *Journal of Sex & Marital Therapy, 19,* 25–40.

Donahue, J. E., et al. (2000). Cells containing immunoreactive estrogen receptor-[alpha] in the human basal forebrain. *Brain Research, 856,* 142–151.

Donnelly, D. A. (1993). Sexually inactive marriages. *Journal of Sex Research, 30,* 171–179.

Donnelly, Denise, et al. (2001). Involuntary celibacy: A life course analysis. *Journal of Sex Research, 38,* 159–169.

Donnerstein, E., Linz, D., & Penrod, S. (1987). *The question of pornography: Research findings and policy implications.* New York: Free Press.

Donohoe, Martin. (2007). Parental notification and consent laws for teen abortion: Overview and 2006 ballot measures. *Medscape Ob/Gyn and Women's Health,* posted 02/09/2007.

Donovan, Basil, Bassett, I., & Bodsworth, N. J. (1994). Male circumcision and common sexually transmissible diseases in a developed nation setting. *Genitourinary Medicine, 70,* 317–320.

Doran, Terence A. (1990). Chorionic villus sampling as the primary diagnostic tool in prenatal diagnosis. *Journal of Reproductive Medicine, 35,* 935–940.

Dorris, Michael. (1989). *The broken cord.* New York: Harper & Row.

Doshi, Mary L. (1986). Accuracy of consumer performed in-home tests for early pregnancy detection. *American Journal of Public Health, 76,* 512–514.

Douglas, Mary. (1970). *Purity and danger: An analysis of concepts of pollution and taboo.* Baltimore: Penguin.

Downs, Barbara. (2003). *Fertility of American women: June 2002.* Washington, DC: U.S. Census Bureau, Current Population Reports, P20–548.

Doyle, James A. (1989). *The male experience* (2nd ed.). Dubuque, IA: Wm. C. Brown.

Drea, Christine, & Wallen, Kim. (2003). Female sexuality and the myth of male control. In Cheryl Travis (Ed.), *Evolution, gender, and rape* (pp. 29–60). Cambridge, MA: MIT Press.

Drey, Eleanor A., et al. (2006). Risk factors associated with presenting for abortion in the second trimester. *Obstetrics & Gynecology, 107,* 128–135.

Dreznick, Michael T. (2003). Heterosocial competence of rapists and child molesters: A meta-analysis. *Journal of Sex Research, 40,* 170–178.

Driscoll, R., Davis, K. E., & Lipetz, M. E. (1972). Parental interference and romantic love: The Romeo and Juliet effect. *Journal of Personality and Social Psychology, 24,* 1–10.

Dryer, P. Christopher, & Horowitz, Leonard. (1997). When do opposites attract? Interpersonal complementarity vs. similarity. *Journal of Personality and Social Psychology, 72,* 592–603.

Du Toit, Brian. (1994). Menstruation: Attitudes and experience of Indian South Africans. In B. M. du Toit (Ed.), *Human sexuality: Cross-cultural readings* (3rd ed., pp. 11–25). New York: McGraw-Hill.

Duncombe, J. A., & Marsden, D. (1994). *Whose orgasm is this anyway? "Sex work" and "emotion work" in long-term couple relationships.* Paper presented at American Sociological Association meetings. Los Angeles, CA.

Dunn, Marian E., & Trost, Jan E. (1989). Male multiple orgasms: A descriptive study. *Archives of Sexual Behavior, 18,* 377–388.

Dunne, E. F., et al. (2007). Prevalence of HPV infection among females in the United States. *Journal of the American Medical Association, 297,* 813–819.

Dutton, Donald G., & Aron, Arthur P. (1974). Some evidence for heightened sexual attraction under conditions of high anxiety. *Journal of Personality and Social Psychology, 30,* 470–517.

East, Patricia. (1998). Racial and ethnic differences in girls' sexual, marital, and birth expectations. *Journal of Marriage and the Family, 60,* 150–162.

Ebel, Charles. (1994). *Managing herpes: How to live and love with a chronic STD.* Research Triangle Park, NC: American Social Health Association.

Ebel, Charles, & Wald, Anna. (2002). *Managing herpes: How to live and love with a chronic STD.* Research Triangle Park, NC: American Social Health Association.

Eder, Donna, et al. (1995). *School talk: Gender and adolescent culture.* New Brunswick, NJ: Rutgers University Press.

Edwards, Weston M., & Coleman, Eli. (2004). Defining sexual health: A descriptive overview. *Archives of Sexual Behavior, 33,* 189–196.

Egan, Jennifer. (2000, December 10). Lonely gay teen seeking same. *New York Times Magazine.*

Ehrhardt, Anke. (1996). Sexual behavior among heterosexuals. In J. Mann & D. Tarantola (Eds.), *AIDS in the world II* (pp. 259–263). New York: Oxford University Press.

Ehrhardt, Anke A., Yingling, Sandra, & Warne, Patricia A. (1991). Sexual behavior in the era of AIDS: What has changed in the United States? *Annual Review of Sex Research, 2,* 25–48.

Eisenberg, M. E., Wagenaar, A., & Neumark-Sztainer, D. (1997). Viewpoints of Minnesota students on school-based sexuality education. *Journal of School Health, 67,* 322–326.

Elder, Glen. (1969). Appearance and education in marriage mobility. *American Sociological Review, 34,* 519–533.

Elias, James, & Gebhard, Paul. (1969). Sexuality and sexual learning in childhood. *Phi Delta Kappan, 50,* 401–405.

Elias, Marilyn. (1997, August 14). Modern matchmaking. *USA Today,* D1–D2.

Elliott, Ann N., & O'Donohue, William T. (1997). The effects of anxiety and distraction on sexual arousal in a nonclinical sample of heterosexual women. *Archives of Sexual Behavior, 26,* 607–624.

Ellis, Henry Havelock. (1939). *My life.* Boston: Houghton Mifflin.

Ellis, Lee. (1996). The role of perinatal factors in determining sexual orientation. In R. C. Savin-Williams & K. M. Cohen (Eds.), *The lives of lesbians, gays, and bisexuals* (pp. 35–70). Fort Worth: Harcourt Brace.

Ellis, Lee, & Cole-Harding, Shirley. (2001). The effects of prenatal stress, and of prenatal alcohol and nicotine exposure, on human sexual orientation. *Physiology and Behavior, 74,* 213–226.

Ellison, Michael. (1999, August 21). Atlanta police smash sex slave ring. *The Guardian.*

Emmers-Sommer, Tara, et al. (2004). A meta-analysis of the relationship between social skills and sexual offenders. *Communication Reports, 17,* 1–10.

Enserink, Martin. (2002). The vanishing promises of hormone replacement. *Science, 297,* 325–326.

Enserink, Martin. (2005). Let's talk about sex—and drugs. *Science, 308,* 1578–1580.

Episcopal Church. (1994). General Convention Statement on Childbirth and Abortion. Resolution 1994–A054. www.episcopalchurch.org.

Epstein, Aaron. (1995, October 8). Court joins gay rights debate. *Wisconsin State Journal,* pp. 1B ff.

Epting, L. Kimberly, & Overman, W. H. (1998). Sex-sensitive tasks in men and women: A search for performance fluctuations across the menstrual cycle. *Behavioral Neuroscience, 112,* 1304–1317.

Equal Employment Opportunity Commission. (1993). *Guidelines on discrimination because of sex.* 29 CFR 1604.11. Washington, DC: U.S. Government Printing Office.

Erikson, Erik H. (1950). *Childhood and society.* New York: Norton.

Erikson, Erik H. (1968). *Identity: Youth and crisis.* New York: Norton.

Ernst, Frederick A., et al. (1991). Condemnation of homosexuality in the Black community: A gender-specific phenomenon? *Archives of Sexual Behavior, 20,* 579–585.

Ernulf, Kurt E., & Innala, Sune M. (1995). Sexual bondage: A review and unobtrusive investigation. *Archives of Sexual Behavior, 24,* 631–654.

Eskanazi, B., et al. (2003). The association of age and semen quality in healthy men. *Human Reproduction, 18,* 447–454.

Espin, Oliva. (1987). Issues of identity in the psychology of Latina lesbians. In Boston Lesbian Psychologies Collective, *Lesbian psychologies.* Urbana: University of Illinois Press.

Esposito, Katherine et al. (2004). Effect of lifestyle changes on erectile dysfunction in obese men: A randomized controlled trial. *Journal of the American Medical Association, 291,* 2978–2984.

Esterberg, Kristin G. (1996). Gay cultures, gay communities: The social organization of lesbians, gay men, and bisexuals. In R. C. Savin-Williams & K. M. Cohen (Eds.), *The lives of lesbians, gays, and bisexuals* (pp. 377–392). Fort Worth: Harcourt Brace.

Evangelical Lutheran Church in America. (2003). *Journey together faithfully: The church and homosexuality.* Chicago: ELCA.

Evans, Donald, & Evans, Marilyn. (1996). Fertility, infertility and the human embryo: Ethics, law, and the practice of human artificial procreation. *Human Reproduction Update, 2,* 208–224.

Evans, Harriet. (1995). Defining differences: The "scientific" construction of sexuality and gender in the People's Republic of China. *Signs, 20,* 357–394.

Everett, Guy M. (1975). Amyl nitrate ("poppers") as an aphrodisiac. In M. Sandler & G. L. Gessa (Eds.), *Sexual behavior: Pharmacology and biochemistry.* New York: Raven.

Everitt, Barry J., & Bancroft, John. (1991). Of rats and men: The comparative approach to male sexuality. *Annual Review of Sex Research, 2,* 77–118.

Exton, M. S., et al. (1999). Cardiovascular and endocrine alterations after masturbation-induced orgasm in women. *Psychosomatic Medicine, 61,* 280–289.

Ezzell, Carol. (1994, October). Breast cancer genes. *Journal of NIH Research, 6,* 33–35.

Ezzell, Carol. (1995, April). Test may detect heritable breast-cancer mutations. *Journal of NIH Research, 7,* 42–44.

Ezzell, Carol. (1996, January). Emergence of the protease inhibitors: A better class of AIDS drugs? *Journal of NIH Research, 8,* 41–43.

Ezzell, Carol. (1996, May). Gene-therapy trial using BRCA1 to begin with ovarian cancer. *Journal of NIH Research, 8,* 24–25.

Fairchild, Halford H., Whitten, Lisa, & Richard, Harriette. (2003). Teaching African American psychology. In P. Bronstein & K. Quina (Eds.), *Teaching gender and multicultural awareness* (pp. 195–200). Washington, DC: American Psychological Association.

Fanburg, Jonathan Thomas, Kaplan, David, & Naylor, Kelly. (1995). Student opinion of condom distribution at a Denver, Colorado high school. *Journal of School Health, 65,* 181–185.

Farkas, G. M., Sine, L. G., & Evans, I. M. (1978). Personality, sexuality, and demographic differences between volunteers and nonvolunteers for a laboratory study of male sexual behavior. *Archives of Sexual Behavior, 7,* 513–520.

Farley, Margaret A. (1994). Sexual ethics. In J. B. Nelson & S. P. Longfellow (Eds.), *Sexuality and the sacred* (pp. 54–67). Louisville, KY: Westminster/John Knox Press.

Farris, Coreen, et al. (2006). Heterosocial perceptual organization: Application of the choice model to sexual coercion. *Psychological Science, 17,* 869–875.

Farvid, Pantea, & Braun, Virginia. (2006). "Most of us guys are raring to go anytime, anyplace, anywhere": Male and female sexuality in *Cleo* and *Cosmo. Sex Roles, 55,* 295–310.

Fasteau, Marc F. (1974). *The male machine.* New York: McGraw-Hill.

Faulkner, S. L. (2003). Good girl or flirt girl: Latinas' definitions of sex and sexual relationships. *Hispanic Journal of Behavioral Sciences, 25,* 174–200.

FBI. (2003). *Crime in the United States, 2002.* www.fbi.gov/ucr.

FBI. (2006). *Uniform crime reports: Crime in the United States, 2005.* www.fbi.gov.

Feder, H. H. (1984). Hormones and sexual behavior. *Annual Review of Psychology, 35,* 165–200.

Federman, Daniel D. (2006). The biology of human sex differences. *New England Journal of Medicine, 354,* 1507–1514.

Feeney, Judith. (1999). Adult romantic attachment and couple relationships. In J. Cassidy & P. R. Shaver (Eds.), *The handbook of attachment: Theory, research, and clinical applications* (pp. 355–377). New York: Guilford.

Feingold, Alan. (1988). Matching for attractiveness in romantic partners and same-sex friends: A meta-analysis and theoretical critique. *Psychological Bulletin, 104,* 226–235.

Feingold, Alan. (1990). Gender differences in effects of physical attractiveness on romantic attraction. *Journal of Personality and Social Psychology, 59,* 981–993.

Feinleib, Joel A., & Michael, Robert T. (2001). Reported changes in sexual behavior in response to AIDS in the United States. In E. O. Laumann & R. T. Michael (Eds.), *Sex, love, and health in America* (pp. 302–326). Chicago: University of Chicago Press.

Feldman-Summers, Shirley, & Pope, Kenneth S. (1994). The experience of "forgetting" childhood abuse: A national survey of psychologists. *Journal of Consulting and Clinical Psychology, 62,* 636–639.

Felton, Gary, & Segelman, Florrie. (1978). Lamaze childbirth training and changes in belief about person control. *Birth and the Family Journal, 5,* 141–150.

Feng, Y., et al. (1996). HIV-1 entry cofactor: Functional cDNA cloning of a seven-trans membrane G protein-coupled reception. *Science, 272,* 872.

Ferguson, Tara, et al. (2005). Variation in the application of the "promiscuous female" stereotype and the nature of the application domain: Influences on sexual harassment judgments after exposure to the *Jerry Springer Show. Sex Roles, 52,* 447–488.

Fields, Jessica, & Tolman, Deborah. (2006). Risky business: Sexuality education and research in U.S. schools. *Sexuality Research and Social Policy, 3,* 63–76.

Figueira, I., et al. (2001). Sexual dysfunction: A neglected complication of panic disorder and social phobia. *Archives of Sexual Behavior, 30,* 369–377.

Finer, Lawrence B., et al. (2005). Reasons U.S. Women have abortions: Quantitative and qualitative perspectives. *Perspectives on Sexual and Reproductive Health, 37,* 110–118.

Finer, Lawrence B., & Henshaw, Stanley K. (2003). Abortion incidence and services in the United States in 2000. *Perspectives on Sexual and Reproductive Health, 35,* 6–15.

Fingerhut, Adam W., Peplau, L. Anne, & Ghavami, Negin. (2005). A dual-identity framework for understanding lesbian experience. *Psychology of Women Quarterly, 29,* 129–139.

Fink, Howard, et al. (2002). Sildenafil for male erectile dysfunction: A systematic review and meta-analysis. *Archives of Internal Medicine, 162,* 1349–1360.

Finkelhor, David. (1980). Sex among siblings: A survey on prevalence, variety and effects. *Archives of Sexual Behavior, 9,* 171–194.

Finkelhor, David. (1984). *Child sexual abuse: New theory and research.* New York: Free Press.

Finkelhor, David, Mitchell, K., & Wolak, J. (2000). *Online victimization: A report on the nation's youth.* Washington, DC: National Center for Missing and Exploited Children.

Finkelhor, David, & Russell, D. (1984). Women as perpetrators: Review of the evidence. In D. Finkelhor (Ed.), *Child sexual abuse: New theory and research.* New York: Free Press.

Finzi, Diana, et al. (1997). Identification of a reservoir for HIV-1 in patients on highly active antiretroviral therapy. *Science, 278,* 1295–1300.

Fisher, Deborah, et al. (2004). *Youth and television: Examining sexual content across program genres.* Paper presented at Society for Research on Adolescence, Baltimore, March 2004.

Fisher, Helen. (1992). *Anatomy of love: The mysteries of mating, marriage and why we stray.* New York: Ballantine Books.

Fisher, Helen, Aron, Arthur, & Brown, Lucy. (2006). Romantic love: A mammalian brain system for mate choice. *Philosophical Transactions of the Royal Society, B, 361,* 2173–2186.

Fisher, Ian. (2006, January 26). Benedict's first encyclical shuns strictures of orthodoxy. *New York Times.*

Fisher, William A., Byrne, D., & White, L. A. (1983). Emotional barriers to contraception. In D. Byrne & W. A. Fisher (Eds.), *Adolescents, sex, and contraception.* Hillsdale, NJ: Lawrence Erlbaum.

Fisher, William A., et al. (1988). Erotophobia-erotophilia as a dimension of personality. *Journal of Sex Research, 25,* 123–151.

Fisher, William A., & Grenier, Guy. (1994). Violent pornography, antiwoman thoughts, and antiwoman acts: In search of reliable effects. *Journal of Sex Research, 31,* 23–38.

Fiske, Susan T., & Glick, Peter. (1995). Ambivalence and stereotypes cause sexual harassment: A theory with implications for organizational change. *Journal of Social Issues, 51* (1), 97–115.

Fitch, Roslyn H., & Bimonte, Heather A. (2002). Hormones, brain, and behavior: Putative biological contributions to cognitive sex differences. In A. McGillicuddy-DeLisi & R. DeLisi (Eds.), *Biology, society, and behavior: The development of sex differences in cognition* (pp. 55–92). Westport, CT: Ablex.

Fitzgerald, Louise F. (1993). Sexual harassment. *American Psychologist, 48,* 1070–1076.

Flaskerud, Jacquelyn H., & Ungvarski, Peter J. (1992). *HIV/AIDS: A guide to nursing care.* Philadelphia: Saunders.

Flaxman, S. M., & Sherman, P. W. (2000). Morning sickness: A mechanism for protecting mother and embryo. *Quarterly Review of Biology, 75,* 113–148.

Fleming, C., & Ingrassia, M. (1993, August 16). The Heidi Chronicles. *Newsweek,* pp. 50ff.

Fleming, Douglas T., et al. (1997). Herpes simplex virus type 2 in the United States, 1976 to 1994. *New England Journal of Medicine, 337,* 1105–1111.

Fleming, Jillian, et al. (1999). The long-term impact of child sexual abuse in Australian women. *Child Abuse and Neglect, 23,* 145–159.

Fleming, M., Steinman, C., & Boeknok, G. (1980). Methodological problems in assessing sex reassignment surgery: A reply to Meyer and Reter. *Archives of Sexual Behavior, 9*, 451–456.

Floyd, Frank J., & Bakeman, Roger. (2006). Coming-out across the life course: Implications of age and historical context. *Archives of Sexual Behavior, 35*, 287–296.

Foa, Edna B., Steketee, G., & Olasov, B. (1989). Behavioral/ cognitive conceptualization of post-traumatic stress disorder. *Behavior Therapy, 20*, 155–176.

Forbes. (2001, May 25). How big is porn? *Forbes.*

Ford, Clellan S., & Beach, Frank A. (1951). *Patterns of sexual behavior.* New York: Harper & Row.

Ford, Jeffry G. (2001). Healing homosexuals: A psychologist's journey through the ex-gay movement and the pseudo-science of reparative therapy. In A. Shidlo et al. (Eds.), *Sexual conversion therapy: Ethical, clinical, and research perspectives* (pp. 69–86). New York: Haworth.

Ford, Kathleen, & Norris, Anne. (1991). Methodological considerations for survey research on sexual behavior: Urban African American and Hispanic youth. *Journal of Sex Research, 28*, 539–555.

Ford, Kathleen, & Norris, Anne. (1997). Sexual networks of African-American and Hispanic youth. *Sexually Transmitted Diseases, 24*, 327–333.

Ford, Nicholas, & Koetsawang, Suporu. (1991). The socio-cultural context of the transmission of HIV in Thailand. *Social Science and Medicine, 33*, 405–414.

Fortenberry, J. Dennis. (2002). Clinic-based service programs for increasing responsible sexual behavior. *Journal of Sex Research, 39*, 63–66.

Foster, C. A., Witcher, B. S., Campbell, W. K., & Green, J. D. (1998). Arousal and attraction: Evidence for automatic and controlled processes. *Journal of Personality and Social Psychology, 74*, 86–101.

Foster, Diana G., et al. (2006). Estimates of pregnancies averted through California's family planning waiver program in 2002. *Perspectives on Sexual and Reproductive Health, 38*, 126–131.

Fox, Douglas. (2002). Gentle persuasion. *New Scientist, 173*, (2329), 32.

Fox, Laura. (1983). The 1983 abortion decisions. *University of Richmond Law Review, 18*, 137–159.

Fox, Ronald C. (1995). Bisexual identities. In A. R. D'Augelli & C. J. Patterson (Eds.), *Lesbian, gay, and bisexual identities over the lifespan.* New York: Oxford University Press.

Frank, Katherine. (2003). "Just trying to relax": Masculinity, masculinizing practices, and strip club regulars. *Journal of Sex Research, 40*, 61–75.

Frank, Katherine. (2005). Exploring the motivations and fantasies of strip club customers in relation to legal regulations. *Archives of Sexual Behavior, 34*, 487–504.

Frank, L. K. (1961). *The conduct of sex.* New York: Morrow.

Frayser, Suzanne G. (1985). *Varieties of sexual experience: An anthropological perspective on human sexuality.* New Haven, CT: Human Relations Area Files Press.

Frayser, Suzanne G. (1994). Defining normal childhood sexuality: An anthropological approach. *Annual Review of Sex Research, 5*, 173–217.

Frayser, Suzanne. (2004). Personal communication.

Frazier, Patricia, et al. (2004). Correlates of levels and patterns of positive life changes following sexual assault. *Journal of Consulting and Clinical Psychology, 72*, 19–30.

Freese, Jeremy, & Meland, Sheri. (2002). Seven tenths incorrect: Heterogeneity and change in the waist-to-hip ratios of *Playboy* centerfold models and Miss America pageant winners. *Journal of Sex Research, 39*, 133–138.

Freud, Sigmund. (1920/1948). The psychogenesis of a case of homosexuality in a woman. In *The collected papers* (Vol. II, pp. 202–231). London: Hogarth.

Freud, Sigmund. (1924). *A general introduction to psychoanalysis.* New York: Permabooks, 1953. (Boni & Liveright edition, 1924).

Freund, M., Lee, N., & Leonard, T. (1991). Sexual behavior of clients with street prostitutes in Camden, NJ. *Journal of Sex Research, 28*, 579–591.

Freyd, Jennifer J., (1996). *Betrayal trauma theory.* Cambridge, MA: Harvard University Press.

Freyd, Jennifer J. (2003). Memory for abuse: What can we learn from a prosecution sample? *Journal of Child Sexual Abuse, 12*, 97–103.

Freyd, Jennifer J., et al. (2005). The science of child sexual abuse. *Science, 308*, 501.

Friday, Nancy. (1973). *My secret garden: Women's sexual fantasies.* New York: Simon & Schuster.

Friday, Nancy. (1975). *Forbidden flowers: More women's sexual fantasies.* New York: Simon & Schuster.

Fried, Peter A. (1986). Marijuana use in pregnancy. In I. J. Chasnott (Ed.), *Drug use in pregnancy: Mother and child.* Boston: MTP Press.

Friedrich, W. N., Beilke, R. L., & Urquiza, A. J. (1988). Behavior problems in young sexually abused boys. *Journal of Interpersonal Violence, 3*, 1–12.

Friedrich, William N., et al. (1998). Normative sexual behavior in children: A contemporary sample. *Pediatrics, 101*, e9.

Frisch, R. E., & McArthur, J. W. (1974). Menstrual cycles: Fatness as a determinant of minimum weight for height necessary for their maintenance or onset. *Science, 185*, 949–951.

Frishman, G. (1995). Abortions, miscarriages, and ectopic pregnancies. In D. R. Carstrin, R. V. Hunning Jr., & E. D. B. Singer (Eds.), *Human reproduction: Growth and development.* Boston: Little, Brown.

Frohlich, Penny, & Meston, Cindy. (2002). Sexual functioning and self-reported depressive symptoms among college women. *Journal of Sex Research, 39*, 321–325.

Frohlich, Penny F., & Meston, Cindy M. (2005). Tactile sensitivity in women with sexual arousal disorder. *Archives of Sexual Behavior, 34*, 207–218.

Fromm, Erich. (1956). *The art of loving.* New York: Harper & Row.

Fuleihan, Ghada. (1997). Tissue-specific estrogens—The promise for the future. *New England Journal of Medicine, 337*, 1686–1687.

Fung, S., & Lok, A. (2004). Viral hepatitis in 2003. *Current Opinion in Gastroenterology, 20*, 241–247.

Furman, Wyndol. (2002). The emerging field of adolescent romantic relationships. *Current Directions in Psychological Science, 11*, 177–180.

Furnish, Victor P. (1994). The Bible and homosexuality: Reading the texts in context. In J. S. Siker (Ed.), *Homosexuality in the church* (pp. 18–35). Louisville, KY: Westminster/John Knox Press.

Furstenberg, Frank F., Brooks-Gunn, J., & Morgan, S. P. (1987). *Adolescent mothers in later life.* New York: Cambridge University Press.

Fyfe, B. (1983). "Homophobia" or homosexual bias reconsidered. *Archives of Sexual Behavior, 12*, 549–554.

Gabelnick, Henry L. (1998). Future methods. In R. Hatcher et al. (Eds.), *Contraceptive technology* (17th ed., pp. 615–622). New York: Ardent Media.

Gagnon, John H. (1977). *Human sexualities.* Glenview, IL: Scott, Foresman.

Gagnon, John H. (1990). The explicit and implicit use of the scripting perspective in sex research. *Annual Review of Sex Research, 1*, 1–44.

Gagnon, John H., & Simon, William. (1973). *Sexual conduct: The social origins of human sexuality.* Chicago: Aldine.

Gagnon, John H., & Simon, William. (1987). The sexual scripting of oral-genital contacts. *Archives of Sexual Behavior, 16*, 1–26.

Galbreath, Nathan, Berlin, Fred, & Sawyer, Denise. (2002). Paraphilias and the Internet. In Al Cooper (Ed.), *Sex and the Internet: A guidebook for clinicians* (pp. 187–205). New York: Brunner-Routledge.

Gallant, Sheryle J., et al. (1992). Using daily ratings to confirm premenstrual syndrome/late luteal phase dysphoric disorder, Part II: What makes a "real" difference? *Psychosomatic Medicine, 54*, 167–181.

Galvani, A., & Slatkin, M. (2003). Evaluating plague and smallpox as historical selective pressures for the CCR5-Delta 32 HIV-resistance allele. *PNAS, 100*, 15276–15279.

Gangestad, Steven W., & Buss, David M. (1993). Pathogen prevalence and human mate preferences. *Ethology and Sociobiology, 14*, 89–96.

Gangestad, Steven W., & Thornhill, R. (1997). Human sexual selection and developmental stability. In J. A. Simpson & D. T. Kenrick

(Eds.), *Evolutionary social psychology* (pp. 169–195). Mahwah, NJ: Erlbaum.

Ganju, D., et al. (2004). *The adverse health and social outcomes of sexual coercion: Experiences of young women in developing countries.* New Delhi: Population Council.

Ganz, Tomas. (2002). Versatile defensins. *Science, 298,* 977–979.

Gao, F., et al. (1992). Human infection by genetically diverse SIVSM-related HIV-2 in West Africa. *Nature, 358,* 495–499.

Gao, Fei, et al. (2006). The Wilms tumor gene, Wt1, is required for Sox9 expression and maintenance of tubular architecture in the developing testis. *PNAS, 103,* 11987–11992.

Garcia-Velasco, Jose, & Mondragon, Manuel. (1991). The incidence of the vomeronasal organ in 1,000 human subjects and its possible clinical significance. *Journal of Steroid Biochemistry and Molecular Biology, 39,* 561–563.

Garver-Apgar, Christine, Gangestad, S., Thornhill, R., Miller, R., & Olp, J. (2006). Major histocompatibility complex alleles, sexual responsivity, and unfaithfulness in romantic couples. *Psychological Science, 17,* 830–835.

Gathorne-Hardy, Jonathan. (2000). *Sex the measure of all things: A life of Alfred C. Kinsey.* Bloomington: Indiana University Press.

Gavey, Nicola. (2005). *Just sex? The cultural scaffolding of rape.* London: Routledge.

Gay, Peter. (1984). *The bourgeois experience: Victoria to Freud.* New York: Oxford University Press.

Gebhard, P. H., et al. (1965). *Sex offenders: An analysis of types.* New York: Harper & Row.

Gebhard, Paul H. (1968). Postmarital coitus among widows and divorcees. In P. Bohmann (Ed.), *Divorce and after.* Garden City, NY: Doubleday.

Gebhard, Paul H. (1976). The Institute. In M. S. Weinberg (Ed.), *Sex research: Studies from the Kinsey Institute.* New York: Oxford University Press.

Geer, James H., & Robertson, Gloria. (2005). Implicit attitudes in sexuality: Gender differences. *Archives of Sexual Behavior, 34,* 671–678.

Gender Identity Research and Education Society (GIRES). (2006). Atypical gender development: A review. *International Journal of Transgenderism, 9,* 29–43.

Genel, Myron. (2000). Gender verification no more? *Medscape Women's Health, 5* (3), E2.

Genovesi, Vincent J. (1987). *In pursuit of love: Catholic morality and human sexuality.* Wilmington, DE: Michael Glazier.

Gentile, D. A., et al. (2004). The effects of violent video game habits on adolescent attitudes and behaviors. *Journal of Adolescence, 27,* 5–22.

George, William H., & Stoner, Susan A. (2000). Understanding acute alcohol effects on sexual behavior. *Annual Review of Sex Research, 11,* 92–124.

George, William H., et al. (2006). Postdrinking sexual perceptions and behaviors toward another person: Alcohol expectancy set and gender differences. *Journal of Sex Research, 43,* 282–291.

Georges, Eugenia. (1996). Abortion policy and practice in Greece. *Social Science and Medicine, 42,* 509–519.

Gerbner, George, Gross, L., & Morgan, M. (2002). Growing up with television: Cultivation processes. In J. Bryant & D. Zillman (Eds.), *Media effects: Advances in theory and research* (2nd ed., pp. 43–67). Mahwah, NJ: Erlbaum.

Gijs, Luk, & Gooren, Louis. (1996). Hormonal and psychopharmacological interventions in the treatment of paraphilias. *Journal of Sex Research, 33,* 273–290.

Gilbert, Laura. (2000, August). Cosmo's hugest sex survey ever. *Cosmopolitan,* 186–189.

Gilligan, Carol. (1982). *In a different voice: Psychological theory and women's development.* Cambridge, MA: Harvard University Press.

Gilmartin, Brian G. (1975). The swinging couple down the block. *Psychology Today, 8* (9), 54.

Ginsburg, Faye. (1989). *Contested lives: The abortion debate in an American community.* Berkeley: University of California Press.

Giuliano, F., et al. (2002). Prevalence of erectile dysfunction in France: Results of an epidemiological survey of a representative sample of 1,004 men. *European Urology, 42,* 382–389.

Giuliano, François, & Clement, Pierre. (2005). Neuroanatomy and physiology of ejaculation. *Annual Review of Sex Research, 15,* 190–216.

Gjerdingen, Dwenda. (2003). The effectiveness of various postpartum depression treatments and the impact of antidepressant drugs on nursing infants. *Journal of the American Board of Family Practice 16,* 372–382.

Glascock, Jack, & LaRose, Robert. (1993). Dial-a-porn recordings: The role of the female participant in male sexual fantasies. *Journal of Broadcasting and Electronic Media,* 313–324.

Glaser, Chris. (1994). The love that dares not pray its name: The gay and lesbian movement in America's churches. In J. S. Siker (Ed.), *Homosexuality in the church* (pp. 150–157). Louisville, KY: Westminster/John Knox Press.

Glass, S. J., & Johnson, R. W. (1944). Limitations and complications of organotherapy in male homosexuality. *Journal of Clinical Endocrinology, 4,* 540–544.

Godges, John. (1986). Religious groups meet the San Francisco AIDS challenge. *Christian Century, 103,* 771–775.

Gold, S. N., Hughes, D., & Hohnecker, L. (1994). Degrees of repression of sexual abuse memories. *American Psychologist, 49,* 441–442.

Goldberg, M. (1987). Understanding hypersexuality in men and women. In G. R. Weeks & L. Hof (Eds.), *Integrating sex and marital therapy.* New York: Brunner–Mazel.

Goldberg, Susan. (1983). Parent-infant bonding: Another look. *Child Development, 54,* 1355–1382.

Goldfoot, D. A., et al. (1980). Behavioral and physiological evidence of sexual climax in the female stump-tailed macaque (*Macaca arctoides*). *Science, 208,* 1477–1478.

Golding, J. M. (1999). Sexual assault history and medical care seeking. *Psychology & Health, 14,* 949–957.

Goldman, Ronald J., & Goldman, Juliette D. G. (1982). *Children's sexual thinking.* London: Routledge & Kegan Paul.

Goldstein, Bernard. (1976). *Human sexuality.* New York: McGraw-Hill.

Goldstein, Irwin, et al. (1998). Oral sildenafil in the treatment of erectile dysfunction. *New England Journal of Medicine, 338,* 1397–1404.

Goldstein, Jill M., et al. (2001). Normal sexual dimorphism of the adult human brain assessed by in vivo magnetic resonance imaging. *Cerebral Cortex, 11,* 490–497.

Golombok, Susan, & Tasker, Fiona. (1996). Do parents influence the sexual orientation of their children? Findings from a longitudinal study of lesbian families. *Developmental Psychology, 32,* 3–11.

Golombok, Susan, et al. (2003). Children with lesbian parents: A community study. *Developmental Psychology, 39,* 20–33.

Golub, Sharon. (1992). *Periods: From menarche to menopause.* Newbury Park, CA: Sage.

Gonsiorek, John C. (1996). Mental health and sexual orientation. In R. C. Savin-Williams & K. M. Cohen (Eds.), *The lives of lesbians, gays, and bisexuals* (pp. 462–478). Fort Worth: Harcourt Brace.

Gonzaga, Gian, Turner, Rebecca, Keltner, Dacher, Campos, Belinda, & Altemus, Margaret. (2006). Romantic love and sexual desire in close relationships. *Emotion, 6,* 163–179.

Gonzalez, Francisco, & Espin, Oliva. (1996). Latino men, Latina women, and homosexuality. In R. Cabaj & T. Stein (Eds.), *Textbook of homosexuality and mental health* (pp. 583–601). Washington, DC: American Psychiatric Association.

Gonzalez, Jeffrey S., et al. (2004). Social support, positive states of mind, and HIV treatment adherence in men and women living with HIV/AIDS. *Health Psychology, 23,* 413–418.

Goodchilds, Jacqueline, & Zellman, Gail. (1984). Sexual signaling and sexual aggression in adolescent relationships. In N. Malamuth & E. Donnerstein (Eds.), *Pornography and sexual aggression.* New York: Academic.

Goodman, Gail S., et al. (2003). A prospective study of memory for child sexual abuse. *Psychological Science, 14,* 113–118.

Goodson, Patricia, & Edmundson, Elizabeth. (1994). The problematic promotion of abstinence: An overview of Sex Respect. *Journal of School Health, 64,* 205–210.

Goodstein, Laurie. (2004, February 28). We swept abusers out, bishops say. *New York Times.*

Gooren, Louis, Fliers, E., & Courtney, K. (1990). Biological determinants of sexual behavior. *Annual Review of Sex Research, 1,* 175–196.

Gordon, B. N., Schroeder, C. S., & Abrams, J. M. (1990). Age and social-class differences in children's knowledge of sexuality. *Journal of Clinical Child Psychology, 19,* 33–43.

Gordon, Betty, & Schroeder, Carolyn. (1995). *Sexuality: A developmental approach to problems.* New York: Plenum Press.

Gordon, Linda. (2002). *The moral property of women: A history of birth control politics.* Champaign: University of Illinois Press.

Gosling, Samuel D., et al. (2004). Should we trust Web-based studies? A comparative analysis of six preconceptions about Internet questionnaires. *American Psychologist, 59,* 93–104.

Gosselin, Chris, & Wilson, Glenn. (1980). *Sexual variations: Fetishism, sadomasochism, transvestism.* New York: Simon & Schuster.

Gottlieb, Lori. (2006, March). How do I love thee? *The Atlantic Monthly,* 58–70.

Gottman, John M. (1994). *Why marriages succeed or fail.* New York: Simon & Schuster.

Gottman, John M., & Porterfield, A. L. (1981). Communicative competence in the nonverbal behavior of married couples. *Journal of Marriage and the Family, 43,* 817–824.

Gottman, John, et al. (1976). *A couple's guide to communication.* Champaign, IL: Research Press.

Gottman, John, et al. (1998). Predicting marital happiness and stability from newlywed interactions. *Journal of Marriage and the Family, 60,* 5–22.

Gottman, John, Markman, H., & Notarius, C. (1977). The topography of marital conflict: A sequential analysis of verbal and nonverbal behavior. *Journal of Marriage and the Family, 39,* 461–478.

Gottschall, Jonathan. (2004). Explaining wartime rape. *Journal of Sex Research, 41,* 129–136.

Gould, Stephen J. (1987). *An urchin in the storm.* New York: Norton.

Gow, Haven Bradford. (1994). Condom distribution in high school. *The Clearing House, 67,* 183–184.

Gower, D. B., & Ruparelia, B. A. (1993). Olfaction in humans with special reference to odorous 16-androstenes: Their occurrence, perception and possible social, psychological and sexual impact. *Journal of Endocrinology, 137,* 167–187.

Graham, Cynthia A., et al. (1995). The effects of steroidal contraceptives on the well-being and sexuality of women. *Contraception, 52,* 363–369.

Graham, Cynthia A., et al. (2004). Turning on and turning off: A focus group study of the factors that affect women's sexual arousal. *Archives of Sexual Behavior, 33,* 527–538.

Grammick, Jeannine. (1986). The Vatican's battered wives. *Christian Century, 103,* 17–20.

Grau, Ina, & Kimpf, Martin. (1993). Love, sexuality, and satisfaction: Interventions of men and women. *Zeitschrift fur Sozial Psychologie, 24,* 83–93.

Gray, Nicola S., et al. (2005). An implicit test of the associations between children and sex in pedophiles. *Journal of Abnormal Psychology, 114,* 304–308.

Greeley, Andrew. (1994). Review of the Janus Report on Sexual Behavior. *Contemporary Sociology, 23,* 221–223.

Green, Lesley L., Fullilove, Mindy T., & Fullilove, Robert E. (2005). Remembering the lizard: Reconstructing sexuality in the rooms of Narcotics Anonymous. *Journal of Sex Research, 42,* 28–34.

Green, Richard. (1975). Adults who want to change sex; adolescents who cross-dress; and children called "sissy" and "tomboy." In R. Green (Ed.), *Human sexuality: A health practitioner's text.* Baltimore: Williams & Wilkins.

Green, Richard. (1978). Intervention and prevention: The child with cross-sex identity. In C. B. Qualls et al. (Eds.), *The prevention of sexual disorders* (pp. 75–94). New York: Plenum.

Green, Richard. (1987). *The Sissy Boy Syndrome and the development of homosexuality.* New Haven, CT: Yale University Press.

Green, Richard, & Fleming, Davis T. (1990). Transsexual surgery follow-up: Status in the 1990s. *Annual Review of Sex Research, 1,* 163–174.

Green, Ronald M. (1984). Genetic medicine in Jewish legal perspective. *Annual of the Society of Christian Ethics,* 249–272.

Greenberg, Bradley S., Brown, Jane D., & Buerkel-Rothfuss, Nancy (Eds.). (1993). *Media, sex, and the adolescent.* Cresskill, NJ: Hampton Press.

Greenberg, Bradley S., & Busselle, Rick. (1996). What's old, what's new: Sexuality on the soaps. *SIECUS Report, 24* (5), 14–16.

Greene, Beverly. (1994). African American women. In L. Coma-Diaz & B. Greene (Eds.), *Women of color* (pp. 1–29). New York: Guilford.

Greene, Beverly. (2000). African American lesbian and bisexual women. *Journal of Social Issues, 56,* 239–250.

Greenwald, Evan, & Leitenberg, Harold. (1989). Long-term effects of sexual experiences with siblings and nonsiblings during childhood. *Archives of Sexual Behavior, 18,* 389–400.

Greer, Arlette E., & Buss, David M. (1994). Tactics for promoting sexual encounters. *Journal of Sex Research, 31,* 185–201.

Gregersen, Edgar. (1996). *The world of human sexuality: Behaviors, customs, and beliefs.* New York: Irvington.

Gregor, Thomas. (1985). *Anxious pleasures: The sexual lives of an Amazonian people.* Chicago: University of Chicago Press.

Greiling, Heidi, & Buss, David. (2000). Women's sexual strategies: The hidden dimension of extra-pair mating. *Personality and Individual Differences, 28,* 929–963.

Grello, Catherine M., Welsh, D., & Harper, M. (2006). No strings attached: The nature of casual sex in college students. *Journal of Sex Research, 43,* 255–267.

Grenier, Guy, & Byers, E. Sandra. (1995). Rapid ejaculation: A review of conceptual, etiological, and treatment issues. *Archives of Sexual Behavior, 24,* 447–474.

Grenier, Guy, & Byers, E. Sandra. (2001). Operationalizing premature or rapid ejaculation. *Journal of Sex Research, 38,* 369–378.

Griffin, Susan. (1981). *Pornography and silence.* New York: Harper & Row.

Grodstein, Francine, et al. (1997). Postmenopausal hormone therapy and mortality. *New England Journal of Medicine, 336,* 1769–1775.

Gross, Alan E., & Bellew-Smith, Martha. (1983). A social psychological approach to reducing pregnancy risk in adolescence. In D. Byrne & W. A. Fisher (Eds.), *Adolescents, sex, and contraception.* Hillsdale, NJ: Lawrence Erlbaum.

Grov, Christian, Bimbi, D., Nanín, J., & Parsons, J. (2006). Race, ethnicity, gender, and generational factors associated with the coming-out process among gay, lesbian, and bisexual individuals. *Journal of Sex Research, 43,* 115–121.

Gruenbaum, E. (2000). *The female circumcision controversy: An anthropological perspective.* Philadelphia: University of Pennsylvania Press.

Grumbach, M. M., & Styne, D. M. (1998). Puberty: Ontogeny, neuroendocrinology, physiology, and disorders. In J. D. Wilson et al. (Eds.), *Williams textbook of endocrinology* (9th ed., pp. 1509–1625). Philadelphia: Saunders.

Gruntz, Louis, Jr. (1974). Obscenity 1973: Remodeling the house that Roth built. *Loyola Law Review, 20,* 159–174.

Guay, Jean-Pierre, et al. (2001). Victim-choice polymorphia among serious sex offenders. *Archives of Sexual Behavior, 30,* 521–534.

Guerrero, Laura, Spitzberg, Brian, & Yoshimura, Stephen. (2004). Sexual and emotional jealousy. In John Harvey, Amy Wenzel, & Susan Sprecher (Eds.), *The handbook of sexuality in close relationships* (pp. 311–345). Mahwah, NJ: Lawrence Erlbaum.

Guise, Jeanne-Marie, et al. (2003). The effectiveness of primary care–based interventions to promote breastfeeding: Systematic evidence review and meta-analysis for the U.S. Preventive Services Task Force. *Annals of Family Medicine, 1,* 70–78.

Gummow, Brian M., et al. (2006). Reciprocal regulation of a gluvovorticoid receptor-steroidogenic factor-1 transcription complex on the Dax-1 promoter by glucocorticoids and adrenocorticotropic hormone in the adrenal cortex. *Molecular Endocrinology, 20,* 2711–2723.

Gunderson, B. H., et al. (1981). Sexual behavior of preschool children. In L. L. Constantine & F. M. Martinson (Eds.), *Children and sex* (pp. 45–62). Boston: Little, Brown.

Gursoy, Akile. (1996). Abortion in Turkey: A matter of state, family, or individual decision. *Social Science and Medicine, 42,* 531–542.

Gutek, Barbara A. (1985). *Sex and the workplace.* San Francisco: Jossey-Bass.

Guttmacher Institute. (2006). *Facts on American teens' sexual and reproductive health.* Retrieved February 2, 2007, from www.guttmacher.org.

Guttmacher Institute. (2007). *Facts on induced abortion in the United States.* Retrieved January 31, 2007, from www. guttmacher.org.

Guttmacher Institute. (2007). State policies in brief: Sex and STD/HIV education. Retrieved April 3, 2007, from http://www. guttmacher.org/statecenter/spibs/spib_SE.pdf.

Guttmacher, Sally, et al. (1995). Parents' attitudes and beliefs about HIV/AIDS prevention with condom availability in New York City public high schools. *Journal of School Health, 65,* 101–106.

Hahm, Hyeouk, Lahiff, M., & Barreto, R. (2006). Asian American adolescents' first sexual intercourse: Gender and acculturation differences. *Perspectives on Sexual and Reproductive Health, 38,* 28–36.

Hahn, S. R., & Paige, K. E. (1980). American birth practices: A critical review. In J. E. Parsons (Ed.), *The psychobiology of sex differences and sex roles.* New York: McGraw-Hill, Hemisphere.

Haig, David. (1996). Altercation of generations: Genetic conflicts of pregnancy. *American Journal of Reproductive Immunology, 35,* 226–232.

Halbreich, Uriel. (1996). Reflections on the cause of premenstrual syndrome. *Psychiatric Annals, 26,* 581–585.

Haldeman, Douglas C. (1994). The practice and ethics of sexual orientation conversion therapy. *Journal of Consulting and Clinical Psychology, 62,* 221–227.

Haldeman, Douglas C. (2001). Therapeutic antidotes: Helping gay and bisexual men recover from conversion therapies. In A. Shidlo et al. (Eds.), *Sexual conversion therapy: Ethical, clinical, and research perspectives* (pp. 117–130). New York: Haworth.

Hall, Gordon C. Nagayama. (1995). Sexual offender recidivism revisited: A meta-analysis of recent treatment studies. *Journal of Consulting and Clinical Psychology, 63,* 802–809.

Hall, Gordon C. Nagayama, & Barongan, Christy. (1997). Prevention of sexual aggression. *American Psychologist, 52,* 5–14.

Hall, Gordon C. Nagayama, et al. (2005). Ethnicity, culture, and sexual aggression: Risk and protective factors. *Journal of Consulting and Clinical Psychology, 73,* 830–840.

Hall, Gordon C. Nagayama, et al. (2006). Initiation, desistance, and persistence of men's sexual coercion. *Journal of Consulting and Clinical Psychology, 74,* 732–742.

Hall, Judith A. (1998). How big are nonverbal sex differences? The case of smiling and sensitivity to nonverbal cues. In D. Canary & K. Dindia (Eds.), *Sex differences and similarities in communication* (pp. 155–178). Mahwah, NJ: Erlbaum.

Halpern, Carolyn, et al. (2000). Smart teens don't have sex (or kiss much either). *Journal of Adolescent Health, 26,* 213–225.

Halpern-Felsher, Bonnie, Cornell, J., Kropp, R., & Tschann, J. (2005). Oral versus vaginal sex among adolescents: Perceptions, attitudes, and behaviors. *Pediatrics, 115,* 845–851.

Hamann, Stephan, et al. (2004). Men and women differ in amygdala response to visual sexual stimuli. *Nature Neuroscience, 7,* 411–416.

Hamer, Dean, et al. (1993). A linkage between DNA markers on the X chromosome and male sexual orientation. *Science, 261,* 321–327.

Hames, Barbara. (2000). Religious groups address sexuality issues: The debate to continue. *Center for Sexuality and Religion Connections, 11* (3), 2–3.

Hamilton, Mykol C., et al. (2006). Gender stereotypes and under-representation of female characters in 200 popular children's picture books: A twenty-first century update. *Sex Roles, 55,* 757–766.

Hammer, G. D., & Ingraham, H. A. (1999). Steroidogenic factor-1: Its role in endocrine organ development and differentiation. *Frontiers in Neuroendocrinology, 20,* 199–223.

Handler, A., et al. (1991). Cocaine use during pregnancy: Perinatal outcomes. *American Journal of Epidemiology, 133,* 818–825.

Hanson, R. Karl. (2000). Will they do it again? Predicting sex-offense recidivism. *Current Directions in Psychological Science, 9,* 106–109.

Hanson, R. Karl, & Bussiere, Monique T. (1998). Predicting relapse: A meta-analysis of sexual offender recidivism studies. *Journal of Consulting and Clinical Psychology, 66,* 348–362.

Harbison, R. D., & Mantilla-Plata, B. (1972). Prenatal toxicity, maternal distribution and placental transfer of tetrahydrocannabinol. *Journal of Pharmacology and Experimental Therapeutics, 180,* 446–453.

Harlow, Harry F., Harlow, Margaret K., & Hause, F. W. (1963). The maternal affectional system of rhesus monkeys. In H. L. Rheingold (Ed.), *Maternal behavior in mammals.* New York: Wiley.

Harper, Cynthia C., et al. (2005). The effect of increased access to emergency contraception among young adolescents. *Obstetrics & Gynecology, 106,* 483–491.

Harris, Christine. (2002). Sexual and romantic jealousy in heterosexual and homosexual adults. *Psychological Science, 13,* 7–12.

Harris, Christine. (2003). A review of sex differences in sexual jealousy, including self-report data, psychophysiological responses, interpersonal violence, and morbid jealousy. *Personality and Social Psychology Review, 7,* 102–128.

Harris, Gardiner. (2004, February 28). Pfizer gives up testing Viagra on women. *New York Times.*

Harris, G. W., & Levine, S. (1965). Sexual differentiation of the brain and its experimental control. *Journal of Physiology, 181,* 379–400.

Harris, Norma S., et al. (2002). Zidovudine and perinatal Human Immunodeficiency Virus Type 1 transmission: A population-based approach. *Pediatrics, 109* (4), Art. No. e60.

Harrison, Albert. (1977). Mere exposure. In L. Berkowitz (Ed.), *Advances in experimental social psychology* (Vol. 10). New York: Academic.

Hart, Linda L. (1990). Accuracy of home pregnancy tests. *Annals of Pharmacotherapy, 24,* 712–713.

Hartman, William, & Fithian, Marilyn. (1984). *Any man can: The multiple orgasmic technique for every loving man.* New York: St. Martin's Press.

Hartmann, Katherine, Viswanathan, M., Palmieri, R., Gartlehner, G., Thorp, J., & Lohr, K. (2005). Outcomes of routine episiotomy: A systematic review. *Journal of the American Medical Association, 293,* 2141–2148.

Hartmann, Uwe, & Waldinger, Marcel D. (2007) l. Treatment of delayed ejaculation. In S. Leiblum (Ed.), *Principles and practice of sex therapy* (4th ed., pp. 241–276). New York: Guilford.

Haslam, Nick, & Levy, Sheri R. (2006). Essentialist beliefs about homosexuality: Structure and implications for prejudice. *Personality and Social Psychology Bulletin, 32,* 471–485.

Hass, Aaron. (1979). *Teenage sexuality.* New York: Macmillan.

Hatcher, Robert A., et al. (1994). *Contraceptive technology* (16th ed.). New York: Irvington.

Hatcher, Robert A., et al. (1998). *Contraceptive technology* (17th ed.). New York: Ardent Media.

Hatcher, Robert A., et al. (2004). *Contraceptive technology* (18th ed.). New York: Ardent Media.

Hatfield, Elaine. (1978). Equity and extramarital sexuality. *Archives of Sexual Behavior, 7,* 127–141.

Hatfield, Elaine. (1994). *Passionate love and sexual desire: A cross-cultural perspective.* Paper presented at the annual meeting of the Society for the Scientific Study of Sexuality, Miami.

Hatfield, Elaine, & Rapson, Richard. (1993a). Historical and cross-cultural perspectives on passionate love and sexual desire. *Annual Review of Sex Research, 4,* 67–97.

Hatfield, Elaine, & Rapson, Richard. (1993b). *Love, sex, and intimacy.* New York: HarperCollins.

Hatfield, Elaine, & Sprecher, Susan. (1986). Measuring passionate love in intimate relations. *Journal of Adolescence, 9,* 383–410.

Hatfield, Elaine, & Walster, G. William. (1978). *A new look at love.* Reading, MA: Addison-Wesley.

Hatfield, Elaine, Walster, G. W., & Berscheid, E. (1978). *Equity theory and research.* Boston: Allyn & Bacon.

Hatzichristou, D., et al. (2004). The efficacy and safety of flexible-dose vardenafil (Levitra) in a broad population of European men. *European Urology, 45,* 634–641.

Hausknecht, Richard U. (1995). Methotrexate and misoprostol to terminate early pregnancy. *New England Journal of Medicine, 333,* 537–540.

Hayes, Tyrone B., et al. (2002). Hermaphroditic, demasculinized frogs after exposure to the herbicide atrazine at low ecologically relevant doses. *PNAS, 99,* 5476–5480.

Haynes, Barton F., Pantaleo, Giuseppe, & Fauci, Anthony S. (1996). Toward an understanding of the correlates of protective immunity to HIV infection. *Science, 271,* 324–328.

Hazan, C., & Shaver, P. (1987). Love conceptualized as an attachment process. *Journal of Personality and Social Psychology, 52,* 511–524.

Hearn, Kimberly D., O'Sullivan, Lucia F., & Dudley, Cheryl D. (2003). Assessing reliability of early adolescent girls' reports of romantic and sexual behavior. *Archives of Sexual Behavior, 32,* 513–522.

Heath, Robert C. (1972). Pleasure and brain activity in man. *Journal of Nervous and Mental Disease, 154,* 3–18.

Heaton, Jeremy P. W. (2000). Central neuropharmacological agents and mechanisms in erectile dysfunction: The role of dopamine. *Neuroscience and Biobehavioral Reviews, 24,* 561–569.

Heaton, Jeremy P. W. (2001). Key issues from the clinical trials of apomorphine SL. *World Journal of Urology, 19,* 25–31.

Hebl, Michelle R., et al. (2002). Formal and interpersonal discrimination: A field study of bias toward homosexual applicants. *Personality and Social Psychology Bulletin, 28,* 815–825.

Heilman, Carole A., & Baltimore, David. (1998). HIV-vaccines—where are they going? *Nature Medicine Vaccine Supplement, 4,* 532–534.

Heim, Nikolaus. (1981). Sexual behavior of castrated sex offenders. *Archives of Sexual Behavior, 10,* 11–20.

Heiman, Julia R. (1975). The physiology of erotica: Women's sexual arousal. *Psychology Today, 8* (11), 90–94.

Heiman, Julia R. (2000). Orgasmic disorders in women. In S. Leiblum & R. Rosen (Eds.), *Principles and practice of sex therapy* (3rd cd., pp. 118–153). New York: Guilford.

Heiman, Julia R. (2002a). Sexual dysfunction: Overview of prevalence, etiological factors, and treatment. *Journal of Sex Research, 39,* 73–78.

Heiman, Julia R. (2002b). Psychological treatments for female sexual dysfunction: Are they effective and do we need them? *Archives of Sexual Behavior, 31,* 445–450.

Heiman, Julia R. (2007). Orgasmic disorders in women. In S. Leiblum (Ed.), *Principles and practice of sex therapy* (4th ed., pp. 84–123). New York: Guilford.

Heiman, Julia R., LoPiccolo, Leslie, & LoPiccolo, Joseph. (1976). *Becoming orgasmic: A sexual growth program for women.* Englewood Cliffs, NJ: Prentice-Hall.

Heiman, Julia R., & Meston, Cindy M. (1997). Empirically validated treatment for sexual dysfunction. *Annual Review of Sex Research, 8,* 148–194.

Heine, Steven J., & Norenzayan, Ara. (2006). Toward a psychological science for a cultural species. *Perspectives in Psychological Science, 1,* 251–269.

Heise, Lori. (1993). Violence against women: The hidden health burden. *World Health Statistics Quarterly, 46,* 78–85.

Helgeson, Vicki S., Snyder, Pamela, & Seltman, Howard. (2004). Psychological and physical adjustment to breast cancer over 4 years: Identifying distinct trajectories of change. *Health Psychology, 23,* 3–15.

Helgeson, Vicki, et al. (2001). Long-term effects of educational and peer discussion group interventions on adjustment to breast cancer. *Health Psychology, 20,* 387–392.

Hellerstein, Herman K., & Friedman, Ernst H. (1969, March). Sexual activity and the post-coronary patient. *Medical Aspects of Human Sexuality, 3,* 70–74.

Hellstrom, W. (2003). Three-piece inflatable penile prosthesis components (surgical pearls on reservoirs, pumps, and rear-tip extenders). *International Journal of Impotence Research, 15,* S136–S138.

Hellstrom, W., et al. (2003a). Tadalafil has no detrimental effect on human spermatogenesis or reproductive hormones. *Journal of Urology, 170,* 887–891.

Hellstrom, W., et al. (2003b). Sustained efficacy and tolerability of vardenafil. *Urology, 61,* 8–14.

Helminiak, Daniel A. (2000). *What the Bible really says about homosexuality* (Millennium ed.) New Mexico: Alamo Square Press.

Helminiak, Daniel A. (2001a). Sexual ethics in college textbooks: A survey. *Journal of Sex Education and Therapy, 26,* 106–114.

Helminiak, Daniel A. (2001b). Sexual ethics in college textbooks: A suggestion. *Journal of Sex Education and Therapy, 26,* 320–327.

Helminiak, Daniel A. (2004). The ethics of sex: A call to the gay community. *Pastoral Psychology, 52,* 259–267.

Helminiak, Daniel A. (2006). *Sex and the sacred: Gay identity and spiritual growth.* Binghamton, NY: Harrington Park Press.

Henahan, John. (1984). Honing the treatment of early breast cancer. *Journal of the American Medical Association, 251,* 309–310.

Hendrick, Clyde, & Hendrick, Susan. (2004). Sex and romantic love: Connects and disconnects. In J. Harvey, A. Wenzel, & S. Sprecher (Eds.), *The handbook of sexuality in close relationships* (pp. 159–182). Mahwah, NJ: Lawrence Erlbaum.

Hendrick, Susan. (1981). Self-disclosure and marital satisfaction. *Journal of Personality and Social Psychology, 40,* 1150–1159.

Hendrick, Susan S., & Hendrick, Clyde. (1992). *Liking, loving, and relating* (2nd ed.). Pacific Grove, CA: Brooks/Cole.

Hendrick, Susan S., Hendrick, Clyde, & Adler, N. L. (1988). Romantic relationships: Love, satisfaction, and staying together. *Journal of Personality and Social Psychology, 54,* 980–988.

Henningsson, Susanne, et al. (2005). Sex steroid-related genes and male-to-female transsexualism. *Psychoneuroendocrinology, 30,* 657–664.

Henshaw, Stanley K. (1990). Induced abortion: A world review, 1990. *Family Planning Perspectives, 22,* 76–89.

Henshaw, Stanley K. (1997). Teenage abortion and pregnancy rates by state, 1992. *Family Planning Perspectives, 29,* 115–122.

Henshaw, Stanley, & Finer, Lawrence. (2003). The accessibility of abortion services in the United States, 2001. *Perspectives on Sexual and Reproductive Health, 35,* 16–24.

Henshaw, Stanley, & Van Vort, Jennifer. (1994). Abortion ser-vices in the United States, 1991 and 1992. *Family Planning Perspectives, 26,* 100–106, 112.

Herbert, J. (1966). The effect of estrogen applied directly to the genitalia upon the sexual attractiveness of the female rhesus monkey. *Exerpta Medica International Congress Series, 3,* 212.

Herbst, A. (1972). Clear cell adenocarcinoma of the genital tract in young females. *New England Journal of Medicine, 287* (25), 1259–1264.

Herdt, Gilbert H. (1984). *Ritualized homosexuality in Melanesia.* Berkeley: University of California Press.

Herdt, Gilbert. (1990). Mistaken gender: 5-alpha reductase hermaphroditism and biological reductionism in sexual identity reconsidered. *American Anthropologist, 92,* 433–446.

Herek, Gregory. (2006). Legal recognition of same-sex relationships in the United States: A social science perspective. *American Psychologist, 61,* 607–621.

Herek, Gregory, & Gonzalez-Rivera, Milagritos. (2006). Attitudes toward homosexuality among U.S. residents of Mexican descent. *Journal of Sex Research, 43,* 122–135.

Herek, Gregory M. (2000). The psychology of sexual prejudice. *Current Directions in Psychological Science, 9* (1), 19–22.

Herek, Gregory M. (2002). Heterosexuals' attitudes toward bisexual men and women in the United States. *Journal of Sex Research, 39,* 264–274.

Herek, Gregory M., et al. (1991). Avoiding heterosexist bias in psychological research. *American Psychologist, 46,* 957–963.

Herek, Gregory M., Gillis, J., & Cogan, J. (1999). Psychological sequelae of hate-crime victimization among lesbian, gay, and bisexual adults. *Journal of Consulting and Clinical Psychology, 67,* 945–951.

Herman, Judith L. (1981). *Father-daughter incest.* Cambridge, MA: Harvard University Press.

Herman-Giddens, M. E., et al. (1997). Secondary sexual characteristics and menses in young girls seen in office practice. *Pediatrics, 99,* 505–512.

Herrero, R., et al. (2003). Human papillomavirus and oral cancer: The International Agency for Research on Cancer multicenter study. *Journal of the National Cancer Institute, 95,* 1772–1783.

Heyl, Barbara Sherman. (1979). *The madam as entrepreneur.* New Brunswick, NJ: Transaction Books.

Hill, C. T., Rubin, Z., & Peplau, L. A. (1976). Breakups before marriage: The end of 103 affairs. *Journal of Social Issues, 32* (1).

Hill, Darryl B., et al. (2007). Gender identity disorders in childhood and adolescence: A critical inquiry. *International Journal of Sexual Health, 1,* 95–122.

Hill, Mark. (2002). Skin color and the perception of attractiveness among African Americans: Does gender make a difference? *Social Psychology Quarterly, 65,* 77–91.

Hite, Shere. (1976). *The Hite report.* New York: Macmillan.

Hite, Shere. (1981). *The Hite report on male sexuality.* New York: Alfred Knopf.

HIV CLAPP. (2004). HIV reporting. HIV Criminal Law and Public Policy Project. www.hivcriminallaw.org.

Ho, Gloria Y. F., et al. (1998). Natural history of cervicovaginal papillomavirus infection in young women. *New England Journal of Medicine, 338,* 423–428.

Hobart, C. Q. (1958). The incidence of romanticism during courtship. *Social Forces, 36,* 364.

Hobfoll, Stevan, et al. (1995). Depression prevalence and incidence among inner-city pregnant and postpartum women. *Journal of Consulting and Clinical Psychology, 63,* 445–453.

Hoff, Gerard A., & Schneiderman, Lawrence J. (1985, December). Having babies at home: Is it safe? Is it ethical? *Hastings Center Report,* 19–27.

Hofferth, Sandra L. (1990). Trends in adolescent sexual activity, contraception, and pregnancy in the United States. In J. Bancroft & J. Reinisch (Eds.), *Adolescence and puberty* (pp. 217–233). New York: Oxford University Press.

Hoffmann, Heather, Janssen, Erick, & Turner, Stefanie L. (2004). Classical conditioning of sexual arousal in women and men: Effects of varying awareness and biological relevance of the conditioned stimulus. *Archives of Sexual Behavior, 33,* 43–54.

Hogben, Matthew, & Byrne, Donn. (1998). Using social learning theory to explain individual differences in human sexuality. *Journal of Sex Research, 35,* 58–71.

Hollander, D. (1996). Programs to bring down cesarean section rate prove to be successful. *Family Planning Perspectives, 28,* 182–185.

Holmstrom, Lynda L., & Burgess, Ann W. (1980). Sexual behavior of assailants during reported rapes. *Archives of Sexual Behavior, 9,* 427–440.

Holroyd, Jean C., & Brodsky, Annette M. (1977). Psychologists' attitudes and practices regarding erotic and noneexualic physical contact with patients. *American Psychologist, 34,* 843–849.

Holstege, Gert, et al. (2003). Brain activation during human male ejaculation. *Journal of Neuroscience, 23,* 9185–9193.

Hom, X., et al. (2004). Predictors of virologic response to lamivudine treatment in children with chronic hepatitis B infection. *Pediatric Infectious Disease Journal, 23,* 441–445.

Hong, Lawrence K. (1984). Survival of the fastest: On the origin of premature ejaculation. *Journal of Sex Research, 20,* 109–122.

Hook, Edward W., & Handsfield, H. (1999). Gonococcal infection in adults. In K. Holmes et al. (Eds.), *Sexually transmitted diseases* (3rd ed.). New York: McGraw-Hill.

Hook, Edward W., & Handsfield, H. Hunter. (1990). Gonococcal infections in adults. In K. Holmes et al. (Eds.), *Sexually transmitted diseases* (pp. 149–160). New York: McGraw-Hill.

Hopwood, Nancy J., et al. (1990). The onset of human puberty: Biological and environmental factors. In J. Bancroft & J. M. Reinisch (Eds.), *Adolescence and puberty.* New York: Oxford University Press.

Horney, Karen. (1973). The flight from womanhood (1926). In K. Horney, *Feminine psychology.* New York: Norton.

Horowitz, Carol R., & Jackson, T. Carey. (1997). Female "circumcision": African women confront American medicine. *Journal of General Internal Medicine, 12,* 491–499.

Horrocks, R. (1997). *An introduction to the study of sexuality.* New York: St. Martin's Press.

Hotz, V. Joseph, Sanders, Seth, & McElroy, Susan W. (1999). *Teenage childbearing and its life cycle consequences: Exploiting a natural experiment.* National Bureau of Economic Research, working paper W7397.

House, Carrie. (1997). Navajo warrior women: An ancient tradition in a modern world. In S. Jacobs et al. (Eds.), *Two-spirit people* (pp. 223–227). Urbana: University of Illinois Press.

Houston, L. N. (1981). Romanticism and eroticism among Black and white college students. *Adolescence, 16,* 263–272.

Howard, D. E. (2005). Psychosocial correlates of U.S. adolescents who report a history of forced sexual intercourse. *Journal of Adolescent Health, 36,* 372–379.

Hoyle, C., et al. (2002). Dax1 expression is dependent on steroidogenic factor 1 in the developing gonad. *Molecular Endocrinology, 16,* 747–756.

Hsu, Bing, et al. (1994). Gender differences in sexual fantasy and behavior in a college population: A ten-year replication. *Journal of Sex and Marital Therapy, 20,* 103–118.

Hubacher, David. (2002). The checkered history and bright future of intrauterine contraception in the United States. *Perspectives on Sexual and Reproductive Health, 34,* 98–103.

Hucker, Stephen, & Blanchard, Ray. (1992). Death scene characteristics in 118 fatal cases of autoerotic asphyxia compared with suicidal asphyxia. *Behavioural Sciences and the Law, 10,* 509–523.

Hudson, Walter W., & Ricketts, Wendell A. (1980). A strategy for the measurement of homophobia. *Journal of Homosexuality, 5,* 357–372.

Huffstutter, P. J., & Frammolino, R. (2001, July 6). Lights, camera, Viagra: When the show must go on, sometimes a little chemistry helps. *Los Angeles Times,* p. A1.

Hughes, I. A., et al. (2006). Consensus statement on management of intersex disorders. *Archives of Disease in Childhood, 91,* 554–562.

Hughes, Jean O., & Sandler, Bernice R. (1987). *"Friends" raping friends: Could it happen to you?* Washington, DC: Association of American Colleges.

Hulshoff, Hilleke E., et al. (2006). Changing your sex changes your brain: Influences of testosterone and estrogen on adult human brain structure. *European Journal of Endocrinology, 155,* S107–S114.

Human Rights Watch. (2001). *Hatred in the hallways: Violence and discrimination against lesbian, gay, bisexual, and transgender students in U.S. schools.* New York: Human Rights Watch. www.hrw.org.

Humes, Karen, & McKinnon, Jesse. (2000). *The Asian and Pacific Islander population in the United States.* U.S. Census Bureau. www.census.gov.

Humphreys, Laud. (1970). *Tearoom trade: Impersonal sex in public places.* Chicago: Aldine.

Hunt, Morton. (1974). *Sexual behavior in the 1970s.* Chicago: Playboy Press.

Hunter, Nan, Michaelson, Sherryl, & Stoddard, Thomas. (1992). *The rights of lesbians and gay men: The basic ACLU guide to a gay person's rights.* Carbondale: Southern Illinois University Press.

Huston, T. L., & Levinger, G. (1978). Interpersonal attraction and relationships. In M. R. Rosenzweig & L. W. Porter (Eds.), *Annual Review of Psychology* (Vol. 29). Palo Alto, CA: Annual Reviews.

Hutchinson, Karen A. (1995). Androgens and sexuality. *American Journal of Medicine, 98* (Suppl. 1A), 1A111S–1A115S.

Hyde, Janet S. (1984). How large are gender differences in aggression? A developmental meta-analysis. *Developmental Psychology, 20,* 722–736.

Hyde, Janet S. (2004). *Half the human experience: The psychology of women* (6th ed.). Boston: Houghton-Mifflin.

Hyde, Janet S. (2005). The gender similarities hypothesis. *American Psychologist, 60,* 581–592.

Hyde, Janet S. (2007). *Half the human experience: The psychology of women* (7th ed.). Boston: Houghton-Mifflin.

Hyde, Janet S., DeLamater, John, & Hewitt, Erri. (1998). Sexuality and the dual-earner couple: Multiple roles and sexual functioning. *Journal of Family Psychology, 12,* 354–368.

Hyde, Janet S., et al. (1996). Sexuality during pregnancy and the year postpartum. *Journal of Sex Research, 33,* 143–151.

Hyde, Janet S., & Jaffee, Sara R. (2000). Becoming a heterosexual adult: The experiences of young women. *Journal of Social Issues, 56,* 283–296.

Hynes, H. Patricia, & Raymond, Janice G. (2002). Put in harm's way: The neglected health consequences of sex trafficking in the United States. In J. Silliman & A. Bhattacharjee (Eds.), *Policing the national body: Sex, race, and criminalization* (pp. 197–229). Cambridge, MA: South End Press.

Icard, Larry D. (1996). Assessing the psychosocial well-being of African American gays. In J. F. Longres (Ed.), *Men of color: A context for service to homosexually active men.* New York: Haworth.

Idänpään-Heikkilä, J., et al. (1969). Placental transfer of tritiated-1 tetrahydrocannabinol. *New England Journal of Medicine, 281,* 330.

Ilies, Remus, et al. (2003). Reported incidence rates of work-related sexual harassment in the United States: Using meta-analysis to explain reported rate disparities. *Personnel Psychology, 56,* 607–631.

Ilkkaracan, Pinar. (2001). Islam and women's sexuality. In P. Jung et al. (Eds.), *Good sex: Feminist perspectives from the world's religions* (pp. 61–76). New Brunswick, NJ: Rutgers University Press.

Imperato-McGinley, J., et al. (1974). Steroid 5 reductase deficiency in man: An inherited form of male pseudohermaphroditism. *Science, 186,* 1213–1215.

Impett, Emily, Peplau, L., & Gable, S. (2005). Approach and avoidance sexual motives: Implications for personal and interpersonal well-being. *Personal Relationships, 12,* 465–482.

Innala, Sune M., & Ernulf, Kurt E. (1989). Asphyxiophilia in Scandinavia. *Archives of Sexual Behavior, 18,* 181–190.

Institute of Medicine. (2004). *New frontiers in contraceptive research.* Washington, DC: National Academies Press.

Investigative Staff of the *Boston Globe.* (2002). *Betrayal: The crisis in the Catholic Church.* Boston: Little, Brown.

Iqbal, Mohammad, et al. (2001). Effects of antimanic mood-stabilizing drugs on fetuses, neonates, and nursing infants. *Southern Medical Journal, 94,* 305–322.

Irvine, Janice M. (1995). *Sexuality education across cultures: Working with differences.* San Francisco: Jossey-Bass.

Iwaniuk, Andrew N., et al. (2006). The effects of environmental exposure to DDT on the brain of a songbird: Changes in structures associated with mating and song. *Behavioural Brain Research, 173,* 1–10.

Jaakkola, Jouni, & Gissler, Mika. (2004). Maternal smoking in pregnancy, fetal development and childhood asthma. *American Journal of Public Health, 94,* 136–141.

Jackson, G. (1999). Erectile dysfunction and cardiovascular disease. *International Journal of Clinical Practice, 53,* 363–368.

Jackson, Robert A., & Newman, Meredith A. (2004). Sexual harassment in the federal workplace revisited: Influences on sexual harassment by gender. *Public Administration Review, 64,* 705–717.

Jacob, Kathryn A. (1981). The Mosher report. *American Heritage,* 57–64.

Jacobs, Sue-Ellen, Thomas, Wesley, & Lang, Sabine (Eds.). (1997). *Two-spirit people.* Urbana: University of Illinois Press.

Jacobson, Sandra W., et al. (1993). Prenatal alcohol exposure and infant information processing ability. *Child Development, 64,* 1706–1721.

Jacobson, Sandra W., Jacobson, Joseph L., & Sokol, Robert J. (1994). Effects of fetal alcohol exposure on infant reaction time. *Alcoholism: Clinical and Experimental Research, 18,* 1125–1132.

Jadack, Rosemary A., Keller, Mary L., & Hyde, Janet S. (1990). Genital herpes: Gender comparisons and the disease experience. *Psychology of Women Quarterly, 14,* 419–434.

Jamieson, Denise J., et al. (2002). A comparison of women's regret after vasectomy versus tubal sterilization. *Obstetrics and Gynecology, 99,* 1073–1079.

Janicek, Mike F., & Averette, Hervy E. (2001). Cervical cancer: Prevention, diagnosis, and therapeutics. *CA: Cancer Journal for Clinicians, 51,* 92–114.

Janowsky, Jeri S., et al. (1998). The cognitive neuropsychology of sex hormones in men and women. *Developmental Neuropsychology, 14,* 421–440.

Janssen, E., Vorst, H., Finn, P., & Bancroft, J. (2002). The Sexual Inhibition (SIS) and Sexual Excitation (SES) Scales: I. Measuring sexual inhibition and excitation proneness in men. *Journal of Sex Research, 39* (2), 114–126.

Jantzen, Grace. (1994). AIDS, shame, and suffering. In J. B. Nelson & S. P. Longfellow (Eds.), *Sexuality and the sacred* (pp. 305–313). Louisville, KY: Westminster/John Knox Press.

Janus, Samuel S., & Janus, Cynthia L. (1993). *The Janus report on sexual behavior.* New York: Wiley.

Jay, Karla, & Young, Allen. (1979). *The gay report.* New York: Summit Books.

Jefferson, Elana A. (2005, November 15). Grown up parties are turning up the heat. *Denver Post.*

Jemail, Jay Ann, & Geer, James. (1977). Sexual scripts. In R. Gemme & C. C. Wheeler (Eds.), *Progress in sexology.* New York: Plenum.

Jenkins, J. S., & Nussey, S. S. (1991). The role of oxytocin: Present concepts. *Clinical Endocrinology, 34,* 515–525.

Jenkins, Philip. (1996). *Pedophiles and priests: Anatomy of a contemporary crisis.* New York: Oxford University Press.

Jenks, Richard J. (1985). Swinging: A replication and test of a theory. *Journal of Sex Research, 21,* 199–210.

Jenks, Richard. (1998). Swinging: A review of the literature. *Archives of Sexual Behavior, 27,* 507–521.

Jenny, Carole, Roesler, Thomas A., & Poyer, Kimberly A. (1994). Are children at risk for sexual abuse by homosexuals? *Pediatrics, 94,* 41–44.

Jensen, Gordon D. (1976). Adolescent sexuality. In B. J. Sadock et al. (Eds.), *The sexual experience.* Baltimore: Williams & Wilkins.

John, E. M., Savitz, D. A., & Sandler, D. P. (1991). Prenatal exposure to parents' smoking and childhood cancer. *American Journal of Epidemiology, 133,* 123–132.

Johnson, Anne M., et al. (1992). Sexual lifestyles and HIV risk. *Nature, 360,* 410–412.

Johnson, Anne M., et al. (2001). Sexual behaviour in Britain: Partnerships, practices, and HIV risk behaviours. *The Lancet, 358,* 1835–1842.

Johnson, Brooke R., Horga, Mihai, & Andronache, Laurentia. (1996). Women's perspectives on abortion in Romania. *Social Science & Medicine, 42,* 521–530.

Johnson, Sharon D., Phelps, D., & Cottler, L. (2004). The association of sexual dysfunction and substance use among a community epidemiological sample. *Archives of Sexual Behavior, 33,* 55–64.

Johri, A., Heaton, J., & Morales, A. (2001). Severe erectile dysfunction is a marker for hyperprolactinemia. *International Journal of Impotence Research, 13,* 176–182.

Jones, Hendree. (2006). Drug addiction during pregnancy: Advances in maternal treatment and understanding child outcomes. *Current Directions in Psychological Science, 15,* 126–130.

Jones, James H. (1981). *Bad blood: The Tuskegee syphilis experiment.* New York: Free Press.

Jones, James H. (1997). *Alfred C. Kinsey: A public/private life.* New York: Norton.

Jones, John, Pelham, Brett, Carvallo, Mauricio, & Mirenberg, Matthew. (2004). How do I love thee? Let me count the Js: Implicit egotism and interpersonal attraction. *Journal of Personality and Social Psychology, 87,* 665–683.

Jones, Rachel K., Darroch, J., & Henshaw, S. (2002). Contraceptive use among U.S. women having abortions in 2000–2001. *Perspectives on Sexual and Reproductive Health, 34,* 294–303.

Jones, Rachel K., & Henshaw, Stanley K. (2002). Mifepristone for early medical abortion: Experiences in France, Great Britain and Sweden. *Perspectives on Sexual and Reproductive Health, 34,* 154–161.

Jorgensen, S. R. (1980). Contraceptive attitude-behavior consistency in adolescence. *Population and Environment, 3,* 174–194.

Julien, Danielle, et al. (2003). Conflict, social support, and relationship quality: An observational study of heterosexual, gay male, and lesbian couples' communication. *Journal of Family Psychology, 17,* 419–428.

Jung, Patricia B., Hunt, Mary E., & Balakrishnan, Radhika (Eds.). (2001). *Good sex: Feminist perspectives from the world's religions.* New Brunswick, NJ: Rutgers University Press.

Kabalin, John N., & Kuo, Jeffrey C. (1997). Long-term follow-up of and patient satisfaction with the Dynaflex self-contained inflatable penile prosthesis. *Journal of Urology, 158,* 456–469.

Kabir, Azad, Pridjian, G., Steinmann, W., Herrera, E., & Khan, M. (2005). Racial differences in cesareans: An analysis of U.S. 2001 national inpatient sample data. *Obstetrics and Gynecology, 195,* 710–718.

Kafka, Martin P. (1997). Hypersexual desire in males: An operational definition and clinical implications for males with paraphilias and paraphilia-related disorders. *Archives of Sexual Behavior, 26,* 505–526.

Kaiser Family Foundation. (1997). *National survey of teens: Teens talk about dating, intimacy, and their sexual experiences.* Menlo Park, CA: Kaiser Family Foundation. www.kff.org.

Kaiser Family Foundation. (1998). *Sex in the 90s: 1998 national survey of Americans on sex and sexual health.* Menlo Park, CA: Kaiser Family Foundation, Pub. No. 1430. www.kff.org.

Kaiser Family Foundation. (2000a). *Sex education in America: A view from inside the nation's classrooms.* Menlo Park, CA: Kaiser Family Foundation.

Kaiser Family Foundation. (2000b). *Sex smarts: Decision-making.* Menlo Park, CA: Kaiser Family Foundation, Publication No. 3064.

Kaiser Family Foundation. (2004a). *Sex education in America: General public/parents survey.* Menlo Park, CA: Kaiser Family Foundation. www.kff.org.

Kaiser Family Foundation. (2004b). *Sex education in America: Principals survey.* Menlo Park, CA: Kaiser Family Foundation. www.kff.org.

Kaiser, Jocelyn. (2003). Studies of gay men, prostitutes come under scrutiny. *Science, 300,* 403.

Kalichman, Seth C., & Cain, Demetria. (2004). The relationship between indicators of sexual compulsivity and high risk sexual practices among men and women receiving services from a sexually transmitted infection clinic. *Journal of Sex Research, 41,* 235–241.

Kalichman, Seth C., & Rompa, D. (1995). Sexual sensation seeking and compulsivity scales: Reliability, validity, and predicting HIV risk behavior. *Journal of Personality Assessment, 62,* 586–601.

Kalick, S. Michael, et al. (1998). Does human facial attractiveness honestly advertise health? Longitudinal data on an evolutionary question. *Psychological Science, 9,* 8–13.

Kalil, Kathleen, et al. (1993). Social and family pressures on anxiety and stress during pregnancy. *Pre- and Perinatal Psychology Journal, 8,* 113–118.

Kallstrom-Fuqua, Amanda C., Weston, R., & Marshall, L. (2004). Childhood and adolescent sexual abuse of community women: Mediated effects on psychological distress and social relationships. *Journal of Consulting and Clinical Psychology, 72,* 980–992.

Kambic, Robert T. (1999). The effectiveness of natural family planning methods for birth spacing: A comprehensive review. *Hopkins Population Center Papers on Population,* WP 99–07. www.popctr.jhsph.edu.

Kamel, H. K., Perry, H. M., & Morley, J. E. (2001). Hormone replacement therapy and fractures in older adults. *Journal of the American Geriatrics Society, 49,* 179–187.

Kane, Elizabeth. (1988). *Birth mother: The story of America's first legal surrogate mother.* San Diego: Harcourt Brace Jovanovich.

Kanin, E. J., Davidson, K. D., & Scheck, S. R. (1970). A research note on male-female differentials in the experience of heterosexual love. *Journal of Sex Research, 6,* 64–72.

Kantner, John F., & Zelnik, Melvin. (1972). Sexual experience of young unmarried women in the United States. *Family Planning Perspectives,* 4 (4), 9–18.

Kantner, John F., & Zelnik, Melvin. (1973). Contraception and pregnancy: Experience of young unmarried women in the United States. *Family Planning Perspectives,* 5 (1), 21–35.

Kaplan, Helen S. (1974). *The new sex therapy.* New York: Brunner/Mazel.

Kaplan, Helen S. (1995). *The sexual desire disorders: Dysfunctional regulation of sexual motivation.* New York: Brunner/Mazel.

Kaplan, Helen S., & Owett, Trude. (1993). The female androgen deficiency syndrome. *Journal of Sex and Marital Therapy, 19,* 3–25.

Kaplan, Helen S., & Sager, C. J. (1971, June). Sexual patterns at different ages. *Medical Aspects of Human Sexuality,* 10–23.

Kaplan, Helen Singer. (1979). *Disorders of sexual desire.* New York: Simon & Schuster.

Karama, S., et al. (2002). Areas of brain activation in males and females during viewing of erotic film excerpts. *Human Brain Mapping, 16,* 1–13.

Karr, Rodney K. (1978). Homosexual labeling and the male role. *Journal of Social Issues, 34* (3), 73–83.

Keefe, David L. (2002). Sex hormones and neural mechanisms. *Archives of Sexual Behavior, 31,* 401–404.

Keenan, T., & Ward, T. (2000). A theory of mind perspective on cognitive, affective, and intimacy deficits in child sex offenders. *Sex Abuse, 12,* 49–60.

Kegel, A. H. (1952). Sexual functions of the pubococcygeus muscle. *Western Journal of Surgery, 60,* 521–524.

Kelly, Brian C., & Muñoz-Laboy, Miguel A. (2005). Sexual place, spatial change, and social reorganization of sexual culture. *Journal of Sex Research, 42,* 359–366.

Kempf, D. J., et al. (1995). ABT-538 is a potent inhibitor of human immunodeficiency virus protease. *Proceedings of the National Academy of Sciences, 92,* 2484.

Kempton, Winifred, & Kahn, Emily. (1991). Sexuality and people with intellectual disabilities: A historical perspective. *Sexuality and Disability, 9,* 93–111.

Kendall-Tackett, K., Williams, L., & Finkelhor, D. (1993). Impact of sexual abuse on children: A review and synthesis of recent empirical studies. *Psychological Bulletin, 113,* 164–180.

Kendler, Kenneth S., et al. (2000a). Childhood sexual abuse and adult psychiatric and substance use disorders in women: An epidemiological and cotwin control analysis. *Archives of General Psychiatry, 57,* 953–959.

Kendler, Kenneth S., et al. (2000b). Sexual orientation in a U.S. national sample of twin and nontwin sibling pairs. *American Journal of Psychiatry, 157,* 1843–1846.

Kennedy, Robert, & Suttenfield, Kelley. (2001). Postpartum depression. *Medscape Mental Health 6,* 4.

Kenrick, D., et al. (1980). Sex differences, androgyny and approach responses to erotica: A new variation on an old volunteer problem. *Journal of Personality and Social Psychology, 38,* 517–524.

Kessler, Suzanne. (1998). *Lessons from the intersexed.* New Brunswick, NJ: Rutgers University Press.

Keverne, Eric B. (1999). The vomeronasal organ. *Science, 286,* 716–720.

Kiecolt, K. J., Fossett, M. A., & Smith, W. (1995). Mate availability and marriage among African-Americans: Aggregate- and individual-level analyses. In M. B. Tucker & C. Mitchell-Kerum (Eds.), *The decline in marriage among African-Americans: Causes, consequences, and policy implications* (pp. 103–116). New York: Russell Sage Foundation.

Kiernan, K. (1988). Who remains celibate? *Journal of Biosocial Science, 20,* 253–263.

Kikuras, A. (2004). An interview with Dave Cummings, *Unchain the underground.* www.unchain.com.

Kilmartin, Christopher T. (2000). *The masculine self* (2nd ed.). New York: McGraw-Hill.

Kim, Bryan, Li, Lisa, & Ng, Gladys. (2005). The Asian American values scale. *Cultural Diversity and Ethnic Minority Psychology, 11,* 187–201.

Kim, Bryan S., et al. (2001). Cultural value similarities and differences among Asian American ethnic groups. *Cultural Diversity and Ethnic Minority Psychology, 7,* 343–361.

Kim, N., et al. (1997). Effectiveness of the 40 adolescent AIDS-risk reduction interventions: A quantitative review. *Journal of Adolescent Health, 20,* 204–215.

King, Mary-Claire, Marks, J., & Mandell, J. (2003). Breast and ovarian cancer risks due to inherited mutations in BRCA1 and BRCA2. *Science, 302,* 643–646.

King, Michael, & Woollett, Earnest. (1997). Sexually assaulted males: 115 men consulting a counseling service. *Archives of Social Behavior, 26,* 579–588.

Kinnish, Kelly K., Strassberg, D., & Turner, C. (2005). Sex differences in the flexibility of sexual orientation: A multidimensional retrospective assessment. *Archives of Sexual Behavior, 34,* 173–184.

Kinsey, Alfred C., et al. (1953). *Sexual behavior in the human female.* Philadelphia: Saunders.

Kinsey, Alfred C., Pomeroy, Wardell B., & Martin, Clyde E. (1948). *Sexual behavior in the human male.* Philadelphia: Saunders.

Kiragu, Karungari. (1995, October). Female genital mutilation: A reproductive health concern. *Population Reports* (Supplement), Series J, No. 41, Vol. 23.

Kiragu, Karungari, et al. (2001). Can we avoid catastrophe? Youth and HIV/AIDS. *Population Reports,* Series L, No. 12. Johns Hopkins University School of Public Health.

Kirby, Douglas. (1992). School-based programs to reduce sexual risk-taking behavior. *Journal of School Health, 62*, 281–287.

Kirby, Douglas. (2002). *Do abstinence-only programs delay the initiation of sex among young people and reduce teen pregnancy?* Washington, DC: National Campaign to Prevent Teen Pregnancy.

Kirby, Douglas. (2002). Effective approaches to reducing adolescent unprotected sex, pregnancy, and childbearing. *Journal of Sex Research, 39*, 51–57.

Kirby, Douglas, et al. (1994). School-based programs to reduce sexual risk behaviors: A review of effectiveness. *Public Health Reports, 109*, 339–360.

Kirk, K., et al. (2000). Measurement models for sexual orientation in a community twin sample. *Behavior Genetics, 30*, 345–356.

Kirkpatrick, Lee, & Davis, Keith. (1994). Attachment style, gender, and relationship stability: A longitudinal analysis. *Journal of Personality and Social Psychology, 66*, 502–512.

Kirkpatrick, Martha. (1996). Lesbians as parents. In R. P. Cabaj & T. S. Stein (Eds.), *Textbook of homosexuality and mental health*. Washington, DC: American Psychiatric Press.

Kiselica, Mark, & Scheckel, Steve. (1995). The couvade syndrome (sympathetic pregnancy) and teenage fathers: A brief primer for counselors. *School Counselor, 43*, 42–51.

Klaus, Marshall, & Kennell, John. (1976). Human maternal and paternal behavior. In M. Klaus & J. Kennell (Eds.), *Maternal-infant bonding*. St. Louis, MO: Mosby.

Klebanov, Pamela K., & Jemmott, John B. (1992). Effects of expectations and bodily sensations on self-reports of premenstrual symptoms. *Psychology of Women Quarterly, 16*, 289–310.

Kleinhaus, K., Perrin, M., Friedlander, Y., Paltiel, O., Malaspina, D., & Harlap, S. (2006). Paternal age and spontaneous abortion. *Obstetrics and Gynecology, 108*, 369–377.

Klemetti, R., Gissler, M., Sevon, T., Koivurova, S., Ritvanen, A., & Hemminki, E. (2005). Children born after assisted fertilization have an increased rate of major congenital abnormalities. *Fertility & Sterility, 84*, 1300–1307.

Kline, Galena, Stanley, S., Markman, H., Olmos-Gallo, P. A., St. Peters, M., Whitton, S., & Prado, L. (2004). Timing is everything: Pre-engagement cohabitation and increased risk for poor marital outcomes. *Journal of Family Psychology, 18*, 311–318.

Klitzman, Robert, & Bayer, Ronald. (2003). *Mortal secrets: Truth and lies in the age of AIDS*. Baltimore: Johns Hopkins University Press.

Knafo, Ariel, Iervolino, Alessandra C., & Plomin, Robert. (2005). Masculine girls and feminine boys: Genetic and environmental contributions to atypical gender development in early childhood. *Journal of Personality and Social Psychology, 88*, 400–412.

Kniffin, K. M., & Wilson, D. S. (2004). The effect of nonphysical traits on perception of physical attractiveness: Three naturalistic studies. *Evolution and Human Behavior, 25*, 88–101.

Koch, Patricia B., Mansfield, P., Thurau, D., & Carey, M. (2005). "Feeling frumpy": The relationships between body image and sexual response changes in midlife women. *Journal of Sex Research, 42*, 215–223.

Koelman, C. A., et al. (2000). Correlation between oral sex and a low incidence of preeclampsia: A role for soluble HLA in seminal fluid? *Journal of Reproductive Immunology, 46*, 155–166.

Kolata, Gina. (2001, March 25). Researchers find grave defect risk in cloning animals. *New York Times*, pp. 1ff.

Kolbenschlag, Madonna. (1985). Abortion and moral consensus: Beyond Solomon's choice. *Christian Century, 102*, 179–183.

Kolker, Aliza. (1989). Advances in prenatal diagnosis. *International Journal of Technology Assessment in Health Care, 5*, 601–617.

Kolodny, R. C., et al. (1974). Depression of plasma testosterone levels after chronic intensive marihuana use. *New England Journal of Medicine, 290*, 872–874.

Komisaruk, Barry R., Gerdes, C. A., & Whipple, Beverly. (1997). "Complete" spinal cord injury does not block perceptual responses to genital self-stimulation in women. *Archives of Neurology, 54*, 1513–1520.

Komisaruk, Barry R., & Whipple, Beverly. (2005). Function MRI of the brain during orgasm in women. *Annual Review of Sex Research, 15*, 62–86.

Koonin, Lisa M., et al. (1991). Abortion surveillance, United States, 1988. *Morbidity and Mortality Weekly Report, 40* (SS-1), 15–42.

Korff, Janice, & Geer, James H. (1983). The relationship between sexual arousal experience and genital response. *Psychophysiology, 20*, 121–127.

Kosfeld, Michael, Heinrichs, Markus, Zak, Paul, Fischbacher, Urs, & Fehr, Ernst. (2005). Oxytocin increases trust in humans. *Nature, 435* (June 2), 673–676.

Kosnick, Anthony, et al. (1977). *Human sexuality: New directions in American Catholic thought*. New York: Paulist Press.

Koss, Mary P. (1993). Rape: Scope, impact, interventions, and public policy responses. *American Psychologist, 48*, 1062–1069.

Koss, Mary P., & Cook, Sarah L. (1994). Facing the facts: Date and acquaintance rape are widespread forms of violence. In M. Koss et al. (Eds.), *No safe haven*. Washington, DC: American Psychological Association.

Koss, Mary P., et al. (1988). Stranger and acquaintance rape: Are there differences in the victim's experience? *Psychology of Women Quarterly, 12*, 1–24.

Koss, Mary P., et al. (1994). *No safe haven: Male violence against women at home, at work, and in the community*. Washington, DC: American Psychological Association.

Koss, Mary P., et al. (2003). Restorative justice of sexual violence: Repairing victims, building community, and holding offenders accountable. *Annals of the New York Academy of Sciences, 989*, 133–147.

Koss, Mary P., & Figueredo, Aurelio. (2004). Change in cognitive mediators of rape's impact on psychosocial health across 2 years of recovery. *Journal of Consulting and Clinical Psychology, 72*, 1063–1072.

Koss, Mary P., Gidycz, C. A., & Wisniewski, N. (1987). The scope of rape: Incidence and prevalence in a national sample of higher education students. *Journal of Consulting and Clinical Psychology, 55*, 162–170.

Koss, Mary P., & Heslet, Lynette. (1992). Somatic consequences of violence against women. *Archives of Family Medicine, 1*, 53–59.

Koss, Mary P., Koss, Paul G., & Woodruff, W. Joy. (1991). Deleterious effects of criminal victimization on women's health and medical utilization. *Archives of Internal Medicine, 151*, 342–347.

Kothari, P. (1984). For discussion: Ejaculatory disorders—a new dimension. *British Journal of Sexual Medicine, 11*, 205–209.

Kovacs, Peter. (2002a). Congenital anomalies and low birth weight associated with assisted reproductive technologies. *Medscape Women's Health, 7* (3). www.medscape.com/viewarticle/435963.

Kovacs, Peter. (2002b). Preconception sex selection. *Medscape Ob/Gyn & Women's Health, 7* (2). www.medscape.com/viewarticle/441313.

Kraut, Robert, et al. (2004). Psychological research online: Report of Board of Scientific Affairs' Advisory Group on the Conduct of Research on the Internet. *American Psychologist, 59*, 105–117.

Kreider, Rose. (2006). Marital status in the 2004 American Community Survey. U.S. Bureau of the Census, Working Paper. U.S. Bureau of the Census, Statistical Abstract of the United States, 2007, Table 62.

Kreimer, A., et al. (2004). Oral human papillomavirus infection in adults is associated with sexual behavior and HIV serostatus. *Journal of Infectious Diseases, 189*, 686–698.

Krieger, John N., & Alderete, John F. (1999). *Trichomonas vaginalis* and trichomoniasis. In K. Holmes et al. (Eds.), *Sexually transmitted diseases* (3rd ed., pp. 587–604). New York: McGraw-Hill.

Krimmel, Herbert T. (1983, October). The case against surrogate parenting. *Hastings Center Report*, 35–39.

Krimsky, Sheldon. (2000). *Hormonal chaos: The scientific and social origins of the environmental endocrine hypothesis*. Baltimore: Johns Hopkins University Press.

Kroeber, Alfred L., & Kluckhohn, Clyde. (1963). *Culture: A critical review of concepts and definitions*. New York: Vintage Books.

Kroll, Ken, et al. (1995). *Enabling romance: A guide to love, sex, and relationships for the disabled (and the people who care for them)*. Bethesda, MD: Woodbine House.

Krueger, R. B., & Kaplan, M. S. (2001). Depo-leuprolide acetate for treatment of paraphilias: A report of twelve cases. *Archives of Sexual Behavior, 30*, 409–422.

Kruger, Brody S. (2006). The post-orgasmic prolactin increase following intercourse is greater than following masturbation and suggests greater satiety. *Biological Psychology, 71,* 312–315.

Krüger, T. H. C., et al. (2002). Orgasm-induced prolactin secretion: Feedback control of sexual drive? *Neuroscience and Biobehavioral Reviews, 26,* 31–44.

Kruijver, F., et al. (2000). Male-to-female transsexuals have female neuron numbers in a limbic nucleus. *Journal of Clinical Endocrinology and Metabolism, 85,* 2034–2041.

Kuffel, Stephanie, & Heiman, Julia R. (2006). Effects of depressive symptoms and experimentally adopted schemas on sexual arousal and affect in sexually healthy women. *Archives of Sexual Behavior, 35,* 163–178.

Kumar, R., Brant, H. A., & Robson, K. M. (1981). Childbearing and maternal sexuality: A prospective survey of 119 primiparae. *Journal of Psychosomatic Research, 25,* 373–383.

Kunkel, Dale, Cope, K. M., & Colvin, C. (1996). *Sexual messages on family hour television: Content and context.* Menlo Park, CA: Kaiser Family Foundation.

Kunkel, Dale, et al. (2003). *Sex on TV.* Menlo Park, CA: Henry J. Kaiser Family Foundation.

Kunkel, Dale, et al. (2005). *Sex on TV 4.* Menlo Park, CA: Kaiser Family Foundation. www.kff.org.

Kunkel, Dale., Eyal, K., Finnerty, K., Biely, E., & Donnerstein, E. (2006). *Sex on TV, 2005.* Menlo Park, CA: Kaiser Family Foundation.

Kurdek, Lawrence A. (1995a). Developmental changes in relationship quality in gay and lesbian cohabiting couples. *Developmental Psychology, 31,* 86–94.

Kurdek, Lawrence A. (1995b). Lesbian and gay couples. In A. R. D'Augelli & C. J. Patterson (Eds.), *Lesbian, gay, and bisexual identities over the lifespan* (pp. 243–261). New York: Oxford University Press.

Kurdek, Lawrence A. (2005). What do we know about gay and lesbian couples? *Current Directions in Psychological Science, 14,* 251–254.

L'Engle, K., Jackson, C., & Brown, J. (2006). Early adolescents' cognitive susceptibility to initiating sexual intercourse. *Perspectives on Sexual and Reproductive Health, 38,* 97–105.

Laan, Ellen, & Everaerd, Walter. (1995). Determinants of female sexual arousal: Psychophysiological theory and data. *Annual Review of Sex Research, 6,* 32–76.

Laan, Ellen, et al. (1994). Women's sexual and emotional responses to male- and female-produced erotica. *Archives of Sexual Behavior, 23,* 153–170.

Lackritz, Eve M., et al. (1995). Estimated risk of transmission of the human immunodeficiency virus by screened blood in the United States. *New England Journal of Medicine, 333,* 1721–1725.

LaFromboise, Theresa D., Heyle, Anneliese M., & Ozer, Emily J. (1990). Changing and diverse roles of women in American Indian cultures. *Sex Roles,* 455–476.

Lalumière, M., Blanchard, R., & Zucker, K. (2000). Sexual orientation and handedness in men and women: A meta-analysis. *Psychological Bulletin, 126,* 575–592.

Lalumière, M. L., & Quinsey, V. L. (1998). Pavlovian conditioning of sexual interests in human males. *Archives of Sexual Behavior, 27,* 241–252.

Lamb, Michael. (1982, April). Second thoughts on first touch. *Psychology Today,* 9–10.

Lamb, Michael E., & Hwang, C. (1982). Maternal attachment and mother-neonate bonding: A critical review. In M. E. Lamb & A. L. Brown (Eds.), *Advances in developmental psychology* (Vol. 2). Hillsdale, NJ: Lawrence Erlbaum.

Lambda Legal. (2007). Legal recognition of same-sex relationships by state. Retrieved March 20, 2007, from http://www.lambdalegal.org/ourwork/publications.

Lambert, Tracy A., Kahn, A., & Apple, K. (2003). Pluralistic ignorance and hooking up. *Journal of Sex Research, 40,* 129–133.

Lamberts, Steven W. J., et al. (1997). The endocrinology of aging. *Science, 278,* 419–424.

Lande, Robert E. (1995). New era for injectables. *Population Reports,* Series K, No. 5.

Landry, David, et al. (2003). Factors associated with the content of sex education in U.S. public secondary schools. *Perspectives on Sexual and Reproductive Health, 35,* 261–269.

Landry, David, Kaeser, Lisa, & Richards, Cory. (1999). Abstinence promotion and the provision of information about contraception in public school district sexuality education policies. *Family Planning Perspectives, 31,* 280–286.

Langan, Patrick, Schmitt, Erica, & Durose, Matthew. (2003). *Recidivism of sex offenders released from prison in 1994.* Washington, DC: U.S. Department of Justice, Bureau of Justice Statistics.

Langer, Ellen J., & Dweck, Carol S. (1973). *Personal politics: The psychology of making it.* Englewood Cliffs, NJ: Prentice-Hall.

Langfeldt, Thore. (1981). Childhood masturbation. In L. L. Constantine & F. M. Martinson (Eds.), *Children and sex* (pp. 63–74). Boston: Little, Brown.

Långström, Niklas, & Seto, Michael C. (2006). Exhibitionistic and voyeuristic behavior in a Swedish national population survey. *Archives of Sexual Behavior, 35,* 427–436.

Långström, Niklas, & Zucker, Kenneth J. (2005). Transvestic fetishism in the general population: Prevalence and correlates. *Journal of Sex and Marital Therapy, 31,* 87–95.

Lantz, H. R., Keyes, J., & Schultz, H. (1975). The American family in the preindustrial period: From baselines in history to change. *American Sociological Review, 40,* 21–36.

Laqueur, Thomas W. (2003). *Solitary sex: A cultural history of masturbation.* New York: Zone Books.

Larsen, Sandra A. (1996). Syphilis. In S. Morse et al. (Eds.), *Atlas of sexually transmitted diseases and AIDS* (pp. 21–46). London: Mosby-Wolfe.

Larsson, IngBeth, & Svedin, Carl-Göran (2002). Sexual experiences in childhood: Young adults' recollections. *Archives of Sexual Behavior, 31,* 263–274.

Lasker, Stephanie. (2002). Sex and the city: Zoning "pornography peddlers and live nude shows." *UCLA Law Review, 49,* 1139–1185.

Lattimore, Keri, Donn, S., Kaciroti, N., Kemper, A., Neal, C., & Vasquez, D. (2005). Selective serotonin reuptake inhibitor (SSRI) use during pregnancy and effects on the fetus and newborn: A meta-analysis. *Journal of Perinatology, 25,* 595–604.

Latty-Mann, Holly, & Davis, Keith. (1996). Attachment theory and partner choice: Preference and actuality. *Journal of Social and Personal Relationships, 13,* 5–23.

Laumann, Edward O., et al. (1994). *The social organization of sexuality: Sexual practices in the United States.* Chicago: University of Chicago Press.

Laumann, Edward O., et al. (2004). *The sexual organization of the city.* Chicago: University of Chicago Press.

Laumann, Edward O., et al. (2005). Sexual problems among women aged 40–80: Prevalence and correlates identified in the Global Study of Sexual Attitudes and Behavior. *International Journal of Impotency Research, 17,* 39–57.

Laumann, Edward O., Masi, C., & Zuckerman, E. (1997). Circumcision in the United States: Prevalence, prophylactic effects, and sexual practice. *Journal of the American Medical Association, 277,* 1052–1057.

Laumann, Edward O., Paik, A., & Rosen, R. (1999). Sexual dysfunction in the United States: Prevalence and predictors. *Journal of the American Medical Association, 281,* 537–544.

Laumann, Edward O., & Parish, William. (2004). Chinese Family Health Survey (CFHS). Personal communication.

Laurenceau, J-P., Feldman, Barrett, & Pietromonaco, P. R. (1998). Intimacy as an interpersonal process: The importance of self-disclosure, partner disclosure, and perceived partner responsiveness in interpersonal exchanges. *Journal of Personality and Social Psychology, 74,* 1238–1251.

Lauzen, Martha M., et al. (2006). Genre matters: An examination of women working behind the scenes and on-screen portrayals in reality and scripted prime-time programming. *Sex Roles, 55,* 445–456.

Lavine, Howard, Sweeney, Donna, & Wagner, Stephen. (1999). Depicting women as sex objects in television advertising: Effects on body dissatisfaction. *Personality and Social Psychology Bulletin, 25,* 1049–1058.

Lawrence, Anne A. (2003). Factors associated with satisfaction or regret following male-to-female sex reassignment surgery. *Archives of Sexual Behavior, 32,* 299–316.

Lawrence, Anne A. (2005). Sexuality before and after male-to-female sex reassignment surgery. *Archives of Sexual Behavior, 34,* 147–166.

Lawrence, Anne A., et al. (2005). Measurement of sexual arousal in postoperative male-to-female transsexuals using vaginal photoplethysmography. *Archives of Sexual Behavior, 34,* 135–146.

Lawrence, Kelli-An, & Byers, E. Sandra. (1995). Sexual satisfaction in long-term heterosexual relationships: The interpersonal exchange model of sexual satisfaction. *Personal Relationships, 2,* 267–285.

Lean, Geoffrey. (2006). Pollution: Where have all the baby boys gone? *The Independent.* Retrieved January 15, 2007, from http://lists.ifas.ufl.edu/cgi-bin/wa.exe?A2=ind0604&L=sanet-mg&D=0&T=0&P=315.

Leaper, Campbell, & Friedman, Carly Kay. (2007). The socialization of gender. In J. Grusec & P. Hastings (Eds.), *Handbook of socialization: Theory and research* (pp. 561–587). New York: Guilford.

Leavitt, Fred. (1974). *Drugs and behavior.* Philadelphia: Saunders.

Lebacqz, Karen. (1987). Appropriate vulnerability: A sexual ethic for singles. *Christian Century, 104,* 435–438.

Lebeque, Breck. (1991). Paraphilias in U.S. pornography titles: "Pornography made me do it" (Ted Bundy). *Bulletin of the American Academy of Psychiatry and Law, 19,* 43–48.

Lechner, Suzanne C., et al. (2003). Cognitive-behavioral interventions improve quality of life in women with AIDS. *Journal of Psychosomatic Research, 54,* 253–261.

Lederer, Laura (Ed.). (1980). *Take back the night: Women on pornography.* New York: Morrow.

Lee, J. A. (1979). The social organization of sexual risk. *Alternative Lifestyles, 2,* 69–100.

Lee, Shirley. (2002). Health and sickness: The meaning of menstruation and premenstrual syndrome in women's lives. *Sex Roles, 46,* 25–36.

Leeman, Lawrence, & Leeman, Rebecca. (2003). A Native American community with a 7% cesarean delivery rate: Does case mix, ethnicity or labor management explain the low rate? *Annals of Family Medicine, 1,* 36–43.

Legman, Gershon. (1968). *Rationale of the dirty joke.* New York: Grove.

Lehren, Andrew, & Leland, John. (2006, March 6). Scant drop seen in abortion rate if parents are told. *New York Times,* National.

Leiblum, Sandra R. (1993). The impact of infertility on sexual and marital satisfaction. *Annual Review of Sex Research, 4,* 99–120.

Leiblum, Sandra R. (2000). Vaginismus: A most perplexing problem. In S. Leiblum & R. Rosen (Eds.), *Principles and practice of sex therapy* (3rd ed., pp. 181–204). New York: Guilford.

Leiblum, Sandra R. (Ed.). (2007). *Principles and practice of sex therapy* (4th ed.). New York: Guilford.

Leiblum, Sandra R., & Rosen, Raymond C. (Eds.). (1989). *Principles and practice of sex therapy* (2nd ed.). New York: Guilford.

Leiblum, Sandra R., & Rosen, Raymond. (Eds.). (2000). *Principles and practice of sex therapy* (3rd ed.). New York: Guilford.

Leifer, Myra. (1980). *Psychological effects of motherhood: A study of first pregnancy.* New York: Praeger.

Leitenberg, Harold, & Henning, Kris. (1995). Sexual fantasy. *Psychological Bulletin, 117,* 469–496.

LeMagnen, J. (1952). Les pheromones olfactosexuels chez le rat blanc. *Archives des Sciences Physiologiques, 6,* 295–332.

Leonard, Arthur S. (1993). *Sexuality and the law: An encyclopedia of major legal cases.* New York: Garland Publishing.

Leonard, Leah M., & Follette, Victoria, M. (2002). Sex functioning in women reporting a history of child sexual abuse: Clinical and empirical considerations. *Annual Review of Sex Research, 13,* 346–388.

Leonard, Lori. (2000). Interpreting female genital cutting: Moving beyond the impasse. *Annual Review of Sex Research, 11,* 158–190.

Lerman, Hannah. (1986). From Freud to feminist personality theory. *Psychology of Women Quarterly, 10,* 1–18.

Leshner, Alan I. (2003). Don't let ideology trump science. *Science, 302,* 1479.

Letvin, Norman L., et al. (2006). Preserved CD4+ central memory T cells and survival in vaccinated SIV-challenged monkeys. *Science, 312,* 1530–1533.

LeVay, Simon. (1991). A difference in hypothalamic structure between heterosexual and homosexual men. *Science, 253,* 1034–1037.

LeVay, Simon. (1996). *Queer science: The use and abuse of research into homosexuality.* Cambridge, MA: MIT Press.

Levin, Roy J. (2003). Is prolactin the biological "off switch" for human sexual arousal? *Sexual and Relationship Therapy, 18,* 237–243.

Levin, Roy J. (2005). Sexual arousal—its physiological roles in human reproduction. *Annual Review of Sex Research, 15,* 154–189.

Levine, Carol, & Bermel, Joyce. (Eds.). (1985, August). *AIDS: The emerging ethical dilemmas.* Hastings Center Report Special Supplement, 1–31.

Levine, Carol, & Bermel, Joyce. (Eds.). (1986, December). *AIDS: Public health and civil liberties.* Hastings Center Report Special Supplement, 1–36.

Levine, R., et al. (1995). Love and marriage in eleven cultures. *Journal of Cross-Cultural Psychology, 26,* 554–571.

Levine, S. B., et al. (1998). The standards of care for gender identity disorders. *International Journal of Transgenderism, 2.* www.symposium.com/ijt/ijtc0405.htm.

Levitas, Eliahu, et al. (2003). *Are semen parameters related to abstinence? Analysis of 7,233 semen samples.* Paper presented at European Society for Human Reproduction and Embryology, Madrid.

Levitt, Eugene, Moser, Charles, & Jamison, Karen. (1994). The prevalence and some attributes of females in the sadomasochistic subculture: A second report. *Archives of Sexual Behavior, 23,* 465–473.

Levitt, Eugene E., & Mulcahy, John J. (1995). The effect of intracavernosal injection of papaverine hydrochloride on orgasm latency. *Journal of Sex and Marital Therapy, 21,* 39–41.

Lewis, Jacqueline, et al. (2005). Managing risk and safety on the job: The experiences of Canadian sex workers. *Journal of Psychology and Human Sexuality, 17,* 147–167.

Lewis, Linwood J., & Kertzner, Robert M. (2003). Toward improved interpretation and theory building of African American male sexualities. *Journal of Sex Research, 40,* 383–395.

Lewis, R. W., et al. (2004). Definitions, classification, and epidemiology of sexual dysfunction. In T. Lue et al. (Eds.), *Sexual medicine* (pp. 39–72). Paris: Editions 21.

Lewis, R. W., & Witherington, R. (1997). External vacuum therapy for erectile dysfunction: Use and results. *World Journal of Urology, 15,* 78–82.

Li, Kai, & Poirier, D. J. (2001). Using the National Longitudinal Study of Youth in the U.S. to study the birth process: A Bayesian approach. *Research in Official Statistics, 4,* 127–150.

Liebmann-Smith, Joan. (1987). *In pursuit of pregnancy: How couples discover, cope with, and resolve their fertility problems.* New York: Newmarket Press.

Lief, Harold I., & Hubschman, Lynn. (1993). Orgasm in the postoperative transsexual. *Archives of Sexual Behavior, 22,* 145–156.

Lightfoot-Klein, Hanny. (1989). *Prisoners of ritual: An odyssey into female genital circumcision in Africa.* New York: Haworth.

Liljeros, F., et al. (2001). The web of human sexual contacts. *Nature, 411,* 907–908.

Lindsey, Robert. (1988, February 1). Circumcision under criticism as unnecessary to newborn. *New York Times,* p. A1.

Linz, Daniel. (1989). Exposure to sexually explicit materials and attitudes toward rape: A comparison of study results. *Journal of Sex Research, 26,* 50–84.

Linz, Daniel, Donnerstein, E., & Penrod, S. (1987). The findings and recommendations of the Attorney General's Commission on pornography: Do the psychological "facts" fit the political fury? *American Psychologist, 42,* 946–953.

Lippa, Richard A. (2003). Are 2D:4D finger-length ratios related to sexual orientation? Yes for men, no for women. *Journal of Personality and Social Psychology, 85,* 179–188.

Lippa, Richard. (2007). The relation between sex drive and sexual attraction to men and women: A cross-national study of heterosexual, bisexual, and homosexual men and women. *Archives of Sexual Behavior, 36,* 209–222.

Lisak, David, & Miller, Paul M. (2002). Repeat rape and multiple offending among undetected rapists. *Violence and Victims, 17,* 73–84.

Liskin, Laurie. (1985, November–December). Youth in the 1980s: Social and health concerns. *Population Reports*, XIII, No. 5, M350–M388.

Liu, Chien. (2003). Does quality of marital sex decline with duration? *Archives of Sexual Behavior*, 32, 55–60.

Liu, Peter, & Chan, Connie S. (1996). Lesbian, gay, and bisexual Asian Americans and their families. In J. Laird & R. Green (Eds.), *Lesbians and gays in couples and families*. San Francisco: Jossey-Bass.

Liu, Peter Y., et al. (2006). Rate, extent, and modifiers of spermatogenic recovery after hormonal male contraception: An integrated analysis. *The Lancet*, 367, 1412–1420.

Ljunger, E., Cnattingius, S., Lundin, C., & Anneren, G. (2005). Chromosomal anomalies in first-trimester miscarriages. *Acta Obstetrica et Gynecologica Scandinavica*, 84, 1103–1107.

Lobato, Maria, et al. (2006). Follow-up of sex reassignment surgery in transsexuals: A Brazilian cohort. *Archives of Sexual Behavior*, 35, 711–716.

Loeb, Tamra B., et al. (2002). Child sexual abuse: Associations with the sexual functioning of adolescents and adults. *Annual Review of Sex Research*, 13, 307–345.

Loffreda, Beth. (2000). *Losing Matt Shepard: Life and politics in the aftermath of anti-gay murder*. New York: Columbia University Press.

Loftus, Elizabeth F. (1993). The reality of repressed memories. *American Psychologist*, 48, 518–537.

Loftus, Elizabeth F., Polonsky, Sara, & Fullilove, Mindy T. (1994). Memories of childhood sexual abuse: Remembering and repressing. *Psychology of Women Quarterly*, 18, 67–84.

Lombardi, Emilia L., et al. (2001). Gender violence: Transgender experiences with violence and discrimination. *Journal of Homosexuality*, 42, 89–101.

Longo, D. J., Clum, G. A., & Yaeger, N. J. (1988). Psychosocial treatment for recurrent genital herpes. *Journal of Consulting and Clinical Psychology*, 56, 61–66.

Lonsway, Kimberly A., & Kothari, Chevon. (2000). First-year campus acquaintance rape education: Evaluating the impact of a mandatory intervention. *Psychology of Women Quarterly*, 24, 220–232.

LoPiccolo, Joseph, & Stock, Wendy E. (1986). Treatment of sexual dysfunction. *Journal of Consulting and Clinical Psychology*, 54, 158–167.

LoPiccolo, Leslie. (1980). Low sexual desire. In S. R. Leiblum & L. A. Pervin (Eds.), *Principles and practice of sex therapy*. New York: Guilford Press.

Lorius, Cassandra. (1999). *Tantric sex: Making love last*. London: Thorsons/HarperCollins.

Louis, R. (1997). *Sexpectations: Women talk candidly about sex and dating*. Madison, WI: MPC Press.

Louv, W. C., et al. (1989). Oral contraceptive use and risk of chlamydial and gonococcal infections. *American Journal of Obstetrics and Gynecology*, 160, 396.

Lowery, Shearon, & Wetli, Charles. (1982). Sexual asphyxia: A neglected area of study. *Deviant Behavior*, 3, 19–39.

Lu, M. C., et al. (2001). Provider encouragement of breast-feeding: Evidence from a national survey. *Obstetrics & Gynecology*, 97, 290–295.

Luby, Elliot C., & Klinge, Valerie. (1985). Genital herpes: A pervasive psychosocial disorder. *Archives of Dermatology*, 121, 494–497.

Lucero, Margaret A., et al. (2006). Sexual harassers: Behaviors, motives, and change over time. *Sex Roles*, 55, 331–344.

Luke, Barbara. (1994). Nutritional influences on fetal growth. *Clinical Obstetrics and Gynecology*, 37, 538–549.

Luker, Kristin. (1975). *Taking chances: Abortion and the decision not to contracept*. Berkeley: University of California Press.

Luker, Kristin. (1984). *Abortion and the politics of motherhood*. Berkeley: University of California Press.

Luo, Minmin, Fee, M., & Katz, L. (2003). Encoding pheromonal signals in the accessory olfactory bulb in behaving mice. *Science*, 299, 1196–1201.

Luo, Shanhong, & Klohnen, Eva. (2005). Assortative mating and marital quality in newly weds: A couple-centered approach. *Journal of Personality and Social Psychology*, 88, 304–326.

Luzuriaga, Katherine, et al. (2006). Vaccines to prevent transmission of HIV-1 via breastmilk: Scientific and logistical priorities. *The Lancet*, 368, 511–521.

Lydon-Rochelle, Mona, et al. (2001). Risk of uterine rupture during labor among women with a prior cesarean delivery. *New England Journal of Medicine*, 345, 3–8.

Lytton, Hugh, & Romney, David M. (1991). Parents' differential socialization of boys and girls: A meta-analysis. *Psychological Bulletin*, 109, 267–296.

Maass, Anne, et al. (2003). Sexual harassment under social identity threat: The computer harassment paradigm. *Journal of Personality and Social Psychology*, 85, 853–870.

Maccoby, Eleanor. (1998). *The two sexes: Growing up apart, coming together*. Cambridge, MA: Harvard University Press.

MacDonald, P. T., et al. (1988). Heavy cocaine use and sexual behavior. *Journal of Drug Issues*, 18, 437–455.

MacDougald, D. (1961). Aphrodisiacs and anaphrodisiacs. In A. Ellis & A. Abarbanel (Eds.), *The encyclopedia of sexual behavior* (Vol. I). New York: Hawthorn.

MacFarlane, J. A., et al. (1978). The relationship between mother and neonate. In S. Kitzinger & J. A. Davis (Eds.), *The place of birth*. Oxford: Oxford University Press.

MacLaughlin, David T., & Donahoe, Patricia K. (2004). Sex determination and differentiation. *New England Journal of Medicine*, 350, 367–378.

MacLean, Paul. (1962). New findings relevant to the evolution of psychosexual functions of the brain. *Journal of Nervous and Mental Disease*, 135, 289–301.

MacNamara, Donald E. J., & Sagarin, Edward. (1977). *Sex, crime, and the law*. New York: Free Press.

Madden, Mary, & Lenhart, Amanda. (2006). Online dating. Pew Internet and American Life Project, March 5. http://www.pewinternet.org/pdfs/PIP_Online_Dating.pdf.

Maddock, J. W. (1997). Sexuality education: A history lesson. In J. W. Maddock (Ed.), *Sexuality education in post-secondary and professional training settings* (pp. 1–22). Binghamton, NY: Haworth Press.

Magaña, J. R., & Carrier, J. M. (1991). Mexican and Mexican American male sexual behavior and spread of AIDS in California. *Journal of Sex Research*, 28, 425–441.

Magley, Vicki J., & Shupe, Ellen I. (2005). Self-labeling sexual harassment. *Sex Roles*, 53, 173–190.

Maguire, Daniel C. (1983). Abortion: A question of Catholic honesty. *Christian Century*, 100, 803–807.

Maguire, Daniel C. (2001). *Sacred choices: The right to contraception and abortion in ten world religions*. Minneapolis: Augsburg Fortress.

Mahaffey, Amanda L., Bryan, A., & Hutchison, K. (2005). Sex differences in affective responses to homoerotic stimuli: Evidence for an unconscious bias among heterosexual men, but not heterosexual women. *Archives of Sexual Behavior*, 34, 537–545.

Mahay, Jenna, Michaels, Stuart, & Laumann, Edward O. (1999). Race, gender, and class in sexual scripts. In E. O. Laumann & R. T. Michael (Eds.), *The social organization of sexuality in the United States: Further studies*. Chicago: University of Chicago Press.

Mahoney, E. R. (1983). *Human sexuality*. New York: McGraw-Hill.

Maines, Rachel P. (1999). *The technology of orgasm: "Hysteria," the vibrator, and women's sexual satisfaction*. Baltimore: Johns Hopkins University Press.

Major, Brenda, et al. (2000). Psychological responses of women after first-trimester abortion. *Archives of General Psychiatry*, 57, 777–784.

Malamuth, Neil M. (1998). The confluence model as an organizing framework for research on sexually aggressive men: Risk moderators, imagined aggression and pornography consumption. In R. Geen & E. Donnerstein (Eds.), *Aggression: Theoretical and empirical reviews*. New York: Academic Press.

Malamuth, Neil M., & Brown, Lisa M. (1994). Sexually aggressive men's perceptions of women's communications. *Journal of Personality and Social Psychology*, 67, 699–712.

Malamuth, Neil M., et al. (1991). Characteristics of aggressors against women: Testing a model using a national sample of college students. *Journal of Consulting and Clinical Psychology*, 59, 670–781.

Maletzky, B. M. (1974). "Assisted" covert sensitization in the treatment of exhibitionism. *Journal of Consulting and Clinical Psychology, 42,* 34–40.

Maletzky, B. M. (1977). "Booster" sessions in aversion therapy: The permanency of treatment. *Behavior Therapy, 8,* 460–463.

Maletzky, B. M. (1980). Assisted covert sensitization. In D. J. Cox & R. J. Daitzman (Eds.), *Exhibitionism: Description, assessment, and treatment.* New York: Garland.

Mallory, Tammie E., & Rich, Katherine E. (1986). Human reproductive technologies: An appeal for brave new legislation in a brave new world. *Washburn Law Journal, 25,* 458–504.

Maltz, Wendy, & Boss, Suzie. (1997). *In the garden of desire: The intimate world of women's sexual fantasies.* New York: Broadway Books.

Manlove, Jennifer, Ryan, Suzanne, & Franzetto, Kerry. (2004). Contraceptive use and consistency in U.S. teenagers' most recent sexual relationships. *Perspectives on Sexual and Reproductive Health, 36,* 265–275.

Margolis, Jonathan. (2004). *"O": The intimate history of the orgasm.* London: Century.

Markman, Howard J. (1979). Application of a behavioral model of marriage in predicting relationship satisfaction of couples planning marriage. *Journal of Consulting and Clinical Psychology, 47,* 743–749.

Markman, Howard J. (1981). Production of marital distress: A 5-year follow-up. *Journal of Consulting and Clinical Psychology, 49,* 760–762.

Markman, Howard J., & Floyd, Frank. (1980). Possibilities for the prevention of marital discord: A behavioral perspective. *American Journal of Family Therapy, 8,* 29–48.

Markman, Howard, & Kadushin, Frederick. (1986). Preventive effects of Damage training for first-time parents: A short-term longitudinal study. *Journal of Consulting and Clinical Psychology, 54,* 872–874.

Marot, D., et al. (2006). The tumor suppressor activity induced by adenovirus-mediated BRCA1 overexpression is not restricted to breast cancers. *Gene Therapy, 13,* 235–244.

Marquis, J. N. (1970). Orgasmic reconditioning: Changing sexual object choice through controlling masturbation fantasies. *Journal of Behavior Therapy and Experimental Psychiatry, 1,* 263–272.

Marshall, Donald C. (1971). Sexual behavior on Mangaia. In D. S. Marshall & R. C. Suggs (Eds.), *Human sexual behavior.* New York: Basic Books.

Marshall, Eliot. (1995). NIH's "Gay Gene" study questioned. *Science, 268,* 1841.

Marshall, W. L. (1993). A revised approach to the treatment of men who sexually assault adult females. In G. Nagayama Hall et al. (Eds.), *Sexual aggression* (pp. 143–165). Washington, DC: Taylor & Francis.

Marshall, W. L., & Pithers, W. D. (1994). A reconsideration of treatment outcome with sex offenders. *Criminal Justice and Behavior, 21,* 10–27.

Marsiglio, William, & Diekow, Douglas. (1998). Men and abortion: The gender politics of pregnancy resolution. In L. J. Beckman & S. M. Harvey (Eds.), *The new civil war* (pp. 269–284). Washington, DC: American Psychological Association.

Marszalek, John F., et al. (2004). Comparing gay identity development theory to cognitive development: An empirical study. *Journal of Homosexuality, 48,* 103–123.

Martin, B. V. S., Kirby, D., Hudes, E., Coyle, K., & Gomez, C. (2006). Boyfriends, girlfriends and teenagers' risk of sexual involvement. *Perspectives on Sexual and Reproductive Health, 38,* 76–83.

Martin, Carol L., & Halverson, C. F. (1983). The effects of sex-typing schemas on young children's memory. *Child Development, 54,* 563–574.

Martin, Carol L., Ruble, D., & Szkrybalo, J. (2002). Cognitive theories of early gender development. *Psychological Bulletin, 128,* 903–933.

Martin, Carol, & Ruble, Diane. (2004). Children's search for gender cues: Cognitive perspectives on gender development. *Current Directions in Psychological Science, 13,* 67–70.

Martin, J. A., Hamilton, B. E., Sutton, P. D., Ventura, S. J., Menacker, F., & Kirmeyer, S. (2006). Births: Final Data for 2004. *National Vital Statistics Reports, 55* (1).

Martinez, Gladys M., Chandra, A., Abma, J. C., Jones, J., & Mosher, W. D. (2006). *Fertility, contraception and fatherhood: Data on men and women from cycle 6 (2002) of the National Survey of Family Growth.* National Center for Health Statistics: Vital and Health Statistics, 23 (26).

Martinez-Donate, Ana, Hovell, Melbourne, & Zellner, Jennifer. (2004). Evaluation of two school-based HIV prevention interventions in the border city of Tijuana, Mexico. *Journal of Sex Research, 41,* 267–278.

Martins, Yolanda, Preti, George, et al. (2005). Preference for human body odors is influenced by gender and sexual orientation. *Psychological Science, 16,* 694–701.

Martinson, Floyd M. (1994). *The sexual life of children.* Westport, CT: Bergin & Garvey.

Marx, Jean. (1995). Sharing the genes that divide the sexes for mammals. *Science, 269,* 1824–1827.

Masters, W. H., Johnson, V. E., & Kolodny, R. C. (1982). *Human sexuality.* Boston: Little, Brown.

Masters, William H., & Johnson, Virginia. (1966). *Human sexual response.* Boston: Little, Brown.

Masters, William H., & Johnson, Virginia. (1970). *Human sexual inadequacy.* Boston: Little, Brown.

Masters, William H., & Johnson, Virginia. (1979). *Homosexuality in perspective.* Boston: Little, Brown.

Masterton, Graham. (1993). *Drive him wild: A hands-on guide to pleasuring your man in bed.* New York: Signet Books.

Mathy, Robin, & Cooper, Al. (2003). The duration and frequency of Internet use in a nonclinical sample: Suicidality, behavioral problems, and treatment history. *Psychotherapy: Theory, Research, Practice, Training, 40,* 125–135.

Maticka-Tyndale, Eleanor, Herold, E., & Oppermann, M. (2003). Casual sex among Australian schoolies. *Journal of Sex Research, 40,* 158–169.

Matsumoto, David. (1994). *Cultural influences on research methods and statistics.* Pacific Grove, CA: Brooks/Cole.

Matteson, David R. (1985). Bisexual men in marriage: Is a positive homosexual identity and stable marriage possible? In F. Klein & T. J. Wolf (Eds.), *Bisexualities: Theory and research.* New York: Haworth.

Mattson, Sarah, & Riley, Edward. (1998). A review of the neurobehavioral deficits in children with fetal alcohol syndrome or prenatal exposure to alcohol. *Alcoholism: Clinical and Experimental Research, 22,* 279–294.

Mauck, C., et al. (2001). Recommendations for the clinical development of topical microbicides. *AIDS, 15,* 857–868.

Maurer, Harry. (1994). *Sex: Real people talk about what they really do.* New York: Penguin Books.

Maurice, William L. (2007). Sexual desire disorders in men. In S. Leiblum (Ed.), *Principles and practice of sex therapy* (4th ed., pp. 181–211). New York: Guilford.

May, Rollo. (1974). *Love and will.* New York: Dell Books.

Mayo Clinic. (2007). Weight gain during pregnancy: What's healthy? Retrieved February 2007 from http://www. mayoclinic.com/health/pregnancyweight-gain/PR00111.

Mazur, Allan. (1986). U.S. trends in feminine beauty and overadaptation. *Journal of Sex Research, 22,* 281–303.

McAuliffe, Timothy L., et al. (2007). Effects of question format and collection mode on the accuracy of retrospective surveys of health risk behavior: A comparison with daily sexual activity diaries. *Health Psychology, 26,* 60–67.

McCabe, Edward. (1996). Sex and the single DAX1: Too little is bad, but can we have too much? *Journal of Clinical Investigation, 98,* 881–882.

McCabe, Marita P. (2002). Relationship functioning and sexuality among people with multiple sclerosis. *Journal of Sex Research, 39,* 302–309.

McCabe, Marita P., & Taleporos, George. (2003). Sexual esteem, sexual satisfaction, and sexual behavior among people with physical disability. *Archives of Sexual Behavior, 32,* 359–370.

McCabe, Marita P., & Wauchope, Michelle. (2005). Behavioral characteristics of men accused of rape: Evidence for different types of rapists. *Archives of Sexual Behavior, 34,* 241–254.

McCarthy, Barry, & McCarthy, Emily. (2002). *Sexual awareness: Couple sexuality for the twenty-first century.* New York: Carroll & Graf Publishers.

McClintock, Martha K. (1971). Menstrual synchrony and suppression. *Nature, 229,* 244–245.

McClintock, Martha K. (1998). Whither menstrual synchrony? *Annual Review of Sex Research, 9,* 77–95.

McClintock, Martha K. (2000). Human pheromones: Primers, releasers, signalers, or modulators? In K. Wallen & J. Schneider (Eds.), *Reproduction in context* (pp. 355–420). Cambridge, MA: MIT Press.

McClintock, Martha, & Herdt, Gilbert. (1996). Rethinking puberty: The development of sexual attraction. *Current Directions in Psychological Science, 5,* 178–183.

McClure, Robert, & Brewer, R. Thomas. (1980). Attitudes of new parents towards child and spouse with Lamaze or non-Lamaze methods of childbirth. *Journal of Human Behavior, 17,* 45–48.

McCoy, Norma L. (1996). Menopause and sexuality. In M. K. Beard (Ed.), *Optimizing hormone replacement therapy: Estrogen-androgen therapy in postmenopausal women* (pp. 32–36). Minneapolis: McGraw-Hill Healthcare.

McCoy, Norma L. (1997). Sexual issues for postmenopausal women. *Topics in Geriatric Rehabilitation, 12,* 28–39.

McCoy, Norma L., & Matyas, Joseph R. (1996). Oral contraceptives and sexuality in university women. *Archives of Sexual Behavior, 25,* 73–90.

McCoy, Norma L., & Pitino, Lisa. (2002). Pheromonal influences on sociosexual behavior in young women. *Physiology & Behavior, 75,* 367–375.

McDonagh, Annmarie, et al. (2005). Randomized trial of cognitive-behavioral therapy for chronic posttraumatic stress disorder in adult female survivors of childhood sexual abuse. *Journal of Consulting and Clinical Psychology, 73,* 515–524.

McDowell, Janet Dickey. (1983). Ethical implications of in vitro fertilization. *Christian Century, 100,* 936–938.

McEwen, B. S. (1997). Meeting report—Is there a neurobiology of love? *Molecular Psychiatry, 2,* 15–16.

McEwen, Bruce S. (2001). Estrogen effects on the brain: Multiple sites and molecular mechanisms. *Journal of Applied Physiology, 91,* 2785–2801.

McFadden, Dennis, et al. (2005). A reanalysis of five studies of sexual orientation and the relative length of the 2nd and 4th fingers. (The 2D:4D ratio). *Archives of Sexual Behavior, 34,* 341–356.

McFarlane, Jessica, Martin, Carol L., & Williams, Tannis M. (1988). Mood fluctuations: Women versus men and menstrual versus other cycles. *Psychology of Women Quarterly, 12,* 201–224.

McFarlane, Jessica M., & Williams, Tannis M. (1994). Placing premenstrual syndrome in perspective. *Psychology of Women Quarterly, 18,* 339–374.

McGuire, R. J., Carlisle, J. M., & Young, B. G. (1965). Sexual deviations as conditioned behavior: A hypothesis. *Behavioral Research and Therapy, 2,* 185–190.

McKay, Alexander. (2005). Sexuality and substance use: The impact of tobacco, alcohol, and selected recreational drugs on sexual function. *Canadian Journal of Human Sexuality, 14,* 47–56.

McKee, Alan. (2005). The objectification of women in mainstream pornographic videos in Australia. *Journal of Sex Research, 42,* 277–290.

McKeganey, N. (1994). Why do men buy sex and what are their assessments of the HIV-related risks when they do? *AIDS Care, 6,* 289–301.

McKenna, K. E. (2000). Some proposals regarding the orga-nization of the central nervous system control of penile erection. *Neuroscience and Biobehavioral Reviews, 24,* 535–540.

McKenna, Katelyn, & Bargh, John. (1998). Coming out in the age of the Internet: Identity "demarginalization" through virtual group participation. *Journal of Personality and Social Psychology, 75,* 681–694.

McKenna, Katelyn Y. A., Green, Amie S., & Smith, Pamela K. (2001). Demarginalizing the sexual self. *Journal of Sex Research, 38,* 302–311.

McKenna, Kevin E. (2005). The central control and pharmacological modulation of sexual function. In J. S. Hyde (Ed.), *Biological substrates of human sexuality* (pp. 75–108). Washington, DC: American Psychological Association.

McKinlay, Sonja M., Brambilla, D. J., & Posner, J. G. (1992). The normal menopause transition. *American Journal of Human Biology, 4,* 37–46.

McMahon, C. G., et al. (2004). Disorders of orgasm and ejaculation in men. In T. Lue et al. (Eds.), *Sexual medicine* (pp. 409–468). Paris: Editions 21.

McMillen, Curtis, Zuravin, Susan, & Rideout, Gregory. (1995). Perceived benefit from child sexual abuse. *Journal of Consulting and Clinical Psychology, 63,* 1037–1043.

McNeill, John J. (1987). Homosexuality: Challenging the Church to grow. *Christian Century, 104,* 242–246.

McWhirter, David P., & Mattison, Andrew M. (1980). Treatment of sexual dysfunction in homosexual male couples. In S. R. Leiblum & L. A. Pervin (Eds.), *Principles and practice of sex therapy.* New York: Guilford.

McWilliams, Elaine. (1994). The association of perceived support with birthweights and obstetric complications: Piloting prospective identification and the effects of counseling. *Journal of Reproductive and Infant Psychology, 12,* 115–122.

Mead, Margaret. (1935). *Sex and temperament in three primitive societies.* New York: Morrow.

Meana, Marta, & Nunnink, Sarah E. (2006). Gender differences in the content of cognitive distraction during sex. *Journal of Sex Research, 43,* 59–67.

Meeks, Joshua J., et al. (2003). Dax1 is required for testis determination. *Nature Genetics, 34,* 32–33.

Mehta, Aditi, & Sheth, S. (2006). Postpartum depression: How to recognize and treat this common condition. *Medscape Psychiatry and Mental Health, 11,* article 529930.

Meischke, Hendrika. (1995). Implicit sexual portrayals in the movies: Interpretations of young women. *Journal of Sex Research, 32,* 29–36.

Melman, A., & Tiefer, L. (1992). Surgery for erectile disorders: Operative procedures and psychological issues. In R. C. Rosen & S. R. Leiblum (Eds.), *Erectile disorders* (pp. 255–282). New York: Guilford.

Menacker, Fay. (2005). Trends in cesarean rates for first births and repeat cesarean rates for low-risk women: United States, 1990–2003. *National Vital Statistics Reports, 54* (No. 4). Hyattsville, MD: National Center for Health Statistics.

Menacker, Fay, & Curtin, Sally. (2001). Trends in cesarean birth and vaginal birth after previous cesarean, 1991–1999. Centers for Disease Control and Prevention, *National Vital Statistics Reports, 49* (13).

Merrick, E. N. (1995). Adolescent childbearing as career "choice": Perspective from an ecological context. *Journal of Counseling and Development, 73,* 288–295.

Meseda, C., et al. (2004). DNA immunization with a herpes simplex virus 2 bacterial artificial chromosome. *Virology, 318,* 420–428.

Messe, Madelyn R., & Geer, James H. (1985). Voluntary vaginal musculature contractions as an enhancer of sexual arousal. *Archives of Sexual Behavior, 14,* 13–28.

Messenger, John C. (1993). Sex and repression in an Irish folk community. In D. N. Suggs & A. W. Miracle (Eds.), *Culture and human sexuality.* Pacific Grove, CA: Brooks/Cole.

Meston, Cindy M. (2004). The effects of hysterectomy on sexual arousal in women with a history of benign uterine fibroids. *Archives of Sexual Behavior, 33,* 31–42.

Meston, Cindy M., et al. (2004). Women's orgasm. *Annual Review of Sex Research, 15,* 173–257.

Meston, Cindy M., et al. (2004). Women's orgasm. In T. Lue et al. (Eds.), *Sexual medicine* (pp. 783–850). Paris: Editions 21.

Meston, Cindy M., Rellini, Alessandra H., & Heiman, Julia R. (2006). Women's history of sexual abuse, their sexuality, and sexual self-schemas. *Journal of Consulting and Clinical Psychology, 74,* 229–236.

Meston, Cindy M., Trapnell, Paul D., & Gorzalka, Boris B. (1996). Ethnic and gender differences in sexuality: Variations in sexual behavior between Asian and non-Asian university students. *Archives of Sexual Behavior, 25,* 33–72.

Metz, Michael E., et al. (1997). Premature ejaculation: A psychophysical review. *Journal of Sex & Marital Therapy, 23,* 3–23.

Meyer, Ilan H. (2003). Prejudice, social stress, and mental health in lesbian, gay, and bisexual populations: Conceptual issues and research evidence. *Psychological Bulletin, 129,* 674–697.

Meyer, J. K. (1979). Sex reassignment. *Archives of General Psychiatry, 36,* 1010–1015.

Meyer-Bahlburg, Heino. (1997). The role of prenatal estrogens in sexual orientation. In L. Ellis & L. Ebertz (Eds.), *Sexual orientation: Toward biological understanding.* Westport, CT: Praeger.

Meyer-Bahlburg, Heino, et al. (2004). Prenatal androgenization affects gender-related behavior but not gender identity in 5–12-year-old girls with congenital adrenal hyperplasia. *Archives of Sexual Behavior, 33,* 97–104.

Meyer-Bahlburg, Heino, et al. (2006). Gender development in women with congenital adrenal hyperplasia as a function of disorder severity. *Archives of Sexual Behavior, 35,* 667–684.

Meyer-Bahlburg, Heino F. L. (2005). Gender dysphoria and gender change in persons with intersexuality. *Archives of Sexual Behavior, 34,* 271–274.

Meyer-Bahlburg, Heino F. L., et al. (1995). Prenatal estrogens and the development of homosexual orientation. *Developmental Psychology, 31,* 12–21.

Meyerowitz, Beth E. (1980). Psychosocial correlates of breast cancer and its treatments. *Psychological Bulletin, 87,* 108–131.

Mezzacappa, Elizabeth, & Katkin, Edward. (2002). Breast-feeding is associated with reduced perceived stress and negative mood in mothers. *Health Psychology, 21,* 187–193.

Michael, Robert T., et al. (1994). *Sex in America: A definitive survey.* Boston: Little, Brown.

Michelson, David, et al. (2000). Female sexual dysfunction associated with antidepressant administration. *American Journal of Psychiatry, 157,* 239–243.

Miki, Yoshio, et al. (1994). A strong candidate for the breast and ovarian cancer susceptibility gene BRCA1. *Science, 226,* 66–71.

Milam, Joel. (2006). Posttraumatic growth and HIV disease progression. *Journal of Consulting and Clinical Psychology, 74,* 817–827.

Milan, Richard J., & Kilmann, Peter R. (1987). Interpersonal factors in premarital contraception. *Journal of Sex Research, 23,* 289–321.

Milbauer, Barbara. (1983). *The law giveth: Legal aspects of the abortion controversy.* New York: Atheneum.

Miller, D., & Kernes, M. (2004). HIV outbreak has adult industry facing spector of government regulation. *AVN: Adult Video News.* www.adultvideonews.com/cover0604.02.html.

Miller, Eleanor M. (1986). *Street woman.* Philadelphia: Temple University Press.

Miller, J., & Schwartz, M. (1995). Rape myths and violence against street prostitutes. *Deviant Behavior, 16,* 1–23.

Miller, L. C., & Fishkin, S. A. (1997). On the dynamics of human bonding and reproductive success: Seeking windows on the adapted-for-human-environmental interface. In J. A. Simpson & D. T. Kenrick (Eds.), *Evolutionary social psychology* (pp. 197–235). Mahwah, NJ: Lawrence Erlbaum Associates.

Miller, Neil. (1992). *Out in the world: Gay and lesbian life from Buenos Aires to Bangkok.* New York: Random House.

Miller, Rickey S., & Lefcourt, Herbert M. (1982). The assessment of social intimacy. *Journal of Personality Assessment, 46,* 514–518.

Miller, S. Andrea, & Byers, E. Sandra. (2004). Actual and desired duration of foreplay and intercourse: Discordance and misperceptions within heterosexual couples. *Journal of Sex Research, 41,* 301–309.

Miller, S., Corrales, R., & Wachman, D. B. (1975). Recent progress in understanding and facilitating marital communication. *Family Coordinator, 24,* 143–152.

Millett, Kate. (1969). *Sexual politics.* New York: Doubleday.

Milligan, G. N., et al. (2004). Efficacy of genital T cell responses to herpes simplex virus type 2 resulting from immunization of the nasal mucosa. *Virology, 318,* 507–515.

Miner, Michael, & Coleman, Eli. (2001). Advances in sex offender treatment and challenges for the future. *Journal of Psychology and Human Sexuality, 13,* 5–24.

Minnesota Department of Health. (nd). Minnesota Education Now and Babies Later (MN ENABL): Evaluation Report 1998–2002. St. Paul: Minnesota Department of Health.

Minto, Catherine L., et al. (2003). The effect of clitoral surgery on sexual outcome in individuals who have intersex conditions with ambiguous genitalia: A cross-sectional study. *The Lancet, 361,* 1252–1257.

Moffatt, Michael. (1989). *Coming of age in New Jersey.* Brunswick, NJ: Rutgers University Press.

Mohr, Jonathan J., & Fassinger, Ruth E. (2006). Sexual orientation identity and romantic relationship quality in same-sex couples. *Personality and Social Psychology Bulletin, 32,* 1085–1099.

Molitch, Mark E. (1995). Neuroendocrinology. In P. Felig et al. (Eds.), *Endocrinology and metabolism.* New York: McGraw-Hill.

Mondaini, N., et al. (2003). Sildenafil does not improve sexual function in men without erectile dysfunction but does reduce the postorgasmic refractory time. *International Journal of Impotence Research, 15,* 225–228.

Money, John. (1987). Sin, sickness, or status: Homosexual gender identity and psychoneuroendocrinology. *American Psychologist, 42,* 384–399.

Money, John, & Ehrhardt, Anke. (1972). *Man and woman, boy and girl.* Baltimore: Johns Hopkins. Reissued in a facsimile edition by Jason Aronson, Northvale, NJ, 1996.

Monro, S. (2000). Theorizing transgender diversity: Towards a social model of health. *Sexual and Relationship Therapy, 15,* 33–45.

Monto, Martin. (2001). Prostitution and fellatio. *Journal of Sex Research, 38,* 140–145.

Montorsi, F., & Althof, S. (2004). Partner responses to sildenafil citrate (Viagra) treatment of erectile dysfunction. *Urology, 63,* 762–767.

Montorsi, F., et al. (2003a). Apomorphine-induced brain modulation during sexual stimulation: A new look at central phenomena related to erectile dysfunction. *International Journal of Impotence Research, 15,* 203–209.

Montorsi, F., et al. (2003b). Brain activation patterns during video sexual stimulation following the administration of apomorphine. *European Urology, 43,* 405–411.

Montorsi, F., et al. (2004). Long-term safety and tolerability of tadalafil in the treatment of erectile dysfunction. *European Urology, 45,* 339–345.

Moore, Allen J. (1987). Teenage sexuality and public morality. *Christian Century, 104,* 747–750.

Moore, Thomas. (1999). *The soul of sex: Cultivating life as an act of love.* New York: HarperCollins.

Moore, Todd. (1994, January 3). Porn shop enjoys brisk business year-round. *The Capital Times,* pp. 5A–6A.

Morales, A., et al. (1998). Clinical safety of oral sildenafil (Viagra) in the treatment of erectile dysfunction. *International Journal of Impotence Research, 10,* 69–74.

Morales, A., & Heaton, J. (2001). Hormonal erectile dysfunction: Evaluation and management. *Urologic Clinics of North America, 28,* 279.

Morales, A., Heaton, Jeremy, & Carson, C. (2000). Andropause: A misnomer for a true clinical entity. *Journal of Urology, 163,* 705–712.

Morbidity and Mortality Weekly Report. (1995). Current trends ectopic pregnancy—United States, 1990–1992. *MMWR, 44* (03), 46–48.

Morbidity and Mortality Weekly Report. (2006). Racial and socioeconomic disparities in breastfeeding—United States, 2004. *MMWR, 55* (12), 335–339.

Moreland, Adele A. (1996a). Genital human papilloma-virus infection. In S. A. Morese et al. (Eds.), *Atlas of sexually transmitted diseases and AIDS* (pp. 225–240). London: Mosby-Wolfe.

Moreland, Adele A., et al. (1996b). Genital herpes. In S. Morese et al. (Eds.), *Atlas of sexually transmitted diseases and AIDS* (pp. 207–224). London: Mosby-Wolfe.

Morell, V. (1998). A new look at monogamy. *Science, 281,* 1982–1983.

Morgan, Robin. (1978, November). How to run the pornographers out of town (and preserve the first amendment). *Ms., 55,* 78–80.

Morgan, Robin. (1980). Theory and practice: Pornography and rape. In L. Lederer (Ed.), *Take back the night: Women on pornography.* New York: Morrow.

Morin, Jack. (1981). *Anal pleasure and health*. Burlingame, CA: Down There Press.

Morin, Stephen F., & Rothblum, Esther D. (1991). Removing the stigma: Fifteen years of progress. *American Psychologist, 46,* 947–949.

Morokoff, Patricia J. (1986). Volunteer bias in the psychophysiological study of female sexuality. *Journal of Sex Research, 22,* 35–51.

Morokoff, Patricia J. (1993). Female sexual arousal disorder. In W. O'Donohue & J. H. Geer (Eds.), *Handbook of sexual dysfunctions* (pp. 157–199). Boston: Allyn & Bacon.

Morris, Norval J. (1973, April 18). The law is a busy-body. *New York Times Magazine,* 58–64.

Morrison, Diane M. (1985). Adolescent contraceptive behavior: A review. *Psychological Bulletin, 98,* 538–568.

Morrison, L., et al. (2001). The long-term reproductive health consequences of female genital cutting in rural Gambia: A community-based survey. *Tropical Medicine & International Health, 6,* 643–653.

Morris-Rush, Jeanine, & Bernstein, Peter. (2002). Postpartum depression. *Medscape Women's Health, 7* (1).

Morrow, Kathleen, et al. (2003). The acceptability of an investigational vaginal microbicide, PRO 2000 gel, among women in a Phase I clinical trial. *Journal of Women's Health, 12,* 655–666.

Mortola, Joseph F. (1998). Premenstrual syndrome—Pathophysiologic considerations. *New England Journal of Medicine, 338,* 256–257.

Moser, C. (1998). S/M (Sadomasochistic) interactions in semi-public settings. *Journal of Homosexuality, 36* (2), 19–29.

Moser, Charles, & Levitt, Eugene E. (1987). An exploratory-descriptive study of a sadomasochistically oriented sample. *Journal of Sex Research, 23,* 322–337.

Moses, Stephen, et al. (1990). Geographical patterns of male circumcision practices in Africa: Association with HIV seroprevalence. *International Journal of Epidemiology, 19,* 693–697.

Mosher, Donald, & MacIan, Paula. (1994). College men and women respond to X-rated videos intended for male or female audiences: Gender and sexual scripts. *Journal of Sex Research, 31,* 99–113.

Mosher, William D., Chandra, Anjani, & Jones, Jo. (2005). Sexual behavior and selected health measures: Men and women 15–44 years of age, United States, 2002. *Vital and Health Statistics, 362.* (Centers for Disease Control and Prevention)

Moss, B. F., & Schwebel, A. I. (1993). Marriage and romantic relationships: Defining intimacy in romantic relationships. *Family Relations, 42,* 31–37.

Muehlenhard, Charlene L. (1988). Misinterpreted dating behaviors and the risk of date rape. *Journal of Social and Clinical Psychology, 6,* 20–37.

Mueller, G. O. W. (1980). *Sexual conduct and the law* (2nd ed.). Dobbs Ferry, NY: Oceana Publications.

Mulders, T., & Dieben, T. (2001). Use of the novel combined contraceptive vaginal ring NuvaRing for ovulation inhibition. *Fertility and Sterility, 75,* 865–870.

Muller, James, et al. (1996). Triggering myocardial infarction by sexual activity. *Journal of the American Medical Association, 275,* 1405–1409.

Murnen, Sarah K., & Stockton, Mary. (1997). Gender and self-reported sexual arousal in response to sexual stimuli: A meta-analytic review. *Sex Roles, 37,* 135–154.

Murnen, Sarah K., Wright, Carrie, & Kaluzny, Gretchen. (2002). If "boys will be boys," then girls will be victims? A meta-analytic review of the research that relates masculine ideology to sexual aggression. *Sex Roles, 46,* 359–376.

Murray, Stephen O. (2000). *Homosexualities*. Chicago: University of Chicago Press.

Mustanski, Brian S. (2001). Getting wired: Exploiting the Internet for the collection of valid sexuality data. *Journal of Sex Research, 38,* 292–301.

Mustanski, Brian S., et al. (2005). A genomewide scan of male sexual orientation. *Human Genetics, 116,* 272–278.

Myers, Barbara J. (1984). Mother-infant bonding: The status of this critical-period hypothesis. *Developmental Review, 4,* 240–274.

Najman, Jake M., et al. (2005). Sexual abuse in childhood and sexual dysfunction in adulthood: An Australian population-based study. *Archives of Sexual Behavior, 34,* 517–526.

Nanda, Serena. (1997). The Hijras of India. In M. Duberman (ed.), *A queer world* (pp. 82–86). New York: New York University Press.

Nanula, Peter J. (1987). Protecting confidentiality in the effort to control AIDS. *Harvard Journal of Legislation, 24* (1), 315–349.

Narod, Steven A., et al. (1988). Human mutagens: Evidence from paternal exposure? *Environmental and Molecular Mutagenesis, 11,* 401–415.

National Abortion Federation. (2004). Analysis of trends of violence and disruption against reproductive health care clinics for 2003. www.prochoice.org/violence.

National Abortion Federation. (2007). NAF violence and disruption statistics. http://www.prochoice.org/pubs_research/publications/downloads/about_abortion/violence_statistics.pdf

National Campaign to Prevent Teen Pregnancy. (2007). *Why it matters: Teen pregnancy, poverty, and income disparity.* Retrieved July 29, 2007 from www.teenpregnancy.org/wim/pdf/poverty.

National Center for Health Statistics. (2002). Births: Final data for 2001. *National Vital Statistics Reports, 51* (2).

National Center for Health Statistics. (2004). Live births by birthweight, percent low birthweight and very low birthweight. Table 1–26. www.cdc.gov/nchs/data/statab/t991x26.pdf.

National Center for Victims of Crime. (2004). Spousal rape laws: 20 years later. www.ncvc.org.

National Commission on AIDS. (1994). Preventing HIV/AIDS in adolescents. *Journal of School Health, 64,* 39–51.

National Conference of State Legislatures. (2006). State human cloning laws. www.ncsl.org/programs/health/genetics/rt-shel.htm.

National Opinion Research Center. (2004a). General Social Survey Codebook. webapp.icpsr.umich.edu/GSS.

National Opinion Research Center. (2004b). Codebook variable: sexeduc.webapp.icpsr.umich.edu/GSS/rnd1998/merged/cdbk/sexeduc.htm.

Neiger, S. (1968). Sex potions. *Sexology,* 730–733.

Nelson, Adie, & Robinson, Barrie. (1994). *Gigolos and madames bountiful: Illusions of gender, power and intimacy.* Toronto: University of Toronto Press.

Nelson, James B. (1978). *Embodiment: An approach to sexuality and Christian theology.* Minneapolis: Augsburg.

Nelson, James B. (1992). *Body theology.* Louisville, KY: Westminster/John Knox Press.

Nelson, James B., & Longfellow, Sandra P. (Eds.). (1994). *Sexuality and the sacred: Sources for theological reflection.* Louisville, KY: Westminster.

Neville, Helen A., et al. (2004). General and culturally specific factors influencing Black and white rape survivors' self-esteem. *Psychology of Women Quarterly, 28,* 83–94.

Newton, Niles A. (1972). Childbearing in broad perspective. In Boston Children's Medical Center, *Pregnancy, birth and the newborn baby.* New York: Delacorte Press.

Niemann, Yolanda F., et al. (1994). Use of free responses and cluster analysis to determine stereotypes of eight groups. *Personality and Social Psychology Bulletin, 20,* 379–390.

Nobre, Pedro J., & Pinto-Gouveia, José. (2006). Dysfunctional sexual beliefs as vulnerability factors for sexual dysfunction. *Journal of Sex Research, 43,* 68–75.

Nobre, Pedro J., et al. (2004). Determinants of sexual arousal and the accuracy of its self-estimation in sexually functional males. *Journal of Sex Research, 41,* 363–371.

Noll, Jennie, Trickett, Penelope, & Putnam, Frank. (2003). A prospective investigation of the impact of childhood sexual abuse on the development of sexuality. *Journal of Consulting and Clinical Psychology, 71,* 575–586.

Noller, P. (1984). *Nonverbal communication and marital interaction.* New York: Pergamon.

Norton, Arthur J. (1987, July–August). Families and children in the year 2000. *Children Today,* 6–9.

Noss, John B. (1963). *Man's religions* (3rd ed.). New York: Macmillan.

Notzon, Francis C. (1990). International differences in the use of obstetric interventions. *Journal of the American Medical Association, 263,* 3286–3291.

Novak, Emil, & Novak, Edmund R. (1952). *Textbook of gynecology.* Baltimore: Williams & Wilkins.

Novembre, John, et al. (2005). The geographic spread of the CCR5 Delta 32 HIV-resistance allele. *PloS Biology, 3,* e339. www.plosbiology.org.

Nsiah-Jefferson, Laurie. (1989). Reproductive laws, women of color, and low-income women. In S. Cohen & N. Taub (Eds.), *Reproductive laws for the 1990s* (pp. 23–68). Clifton, NJ: Humana Press.

Nulman, Irena, et al. (1997). Neurodevelopment of children exposed in utero to antidepressant drugs. *New England Journal of Medicine, 336,* 258–262.

O'Brien, Shari. (1986). Commercial conceptions: A breeding ground for surrogacy. *North Carolina Law Review, 65,* 127–153.

O'Connell, Helen E., & DeLancey, John. (2005). Clitoral anatomy in nulliparous, healthy, premenopausal volunteers using unenhanced magnetic resonance imaging. *Journal of Urology, 173,* 2060–2063.

O'Connell, Helen E., et al. (1998). Anatomical relationship between urethra and clitoris. *Journal of Urology, 159,* 1892–1897.

O'Connell, Helen E., Sanjeevan, K., & Hutson, J. (2005). Anatomy of the clitoris. *Journal of Urology, 174,* 1189–1195.

O'Connor, Art. (1987). Female sex offenders. *British Journal of Psychiatry, 150,* 615–620.

O'Connor, Mary J., Sigman, Marian, & Kasari, Connie. (1993). Interactional model for the association among maternal alcohol use, mother-infant interaction, and infant cognitive development. *Infant Behavior and Development, 16,* 177–192.

O'Hara, Michael W., & Swain, Annette M. (1996). Rates and risk of postpartum depression: A meta-analysis. *International Review of Psychiatry, 8,* 37–54.

O'Hare, Elizabeth A., & O'Donohue, William. (1998). Sexual harassment: Identifying risk factors. *Archives of Sexual Behavior, 27,* 561–580.

O'Shea, P. A. (1995). Congenital defects and their causes. In D. R. Constan, R. V. Haning, Jr., & D. B. Singer (Eds.), *Human reproduction: Growth and development.* Boston: Little, Brown.

O'Sullivan, Lucia. (1995). Less is more: The effects of sexual experience on judgments of men's and women's personality characteristics and relationship desirability. *Sex Roles, 33,* 159–181.

O'Sullivan, Lucia., & Brooks-Gunn, Jeanne. (2005). The timing of changes in girls' sexual cognitions and behaviors in early adolescence: A prospective cohort study. *Journal of Adolescent Health, 37,* 211–219.

O'Sullivan, Lucia, & Meyer-Bahlburg, Heino. (2003). African-American and Latina inner-city girls' reports of romantic and sexual development. *Journal of Social and Personal Relationships, 20,* 221–238.

Obzrut, L. (1976). Expectant fathers' perceptions of fathering. *American Journal of Nursing, 76,* 1440–1442.

Ochs, Eric P., Mah, K., & Binik, Y. (2002). Obtaining data about human sexual functioning from the Internet. In A. Cooper (Ed.), *Sex and the Internet: A guidebook for clinicians* (pp. 245–262). New York: Routledge.

Oesterling, Joseph E. (1995). Benign prostatic hyperplasia. *New England Journal of Medicine, 332,* 99–109.

Ogletree, Shirley M., & Ginsburg, Harvey J. (2000). Kept under the hood: Neglect of the clitoris in common vernacular. *Sex Roles, 43,* 917–926.

Okami, Paul. (1995). Childhood exposure to parental nudity, parent-child co-sleeping, and "primal scenes": A review of clinical opinion and empirical evidence. *Journal of Sex Research, 32,* 51–64.

Okami, Paul, Olmstead, Richard, & Abramson, Paul. (1997). Sexual experiments in early childhood: 18-year longitudinal data from the UCLA Family Lifestyles Project. *Journal of Sex Research, 34,* 339–347.

Okazaki, Sumie. (2002). Influences of culture on Asian Americans' sexuality. *Journal of Sex Research, 39,* 34–41.

Okwumabua, T. M., Okwumabua, J. O., & Elliott, V. (1998). "Let the circle be unbroken" helps African-Americans prevent teen-pregnancy. *SIECUS Report, 26,* 12–17.

Oliver, Mary Beth, & Hyde, Janet S. (1993). Gender differences in sexuality: A meta-analysis. *Psychological Bulletin, 114,* 29–51.

Olson, Beth, & Douglas, William. (1997). The family on television: Evaluation of gender roles in situation comedy. *Sex Roles, 36,* 409–427.

Olsson, Stig-Eric, & Möller, Anders R. (2003). On the incidence and sex ratio of transsexualism in Sweden, 1972–2002. *Archives of Sexual Behavior, 32,* 381–386.

Oosterhuis, Harry. (2000). *Step children of nature: Krafft-Ebing, psychiatry, and the making of sexual identity.* Chicago: University of Chicago Press.

Osman, Suzanne L. (2003). Predicting men's rape perceptions based on the belief that "no" really means "yes." *Journal of Applied Social Psychology, 33,* 683–692.

Ostensten, Monika. (1994). Optimisation of antirheumatic drug treatment in pregnancy. *Clinical Pharmacokinetics, 27,* 486–503.

Ott, Mary, Millstein, S., Ofner, S, & Halpern-Felsher, B. (2006). Greater expectations: Adolescents' positive motivations for sex. *Perspectives on Sexual and Reproductive Health, 38,* 84–89.

Otto, H. A. (1963). Criteria for assessing family strengths. *Family Process, 2,* 329–337.

Pachankis, John E. (2007). The psychological implications of concealing a stigma: A cognitive-affective-behavioral model. *Psychological Bulletin, 133,* 328–345.

Packer, H. L. (1968). *The limits of the criminal sanction.* Stanford, CA: Stanford University Press.

Padma-Nathan, H., et al. (2001). On-demand IC351 (Cialis) enhances erectile function in patients with erectile dysfunction. *International Journal of Impotence Research, 13,* 2–9.

Page, David C., et al. (1987). The sex-determining region of the human Y chromosome encodes a finger protein. *Cell, 51,* 1091–1104.

Page, Stephanie T., et al. (2006). Testosterone gel combined with depomedroxyprogesterone acetate is an effective male hormonal contraceptive regimen and is not enhanced by the addition of a GnRH antagonist. *Journal of Clinical Endocrinology and Metabolism, 91,* 4374–4380.

Paige, Karen E. (1971). Effects of oral contraceptives on affective fluctuations associated with the menstrual cycle. *Psychosomatic Medicine, 33,* 515–537.

Pakenham, Kenneth I., Dadds, Mark R., & Terry, Deborah J. (1994). Relationships between adjustment to HIV and both social support and coping. *Journal of Consulting and Clinical Psychology, 62,* 1194–1203.

Palace, Eileen M. (1995a). A cognitive-physiological process model of sexual arousal and response. *Clinical Psychology: Science and Practice, 2,* 370–384.

Palace, Eileen M. (1995b). Modification of dysfunctional patterns of sexual response through autonomic arousal and false physiological feedback. *Journal of Consulting and Clinical Psychology, 63,* 604–615.

Paredes, Raul G., & Baum, Michael J. (1997). Role of the medial preoptic area/anterior hypothalamus in the control of masculine sexual behavior. *Annual Review of Sex Research, 8,* 68–101.

Parents Television Council. (2000). *What a difference a decade makes: A comparison of prime time sex, language, and violence in 1989 and '99.* Special report. www.parentstv.org/publications/reports/Decadestudy/decadestudy.html.

Parish, William L., Das, A., & Laumann, E. (2006). Sexual harassment of women in urban China. *Archives of Sexual Behavior, 35,* 411–425.

Park, K., et al. (2001). A new potential of blood oxygenation level dependent (BOLD) functional MRI for evaluating cerebral centers of penile erection. *International Journal of Impotence Research, 13,* 73–81.

Parker, Graham. (1983). The legal regulation of sexual activity and the protection of females. *Osgoode Hall Law Journal, 21,* 187–244.

Parker, Richard, et al. (2004). Global transformations and intimate relations in the 21st century: Social science research on sexuality and the emergence of Sexual Health and Sexual Rights frameworks. *Annual Review of Sex Research, 15,* 362–398.

Parks, Cheryl A., Hughes, Tonda L., & Matthews, Alicia K. (2004). Race/ethnicity and sexual orientation: Intersecting identities. *Cultural Diversity & Ethnic Minority Psychology, 10,* 241–254.

Parlee, Mary Brown. (1973). The premenstrual syndrome. *Psychological Bulletin, 80,* 454–465.

Parnas, Raymond I. (1981). Legislative reform of prostitution laws: Keeping commercial sex out of sight and out of mind. *Santa Clara Law Review, 21,* 669–696.

Parrado, Emilio, Flippen, Chenoa, & McQuiston, Chris. (2004). Use of commercial sex workers among Hispanic migrants in North Carolina: Implications for the spread of HIV. *Perspectives on Sexual and Reproductive Health, 36,* 150–156.

Parrinder, Geoffrey. (1980). *Sex in the world's religions.* New York: Oxford University Press.

Parrinder, Geoffrey. (1996). *Sexual morality in the world's religions.* Oxford: Oneworld.

Pathela, Preeti, et al. (2006). Discordance between sexual behavior and self-reported sexual identity: A population-based survey of New York City men. *Annals of Internal Medicine, 145,* 416–425.

Patrick, David, Wong, Thomas, & Jordan, Robbie. (2000). Sexually transmitted infections in Canada: Recent resurgence threatens national goals. *Canadian Journal of Human Sexuality, 9,* 149–168.

Patterson, Charlotte. (1992). Children of lesbian and gay parents. *Child Development, 63,* 1025–1042.

Patterson, Charlotte J. (1995). Families of the lesbian baby boom: Parents' division of labor and children's adjustment. *Developmental Psychology, 31,* 115–123.

Patterson, Charlotte J. (1996). Lesbian mothers and their children: Findings from the Bay Area Families Study. In J. Laird & R. Green (Eds.), *Lesbians and gays in couples and families* (pp. 420–438). San Francisco: Jossey-Bass.

Patterson, Charlotte J. (2000). Family relationships of lesbians and gay men. *Journal of Marriage and the Family, 62,* 1052–1069.

Patterson, Charlotte J. (2004). What difference does a civil union make? *Journal of Family Psychology, 18,* 287–289.

Patterson, Charlotte J. (2006). Children of lesbian and gay parents. *Current Directions in Psychological Science, 15,* 241–244.

Paul, Elizabeth, McManus, Brian, & Hayes, Allison. (2000). "Hookups": Characteristics and correlates of college students' spontaneous and anonymous sexual experiences. *Journal of Sex Research, 37,* 76–88.

Paul, Eva W., & Klassel, Dara. (1987). Minors' rights to confidential contraceptive services. *Women's Rights Law Reporter, 10,* 45–64.

Paulson, Richard, et al. (2001). *American Journal of Obstetrics and Gynecology, 184,* 818–824.

Pawelski, James, Perrin, Ellen, Foy, Jane, et al. (2006). The effects of marriage, civil union, and domestic partnership laws on the health and well-being of children. *Pediatrics, 118,* 349–364.

Pedersen, William, et al. (2002). Evolved sex differences in the number of partners desired? The long and short of it. *Psychological Science, 13,* 157–159.

Pennisi, Elizabeth. (1996). Homing in on a prostate cancer gene. *Science, 274,* 1301.

Peplau, L. Anne. (2003). Human sexuality: How do men and women differ? *Current Directions in Psychological Science, 12,* 37–40.

Peplau, L. Anne, Cochran, Susan D., & Mays, Vickie M. (1997). A national survey of the intimate relationships of African American lesbians and gay men. In B. Greene (Ed.), *Ethnic and cultural diversity among lesbians and gay men* (pp. 11–38). Thousand Oaks, CA: Sage.

Peplau, L. Anne, et al. (1998). A critique of Bem's "exotic becomes erotic" theory of sexual orientation. *Psychological Review, 105,* 387–394.

Peplau, L. Anne, Veniegas, Rosemary C., & Campbell, Susan M. (1996). Gay and lesbian relationships. In R. C. Savin-Williams & K. M. Cohen (Eds.), *The lives of lesbians, gays, and bisexuals* (pp. 250–273). Fort Worth: Harcourt Brace.

Pepper, Gillian, & Roberts, S. Craig. (2006). Rates of nausea and vomiting in pregnancy and dietary characteristics across populations. *Proceedings of the Royal Society B,* published online, doi:10.1098/3633.

Perelman, Michael A., & Rowland, David L. (2006). Retarded ejaculation. *World Journal of Urology, 24,* 645–652.

Perez, Martin A., Skinner, Eila C., & Meyerowitz, Beth E. (2002). Sexuality and intimacy following radical prosta-tectomy: Patient and partner perspectives. *Health Psychology, 21,* 288–293.

Perkins, D. F., et al. (1998). An ecological risk-factor examination of adolescents' sexual activity in three ethnic groups. *Journal of Marriage and the Family, 60,* 660–673.

Perkins, Roberta, & Bennett, Garry. (1985). *Being a prostitute: Prostitute women and prostitute men.* London: Allen & Unwin.

Perlman, Daniel, & Fehr, B. (1987). The development of intimate relationships. In D. Perlman & S. Duck (Eds.), *Intimate relationships: Development, dynamics, and deterioration.* Newbury Park, CA: Sage.

Perrin, Ellen C., et al. (2002). Technical report: Coparent or second-parent adoption by same-sex parents. *Pediatrics, 109,* 341–344.

Perry, C. D. (1980). Right of privacy challenges to prostitution statutes. *Washington University Law Quarterly, 58,* 439–480.

Perry, John D., & Whipple, Beverly. (1981). Pelvic muscle strength of female ejaculators: Evidence in support of a new theory of orgasm. *Journal of Sex Research, 17,* 22–39.

Persson, Goran. (1980). Sexuality in a 70-year-old urban population. *Journal of Psychosomatic Research, 24,* 335–342.

Peterson, J., & Marin, G. (1988). Issues in the prevention of AIDS among Black and Hispanic men. *American Psychologist, 43,* 871–877.

Peterson, J. L., et al. (1992). High-risk sexual behavior and condom use among gay and bisexual African American men. *American Journal of Public Health, 82,* 1490–1494.

Peterson, Kavan. (2004). *Fifty-state rundown on gay marriage laws.* www.stateline.org.

Peterson, Maxine E., & Dickey, Robert. (1995). Surgical sex reassignment: A comparative survey of international centers. *Archives of Sexual Behavior, 24,* 135–156.

Petkovich, A. (2004). From gonzo porn to mainstream? Porn starlet Sienna. *Spectator,* www.spectator.net/1196/1196_sienna.html.

Pfeiffer, E., Verwoerdt, A., & Wang, H. S. (1968). Sexual behavior in aged men and women. *Archives of General Psychiatry, 19,* 753–758.

Pfeiffer, Eric. (1975). Sex and aging. In L. Gross (Ed.), *Sexual issues in marriage.* New York: Spectrum.

Phelps, Jerry, et al. (2001). Spinal cord injury and sexuality in married or partnered men: Activities, function, needs, and predictors of sexual adjustment. *Archives of Sexual Behavior, 30,* 591–602.

Phibbs, C. S., Bateman, D. A., & Schwartz, R. M. (1991). The neonatal costs of maternal cocaine use. *Journal of the American Medical Association, 266,* 1521–1526.

Phillip, M., & Lazar, L. (2003). The regulatory effect of hormones and growth factors on the pubertal growth spurt. *Endocrinologist, 13,* 465–469.

Phoenix, C. H., et al. (1959). Organizing action of prenatally administered testosterone propionate on the tissues mediating mating behavior in the female guinea pig. *Endocrinology, 65,* 369–382.

Phoolcharoen, Wiput. (1998). HIV/AIDS prevention in Thailand: Success and challenges. *Science, 280,* 1873–1874.

Piccinino, Linda J., & Mosher, William D. (1998). Trends in contraceptive use in the United States: 1982–1995. *Family Planning Perspectives, 30,* 4–10.

Pick, Susan, Givaudan, Martha, & Poortinga, Ype. (2003). Sexuality and life skills education: A multistrategy intervention in Mexico. *American Psychologist, 58,* 230–234.

Pillard, Richard C., & Weinrich, James D. (1987). Periodic table model of transpositions. *Journal of Sex Research, 23,* 425–454.

Pithers, W. D. (1993). Treatment of rapists. In G. Nagayama Hall et al. (Eds.), *Sexual aggression* (pp. 167–196). Washington, DC: Taylor & Francis.

Pittenger, W. Norman. (1970). *Making sexuality human.* Philadelphia: Pilgrim Press.

Pittman, Frank, III. (1993, May–June). Beyond betrayal: Life after infidelity. *Psychology Today,* 32–38ff.

Pitts, Marian K., Smith, Anthony, Grierson, Jeffrey, O'Brien, Mary, & Mission, Sebastian. (2004). Who pays for sex and why? An analysis of social and motivational factors associated with male clients of sex workers. *Archives of Sexual Behavior, 33,* 353–368.

Plant, T. M., et al. (1993). The follicle stimulating hormone—Inhibin feedback loop in male primates. *Human Reproduction, 8,* Suppl. 2, 41–44.

Pollack, Andrew. (2004, February 13). Medical and ethical issues cloud plans to clone for therapy. *New York Times.*

Polonsky, Derek C. (2000). Premature ejaculation. In S. Leiblum & R. Rosen (Eds.), *Principles and practice of sex therapy* (3rd ed., pp. 305–334). New York: Guilford.

Pomeroy, Wardell B. (1972). *Dr. Kinsey and the Institute for Sex Research.* New York: Harper & Row.

Pomeroy, Wardell B. (1975). The diagnosis and treatment of transvestites and transsexuals. *Journal of Sex and Marital Therapy, 1,* 215–224.

Pope Paul VI. (1968, July 30). *Humanae vitae.* (English text in the *New York Times,* 20.)

Pope, Ken. (2001). Sex between therapists and clients. In J. Worell (Ed.), *Encyclopedia of women and gender* (pp. 955–862). New York: Academic Press.

Population Information Program. (1983). Vasectomy—Safe and simple. *Population Reports,* Series D, No. 4, D61–D100.

Posner, Richard. (1992). *Sex and reason.* Cambridge, MA: Harvard University Press.

Posner, Richard, & Silbaugh, Katherine. (1996). *A guide to America's sex laws.* Chicago: University of Chicago Press.

Potts, A., et al. (2003). The downside of Viagra: Women's experiences and concerns. *Sociology of Health and Illness, 25,* 697–719.

Powdermaker, Hortense. (1933). *Life in Lesu.* New York: Norton.

Prather, Randall S. (2000). Pigs is pigs. *Science, 289,* 1886–1887.

Prause, N., & Graham, C. A. (2007). Asexuality: Classification and characterization. *Archives of Sexual Behavior, 36,* in press.

President's Council on Bioethics. (2004). Reproduction and responsibility: The regulation of new biotechnologies. http://bioethicsprint.bioethics.gov/reports.

Price, James, Allensworth, Diane, & Hillman, Kathleen. (1985). Comparison of sexual fantasies of homosexuals and heterosexuals. *Psychological Reports, 57,* 871–877.

Pridal, Cathryn G., & LoPiccolo, Joseph. (2000). Multielement treatment of desire disorders: Integration of cognitive, behavioral, and systemic therapy. In S. Leiblum & R. Rosen (Eds.), *Principles and practice of sex therapy* (3rd ed., pp. 57–84). New York: Guilford.

Propper, C. R. (2005). The study of endocrine-disrupting compounds: Past approaches and new directions. *Integrative and Comparative Biology, 45,* 194–200.

Prostitutes Education Network. (1998). Prostitution in the United States—the statistics. www.bayswan.org/stats.html.

Puar, Jasbir K. (2001). Global circuits: Transnational sexualities and Trinidad. *Signs: Journal of Women in Culture and Society, 26,* 1039–1065.

Purdon, Christine, & Holdaway, Laura. (2006). Non-erotic thoughts: Content and relation to sexual functioning and sexual satisfaction. *Journal of Sex Research, 43,* 154–162.

Purnine, Daniel, & Carey, Michael. (1997). Interpersonal communication and sexual adjustment: The roles of understanding and agreement. *Journal of Consulting and Clinical Psychology, 65,* 1017–1025.

Quadagno, D., et al. (1991). The menstrual cycle: Does it affect athletic performance? *Physician and Sports Medicine, 19,* 121–124.

Quadagno, David, et al. (1995). Cardiovascular disease and sexual functioning. *Applied Nursing Research, 8,* 143–146.

Quadagno, David, et al. (1998). Ethnic differences in sexual decisions and sexual behavior. *Archives of Sexual Behavior, 27,* 57–75.

Qualls, C. B., Wincze, J. P., & Barlow, D. H. (1978). *The prevention of sexual disorders.* New York: Plenum.

Quas, Jodi A., et al. (2005). Childhood sexual assault victims: Long-term outcomes after testifying in criminal court. *Monographs of the Society for Research in Child Development, 70* (2), 1–127.

Quinn, T. C., et al. (2000). Viral load and heterosexual transmission of human immunodeficiency virus type 1. *New England Journal of Medicine, 342,* 921.

Quinn, Thomas C., & Overbaugh, Julie. (2005). HIV/AIDS in women: An expanding epidemic. *Science, 308,* 1582–1583.

Quittner, Joshua. (1997, April 14). Divorce, Internet style. *Time,* 72.

Rachman, S. (1966). Sexual fetishism: An experimental analogue. *Psychological Record, 16,* 293–296.

Raffaelli, Marcela, & Ontai, Lenna L. (2004). Gender socialization in Latino/a families: Results from two retrospective studies. *Sex Roles, 50,* 287–300.

Raghavan, Ramesh, et al. (2004). Sexual victimization among a national probability sample of adolescent women. *Perspectives on Sexual and Reproductive Health, 36,* 225–232.

Ragona, Steven. (1993). *City of National City v. Wiener:* The further erosion of First Amendment protection for adult businesses. *Loyola of Los Angeles Entertainment Law Journal, 14,* 331–355.

Raine, Nancy V. (1998). *After silence: Rape and my journey back.* New York: Crown.

Rako, Susan, & Friebely, Joan. (2004). Pheromonal influences on sociosexual behavior in postmenopausal women. *Journal of Sex Research, 41,* 372–380.

Ramchandani, Paul, Stein, A., Evans, J., O'Connor, T., & the ALSPAC Study Team. (2005). Paternal depression in the postnatal period and child development: A prospective population study. *The Lancet, 365,* 2201–2205.

Rasmussen, Stephanie J. (1998). Chlamydia immunology. *Current Opinion in Infectious Diseases, 11,* 37–41.

Rawicki, H. B., & Hill, S. (1991). Semen retrieval in spinal cord injured men. *Paraplegia, 29,* 443–446.

Raymond, E., Chen, P., & Luoto, J. (2004). Contraceptive effectiveness and safety of five nonoxynol-9 spermicides: A randomized trial. *Obstetrics and Gynecology, 103,* 430–439.

Raymond, N. C., et al. (2002). Treatment of compulsive sexual behaviour with naltrexone and serotonin reuptake inhibitors: Two case studies. *International Clinical Psychopharmacology, 127,* 201–205.

Ream, Geoffrey, & Savin-Williams, Ritch. (2005). Reciprocal associations between adolescent sexual activity and quality of youth-parent interactions. *Journal of Family Psychology, 19,* 171–179.

Reamy, Kenneth J., & White, Susan E. (1987). Sexuality in the puerperium: A review. *Archives of Sexual Behavior, 16,* 165–186.

Reddy, K. J., et al. (2004). Induction of immune responses against human papillomaviruses by hypervariable epitope constructs. *Immunology, 112,* 321–327.

Rederstorff, Juliette C., et al. (2007). The moderating roles of race and gender-role attitudes in the relationship between sexual harassment and psychological well-being. *Psychology of Women Quarterly, 31,* 50–61.

Reece, Michael, Herbenick, D., & Sherwood-Puzzello, C. (2004). Sexual health promotion and adult retail stores. *Journal of Sex Research, 41,* 173–180.

Regan, Pamela. (2004). Sex and the attraction process: Lessons from science (and Shakespeare) on lust, love, chastity, and fidelity. In J. Harvey et al. (Eds.), *The handbook of sexuality in close relationships* (pp. 115–133). Mahwah, NJ: Lawrence Erlbaum.

Reichert, T., & Carpenter, C. (2004). An update on sex in magazine advertising: 1983 to 2003. *Journalism and Mass Communication Quarterly, 81,* 823–837.

Reichert, Tom. (2002). Sex in advertising research: A review of content, effects, and functions of sexual information in consumer advertising. *Annual Review of Sex Research, 13,* 241–273.

Reid, Pamela T., & Bing, Vanessa M. (2000). Sexual roles of girls and women: An ethnocultural lifespan perspective. In C. Travis & J. White (Eds.), *Sexuality, society, and feminism* (pp. 141–166). Washington, DC: American Psychological Association.

Reimers, Stan. (2007). The BBC Internet Study: General methodology. *Archives of Sexual Behavior, 36,* 147–161.

Reinharz, Shulamit. (1992). *Feminist methods in social research.* New York: Oxford University Press.

Reisenzein, Rainer. (1983). The Schachter theory of emotion: Two decades later. *Psychological Bulletin, 94,* 239–264.

Reiss, Ira L. (1960). *Premarital sexual standards in America.* New York: Free Press.

Reiss, Ira L. (1967). *The social context of premarital sex permissiveness.* New York: Holt.

Reiss, Ira L. (1986). *Journey into sexuality: An exploratory voyage.* Englewood Cliffs, NJ: Prentice-Hall.

Reissing, Elke E., et al. (2004). Vaginal spasm, pain, and behavior: An empirical investigation of the diagnosis of vaginismus. *Archives of Sexual Behavior, 33,* 5–18.

Rekart, Michael. (2005). Sex-work harm-reduction. *The Lancet, 366,* 2123–2134.

Religious Coalition for Reproductive Choice. (2004). *We affirm: Religious organizations support reproductive choice.* www.ncrc.org.

Renaud, Cheryl, & Byers, E. Sandra. (1997). Sexual and relationship satisfaction in mainland China. *Journal of Sex Research, 34,* 399–410.

Renne, Elisha P. (1996). The pregnancy that doesn't stay: The practice and perception of abortion by Ekiti Yoruba women. *Social Science and Medicine, 42,* 483–494.

Repke, John T. (1994). Calcium and vitamin D. *Clinical Obstetrics and Gynecology, 37,* 550–557.

Reuther, Rosemary Radford. (1985). Catholics and abortion: Authority vs. dissent. *Christian Century, 102,* 859–862.

Reynolds, Meredith, Herbenick, Debra, & Bancroft, John. (2003). The nature of childhood sexual experiences: Two studies 50 years apart. In John Bancroft (Ed.), *Sexual development in childhood* (pp. 134–155). Bloomington: Indiana University Press.

Rhoades, Galena K., Stanley, S., & Markman, H. (2006). Pre-engagement cohabitation and gender asymmetry in marital commitment. *Journal of Family Psychology, 20,* 553–560.

Rice, Berkeley. (1974). Rx: Sex for senior citizens. *Psychology Today, 8* (1), 18–20.

Rice, George, et al. (1999). Male homosexuality: Absence of linkage to microsatellite markers at Xq28. *Science, 284,* 665–667.

Rich, Frank. (2001, May 20). Naked capitalists. *New York Times Magazine.*

Richardson, Chinue, & Nash, Elizabeth. (2006). Misinformed consent: The medical accuracy of state-developed abortion counseling materials. *Guttmacher Policy Review, 9* (No. 4), 6–11.

Richardson, J. Derek. (1991). I. Medical causes of male sexual dysfunction. *Medical Journal of Australia, 155,* 29–33.

Richters, Juliet, de Visser, R., Rissel, C., & Smith, A. (2006). Sexual practices at last heterosexual encounter and occurrence of orgasm in a national survey. *Journal of Sex Research, 43,* 217–226.

Rideout, Victoria, et al. (2005). *Generation M: Media in the lives of 8–18-year-olds.* Menlo Park, CA: Kaiser Family Foundation. www.kff.org.

Ridley, Carl A., et al. (2006). The ebb and flow of marital lust: A relational approach. *Journal of Sex Research, 43,* 144–153.

Rieger, Gerulf, Chivers, Meredith L., & Bailey, J. Michael. (2005). Sexual arousal patterns of bisexual men. *Psychological Science, 16,* 579–584.

Rigdon, Susan M. (1996). Abortion law and practice in China: An overview with comparisons to the United States. *Social Science and Medicine, 42,* 543–560.

Rimm, Marty. (1995). Marketing pornography on the information superhighway: A survey of 917,410 images. *Georgetown Law Journal, 83,* 1849–1925.

Rind, Bruce, Tromovitch, Philip, & Bauserman, Robert. (1998). A meta-analytic examination of assumed properties of child sexual abuse using college samples. *Psychological Bulletin, 124,* 22–53.

Rini, Christine, Dunkel Schetter, C., Hobel, C., Glynn, L., and Sandman, C. (2006). Effective social support: Antecedents and consequences of partner support during pregnancy. *Personal Relationships, 13,* 207–229.

Riportella-Muller, Roberta. (1989). Sexuality in the elderly: A review. In K. McKinney & S. Sprecher (Eds.), *Human sexuality: The societal and interpersonal context* (pp. 210–236). New York: Ablex.

Roberson, Bruce, & Wright, Rex. (1994). Difficulty as a determinant of interpersonal appeal: A social-motivational application of energization theory. *Basic and Applied Social Psychology, 15,* 373–388.

Roberts, C., et al. (2003). Increasing proportion of herpes simplex virus type I as a cause of genital herpes infection in college students. *Sexually Transmitted Diseases, 30,* 797–800.

Roberts, D. (2000). Media and youth: Access, exposure, and privatization. *Journal of Adolescent Health, 27* (2), 8–14.

Roberts, Dorothy E. (1993). Crime, race, and reproduction. *Tulane Law Review, 67,* 1945–1977.

Robertson, David L., Hahn, Beatrice, & Sharp, Paul M. (1995). Recombination in AIDS viruses. *Molecular Evolution, 40,* 249–259.

Robertson, John A. (1986). Embryos, families and procreative liberty: The legal structure of the new reproduction. *Southern California Law Review, 59,* 942–1041.

Robertson, Sarah, & Sharkey, David. (2001). The role of semen in induction of maternal immune tolerance to pregnancy. *Seminars in Immunology, 13,* 243.

Robinson, D., & Rock, J. (1967). Intrascrotal hyperthermia induced by scrotal insulation: Effect on spermatogenesis. *Obstetrics and Gynecology, 29,* 217.

Roehr, Bob. (2007). Dramatic drop in HIV infections halts circumcision trials. *British Medical Journal, 334,* 11.

Roisman, Glenn, et al. (2004). Salient and emerging developmental tasks in the transition to adulthood. *Child Development, 75,* 123–133.

Romer, Daniel, et al. (1997). "Talking computers": A reliable and private method to conduct interviews on sensitive topics with children. *Journal of Sex Research, 34,* 3–9.

Rondeaux, Candace. (2006, July 5). Can castration be a solution for sex offenders? *Washington Post.*

Root, Maria P. (1995). The psychology of Asian American women. In H. Landrine (Ed.), *Bringing cultural diversity to feminist psychology: Theory, research, and practice* (pp. 265–302). Washington, DC: American Psychological Association.

Roper Center, The. (2004). U.S. public opinion on homosexual marriages. www.ropercenter.uconn.edu.

Rosaldo, Michelle A. (1974). Woman, culture, and society: A theoretical overview. In M. S. Rosaldo & L. Lamphere (Eds.), *Woman, culture, and society.* Stanford, CA: Stanford University Press.

Rosario, Margaret, et al. (1996). The psychosexual development of urban lesbian, gay and bisexual youths. *Journal of Sex Research, 33,* 113–126.

Rosario, Margaret, et al. (2004). Ethnic/racial differences in the coming-out process of lesbian, gay, and bisexual youths: A comparison of sexual identity development over time. *Cultural Diversity & Ethnic Minority Psychology, 10,* 215–228.

Rosario, Margaret, Schrimshaw, E., Hunter, J., & Braun, L. (2006). Sexual identity development among gay, lesbian, and bisexual youths: Consistency and change over time. *Journal of Sex Research, 43,* 46–58.

Roscoe, B., Cavanaugh, L., & Kennedy, D. (1988). Dating infidelity: Behaviors, reasons, and consequences. *Adolescence, 89,* 36–43.

Roscoe, Bruce, Kennedy, Donna, & Pope, Tony. (1987). Adolescents' views of intimacy: Distinguishing intimate from nonintimate relationships. *Adolescence, 22,* 511–516.

Rose, S., & Frieze, I. H. (1993). Young singles' contemporary dating scripts. *Sex Roles, 28,* 499–509.

Roselli, Charles E., Resko, J., & Stormshak, F. (2002). Hormonal influences on sexual partner preference in rams. *Archives of Sexual Behavior, 31,* 43–50.

Rosen, David H. (1974). *Lesbianism: A study of female homosexuality.* Springfield, IL: Charles C. Thomas.

Rosen, Raymond C. (2007). Erectile dysfunction: Integration of medical and psychological approaches. In S. Leiblum (Ed.), *Principles and practice of sex therapy* (4th ed., pp. 277–312). New York: Guilford.

Rosen, Raymond C., & Leiblum, Sandra R. (1995a). Hypoactive sexual desire. *Psychiatric Clinics of North America, 18,* 107–121.

Rosen, Raymond C., & Leiblum, Sandra R. (1995b). Treatment of sexual disorders in the 1990s: An integrated approach. *Journal of Consulting and Clinical Psychology, 63,* 877–890.

Rosen, Raymond C., Leiblum, Sandra R., & Spector, Ilana P. (1994). Psychologically-based treatment for male erectile disorder: A cognitive-interpersonal model. *Journal of Sex and Marital Therapy, 20,* 67–85.

Rosen, Raymond C., & McKenna, Kevin E. (2002). PDE-5 inhibition and sexual response: Pharmacological mechanisms and clinical outcomes. *Annual Review of Sex Research, 13,* 36–88.

Rosenberg, E. S., et al. (2000). Immune control of HIV-1 after early treatment of acute infection. *Nature, 407,* 523–526.

Rosenberg, Lynn. (1993). Hormone replacement therapy: The need for reconsideration. *American Journal of Public Health, 83,* 1670–1673.

Rosenblatt, Karin A., Wicklund, K., & Stanford, J. (2001). Sexual factors and the risk of prostate cancer. *American Journal of Epidemiology, 153,* 1152–1158.

Rosenbleet, C., & Pariente, B. J. (1973). The prostitution of the criminal law. *American Criminal Law Review, 11,* 373–427.

Rosler, Ariel, & Witztum, Eliezer. (1998). Treatment of men with paraphilia with a long-lasting analogue of gonadotropin-releasing hormone. *New England Journal of Medicine, 338,* 416–422.

Rosner, Fred. (1983). In vitro fertilization and surrogate motherhood: The Jewish view. *Journal of Religion and Health, 22,* 139–160.

Ross, David, & Stevenson, John. (1993, November–December). HRT and cardiovascular disease. *British Journal of Sexual Medicine,* 10–13.

Ross, Michael, & Williams, Mark. (2002). Effective targeted and community HIV/STD prevention programs. *Journal of Sex Research, 39,* 58–62.

Ross, Michael N., Paulsen, J. A., & Stalstrom, O. W. (1988). Homosexuality and mental health: A cross-cultural review. *Journal of Homosexuality, 15,* 131–152.

Ross, Michael W. (2005). Typing, being, and doing: Sexuality and the Internet. *Journal of Sex Research, 42,* 342–354.

Rotello, Gabriel. (1997). *Sexual ecology: AIDS and the destiny of gay men.* New York: Dutton.

Rothbaum, B. O., et al. (1992). A prospective examination of post-traumatic stress disorder in rape victims. *Journal of Traumatic Stress, 5,* 455–475.

Rothblum, Esther D. (1994). "I only read about myself on bathroom walls": The need for research on the mental health of lesbians and gay men. *Journal of Consulting and Clinical Psychology, 62,* 213–220.

Rothblum, Esther D. (2007). Personal communication.

Rothblum, Esther D., & Bond, Lynne A. (Eds.). (1996). *Preventing heterosexism and homophobia.* Thousand Oaks, CA: Sage.

Rousseau, S., et al. (1983). The expectancy of pregnancy for "normal" infertile couples. *Fertility and Sterility, 40,* 768–772.

Rowland, David A., & Slob, A. Koos. (1997). Premature ejaculation: Psychophysiological considerations in theory, research, and treatment. *Annual Review of Sex Research, 8,* 224–253.

Rowland, David L., & Burnett, Arthur L. (2000). Pharmacotherapy in treatment of male sexual dysfunction. *Journal of Sex Research, 37,* 226–243.

Rozée, Patricia D., & Koss, Mary P. (2001). Rape: A century of resistance. *Psychology of Women Quarterly, 25,* 295–311.

Ruan, Fang-fu. (1991). *Sex in China.* New York: Plenum.

Ruan, Fang-fu, & Lau, M. P. (1998). China. In R. Francoeur (Ed.), *The international encyclopedia of sexuality* (Vol. 1, pp. 344–399). New York: Continuum.

Rubin, Isadore. (1966). Sex after forty—and after seventy. In Ruth Brecher & Edward Brecher (Eds.), *An analysis of human sexual response.* New York: Signet Books, New American Library.

Rubin, Lillian B. (1979). *Women of a certain age: The midlife search for self.* New York: Harper & Row.

Rubin, Robert T., Reinisch, J. M., & Haskett, R. F. (1981). Postnatal gonadal steroid effects on human behavior. *Science, 211,* 1318–1324.

Rubin, Zick. (1973). *Liking and loving: An invitation to social psychology.* New York: Holt.

Rubin, Zick, et al. (1980). Self-disclosure in dating couples: Sex roles and the ethic of openness. *Journal of Marriage and the Family, 42,* 305–317.

Ruble, Diane N. (1977). Premenstrual symptoms: A reinterpretation. *Science, 197,* 291–292.

Ruble, Diane N., & Stangor, Charles. (1986). Stalking the elusive schema: Insights from developmental and social-psychological analyses of gender schemas. *Social Cognition, 4,* 227–261.

Rusbult, Caryl. (1983). A longitudinal test of the investment model: The development (and deterioration) of satisfaction and commitment in heterosexual involvements. *Journal of Personality and Social Psychology, 45,* 101–117.

Rusbult, Caryl, Johnson, D. J., & Morrow, G. D. (1986). Predicting satisfaction and commitment in adult romantic involvements: An assessment of the generalizability of the investment model. *Social Psychology Quarterly, 49,* 81–89.

Russell, Diana E. H. (1980). Pornography and violence: What does the new research say? In L. Lederer (Ed.), *Take back the night: Women on pornography.* New York: Morrow.

Russell, Diana E. H. (1983). *Rape in marriage.* New York: Macmillan.

Russell, Diana E. H. (1990). *Rape in marriage* (rev. ed.). Bloomington: Indiana University Press.

Rust, Paula C. Rodriguez. (2002). Bisexuality: The state of the union. *Annual Review of Sex Research, 13,* 180–240.

Ruth, Sheila. (Ed.). (1990). *Issues in feminism: An introduction to women's studies* (2nd ed.). Mountain View, CA: Mayfield.

Ryan, G. L., Sparks, A. E. T., Sipe, C. S., Syrop, C. H., Dokras, A., & Van Voorhis, B. J. (2007). A mandatory single blastocyst transfer policy with educational campaign in a United States IVF program reduces multiple gestation rates without sacrificing pregnancy rates. *Fertility and Sterility,* in press.

Rye, B. J., & Meaney, G. (2007). Voyeurism: It is good as long as we do not get caught. *International Journal of Sexual Health, 1,* 77–93.

Rylko-Bauer, Barbara. (1996). Abortion from a cross-cultural perspective. *Social Science and Medicine, 42,* 479–482.

Sabatelli, R. M., Buck, R., & Dreyer, A. (1982). Nonverbal communication accuracy in married couples: Relationships with marital complaints. *Journal of Personality and Social Psychology, 43,* 1088–1097.

Sachs-Ericsson, Natalie et al. (2005). Childhood sexual and physical abuse and the 1-year prevalence of medical problems in the National Comorbidity Survey. *Health Psychology, 24,* 32–40.

Sackellares, Stephanie N. (2005). From Bosnia to Sudan: Sexual violence in modern armed conflict. *Wisconsin Women's Law Journal, 20,* 137–166.

Sacks, S. L. (2004). Famciclovir suppression of asymptomatic and symptomatic recurrent anogenital herpes simplex virus shedding in women. *Journal of Infectious Diseases, 189,* 1341–1347.

Sacred Congregation for the Doctrine of the Faith. (1976, January 16). *Declaration on certain questions concerning sexual ethics.* English text in the *New York Times,* p. 2.

Sadock, Benjamin J., & Sadock, Virginia A. (1976). Techniques of coitus. In B. J. Sadock et al. (Eds.), *The sexual experience.* Baltimore: Williams & Wilkins.

Saegert, S., Swap, W., & Zajonc, R. B. (1973). Exposure, context, and interpersonal attraction. *Journal of Personality and Social Psychology, 25,* 234–242.

Sáenz de Tejada, I., et al. (2004). Physiology of erectile dysfunction and pathophysiology of erectile dysfunction. In T. Lue et al. (Eds.), *Sexual medicine* (pp. 287–343). Paris: Editions 21.

Sagarin, Edward. (1973). Power to the peephole. *Sexual Behavior, 3,* 2–7.

Salamon, Edna. (1989). The homosexual escort agency: Deviance disavowal. *British Journal of Sociology, 40,* 1–21.

Saleh, Fabian M., & Berlin, F. S. (2003). Sex hormones, neurotransmitters, and psychopharmacological treatments in men with paraphilic disorders. *Journal of Child Sexual Abuse, 12,* 233–253.

Saleh, Fabian M., Niel, T., & Fishman, M. J. (2004). Treatment of paraphilia in young adults with leuprolide acetate: A preliminary case report series. *Journal of Forensic Science, 49,* 1343–1348.

Salem, Ruwaida N. (2005). World Health Organization updates guidance on how to use contraceptives. *INFO Reports, 4.* Baltimore: Johns Hopkins University.

Salgado de Snyder, et al. (2000). Understanding the sexuality of Mexican-born women and their risk for HIV/AIDS. *Psychology of Women Quarterly, 24,* 100–109.

Salonia, Andrea, et al. (2003). Sildenafil in erectile dysfunction: A critical review. *Current Medical Research Opinion, 19,* 241–262.

Saltik-Temizel, I., Kocak, N., & Demit, H. (2004). Interferon-alpha and lamivudine combination therapy of children with chronic hepatitis B infection who were interferon-alpha nonresponders. *Pediatric Infectious Disease Journal, 23,* 466–468.

San Francisco Task Force on Prostitution. (1996). *Final report.* www.bayswan.org.

Sanchez, Diana T., Kiefer, Amy K., & Ybarra, Oscar. (2006). Sexual submissiveness in women: Costs for sexual autonomy and arousal. *Personality and Social Psychology Bulletin, 32,* 512–524.

Sanday, Peggy R. (1981). The socio-cultural context of rape: A cross-cultural study. *Journal of Social Issues, 37* (4), 5–27.

Sanday, Peggy R. (1990). *Fraternity gang rape.* New York: New York University Press.

Sanders, G., & Mullis, R. (1988). Family influences on sexual attitudes and knowledge as reported by college students. *Adolescence, 23,* 837–845.

Sandfort, Theo, & Ehrhardt, Anke. (2004). Sexual health: A useful public health paradigm or a moral imperative? *Archives of Sexual Behavior, 33,* 181–187.

Sanghavi, Darshak M. (2006, October 17). Preschool puberty, and a search for the causes. *New York Times.*

Santen, Richard J. (1995). The testis. In P. Felig, J. D. Baxter, & L. A. Frohman (Eds.), *Endocrinology and metabolism* (3rd ed.). New York: McGraw-Hill.

Santora, Marc. (2005, January 30). U.S. is close to eliminating AIDS in infants, officials say. *New York Times.*

Santtilla, Pekka, et al. (2002). Investigating the underlying structure in sadomasochistically oriented behavior. *Archives of Sexual Behavior, 31,* 185–196.

Sarrel, Lorna, & Sarrel, Philip. (1984). *Sexual turning points: The seven stages of adult sexuality.* New York: Macmillan.

Savage, Olayinka M. N., & Tchombe, Therese M. (1994). Anthropological perspectives on sexual behaviour in Africa. *Annual Review of Sex Research, 5,* 50–72.

Savin-Williams, Ritch. (2001). Suicide attempts among sexual-minority youths: Population and measurement issues. *Journal of Consulting and Clinical Psychology, 69,* 983–991.

Savin-Williams, Ritch, & Diamond, Lisa. (1999). Sexual orientation. In Wendy Silverman & Thomas Ollendick (Eds.), *Developmental issues in the clinical treatment of children* (pp. 241–258). Needham Heights, MA: Allyn & Bacon.

Savin-Williams, Ritch C. (2005). *The new gay teenager.* Cambridge, MA: Harvard University Press.

Savin-Williams, Ritch C. (2006). Who's gay? Does it matter? *Current Directions in Psychological Science, 15,* 40–44.

Savin-Williams, Ritch C., & Ream, Geoffrey L. (2003). Suicide attempts among sexual-minority male youth. *Journal of Clinical Child and Adolescent Psychology, 32,* 509–522.

Savolainen, Vincent, & Lehmann, Laurent. (2007). Genetics and bisexuality. *Nature, 445,* 158–159.

Sayle, A. E., et al. (2001). Sexual activity during late pregnancy and risk of preterm delivery. *Obstetrics and Gynecology, 97,* 283–289.

Sbraga, Tamara P., & O'Donohue, William. (2000). Sexual harassment. *Annual Review of Sex Research, 11,* 258–285.

Schachter, Stanley. (1964). The interaction of cognitive and physiological determinants of emotional state. In L. Berkowitz (Ed.), *Advances in experimental social psychology* (Vol. I). New York: Academic Press.

Schaefer, Mark T., & Olson, David H. (1981). Assessing intimacy: The PAIR Inventory. *Journal of Marital and Family Therapy,* 47–60.

Schaffer, H. R., & Emerson, Peggy E. (1964). Patterns of response to physical contact in early human development. *Journal of Child Psychology and Psychiatry, 5,* 1–13.

Schaffir, Jonathan. (2006). Sexual intercourse at term and onset of labor. *Obstetrics and Gynecology, 107,* 1310–1314.

Scharfe, Elaine, & Bartholomew, Kim. (1995). Accommodation and attachment representations in young couples. *Journal of Social and Personal Relationships, 12,* 389–401.

Schatz, B. (1987). The AIDS insurance crisis: Underwriting or overreaching? *Harvard Law Review, 100* (7), 1782–1805.

Schenker, J. G., & Evron, S. (1983). New concepts in the surgical management of tubal pregnancy and the consequent postoperative results. *Fertility and Sterility, 40,* 709–723.

Schiavi, Raul C. (1990). Sexuality in aging men. *Annual Review of Sex Research, 1,* 227–250.

Schiavi, Raul C., et al. (1994). Sexual satisfaction in healthy aging men. *Journal of Sex and Marital Therapy, 20,* 3–13.

Schieffelin, E. L. (1976). *The sorrow of the lonely and the burning of the dancers.* New York: St. Martin's Press.

Schlenker, Jennifer A., Caron, Sandra L., & Halteman, William A. (1998). A feminist analysis of *Seventeen* magazine: Content analysis from 1945 to 1995. *Sex Roles, 38,* 135–150.

Schmidt, L. (2006). Psychosocial burden of infertility and assisted reproduction. *The Lancet, 367,* 379–380.

Schmiege, Sarah, & Russo, Nancy F. (2005). Depression and unwanted first pregnancy: Longitudinal cohort study. *British Medical Journal, 331,* 1303.

Schmitt, David P. (2003). Universal sex differences in the desire for sexual variety: Tests from 52 nations, 6 continents, and 13 islands. *Journal of Personality and Social Psychology, 85,* 85–104.

Schmitt, David, & Buss, David. (1996). Strategic self-promotion and competitor derogation: Sex and content effects on the perceived effectiveness of mate attraction tactics. *Journal of Personality and Social Psychology, 70,* 1185–1204.

Schneider, Edward D. (Ed.). (1985). *Questions about the beginning of life.* Minneapolis: Augsburg.

Schofield, Alfred T., & Vaughan-Jackson, Percy. (1913). *What a boy should know.* New York: Cassell.

Schooler, Deborah, Ward, L. Monique, Merriwether, Ann, & Caruthers, Allison. (2005). Cycles of shame: Menstrual shame, body shame, and sexual decision-making. *Journal of Sex Research, 42,* 324–334.

Schooley, R. T., et al. (2000). Two double-blinded, randomized, comparative trials of 4 human immunodeficiency virus type 1 (HIV-1) envelope vaccines in HIV-1-infected individuals across a spectrum of disease severity. *Journal of Infectious Diseases, 182,* 1357–1364.

Schrock, Douglas P., & Reid, Lori L. (2006). Transsexuals' sexual stories. *Archives of Sexual Behavior, 35,* 75–86.

Schroeder, Patricia. (1994). Female genital mutilation—A form of child abuse. *New England Journal of Medicine, 331,* 739–740.

Schubach, Gary. (2002). The G-spot is the female prostate. *American Journal of Obstetrics and Gynecology, 186,* 850.

Schultz, W. C. M., et al. (1989). Vaginal sensitivity to electric stimuli: Theoretical and practical implications. *Archives of Sexual Behavior, 18,* 87–96.

Schultz, Willibrord W., et al. (1999). Magnetic resonance imaging of male and female genitals during coitus and female sexual arousal. *British Medical Journal, 319,* 1596–1600.

Schwartz, Lisa Barrie. (1997, December 20/27). Understanding human parturition. *The Lancet, 350,* 1792–1793.

Schwartz, Lita. (2003). A nightmare for King Solomon: The new reproductive technologies. *Journal of Family Psychology, 17,* 229–237.

Sciarra, John J. (1991). Infertility: A global perspective on the role of infection. *Annals of the New York Academy of Sciences, 626,* 478–483.

Scott, Charles, & Holmberg, T. (2003). Castration of sex offenders: Prisoners' rights versus public safety. *Journal of the American Academy of Psychiatry and the Law, 31,* 502–509.

Scott, John Paul. (1964). The effects of early experience on social behavior and organization. In W. Etkin (Ed.), *Social behavior and organization among vertebrates.* Chicago: University of Chicago Press.

Scroggs, Robin. (1983). *The New Testament and homosexuality.* Philadelphia: Fortress.

Seal, David W., & Ehrhardt, A. E. (2003). Masculinity and urban men: Perceived scripts for courtship, romantic, and sexual interactions with women. *Culture, Health, and Sexuality, 5,* 295–319.

Segraves, Robert T., & Balon, Richard. (2003). *Sexual pharmacology: Fast facts.* New York: Norton.

Sell, Randall L. (1997). Defining and measuring sexual orientation: A review. *Archives of Sexual Behavior, 26,* 643–658.

Sell, Randall L., Wells, James A., & Wypij, David. (1995). The prevalence of homosexual behavior and attraction in the United States, the United Kingdom and France. *Archives of Sexual Behavior, 24,* 235–248.

Semple, S. J., Patterson, T. L., & Grant, I. (2004). The context of sexual risk behavior among heterosexual methamphetamine users. *Addictive Behaviors, 29,* 807–810.

Seto, Michael C. (2004). Pedophilia and sexual offenses against children. *Annual Review of Sex Research, 15,* 321–361.

Seto, Michael C., Cantor, James M., & Blanchard, Ray. (2006). Child pornography offenses are a valid diagnostic indicator of pedophilia. *Journal of Abnormal Psychology, 115,* 610–615.

Setty-Venugopal, Vidya, & Upadhyay, Ushma D. (2002). Three to five saves lives. *Population Reports,* Series L, Number 13. Baltimore: Johns Hopkins University School of Public Health.

Sex Industry, The. (1998, February 14). *The Economist,* 21–23.

Shabsigh, R., et al. (2000). Intracavernous alprostadil alfadex (Edex/viridal) is effective and safe in patients with erectile dysfunction after failing sildenafil (Viagra). *Urology, 55*, 477–480.

Shackelford, Todd, & Buss, David. (1997). Cues to infidelity. *Personality and Social Psychology Bulletin, 23*, 1034–1045.

Shandera, K. C., & Thompson, I. M. (1994). Urologic prostheses. *Emergency Medicine Clinics of North America, 12*, 729–748.

Shapiro, Craig N., & Alter, Miriam J. (1996). Syphilis. In S. A. Morse et al. (Eds.), *Atlas of sexually transmitted diseases* (pp. 241–268). London: Mosby-Wolfe.

Shapiro, E. Donald. (1986). New innovations in conception and their effects upon our law and morality. *New York Law Review, 21*, 37–59.

Shapiro, Harold T. (1997). Ethical and policy issues in human cloning. *Science, 277*, 195–196.

Sharpstein, Don J., & Kirkpatrick, Lee. (1997). Romantic jealousy and adult romantic attachment. *Journal of Personality and Social Psychology, 72*, 627–640.

Shattuck-Eidens, Donna, et al. (1995). A collaborative survey of 80 mutations in the BRCA1 breast and ovarian cancer susceptibility gene. *Journal of the American Medical Association, 273*, 535–541.

Sheff, Elisabeth. (2005). Polyamorous women, sexual subjectivity, and power. *Journal of Contemporary Ethnographics, 34*, 251–283.

Shepherd, Gordon M. (2006). Smells, brains and hormones. *Nature, 439*, 149–151.

Sherrard, J., & Barlow, D. (1996). Gonorrhoea in men: Clinical and diagnostic aspects. *Genitourinary Medicine, 72*, 422–426.

Sherwin, Barbara B. (1991). The psychoendocrinology of aging and female sexuality. *Annual Review of Sex Research, 2*, 181–198.

Shewaga, Duane. (1983). Note on *New York v. Ferber. Santa Clara Law Review, 23*, 675–684.

Shidlo, Ariel, Schroeder, M., & Drescher, J. (Eds.). (2002). *Sexual conversion therapy: Ethical, clinical, and research perspectives.* New York: Haworth.

Shifren, Jan L., et al. (2000). Transdermal testosterone treatment in women with impaired sexual function after oophorectomy. *New England Journal of Medicine, 343*, 682–688.

Shifren, Jan L., Nahum, R., & Mazer, N. A. (1998). Incidence of sexual dysfunction in surgically menopausal women. *Menopause, 5*, 189–190.

Shostak, Arthur B. (1984). *Men and abortion: Lessons, losses, and love.* New York: Praeger.

Shouvlin, David P. (1981). Preventing the sexual exploitation of children: A model act. *Wake Forest Law Review, 17*, 535–560.

SIECUS (Sex Information and Education Council of the United States). (1996). *Guidelines for comprehensive sexuality education, rev.* New York: Sexuality Information and Education Council of the United States.

SIECUS. (2004). *Guidelines for comprehensive sexuality education* (3rd ed.). New York: SIECUS. http://www.siecus.org/pubs/guidelines/guidelines.pdf.

SIECUS. (2004a). *Is there research that supports condom availability?* New York: SIECUS. www.siecus.org.

SIECUS. (2004b). *SIECUS state profiles: A portrait of sexuality education and Abstinence-Only-Until-Marriage programs in the states.* New York: SIECUS.

Siegel, Karolynn, Krauss, Beatrice J., & Karus, Daniel. (1994). Reporting recent sexual practices: Gay men's disclosure of HIV risk by questionnaire and interview. *Archives of Sexual Behavior, 23*, 217–230.

Siegel, Karolynn, & Scrimshaw, Eric. (2003). Reasons for the adoption of celibacy among older men and women living with HIV/AIDS. *Journal of Sex Research, 40*, 189–200.

Sieving, Renee, Eisenberg, M., Pettingel, S., & Skay, C. (2006). Friends' influence on adolescents' first sexual intercourse. *Perspectives on Sexual and Reproductive Health, 38*, 13–19.

Signorielli, Nancy. (1990). Children, television, and gender roles. *Journal of Adolescent Health Care, 11*, 50–58.

Signorile, Michelangelo. (1997). *Life on the outside: The Signorile report on gay men.* New York: HarperCollins.

Sik Ying Ho, P. (2006). The (charmed) circle game: Reflections on sexual hierarchy through multiple sexual relationships. *Sexualities, 9*, 547–564.

Siker, Jeffrey S. (Ed.). (1994). *Homosexuality in the church: Both sides of the debate.* Louisville, KY: Westminster/John Knox Press.

Silbaugh, Katharine. (2002). Sex offenses: Consensual. In J. Dressler (Ed.), *Encyclopedia of crime and justice* (pp. 1465–1475). New York: Macmillan Reference USA.

Silvestre, Louise, et al. (1990). Voluntary interruption of pregnancy with mifepristone (RU-486) and a prostaglandin analogue: A large-scale French experience. *New England Journal of Medicine, 322*, 645.

Simon, Viviana, Ho, David, & Karim, Quarraisha. (2006). HIV/AIDS epidemiology, pathogenesis, prevention, and treatment. *The Lancet, 368*, 489–504.

Simpson, J. A. (1990). Influence of attachment styles on romantic relationships. *Journal of Personality and Social Psychology, 59*, 971–980.

Simpson, J. A., Campbill, B., & Berscheid, E. (1986). The association between romantic love and marriage. *Personality and Social Psychology Bulletin, 12*, 363–372.

Singer, D. B. (1995). Human embryogenesis. In D. R. Coustan, R. V. Haning, Jr., & D. B. Singer (Eds.), *Human reproduction: Growth and development.* Boston: Little, Brown.

Singer, Dani, & Hunter, Myra (Eds.). (2003). *Assisted human reproduction: Psychological and ethical dilemmas.* London: Whurr Publishers.

Singer, Lynn, et al. (2002). Cognitive and motor outcomes in cocaine-exposed infants. *Journal of the American Medical Association, 287*, 1952–1960.

Singh, D. (1993). Adaptive significance of female physical attractiveness: Role of waist-to-hip ratio. *Journal of Personality and Social Psychology, 65*, 293–307.

Siosteen, A., et al. (1990). Sexual ability, activity, attitudes and satisfaction as part of adjustment in spinal cord-injured subjects. *Paraplegia, 28*, 285–295.

Sipe, A. W. Richard. (1995). *Sex, priests, and power: Anatomy of a crisis.* New York: Brunner/Mazel.

Sipski, Marca L. (2002). Central nervous system based neurogenic female sexual dysfunction: Current status and future trends. *Archives of Sexual Behavior, 31*, 421–424.

Sipski, Marca L., & Alexander, Craig J. (Eds.). (1997). *Sexual function in people with disability and chronic illness.* Gaithersburg, MD: Aspen.

Sipski, Marca L., Alexander, C., & Rosen, R. (2001). Sexual arousal and orgasm in women: Effects of spinal cord injury. *Annals of Neurology, 49*, 35–44.

Sipski, Marca L., Rosen, R., Alexander, C., & Gómez-Marín, O. (2004). Sexual responsiveness in women with spinal cord injuries: Differential effects of anxiety-eliciting stimulation. *Archives of Sexual Behavior, 33*, 295–302.

Skaletsky, Helen, et al. (2003). The male-specific region of the human Y chromosome is a mosaic of discrete sequence classes. *Nature, 423*, 825–837.

Slovenko, Ralph. (1965). *Sexual behavior and the law.* Springfield, IL: Charles C. Thomas.

Small, Meredith F. (1993). *Female choices: Sexual behavior of female primates.* Ithaca, NY: Cornell University Press.

Smallwood, G., et al. (2001). Efficacy and safety of a transdermal contraceptive system. *Obstetrics and Gynecology, 98*, 799–805.

Smiler, Andrew P. (2006). Living the image: A quantitative approach to delineating masculinities. *Sex Roles, 55*, 621–632.

Smith, Anthony, et al. (2003). Sex in Australia. *Australian and New Zealand Journal of Pubic Health, 27*, No. 2 (whole).

Smith, Edward, Dariotis, J., & Potter S. (2004). *Evaluation of Pennsylvania Abstinence Education and Related Services Initiative.* Final Report to Commonwealth of Pennsylvania.

Smith, George, Frankel, Stephen, & Yarnell, John. (1997). Sex and death: Are they related? Findings from the Caerphilly cohort study. *British Medical Journal, 315*, 1641–1645.

Smith, Jeffrey R., et al. (1996). Major susceptibility locus for prostate cancer on chromosome 1 suggested by a genome-wide search. *Science, 274*, 1371–1373.

Smith, Tom. (2003). *American sexual behavior: Trends, sociodemographic differences, and risk behavior.* University of Chicago, National Opinion Research Center, GSS Topical Report No. 25.

Smyth, L. J. C., et al. (2004). Immunological responses in women with human papillomavirus type 16 (HPV-16) associated anogenital intraepithelial neoplasia induced by heterologous prime-boost HYP-16 oncogene vaccination. *Clinical Cancer Research, 10,* 2954–2961.

Snowdon, Charles T., et al. (2006). Social odours, sexual arousal and pairbonding in primates. *Philosophical Transactions of the Royal Society B, 361,* 2079–2089.

Sokol, R. J., Janisse, J. J., Louis, J. M., Bailey, B. N., Ager, J., Jacobson, S. W., & Jacobson, J. L. (2007). Extreme prematurity: An alcohol-related birth effect. *Alcoholism: Clinical and Experimental Research, 31,* 1031–1037.

Soley, Lawrence C., & Kurzbard, Gary. (1986). Sex in advertising: A comparison of 1964 and 1984 magazine advertisements. *Journal of Advertising, 15* (3), 46–54.

Solms, Mark. (1997). *The neuropsychology of dreams: A clinico-anatomical study.* Mahwah, NJ: Erlbaum.

Solomon, Sondra E., Rothblum, Esther D., & Balsam, Kimberly F. (2004). Pioneers in partnership: Lesbian and gay male couples in civil unions compared with those not in civil unions and married heterosexual siblings. *Journal of Family Psychology, 18,* 275–286.

Solomon, Sondra E., Rothblum, Esther, & Balsam, Kimberly. (2005). Money, housework, sex, and conflict: Same-sex couples in civil unions, those not in civil unions, and heterosexual married siblings. *Sex Roles, 52,* 561–576.

Sommers-Flanagan, Rita, Sommers-Flanagan, John, & Davis, Britta. (1993). What's happening on music television? A gender role content analysis. *Sex Roles, 28,* 745–753.

Song, Y. I. (1991). Single Asian women as a result of divorce: Depressive affect and changes in social support. *Journal of Divorce and Remarriage, 14,* 219–230.

Sorensen, Robert C. (1973). *Adolescent sexuality in contemporary America.* New York: World.

Sorenson, Susan B., & Siegel, Judith M. (1992). Gender, ethnicity, and sexual assault: Findings from a Los Angeles study. *Journal of Social Issues, 48* (1), 93–104.

Spalding, Leah R., & Peplau, L. Anne. (1997). The unfaithful lover: Heterosexuals' perceptions of bisexuals and their relationships. *Psychology of Women Quarterly, 21,* 611–625.

Spark, R. F. (2002). Dehydroepiandrosterone: A springboard hormone for female sexuality. *Fertility and Sterility, 77,* S19–S25.

Specter, Michael. (1998, January 11). Contraband women: A special report. *New York Times,* p. 6.

Spector, Ilana P., & Carey, Michael P. (1990). Incidence and prevalence of the sexual dysfunctions: A critical review of the empirical literature. *Archives of Sexual Behavior, 19,* 389–408.

Spehr, Marc, et al. (2003). Identification of a testicular odorant receptor mediating human sperm chemotaxis. *Science, 299,* 2054–2058.

Spencer, Natasha A., McClintock, Martha K., et al. (2004). Social chemosignals from breastfeeding women increase sexual motivation. *Hormones and Behavior, 46,* 362–370.

Spitz, Irving M., et al. (1998). Early pregnancy termination with mifepristone and misoprostol in the United States. *New England Journal of Medicine, 338,* 1241–1247.

Spitz, Rene A. (1949). Autoeroticism: Some empirical findings and hypotheses on three of its manifestations in the first year of life. *Psychoanalytic Study of the Child* (Vols. III–IV, pp. 85–120). New York: International Universities Press.

Sprecher, Susan. (1987). The effects of self-disclosure given and received on affection for an intimate partner and stability of the relationship. *Journal of Social and Personal Relationships, 4,* 115–127.

Sprecher, Susan, Barbee, Anita, & Schwartz, Pepper. (1995). "Was it good for you, too?": Gender differences in first sexual intercourse experiences. *Journal of Sex Research, 32,* 3–15.

Sprecher, Susan, & Hatfield, Elaine. (1996). Premarital sexual standards among U.S. college students: Comparison with Russian and Japanese students. *Archives of Sexual Behavior, 25,* 261–288.

Sprecher, Susan, & McKinney, Kathleen. (1993). *Sexuality.* Newbury Park, CA: Sage.

Sprecher, Susan, Sullivan, Quintin, & Hatfield, Elaine. (1994). Mate selection preferences: Gender differences examined in a national sample. *Journal of Personality and Social Psychology, 66,* 1074–1080.

Springen, Karen, & Noonan, David. (2002). *Sperm banks go online.* MSNBC News 899016.

St. Louis, Michael F., & Wasserheit, Judith N. (1998). Elimination of syphilis in the United States. *Science, 281,* 353–354.

Stack, Steven, & Gundlach, James H. (1992). Divorce and sex. *Archives of Sexual Behavior, 21,* 359–368.

Stanton, Annette L., et al. (2002). Psychosocial aspects of selected issues in women's reproductive health: Current status and future directions. *Journal of Consulting and Clinical Psychology, 70,* 751–770.

Stark, Philip. (2006). Expert Report of Philip B. Stark, Ph.D. *ACLU v Gonzales.* Civ. Action No. 98–5591 (E.D. Pa.)

Starks, Kay J., & Morrison, Eleanor S. (1996). *Growing up sexual* (2nd ed.). New York: HarperCollins.

Steege, J. F., Stout, A. L., & Carson, Culley C. (1986). Patient satisfaction in Scott and Small-Carrion penile implant recipients. *Archives of Sexual Behavior, 15,* 393–400.

Steinberg, Jennifer. (1993, February). CDC broadens AIDS definition. *Journal of NIH Research, 5,* 32.

Steinberg, Karen K., et al. (1991). A meta-analysis of the effect of estrogen replacement therapy on the risk of breast cancer. *Journal of the American Medical Association, 265,* 1985–1990.

Steinberg, Laurence. (2002). *Adolescence* (6th ed). New York: McGraw-Hill.

Steinberg, Laurence. (2005). *Adolescence* (7th ed.). New York: McGraw-Hill.

Steiner, Markus J., & Cates, Willard. (2006). Condoms and sexually-transmitted infections. *New England Journal of Medicine, 354,* 2642–2643.

Steinman, Debra L., et al. (1981). A comparison of male and female patterns of sexual arousal. *Archives of Sexual Behavior, 10,* 529–548.

Stern, Kathleen, & McClintock, Martha K. (1998). Regulation of ovulation by human pheromones. *Nature, 392,* 177–179.

Sternberg, Robert J. (1986). A triangular theory of love. *Psychological Review, 93,* 119–135.

Sternberg, Robert J. (1987). Liking versus loving: A comparative evaluation of theories. *Psychological Bulletin, 102,* 331–345.

Sternberg, Robert. (1997). Construct validation of a triangular love scale. *European Journal of Social Psychology, 27,* 313–335.

Sternberg, Robert. (1998). *Love is a story: A new theory of relationships.* New York: Oxford University Press.

Stevenson, Michael R. (1995). Searching for a gay identity in Indonesia. *Journal of Men's Studies, 4,* 93–108.

Stiles, William B., et al. (1996). Attractiveness and disclosure in initial encounters of mixed-sex dyads. *Journal of Social and Personal Relationships, 13,* 303–312.

Stodghill II, Ron. (1998, June 15). Where'd you learn that? *Time,* 52–59.

Stone, K. M. (1994). HIV, other STDs, and barriers. In C. Mauck et al. (Eds.), *Barrier contraceptives: Current status and future prospect* (pp. 203–212). New York: Wiley.

Stoneburner, Rand L., et al. (1994). The global HIV pandemic. *Acta Paediatrica,* Suppl. 400, 1–4.

Stoneburner, Rand L., & Low-Beer, Daniel (2004). Population-level HIV declines and behavioral risk avoidance in Uganda. *Science, 304,* 714–718.

Storey, Anne E., et al. (2000). Hormonal correlates of paternal responsiveness in new and expectant fathers. *Evolution and Human Behavior, 21,* 79–95.

Storms, Michael D. (1980). Theories of sexual orientation. *Journal of Personality and Social Psychology, 38,* 783–792.

Strachan, Tom, & Read, Andrew P. (2004). *Human molecular genetics* (3rd ed.). New York: Garland Science.

Strassberg, Donald S., & Lowe, Kristi. (1995). Volunteer bias in sex research. *Archives of Sexual Behavior, 24,* 369–382.

Streissguth, Ann P., et al. (1999). The long-term neurocognitive consequences of prenatal alcohol exposure: A 14-year study. *Psychological Science, 10,* 186–190.

Strickland, Bonnie R. (1995). Research on sexual orientation and human development. *Developmental Psychology, 31,* 137–140.

Striegel-Moore, Ruth, et al. (1996). A prospective study of somatic and emotional symptoms of pregnancy. *Psychology of Women Quarterly, 20,* 393–408.

Strong, Carson. (1997). *Ethics in reproductive and perinatal medicine.* New Haven, CT: Yale University Press.

Struckman-Johnson, Cindy, et al. (1996). Sexual coercion reported by men and women in prison. *Journal of Sex Research, 33,* 67–76.

Struckman-Johnson, Cindy, Struckman-Johnson, D., & Anderson, P. B. (2003). Tactics of sexual coercion: When men and women won't take no for an answer. *Journal of Sex Research, 40,* 76–86.

Stryker, Sheldon. (1987). The vitalization of symbolic interactionism. *Social Psychology Quarterly, 50,* 83–94.

Stulhofer, Aleksandar, & Sandfort, Theo. (2005). *Sexuality and gender in postcommunist Eastern Europe and Russia.* New York: Haworth.

Sudarkasa, Niara. (1997). African American families and family values. In H. P. McAdoo (Ed.), *Black families* (3rd ed., pp. 9–40). Thousand Oaks, CA: Sage.

Sun, Shumei S., et al. (2002). National estimates of the timing of sexual maturation and racial differences among US children. *Pediatrics, 110,* 911–919.

Sun, Shumei S., et al. (2005). Is sexual maturity occurring earlier among U.S. children? *Journal of Adolescent Health, 37,* 345–355.

Swaab, Dick F., (2005). The role of the hypothalamus and endocrine system in sexuality. In J. S. Hyde (Ed.), *Biological substrates of human sexuality* (pp. 21–74). Washington, DC: American Psychological Association.

Swaab, Dick F., et al. (2001). Structural and functional sex differences in the human hypothalamus. *Hormones and behavior, 40,* 93–98.

Swaab, D. F., Gooren, L. J. G., & Hofman, M. A. (1995). Brain research, gender, and sexual orientation. *Journal of Homosexuality, 28,* 283–301.

Swerdloff, Ronald S., & Wang, Christina. (2000). Causes of male infertility. *Up to Date: Electronic Clinical Reference Library.* Medscape. www.medscape.com.

Swygard, H., et al. (2004). Trichomoniasis: Clinical manifestations, diagnosis, and management. *Sexually Transmitted Infections, 80,* 91–95.

Symons, Donald. (1979). *The evolution of human sexuality.* New York: Oxford University Press.

Symons, Donald. (1987). An evolutionary approach: Can Darwin's view of life shed light on human sexuality? In J. H. Geer & W. T. O'Donohue (Eds.), *Theories of human sexuality* (pp. 91–126). New York: Plenum.

Szasz, Thomas S. (1965). Legal and moral aspects of homosexuality. In J. Marmor (Ed.), *Sexual inversion: The multiple roots of homosexuality.* New York: Basic Books.

Szasz, Thomas S. (1980). *Sex by prescription.* Garden City, NY: Anchor Press/Doubleday.

Taberner, Peter V. (1985). *Aphrodisiacs: The science and the myth.* Philadelphia: University of Pennsylvania Press.

Tabet, S., et al. (2003). Safety and acceptability of penile application of 2 candidate topic microbicides: BufferGel and PRO 2000 Gel. *Journal of Acquired Immune Deficiency Syndromes, 33,* 476–483.

Taffel, Selma M., et al. (1991, June). 1989 U.S. cesarean section rate steadies—VBAC rate rises to nearly one in five. *Birth, 18,* 73–77.

Tafoya, Terry. (1989). Pulling coyote's tale: Native American sexuality and AIDS. In V. M. Mays et al. (Eds.), *Primary prevention of AIDS* (pp. 280–289). Newbury Park, CA: Sage.

Tafoya, Terry, & Wirth, Douglas A. (1996). Native American two-spirit men. In J. F. Longres (Ed.), *Men of color* (pp. 51–67). New York: Haworth.

Talamini, John T. (1982). *Boys will be girls: The hidden world of the heterosexual male transvestite.* Washington, DC: University Press of America.

Talge, N. M., Neal, C., Glover, V., et al. (2007). Antenatal maternal stress and long-term effects on child neurodevelopment: How and why? *Journal of Child Psychology and Psychiatry, 48,* 245–261.

Tan, Robert S., & Culberson, John W. (2003). An integrative review on current evidence of testosterone replacement therapy for the andropause. *Maturitas, 45,* 15–27.

Tanfer, Koray, & Schoorl, Jeannette J. (1992). Premarital sexual careers and partner change. *Archives of Sexual Behavior, 21,* 45–68.

Tannen, Deborah. (1986). *That's not what I meant: How conversational style makes or breaks relationships.* New York: Ballantine Books.

Tannen, Deborah. (1991). *You just don't understand: Women and men in conversation.* New York: William Morrow.

Tanner, James M. (1967). Puberty. In A. McLaren (Ed.), *Advances in reproductive physiology* (Vol. II). New York: Academic.

Taub, Nadine. (1987). Amicus brief: In the matter of Baby M. *Women's Rights Law Reporter, 10,* 7–24.

Taylor, Diana. (2006). From "It's all in your head" to "Taking back the month": Premenstrual syndrome (PMS) research and the contributions of the Society for Menstrual Cycle Research. *Sex Roles, 54,* 377–392.

Taylor, Humphrey. (2004). *Online activity grows as more people use Internet for more purposes.* Retrieved January 25, 2004, from www.harrisinteractive.com.

Taylor, Laramie D. (2005). All for him: Articles about sex in American lad magazines. *Sex Roles, 52,* 153–164.

Taylor, Laramie D. (2006). College men, their magazines, and sex. *Sex Roles, 55,* 693–702.

Taylor, Robert. (1994, April). Quiet clues to HIV-1 immunity: Do some people resist infection? *Journal of NIH Research, 6,* 29–31.

Teachman, J. D., Tedrow, L. M., & Crowder, K. D. (2000). The changing demography of America's families. In R. M. Milardo (Ed.), *Understanding families into the new millennium: A decade in review* (pp. 453–465). Minneapolis: National Council on Family Relations.

Technical Working Group. (2002). *Evaluation of abstinence education programs funded under Title V, Section 510: Interim Report.* U.S. Department of Health and Human Services: Office of the Assistant Secretary for Planning and Evaluation.

Templeman, Terrel L., & Stinnett, Ray D. (1991). Patterns of sexual arousal and history in a "normal" sample of young men. *Archives of Sexual Behavior, 20,* 137–150.

Terman, Lewis M. (1948). Kinsey's *Sexual Behavior in the Human Male:* Some comments and criticisms. *Psychological Bulletin, 45,* 443–459.

Terman, Lewis, et al. (1938). *Psychological factors in marital happiness.* New York: McGraw-Hill.

Testa, Maria, et al. (2007). Prospective prediction of women's sexual victimization by intimate and nonintimate male perpetrators. *Journal of Consulting and Clinical Psychology, 75,* 52–60.

Testa, Maria, VanZile-Tamsen, Carol, & Livingston, Jennifer A. (2005). Childhood sexual abuse, relationship satisfaction, and sexual risk taking in a community sample of women. *Journal of Consulting and Clinical Psychology, 73,* 1116–1124.

Thibaut, John, & Kelley, Harold. (1959). *The social psychology of groups.* New York: Wiley.

Thielicke, Helmut. (1964). *The ethics of sex.* New York: Harper & Row.

Thomas, S., & Quinn, S. (1991). The Tuskegee Syphilis Study 1932–1972: Implications for HIV education and AIDS risk education programs in the African American community. *American Journal of Public Health, 81,* 1498–1505.

Thompson, Anthony P. (1983). Extramarital sex: A review of the research literature. *Journal of Sex Research, 19,* 1–22.

Thorne, Barrie. (1993). *Gender play: Girls and boys in school.* New Brunswick, NJ: Rutgers University Press.

Thorne, Natasha, & Amrein, H. (2003). Vomeronasal organ: Pheromone recognition with a twist. *Current Biology, 13,* R220–R222.

Thornhill, Randy, & Palmer, Craig T. (2000). *A natural history of rape: Biological bases of sexual coercion.* Cambridge, MA: MIT Press.

Thornton, Michael C., & Wason, Suzanne. (1995). Intermarriage. In D. Levinson (Ed.), *Encyclopedia of marriage and the family* (Vol. 2, pp. 396–402). New York: Macmillan.

Thorpe, L. P., Katz, B., & Lewis, R. T. (1961). *The psychology of abnormal behavior.* New York: Ronald Press.

Tiefer, Leonore. (1991). Historical, scientific, clinical, and feminist criticisms of "The Human Sexual Response Cycle" model. *Annual Review of Sex Research, 2,* 1–24.

Tiefer, Leonore. (1994). Three crises facing sexology. *Archives of Sexual Behavior, 23,* 361–374.

Tiefer, Leonore. (2000). Sexology and the pharmaceutical industry: The threat of co-optation. *Journal of Sex Research, 37,* 273–283.

Tiefer, Leonore. (2001). A new view of women's sexual problems: Why new? Why now? *Journal of Sex Research, 38,* 89–96.

Tiefer, Leonore. (2004). *Sex is not a natural act and other essays* (2nd ed.). Boulder, CO: Westview Press.

Timmerman, Greetje. (2003). Sexual harassment of adolescents perpetrated by teachers and by peers; An exploration of the dynamics of power, culture, and gender in secondary schools. *Sex Roles, 48,* 231–244.

Tjaden, P., & Thoennes, N. (1998, November). *Prevalence, incidence, and consequences of violence against women: Findings from the National Violence Against Women Survey.* National Institute of Justice, Centers for Disease Control and Prevention Research Brief.

Todosijevic, Jelica, Rothblum, Esther, & Solomon, Sondra. (2005). Relationship satisfaction, affectivity, and gay-specific stressors in same-sex couples joined in civil unions. *Psychology of Women Quarterly, 29,* 158–166.

Tone, Andrea. (2001). *Devices and desires: A history of contraceptives in America.* New York: Hill & Wang.

Toubia, Nahid. (1994). Female circumcision as a public health issue. *New England Journal of Medicine, 331,* 712–716.

Toubia, Nahid. (1995). *Female genital mutilation: A call for global action.* New York: Women Ink.

Touchette, Nancy. (1991, July). HIV-1 link prompts circumspection on circumcision. *Journal of NIH Research, 3,* 44–46.

Townsend, John W. (2003). Reproductive behavior in the context of global population. *American Psychologist, 58,* 197–204.

Traish, Abdulmaged M., et al. (2002). Biochemical and physiological mechanisms of female genital sexual arousal. *Archives of Sexual Behavior, 31,* 393–400.

Traven, Sheldon, Cuyllen, Ken, & Protter, Barry. (1990). Female sexual offenders: Severe victims and victimizers. *Journal of Forensic Sciences, 35,* 140–150.

Treiman, Katherine, et al. (1995). IUDs—An update. *Population Reports,* Series B, No. 6. Baltimore: Johns Hopkins School of Public Health.

Triandis, H. C., McCusker, C., & Hui, C. H. (1990). Multimethod probes of individualism and collectivism. *Journal of Personality and Social Psychology, 59,* 1006–1020.

Troy, Ann. (2007, March 14). Sharp drop in gays discharged from military tied to war need. *Washington Post,* p. A03.

Truitt, William A., & Coolen, L. (2002). Identification of a potential ejaculation generator in the spinal cord. *Science, 297,* 1566–1569.

Trussell, James, et al. (2004). The role of emergency contraception. *American Journal of Obstetrics and Gynecology, 190,* Suppl. S, 530–538.

Trussell, James, & Vaughan, Barbara. (1991). *Selected results concerning sexual behavior and contraceptive use from the 1988 National Survey of Family Growth and the 1988 National Survey of Adolescent Males.* Working paper 91–12. Princeton, NJ: Office of Population Research.

Tsai, Mavis, & Uemura, Anne. (1988). Asian Americans: The struggles, the conflicts, and the successes. In P. Bronstein & K. Quina (Eds.), *Teaching a psychology of people.* Washington, DC: American Psychological Association.

Tullman, Gerald M., et al. (1981). The pre- and post-therapy measurement of communication skills of couples undergoing sex therapy at the Masters & Johnson Institute. *Archives of Sexual Behavior, 10,* 95–109.

Turkle, S. (1995). *Life on the screen: Identity in the age of the Internet.* New York: Simon & Schuster.

Turner, Charles F., et al. (2005). Same-gender sex among U.S. adults: Trends across the twentieth century and during the 1990s. *Public Opinion Quarterly, 69,* 439–462.

Tutin, C. E. G., & McGinnis, P. R. (1981). Chimpanzee reproduction in the wild. In C. E. Graham (Ed.), *Reproductive biology of the great apes* (pp. 239–264). New York: Aca-demic Press.

Tutuer, W. (1984). Dangerousness of peeping toms. *Medical Aspects of Human Sexuality, 18,* 97.

Tyson, Ann. (2007, March 14). Sharp drop in gays discharged from military tied to war need. *Washington Post,* p. A3.

U.S. Bureau of the Census. (1997). *Statistical abstract of the United States 1997.* Washington, DC: Bureau of the Census.

U.S. Bureau of the Census. (2000a). *The Hispanic population in the United States.* www.census.gov.

U.S. Bureau of the Census. (2000b). *Statistical abstract of the United States: 1999* (119th ed.). Washington, DC: Bureau of the Census.

U.S. Bureau of the Census. (2002). *Statistical abstract of the United States.* Population, Table No. 14. www.census.gov.

U.S. Bureau of the Census. (2003). *Statistical abstract of the United States.* National Defense and Veterans Affairs, Table No. 517, Department of Defense Manpower: 1950–2002.

U.S. Bureau of the Census. (2004). Estimated median age of first marriage, by sex: 1890 to present.

U.S. Bureau of the Census. (2006). *Families and living arrangements.* Washington, DC: US Census Bureau News, May 25, 2006.

U.S. Bureau of Labor Statistics. (2001). Labor force statistics from the current population survey. www.stats.bls.gov.

U.S. Bureau of Labor Statistics. (2004). Table D-16, Unemployment rates by age, sex, race, and Hispanic or Latino ethnicity. www.bls.gov.

U.S. Bureau of Labor Statistics. (2007). *Unemployed persons by marital status, race, Hispanic or Latino ethnicity, age, and sex.* Retrieved February 17, 2007, from www.bls.gov/cps/cpsaat24.pdf.

U.S. Department of Justice. (1986). *The Attorney General's Commission on Pornography: Final Report.* Washington, DC: U.S. Department of Justice.

U.S. House of Representatives Committee on Government Reform— Minority Staff, Special Investigations Division. (2003). *Politics and science in the Bush administration.* www.reform.house. gov.min.

U.S. National Commission for the Protection of Human Subjects of Biomedical and Behavioral Research. (1978). *The Belmont Report: Ethical principles and guidelines for the protection of human subjects of research.* Washington, DC: U.S. Government Printing Office.

Udry, J. Richard. (1988). Biological predispositions and social control in adolescent sexual behavior. *American Sociological Review, 53,* 709–722.

Udry, J. Richard, & Eckland, Bruce K. (1984). Benefits of being attractive: Differential payoffs for men and women. *Psychological Reports, 54,* 47–56.

Udry, J. Richard, et al. (1985). Serum androgenic hormones motivate sexual behavior in adolescent boys. *Fertility and Sterility, 43,* 90–94.

Ullman, Sarah E. (2004). Sexual assault victimization and suicidal behavior in women: A review of the literature. *Aggression & Violent Behavior, 9,* 331–351.

Ullman, Sarah E., et al. (2007). Structural models of the relations of assault severity, social support, avoidance coping, self-blame, and PTSD among sexual assault survivors. *Psychology of Women Quarterly, 31,* 23–27.

Ullman, Sarah E., & Knight, Raymond A. (1993). The efficacy of women's resistance strategies in rape situations. *Psychology of Women Quarterly, 17,* 23–38.

Ulmann, A., Teutsch, G., & Philibert, D. (1990, June). RU-486. *Scientific American, 262,* 42–48.

Ulrich's. (2001). *International periodical directory.* www.ulrichsweb. com.

UNAIDS—United Nations Program on HIV/AIDS. (1997). *Impact of HIV and sexual health education on the sexual behavior of young people.* Geneva, SU.

Union for Reform Judaism. (2004). *What is the Reform perspective on abortion?* http://uahc.org.

United Church of Christ. (2004). *Reproductive rights.* www.ucc.org.

United Synagogue of Conservative Judaism. (1989). www.ncrc.org.

Upadhyay, Ushma. (2005). New contraceptive choices. *Population Reports*, Series M, 19. Baltimore: Johns Hopkins Bloomberg School of Public Health. http://www.populationreports.org/m19.

Upadhyay, Ushma, et al. (2005). Microbicides: New potential for protection. *Inforeports, 3.* Johns Hopkins School of Public Health. www.infoforhealth.org.

Upadhyay, Ushma D., & Robey, Bryant. (1999). Why family planning matters. *Population Reports*, Series J, No. 49. Baltimore: Johns Hopkins University School of Public Health.

Upchurch, Dawn, et al. (1998). Gender and ethnic differences in the timing of first sexual intercourse. *Family Planning Perspectives, 1998, 30,* 121–127.

UPI (1981, November 5). Toxicologist warns against butyl nitrite. *Delaware Gazette,* p. 3.

U.S. Bureau of the Census. (2004). Estimated median age of first marriage, by sex: 1890 to present.

Urbina, A., & Jones, K. (2004). Crystal methamphetamine, its analogues, and HIV infection; Medical and psychiatric aspects of a new epidemic. *Clinical Infectious Diseases, 38,* 890–894.

USDHHS. (1999). *A National Strategy to Prevent Teen Pregnancy: Annual Report 1998–99.* Washington, DC: U.S. Department of Health and Human Services.

Vacca, J. P., et al. (1994). L-735, 524: An orally bioavailable human immunodeficiency virus type I protease inhibitor. *Proceedings of the National Academy of Sciences USA, 91,* 4096.

Van Damme, Lut, et al. (2000). Penile application of dextrin sulphate gel (Emmelle). *Contraception, 66,* 133–136.

Van Damme, Lut, et al. (2002). Effectiveness of COL-1492, a nonxynol-9 vaginal gel, on HIV-1 transmission in female sex workers: A randomised controlled trial. *The Lancet, 360,* 971–977.

Van Dis, H., & Larsson, K. (1971). Induction of sexual arousal in the castrated male rat by intracranial stimulation. *Physiology & Behavior, 6,* 85–86.

Van Goozen, Stephanie H. M., et al. (1997). Psychoendocrinological assessment of the menstrual cycle: The relationship between hormones, sexuality, and mood. *Archives of Sexual Behavior, 26,* 359–382.

Van Lankveld, Jacques. (1998). Bibliotherapy in the treatment of sexual dysfunctions: A meta-analysis. *Journal of Consulting and Clinical Psychology, 66,* 702–708.

Van Lankfeld, Jacques, et al. (2006). Cognitive-behavioral therapy for women with lifelong vaginismus: A randomized waiting-list controlled trial of efficacy. *Journal of Consulting and Clinical Psychology, 74,* 168–178.

Van Lankveld, Jacques, Everaerd, Walter, & Grotjohann, Yvonne. (2001). Cognitive-behaviorial bibliotherapy for sexual dysfunctions in heterosexual couples: A randomized waiting-list controlled clinical trial in the Netherlands. *Journal of Sex Research, 38,* 51–67.

Van Lent, P. (1996). Her beautiful savage: The current sexual image of the Native American male. In S. E. Bird (Ed.), *Dressing in feathers: The construction of the Indian in American popular culture* (pp. 211–228). Boulder, CO: Westview.

Van Preagh, P. (1982). The Hamilton birth control clinic. In response to need. *News/Nouvelles, Journal of Planned Parenthood Federation of Canada, 3* (2).

Vance, Ellen B., & Wagner, Nathaniel N. (1976). Written descriptions of orgasm: A study of sex differences. *Archives of Sexual Behavior, 5,* 87–98.

Vanwesenbeeck, Ine. (1994). *Prostitutes' well-being and risk.* Amsterdam: VU University Press.

Vanwesenbeeck, Ine. (2001). Another decade of social scientific work on sex work: A review of research 1990–2000. *Annual Review of Sex Research, 12,* 242–289.

Vanwesenbeeck, Ine. (2005). Burnout among female indoor sex workers. *Archives of Sexual Behavior, 34,* 627–640.

Varghese, Beena, et al. (2002). Reducing the risk of sexual HIV transmission. *Sexually Transmitted Diseases, 29,* 38–43.

Vasey, Paul L. (2002a). Same-sex sexual partner preference in hormonally and neurologically unmanipulated animals. *Annual Review of Sex Research, 13,* 141–179.

Vasey, Paul L. (2002b). Sexual partner preference in female Japanese macaques. *Archives of Sexual Behavior, 31,* 51–62.

Vasey, Paul L., et al. (2006). Male-female and female-female mounting in Japanese macaques: A comparative study. *Archives of Sexual Behavior, 35,* 117–130.

Ve Ard, Cherie, & Veaux, Franklin. (2003). *Polyamory 101.* www.xeromag.com/poly101.pdf.

Venicz, L., & Vanwesenbeeck, I. (2000). *Something is going to change in prostitution: Social position and psychological well being of indoor prostitutes before the law reform.* Utrecht/The Hague, The Netherlands: NISSO/Ministry of Justice.

Veronesi, Umberto, et al. (1981). Comparing radical mastectomy with quadrantectomy, axillary dissection, and radiotherapy in patients with small cancers of the breast. *New England Journal of Medicine, 305,* 6–11.

Vicioso, Kalil J., Parsons, J., Nanin, J., Purcell, D., & Woods, W. (2005). Experiencing release: Sex environments and escapism for HIV-positive men who have sex with men. *Journal of Sex Research, 42,* 13–19.

Vickberg, Suzanne, & Deaux, Kay. (2005). Measuring the dimensions of women's sexuality: The women's sexual self-concept scale. *Sex Roles, 53,* 361–370.

Vigil, Jacob M., Geary, David C., & Byrd-Craven, Jennifer. (2005). A life history assessment of early childhood sexual abuse in women. *Developmental Psychology, 41,* 553–561.

Vilain, Eric. (2000). The genetics of sexual development. *Annual Review of Sex Research, 11,* 1–25.

Villa, L. L., et al. (2006). High sustained efficacy of a prophylactic quadrivalent human papillomavirus types 6/11/16/18 L1 virus-like particle vaccine through 5 years of follow-up. *British Journal of Cancer, 95,* 1459–1466.

Vincent, J. P., et al. (1979). Demand characteristics in observations of marital interaction. *Journal of Consulting and Clinical Psychology, 47,* 557–566.

Von Hertzen, Helena, et al. (2002). Low dose mifepristone and two regimens of levonorgestrel for emergency contraception: A WHO multicentre randomised trial. *The Lancet, 360,* 1803–1810.

Von Hertzen, Helena, & Van Look, Paul. (1996). Research on new methods of emergency contraception. *Family Planning Perspectives, 28,* 52–57.

Von Krafft-Ebing, Richard. (1886). *Psychopathia sexualis.* (Reprinted by Putnam, New York, 1965).

Von Kries, Rudifer, et al. (1999). Breast feeding and obesity: Cross sectional study. *British Medical Journal, 319,* 147–150.

von Sydow, Kirsten. (1999). Sexuality during pregnancy and after childbirth: A metacontent analysis of 59 studies. *Journal of Psychosomatic Research, 47,* 27–49.

Wabrek, Alan J., & Burchell, R. Clay. (1980). Male sexual dysfunction associated with coronary heart disease. *Archives of Sexual Behavior, 9,* 69–75.

Wade, Lisa, & DeLamater, John. (2002). Relationship dissolution as a life stage transition: Effects on sexual attitudes and behaviors. *Journal of Marriage and the Family, 64,* 898–914.

Waite, Linda, & Joyner, Kara. (2000). Emotional and physical satisfaction with sex in married, cohabitating, and dating sexual unions: Do men and women differ? In Edward Laumann & Robert Michael (Eds.), *Sex, love, and health in America: Private choices and public policy* (pp. 239–269). Chicago: University of Chicago Press.

Waite, Linda, & Joyner, Kara. (2001). Men's and women's general happiness and sexual satisfaction in marriage, cohabitation, and single living. In E. O. Laumann & R. Michael (Eds.), *The social organization of sexuality: Further studies.* Chicago: University of Chicago Press.

Wald, Anna, et al. (2001). Effect of condoms on reducing the transmission of herpes simplex virus type 2 from men to women. *Journal of the American Medical Association, 285,* 3100–3106.

Wald, Anna, et al. (2005). The relationship between condom use and herpes simplex virus acquisition. *Annals of Internal Medicine, 143,* 707–713.

Wald, Anna, et al. (2006). Comparative efficacy of famciclovir and valacyclovir for suppression of recurrent genital herpes and viral shedding. *Sexually Transmitted Diseases, 33,* 529–533.

Walen, Susan R., & Roth, David. (1987). A cognitive approach. In J. H. Geer & W. T. O'Donohue (Eds.), *Theories of human sexuality*. New York: Plenum.

Walker, Jayne, Archer, J., & Davies, M. (2005). Effects of rape on men: A descriptive analysis. *Archives of Sexual Behavior, 34*, 69–80.

Wallen, Kim. (2001). Sex and context: Hormones and primate sexual motivation. *Hormones and Behavior, 40*, 339–357.

Wallen, Kim, & Parsons, William A. (1997). Sexual behavior in same-sexed nonhuman primates: Is it relevant to understanding human homosexuality? *Annual Review of Sex Research, 8*, 195–223.

Wallen, Kim, & Zehr, Julia L. (2004). Hormones and history: The evolution and development of primate female sexuality. *Journal of Sex Research, 41*, 101–112.

Wallerstein, Edward. (1980). *Circumcision: An American health fallacy*. New York: Springer.

Wallin, Paul. (1949). An appraisal of some methodological aspects of the Kinsey report. *American Sociological Review, 14*, 197–210.

Walsh, Terri L., et al. (2003). Evaluation of the efficacy of a nonlatex condom: Results from a randomized, controlled clinical trial. *Perspectives on Sexual and Reproductive Health, 35*, 79–86.

Walster, Elaine, et al. (1973). "Playing hard-to-get": Understanding an elusive phenomenon. *Journal of Personality and Social Psychology, 26*, 113–121.

Walster [Hatfield], Elaine, Walster, William, & Berscheid, Ellen. (1978). *Equity: Theory and research*. Boston, Allyn & Bacon.

Walther, Carol S., & Poston, Dudley L. (2004). Patterns of gay and lesbian partnering in the larger metropolitan areas of the United States. *Journal of Sex Research, 41*, 201–214.

Wang, L. Y., et al. (2000). Economic evaluation of Safer Choices: A school-based human immunodeficiency virus, other sexually transmitted diseases, and pregnancy prevention program. *Archives of Pediatrics & Adolescent Medicine, 154*, 1017–1024.

Wang, P. Jeremy, et al. (2001). An abundance of X-linked genes expressed in spermatogonia. *Nature Genetics, 27*, 422–426.

Ward, L. Monique. (2002). Does television exposure affect emerging adults' attitudes and assumptions about sexual relationships? Correlational and experimental confirmation. *Journal of Youth and Adolescence, 31*, 1–15.

Ward, L. Monique, Hansbrough, E., & Walker, E. (2005). Contributions of music video exposure to Black adolescents' gender and sexual schemas. *Journal of Adolescent Research, 20*, 143–166.

Ward, O. Byron, et al. (2002). Hormonal mechanisms underlying aberrant sexual differentiation in male rats prenatally exposed to alcohol, stress, or both. *Archives of Sexual Behavior, 31*, 9–16.

Warnock, Julia K., Bundren, J. Clark, & Morris, David W. (1997). Female hypoactive sexual desire disorder due to androgen deficiency: Clinical and psychometric issues. *Psychopharmacology Bulletin, 33*, 761–766.

Warr, M. (1985). Fear of rape among urban women. *Social Problems, 32*, 239–250.

Wass, Debbie M., et al. (1991). Completed follow-up of 1,000 consecutive transcervical chorionic villus samplings performed by a single operator. *Australia New Zealand Journal of Obstetrics and Gynecology, 31*, 240–245.

Weaver, Angela, et al. (2002). Sexual health education at school and at home: Attitudes and experiences of New Brunswick parents. *Canadian Journal of Human Sexuality, 11*, 19–31.

Weaver, Hilary N. (1999). Through indigenous eyes: Native Americans and the HIV epidemic. *Health and Social Work, 24*, 27–24.

Weber, Robert P. (1990). *Basic content analysis* (2nd ed.). Newbury Park, CA: Sage.

Weideger, Paula. (1976). *Menstruation and menopause*. New York: Knopf.

Weight gain during pregnancy. (2003). *Journal of Midwifery and Women's Health, 48*, 229–230.

Weinberg, Martin, Williams, Colin, & Calhan, Cassandra. (1995). "If the shoe fits . . .": Exploring male homosexual foot fetishism. *Journal of Sex Research, 32*, 17–27.

Weinberg, Martin S., Williams, Colin J., & Pryor, Douglas W. (1994). *Dual attraction: Understanding bisexuality*. New York: Oxford University Press.

Weinberg, Martin S., Williams, C., & Pryor, D. (2001). Bisexuals at midlife: Commitment, salience, and identity. *Journal of Contemporary Ethnography, 30*, 180–208.

Weinberg, Samuel K. (1955). *Incest behavior*. New York: Citadel Press.

Weinberg, Thomas S. (1987). Sadomasochism in the United States: A review of recent sociological literature. *Journal of Sex Research, 23*, 50–69.

Weinberg, Thomas S. (1994). Research in sadomasochism: A review of sociological and social psychological literature. *Annual Review of Sex Research, 5*, 257–279.

Weinberger, L. E., Sreenivasan, S., Garrick, T., & Osran, H. (2005). The impact of surgical castration on sexual recidivism risk among sexually violent predatory offenders. *Journal of the American Academy of Psychiatry and the Law, 33*, 16–36.

Weinhardt, Lance S., & Carey, Michael P. (1996). Prevalence of erectile disorder among men with diabetes mellitus. *Journal of Sex Research, 33*, 205–214.

Weinstock, Hillard, Berman, S., & Cates, W. (2004). Sexually transmitted diseases among American youth: Incidence and prevalence estimates, 2000. *Perspectives on Sexual and Reproductive Health, 36*, 6–10.

Weinstock, Hillard, Dean, Deborah, & Bolan, Gail. (1994). Chlamydia trachomatis infections. *Infectious Disease Clinics of North America, 8*, 797–819.

Weisberg, D. Kelly. (1985). *Children of the night: A study of adolescent prostitution*. Lexington, MA: Lexington Books.

Weller, Leonard, Weller, Aron, & Avinir, Ohala. (1995). Menstrual synchrony: Only in roommates who are close friends? *Physiology and Behavior, 58*, 883–889.

Wells, B., & Twenge, J. (2005). Changes in young people's sexual behavior and attitudes, 1943–1999: A cross-temporal meta-analysis. *Review of General Psychology, 9*, 249–261.

Welsh, Sandy. (1999). Gender and sexual harassment. *Annual Review of Sociology, 25*, 169–190.

Wenk, Melanie, & Nieschlag, Eberhard. (2006). Male contraception: A realistic option? *The European Journal of Contraception and Reproductive Health Care, 11*, 69–80.

Wertz, R. W., & Wertz, D. C. (1977). *Lying-in: A history of childbirth in America*. New York: Free Press.

West, Suzanne L., Vinikoor, Lisa C., & Zolnoum, Dennis. (2004). A systematic review of the literature on female sexual dysfunction prevalence and predictors. *Annual Review of Sex Research, 15*, 40–172.

Wethington, Elaine. (2000). Expecting stress: Americans and the "midlife crisis." *Motivation and Emotion, 24*, 85–103.

Whatley, Mariamne H., & Henken, Elissa R. (2001). *Did you hear about the girl who . . . ? Contemporary legends, folklore, and human sexuality*. New York: New York University Press.

Wheeler, Garry D., et al. (1984). Reduced serum testosterone and prolactin levels in male distance runners. *Journal of the American Medical Association, 252*, 514–516.

Whipple, Beverly, Ogden, Gina, & Komisarak, Barry. (1992). Physiological correlates of imagery-induced orgasm in women. *Archives of Sexual Behavior, 21*, 121–133.

Whitam, Frederick L. (1983). Culturally invariable properties of male homosexuality: Tentative conclusions from cross-cultural research. *Archives of Sexual Behavior, 12*, 207–226.

Whitam, Frederick L., & Mathy, Robin M. (1991). Childhood cross-gender behavior of homosexual females in Brazil, Peru, the Philippines, and the United States. *Archives of Sexual Behavior, 20*, 151–170.

White, Gregory L., Fishbein, S., & Rutstein, J. (1981). Passionate love and the misattribution of arousal. *Journal of Personality and Social Psychology, 41*, 56–62.

White, Gregory L., & Mullen, Paul E. (1989). *Jealousy: Theory, research, and clinical strategies*. New York: Guilford.

White, Jacquelyn W., & Sorenson, Susan B. (1992). Adult sexual assault. *Journal of Social Issues, 48* (1), 1–8.

White, L., & Edwards, J. N. (1990). Emptying the nest and parental well-being: An analysis of national panel data. *American Sociological Review, 55*, 235–242.

White, Leland J. (2001). Romans 1:26–27: The claim that homosexuality is unnatural. In P. Jung & J. Coray (Eds.), *Sexual diversity and Catholicism* (pp. 133–149). Collegeville, MN: The Liturgical Press.

Whitley, Bernard, Jr. (1993). Reliability and aspects of the construct validity of Sternberg's Triangular Love Scale. *Journal of Social and Personal Relationships, 10,* 475–480.

Whittington, William, Ison, Catherine, & Thompson, Sumner. (1996). Gonorrhea. In S. Morse et al. (Eds.), *Atlas of sexually transmitted diseases and AIDS* (pp. 99–118). London: Mosby-Wolfe.

Wichstrøm, Lars, & Hegna, Kristinn. (2003). Sexual orientation and suicide attempt: A longitudinal study of the general Norwegian adolescent population. *Journal of Abnormal Psychology, 112,* 144–151.

Wickham, DeWayne. (2001, September 3). Castration often fails to halt offenders. *USA Today.*

Wickler, Wolfgang. (1973). *The sexual code.* New York: Anchor Books. (Original in German, 1969)

Widmer, M., Villar, J., Benigni, A., Conde-Agudelo, A., Karumanchi, S. A., & Lindheimer, M. (2007). Mapping the theories of preeclampsia and the role of angiogenic factors: A systematic review. *Obstetrics & Gynecology, 109* (1), 168–180.

Wiederman, Michael W. (1993). Demographic and sexual characteristics of nonresponders to sexual experience items in a national survey. *Journal of Sex Research, 30,* 27–35.

Wiederman, Michael W. (2001). *Understanding sexuality research.* Belmont, CA: Wadsworth.

Wiederman, Michael W., Weis, David L., & Allgeier, Elizabeth R. (1994). The effect of question preface on response rates to a telephone survey of sexual experience. *Archives of Sexual Behavior, 23,* 203–216.

Wiesenfeld, H. C., et al. (2001). Self-collection of vaginal swabs for the detection of Chlamydia, gonorrhea, and tricho-moniasis: Opportunity to encourage sexually transmitted disease testing among adolescents. *Sexually Transmitted Diseases, 28,* 321–325.

Wilcox, A. J., Weinberg, C. R., & Baird, D. D. (1995). Timing of sexual intercourse in relation to ovulation. *New England Journal of Medicine, 333,* 1517–1521.

Wilcox, Brian L., Robbenoit, J. K., & O'Keefe, J. E. (1998). Federal abortion policy and politics: 1973 to 1996. In L. J. Beckman & S. M. Harvey (Eds.), *The new civil war: The psychology, culture and politics of abortion* (pp. 3–24). Washington, DC: American Psychological Association.

Wilcox, Brian L., & Wyatt, J. (1997). *Adolescent abstinence education programs: A meta-analysis.* Presented at the annual meeting, Society for the Scientific Study of Sexuality, Arlington, VA.

Wilkinson, Ross. (1995). Changes in psychological health and the marital relationship through child bearing: Transition or process as stressor. *Australian Journal of Psychology, 47,* 86–92.

Willetts, Marion, Sprecher, Susan, & Beck, Frank. (2004). Overview of sexual practices and attitudes within relational contexts. In J. H. Harvey, A. Wenzel, & S. Sprecher (Eds.), *The handbook of sexuality in close relationships* (pp. 57–85). Mahwah, NJ: Lawrence Erlbaum.

Williams, Colin, & Weinberg, Martin. (2003). Zoophilia in men: A study of sexual interest in animals. *Archives of Sexual Behavior, 32,* 523–535.

Williams, Letitia, et al. (2003). Surveillance for selected maternal behaviors and experiences before, during, and after pregnancy. *Morbidity and Mortality Weekly Report, 52* (SS11), 1–14.

Williams, Linda M. (1994). Recall of childhood trauma: A prospective study of women's memories of child sexual abuse. *Journal of Consulting and Clinical Psychology, 62,* 1167–1176.

Williams, Lindy, & Sobieszczyk, Teresa. (1997). Attitudes surrounding the continuation of female circumcision in the Sudan: Passing tradition to the next generation. *Journal of Marriage and the Family, 59,* 966–981.

Williams, Tricia, Taradash, Ali, & Connolly, Jennifer. (2004). *Sexual behavior and dating activities among young Canadian adolescents: Normative patterns and biosocial links.* Presented at Society for Research on Adolescence, Baltimore, MD.

Wilson, E. O. (1975). *Sociobiology: The new synthesis.* Cambridge, MA: Harvard University Press.

Wilson, Glenn D. (1987). An ethological approach to sexual deviation. In G. D. Wilson (Ed.), *Variant sexuality: Research and theory.* Baltimore: Johns Hopkins University Press.

Wilson, Glenn. (1997). Gender differences in sexual fantasy: An evolutionary analysis. *Personality and Individual Differences, 22,* 27–31.

Wilson, W. Cody. (1973). Pornography: The emergence of a social issue and the beginning of psychological study. *Journal of Social Issues, 29,* 7–17.

Wilstein, Steve. (2002, October 31). Tuaolo announces he's gay. *Associated Press.*

Wimberly, Sarah R., et al. (2005). Perceived partner reactions to diagnosis and treatment of breast cancer: Impact on psychosocial and psychosexual adjustment. *Journal of Consulting and Clinical Psychology, 73,* 300–311.

Wincze, John P., & Carey, Michael P. (1991). *Sexual dysfunction: A guide for assessment and treatment.* New York: Guilford.

Windmeyer, Shane L. (2006). *The Advocate college guide for LGBT students.* New York: Alyson Books.

Winer, Rachel L., et al. (2006). Condom use and the risk of genital human papillomavirus infection in young women. *New England Journal of Medicine, 354,* 2645–2654.

Wingert, Pat. (2002, February 11). Sex education: "Values trump data." *Newsweek,* 8.

Winn, Rhonda L., & Newton, Niles. (1982). Sexuality in aging: A study of 106 cultures. *Archives of Sexual Behavior, 11,* 283–298.

Winter, Jeremy S. D., & Couch, Robert M. (1995). Sexual differentiation. In P. Felig, J. D. Baxter, & L. A. Frohman (Eds.), *Endocrinology and metabolism* (3rd ed., pp. 1053–1104). New York: McGraw-Hill.

Wise, Phyllis M., Krajnak, Kristine M., & Kashon, Michael L. (1996). Menopause: The aging of multiple pacemakers. *Science, 273,* 67–70.

Wisniewski, A. B., et al. (2000). Complete androgen insensitivity syndrome: Long-term medical, surgical, and psychosexual outcome. *Journal of Clinical Endocrinology & Metabolism, 85,* 2664–2669.

Wisniewski, Amy B., et al. (2001). Congenital micropenis: Long-term medical, surgical, and psychosexual follow-up of individuals raised male or female. *Hormone Research, 56,* 3–11.

Wiswell, Thomas E., et al. (1987). Declining frequency of circumcision: Implications for changes in the absolute incidence and male to female sex ratio of urinary tract infections in early infancy. *Pediatrics, 79,* 338–342.

Witte, Florence M., Stratton, Terry D., & Nora, Lois M. (2006). Stories from the field: Students' descriptions of gender discrimination and sexual harassment during medical school. *Academic Medicine, 81,* 648–654.

Wohl, A. R., et al. (2002). HIV risk behaviors among African American men in Los Angeles County who self-identify as heterosexual. *Journal of Acquired Immune Deficiency Syndromes, 31,* 354–360.

Wolak, Janis, Mitchell, Kimberly, & Finkelhor, David. (2003). *Internet sex crimes against minors: The response of law enforcement.* Alexandria, VA: National Center for Missing and Exploited Children.

Wolchik, Sharlene A., Spencer, S. L., & Lisi, I. S. (1983). Volunteer bias in research employing vaginal measures of sexual arousal. *Archives of Sexual Behavior, 12,* 399–408.

Wolf, Timothy J. (1985). Marriages of bisexual men. In F. Klein & T. J. Wolf (Eds.), *Bisexualities: Theory and research.* New York: Haworth.

Wonders, N. A., & Michalowski, R. (2001). Bodies, borders and sex tourism in a globalized world: A tale of two cities—Amsterdam and Havana. *Social Problems, 48,* 545–571.

Wong, Joseph K., et al. (1997). Recovery of replication-competent HIV despite prolonged suppression of plasma viremia. *Science, 278,* 1291–1295.

Wood, Jill M., Koch, Patricia B., & Mansfield, Phyllis K. (2006). Women's sexual desire: A feminist critique. *Journal of Sex Research, 43,* 236–244.

Wood, Julia T. (1994). *Gendered lives: Communication, gender, and culture.* Belmont, CA: Wadsworth.

Wood, N. S., et al. (2000). Neurologic and developmental disability after extremely preterm birth. *New England Journal of Medicine, 343,* 378–384.

Woods, Scott, & Raju, Uma. (2001). Maternal smoking and the risk of congenital birth defects: A cohort study. *Journal of the American Board of Family Practice, 14,* 330–334.

Woodzicka, Julie A., & LaFrance, Marianne. (2005). The effects of subtle sexual harassment on women's perfor-mance in a job interview. *Sex Roles, 53,* 67–78.

Woollett, Anne, et al. (1995). The ideas and experiences of pregnancy and childbirth of Asian and non-Asian women in East London. *British Journal of Medical Psychology, 68,* 65–84.

World Health Organization. (2002). Sexual health. Retrieved January 7, 2007, from http://who.int/reproductiv-health/gender/sexual_health.html.

Worthington, Everett, et al. (1983). The effect of brief Lamaze training and social encouragement on pain endurance in a cold pressor task. *Journal of Applied Social Psychology, 13,* 223–233.

Wright, Alexi A., & Katz, Ingrid T. (2006). *Roe* versus reality—abortion and women's health. *New England Journal of Medicine, 355,* 1–9.

Wright, V. C., Chang, J., Jeng, G., Chen, M., & Macaluso, M. (2007). Assisted reproductive technology surveillance—United States, 2004. *Morbidity and Mortality Weekly Report, 56* (Surveillance Summary 06).

Wright, Victoria Clay, et al. (2004). Assisted reproductive technology surveillance—United States, 2001. *Morbidity and Mortality Weekly Report, 53* (SS01).

Wright, Victoria, Schieve, L., Reynolds, M., & Jeng, G. (2005). Assisted reproductive technology surveillance—United States, 2002. *Morbidity and Mortality Weekly Report, 54* (SS02), 1–24.

Wyatt, Gail E. (1992). The sociocultural context of African American and white American women's rape. *Journal of Social Issues, 48* (1), 77–92.

Wyatt, Gail E. (1997). *Stolen women: Reclaiming our sexuality, taking back our lives.* New York: Wiley.

Wyatt, Gail E., Peters, S. D., & Guthrie, D. (1988). Kinsey revisited, Part I: Comparisons of the sexual socialization and sexual behavior of white women over 33 years. *Archives of Sexual Behavior, 17,* 201–240.

Wyatt, Tristram D. (2003). *Pheromones and animal behaviour.* New York: Cambridge University Press.

Wylie, Kevan R., Jones, R., & Walters, S. (2003). The potential benefit of vacuum devices augmenting psychosexual therapy for erectile dysfunction: A randomized controlled trial. *Journal of Sex and Marital Therapy, 29,* 227–236.

Wyrobek, A., Eskenazi, B., Young, W. S., Arnheim, N., Tiemann-Boegr, I., Jabs, E., Glaser, R., Pearson, F., & Evenson, D. (2006). Advancing age has different effects on DNA damage, chromatin integrity, gene mutations, and aneuploidies in sperm. *Proceedings of the National Academy of Sciences, 103,* 9601–9606.

Wysocki, Charles J., & Lepri, John J. (1991). Consequences of removing the vomeronasal organ. *Journal of Steroid Biochemistry and Molecular Biology, 39,* 661–669.

Xu, Fujie, et al. (2006). Trends in herpes simplex virus type 1 and type 2 seroprevalence in the United States. *Journal of American Medical Association, 296,* 964–973.

Yalom, Irvin D. (1960). Aggression and forbiddenness in voyeurism. *Archives of General Psychiatry, 3,* 317.

Yeh, Hsiu-Chen, Lorenz, F., Wickrama, K. A. S., Conger, R., and Elder, G. H., Jr., (2006). Relationships among sexual satisfaction, marital quality and marital instability at midlife. *Journal of Family Psychology, 20,* 336–343.

Yellowlees, P. M., & Marks, S. (2007). Problematic Internet use or Internet addiction? *Computers in Human Behavior, 23,* 1447–1453.

Yoder, P. Stanley, et al. (2004). *Female genital cutting in the demographic and health surveys: A critical and comparative analysis.* DHS Comparative Reports No. 7. Calverton, MD: ORC Macro.

Yost, Lisa. (1991). Bisexual tendencies. In L. Hutchins & L. Kaahumanu (Eds.), *Bi any other name: Bisexual people speak out.* Boston: Alyson.

Yost, Megan R., & Zurbriggen, Eileen L. (2006). Gender differences in the enactment of sociosexuality: An examination of implicit social motives, sexual fantasies, coercive sexual attitudes, and aggressive sexual behavior. *Journal of Sex Research, 43,* 163–173.

Young, Ian. (1996). Education for sexuality—the role of the school. *Journal of Biological Education, 30,* 250–255.

Young, Kimberly, et al. (2000). Online infidelity: A new dimension in couple relationships with implications for evaluation and treatment. *Sexual Addiction and Compulsivity, 7,* 59–74.

Zabin, L. S., et al. (1984). Adolescent sexual attitudes and behaviors: Are they consistent? *Family Planning Perspectives, 4,* 181–185.

Zak, P. J., Kurzban, R. O., & Matzner, W. L. (2003). The neurobiology of trust. Society for Neuroscience Annual Meeting. Program No. 195.27.

Zala, Sarah M., & Penn, Dustin J. (2004). Abnormal behaviours induced by chemical pollution: A review of the evidence and new challenges. *Animal Behaviour, 68,* 649–664.

Zaslow, Martha J., et al. (1985). Depressed mood in new fathers: Association with parent-infant interaction. *Genetic, Social, and General Psychology Monographs, 111* (2), 133–150.

Zaviačič, M. (1994). Sexual asphyxiophilia (Koczwarism) in women and the biological phenomenon of female ejaculation. *Medical Hypotheses, 42,* 318–322.

Zaviačič, M., et al. (2000a). Immunohistochemical study of prostate-specific antigen in normal and pathological human tissues: Special reference to the male and female prostate and breast. *Journal of Histotechnology, 23,* 105–111.

Zaviačič, M., et al. (2000b). Weight, size, macroanatomy, and histology of the normal prostate in the adult human female: A minireview. *Journal of Histotechnology, 23,* 61–69.

Zax, M., Sameroff, A., & Farnum, J. (1975). Childbirth education, maternal attitude and delivery. *American Journal of Obstetrics and Gynecology, 123,* 185–190.

Zhang, Heping, & Bracken, M. B. (1995). Tree-based risk factor analysis of preterm delivery and small-for-gestational-age birth. *American Journal of Epidemiology, 141,* 70–78.

Zhou, Jiang-Ning, et al. (1995). A sex difference in the human brain and its relation to transsexuality. *Nature, 378,* 68–70.

Zilbergeld, Bernie. (1978). *Male sexuality.* Boston: Little, Brown.

Zilbergeld, Bernie. (1992). *The new male sexuality.* New York: Bantam Books.

Zilbergeld, Bernie. (1999). *The new male sexuality* (rev. ed.). New York: Bantam.

Zilbergeld, Bernie, & Ellison, Carol Rinklieb. (1980). Desire discrepancies and arousal problems in sex therapy. In S. R. Leiblum & L. A. Pervin (Eds.), *Principles and practice of sex therapy* (pp. 65–104). New York: Guilford.

Zilbergeld, Bernie, & Evans, Michael. (1980, August). The inadequacy of Masters and Johnson. *Psychology Today, 14* (3), 28–43.

Zillmann, Dolf, Schweitzer, Karla J., & Mundorf, Norbert. (1994). Menstrual cycle variations of women's interest in erotica. *Archives of Sexual Behavior, 23,* 579–598.

Zimmer, D. (1983). Interaction patterns and communication skills in sexually distressed and normal couples: Two experimental studies. *Journal of Sex and Marital Therapy, 9,* 251–265.

Zimmerman-Tansella, Christa, et al. (1994). Marital relationships and somatic and psychological symptoms in pregnancy. *Social Science and Medicine, 38,* 559–564.

Zlidar, Vera M., et al. (2003). The reproductive revolution continues. *Population Reports,* Series M, No. 17. Baltimore: Johns Hopkins University School of Public Health.

Zoldbrod, Aline P. (1993). *Men, women, and infertility: Intervention and treatment strategies.* New York: Lexington Books.

Zoucha-Jensen, J. M., & Coyne, A. (1993). The effects of resistance strategies on rape. *American Journal of Public Health, 83,* 1633–1634.

Zucker, Kenneth J. (2000). Gender identity disorder. In A. J. Sameroff et al. (Eds.), *Handbook of developmental psychopathology* (2nd ed., pp. 671–686). New York: Kluwer Academic/Plenum.

Zucker, Kenneth J., et al. (2002). Gender-dysphoric children and adolescents: A comparative analysis of demographic characteristics and behavioral problems. *Clinical Child Psychology and Psychiatry, 7,* 398–411.

Zuger, Abigail. (1987, June). AIDS on the wards: A residency in medical ethics. *Hastings Center Report,* June 16–20.

Zuk, Marlene. (2002). *Sexual selections: What we can and can't learn about sex from animals.* Berkeley: University of California Press.

Zumpe, Doris, & Michael, R. P. (1968). The clutching reaction and orgasm in the female rhesus monkey (*Macaca mulatta*). *Journal of Endocrinology, 40,* 117–123.

Zumwalt, Rosemary. (1976). Plain and fancy: A content analysis of children's jokes dealing with adult sexuality. *Western Folklore, 35,* 258–267.

Zurbriggen, Eileen, & Morgan, E. (2006). Who wants to marry a millionaire? Reality dating television programs, attitudes toward sex, and sexual behaviors. *Sex Roles, 54,* 1–17.

Zurbriggen, Eileen, & Yost, Megan R. (2004). Power, desire, and pleasure in sexual fantasies. *Journal of Sex Research, 41,* 288–300.

Zussman, Leon, et al. (1981). Sexual response after hysterectomy-oophorectomy. *American Journal of Obstetrics and Gynecology, 140,* 725–729.

Zweifler, John, Garza, A., Hughes, S., Stanich, M., Hierholzer, A., & Lau, M. (2006). Vaginal birth after cesarean in California: Before and after a change in guidelines. *Annals of Family Medicine, 4,* 228–234.

Glossary

Abortion The termination of a pregnancy.

Abstinence (sexual) Not engaging in sexual activity.

Acculturation The process of incorporating the beliefs and customs of a new culture.

Acquired erectile disorder Cases of erectile disorder in which the man at one time was able to have satisfactory erections but now can no longer do so.

Acquired Immune Deficiency Syndrome (AIDS) A sexually transmitted disease that destroys the body's natural immunity to infection so that the person is susceptible to and may die from a disease such as pneumonia or cancer.

Acquired orgasmic disorder A case of female orgasmic disorder in which the woman had orgasms at some time in her life but no longer does so.

Acquired sexual disorder A sexual disorder that develops after a period of normal functioning.

Activating effects of hormones Effects of sex hormones in adulthood, resulting in the activation of behaviors, especially sexual behaviors and aggressive behaviors.

Adrenal glands Endocrine glands located just above the kidneys; in the female they are major producer of androgens.

Adrenarche A time of increased secretion of adrenal androgens, usually just before age 8.

Adultery Voluntary sexual intercourse by a husband or wife with someone other than one's spouse; thus betrayal of one's marriage vows.

Agenda setting In communications theory, the idea that the media define what is important and what is not by which stories they cover.

AIDS See *Acquired Immune Deficiency Syndrome.*

Amenorrhea The absence of menstruation.

Amniocentesis A test done to determine whether a fetus has birth defects; done by inserting a fine tube into the woman's abdomen in order to obtain a sample of amniotic fluid.

Amniotic fluid The watery fluid surrounding a developing fetus in the uterus.

Anal intercourse Insertion of the penis into the partner's rectum.

Analogous organs Organs in the male and female that have similar functions.

Anaphrodisiac A substance that decreases sexual desire.

Androgen-insensitivity syndrome (AIS) A genetic condition in which the body is unresponsive to androgens so that a genetic male may be born with a female-appearing body.

Anilingus Mouth stimulation of the partner's anus.

Antigay prejudice Negative attitudes and behaviors toward gays and lesbians. Also termed *sexual prejudice.*

Aphrodisiac A substance that increases sexual desire.

Artificial insemination A procedure in which sperm are placed into the vagina by means other than sexual intercourse.

Asceticism An approach to life emphasizing discipline and impulse control.

Asexuality Having no sexual attraction to a person of either sex.

Asphyxiophilia The desire to induce in oneself a state of oxygen deficiency in order to create sexual arousal or to enhance excitement and orgasm.

Asymptomatic Having no symptoms.

Attachment A psychological bond that forms between an infant and the mother, father, or other caregiver.

Autoeroticism Sexual self-stimulation; for example, masturbation.

AZT A drug used to treat HIV-infected persons; also called *ZDV.*

Bartholin glands Two tiny glands located on either side of the vaginal entrance.

Basal body temperature (BBT) method A type of rhythm method of birth control in which the woman determines when she ovulates by keeping track of her temperature.

Behavior modification A set of operant conditioning techniques used to modify human behavior.

Behavior therapy A system of therapy based on learning theory, in which the focus is on the problem behavior and how it can be modified or changed.

Bibliotherapy The use of a self-help book to treat a disorder.

Bisexual A person whose sexual orientation is toward both men and women.

Body-centered sex Sexual expression in which the emphasis is on the body and physical pleasure.

Bondage and discipline The use of physical or psychological restraint to enforce servitude, from which both participants derive sensual pleasure.

Braxton-Hicks contractions Contractions of the uterus during pregnancy that are not part of actual labor.

Brothel A house of prostitution.

Buccal smear A test of genetic sex, in which a small scraping of cells is taken from the inside of the mouth, stained, and examined under a microscope.

Calendar method A type of rhythm method of birth control in which the woman determines when she ovulates by keeping a calendar record of the length of her menstrual cycles.

Call girl The most expensive and exclusive category of prostitutes.

Celibacy The practice of remaining celibate or unmarried. Sometimes used to refer to abstaining from sexual intercourse, the correct term for which is *chastity.*

Cervical mucus method A type of rhythm method of birth control in which the woman determines when she ovulates by checking her cervical mucus.

Cesarean section (C-section) A method of delivering a baby surgically by an incision in the abdomen.

Chancre A painless, ulcerlike lesion with a hard, raised edge that is an early symptom of syphilis.

Chlamydia An organism causing a sexually transmitted disease. The symptoms in males are a thin, clear discharge and mild pain on urination; females are frequently asymptomatic.

Chorionic villus sampling (CVS) A technique for prenatal diagnosis of birth defects, involving taking a sample of cells from the chorionic villus and analyzing them.

Circumcision Surgical removal of the foreskin of the penis.

Classical conditioning The learning process in which a previously neutral stimulus (conditioned stimulus) is repeatedly paired with an unconditioned stimulus that reflexively elicits an unconditioned response. Eventually the conditioned stimulus itself will evoke the response.

Clitoral orgasm Freud's term for orgasm in the female resulting from stimulation of the clitoris.

Clitoris A small, highly sensitive sexual organ in the female, found in front of the vaginal entrance.

Cognitive interference Negative thoughts that distract a person from focusing on the erotic experience.

Cognitive–behavioral therapy A form of therapy that combines behavior therapy and restructuring of negative thought patterns.

Cohabitation Unmarried persons living together (with sexual relations assumed).

Coitus Sexual intercourse; insertion of the penis into the vagina.

Colostrum A watery substance that is secreted from the breasts at the end of pregnancy and during the first few days after delivery.

Combination birth control pills Birth control pills that contain a combination of estrogen and progestin (progesterone).

Coming out The process of acknowledging to oneself, and then to others, that one is gay or lesbian.

Companionate love A feeling of deep attachment and commitment to a person with whom one has an intimate relationship.

Compulsive sexual behavior (CSB) A disorder in which the individual experiences intense, uncontrollable sexually arousing fantasies, urges, and associated sexual behaviors.

Computer-assisted self-interview (CASI) A method of administering questionnaires that gives respondents maximum privacy because they answer on a computer.

Congenital adrenal hyperplasia (CAH) A condition in which a genetic female produces abnormal levels of androgens prenatally and therefore has male-appearing genitals at birth.

Congenital syphilis A syphilis infection in a newborn baby resulting from transmission from an infected mother.

Content analysis A set of procedures used to make valid inferences about text.

Conversion therapy Any one of a number of treatments designed to turn LGBs into heterosexuals; also called *reparative therapy.*

Coprophilia Deriving sexual satisfaction from contact with feces.

Corpora cavernosa Spongy bodies running the length of the top of the penis; also found in the clitoris.

Corpus luteum The mass of cells of the follicle remaining after ovulation; it secretes progesterone.

Corpus spongiosum A spongy body running the length of the underside of the penis.

Correlation A number that measures the relationship between two variables.

Correlational study A study in which the researcher does not manipulate variables but rather studies naturally occurring relationships (correlations) among variables.

Cost-benefit approach An approach to analyzing the ethics of a research study, based on weighing the costs of the research (the participants' time, the stress to participants, and so on) against the benefits of the research (gaining knowledge about human sexuality).

Covert homosexual A homosexual who is "in the closet," who keeps his or her sexual orientation a secret.

Cowper's glands Glands that secrete a clear alkaline fluid into the male's urethra.

Cryptorchidism Undescended testes; the condition in which the testes do not descend to the scrotum as they should during prenatal development.

Cultivation In communications theory, the view that exposure to the mass media makes people think that what they see there represents the mainstream of what really occurs.

Culture Traditional ideas and values transmitted to members of the group by symbols such as language.

Cunnilingus Mouth stimulation of the female genitals.

Cyberaffair A romantic or sexual relationship initiated by online contact and maintained primarily via online communication, involving a person who is married/in a committed relationship.

Cystitis An infection of the urinary bladder in women, causing painful, burning urination.

Decriminalization Removing an act from those prohibited by law, ceasing to define it as a crime.

Deprivation homosexuality Homosexual activity that occurs in certain situations, such as prisons, when people are deprived of their regular heterosexual activity.

Diaphragm A cap-shaped rubber contraceptive device that fits inside a woman's vagina over the cervix.

Dilation An opening up of the cervix during labor; also called *dilatation*.

Dildo A rubber or plastic cylinder, often shaped like a penis.

Discrepancy of sexual desire A sexual disorder in which the partners have considerably different levels of sexual desire.

Disorders of sex development (DSD) A newer term for intersex conditions.

Documenting Giving specific examples of the issue being discussed.

Dominance and submission The use of power consensually given to control the sexual stimulation and behavior of the other person.

Don Juanism See *satyriasis*.

Double standard A standard in which premarital intercourse is considered acceptable for males but not for females.

Douching Flushing out the inside of the vagina with a liquid.

Drag queen A male homosexual who dresses in women's clothing.

Dualism A religious or philosophical belief that body and spirit are separate and opposed to each other and that the goal of life is to free the spirit from the bondage of the body; thus a depreciation of the material world and the physical aspect of humanity.

Dysmenorrhea Painful menstruation.

Dyspareunia Painful intercourse.

Ectopic pregnancy A pregnancy in which the fertilized egg implants somewhere other than the uterus.

Edema Excessive fluid retention and swelling.

Editing Censoring or not saying things that would be deliberately hurtful to your partner or that are irrelevant.

Effacement A thinning out of the cervix during labor.

Effective communicator A communicator whose impact matches his or her intent.

Ego According to Freud, the part of the personality that helps the person have realistic, rational interactions.

Electra complex According to Freud, the sexual attraction of a little girl for her father.

Embryo transfer A procedure in which an embryo is transferred from the uterus of one woman into the uterus of another.

Endometriosis A condition in which the endometrium grows abnormally outside the uterus; the symptom is unusually painful periods with excessive bleeding.

Epididymis A highly coiled tube located on the edge of the testes; where sperm mature.

Episiotomy An incision made in the skin just behind the vagina, allowing the baby to be delivered more easily.

Equity theory A theory that states that people mentally calculate the benefits and costs for them in a relationship; their behavior is then affected by whether they feel there is equity or inequity, and they will act to restore equity if there is inequity.

Erectile disorder The inability to have or maintain an erection.

Erogenous zones Areas of the body that are particularly sensitive to sexual stimulation.

Erotica Sexually arousing material that is not degrading to women, men, or children.

Erotophiles People who feel comfortable with sex, lacking in feelings of guilt and fear about sex.

Erotophobes People who feel guilty and fearful about sex.

Estrogens The group of "female" sex hormones.

Ethics A system of moral principles; a way of determining right and wrong.

Ethnocentrism The tendency to regard one's own ethnic group and culture as superior to others and to believe that its customs and way of life are the standards by which other cultures should be judged.

Evolution A theory that all living things have acquired their present forms through gradual changes in their genetic endowment over successive generations.

Evolutionary psychology The study of psychological mechanisms that have been shaped by natural selection.

Excitement The first stage of sexual response, during which erection in the male and vaginal lubrication in the female occur.

Exhibitionism Showing one's genitals in a public place, to passersby; indecent exposure.

Exhibitionist A person who derives sexual gratification from exposing his genitals to others in situations in which this is inappropriate.

Experiment A type of research study in which one variable (the independent variable) is manipulated by the experimenter while all other factors are held constant; the researcher can then study the effects of the independent variable on some measured variable (the dependent variable); the researcher is permitted to make causal inferences about the effects of the independent variable on the dependent variable.

Extinction The process of repeatedly pairing a behavior with an aversive stimulus, leading to a decrease in the frequency of a behavior.

Extramarital sex Sexual activity by a married person with someone other than that person's spouse; adultery.

Failure rate The pregnancy rate occurring using a particular contraceptive method; the percentage of women who will be pregnant after a year of use of the method.

Fallopian tubes The tubes extending from the uterus to the ovary; also called the *oviducts*.

Fellatio Mouth stimulation of the male genitals.

Female impersonator A man who dresses up as a woman as part of a job in entertainment.

Female orgasmic disorder A sexual disorder in which the woman is unable to have an orgasm.

Female sexual arousal disorder (FSAD) A sexual disorder in which there is a lack of response to sexual stimulation.

Female-to-male transsexual (FTM) A person born with a female body whose gender identity is male and who wishes to undergo gender reassignment.

Fertility cult A form of nature religion in which the fertility of the soil is encouraged through various forms of ritual magic, often including ritual sexual intercourse.

Fetal alcohol syndrome (FAS) Serious growth deficiency and malformations in the child of a mother who abuses alcohol during pregnancy.

Fetishism A person's sexual fixation on some object other than another human being and attachment of great erotic significance to that object.

Fighting fair A set of rules designed to make arguments constructive rather than destructive.

First-stage labor The beginning of labor, during which there are regular contractions of the uterus; the stage lasts until the cervix is dilated 8 centimeters (3 inches).

Follicle-stimulating hormone (FSH) A hormone secreted by the pituitary; it stimulates follicle development in females and sperm production in males.

Follicular phase The first phase of the menstrual cycle, beginning just after menstruation, during which an egg matures in preparation for ovulation.

Foreskin A layer of skin covering the glans or tip of the penis in an uncircumcised male; also called the *prepuce.*

Form fetish A fetish whose object is a particular shape, such as high-heeled shoes.

Fornication The biblical term for sex by unmarried persons and, more generally, all immoral sexual behavior.

Frequency How often a person does something.

Frotteurism Rubbing one's genitals against the body of a nonconsenting person.

Gay Homosexual; especially male homosexuals.

Gay baths Clubs where gay men can socialize; features include a swimming pool or whirlpool and access to casual sex.

Gender The state of being male or female.

Gender dysphoria Unhappiness with one's gender; another term for *transsexualism.*

Gender identity disorder (GID) A strong and persistent cross-gender identification.

Gender reassignment The process for transsexuals to change their body to the other gender.

Gender role A set of norms, or culturally defined expectations, that define how people of one gender ought to behave.

Gender-segregated social organization The tendency of children to play and associate only with members of their own gender; all-boys groups and all-girls groups predominate.

Genital herpes A sexually transmitted disease, the symptoms of which are small, painful bumps or blisters on the genitals.

Genital warts A sexually transmitted infection causing warts on the genitals.

GIFT Gamete intrafallopian transfer, a procedure in which sperm and eggs are collected and then inserted together into the fallopian tube.

Gigolo A male who provides companionship and sexual gratification on a continuing basis to a woman in exchange for money.

GnRH (gonadotropin-releasing hormone) A hormone secreted by the hypothalamus that regulates the pituitary's secretion of gonad-stimulating hormones.

Gonorrhea A sexually transmitted infection that usually causes symptoms of a puslike discharge and painful, burning urination in the male but is frequently asymptomatic in the female.

Gräfenberg spot (G spot) A small gland on the front wall of the vagina that is responsible for female ejaculation; it empties into the urethra.

Hedonism A moral system based on maximizing pleasure and avoiding pain.

Heterosexism The belief that everyone is heterosexual and that heterosexuality is the norm; homosexuality is denigrated.

Heterosexual A person whose sexual orientation is toward members of the other gender.

HIV Human immunodeficiency virus; the virus that causes AIDS.

Homologous organs Organs in the male and female that develop from the same embryonic tissue.

Homophily The tendency to have contact with people equal in social status.

Homophobia A strong, irrational fear of homosexuals; negative attitudes and reactions to homosexuals.

Homosexual A person whose sexual orientation is toward members of the same gender.

Hooking up A sexual encounter that usually occurs on one occasion involving people who are strangers or acquaintances.

HPG axis Hypothalamus–pituitary–gonad axis, the negative feedback loop that regulates sex-hormone production.

HPV Human papillomavirus, the organism that causes genital warts.

Human chorionic gonadotropin (hCG) A hormone produced by the placenta; it is the hormone detected in pregnancy tests.

Humanism A philosophical system that denies a divine origin for morality and holds that ethical judgments must be made on the basis of human experience and human reason.

Hustler A male sex worker who sells his services to men.

Hyaluronidase An enzyme secreted by the sperm that allows one sperm to penetrate the egg.

Hymen A thin membrane that may partially cover the vaginal entrance.

Hypersexuality An excessive, insatiable sex drive in either men or women.

Hypoactive sexual desire (HSD) A sexual disorder in which there is a lack of interest in sexual activity; also termed *inhibited sexual desire* or *low sexual desire.*

Hypothalamus A small region of the brain that is important in regulating many body functions, including the functioning of the sex hormones.

Hysterectomy Surgical removal of the uterus.

Hysterotomy A surgical method of abortion done in the late second trimester.

"I" language Speaking for yourself, using the word "I," not mind reading.

Id According to Freud, the part of the personality containing the libido.

Immediate causes Various factors that occur in the act of lovemaking that inhibit sexual response.

Impact What someone else understands the speaker to mean.

In vitro fertilization (IVF) A procedure in which an egg is fertilized by sperm in a laboratory dish.

In-call service A residence in which prostitutes work regular shifts, selling sexual services on an hourly basis.

Incest Sexual activity between relatives.

Incest taboo A regulation prohibiting sexual interaction between blood relatives, such as brother and sister or father and daughter.

Incidence The percentage of people giving a particular response.

Infertility A woman's inability to conceive and give birth to a child, or a man's inability to impregnate a woman.

Informed consent An ethical principle in research, in which people have a right to be informed, before participating, of what they will be asked to do in the research.

Inhibin A substance secreted by the testes and ovaries which regulates FSH levels.

Inner lips Thin folds of skin on either side of the vaginal entrance.

Intent What the speaker means.

Intercoder reliability In content analysis, the correlation or percent of agreement between two coders independently rating the same texts.

Interfemoral intercourse A sexual technique used by gay men in which one man moves his penis between the thighs of the other.

Intersex An individual who has a mixture of male and female reproductive structures, so that it is not clear at birth whether the individual is a male or a female. Also called a *pseudohermaphrodite*.

Interstitial cells Cells in the testes that manufacture testosterone.

Intimacy A quality of relationships characterized by commitment, feelings of closeness and trust, and self-disclosure.

Intrauterine device (IUD) A plastic device sometimes containing metal or a hormone that is inserted into the uterus for contraceptive purposes.

Introitus Another word for the vaginal entrance.

Kegel exercises A part of sex therapy for women with orgasmic disorder, in which the woman exercises the muscles surrounding the vagina; also called *pubococcygeal* or *PC muscle exercises*.

Kiddie porn Pictures or films of sexual acts involving children.

Labia majora See *outer lips*.

Lamaze method A method of "prepared" childbirth involving relaxation and controlled breathing.

Late syphilis The fourth and final stage of syphilis, during which the disease does damage to major organs of the body such as the lungs, heart, or brain.

Latent syphilis The third stage of syphilis, which may last for years, during which symptoms disappear although the person is still infected.

Latinos People of Latin American heritage.

Legalism Ethics based on the assumption that there are rules for human conduct and that morality consists of knowing the rules and obeying them.

Leptin A hormone produced in the body that is related to the onset of puberty.

Lesbian A woman whose sexual orientation is toward other women.

Leveling Telling your partner what you are feeling by stating your thoughts clearly, simply, and honestly.

Libido In psychoanalytic theory, the term for the sex energy or sex drive.

Lifelong erectile disorder Cases of erectile disorder in which the man has never had an erection sufficient to have intercourse.

Lifelong orgasmic disorder A case of female orgasmic disorder in which the woman has never in her life had an orgasm.

Lifelong sexual disorder A sexual disorder that has been present ever since the person began sexual functioning.

Life-span development Development from birth through old age.

Limbic system A set of structures in the interior of the brain, including the amygdala, hippocampus, and fornix; believed to be important for sexual behavior in both animals and humans.

Love story A story about what love should be like, including characters, a plot, and a theme.

Lumpectomy A surgical treatment for breast cancer in which only the lump and a small bit of surrounding tissue are removed.

Luteal phase The third phase of the menstrual cycle, following ovulation.

Luteinizing hormone (LH) A hormone secreted by the pituitary; it regulates estrogen secretion and ovum development in the female and testosterone production in the male.

Madam A woman who manages a brothel, in-call, out-call, or escort service.

Male condom A contraceptive sheath that is placed over the penis.

Male orgasmic disorder A sexual disorder in which the male cannot have an orgasm, even though he is highly aroused and has had a great deal of sexual stimulation.

Male-to-female transsexual (MTF) A person who is born with a male body but who has a female identity and wishes to become a female biologically in order to match her identity.

Marital rape The rape of a person by her or his current or former spouse.

Massage parlor A place where massages, as well as sexual services, can generally be purchased.

Masturbation Stimulation of one's own genitals with the hand or with some object, such as a pillow or vibrator.

Matching phenomenon The tendency for men and women to choose as partners people who match them, that is, who are similar in attitudes, intelligence, and attractiveness.

Mean The average of respondents' scores.

Media fetish A fetish whose object is anything made of a particular substance, such as leather.

Median The middle score.

Medical model A theoretical model in psychology and psychiatry in which mental problems are thought of as sickness or mental illness; the problems in turn are often thought to be due to biological factors.

Medicalization of sexuality The tendency to give medical treatment to problematic experiences and to define certain conditions in terms of health or illness.

Menopause The cessation of menstruation.

Menstrual synchrony The convergence, over several months, of the dates of onset of menstrual periods among women who are in close contact with each other.

Menstruation The fourth phase of the menstrual cycle, during which the endometrium of the uterus is sloughed off in the menstrual discharge.

Mere-exposure effect The tendency to like someone more if we have been exposed to him or her repeatedly.

Mifepristone The "abortion pill." Also called *RU-486*.

Mind reading Making assumptions about what your partner thinks or feels.

Minilaparotomy A method of female sterilization.

Misattribution of arousal When one is in a stage of physiological arousal (e.g., from exercising or being in a frightening situation), attributing these feelings to love or attraction to the person present.

Miscarriage The termination of a pregnancy before the fetus is viable, as a result of natural causes (not medical intervention).

Monilia A form of vaginitis causing a thick, white discharge; also called *candida* or *yeast infection.*

Mons pubis The fatty pad of tissue under the pubic hair.

Moralism A religious or philosophical attitude that emphasizes moral behavior, usually according to strict standards, as the highest goal of human life. Moralists tend to favor strict regulation of human conduct to help make people good.

Müllerian ducts Ducts found in both male and female fetuses; in males they degenerate and in females they develop into the fallopian tubes, the uterus, and the upper part of the vagina.

Multiple orgasm A series of orgasms occurring within a short period of time.

Myotonia Muscle contraction.

Natural selection A process in nature resulting in greater rates of survival of those plants and animals that are adapted to their environment.

Necrophilia Deriving sexual satisfaction from contact with a dead person.

Nonverbal communication Communication not through words, but through the body; for example, eye contact, tone of voice, touching.

Nymphomania An excessive, insatiable sex drive in a woman.

Obscenity That which is offensive to decency or modesty, or calculated to arouse sexual excitement or lust.

Oedipus complex According to Freud, the sexual attraction of a little boy for his mother.

Oophorectomy Surgical removal of the ovaries.

Operant conditioning The process of changing the frequency of a behavior (the operant) by following it with positive reinforcement (which will make the behavior more frequent in the future) or punishment (which should make the behavior less frequent in the future).

Operational definition Defining some concept or term by how it is measured, for example, defining intelligence as those abilities that are measured by IQ tests.

Organic factors of sexual disorders Physical factors, such as disease or injury, that cause sexual disorders.

Organizing effects of hormones Effects of sex hormones early in development, resulting in a permanent change in the brain or reproductive system.

Orgasm The second stage of sexual response, an intense sensation that occurs at the peak of sexual arousal and is followed by release of sexual tensions.

Orgasmic platform A tightening of the entrance to the vagina caused by contractions of the bulbospongiosus muscle (which covers the vestibular bulbs) that occur during the excitement stage of sexual arousal.

Out-call service A service that sends a prostitute or sex worker to a location specified by the client to provide sexual services.

Outer lips Rounded pads of fatty tissue lying on either side of the vaginal entrance.

Ovaries Two organs in the female that produce eggs and sex hormones.

Overt homosexual A homosexual who is "out of the closet," who is open about his or her sexual orientation.

Ovulation Release of an egg from the ovaries; the second phase of the menstrual cycle.

Paraphilia Recurring, intense, unconventional sexual fantasies, urges, or behavior that is obsessive and compulsive.

Paraphrasing Saying, in your own words, what you thought your partner meant.

Participant-observer technique A research method in which the scientist becomes part of the community to be studied and makes observations from inside the community.

Passionate love A state of intense longing for union with the other person and of intense physiological arousal.

Pederasty Sex between an older man and a younger man, or a boy; sometimes called *boy love.*

Pedophilia Child molesting, an adult having sexual activity with a prepubescent child.

Peggy Lee syndrome The feelings of disappointment experienced by teenage girls at first intercourse when it is not as thrilling as they expected.

Pelvic inflammatory disease (PID) An infection and inflammation of the pelvic organs, such as the fallopian tubes and the uterus, in the female.

Penile prosthesis A surgical treatment for erectile dysfunction, in which inflatable tubes are inserted into the penis.

Penile strain gauge A device used to measure physiological sexual arousal in the male; it is a flexible loop that fits around the base of the penis.

Penis The male external sexual organ, which functions both in sexual activity and in urination.

Perineum The skin between the vaginal entrance and the anus.

Permissiveness with affection A standard in which premarital intercourse is considered acceptable if it occurs in the context of a loving, committed relationship.

Permissiveness without affection A standard in which premarital intercourse is acceptable without emotional commitment.

Person-centered sex Sexual expression in which the emphasis is on the relationship and emotions between the two people.

Pheromones Biochemicals secreted outside the body that are important in communication between animals and that may serve as sex attractants.

Photoplethysmograph An acrylic cylinder that is placed inside the vagina in order to measure physiological sexual arousal in the female. Also called a photometer.

Pimp A prostitute's companion, protector, and master.

Pituitary gland A small endocrine gland located on the lower side of the brain below the hypothalamus; the pituitary is important in regulating levels of sex hormones.

Placenta An organ formed on the wall of the uterus through which the fetus receives oxygen and nutrients and gets rid of waste products.

Pluralism A philosophical or political attitude that affirms the value of many competing opinions and believes that the truth is discovered in the clash of diverse perspectives. Pluralists, therefore, believe in the maximum human freedom possible.

Polyamory The nonpossessive, honest, responsible and ethical philosophy of loving multiple persons at the same time.

Population A group of people a researcher wants to study and make inferences about.

Pornography Sexually arousing art, literature, or films.

Postpartum depression Mild to moderate depression in women following the birth of a baby.

Posttraumatic growth Positive life changes and psychological development following exposure to trauma.

Posttraumatic stress disorder (PTSD) Long-term psychological distress suffered by someone who has experienced a terrifying event.

Preeclampsia A serious disease of pregnancy, marked by high blood pressure, severe edema, and proteinuria.

Premature (early) ejaculation A sexual disorder in which the man ejaculates too soon and believes he cannot control when he ejaculates.

Premenstrual dysphoric disorder (PMDD) A tentative diagnostic category in the DSM, characterized by symptoms such as sadness, anxiety, and irritability in the week before menstruation.

Premenstrual syndrome (PMS) A combination of severe physical and psychological symptoms, such as depression and irritability, occurring just before menstruation.

Prenatal period The time from conception to birth.

Primary-stage syphilis The first few weeks of a syphilis infection during which the chancre is present.

Primipara A woman having her first baby.

Prior learning Things that people have learned earlier—for example, in childhood—that now affect their sexual response.

Probability sampling An excellent method of sampling in research, in which each member of the population has a known probability of being included in the sample.

Problem of refusal or nonresponse The problem that some people will refuse to participate in a sex survey, thus making it difficult to have a random sample.

Progesterone A female sex hormone secreted by the ovaries.

Prostaglandins Chemicals secreted by the uterus that cause the uterine muscles to contract; they are a likely cause of painful menstruation.

Prostate The gland in the male, located below the bladder, that secretes some of the fluid in semen.

Prostatectomy Surgical removal of the prostate.

Prostatitis An infection or inflammation of the prostate gland.

Prostitutes / commercial sex workers Persons who engage in sexual acts in return for money or drugs and do so in a promiscuous, fairly nondiscriminating fashion.

Prostitution The exchange of sex for money or other payment such as drugs.

Pseudocyesis False pregnancy, in which the woman displays the signs of pregnancy but is not pregnant.

Psychoanalytic theory A psychological theory originated by Sigmund Freud; it contains a basic assumption that part of the human personality is unconscious.

Puberty The time during which there is sudden enlargement and maturation of the gonads, other genitalia, and secondary sex characteristics, so that the individual becomes capable of reproduction.

Pubic lice Tiny lice that attach themselves to the base of pubic hairs and cause itching; also called *crabs* or *pediculosis pubis.*

Pubococcygeus muscle A muscle around the vaginal entrance.

Purposeful distortion Purposely giving false information in a survey.

Radical mastectomy A surgical treatment for breast cancer in which the entire breast, as well as underlying muscles and lymph nodes, is removed.

Random sampling An excellent method of sampling in research, in which each member of the population has an equal chance of being included in the sample.

Rape trauma syndrome The emotional and physical effects a woman undergoes following a rape or attempted rape.

Rape Nonconsenting oral, anal, or vaginal penetration obtained by force, by threat of bodily harm, or when the victim is incapable of giving consent.

Refractory period The period following orgasm during which the male cannot be sexually aroused.

Resolution Masters and Johnson's term for the last phase of sexual response, in which the body returns to the unaroused state.

Retrograde ejaculation A condition in which orgasm in the male is not accompanied by an external ejaculation; instead, the ejaculate goes into the urinary bladder.

Rhythm (fertility awareness) method A method of birth control that involves abstaining from intercourse around the time the woman ovulates.

Saliromania A desire to damage or soil a woman or her clothes.

Sample A part of a population.

Satyriasis An excessive, insatiable sex drive in a man; also called *Don Juanism.*

Schema A general knowledge framework that a person has about a particular topic.

Scoptophilia A sexual variation in which the person becomes sexually aroused by observing others' sexual acts and genitals.

Scrotum The pouch of skin that contains the testes in the male.

Secondary-stage syphilis The second stage of syphilis, occurring several months after infection, during which the chancre has disappeared and a generalized body rash appears.

Second-stage labor The stage during which the baby moves out through the vagina and is delivered.

Self-disclosure Telling personal things about yourself.

Self-efficacy A sense of competence at performing an activity.

Seminal vesicles Saclike structures that lie above the prostate which produce about 70 percent of the seminal fluid.

Seminiferous tubules Tubules in the testes that manufacture sperm.

Sensate focus exercise A part of the sex therapy developed by Masters and Johnson in which one partner caresses the other, the other communicates what is pleasurable, and there are no performance demands.

Serial monogamy A premarital sexual pattern in which there is an intention of being faithful to the partner, but the relationship may end and the person may then move on to another partner.

Sex tourism Leisure travel with the purpose of purchasing sexual services.

Sex trafficking The recruitment and control of persons for sexual exploitation.

Sexual behavior Behavior that produces arousal and increases the chance of orgasm.

Sexual disorder A problem with sexual response that causes a person mental distress.

Sexual fantasy Sexual thoughts or images that alter the person's emotions or physiological state.

Sexual health The state of having physical, emotional, mental, and social well-being in relation to sexuality.

Sexual identity One's self-identity as homosexual, heterosexual, or bisexual.

Sexual masochist A person who derives sexual satisfaction from experiencing pain.

Sexual orientation A person's erotic and emotional orientation toward members of his or her own gender or members of the other gender.

Sexual rights Basic, inalienable rights regarding sexuality, both positive and negative, such as rights to reproductive self-determination and sexual self-expression and freedom from sexual abuse and violence.

Sexual sadist A person who derives sexual satisfaction from inflicting suffering or humiliation on another person.

Sexual selection Processes by which members of one gender (usually males) compete with each other for mating privileges with members of the other gender (usually females) and members of the other gender (females) choose to mate only with certain preferred members of the first gender (males).

Sexualization Occurs when a person is valued only for sex appeal or behavior, is held to a standard that equates physical attractiveness with being sexy, or is sexually objectified; or when sexuality is inappropriately imposed upon a person.

Singleism The stigmatizing and stereotyping of people who are not in a socially recognized couple relationship.

Situational orgasmic disorder A case of orgasmic disorder in which the woman is able to have an orgasm in some situations (e.g., while masturbating) but not in others (e.g., while having sexual intercourse).

Situationism Ethics based on the assumption that there are no absolute rules, or at least very few, and that each situation must be judged individually.

Sixty-nining Simultaneous mouth–genital stimulation; also called *soixante-neuf.*

Skene's glands Glands opening into the urethra.

Social exchange theory The theory, based on the principle of reinforcement, that assumes that people choose those behaviors that maximize rewards and minimize costs.

Social learning The theory that behavior is learned through processes such as reinforcement and punishment and imitation.

Socialization The ways in which society conveys to the individual its norms or expectations for his or her behavior.

Sociobiology The application of evolutionary biology to understanding the social behavior of animals, including humans.

Sodomy Originally "crimes against nature"; in contemporary laws, oral and anal intercourse.

Somatic cell nuclear transfer A cloning technique that involves substituting genetic material from an adult's cell for the nucleus of an egg.

Spectatoring Masters and Johnson's term for acting as an observer or judge of one's own sexual performance; hypothesized to contribute to sexual disorders.

Sperm The mature male reproductive cell, capable of fertilizing an egg.

Spermicide A substance that kills sperm.

SRY Sex-determining region, Y chromosome.

Stereotype A generalization about a group of people (e.g., men) that distinguishes them from others (e.g., women).

Sterilization A surgical procedure by which an individual is made sterile, that is, incapable of reproducing.

Straight Heterosexual; that is, a person whose sexual orientation is toward members of the opposite gender.

Streetwalker A lower-status prostitute or sex worker who walks the streets selling sexual services.

Subincision A form of male genital cutting in which a slit is made on the lower side of the penis along its entire length.

Supercision A form of male genital cutting in which a slit is made the length of the foreskin on top.

Superego According to Freud, the part of the personality containing the conscience.

Swinging A form of extramarital sex in which married couples exchange partners with each other.

Symbolic interaction theory A theory that a person's behavior is constructed through interaction and symbolic communication with others.

Sympto-thermal method A type of rhythm method birth control combining the basal body temperature method and the cervical mucus method.

Syphilis A sexually transmitted infection that causes a chancre to appear in the primary stage.

Teratogen A substance that produces defects in a fetus.

Testes The pair of glands in the scrotum that manufacture sperm and sex hormones.

Testosterone A hormone secreted by the testes in the male (and also present at lower levels in the female).

Test-retest reliability A method for testing whether self-reports are reliable or accurate; participants are interviewed (or given a questionnaire) and then interviewed a second time sometime later to determine whether their answers are the same both times.

Therapeutic cloning Creating cells or tissues that are genetically identical to those of a patient, who needs them to treat a disease.

Third-stage labor The stage during which the afterbirth is expelled.

Toxic shock syndrome A sometimes fatal bacterial infection associated with tampon use during menstruation.

Transgender A category including transsexuals, those who think of themselves as a third gender, transvestites, gender benders, and others.

Transition The difficult part of labor at the end of the first stage, during which the cervix dilates from 8 to 10 centimeters (3 to 4 inches).

Transsexual A person who feels that he or she is trapped in the body of the other gender. See also *transgender* and *gender reassignment process.*

Transvestism The practice of deriving sexual gratification from dressing as a member of the other gender.

Tribadism A sexual technique used by lesbians in which one woman lies on top of another and moves rhythmically in order to produce sexual pleasure, particularly clitoral stimulation.

Trichomoniasis A form of vaginitis causing a frothy white or yellow discharge with an unpleasant odor.

Triphasic model Kaplan's model of sexual response in which there are three components: vasocongestion, muscular contractions, and sexual desire.

Triphasic pill A birth control pill containing a steady level of estrogen and three phases of progesterone, intended to mimic more closely women's natural hormonal cycles.

Troilism Three people having sex together.

Two-component theory of love Berscheid and Walster's theory that two conditions must exist simultaneously for passionate love to occur: physiological arousal and attaching a cognitive label ("love") to the feeling.

Umbilical cord The tube that connects the fetus to the placenta.

Urethra The tube through which urine leaves the bladder and passes out of the body; in males, also the tube through which semen is discharged.

Urophilia Deriving sexual satisfaction from contact with urine.

Uterus The organ in the female in which the fetus develops.

Vacuum aspiration A method of abortion that is performed during the first trimester and involves suctioning out the contents of the uterus; also called *suction curettage*.

Vagina The tube-shaped organ in the female into which the penis is inserted during coitus and through which a baby passes during birth.

Vaginal orgasm Freud's term for orgasm in the female resulting from stimulation of the vagina in heterosexual intercourse; Freud considered vaginal orgasm to be more mature than clitoral orgasm.

Vaginismus A sexual disorder in which there is a spastic contraction of the muscles surrounding the entrance to the vagina, in some cases so severe that intercourse is impossible.

Vaginitis An irritation or inflammation of the vagina, usually causing a discharge.

Validation Telling your partner that, given his or her point of view, you can see why he or she thinks a certain way.

Vas deferens The tube through which sperm pass on their way from the testes and epididymis, out of the scrotum, and to the urethra.

Vasectomy A surgical procedure for male sterilization involving severing of the vas deferens.

Vasocongestion An accumulation of blood in the blood vessels of a region of the body, especially the genitals; a swelling or erection results.

Vestibular bulbs Erectile tissue running under the inner lips.

Viagra A drug used in the treatment of erectile disorder. Sildenafil.

Victim-precipitated rape The view that rape is a result of a woman "asking for it."

Victorian compromise The decision not to criminalize behavior per se and instead criminalize conduct that is visible to the outside world.

Volunteer bias A bias in the results of sex surveys that arises when some people refuse to participate, so that those who are in the sample are volunteers who may in some ways differ from those who refuse to participate.

Voyeur A person who becomes sexually aroused from secretly viewing nudes.

Voyeurism Secretly watching people who are nude.

Vulva The collective term for the external genitals of the female.

Withdrawal A method of birth control in which the man withdraws his penis from his partner's vagina before he has an orgasm.

Wolffian ducts Ducts found in both male and female fetuses; in females they degenerate and in males they develop into the epididymis, the vas deferens, and the ejaculatory duct.

Zoophilia Sexual contact with an animal; also called *bestiality* or *sodomy*.

Zygote A fertilized egg.

Acknowledgments

PHOTOGRAPHS

Chapter 1
p. 1: Royalty-Free/Corbis; p. 4 (left): AP Images; p. 4 (right): Culver Pictures, Inc.; p. 5 (left): Reprinted by permission of the Kinsey Institute for Research in Sex, Gender and Reproduction, Inc. Photo by Bill Dellenback; p. 5 (right): Courtesy of A.L. Enterprises; p.7: © David Young-Wolff/PhotoEdit; p. 9: AP Images; p. 12 (left): © Art Wolfe/Getty Images; p. 12 (right): © Staff/Getty Images; p. 15 (top): © Myrleen Ferguson Cate/PhotoEdit; p. 15 (bottom): © Martha Cooper/Peter Arnold; p. 19 (left): © Meredith F. Small; p. 19 (right): © Thomas Michael Corcoran/PhotoEdit.

Chapter 2
p. 23: Getty Images/PunchStock; p. 25 (left): © J.H. Robinson/Photo Researchers; p. 25 (right): © SuperStock, Inc.; p. 29: © Lester Lefkowitz/Taxi/Getty Images; p. 32: © Joel Gordon; p. 36: © Bill Aron/PhotoEdit; p. 39: © Steve Mason/Getty Images; p. 40: © Suzanne Arms/The Image Works.

Chapter 3
p. 43: Pixtal/PunchStock; p. 46: © David Young-Wolff/PhotoEdit; p. 53 (left): Reprinted by permission of the Kinsey Institute for Research in Sex, Gender and Reproduction, Inc., photo by Bill Dellenback; p. 53 (right): © Matthew Peyton/Getty Images; p. 56 (left): Courtesy of Edward Laumann; p. 56 (right): © Thinkstock/Getty Images; p. 59: © Bob Daemmrich; p. 63: © David Young-Wolff/PhotoEdit.

Chapter 4
p. 68: Digital Vision/Getty Images; p. 73: © Lori Grinker/Contact Press Images; p. 74: © Thomas Michael Corcoran/PhotoEdit; p. 78 (top): © Jessica Abad de Gail/AGE Fotostock; pp. 78, 80: © Joel Gordon; p. 85: © Susan Lerner/ Joel Gordon Photography; p. 88: © Joel Gordon.

Chapter 5
p. 85: © Lennart Nilsson; p. 100: © José Villarrubia. Photo Courtesy of John Money; p. 103: © Michael Geissinger; p. 106 (left): © Elizabeth Crews/The Image Works; p. 106 (right): © ChromoSohm Media/The Image Works; p. 107 (left): © Blair Seitz/Photo Researchers; p. 107 (right): © Jason Laure/Woodfin Camp; p. 110: © C. Edelmann/Photo Researchers, Inc.; p. 116: © Amy Etra/PhotoEdit.

Chapter 6
p. 119: Brand X; p. 122: © 3D4Medical.com/Getty Images; p. 124 (top left): © Petit Format/Nestle/Science Source/Photo Researchers; p. 124 (top right, bottom left, bottom right): Lennart Nilsson, from *A Child Is Born*, Dell Publishing Company; p. 130: © Spencer Grant/Photo Researchers; p. 133 (left): Streissguth, A.P., Landesman-Dwyer, S., Martin, J.C., & Smith, D.W. (1980). "Teratogenic effects of alcohol in humans and laboratory animals," *Science, 209,* 353–361; p. 133 (right): © John Chiasson/Gamma Liaison/Getty Images; p. 136 (top): © D. Van Rossum/Petit Format/Photo Researchers, Inc.; p. 136 (bottom): © O.V.N./Petit Format/Photo Researchers, Inc.; p. 138: © Lawrence Migdale/Photo Researchers, Inc.; p. 140 (left, right): © Byron/Monkmeyer/Photo Researchers, Inc.; p. 143: © Digital Vision/Getty Images; p. 151 (top): © ISM/Phototake; p. 151 (bottom): © Stefano Paltera/Gamma NY.

Chapter 7
p. 155: Jack Star/PhotoLink/Getty Images; p. 159: Bettmann/Corbis; p. 161: © Tony Freeman/PhotoEdit; p. 162: © Joel Gordon; p. 163: © Mauritius, GMBH/Phototake; p. 166: © The McGraw-Hill Companies, Inc./Bob Coyle; pp. 167, 168, 169: © Joel Gordon; p. 171: © The McGraw-Hill Companies, Inc./Jill Braaten, photographer; p. 172: Courtesy of National Campaign to Prevent Teen Pregnancy; p. 182 (right): © John Berry.

Chapter 8
p. 190: Stockbyte/PunchStock; p. 198: Bettmann/Corbis; p. 200: © Owen Franken/Corbis; p. 202 (left): © Mark Richards/PhotoEdit; p. 202 (right): Courtesy of Ellen Stohl; p. 207: © Dr. Scott T. Grafton/Visuals Unlimited; p. 209: © Bob Daemmrich/Stock Boston; p. 210 (top): © Betts Loman/PhotoEdit; p. 210 (bottom): © Luis Fernandez/SuperStock; p. 212 (top, bottom): © Joel Gordon; p. 214: © Mark Antman/The Image Works; p. 217: Luiz C. Marico/Peter Arnold, Inc.

Chapter 9

p. 230: Digital Vision; p. 232 (left): © Amy C. Etra/PhotoEdit; p. 232 (right): © Maya Barnes/The Image Works; p. 234: © Cassy Cohen/PhotoEdit; p. 238: © Greg Ceo/Getty Images; p. 243: © SW Productions/Photodisc/Getty Images; p. 246: © Francesco Venturi/Corbis; p. 249: © Stephen Ferry/Liaison/Getty Images.

Chapter 10

p. 256: Comstock Images; p. 258: © SuperStock, Inc.; p. 261 (left): © Johnny Crawford/The Image Works; p. 261 (right): © Photodisc Collection/Getty Images; p. 266 (left): © Ryan McVay/Getty Images; p. 266 (right): © Paul Vozdic/The Image Bank/Getty Images; p. 272: © Frank Siteman/PhotoEdit; p. 276: © Mike Siluk/The Image Works; p. 279: © Network Productions/The Image Works.

Chapter 11

p. 282: Brand X Pictures/PunchStock; p. 287: © Wayne Levin/Getty Images; p. 289: © Richard Lord Enterprises, Inc./The Image Works; p. 295: © Michael Krasowitz/Taxi/Getty Images; p. 300: © David Young-Wolff/PhotoEdit; p. 301: © Jerry Cooke/Photo Researchers; p. 307 (left): © Tim Hall/Taxi/Getty Images; p. 307 (right): © Bruce Ayres/Tony Stone/Getty Images; p. 309: © Bill Aron/PhotoEdit.

Chapter 12

p. 313: Yao Yongqiang/ChinaFotoPress/Getty Images; p. 316: © Johnny Nunez/WireImage/Getty Images; p. 317: Photofest; p. 318: © F.A. Rinehart for B.A.E./Smithsonian Institute; p. 319 (left): © George Simian/Corbis; p. 319 (right): © Anne Flinn Powell/Index Stock Imagery; p. 322: Photo courtesy of J.R. Heiman; p. 328: © Pascal Le Segretain/Getty Images; pp. 330, 331: photo courtesy of Dr. Daniel Greenwald; p. 333: © Philip Blenksop/Agence VU; p. 333 (bottom left): © Hulton Archive/Getty Images; p. 333 (bottom right): AP Images.

Chapter 13

p. 336: Thinkstock LLC; p. 339: © Bettmann/Corbis; p. 342: © Gabe Palacio/Getty Images; p. 344: © Plush Studios/Brand X Pictures/Getty Images; p. 346 (top): © Geoff Manasse/IPN/Aurora; p. 346 (bottom): © Colin McPherson/Corbis Sygma; p. 351: Courtesy of John Michael Bailey, Northwestern University; p. 358: © Jeff Greenberg/PhotoEdit.

Chapter 14

p. 364: Digital Vision/PunchStock; p. 368: © Joel Gordon; p. 369 (left): © Photofest; p. 369 (right): © Kevin Winter/Getty Images; p. 374: © Jacques Prayer/Gamma; p. 376: © Jutta Klee/Corbis; p. 378: © Christie's Images/SuperStock; p. 382: © CBS Photo Archive/Getty Images; p. 385: © David Harry Stewart/Tony Stone/Getty Images.

Chapter 15

p. 388: Brand X Pictures/PunchStock; p. 391: © Rhonda Sidney/PhotoEdit; p. 399: © Colin McPherson/Corbis Sygma; p. 400: National Center for Victims of Crime © 2007; p. 406 (left, right): Brad Markel/Gamma Liaison/Getty Images; p. 407: © Richard Townshend/Corbis.

Chapter 16

p. 410: © Jonkmanns/laif/Aurora; p. 412: © The McGraw-Hill Companies, Inc./Christopher Kerrigan, photographer; p. 419: © Joel Gordon; p. 421: Axel Koester for the New York Times; p. 422: © P. Chevillot/Gamma US; p. 424: © Joel Gordon;

p. 426: © Deanpictures/The Image Works; p. 427: © Dan Callister/Online USA/Getty Images; p. 430: Photofest; p. 431 (left): © Charles Gatewood/The Image Works; p. 431 (right): © Myrleen Ferguson/PhotoEdit.

Chapter 17

p. 433: Ryan McVay/Getty Images; p. 441 (left): © Jeff Greenberg/PhotoEdit; p. 441 (right): © David Young-Wolff/PhotoEdit; p. 451: © Larry Mulvehill/The Image Works.

Chapter 18

p. 458: Courtesy New York Department of Health and Mental Hygiene, www.nyccondom.org; p. 461 (top): © Science VU/Visuals Unlimited; p. 461 (bottom): © Bart's Medical Library/Phototake; p. 462 (top, bottom): © Biophoto Associates/Photo Researchers, Inc.; p. 466: © Bill Aron/PhotoEdit; p. 468 (top): © Thomas Bowman/PhotoEdit; p. 468 (bottom): © Karen Kasmauski/Corbis; p. 471: AP Images; p. 473: © Wilson Chu/Reuters/Corbis; pp. 474, 476 (top, bottom): Centers for Disease Control; p. 478: © E. Gray/Science Photo Library/Photo Researchers.

Chapter 19

p. 482: Royalty-Free/Corbis; p. 484: The Metropolitan Museum of Art, Rogers Fund, 1941 (41.162.101) Neg. #177754; p. 487: Ognissanti Church, Florence, Italy/Bridgeman Art Library, London/SuperStock, Inc.; p. 488: Hermitage Museum, St. Petersburg, Russia/SuperStock, Inc.; p. 491: Frances M. Roberts; p. 492: © Lauren Goodsmith/The Image Works; p. 493: © Sujoy Das/Stock Boston; p. 497 (top): © Stephen J. Boitano/Gamma; p. 497 (bottom): © Joel Gordon; p. 500: National Gallery of Art, Washington, D.C./SuperStock; p. 502: © Rick Gerharter; p. 504: © Najlah Feanny/Stock Boston.

Chapter 20

p. 508: Creatas/PunchStock; p. 515: © Ira Schwarz/Reuters/Corbis; p. 516: © Rachel Epstein/The Image Works; p. 518: © Mark Richards/PhotoEdit; p. 522: © Reagan Louie; p. 528: © Joel Gordon.

TEXT AND LINE ART CREDITS

Chapter 1

Table 1.1, Edward O. Laumann, et al., *The Social Organization of Sexuality: Sexual Practices in the United States*, 1994. Reprinted by permission of the University of Chicago Press.

Table 1.2, Edward O. Laumann, et al., *The Social Organization of Sexuality: Sexual Practices in the United States*, 1994. Reprinted by permission of the University of Chicago Press.

Chapter 3

Table 3.1, Review of the *Janus Report* on Sexual Behavior by Andrew M. Greeley in *Contemporary Sociology*, Vol. 23, No. 2 (March 1994), pp. 221–223. Reprinted by permission of the American Sociological Association and Andrew M. Greeley.

Chapter 5

p. 92 "This Way" by Sherri Groveman from *Hermaphrodites with Attitude*, 1995, p. 2. Reprinted by permission of the author.

Chapter 7

p. 184 Elisha P. Renne, "The pregnancy that doesn't stay: The practice and perception of abortion by Ekiti Yoruba women," *Social Science and Medicine, 42,* Issue 4, p. 487. Copyright 1996 with permission from Elsevier via the Copyright Clearance Center.

Table 7.5, Robert A. Hatcher et al., *Contraceptive technology* (18th ed.), 2007. Adapted by permission of Irvington Publishers.

Chapter 8

p. 217 From Harry Maurer, *Sex: An Oral History,* © 1994 by Harry Maurer. Used by permission of Viking Penguin, a division of Penguin Group USA Inc., and by permission of International Creative Management, Inc.

Chapter 9

p. 231 From Sandra L. Bem, 1989, Genital knowledge and gender consistency in preschool children. *Child Development, 60,* 649–662. Blackwell Publishing Ltd.

pp. 232, 234, 235 Floyd M. Martinson, *The Sexual Life of Children,* 1994, Greenwood Publishing Group, Inc., pp. 37, 59, 62. Copyright © 1994 by Floyd M. Martinson. Reproduced with permission of Greenwood Publishing Group, Inc., Westport, CT.

pp. 235, 243 Kay J. Starks & Eleanor S. Morrison, *Growing up Sexual,* 2e, 1996, HarperCollins; Pearson Education.

pp. 236, 241, 247 Reproduced with permission from Playboy Enterprises, Inc. from *Sexual Behavior in the 1970s* by Morton Hunt. © 1974, 2005 by Morton Hunt.

Figure 9.7, Figure from Brooke E. Wells & Jean M. Twenge, "Changes in young people's sexual behavior and attitudes, 1943–1999: A cross-temporal meta-analysis," *Review of General Psychology, 9,* 2005, 249–261 (Figure 2). Reprinted with permission of the American Psychological Association.

Chapter 10

pp. 264, 265, 277 From *The Janus Report on Sexual Behavior* by Samuel S. Janus & Cynthia L. Janus, 1993, pp. 8, 191, 383, John Wiley & Sons, Inc., pp. 8, 191, 383.

pp. 265, 267, 268, 269, 277 From Harry Maurer, *Sex: An Oral History,* © 1994 by Harry Maurer. Used by permission of Viking Penguin, a division of Penguin Group USA Inc., and by permission of International Creative Management, Inc.

Chapter 11

p. 310 From *Why Marriages Succeed or Fail: What You Can Learn from the Breakthrough Research to Make Your Marriage Last* by John Gottman, Ph.D. Copyright © 1994 by John Gottman. All rights reserved. Reprinted with permission of Simon & Schuster Adult Publishing Group, and by permission of Bloomsbury Publishing Ltd.

Table 11.1, Edward O. Laumann, et al., *The Social Organization of Sexuality: Sexual Practices in the United States,* 1994. Reprinted by permission of the University of Chicago Press.

Chapter 12

Table 12.1, Yolanda F. Niemann et al., "Use of Free Responses and Cluster Analysis to Determine Stereotypes of Eight Groups." In Judith M. Harackiewicz (Ed.), *Personality and Social Psychology Bulletin,* Vol. 20, Issue 4, 1994, pp. 379–390, copyright 1994 Sage Publications Inc. Reprinted by permission of Sage Publications Inc.

Chapter 13

p. 337 Jennifer Egan, "Lonely Gay Teen Seeking Same." *The New York Times Magazine* © 2000 Jennifer Egan. Reprinted by permission.

p. 360 Condensed from Lisa Yost, "Bisexual Tendencies," in *Bi Any Other Name: Bisexual People Speak Out,* L. Hutchins & L. Kaahumanu (Eds.), 1991, Alyson Publications. Reprinted by permission of Alyson Publications.

Table 13.1, J. A. Davis & T. Smith, *General Social Survey,* National Opinion Research Center, 1972, 2004, http://webapp.icpsr.umich.edu/GSS. Reprinted by permission of the National Opinion Research Center.

Chapter 15

Table 15.1, Edward O. Laumann, et al., *The Social Organization of Sexuality: Sexual Practices in the United States,* 1994. Reprinted by permission of the University of Chicago Press.

pp. 392, 393, 398 Jean O. Hughes and Bernice R. Sandler, appeared originally in "On Campus With Women," 1987, Project on Status and Education of Women, Association of American Colleges, Washington, DC. For further information, contact Bernice R. Sandler (sandler@bernicesandler.com). Reprinted with permission.

p. 397 C. Struckman-Johnson, D. Struckman-Johnson, & P. B. Anderson, 2003, "Tactics of sexual coercion: When men and women won't take no for an answer," *Journal of Sex Research, 40.* Used by permission of The Society for the Scientific Study of Sexuality.

Chapter 16

pp. 422, 423 From Harry Maurer, *Sex: An Oral History,* © 1994 by Harry Maurer. Used by permission of Viking Penguin, a division of Penguin Group USA Inc., and by permission of International Creative Management, Inc.

Table 16.1, Martin Rimm, "Marketing Pornography on the Information Superhighway," *Georgetown Law Journal,* Vol. 83, 1995, p. 1891. Reprinted with permission of the publisher, Georgetown Law Journal © 1995.

Table 16.2, From Frontline / WGBH Educational Foundation Copyright © 1995–2005 WGBH/Boston.

Chapter 17

Figure 17.3, David H. Barlow, "Causes of sexual dysfunction: The role of cognitive interference," 1986, *Journal of Consulting and Clinical Psychology, 54,* 140–148. Reprinted with permission of the American Psychological Association.

p. 447 From Rosemary Basson, "Sexual Desire/Arousal Disorders in Women," in S. Leiblum (Ed.), *Principles and Practice of Sex Therapy* 4e, 2007, pp. 42–43. Reprinted by permission of the Guilford Press.

Chapter 18

Table 18.1, From *Barrier Contraceptives: Current Status and Future Prospects* by Katherine M. Stone. In Christine K. Mauck et al. (Eds.), 1994, John Wiley & Sons, Inc., pp. 203–212. Copyright © 1994 Wiley-Liss, Inc., a subsidiary of John Wiley & Sons, Inc. Reprinted with permission of John Wiley & Sons, Inc.

p. 479 Used with permission from Planned Parenthood® Federation of America, Inc. © 2007 PPFA. All rights reserved.

Chapter 20

p. 510 Graham Parker, "The legal regulation of sexual activity and the protection of females," 1983, *Osgoode Hall Law Journal, 21*, p. 190.

Figure 20.1, R. A. Posner and K.B. Silbaugh, *A Guide to America's Sex Laws*, 1996, The University of Chicago Press. Reprinted by permission of the University of Chicago Press.

p. 514 E.M.L. Ng, J.J. Borras-Vallas, M. Perez-Conchillo, and E. Coleman (Eds.), *Sexuality in the New Millennium*, 2000. Bologna, Editrice Compositori. P. xii. Reprinted by permission.

Figure 20.4, Copyright © 2004 Lambda Legal Defense and Education Fund. Reprinted by permission.

p. 521 Norval J. Morris, "The Law Is a Busy-Body" (1973, April 18). From *The New York Times Magazine.* © 1973 The New York Times. All rights reserved. Used by permission and protected by the Copyright Laws of the U.S. The printing, copying, redistribution, or retransmission of the Material without express written permission is prohibited.

Figure 20.9, R. A. Posner and K.B. Silbaugh, *A Guide to America's Sex Laws*, 1996, The University of Chicago Press. Reprinted by permission of the University of Chicago Press.

Index

H

Directory of Resources in Human Sexuality

(*continued from front inside cover*)

III. Lifestyle Issues

Harry Benjamin International Gender Dysphoria Association
1300 South 2nd St., #180
Minneapolis, MN 55454
Society for professionals interested in the study and care of transsexualism and gender dysphoria.

Intersex Society of North America
4500 Ninth Ave. NE #300
Seattle, WA 98105
email: info@isna.org
www.isna.org
ISNA is a peer support and advocacy group for intersexuals (persons born with mixed sexual anatomy).

J2CP Information Services
P.O. Box 184
San Juan Capistrano, CA 92693-0184
Information on transsexualism and professional referrals.

Lambda Legal Defense and Education Fund
120 Wall Street, Suite 1500
New York, NY 10005-3904
(212) 809-8585
and
3325 Wilshire Blvd., Suite 1300
Los Angeles, CA 90010-1729
(213) 382-7600
www.lambdalegal.org
Advances the legal rights of lesbians, gay men, and people with AIDS through test case litigation and public education. Publishes many resource manuals, newsletters, bibliographies, and articles on current topics for lesbians, gay men, and people with HIV/AIDS.

National Gay and Lesbian Task Force (NGLTF)
1325 Massachusetts Ave., NW
Washington, DC 20500
(202) 393-8579
The oldest national gay and lesbian civil rights advocacy organization. Lobbying, grassroots organizing, publications (call or write for listing), and referrals.

Society for the Second Self
Box 194
Tulare, CA 93275
(209) 688-9246
email: trichil@aol.com
members.aol.com/chitriess/triss/chimain.htm
An organization for heterosexual men who cross-dress and their wives.

IV. Media

Multi-Focus, Inc.
1525 Franklin Street
San Francisco, CA 94109-4592
1-800-821-0514
Has one of the largest selections of sexuality education and sex therapy films and videos available for rent or purchase.

Sinclair Intimacy Institute
P.O. Box 8865
Chapel Hill, NC 27514
Another organization with a large selection of sexuality education and sex therapy films and videos.